West's Law School Advisory Board

JESSE H. CHOPER
Professor of Law,
University of California, Berkeley

DAVID P. CURRIE
Professor of Law, University of Chicago

YALE KAMISAR
Professor of Law, University of San Diego
Professor of Law, University of Michigan

MARY KAY KANE
Chancellor, Dean and Distinguished Professor of Law,
University of California,
Hastings College of the Law

LARRY D. KRAMER
Dean and Professor of Law, Stanford Law School

WAYNE R. LaFAVE
Professor of Law, University of Illinois

JONATHAN R. MACEY
Professor of Law, Yale Law School

ARTHUR R. MILLER
Professor of Law, Harvard University

GRANT S. NELSON
Professor of Law,
University of California, Los Angeles

JAMES J. WHITE
Professor of Law, University of Michigan

*TO HAROLD, OUR CHILDREN AND SPOUSES,
PAT AND CARA, SCOTT AND LAURA,
KIM AND ROBERT*

M.E.P.

TO ANNE

R.J.D.

*

Preface

Representation of nonprofit organizations has become an increasingly important area of legal practice given the extensive growth of the nonprofit sector. This casebook provides a comprehensive coverage of the laws related to nonprofit organizations to provide the law student with the expertise needed to represent these organizations. Because tax exempt status is an important reason to establish a nonprofit organization, an attorney must be knowledgeable of the tax laws applicable to nonprofit organizations. The casebook presents these tax laws in a brief historical and interpretive form so that the tax laws can be grasped easily enough by the student or by an attorney who is not a tax expert. Still, the casebook is not limited to tax provisions. It covers other laws relating to nonprofit organizations. Thus, the casebook can serve as a hornbook for persons who have expertise in the area of nonprofit law but also somewhat as a primer for first-time readers.

The first three chapters provide an overview of the nonprofit sector. The first chapter includes a discussion of the different organizational structures available for a nonprofit organization and contains a description of the global third sector, to include a discussion of NGOS and some foreign nonprofit organizations. The second chapter describes the corporate structure for a nonprofit organization, including the creation and operation of a nonprofit corporation. It consider the status and rights of directors and members. The third chapter covers the governance of a nonprofit organization. It includes a discussion of the standards of care and loyalty applicable to directors and trustees of nonprofit organizations as well as the means to enforce fiduciary obligations. This chapter also considers the penalty taxes imposed by the Internal Revenue Code for individuals' acts of self-dealing and involvement in excess benefit transactions with charitable organizations.

The next five chapters address issues relating specifically to charitable organizations. The fourth chapter is a general discussion of the charitable organization and the requirements for obtaining § 501(c)(3) status. It also compares charitable organizations to social welfare organizations exempt under § 501(c)(4) of the Internal Revenue Code. The fifth chapter further addresses the charitable organization by setting out the requirements to maintain § 501(c)(3) status and by delineating those activities that can cause loss of exempt status, such as substantial involvement in commercial activities, inurement, conferring a private benefit on individuals or for-profit entities, substantial involvement in lobbying, and any involvement in political activities. The sixth chapter reviews the requirements for a charitable organization to obtain and maintain public charity status. The seventh chapter then discusses the effects of a charitable organization failing to qualify as a public charity and, thus, being designated as a private foundation for tax purposes. It covers the excise tax imposed on private foundations and the penalty taxes applicable to private foundations that engage in certain prohibited activities. The eighth chapter covers laws relating to fund raising. It includes a discussion of the charitable contribution deduction—when a donor is entitled to a deduction for a charitable contribution, the amount of the deduction when the donation is in the form of property, the annual limitations on the amount of the deduction, and issues related to deferred giving. The chapter also covers the laws regulating charitable solicitations and the effect of restrictions on gifts to include a discussion of the cy pres doctrine and the doctrine of deviation.

The ninth chapter sets out the commercial activities of nonprofit organizations that are subject to tax and explains how and why these activities are taxed. It reviews the history of the unrelated business income tax (UBIT).

Chapters 10 through 16 address legal issues specific to some of the different types of nonprofit organizations. For example, chapter 10 covers laws relating to religious organizations. It addresses First Amendment constraints, involvement of religious organizations in political activities, tax audits of religious organizations, and problems relating to property ownership and liability of members because of the associational status of many churches and other religious organizations. Chapter 11 addresses certain legal and tax issues that affect private schools, such as nondiscrimination requirements for tax exempt status, rights of students, voucher systems, and First Amendment concerns for private religious schools. Chapter 12 covers specific issues unique to hospitals, such as physician recruitment, involvement in partnerships with for-profit entities, hospital reorganizations, and legal and tax concerns when hospitals seek to convert to for-profit status. Chapter 13 covers special taxation issues relating to social clubs and to the status of fraternities and sororities as social clubs. The chapter also addresses members' rights of association and expands the issue to apply it to members of charitable organizations. Chapter 14 covers specialized legal issues relating to trade and professional organizations, such as the proxy tax, antitrust regulations, and members's rights. Chapter 15 gives students a further insight into the problem of nonprofit organizations being involved in political campaigns as it addresses regulation of, and specific legal requirements and tax issues related to, political organizations. The last chapter addresses the home owners' association, its nature as well as the rights and obligations of members.

[The reader who is interested in other areas of the law pertaining to nonprofit organizations is encouraged to refer to Marilyn Phelan, *Nonprofit Enterprises: Corporations, Trusts, and Associations*, a three volume treatise published by Thomson/West. It is online at Westlaw, database NPECTA. The treatise covers the tax and other legal issues that are addressed in this casebook, but it also discusses many other issues of importance to representatives of nonprofit organizations. For example, it has additional separate chapters covering laws relating to museums, cemetery organizations, exempt cooperatives, labor organizations, and family foundations. It also contains a more expansive coverage of laws relating to religious organizations, schools, hospitals, trade and professional organizations, and political organizations. It discusses how copyright and securities laws apply to nonprofit organizations, and contains a discussion of accounting considerations for nonprofit organizations, mergers and dissolution of nonprofit organizations, application for tax exempt status for the many other nonprofit organizations, and a summary of each state's nonprofit corporation acts. It contains sample forms, with explanations, for applying for exempt status and for meeting annual reporting requirements, i.e., Forms 1023, 1024, 1028, 990, 990EZ, Schedules A and B for Forms 990 and 990EZ, 990C, 990PF, and 990T.]

Although this casebook does not include all the laws relating to nonprofit organizations, it is comprehensive enough that it will provide the reader with a basic understanding of the principal issues that confront all types of nonprofit organizations. Thus, we think that the materials in the book will be of interest and will be very helpful both to laws students and to attorneys who represent nonprofit organizations. Readers are encouraged to refer questions and comments to Marilyn Phelan, Texas Tech University School of Law, 1802 Hartford, Lubbock, Texas, 79409, telephone 806-742-3787, Ext. 251, e-mail { and Robert Desiderio, University of New Mexico School of Law, 1117 Stanford Drive, N.E., Albuquerque, New Mexico, 87131, telephone 505-247-9355, e-mail {

We wish to extend special thanks to Salli Anne Swartz, Avocat a la Cour, Paris, France, for submitting a synopsis on laws in France relating to nonprofit organizations and to Marie Pierre Gay, Avocat a la Cour, for her contribution and assistance. We also thank Professor Giovanni Maria Riccio, Professor of Law, University of Salerno, for preparing a synopsis on the laws in Italy relating to nonprofit organizations, and we thank Ileana Ippolito and Frank Z. Elmer for translating his synopsis.

We thank Texas Tech University School of Law and University of New Mexico School of Law for their financial and scheduling support of this project. We also are grateful to the production staff of Thomson/West for their help. Special thanks to those who saw us through the project: Harold Phelan and Anne Desiderio.

MARILYN PHELAN
ROBERT DESIDERIO

*

Summary of Contents

	Page
PREFACE	v
TABLE OF CASES	xxiii

Chapter 1. Overview of the Nonprofit Sector — 1
- I. Nature of a Nonprofit Organization — 1
- II. Organizational Structure of a Nonprofit Organization — 27
  - A. Trust — 27
  - B. Association — 28
  - C. Nonprofit Corporation — 30
- III. Nongovernmental Organization (NGO) — 46
- IV. Foreign Nonprofit Organizations and Philanthropy Abroad — 47
  - A. Synopsis of French Law on Non–Profit Organizations — 48
  - B. Synopsis of Italian Law on Nonprofit Organizations — 53

Chapter 2. The Nonprofit Corporation — 61
- I. Nature of a Nonprofit Corporation — 61
- II. Creation of a Nonprofit Corporation — 64
  - A. Articles of Incorporation — 64
  - B. Bylaws — 65
  - C. Authorization to Conduct Affairs in Another State — 66
  - D. Obtaining Tax–Exempt Status — 66
- III. Directors — 66
  - A. Management of a Nonprofit Corporation — 66
  - B. Meetings of Directors — 71
  - C. Removal of Directors — 72
- IV. Members — 76
  - A. Rights of Members — 77
  - B. Meetings — 81
  - C. Removal of Members — 82
  - D. Members' Derivative Actions — 89

Chapter 3. Governance of a Nonprofit Organization — 91
- I. State Standards of Conduct — 91
  - A. Fiduciary Obligations — 92
  - B. Indemnification of Directors — 115
  - C. Disposition of Assets upon Dissolution — 119
  - D. Enforcement of Fiduciary Obligations — 125
  - E. Volunteer Immunity from Liability — 154
- II. Federal Standards of Conduct — 154
  - A. Self–Dealing — 155
  - B. Excess Benefits Transactions — 161

SUMMARY OF CONTENTS

	Page
Chapter 4. Charitable Organizations	**176**
I. Background	176
II. Section 501(c)(3) Elements	177
III. Organizational and Operational Tests	177
IV. The Charitable Purpose Test	182
V. Social Welfare Organizations	199
Chapter 5. Obtaining and Maintaining Tax Exempt Status	**212**
I. Obtaining Tax Exempt Status	213
II. Maintaining Tax Exempt Status	213
A. Commercial Activity	214
B. Private Benefit	226
C. Private Inurement	245
D. Excess Benefit Transaction	262
E. Action Organization	265
F. Public Policy	280
Chapter 6. Public Charities	**281**
I. Requirements for Public Charity Status	281
II. Section 509(a) Organizations	282
A. Section 509(a)(1) Organizations	283
B. Section 509(a)(2) Organizations	288
C. Section 509(a)(3) Organizations	291
D. Section 509(a)(4) Organizations	301
E. Filing Requirements	301
Chapter 7. Private Foundations	**303**
I. Private Operating Foundation	304
II. Excise Tax	305
III. Self–Dealing	315
IV. Failure to Distribute Income	319
V. Excess Business Holdings	325
VI. Jeopardizing Investments	326
VII. Taxable Expenditures	327
VIII. Termination of Private Foundation Status	338
Chapter 8. Fundraising	**346**
I. The Importance of Fundraising	346
II. Regulation of Charitable Solicitations	347
III. Charitable Contribution Deductions	368
A. Quid Pro Quo	369
B. Services	385
C. Timing	386
D. Unconditional Gift	386
E. Amount of Deduction	386
F. Appraisals of Donated Property	391
G. Substantiation	395
H. Deferred Giving	396
IV. Cy Pres Doctrine	408

SUMMARY OF CONTENTS

	Page
Chapter 9. Unrelated Business Taxable Income	**429**
I. History of the Unrelated Business Income Tax	430
A. Pre-Revenue Act of 1950	430
B. The Revenue Act of 1950	431
C. The Regulations	432
II. Organizations to Which 'UBIT' Applies	433
III. Elements of the Unrelated Business Income Tax (UBIT)	433
A. Unrelated Trade or Business	434
B. Regularly Carried On	446
C. Substantially Related	454
D. Exceptions to "UBIT"	464
E. Modifications	466
Chapter 10. Churches and Other Religious Organizations	**491**
I. Definition of a "Church"	491
II. Membership	514
III. Association Status	522
A. Liability of Members of a Religious Organization	522
B. Property Ownership	528
IV. Incorporation of Religious Associations	543
V. Specialized Tax Issues Relating to Religious Organizations	549
A. Involvement in Political Activities	549
B. Tax Audits of Churches	557
C. Other Tax Issues	559
Chapter 11. Schools	**561**
I. Role of Private Schools	561
II. Tax Exempt Status of Private Schools	584
III. Rights of Students	605
A. Suspension of Students	605
B. Privacy Rights	611
C. Right of Expression	612
Chapter 12. Hospitals	**619**
I. Organizational Structure	619
II. Reorganizations of Nonprofit Hospitals	627
III. Exemption From Property Taxes	655
IV. Abandonment of Nonprofit Hospital Status	673
V. Conversion to For-Profit Status	676
Chapter 13. Social Clubs	**680**
I. Nature of Social Clubs	680
II. Right of Association	683
III. Taxation of Social Clubs	706
IV. Business Use of a Social Club	713
V. Fraternities and Sororities	717

	Page
Chapter 14. Trade and Professional Organizations	**726**
I. Trade Association Status	726
II. Trade Shows	734
III. Political Activities	734
IV. Antitrust Regulations	740
V. Membership in Trade Associations	757
Chapter 15. Political Organizations	**761**
I. Regulation of Political Organizations	761
II. Taxation of Political Organizations	770
III. Separate Fund for Political Expenditures of Nonprofit Organizations	771
IV. Political Activities of § 501(c)(3) Organizations	773
V. Registration Requirements for Tax Exempt Political Organizations	777
Chapter 16. Homeowners' Associations	**781**
I. Nature of Homeowners' Associations	781
II. Rights and Liabilities of Members	782
INDEX	799

Table of Contents

	Page
PREFACE	v
TABLE OF CASES	xxiii

Chapter 1. Overview of the Nonprofit Sector 1
- I. Nature of a Nonprofit Organization 1
  - Note 2
  - Questions 3
  - *Association for Preservation of Freedom of Choice v. Shapiro* 3
  - Note 6
  - Questions 6
  - *Slee v. Commissioner* 6
  - Questions 8
  - *Haring v. Blumenthal* 8
  - Note 14
  - Questions 15
  - *Big Mama Rag v. United States* 15
  - *National Alliance v. United States* 20
  - Questions 24
  - *Nationalist Foundation v. Commissioner* 25
  - Problem 27
- II. Organizational Structure of a Nonprofit Organization 27
  - A. Trust 27
    - Restatement, Trusts 28
      - § 348. Definition of Charitable Trust 28
      - § 364. Indefinite Beneficiaries 28
      - § 380. Extent of Trustee's Powers 28
  - B. Association 28
    - Uniform Unincorporated Nonprofit Association Act 29
      - Section 4 29
      - Section 6 29
    - Problem 29
    - Note 30
  - C. Nonprofit Corporation 30
    1. Model Nonprofit Corporation Acts 30
    2. Status of a Nonprofit Corporation as a Charitable Trust 31
       - Uniform Supervision of Trustees for Charitable Purposes Act 31
       - California Government Code 32
         - § 12580 32
         - § 12581 32

xiii

	Page
II. Organizational Structure of a Nonprofit Organization—Continued	
Younger v. Wisdom Society	32
People v. George F. Harding Museum	36
Question	39
Commonwealth of Virginia v. The JOCO Foundation	39
Questions	45
Problem	46
III. Nongovernmental Organization (NGO)	46
IV. Foreign Nonprofit Organizations and Philanthropy Abroad	47
Notes	47
A. Synopsis of French Law on Non-Profit Organizations	48
1. Associations	48
2. Foundations	50
3. Public Interest Foundations	51
4. Corporate Foundations	51
B. Synopsis of Italian Law on Nonprofit Organizations	53
Note	53
Revenue Ruling 63–252	54
Revenue Ruling 66–79	57
Question	60
Note	60
Chapter 2. The Nonprofit Corporation	**61**
I. Nature of a Nonprofit Corporation	61
In re Mt. Sinai Hospital	61
II. Creation of a Nonprofit Corporation	64
A. Articles of Incorporation	64
B. Bylaws	65
C. Authorization to Conduct Affairs in Another State	66
D. Obtaining Tax–Exempt Status	66
III. Directors	66
A. Management of a Nonprofit Corporation	66
Bailey v. American Soc. for Prevention of Cruelty to Animals	66
Solomon v. Hall–Brooke Foundation, Inc.	69
B. Meetings of Directors	71
C. Removal of Directors	72
Grace v. Grace Institute	72
Collins v. Beinecke	75
IV. Members	76
Note	77
A. Rights of Members	77
In re Mt. Sinai Hospital	77
Harris v. Board of Directors of Community Hospital	78
B. Meetings	81
C. Removal of Members	82
Raulston v. Everett	82
Question	85
Bartley v. Augusta Country Club, Inc.	85

TABLE OF CONTENTS

	Page
IV. Members—Continued	
Rowland v. Union Hills Country Club	87
D. Members' Derivative Actions	89
Notes	89
Chapter 3. Governance of a Nonprofit Organization	**91**
I. State Standards of Conduct	91
A. Fiduciary Obligations	92
Litwin v. Allen	92
Questions	93
Stern v. Lucy Webb Hayes Nat'l Training School–Deaconesses, Missionaries	94
Louisiana World Exposition v. Federal Insurance Co.	101
Note	105
Questions	106
Uniform Management of Institutional Funds Act (Currently Uniform Prudent Management of Institutional Funds Act)	106
Uniform Prudent Investor Act (Currently Uniform Prudent Management of Institutional Funds Act)	107
Model Nonprofit Corporation Act of 1987	108
Section 8.30. General Standards for Directors	108
Section 8.32. Director Conflict of Interest	108
Questions	109
Northeast Harbor Golf Club v. Harris	109
B. Indemnification of Directors	115
John v. John	115
Note	119
C. Disposition of Assets upon Dissolution	119
Holden Hospital Corp. v. Southern Illinois Hosp. Corp.	120
Note	122
Sharpless v. Religious Society of Friends	122
Question	125
D. Enforcement of Fiduciary Obligations	125
In re Estate of Stern	126
Questions	128
In re Milton Hershey School	129
Note	140
Question	140
Herzog Foundation, Inc. v. University of Bridgeport	141
Russell v. Yale University	148
Cornyn v. Fifty–Two Members of the Schoppa Family	150
E. Volunteer Immunity from Liability	154
II. Federal Standards of Conduct	154
A. Self–Dealing	155
Estate of Reis	155
B. Excess Benefits Transactions	161
Caracci v. Commissioner	161
Questions	172
Notes	173
Problem	175

	Page
Chapter 4. Charitable Organizations	**176**
I. Background	176
II. Section 501(c)(3) Elements	177
III. Organizational and Operational Tests	177
Better Business Bureau v. United States	178
Questions	181
IV. The Charitable Purpose Test	182
Monterey Public Parking Corp. v. United States	182
Note	186
Columbia Park and Recreation Ass'n v. Commissioner	186
Questions	199
Notes	199
V. Social Welfare Organizations	199
Regan v. Taxation With Representation	200
People's Educational Camp Society, Inc. v. Commissioner	204
Chapter 5. Obtaining and Maintaining Tax Exempt Status	**212**
I. Obtaining Tax Exempt Status	213
II. Maintaining Tax Exempt Status	213
A. Commercial Activity	214
Note	214
Note	215
Living Faith, Inc. v. Commissioner	216
Questions	225
Note	226
B. Private Benefit	226
American Campaign Academy v. Commissioner	226
Question	243
Plumstead Theatre Society v. Commissioner	244
Note	245
C. Private Inurement	245
Church of Scientology of California v. Commissioner	245
Note	255
United Cancer Council, Inc. v. Commissioner	255
Note	262
D. Excess Benefit Transaction	262
E. Action Organization	265
1. Lobbying Activity	265
Christian Echoes National Ministry, Inc. v. United States	266
Notes	272
General Counsel Memorandum	272
Notes	276
Problem	277
Note	277
Problem	278
2. Political Campaigns	279
Note	279
Notes	279
F. Public Policy	280
Questions	280

	Page
Chapter 6. Public Charities	**281**
I. Requirements for Public Charity Status	281
II. Section 509(a) Organizations	282
A. Section 509(a)(1) Organizations	283
1. Churches	283
2. Educational Organizations	283
3. Hospitals and Medical Research Organizations	284
4. Organizations for the Benefit of Colleges and Universities	284
5. Governmental Units	285
6. Publicly Supported Organizations	285
One–Third Support Test	285
Facts and Circumstances Test	287
Unusual Grants	288
Problem	288
B. Section 509(a)(2) Organizations	288
1. One–Third Support Test	289
Questions	290
2. One–Third Investment Income Test	290
Note	290
Problem	291
C. Section 509(a)(3) Organizations	291
1. Organizational Test	291
2. Operational Test	291
Lapham Foundation, Inc. v. Commissioner	293
Note	300
Note	300
D. Section 509(a)(4) Organizations	301
E. Filing Requirements	301
Note	302
Chapter 7. Private Foundations	**303**
I. Private Operating Foundation	304
II. Excise Tax	305
Note	306
Problem	306
Zemurray Foundation v. United States	306
Greenacre Foundation v. United States	312
Note	315
III. Self–Dealing	315
Notes	315
Estate of Reis v. Commissioner	316
Problems	319
IV. Failure to Distribute Income	319
Note	320
Problem	320
Note	320
In re Estate of John A. Hermann	321
Question	325

	Page
V. Excess Business Holdings	325
Note	326
VI. Jeopardizing Investments	326
Note	326
VII. Taxable Expenditures	327
Mannheimer Charitable Trust v. Commissioner	327
VIII. Termination of Private Foundation Status	338
Gladney v. Commissioner	338
Note	344
Problem	345

Chapter 8. Fundraising — 346

	Page
I. The Importance of Fundraising	346
II. Regulation of Charitable Solicitations	347
Riley v. National Federation of Blind of North Carolina	347
Question	356
Madigan v. Telemarketing Associates, Inc.	357
Note	363
Questions	363
United Cancer Council Inc. v. Commissioner	363
Question	368
III. Charitable Contribution Deductions	368
A. Quid Pro Quo	369
United States v. American Bar Endowment	370
Revenue Ruling 67–246	373
Revenue Procedure 90–12	381
Notes	385
B. Services	385
C. Timing	386
D. Unconditional Gift	386
E. Amount of Deduction	386
1. Amount of Contribution	387
2. Long–Term Capital Gain Property	387
Note	388
3. Ordinary Income Producing Property	388
4. Percentage Limitations	389
5. Carryforward of Charitable Contribution Deduction	390
F. Appraisals of Donated Property	391
Revenue Procedure 66–49	391
Note	395
G. Substantiation	395
Note	396
H. Deferred Giving	396
1. Charitable Remainder Trusts	397
Revenue Procedure 2005–52	399
Revenue Procedure 2005–53	403
Note	407
2. Charitable Gift Annuity	407

	Page
IV. Cy Pres Doctrine	408
United States v. Cerio	408
Notes	421
Questions	421
Note	422
Niemann v. Vaughn Community Church	422

Chapter 9. Unrelated Business Taxable Income — 429

Note — 429
- I. History of the Unrelated Business Income Tax — 430
  - A. Pre–Revenue Act of 1950 — 430
  - B. The Revenue Act of 1950 — 431
  - C. The Regulations — 432
    - Questions — 433
- II. Organizations to Which 'UBIT' Applies — 433
- III. Elements of the Unrelated Business Income Tax (UBIT) — 433
  - A. Unrelated Trade or Business — 434
    - *Professional Insurance Agents v. Commissioner* — 434
    - *United States v. American Bar Endowment* — 442
    - Question — 446
    - Note — 446
  - B. Regularly Carried On — 446
    - *National Collegiate Athletic Ass'n v. Commissioner* — 447
    - Question — 454
  - C. Substantially Related — 454
    - *United States v. American College of Physicians* — 455
    - Notes — 463
    - Problems — 464
  - D. Exceptions to "UBIT" — 464
    - Problems — 465
  - E. Modifications — 466
    - 1. Rents — 466
      - Note — 467
    - 2. Royalties — 467
      - *Sierra Club, Inc. v. Commissioner* — 468
      - Note — 473
    - 3. Unrelated Debt–Financed Income — 473
      - *University Hill Foundation v. Commissioner* — 474
      - Note — 486
      - Problem — 487
      - Question — 487
      - *Mose and Garrison Siskin Memorial Foundation v. United States* — 487
      - Note — 490

Chapter 10. Churches and Other Religious Organizations — 491
- I. Definition of a "Church" — 491
  - *Foundation of Human Understanding v. Commissioner* — 491
  - Question — 498
  - *Lutheran Social Service of Minnesota v. United States* — 499
  - Question — 505

	Page
I. Definition of a "Church"—Continued	
Strayhorn v. Ethical Society of Austin	505
Question	514
II. Membership	514
Serbian Eastern Orthodox Diocese v. Milivojevich	514
Note	522
III. Association Status	522
A. Liability of Members of a Religious Organization	522
Notes	522
Smith v. Calvary Christian Church	522
Notes	527
B. Property Ownership	528
Presbyterian Church in United States v. Hull Presbyterian Church	529
Holiman v. Dovers	534
Mills v. Baldwin	537
Note	540
Wood v. Benedictine Society of Alabama	541
IV. Incorporation of Religious Associations	543
Murphy v. Traylor	543
Notes	548
V. Specialized Tax Issues Relating to Religious Organizations	549
A. Involvement in Political Activities	549
Branch Ministries v. Rossotti	549
Notes	556
B. Tax Audits of Churches	557
C. Other Tax Issues	559
Problem	560
Chapter 11. Schools	**561**
I. Role of Private Schools	561
Pierce v. Society of the Sisters of Holy Names of Jesus and Mary	561
Questions	564
New Life Baptist Church Academy v. East Longmeadow	564
Question	574
Zelman v. Simmons–Harris	575
Notes	583
II. Tax Exempt Status of Private Schools	584
Bob Jones University v. United States	584
Question	595
Notes	595
Doe v. Kamehameha Schools/Bernice Pauahi Bishop Estate	596
Note	605
III. Rights of Students	605
A. Suspension of Students	605
Harris v. Trustees of Columbia University	605
Note	611
B. Privacy Rights	611
Note	612
C. Right of Expression	612

TABLE OF CONTENTS

Page

III. Rights of Students—Continued
    Question 612
        Rumsfeld v. Forum for Academic and Institutional Rights, Inc. 612
        Note 618

Chapter 12. Hospitals 619
  I. Organizational Structure 619
    Questions 619
    American Hospital Association v. Hansbarger 620
    Notes 627
  II. Reorganizations of Nonprofit Hospitals 627
    Question 628
    Revenue Ruling 97–21 629
    Question 636
    Revenue Ruling 98–15 636
    Redlands Surgical Services v. Commissioner 643
    Note 653
    Question 654
    Notes 654
  III. Exemption From Property Taxes 655
    Question 655
    Lamb County Appraisal District v. South Plains Hospital–Clinic 655
    Utah County v. Intermountain Health Care 660
    Notes 672
  IV. Abandonment of Nonprofit Hospital Status 673
    Queen of Angels Hospital v. Younger 673
  V. Conversion to For–Profit Status 676
    State of Florida v. Anclote Manor Hospital 676
    Questions 679
    Notes 679

Chapter 13. Social Clubs 680
  I. Nature of Social Clubs 680
    Revenue Ruling 58–501 680
    Note 683
  II. Right of Association 683
    Board of Directors, Rotary International v. Rotary Club of Duarte 683
    Question 689
    New York State Club Association, Inc. v. City of New York 689
    Questions 696
    Boy Scouts of America v. Dale 696
    Note 705
  III. Taxation of Social Clubs 706
    Portland Golf Club v. Commissioner 707
    Notes 713
  IV. Business Use of a Social Club 713
    Revenue Procedure 71–17 714
    Note 717

	Page
V. Fraternities and Sororities	717
Zeta Beta Tau Fraternity v. Commissioner	717
Problem	725

Chapter 14. Trade and Professional Organizations **726**

- I. Trade Association Status 726
  - *National Muffler Dealers Association, Inc. v. United States* 726
  - *Guide International Corporation v. United States* 732
- II. Trade Shows 734
- III. Political Activities 734
  - *American Society of Association Executives v. United States* 735
- IV. Antitrust Regulations 740
  - *Goldfarb v. Virginia State Bar* 740
  - *National Collegiate Athletic Assoc. v. University of Oklahoma* 747
- V. Membership in Trade Associations 757
  - *Austin v. American Association of Neurological Surgeons* 757

Chapter 15. Political Organizations **761**

- I. Regulation of Political Organizations 761
  - *Federal Election Commission v. Beaumont* 762
  - Note 769
- II. Taxation of Political Organizations 770
- III. Separate Fund for Political Expenditures of Nonprofit Organizations 771
  - Note 772
- IV. Political Activities of § 501(c)(3) Organizations 773
  - Note 773
  - *Branch Ministries v. Rossotti* 773
  - Notes 776
- V. Registration Requirements for Tax Exempt Political Organizations 777
  - § 527. Political Organizations 778
  - Note 779

Chapter 16. Homeowners' Associations **781**

- I. Nature of Homeowners' Associations 781
  - Note 782
- II. Rights and Liabilities of Members 782
  - *Inwood North Homeowners' Association, Inc. v. Harris* 783
  - Question 786
  - *Brooks v. Northglen Association* 786
  - *Trustees of the Prince Condominium Trust v. Prosser* 790
  - Question 791
  - *Ashcreek Homeowner's Association, Inc. v. Smith* 792
  - Texas Residential Property Owners Protection Act—Selected Sections 794
  - Question 796
  - Oregon Revised Statutes § 94.560 796

INDEX 799

Table of Cases

The principal cases are in bold type. Cases cited or discussed in the text are roman type. References are to pages. Cases cited in principal cases and within other quoted materials are not included.

Alumni Ass'n of University of Oregon, Inc. v. Commissioner, T.C. Memo. 1996-63 (U.S.Tax Ct.1996), 468
American Bar Endowment, United States v., 477 U.S. 105, 106 S.Ct. 2426, 91 L.Ed.2d 89 (1986), **370, 442**
American Campaign Academy v. Commissioner, 92 T.C. No. 66, 92 T.C. 1053 (U.S.Tax Ct.1989), 199, **226**
American College of Physicians, United States v., 475 U.S. 834, 106 S.Ct. 1591, 89 L.Ed.2d 841 (1986), **455**
American Hosp. Ass'n v. Hansbarger, 600 F.Supp. 465 (N.D.W.Va.1984), **620**
American Soc. of Ass'n Executives v. United States, 195 F.3d 47, 338 U.S.App.D.C. 432 (D.C.Cir.1999), **735**
Anclote Manor Hosp., Inc., State ex rel. Butterworth v., 566 So.2d 296 (Fla. App. 2 Dist.1990), **676**
Anclote Psychiatric Center, Inc. v. Commissioner, T.C. Memo. 1998-273 (U.S.Tax Ct.1998), 679
Ashcreek Homeowner's Ass'n, Inc. v. Smith, 902 S.W.2d 586 (Tex.App.-Hous. (1 Dist.) 1995), **792**
Association for Preservation of Freedom of Choice, Inc. v. Shapiro, 214 N.Y.S.2d 388, 174 N.E.2d 487 (N.Y. 1961), **3**
Austin v. American Ass'n of Neurological Surgeons, 253 F.3d 967 (7th Cir. 2001), **757**

Bailey v. American Soc. for Prevention of Cruelty to Animals, 282 A.D. 502, 125 N.Y.S.2d 18 (N.Y.A.D. 1 Dept.1953), **66**
Bartley v. Augusta Country Club, Inc., 254 Ga. 144, 326 S.E.2d 442 (Ga.1985), **85**
Beach, Estate of, No. 23257 (Cal.Super.1986), 422
Bethel School Dist. No. 403 v. Fraser, 478 U.S. 675, 106 S.Ct. 3159, 92 L.Ed.2d 549 (1986), 612
Better Business Bureau of Washington, D.C., v. United States, 326 U.S. 279, 66 S.Ct. 112, 90 L.Ed. 67 (1945), **178,** 430
Big Mama Rag, Inc. v. United States, 631 F.2d 1030, 203 U.S.App.D.C. 448 (D.C.Cir.1980), **15**
Bishop College, In re, 151 B.R. 394 (Bkrtcy. N.D.Tex.1993), 421
Board of Directors of Rotary Intern. v. Rotary Club of Duarte, 481 U.S. 537, 107 S.Ct. 1940, 95 L.Ed.2d 474 (1987), **683**
Bob Jones University v. Simon, 416 U.S. 725, 94 S.Ct. 2038, 40 L.Ed.2d 496 (1974), 6, 214
Bob Jones University v. United States, 461 U.S. 574, 103 S.Ct. 2017, 76 L.Ed.2d 157 (1983), 280, **584**
Boy Scouts of America v. Dale, 530 U.S. 640, 120 S.Ct. 2446, 147 L.Ed.2d 554 (2000), **696**
Branch Ministries v. Rossotti, 211 F.3d 137, 341 U.S.App.D.C. 166 (D.C.Cir. 2000), 8, **549, 773**
Brooks v. Northglen Ass'n, 141 S.W.3d 158 (Tex.2004), **786**
Brown, Commissioner v., 380 U.S. 563, 85 S.Ct. 1162, 14 L.Ed.2d 75 (1965), 486
Buckley v. Valeo, 424 U.S. 1, 96 S.Ct. 612, 46 L.Ed.2d 659 (1976), 770
Burton v. William Beaumont Hosp., 347 F.Supp.2d 486 (E.D.Mich.2004), 672
Butterworth, State ex rel. v. Anclote Manor Hosp., Inc., 566 So.2d 296 (Fla. App. 2 Dist.1990), **676**

Calhoun Academy v. Commissioner, 94 T.C. No. 17, 94 T.C. 284 (U.S.Tax Ct.1990), 596
Caracci v. Commissioner, 118 T.C. No. 25, 118 T.C. 379 (U.S.Tax Ct.2002), **161,** 172, 679

Cerio, United States v., 831 F.Supp. 530 (E.D.Va.1993), **408**

C.F. Mueller Co. v. Commissioner, 190 F.2d 120 (3rd Cir.1951), 215, 430

Chamber of Commerce of the United States v. Federal Election Com'n, 540 U.S. 93, 124 S.Ct. 619, 157 L.Ed.2d 491 (2003), 770

Christian Echoes Nat. Ministry, Inc. v. United States, 470 F.2d 849 (10th Cir. 1972), **266**

Church By Mail, Inc. v. Commissioner, 765 F.2d 1387 (9th Cir.1985), 182

Church of Eternal Life and Liberty, Inc. v. Commissioner, 86 T.C. No. 54, 86 T.C. 916 (U.S.Tax Ct.1986), 262

Church of Scientology of California v. Commissioner, 823 F.2d 1310 (9th Cir. 1987), 6, **245**

Collins v. Beinecke, 504 N.Y.S.2d 72, 495 N.E.2d 335 (N.Y.1986), **75**

Colorado State Chiropractic Soc. v. Commissioner, 93 T.C. No. 39, 93 T.C. 487 (U.S.Tax Ct.1989), 178

Columbia Park and Recreation Ass'n., Inc. v. Commissioner, 88 T.C. No. 1, 88 T.C. 1 (U.S.Tax Ct.1987), **186**

Commissioner v. _____ (see opposing party)

Common Cause v. Commissioner, 112 T.C. No. 23, 112 T.C. 332 (U.S.Tax Ct.1999), 467

Commonwealth v. _____ (see opposing party)

Community Services, United States v., 189 F.2d 421 (4th Cir.1951), 430

Cornyn v. Fifty–Two Members of Schoppa Family, 70 S.W.3d 895 (Tex. App.-Amarillo 2001), **150**

Dillingham Transp. Bldg. Ltd. v. United States, 137 Ct.Cl. 389, 146 F.Supp. 953 (Ct.Cl.1957), 178

Disabled American Veterans v. Commissioner, 227 Ct.Cl. 474, 650 F.2d 1178 (Ct.Cl.1981), 468

Doe v. Corp. of President of Church of Jesus Christ of Latter Day Saints, 98 P.3d 429 (Utah App.2004), 527

Doe v. Kamehameha Schools/Bernice Pauahi Bishop Estate, 416 F.3d 1025 (9th Cir.2005), **596**

Doe ex rel. Doe v. Kamehameha Schools/Bernice Pauahi Bishop Estate, 441 F.3d 1029 (9th Cir.2006), 605

Elvig v. Ackles, 123 Wash.App. 491, 98 P.3d 524 (Wash.App. Div. 1 2004), 527

Elvig v. Calvin Presbyterian Church, 375 F.3d 951 (9th Cir.2004), 528

Estate of (see name of party)

Eulitt ex rel. Eulitt v. Maine, Dept. of Educ., 386 F.3d 344 (1st Cir.2004), 584

Federal Election Com'n v. Beaumont, 539 U.S. 146, 123 S.Ct. 2200, 156 L.Ed.2d 179 (2003), **762**

Fides Publishers Ass'n v. United States, 263 F.Supp. 924 (N.D.Ind.1967), 430

Financial Industrial Fund, Inc. v. McDonnell Douglas Corp., 474 F.2d 514 (10th Cir.1973), 106

Foundation of Human Understanding v. Commissioner, 88 T.C. No. 75, 88 T.C. 1341 (U.S.Tax Ct.1987), **491**

George F. Harding Museum, People ex rel. Scott v., 58 Ill.App.3d 408, 15 Ill. Dec. 973, 374 N.E.2d 756 (Ill.App. 1 Dist.1978), **36**

Gladney v. Commissioner, 745 F.2d 955 (5th Cir.1984), **338**

Golden Rule Church Ass'n v. Commissioner, 41 T.C. 719 (Tax Ct.1964), 430

Goldfarb v. Virginia State Bar, 421 U.S. 773, 95 S.Ct. 2004, 44 L.Ed.2d 572 (1975), **740**

Gonzaga University v. Doe, 536 U.S. 273, 122 S.Ct. 2268, 153 L.Ed.2d 309 (2002), 612

Grace v. Grace Institute, 279 N.Y.S.2d 721, 226 N.E.2d 531 (N.Y.1967), **72**

Greenacre Foundation v. United States, 762 F.2d 965 (Fed.Cir.1985), **312**

Groetzinger, Commissioner v., 480 U.S. 23, 107 S.Ct. 980, 94 L.Ed.2d 25 (1987), 446

Guide Intern. Corp. v. United States, 948 F.2d 360 (7th Cir.1991), **732**

Haring v. Blumenthal, 471 F.Supp. 1172 (D.D.C.1979), **8**

Harris v. Board of Directors of Community Hospital of Evanston, 55 Ill. App.3d 392, 13 Ill.Dec. 94, 370 N.E.2d 1121 (Ill.App. 1 Dist.1977), **78**

Harris v. Trustees of Columbia University in City of New York, 98 A.D.2d 58, 470 N.Y.S.2d 368 (N.Y.A.D. 1 Dept. 1983), **605**

Haswell v. United States, 205 Ct.Cl. 421, 500 F.2d 1133 (Ct.Cl.1974), 278

Hermann's Estate, In re, 454 Pa. 292, 312 A.2d 16 (Pa.1973), **321**

Herzog Foundation, Inc. v. University of Bridgeport, 243 Conn. 1, 699 A.2d 995 (Conn.1997), **141**

Holden Hospital Corp. v. Southern Ill. Hospital Corp., 22 Ill.2d 150, 174 N.E.2d 793 (Ill.1961), **120**

Holiman v. Dovers, 236 Ark. 211, 236 Ark. 460, 366 S.W.2d 197 (Ark.1963), 522, **534**

Holt v. College of Osteopathic Physicians and Surgeons, 61 Cal.2d 750, 40 Cal. Rptr. 244, 394 P.2d 932 (Cal.1964), 128

Holy Land Foundation for Relief and Development v. Ashcroft, 333 F.3d 156, 357 U.S.App.D.C. 35 (D.C.Cir.2003), 3

TABLE OF CASES

In re (see name of party)
Inwood North Homeowners' Ass'n, Inc. v. Harris, 736 S.W.2d 632 (Tex.1987), **783**
Iowa State University of Science and Technology v. United States, 205 Ct.Cl. 339, 500 F.2d 508 (Ct.Cl.1974), 433

Jackson v. Birmingham Bd. of Educ., 544 U.S. 167, 125 S.Ct. 1497, 161 L.Ed.2d 361 (2005), 611
John v. John, 153 Wis.2d 343, 450 N.W.2d 795 (Wis.App.1989), **115**

Kemper Military School v. Crutchley, 274 F. 125 (W.D.Mo.1921), 262
Kizzire v. Baptist Health Systems, Inc., 343 F.Supp.2d 1074 (N.D.Ala.2004), 672

Lamb County Appraisal Dist. v. South Plains Hospital–Clinic, Inc., 688 S.W.2d 896 (Tex.App.-Amarillo 1985), **655**
Lapham Foundation, Inc. v. Commissioner, 389 F.3d 606 (6th Cir.2004), **293**
Litwin v. Allen, 25 N.Y.S.2d 667 (N.Y.Sup.1940), **92**
Living Faith, Inc. v. Commissioner, 950 F.2d 365 (7th Cir.1991), **216**
Locke v. Davey, 540 U.S. 712, 124 S.Ct. 1307, 158 L.Ed.2d 1 (2004), 583
Lorens v. Catholic Health Care Partners, 356 F.Supp.2d 827 (N.D.Ohio 2005), 672
Louisiana World Exposition v. Federal Ins. Co., 864 F.2d 1147 (5th Cir.1989), **101**
Lutheran Social Service of Minnesota v. United States, 758 F.2d 1283 (8th Cir.1985), **499**

Madigan v. Telemarketing Associates, Inc., 538 U.S. 600, 123 S.Ct. 1829, 155 L.Ed.2d 793 (2003), **357**
Mannheimer Charitable Trust v. Commissioner, 93 T.C. No. 5, 93 T.C. 35 (U.S.Tax Ct.1989), **327**
Mills v. Baldwin, 362 So.2d 2 (Fla.1978), **537**
Milton Hershey School, In re, 867 A.2d 674 (Pa.Cmwlth.2005), **129**
Mississippi State University Alumni, Inc. v. Commissioner, T.C. Memo. 1997-397 (U.S.Tax Ct.1997), 468
Monterey Public Parking Corp. v. United States, 321 F.Supp. 972 (N.D.Cal.1970), **182**
Mose and Garrison Siskin Memorial Foundation, Inc. v. United States, 790 F.2d 480 (6th Cir.1986), **487**
Mt. Sinai Hospital, In re, 250 N.Y. 103, 164 N.E. 871 (N.Y.1928), **61, 77**
Murphy v. Traylor, 292 Ala. 78, 289 So.2d 584 (Ala.1974), **543**

National Alliance v. United States, 710 F.2d 868, 228 U.S.App.D.C. 357 (D.C.Cir.1983), **20**
National Collegiate Athletic Ass'n v. Board of Regents of University of Oklahoma, 468 U.S. 85, 104 S.Ct. 2948, 82 L.Ed.2d 70 (1984), **747**
National Collegiate Athletic Ass'n v. Commissioner, 914 F.2d 1417 (10th Cir.1990), **447**
Nationalist Foundation v. Commissioner, T.C. Memo. 2000-318 (U.S.Tax Ct.2000), **25**
Nationalist Movement v. Commissioner, 102 T.C. No. 22, 102 T.C. 558 (U.S.Tax Ct.1994), 272
National Muffler Dealers Ass'n, Inc. v. United States, 440 U.S. 472, 99 S.Ct. 1304, 59 L.Ed.2d 519 (1979), **726**
National Water Well Ass'n, Inc. v. Commissioner, 92 T.C. No. 7, 92 T.C. 75 (U.S.Tax Ct.1989), 468
New Life Baptist Church Academy v. East Longmeadow, 885 F.2d 940 (1st Cir.1989), **564**
New York State Club Ass'n, Inc. v. City of New York, 487 U.S. 1, 108 S.Ct. 2225, 101 L.Ed.2d 1 (1988), **689**
Niemann v. Vaughn Community Church, 154 Wash.2d 365, 113 P.3d 463 (Wash.2005), **422**
Northeast Harbor Golf Club, Inc. v. Harris, 725 A.2d 1018 (Me.1999), **109**

Oregon State University Alumni Ass'n, Inc. v. Commissioner, T.C. Memo. 1996-34 (U.S.Tax Ct.1996), 468

Panter v. Marshall Field & Co., 646 F.2d 271 (7th Cir.1981), 105
People ex rel. v. _____ (see opposing party and relator)
People's Educational Camp Soc. Inc. v. Commissioner, 331 F.2d 923 (2nd Cir. 1964), **204**
Pierce v. Society of the Sisters of the Holy Names of Jesus and Mary, 268 U.S. 510, 45 S.Ct. 571, 69 L.Ed. 1070 (1925), **561**
Plumstead Theatre Soc., Inc. v. Commissioner, 675 F.2d 244 (9th Cir.1982), **244**
Portland Golf Club v. Commissioner, 497 U.S. 154, 110 S.Ct. 2780, 111 L.Ed.2d 126 (1990), **707**
Presbyterian Church in United States v. Hull Memorial Presbyterian Church, 393 U.S. 440, 89 S.Ct. 601, 21 L.Ed.2d 658 (1969), **529**
Professional Ins. Agents of Michigan v. Commissioner, 726 F.2d 1097 (6th Cir. 1984), **434**

Queen of Angels Hospital v. Younger, 66 Cal.App.3d 359, 136 Cal.Rptr. 36 (Cal.App. 2 Dist.1977), **673**

Raulston v. Everett, 561 S.W.2d 635 (Tex.Civ.App.-Texarkana 1978), **82**

Redlands Surgical Services v. Commissioner, 113 T.C. No. 3, 113 T.C. 47 (U.S.Tax Ct.1999), **643,** 654

Regan v. Taxation With Representation of Washington, 461 U.S. 540, 103 S.Ct. 1997, 76 L.Ed.2d 129 (1983), **200**

Reis, Estate of, 87 T.C. No. 64, 87 T.C. 1016 (U.S.Tax Ct.1986), **155, 316**

Riley v. National Federation of the Blind of North Carolina, Inc., 487 U.S. 781, 108 S.Ct. 2667, 101 L.Ed.2d 669 (1988), **347**

Roche's Beach v. Commissioner, 96 F.2d 776 (2nd Cir.1938), 430

Rowland v. Union Hills Country Club, 157 Ariz. 301, 757 P.2d 105 (Ariz.App. Div. 2 1988), **87**

Rumsfeld v. Forum for Academic and Institutional Rights, Inc., ___ U.S. ___, 126 S.Ct. 1297, 164 L.Ed.2d 156 (2006), **612**

Russell v. Yale University, 54 Conn.App. 573, 737 A.2d 941 (Conn.App.1999), **148**

Samuel Friedland Foundation v. United States, 144 F.Supp. 74 (D.N.J.1956), 178

Sand Springs Home v. Commissioner, 6 B.T.A. 198 (B.T.A.1927), 430

Scott, People ex rel. v. George F. Harding Museum, 58 Ill.App.3d 408, 15 Ill.Dec. 973, 374 N.E.2d 756 (Ill.App. 1 Dist.1978), **36**

Scripture Press Foundation v. United States, 152 Ct.Cl. 463, 285 F.2d 800 (Ct.Cl.1961), 430

Seasongood v. Commissioner, 227 F.2d 907 (6th Cir.1955), 278

Serbian Eastern Orthodox Diocese for United States of America and Canada v. Milivojevich, 426 U.S. 696, 96 S.Ct. 2372, 49 L.Ed.2d 151 (1976), **514**

Sharpless v. Religious Soc. of Friends, 228 N.J.Super. 68, 548 A.2d 1157 (N.J.Super.A.D.1988), **122**

Sherwin–Williams Co. v. United States, 403 F.3d 793 (6th Cir.2005), 429

Sierra Club Inc. v. Commissioner, 86 F.3d 1526 (9th Cir.1996), 467

Sierra Club, Inc. v. Commissioner (Sierra Club II), 103 T.C. No. 17, 103 T.C. 307 (U.S.Tax Ct.1994), **468**

Sierra Club, Inc. v. Commissioner (Sierra Club I), T.C. Memo. 1993-199 (U.S.Tax Ct.1993), 468

Slee v. Commissioner, 42 F.2d 184 (2nd Cir.1930), **6**

Smith v. Calvary Christian Church, 462 Mich. 679, 614 N.W.2d 590 (Mich.2000), **522**

Solomon v. Hall–Brooke Foundation, Inc., 30 Conn.App. 129, 619 A.2d 863 (Conn.App.1993), **69**

State ex rel. v. _____ (see opposing party and relator)

St. David's Health Care System v. United States, 349 F.3d 232 (5th Cir.2003), 653

Stern, In re Estate of, 240 Ill.App.3d 834, 181 Ill.Dec. 461, 608 N.E.2d 534 (Ill. App. 1 Dist.1992), **126**

Stern v. Lucy Webb Hayes Nat. Training School for Deaconesses and Missionaries, 381 F.Supp. 1003 (D.D.C. 1974), **94**

Strayhorn v. Ethical Soc. of Austin, 110 S.W.3d 458 (Tex.App.-Austin 2003), **505**

Tax Analysts v. I.R.S., 410 F.3d 715, 366 U.S.App.D.C. 208 (D.C.Cir.2005), 557

Tinker v. Des Moines Independent Community School Dist., 393 U.S. 503, 89 S.Ct. 733, 21 L.Ed.2d 731 (1969), 612

Tressler v. Commissioner, 206 F.2d 538 (4th Cir.1953), 53

Trinidad v. Sagrada Orden de Predicadores, etc., 263 U.S. 578, 44 S.Ct. 204, 68 L.Ed. 458 (1924), 430

Trustees of Dartmouth College v. Woodward, 17 U.S. 518, 4 L.Ed. 629 (1819), 61

Trustees of Prince Condominium Trust v. Prosser, 412 Mass. 723, 592 N.E.2d 1301 (Mass.1992), **790**

United Cancer Council, Inc. v. Commissioner, 165 F.3d 1173 (7th Cir. 1999), **255, 363**

United States v. _____ (see opposing party)

Universal Life Church, Inc. v. United States, 13 Cl.Ct. 567 (Cl.Ct.1987), 182

University Hill Foundation v. Commissioner, 446 F.2d 701 (9th Cir.1971), 486

University Hill Foundation v. Commissioner, 51 T.C. 548 (Tax Ct.1969), **474**

Utah County v. Intermountain Health Care, Inc., 709 P.2d 265 (Utah 1985), **660**

Valencia v. Mississippi Baptist Medical Center, Inc., 363 F.Supp.2d 867 (S.D.Miss. 2005), 672

Virginia, Commonwealth of v. JOCO Foundation, 263 Va. 151, 558 S.E.2d 280 (Va.2002), **39**

Virginia Educ. Fund v. Commissioner, 85 T.C. No. 44, 85 T.C. 743 (U.S.Tax Ct.1985), 280

Waco Lodge No. 166, Benev. & Protective Order of Elks v. Commissioner, T.C. Memo. 1981-546 (U.S.Tax Ct.1981), 465

Wood v. Benedictine Soc. of Alabama, Inc., 530 So.2d 801 (Ala.1988), **541**

Younger v. Wisdom Society, 121 Cal. App.3d 683, 175 Cal.Rptr. 542 (Cal.App. 2 Dist.1981), **32**

Zelman v. Simmons–Harris, 536 U.S. 639, 122 S.Ct. 2460, 153 L.Ed.2d 604 (2002), **575**

Zemurray Foundation v. United States, 687 F.2d 97 (5th Cir.1982), **306**

Zeta Beta Tau Fraternity, Inc. v. Commissioner, 87 T.C. No. 23, 87 T.C. 421 (U.S.Tax Ct.1986), **717**

NONPROFIT ORGANIZATIONS LAW AND POLICY

Second Edition

Chapter 1

OVERVIEW OF THE NONPROFIT SECTOR

I. NATURE OF A NONPROFIT ORGANIZATION

The role of the third sector in society, even the concept of the nonprofit organization, is somewhat unclear. Although one expert on nonprofit law calculated some years ago that almost half of the organizations and enterprises in the United States at that time were nonprofit in nature,[1] there remains a misconception of the nonprofit sector. The types and forms of nonprofit enterprises are varied, and they serve many and diverse purposes in a community. Some are formed to further the general welfare of members of a community. Some are organized for specific charitable purposes—whether educational, religious, artistic, literary, or scientific.[2] Some are formed to benefit their members exclusively. The charitable organization, funded for the most part through donations, is the type of organization the public generally associates with nonprofit status. There are, however, many nonprofit organizations that are not charitable organizations. Political organizations, professional and trade organizations, social clubs, homeowners' associations, and employee organizations are a few examples. There are numerous nonprofit organizations of a commercial nature that derive most of their funds from profits generated by operations. Hospitals, day care centers, retirement villages, country clubs, and farmers' cooperatives are examples of profit-making entities often established as nonprofit corporations. Some nonprofit organizations have been identified as nongovernmental organi-

---

1. See Howard Oleck, Nature of Nonprofit Organizations, 10 U. Tol. L. Rev. 962 (1979). In 2002 Statistics of Income, the Internal Revenue Service reported that assets of charitable organizations rose, from $423 billion in 1985 to $1.733 trillion in 2002. The five percent of organizations with assets of $10 million or more held 89% of these assets. See data at www.irs.gov/taxstats.

Lester M. Salamon reported that there were 1.6 million identifiable nonprofit organizations in 1995 with revenues as of 1996 of $670 billion. See Lester M. Salamon, "Scope and Structure: The Anatomy of America's Nonprofit Sector," in The Nature of the Nonprofit Sector, J. Steven Ott, ed., Westview Press, 2001, p. 23.

2. These organizations seek tax exempt status as § 501(c)(3) organizations. Discussion in Chapters 4, 6, and 7.

zations (NGOs) and serve a global purpose to address issues of human rights and social justice around the world.

Unfortunately, the law relating to nonprofit organizations is fragmented and to some extent uncertain. Some states have separated the diverse nonprofit organizations into different categories in order to address legal issues related to, and to regulate more effectively, the dissimilar types of organizations. Nonprofit corporations have been classified as public benefit corporations (those benefitting the public, such as charitable organizations) and mutual benefit corporations (those benefitting their members, such as social clubs).[3] The two other general categories are the donative nonprofits, those that obtain their funding from sources other than revenues, generally from donations, and the commercial nonprofits, those that obtain most of their financial resources from the selling of merchandise or from the rendering of services.

A nonprofit organization, whether incorporated or operated as a trust or as an association, is defined as an organization in which no part of the income can be distributed to members, directors, or officers. Nonprofit organizations are not prohibited from making a profit. The prohibition is against the distribution of any profits to members, officers, or directors of the organization, or to other private individuals or entities.[4]

Note

Nonprofit organizations generally seek tax exempt status. In this context, nonprofit organizations are subsidized by the government. Further, those nonprofits that qualify as charitable organizations under § 501(c)(3) of the Internal Revenue Code, as nonprofit cemetery organizations under § 501(c)(13) of the Code, or as war veteran's organizations under § 501(c)(19), provide their donors with charitable contribution deductions for their donations.(See discussion of provisions in the Internal Revenue Code, which characterize the tax exempt status for the many and varied nonprofit organizations, in Chapter 5.) It can be stated that these nonprofits have a double governmental subsidy. Governmental subsidy of the nonprofit sector via tax benefits has been justified on the theory that nonprofit organizations provide benefits to society the government otherwise would be

---

3. See, e. g., Cal. Corp. Code §§ 5110, 7110, and 9110. California has separate provisions for "public benefit" corporations, "mutual benefit" corporations, and religious corporations. A public benefit corporation may be formed in California for any public or charitable purpose whereas a mutual benefit corporation may be formed for any lawful purpose. Both types have authority to issue memberships and to levy dues, assessments, and admission fees.

The Model Nonprofit Corporation Act of 1987 recognizes the two categories of nonprofit corporations, the public benefit and the mutual benefit corporation. Under the Act, all § 501(c)(3) organizations (charitable nonprofits) must be public benefit corporations. Mutual benefit corporations are those organized for the mutual benefit of their members and may make distributions to members upon dissolution. See Mod. Nonprofit Corp. Act §§ 1.40(23), 14.06(a)(7), 17.07.

4. Model Nonprofit Corporation Act §§ 2(c) and 26 (1964).

required to furnish. Supposedly, the nonprofit organization, particularly a "charitable" entity, "lessens the burdens of government."5

Questions

1. What is a "nonprofit" purpose? Would the following organizations have a nonprofit purpose: the State Rifle Association, an Abortion Rights State Organization, the National Atheist Foundation, the Center to Advance Rights of Aryan Persons, and the Holy Land Freedom Foundation (which funnels donations to terrorist groups in the Middle East)?

In *Holy Land Foundation for Relief and Development v. Ashcroft*, 333 F.3d 156 (D.C.Cir.2003), cert. denied, 540 U.S. 1218, 124 S.Ct. 1506, 158 L.Ed.2d 153 (2004), the D.C. Court of Appeals ruled that the Office of Foreign Asset Control did not act arbitrarily and capriciously in designating a Muslim charitable foundation as a terrorist organization and blocking its assets.

2. Section 501(p), which was added to the Internal Revenue Code in 2003, provides for the suspension of the tax exempt status of any organization that is designated or otherwise identified as a terrorist organization or a foreign terrorist organization. In Announcement 2003–74, 2003–2 C.B. 1171, the Service announced it was suspending, pursuant to § 501(p), the tax exemption of certain organizations that have been designated as supporting or engaging in terrorist activities or supporting terrorism.

3. What is a "charity?" Would any of the organizations listed in question 1 qualify as a "charitable" organization?

4. Should there be restrictions on the ability of individuals and groups to establish nonprofit organizations?

5. Who decides whether an organization has an "acceptable" nonprofit purpose? Should a governmental official be given discretion to deny an application for incorporation of a nonprofit corporation if the official takes issue with the stated purpose of the organization?

Consider these issues in the following case.

ASSOCIATION FOR PRESERVATION OF FREEDOM OF CHOICE v. SHAPIRO

Court of Appeals, New York, 1961
9 N.Y.2d 376, 214 N.Y.S.2d 388, 174 N.E.2d 487

* * *

FOSTER, Judge.

* * *

---

5. Treas. Reg. § 1.501(c)(3)–1(d)(2). The Regulation identifies a charitable organization as one whose purposes include: relief of the poor and distressed or of the underprivileged; advancement of religion; advancement of education or science; erection or maintenance of public buildings, monuments, or works; lessening of the burdens of government; promotion of social welfare; lessening of neighborhood tensions; elimination of prejudice and discrimination; defending human and civil rights secured by law; and combating community deterioration and juvenile delinquency.

The proposed certificate of incorporation, as presented for the approval of a Justice of the Supreme Court, listed the following charter purposes:

'(a) to promote the right to individual freedom of choice and association, constituting the right of the individual to associate with only those persons with whom he desires to associate;

'(b) to conduct itself, and to encourage, promote, and aid in scientific research into problems engendered by a multicultural society, into problems of intergroup relations, in areas of ethnic characteristics and patterns, and into the implications and effects of such problems on freedom of choice and association, and to publish and to encourage, promote, aid and assist in publication of the results of such research in suitable scholarly periodicals and other publications;

'(c) to assist in the elimination of barriers to individual freedom of choice and its exercise in specific instances, as well as preventing and guarding against deprivation of this right at large; and

'(d) to find and promote the means through freedom of choice and association by which the numerous groups in our multicultural society can find their fullest development.'

* * *

Approval was denied. * * *

* * *

We agree with the courts below that the purposes expressed in the proffered certificate of incorporation are not unlawful, and hence we can find no legal basis for its rejection. The reasons assigned by the courts below are, in our opinion, untenable. It is perfectly lawful for an individual or group of individuals to agitate for the repeal or modification of any law on the statute books of the State; or even for a change in the form of the State government itself, provided such agitation is not coupled with the advocacy of force and violence. Such activity is not against public policy whether indulged in by an individual or a membership corporation, but of course approval of a corporate charter devoted to such a purpose does not imply approval of the views of its sponsors. It simply means that their expression is lawful, and their sponsors entitled to a vehicle for such expression under a statute which cannot constitutionally be made available only to those who are in harmony with the majority viewpoint. Dissenting organizations have equal rights, so far as freedom of expression is concerned, as any other groups, and are entitled to an equal and objective application of the statute.

BURKE, Judge (dissenting).

I dissent and vote to affirm. * * *

That which is sought here is not solely permission to accomplish a simple act of business, to organize for political purposes and exercise freedom of speech, but rather to obtain 'the imprimatur of incorporation', bearing the blessing of the Supreme Court, the benediction of the Secretary of State, and the right to affix the characterization 'Incorporated under the Laws of the State of New York' to public matter so as to enable the organizers to assure themselves the prestige which accompanies the privilege.* * *

* * *

The use of the word 'lawful', as describing the purposes for which a membership corporation may be formed (Membership Corporations Law, s 10), does not restrict the Justice of the Supreme Court merely to the performance of a ministerial act, but rather requires the exercise of a judicial function. 'That is LAWFUL which is in conformity with the principle or spirit of the law, whether moral or juridical; that is LEGAL which is in conformity with the letter or rules of law as it is administered in the courts' (Webster's New International Dictionary (2d ed., Unabridged), p. 1401; * * *. A 'lawful purpose' hence must be in conformity not only with the letter but also the spirit of the law. To be 'lawful' then, the purposes of a proposed incorporation, although legal, must also be in harmony with an explicitly defined public policy of a State.

The purposes of the applicant are in conflict with a well-known and recognized public policy of the State of New York, which finds expression in numerous statutes. Consequently the denial of this application by the courts below does not rest on an unconstitutionally vague notion of 'what is wholesome public policy' or on any other vague personal philosophy, but on a definite standard of conduct mandated by the Legislature in various statutes. (Section 290 of the Executive Law, Consol. Laws, c. 18, states: '(T)he legislature hereby finds and declares that practices of discrimination against any of its inhabitants because of race, creed, color or national origin are a matter of state concern, that such discrimination threatens not only the rights and proper privileges of its inhabitants but menaces the institutions and foundation of a free democratic state.') Incorporation, moreover, is a privilege which may be withheld.* * *

Each of the individual members of this proposed corporation has all of those rights of freedom of speech and association as may be guaranteed by either the State or Federal Constitution. Special Term did not prohibit or limit them in any such protected activity. They may continue, as they have undoubtedly done, to gather together and exercise their rights in all permissible forms. But the 'constitutionally protected right of association' is not tantamount to a right of incorporation* * *

Although we respect the right of petitioners to share a belief that the exercise of freedom of choice is one of the constitutionally protected, inalienable rights referred to in the Declaration of Independence, we may give effect not only to our State public policy but also to the decisions of the United States Supreme Court, all of which are to the contrary.* * *

Note

Two experts on the nonprofit sector concluded that freedom of association is "the foundation for voluntary organizations and citizen participation." See Virginia Hodgkinson and Russy Sumariwalla, "The Nonprofit Section and the New Global Community: Issues and Challenges," in *The Nonprofit Sector in the Global Community*, Kathleen D. McCarthy, Viginia A. Hodgkinson, Russy D. Smuariwalla, eds., Jossey–Bass Publishers, San Francisco, 1992, p. 494. They concluded that this "freedom must be guaranteed under law and protected as a fundamental right." Id.

Dictatorial systems, both past and current, have viewed a freedom of association as being "dangerous." The 1791 Law of Chapelier in France is an example along with the Italian code adopted by Italy's fascist dictatorship in 1942. Article 18 of the present Italian Constitution now guarantees a freedom of association for its citizens so long as they are not organized for a purpose that is prohibited by penal laws or have not created a secret association or a military organization that pursues a political end.

Questions

1. Should individuals have a protected "right of association" through a vehicle in the form of a nonprofit corporation? Does the "right of association" necessarily implicate a "right to discriminate" that too can be "dangerous?" The "right of association" is discussed in Chapter 13.

2. Should a nonprofit organization be denied tax exempt status on the basis of public policy? See *Church of Scientology of California v. Commissioner*, 823 F.2d 1310 (9th Cir.1987), cert. den., 486 U.S. 1015, 108 S.Ct. 1752, 100 L.Ed.2d 214 (1988), discussed in chapter 5, and *Bob Jones University v. Simon*, 416 U.S. 725, 94 S.Ct. 2038, 40 L.Ed.2d 496 (1974), discussed in Chapters 5 and 11.

3. Is the involvement of a "charitable" organization in political activities antithetical to an organization's charitable purpose? Consider the following case.

SLEE v. COMMISSIONER

United States Court of Appeals, Second Circuit, 1930
42 F.2d 184

L. HAND, Circuit Judge.

During each of the years in question Slee, the petitioner, made gifts to the American Birth Control League, which he deducted from his income. The Commissioner, and later the Board, disallowed these, and the only question is whether section 214(a)(11)(B) of the Internal Revenue Act of 1921 (42 Stat. 227), and section 214(a)(10) of the Revenue Acts of 1924 and 1926 (26 USCA § 955(a)(10), include the League. Those sections allow the deduction of gifts made to 'any corporation * * * organized and operated exclusively for religious, charitable, scientific, literary or educational purposes, including posts of the American Legion or * * * for the prevention of cruelty to children or animals.' The question is whether the League is organized for charitable, scientific or educational purposes and, if so, whether those are its exclusive purposes.

It at first was an unincorporated association, but secured incorporation in New York in September, 1922, and its declared objects were as follows: 'To collect, correlate, distribute and disseminate lawful information regarding the political, social and economic facts of uncontrolled procreation. To enlist the support and co-operation of legal advisors, statesmen and legislators in effecting the lawful repeal and amendment of state and federal statutes which deal with the prevention of conception.' To publish a magazine 'in which shall be contained reports and studies of the relationship of controlled and uncontrolled procreation to national and world problems.' In operation it has gone somewhat further than these projects. It maintains a 'research department' in New York in charge of a physician, a medical, and a clinical, director. Married women come to the clinic for advice, are examined, and if in the judgment of the physician their health demands but not otherwise, are told how to prevent conception. Unmarried women are not received. The officials keep elaborate records of the work, follow up the cases, and publish the results at large to the medical profession. At times patients are charged for the service, but the work as a whole goes on at a loss and has to be supported by gifts. The only part of its activities which can be thought to touch upon legislation is in directing persons how best to prepare proposals for changes in the law, and in distributing leaflets to legislators and others recommending such changes, chiefly by bringing before them such information as is supposed to 'enlighten' their minds. These suggest and advocate a relaxation in existing restraints.

That the League is organized for charitable purposes seems to us clear and the Board did not find otherwise. A free clinic, or one where only those pay who can, is a part of nearly every hospital, a recognized form of charitable venture. We can see no difference that this is confined to married women who ought not bear children both for their own, and the children's, sake. Health is as much at stake as though it attempted the general prevention of sickness. Nor does it matter that there are many who think the cure worse than the disease; there are people who object to venereal prophylaxis. It is enough that the object was to maintain health without profit by lawful means; that has been a recognized kind of charity from time immemorial. The collection and publication of the information so obtained was also a legitimate scientific enterprise, like any collection of medical data. We cannot discriminate unless we doubt the good faith of the enterprise.

* * *

So far as the society at bar sought to relieve itself of the restraints of law in order the better to conduct its charity, we might indeed hold that it fell within the class of which we have just given some instances. So far, however, as its political activities were general, it seems to us, regardless of how much we might be in sympathy with them, that its purposes cannot be said to be 'exclusively' charitable, educational or scientific. It may indeed be for the best interests of any community voluntarily to control the procreation of children, but the question before us is whether the statute covers efforts to proselytize in that or other causes. Of the purposes it defines 'educational' comes the closest, and when people organize to secure the more general acceptance of beliefs which they think beneficial to the community at large, it is common enough to say that the public must be 'educated' to their views. In a sense that is indeed true, but it would be a perversion to stretch the meaning of the statute to such cases; they are indistinguishable from societies to promote or defeat prohibition, to adhere to the League of Nations, to increase the Navy, or any other of the many causes in which ardent persons engage.

Our review is limited to the correction of obvious errors; we cannot say that the Board committed any here.

Decision affirmed.

Questions

1. A § 501(c)(3) organization may not participate or intervene in any political campaign on behalf of or in opposition to any candidate for public office. See I.R.C. § 501(c)(3) and discussion in Chapters 5 and 15. Is the prohibition against a charitable organization's involvement in political campaigns a violation of the members' First Amendment rights? See *Branch Ministries v. Rossotti*, 211 F.3d 137 (D.C.Cir.2000), discussed in Chapter 10.

2. Should an employee of the Internal Revenue Service on her own volition be permitted to deny § 501(c)(3) status to a nonprofit organization? May a taxpayer challenge a decision of the IRS either to grant or to deny tax exempt status to a nonprofit organization? Consider the following case.

HARING v. BLUMENTHAL

United States District Court, District of Columbia, 1979
471 F.Supp. 1172

HAROLD H. GREENE, District Judge.

In this action plaintiff requests relief from alleged religious discrimination in violation of Title VII of the Civil Rights Act of 1964, and an injunction to restrain defendant from classifying "abortion clinics and other organizations promoting abortion and homosexuality as tax exempt organizations."

Plaintiff is an employee of the Internal Revenue Service.* * * He applied for promotion to Tax Law Specialist,* * * but was turned down, allegedly on account of his Catholic religious belief and conduct. The government contends that there also were other reasons for plaintiff's failure to achieve promotion, but for purposes of the present motion it concedes that plaintiff was not promoted solely because of his inability or unwillingness to abide by Internal Revenue Service policies on abortion. After receiving the agency's final decision on December 19, 1977, plaintiff filed the instant action which, as indicated, challenges the tax-exempt status of various organizations and alleges violations of his rights under Title VII.* * *

I

Under section 501(a) of the Internal Revenue Code, 26 U.S.C. § 501(a), organizations more specifically designated in sections 501(c)(3) and (c)(4) as being organized for religious, charitable, educational, or social welfare purposes, are exempt from income taxation. Within the framework of these statutory provisions, the Internal Revenue Service has granted tax-exempt status to abortion clinics and to various organizations involved with homosexual rights, and additional Revenue Rulings dealing with abortion clinics may be issued at future dates. One portion of plaintiff's suit challenges these present and expected rulings, and defendant has moved to dismiss that part of the complaint on several grounds, principally plaintiff's alleged lack of standing to bring the action.

The requirement in the law that only a person with "standing" may pursue a lawsuit in the courts stems from the requirement in Article III of the Constitution that the federal courts may hear and decide only actual "cases" and "controversies." Flast v. Cohen, 392 U.S. 83, 95, 88 S.Ct. 1942, 20 L.Ed.2d 947 (1968). While the issue of standing has been much mooted and has witnessed several shifts in perspective, it is now clear that the "gist of the question of standing" is whether the party seeking relief has "alleged such a personal stake in the outcome of the controversy as to assure that concrete adverseness which sharpens the presentation of issues upon which the court so largely depends for illumination of difficult constitutional questions." * * * Baker v. Carr, 369 U.S. 186, 204, 82 S.Ct. 691, 703, 7 L.Ed.2d 663 (1962). If a plaintiff is unable to make such an allegation, he lacks standing; the case then is deemed not to involve an actual controversy but to call merely for an advisory opinion; and the court lacks jurisdiction. Simon v. Eastern Kentucky Welfare Rights Organization, 426 U.S. 26, 37 note 15, 96 S.Ct. 1917, 48 L.Ed.2d 450 (1976); Sierra Club v. Morton, 405 U.S. 727, 92 S.Ct. 1361, 31 L.Ed.2d 636 (1972). The government asserts that this is precisely the situation here.

Plaintiff in this case concedes, as he must, that he does not have standing to challenge the exemption rulings at issue here merely because he is a citizen or taxpayer * * * and claims instead to find a basis for his ability to bring this lawsuit in his employment status.

In order to achieve standing in his capacity as an employee of the Internal Revenue Service, plaintiff must be able to allege that the challenged actions of that Service are causing him an "injury in fact" and that his interests are arguably within "the zone of interests to be protected or regulated by the statute or constitutional guarantee in question." * * * In the view of this Court, he cannot satisfy either test.

Plaintiff claims that he is suffering an injury in fact in that, but for the existence of IRS tax policies which exempt abortion clinics from taxation, he would not be subjected to the alleged discrimination with respect to promotions which stems from his objection to these exemptions. However, there clearly is an insufficient nexus between the exemption rulings plaintiff complains about and the alleged harm to his beliefs and practices to satisfy the injury in fact standard. It is the action of the promotion panel, not the exemption rulings of IRS, which is the direct cause of the injury to plaintiff; he is able to challenge that action in a Title VII suit; he has in fact done so; and under the law his action pursuant to that statute constitutes his exclusive remedy for discrimination in employment. * * *

Plaintiff's allegation of injury in fact is thus on its face insufficient, for there would still be no cognizable injury even if the allegation were proved. Indeed, if the requisite nexus were found to exist here, every employee of every governmental organization would automatically be deemed to have standing to challenge any action of government, or at least any action of the department or agency which employs him, for he could acquire such standing by the simple device of refusing to implement the particular governmental policy and await the inevitable adverse personnel action. Were the Court to entertain such a doctrine, the consequence would be that only government employees, but not other citizens or taxpayers, would be able to challenge in court governmental action with which they disagree ... * * *

Plaintiff has also failed to show that his interest in reversing the exemption policies is arguably within the zone of interests protected by the First Amendment. The abortion clinics themselves obviously are not vested with the requisite governmental authority for a valid constitutional deprivation claim, nor do they in any way impede or interfere with plaintiff's freedom of speech or religion. Insofar as the grant of tax exemptions for such clinics are concerned, while they of course constitute governmental action, it is action which does not violate the Constitution.

Tax exemptions for religious organizations in general have long been held not to constitute an impermissible government sponsorship of religion. * * * More specifically, the grant of an exemption from taxation which is otherwise appropriate, e. g. to providers of health care, does not impermissibly infringe upon the Establishment Clause of the First Amendment merely because abortions are or are not performed by the particular health care organization. * * * Such exemptions do not foster an excessive governmental entanglement with religion, inhibit the free exercise of religion, or fail to reflect a secular purpose. * * * Different religions take different views on abortion (Roe v. Wade, 410 U.S. 113, 160–61, 93 S.Ct. 705, 35 L.Ed.2d 147 (1973)) and the Constitution neither requires nor prohibits governmental funding of abortions. Maher v. Roe, 432 U.S. 464, 480, 97 S.Ct. 2376, 53 L.Ed.2d 484 (1977). For these reasons, plaintiff's claimed interest cannot be regarded as being within the zone of interests protected by the First Amendment.

* * *

For these reasons, defendant's motion to dismiss the claim which challenges the validity of tax exemptions to abortion clinics and other organizations will be granted.

II

Plaintiff's second claim is that he was denied a promotion to the position of a reviewer position in IRS's Exempt Organizations Branch in violation of the Constitution of the United States and of Title VII of the Civil Rights Act of 1964, as amended, 42 U.S.C. § 2000e–2(a)(1). In support of this claim, plaintiff argues, first, that the grant of tax exemptions to groups favoring abortions is illegal and that for this reason he should not be denied promotion for failing to implement the policy which establishes such grants, and second, that to deny him a promotion solely because of his unwillingness to process tax exemption applications for purposes which he regards as repugnant to his religious principles violates his rights under Title VII. The first of these contentions has little merit; the second presents a far more substantial question.

III

In order to prevail on his "illegality" argument, plaintiff must demonstrate, first, that the legality of the decisions of the Internal Revenue Service to grant tax exemption to abortion clinics and to organizations advocating free choice with respect to abortions may be determined by an employee of IRS, that is, by his refusal to implement them; and second, if the answer to the first question is in the affirmative, that the IRS decisions in fact violate the Constitution or laws of the United States. He has failed in both respects. As has been noted, plaintiff lacks standing to contest the validity of IRS rulings. Unless and until the Congress, or a court of competent jurisdiction in an action by an individual with the requisite standing to sue, determines that a particular tax exemption ruling is invalid, the employees of the Service, as long as they wish to remain in that status, are obliged to implement that ruling. Not merely the concept of a uniform tax policy but the effectiveness of the government of the United States as a functioning entity would be in jeopardy if each employee could take it upon himself to decide which particular laws, regulations, and policies are legal or illegal, and to base his official actions upon that private determination.

* * *

Section 703(a)(1) of the Civil Rights Act, 42 U.S.C. § 2000e–2(a)(1), 42 U.S.C. § 2000e(j) (1970 ed., Supp. V), provides that it "shall be an unlawful employment practice for an employer ... to discriminate against any individual with respect to his compensation, terms, conditions, or privileges of employment, because of such individual's race, color, religion, sex, or national origin." In its 1972 amendments to the Act, Congress added the following definition. The term 'religion' includes all aspects of religious observance and practice, as well as belief, unless an employer demonstrates that he is unable to reasonably accommodate to an employee's or prospective employee's religious observance or practice without undue hardship on the conduct of the employer's business.

On this motion for partial summary judgment, plaintiff claims that the Internal Revenue Service is able without undue hardship to accommodate its operations to his practices, while the government argues that, for a variety of reasons it cannot do so.

First. The Internal Revenue Service contends that plaintiff's refusal to handle applications for exemptions from persons or groups which advocate abortion or other practices to which he objects creates problems with the efficient and expeditious operations of the office in which he works.

As indicated, plaintiff seeks promotion to the position of reviewer in the Exempt Organizations Division. Such reviewers have considerable independent or quasi-judicial authority, for when a reviewer agrees with a tax law specialist recommendation to grant tax exempt status to an organization, he is authorized to issue a final favorable ruling. Additionally, reviewers have administrative authority for they supervise a number of other persons. Currently, two reviewers are assigned to each group of 8–12 tax law specialists, and sometimes a reviewer must also substitute as an acting supervisor, leaving only one active reviewer available for the group. The Service contends that because of these staffing patterns plaintiff's refusal to process applications he considers objectionable would make it difficult to operate the Exempt Organizations Division were he to be promoted to one of the reviewer positions.

Plaintiff's affidavit, which for present purposes must be assumed to be true, asserts that in his experience the types of cases with which he might have a moral or religious problem constitute only a minute percentage of the total volume of applications for exemption processed by a reviewer in the Exempt Organizations Division. He estimates that percentage to constitute "a fraction of 1% of the total cases or at most less than 2%." Assuming this volume of cases to be accurate, it appears that the Internal Revenue Service should have no difficulty, on a purely mechanical level, to accommodate itself to the overt manifestations of plaintiff's beliefs. The applications for exemption which plaintiff refuses to handle could clearly be processed without undue hardship or burden to the Service, or any significant expense or loss of time, by another reviewer. On this basis, therefore, defendant cannot meet the "undue hardship" test of section 703(a)(1).

Second. Defendant's next set of arguments may be grouped together for purpose of analysis, for all of them relate in one way or another to the Internal Revenue Service's fears that a precedent here would eventually come to complicate its operations to an unreasonable degree. Thus, it is claimed that, if this plaintiff were permitted to become a reviewer notwithstanding his refusal to handle certain types of cases, others will be encouraged to do likewise, and a point will soon be reached where the agency will be faced with very real and substantial practical problems. Alternatively, it is contended that plaintiff's own views appear to be subject to change and amplification; that he began by refusing to deal with abortion and homosexuality, an area which he has now expanded to encompass "any organization which violates or promotes and encourages violations of the Ten Commandments of God and violations of God's Natural Law." * * *

Finally, defendant suggests that, if plaintiff must be promoted to a reviewer position notwithstanding his announced policies, a precedent will be set for his promotion, or that of others like him, to higher and yet higher supervisory levels, where both from the point of view of administrative efficiency and of policy it will become less and less possible to avoid undue hardship to the Service. In short, defendant suggests, a line must be drawn at some time, and it might as well be here and now.

* * *

Under the Act, employers must make "reasonable accommodation" to the religious beliefs of their employees, a relative term which depends upon the facts and circumstances. * * * Unless the statutory mandate is to be rendered meaningless, it must be held to provide that until facts or circumstances arise from which it may be concluded that there can no longer be an accommodation without undue hardship, the employee's religious practices are required to be tolerated. This Court is not prepared to adopt a construction which would emasculate this law designed to protect religious liberty and the free exercise of religious practices and, to the extent that any of the decisions cited may be construed as calling for such an interpretation, I decline to follow them.

There is, moreover, no reason to believe either that this plaintiff's zone of objectionable policies will grow significantly or that his stand will have a mushroom effect on other IRS reviewers. Irrespective of how plaintiff's objections to IRS policies are phrased, it appears, on this record at least, that they will still constitute only a small segment of his workload. Most IRS exemption decisions, it may safely be assumed, are in the more pedestrian realms of the financial world, and even when they involve other public policy issues, they are not likely very often to touch upon plaintiff's category of objectionable policies, however much those policies may have been inflated most recently to give them their broadest and most diffuse expression. Further unlike, for example, the typical Saturday workday problem which has been before the courts in so many different guises, there is little real incentive for others to emulate this plaintiff. It is not probable that many employees will carry convictions of a sufficiently stubborn nature as would cause them to take the fairly extreme route this plaintiff has chosen. Unlike prohibitions on laboring during certain days of the week, the refusal to make decisions with respect to specific issues does not appear to be a widespread and deeply ingrained religious tenet.

In any event, however, if, contrary to the assumptions made by the Court, it subsequently develops either that plaintiff enlarges the zone of his objections to such an extent that it encompasses a significant part of his assigned workload, or that other IRS employees follow his example and refuse to handle a significant number of applications for tax exemptions on grounds of offensiveness to religious belief, then at some point the level of "undue hardship" provided for in the statute will have been reached, and defendant will then be free to take all appropriate and necessary action. Should such an eventuality develop, the employee or employees involved would not be protected by section 703(a)(1) of the Act from failures or refusals to hire, discharge, or take other action to protect the efficient conduct of the employer's business.

Third. The government raises a fundamental question of principle. It argues that what is at stake here is the integrity of the Internal Revenue Service and, indeed, of the Nation's uniform tax system itself. Citizens are entitled to have confidence in that Service and that system, and this confidence, so it is claimed, would be jeopardized if plaintiff's insistence on his interpretation of law and public policy were allowed to prevail. The Service also argues in this connection that different standards must be applied to judicial or quasi-judicial officers than to employees who carry out mere ministerial functions, and that any deviation by such an officer from duly promulgated law and policy must be regarded as per se inflicting an undue hardship on the government which employs him.

Those arguments would be extremely persuasive, even conclusive, if plaintiff were taking the position that he would deny tax exemptions to organizations to whose policies he objects. Indeed it may be that, at one time in the course of the administrative proceedings, he took that very position. But that is not the posture of this case now. Plaintiff does not assert that he will tailor his decisions to his beliefs but merely that, when there is a conflict between his beliefs and what the law would require him to decide, he will in effect disqualify himself and request that the matter be reassigned to another reviewer. It is difficult to see how that stand could impair taxpayer confidence in the tax system or the impartiality of the IRS. * * *

The government also suggests that it should not have to accommodate itself to the kind of internal dissent from its policies exemplified by plaintiff's refusal to process applications for tax exemption from abortion clinics. The short answer is that provided in the Civil Rights Act itself which directs that, absent undue hardship to its operations, the Internal Revenue Service, like any other covered employer, must accommodate itself to dissent based on religious belief.

* * *

Note

If an organization receives an adverse determination from the IRS as to the exempt status of the organization, or the failure to qualify as a § 501(c)(3) organization, it will be advised of its right to protest the determination by requesting the Appeals Office of the Service to consider the case. A protest must be submitted to the District Director within 30 days from the date of the adverse determination.[6] The Appeals Office must request technical advice from the IRS national Office in Washington, D.C. concerning qualifications for exemption if there is no published precedent or if there is reason to believe nonuniformity exists.[7] If an application is referred to the National Office, the organization is entitled to a conference with the National Office should it issue an adverse ruling.

In addition to administrative remedies, an organization may file a suit for declaratory judgment in the United States Tax Court, the United States Claims Court, or the United States district Court for the District of Columbia,[8] but only after all administrative remedies have been exhausted.[9]

Questions

1. The court in *Haring* pointed out that a person does not have standing to challenge tax exemption rulings merely because she is a citizen or taxpayer. How may a citizen challenge governmental subsidies of nonprofit organizations via tax exemptions? (See discussion of standing to sue in Chapter 3.)

2. Do advocacy groups serve a nonprofit purpose? Should they qualify for tax exempt status? If so, in what context?

Consider the issues in the following cases.

BIG MAMA RAG v. UNITED STATES
United States Court of Appeals, D.C. Circuit, 1980
631 F.2d 1030

* * *

MIKVA, Circuit Judge:

Plaintiff, Big Mama Rag, Inc. (BMR, Inc.), appeals from the order of the court below granting summary judgment to defendants and upholding the IRS's rejection of plaintiff's application for tax-exempt status. Specifically, BMR, Inc. questions the finding that it is not entitled to tax exemption as an educational or charitable organization under section 501(c)(3) of the Internal Revenue Code, 26 U.S.C. § 501(c)(3) (1976), and Treas.Reg. § 1.501(c)(3)–1(d) (2) & (3) (1959). Appellant also challenges the constitutionality of the regulatory scheme, arguing that it violates the First Amendment and the equal protection component of the Fifth Amendment and that it unconstitutionally conditions tax-exempt status on the waiver of constitutional rights.

---

6. Treas. Reg. § 601.201(n)(5)(i), (6)(ii)(b). See Rev. Proc. 90–27, 1990–1 C.B. 514, 517.

7. Id. See also Rev. Proc. 2003–8, 2003–1 I.R.B. 236.

8. I.R.C. § 7428.

9. An organization requesting the determination is deemed to have exhausted its administrative remedies if the IRS fails to make a determination as to its exempt status or if 270 days have expired after the day on which the organization made a request for such a determination. See IRC § 7428(b)(2). The organization must take all reasonable steps to secure such determination. If the IRS has mailed a notice of its final determination, a proceeding for a declaratory judgment must be initiated on or before 90 days after the date of such mailing. IRC § 7428(b)(3).

Because we find that the definition of "educational" contained in Treas. Reg. § 1.501(c)(3)–1(d)(3) is unconstitutionally vague in violation of the First Amendment, we reverse the order of the court below.

I. BACKGROUND

BMR, Inc. is a nonprofit organization with a feminist orientation. Its purpose is "to create a channel of communication for women that would educate and inform them on general issues of concern to them." To this end, it publishes a monthly newspaper, Big Mama Rag (BMR), which prints articles, editorials, calendars of events, and other information of interest to women. BMR, Inc.'s primary activity is the production of that newspaper, but it also devotes a considerable minority of its time to promoting women's rights through workshops, seminars, lectures, a weekly radio program, and a free library. BMR, Inc. has a predominantly volunteer staff and distributes free approximately 2100 of 2700 copies of Big Mama Rag's monthly issues. Moreover, the organization has severely limited the quantity and type of paid advertising. As the district court found, BMR, Inc. neither makes nor intends to make a profit and is dependent on contributions, grants, and funds raised by benefits for over fifty percent of its income. * * *

Because of its heavy reliance on charitable contributions, BMR, Inc. applied in 1974 for tax-exempt status as a charitable and educational institution. That request was first denied by the IRS District Director in Austin, Texas, on the ground that the organization's newspaper was indistinguishable from an "ordinary commercial publishing practice." After BMR, Inc. filed a protest and a hearing was held in the IRS National Office, the denial of tax-exempt status was affirmed on three separate grounds:

> 1. the commercial nature of the newspaper; 2. the political and legislative commentary found throughout; and 3. the articles, lectures, editorials, etc., promoting lesbianism.

II. THE REGULATORY SCHEME

Tax exemptions are granted under section 501(c) of the Internal Revenue Code to a variety of socially useful organizations, including the charitable and the educational. The Code forbids exemption of an organization if any part of its net earnings inures to the benefit of private persons or if it is an "action organization"—one that attempts to influence legislation or participates in any political campaign. Treasury regulations impose additional requirements: exempt status is accorded only to applicants whose articles of organization limit their activities to furtherance of exempt purposes (the "organizational test") or whose activities are in fact aimed at accomplishment of exempt purposes (the "operational test"). Treas.Reg. § 1.501(c)(3)–1(b) & (c) (1959).

The Treasury regulations also define some of the exempt purposes listed in section 501(c)(3) of the Code, including "charitable" and "educational." The definition of "educational" is the one at issue here: The term "educational," as used in section 501(c)(3), relates to—

>(a) The instruction or training of the individual for the purpose of improving or developing his capabilities; or

>(b) The instruction of the public on subjects useful to the individual and beneficial to the community.

An organization may be educational even though it advocates a particular position or viewpoint so long as it presents a sufficiently full and fair exposition of the pertinent facts as to permit an individual or the public to form an independent opinion or conclusion. On the other hand, an organization is not educational if its principal function is the mere presentation of unsupported opinion. Treas.Reg. § 1.501(c)(3)–1(d)(3)(i) (1959).

The district court found that BMR, Inc. was not entitled to tax-exempt status because it had "adopted a stance so doctrinaire" that it could not meet the "full and fair exposition" standard articulated in the definition quoted above. * * *

Even though tax exemptions are a matter of legislative grace, the denial of which is not usually considered to implicate constitutional values, tax law and constitutional law are not completely distinct entities. In fact, the First Amendment was partly aimed at the so-called "taxes on knowledge," which were intended to limit the circulation of newspapers and therefore the public's opportunity to acquire information about governmental affairs. * * * In light of their experience with such taxes, the framers realized, in the words of Mr. Justice Douglas, that "(t)he power to tax the exercise of a privilege is the power to control or suppress its enjoyment." Murdock v. Pennsylvania, 319 U.S. 105, 112, 63 S.Ct. 870, 874, 87 L.Ed. 1292 (1943). Thus, although First Amendment activities need not be subsidized by the state, the discriminatory denial of tax exemptions can impermissibly infringe free speech. * * * Similarly, regulations authorizing tax exemptions may not be so unclear as to afford latitude for subjective application by IRS officials. We find that the definition of "educational," and in particular its "full and fair exposition" requirement, is so vague as to violate the First Amendment and to defy our attempts to review its application in this case.

III. VAGUENESS ANALYSIS

Vague laws are not tolerated for a number of reasons, and the Supreme Court has fashioned the constitutional standards of specificity with these policies in mind.

* * *

We do not minimize the difficulty and delicacy of the task delegated to the Treasury by Congress under section 501(c)(3) of the Code. Words such as "religious," "charitable," "literary," and "educational" easily lend themselves to subjective definitions at odds with the constitutional limitations we describe above. Treasury bravely made a pass at defining "educational," but the more parameters it tried to set, the more problems it encountered.

The first portion of the regulation relied upon to deny BMR, Inc.'s request for tax-exempt status measures an applicant organization by whether it provides "instruction of the public on subjects useful to the individual and beneficial to the community." Treas.Reg. § 1.501(c)(3)-1(d)(3)(i)(b) (1959). The district court rejected that test with barely a murmur of disagreement from appellees. That standard, held the court below, "would be far too subjective in its application to pass constitutional muster." * * *

We find similar problems inherent in the "full and fair exposition" test, on which the district court based affirmance of the IRS's denial of tax-exempt status to BMR, Inc. That test lacks the requisite clarity, both in explaining which applicant organizations are subject to the standard and in articulating its substantive requirements.

A. Who is Covered by the "Full and Fair Exposition" Test?

According to the terms of the Treasury regulation, only an organization that "advocates a particular position or viewpoint" must clear the "full and fair exposition" hurdle. Appellant maintains that the definition of an advocacy organization is to be found in the preceding subsection of the regulation, which defines the term "charitable": The fact that an organization, in carrying out its primary purpose, advocates social or civic changes or presents opinion on controversial issues with the intention of molding public opinion or creating public sentiment to an acceptance of its views does not preclude such organization from qualifying under section 501(c)(3) so long as it is not an "action" organization of any one of the types described in paragraph (c)(3) of this section. Treas.Reg. § 1.501(c)(3)–1(d)(2) (1959). The district court held that this part of the regulation was designed to cover charitable institutions and that BMR, Inc., an educational rather than a charitable organization, must meet the "full and fair exposition" standard rather than the more lenient "action organization" standard of section 1.501(c)(3)–1(d)(2). Obviously, if BMR, Inc. is an advocacy group and is not a charitable organization, it may not take cover under the "action organization" standard but must instead meet the "full and fair exposition" test.

The initial question, however, is whether or not BMR, Inc. is an advocacy group at all. What appellant turns to Treas.Reg. § 1.501(c)(3)–1(d)(2) for is the definition of "advocacy," not for the appropriate standard to be applied to advocacy organizations seeking tax-exempt status. The district court did not deal with that question, and, indeed, it is difficult to ascertain from the language of the regulation defining "educational" exactly what organizations are intended to be covered by the "full and fair exposition" standard and whether or not the definitions of advocacy groups are the same for both educational and charitable organizations.

The uncertainty of the coverage of the "full and fair exposition" standard is evidenced by its application over the years by the IRS. The Treasury Department's Exempt Organizations Handbook has defined "advocates a particular position" as synonymous with "controversial." Such a gloss clearly cannot withstand First Amendment scrutiny. It gives IRS officials no objective standard by which to judge which applicant organizations are advocacy groups-the evaluation is made solely on the basis of one's subjective notion of what is "controversial." And, in fact, only a very few organizations, whose views are not in the mainstream of political thought, have been deemed advocates and held to the "full and fair exposition" standard. The one tax-exempt homosexual organization cited by the Government as evidence that the IRS does not discriminate on the basis of sexual preference was required to meet the "full and fair exposition" standard even though it admittedly did not "advocate or seek to convince individuals that they should or should not be homosexuals." Rev.Rul. 78–305, 1978–2 C.B. 172, 173.

The Treasury regulation defining "educational" is, therefore, unconstitutionally vague in that it does not clearly indicate which organizations are advocacy groups and thereby subject to the "full and fair exposition" standard. And the latitude for subjectivity afforded by the regulation has seemingly resulted in selective application of the "full and fair exposition" standard-one of the very evils that the vagueness doctrine is designed to prevent.

B. *What Does the "Full and Fair Exposition" Test Require?*

The Treasury definition of "educational" may also be challenged on the ground that it fails to articulate with sufficient specificity the requirements of the "full and fair exposition" standard. The language of the regulation gives no aid in interpreting the meaning of the test: An organization may be educational even though it advocates a particular position or viewpoint so long as it presents a sufficiently full and fair exposition of the pertinent facts as to permit an individual or the public to form an independent opinion or conclusion. On the other hand, an organization is not educational if its principal function is the mere presentation of unsupported opinion. Treas.Reg. § 1.501(c)(3)–1(d)(3) (1959). What makes an exposition "full and fair"? Can it be "fair" without being "full"? Which facts are "pertinent"? How does one tell whether an exposition of the pertinent facts is "sufficient ... to permit an individual or the public to form an independent opinion or conclusion"? And who is to make all of these determinations?

The regulation's vagueness is especially apparent in the last clause quoted above. That portion of the test is expressly based on an individualistic-and therefore necessarily varying and unascertainable-standard: the reactions of members of the public.

* * *

IV. CONCLUSION

The definition of "educational" contained in Treas.Reg. § 1.501(c)(3)–1(d)(3) lacks sufficient specificity to pass constitutional muster. Its "full and fair exposition" standard, on the basis of which the denial of BMR, Inc.'s application for tax exemption was upheld by the court below, is vague both in describing who is subject to that test and in articulating its substantive requirements. The history of appellant's application for tax-exempt status attests to the vagueness of the "full and fair exposition" test and evidences the evils that the vagueness doctrine is designed to avoid. The district court's decision was based on the value-laden conclusion that BMR was too doctrinaire. Similarly, IRS officials earlier advised appellant's counsel that an exemption could be approved only if the organization "agree(d) to abstain from advocating that homosexuality is a mere preference, orientation, or propensity on par with heterosexuality and which should otherwise be regarded as normal." Whether or not this view represented official IRS policy is irrelevant. It simply highlights the inherent susceptibility to discriminatory enforcement of vague statutory language.

* * *

We are not unmindful of the burden involved in reformulating the definition of "educational" to conform to First Amendment requirements. But the difficulty of the task neither lessens its importance nor warrants its avoidance. Objective standards are especially essential in cases such as this involving those espousing nonmajoritarian philosophies. In this area the First Amendment cannot countenance a subjective "I know it when I see it" standard. And neither can we.

Reversed and remanded.

NATIONAL ALLIANCE v. UNITED STATES
United States Court of Appeals, D. C. Circuit, 1983
710 F.2d 868

FAIRCHILD, Senior Circuit Judge:

On July 28, 1977, National Alliance applied to the IRS for a tax exemption as a charitable and educational institution under 26 U.S.C. § 501(c)(3). The IRS District Director in Arlington, Virginia denied the corporation's application on March 31, 1978, concluding that National Alliance was neither "charitable" nor "educational" as those terms are applied by Treas.Reg. § 1.501(c)(3)–(1)(d)(2) & (3).

National Alliance, a Virginia corporation, publishes a monthly newsletter and membership bulletin, organizes lectures and meetings, issues occasional leaflets, and distributes books; all for the stated purpose of arousing in white Americans of European ancestry "an understanding of and a pride in their racial and cultural heritage and an awareness of the present dangers to that heritage." The Treasury Regulation sometimes said to "define" the statutory term "educational" provides that:

"[a]n organization may be educational even though it advocates a particular position or viewpoint so long as it presents a sufficiently full and fair exposition of the pertinent facts as to permit an individual or the public to form an independent opinion or conclusion. On the other hand, an organization is not educational if its principal function is the presentation of unsupported opinion."

The District Director's proposed determination letter quoted extensively from National Alliance publications, and concluded they fell substantially short of satisfying this "full and fair exposition" standard.

National Alliance appealed the District Director's proposed determination letter arguing that the refusal to grant its application for tax-exempt status was based on the content of its publications in violation of the First Amendment. An Assistant Regional Commissioner denied the appeal on January 12, 1979. The IRS issued a final adverse determination letter on April 23, 1979. Having exhausted its available administrative remedies, National Alliance filed suit in federal district court for declaratory judgment pursuant to 26 U.S.C. § 7428.

The parties filed cross-motions for summary judgment.

This court had then recently decided Big Mama Rag, Inc. v. United States, 631 F.2d 1030 (D.C.Cir.1980). This court there reversed a judgment upholding a denial of tax exemption, and held the IRS regulation defining the term "educational" unconstitutionally vague. The regulation in effect at the time of the IRS National Alliance decision was the same regulation held unconstitutional in *Big Mama*. * * *

* * *

I.

In response to an IRS request, National Alliance supplemented its application for exemption with back copies of its monthly newsletter, *Attack!*, and its membership bulletin, *Action*. It is these materials the IRS found noneducational.

The nature of these publications may be summarized as follows. *Attack!* is the organization's principal publication; it contains stories, pictures, feature articles and editorials in a form resembling a newspaper. The general theme of the newsletter is that "non-whites"—principally blacks—are inferior to white Americans of European ancestry ("WAEA"), and are aggressively brutal and dangerous; Jews control the media and through that means—as well as through political and financial positions and other means—cause the policy of the United States to be harmful to the interests of WAEA. A subsidiary proposition is that communists have persuaded "neo-liberals" of equality among human beings, the desirability of racial integration, and the evil of discrimination on racial grounds.

In support of these themes, each newsletter contains one or two news stories reporting incidents of murder or other violence by black persons, and identifying as Jews persons holding important media or other positions. Reports of black violence are presented as brief factual accounts—though usually without reference to source—accompanied by assertions of a media coverup and the inborn savagery of blacks. Identifications as Jews of individuals holding significant positions are accompanied by assertions of resulting Jewish manipulation of American society. Other articles and editorials attribute political and social events deemed detrimental to WAEA to the integration of non-whites into society or to Jewish manipulation of society.

The organization's newsletter describes its themes of black savagery or Jewish manipulation as warnings to WAEA of the "dangers which arise from the presence of so many alien groups in our midst." * * * A National Alliance membership bulletin states that these perceived dangers can only be averted by the removal of non-whites and Jews from society.

In sum, National Alliance repetitively appeals for action, including violence, to put to disadvantage or to injure persons who are members of named racial, religious, or ethnic groups. It both asserts and implies that members of these groups have common characteristics which make them sufficiently dangerous to others to justify violent expulsion and separation.

Even under the most minimal requirement of a rational development of a point of view, National Alliance's materials fall short. The publications before us purport to state demonstrable facts—such as the occurrence of violent acts, perpetrated by black persons, the presence of Jews in important positions, and other events consistent with National Alliance themes. The real gap is in reasoning from the purported facts to the views advocated; there is no more than suggestion that the few "facts" presented in each issue of *Attack!* justify its sweeping pronouncements about the common traits of non-whites and Jews or the need for their violent removal from society. It is the fact that there is no reasoned development of the conclusions which removes it from any definition of "educational" conceivably intended by Congress. The material may express the emotions felt by a number of people, but it cannot reasonably be considered intellectual exposition.

* * *

We recognize the inherently general nature of the term "educational" and the wide range of meanings Congress may have intended to convey. In attempting a definition suitable for all comers, IRS, or any legislature, court, or other administrator is beset with difficulties which are obvious. We do not attempt a definition, but we are convinced that the National Alliance material is far outside the range Congress could have intended to subsidize in the public interest by granting tax exemption.

II.

Aside from vagueness, it is clear that in formulating its regulation, IRS was attempting to include as educational some types of advocacy of views not generally accepted. But in order to be deemed "educational" and enjoy tax exemption some degree of intellectually appealing development of or foundation for the views advocated would be required. Hence, portion of the Regulation requires that the organization: "present a sufficiently full and fair exposition of the pertinent facts as to permit an individual or the public to form an independent opinion or conclusion. On the other hand, an organization is not educational if its principal function is the mere presentation of unsupported opinion." It is clear that the National Alliance material is not educational under that test.

One of the concerns in this area, because of First Amendment considerations, is that the government must shun being the arbiter of "truth." Material supporting a particular point of view may well be "educational" although a particular public officer may strongly disagree with the proposition advocated. Accordingly IRS has attempted to test the method by which the advocate proceeds from the premises he furnishes to the conclusion he advocates rather than the truth or accuracy or general acceptance of the conclusion.

Thus the Methodology Test presented in this proceeding contains the following four criteria:

1. Whether or not the presentation of viewpoints unsupported by a relevant factual basis constitutes a significant portion of the organization's communications.

2. To the extent viewpoints purport to be supported by a factual basis, are the facts distorted?

3. Whether or not the organization makes substantial use of particularly inflammatory and disparaging terms, expressing conclusions based more on strong emotional feelings than objective factual evaluations.

4. Whether or not the approach to a subject matter is aimed at developing an understanding on the part of the addressees, by reflecting consideration of the extent to which they have prior background or training.

Nothing in these criteria would suggest that the National Alliance material could be deemed educational.

III.

Nothing in this court's decision in *Big Mama Rag, Inc. v. United States,* 631 F.2d 1030 (D.C.Cir.1980), compels our reaching a different conclusion. * * *

We assume that the court in *Big Mama* viewed the activity of BMR, Inc. as falling within the range of reasonable interpretation of "educational" as used in the statute, or at least not clearly outside such range. Thus the vague test posed a real risk that BMR, Inc. might have been denied exemption under the test while others not distinguishable on any principled objective basis might be granted exemption.

In the present case we see no possibility that the National Alliance publication can be found educational within any reasonable interpretation of the term.

Relying on the Supreme Court's decision in *Speiser v. Randall*, 357 U.S. 513, 518, 78 S.Ct. 1332, 1338, 2 L.Ed.2d 1460 (1958), the *Big Mama* court noted that while First Amendment activities need not be subsidized, the discriminatory denial of tax exemptions for engaging in particular speech can impermissibly infringe constitutionally protected rights. 631 F.2d at 1034. As a consequence the court held invalid a standard so vague that it might permit an IRS official to discriminate between applications on the basis of approval or rejection of the ideas expressed by the applying organizations. Neither *Speiser* nor *Big Mama*, however, stand for the proposition that an exemption may not be denied on criteria neutral with regard to viewpoint. * * *

We have no doubt that publication of the National Alliance material is protected by the First Amendment from abridgement by law. * * * But it does not follow that the First Amendment requires a construction of the term "educational" which embraces every continuing dissemination of views. * * *

Based on a careful review of National Alliance's publications in the record before us, we are convinced that the IRS denial of exemption was not arbitrary or discriminatory, and was consistent with any reasonable interpretation of the statutory term "educational."

* * *

The judgment appealed from is reversed and the cause remanded with directions to enter judgment declaring National Alliance not tax-exempt.

Questions

1. Must First Amendment rights be subsidized by the government to be "realized fully?"

2. Can you prepare a sufficient, objective standard to determine which "communication to the public" made through a nonprofit organization should qualify for governmental subsidy via tax benefits?

The court in *Big Mama Rag* stated it could not "countenance a subjective 'I know it when I see it' standard" to determine what organizations qualified as "educational" in nature. The court in *National Alliance* decided it would not attempt a definition of educational but it was "convinced that the *National Alliance* material is far outside the range Congress could have intended to subsidize in the public interest by granting tax exemption." Is the court's test in National Alliance more than a subjective "I know it when I see it" standard? How does the standard used in *National Alliance* to affirm the IRS' denial of tax exempt status differ from the standard the court used in Big Mama Rag to reverse the IRS' denial of tax exemption?

NATIONALIST FOUNDATION v. COMMISSIONER
United States Tax Court, 2000
80 T.C.M. 507, T.C. Memo 2000-318

COHEN, J.

Respondent determined that The Nationalist Foundation (petitioner) does not qualify as a section 501(c)(3) charitable organization and, therefore, is not exempt from Federal taxation under section 501(a). Pursuant to section 7428 and title XXI of the Tax Court Rules of Practice and Procedure, petitioner seeks a declaratory judgment that it is a qualified organization under section 501(c)(3). The issues for decision are whether petitioner operates exclusively for charitable and/or educational purposes and whether the Commissioner treated petitioner differently from other similarly situated organizations in violation of petitioner's due process and equal protection rights under the 5th and 14th Amendments to the Constitution. * * *

* * *

On Form 1023, Application for Recognition of Exemption Under Section 501(c)(3) of the Internal Revenue Code, petitioner stated that its principal activities are: Conducting forums to discuss Constitutional rights' issues, stressing the First Amendment; conducting public access cable television and internet programs featuring guests, interviews and documentaries on current issues stressing the use of lawful, peaceful and positive means to achieve democratic ends, conducting litigation (or amicus curiae) to lessen the burdens of government under the "private attorney general" method to secure and advance civil, constitutional and First Amendment rights. According to petitioner, "private attorney general" means that "citizens assist in enforcement of the laws, saving the government time and expense of doing so, such as by private litigation." Petitioner's constitution states that it shall be a nonprofit charitable and educational organization dedicated to advancing American freedom, American democracy, and American nationality.

Petitioner seeks to become the legal and educational arm of rightist and promajority Americans. Petitioner states, in a letter soliciting donations from the public, that it will use the courts to bring "terrorists" who attack promajority demonstrators to justice. The letter cites two examples of events where petitioner would bring litigation using the "private attorney general" technique:

In Simi Valley, self-described communists advertised in the newspaper that they would kill patriots assembled to thank the jury that acquitted Officers Koon and Powell (Police officers accused of beating Rodney King). In New Hampshire, avowed homosexuals advertised that they would attack patriots calling for abolishing the * * * [Martin Luther King, Jr.] Holiday. It took massive intervention by riot police to back them off.

Both of these events were assemblies organized by Barrett, in which promajority demonstrators were attacked by counter demonstrators. Petitioner also plans to file amicus curiae briefs in cases involving the First Amendment rights of promajority-minded Americans and to use 42 U.S.C. sec. 3604(e) as an antiblockbusting law to "save" neighborhoods by suing incoming minorities.

Petitioner will use the internet to conduct seminars for teaching skills for more effective social action. The administrative record contains a transcript from only one seminar, which was conducted February 18, 1997. The seminar, recounted on the website of petitioner, gives students instruction on how to advocate peacefully without violating laws pertaining to hate crimes, housing violations, harassment, and racketeering. Petitioner's home page also contains links to other articles entitled "Constitutional Protection", "Educational Outreach", "Nationalist Ideology", "Private Attorney–General", "Pro–Democracy Methodology", "Relief for the Poor", and "Using the First Amendment as Democracy's Shield and Sword". The administrative record, however, does not contain copies of these articles despite attempts by the Commissioner to obtain them from petitioner.* * *

* * *

The actions of petitioner are designed to counteract the work of organizations such as the NAACP Legal Defense Fund, Inc., and the American Civil Liberties Union. Petitioner characterizes these groups as "the leftist threat to our liberties."

Petitioner's donation solicitation material contains several distortions of fact. Petitioner's statement, in its solicitation letter, that "avowed homosexuals advertised that they would attack patriots" was fabricated from a newspaper article that reads "Members of the National Peoples Campaign plan to *shadow* Barrett outside the State House beginning at 8 a.m. to oppose his ultra-conservative views. And they are looking for all the picketers they can get." (Emphasis added.) The same solicitation letter also claims that petitioner has in its possession "actual photos of the terrorists in the act of attacking the Anti–King Rally at the State Capitol." Petitioner, however, has only one photograph of three individuals holding a banner, which opposes the views of petitioner. The individuals depicted in the photograph are not engaged in any kind of attack on Barrett or his fellow demonstrators.

* * *

Petitioner argues that its activities, which promote free speech and create forums for the exchange of ideas and information, are charitable and educational by nature. The rationale of petitioner is that freedom of speech is the highest national priority, and, if freedom is extended to even one group or individual, all Americans benefit. Respondent claims that petitioner has failed to prove that its activities are charitable and educational within the meaning of section 501(c)(3).

* * *

The few activities of petitioner that have been disclosed fall outside of the definitions of "charitable" and "educational" under section 501(c)(3). Section 1.501(c)(3)–1(d)(2), Income Tax Regs., specifically states that examples of charitable activities are ones designed "to lessen neighborhood tension" and "to eliminate prejudice and discrimination." Petitioner's actions serve the purpose of increasing social activism of promajority and rightist beliefs and are antithetical to these examples.

* * *

For the reasons stated, we conclude that petitioner is not operated as a section 501(c)(3) organization. We have considered the remaining arguments of petitioner, and they are either irrelevant or otherwise lack merit.

Decision will be entered upholding respondent's determination.

Problem

You are an employee of the IRS and, as such, you are reviewing the application for tax exempt § 501(c)(3) status of the Satanic Society of America. The organization prints a monthly newsletter and devotes considerable time promoting Satanic worship and rituals through workshops, seminars, lectures, and a weekly radio program. Would you grant or deny exemption? On what basis?

II. ORGANIZATIONAL STRUCTURE OF A NONPROFIT ORGANIZATION

Nonprofit organizations have one of three forms—trust, association, or corporation. Many small nonprofits are unincorporated associations. Although a nonprofit organization can be organized as a trust or an unincorporated association, the preferable organizational structure is the nonprofit corporation.

A. Trust

A nonprofit charitable organization can be established as a charitable trust. A trust is not a statutory organization and, thus, does not report to the state (absent mandatory reporting for charities in a particular state). Few formalities are required in creating a trust, and the enabling document is not filed with the secretary of state (as is the case for a nonprofit corporation). As a result, a trust structure may provide the organization more privacy than would organization and operation as a nonprofit corporation.

The procedures to create a trust are not complicated. The grantor or trustor must execute a declaration of trust to transfer property to another person, the trustee (or trustees), who holds the property upon a charitable trust. Legal title to the trust property is vested in the trustee, while equitable title is in the beneficiary or beneficiaries.

Restatement, Trusts

§ 348. Definition of Charitable Trust

A charitable trust is a fiduciary relationship with respect to property arising as a result of a manifestation of an intention to create it, and subjecting the person by whom the property is held to equitable duties to deal with the property for a charitable purpose.

Often there are no definitely ascertainable beneficiaries of a charitable trust. If a charitable trust does not designate a particular charity or charities as its beneficiary, the public is the beneficiary. However, if a charitable trust is created to support a particular charity, the named charity would be the designated beneficiary.

Restatement, Trusts

§ 364. Indefinite Beneficiaries

A charitable trust can be created although there is no definite or definitely ascertainable beneficiary designated.

Although most operating charities are not organized as trusts, a trust can be an effective form of organization for a supporting foundation for an operating charity. Because a trust structure requires few formalities and the declaration of trust is not filed with the secretary of state as is required for articles of incorporation for a nonprofit corporation, some donors prefer a trust arrangement as the means by which they channel their contributions to operating charities.

A declaration of trust for a charitable trust would include the name of the grantor, the names of the original trustees, the charitable purposes of the trust, the period of duration of the trust, the manner in which successor trustees will be selected, and a provision that assets of the trust will be distributed to charitable organizations upon termination of the trust. A schedule attached to the trust document would list property transferred to the trust.

Restatement, Trusts

§ 380. Extent of Trustee's Powers

... the trustee of a charitable trust can properly exercise such powers ... as

(a) are conferred upon him in specific words by the terms of the trust, or

(b) are necessary or appropriate to carry out the purposes of the trust and are not forbidden by the terms of the trust.

B. Association

A nonprofit organization that is not formed as a trust and that is not incorporated is an association. The formation of an association is elementary. An association is created when members agree to perform a common purpose. An enabling document is not necessary.

Despite the simplicity in creating an association, an association may not be an acceptable form of organization as few states have statutes dealing with the formation and operation of an association. The lack of statutory law in most states defining the legal status and the boundaries of an unincorporated association make operation of an association uncertain. Because an association is not a legal entity separate from its members, in the absence of specific state statutory authority, an association does not have perpetual duration, cannot contract, and cannot hold title to property. Members of an association may have vicarious liability for actions of the association. They may be liable individually for their actions and for actions of other members. Liability of members of an association generally is determined by the principles of agency.

A few states have adopted the Uniform Unincorporated Nonprofit Association Act,[10] which permits nonprofit associations to acquire and hold property and provides that members are not liable as such for debts of the association.

Uniform Unincorporated Nonprofit Association Act

Section 4.

(a) A nonprofit association is a legal entity separate from its members for the purposes of acquiring, holding encumbering, and transferring real and personal property.

(b) A nonprofit association in its name may acquire, hold, encumber, or transfer an estate or interest in real or personal property.

Section 6.

(a) A nonprofit association is a legal entity separate from its members for the purposes of determining and enforcing rights, duties, and liabilities in contract and tort.

(b) A person is not liable for a breach of a nonprofit association's contract merely because the person is a member, is authorized to participate in the management of the affairs of the nonprofit association, or is a person considered to be a member by the nonprofit association.

Problem

A member of an unincorporated nonprofit association signed a contract on behalf of the association to construct a building that would contain offices for the association. The association later is without sufficient funds to pay the building contractor. The contractor has threatened to file suit against the association member who executed the

---

10. See copy of Uniform Unincorporated Nonprofit Association Act at 3 Marilyn Phelan, *Nonprofit Enterprises*, App. F.

contract on behalf of the association. Would the contractor have a cause of action against the member in a state that had adopted the Uniform Unincorporated Nonprofit Association Act?

Note

The National Conference on Commissioners on Uniform State Laws is in the process of replacing the Uniform Unincorporated Nonprofit Association Act with an act that contains more default rules for unincorporated associations and that will be compatible with uniform acts for unincorporated associations in Canada and Mexico.

C. Nonprofit Corporation

Most nonprofit organizations seek corporate status. The law relating to nonprofit corporations is more defined and more flexible than that relating to trusts and unincorporated associations. Further, because most nonprofit corporations are tax exempt, the double taxation factor, which has discouraged incorporation of for-profit entities, has not been a problem.

1. Model Nonprofit Corporation Acts

Several states have adopted, either in whole or in modified form, the Model Nonprofit Corporation Act, which was drafted originally in 1952 by the Committee on Corporate Laws of the Section of Corporation, Banking and Business Law of the American bar Association. The Act was revised in 1964 to make it more compatible with the Model Business Corporation Act. The intent of the drafters of the Model Act was that decisions interpreting the Business Corporation Act would become applicable and helpful in interpreting provisions of the Model Act.[11]

The committee adopted the Revised Model Nonprofit Corporation Act in 1987, which was patterned after the 1984 Model Business Corporation Act. The Revised Act classified nonprofit corporations into public benefit corporations and mutual benefit corporations. It incorporated legal standards applicable to corporate directors in determining legal liability of nonprofit corporations (discussion in Chapter 3).

The American Bar Association has drafted a proposed Model Nonprofit Corporation Act, Third Edition. The Third Edition incorporated many provisions of the Model Business Corporation Act, Third Edition, that was adopted by the American Bar Association in 2002; however, the current proposed Third Edition Model Nonprofit Corporation Act (as of the date of publication of this casebook) does not classify nonprofit corporations into public benefit and mutual benefit corporations. The proposed Act does provide for a "select exempt organization," which is a nonprofit corporation that is exempt from Federal income taxation under Section 501(c)(3) or (4) of the Internal Revenue Code.

Drafters of the Model Acts recognized that nonprofit corporations may have incidental income or profit in performing their nonprofit

---

11. See copies of Model Nonprofit Corporation Act and Revised Model Corporation Act at 3 Marilyn Phelan, *Nonprofit Enterprises*, Apps. D and E.

purposes. Because a minority of the drafters of the original Model Act thought a nonprofit corporation should have any permitted purpose not prohibited in its bylaws, the Model Act provided an alternative purpose section that would permit a nonprofit corporation to be organized for any lawful purpose. The drafters of the original act were of the opinion there would be a safeguard through § 26 of the Act, which provides that no dividends can be paid and that no part of the income of a corporation can be distributed to members, directors, or officers, except as reasonable compensation for services rendered.

There are common elements of all state statutes governing nonprofit corporations. Most states prohibit nonprofit corporations from issuing stock, and although state statutes do not prohibit a nonprofit corporation from making a profit, all state statutes prohibit nonprofits from paying dividends. Most state statutes provide for payment of a reasonable compensation to officers and directors and for the payment of other noncash benefits to their members. Most states prohibit charitable nonprofit corporations from distributing their assets upon dissolution except to charitable organizations. Some states provide standards of conduct for officers and directors and some provide immunity from liability for volunteers in certain circumstances. (See discussion in Chapter 3.)

State nonprofit corporate statutes provide benefits of limited liability for members, centralized management, and, in many states, standards relating to liability of officers and directors. Standards of conduct applicable to directors of nonprofit corporations make it less likely that directors will be subject to liability for their inadvertent acts than trustees of trusts and members of associations and, thus, provide additional reason to incorporate a nonprofit organization. (See discussion in Chapter 3.)

2. Status of a Nonprofit Corporation as a Charitable Trust

The property of a nonprofit organization that is exempt from federal taxation under § 501(c)(3) of the Internal Revenue Code is held for a charitable purpose; thus, these organizations generally are treated as charitable trusts regardless of their organizational structure. As such, charitable organizations are subject to state statutes governing administration of property held for charitable purposes. Because the public is the general beneficiary of a charitable trust, property in the trust must be devoted to purposes beneficial to the public. Members of the governing board of a charitable organization must manage the charity's property and operate the charity for the public welfare. In most states, the attorney general, as representative of the community, has the duty to protect the public interest in such charitable trusts.

Uniform Supervision of Trustees for Charitable Purposes Act

Section 1. This act applies to all trustees holding property for charitable purposes over which the State of the Attorney General has enforcement or supervisory powers.

Section 2. "Trustee" means (a) any individual, group of individuals, corporation, or other legal entity holding property in trust pursuant to any charitable trust, (b) any corporation which has accepted property to be used for a particular charitable corporate purpose as distinguished from the general purposes of the corporation, and (c) a corporation formed for the administration of a charitable trust, pursuant to the directions of the settlor or at the instance of the trustee.

Section 6.

(a) Except as otherwise provided, every trustee subject to this act shall, in addition to filing copies of the instruments ... file with the Attorney General periodic written reports, under oath, setting forth information as to the nature of the assets held for charitable purposes and the administration thereof by the trustee, in accordance with rules and regulations of the Attorney General.

(b) The Attorney General shall make rules and regulations as to the time for filing reports, the contents thereof, and the manner of executing and filing them ...

Section 8. The Attorney General may investigate transactions and relationships of trustees subject to this act for the purpose of determining whether the property held for charitable purposes is properly administered.

California Government Code

§ 12580

This article may be cited as the Uniform Supervision of Trustees and Fundraisers for Charitable Purposes Act.

§ 12581

This article applies to all charitable corporations and trustees holding property for charitable purposes, commercial fundraisers for charitable purposes, fundraising counsel for charitable purposes, and commercial coventurers, over which the state or the Attorney General has enforcement or supervisory powers ...

YOUNGER v. WISDOM SOCIETY
Court of Appeals, California, 1981
121 Cal.App.3d 683, 175 Cal.Rptr. 542

Attorney General filed action seeking to have nonprofit educational corporation declared "charitable corporation" and subject to reporting and other regulations related to charitable corporations.* * *

KINGSLEY, Acting Presiding Justice.

Respondent Attorney General filed an action for enforcement of Governmental Code sections 12585 and 12586(a) against the Wisdom

Society and Leon Gutterman, (president and editor-in-chief), and Betty Jane Lang, (vice-president and editorial and research director), to require the Wisdom Society and its trustees to file with the Attorney General certain documents, including annual financial reports. The Attorney General sought to have the Wisdom Society declared a "charitable corporation" within the meaning of Government Code section 12582.1 and therefore subject to reporting and other regulations related to charitable corporations. The trial court found that the Wisdom Society is a nonprofit educational corporation operated exclusively for educational purposes and made a conclusion of law that the "Wisdom Society" is a "charitable corporation" within Government Code section 12582.1. The court ordered the Wisdom Society, Gutterman and Lang to comply retroactively with the reporting requirement of Government Code section 12586, and ordered Gutterman and Lang to pay reasonable expenses incurred by the office in investigation and prosecution of the action. Appellants' motion for new trial was denied and they appeal.

* * *

The society's work involved interpretation of the wisdom of great scholars and of persons of historical importance. The publications dealt with such persons and subjects as William Shakespeare, Carl Sandburg, Robert Frost, Thomas Edison, Moses, Jesus, the Holy Bible, Will Durant, Felix Frankfurter, Arnold Toynbee, Picasso, Ernest Hemingway, Pope Pius XII, Eleanor Roosevelt, Dwight Eisenhower, Bertrand Russell, Dr. Jonas Salk, Nehru, Walt Disney, Winston Churchill and others. Gutterman himself conducted interviews with many of the living subjects of his articles.

The Wisdom Society through its attorney applied to the State Franchise Tax Board for an exemption from California State Franchise tax when the society was formed, and the exception was granted on the ground that the Wisdom Society was organized and operated exclusively as an educational organization. The letter from the Franchise Tax Board granting the exemption stated that the contributions to the Wisdom Society are deductible to the donor. The society never claimed contributions to it were deductible for federal income tax purposes and no federal income tax exemptions were sought. The society filed federal and state tax returns as any nonprofit corporation would do. The money given by recipients of the awards were not deductible on the recipient's tax returns.

The Wisdom Society did not file articles of incorporation under Government Code section 12585 (which deals with charitable corporations) nor did it file any periodic reports under Government Code section 12586(a). The society has never paid income tax but it did file federal and state tax returns as a "nonprofit corporation."

The articles of incorporation set forth as its purpose the following: "To promote, stimulate and encourage public interest in support of knowledge, learning and education and to search for new knowledge and understanding by advancing the educational welfare of mankind; and to create and publish educational magazines and books dedicated to the development of the human mind and to the betterment of mankind."

* * *

The sole question presented by the appeal is whether the trial court properly concluded that the Wisdom Society is a "charitable corporation" within the meaning of Government Code section 12582.1 and is, therefore, subject to the reporting requirements of the Government Code sections dealing with charitable corporations.

Sections 12585 and 12586(a) impose on charitable corporations and their trustees the following requirements:

> Section 12585: "Every charitable corporation and trustee subject to this article who has received property for charitable purposes shall file with the Attorney General, within six months after any part of the income or principal is authorized or required to be applied to a charitable purpose, a copy of the articles of incorporation or other instrument providing for his title, powers or duties."

> Section 12586(a): "Except as otherwise provided and except corporate trustees which are subject to the jurisdiction of the Superintendent of Banks of the State of California or to the Comptroller of Currency of the United States, every charitable corporation and trustee subject to this article shall, in addition to filing copies of the instruments previously required, file with the Attorney General periodic written reports, under oath, setting forth information as to the nature of the assets held for charitable purposes and the administration thereof by the corporation or trustee, in accordance with rules and regulations of the Attorney General."

Therefore, if the Wisdom Society is a "charitable corporation" within section 12582.1, the society must comply with the above reporting and registration requirements of sections 12585 and 12586(a).

Section 12582 reads as follows: "'Trustee' means (a) any individual group of individuals, corporation, or other legal entity holding property in trust pursuant to any charitable trust, (b) any corporation which has accepted property to be used for a particular charitable corporate purpose as distinguished from the general purposes of the corporation, and (c) a corporation formed for the administration of a charitable trust, pursuant to the directions of the settlor or at the instance of the trustee."

Section 12582.1 defines charitable corporations as follows: "'Charitable corporation' means any nonprofit corporation organized under the laws of this State for charitable or eleemosynary purposes and any similar foreign corporation doing business or holding property in this State for such purposes."

Thus, the question before us becomes whether the Wisdom Society was organized for "charitable or eleemosynary purposes."

The law is clear that a nonprofit corporation organized for the advancement of the education is a charitable corporation. * * *

A reading of the articles of incorporation as a whole should determine the real purpose of a particular institution, but its character is not to be determined alone by the powers and purposes defined in its articles, but also by the method of transacting business. * * * The court can take into consideration the actual conduct of the corporation in its method of operation. * * * In the case at bar, a reading of the Wisdom Society's articles of incorporation as a whole, indicates that the Wisdom Society was formed for educational purposes, for the advancement of knowledge, and the educational welfare of mankind. And when we examine the actual conduct of the Wisdom Society, its method of operation and its procedure for transacting business, we see that the corporation was conducted as a charitable corporation in that it was dedicated to disseminating publications of strictly an educational nature, i. e., its publications were limited to informing readers on many literary, philosophical, religious, scientific, historical, political and other subjects.

In the case at bench, both the purposes as set forth in articles of incorporation and also the actual conduct of Wisdom were more than sufficient to sustain the action of the trial court in its conclusion that the Wisdom Society is a charitable corporation.

* * *

Although nonprofit corporations are certainly not synonymous with charitable corporations, a nonprofit corporation whose purpose is educational has been held a charitable corporation in Estate of Connolly (1975) 48 Cal.App.3d 129, 121 Cal.Rptr. 325. Furthermore, an educational purpose related to learning has been held to be a charitable use, * * * and a trust for promotion of education generally is charitable in nature. * * * Therefore, the conclusion of law that a corporation is a charitable corporation follows from the fact that a nonprofit corporation is created for or devoted to educational purposes. * * *

Appellants argue that the statutory scheme classifying nonprofit corporations differentiates between educational corporations and charitable corporations, and that the Wisdom Society was formed under Government Code section 9000 et seq., related to nonprofit corporations, and was not formed under Corporations Code section 10200 et seq., related to charitable corporations. Appellants argue that the Legislature necessarily meant charitable corporations to be something different from other nonprofit corporations or they would not have had a separate section for charitable corporations.

The particular sections under which the corporation was formed is not conclusive on the issue of whether a corporation is charitable or not. In determining whether a corporation was organized exclusively for charitable purposes and therefore was exempt from unemployment contributions, the trial court in California Employment Commission v. Betthesda Foundation (1942) 54 Cal.App.2d 348, 128 P.2d 874, was not bound either by the articles of incorporation or by the particular code section that the corporation was formed under, but the court could consider the corporation's actual conduct and method of operation. * * * Therefore, appellants' argument that Wisdom was formed under former code section 9200 dealing with nonprofit corporations having only three incorporators, rather than under former code section 10200, dealing with charitable corporations, requiring 25 incorporators, for a charitable corporation, would not be decisive on the issue of whether or not the corporation is a charitable corporation. The court is not bound by the particular code section the corporation was formed under. * * *

* * *

The judgment is affirmed.

PEOPLE v. GEORGE F. HARDING MUSEUM

Court of Appeals, Illinois, 1978
58 Ill.App.3d 408, 15 Ill.Dec. 973, 374 N.E.2d 756

DOWNING, Justice:

This is a case brought by the Attorney General of Illinois to enforce the terms of a charitable trust under the Illinois Charitable Trust Act (Act) (Ill.Rev.Stat.1969, ch. 14, pars. 51 through 64). The trial court granted defendants' motion to strike and dismiss the complaint for failure to state a claim upon which relief may be granted (Ill.Rev.Stat. 1971, ch. 110, par. 45). The Attorney General appeals from the dismissal of the complaint. Defendants have filed a cross-appeal from that portion of the trial court's order which upheld the constitutionality of the Act. The issues on appeal are whether defendants are "trustees" within the meaning of the Act, and whether the Act is constitutional.

* * * The purposes of the George F. Harding Museum, the successor to the George F. Harding Collection, Inc., incorporated on September 30, 1930, are set forth in its articles of incorporation as:

> "(F)or the accumulation and dissemination of knowledge and the perpetuation of knowledge of ancient arts and sciences, for the improvement of the mind by the collection, preservation and exhibition of ancient and authentic objects illustrating art, science, and history, painting, sculpture, armor, weapons, objects of art and other objects and antiques bringing to the mind activities of mankind of earlier periods of time; to found, build, maintain and operate a museum for the exhibition of the collection; to receive gifts, donations and endowments and to receive in trust property of all kinds and to exercise all necessary powers as aforesaid for such trust estates where the purpose of the trust is for the furtherance of the above objects only."

George F. Harding provided additional funding for the collection in his last will and testament admitted to probate on April 6, 1939.

Originally, the George F. Harding Museum was located at 4853 S. Lake Park Avenue in Chicago, and was open to the public. In January of 1965, the collection was moved to 84–86 E. Randolph. After relocating, the museum ceased to be open to the public. Since that time, it is alleged, the collection has not been used to promote the purposes set forth in the articles of incorporation. Count I further alleged that the corporate defendant is a "trustee" within the meaning of the Act, as a legal entity holding property for charitable purposes, and that defendants have failed to comply with the Act.

* * *

The purpose of the Charitable Trust Act is to assist the Attorney General in carrying out his common law powers and duties to enforce charitable trusts and to see to the application of their funds to their intended charitable uses. (See Ill.Ann.Stat., ch. 14, par. 51, General Commentary, at 292 (Smith–Hurd 1963).) Prior to enactment of the Charitable Trust Act, trustees of charitable trusts had no duty to make the Attorney General aware of the existence of charitable trusts or of the manner of their operation. The Act is intended to give the Attorney General the tools with which to discharge his responsibilities. The 1963 amendments to section 3 of the Act, which redefined "trustee," were intended to bring all foundations and not-for-profit corporations "holding property for any charitable purpose" within the scope of the Act. * * *

It has long been the rule that a trust for the promotion of "educational" purposes may be considered to be "charitable" in nature. Scott, in his treatise on the law of trusts, states:

> "Trusts for the advancement of education are charitable. In the Statute of Charitable Uses the enumeration of charitable purposes includes 'schools of learning, free schools, and scholars in universities.' * * * The cases in which trusts for the advancement of education have been upheld as charitable are numerous. * * * A trust is a valid charitable trust as one for the advancement of education although it is not connected with an educational institution. Thus trusts to establish or maintain public libraries, art museums or botanical or zoological or similar institutions are charitable. * * * So too are trusts for the dissemination of knowledge or beliefs through the publication or distribution of books or pamphlets or the delivery of lectures." (IV Scott on Trusts, 3d ed. 1967, s 370, at 2866 and 2871.) * * *

Professor Bogert, in his treatise on trusts, states:

> "There is a wide difference between the popular and legal meanings of the word 'charity.' To the non-legal mind the word often means 'almsgiving,' or 'liberality to the poor,' or 'that which is given to relieve the needy'; whereas in the law the word has a much broader meaning and includes a large number of other acts working toward

the social welfare." (Bogert, Trusts and Trustees, § 369, at 62 (Revised 2d ed. 1977).)

Bogert goes on to define a charitable trust:

"A charitable trust may be briefly defined as one which is for the public benefit. It is impractical to attempt to frame a definition which includes a description of all the types of activity which the courts regard as of advantage to the community. The list would be long and it would be impossible to classify many of the objects which the courts have approved. Furthermore it would be inadvisable to attempt to bind the courts by a rigid formula. They should have latitude to include new purposes as society develops and public opinion changes and to exclude objectives which have become obsolete or unsuited to prevailing conditions." (Bogert, § 69, at 65.)* * *

The second Restatement of the Law of Trusts defines the nature of charitable purposes in the following manner:

"A purpose is charitable if its accomplishment is of such social interest to the community as to justify permitting the property to be devoted to the purpose in perpetuity." (Restatement (Second) of Trusts, § 368, comment b., at 248.)

Comment a. to section 370 of the Restatement lists the methods by which a charitable trust may promote education, including the establishment of "public libraries, art museums or other museums." (Restatement (Second) of Trusts, § 370, comment a., at 251.) (Emphasis added.)

The courts in Illinois are in accord in applying a broad definition of "charity":

"This court approved and adopted the following legal definition of a charity in Crerar v. Williams, 145 Ill. 625, 34 N.E. 467: 'A charity, in a legal sense, may be more fully defined as a gift, to be applied consistently with existing laws, for the benefit of an indefinite number of persons, either by bringing their hearts under the influence of education or religion, by relieving their bodies from disease, suffering or constraint, by assisting them to establish themselves for life, or by erecting or maintaining public buildings or works or otherwise lessening the burthens of government.' In Congregational Sunday School and Publishing Society v. Board of Review, 290 Ill. 108, 125 N.E. 7, it was said that charity, in a legal sense, is not confined to mere almsgiving or the relief of poverty and distress, but has a wider signification, which embraces the improvement and promotion of the happiness of man. A charitable use, where neither law nor public policy forbids, may be applied to almost anything that tends to promote the well-doing and well-being of social man." (School of Domestic Arts v. Carr (1926), 322 Ill. 562, 568–569, 153 N.E. 669, 671.)

In Morgan v. National Trust Bank (1928), 331 Ill. 182, 186, 162 N.E. 888, 890, our supreme court stated that "(t)he test as to whether an enterprise is charitable is whether it exists to carry out a purpose recognized in law as charitable or whether it is maintained for gain, profit, or private advantage. (11 Corpus Juris 303.)" Clearly, the broad legal concept of charitable purposes embraces the corporate purpose of the George F. Harding Museum, as set forth in its articles of incorporation. There can be no question that the intent of Harding was to promote the well being of social man through the various purposes set forth in the articles of incorporation. In the establishment of this museum, the express intent of the donor was the "collection, preservation and exhibition of ancient and authentic objects illustrating art, science, history, painting, sculpture, * * * to found, maintain and operate a museum for the exhibition of the collection; * * *." It is obvious that George F. Harding did not intend to distinguish between educational and charitable purposes. * * * Indeed, except for the sophistical reading of the purpose clause of the articles of incorporation suggested by defendants, whose interests in this case could be adverse to the original intentions of George F. Harding, there is nothing in the record to even suggest that the George F. Harding Museum was intended to be an educational institution. For all these reasons we conclude it was error for the trial court to grant defendants' motion to dismiss the complaint.

* * *

Accordingly, the circuit court of Cook County's judgment that the Act is constitutional is affirmed. The circuit court's judgment that the Act is inapplicable to defendants is reversed.

Question

The court in *George F. Harding Museum* assumed that the Attorney General has common law powers and duties to enforce charitable trusts and to see to the application of their funds to their intended charitable uses. Does the Attorney General of a state have "inherent" power to regulate all nonprofit organizations?

COMMONWEALTH OF VIRGINIA v. THE JOCO FOUNDATION

Supreme Court, Virginia, 2002
263 Va. 151, 558 S.E.2d 280

Opinion by Senior Justice A. CHRISTIAN COMPTON.

The question presented in this appeal is whether the circuit court has subject matter jurisdiction over this suit instituted by the Attorney General of Virginia, in the name of the Commonwealth. The suit involves a Virginia corporation duly established by the State Corporation Commission under the Virginia Nonstock Corporation Act, Code §§ 13.1–801 through–944 (the Act). The crux of the question is whether the State Corporation Commission is the proper forum for decision of the matters raised in the suit, or whether the Attorney General may proceed in the circuit court under some "inherent power" of the circuit court or under the common law to obtain the relief requested.

This proceeding is one of a series of lawsuits stemming from the 1996 death of Reid Jones, Jr., a philanthropist of Moneta, Virginia.

In January 2001, the Attorney General filed this suit in a pleading labeled "Bill of Complaint for Reformation and Removal of Directors." Among the defendants are The JOCO Foundation, Dianne E.H. Wilcox, Judy Jarrells, William John Killinger, SunTrust Bank, SunTrust Securities, Inc., and the Phoenix Foundation, Inc.

In the bill, the Attorney General asserts that he sues "in his official capacity . . . as legal representative of the charitable beneficiaries of the JOCO Foundation, Inc., a charitable foundation established under the will of Reid Jones." He asserts that "under the common law and by statute," he "is the legal representative of the beneficiaries of all charitable trusts and charitable assets in the Commonwealth." According to the pleading, the "Attorney General possesses the common law authority to act on behalf of the public in matters involving charitable assets."

Further, the Attorney General asserts that The JOCO Foundation "is a Virginia corporation organized under § 501(c)(3) of the Internal Revenue Code to benefit community organizations and created under" the Jones will. He alleges that defendants Wilcox, Killinger, and Jarrells are JOCO's corporate directors, residing in Bedford County.

The bill of complaint states that the SunTrust defendants are named parties "because they currently hold the assets" of JOCO. The Attorney General alleges that, "on behalf of the intended beneficiaries" of JOCO, "he asserts this claim to the assets of the Foundation held by SunTrust to ensure that those assets are distributed as Reid Jones, Jr., intended when he created JOCO Foundation."

Additionally, the Attorney General alleges that "The Phoenix Foundation Inc., is a non-stock corporation created by Wilcox as a charitable foundation under her control and funded by money transferred from the JOCO Foundation. [Defendants] Wilcox, Killinger and Jarrells are all directors of the Phoenix Foundation, Inc. The Phoenix Foundation is an offshoot or 'alter ego' of the JOCO Foundation."

Also, the Attorney General asserts that he is "informed and believe[s]" that the individual defendants "have breached their fiduciary duties owed to the JOCO Foundation by acts of self-dealing, by engaging in actions which create conflicts of interest, by accepting and/or paying excessive fees for services rendered, and by taking actions and using assets of the JOCO Foundation for non-charitable purposes and/or purposes that conflict with the stated intentions of the testator, Reid Jones, Jr., all to the detriment of the intended beneficiaries of the JOCO Foundation."

Additionally, the Attorney General alleges that "the actions and/or inaction" of the individual defendants "have caused the assets of the JOCO Foundation to be jeopardized and threaten to frustrate the stated intent" of Jones.

The Attorney General further alleges that the "original Articles of Incorporation of the JOCO Foundation reflect ... Jones' express intention to use Foundation proceeds to benefit existing charities in the United States and particularly charities in the Roanoke, Virginia community." Instead, according to the allegations, the individual defendants have removed JOCO's assets from the United States to the Dominican Republic, either directly or by channeling the assets through the Phoenix Foundation, Inc.

Also, the Attorney General alleges that the individual defendants have authorized unnecessary or excessive expenditures of JOCO assets both in the United States and in the Dominican Republic, and that they will continue to remove assets "to be used, among other things for construction of a school in the Dominican Republic."

Continuing, the Attorney General lists certain conduct of the individual defendants under the heading "Breaches of Fiduciary Duties and Acts of Self Dealing." Included in the list are: Appointing JOCO directors "who are closely related to or are indebted to Wilcox or subject to her control;" employing Killinger and his company to perform construction work for JOCO, and using JOCO assets to pay Killinger fees and costs in excess of the market rate for services or materials provided; "hiring family members or friends to perform unnecessary services" for JOCO, and paying those persons with JOCO funds; creating in 1999 the Phoenix Foundation for the purpose of using JOCO assets "to travel to and spend time at a resort in the Dominican Republic and to build a school" there, thus contravening Jones' intent in establishing JOCO to benefit existing charities in the United States and in the Roanoke area; and, amending the JOCO articles of incorporation "to delete the geographic limitation ... and give the Board of Directors nearly unlimited discretion in distributing the funds of the JOCO Foundation."

In the prayer for relief, the Attorney General specifically seeks: Removal of the individual defendants as JOCO directors and replacement with "new, independent directors;" rescission or reformation of the JOCO articles of incorporation; appointment of a receiver to conduct audits of JOCO's and Phoenix's financial records; an injunction against SunTrust from releasing or distributing corporate funds; an injunction against the individual defendants prohibiting distribution of Phoenix funds; and, an order requiring Phoenix "to return all funds transferred to it or 'donated' to it by the JOCO Foundation."

In the prayer, the Attorney General also asks the court to "order such terms and conditions as it deems appropriate to protect the public's interest in the charitable assets of the JOCO Foundation."

* * *

He [the Attorney General] also acknowledges that generally only members or shareholders of a corporation have standing to challenge internal management decisions of a corporation. However, he argues, this rule does not apply "where the Corporation is also a charitable foundation." The Attorney General principally relies upon *Tauber v. Commonwealth*, 255 Va. 445, 499 S.E.2d 839 (1998), as authority for the latter proposition. He opines that "[i]nasmuch as JOCO is a charitable foundation, it is essentially a trust as well as a non-stock corporation," and that he has the common law authority to act on behalf of the public in such a case.

Summarizing, the Attorney General argues that the circuit court has the authority to consider claims brought by the Commonwealth against directors of a charitable foundation, organized as a nonstock corporation, alleging the directors have breached fiduciary duties, engaged in acts of self dealing, and wasted foundation assets. The court has the power, the argument continues, to order an accounting to ensure the funds are being distributed in a way that satisfies the charitable purposes set forth in the original articles of incorporation. Also, the Attorney General contends, the circuit court "has inherent ancillary authority" to award injunctive relief and appoint a receiver.

Finally, the Attorney General argues that if "Dianne Wilcox and the other individual directors of JOCO breached their fiduciary duties when they amended the original Articles of Incorporation to delete the geographic restriction on charitable donations," the circuit court "may enter an order striking the amendment and restoring the original Articles of Incorporation."

We do not agree with the Attorney General. We hold that the trial court correctly ruled that it lacked subject matter jurisdiction over the matters raised in this suit.

Initially, applicable general principles should be reviewed. The phrase "subject matter jurisdiction" means the power of a court to adjudicate a specified class of cases. Subject matter jurisdiction is granted by constitution or statute, and cannot be waived. *Nelson v. Warden*, 262 Va. 276, 281, 552 S.E.2d 73, 75 (2001). Whether a plaintiff has a common law remedy is a question of subject matter jurisdiction. * * *

A circuit court has "original and general jurisdiction of all cases in chancery" except for cases "assigned to some other tribunal." Code § 17.1–513. Every circuit court has jurisdiction to award injunctions. Code § 8.01–620.

Among the powers and duties of the State Corporation Commission (Commission) is the "duty of administering the laws made in pursuance of [the Constitution of Virginia] for the regulation and control of corporations doing business in this Commonwealth." Va. Const. art. IX, § 2. "No court within or without Virginia, except the Supreme Court by way of appeal as authorized by law, shall have jurisdiction to review, reverse, correct or annul any action of the Commission, within the scope of its authority, ... or to enjoin, restrain or interfere with the Commission in the performance of its official duties." Code § 13.1–813, a part of the Act. "In the administration and enforcement of all laws within its jurisdiction, the Commission shall have the power ... to issue temporary and permanent injunctions." Code § 12.1–13.

As we commence the analysis of the issue presented, certain basic, undisputed circumstances should be made clear. First, there has been no dissolution of either JOCO or Phoenix. According to this record, those domestic corporations, duly established by the Commission, are lawful, viable entities with full power to operate within the authority granted by the Commission.

Second, the gist of the plaintiffs' claim is an attempt to inject the circuit court at the behest of the Attorney General into the operating machinery of established corporate entities. While the General Assembly, in Code § 55-532, has authorized the Attorney General to "exercise his common law and statutory authority" regarding certain nonprofit health care entities, and to become involved in the disposition of assets, no such specific power has been granted by the legislature regarding nonprofit corporations devoted to charitable purposes.

Third, and to state the obvious, this suit is brought by the Attorney General, and not by any director or other person or entity with statutory standing having the authority to tinker with corporate machinery.

And, fourth, the Attorney General's contention that the circuit court has subject matter jurisdiction in this matter advances the theory that a Virginia nonstock corporation devoted to charitable purposes "essentially" is a charitable trust. No direct authority is cited for this proposition and we have found none. * * *

We shall now turn to the Attorney General's prayer for relief and will demonstrate that the General Assembly has decided that the forum for each type of relief sought is in the Commission, and not the circuit court.

Significantly, the bill is labeled "Bill of Complaint for Reformation and Removal of Directors," and the plaintiffs pray for an order granting reformation and removal. Specifically, the bill asks "that the current Articles of Incorporation of the JOCO Foundation be rescinded and reformed ... ," and "that the court remove ... Wilcox, Killinger and Jarrells as directors of the JOCO Foundation and replace them with new, independent directors."

The Act, in Code § 13.1-860, sets forth detailed procedures for removal of directors, and the General Assembly has not authorized the Attorney General to participate in that exercise by prosecuting a suit in a circuit court. Code § 13.1-861 permits any member or director, not the Attorney General, to contest an election of directors in an appropriate circuit court. Code § 13.1-874 provides for removal of officers of nonstock corporations, without any mention of the participation of the Attorney General. Code §§ 13.1-884 through-893 control the amendment of articles of incorporation, including addition or deletion of provisions, under the supervision of the Commission, without any participation in such reformation in a circuit court at the relation of the Attorney General.

The prayer for relief also asks for appointment of a receiver to conduct an accounting and to manage JOCO and Phoenix until this suit is resolved, and for injunctive relief. In Code § 13.1–909, the General Assembly has given circuit courts subject matter jurisdiction in the process of the dissolution of nonstock corporations, but only after termination of corporate existence. A circuit court has "full power to liquidate the assets and business of the corporation at any time after the termination of corporate existence ... upon the application of any person, for good cause, with regard to any assets or business that may remain." § 13.1–909(B). In a proceeding brought to dissolve such a corporation, a court "may issue injunctions, appoint a receiver or custodian pendente lite with such powers and duties as the court may direct, take other action required to preserve the corporate assets where located, and carry on the business of the corporation until a full hearing can be held." § 13.1–909(E). Of course, in this case there has been no termination of corporate existence, according to the statutes providing for dissolution, to furnish the predicate for appointment of a receiver to conduct the corporate affairs.

The corporate existence of a nonstock corporation may be terminated involuntarily by order of the Commission "when it finds that the corporation (i) has continued to exceed or abuse the authority conferred upon it by law...." Code § 13.1–915. Before entering such order, the Commission must issue a rule to show cause against the corporation. The Commission may issue the rule on its own "or on motion of the Attorney General." Of course, that has not happened here.

But, as we have said, the Attorney General maintains that a proper forum for the relief he seeks in the prayer of the bill is in the circuit court, principally relying on *Tauber*. In that case, we said, "This Court long ago recognized the common law authority of the Attorney General to act on behalf of the public in matters involving charitable assets." * * * There, we held that the Attorney General could properly assert jurisdiction in a circuit court over assets located in Virginia held by trustees in dissolution of a foreign charitable corporation. The trustees had been directors of the corporation, which operated a hospital in the Commonwealth.

In that case, the charter of a Maryland charitable corporation had been revoked by that state, which converted its directors by operation of law to trustees in dissolution. * * * Because the charter revocation terminated the entity's corporate existence, it could no longer function as a corporation. The corporate assets, located in Virginia, had automatically transferred to the directors as trustees. * * * There, unlike this case, charitable assets were abroad in this State in the hands of individuals who were trustees in dissolution; those assets were not being held, as here, by a viable, lawful Virginia corporation. Thus, we decided the Attorney General could act on behalf of the public regarding the *Tauber* assets.

Addressing another issue in *Tauber,* we rejected the defendants' contention that the litigation, dealing with appropriation of charitable assets by directors for their personal gain, involved impermissible interference by Virginia with the internal affairs of a foreign corporation. * * * In that context, we said, quoting *Hanshaw v. Day,* 202 Va. 818, 824, 120 S.E.2d 460, 464 (1961), that contributions made to a charitable corporation and "the assets realized therefrom were dedicated to those purposes and stamped with a public interest by the charter, the laws of this State, sound reason and public policy." * * * We also stated that "[t]he members acquired no property rights in, nor were they equitably entitled to such assets, either during the lifetime of the corporation or upon dissolution." *Id.* "To hold otherwise," we said, "would convert the public nature and purpose of the corporation into a vehicle for the personal pecuniary gain of the members."

Contrary to the Attorney General's argument, the fact that members of a charitable corporation have no personal property rights in corporate assets is not authority for permitting the Attorney General, in a circuit court suit like this, effectively to penetrate the corporate veil of an existing Virginia corporation, or as the Attorney General urges, "disregard, to some extent, the corporate form."

* * *

In sum, the General Assembly has provided in Code § 13.1–813 that "[n]o court within or without Virginia ... shall have jurisdiction to review, reverse, correct or annul any action of the Commission, within the scope of its authority ... or to enjoin, restrain or interfere with the Commission in the performance of its official duties." If circuit courts, at the request of the Attorney General, are to have subject matter jurisdiction over claims like those made in this suit, the General Assembly has the power to so provide, as it did in Code § 55–532 when it authorized the Attorney General to exercise his common law authority regarding certain nonprofit health care entities. Under the existing common law and present statutory scheme, however, the circuit court lacks subject matter jurisdiction over this suit.

Consequently, finding that the trial court did not err in denying the plaintiffs' motion for a preliminary injunction and appointment of a receiver, the May 2001 order will be affirmed.

Affirmed.

Questions

Do you agree with the Virginia Supreme Court that the state's Attorney General should not be permitted to intervene in the disposition of assets of nonprofit corporations devoted to charitable purposes in the absence of a specific power granted by the state legislature? The Virginia Court decided the State Corporation Commission should be the proper forum for issues involving management of charitable assets and that the Attorney General does not have "inherent power" to act of behalf of the public in such matters. The Court disputed the Attorney General's position that a Virginia nonstock corporation devoted to charitable purposes is "essentially" a charitable trust. Would a state corporation commission better serve the public than a state's Attorney General?

Problem

John and Mary Barry want to operate a day care center. They approach you for your opinion as to the structure they should choose for the center. They ask whether they should incorporate. In addition, they ask whether the center should be for-profit or nonprofit. Profits from the center will be their sole source of income. They also ask you for your advice as to how profits can be distributed to them.

III. NONGOVERNMENTAL ORGANIZATION (NGO)

Some nonprofit organizations have sought status as a nongovernmental organization (NGO) in what has been termed the global third sector. The nongovernmental organization, the NGO, is a nonprofit organization that is concerned with the social development of communities[12] and one that plays a direct role in the development of international law. Examples of NGOs include Greenpeace, Amnesty International, Oxford Committee for Famine Relief (Oxfam), which is a British organization whose objectives are to "relieve poverty, distress and suffering in any part of the world, and to educate the public concerning the nature, causes and effects of poverty,"[13] the International Red Cross, the International Campaign to Ban Landmines, and the International Senior Lawyers Project, which provides a vehicle by which skilled and experienced senior lawyers can provide volunteer legal services to the world community. These organizations seek enforcement of international law and, in this context, monitor State compliance with international laws in the areas of environmental protection, international human rights, and humanitarian law.[14] As one author concluded, the principle function of NGOs is their participation in the international decision making process.[15] They seek to find solutions for global problems and to develop and strengthen international law.

One of the major contributions of NGOs is the communicating of information to governments, including the United Nations.[16] Although NGOs in their present form came into existence after World War II

---

12. See Chiara Giorgetti, "The Role of Nongovernmental Organizations in the Climate Change Negotiations," 9 Colo. J. Int'l Envtl. L. & Pol'y. 115, 116. The author noted that NGOs have become important actors in international and national politics. Id. at 136.

13. See OXFAM, http://www.who.org/programmes/ina/ngo/ngo147.htm.

14. Karsten Nowrot, "Legal Consequences of Globalization: The Status of Non–Governmental Organizations under International Law," 6 Ind. J. Global Leg. Stud. J. 579, 580.

15. Id. at 590.

16. See John King Gamble and Charlotte Ku, "International Law—New Actors and New Technologies: Center Stage for NGOs?," 31 L. & Pol. in Int'l. Bus. 221, 320.

because of their activities following the creation of the United Nations,[17] the propagation and refinement of NGOs is a more recent phenomenon.

IV. FOREIGN NONPROFIT ORGANIZATIONS AND PHILANTHROPY ABROAD

Two preeminent authors on the role of the nonprofit sector in the global community summarized voluntary sector activities currently existing outside the United States in a book they edited on the subject.[18] They concluded that the distinction between governmental and nongovernmental institutions is often blurred and that the nonprofit sector is generally more independent in common law countries than civil law States. They noted that in many Catholic countries, the voluntary sector has evolved from the church whereas nonprofit groups in socialist countries, if they exist, are controlled by the government. They pointed out that NGOs provide services to impoverished groups and support projects in developing countries. The authors noted that because state subsidies may be limited in these countries and because corporations and individuals may have little disposable income, the nonprofit organization in developing countries may have few resources.

Notes

1. An example of the expanding role of nonprofit organizations in former Communist countries is the Act on Organizing and Conducting Cultural Activities enacted in Poland in 1991 to define methods and procedures for establishing cultural (national, state-owned and community-owned institutions).[19] The Act provides that supreme and central governmental administrative agencies and voivods (district or provincial governments) may establish cultural institutions, such as theaters, museums, cinemas, libraries, and art galleries. A local community or a community union may establish community-owned cultural institutions for which cultural activities constitute the primary goals under their charters.[20] The deed to establish a cultural institution is issued by its founder (the entity that forms the cultural institution). The founder provides the cultural institution with the necessary means to commence and carry out cultural activities and to maintain premises where the activities are conducted. The Act confers the status of incorporation on cultural institutions as of the date of their entry in the register maintained by the founder. Founders may include local communities and community unions, and supreme and central government administrative agencies.[21] Donations to cultural institutions are exempted from the income tax basis.

17. See Karsten Nowrot, cited in note 14, p. 581.

18. Virginia Hodgkinson and Kathleen McCarty, "The Voluntary Sector in International Perspective: an Overview," Chapter 1 in Kathlen McCarthy, Virginia Hodgkinson, and Russy Sumariwalla, The Nonprofit Sector in the Global Community, Jossey–Bass Publishers, 1992.

19. Discussion by Teresa Drozdowska, "Legal Foundations for Protection of Cultural Property in Poland," Chapter 17 in Law of Cultural Property, Marilyn Phelan, Gary Edson, and Kimberly Mayfield, eds., Kalos Kapp Press, 1998.

20. See Articles 2, 8–10, and 18–20, Section 1, Journal of Laws No. 60/91, Item 253.

21. Id., Articles 8 and 9. Article 21, Section 1 of the Act permits founders such as

2. An example of a progressive NGO law in an Arab country is a law enacted in Yemen in 2001 related to associations and foundations.[22] The law improves the legal framework for NGOs by simplifying the procedures for establishing them. Foreign associations and foundations may register offices in Yemen.

3. The United Kingdom encourages philanthropy through the voluntary sector and by private public partnerships (PPPs). The concept of the PPP is that private enterprise should invest in major projects carried out by public entities.

The U.K. is introducing measures to provide income tax relief for donors of gifts of cash, but not assets, to charities. The Private Treaty Sales plan permits owners of artworks and antiquities to negotiate a reduced sale price with an approved charity for their works in exchange for an agreed deduction in their inheritance tax. The transfer of works of art, which satisfy a "pre-eminence" test, will eliminate part or all of the inheritance tax.

A. Synopsis of French Law on Non–Profit Organizations

Consider the laws in France relating to nonprofits from the following summary of French laws on nonprofit associations and foundations prepared by Salli Swartz,[23] an attorney who practices in Paris.

1. Associations

The laws of June 14 and 17, of 1791, enacted during the French Revolution (and which were called the laws "Le Chapelier) prohibited individuals from forming groups to defend their "alleged mutual interests." In furtherance of this prohibition, Articles 291–294 of the Napoleonic Code created and punished the crime of association. Although Article 8 of the Constitution of 1848 recognized the right to associate, it did not repeal the Articles of the Napoleonic Code. This situation remained until the enactment of the law of July 1, 1901 (the "Association Law") which created the right to form groups or associations.

The Association Law created a right to create associations, but it did not create a legal entity specific to associations. Article 1 of the Association Law defines an association as an agreement by which two or more persons mutually and permanently make available to themselves their knowledge and activities for a purpose other than making profit.

To be construed as an association under French law, the group of persons must be independent and the association must be created permanently and indefinitely. Groups that are created for the sole purpose of promoting one event, or to lobby for a particular mission, are not considered to be an association under French law and case law.

voivods and supreme and central government administrative agencies to establish cultural institutions pursuant to agreements with natural persons, legal persons, or unincorporated organizational entities.

22. Law No. 1 for the Year 2001, Feb., 2001.

23. Salli Anne Swartz, Phillips, Giraud, Naud & Swartz, Avocats a la Cour, Paris, France. Ms. Swartz would like to thank Marie Pierre Gay, Avocat a la Cour, for her contribution and assistance in preparing this synopsis.

An association, which can take the form of a mere agreement between two or more persons, does not have to be publicly registered with the authorities. However, if an association is declared and registered with the authorities, it will benefit from the attributes of a legal entity. To register an association, the association must have by-laws drafted in accordance with the Association Law and certain written formalities must be carried out with the local police and administrative authorities (the "Préfecture") at the place of the association's registered office.

There is a distinction under French law between an association and a foundation: the purpose of an association is to permit a group of persons to pursue a common objective for non profit reasons, whereas pursuant to the Law nË 87–571 of July 23, 1987, the purpose of a foundation is to receive assets irrevocably for the furtherance of the goal of the foundation. A foundation does not have members.

The legal concept of a trust does not exist under French law. Consequently, there is no such entity as a charitable trust in France.

There are several different types of nonprofit associations in France, such as public interest associations and associations which are subject to administrative approval.

A public interest association is one which meets two criteria: first it must have a general public interest mission as its goal, such as sports federations, a musical orchestra, tourism, education and culture, and second, it must allow for administrative oversight to assure that the association is furthering its purpose. There is no fixed manner in which this latter criteria must be met, but the by-laws must provide for some oversight mechanism, for example, the appointment of governmental representatives to the board of directors.

Associations which are subject to administrative approval include, for example, associations the purposes of which are consumer protection, environmental protection, financing political parties, and sporting associations. In order to obtain approval, certain formalities must be accomplished with the governmental entity or ministry which is responsible for the subject matter of the association. For example, an association which promotes tourism will require the authorization of the local police authorities and the Ministry of Tourism.

The advantage of obtaining an administrative authorization is that it confers to the association certain benefits such as standing to file judicial actions to defend or further its goals, the possibility of receiving state grants, and the possibility of receiving gifts or donations and certain tax advantages. To obtain and maintain such administrative authorization, the association must fulfill the following criteria:

- The association's purpose must not include the generating of profit and its directors and/or managers cannot be remunerated;

- Its activity must be carried out in a manner so as to benefit the general interest of the users/members of the association; and

- The exercise of its activity must contribute to its purpose and should not generate significant direct or indirect profit either for the association itself or for any of its directors, founders, managers or members.

- It should not carry out activities or be managed in such a manner so as to systematically result in its turnover exceeding its operating costs and if such a situation should arise, the profit should be reinvested in the activity of the association and not distributed;

- The work of the association should have some social benefit and should provide a service or meet needs that are not met by the market/commercial sector.

With regard to the value added tax ("VAT"), unless the association's purpose is specifically excepted by law from the application of value added tax, such tax may apply to certain of the activities of certain associations. The associations which are exempt from VAT are those the purposes of which are philosophical, religious, political, patriotic, or which are related to union or civil society activities. Social, educational, cultural or sports associations will be exempt if the services rendered to their members and/or the sales made to such members does not exceed 10% of the total turnover of the association concerned. Charitable associations which have social functions open to the public will not be liable for VAT provided that the prices have been approved by the public authorities or if such prices are below market prices for comparable events carried out by commercial enterprises.

Tax deductions to nonprofit organizations are fairly limited under the French Tax Code.

2. Foundations

Foundations have been in existence since antiquity and have been subject to administrative oversight commencing in the fifteenth century. Foundations were then prohibited during the French Revolution and the term "foundation" was not even mentioned in the Napoleonic Code. Although foundations reappeared in the eighteenth century, the Law nË 87–571 of July 23, 1987, modified by the Law nË 90–559 of July 4, 1990, was the first law to provide legal status for foundations and to define the tax system to which foundations are subject.

A foundation is the agreement by which one or several individuals or entities decide to assign irrevocably goods, rights or resources to a group or legal entity in order to further a general interest mission (such as a cultural or a charitable goal, for instance) and for a purpose other than generating profit. Unlike associations and companies, a foundation consists of a group of assets and not of a group of persons.

A foundation can either take the form of an agreement between one individual (or an entity) and another entity or the form of a legal entity.

A foundation which takes the form of a simple agreement is usually a grant by which a person (or an entity) decides to make a donation to an entity which is entitled to receive such grant or donation. Entities which are entitled to receive grants or donations include public institutions, publicly owned corporations and associations which have been duly registered with and authorized by the authorities.

A foundation, which takes the form of a legal entity, can be formed by individuals, or several publicly-owned or private entities. In addition, this type of foundation can be set up for the purpose of receiving grants and/or donations.

Foundations which benefit from the attributes of a legal entity are few in France because it is difficult for them to meet the criteria to which their formation is subject.

There are two types of foundations which can be constituted as legal entities: public interest foundations and corporate foundations ("fondation d'entreprise").

3. Public Interest Foundations

This type of foundation needs to be approved by the French Administrative Supreme Court (the "Conseil d'Etat") in order to have the right to be called a "foundation" and to benefit from the attributes of a legal entity. Once it receives such approval, the foundation is recognized as serving the public interest ("fondation reconnue d'utilité publique").

In order to obtain such administrative approval, the foundation must meet three criteria:

- the purpose of the foundation must be philanthropic or altruistic;
- the founders must grant to the foundation sufficient assets so that such assets can ensure adequate income for the foundation, and
- its by-laws must conform to the standard ones which have been drafted by the "Conseil d'Etat".

The by-laws must specify in particular the purpose of the foundation, its means of action and the composition of its Board of Directors.

The directors must include governmental representatives and persons who have expertise with respect to the purpose of the foundation. In addition, this type of foundation is subject to administrative oversight. For example, the sale of any foundation's assets or any contribution made to the foundation is subject to administrative approval.

In France, a national body, the National Council of Foundations ("Conseil National des Fondations"), exists to gather information on foundations, draft an annual report for the Government and propose to the Government actions for the development of philanthropy through foundations.

4. Corporate Foundations

A corporate foundation can be formed by civil or commercial companies or publicly owned industrial or commercial companies, the purpose of which is to provide a structure for corporate sponsorship by such entities.

Although no standard by-laws are imposed by the French administration for this type of foundation, a corporate foundation must meet the following three criteria:

- First, like any foundation, the foundation must consist of a group of assets which must be devoted to the furtherance of a general interest mission and for a purpose other that making a profit, i. e., the foundation must have an altruistic or philanthropic purpose;

- Second, the setting up of a corporate foundation is subject to administrative approval;

- Third, the founders must contribute an amount of capital which is fixed by a Decree. This capital contribution must be irrevocably donated to the foundation and may be used only to carry out the purpose of the foundation. In addition, the founders must commit to make payments on a regular basis, over a period of five years maximum, to the foundation.

These commitments must be provided in the by-laws and must be secured by a bank guarantee.

Unlike the public interest foundation, there is no requirement for governmental representatives to sit on the Board of Directors.

Corporate foundations must file annual accounts and unlike the other types of foundations, they can be formed for a short period of time (but not less than five years).

Most foundations are subject to corporate income tax pursuant to the same conditions as commercial enterprises. However, those foundations which carry out their activity free of charge (i. e., they have no income) or those whose expenses exceed income are exempt from corporate tax.

With regard to the value added tax ("VAT"), as is the case for associations, this tax may apply to certain activities of certain types of foundations.

Foundations which are exempt from VAT are those the purpose of which is charitable or philanthropic, and only provided that the prices which they charge have been approved by the public authorities, or if the prices are below market prices for comparable services, or if the services performed by the foundation are not available by commercial enterprises.

Finally, like associations, payments which are made by individuals to a public interest foundation are deductible from taxable income within certain limits which are set by the Tax Law enacted each year by the legislature.

B. Synopsis of Italian Law on Nonprofit Organizations

Professor Giovanni Riccio[24] summarized laws in Italy on nonprofit organizations as follows. Italy reorganized the fiscal legal principles of nonprofit organizations in 1997.[25] The 1997 law created ONLUS (Organizzazione non lucrativa di utilita or Non-profit organization of social utility), which is a nonprofit organization with social benefit purposes. These separate and autonomous category of entities have fiscal benefits in that they may receive donations from the state. Further, individuals and companies receive tax deductions for their donations. Donations to the ONLUS foundations are deductible up to a certain percentage of gross tax, and the transfer of goods as gifts to ONLUS is VAT exempt. Activities of ONLUS center around benefitting persons disadvantaged by economic, physical, mental, social or family conditions and include providing humanitarian aid to members of foreign groups. These corporate bodies may not distribute their profits to members or other entities nor may they distribute assets to their members upon dissolution (the non-distribution constraint principle).

The Italian Civil code recognizes two forms of nonprofit organizations: associations and foundations. Associations and foundations are set up by a public document, by a notarial act, or by another public official, but foundations, unlike associations, may be created by will. The law relating to associations and foundations is similar to that in the United States in many respects. These organizations have private autonomy and, in effect, become corporations by filing a memorandum of association that sets out the purpose of the corporation, its name, location, and rules regarding its administration. An association must set out the rights and duties of its members and the conditions for its administration. Foundations must set out the criteria and the income donations procedures. The law prohibits the distribution of profits and in the case of dissolution, any remaining property, after liquidation, must be assigned to other nonprofit organizations that have similar purposes.

Note

In the United States, foreign governments and international organizations qualify for exemption from taxation under § 892 of the Internal Revenue Code. Thus, foreign nonprofit organizations, like their U.S. counterparts, are exempt from U.S. income taxation. However, donors in the United States may not receive a charitable contribution deduction for contributions to organizations organized outside the United States.[26]

---

24. Professor Giovanni Maria Riccio, Professor of Law, University of Salerno (Italy); translated by Ileana Ippolito and Frank Z. Elmer.

25. Legislative Decree 460.

26. Section 170 grants a taxpayer a charitable deduction for contributions to organizations described in § 170(c). Section 170(c) requires these entities to be organized within the United States. See also *Tressler v. Commissioner*, 206 F.2d 538 (4th Cir.1953). The theory is that tax subsidies for nonprofit organizations are justified because these organizations relieve the government of some costs associated with general welfare. The state and federal governmental costs of providing benefits to the public is not alleviated by organizations in foreign countries.

Nonetheless donations that benefit charitable causes in foreign countries, under certain circumstances, can qualify for charitable contribution deductions when they are funneled through an organization based in the United States.

REVENUE RULING 63–252
1963–2 C.B. 101

Advice has been requested as to the deductibility, under section 170 of the Internal Revenue Code of 1954, of contributions by individuals to a charity organized in the United States which thereafter transmits some or all of its funds to foreign charitable organization.

Section 170 of the Code provides, in material part, as follows:

(a) ALLOWANCE OF DEDUCTION.—

(1) GENERAL RULE.—There shall be allowed as a deduction any charitable contribution (as defined in subsection (c)) payment of which is made within the taxable year. A charitable contribution shall be allowable as a deduction only if verified under regulations prescribed by the Secretary or his delegate. * * *

(c) CHARITABLE CONTRIBUTION DEFINED.—For purposes of this section, the term 'charitable contribution' means a contribution or gift to or for the use of—* * *

(2) A corporation, trust, or community chest, fund, or foundation—

(A) created or organized in the United States or in any possession thereof, or under the law of the United States, any State or Territory, the District of Columbia, or any possession of the United States;

(B) organized and operated exclusively for religious, charitable, scientific, literary, or educational purposes or for the prevention of cruelty to children or animals;

(C) no part of the net earnings of which inures to the benefit of any private shareholder or individual; and

(D) no substantial part of the activities of which is carrying on propaganda, or otherwise attempting, to influence legislation.

A contribution or gift by a corporation to a trust, chest, fund, or foundation shall be deductible by reason of this paragraph only if it is to be used within the United States or any of its possessions exclusively for purposes specified in subparagraph (B).

In determining whether contributions to or for the use of a particular corporation, trust, community chest, fund, or foundation are deductible, it must first be determined that the recipient organization was validly created or organized in the United States, a state or territory, the District of Columbia or a possession of the United States, as required by section 170(c)(2)(A) of the Code. If the organization does not qualify

Sec. IV FOREIGN NONPROFIT ORGANIZATIONS 55

under section 170(c)(2)(A) of the Code—that is, it was not created or organized in the United States, etc.—a contribution thereto is not deductible under section 170 of the Code. Dora F. Welti v. Commissioner, 1 T.C. 905 (1943); Muzaffer Erselcuk et al. v. Commissioner, 30 T.C. 962 (1958). It must further be found that the recipient was organized and operated exclusively for one of the purposes stated in section 170(c)(2)(B) of the Code, namely, religious, charitable, scientific, literary, or educational purposes or for the prevention of cruelty to children or animals, and that it meets the remaining requirements of section 170(c)(2) of the Code. Assuming that an organization otherwise meets the requirements set forth in section 170(c)(2) of the Code, a further problem arises where that organization is required to turn all or part of its funds over to a foreign charitable organization. As noted above, contributions directly to the foreign organization would not be deductible. The question presented here is whether the result should differ when funds are contributed to a domestic charity which then transmits those funds to a foreign charitable organization.

Prior to the passage of the Revenue Act of 1938 there were no restrictions as to the place of creation of charitable organizations to which individuals might make deductible contributions. (Section 102(c) of the Revenue Act of 1935, which first permitted a deduction for corporate charitable contributions, limited that deduction to contributions to 'domestic' organizations which used such contributions within the United States.) The rule as to individual contributions was changed with the passage of the Revenue Act of 1938. Section 23(*o*) of that Act provided that contributions by individuals were deductible only if the recipient was a 'domestic' organization. See discussion of that section in Ways and Means Committee Report, H.R. Report No. 1860, Seventy-fifth Congress, Third Session, C.B. 1939–1 (Part 2), 728, at 742. Section 224 of the Revenue Act of 1939 substituted for the requirement that a qualifying organization be 'domestic,' the requirement that it have been 'created or organized in the United States or in any possession thereof,' etc. In substantially the same form, this requirement was re-enacted as section 170(c)(2)(A) of the 1954 Code.

At the outset, it should be noted that section 170(c)(2) (A) of the Code relates only to the place of creation of the charitable organization to which deductible contributions may be made and does not restrict the area in which deductible contributions may be used. Compare the last sentence in section 170(c)(2) of the Code, which requires that certain corporate contributions be used within the United States. Accordingly, the following discussion should not be construed as limiting in any way the geographical areas in which deductible contributions by individuals may be used.

The deductibility of the contributions here at issue will be discussed in connection with five illustrative examples set out below. The 'foreign organization' referred to in each of the examples is an organization which is chartered in a foreign country and is so organized and operated that it meets all the requirements of section 170(c)(2) of the Code excepting the requirement set forth in section 170(c)(2)(A) of the Code. The 'domestic organization' in each example is assumed to meet all the requirements in section 170(c)(2) of the Code. In each case, the question to be decided is whether the amounts paid to the domestic organization are deductible under section 170(a) of the Code.

(1) In pursuance of a plan to solicit funds in this country, a foreign organization caused a domestic organization to be formed. At the time of formation, it was proposed that the domestic organization would conduct a fund-raising campaign, pay the administrative expenses from the collected fund and remit any balance to the foreign organization.

(2) Certain persons in this country, desirous of furthering a foreign organization's work, formed a charitable organization within the United States. The charter of the domestic organization provides that it will receive contributions and send them, at convenient intervals, to the foreign organization.

(3) A foreign organization entered into an agreement with a domestic organization which provides that the domestic organization will conduct a fund-raising campaign on behalf of the foreign organization. The domestic organization has previously received a ruling that contributions to it are deductible under section 170 of the Code. In conducting the campaign, the domestic organization represents to prospective contributors that the raised funds will go to the foreign organization.

(4) A domestic organization conducts a variety of charitable activities in a foreign country. Where its purposes can be furthered by granting funds to charitable groups organized in the foreign country, the domestic organization makes such grants for purposes which it has reviewed and approved. The grants are paid from its general funds and although the organization solicits from the public, no special fund is raised by a solicitation on behalf of particular foreign organizations.

(5) A domestic organization, which does charitable work in a foreign country, formed a subsidiary in that country to facilitate its operations there. The foreign organization was formed for purposes of administrative convenience and the domestic organization controls every facet of its operations. In the past the domestic organization solicited contributions for the specific purpose of carrying out its charitable activities in the foreign country and it will continue to do so in the future. However, following the formation of the foreign subsidiary, the domestic organization will transmit funds it receives for its foreign charitable activities directly to that organization.

It is recognized that special earmarking of the use or destination of funds paid to a qualifying charitable organization may deprive the donor of a deduction. In S. E. Thomason v. Commissioner, 2 T.C. 441 (1943), the court held that amounts paid to a charitable organization were not deductible where the contributions were earmarked for the benefit of a particular ward of the organization. Similarly, see Revenue Ruling 54–580, C.B. 1954–2, 97. These cases indicate that an inquiry as to the deductibility of a contribution need not stop once it is determined that an amount has been paid to a qualifying organization; if the amount is earmarked, then it is appropriate to look beyond the fact that the immediate recipient is a qualifying organization to determine whether the payment constitutes a deductible contribution.

Similarly, if an organization is required for other reasons, such as a specific provision in its charter, to turn contributions, or any particular contribution it receives, over to another organization, then in determining whether such contributions are deductible it is appropriate to determine whether the ultimate recipient of the contribution is a qualifying organization. * * * Moreover, it seems clear that the requirements of section 170(c)(2)(A) of the Code would be nullified if contributions inevitably committed to go to a foreign organization were held to be deductible solely because, in the course of transmittal to the foreign organization, they came to rest momentarily in a qualifying domestic organization. In such cases the domestic organization is only nominally the donee; the real donee is the ultimate foreign recipient.

Accordingly, the Service holds that contributions to the domestic organizations described in the first and second examples set forth above are not deductible. Similarly, those contributions to the domestic organization described in the third example which are given for the specific purpose of being turned over to the foreign organization are held to be nondeductible.

On the other hand, contributions received by the domestic organization described in the fourth example will not be earmarked in any manner, and use of such contributions will be subject to control by the domestic organization. Consequently, the domestic organization is considered to be the recipient of such contributions for purposes of applying section 170(c) of the Code. Similarly, the domestic organization described in the fifth example is considered to be the real beneficiary of contributions it receives for transmission to the foreign organization. Since the foreign organization is merely an administrative arm of the domestic organization, the fact that contributions are ultimately paid over to the foreign organization does not require a conclusion that the domestic organization is not the real recipient of those contributions. Accordingly, contributions by individuals to the domestic organizations described in the fourth and fifth examples are considered to be deductible.

* * *

REVENUE RULING 66–79
1966–1 C.B. 48

Contributions to a domestic charity described in section 170(c)(2) of the Internal Revenue Code of 1954 which are solicited for a specific project of a foreign charitable organization are deductible under section 170 of the Code where the domestic charity has reviewed and approved the project as being in furtherance of its own exempt purposes and has control and discretion as to the use of the contributions. Revenue Ruling 63–252, C.B. 1963–2, 101, amplified.

The Internal Revenue Service has been requested to clarify Revenue Ruling 63–252, C.B. 1963–2, 101 with respect to the deductibility of contributions to a domestic charitable corporation which may solicit contributions for a specific project of a foreign charity in the manner presented below.

X corporation is a domestic charitable organization formed under the nonprofit laws of the state of Y. It is exempt from Federal income tax as being organized and operated exclusively for charitable, educational, and scientific purposes described in section 501(c)(3) of the Internal Revenue Code of 1954. Contributions to it are deductible since it is an organization described in section 170(c)(2) of the Code.

The corporation's charter provides, in part, that in furtherance of its educational, scientific, and charitable purposes it shall have the power to receive and allocate contributions, within the discretion of the board of directors, to any organization organized and operated exclusively for charitable or educational purposes within the meaning of section 501(c)(3) of the Code.

In contrast to the broad generality of the purposes stated in its charter, the name X corporation suggests a purpose to assist a named foreign organization. The individuals who organized X corporation had become interested in furthering the work of the named foreign organization, a corporation organized and operated in a foreign country exclusively for charitable, scientific, and educational purposes. The individuals concerned, who are United States citizens not acting on behalf of the foreign organization, did not wish X corporation to function simply as a fund raising medium for the foreign organization. Instead, they were interested in raising funds for specific projects, such as scientific research projects, to be carried out by the foreign organization, or individuals connected with the foreign organization, pursuant to grants previously reviewed and approved by the board of directors of X corporation.

The bylaws of X corporation provide, in part, that: (1) The making of grants and contributions and otherwise rendering financial assistance for the purposes expressed in the charter of the organization shall be within the exclusive power of the board of directors; (2) in furtherance of the organization's purposes, the board of directors shall have power to make grants to any organization organized and operated exclusively for charitable, scientific or educational purposes within the meaning of section 501(c)(3) of the Code; (3) the board of directors shall review all requests for funds from other organizations, shall require that such requests specify the use to which the funds will be put, and if the board of directors approves the request, shall authorize payment of such funds to the approved grantee; (4) the board of directors shall require that the grantees furnish a periodic accounting to show that the funds were expended for the purposes which were approved by the board of directors; and (5) the board of directors may, in its absolute discretion, refuse to make any grants or contributions or otherwise render financial assistance to or for any or all the purposes for which funds are requested.

The bylaws also provide that after the board of directors has approved a grant to another organization for a specific project or purpose, the corporation may solicit funds for the grant to the specifically approved project or purpose of the other organization. However, the board of directors shall at all times have the right to withdraw approval of the grant and use the funds for other charitable, scientific or educational purposes.

In accordance with the provisions of its charter and bylaws, X corporation at times solicits contributions which are to be used to provide grants to the foreign organization mentioned above, or to individuals connected with such foreign organization, for specific purposes approved by X corporation's board of directors in accordance with its bylaws. At all times all of the pertinent facts, including the fact that the board of directors may withdraw its approval of a particular grant even after it has been made, are available to any contributor not previously informed of such facts should the contributor so request either before or after a contribution has been made. The corporation refuses to accept contributions so earmarked that they must in any event go to the foreign organization.

* * *

Revenue Ruling 63–252, C.B. 1963–2, 101, discusses the deductibility of contributions by individuals to a charity organized in the United States which thereafter transmits some or all of its funds to a foreign charitable organization. Example (4) of that ruling concerns a domestic organization described in section 170(c) of the Code which makes grants to a foreign organization for purposes which the domestic organization has reviewed and approved as in furtherance of its purposes. Contributions to the domestic organization are not earmarked in any manner for a foreign organization and the use of such contributions is subject to control by the domestic organization. For these reasons, the domestic organization is considered to be the recipient of such contributions within the meaning of section 170(c)(2) of the Code.

Under the provisions of its charter and bylaws, X corporation may make grants to any organization organized and operated exclusively for charitable, scientific, or educational purposes within the meaning of section 501(c)(3) of the Code. An organization described in that section can be either a domestic or a foreign organization. The operations of X corporation bring it within the purview of example (4) of Revenue Ruling 63–252 except for the manner in which it may solicit contributions for its foreign grants. This raises a question as to whether the contributions are earmarked for the foreign organization so as to prohibit a deduction under section 170 of the Code.

Revenue Ruling 62–113, C.B. 1962–2, 10, holds that where gifts to an organization described in section 170(c) of the Code are not earmarked by the donor for a particular individual, the deduction will be allowable where it is established that a gift is intended by the donor for the use of the organization and not as a gift to an individual for whose benefit the amount given may be used by the donee organization. The test in each case is whether the organization has full control of the donated funds, and discretion as to their use, so as to insure that they will be used to carry out its functions and purposes.

In the instant case the domestic corporation may only solicit for specific grants when it has reviewed and approved them as being in furtherance of its purposes. Furthermore, under the terms of its bylaws the domestic corporation may make such solicitations only on the condition that it shall have control and discretion as to the use of the contributions received by it. Therefore, contributions received by the domestic organization from such solicitations are regarded as for the use of the domestic corporation and not for the organization receiving the grant from the domestic organization.* * *

Question

Do you agree that donations by U.S. taxpayers to charitable entities organized in foreign countries or donations to domestic charities but earmarked for use in a foreign country should not be deductible for federal income tax purposes?

Note

The IRS has expressed concern that there may be a diversion of assets for noncharitable purposes with respect to international grant-making and other international activities. In November 2002, the Treasury Department released "Anti–Terrorist Financing Guidelines: Voluntary Best Practices for U.S.-Based Charities." These guidelines were developed to help charities reduce the risk that their funds would be frozen in connection with any ongoing anti-terrorism investigation. The Service pointed out in Announcement 2003–29, 2003–1 C.B. 928, that investigative and law enforcement initiatives have identified situations in which charitable organizations have been a significant source of terrorist funding. In Announcement 2003–29, the Service pointed out that private foundations must exercise expenditure responsibility with respect to grants to organizations that are not public charities for tax purposes. (See Chapters 6 and 7 for a discussion of public charities and private foundations.) Failure to establish adequate procedures (1) to see that a grant is spent solely for the purpose for which it was made, (2) to obtain full and complete reports from the grantee on how the funds were spent, and (3) to make full and detailed reports to the IRS with respect to these expenditures will cause a private foundation to be subject to the excise tax of § 4945. (See discussion of § 4945 excise tax in Chapter 7.)

Chapter 2

THE NONPROFIT CORPORATION

I. NATURE OF A NONPROFIT CORPORATION

Most nonprofit organizations seek corporate status. The law relating to corporations is more defined, and corporate status provides for limited liability for members of the organization, for centralized management, and for more definite standards relating to liability of officers and directors.

A corporation has been defined as "an artificial being, invisible, intangible, and existing only in contemplation of law."[1] Because it is a creature of law, it cannot be created by agreement of interested parties or members but rather can be created and corporate powers granted only by or under authority of an act of a state legislature. The legislature of the state, as the state sovereignty, has inherent power to create corporations, to determine the procedures for incorporation, the purposes for which a corporation can be created, and the powers to be conferred upon a corporation.

Corporations can be private, public, quasi-public, profit and nonprofit. Public corporations are those corporations, connected with the administration of the government, that are created for public purposes only. The fact that a private corporation serves a public interest does not make it a public corporation. Thus, a nonprofit corporation created by individuals is a private corporation even though it was created to administer a public charity. A quasi-public corporation is a private corporation that has been given powers of a public nature in order that it may fulfill duties of a public nature.

IN RE MT. SINAI HOSPITAL
Court of Appeals, New York, 1928
250 N.Y. 103, 164 N.E. 871

POUND, J.

Mt. Sinai Hospital is a charitable corporation. It was incorporated in the year 1852 under the name of 'The Jews Hospital in New York,'

---

[1] Trustees of Dartmouth College v. Woodward, 17 U.S. 518 (1819).

under a general act (L. 1848, c. 319) entitled: 'An Act for the incorporation of benevolent, charitable, scientific and missionary societies.' The affairs of such a corporation are, under such act, controlled and managed by a board of trustees or directors. The purpose of the incorporation, as stated in the certificate, was 'medical and surgical aid to persons of the Jewish persuasion and for all other purposes appertaining to Hospitals and Dispensaries.' Its name was changed by a special act of the Legislature (L. 1866, c. 627) to 'The Mount Sinai Hospital.' The act of 1848 provided: 'The society so incorporated may annually elect from its members its trustees, directors or managers, at such time and place, and in such manner as may be specified in its by-laws.'

* * *

Laws of 1925, c. 17, provides: 'The various classes of the board of trustees of the Mount Sinai Hospital, as now constituted, shall continue in office until the expiration of their respective terms, and the successors of said respective classes shall be elected *by a majority vote of the remaining members of the board of trustees* annually upon the expiration of the terms of said respective classes.'

The election of the members of the board in the year 1925 was held under the provisions of this act. The constitutionality of the statute is challenged in this proceeding, not by the corporation, but by two members of the society, paying annual dues, one as a $10 member and the other as a donor or $25 member. Membership consists of 'those persons who have enrolled their names' in one of several classes of members; the classification being dependent on the amount received. It is also provided that a member in arrears for one year may be dropped. The only question is whether the act violates any of the appellants' constitutional rights to have their contracts unimpaired and their property and liberty uninterfered with, except by due process of law, and to the protection of equal laws.

The change is not arbitrary or unreasonable. A board of trustees once elected by the members of the corporation becomes self-perpetuating. The purpose of the enactment may be regarded as twofold: First, to meet the situation of a possible falling membership; and, secondly, to make certain the self-perpetuating control of the society by the board as against the possible dangers of popular elections. Such a change must be upheld, unless, under the circumstances, it violates fundamental principles of justice, inconsistently with constitutional limitations on the legislative power.

The certificate of incorporation is subject to alteration by the Legislature. Not only did the Constitution of New York of 1846, in force when the hospital was incorporated, provide, as does the present Constitution (article 8, § 1), 'All general laws and special acts passed pursuant to this section may be altered from time to time or repealed;' but the act of 1848 (section 10) also contained a provision, 'The legislature may at any time amend, annual or repeal any incorporation formed or created under this act.' This reservation is a part of the charter. * * * Furthermore, the Legislature may, when in its judgment the objects of the corporation cannot be attained under general laws, create corporations by special act. Article 8, § 1. Thus we have the Mt. Sinai Hospital with a charter consisting of its certificate of incorporation as amended by special acts. We have such special acts accepted by the corporation. We have the act of 1925, challenged as unconstitutional by two members who assert that the board of trustees may not accept the amendment without their consent. They rest on the proposition that, so long as they choose to remain members of the corporation, the Legislature may not, under the reserved power to amend the corporate charter, without their consent, deprive them of their right to vote for trustees.

The reserved power to amend corporate charters prevents the charter from becoming a contract between state and corporation protected from impairment by the Constitution. * * * Under it anything may be done by the Legislature that could be done if the Federal Constitution did not prohibit a state from passing a law impairing the obligation of contracts. Const. U. S. art. 1, § 10. Any alteration may be made 'which will not defeat or substantially impair the object of the grant, or any rights * * * vested under it, and which the legislature may deem necessary to secure either' that object 'or any public right' or 'to promote due administration of the affairs of the corporation.' * * * A state may not, by using the form of charter amendment, deprive a corporation of any of its substantial property or property rights, except in the legitimate exercise of the legislative or police power, under the due process and equal protection clauses of the State and Federal Constitutions. * * * In other words, a corporate charter is no longer a contract between the corporation and the state which the state may not alter without the consent of the corporation; but the corporation and its members are not subject to any kind of confiscatory legislation or discriminatory burden which takes the guise of an amendment to the charter. 'The alterations [under the reserved power] must be reasonable; * * * and be consistent with the scope and object of the act of incorporation.' * * * Tested by this rule, the amendment is unobjectionable on constitutional grounds and is a proper exercise of the reserved power to alter charters, wholly independent of the exercise of the police power of the state. * * *

The grant of a special charter to a corporation does not deny to it or to other corporations 'the equal protection of the laws.' U. S. Const. Fourteenth Amendment, § 1. A corporate charter creates a legal entity, distinct from its members and from other corporations. The trustees of one charitable or educational corporation may be elected by the members; of another by the board itself; of a third by co-optation. Education Law (Cons. Laws, c. 16) § 1031. One corporation may have many and great powers; another few and small powers. They differ as individuals differ. The effort to require incorporation under general laws has proved both half-hearted and ineffective. The monition contained in the New York Constitution that 'corporations may be formed under general laws' has been heeded by the Legislature only so far as it has been deemed expedient by the Legislature itself to do so and the determination of the

Legislature is controlling on the courts. * * * The act of 1925, even though the corporation sought to reject it, as it does not, is not discriminatory legislation placing an unequal burden on the Mt. Sinai Hospital or on its members. * * * It is a governmental regulation of the method of electing trustees, as to which no rule of uniformity exists and which is a common regulation of charitable corporate charters. If the Legislature, in its wisdom, deems it necessary or appropriate, on grounds of public policy, to enact such a statute to carry into execution its power over the conduct of the business of its creature, the equal protection of the laws is not thereby withheld.

The corporation itself has been deprived of no property 'without due process of law' (U. S. Const. Fourteenth Amendment, § 1), for the provision that the trustees should be elected by its members, although a contractual right between state and corporation, subject to amendment under the reserved power, is not a property right of the corporation of which it could not be deprived without its consent. It has, moreover, sought the change in the law for its benefits and accepted and acted on it; so that the test is not, What are its rights in this regard, but what are the rights of the appellants as members of the corporation? * * * They had the bare right to vote for trustees because they were mere members of the corporation paying an annual membership fee. When they became members of the corporation they consented in advance to everything that could be done by legislative amendment to the charter which did not deprive them of their constitutional rights. * * * They took the risk of a true amendment.

* * *

If appellants are not satisfied with the amendment, they have an ample remedy in the right to refrain from paying membership dues in the future.

The order should be affirmed, with costs.

II. CREATION OF A NONPROFIT CORPORATION

Most states have separate statutes for nonprofit corporations although a few states have one general corporation act that governs both nonprofit and profit corporations. Most states prohibit nonprofit organizations from issuing shares of stock to their members. While a few do permit the issuance of stock certificates, all states prohibit nonprofit organizations from paying dividends to members. No states prohibit a nonprofit corporation from making a profit, but all states prohibit a distribution of assets to individuals or to for-profit entities other than the payment of reasonable compensation for services rendered.

A. Articles of Incorporation

The first step in creating a corporation is the filing of articles of incorporation with the Secretary of State.[2] The contents of the articles of incorporation are determined by the statutes of the state of incorporation. Generally, the articles for a nonprofit corporation would include the following information:

1. The name of the corporation.
2. The period of duration, which may be perpetual.
3. The purpose or purposes for which the corporation is organized.
4. The street address of the corporation's registered office and the name of its initial registered agent at that office.
5. The name and address of each incorporator.
6. A statement as to whether the corporation will have members.
7. Any provisions not inconsistent with law regarding the distribution of assets on dissolution.
8. The names and addresses of the individuals who are to serve as the initial directors.

If the nonprofit corporation seeks federal tax exempt status under § 501(c)(3), its articles must limit the purposes of the corporation to one or more of the exempt purposes set out in § 501(c)(3) of the Code. The articles of a § 501(c)(3) organization must provide that upon dissolution, all assets of the corporation will be distributed for one or more exempt purposes, or to the federal government, or to a state or local government, for a public purpose. The articles, or the law of the state in which the corporation is created, may not provide that the assets, upon dissolution, may be distributed to the corporation's members or shareholders. The articles for a charitable corporation, that is a private foundation for tax purposes (discussion in Chapter 7), must include provisions requiring the corporation to act or to refrain from acting in a manner that would cause it to become liable for penalty taxes imposed by §§ 4941–45 of the Internal Revenue Code (discussion in Chapter 7). However, this requirement is satisfied if state law contains such provisions.

If the Secretary of State finds that the articles comply with the law, the Secretary will file one of the duplicate originals of the articles in the office of the Secretary and attach the other to a certificate of incorporation, or charter, which is returned to the incorporators. Upon issuance of the certificate of incorporation, or charter, the corporation begins existence.

B. Bylaws

After a nonprofit corporation receives its charter, it would have an organizational meeting during which it would adopt corporate bylaws.

---

2. The New York Not-for-Profit Corporation Law, § 404, requires that most nonprofit entities obtain various approvals or consents prior to incorporation.

The Texas Business Organizations Code, V.T.C.A, Bus. Organ. Code § 1.002(6), refers to the Articles of Incorporation as "Certificate of Formation."

The bylaws of a corporation determine the rights and duties of the members with reference to the internal governance of the corporation and the management of its affairs. A bylaw is an agreement or contract between the corporation and its members to conduct the corporate affairs. It includes all regulations of the corporation, and until repealed, constitutes continuing rules for the governance of the corporation and its officers and directors. The bylaws may contain any provisions for the regulation and management of corporate affairs that are not inconsistent with the law or with the articles of incorporation.

The power to make bylaws generally resides in the corporate members or the corporate directors if the corporation does not have members. The power to alter, amend, or repeal the bylaws or to adopt new bylaws is vested in the board of directors unless otherwise provided in the articles of incorporation or in the bylaws.

C. Authorization to Conduct Affairs in Another State

A corporation makes application for authorization to conduct transactions in another state by filing an application for a Certificate of Authority with the Secretary of State of that state.

D. Obtaining Tax-Exempt Status

After obtaining its charter, having its organizational meeting, and adopting bylaws, a nonprofit corporation would apply for tax exempt status, first, with the Internal Revenue Service, and then, with the comptroller of the state in which it is organized. (See further discussion in Chapter 5.)

III. DIRECTORS

A. Management of a Nonprofit Corporation

The affairs of a nonprofit corporation are managed by a board of directors. Generally, directors need not be residents of the state of incorporation unless the articles of incorporation or the bylaws provide otherwise. The number of directors, which in most states is three, is fixed by the bylaws for most nonprofit corporations. A change in the number then is made by amending the bylaws.

As a general rule, directors are elected or appointed in the manner prescribed in the bylaws. A vacancy occurring on the board would be filled by vote of a majority of the remaining directors.

BAILEY v. AMERICAN SOC. FOR PREVENTION OF CRUELTY TO ANIMALS

Supreme Court, Appellate Division, New York, 1953
282 A.D. 502, 125 N.Y.S.2d 18

CALLAHAN, Justice.

Defendant, Society, appeals from an order denying defendant's motion to dismiss the complaint for insufficiency and for summary judg-

Sec. III **DIRECTORS** 67

ment in defendant's favor. Twenty members, a small minority of defendant Society, sue the Society for a judgment declaring certain by-laws of the Society void and for a judicial determination of the rights of the parties.

The Society was organized in 1866 by a special act of the legislature, Chap. 469, L.1866, for a non-profit and humane purpose. Plaintiffs are among those who pay dues as patrons or members of various classes. Certain functions of a public nature in the way of enforcement of laws against cruelty to animals and licensing of animals have been delegated to the Society.

The act of incorporation gave the Society the right to adopt a code of by-laws not inconsistent with the laws of the State or the United States, which code until modified or rescinded was to be as binding on the Society, its officers and members as the Act itself. Pursuant to this power defendant did adopt by-laws from time to time. It is largely with relation to by-laws adopted in 1900 and 1907 that plaintiffs complain, contending, *inter alia*, that there has been an unlawful usurpation of power by the Board of Managers of the Society in various respects to the injury and deprivation of plaintiffs' rights. There is also complaint as to the procedure under which these by-laws were adopted. The complaint prays this Court to declare the by-laws of 1907 unlawful and to enjoin action under them and for such other relief as may be necessary and proper.

The complaint also recites that an actual controversy exists in the Society as to the failure of the Board of Managers to oppose a certain statute enacted by the legislature of this State with respect to the requisition of dumb animals for scientific experimentation and that the Board of Managers refused to follow the desires and requests of a majority of the members to oppose this law. No specific relief is asked from the Court with respect to this phase of the controversy. In any event, it is plain that the policy of a corporation with respect to a law of this State is to be determined in the discretion of the directors or managers as to which the courts would not interfere.

We thus have an action in which the sole question presented for judicial determination is whether certain by-laws are in conflict with the law of the land or were illegally adopted. Thus, only questions of law are presented which we should now determine. We have examined the complaint and find no actionable violation of plaintiffs' rights sufficiently alleged. Among the contentions of plaintiffs is that defendant is subject to the provisions of the membership corporations law and certain of its by-laws conflict with such statute. We think it is clear that Section 2 of the Membership Corporations Law excludes this Society from its provisions as a corporation created by special law.

There appears to be no present justiciable issue as to whether the by-laws were illegally or improperly adopted.

In fact, both the 1900 and the 1907 amendments appear to have been adopted or ratified at a meeting of the members of the Society.

Whether these amendments had been properly introduced, or proper preliminary steps initiated with respect thereto at some earlier meeting, would seem to us to be academic. The propriety of the preliminaries would appear to be a matter for the members to decide before voting, and since they adopted the amendments, the inference is warranted that they waived any possible procedural irregularity. At least, the matter would hardly appear to be available to members who joined the Society many years after 1907. The lapse of almost fifty years would seem to make any present complaint as to procedure in adoption untenable, and we find that plaintiffs' contentions as to the impropriety in adopting the 1900 or 1907 by-laws are not shown. In any event, summary judgment would have to be awarded defendant concerning any claim as to the improper adoption of these by-laws if the controversy be assumed to present a justiciable issue. Further, the adoption of the 1907 by-laws would eliminate as immaterial complaint of impropriety in adopting the 1900 by-laws.

Aside from impropriety in adoption, the plaintiffs' principal complaint is that the Board of Managers has unlawfully usurped too much power to itself with respect to acceptance of new members and expulsion of present members and in respect to self-perpetuation of control by selection of successors when vacancies occur in the Board of Managers. In the absence of any complaint that any particular applicants were improperly excluded from membership or any members unlawfully expelled—and no such claims are made—it would appear that the complaint asserts no actionable wrong in these matters.

As to the so-called 'self-perpetuation' by the Board controlling election of their successors, it is clear that in the case of a membership corporation organized for charitable or non-profit purposes such provisions in corporate by-laws do not infringe on any property or other enforceable right of ordinary members and are not illegal. * * *

It is true that the Mt. Sinai case represented a change in corporate powers by legislative action, and, of course, the only restriction on the legislature would be one of constitutional limitation. We deem, however, that what was said in that case as to the reasons why some degree of self-perpetuation is permissible in the governing bodies of charitable corporations to be equally applicable here where the so-called 'perpetuation' was provided by amendments to by-laws.

Perhaps the provisions in the by-laws that five managers would constitute a quorum of its Board run counter to the present requirements of Section 27 of the General Corporation Law, and, therefore, it might be improper for the Board to attempt to act by a vote of five though the by-laws were lawful when adopted. But there is no claim that defendant has ever attempted to adopt any resolution by a vote of five, and until it does so, there appears to be no necessity for judicial action or declaration on the subject.

* * *

SOLOMON v. HALL–BROOKE FOUNDATION, INC.

Court of Appeals, Connecticut, 1993
30 Conn.App. 129, 619 A.2d 863

HEIMAN, Judge.

The plaintiff appeals from the trial court's judgment rendered in favor of the defendant on an action for the recission of a trust instrument and for breach of contract. On appeal, the plaintiff asserts that (1) as a matter of both law and sound public policy, the court failed to accord proper consideration to her intent as creator conditioning her gift to the charity and (2) even if she did not condition her charitable donation upon her continued employment, the trial court incorrectly disregarded her employment contract with the defendant. We disagree and affirm the judgment of the trial court.

The trial court found the following facts. In 1964, the plaintiff purchased the Hall–Brooke Hospital in Westport. Upon acquiring the hospital, the plaintiff established two corporations. One corporation owned the land on which the private hospital was situated and the other owned the hospital and its assets. In 1966, the plaintiff with the advice of various professionals in the areas of health care and nonprofit institutions set up Hall–Brooke as a nonprofit corporation. She made a gift of assets to the defendant, the Hall–Brooke Foundation, Inc. (foundation), but retained control of the real estate on which the hospital was situated. She understood that once she established this foundation, it would exist in perpetuity, and would not be dependent on any one person's life or ownership, but would be governed by a self-perpetuating board of trustees. As a not-for-profit foundation, its board would have the power to run the organization. The plaintiff knew that she no longer would control its operations and that the board was obligated to act in the foundation's best interests without concern for what might be beneficial to her.

The plaintiff, as a trustee, actively participated in the affairs of the foundation. She also signed an employment contract with the newly created foundation that provided for her to serve as executive director until the age of sixty-five or retirement, whichever occurred sooner, to render services to the foundation at an annual salary of $35,000 to be "increased proportionately with any increases in salary given to the highest medical staff members of Hall–Brooke Hospital." The contract also provided that the "[f]oundation may terminate this agreement if Solomon has been adjudicated in a criminal court of competent jurisdiction as guilty of theft, fraud, or embezzlement regarding the assets of the foundation or regarding her employment."

In 1980, the defendant removed the plaintiff from all of her positions at the foundation. The plaintiff subsequently brought an action to rescind her gift to create the foundation because she felt that her intent was frustrated by the board of trustees, and specifically to enforce her employment contract with the defendant. She also included a prayer for "such other relief as the court deems necessary and just."

After a trial on the merits, the trial court found that the plaintiff's gift to create the foundation was absolute. It also found that the plaintiff's employment contract with the defendant violated public policy and that she was thus an at-will employee of the foundation whose employment could be terminated with or without cause. This appeal followed.

The plaintiff asserts that the trial court failed to accord proper consideration to her intent as the creator of the defendant. She argues that the trial court made several errors with respect both to finding and to enforcing her true intention at the time she created the foundation. She posits that the court's findings "not only lack authority but [are] emblematic of much of the confusion which has corrupted the operation of charities in the current era."

While we acknowledge the plaintiff's invitation to take "an unusual opportunity to clarify the law of charitable corporations at a moment when it very much needs clarification and, in the process, to remind those charged with the responsibility of managing such corporations that fidelity to the intentions of their founders is among the first of their obligations," we decline to do so since we conclude that the trial court's findings were not clearly erroneous.

* * *

Here, the trial court conducted extensive factfinding. It found an absence of written documentation conditioning the creation of the foundation on either the plaintiff's employment contract with the foundation or her lifetime trustee status at the foundation. In fact, the trial court found that several of the founding documents contradicted the plaintiff's claim that the creation of the foundation was so conditioned. The court extensively considered the evidence that the plaintiff hoped would reveal that the creation of the foundation was conditioned on her employment contract and lifetime trusteeship. In particular, the court reviewed the plaintiff's correspondence with a trustee who was also her personal attorney. In examining this correspondence, the court found that there was no evidence that her gift was conditional. It also found no evidence that the plaintiff shared with anyone other than her attorney her feeling that her employment was an important factor in the creation of the foundation. The trial court thus found that the creation of the foundation was an absolute rather than a conditional grant. The trial court's findings were not clearly erroneous.

* * *

The plaintiff also argues that even if the court properly found that the creation of the charitable foundation was not conditioned on her continued employment, the court cannot disregard her employment contract. She concedes that in this action, she primarily seeks the specific enforcement of the contract. In the alternative, she asserts that her claim for "such other relief as the court deems necessary and just" encompasses money damages for the breach of her employment contract. We disagree.

* * *

The plaintiff asserts that her contract with the defendant was valid and enforceable. She argues that the defendant ignored the plain language of the contract, which permitted the defendant to fire her only if she were adjudicated in a criminal court of competent jurisdiction to be guilty of theft, fraud or embezzlement regarding the defendant's assets. The court, however, found that her employment contract with the defendant was unenforceable as a matter of public policy. See *Osborne v. Locke Steel Chain Co.*, 153 Conn. 527, 537, 218 A.2d 526 (1966).[5] Her employment with the foundation was thus at will. The defendant could terminate her employment with or without just cause pursuant to General Statutes §§ 33–451(b) and 33–453(b).[6] The plaintiff has failed to demonstrate that the trial court's finding was clearly erroneous.

The judgment is affirmed.

B. Meetings of Directors

Meetings of the board, whether regular or special, may be held within or without the state of incorporation. Attendance of a director at a meeting constitutes a waiver of notice of the meeting unless a director is in attendance for the purpose of objecting to any transactions of the board because the meeting was not lawfully convened.

Generally, the board of directors may delegate the management of activities of the corporation to committees, but all activities and affairs of the corporation must be managed, and all corporate power exercised, under the ultimate direction of the board.

A member of the board cannot act alone on behalf of the corporation. An act of the majority of the directors present at a meeting at which a quorum is present constitutes an act of the board unless the articles or bylaws provide for a greater number. A majority of the

---

5. Our Supreme Court stated that "[t]here is some authority for the proposition that directors have no power to hire an employee on a lifetime basis.... Such cases are generally based on the theory that a board of directors, in selecting the management personnel of the corporation, should not be allowed to hamstring future boards in the overall supervision of the enterprise and the implementation of changing corporate policy." *Osborne v. Locke Steel Chain Co.*, 153 Conn. 527, 537, 218 A.2d 526 (1966).

6. General Statutes § 33–451(b) provides in pertinent part: "A director shall cease to be in office upon ... (3) [her] removal from office in accordance with bylaws adopted by members or, if there are no such bylaws, at a meeting of the members or directors entitled to fill such directorship called expressly for the purpose of considering such removal, with or without cause, by such vote as would suffice for [her] election as a director...."

General Statutes § 33–453(b) provides: "Officers may be removed, with or without cause, but without prejudice to their contract rights, if any. The appointment or election of an officer for a given term, or a general provision in the bylaws or certificate of incorporation with respect to the term of the office, shall not of itself create contract rights."

number of directors generally constitutes a quorum for the transaction of corporate affairs.

C. Removal of Directors

A director may be removed from office pursuant to any procedure provided for in the articles or in the bylaws. If a nonprofit corporation has members, a director generally can be removed without cause by members of the corporation. Usually a director can be removed only if the number of votes cast to remove the director would be sufficient to elect the director. In the absence of provisions in the articles or the bylaws or in the state's statutes, a director cannot be removed or suspended from office without cause until the end of the director's term.

GRACE v. GRACE INSTITUTE
Court of Appeals, New York, 1967
19 N.Y.2d 307, 279 N.Y.S.2d 721, 226 N.E.2d 531

KEATING, Judge.

The Grace Institute was incorporated by an act of the Legislature (L. 1897, ch. 285) for the purpose of furnishing women and girls instruction in trades and occupations and in branches of domestic arts and science.

Three named members of the Grace family and their successors were constituted the body corporate. The corporation was granted 'all the powers and privileges and (was) subject to the liabilities of a corporation conferred by chapter thirty-five of the general laws known as the general corporation law.'

By virtue of section 3 of the incorporating statute all the powers and privileges of the corporation were to be exercised by the three life members 'together with such other persons as they may select and such members and the persons selected by them shall be known as trustees.'

The petitioner in this action, Michael P. Grace, II, was a successor to one of the original life members and, by virtue of that position, a member of the board of trustees of the Institute. During his tenure in those positions Michael, among other things, commenced several actions against the Institute—actions in which he was uniformly unsuccessful. Largely, as a result of the commencement of these actions, charges were drawn up against him and a hearing was held. Thereafter Michael was removed as a trustee and life member of the Institute. This removal was accomplished, despite the fact that there was no provision in the incorporating statute or the by-laws of the corporation relating to the removal of a life member.

Following his removal, Michael commenced an article 78 proceeding seeking judicial review and annulment of the determination made by the life members and trustees of the Institute whereby he was removed as a life member and trustee.

* * *

The law is settled that a corporation possesses the inherent power to remove a member, officer or director for cause, regardless of the presence of a provision in the charter or by-laws providing for such removal. * * *

The question with which we are presented in this case is whether there exists any triable issues relating to the manner in which this petitioner was removed from his position as a life member and trustee.

It has been the consistent policy of the courts of this State to avoid interference with the internal management and operation of corporations. * * * Although we are dealing here with a charitable corporation over which the Supreme Court is vested with supervisory powers, the Legislature in creating it set up a governing board of trustees and vested in them the power and authority necessary for the management and operation of the Institute. That body, after hearings and deliberation, has decided that the petitioner's conduct was so inimical to the corporate interests as to require his removal. In reaching that conclusion, the trustees had before them evidence of a series of lawsuits commenced by the petitioner against the corporation in each of which he was unsuccessful and in none of which did any of the 13 jurists who took part find even so much as a single triable issue.

After reviewing each of these actions and after studying the entire record in this case, we have reached the conclusion that the evidence clearly supported the finding of the trustees that Michael had embarked on a course of conduct designed to involve the Institute in endless and costly litigation and that the suits were undertaken for the purpose of harassing the Institute and its members. Under these circumstances, courts should not substitute their judgment for the judgment of those charged by the Legislature with the responsibility of running the corporation and seeing to it that it fulfills the purposes for which it was created.

In addition, we have examined the procedure by which the petitioner was removed and we have concluded there is no question but that he was given a reasonable opportunity to be heard and to answer the charges leveled against him. At the hearing during which the charges were aired, he was represented by three attorneys and a law assistant. His attorneys were permitted to cross-examine one of the parties who had been instrumental in preparing the charges against Michael and they could have exercised their right to examine others. Yet despite this opportunity to be heard and to present evidence, Michael never took the stand and never even attempted to answer the charges. The objections of Michael to the hearing we find to be without merit. The things to which he objects in no way detracted from his opportunity to be heard or the validity of his removal.

Michael argues, however, that the position of life member was created by the Legislature and 'only the Legislature has the power to change the rights and privileges specifically granted by the act of incorporation.' Michael obviously misapprehends the nature of the rights

and privileges accorded to him. The Legislature surely could not have intended that a life member retain his position regardless of the manner in which he acted and regardless of the manner in which he abused his trust. The petitioner may not be removed so long as he adheres to what must be regarded as an implied condition of his position—that is so long as he faithfully serves the Institute. Once he breaches that condition and engages in activities that obstruct and interfere with the operation of the corporation and the purposes for which the Legislature created it, he may be removed. Indeed, the statute creating the corporation appears to recognize that a member may leave his position through ways other than death or voluntary resignation. Section 4 provides that a member may designate a successor 'who shall take the place made vacant by the death, resignation or otherwise of the person making such nomination.'
* * *

For the reasons stated, we reach the conclusion that there are no issues requiring a trial and that the petition of Michael Grace should be dismissed.

In addition to the prayer of Michael for the annulment of the action taken by the trustees, Corinne Grace petitions that, if the relief requested by Michael is denied, she be declared his lawful successor as a life member and trustee. This request was not considered by either of the courts below and we do not feel that we should summarily grant the relief requested in the first instance. Nevertheless, since both sides have asked us to consider the issue, we have decided to indicate our view for the guidance of the lower court and in the interest of avoiding future appellate litigation.

As noted earlier, section 4 of the incorporating statute gave the life members the right to designate their successors in the event of 'death, resignation or otherwise'. Prior to his removal, Michael designated Corinne Grace to succeed him in the event of his death, resignation 'or for any reason'. We believe that the word 'otherwise' in the incorporating act encompasses his involuntary removal.

The Institute argues that, if Michael's removal was valid, it terminated his right to appoint his successor. This argument overlooks the fact that Corinne Grace was designated by Michael prior to his removal in accordance with the provisions of the incorporating statute. If the contention of the Institute is adopted, then all designations would be invalid since the death or resignation of the life member after he designates someone to succeed him would, according to this reasoning, terminate his right to appoint.

If Corinne chooses to emulate the conduct of her spouse, then the corporation may remove her from office and, if necessary, petition the Legislature to amend the incorporating act so as to eliminate the position of life member—a position hardly essential to the effective operation of the corporation.

Unless additional evidence is forthcoming when the matter is considered by Special Term, we believe that the relief requested in the petition of Corinne Grace should be granted.

* * *

COLLINS v. BEINECKE
Court of Appeals, New York, 1986
67 N.Y.2d 479, 504 N.Y.S.2d 72, 495 N.E.2d 335

PER CURIAM.

This is an action for declaratory judgment and injunctive relief seeking a judicial determination of questions concerning the control and management of defendant S & H Foundation, Inc. Plaintiffs represent the interests of Baldwin–United Corporation which now indirectly owns all the stock of the former Sperry & Hutchinson Company, Inc. The individual defendants are former officers and stockholders of Sperry & Hutchinson Company, Inc. and are members and directors of the foundation. Plaintiffs seek to remove them and install representatives of Baldwin–United Corporation in their place.

The S & H Foundation was formed in 1962 as a type-B not-for-profit corporation and has, since its creation, received its sole financial support from the Sperry & Hutchinson Company, a company well known for its S & H green stamps. The foundation is and always has been a separate legal entity with its own bylaws and certificate of incorporation. Throughout the years, however, a substantial portion of the foundation's grants benefitted company employees directly or indirectly and many of its charitable programs were continuations of programs established and conducted by the company prior to 1962. Neither the certificate of incorporation nor the bylaws of the S & H Foundation contain any qualifications for membership or holding office. From its inception in 1962, however, a practice developed that only officers, directors or agents of the company served as members and directors of the foundation.

In 1981 Baldwin–United Corporation purchased all of the outstanding stock of the company, including all of the stock of the Beinecke defendants. Although the Beineckes' connection with the company terminated with this stock sale, they have refused to resign as members of the foundation or to second the nomination for membership of three individuals associated with Baldwin–United. Accordingly, plaintiffs instituted this action seeking to compel them to do so, claiming that this is a "company" foundation and that individual defendants therefore have a fiduciary duty not to act contrary to the established practices and purposes of Sperry & Hutchinson Company, Inc. but that they are in fact doing so by blocking the personnel changes proposed by Baldwin–United.

As plaintiffs point out, the creation of company foundations is a recognized business practice. Such foundations provide a company with an opportunity to integrate and institutionalize its long-range charitable giving to further corporate goals and objects, and permit the company to create goodwill while doing so. Moreover, there are definite tax advantages to a company in using a foundation because it may use its gifts to smooth out its earnings picture by making large gifts in profitable years and smaller gifts in lean years * * *. Except for special tax treatment, however, the law does not accord any special status to company foundations, as plaintiffs concede.

The S & H Foundation exhibits many of the indicia common to "company" foundations: it bears the name of the company that created it; its charitable programs, involving as they frequently do the company's employees and clientele, publicize the company's generosity and contribute to the company's goodwill; its organization and administration are intimately intertwined with that of the company; and the company is the sole source of its funds.

However, the foundation's certificate of incorporation and bylaws and the annual gift instruments from the company contain no specific limitations requiring the foundation to expend its resources as the company directs or limiting membership in the foundation to persons affiliated with the company. Nor did the sale documents contain any provisions to ensure Baldwin–United's future control over the foundation.

Plaintiffs assert, however, that due to the past practices and relations between the corporations and the substantial assets that the company has contributed to the foundation, which now total over six million dollars, equity must intervene to remove the individual defendants and thus prevent them from diverting these funds to their own purposes. We agree with plaintiffs that the sale of a business imposes a duty upon the seller not to impair the goodwill of that business * * *, and that defendants may not act in a manner that is inimical to the charitable purposes of the foundation * * *. The customs and practices of the past are not enough, however, to impose a fiduciary duty on them to resign or to install plaintiffs' representatives in their places * * *. Absent evidence that defendants have misused the foundation's assets or a showing that their acts are 'unfair, oppressive or manifestly detrimental to the [foundation's] interests' * * *, we find no basis for the invocation of equitable power to annul defendants' acts and interfere in the legal relationship that the parties have structured for themselves.

* * *

IV. MEMBERS

A nonprofit corporation may have one or more classes of members or it may have no members. If the corporation has members, the designation of the class of membership, the manner of election or appointment and the qualifications and rights of the members of each class must be set out in the articles of incorporation or in the bylaws.

Note

Nonprofit corporations in California have no members unless the articles of incorporation or the bylaws provide otherwise. See Cal. Corp. Code §§ 5310, 7310. If the corporation has no members, approval of the board is required of transactions otherwise requiring approval of the members.

A. Rights of Members

Members of nonprofit corporations are treated much the same as members of unincorporated associations. As a general rule, a member of a nonprofit corporation does not acquire a severable right to any of the property or funds of the corporation.

The right of members to vote may be limited, enlarged or denied to the extent provided for in the articles of incorporation or in the bylaws. Unless limited, each member is entitled to one vote on each matter submitted to a vote of the members.

IN RE MT. SINAI HOSPITAL

Court of Appeals, New York, 1928
250 N.Y. 103, 164 N.E. 871

POUND, J.

* * *

A member's right to a voice in the management of a corporation may under conditions not presented here be a vested interest entitled to protection under the Constitution. What vested interest does a mere voting member of a charitable corporation, devoted in part, at least, to public uses, have to protect of which he is deprived when he is deprived of his right to vote? Not, as in the case of the stockholders of a business corporation, property interests of his own * * *, because he has no interest in the property of the corporation. If the corporation were dissolved, the funds would not be awarded to the individual members. * * * The members do not invest their money. They give it to charity. Not the right of a founder, or one who contributes money under express conditions, to have the statutes of his foundation as to the powers of trustees or the terms of his conditions, strictly adhered to, except so far as he consents to their alteration. * * * Appellants are not founders, nor did they attach any express conditions to the payment of their membership dues. Appellants are not asserting the right of the corporation to prevent the transfer of the corporate property from one board of trustees to another by the creation of a new corporation under a new charter, * * * for no such transfer is attempted. The corporation continues to elect its own trustees. Nor are they asserting the right of the corporation to prevent diversion of the funds raised for the corporation * * *; the corporation and its purposes remain intact. The voting power was exercised by the members for the benefit of the corporation. Appellants have no beneficial interest of their own to protect * * *.

Under the reserved power of amendment, when in the judgment of the Legislature the interests of a charitable corporation will be promoted by a change in the method of electing trustees, once intrusted to the members, whereby the members are disfranchised and the board is made self-perpetuating, no one's property is taken; no one is deprived of his liberty, except by the rightful exercise of the reserved power. * * *

As was pointedly said in Looker v. Maynard, 179 U. S. 46, 54, 21 S. Ct. 21, 24 (45 L. Ed. 79): 'Remembering that the Dartmouth College Case [4 Wheat. 518, 4 L. Ed. 629] (which was the cause of the general introduction into the legislation of the several States of a provision reserving the power to alter, amend or repeal acts of incorporation), concerned the right of a Legislature to make a change in the number and mode of appointment of the trustees or managers of a corporation, we cannot assent to the theory that an express reservation of the general power does not secure to the Legislature the right to exercise it in this respect.'

The appellants' case has been presented to the court from many different angles, none of which has been overlooked. The court has carefully considered all their points. It has reached the conclusion that the right of a member of a charitable corporation to participate in the control of the corporation by voting for trustees must, under the reserved power, yield to the greater right of the state and the corporation to provide for the more efficient administration of the affairs of the corporation, as their judgment dictates.

It would be contrary to all correct ideas of the reserved power to say that one who once becomes, by the payment of annual dues, a voting member of a charitable corporation of 4,000 members, becomes also a party to a perpetual contract that he shall not be divested of his voting rights without his consent so that he may insist on retaining his membership to bar the adoption of a detail of administration, such as the method of electing trustees, which is deemed salutary by the Legislature and the corporation. Such is the substance of appellants' claim. We find no authority which compels such a conclusion.

HARRIS v. BOARD OF DIRECTORS OF COMMUNITY HOSPITAL

Court of Appeals, Illinois, 1977
55 Ill.App.3d 392, 13 Ill.Dec. 94, 370 N.E.2d 1121

PUSATERI, Justice:

Plaintiffs, members of the Community Hospital of Evanston, commenced this action to remove the defendants, who are members of the Board of Directors of the hospital. The hospital is a not-for-profit corporation.

Under the provisions of the by-laws of the hospital, a meeting of the members was to be held annually on a day in January or February. During such meeting, eight Directors were to be elected for a period of three years by the members voting in person or by proxy. The twenty-four Directors were divided into three classes of eight members, the three year term of one class expiring each year. The elected Board members were also to manage and control the affairs of the hospital. Pursuant to growing disagreement and resentment between some of the members and the Board, these members sent out a notice on December 31, 1974, calling a meeting on January 14, 1975, stating that their general purpose was among other reasons to remove the Board members.

In response to this notification, the Board distributed a letter dated January 8, 1975, to all of the members of the hospital, explaining that the Board was engaged in extensive hearings on a personnel matter and therefore could not prepare for or attend the meeting of January 14, 1975. The Board further advised the members that under Illinois law, the members could not remove the Board of Directors whether or not the Board was present at such a meeting. Notice was also given at this time that the annual membership meeting would be held on March 28, 1975.

Despite the above correspondence, the January 14, 1975, meeting was held and resulted in a resolution that the Board should show cause why it should not be removed, and it was also resolved that all power and control of the Board should be subject to approval of the members. The President of the Board, in a letter to the dissident members dated January 24, 1975, stated that the so-called resolution was illegal, but did acknowledge that the Board was anxious to meet with the members at a mutually agreed upon time.

Subsequently, the President of the Board drafted a response to the removal resolution, reiterating the Board's legal position, while emphasizing that a number of Board members were never given notice of the January 14, 1975, meeting as required by the by-laws.

On February 10, 1975, the Board of Directors amended the corporate by-laws to disallow proxy voting, limit the vote of corporate members and to permit the Board of Directors to elect its own membership.

Another meeting was called on February 28, 1975, by the members, and at that time it was decided to permanently remove the Board of Directors, and in their place a disputed interim board was elected. The original Board of Directors, however, continued in its refusal to recognize the removal resolution.

Pursuant to a second notice to all members on March 17, 1975, the annual members meeting commenced on March 27, 1975, and abruptly adjourned over a dispute regarding who were to be the members of the legal Board of Directors. Shortly thereafter, plaintiffs commenced this action to remove the Board of Directors. Following a full hearing, the circuit court of Cook County resolved the issue in favor of the defendants Board of Directors and decreed that the cause be dismissed. Plaintiffs prosecute this appeal, contending that the February 10, 1975, amendments to the by-laws are invalid.

In making its determination, the trial court first referred to the by-laws of the hospital, and specifically Article XI, which states as follows:

AMENDMENTS

These by-laws may be altered, amended or repealed and new by-laws may be adopted by the affirmative vote of two-thirds (2/3) of the members of the Board of Directors present at any regular or special meeting, provided that the proposed alteration, amendment, action for repeal or form of new by-laws is submitted in writing to each Director at least five (5) days prior to the meeting at which the same is to be considered.

The trial court correctly concluded that the aforementioned by-law provision places the exclusive power to amend the by-laws in the Board of Directors. Section 9 of the General Not for Profit Corporation Act (Ill.Rev.Stat.1975, ch. 32, par. 163a8) provides " * * * The power to alter, amend or repeal the by-laws or adopt new by-laws shall be vested in the board of directors unless otherwise provided in the articles of incorporation or the by-laws. * * * "

There is no provision, either in the by-laws or articles of incorporation of the hospital, that concerns amendments to the by-laws, other than the aforementioned Article XI. A further study of by-laws discloses that not less than fifteen members could call a special meeting; however, the by-laws do not authorize the members to remove directors by way of resolution at such meetings.

In Westlake Hospital Ass'n v. Blix (1958), 13 Ill.2d 183, 148 N.E.2d 471, * * *, our supreme court was confronted with a similar factual situation and the determination as to which group of directors and which set of by-laws constituted the legal board of directors and by-laws of the Westlake Hospital Association, a not-for-profit corporation. The by-law provision dealing with amendments to the by-laws was very similar to that in the case at bar and provided for amendment by a majority vote of the board of directors.

The court, in reversing the trial court and ruling in favor of the original board of directors and against the members, stated as follows:

* * * We find neither a constitutional right in the members to vote for directors, nor a constitutional prohibition of the staggered election of directors, in that not-for-profit corporations are not governed by the constitutional mandate of section 3 of Article XI of the Illinois constitution of 1870. American Aberdeen–Angus Breeders' Ass'n v. Fullerton, 325 Ill. 323, 156 N.E. 314; Cf. Wolfson v. Avery, 6 Ill.2d 78, 126 N.E.2d 701. Westlake Hospital Ass'n, at 191–92, 148 N.E.2d at 476.

It is well established in this State that the right of members of a not-for-profit corporation to vote is not constitutionally protected. * * * "Since the State, through the legislature, retained the right to amend the statutes, and the corporation, pursuant to statute, reserved the power to amend its bylaws, and the right of members of a charitable corporation to vote is not constitutionally protected, it follows that the amendments in issue did not deprive plaintiffs of their constitutional rights." * * *

Section 3 of Article XI of the Illinois constitution of 1870 (Ill. Const.1870, art. XI, § 3) has been replaced by section 6 of Article XIII of the Illinois constitution of 1970 (Ill.Const.1970, art. XIII, s 6). However, we conclude that irrespective of this new constitutional provision that the reasoning and holding in Westlake Hospital Ass'n is still applicable to the facts in the case at bar.

The statute referred to in Westlake Hospital Ass'n is the General Not for Profit Corporation Act (Ill.Rev.Stat.1975, ch. 32, par. 163a et seq.) Section 15 of the Act provides as follows:

> The right of the members, or any class or classes of members, to vote may be limited, enlarged or denied to the extent specified in the articles of incorporation or the by-laws. * * * A member may vote in person or, unless the articles of incorporation or the by-laws otherwise provide, by proxy executed in writing by the member or by his duly authorized attorney-in-fact. * * * Ill.Rev.Stat.1975, ch. 32, par. 163a14.

We conclude that the Board of Directors in the instant case alone had the power to amend the by-laws at all times in this litigation, and it had the right to amend the by-laws to disallow proxy voting and to limit the members' vote. Further, it had the right to amend the by-laws to provide for a self-perpetuating directorate. * * *

No matter how sympathetic we may be with the members in this proceeding, or how well intentioned their actions may be, we feel that we must concur with the conclusion of our supreme court in the Westlake Hospital Ass'n case that the wisdom and desirability of a co-optating or self-perpetuating board of directors for a charitable corporation is a question which should be addressed to the legislature and not to the court. Westlake Hospital Ass'n, at 196. It is also to be noted that in the case at bar no question of fraud has been raised or suggested in the record or briefs, and plaintiffs' counsel acknowledged the absence of same at the time of oral argument.

The plaintiff members rely in great part upon the decision of the court in West Side Hospital v. Steele (1st Dist. 1906), 124 Ill.App. 534. However, examination of this decision reveals clearly that it is inapposite to the case at bar since it did not involve a not-for-profit corporation; rather it involved a for-profit corporation with the ownership vested in the shareholders.

For all of the foregoing reasons, the judgment of the trial court dismissing the complaint herein is affirmed.

Affirmed.

B. Meetings

Meetings of members generally are held at the place designated in the bylaws and at the time provided for in the bylaws. Should the board of directors fail to call an annual meeting at the designated time, some state statutes provide that any member may demand that a meeting be held within a reasonable time.

At least one general meeting of members should be held annually to elect directors and to approve annual reports. Meetings are required when the approval of members is necessary to enter into a transaction or to adopt or amend the bylaws.

A quorum is the number of members required to be present at a meeting to bind the corporation as to any business undertaken at the meeting. Generally, this is a majority of the members, but it can be a majority of the voting members present at a particular meeting. The bylaws should specify the number of members constituting a quorum.

Written notice stating the place, day and hour of a meeting of the members must be delivered to the members within a certain period of time before the meeting date. The Model Nonprofit Corporation Act, § 14, specifies that notice should be delivered to the members not less than 10 nor more than 50 days before the meeting. If the meeting is a special meeting, the purpose or purposes for which the meeting is called should be part of the notice.

C. Removal of Members

Most state statutes do not have provisions relating to the removal of members of a nonprofit corporation. Courts are reluctant to interfere with the internal affairs of a membership corporation with regard to its disciplinary proceedings.

RAULSTON v. EVERETT
Court of Civil Appeals, Texas, 1978
561 S.W.2d 635

CORNELIUS, Chief Justice.

In 1967 the plaintiffs O. L. Ford, Thomas Welch, Tinnie Garrison and Conde Rodriques, together with several other persons, formed the Dimple Grazing Association and incorporated it as a Texas non-profit corporation. It was created under the supervision of and in cooperation with the Farmers Home Administration of the U. S. Department of Agriculture for the purposes of purchasing and holding grazing lands for the joint use of its members. The organization was a membership corporation, as distinguished from a stock corporation, each member being issued a "membership certificate" to evidence his status as a member. The corporation began its existence with some thirteen members. A $411,550.00 loan was obtained from the Farmers Home Administration and was used to purchase approximately 2600 acres of grazing lands. A set of by-laws was adopted which provided, inter alia, that each member would be obligated to graze a specified number of cattle on the land each year and pay the sum of $40.27 per animal grazing unit (being one cow with calf or one bull) per year as grazing fees. The fees were to be used to pay the expenses of the organization and to retire the land purchase note. The by-laws further provided that other assessments could be imposed upon the members by a vote of the directors. According to the by-laws a member's status could be terminated by a voluntary surrender of his membership certificate or by forfeiture of the same by vote of the directors for failure to pay assessments (as distinguished from grazing fees). The number of members fluctuated through the years, with several members surrendering their certificates and others failing or refusing to graze cattle on the corporation's land and to participate in the affairs of the organization. The corporation experienced increasing financial difficulties and loss of member participation, and by 1971 only four members, the defendants Kenneth Bishop, Richard Boggess, Jack Pollock and Kenneth Raulston, were grazing cattle on the land, attending meetings and actively participating in the management. At the January 12, 1972, meeting a resolution was adopted asserting that those four persons were the only remaining members of the association, and a sale of the corporation's land was discussed. On February 14, 1973, the sale was effected. The sale of the land produced a net profit of $130,408.20, which was divided equally among the four defendants. On March 16, 1973, a resolution ratifying the sale of the land and purporting to dissolve the corporation was adopted. Thereafter, the plaintiffs Ford, Welch, Garrison and Rodriques, contending that they were still members of the organization on March 16, 1973, filed suit against the defendants individually to recover their pro rata share of the profits from the land sale. Trial was to a jury which found that each of the plaintiffs had waived his membership in the corporation prior to January 1, 1973. The trial court, however, disregarded the jury's verdict and rendered judgment non obstante veredicto, awarding each plaintiff the sum of $19,561.23, allegedly being one-eighth of the profits realized from the land sale.

The defendants have appealed from the judgment below contending that the membership rights of the plaintiffs were subject to loss by waiver, and that inasmuch as the jury found that such rights had been waived, the trial court should have entered a take-nothing judgment. The plaintiffs contend that, as a matter of law, they were still lawful members of the corporation at the time the land was sold, and there was no waiver. It was undisputed that plaintiffs' membership certificates had not been physically surrendered or forfeited or cancelled in accordance with the applicable provisions of the by-laws.

To sustain the trial court's action in disregarding the jury verdict and rendering judgment non obstante veredicto, we must find either (1) that, as a matter of law, the plaintiffs could not waive or abandon their membership in the Dimple Grazing Association, Inc. short of a surrender or legal cancellation of their membership certificates, or (2) that, if such membership were subject to loss by waiver or abandonment, there is no evidence that such a waiver or abandonment was in fact accomplished.

There are two types of corporations, stock corporations and non-stock or membership corporations. * * * The entity involved here is of the latter type. A non-profit membership corporation, although a corporate entity, is in other respects similar to an unincorporated association, and generally speaking, the same rules concerning members and their rights apply to both. * * * A member of such an organization acquires not a severable right to any of its property or funds, but merely a right to the joint use and enjoyment thereof so long as he continues to be a member. * * * Usually, if a member withdraws from or abandons the organization, his membership is terminated, his right to share in the association's property upon dissolution is lost, and those who remain and succeed him are entitled to his interest. * * * rule has likewise been applied to incorporated non-profit membership organizations. * * * Generally speaking, the termination of one's membership must be by voluntary act of the member or by act of the organization pursuant to authority granted by the charter or the by-laws. * * * But it may also be terminated by waiver or abandonment, provided there is sufficient proof thereof. * * * general, every right may be lost by waiver or abandonment, whether such right is secured by contract, conferred by statute or guaranteed by the Constitution. * * * An abandonment or waiver must be voluntary and intentional, but it need not be proved by express declaration, but may be inferred from the surrounding circumstances. * * *

With the foregoing principles in mind, we note the following evidence presented by the defendants: O. L. Ford ceased to participate in the corporation's affairs after 1969. He grazed no cattle after 1969, neither paid nor offered to pay any grazing fees since 1969, attended no meetings since 1969, and "just left it up to the fellows that were left there to run it ...". Thomas Welch grazed no cattle after 1968, neither paid nor offered to pay any grazing fees after 1968 and attended only one meeting after 1968, which was in the spring of 1969. Tinnie Garrison removed his cattle from the corporation's lands in 1970, never thereafter grazed any cattle or paid or offered to pay any grazing fees, and never attended any meeting after 1970. Conde Rodriques grazed no cattle after 1970, never attended any meeting after 1970, neither paid nor offered to pay any grazing or other fees after 1970, told Jack Pollock that he was quitting the organization, and "just left it up to someone else" to take care of the corporation and its obligations. All of the plaintiffs acknowledged that they knew the corporation was required to make the payments on the FHA mortgage or lose the land, and that the grazing fees which each member was obligated to pay were depended upon for that purpose. On the other hand, the evidence showed that each of the defendants remained active in the organization from the time he became a member, participated in the meetings, served as a director and/or officer, was active in managing the corporation and maintaining its property, and faithfully grazed his cattle on the corporation's lands each year and paid the applicable grazing fees. The jury, upon such evidence, found that each of the plaintiffs had waived his membership rights in the association.

The authorities speak of losing one's membership rights by abandoning the organization and its purposes, whereas the jury issues here inquired if plaintiffs "waived" their membership rights, but in a case of this type, waiver and abandonment are almost identical. * * * Indeed, the definition of waiver which the trial court gave to the jury was the same as that for abandonment, i. e., "... the intentional relinquishment of a known right." That definition has been approved in Texas for both waiver and abandonment. * * * Thus, the jury's findings of waiver can be deemed the equivalent of findings that the plaintiffs abandoned the organization and their membership rights therein.

We recognize that the by-laws of the corporation provided for the termination of a member's status by voluntary surrender of his certificate of membership or by the forfeiture of that certificate by act of the directors for failure to pay lawful assessments, and that neither was literally done in this case, unless it can be said that by abandoning the organization and its purposes, a member has, in effect, voluntarily surrendered his certificate. But the physical surrender of the certificate itself is not absolutely necessary for a termination of one's membership. The certificate does not constitute the membership relation; it is but the evidence of that relation. * * * Obviously, in a proper case, that relation may be terminated without a physical surrender of the certificate. For example, can it be doubted that a letter of resignation delivered by a member to the corporation, although unaccompanied by a physical delivery of the certificate, would be an effective termination of a member's status? We think not. Compare Wall v. Bureau of Lathing & Plaster. of Dade County, supra.

Plaintiffs' membership rights being subject to loss by waiver or abandonment, and the jury having found such waiver upon sufficient evidence, the trial court should have rendered a judgment that the plaintiffs take nothing. For the reasons stated, the judgment of the trial court is reversed and judgment is here rendered that the plaintiffs take nothing.

Question

Why were the persons who were members in good standing of the grazing association at the time of its dissolution entitled to the assets of the nonprofit upon its dissolution?

BARTLEY v. AUGUSTA COUNTRY CLUB, INC.

Supreme Court, Georgia, 1985
254 Ga. 144, 326 S.E.2d 442

MARSHALL, Presiding Justice.

The plaintiff-appellant appeals from the trial court's award of summary judgment in favor of the defendant-appellee incorporated, private, nonprofit social club, in the appellant former member's action to enjoin the club from prohibiting him from being a member of the club after the club had expelled him from membership pursuant to its bylaws for conduct "endangering the good order, welfare or character of the club."

The showing on the motion for summary judgment was that the conduct in question consisted of assisting his wife to sue the club, thereby putting its reputation and financial resources in jeopardy * * *; assisting his wife in preparing and distributing a letter derogatory of the club's actions; causing disruption within the club's membership by actively advocating his wife's lawsuit; making continuous complaints about the operation of the club; and becoming involved in a locker-room fracas regarding those complaints. *Held:*

> 1. Some of the appellant's claims are based on various alleged ways in which the club's action in expelling him violated his constitutional rights. "However, disciplinary actions taken by a private, social club against its members are not matters of constitutional law. Appellant's rights, if any, are governed by the by-laws, which constitute the agreement between the corporation and its members. * * * "[J]udicial inquiry into the suspension or expulsion of a member of an incorporated, private, social club is limited to a determination of whether the club has acted 'in good faith under the by-laws adopted by it.' * * * [T]he courts should not interfere with a club's authorized, good[-]faith exercise of discretion in disciplining members." * * * The appellant was afforded the process provided for in the by-laws, i.e., ten-days' notice and a hearing. There is no evidence that the club's action in expelling the appellant was not in good faith, nor that it was not authorized within the club's discretion under the by-law permitting expulsion for conduct "endangering the good order, welfare or character of the club."
>
> 2. "Unless the articles of incorporation or the bylaws grant property rights in the assets of the [nonprofit] corporation to expelled members, expelled members shall have no right to any part of such assets." OCGA § 14–3–80(b). Neither the articles of incorporation nor the bylaws of the appellee corporation grant property rights in the assets of the corporation to expelled members.

Waring v. Ga. Medical Society, 38 Ga. 608 (1869), cited by the appellant, involved a dispute over a physician's membership in a state-chartered medical society. Although the court designated the society as "a private civil corporation," as is the appellee here, and held that the corporators had a "property in the franchise," of which they could not be deprived without due process of law, it was alleged there that membership in the society was important to the physician's practice of his profession, and that the association played a significant role in the individual's trade or profession. It was also made clear that the medical society was organized not for private benefit, as is a social club such as the appellee here, but for the public purpose of "lessening the fatality induced by climate and incidental causes, and improving the science of medicine." Id. at p. 628. Accordingly, the court found it appropriate to inquire into the sufficiency of the physician's conduct to warrant expulsion.

The trial court did not err in granting summary judgment in favor of the appellee.

Judgment affirmed.

ROWLAND v. UNION HILLS COUNTRY CLUB

Court of Appeals, Arizona, 1988
157 Ariz. 301, 757 P.2d 105

HOWARD, Presiding Judge.

This is an appeal from an order granting summary judgment in the defendants' favor on all counts and denying plaintiffs' cross-motion for summary judgment on a breach of contract claim.

* * *

At the time of the events in question, defendant Collins was president of the board of directors of defendant Union Hills Country Club. The plaintiffs were members of the country club. The plaintiffs were expelled on February 26, 1986, for "conduct unbecoming a member." It is this expulsion and the defendants' alleged motivation for it on which the plaintiffs base their claims. * * *

Union Hills Country Club (UHCC or Club) is an Arizona corporation with approximately 900 shareholder-members. Its by-laws provide for selection of a board of directors by member vote, a process for amending the by-laws and a nominating procedure for candidates for the board of directors. The plaintiffs contend that the "conduct unbecoming a member" on which their expulsion was based was their attempt, undertaken in accordance with the by-laws, to elect a new board of directors and, ultimately, to amend the by-laws to permit governance by the general membership rather than by a board of directors. In effect, the plaintiffs contend that no specific conduct other than this supports the charges against them and that this conduct alone, which is authorized by the by-laws, cannot be characterized as "conduct unbecoming a member."

* * *

The facts are as follows. The plaintiffs, members of UHCC, formed a lobbying organization, The Independent Members Electorate (TIME). TIME representatives began lobbying the general membership in an effort to amend the by-laws. The proposed amendments were intended ultimately to permit replacement of the board of directors. A meeting between the board of directors and TIME representatives was held on February 11, 1986. Defendant Collins reported by letter to the general membership that the meeting revealed no disagreement on major issues. However, on February 20, Collins, as president of the board, sent letters to the plaintiffs advising them to appear on February 25 for an "opportunity to be heard" on charges of "violation of UHCC by-laws and unbecoming conduct as a member as required by Article IV, Section 4." The letter informed the plaintiffs that the board would be acting on the charges whether the plaintiffs appeared or not.

The charges against the plaintiffs were set forth in an attachment to the letter which provided:

"You are called before this Special Meeting of the Board of Directors under the provisions of Article III, Section 1, par. f and Article IV, Section 4 of the By–Laws of U.H.C.C.

1. You have fostered an alienating and contemptuous attitude toward the Board of Directors which 'creates problems for the members of the Club.'

2. You have helped develop and distribute both orally and in writing a program of misinformation which 'creates problems for the members of the Club'.

3. Unsupported accusations have caused untold wasted time and effort on the part of Board members and employees. This type of harassment has made the work of our Board more difficult than necessary. It has also made it increasingly difficult to obtain qualified candidates for the Board which is 'conduct unbecoming a member in his or her relation with other members'.

4. You have refused to meet your membership responsibility of making your complaints in writing as required by Art. XIV, Sec. 3, which is in violation of our By–Laws.

Through these and other actions and behavior, you have been able to foment and foster an attitude of suspicion and mistrust toward the Board. This has been detrimental to the patronage of the Club and has cost the Club some candidates for membership. This is a threat to the financial health of our Corporation."

Plaintiff Rowland appeared at his appointed time, 8:30 a.m. on February 25. After reading his own letter to the board, in which he asked for a "Bill of Particulars," he stated that he was unable to identify the acts or words that formed the basis for the charges. He brought to the board letters from other TIME members similarly charged, who felt it futile to appear, which also requested a "Bill of Particulars." Collins, in reply, asked Rowland whether he had anything more to say. Rowland replied that he did not and was excused. Before the meeting adjourned at 9:45 a.m., the board voted to expel Rowland. The other plaintiffs were expelled as the time set for their hearing passed and they did not appear.

* * *

The rights of members of a private organization are governed by the articles of incorporation and by-laws, which constitute a contract between the members and the organization, and among the members themselves. * * * Although defendants concede this, they argue that because the relationship is "social" in nature, judicial scrutiny does not extend to substantive claims of breach and is limited to determining whether the organization followed its own procedures in expelling a member. Defendants rely on this court's decision, in *Aspell v. American Contract Bridge League of Memphis, Tennessee,* 122 Ariz. 399, 595 P.2d 191 (App.1979), where we stated:

> "Courts have not yet been willing to extend legal protection from ostracism ... or provide compensation for 'mere insults, indignities, threats, annoyances, petty oppressions, or other trivialities.' ... The decision to exclude a person from one's social activities should be one of the more remote objects of judicial scrutiny. The fact that the parties voluntarily agree to associate with each other should not create for the courts the obligation to adjudicate such injuries, or impose liability beyond that which was within the range of contemplation of the contracting parties." 122 Ariz. at 403, 595 P.2d at 195 (citations omitted).

We note, however, that the cause of action in *Aspell* was not for breach of contract, but rather in tort. In affirming a directed verdict for the defendants, we merely refused to find that the law imposed a duty on the relationship created by the parties' contract which existed apart from that contract.

We do not agree with defendants' characterization of the scope of our review. While it is generally true that courts will not become involved in the internal disputes of a social organization resulting in the suspension or expulsion of its members, redress may be had where it is established that the action taken violated the organization's by-laws or was in bad faith, fundamentally unfair, fraudulent or utterly unsupported by any evidence. * * *

D. Members' Derivative Actions

Some states provide members of a nonprofit corporation with a right to bring a member's derivative action. This right permits a member of a nonprofit corporation to institute a lawsuit for the corporation to secure a judgment in favor of the corporation for restoration of corporate property or for compensation to the corporation for losses suffered. A member's derivative action may be brought to secure damages for an improper distribution of property of the corporation, for a self-dealing transaction between the corporation and one of its directors, and for breach of a charitable trust.

Notes

1. New York statutes provide that a member's derivative action may be brought by five percent or more of any class of members, capital certificate holders, or owners of a beneficial interest in the capital certificates of the corporation. See N.Y. Not-for-Profit Corp. Law. § 623. If the action is successful, the court may award the complaining members reasonable expenses, including reasonable attorneys' fees.

2. In California, a member must demonstrate that she had informed the corporation or the board in writing of the ultimate facts of each cause of action, or had delivered a copy of the complaint to the corporation, and must allege the member's efforts to cause the board to bring the action. See Cal. Corp. Code §§ 5710(b)(2), 7710(b)(2). The member must have been a member of the corporation at the time the particular transaction of which that member is complaining occurred.

Chapter 3

GOVERNANCE OF A NONPROFIT ORGANIZATION

Nonprofit organizations are regulated both by the states, often through provisions set out in state nonprofit corporation acts that prescribe standards of conduct for officers and directors, and by the Internal Revenue Service, vis-a-vis conditions set out in the Internal Revenue Code to obtain and maintain tax exempt status and by penalty taxes imposed on officers and directors for certain conflict of interest transactions. The requirements set out in the Internal Revenue Code to maintain tax exempt status and to avoid penalty taxes often have the effect of imposing more exacting standards of conduct on directors and trustees than those imposed by state legislatures or by the courts.

I. STATE STANDARDS OF CONDUCT

Because ethical standards alone often are inadequate to assure ethical conduct on the part of board members of nonprofit organizations, some states have imposed legal constraints in the form of required standards of conduct, applicable to trustees and directors in the performance of their duties, to insure at least a minimum level of ethical performance. The question courts and state legislatures must consider is how comprehensive and far-reaching the legal standards should be.

State laws relating to the governance of nonprofit organizations are somewhat imprecise. Because the law relating to nonprofit organizations has not been well defined, courts have looked to laws applicable to for-profit entities to decide issues relating to the liability of directors of nonprofit enterprises for improper discharge of duties.

A. Fiduciary Obligations

LITWIN v. ALLEN
Supreme Court, New York, 1940
25 N.Y.S.2d 667

SHIENTAG, Justice.

* * *

It has sometimes been said that directors are trustees. If this means that directors in the performance of their duties stand in a fiduciary relationship to the company, that statement is essentially correct. * * * 'The directors are bound by all those rules of conscientious fairness, morality, and honesty in purpose which the law imposes as the guides for those who are under the fiduciary obligations and responsibilities. They are held, in official action, to the extreme measure of candor, unselfishness, and good faith. Those principles are rigid, essential, and salutary.' * * *

It is clear that a director owes loyalty and allegiance to the company—a loyalty that is undivided and an allegiance that is influenced in action by no consideration other than the welfare of the corporation. Any adverse interest of a director will be subjected to a scrutiny rigid and uncompromising. He may not profit at the expense of his corporation and in conflict with its rights; he may not for personal gain divert unto himself the opportunities which in equity and fairness belong to his corporation. He is required to use his independent judgment. In the discharge of his duties a director must, of course, act honestly and in good faith, but that is not enough. He must also exercise some degree of skill and prudence and diligence.

In a leading case the Court of Appeals, in referring to the duties of directors, said: 'They should know of and give direction to the general affairs of the institution and its business policy, and have a general knowledge of the manner in which the business is conducted, the character of the investments, and the employment of the resources. No custom or practice can make a directorship a mere position of honor void of responsibility, or cause a name to become a substitute for care and attention. The personnel of a directorate may give confidence and attract custom; it must also afford protection.' * * *

In other words, directors are liable for negligence in the performance of their duties. Not being insurers, directors are not liable for errors of judgment or for mistakes while acting with reasonable skill and prudence. It has been said that a director is required to conduct the business of the corporation with the same degree of fidelity and care as an ordinarily prudent man would exercise in the management of his own affairs of like magnitude and importance. General rules, however, are not altogether helpful. In the last analysis, whether or not a director has discharged his duty, whether or not he has been negligent, depends upon the facts and circumstances of a particular case, the kind of corporation involved, its size and financial resources, the magnitude of the transaction, and the immediacy of the problem presented. A director is called upon 'to bestow the care and skill' which the situation demands. * * *

Undoubtedly, a director of a bank is held to stricter accountability than the director of an ordinary business corporation. A director of a bank is entrusted with the funds of depositors, and the stockholders look to him for protection from the imposition of personal liability. * * * But clairvoyance is not required even of a bank director. The law recognizes that the most conservative director is not infallible, and that he will make mistakes, but if he uses that degree of care ordinarily exercised by prudent bankers he will be absolved from liability although his opinion may turn out to have been mistaken and his judgment faulty.

Finally, in order to determine whether transactions approved by a director subject him to liability for negligence, we must 'look at the facts as they exist at the time of their occurrence, not aided or enlightened by those which subsequently take place'. * * * 'A wisdom developed after an event, and having it and its consequences as a source, is a standard no man should be judged by.' * * *

* * *

A director of a corporation is in the position of a fiduciary. He will not be permitted improperly to profit at the expense of his corporation. Undivided loyalty will ever be insisted upon. Personal gain will be denied to a director when it comes because he has taken a position adverse to or in conflict with the best interests of his corporation. The fiduciary relationship imposes a duty to act in accordance with the highest standards which a man of the finest sense of honor might impose upon himself. 'Uncompromising rigidity has been the attitude of courts of equity when petitioned to undermine the rule of undivided loyalty by the 'disintegrating erosion' of particular exceptions. * * * Only thus has the level of conduct for fiduciaries been kept at a level higher than that trodden by the crowd. It will not consciously be lowered by any judgment of this court. * * * While there is a lofty moral ideal implicit in this rule, it actually accomplishes a practical beneficent purpose. It recognizes the frailty of human nature; it realizes that where a man's immediate fortunes are concerned he may sometimes be subject to a blindness often intuitive and compulsive. The rule is designed on the one hand to prevent clouded conception of fidelity and a moral indifference that blurs the vision, and on the other hand to stimulate the most luminous critical sense and the finest exercise of judgment uncontaminated by the dross of prejudice, of divided allegiance or of self interest. * * *

Questions

1. The court in *Litwin* recognized that a corporate director, like a trustee, is a fiduciary. Fiduciaries are subject to standards of care and loyalty. What are the standards of care and loyalty for a trustee? For a corporate director? Should the same standards apply to corporate directors as are applicable to trustees? Why or why not?

2. Should the standards of care and loyalty imposed on directors of nonprofit entities differ from those imposed on directors of for-profit entities?

3. Should a higher standard of conduct be imposed on directors of "charitable" corporations than on directors of other nonprofit corporations?

Consider these issues in the following case.

STERN v. LUCY WEBB HAYES NAT'L TRAINING SCHOOL–DEACONESSES, MISSIONARIES

United States District Court, District of Columbia, 1974
381 F.Supp. 1003

GESELL, District Judge.

This is a class action which was tried to the Court without a jury. Plaintiffs were certified as a class under Rule 23(b)(2) of the Federal Rules of Civil Procedure and represent patients of Sibley Memorial Hospital, a District of Columbia non-profit charitable corporation organized under D.C.Code § 29–1001 et seq. They challenge various aspects of the Hospital's fiscal management. The amended complaint named as defendants nine members of the Hospital's Board of Trustees, six financial institutions, and the Hospital itself.* * *

* * *

The two principal contentions in the complaint are that the defendant trustees conspired to enrich themselves and certain financial institutions with which they were affiliated by favoring those institutions in financial dealings with the Hospital, and that they breached their fiduciary duties of care and loyalty in the management of Sibley's funds. The defendant financial institutions are said to have joined in the alleged conspiracy and to have knowingly benefitted from the alleged breaches of duty. The Hospital is named as a nominal defendant for the purpose of facilitating relief.

I. Corporate History.

The Lucy Webb Hayes National Training School for Deaconesses and Missionaries was established in 1891 by the Methodist Women's Home Missionary Society for the purpose, in part, for providing health care services to the poor of the Washington area. The School was incorporated under the laws of the District of Columbia as a charitable, benevolent and educational institution by instrument dated August 8, 1894. During the following year, the School built the Sibley Memorial Hospital on North Capitol Street to facilitate its charitable work. Over the years, operation of the Hospital has become the School's principal concern, so that the two institutions have been referred to synonymously by all parties and will be so treated in this Opinion. As increasing demands were made upon Sibley's facilities, the Hospital was renovated several times. Finally, in the mid–1950's, it was decided to move the Hospital to a new location on Loughboro Road in Northwest Washington. The nearby Hahnemann Hospital, another Methodist charity, was merged with Sibley in 1956 in anticipation of this move. The new Sibley Memorial Hospital was dedicated on June 17, 1962.

In 1960, shortly after ground was broken for the new building, the Sibley Board of Trustees revised the corporate by-laws in preparation for an expected increase in the volume and complexity of Hospital business following the move. Under the new by-laws, the Board was to consist of from 25 to 35 trustees, who were to meet at least twice each year. Between such meetings, an Executive Committee was to represent the Board, and was authorized, inter alia, to open checking and savings accounts, approve the Hospital budget, renew mortgages, and enter into contracts. A Finance Committee was created to review the budget and to report regularly on the amount of cash available for investment. Management of those investments was to be supervised by an Investment Committee, which was to work closely with the Finance Committee in such matters.

In fact, management of the Hospital from the early 1950's until 1968 was handled almost exclusively by two trustee officers: Dr. Orem, the Hospital Administrator, and Mr. Ernst, the Treasurer. Unlike most of their fellow trustees, to whom membership on the Sibley Board was a charitable service incidental to their principal vocations, Orem and Ernst were continuously involved on almost a daily basis in the affairs of Sibley. They dominated the Board and its Executive Committee, which routinely accepted their recommendations and ratified their actions. Even more significantly, neither the Finance Committee nor the Investment Committee ever met or conducted business from the date of their creation until 1971, three years after the death of Dr. Orem. As a result, budgetary and investment decisions during this period, like most other management decisions affecting the Hospital's finances, were handled by Orem and Ernst, receiving only cursory supervision from the Executive Committee and the full Board.

Dr. Orem's death on April 5, 1968, obliged some of the other trustees to play a more active role in running the Hospital. The Executive Committee, and particularly defendant Stacy Reed (as Chairman of the Board, President of the Hospital, and ex officio member of the Executive (Committee), became more deeply involved in the day-to-day management of the Hospital while efforts were made to find a new Administrator. The man who was eventually selected for that office, Dr. Jarvis, had little managerial experience and his performance was not entirely satisfactory. Mr. Ernst still made most of the financial and investment decisions for Sibley, but his actions and failures to act came slowly under increasing scrutiny by several of the other trustees, particularly after a series of disagreements between Ernst and the Hospital Comptroller which led to the discharge of the latter early in 1971.

Prompted by these difficulties, Mr. Reed decided to activate the Finance and Investment Committee in the Fall of 1971. However, as Chairman of the Finance Committee and member of the Investment

Committee as well as Treasurer, Mr. Ernst continued to exercise dominant control over investment decisions and, on several occasions, discouraged and flatly refused to respond to inquiries by other trustees into such matters. It has only been since the death of Mr. Ernst on October 30, 1972, that the other trustees appear to have assumed an identifiable supervisory role over investment policy and Hospital fiscal management in general.

Against this background, the basic claims will be examined.

II. Conspiracy.

Plaintiffs first contend that the five defendant trustees and the five defendant financial institutions were involved in a conspiracy to enrich themselves at the expense of the Hospital. They point to the fact that each named trustee held positions of responsibility with one or more of the defendant institutions as evidence that the trustees had both motive and opportunity to carry out such a conspiracy.* * *

* * *

Basically, the trustees are charged with mismanagement, nonmanagement and self-dealing. The applicable law is unsettled. The charitable corporation is a relatively new legal entity which does not fit neatly into the established common law categories of corporation and trust. As the discussion below indicates, however, the modern trend is to apply corporate rather than trust principles in determining the liability of the directors of charitable corporations, because their functions are virtually indistinguishable from those of their 'pure' corporate counterparts.

* * *

Both trustees and corporate directors are liable for losses occasioned by their negligent mismanagement of investments. However, the degree of care required appears to differ in many jurisdictions. A trustee is uniformly held to a high standard of care and will be held liable for simple negligence, while a director must often have committed 'gross negligence' or otherwise be guilty of more than mere mistakes of judgment. * * *

* * *

This distinction may amount to little more than a recognition of the fact that corporate directors have many areas of responsibility, while the traditional trustee is often charged only with the management of the trust funds and can therefore be expected to devote more time and expertise to that task. Since the board members of most large charitable corporations fall within the corporate rather than the trust model, being charged with the operation of ongoing businesses, it has been said that they should only be held to the less stringent corporate standard of care. * * * More specifically, directors of charitable corporations are required to exercise ordinary and reasonable care in the performance of their duties, exhibiting honesty and good faith. * * *

Plaintiffs allege that the individual defendants failed to supervise the management of hospital investments or even to attend meetings of the committees charged with such supervision. Trustees are particularly vulnerable to such a charge, because they not only have an affirmative duty to 'maximize the trust income by prudent investment,' * * *, but they may not delegate that duty, even to a committee of their fellow trustees. * * * A corporate director, on the other hand, may delegate his investment responsibility to fellow directors, corporate officers, or even outsiders, but he must continue to exercise general supervision over the activities of his delegates. * * * Once again, the rule for charitable corporations is closer to the traditional corporate rule: directors should at least be permitted to delegate investment decisions to a committee of board members, so long as all directors assume the responsibility for supervising such committees by periodically scrutinizing their work. * * *

* * *

Total abdication of the supervisory role, however, is improper even under traditional corporate principles. A director who fails to acquire the information necessary to supervise investment policy or consistently fails even to attend the meetings at which such policies are considered has violated his fiduciary duty to the corporation. * * * While a director is, of course, permitted to rely upon the expertise of those to whom he has delegated investment responsibility, such reliance is a tool for interpreting the delegate's reports, not an excuse for dispensing with or ignoring such reports. * * * A director whose failure to supervise permits negligent mismanagement by others to go unchecked has committed an independent wrong against the corporation; he is not merely an accessory under an attenuated theory of respondent superior or constructive notice. * * *

* * *

Under District of Columbia Law, neither trustees nor corporate directors are absolutely barred from placing funds under their control into a bank having an interlocking directorship with their own institution. In both cases, however, such transactions will be subjected to the closest scrutiny to determine whether or not the duty of loyalty has been violated. * * * A deliberate conspiracy among trustees or Board members to enrich the interlocking bank at the expense of the trust or corporation would, for example, constitute such a breach and render the conspirators liable for any losses. * * * In the absence of clear evidence of wrongdoing, however, the courts appear to have used different standards to determine whether or not relief is appropriate, depending again on the legal relationship involved. Trustees may be found guilty of a breach of trust even for mere negligence in the maintenance of accounts in banks with which they are associated, * * *, while corporate directors are generally only required to show 'entire fairness' to the corporation and 'full disclosure' of the potential conflict of interest to the Board. * * *

Most courts apply the less stringent corporate rule to charitable corporations in this area as well. * * * It is, however, occasionally added that a director should not only disclose his interlocking responsibilities but also refrain from voting on or otherwise influencing a corporate decision to transact business with a company in which he has a significant interest or control. See, e.g., Gilbert v. McLeod Infirmary, supra.

* * *

Having surveyed the authorities as outlined above and weighed the briefs, arguments and evidence submitted by counsel, the Court holds that a director or so-called trustee of a charitable hospital organized under the Non–Profit Corporation Act of the District of Columbia (D.C.Code § 29–1001 et seq.) is in default of his fiduciary duty to manage the fiscal and investment affairs of the hospital if it has been shown by a preponderance of the evidence that:

(1) while assigned to a particular committee of the Board having general financial or investment responsibility under the by-laws of the corporation, he has failed to use due diligence in supervising the actions of those officers, employees or outside experts to whom the responsibility for making day-to-day financial or investment decisions has been delegated; or

(2) he knowingly permitted the hospital to enter into a business transaction with himself or with any corporation, partnership or association in which he then had a substantial interest or held a position as trustee, director, general manager or principal officer without having previously informed the persons charged with approving that transaction of his interest or position and of any significant reasons, unknown to or not fully appreciated by such persons, why the transaction might not be in the best interests of the hospital; or

(3) except as required by the preceding paragraph, he actively participated in or voted in favor of a decision by the Board or any committee or subcommittee thereof to transact business with himself or with any corporation, partnership or association in which he then had a substantial interest or held a position as trustee, director, general manager or principal officer; or

(4) he otherwise failed to perform his duties honestly, in good faith, and with a reasonable amount of diligence and care.

* * *

Applying these standards to the facts in the record, the Court finds that each of the defendant trustees has breached his fiduciary duty to supervise the management of Sibley's investments. All except Mr. Jones were duly and repeatedly elected to the Investment Committee without ever bothering to object when no meetings were called for more than ten years. Mr. Jones was a member of the equally inactive Finance Committee, the failure of which to report on the existence of investable funds was cited by several other defendants as a reason for not convening the Investment Committee. In addition, Reed, Jones and Smith were, for varying periods of time, also members of the Executive Committee, which was charged with acquiring at least enough information to vote intelligently on the opening of new bank accounts. By their own testimony, it is clear that they failed to do so. And all of the individual defendants ignored the investment sections of the yearly audits which were made available to them as members of the Board. In short, these men have in the past failed to exercise even the most cursory supervision over the handling of Hospital funds and failed to establish and carry out a defined policy.

The record is unclear on the degree to which full disclosure preceded the frequent self-dealing which occurred during the period under consideration. It is reasonable to assume that the Board was generally aware of the various bank affiliations of the defendant trustees, but there is no indication that these conflicting interests were brought home to the relevant committees when they voted to approve particular transactions. Similarly, while plaintiffs have shown no active misrepresentation on defendants' part, they have established instances in which an interested trustee failed to alert the responsible officials to better terms known to be available elsewhere.

It is clear that all of the defendant trustees have, at one time or another, affirmatively approved self-dealing transactions. Most of these incidents were of relatively minor significance: one interested trustee would join a dozen disinterested fellow members of the Executive Committee in unanimously approving the opening of a bank account; two or three interested trustees would support a similarly large group in voting to give or renew the mortgage. Others cannot be so easily disregarded. Defendant Ferris' advice and vote in the relatively small Investment Committee to recommend approval of the investment contract with Ferris & Co. may have been crucial to that transaction. Defendant Reed assumed principal responsibility for account levels between 1969 and 1971, during which period the Security checking account grew to more than a million dollars. And defendant Smith, in his capacity as President of Jefferson Federal, personally negotiated the interest rates on a $230,000 certificate account with the Hospital.

That the Hospital has suffered no measurable injury from many of these transactions—including the mortgage and the investment contract—and that the excessive deposits which were the real source of harm were caused primarily by the uniform failure to supervise rather than the occasional self-dealing vote are both facts that the Court must take into account in fashioning relief, but they do not alter the principle that the trustee of a charitable hospital should always avoid active participation in a transaction in which he or a corporation with which he is associated has a significant interest.

* * *

While it is thus established that the named trustees acted in breach of fiduciary duty, the institutional defendants are not liable simply because they benefitted from those breaches. Under the prevailing rule of law, a bank or other financial institution is only liable for losses sustained by a trust by reason of its dealings with a trustee if the institution had actual or constructive knowledge that the transaction was in breach of the trustee's fiduciary duty. * * *

* * *

Removal of the defendant trustees from the Sibley Board would be unduly harsh, and this will not be ordered. These trustees are now completing long years of service and they will soon become less active in the day-to-day affairs of the Hospital because of age or illness. It would unduly disrupt the affairs of the Hospital abruptly to terminate their relationship with that institution. Others must soon take over their roles in carrying forward the Hospital's affairs, and it is therefore unnecessary to interfere by order of removal or disqualification with a transition that is necessarily already taking place due to other immutable factors.

The management of a non-profit charitable hospital imposes a severe obligation upon its trustees. A hospital such as Sibley is not closely regulated by any public authority, it has no responsibility to file financial reports, and its Board is self-perpetuating. The interests of its patients are funneled primarily through large group insurers who pay the patients' bills, and the patients lack meaningful participation in the Hospital's affairs. It is obvious that, in due course, new trustees must come to the Board of this Hospital, some of whom will be affiliated with banks, savings and loan associations and other financial institutions. The tendency of representatives of such institutions is often to seek business in return for advice and assistance rendered as trustees. It must be made absolutely clear that Board membership carries no right to preferential treatment in the placement or handling of the Hospital's investments and business accounts. The Hospital would be well advised to restrict membership on its Board to the representatives of financial institutions which have no substantial business relationship with the Hospital. The best way to avoid potential conflicts of interest and to be assured of objective advice is to avoid the possibility of such conflicts at the time new trustees are selected.

As an additional safeguard, the Court will require that each newly-elected trustee read this Opinion and the attached Order. Compliance with this requirement must appear in a document signed by the new trustee or in the minutes of the Sibley Board. In view of the circumstances disclosed by the record it will be desirable, in addition, to require public disclosure which will further insure that the Board's recently-avowed good intentions are faithfully carried out. To this end, the Court will direct that prior to each meeting of the full Board the members of the Board shall receive, at least one week in advance, a formal written statement prepared by the Hospital's Treasurer or Comptroller disclosing in detail the full extent of all business done by the Hospital since the last Board meeting with any bank, savings and loan association, investment service or other financial institution with which any trustee or officer of the Hospital is affiliated as a trustee, director, principal officer, partner, general manager or substantial shareholder. Moreover, all such dealings shall be summarized by the Hospital's auditors in their annual audit and a copy of the annual audit shall be made available on request for inspection by any patient of the Hospital at the Hospital's offices during business hours. Such arrangements should continue for a period of five years.

* * *

LOUISIANA WORLD EXPOSITION v. FEDERAL INSURANCE CO.

United States Court of Appeals, Fifth Circuit, 1989
864 F.2d 1147

NG, Circuit Judge:

The standard of care applicable to the officers and directors of a nonprofit Louisiana corporation is a statutory one, and one in which the words "negligence" and "gross negligence" do not appear. The statute reads in pertinent part:

> Officers and directors shall be deemed to stand in a fiduciary relation to the corporation and its members, and shall discharge the duties of their respective positions in good faith, and with that diligence, care, judgment and skill which ordinarily prudent men would exercise under similar circumstances in like positions. La.Rev. Stat.Ann. § 12:226(A) (West 1969).

We emphasize that we do not seek here to depart from that explicit standard. Our task is simply to interpret the standard as it is written. The necessity for our inquiry into whether simple negligence would suffice to create liability under section 12:226(A) is occasioned by judicial interpretations of the statute and its predecessors.

Although the language in the statutory standard makes no reference to concepts of ordinary or gross negligence, the courts have turned to these concepts to guide them in determinations of what the standard means. Our task here, then, is to clarify the meaning of the Louisiana statutory standard of care in terms of gross and ordinary negligence to give greater guidance to the district court on remand.

As we indicated in our original opinion, *LWE*, 858 F.2d at 237, section 12:226(A) is virtually identical to the analogous provision in the Louisiana Business Corporation Law. La.Rev.Stat.Ann. § 12:91 (West 1969). We are therefore properly guided by interpretations of the latter statute. Similarly, we can look to the judicial interpretations of the predecessor statutes to section 12:91 for guidance because the earlier statutes are in pertinent part identical to section 12:91. Further, section 12:91 is also very similar to the analogous provision in the original

Model Business Corporation Act (1950). Therefore, we also look to commentary discussing the original Model Act for guidance in our inquiry.

* * *

In our original opinion, we discussed in some detail the Louisiana case law regarding the duty owed by directors and officers to the corporation. * * * Our conclusion was that allegations of fraud were not necessary to establish a cause of action against directors or officers by the corporation and that because LWE's complaint could be read to state a cause of action for gross negligence, the complaint could be maintained. We will not reiterate that summary of the case law, but will instead highlight those cases which explain the duty in terms of gross or simple negligence.

In *Pool v. Pool,* 16 So.2d 132 (La.App.1943) (interpreting Act No. 250 of 1928 § 36), after repeating the statutory standard of care, * * * the court goes on to say: Directors are not liable for mere errors of judgment on their part where they act in good faith. They are only required to exercise reasonable care and diligence and act in good faith. But they are liable for wilful neglect of duty, gross negligence or their fraudulent breach of trust.

Thus, rather than simplifying the statutory standard, *Pool* complicates it by adding to the analysis this additional gloss, including the concept of gross negligence. Further, it is unclear from this language whether simple negligence would be sufficient to hold a corporate principal liable. * * *

In *Mansfield Hardwood Lumber Co. v. Johnson,* 263 F.2d 748 (5th Cir.) (applying Louisiana law and interpreting La.Rev.Stat. § 12:36 (1950)), *cert. denied,* 361 U.S. 885, 80 S.Ct. 156, 4 L.Ed.2d 120 (1959), we discuss the duty owed by Louisiana corporate officers and directors to the corporation and its shareholders:

> Whether this relationship between officers and directors and their stockholders is termed fiduciary or quasi-fiduciary or trust or confidence is immaterial, and, likewise, it is immaterial whether its breach is described as constructive fraud, unjust enrichment, fraudulent breach of trust, breach of fiduciary obligation, gross negligence, or otherwise, and whether the remedy is given by a constructive trust, restitution, or accounting.... The standard of a fiduciary's duty to his beneficiary, depending on the instant relation and the facts of the particular case, lies somewhere between simple negligence and willful misconduct or fraud with intent to deceive.

* * * This language suggests—albeit ambiguously—that something more than simple negligence will be required to hold a corporate officer or director liable to the corporation.

Recently, the Court of Appeal of Louisiana has again used the opportunity to interpret this standard with the application of concepts of negligence. In *Bordelon v. Cochrane*, 533 So.2d 82 (La.App.1988) (interpreting La.Rev.Stat.Ann. § 12:91 (West 1969)), the plaintiff sought to recover individually as a shareholder, and alternatively to bring a derivative suit against the corporation's officers and directors for breach of their fiduciary duty. After denying the plaintiff relief as an individual shareholder, the court went on to refuse him the right to sue derivatively, saying: "in the absence of usurpation, of fraud, or of gross negligence [courts] will not interfere...." * * *.

These cases suggest, if not compel, an interpretation of the statutory standard which stops short of finding liability when the evidence suggests only simple negligence on the part of a corporate principal. The cases which use negligence and gross negligence as concepts to aid in interpreting the duty owed simply have not gone so far as to find liability where a director or officer has been merely negligent.

This interpretation is also consistent with commentary on the subject of officer and director liability. The Louisiana statute was specifically analyzed in these terms in Veasy and Manning, *Codified Standard—Safe Harbor or Uncharted Reef? An Analysis of the Model Act Standard of Care Compared with Delaware Law*, 35 Bus.Law. 920, 927 (1980) [hereinafter "*Codified Standard*"]. The authors discuss *Pool* and characterize it as adding to the confusion surrounding the subject of director liability and concepts of negligence and gross negligence. Arsht and Hinsey, in an article responding to *Codified Standard,* say:

> [T]he discrepancy in standards suggested by the *dicta* of a Louisiana Court in *Pool v. Pool* is more apparent than real. In stating that directors must exercise such "diligence, care, judgment and skill which ordinarily prudent men would exercise under similar circumstances in like positions," and then stating that directors are liable for their "gross negligence," the court did not use the term "gross negligence" to lower the articulated standard of care—but rather to refer to conduct that failed to satisfy the articulated standard. This use is confirmed by reference to the first authority cited by the court which states:
>
> In some jurisdictions the only negligence for which directors are liable is gross negligence, or gross negligence which would warrant an imputation of fraud, but both in these and other jurisdictions, the measure of care required is ordinary and reasonable care, such as a reasonably prudent, careful, and skillful man exercises in the conduct of his own affairs, and they are liable for losses when they fail to exercise such care, and only when they fail to exercise such care. *A failure to conform to this standard is held to constitute gross negligence.* (Citations omitted and emphasis added).

Arsht and Hinsey, *Codified Standard—Same Harbor but Chartered Channel: A Response,* 35 Bus.Law. 947, 949 (1980) (footnotes omitted).

Thus, the Louisiana cases and the commentary thereon indicate that in the case of a for-profit business the statutory standard of care should be interpreted as requiring at least gross negligence. Simple negligence alone is insufficient for a finding of personal liability of an officer or director to the corporation.

* * *

As we noted, Louisiana jurisprudence has not interpreted the standard of care of corporate officers and directors as applied to nonprofit corporations. We therefore look to decisions from other jurisdictions for guidance. The standard of care for a director of a nonprofit corporation was long held to be more demanding than that for a director of a for-profit business. The theory was that a nonprofit corporation was analogous to a public trust, and its directors were deemed its trustees. However, modern statutes and case law have altered that, and now the standard for nonprofit corporate directors is usually the same as that of their for-profit counterparts.

The leading case to indicate the change away from the higher standard of care for nonprofit corporate directors is *Stern v. Lucy Webb Hayes Nat. Training Sch. for Deaconesses and Missionaries,* 381 F.Supp. 1003 (D.D.C.1974). In *Stern,* the defendant hospital was sued by a class of patients for its alleged failure to invest its liquid assets in prudent ways, often failing to earn interest on very large sums of money. In finding liability on the parts of the corporation's "trustees" (who acted as corporate directors), the court stated:

> [t]he charitable corporation is a relatively new legal entity which does not fit neatly into the established common law categories of corporation and trust. As the discussion below indicates, however, the modern trend is to apply corporate rather than trust principles in determining the liability of the directors of charitable corporations, because their functions are virtually indistinguishable from those of their "pure" corporate counterparts.

* * * The court went on to note that a trustee is held to a higher standard of care than a corporate director; the former is liable for simple negligence, while the latter is liable only when he has committed gross negligence. *Id.* Because the corporation's "trustees" acted as directors, the court held them to the lower standard of care applicable to directors. On the facts before it, the court found the corporation's trustees liable for their failure to object when no meeting of the board was held for more than ten years, their failure to acquire adequate knowledge to vote intelligently on corporate funds, and their failure to "exercise even the most cursory supervision of Hospital funds." * * *

In a variety of other cases courts have refused to impose the trustee standard of care on directors of nonprofit organizations, and instead they have used the more lenient standard of a corporate director. *Rywalt v. Writer Corp.,* 34 Colo.App. 334, 526 P.2d 316 (1974), involves a Colorado nonprofit corporation. The court refused to impose a higher standard on the board of a nonprofit homeowners' association than that imposed on principals of for-profit businesses. It denied the plaintiffs the injunctive relief they sought against the board of the association, holding that where the acts of the board are in good faith and within the exercise of honest business judgments, the courts will not interfere. In *Midatlantic Nat. Bank v. Frank G. Thompson Found.*, 170 N.J.Super. 128, 405 A.2d 866 (1979), the members of the governing board of a nonprofit corporation petitioned the court for advice as to whether it could engage in certain transactions. In holding that the transactions in question were permissible, the court stated "the responsibilities of members of governing boards of charitable corporations are to be considered more under the developed law of corporations than of trusts." * * *

* * *

We emphasize what we indicated at the outset: the standard of care owed by the director or officer of a Louisiana nonprofit corporation is that expressed by the statute. With respect to the specific issue addressed in this opinion,* * * officers and directors are required to discharge the duties of their respective positions with that diligence, care, judgment and skill which ordinarily prudent men would exercise under similar circumstances in like positions. On remand, in order to recover against any defendant, the plaintiff must establish at least gross negligence on the part of that defendant.

* * *

Note

Courts have ruled that while directors are liable for negligence in the performance of their duties, they are not insurers and, thus, are not liable for errors of judgment or for mistakes so long as they act with reasonable skill and prudence. This "business judgment rule" rule was described in Panter v. Marshall Field & Company, 646 F.2d 271 (7th Cir.1981) as establishing that:

"(d)irectors of corporations discharge their fiduciary duties when in good faith they exercise business judgment in making decisions regarding the corporation. When they act in good faith, they enjoy a presumption of sound business judgment, reposed in them as directors, which courts will not disturb if any rational business purpose can be attributed to their decisions. In the absence of fraud, bad faith, gross overreaching or abuse of discretion, courts will not interfere with the exercise of business judgment by corporate directors."

The court in Panter decided that if directors were held to the same standard as ordinary fiduciaries a corporation could not conduct business. It stated:

"(a)n ordinary fiduciary may not have the slightest conflict of interest in any transaction he undertakes on behalf of the trust. Yet by the very nature of corporate life a director has a certain amount of self-interest in everything he does. The very fact that the director wants to enhance corporate profits is in part attributable to his desire to keep shareholders satisfied so that they will not oust him.

The business judgment rule seeks to alleviate this problem by validating certain situations that otherwise would involve a conflict of interest for the ordinary fiduciary. The rule achieves this purpose by postulating that if actions are arguably taken for the benefit of the corporation, then the directors are presumed to have been exercising their sound business judgment rather than responding to any personal motivations."

The business judgment rule, called the best judgment rule with respect to directors of nonprofit organizations, evolved from a determination that in order to make a corporation function effectively, those having management responsibility must have the freedom to make in good faith the many necessary decisions quickly and finally without the impairment of having to be liable for an honest error in judgment. See Financial Industrial Fund, Inc. v. McDonnell Douglas Corp. 474 F.2d 514 (10th Cir.1973). Application of this rule to actions of members of a board of directors, in effect, causes directors of corporations to be liable for their negligent acts only if they are grossly negligent.

Questions

1. Shareholders of for-profit corporations oversee actions of members of their board of directors, but members of the public, the beneficiaries of charitable corporations, cannot monitor adequately actions of members of boards of directors of these corporations. Do you think the public's lack of ability to hold members of a board of a charitable corporation accountable for their actions would justify imposing a higher trust standard of care on directors of charitable corporations? The court in *Litwin* opined that a director of a bank should be held to a stricter accountability than a director of an ordinary business corporation. Are directors of charitable corporation subject to a public trust that should hold them to stricter accountability than directors of "ordinary business corporations?"

2. Because a lesser standard of conduct is applicable to corporate directors, directors are less likely to be liable for negligent acts than are trustees of a charitable trust. Would this be a factor that would influence you in determining whether to structure a charitable organization as a nonprofit corporation or as a charitable trust?

3. The court in *Lucy Webb Hayes Nat'l School for Deaconesses* would find board members of a nonprofit corporation negligent and in violation of the standard of care if members of the board failed to invest funds of the nonprofit in a prudent manner. What guidance does a board member have in making prudent investment decisions?

Uniform Management of Institutional Funds Act (Currently Uniform Prudent Management of Institutional Funds Act)

A number of states have adopted the Uniform Management of Institutional Funds Act which provides a standard of business care and prudence in the investment of funds of nonprofit organizations. The Act requires governing boards to exercise "ordinary business care and prudence" considering the facts and circumstances existing at the time of their action. It authorizes the delegation of investment decisions and provides for the expenditure of the appreciation of invested funds. The standard of care is that of a reasonable and prudent director of a nonprofit corporation. The Act requires that, in the course of administering investment funds, individual investments must be considered as part of an overall investment strategy. The Act states that, in making investments, members of the governing board must consider the long- and short-term needs of the institution in carrying out its charitable purposes, its present and anticipated financial requirements, the expected total return on its investments, general economic conditions, the appropriateness of a reasonable proportion of higher risk investment with respect to institutional funds as a whole, income, growth, and long-term net appreciation, as well as the probable safety of funds.

The Act provides that the governing board of a charitable organization may release a restriction imposed by the applicable gift instrument on the use or investment of an institutional fund with the written consent of the donor or, if written consent cannot be obtained, by application to a court of the county in which the principal activities of the institution are conducted for release of a restriction or use of the funds. The Act requires that the Attorney General be a party to the proceedings and states that provisions in the Act do not limit the application of the cy pres doctrine, discussed below.

The Act adopts corporate standards based on a concern by the drafters that use of the trustee standard could have a debilitating effect upon members of a governing board of a nonprofit corporation, most of whom would be "uncompensated public minded citizens."[1]

The Uniform Management of Institutional Funds Act was drafted about 35 years ago and now is considered to be out of date. Accordingly, the National Conference of Commissioners on Uniform State Laws has replaced the act with the Uniform Prudent Management of Institutional Funds Act (UPMIFA). This act (UPMIFA) combines the Uniform Management of Institutional Funds Act with the Uniform Prudent Investor Act (UPIA), discussed below. It also updates provisions of UPIA to apply its investment decision making rules to nonprofit corporations as well as to trusts.

Uniform Prudent Investor Act
(Currently Uniform Prudent Management of Institutional Funds Act)

The Uniform Prudent Investor Act (UPIA) has been enacted in 43 jurisdictions. It updated rules on investment decision making for trusts. The Act provides that the standard of care applicable to investments is directed toward the investment portfolio as a whole, and as part of an overall investment strategy, rather than to any particular investment. The Act directs a trustee of funds to invest and manage assets prudently by considering the purposes, distribution requirements, and other circumstances of the entity. A trustee generally must diversify the charity's investments. Circumstances appropriate to consider in investing and

---

1. Unif. Management of Institutional Funds Act, Commissioners' Prefatory Note.

managing funds include general economic conditions, effects of inflation and deflation, the role that each investment or course of action plays with the overall portfolio, and the entity's needs for liquidity, regularity of income, and preservation or appreciation of capital. Compliance with the prudent investor rule is determined in light of the facts and circumstances existing at the time of a trustee's decision or action and not by hindsight. An institution may delegate the management and investment of an institutional fund to an external agent but must exercise prudence in selecting an agent and in reviewing periodically the agent's overall performance and compliance with terms of the delegation.

The Uniform Prudent Management of Institutional Funds Act (UPMIFA) extends the rules and duties set out in UPIA to charities organized as corporations. It also provides that in addition to identifying facts a charity must consider in making management and investment decisions, including the general requirement to diversify investments and to make decisions about each asset in the context of the portfolio of investments, those who manage and invest charitable funds must give primary consideration to donor intent as expressed in a gift instrument, must incur only reasonable costs in investing and managing charitable funds, must dispose of unsuitable assets, and, in general, must develop an investment strategy appropriate for the fund and the charity.

Model Nonprofit Corporation Act of 1987

While the original Model Nonprofit Corporation Act was silent with respect to standards of conduct for corporate directors, the 1987 Model Act sets out standards of conduct to define a duty of care and a duty of loyalty for a director of a nonprofit corporation.

Section 8.30. General Standards for Directors

(a) A director shall discharge his or her duties as a director, including his or her duties as a member of a committee:

(1) in good faith;

(2) with the care an ordinarily prudent person in a like position would exercise under similar circumstances; and

(3) in a manner the director reasonably believes to be in the best interests of the corporation.

* * *

Section 8.32. Director Conflict of Interest

(a) A conflict of interest transaction is a transaction with the corporation in which a director of the corporation has a direct or indirect interest. A conflict of interest transaction is not voidable or the basis of imposing liability on the director if the transaction was fair at the time it was entered into or is approved as provided in subsections (b) or (c).

(b) A transaction in which a director of a public benefit or religious corporation has a conflict of interest may be approved:

(1) in advance by the vote of the board of directors of a committee of the board if

(i) the material facts of the transaction and the director's interest are disclosed or known to the board of committee of the board, and

(ii) the directors approving the transaction in good faith reasonably believe that the transaction is fair to the corporation; or

(2) before or after it is consummated by obtaining approval of the

(i) attorney general, or

(ii) court in an action in which the attorney general is joined as a party; or

(c) A transaction in which a director of a mutual benefit corporation has a conflict of interest may be approved if:

(1) the material facts of the transaction and the director's interest were disclosed or known to the board of directors or a committee of the board and the board or committee of the board authorized, approved, or ratified the transaction; or

(2) the material facts of the transaction and the director's interest were disclosed or known to the members and they authorized, approved or ratified the transaction.

* * *

Questions

1. The 1987 Model Act sets out different procedures for approving a director conflict of interest transaction for public benefit and mutual benefit corporations. What is the difference? Should there be a difference?

2. Should a director of a charitable nonprofit corporation be precluded from involvement in any conflict of interest transactions? Or should such transactions be approved so long as they are "fair" to the corporation?

3. The court in *Litwin* discussed the "corporate opportunity" doctrine. Does the doctrine apply to a director of a nonprofit organization?

NORTHEAST HARBOR GOLF CLUB v. HARRIS

Supreme Court, Maine, 1999
725 A.2d 1018

CLIFFORD, J.

Nancy Harris appeals from a judgment ordering equitable relief entered in the Superior Court (Hancock County, *Atwood, J.*) in favor of Northeast Harbor Golf Club, Inc., following a non-jury trial. Harris contends that the court incorrectly determined that her purchase and development of property surrounding the Club was a corporate opportunity that she usurped, and further contends that any cause of action against her is barred by the statute of limitations and by laches. The Club cross-appeals, contending that, independent of usurping a corporate opportunity, Harris breached her fiduciary duty to the Club when she began developing the property in 1988. Because we conclude that the court correctly determined that Harris usurped a corporate opportunity, but that the statute of limitations period within which the Club could have brought an action against Harris expired, and that laches applies to preclude any action not barred by the expiration of the limitations period, and that no other cause of action arose, we vacate the judgment.

The Northeast Harbor Golf Club is a Maine corporation operating a golf course located in Mt. Desert. Nancy Harris served as president of the Club from 1971 until August of 1990. The Club is managed by the president and a board of directors. Although the board of directors was empowered to approve policy decisions, it was content to have Harris assume much of the responsibility for the Club's operation. Harris generously contributed to the Club throughout her tenure as president. In addition to her duties as president, she performed other tasks, including mowing and gardening. Moreover, to alleviate the Club's financial difficulties, Harris often purchased equipment for the Club with her own money and either leased or sold it to the corporation for a reduced price to ensure that the Club would not be forced to make substantial cash outlays.

From 1972 until 1984, the board, at Harris's insistence, discussed either purchasing and developing land surrounding the Club or developing some of the Club's real estate in order to raise money. At the 1976 annual meeting, the Club was informed that a consultant, after investigating the matter, had concluded that the Club's land, surrounding the golf course, was suitable for development. In 1977, the board authorized Harris to form a committee to study in more detail developing some of the Club's land. The purpose of development was to improve the financial condition of the Club.

At the 1982 meeting, Harris made it clear that she strongly advocated housing development on Club property and volunteered to finance construction of the first house. Although some directors opposed development, the board eventually approved building houses on Club property by a 14 to 4 vote. At the 1984 annual meeting, Harris presented an "Outline of Proposal for Sale and Management of Excess Land" and the board approved her proposal to sell two lots of Club land to raise revenue. No lots were ever sold.

The subject of this lawsuit is land surrounding the Club that Harris purchased in her own name, some in 1979, and more in 1985. In 1979, in her capacity as Club president, Harris learned of an opportunity to purchase property owned by Lucy Gilpin. The Gilpin property adjoins Club property, including the driveway which provided access to the golf course, the clubhouse, and a portion of the Club's parking lot. Moreover, the Gilpin property is encumbered by an easement that allows golfers to travel from the green of one hole to the tee area of the next hole.

Harris purchased the Gilpin property in her own name for $45,000. She did not disclose her plans to the board prior to acquiring the property. The minutes from the Club's 1979 Board of Directors' meeting stated that "Harris reported that she had recently acquired the Gilpin land adjacent to the old first, second and third holes. Though she intends to hold the land for herself, the golf club will be protected." Harris contends that her statements were made to assure the Club that she would act responsibly, not that she would never develop the land. The board took no action in response to Harris's purchase. Harris testified that at the time she bought the land she had no plans to develop the property and that no such plans were formulated until 1988.

In 1984, Harris, independent of her position with the Club, learned of the availability of property owned by the Smallidge family. The property was surrounded on three sides by the Club and on the fourth side by a house. Harris contracted to purchase eight of the ten interests of the Smallidge heirs in February of 1985, another in March, and the last in June of 1985, for a total of $60,000. Harris disclosed the purchase to the board of directors at the Club's annual meeting on August 28, 1985. At the meeting, she apologized for delaying the construction of a shed approved the previous year, explaining that the construction was delayed because the site was adjacent to the Smallidge property and she did not want to "rock the boat" in her negotiations to purchase the land. She justified the purchase by stating that she wanted the land to remain in "friendly hands." The board took no formal action with respect to Harris's purchase.

In December of 1988, Harris's son filed an application with the Mt. Desert Planning Board to subdivide part of the Gilpin property into five house lots to be named Bushwood. The plan was approved in June of 1991. The board of directors of the Club took no action to oppose the subdivision. A group of the Club's directors, however, formed a separate organization to oppose the subdivision, contending that it violated local zoning ordinances.

The effort to oppose the subdivision did not succeed. Eventually the board became divided over development. In 1989, however, the board agreed that it "would not adopt any position" on Harris's son's pending subdivision application. Harris was asked for and gave her resignation in 1990. In 1991, the Club voted to challenge the Bushwood subdivision. The challenge, however, was not successful. * * * The Club commenced this suit against Harris, on May 23, 1991, alleging that by purchasing the Gilpin and Smallidge properties she usurped an opportunity that belonged to the Club.

The Superior Court initially concluded that Harris had not usurped a corporate opportunity because it found that the Club was not in the business of purchasing property and lacked the financial ability to do so.

The Club appealed, and we adopted the American Law Institute's (ALI) definition of taking a corporate opportunity, vacated the judgment, and remanded the case to the Superior Court for trial of the facts pursuant to the ALI definition. * * * After remand, the Superior Court found that Harris had usurped a corporate opportunity and that the Club's claim was not barred by the statute of limitations. The court entered a judgment for the Club, imposed a constructive trust on the property owned by Harris, and ordered Harris to convey the properties to the Club on payment of the purchase price and interest and taxes. These appeals by Harris and the Club followed.

* * *

A. Corporate Opportunity

Harris concedes that, because she learned of the opportunity to purchase the Gilpin property in her capacity as president of the Club, her purchase of that property in 1979 constituted the taking of a corporate opportunity. * * * She disputes liability, relying on the statute of limitations and laches. Harris contends that because she learned of the availability of the Smallidge property independent of her position as an officer of the Club, and because the purchase of that land was not closely related to the Club's business, that there was no usurpation of a corporate opportunity. In reviewing the decision of the Superior Court, we defer to the historical factual findings of the court, but the determination of whether an opportunity is a "corporate opportunity" is a question of law that we review *de novo*. * * *

Even if the opportunity to engage in a business activity, in which the officer or director becomes involved, is not learned of through her connection to the business of the corporation, nevertheless, such an opportunity may be considered a corporate opportunity if the officer or director knows it "is closely related to a business in which the corporation is engaged or expects to engage." PRINCIPLES OF CORPORATE GOVERNANCE § 5.50(b)(2).[4]

---

4. The ALI defines corporate opportunity as:

(1) Any opportunity to engage in a business activity of which a director or senior executive becomes aware, either:

(A) In connection with the performance of functions as a director or senior executive, or under circumstances that should reasonably lead the director or senior executive to believe that the person offering the opportunity expects it to be offered to the corporation; or

(B) Through the use of corporate information or property, if the resulting opportunity is one that the director or senior executive should reasonably be expected to believe would be of interest to the corporation; or

(2) Any opportunity to engage in a business activity of which a senior executive becomes aware and knows is *closely related* to a business in which the corporation is *engaged or expects to engage*.

PRINCIPLES OF CORPORATE GOVERNANCE § 5.05(b) (emphasis added). Section 505(b)(1) applies to Harris's purchase of the Gilpin property. Because Harris did not become aware that the Smallidge property was available for purchase in her capacity as Club president, section 5.05(b)(2) is applicable to the purchase of that property.

"The central feature of the ALI test is the strict requirement of full disclosure prior to taking advantage of any corporate opportunity." * * * This feature was designed to prevent individual directors and officers from substituting their own judgment for that of the corporation when determining whether it would be in the corporate interest, or whether the corporation is financially or otherwise able to take advantage of an opportunity. * * * Doubt about the financial capacity of a corporation to pursue an opportunity may affect the incentive of a director or officer to solve corporate financing problems, and evidence regarding the corporation's financial status is often controlled by the usurping corporate director or officer. * * * The ALI approach recognizes the danger in allowing an individual director or officer to determine whether a corporation has the ability to take an opportunity, and accordingly disclosure to the corporation is required.

Full disclosure is likewise important to prevent individual directors and officers from using their own unfettered judgment to determine whether the business opportunity is related to the corporation's business, such that it would be in the corporate interest to take advantage of that opportunity. "The appropriate method to determine whether or not a corporate opportunity exists is to let the corporation decide at the time the opportunity is presented." 3 FLETCHER CYC. CORP. § 861.10, p. 285 (1994). This rule protects individual directors and officers because after disclosing the potential opportunity to the corporation, they can pursue their own business ventures free from the possibility of a lawsuit. If there is doubt as to whether a business opportunity is closely related to the business of the corporation, that doubt must be resolved in favor of the corporation so that the officer or director will have a strong incentive to disclose any business opportunity even remotely related to the business of the corporation.

In this case, the Club's normal business is maintaining and operating a golf course. That business is dependent on having sufficient land for the course itself and ensuring that the activity of golf is not hindered or affected by development of adjacent and surrounding property. The Club had frequently discussed developing some of its own land and on one occasion talked about the possibility of purchasing and developing adjacent land. The purchase of the Smallidge land, surrounded as it is on three sides by the Club's land and adjacent to three of its golf holes, land that could be developed, is, in the circumstances of this case, sufficiently related to the Club's business to constitute a corporate opportunity. Accordingly, Harris would be liable to the Club for taking advantage of a corporate opportunity for purchases of both the Gilpin and Smallidge properties unless the Club's action is barred by the statute of limitations, or is otherwise barred by laches.

B. STATUTE OF LIMITATIONS

Harris contends that the statute of limitations bars both claims. The statute of limitations is an affirmative defense and the burden of establishing the expiration of the limitations period is on the party asserting it. * * * Determining whether the statutory limitations period has expired requires a determination of when a cause of action for taking a corporate opportunity accrues. * * *

The limitations period applicable to the Club's action for usurping a corporate opportunity is six years. "All civil actions shall be commenced within 6 years after the cause of action accrues and not afterwards." * * * A cause of action accrues "the moment when a wrongful action produces an injury for which a plaintiff is entitled to seek vindication." * * * The gravamen of the cause of action of usurping a corporate opportunity is the taking advantage of a such an opportunity without first offering it to the corporation. * * * The Club had a cause of action for taking a corporate opportunity entitling it to seek judicial vindication against Harris, when Harris, as an officer of the Club, took the opportunity to purchase the Gilpin and Smallidge properties in 1979 and 1985 respectively, without first offering those properties to the corporation. * * *

The Club filed its complaint on May 23, 1991, twelve years after Harris purchased the Gilpin property. Harris notified the board of directors of the purchase in 1979. The statute of limitations bars the Club's claim against Harris for the purchase of the Gilpin property.

In 1985, Harris contracted to purchase the Smallidge property in three separate transactions. In the first two transactions in February and March of 1985, she contracted to purchase nine of the ten interests from the owners of the land. Applying the six year statute of limitations, any action against Harris for purchasing these nine interests had to be filed by February and March of 1991 respectively. Because the Club did not bring suit against Harris until May 23, 1991, the Club's action with respect to those interests is barred because it was not brought within the limitations period.

The only portion of the Smallidge property purchased within the limitations period was the one-tenth interest that Harris purchased on June 11, 1985. Harris contends that the Club's actions as to that one-tenth interest is barred by laches. She argues that the Club unreasonably delayed in filing a claim against her, and that because she invested substantial money in developing the Smallidge property she would suffer substantial prejudice were the Club's suit allowed to proceed. We agree. "Laches is the omission to assert a right for an unreasonable and unexplained length of time...." *Longley v. Knapp*, 1998 ME 142, ¶ 10, 713 A.2d 939. "It exists when the omission to assert the right has continued for an unreasonable and unexplained lapse of time, and under circumstances where the delay has been prejudicial to an adverse party, and where it would be inequitable to enforce the right." * * * Whether the equitable doctrine of laches applies in a given circumstance is a question of law. * * *

Harris notified the board at the annual meeting in August 1985 that she had purchased the Smallidge property. The board took no action with respect to the purchase. Even after learning that Harris intended to develop the property, the board agreed that it "would not adopt any position" on Harris's son's pending subdivision application. In 1990, in reliance on the Club's position and to further her plans to develop the Smallidge property, Harris purchased property separating the Smallidge property from the road for $275,000. There is nothing to indicate that Harris would have purchased the property in the absence of her plans for development. Should the board prevail in its claim for taking a corporate opportunity, that investment, made to ensure that the Bushwood development would not be landlocked, would be substantially wasted. The Club's claim regarding the one-tenth interest of the Smallidge property is barred by laches.

The Superior Court concluded that the Club's claim is not barred by the statute of limitations because the cause of action for usurping a corporate opportunity did not accrue as to any of the property until Harris began to actively develop the property in 1988. The court relied on the fact that Harris was an influential club member; on Harris's statement to the board of directors in 1979, when she purchased the Gilpin property, that the "Club will be protected;" that she had often purchased equipment for the Club and either leased it or sold it to the Club to prevent it from having to make large cash outlays; and that she told the Club after purchasing the Smallidge property that "she wanted the property to remain in friendly hands." The court found that the Club could reasonably have believed that Harris bought the property solely for the benefit of the Club.

The limitations period, however, begins to run as soon as a cause of action accrues, and in the absence of fraud, its running is not delayed even if the cause of action is not immediately discovered. * * * The court's ruling in effect applies the discovery rule to extend the statute of limitations beyond the six year period with respect to the Smallidge property, and indeed well beyond the six years in the case of the Gilpin property. * * *

* * *

B. Indemnification of Directors

Because there is no common-law right of indemnification for corporate directors, some states have added provisions providing for indemnification for directors for liability for damages and for expenses to defend an action brought against the director.

JOHN v. JOHN
Court of Appeals, Wisconsin, 1989
153 Wis.2d 343, 450 N.W.2d 795

SULLIVAN, Judge.

Harry G. John appeals from a judgment permanently enjoining him from serving as a director and trustee of De Rance, Inc.* * *

* * *

De Rance, a non-stock corporation organized under Chapter 181, Stats., was established in 1946. John funded it in the early 1950's by three deeds of gift valued at $14 million, consisting of his inherited stock in the Miller Brewing Company. De Rance was organized to provide financial support for religious, charitable and educational causes. Until 1970, De Rance grants were paid from Miller stock dividends. In 1970 De Rance sold its 47% equity position in Miller to the Philip Morris Company for $97 million. From 1970 to 1984, grants totaled $125 million and were made principally, but not exclusively, to Roman Catholic charities and institutions. The market value of De Rance's assets was $188 million in 1983.

From its creation until September of 1982, De Rance operated exclusively as a grant-making organization. In September of 1982, John incorporated Santa Fe as a non-profit, non-stock corporation under Chapter 181, Stats. It was organized for the purpose of producing and broadcasting radio, television, and cinema programs and publishing printed matter of a religious and educational nature consistent with the teachings of the Holy See.

Through Santa Fe, John hoped to establish a national television and satellite communications empire. To that end, John caused De Rance, Santa Fe, and HBIAC to acquire substantial interests in television and radio stations and to establish several production facilities with all funds provided by De Rance. The trial court found that John's mismanagement caused De Rance to accumulate more than $86 million in unnecessary and wasteful expenses related to these investments.

Until October of 1984, John was the sole donor, trustee, chairman of the board of directors, president and chief executive officer, and treasurer and chief financial officer of De Rance. The trial court characterized John as De Rance's "dominant authority" * * *

* * *

The procedural history of the case is succinctly set forth in the trial court's findings of fact:

> On October 5, 1984, defendant was suspended as an officer, director and trustee of De Rance by an ex-parte order of this Court upon a showing of an appearance of abuse of his trust pursuant to Section 776.32(3), Wis.Stats. On October 15, 1984, defendant was removed from his positions as president and treasurer of De Rance by action of the board of directors of De Rance. This removal was ratified and confirmed at a special meeting of the board of directors of De Rance on January 2, 1985.

Plaintiffs used proper corporate procedures to remove defendant from his positions as president and treasurer. Defendant's suspension as a director and trustee of De Rance was continued through the trial by virtue of a stipulation for the entry of a preliminary injunction in this action which was signed by the Court on February 11, 1985. Defendant was permanently removed from his positions as trustee and director of De Rance by decision of this court on August 21, 1986.

* * *

JOHN'S REMOVAL: GROSS MISCONDUCT

John argues that the trial court's finding of his gross misconduct is clearly erroneous because: (1) his business judgment, however imprudent, was essentially honest; and (2) Erica John and Gallagher waived any objection to his transactions because they acquiesced to them.

Section 776.32(4), Stats., vested the trial court with the power to remove a director or officer upon proof of gross misconduct. However, the term "gross misconduct" is not defined in the statutes. The Wisconsin Supreme Court has declared that as a well-established rule courts will not interfere in corporate affairs in the absence of allegations clearly disclosing abuse of power by the corporate officers, bad faith, willful abuse of discretion, or positive fraud. * * * We conclude that the term "gross misconduct" found in sec. 776.32(4), Stats., embraces the concepts of an officer's abuse of power, bad faith, willful abuse of discretion, or positive fraud. Gross misconduct contains the element of intentional wrongdoing or failure to act consistently with the officer's duty to the corporation. In this case, the findings of the trial court establish John's abuse of power, and, in some instances, his practice of positive fraud upon De Rance. Thus, his conduct may not be excused under the guise of "honest business judgment."

* * *

As a defense, John argues that Erica John and Gallagher acquiesced in these activities. The trial court rejected this argument by its finding, based on credible evidence not contrary to the great weight and clear preponderance of the evidence, that Gallagher and Erica John did not have knowledge of John's self-dealing, securities infractions, tax misrepresentations, voucher misstatements and other breaches of duty, much less acquiesce in or authorize them. Upon certain occasions they authorized John to proceed, but only after John misadvised or withheld information from them.

John complains that the trial court erred by not at least allowing him to continue as a De Rance trustee. John, however, violated his superintending duty as trustee when he tolerated his shortcomings as a director. The trial court did not abuse its discretion in removing John from both of his fiduciary positions when his gross misconduct in one position implicated the other. * * *

John argues that Gallagher and Erica John lacked corporate authorization to bring and maintain this action. He bases this argument on section 181.20(1), Stats., which prescribes a minimum of three directors in a corporation. However, no corporate authorization was required. Although this action was brought by the plaintiffs in their capacities as representatives of De Rance, it was not brought by De Rance, and, therefore, does not constitute a corporate act.

* * *

The trial court approved a $25,000 loan to fund John's defense of this action. He contends that De Rance should have fully indemnified him for this expense. He argues that the court violated the principle of corporate neutrality by authorizing huge outlays to launch and support this action while simultaneously denying him all but a relatively small loan for his defense.

In its analysis of this issue, the trial court applied section 181.045, Stats. (1983–84).[10] Again, the facts relating to the indemnification and neutrality issues are either undisputed or have been determined by the trial court and are not contrary to the great weight and clear preponderance of the credible evidence. Application of the statute and related case law to these facts presents a legal issue which we decide without deference to the conclusions of the trial court. * * *

John's claim for indemnification is defeated by section 181.045(1) and (3), Stats. (1983–84). As the trial court determined, John did not exercise good faith during the period in question and has not been successful on the merits. John not only failed in the defense of what he considered to be his interest in De Rance, but his activities were inimical to De Rance's interest. He was entitled to no advance for defense costs, and, once losing, is entitled to no indemnification.[11]

Case law also supports this result. *Jesse v. Four Wheel Drive Auto Co.*, 177 Wis. 627, 189 N.W. 276 (1922), was a suit to compel corporate directors to reimburse the company for funds used to defend a minority shareholder suit against the directors and to enjoin further distributions. The supreme court affirmed the trial court's judgment ordering reimbursement and restraining future expenditures. The supreme court reasoned that the defense was to protect the director's rights and did not pertain to any interest of the company, and, therefore, the distributions were invalid. Addressing the shareholders' resolution which authorized the distributions the supreme court said: "From no standpoint, legal,

---

10. Sections 181.045(1) and (3), Stats. (1983–84), provide in part:

181.045 Indemnification of officers, directors, employees and agents. (1) A corporation may indemnify any person who was or is a party ... to any suit threatened, pending or completed action, or proceeding, whether civil, criminal, administrative or investigative ... if the person acted in good faith and in a manner he or she reasonably believed to be in or not opposed to the best interests of the corporation....

(3) To the extent that a director, officer, employee or agent of a corporation has been successful on the merits or otherwise in defense of any action, suit or proceeding referred to in sub. (1) or (2), or in defense of any claim, issue or matter therein, he shall be indemnified against expenses, including attorneys' fees, actually and reasonably incurred by him in connection therewith.

11. *See* Note, *Corporations: Directors: Indemnification for Litigation Expenses*, 37 Cornell L.Q. 78, 79–80 (1951), "American jurisdictions universally hold that directors who are unsuccessful in their defense to civil actions based upon their misconduct are not entitled to reimbursement from the corporation for litigation expenses."

equitable, or moral, can less than all the shareholders authorize the use of the funds of the corporation for purposes not germane to the business of the corporation." * * *

John also relies on De Rance's By–Law Seventeen which provides, *inter alia,* that De Rance will indemnify a party to a civil suit by reason of the fact that he is a De Rance officer or director. Such officer or director may recover expenses, including attorney fees, "actually and reasonably incurred in connection with such action . . . to the full extent *permitted under the law....*" [Emphasis added.] Because secs. 181.045(1) and (3), Stats. (1983–84), conditioned indemnification upon an individual's good faith actions, and upon his or her success on the merits, John does not qualify as "permitted under the law." Therefore, the by-law does not provide John with a right to indemnification.

In addition, De Rance had no duty to maintain a stance of corporate neutrality in this litigation. This suit was not purposed to protect or establish any personal interest of the plaintiffs. It was brought to abate John's continued depredation of De Rance. John's reliance on *Jesse v. Four Wheel Drive Auto Co.* fails because the directors there retained counsel to defend a suit against their personal account, rather than to defend any interest of the corporation. * * *

John cites no pertinent authority to establish his right to defense funds based on the doctrine of corporate neutrality. We decline to adopt John's position on the basis of the record before us.* * *

* * *

Note

While the expenditure of a reasonable amount to defend a suit brought against a nonprofit corporation has been held to be an expenditure for the carrying on of the ordinary business of the organization, a court may determine that the payment of attorneys' fees to defend directors prior to a determination that the directors were not guilty of negligence or misconduct in the performance of their duties is an unauthorized transfer of funds of the corporation which is not in conformity with the corporation's nonprofit purposes. A nonprofit organization might consider adopting a bylaw to provide indemnification for its officers and directors. In compliance with the bylaw, the board of directors may purchase errors and omission insurance to protect directors should they be sued for breach of their duties.

C. Disposition of Assets upon Dissolution

A nonprofit organization may dissolve if provisions of state statutes are followed. Both state statutes and federal tax provisions impose certain restrictions on the manner in which assets of a nonprofit corporation can be distributed. For example, Treasury Regulations, Reg. § 1.501(c)(3)–4, require that upon dissolution of a § 501(c)(3) organization, all assets must be distributed for one or more exempt purposes, or to the federal government, or to a state or local government, for public purposes. Most state statutes require that assets held in trust, or upon certain conditions, be returned, transferred or conveyed in accordance with requirements of conditions imposed on the assets.[2] State statutes require that assets held for charitable, religious, eleemosynary, benevolent, education, or similar purposes, but not held upon a condition requiring return, transfer, or conveyance by reason of a dissolution, be transferred or conveyed to one or more nonprofit organization engaged in activities substantially similar to those of the dissolving corporation.[3] Other assets must be distributed in accordance with provisions of the articles of incorporation or bylaws to the extent the articles or bylaws determine the distribution rights of members or provide for distribution to others.[4]

HOLDEN HOSPITAL CORP. v. SOUTHERN ILLINOIS HOSP. CORP.

Supreme Court, Illinois, 1961
22 Ill.2d 150, 174 N.E.2d 793

SCHAEFER, Chief Justice.

Holden Hospital Corporation (Holden) brought this action to secure approval of a contract to sell all of its assets and to obtain instructions as to the distribution of the proceeds of the sale. Both Holden and the vendee, Southern Illinois Hospital Corporation (Southern), are charitable corporations. The defendants were Southern, the Attorney General of Illinois, The Southern Illinois Conference of the Methodist Episcopal Church (Methodist Conference) and The Southern Illinois Conference Woman's Society of Christian Service (Woman's Society). Both the Attorney General and a group of intervenors who alleged themselves to be 'adversely affected' by the proposed sale filed counterclaims. The trial court dismissed the complaint for want of equity and, in accord with the prayer of the counterclaims, ordered Holden to continue to operate its hospital. The court also retained jurisdiction of 'this cause and all parties hereto' for an indefinite period of time. Holden, Southern, Methodist Conference and Woman's Society have appealed directly to this court. The contract contemplated the sale of Holden's real estate, and a freehold is involved. McDonough County Orphanage v. Burnhart, 5 Ill.2d 230, 125 N.E.2d 625; Catholic Bishop of Chicago v. Murr, 3 Ill.2d 107, 120 N.E.2d 4; Altschuler v. Chicago City Bank & Trust Co., 380 Ill. 137, 43 N.E.2d 673. The controversy arose in the following factual context. In 1912 Carrie Holden donated her house in Litchfield, Illinois, to the Home Missionary Society of the Methodist Church. For some time the Society used it for a hospital, but when it subsequently appeared that it was impractical to maintain a hospital in Litchfield, the Society first leased, and then bought, the former Amy Lewis hospital in Carbondale. The Society operated the hospital until 1925.

---

2. See Model Nonprofit Corp. Act § 64 (1964) and Rev. Model Nonprofit Corporation Act § 14.06.

3. Id.

4. Id.

In that year, Holden Hospital Corporation was organized under the not-for-profit provisions of the Corporation Act of 1872. (Cahill's Ill.Rev. Stat.1923, chap. 32, pars. 159–164, Ill.Rev.Stat.1923, c. 32, ss 158–163.) Its charter stated its purposes in these terms: 'The object for which it is formed is to own and maintain hospitals and equipment for the relief of the sick, needy and destitute, and conduct in connection therewith schools and homes for nurses; to maintain and conduct classes for first aid, education and relief, and maintain and conduct clinics and traveling instructors.' * * *

* * *

The suggestion of the trial court that dissolution and sale are improper because the purposes of the corporation can still be carried out is based upon the doctrine of judicial cy pres, which we think is not controlling, and it fails to take into account the statute that governs here. That doctrine rests upon the conviction that the donor's intent should be law unless it is impossible, impracticable, or illegal that it should be so. It contemplates that the court will decree that property which can no longer be applied to a specific purpose selected by the donor, will be applied instead to some different purpose, as near as may be to the one which he selected, within the scope of his general charitable intent. Here there is no specific purpose that can not be carried out, and the doctrine is not applicable. There is nothing to prevent this property from being used for the operation of hospitals. Indeed, the property must remain devoted to those ends. Cy pres is only of importance when there is a need to divert property from one purpose to another; here, the statutory scheme permits the property to remain devoted to the basic purposes that were set forth in Holden's charter. It should be of little consequence to anyone that Holden's assets are administered in the future not by Holden but by some other corporation under similar restrictions. We do not face the problem of violating the intent of the grantor.

We come now to the question of distribution of the proceeds of sale and the validity of Holden's bylaw which purported to establish a 'trust' for the Methodist Conference and the Woman's Society. The bylaw expresses a relationship which finds support in a statute (not repealed by the General Act) enacted in 1903 (Ill.Rev.Stat.1959, chap. 32, par. 201), which provides that when the purposes of a charitable corporation can no longer be carried out, it may be dissolved and the assets distributed to the religious denomination having 'care or patronage' of the corporation. Since Holden's purposes are so general as to be easily carried out, we can give this statute no effect here.

The General Act establishes other standards to deal with situations in which the purposes remain capable of fulfillment, which are the same regardless of whether the corporation is carrying out its dissolution without aid of a court or has made 'application * * * to have its dissolution continued under the supervision of the court.' (Ill.Rev.Stat. 1959, chap. 32, par. 163a53(c). Sections 45(c) and 55(c) of the General

Act provide that 'Assets held for a charitable * * * use * * * shall be transferred or conveyed to one or more domestic or foreign corporations, societies or organizations engaged in activities substantially similar' to those of the dissolving corporation. In short, the statute sets up specific standards to be applied in determining the disposition of assets of dissolving charitable corporations. There is no provision for evading this standard by means of a bylaw. The more general provisions in the statute, such as section 45(d) (par. 163a44(d) which says that 'other assets' may be distributed in accordance with the bylaws, are not applicable here, for all of Holden's assets are held for a charitable use. Many kinds of corporations are involved, and some of the provisions of the General Act are of necessity very broad. They should not be read to destroy specific limitations imposed for a limited class of corporations elsewhere in the act. We do not believe that the statute is intended to authorize the directors to enact bylaws which will remove the restrictions on their own authority imposed by section 45(c).

Holden has, in its complaint, sought approval of a course of action which explicitly involves sale and distribution of the proceeds and implicitly involves dissolution. We see no legal impediment to sale and dissolution. However, we cannot rule on the question of distribution except as we have rejected the bylaw. There is no evidence in the record to show that the proposed distributees are carrying on 'substantially similar' activities. Furthermore, Holden's complaint can hardly be deemed an 'application * * * to have its dissolution continued under the supervision of the court.' Only in that circumstance is the court given full power to apply the 'substantially similar' standard. (Ill.Rev.Stat. 1959, chap. 32, pars. 163a54, 163a55.) Otherwise, the assets are to be distributed in accordance with a plan of distribution, subject to that standard, adopted by the members and directors. Ill.Rev.Stat.1959, chap. 32, pars. 163a44(c), 163a45.

Therefore, we hold no more than that sale and dissolution are permitted. Holden is free to distribute the proceeds of the sale to the Methodist Conference or the Woman's Society only if one or both of them meet the statutory standard. * * *

Note

The court in *Holden Hospital* discussed the cy pres doctrine, which may be applicable in dissolution proceedings to determine the distribution of assets. Consider the applicability of the doctrine in the following case.

SHARPLESS v. RELIGIOUS SOCIETY OF FRIENDS

Superior Court, Appellate Division, New Jersey, 1988
228 N.J.Super. 68, 548 A.2d 1157

HAVEY, J.A.D.

Plaintiffs appeal from a final judgment permitting defendant Medford Monthly Meeting of the Religious Society of Friends (Medford

Meeting) to combine graveyard trust funds and to apply part of the trust income for meeting purposes other than the maintenance of graveyard sites. The issue raised is whether the doctrine of *cy pres* may be applied to the surplus trust income so as to permit Medford Meeting, as trustee, to utilize the surplus for general meeting purposes. We conclude that the doctrine does apply and therefore affirm.

Plaintiff Francis Sharpless was a member of the former Upper Evesham Preparative Meeting (Union Street Meeting), a Quaker preparative meeting which owned a meeting house and graveyard situate on Union Street in Medford. Plaintiffs Edward C. Jennings and Joseph B. Engle were members of the former Medford Preparative Meeting of Friends (Main Street Meeting), which owned and maintained a meeting house and graveyard on Main Street in Medford. Both meetings existed as separate entities prior to 1971 because of a doctrinal schism which existed within Quakerism.

The Union Street Meeting established a graveyard fund in 1911 by soliciting contributions from members to care for and maintain its graveyard. A trust for that purpose was created with the Burlington County National Bank of Medford in 1943. Thereafter, the trust received bequests and gifts which, according to Sharpless, were made for the specific purpose of maintaining the graveyard. In 1986, the trust had income of $18,412.57 and expenses of $1,376.34. As of January 26, 1987, the estimated market value of the Union Street graveyard trust was $177,026.01.

The Main Street Meeting graveyard fund was originated in 1922 when a specific bequest of $2,000 was made by the will of Elizabeth J. Shreve for the purpose of keeping the Main Street burial ground in good order "and any balance of income left over to assist in keeping the Meeting House and grounds ... in good order and repair." A trust was created in 1970 for the purpose of "the upkeep of the graveyard" with a proviso that if the meeting house was in need of repairs, monies could be used from the trust under carefully circumscribed conditions. In 1986, the Main Street trust produced income of $9,898.25 and incurred expenses of $934.73. As of January 26, 1987 the trust had a total value of $85,177.

In 1971, doctrinal differences between the meetings were resolved and they merged under the corporate charter of the Society of Friends of Medford, which later changed its name to defendant Medford Monthly Meeting of the Religious Society of Friends. Medford Meeting adopted as its bylaws the Book of Faith and Practice, which in part recited the manner by which its trustees would retain meeting assets and administer meeting funds.

In 1985, Medford Meeting discussed the possibility of using the excess income from the two funds for purposes other than the maintenance of the two graveyards. Sharpless took an unbending position that the Union Street fund, which he administered, could not be used for any purpose other than the maintenance of the Union Street graveyard.

Plaintiffs thereupon filed the present declaratory judgment action seeking permanent restraints and to determine the rights and obligations of the respective parties with respect to graveyard funds. Medford Meeting counterclaimed seeking a declaration that excess income could be used for general meeting purposes, that the two funds could be combined, and naming it as trustee of the combined funds.

* * *

Judge Wells' broad construction of the probable intent of the donors to encompass use of excess funds for general meeting purposes is, in our view, supportable by substantial credible evidence on the record. * * * The Shreve bequest in 1922, for example, which created the Main Street fund, expressly provided for the use of excess income for repair of the Union Street meeting house, if necessary.

However, we are also satisfied that the judge's determination is sustainable by application of the equitable doctrine of *cy pres*. *Cy pres* is a judicial mechanism for the preservation of a charitable trust when accomplishment of the particular purpose of the trust becomes impossible, impracticable or illegal. * * * If the settlor manifests an intent to devote the trust to a charitable purpose more general than the frustrated purpose, a court may apply the trust funds to a charitable purpose as similar as possible to the particular purpose of the settlor instead of allowing the trust to fail. * * * If income from the charitable trust exceeds that which is necessary to achieve the donor's charitable objective, *cy pres* may be applied to the surplus income "since there is an impossibility of using the income to advance any of the charitable purposes of the settlor." * * *

Here, no one disputes that the graveyard funds constitute charitable trusts. The particular purpose of the trusts, as found by Judge Wells, was to maintain and preserve the respective graveyard sites. To the extent that the trust income exceeds maintenance and preservation costs, application of *cy pres* is appropriate since there is an impossibility of using the excess income to advance the particular charitable purpose expressed by the donors. * * *

The question then becomes whether the settlor manifested an intent to devote the excess income to a charitable purpose more general than maintenance and preservation of the graveyard sites. As Judge Wells correctly found, a general charitable purpose can be inferred. Since the donations were made for the perpetual maintenance of the graveyards, it is logical to conclude the donors expected excess income would be used, as the judge noted, "to strengthen the very institution to which [the donors] entrusted their money" to permit it to survive in perpetuity in order to carry out the donors' intent. A contrary result, that the income be held in each trust and accumulate in perpetuity for maintenance of the graveyards, is both illogical and contrary to the probable intent of the donors. The only sensible conclusion to be reached is that the donors did not intend that the trusts would grow while the meeting itself may cease to exist because of lack of funds. We are also convinced that use of the funds for general meeting purposes is sufficiently similar to the particular purpose of the settlors to apply the *cy pres* doctrine. * * *

* * *

In our view, vesting the discretionary power with the trustees rather than the Superior Court was a sensible and cost-saving device. In the absence of contrary evidence, the law presumes that a trustee intends to perform, rather than violate his duties, and that he will not misappropriate trust properties or funds. * * * No one suggests that the trustees may act in bad faith or will be incapable of administering the trust. According to the judgment, the trustees are compelled to apply income in the first instance for care and preservation of the graveyard sites, and are prohibited from invading corpus for general meeting purposes. They are also duty-bound to follow the provisions of the Book of Faith and Practice which provide for yearly audits, inspection of the trusts by certified public accountants and appropriate committees, and the creation of a committee to assure that the burial grounds are kept in good order. We have no reason to conclude that the trustees will not adhere to that standard.

For the same reasons, we cannot take issue with the judge's directive that the trust funds be combined for purposes of administration. The separate funds were vestiges of the doctrinal schism which no longer exists, and thus there is no apparent policy reason to keep the funds separate. Combining the funds provides a cost-saving method of administering the funds, subject to careful monitoring in accordance with the Book of Faith and Practice. Plaintiffs and other members of the Medford Meeting, of course, have their remedy if the trustees violate their fiduciary duties.

AFFIRMED.

Question

Are assets of a charitable corporation subject to a public trust that would prevent them from being distributed to creditors of the corporation should the corporation have financial problems?

D. Enforcement of Fiduciary Obligations

Although the public has an interest in enforcement of fiduciary responsibilities imposed on trustees and directors of nonprofit organizations, the Attorney General is the representative of the general public in compelling trustees and directors to perform their duties properly, and most courts preclude members of the general public from proceeding against negligent trustees and directors.

IN RE ESTATE OF STERN

Court of Appeals, Illinois, 1992
240 Ill.App.3d 834, 181 Ill.Dec. 461, 608 N.E.2d 534

Presiding Justice JIGANTI delivered the opinion of the court:

This appeal arises from an action filed by the Attorney General of Illinois seeking to contest the will of Lotta Stern. The trial court granted the Stern estate executor's section 2–619(a)(9) motion to dismiss based upon the executor's affirmative defense that the Attorney General lacked standing to bring the action. The central issue on appeal is whether the Attorney General has standing to file a will contest action in which specifically named charities are affected by the outcome of the contest.

We first summarize the pertinent facts. On May 23, 1980, Lotta Stern executed a trust entitled the "Lotta Stern Trust," in which she designated herself as trustee and the Northern Trust Company as successor trustee. Pursuant to the terms of the trust, the trustee, upon her death, was to distribute $2,000 of the trust principal to each of the following named charities: the American Cancer Society, the American Red Cross, the Art Institute of Chicago, the Heart Association of Chicago, the Ravinia Festival Association, the Orchestral Association, and the Field Museum of Natural History. The trust agreement further provided that any remaining balance was to be distributed in equal shares to the American Cancer Society, the Art Institute of Chicago, the Ravinia Festival Association, the Orchestral Association, and the Field Museum of Natural History.

Stern executed a will on the same day that she executed the trust agreement. In her will, Stern devised the residue of her estate to the Stern Trust.

On September 1, 1989, Stern executed a second will which revoked the 1980 will and named Wanda Gibbs, Stern's housekeeper, as her executor. The 1989 will devised $1,000 to each of the named charities: the American Cancer Society, the American Red Cross, the Art Institute of Chicago, the Heart Association of Chicago, the Ravinia Festival Association, the Orchestral Association, and the Field Museum of Natural History. Stern devised her books to the Glencoe Public Library and $1,000 to St. Jude Temple. Additionally, in contrast to the 1980 will which devised the residue of her estate to the Stern Trust, the 1989 will devised the residue of her estate to Wanda Gibbs.

Stern died on December 30, 1989, and her 1989 will was admitted to probate. The Attorney General filed a petition to contest the 1989 will and claimed that Stern was unduly influenced by Gibbs and asked the court to set aside that will. The Attorney General's action was dismissed for lack of standing.

We begin by addressing the primary issue in this appeal, the scope of the Attorney General's power. The powers originate in common law and have been incorporated into our State's constitution, codified in various statutes, and interpreted by our courts. * * * The Attorney General is held to be the sole officer authorized to represent the People of this State in any litigation in which the People of the State are the real party in interest, absent a contrary constitutional directive. * * *

As it pertains to charities and the funds appropriated to them, the Charitable Trust Act provides the Attorney General with the authority to enforce and supervise charitable trusts. (Ill.Rev.Stat. 1989, ch. 14, par. 51 *et seq.*) Prior to the enactment of the Charitable Trust Act, trustees of charitable trusts had no duty to make the Attorney General aware of the existence of the trusts or of the manner in which they were being operated. The purpose of the Act was to assist the Attorney General in carrying out its common law powers and duties to enforce charitable trusts and to assure that their funds were applied to their intended charitable use. * * *

Our supreme court has discussed the Attorney General's authority with reference to litigation involving charitable trusts in *In re Estate of Tomlinson* (1976), 65 Ill.2d 382, 3 Ill.Dec. 699, 359 N.E.2d 109.

> "He has the authority to protect a charitable trust and its property either defensively, where an attack is made on its validity, or by an action as plaintiff, by securing the construction of the trust instrument. In a suit by others where the validity or the enforcement of a charitable trust may come into question the Attorney General should be made a party defendant." * * *

In the instant case, Gibbs argues that the Attorney General does not have the authority to contest Stern's will because the Stern Trust is not a charitable trust. Gibbs classifies the trust as a "simple, uncomplicated inter-vivos trust, whose beneficiaries are specific, existing charities." According to Gibbs, this distinction is predicated upon the fact that the trust language does not specify that the funds are to be used for a charitable purpose.

We do not believe that there is any merit to Gibbs' assertion. A charitable purpose has been broadly defined to include almost anything that tends to promote the improvement or well being of social man. * * * Moreover, under the Charitable Trust Act, a corporation is considered a trustee of a charitable trust if it holds property "for any charitable purpose." Ill.Rev.Stat.1989, ch. 14, par. 53.

Thus, funds which are appropriated for the benefit of society at large are considered to be held in a charitable trust, over which the Attorney General has regulatory authority. There is no requirement that express trust language be used to qualify the funds as a "charitable trust."

Lotta Stern made monetary bequests to specified charities which promote the improvement and well-being of society. The charities encompass medical, cultural, educational, and social benefits. We believe the Attorney General has common law power and authority to safeguard these charitable assets.

Gibbs has further argued that the Attorney General has no standing to initiate a will contest because he only has authority in cases which involve the construction, enforcement, validity, or administration of charitable trusts. We find no merit to this argument. The essence of the Attorney General's action to contest Stern's 1989 will is to protect the monies which were allocated in Stern's 1980 will that poured over into the Stern Trust. The Stern Trust appropriated the residue of Stern's 1980 will to the specified charities. The Attorney General's role in the will contest is to protect charitable assets, and he is vested with that authority. By initiating a will contest, the Attorney General was properly attempting to assure that the funds which were initially bequeathed to the charities were applied to their intended charitable use.

Applying these principles to the case at bar leads us to conclude that the trial court erred in granting Gibbs' motion to dismiss the Attorney General's complaint for lack of standing. The Attorney General has authority to contest Stern's will in which funds appropriated for a charitable purpose are at issue.

* * *

Reversed and remanded.

Questions

1. The court in *Stern* stated that funds "appropriated for the benefit of society at large are considered to be held in a charitable trust, over which the Attorney General has regulatory authority." Can you reconcile this statement of the Illinois court in *Stern* with the decision of the Virginia Supreme Court in *Commonwealth of Virginia v. The Joco Foundation*, cited in Chapter 1, wherein the Virginia Supreme Court ruled that the state's Attorney General could not intervene in the disposition of assets devoted to charitable purposes in the absence of a specific power granted by the state's legislature?

2. Suppose the Attorney General of a state elects not to proceed against negligent directors of a nonprofit corporation. Should there be a special class of beneficiaries of nonprofit organizations that also would have standing to challenge actions of directors or trustees? See Cal. Corp. Code § 7142 which permits relator actions. A relator is a private individual who is granted permission to pursue litigation on behalf of the attorney general of the state. In California, these persons include those with reversionary, contractual, or property interests in assets subject to the charitable trust. For public benefit corporations, a relator steps into the shoes of the attorney general. The attorney general gives consent to the relator filing an action against a public benefit corporation. For public benefit charitable trusts, a minority of co-trustees, as well as beneficiaries, have standing to sue independently of the attorney general. See *Holt v. College of Osteopathic Physicians and Surgeons*, 61 Cal.2d 750, 40 Cal.Rptr. 244, 394 P.2d 932 (1964).

3. Should courts grant standing to persons or entities with "special interests" in actions by trustees or directors of nonprofit organizations? Consider the issues in the following case.

IN RE MILTON HERSHEY SCHOOL

Commonwealth, Pennsylvania, 2005
867 A.2d 674

OPINION BY Judge PELLEGRINI.

I.

The Milton Hershey School Alumni Association (Association) appeals an order of the Court of Common Pleas of Dauphin County (trial court) dismissing for lack of standing the Association's challenge to the rescission of an agreement between the Office of Attorney General (OAG), the Milton Hershey School (School) and the Hershey Trust Company (Trust Company) that prohibited conflicts of interests and other actions by the trust managers that were deemed inimical to the interests of the orphan beneficiaries.

A.

Because standing is largely determined by the type of interest a party is asserting, it is necessary to determine the sufficiency of the interest and to set forth in some detail what the object of that interest is-in this case, the School and the Trust Company.

In 1909, Milton and Catherine Hershey (the Hersheys established the Milton Hershey School, a charitable institution funded by the Milton Hershey School Trust (Trust). The School provides residential care for dependent and at-risk children, or "orphan" children as the term was then used. The Hersheys originally contributed 12,000 acres of land to the corpus of the trust and bequeathed virtually their entire fortune for the purpose of saving orphan children.

The deed of trust is the original agreement between the Hersheys, the Hershey Trust Company as Trustee of the Trust, and the Managers of the Trust (originally, Milton Hershey, W.H. Lebkichner and John E. Snyder). The original deed was amended in 1976 and provides that the School is to be administered by the Trust Company and the Board of Managers. It states that the School was organized to "receive and admit to the School as many poor, healthy children as may from time to time be determined by the Managers, to the extent, capacity, and income of the School will provide for and shall be adequate to maintain." * * *

* * *

'The deed of trust provides that the beneficiaries of the Trust are the orphan children attending the School. Children cared for by the Trust within the orphan parameters established by the Hersheys have a high degree of social and financial need and would otherwise require residential care in other facilities, such as foster care. Once enrolled, these children have all of their educational, physical, spiritual and other needs met by the Trust in a setting commonly referred to as the children's home. Those within the care of the Trust establish familial bonds with each other, viewing the School as a home and viewing other children at the School as a type of surrogate family. These bonds cross generational lines, and adults who had been within the care of the School have shown a devotion and commitment to the welfare of children later entering the School's care.

At the direction of Milton Hershey, the Association was created 74 years ago and is comprised entirely of orphan graduates of the School. It is a tax-exempt organization under Section 501(c)(3) of the Internal Revenue Code, 26 U.S.C. section 501(c)(3), and incorporated under the laws of Pennsylvania. One of its functions is to directly serve orphan beneficiaries and to continue the bonds that form in orphanhood while under the care of the School.

Pursuant to the Association's Articles of Incorporation, its purpose includes: the promoting in every proper way of the interests of Milton Hershey School, including ... the establishment and maintenance of supplemental educational programs and activities for students ... that encourage habits of thrift, industry, leadership, scholarly achievement, and other attributes of good citizenship; and to foster among its graduates an attachment to their Alma Mater. * * *

From its office on the School's property (owned by the Trust), the Association provides student-related functions and young graduate assistance programs, including programs directed at mentoring, job shadowing, transitioning, general graduate assistance and graduate crisis services. Orphan children that graduate from the School often become members of the Association.

The Association is not a division of the School or of the Trust Company. It was not named in the deed of trust and is not an intended beneficiary of the Trust. As the deed states, "[a]ll children shall leave the institution and cease to be the recipients of its benefits upon the completion of the full course of secondary education being offered at the School." * * * The Managers of the Trust may, in their discretion, contribute to the higher education of a graduate of the School, in which case the graduates would continue to be beneficiaries of the Trust, but generally, once orphans graduate from the School, they are no longer Trust beneficiaries.

Though the Association is not a division of the School, a division of the Trust, or a beneficiary of the Trust, it has participated in many efforts aimed at protecting the charitable intent of the Trust, i.e., to assure that Trust assets are used to promote the child-saving mission of the Hersheys. It has made efforts in the past to prevent Trust resources from being diverted to non-child purposes and has lobbied the OAG and the Trust Company for assistance in this regard.

Another participant in the affairs of the Trust is the OAG. The OAG is charged with enforcing the duties of charitable trustees and protecting the public. In addition to overseeing the Trust administration, the OAG also holds the position that in exercising that duty, it is seeking to protect the community and general public in addition to the orphan beneficiaries designated as such under the terms of the deed of trust.

From 1970 to 2003, Trust assets grew from $200 million to $5.5 billion (at the time this action was filed with the trial court).* * * It is currently the largest residential childcare charity in the world, dwarfing any comparable facility in asset size. Other entities owned by, controlled by or affiliated with the Trust, such as Hershey Entertainment & Resort Company (HERCO) and the Hershey Medical Center (HMC), also enjoyed tremendous growth during this period.

B.

While Trust assets grew during this period, the number of children served by the Trust decreased, as did the amount of land appropriated to house the orphaned children (from approximately 10,000 acres to 2,000 acres). To illustrate, some of the land formerly designated for the School use was closed, sold, abandoned or transferred to HERCO, thereby reducing the amount of homes that could house roughly 310 orphans. Another example dates back to 1963, where the OAG and the Trust Company successfully sought removal of 500 acres of land and $50 million in cash from the Trust to build HMC for Penn State University.

Beginning in 1990, the Association began observing what it believed were Trust activities that diverted from the Trust's charitable intent to help orphan children. As alleged in its petition before the trial court, the Association noticed that School enrollment policies were altered to disfavor or turn away children requiring year-round residential care. In addition, it observed that education, housing and other policies were similarly altered to reflect the differing needs of the enrolled children who increasingly did not require substantially year-round residential care. It also observed that the childcare facilities at the School reached crisis levels in 2001 because of overcrowding, safety concerns and incidents of physical or sexual abuse resulting in a one-year moratorium on enrollment.

The Association became actively involved in efforts to quell what it believed were gross deviations from the charitable intent of the Trust. For instance, the Association reacted to an attempt by the Trust to end entirely the vocational education program mandated by the deed of trust, a program that targets on-college bound students. The Association's efforts resulted in an agreement signed by the OAG and the Trust compelling the Trust to preserve some form of vocational education at the School. The Association also participated as amicus curiae in a proceeding initiated by the Trust Company to create the Catherine Hershey Institute of Learning and Development (CHILD) and to divert land to public use that was ultimately rejected by the trial court because it found that CHILD would have violated the Trust's charitable intent.

With the Association's concerns elevating, it alerted the OAG to what the Association believed were serious improprieties associated with the administration of the Trust. The Association alleged that conflicts of interest among the Trust Managers mired their ability to properly administer the Trust to carry out its charitable intent of saving orphan children. It also alleged that there were improper enrollment policies, improper and unsafe residential policies, and improper utilization of Trust assets to serve only orphan children and as many of them as possible. The Association believed that these actions taken as a whole constituted a perversion of the Trust's charitable intent.

Responding to the concerns raised by the Association, the OAG initiated and conducted an exhaustive 12–month investigation into the administration of the Trust.* * * On December 5, 2001, the OAG determined that the Trust Company was diverting from the Trust's charitable intent and called for broad reforms.

The OAG made clear that conflicts of interest burdened the Trust Company's decisions and emphasized that personnel changes would be inadequate to address the failures of the Trust, requiring instead structural reforms to obtain lasting improvements to Trust administration. The OAG threatened legal action if necessary to obtain the reforms. As a result, the parties (the OAG, the School and the Trust Company) participated in negotiations. The Association participated in an advisory role and contributed millions of dollars to the process. Though it was not a party to the ultimate agreement, the Association acted to protect its own central purpose of preserving bonds formed in orphanhood and furthering the child-saving mission of the Trust.

On July 31, 2002, the parties reached an agreement * * * outlining the reforms that the parties negotiated. The Reform Agreement purported to (1) end all conflicts of interests; * * * (2) ensure the admission of needy children; * * *(3) mandate a foster care program; * * *(4) restrict land transfers and land uses that focused on anything but childcare; * * *(5) reform academic standards for admissions and expulsions; * * * and (6) require biannual status reports to the OAG. * * *

C.

After the Reform Agreement was executed, the highly publicized litigation over the controversial sale of a controlling interest in Hershey Foods Corporation (HFC) took place. See In re Milton Hershey School Trust, 807 A.2d 324 (Pa.Cmwlth.2002). Though, ultimately, there was no sale of HFC, there was a significant reorganization of leadership within the Trust Managers shortly after the attempted sale. As a result of the reorganization of leadership within the Trust Company and the Board of Managers of the School, the OAG, the School and the Trust Company determined that the Reform Agreement should be modified.

On June 27, 2003, the OAG, the School and the Trust executed an agreement. * * * The background statement included within that agreement indicated that because personnel changes in the Trust Company resulting from the attempted sale of HFC obviated the need for the reforms as they were presented in the original July 2002 Reform Agreement, the parties needed to modify that agreement. By comparison, the June 2003 Agreement (1) modified the provisions relating to conflicts of interest; (2) deleted the income and poverty level guidelines set forth in the July 2002 Agreement aimed at assuring the admission of truly needy children; (3) deleted the foster care program; (4) modified the restriction on land transfers to "sales" and exempting the notice requirement for the sale of land that is already commercially used; (5) modified the academic standards; and (6) changed the status report requirement from biannual, face-to-face meetings to annual written reports.

On September 4, 2003, the Association filed the petition for rule to show cause at issue in this case, seeking rescission of the June 2003 Agreement, reinstatement of the July 2002 Reform Agreement, appointment of a guardian, and appointment of a trustee ad litem. The School and the Trust Company filed preliminary objections to the petition, alleging that the Association lacked standing to challenge the rescission of the July 2002 Agreement.

The trial court granted the preliminary objections of the School and the Trust. In finding that the Association lacked standing, the trial court rejected the Association's contention that it was bringing suit on behalf of current and potential students because the Association's composition was limited to past members of the School. It also rejected the Association's contention that it was the only party that could protect current and potential students because it argued that the OAG's interest in the Trust was to benefit the public at large, not just the students at the School. Noting that the Association was not part of the original deed of trust, was not a party to any of the agreements, and was merely an advisor during the negotiations that led to the July 2002 Reform Agreement, the trial court refused to confer standing upon the Association because there was no evidence of a complete perversion of the charitable purpose of the Trust and no evidence that the OAG would fail in its purpose of supervising the Trust.

The Association has appealed that determination to this Court. The sole issue on appeal is whether the Association has standing to bring an action to rescind the July 2003 Agreement and reinstate the June 2002 Reform Agreement.

II.

Now that we have the factual background that led to the dispute, it is also necessary to describe the legal terrain on which the issue of standing will be resolved. This involves a discussion of the law of trusts in general and the law of charitable trusts in particular followed by a discussion on the concept of standing.

A.

Generally, a trust is a legal instrument created by one person or entity (the "settlor") purporting to transfer property (the "trust res" or "trust property") to another person or entity (the "trustee") to hold in trust for the benefit of another (the "beneficiary"). * * *

The ability to convey property to another to hold in trust has been in existence since the enactment of the Statute of Uses in mid–14th Century England and the enactment of the Statute of Charitable Uses in 1601, * * * both allowing for the transfer of real property to hold as a "use" for the benefit of another. * * * The former commonly dealt with the transfer of real property among private citizens, while the latter, as the name suggests, dealt with the transfer of real property for the benefit of the people. These statutes served as the foundation for modern American trust law and have long been recognized and applied in some form as the law of every state, including Pennsylvania. * * *

Though the Hershey Trust is a charitable trust, the distinctions between private trusts and charitable trusts are important for comparison and contextual reasons. To create a typical "private" trust, * * * the settlor must have the intent to transfer trust property to the trustee for the benefit of a definite and specific beneficiary or beneficiaries named in the trust. * * * The trustee, consequently, is bestowed with legal title to the property in order to manage and transfer the property for the benefit of the beneficiary, while the beneficiary has an equitable interest in the trust property and an actual property interest in the subject matter of the trust. * * * Because the role of the trustee involves the management of another's wealth for the benefit of a third party, the trustee has a fiduciary responsibility to act in the best interests of the beneficiaries consistent with the purpose of the trust and the powers granted to the trustee.

A charitable trust differs from an ordinary private trust in several important respects, the first being that a private trust can serve any purpose for which the settlor determines, whereas the charitable trust serves some type of recognizable, charitable purpose. * * * Under Section 28 of the Third Restatement of Trusts, the purposes of charitable trusts include, but are not limited to, the following:

(a) the relief of poverty;

(b) the advancement of knowledge or education;

(c) the advancement of religion;

(d) the promotion of health;

(e) governmental or municipal purposes; and

(f) other purposes that are beneficial to the community.

Restatement (Third) Trusts section 28, at 9–10. As the General Comment to the Third Restatement of Trusts indicates, this list is not exhaustive: The common element of charitable purposes is that they are designed to accomplish objects that are beneficial to the community—i.e., to the public or indefinite members thereof—without also serving what amount to private trust purposes.... As long as the purposes to which the property of the trust is to be devoted are charitable, however, the motives of the settlor in creating the trust are immaterial. * * *

Second, the beneficiaries of a charitable trust are indefinite in identity and in number, whereas the beneficiaries of a private trust are specific, often few in number, and readily ascertainable. * * * Though the beneficiary of a charitable trust is often said to be the public at large, it does not matter that each and every member of the entire public receive a direct benefit from a charitable trust so long as the trust benefits an indefinite class of people to a degree where the performance of the trust substantially benefits the community as a whole. * * * For instance, a trust created to establish a shelter for the poor and homeless in a given community does not directly benefit those in that community with a steady job, a steady income, and a home because they would have no need to actually use the shelter. In that situation, however, everyone in that community incidentally benefits from such a trust because it is in the public interest to shelter the poor and the homeless.

B.

With these principles of trust law in mind, we turn to the difficult concept of standing. In simple terms, "standing to sue" is a legal concept assuring that the interest of the party who is suing is really and concretely at stake to a degree where he or she can properly bring an action before the court. * * * Pennsylvania has its own standing jurisprudence, although the doctrine of standing in this Commonwealth is recognized primarily as a doctrine of judicial restraint and not one having any basis in the Pennsylvania Constitution. * * *

Fundamentally, the standing requirement in Pennsylvania "is to protect against improper plaintiffs." * * * Juxtaposed against the federal standards, * * * the test for standing in Pennsylvania is a flexible rule of law, perhaps because the lack of standing in Pennsylvania does not necessarily deprive the court of jurisdiction, whereas a lack of standing in the federal arena is directly correlated to the ability of the court to maintain jurisdiction over the action. * * * Thus, Pennsylvania courts are much more expansive in finding standing than their federal counterparts.

In William Penn Parking Garage, Inc. v. City of Pittsburgh, 464 Pa. 168, 346 A.2d 269 (1975), our Supreme Court held that a party has standing to sue if he or she has a "substantial, direct, and immediate interest" in the Subject matter of the litigation. * * * In William Penn, residents, taxpayers and operators of parking lots were affected by a tax ordinance that imposed a tax on patrons of non-residential parking places. The plaintiffs challenged the ordinance and were held to have standing because they were aggrieved by the ordinance. In other words, those challenging the taxing ordinances in that case were parking lot taxpayers and were able to bring their action for that reason because they showed a substantial, direct and immediate interest in the imposition of the tax. Guided by much of our Supreme Court's discussion in

William Penn, cases that followed elaborated on the substantial-direct-immediate test. The elements have been defined as follows: A "substantial" interest is an interest in the outcome of the litigation which surpasses the common interest of all citizens in procuring obedience to the law.... A "direct" interest requires a showing that the matter complained of caused harm to the party's interest.... An "immediate" interest involves the nature of the causal connection between the action complained of and the injury to the party challenging it, ... and is shown where the interest the party seeks to protect is within the zone of interests sought to be protected by the statute or constitutional guarantee in question. * * * Although the substantial-direct-immediate test is the general rule for determining the standing of a party before the court, there have been a number of cases following William Penn that have granted standing to parties who otherwise failed to meet this test. These so-called "taxpayer standing" cases are best described as relaxations of the general standing rule where the party asserting the action can show that (1) government action will otherwise go unchallenged unless standing is granted; (2) those most directly affected by government action would benefit and would not challenge the action; (3) judicial relief is appropriate; (4) alternative remedies are not available; and (5) no one other than the party asserting the action is better suited to demonstrate an injury distinct from that of an ordinary taxpayer.* * * This exception has been utilized by our courts to grant standing to taxpayers challenging a variety of governmental actions. For example, the courts have granted standing to taxpayers challenging judicial elections on the grounds that those elections were scheduled in a year contrary to that prescribed by Pennsylvania's Constitution; * * * to the state bar association, Pennsylvania attorneys, taxpayers and electors challenging the placement of a proposed state constitutional amendment on the ballot; * * * and to a state senator challenging the governor's failure to submit nominations to the state senate within the constitutional period. * * * The theory underlying these cases is that public policy considerations favor a relaxed application of the substantial-direct-immediate test, particularly the "direct" element that requires the party bringing the action to have an interest that surpasses that of the common people. * * *

Finally, certain public officials have standing to represent the interest of the public both under their authority as representatives of the public interest and under the doctrine of parens patriae. The doctrine of "parens patriae" refers to the "ancient powers of guardianship over persons under disability and of protectorship of the public interest which were originally held by the Crown of England as 'father of the country,' and which as part of the common law devolved upon the states and federal government." * * * Under parens patriae standing, the attorney general is asserting and protecting the interest of another, not that of the Commonwealth. For example, public officials have an interest as parens patriae in the life of an unemancipated minor. * * *

III.

All of that leads us to the question before us: who has an interest in challenging the actions of the board of directors of a charitable trust? As mentioned above, because charitable trusts benefit a class of the public and not specific individuals, a guardian of the public interest is ordinarily charged with supervising and overseeing the administration of a charitable trust. In Pennsylvania, and all other states, for that matter, the attorney general under its parens patriae authority is the watch dog that supervises the administration of charitable trusts to ensure that the object of the trust remains charitable and to ensure that the charitable purpose of the trust is carried out. * * * The attorney general has the power and duty to oversee the administration of the trust and, consequently, has standing in any case involving a charity. * * * In fact, no trust can declare itself charitable without submitting to the supervision and inspection of the attorney general, * * * and the attorney general may intervene in any action involving charitable bequests and trusts under Section 204(c) of the Commonwealth Attorneys Act. * * *

Unlike other states, however, the OAG takes the position that it has the power to oppose that which may be in the best interests of the trust and examine the effects that the actions of the trust have on the larger community. * * * In its petition opposing the Trust's proposed sale of its controlling interest in HFC, the OAG acknowledged that the sale would likely diversify and increase the assets of the Trust, but nonetheless objected to the sale because any sale would have profound negative consequences for the Hershey community and surrounding areas, including but not limited to the closing and/or withdrawal of HFC from the local community, together with a dramatic loss of the region's employment opportunities, related businesses and tax base. Agreeing with that view, the trial court, in that case, held that the OAG could take those views into consideration and ordered that those concerns were sufficient to stop any efforts by the Trust to sell its interest in HFC. As defined by the OAG, its role, in certain circumstances, is to protect the interests of both the beneficiaries of the Trust and the surrounding community and, where necessary, to balance those interests. * * *

While an attorney general is the only person that has automatic standing in the enforcement of charitable trusts, Pennsylvania and other states have expanded the class of plaintiffs who can intervene and challenge the actions of a charity so long as the potential plaintiff shows a "special interest" in the proceeding. Previously, it was thought that the attorney general should have the exclusive power to enforce charitable trusts (1) to protect trustees from frequent, unreasonable and vexatious litigation by parties who have no stake in the charity at all; (2) to prevent harassment; and (3) to safeguard the assets of the charity from loss due to needless litigation. * * * However, criticisms of exclusive attorney general enforcement power gave rise to the need for courts to give third parties the ability to bring enforcement actions against charitable organizations. As Section 391 of the Second Restatement of Trusts states:

A suit can be maintained for the enforcement of a charitable trust by the Attorney General or other public officer, or by a co-trustee, or by a person who has a special interest in the enforcement of the charitable trust, but not by persons who have no special interest or by the settlor or his heirs, personal representatives or next of kin.* * *

* * *

It is clear that courts often use the "special interest" doctrine to ensure that charities are subject to some form of effective scrutiny, especially on important issues. This mechanism will increase in fairness and predictability, and consequently in value, if courts adhere to a specific formulation of the doctrine. The multi-factor test used so far by only a few courts seems to be an effective approach. It is flexible and can readily accommodate factual variations such as the level of activity of the relevant attorney general or the crucial quality of the complained-of actions. Certain factors should always play important roles. In particular, the presence of sincere allegations of managerial bad faith, and a request for a limited remedy should favor a grant of standing to private parties. A claim that the complained-of acts will have an extraordinary impact on the charity should be especially persuasive in the plaintiffs' favor.* * *

The nature of the relationship between the charity and the plaintiffs probably will remain a less easily measured factor, but the existence of a well-defined and limited group of plaintiffs who have a clear interest in the operation of the charity should favor a grant of standing. If courts allow suits by larger groups of plaintiffs with more vague interests, they should understand that this could substantially expand the range of potential plaintiffs in charitable abuse cases.

In short, we recommend that courts explicitly adopt the multi-factor approach* * * This method would allow courts to grant standing to private plaintiffs needed to keep charities accountable on important matters while avoiding excessive and undesirable litigation burdens on those charities, all with greater consistency and predictive value than is currently the case.* * *

IV.

The Association argues that it has met the special interest test for challenging the modification of the July 2002 Reform Agreement. * * * The Association points out that it was instrumental in bringing to the OAG's attention the substantial growth in Trust assets (exceeding $5 or $6 billion) concomitantly with a decrease in the number of orphan children served. In addition, the Association also raised concerns about potential conflicts of interest amongst the Trust directors and potential mismanagement of trust funds that led to a decline in serving orphan children at the School. The Association was instrumental in having the OAG seek the July 2002 Reform Agreement that sought to remedy these problems, problems that were acknowledged by the OAG, by eliminating conflicts of interest, by reworking admissions and academic standards, by restricting land transfers and sales, and by requiring status reports to the OAG. Given the nature of these events, given the enormous amount of money at stake, and given that the Association merely seeks to determine whether the July 2002 Reform Agreement will better serve the charitable purpose of the Trust instead of the June 2003 Agreement struck by the OAG, the School, and the Trust, the Association has pled a special interest in this matter. * * *

The Association also has a special interest because of its relationship with the benefitted class and the charity itself. * * * The Association has historically maintained a close, cordial relationship with the Trust for over 70 years, and it has made monetary contributions to the School on a number of occasions. The members of the Association are all successful participants of the School, and the Association has its office on Trust lands where it conducts student-related activities and graduate assistance programs for students at the School. The Association was created by Mr. Hershey, settlor of the Trust, and the Association's articles of incorporation and bylaws require that it maintain the common bonds formed during orphanhood and preserve the charitable, child-saving purpose of the Trust. In addition, the Association is particularly well-suited to evaluate the performance of this Trust because of its intimate knowledge of orphanhood, poverty and other alternative foster care facilities. At bottom, the Association, whose membership consists exclusively of past beneficiaries of the Hershey Trust, is the only other party with a sufficient relationship to the Trust that would have any interest in assuring that its charitable purpose was achieved.

Furthermore, the risk of vexatious or unreasonable litigation by the Association is virtually non-existent in this case. This is not a situation where a mere potential beneficiary with a speculative interest in the charity is seeking to interfere with the administration of the Trust or where a member of the general public is disagreeing with the administration of the Trust.

This is also not a situation where the Association wishes to drain Trust assets by litigating each and every decision made by trust managers. The Association only seeks the reasons why the July 2002 Reform Agreement was replaced by the June 2003 Agreement when the Reform Agreement was the result of an extensive investigation funded in part by the Association to aid the OAG, which concluded that potential conflicts of interests amongst trust managers and potential asset mismanagement interfered with the Trust's charitable mission. That inquiry is neither vexatious nor unreasonable.

Given the nature of this Trust, its status as the largest residential childcare charity in the world, and the fact that the OAG agreed to modify the July 2002 Reform Agreement, this scrutiny will serve the public interest in assuring that the Trust is operating efficiently and effectively to serve its beneficiaries.* * * Accordingly, because the Association has a "special interest" in this proceeding, it should have been allowed to challenge the modification of the July 2002 Reform Agreement, and for the foregoing reasons, the order of the trial court is reversed and the matter is remanded for hearings on the Association's petition. * * *

Dissenting Opinion by President Judge COLINS, joined by Judges COHN JUBELIRER and SIMPSON.

Dissenting Opinion by President Judge COLINS.

I must respectfully dissent from the majority opinion while, at the same time, comment that it is one of the finest pieces of legal scholarship that I have read in my 25 years on the bench.

The reasons for my dissent follow briefly.

* * *

It is clear from the historical background of this saga that the Settlors in no way intended to give the Alumni Association standing in the administration of the Trust. The Settlor, Milton Hershey, was also the creator of the Alumni Association. To now give the Association legal rights that were expressly excluded by the Settlor of the Trust is a dangerous expansion of standing not supported by over 300 years of case law within the Commonwealth.

The Attorney General of the Commonwealth, pursuant to well-accepted principles of "parens patriae," as noted by the majority, is the watch dog that supervises the administration of charitable trusts to ensure that the object of the trust remains charitable and to ensure that the charitable purpose of the trust is carried out.* * * The attorney general has the power to oversee the administration of the trust and, consequently, has standing in any case involving charity.* * * To allow the Alumni Association standing, no matter how eleemosynary its purpose may be, interferes with the efficient performance of the Attorney General's statutorily-mandated duties, as well as being violative of the wishes of the Settlor of the Trust and founder of the Alumni Association. Such a quantum leap away from historical concepts of standing, based upon public policy considerations, and a judicially-created "special interest," may only be undertaken by the Supreme Court of the Commonwealth.

Note

The Supreme Court of Pennsylvania, 586 Pa. 717, 889 A.2d 1219 (2005), granted appeal in the above case.

Question

Should a donor of funds to a charitable organization be permitted to enforce terms of the gift?

HERZOG FOUNDATION, INC. v. UNIVERSITY OF BRIDGEPORT

Supreme Court, Connecticut, 1997
243 Conn. 1, 699 A.2d 995

NORCOTT, Associate Justice.

The sole issue in this certified appeal is whether the Connecticut Uniform Management of Institutional Funds Act (CUMIFA), General Statutes §§ 45a–526 through 45a–534, establishes statutory standing for a donor to bring an action to enforce the terms of a completed charitable gift. Because we conclude that the legislature did not intend to establish donor standing under the circumstances of this case, we reverse the judgment of the Appellate Court.

The facts and procedural history of this case are aptly set forth in the Appellate Court opinion from which this appeal ensues. The plaintiff [Carl J. Herzog Foundation, Inc.] commenced an action against the defendant, the University of Bridgeport, seeking injunctive and other relief in connection with a gift made by it to the defendant. The plaintiff alleged in its revised complaint that prior to August 12, 1986, it made various grants to the defendant 'to provide need-based merit scholarship aid to disadvantaged students for medical related education.' On August 12, 1986, the plaintiff agreed, by letter, to participate in a matching grant program that would provide need-based merit scholarships to disadvantaged students for medical related education on a continuing basis. On September 9, 1986, the defendant wrote a letter accepting the offer of a matching grant of up to $250,000.

Over a period of time, the defendant raised the necessary $250,000, which the plaintiff matched in accordance with the agreement. The plaintiff transferred $144,000 on June 26, 1987, and $106,000 on June 28, 1988, to the defendant. The grants were used to provide scholarships to students in the defendant's nursing program. On November 21, 1991, however, the plaintiff was informed that the defendant had closed its nursing school on June 20, 1991.

* * *

The plaintiff's alleged injury is that the funds are no longer being used for their specified purpose. Paragraph fourteen of the revised complaint states: 'The [plaintiff] has been given to understand and believes that the said institutional funds have been co-mingled with the general funds of the [defendant], that said institutional funds are not being used in accordance with the "Gift Instrument" under which said institutional funds were transferred to [the defendant], and that said institutional funds have in fact been spent for general purposes of [the defendant].'

* * *

"Standing is established by showing that the party claiming it is authorized by statute to bring suit or is classically aggrieved." * * * The sole basis for standing claimed by the plaintiff is CUMIFA, more particularly, § 45a–533 (a). Our task, therefore, devolves into a question of statutory construction. We must determine whether the legislature intended CUMIFA to provide a donor that has made a completed charitable gift to an "institution" as defined by § 45a–527 (1), with standing to bring an action to enforce the terms of that gift where, as here, the gift instrument contained no express reservation of control over the disposition of the gift, such as a right of reverter or a right to redirect.

* * *

At common law, a donor who has made a completed charitable contribution, whether as an absolute gift or in trust, had no standing to bring an action to enforce the terms of his or her gift or trust unless he or she had expressly reserved the right to do so. "Where property is given to a charitable corporation and it is directed by the terms of the gift to devote the property to a particular one of its purposes, it is under a duty, *enforceable at the suit of the [a]ttorney [g]eneral*, to devote the property to that purpose." (Emphasis added.) 2 Restatement (Second), Trust § 348, comment (f), p. 212 (1959); * * * At common law, it was established that "[e]quity will afford protection to a donor to a charitable corporation in that *the [a]ttorney [g]eneral may maintain a suit* to compel the property to be held for the charitable purpose for which it was given to the corporation." * * * "The general rule is that charitable trusts or gifts to charitable corporations for stated purposes are [enforceable] at the instance of the [a]ttorney [g]eneral.... It matters not whether the gift is absolute or in trust or whether a technical condition is attached to the gift."³ * * *

"The theory underlying the power of the [a]ttorney [g]eneral to enforce gifts for a stated purpose is that a donor who attaches conditions to his gift has a right to have his intention enforced." * * * The donor's right, however, is enforceable only at the instance of the attorney general; *Wier v. Howard Hughes Medical Institute*, 407 A.2d 1051, 1057 (Del.Ch.1979) (attorney general "has the *exclusive* power to bring actions to enforce charitable trusts" [emphasis added]; *Lopez v. Medford Community Center, Inc.*, 384 Mass 163, 167, 424 N.E.2d 229 (1981) (common law rule that "it is the *exclusive* function of the [a]ttorney

---

3. Public officials, such as the attorney general, had common law standing to enforce charitable trust because, by virtue of their positions, they are closely associated with the public nature of charities. A leading treatise on the subject states that "[t]he public benefits arising from the charitable trust justify the selection of some public official for its enforcement. Since the [a]ttorney [g]eneral is the governmental officer whose duties include the protection of the rights of the people of the state in general, it is natural that he has been chosen as the prosecutor, supervisor, and enforcer of charitable trusts, both in England and in the several states...." G. Bogert & G. Bogert, Trusts and Trustees (2d Rev. Ed.1991) § 411, pp. 2–3. Connecticut is among the majority of jurisdictions which have codified this common law rule and has entrusted the attorney general with the responsibility and duty to "represent the public interest in the protection of any gifts, legacies or devises intended for public or charitable purposes...." General Statutes § 3–125.

[g]eneral to correct abuses in the administration of a public charity by the institution of proper proceedings" [emphasis added]); and the donor himself has no standing to enforce the terms of his gift when he has not retained a specific right to control the property, such as a right of reverter, after relinquishing physical possession of it. See, e.g., *Marin Hospital District v. State Dept. of Health*, 92 Cal.App.3d 442, 448, 154 Cal.Rptr. 838 (1979) (fact that charity is bound to use contributions for purposes for which they were given does not confer to *donor* standing to bring action to enforce terms of gift).[4] As a matter of common law, when a settlor of a trust or a donor of property to a charity fails specifically to provide for a reservation of rights in the trust or gift instrument, " 'neither the donor nor his heirs have any standing in court in a proceeding to compel the proper execution of the trust, except as relators.' " * * * "There is no such thing as a resulting trust with respect to a charity.... Where the donor has effectually passed out of himself all interest in the fund devoted to a charity, neither he nor those claiming under him have any standing in a court of equity as to its disposition and control." * * * On the basis of the weight of the foregoing authorities, we conclude that it is clear that the general rule at common law was that a donor had no standing to enforce the terms of a completed charitable gift unless the donor had expressly reserved a property interest in the gift.[5]

Having concluded that the plaintiff would have had no standing at common law, we now turn to its contention that the common law has been altered by the legislature's adoption of CUMIFA, specifically that portion codified at § 45a–533.[6] Subsection (a) of § 45a–533 empowers

---

4. We note that it is well established in the context of charitable trusts that there are others, in addition to the attorney general, who may enforce the terms of a trust. Section 391 of the Restatement (Second) of Trusts provides: "Who Can Enforce a Charitable Trust."
"A suit can be maintained for the enforcement of a charitable trust by the [a]ttorney [g]eneral or other public officer, or by a co-trustee, or by a person who has a special interest in the enforcement of the charitable trust, but not by persons who have no special interest or by the settlor or heir heirs, personal representatives or next of kin." Fiduciaries, such as trustees or co-trustees, have historically been deemed to have a "special interest" so as to possess standing. See *Hartford v. Larrabee Fund Assn.*, 161 Conn. 312, 288 A.2d 71 (1971) (declaratory action by trustee to determine constitutionality of special legislative act affecting terms of charitable trust). Still, the attorney general must be joined as a party to protect the public interest. General Statutes § 3–125; 2 Restatement (Second), supra, § 391. Those who have no "special interest" have no standing to bring an action to enforce the conditions of the gift.

These include persons within the general class of beneficiaries of the general public. See *Steeneck v. University of Bridgeport*, supra, 235 Conn. at 588, 668 A.2d 688.

5. By expressly reserving a property interest such as a right of reverter, the donor of the gift or the settlor of the trust may bring himself and his heirs within the "special interest" exception to the general rule that beneficiaries of a charitable trust may not bring an action to enforce the trust, but rather are represented exclusively by the attorney general. See *Steeneck v. University of Bridgeport*, supra, 235 Conn. at 588, 668 A.2d 688, citing *Jones v. Grant*, 344 So.2d 1210, 1212 (Ala.1977) (adopting rule that "beneficiaries with a sufficient special interest in the enforcement of a charitable trust can institute a suit as to that trust"); *Hooker v. Edes Home*, 579 A.2d 608, 612–15 (D.C.App.1990) (beneficiaries with "special interest" in charitable trust may bring action to enjoin breach of trust); *Young Men's Christian Assn. of Washington v. Covington*, 484 A.2d 589, 591 (D.C.App.1984) (same).

6. General Statutes § 45a–533 provides: "Release of restriction in gift instrument: Written consent, court order. Limitations.

the governing board of an institution to seek a release of an onerous or obsolete restriction without resort to the courts by obtaining the donor's consent. Subsection (b) of § 45a–533 empowers the board to apply to the courts for such release in the event of the donor's death, disability or other unavailability.[7] Subsection (c) of § 45a–533 precludes the governing board from using a gift unburdened by a restriction for anything other than the "educational, religious, charitable or other eleemosynary purposes" of the institution. Subsection (d) of § 45a–533 confirms that the statute was not enacted to supplant but to supplement the doctrines of cy pres and approximation.[8]

* * *

The plaintiff concedes, as it must, that nothing in the plain language of § 45a–533(a) or any other portion of CUMIFA expressly provides statutory standing for donors to charitable institutions who have not somehow reserved a property interest in the gift such as a right of reverter. In order to demonstrate that the legislature intended to abrogate the common law, therefore, the plaintiff is left only with the legislative history of CUMIFA and the circumstances surrounding its enactment. The history and background of CUMIFA, however, not only do not support the plaintiff's claim of statutory standing, they directly refute it.

Faced with similar problems of statutory construction of CUMIFA provisions, we have stated that [i]n the absence of prior authority to aid in the interpretation § 45a–527(2)(B), we are guided by the meaning ascribed by its drafters to the parallel provision of the Uniform Management of Institutional Funds Act (UMIFA). * * * We agree with the

---

Doctrine of cy pres applicable. (a) With the written consent of the donor, the governing board may release, in whole or in part, a restriction imposed by the applicable gift instrument on the use or investment of an institutional fund." (b) If written consent of the donor cannot be obtained by reason of his death, disability, unavailability or impossibility of identification, the governing board may apply, in the name of the institution, to the Superior Court for a judicial district in which the institution conducts its affairs for release of a restriction imposed by the applicable gift instrument on the use or investment of an institutional fund. The Attorney General shall be notified of the application and shall be given an opportunity to be heard. If the court finds that the restriction is obsolete, inappropriate or impracticable, it may by order release the restriction in whole or in part. A release under this subsection may not change an endowment fund to a fund that is not an endowment fund.

"(c) A release under this section may not allow a fund to be used for purposes other than the educational, religious, charitable or other eleemosynary purposes of the institution affected.

"(d) This section does not limit the application of the doctrine of cy pres or approximation."

7. When the donor is unavailable, under § 45a–533 (b), the governing board need only give notice to the attorney general who operates to protect the public interest.

8. "The rule of cy-pres is a rule for the construction of instruments in equity, by which the intention of the party is carried out *as near as may be,* when it would be impossible or illegal to give it literal effect...." (Emphasis added.) Black's Law Dictionary (6th Ed.1990) p. 387. The doctrine of cy pres may be applied without the consent of the donor. See 2 Restatement (Second), supra, § 399, comment (g).

The fact that the drafters of the Uniform Management of Institutional Funds Act and CUMIFA incorporated reference to the continued validity of the doctrine reflects that the provisions of CUMIFA were meant to supplement and not supplant cy pres.

defendant that the drafters of UMIFA did not intend to confer donor standing in the matter of the release of gift restrictions, and that our legislature provided no indication when it enacted CUMIFA that it intended any other result.

First, it is unmistakable that the drafters of UMIFA regarded charitable institutions, particularly colleges and universities, as the principal beneficiaries of their efforts. The drafters set forth the explanation of their purpose in the prefatory note to UMIFA. "Over the past several years the governing boards of eleemosynary institutions, particularly colleges and universities, have sought to make more effective use of endowment and other investment funds. They and their counsel have wrestled with questions as to permissible investments, delegation of investment authority, and use of the total return concept in investing endowment funds. Studies of the legal authority and responsibility for the management of the funds of an institution have pointed up the uncertain state of the law in most jurisdictions. There is virtually no statutory law regarding trustees or governing boards of eleemosynary institutions, and case law is sparse.... One further problem regularly intruded upon the discussion of efforts to free trustees and managers from the alleged limitations on their powers to invest for growth and meet the financial needs of their institutions. Some gifts and grants contained restrictions on use of funds or selection of investments which imperiled the effective management of the fund. An expeditious means to modify obsolete restrictions seemed necessary." UMIFA, prefatory note, 7A U.L.A. 706 (1985).

UMIFA, drafted in the early 1970s, was set against the backdrop of a state of flux for colleges and universities. In a time of dramatic social change that cast new light on many older charitable gift restrictions, these institutions saw their operating costs rise significantly without a similar increase in endowment funds. W. Cary & C. Bright, The Law and Lore of Endowment Funds (1969) p. 1. In the late 1960s, the Ford Foundation commissioned Professors Cary and Bright "to examine the legal restrictions on the powers of trustees and managers of colleges and universities to invest endowment funds to achieve growth, to maintain purchasing power, and to expend a prudent portion of appreciation in endowment funds." UMIFA, prefatory note, 7A U.L.A. 706 (1985). It is evident that the drafters of UMIFA paid heed to the concerns expressed in the Ford Foundation report as their final draft of UMIFA attempted to offer as much relief as possible *to charitable institutions,* without any mention of concern regarding a donor's ability to bring legal action to enforce a condition on a gift.

The specific area of relief to institutions focused upon by the Appellate Court and the plaintiff is that embodied in § 7, of UMIFA, entitled "Release of Restrictions on Use or Investment."[9] The prefatory note to that section provides: "It is established law that the donor may place restrictions on his largesse which the donee institution must

9. Section 7 of UMIFA is codified in CUMIFA at § 45a–533.

honor. Too often, the restrictions on use or investment become outmoded or wasteful or unworkable. There is a need for review of obsolete restrictions and a way of modifying or adjusting them. The Act authorizes the governing board to obtain the acquiescence of the donor to a release of restrictions and, in the absence of the donor, to petition the appropriate court for relief in appropriate cases." * * * In the comment to § 7, the drafters of UMIFA expressly provided that the donor of a completed gift would not have standing to enforce the terms of the gift. *"The donor has no right to enforce the restriction, no interest in the fund and no power to change the eleemosynary beneficiary of the fund. He may only acquiesce in a lessening of a restriction already in effect."* * * *

These clear comments regarding the power of a donor to enforce restrictions on a charitable gift arose in the context of debate concerning the creation of potential adverse tax consequences for donors, if UMIFA was interpreted to provide donors with control over their gift property after the completion of the gift. Pursuant to § 170(a) of the Internal Revenue Code and § 1.170A–1(c) of the Treasury Regulations, an income tax deduction for a charitable contribution is disallowed unless the taxpayer has permanently surrendered "dominion and control" over the property or funds in question. Where there is a possibility not "so remote as to be negligible" that the charitable gift subject to a condition might fail, the tax deduction is disallowed. See also I.R.C. § 2055; Treas. Reg. § 20.2055–2(b) (similar provisions for estate tax deductions).

The drafters of UMIFA worked closely with an impressive group of professionals, including tax advisers, who were concerned with the federal tax implications of the proposed act. The drafters' principal concern in this regard was that the matter of donor restrictions not affect the donor's charitable contribution deduction for the purposes of federal income taxation. In other words, the concern was that the donor not be so tethered to the charitable gift through the control of restrictions in the gift that the donor would not be entitled to claim a federal charitable contribution exemption for the gift. See I.R.C. § 170(a); Treas. Reg. § 1.170A–1(c).

In resolving these concerns, the drafters of UMIFA clearly stated their position in the commentary. "No federal tax problems for the donor are anticipated by permitting release of a restriction. *The donor has no right to enforce the restriction, no interest in the fund and no power to change the eleemosynary beneficiary of the fund.* He may only acquiesce in a lessening of a restriction already in effect." * * * The Appellate Court dismissed this language, reasoning that it is limited to "tax implications when a donor does consent in writing to a release of a restriction" and does not answer the question of whether the sole right to speak to the donor's interest in the release of a restriction "lies with the attorney general, to the exclusion of a donor." *Carl J. Herzog Foundation, Inc. v. University of Bridgeport,* supra, 41 Conn.App. at 800, 677 A.2d 1378. We disagree. Although the comments and the prefatory note to UMIFA do recognize that a donor has an interest in a restriction, as analyzed herein, we find no support in any source for the proposition that the drafters of either UMIFA or CUMIFA intended that a donor or his heirs would supplant the attorney general as the designated enforcer of the terms of completed and absolute charitable gifts.

Indeed, it would have been anomalous for the drafters of UMIFA to strive to assist charitable institutions by creating smoother procedural avenues for the release of restrictions while simultaneously establishing standing for a new class of litigants, donors, who would defeat this very purpose by virtue of the potential of lengthy and complicated litigation.[11]

* * *

Finally, the legislative history of CUMIFA indicates that the legislature was aware of the question of donor standing regarding restrictions, but chose not to establish it. During the legislative debate regarding House Bill No. 8268, Representative James T. Healey stated, "if the donor has seen fit to spell out restrictions, then those restrictions govern. This bill steps in only in the event that he has not spelled out the restrictions." 16 H.R. Proc., Pt. 11, 1973 Sess., p. 5732. Representative David Neiditz added that "the bill generally leaves it to the donor to make his own provisions for the matters covered in the bill. The bill applies when the donor has not specified another way." * * *

On the basis of our careful review of the statute itself, its legislative history, the circumstances surrounding its enactment, the policy it was intended to implement, and similar common law principles governing the same subject matter, we conclude that CUMIFA does not establish a new class of litigants, namely donors, who can enforce an unreserved restriction in a completed charitable gift. Nothing in our review supports the conclusion that the legislature, in enacting CUMIFA, implicitly intended to confer standing on donors.

* * *

McDONALD, Associate Justice, with whom BERDON, J., joins, dissenting.

I would affirm the thoughtful and well reasoned opinion of the Appellate Court. *Carl J. Herzog Foundation, Inc. v. University of Bridgeport,* 41 Conn.App. 790, 677 A.2d 1378 (1996).

The majority here holds that the donor itself may not enforce a restriction in a gift to an educational institution when the institution had specifically agreed to that restriction. This decision is simply an approval of a donee, in the words of the donor, "double crossing the

---

11. The brief of the amici curiae in this appeal, the Connecticut Conference of Independent Colleges, Inc., the Connecticut Association of Independent Schools, Inc., and the National Association of Independent Colleges and Universities persuasively posits that, should the establishment of donor standing become the law, the infinite variety of charitable gift restrictions that affect educational institutions would create the potential for a flood of "time-consuming, fact-sensitive litigation." This "mischief," they argue, would harm the very institutions that the CUMIFA intended to protect. We agree.

donor," and doing it with impunity unless an elected attorney general does something about it.

This decision will not encourage donations to Connecticut colleges and universities. I fail to see why Connecticut, the home of so many respected schools that would honor their promises, should endorse such sharp practices and create a climate in this state that will have a chilling effect on gifts to its educational institutions.

Accordingly, I respectfully dissent.

RUSSELL v. YALE UNIVERSITY

Court of Appeals, Connecticut, 1999
54 Conn.App. 573, 737 A.2d 941

LAVERY, J.

The plaintiffs, an heir of the settlor of a charitable trust, alumni donors and students of the named defendant, Yale University (Yale), appeal from the judgment of dismissal rendered by the trial court in granting the Yale's motion to dismiss, which asserted that the trial court lacked subject matter jurisdiction on the ground that the plaintiffs lacked standing. On appeal, the plaintiffs claim that the trial court improperly granted Yale's motion to dismiss because, where the attorney general elects not to participate in a proceeding involving a charitable trust, a person with a "special interest" may appear on behalf of the trust to protect the interests of the beneficiaries and that the plaintiff heir, alumni donors and students have the special interest necessary to confer standing on them. We affirm the judgment of the trial court.

The following facts are necessary for our resolution of this appeal. Yale is a nonprofit corporation organized pursuant to a 1745 charter, which was reconfirmed in article eighth, § 3, of the constitution of Connecticut in 1965. The settlor, John W. Sterling, died in 1918. At that time, he left, in trust, money for the erection of a building or buildings that would constitute a fitting memorial reflecting his gratitude and affection for his alma mater, Yale. The trustees were given broad discretion in the disposition of these funds and directed, if their discretion made it advisable, to consult with Sterling's sisters with regard to the use of the funds. The will directed that the money not be used for the purchase of land or as part of Yale's general fund. In 1930, the Sterling trustees voted to contribute money for the erection and maintenance of the divinity school quadrangle that bears Sterling's name. No other restrictions existed in the will and no property rights were reserved for Sterling's heirs by the will.

The divinity school is one of Yale's graduate professional schools, which educates men and women for the Christian ministry and provides theological education for persons engaged in other professions. Prior to the commencement of this action, the president of Yale appointed a committee to undertake a comprehensive study of the divinity school and its future. In late 1996, the Fellows of the Yale Corporation approved certain recommendations, as made to them by the president and dean of the divinity school, calling for the reorganization of the divinity school, including the demolition of large portions of the Sterling Divinity Quadrangle.

The plaintiffs took exception to the reorganization and instituted this action seeking a temporary and permanent injunction enjoining Yale from carrying out the reorganization, a declaratory judgment that Yale's reorganization plan constitutes an abuse of discretion as a trustee of a public charitable trust, and an accounting of all gifts and donations Yale received for the benefit of the divinity school and of charges against the divinity school's endowment. Yale moved to dismiss the complaint on the ground that the plaintiffs lack standing to bring suit. The trial court granted the motion to dismiss and the plaintiffs appealed. Additional facts will be addressed as necessary.

"It is a basic principle of our law ... that the plaintiffs must have standing in order for a court to have jurisdiction to render a declaratory judgment.... A party pursuing declaratory relief must ... demonstrate, as in ordinary actions, a justiciable right in the controversy sought to be resolved, that is, contract, property or personal rights ... as such will be affected by the [court's] decision.... When standing is put in issue, the question is whether the person whose standing is challenged is a proper party to request an adjudication of the issue and not whether the controversy is otherwise justiciable, or whether, on the merits, the plaintiff has a legally protected interest that the defendant's action has invaded.... Standing is established by showing that the party claiming it is authorized by statute to bring suit or is classically aggrieved.... The fundamental test for determining aggrievement encompasses a well-settled twofold determination: first, the party claiming aggrievement must successfully demonstrate a specific, personal and legal interest in [the challenged action], as distinguished from a general interest, such as is the concern of all members of the community as a whole. Second, the party claiming aggrievement must successfully establish that this specific personal and legal interest has been specially and injuriously affected by the [challenged action].... The determination of aggrievement presents a question of fact for the trial court and a plaintiff has the burden of proving that fact.... The conclusions reached by the trial court cannot be disturbed on appeal unless the subordinate facts do not support them.... Where a plaintiff lacks standing to sue, the court is without subject matter jurisdiction." * * *

Although *Carl J. Herzog Foundation, Inc. v. University of Bridgeport,* 243 Conn. 1, 699 A.2d 995 (1997), concerns the interpretation of a statute, in that case, our Supreme Court set out, at length, the common-law rule with regard to standing to bring suit against a charitable entity, which controls the issues here.* * *

* * *

The trial court found the facts noted previously in this opinion and concluded that if Sterling were alive today, he would have no right to enforce conditions of his gift, and that, therefore, his heir and successor lacks standing to bring this suit, as well. We agree. See *id.*, at 5–6, 699 A.2d 995.

For the same reasons, the trial court also concluded that the plaintiff alumni donors also lack standing as contributors of unrestricted charitable gifts to their alma mater and nothing about the fact that they are graduates of the divinity school gives them standing. We agree with that conclusion as well. See *id.*

With regard to the third group of plaintiffs, the students, the trial court determined that they also lack standing. We agree with the trial court and hold that, absent special injury to a student or his or her fundamental rights, students do not have standing to challenge the manner in which the administration manages an institution of higher education. * * * The plaintiff students lack standing because they alleged no injuries to themselves or to any of their fundamental rights, collectively or individually.

We hold, therefore, that the trial court properly concluded that, although the plaintiffs are sincere in their efforts to maintain the divinity school as a leader in theological education and preparation for the Christian ministry and they acted in good faith based on motives that are beyond question, the plaintiffs, as a matter of law, lack standing to adjudicate the equitable remedies they seek.

The judgment is affirmed.

CORNYN v. FIFTY–TWO MEMBERS OF THE SCHOPPA FAMILY

Court of Appeals, Texas, 2001
70 S.W.3d 895

JOHN T. BOYD, Chief Justice.

In this interlocutory appeal, the Attorney General, appellant, challenges the denial by the trial court of his special exceptions and motion to deny the claims of appellees. The suit arises out of an action brought by 52 members of the Schoppa family, Marilyn and Tom Davis, Maxine Cato, the N.L. Douglas family, the George Weiss family, and 168 other named individuals on behalf of their families, living and deceased, herein appellees. In their action, appellees sought to enjoin Texas Tech University Health Sciences Center (TTUHSC) or Texas Tech University (the University) from destroying DNA samples, brain tissue, and medical records collected in furtherance of research on Alzheimer's disease.* * * Appellees, who are individual donors and representatives of deceased donors, also sought the return of samples given at the request of TTUHSC if it "was unwilling or unable to continue genetic based research." We reverse the order of the trial court and remand the cause for further proceedings in accordance with this opinion.

The research project in question was begun by Dr. Shirley Poduslo in 1994. She proposed the research to examine the influence of genetic factors in the development of Alzheimer's, Parkinson's, and Multiple Sclerosis conditions. The research required the collection of DNA samples, brain tissue, and detailed medical records on large numbers of people, with a particular emphasis on family groups. The University obtained written consent from each donor or representative to conduct this research. The consent forms specified that Dr. Poduslo was the primary researcher responsible for the project and that the subjects' medical records would be available to her. The forms also provided that the donors could "discontinue ... participation in the study at any time." The research project was funded by a specific appropriation from the Texas legislature. By January 2000, the project had accumulated a DNA bank with over 10,000 samples from 2,200 family lines, 150 brains (137 from patients diagnosed with Alzheimer's disease), as well as a large collection of medical records. The project had received favorable reviews from researchers at other institutions. However, the 1999 legislature did not make a separate appropriation for the project.

In 1999, the University discovered that 140 consent forms were missing. In the fall of that year, the Department Chair, R.B. Schiffer, had Dr. Guy McKhann of Johns Hopkins review the program. After doing so, by letter dated January 14, 2000, Dr. McKhann referred to Dr. Poduslo's efforts to develop the DNA databank as "herculean" and only recommended that she collaborate with more researchers from other disciplines. The parties differ on the details of what transpired in late 1999 and early 2000 and the record as to that time is not fully developed. However, it is undisputed that Schiffer wrote a letter to Poduslo "relieving her" as head of research and assuming acting directorship of the program. Poduslo was not permitted access to the lab or to the donor charts. One month later, Schiffer wrote to the program donors notifying them that he would act as program director and Poduslo would "continue as an active senior investigator." In the letter, he notified donors that TTUHSC "is committed to continuing and expanding our research efforts."

* * *

In the suit underlying this appeal, appellees sued Dr. Joel Kupersmith in his capacity as dean of the TTUHSC School of Medicine and Dr. Schiffer in his capacity as Chair of the Department of Psychiatry. *Inter alia*, they alleged the research project was a charitable trust and they sought an injunction preventing TTUHSC from the "destruction of any DNA samples, brains or medical records associated with the DNA Alzheimer's Bank." They also sought a holding that upon "a determination that [TTUHSC] is unable or unwilling to continue genetic based research with Dr. Poduslo as the principal investigator," the school must return the DNA samples to those donors who no longer wished to participate in the research. In the alternative, they requested the appointment of a new trustee and the transfer of all DNA samples to that trustee.

* * *

We must next determine appellant's contention that appellees, the parties seeking to invoke the jurisdiction of the trial court, lack standing to do so. It is well established that standing is implicit in the concept of subject matter jurisdiction. * * * The core of appellant's argument on appeal is that he is the only proper party to protect the public interest in this project which all parties characterize as being in the nature of a charitable trust. That being so, we will refer to the project as a trust. Implicit in appellant's argument is the assumption that the public's interest in the trust is the only interest that is affected by this litigation. He premises that argument on the characterization that in their suit, appellees "request a court order allowing them to control the research without interference from Texas Tech." Bottomed on that premise, he concludes that appellees have no standing to assert claims "in matters pertaining to how the charity operates or effectuates its charitable mission. That is what the Donor plaintiffs want to do in this case" and neither the consent form or any other authority allows them to exercise such control.

However, the plain language of the relief sought by appellees in their amended petition does not show they are trying to direct or control the research in this suit. Rather, they allege that they provided blood and brain samples and personal medical records for a specific research project and if TTUHSC is not going to pursue that research, or is not going to make use of specific samples, they seek a return of those samples. The only portion of the relief sought by appellees which arguably appears to seek control of any part of the research project is the reference to "Dr. Poduslo as the principal investigator." The reason for this qualification seems clear, as she is the only person listed on the consent forms as the investigator responsible for the project and to whom medical records could be released. For this reason, and under this record, the authorities cited by appellant on the issue of donors seeking to exercise control over the administration of a charitable trust are not applicable. * * *

The existence of a public interest in a public trust does not necessarily preclude private interests in the same trust. The distinction between public and private interests was discussed in *Carroll,* in which the court used as examples of private interests in a public trust situations in which donors were "claiming a reversionary interest by reason of a forfeiture for the breach of the trust, the termination of the trust for some reason, such as the heirs of the donor or someone entitled in private right to the property as a result of a revision." * * * The facts alleged by appellees here, which we must accept as true for the purpose of determining their standing, * * *, essentially allege a termination of the trust by reason of TTUHSC's apparent decision to discontinue the research for which the donations were made. Thus, if the trial court were to find that the evidence justified a finding of termination of the research, and thereby termination of the trust because of a failure of purpose, it could also find that appellees had a reversionary interest that would support standing. * * * Such a disposition would be consistent with the rule applicable to failures of express trusts, the effect of which is to create a resulting trust in favor of the settlor. * * *

* * *

In challenging appellees' standing, appellant argues their only interest is in the discovery of treatment or a cure for Alzheimer's disease. That is true as to some appellees. For those living appellees who have provided blood samples and access to their medical records, the destruction of those samples would cause no direct injury, because their desire to support Alzheimer's research by providing DNA samples and medical records would not be foreclosed by TTUHSC's decision to discontinue the research or not to use the samples provided. It is not clear how they would be harmed by any misrepresentation by TTUHSC about continuing the research. It appears that the only harm those particular appellees would suffer would be to be denied the opportunity to discover if they had a genetic predisposition to the disease. That harm would be highly speculative in nature in that it was not established that such genetic markers were identified in individual appellees and, even if they were, there is nothing to show that those particular appellees could not have their DNA examined elsewhere for that purpose.

Even so, as to those appellees who have authorized the use of blood samples from deceased relatives or, more particularly, might have donated part or all of a deceased relative's brain, their interest would be very different from that of the general public. The decision by those appellees to donate those type of samples may well have been the result of difficult personal decisions regarding the disposition of their deceased relative's remains. The donation of such remains would also preclude participation in any other research projects.

Additionally, the consent forms do not purport to be integrated agreements between the parties. Therefore, evidence of other agreements or representation could be introduced. If that evidence should reveal that the donations were motivated by representations concerning TTUHSC's commitment to the research and those representations were false, those donors would have suffered direct harm as a result of such conduct. They may also be able to show that religious considerations motivated the disposition of the brain material in a manner different from the ordinary practices of a research university. As to those individual appellees, appellant would not be the proper party to litigate those issues.

We also note that the donor consent forms specifically provide donors with the right to "discontinue my participation in this study at any time I choose," and did not specify the effect of the donor's election to "discontinue" participation. When the evidence is more fully developed, a factfinder might find that the participants have a reversionary interest in the samples supplied. Such an interest would support standing. * * *

* * *

E. Volunteer Immunity from Liability

Some states became concerned that volunteer philanthropists might not provide their services to nonprofits if strict standards of care were imposed on them. Thus, several state legislatures adopted statutes granting volunteers immunity from liability unless they engage in willful conduct or are grossly negligent.[5]

Congress enacted the Federal Volunteer Protection Act[6] in 1997 to provide additional protection from liability for volunteers in the performance of services for nonprofit organizations. Congress had become concerned that many nonprofit public and private organizations and governmental entitles had been affected adversely by the withdrawal of volunteers from boards and from service in other capacities.

The Federal Volunteer Protection Act provides that no volunteer of a nonprofit organization or governmental entity will be liable for harm caused by an act or omission of the volunteer on behalf of the organization or entity if: (1) the volunteer was acting within the scope of her responsibilities in the nonprofit or governmental entity at the time of the act or omission; (2) the volunteer was properly licensed, certified, or authorized (if appropriate or required) by the appropriate authorities for the activities or practice in the state in which the harm occurred; (3) the harm was not caused by willful or criminal misconduct, gross negligence, reckless misconduct, or a conscious, flagrant indifference to the rights or safety of the individual harmed by the volunteer; and (4) the harm was not caused by the volunteer operating a motor vehicle, vessel, aircraft, or other vehicle for which the state requires an operator's license or insurance.[7]

The federal immunity statute preempts the laws of any state to the extent state laws are inconsistent.[8]

II. FEDERAL STANDARDS OF CONDUCT

Congress, through conditions it has imposed upon tax exempt organizations, demands a strict accountability for directors of some tax exempt

---

5. See, e.g., Ark. Code Ann. § 16–120–102; N. Mex. Stat. Ann. § 53–8–25.1; Tex. Civ. Prac. & Rem. Code §§ 84.001–84.008; Vt. Stat. Ann. tit. 12, § 5781, and Wis. Stat. § 181.287.

6. 42 U.S.C. §§ 14501–5.

7. 42 U.S.C. § 14503(a). There are exceptions to limitation of liability. The limitations will not apply to any misconduct that constitutes a crime of violence, constitutes a hate crime, involves a sexual offense, involves misconduct for which the volunteer was found to have violated a Federal or state civil rights law, or where the volunteer was under the influence of intoxicating alcohol or any drug at the time of the misconduct. 42 U.S.C. § 14503(f).

The Act provides that punitive damages may not be awarded against a volunteer unless the claimant establishes by clear and convincing evidence that the harm was proximately caused by an action of a volunteer that constitutes willful or criminal misconduct, or a conscious, flagrant indifference to the rights or safety of the individual harmed. 42 U.S.C. § 14503(e). Further, if a volunteer is found liable for harm caused an individual, the volunteer will be liable only for the noneconomic loss allocated to the volunteer in direct proportion to the percentage of responsibility of that volunteer. 42 U.S.C. § 14504.

8. 42 U.S.C. § 14502. It does not preempt any state law that provides additional protection from liability relating to volunteers in the performance of services for a nonprofit organization or governmental entity.

organizations. (See discussion of regulation of tax exempt organizations by the Internal Revenue Service in Chapters 5–9.) Directors of tax-exempt charitable or social welfare organizations can be subject individually to substantial penalty taxes if they engage in self-dealing (applicable to those charitable organizations that are classified as private foundations for tax purposes, discussed in Chapter 7) or receive excess benefits (applicable to charitable organizations that qualify as public charities, discussed in Chapter 6, and to social welfare organizations that are tax exempt under § 501(c)(4) of the Code, discussed in Chapter 4).

A. Self–Dealing

Directors of § 501(c)(3) organizations that do not qualify for public charity status and, thus, are classified for tax purposes as private foundations (discussion in Chapter 7), are subject to a penalty tax under § 4941 of the Internal Revenue Code if they engage in any conflict of interest transaction with the organization. A director's participation in a conflict of interest transaction would be an act of self-dealing regardless of whether the transaction was fair to the organization and regardless of whether the person involved was aware that the act constituted self-dealing.

The self-dealing tax is imposed upon the person who participated in the act (rather than on the nonprofit organization). The tax on self-dealing is a two-tier tax: 5 percent of the amount involved for each year, but if the act is not corrected, 200 percent of the amount involved. (See further discussion in Chapter 7.)

ESTATE OF REIS
United States Tax Court, 1986
87 T.C. 1016

In 1970, Mark Rothko, a well-known American painter, died. The bulk of his estate (including many of his original paintings) was bequeathed to the Mark Rothko Foundation. Shortly after Rothko's death, the decedent Bernard J. Reis and the other executors of the Mark Rothko estate entered into contracts on behalf of the estate for the sale of the paintings through the Marlborough Gallery, Inc., or one of its affiliated companies.

Individual executors of the Mark Rothko estate (including decedent Bernard J. Reis) also were directors of the Mark Rothko Foundation and were employees of the Marlborough Gallery. After extensive New York state court litigation concerning the terms of the contracts with the Marlborough Gallery, the contracts were avoided, the executors of the estate were removed, and damages were awarded to the estate.

Respondent determined that individual directors of the Mark Rothko Foundation (including decedent Bernard J. Reis) were disqualified persons who had engaged in acts of self-dealing under sec. 4941, I.R.C. 1954, as amended. Each party now moves for summary judgment herein.

* * *

SWIFT, JUDGE:

This matter is before the Court on cross motions for summary judgment.* * *

The issues in this case arise out of the widely publicized and much litigated Estate of Mark Rothko (hereinafter sometimes referred to as the 'Estate'). Mark Rothko was a well-known American abstract expressionist painter who died in 1970. Bernard J. Reis, decedent ('Reis'), was one of the executors of the Estate of Mark Rothko. Reis also was one of the directors of the Mark Rothko Foundation (the 'Foundation'). The Foundation was established by Mark Rothko in 1967. In his will, after making certain specific bequests to family members, Mark Rothko bequeathed all of his remaining property to the Foundation.

Reis also was an officer and employee of the Marlborough Gallery, Inc. (the 'Gallery'). In May of 1970, shortly after Mark Rothko's death, the executors of the Estate, including Reis, entered into contracts on behalf of the Estate with the Gallery under which the paintings of Mark Rothko (which comprised the bulk of the Estate's assets) could be sold only by the Gallery or its affiliated corporations, offices of which were located throughout the world. The contracts were to last 12 years, and the Gallery was to receive a commission of 50 percent of the proceeds from the sale of each painting.

In New York state courts, the surviving members of Mark Rothko's family sued the Estate, the executors thereof (including Reis), and the Gallery. The Foundation intervened and became a party to the state court proceedings. The litigation, insofar as pertinent to the motions before us, sought to void the 12–year exclusive sales contract between the Estate and the Gallery, to remove Reis as an executor of the Estate, and to recover monetary damages. * * *

Much of the legal relief sought by the surviving family of Mark Rothko was granted in the New York litigation. Reis and the other executors of the Estate were removed, the contract with the Gallery was voided, and monetary damages were awarded to the Estate.

The New York litigation did not go unnoticed by the Internal Revenue Service. Respondent's representatives audited the Foundation and determined that Reis was liable for various self-dealing excise taxes under section 4941 for the years 1970 through 1974 in the total amount of $18,582,500, and additions to tax under sections 6651 and 6684 for the same years in the respective total amounts of $518,125 and $2,112,500.

Petitioner's motion for summary judgment is based on the following three alternative legal arguments: (1) That section 4941(d)(1)(E) and the related provisions are so vague and imprecise that they are unconstitutional and void; (2) that the assets of the Estate were separate and distinct from the assets of the Foundation and therefore that any improper, non-arm's-length conduct that occurred in administering the assets of the Estate do not also constitute self-dealing in the use of the assets of the Foundation; and (3) that whatever misuse of the assets of the Foundation may have occurred, under the undisputed facts of this case, such misuse did not constitute self-dealing by Reis because the assets of the Foundation were not used for the benefit of or transferred to Reis.

In his determination concerning petitioner's liability for the self-dealing excise taxes, and in his motion for summary judgment herein, respondent relies heavily on specific findings of fact made by the New York state courts in the New York litigation. Respondent contends that under Fed. R. Evid. 201 this Court is entitled to take judicial notice of those findings. If so, those findings would be deemed to be conclusively established herein and would serve as the factual basis for respondent's motion for summary judgment.

* * *

CONSTITUTIONALITY OF THE SELF–DEALING EXCISE TAXES

Petitioner argues that in light of the large amounts of Federal excise taxes (e.g., the approximate $21 million at issue herein) that can be assessed against an individual for self-dealing with respect to the assets of a private foundation, it is particularly important that the statutory language be clear and precise. If ambiguous, petitioner argues that the Court should not be hesitant to void the statute as unconstitutional. Petitioner submits that subparagraph (E) of section 4941(d)(1) is so vague that it should be held unconstitutional.[2]

Although based on slightly different reasons, the constitutionality of the self-dealing excise taxes of section 4941 and the underlying regulations previously have been upheld. * * * A number of court opinions have discussed the statutory scheme of the self-dealing excise taxes, and each opinion has recognized those provisions as a valid legislative response to perceived abuses in the use of private foundations.* * * We find no basis for holding any of the provisions of section 4941 unconstitutional.

ESTATE PROPERTY VERSUS FOUNDATION PROPERTY

Petitioner contends that under New York law the paintings of Mark Rothko that were the subject matter of the May 1970 contracts entered

---

2. The relevant statutory language provides as follows:

SEC. 4941. TAXES ON SELF–DEALING

* * *

(d) Self–Dealing.—

(1) In general.—For purposes of this section, the term 'self-dealing' means any direct or indirect—

* * *

(E) transfer to, or use by or for the benefit of, a disqualified person of the income or assets of a private foundation;

into by Reis and the other executors on behalf of the Estate and the Gallery constituted, at that time, property of the Estate, not assets of the Foundation. Petitioner thus contends that regardless of the propriety of those contracts, as a matter of law, the contracts could not have constituted acts of self-dealing by Reis with respect to assets of the Foundation.

Respondent contends that because the Foundation was a beneficiary under Mark Rothko's will, the Foundation had a vested beneficial interest in the property of the Estate. Respondent contends that Reis' acts with respect to the property of the Estate simultaneously and adversely affected the Foundation's beneficial interest therein and thereby constituted an indirect use by or for the benefit of Reis of the assets of the Foundation. Respondent cites section 53.4941(d)–1(b)(3), Excise Tax Regs., as authority for the general proposition that acts of self-dealing with respect to property of an estate also will be regarded as acts of self-dealing with respect to assets of a private foundation that has a beneficial interest in the property of the estate. For the reasons explained below, we agree with respondent on this issue.

Section 53.4941(d)–1(b)(3), Excise Tax Regs., clearly contemplates that the interest of a private foundation in the property of an estate, as a beneficiary thereof, will be treated as an 'asset' of the private foundation under section 4941(d)(1)(E). Accordingly, acts of self-dealing with respect to property of an estate may also constitute acts of self-dealing with respect to assets of a private foundation which is a beneficiary of the Estate. Section 53.4941(d)–1(b)(3), Excise Tax Regs., provides, however, an exception to what otherwise is considered acts of self-dealing if, among other requirements, the transaction is approved by a probate court and if the transaction reflects an exchange at fair market value.[3]

---

3. Insofar as pertinent, section 53.4941(d)–1(b)(3, Excise Tax Regs., provides as follows:

(3) Transactions during the administration of an estate or revocable trust. The term 'indirect self-dealing' shall not include a transaction with respect to a private foundation's interest or expectancy in property (whether or not encumbered) held by an estate (or revocable trust, including a trust which has become irrevocable on a grantor's death), regardless of when title to the property vests under local law, if—

(i) The administrator or executor of an estate or trustee of a revocable trust either—

(a) Possesses a power of sale with respect to the property,

(b) Has the power to reallocate the property to another beneficiary, or

(c) Is required to sell the property under the terms of any option subject to which the property was acquired by the estate (or revocable trust);

(ii) Such transaction is approved by the probate court having jurisdiction over the estate (or by another court having jurisdiction over the estate (or trust) or over the private foundation);

(iii) Such transaction occurs before the estate is considered terminated for Federal income tax purposes pursuant to paragraph (a) of section 1.641(b)–3 of this chapter (or in the case of a revocable trust, before it is considered subject to section 4947);

(iv) The estate (or trust) receives an amount which equals or exceeds the fair market value of the foundation's interest or expectancy in such property at the time of the transaction, taking into account the terms of any option subject to which the the property was acquired by the estate (or trust);* * *

Petitioner concedes that the contracts entered into between the Estate and the Gallery do not qualify for the exception allowed in the section 53.4941(d)–1(b)(3), Excise Tax Regs. The sales contracts were not approved by the probate court and the terms of the contracts apparently did not reflect the fair market value of the paintings. Petitioner argues, however, that because section 53.4941(d)–1(b)(3), Excise Tax Regs., is written in the negative form (i.e., because it explains what transactions are excluded from being treated as acts of self-dealing under section 4941), the regulation does not cover transactions that are to be treated as acts of self-dealing under section 4941. We disagree.

It is obvious to us that the only reason section 53.4941(d)–1(b)(3), Excise Tax Regs., takes a negative approach and describes certain exceptions to acts of self-dealing is that in the absence of those exceptions, such transactions would have been covered by section 4941. In other words, in light of the terms of section 53.4941(d)–1(b)(3), Excise Tax Regs., it is clear that transactions affecting the assets of an estate generally are treated also as affecting the assets of any private foundation which, as a beneficiary of the estate, has an expectancy interest in the assets of the estate.

As previously mentioned, the validity of section 53.4941(d)–1(b)(3), Excise Tax Regs., has been sustained. See Rockefeller v. United States, supra. The general purpose of the regulation was explained as follows:

> It logically follows that Congress would be concerned about the circumvention of an estate's assets which are earmarked for a private foundation, especially in a case such as this, where the bulk of the estate is bequeathed to a charitable trust. It is also reasonable to subject such an estate, in part, to the statutory checks which Congress has deemed fit for private foundations. Rockefeller v. United States, 572 F. Supp. 9, 14 (E.D.Ark.1982).

In summary, regardless of whether the Foundation is considered to have had a vested or merely an expectancy interest under New York law in the property of the Mark Rothko Estate, under section 4941 and the relevant Treasury regulations, the expectancy interest the Foundation had in the Estate is treated as an asset of the Foundation, and transactions affecting property of the Estate are treated as affecting assets of the Foundation. Such transactions are excepted from the definition of acts of self-dealing under section 4941 only if they qualify for the exception described in section 53.4941(d)–1(b)(3), Excise Tax Regs., or under one of the other available exceptions (e.g., the exception for transactions which provide only incidental benefits to disqualified persons). Sec. 53.4941(d)–2(f)(2), Excise Tax Regs.

BENEFIT TO PETITIONER

Petitioner's third argument in support of her motion for summary judgment is that the alleged acts of self-dealing only could have benefitted Reis in a nonpecuniary manner and that under any proper reading of section 4941, that section does not reach nonpecuniary benefits. We disagree.

The language of section 4941(d)(1)(E) * * * does not suggest that it is limited to pecuniary benefits, and we find no basis for imposing such a limitation. Section 4941(d) enumerates in detail those categories of activities that will constitute acts of self-dealing. The purpose of that enumeration was to clarify what acts would be considered acts of self-dealing and to minimize the need to use subjective standards in evaluating potential acts of self-dealing. S. Rept. No. 91–552, 1969–3 C.B. 423, 442–443; Rockefeller v. United States, 572 F. Supp. 9, 12–13 (E.D.Ark. 1982).

Petitioner argues that respondent's interpretation of section 4941(d)(1)(E) is erroneous because it is too broad and fails adequately to distinguish between significant and insignificant personal benefits accruing to a disqualified person. We again disagree. Implicit in the statutory language of subparagraph (E) of section 4941(d)(1) is the requirement that the benefits accruing to the disqualified person be significant. That reading of the statute is supported by Treasury regulations which expressly provide that incidental or tenuous benefits accruing to a disqualified person will not constitute acts of self-dealing. See sec. 53.4941(d)-2(f)(2), Excise Tax Regs.[4]

We also note that respondent contends that the benefits accruing to Reis as a result of the alleged acts of self-dealing were pecuniary in nature and were substantial. Although such allegation does not establish either of those facts, we must assume such facts to be true for purposes

---

4. Sec. 53.4941(d)–2(f)(2), Excise Tax Regs., provides—

(2) Certain incidental benefits. The fact that a disqualified person receives an incidental or tenuous benefit from the use by a foundation of its income or assets will not, by itself, make such use an act of self-dealing. Thus, the public recognition a person may receive, arising from the charitable activities of a private foundation to which such person is a substantial contributor, does not in itself result in an act of self-dealing since generally the benefit is incidental and tenuous. For example, a grant by a private foundation to a section 509(a)(1), (2), or (3) organization will not be an act of self-dealing merely because such organization is located in the same area as a corporation which is a substantial contributor to the foundation, or merely because one of the section 509(a)(1), (2), or (3) organization's officers, directors, or trustees is also a manager of or a substantial contributor to the foundation. Similarly, a scholarship or a fellowship grant to a person other than a disqualified person, which is paid or incurred by a private foundation in accordance with a program which is consistent with—

(i) The requirements of the foundation's exempt status under section 501(c)(3),

(ii) The requirements for the allowance of deductions under section 170 for contributions made to the foundation, and

(iii) The requirements of section 4945(g)(1), will not be an act of self-dealing under section 4941(d)(1) merely because a disqualified person indirectly receives an incidental benefit from such grant. Thus, a scholarship or a fellowship grant made by a private foundation in accordance with a program to award scholarships or fellowship grants to the children of employees of a substantial contributor shall not constitute an act of self-dealing if the requirements of the preceding sentence are satisfied. For an example of the kind of scholarship program with an employment nexus that meets the above requirements, see (53.4945–4(b)(5) (Example 1).

of deciding petitioner's motion for summary judgment. Espinoza v. Commissioner, 78 T.C, 412 (1982). If petitioner establishes in a subsequent trial herein that Reis, as a disqualified person, received tenuous benefits from his use of the assets of the Foundation, section 53.4941(d)–2(f)(2), Excise Tax Regs., will protect petitioner from imposition of the self-dealing taxes.

For the reasons set forth above, petitioner's motion for summary judgment against respondent will be denied.

* * *

B. Excess Benefits Transactions

Until 1996, only directors of § 501(c)(3) organizations that were classified as private foundations for tax purposes were subject to self-dealing penalties. Section 4958 was added to the Code in 1996 to provide that officers and directors of § 501(c)(3) organizations that qualify as public charities and § 501(c)(4) organizations (social welfare organizations) are subject to a penalty tax on "excess benefit transactions." An "excess benefit transaction" is any transaction in which the covered organization provides an economic benefit directly or indirectly to or for the use of any disqualified person if the value of the economic benefit provided exceeds the value of the consideration (including the performance of services) received for providing the benefit. The tax on an excess benefit transaction is 25 percent of the excess benefit and is imposed on the person receiving the benefit. If the excess benefit is not corrected, the tax becomes 200 percent of the excess benefit.

CARACCI v. COMMISSIONER
United States Tax Court, 2002
118 T.C. 379

LARO, J.

* * *

FINDINGS OF FACT

Some facts have been stipulated. We incorporate herein by this reference the parties' stipulation of facts and the exhibits submitted therewith. We find the stipulated facts accordingly. The couples, Michael and Cindy Caracci, Victor and Joyce Caracci, Vincent and Denise Caracci, and Christina and David McQuillen, are husband and wife, each of whom resided in Mississippi when the petitions were filed. Christina McQuillen is the sister of Michael and Vincent Caracci, and the three of them are the children of Vincent and Joyce Caracci (the father, mother, and three children are referred to collectively as the Caracci family). The principal place of business of the various Sta–Home entities also was in Mississippi at that time.

From 1973 to 1976, Joyce Caracci served as a consulting nurse for the State of Mississippi Board of Health, surveying healthcare facilities for participation in the Medicare/Medicaid programs. On May 3, 1976, Joyce Caracci, Victor Caracci, and a third individual not relevant herein started Sta–Home Home Health Agency, Inc. Approximately 1 year later, Joyce Caracci, Victor Caracci, and a third individual not relevant herein formed the other two Sta–Home tax-exempt entities. Each of the Sta–Home tax-exempt entities was formed as a nonstock corporation under Mississippi law, with Victor and Joyce Caracci as the owners during all relevant times. In the early years of their business, Victor and Joyce Caracci borrowed money collateralized by their residence to fund the Sta–Home tax-exempt entities' operations, and they (the individuals) guaranteed the extension of credit to the entities. Throughout the years, the managers of the three separate entities generally operated the entities as one integrated unit. (Because the parties also generally treat the three separate entities as one integrated unit, so do we.) During the subject year, Joyce Caracci, Michael Caracci, and Christina McQuillen were the Sta–Home tax-exempt entities' only directors and officers.

The Sta–Home tax-exempt entities participated in the Medicare program. Medicare was established in title XVIII of the Social Security Act, Pub.L. 89–97, 79 Stat. 291 (1965), and is the principal healthcare insurance for individuals who are either disabled or aged 65 or older. It is administered by the Healthcare Financing Administration (HCFA), a division of the U.S. Department of Health and Human Services, with whom private insurance companies in different regions of the country have contracted to serve as fiscal intermediaries.

* * *

During 1994 and 1995, the prospect arose of Medicare's shifting from a PIP cost reimbursement system to a prospective payment system (PPS). Several groups discussed the proposal in theory, but no one knew exactly what form PPS might take. The Sta–Home tax-exempt entities, through Vincent Caracci, an attorney whose job included keeping abreast of current events, learned of these proposed changes. Petitioners came to understand that the Sta–Home tax-exempt entities would not under a PPS receive a check every 2 weeks but would have to file a claim for every service rendered and wait for the claim to be processed and paid. Petitioners became concerned about the lack of cashflow under a PPS. They also believed that a PPS would reduce the Sta–Home tax-exempt entities' income.

Late in December 1994, the Caracci family consulted an attorney named Thomas Kirkland (Kirkland) about converting the Sta–Home tax-exempt entities into for-profit corporations. Kirkland's firm represented many home health care agencies, and he had recommended that all of those agencies make such a conversion. Kirkland's recommendation was based, in part, on his discussions with bankers who were reluctant to lend money to nonprofit home healthcare agencies. By 1991, petitioners' regular accountant, Danny Hart (Hart), also recommended that the Sta–Home tax-exempt entities convert to nontax-exempt status.

Kirkland retained a tax attorney named James Pettis (Pettis) to help Kirkland convert the Sta–Home tax-exempt entities into for-profit entities. Subsequently, Pettis learned that Kirkland's firm had not obtained an appraisal for any of its previous conversions. Pettis informed Kirkland that Pettis "strongly [disagreed]" with that approach. By letter dated July 7, 1995, Kirkland's firm retained Hart's accounting firm to appraise the Sta–Home tax-exempt entities' net assets as of a proposed transaction date of October 1, 1995.

The appraisal was slow in coming. Pettis, the tax adviser, insisted on seeing the appraisal before proceeding with any transaction that would effect a conversion. After reading the appraisal, Pettis was concerned that it failed to deal with issues concerning intangible assets. He believed that the mere fact that an entity had lost money or had a negative cashflow did not mean that the entity was worthless. He also was concerned that the appraisal failed to address Rev. Rul. 59–60, 1959–1 C.B. 237, where the Commissioner has set forth standards on valuation for Federal income tax purposes. Upon Pettis's request, he received a second appraisal. Because some of his concerns as to intangible assets remained after reading the second appraisal, he sought and received assurance that the Sta–Home tax-exempt entities' liabilities far exceeded the value of their assets and that the value of the intangibles would not give the entities a positive fair market value.

On July 11, 1995, the Sta–Home tax-exempt entities' boards of directors authorized the conversion of those entities into S corporations. The S status was chosen so that the shareholders could deduct the new entities' future losses. On August 22, 1995, in anticipation of a transfer of the Sta–Home tax-exempt entities' assets, Kirkland's firm, with petitioners' approval, formed the Sta–Home for-profit entities under Mississippi law. Each of those corporations subsequently elected to be taxed as an S corporation for Federal income tax purposes. Since their formation, the only shareholders of each of the Sta–Home for-profit entities have been Joyce Caracci (17.5 percent), Victor Caracci (17.5 percent), Michael Caracci (30 percent), Christina McQuillen (17.5 percent) and Vincent Caracci (17.5 percent). The only directors and officers have been members of the Caracci family.

On August 28, 1995, Hart's accounting firm tendered an appraisal stating that the value of the Sta–Home tax-exempt entities' assets was less than their liabilities. Kirkland had assumed that this would be the case. On September 1, 1995, Kirkland executed and filed on behalf of each of the Sta–Home tax-exempt entities "Notices of Intent to Change Ownership" with the State of Mississippi Department of Health.

Effective October 1, 1995, Sta–Home Home Health Agency, Inc., transferred all of its tangible and intangible assets to Sta–Home Health Agency of Jackson, Inc., Sta–Home Home Health Agency, Inc., of Forest, Mississippi, transferred all of its tangible and intangible assets to Sta–Home Health Agency of Carthage, Inc., and Sta–Home Home Health Agency, Inc., of Grenada, Mississippi, transferred all of its assets to Sta–

Home Health Agency of Greenwood, Inc. The consideration paid by each transferee was the assumption of the related transferor's liabilities. Since the transfers, the transferors have not engaged in any activities, charitable or otherwise; nor have they been dissolved under Mississippi law.

* * *

Other than State and Federal filing requirements and the slight changes in the names of the entities, the Sta–Home operations remained the same after the transfer as they were before. The Sta–Home for-profit entities continued to use a fiscal year ending on September 30 for financial accounting and Medicare reporting purposes, although not for tax purposes. As part of the transfers, the Sta–Home for-profit entities accepted assignment of the Sta–Home tax-exempt entities' Medicare provider agreements and continued to use the provider numbers of the Sta–Home tax-exempt entities. The Sta–Home for-profit entities continued to receive PIP payments and lump-sum settlements from the Medicare program, including quarterly payments based on quarterly PIP reports. The Sta-Home for-profit entities received a net preacquisition payment relating to settlement of the Sta–Home tax-exempt entities' 1987 fiscal year. Substantially, the same employees continued to do the same work, and the same assets were used in the same three locations. The Caracci family members continued to be employed by the Sta–Home for-profit entities in the same positions in which they were employed by the Sta–Home tax-exempt entities, and each member's compensation and employment benefits remained subject to review by HCFA through the cost reporting process.* * *

* * *

OPINION

I. *Introduction*

Respondent has determined that petitioners' participation in the asset transfer made them liable for deficiencies totaling $256,114,435.[6] Respondent's determination rests on his expert's determination that the fair market value of the transferred assets exceeded the assumed liabilities by approximately $20 million. Petitioners argue that the assumed liabilities exceeded the fair market value of the transferred assets. Petitioners rely on their expert, who concluded similarly. It is with this backdrop that we proceed to decide the assets' value at the time of the transfer. We bear in mind the wide difference in values ascertained by the experts.

---

6. Of course, were the respondent to prevail in full, he would be entitled to only $46,460,477 of approximately $256,114,435. The lion's share of the $256,114,435 is attributable to excise taxes under sec. 4958(a)(1) and (2) and (b) totaling $41,753,311 ($4,635,923 + $30,000 + $37,087,388), for all or part of which respondent has determined that eight petitioners are jointly and severally liable.

II. *Fair Market Value*

A. *Overview*

A determination of fair market value is factual, and a trier of fact must weigh all relevant evidence of value and draw appropriate inferences. * * * Fair market value is the price that a willing buyer would pay a willing seller, both persons having reasonable knowledge of all relevant facts and neither person being under any compulsion to buy or to sell. * * * The willing buyer and the willing seller are hypothetical persons, rather than specific individuals or entities, and the characteristics of these hypothetical persons are not necessarily the same as the personal characteristics of the actual seller or a particular buyer. * * *

* * *

B. *Role of the Expert*

As typically occurs in a case of valuation, each party relies primarily upon an expert's testimony and report to support the respective positions on valuation. A trial judge bears a special gatekeeping obligation to ensure that any and all expert testimony is relevant and reliable. * * *

The Court has broad discretion to evaluate the cogency of an expert's analysis. * * * Sometimes, an expert will help us decide a case. * * * Other times, he or she will not. * * * O Aided by our common sense, we weigh the helpfulness and persuasiveness of an expert's testimony in light of his or her qualifications and with due regard to all other credible evidence in the record. * * *

C. *Expert Testimony for Petitioners*

To support their contention that the value of the Sta–Home tax-exempt entities' assets was less than the liabilities assumed, petitioners rely upon the report and testimony of Hahn. Hahn, a director in PricewatershouseCoopers Northeast Region Corporation Valuation Consulting Group, has written extensively on the valuation of home healthcare agencies and has frequently appeared as an expert witness.

Hahn started by noting that because of the predominance of Medicare in the payor mix of most home health agencies, a conventional cash flow or earnings approach to valuation would produce "a very different result from other, more appropriate approaches." This is so because home health agencies, with a preponderance of Medicare-eligible patients, earn little if any profit.[7]

* * *

D. *Expert Testimony for Respondent*

Charles A. Wilhoite (Wilhoite) presented expert testimony on behalf of respondent. Wilhoite, a certified public accountant, is a principal of Willamette Management Associates and codirector of that firm's office in

---

7. The evidence includes an article written by Hahn wherein he reports that his firm's database reflects that "more than 75 percent of home health agency acquisitions involved agencies that recorded losses." Hahn, "Payment Reform Will Shift Home Health Agency Valuation Parameters", Healthcare Financial Management (Dec. 1998).

Portland, Oregon. He has performed a number of assignments involving the analysis and appraisal of professional practices, with a heavy concentration in the health care field. He has been involved with assignments requiring the valuation of intangible assets, including CONs, customer relationships, goodwill, and workforces.

* * *

E. *Our Valuation of the Sta–Home Tax–Exempt Entities*

The traditional determinants of fair market value persist even when valuing a nonprofit, tax-exempt company. There are differences, however, in the amount of weight usually given to the earnings and profits of regular business organizations and those of tax-exempt entities. Earnings and profits are obviously less meaningful in the case of nonprofit organizations. Here, Medicare funded 95 percent of the Sta–Home tax-exempt entities' operations. As applicable herein, the Medicare program was not designed to produce corporate profits nor to contribute to the capital growth of healthcare organizations. It was designed to reimburse providers of home health care services for their costs, including administrative salaries and overhead. The system nevertheless permitted the operators of such agencies to generate executive-level salaries and benefits for themselves. It also permitted them to accumulate substantial assets in their businesses without paying income taxes on any of their earnings.

* * *

We believe that the best evidence of the value of the Sta–Home tax-exempt entities arises from the use of the comparable value method employed by both experts.

* * *

When we take these modifications into account, we arrive at a fair market value of $18,675,000 * * *

* * *

F. *Excess Value*

Having found the fair market value of the Sta–Home tax-exempt entities, we turn to decide the value in excess of the assumed liabilities. We are satisfied that the Sta–Home for-profit entities intended to, and did, assume all of the liabilities of the predecessor businesses. The evidence includes an audited balance sheet, prepared for purposes of this case, which indicates that the total liabilities as of September 30, 1995, were $13,310,860. To this amount we think there is properly added $201,000, as ascertained by Hahn, representing a reserve account for cost claims disallowed by Medicare. Total liabilities assumed were therefore $13,511,000. Subtracting the total liabilities from the fair market value we have decided, results in an excess of $5,164,000:

Fair market value	$18,675,000
Assumed liabilities	(13,511,000)
Excess	5,164,000

III. *Excise Taxes Under Section 4958*

Section 4958, the provisions of which are set forth in the appendix to this report, was added to the Internal Revenue Code by the Taxpayer Bill of Rights 2, Pub.L. 104–168, sec. 1311(a), 110 Stat. 1452, 1475 (1996). Section 4958 is patterned after section 4941, which applies to acts of self-dealing between private foundations and disqualified persons. Section 4958 applies to public charities and social welfare organizations which are exempt from Federal income taxes.* * *

* * *

Section 4958 was enacted to impose penalty excise taxes as "intermediate" sanctions in cases where organizations exempt from tax under section 503(c) engage in "excess benefit transactions." H. Rept. 104–506, at 56 (1996), 1996–3 C.B. 49, 104. An excess benefit transaction is one in which a tax-exempt organization provides an economic benefit to one or more of the organization's insiders, called "disqualified persons", if the fair market value of the benefit exceeds the value of what the organization receives in return. Sec. 4958(c)(1)(A); H. Rept. 104–506, *supra* at 56, 1996–3 C.B. at 104. Disqualified persons include not only those who are able to exercise substantial influence over the tax-exempt organization, but also their family members and entities in which those individuals have 35 percent of the voting power. Disqualified persons are subject to the excise penalties, whether the excess benefit transactions are accomplished "directly or indirectly." Sec. 4958(c).

Before the enactment of section 4958, if an organization within its purview did not comply with the rules regarding tax exemption, the Commissioner's only recourse was to revoke the organization's exemption. The Treasury Department realized that such a response might be inappropriate when the exempt organization did not conform to all the applicable rules but was nevertheless capable of functioning for a charitable purpose.* * *

A disqualified person who receives an excess benefit from an excess benefit transaction is liable for an initial excise tax equal to 25 percent of the excess benefit. Sec. 4958(a)(1). If the initial tax is imposed and the transaction is not corrected within the taxable period, then the disqualified person is liable for an additional tax of 200 percent of the excess benefit. Sec. 4958(b).

Here, the fair market value of the Sta–Home tax-exempt entities' transferred assets far exceeded the consideration paid by the Sta–Home for-profit entities. Thus, the asset transfers were excess benefit transactions which directly benefited the transferees (i.e., the Sta–Home for-profit entities) and indirectly benefited the Sta–Home for-profit entities' shareholders (i.e., the Caracci family members). Petitioners do not seriously dispute that they are disqualified persons with respect to the Sta–Home tax-exempt entities. Joyce P. Caracci, Michael Caracci, and Christina C. McQuillen, as directors and officers of each of the three Sta–Home tax-exempt entities, are disqualified persons because they were in positions to exercise substantial influence over the entities' affairs. Sec. 4958(f)(1)(A). Victor Caracci and Vincent Caracci are disqualified persons because of their familial relationships to Joyce P. Caracci, Michael Caracci, and Christina C. McQuillen. Sec. 4958(f)(1)(B). Sta–Home Health Agency of Carthage, Inc., Sta–Home Health Agency of Greenwood, Inc., and Sta–Home Health Agency of Jackson, Inc., are disqualified persons because they are entities that are 35–percent controlled by disqualified persons; in fact, members of the Caracci family own 100 percent of the Sta–Home for-profit entities' voting stock. Sec. 4958(f)(1)(C). Accordingly, petitioners are subject to excess benefit taxes under section 4958.

Because we have decided the value of the Sta–Home tax-exempt entities' assets on the basis of a revenue multiple, it is appropriate to ascribe the excess benefit to each of the Sta–Home for-profit entities in proportion to the amounts the 1995 revenues of their respective predecessors bore to the total revenue.* * *

* * *

We conclude that each of the disqualified person/petitioners is jointly and severally liable for the initial and additional taxes under section 4958(a)(1) and (b) as to the excess benefits. The effect of our holding is that the individual petitioners are jointly and severally liable for the total excess benefit of $5,164,000 from the three Sta–Home entities, while the Sta-Home for profit entities are liable for taxes as specified in the above table. In so concluding, we decline at this time petitioners' invitation to abate the initial and additional excise taxes pursuant to section 4961 (second-tier tax abatement) and section 4962(a) (first-tier tax abatement). Because the excess benefit transactions have never been corrected for purposes of section 4958(f)(6), petitioners' invitation is, at best, premature. Petitioners have not as of yet met the prerequisite for the requested abatement; i.e., a timely correction. In this regard, however, we note that sections 4961(a) and 4963(e)(1) generally allow for the abatement of a section 4958 excise tax if the excess benefit transaction giving rise thereto is corrected within 90 days after our decision sustaining the tax becomes final. Cf. *Morrissey v. Commissioner,* T.C. Memo. 1998–443. Because the issue of whether petitioners will or would qualify for an abatement is not yet ripe for decision, we express no opinion on this issue.

IV. *Revocation of Tax–Exempt Status*

Section 501(c)(3) requires, among other things, that an organization be operated exclusively for one or more specified exempt purposes. An organization is not operated exclusively for one or more exempt purposes unless it serves a public rather than a private interest and its net earnings do not inure to the benefit of any shareholder or individual. Sec. 1.501(c)(3)–1, Income Tax Regs.

* * *

With the enactment of section 4958, * * * the issue whether the tax-exempt status of the Sta–Home tax-exempt entities should be revoked must now be considered in the context of the "intermediate sanction" provisions. As noted above, the intermediate sanction regime was enacted in order to provide a less drastic deterrent to the misuse of a charity than revocation of that charity's exempt status. The legislative history explains that "the intermediate sanctions for 'excess benefit transactions' may be imposed by the IRS in lieu of (or in addition to) revocation of an organization's tax-exempt status." H. Rept. 104–506, *supra* at 59, 1996–3 C.B. at 107. A footnote to this statement explains: "In general, the intermediate sanctions are the sole sanction imposed in those cases in which the excess benefit does not rise to a level where it calls into question whether, on the whole, the organization functions as a charitable or other tax-exempt organization". *Id.* n. 15, 1996–3 C.B. at 107. Although the imposition of section 4958 excise taxes as a result of an excess benefit transaction does not preclude revocation of the organization's tax-exempt status, the legislative history indicates that both a revocation and the imposition of intermediate sanctions will be an unusual case.

We do not believe that this is such an unusual case. The dormant state of the Sta–Home tax-exempt entities precludes calling into question whether, on the whole, they are functioning tax-exempt entities. Moreover, we perceive three reasons why it is not appropriate to remove their tax-exempt status at this time. First, the excess benefit represented the fair market value of the Sta-Home tax-exempt entities' assets less the liabilities assumed by the Sta–Home for-profit entities. Given that we have already sustained the imposition of intermediate sanctions as to this excess value, we do not believe it appropriate under the facts herein to conclude that the single transaction (as to each entity) underlying the excess value also requires our revocation of each entity's tax-exempt status. Second, the Sta–Home tax-exempt entities have not since the transfers been operated contrary to their tax-exempt purpose. Third, we find some credence in petitioners' suggestion that maintenance of the tax exemption may enable them to utilize the correction provisions made available in sections 4961 through 4963. While the issue is not ripe for us to decide at this time, we note that a permissible correction may require that the Sta–Home for-profit entities transfer the assets back to the Sta–Home tax-exempt entities. If we were to remove the Sta–Home tax-exempt entities' tax-exempt status at this stage, however, those entities would no longer be tax-exempt entities available to receive the assets.

The legislative history quoted above indicates that "the term 'correction' means undoing the excess benefit to the extent possible and taking any additional measures necessary to place the organization in a financial position not worse than that in which it would be if the disqualified person were dealing under the highest fiduciary standards." H. Rept. 104–506, *supra* at 59, 1996–3 C.B. at 107. Petitioners suggest that preserving the tax-exempt status of the now-dormant tax-exempt Sta–Home entities may leave petitioners with a means of correction by placing the entities back into a "financial position not worse than it would be" if the disqualified persons had observed the proper standards. While, as noted above, we do not address the issue of timely corrections, we believe that leaving the exemptions intact is consistent with both the legislative history underlying section 4958 and the provisions for abatement in sections 4961 through 4963.

* * *

APPENDIX

SEC. 4958. TAXES ON EXCESS BENEFIT TRANSACTIONS

(a) Initial Taxes.—

(1) On the disqualified person.—There is hereby imposed on each excess benefit transaction a tax equal to 25 percent of the excess benefit. The tax imposed by this paragraph shall be paid by any disqualified person referred to in subsection (f)(1) with respect to such transaction.

(2) On the management.—In any case in which a tax is imposed by paragraph (1), there is hereby imposed on the participation of any organization manager in the excess benefit transaction, knowing that it is such a transaction, a tax equal to 10 percent of the excess benefit, unless such participation is not willful and is due to reasonable cause. The tax imposed by this paragraph shall be paid by any organization manager who participated in the excess benefit transaction.

(b) Additional Tax on the Disqualified Person.—In any case in which an initial tax is imposed by subsection (a)(1) on an excess benefit transaction and the excess benefit involved in such transaction is not corrected within the taxable period, there is hereby imposed a tax equal to 200 percent of the excess benefit involved. The tax imposed by this subsection shall be paid by any disqualified person referred to in subsection (f)(1) with respect to such transaction.

(c) Excess Benefit Transaction; Excess Benefit.—For purposes of this section—

(1) Excess benefit transaction.—

(A) In general.—The term "excess benefit transaction" means any transaction in which an economic benefit is provided by an applicable tax-exempt organization directly or indirectly to or for the use of any disqualified person if the value of the economic benefit provided exceeds the value of the consideration (including the performance of services) received for providing such benefit. For purposes of the preceding sentence, an economic benefit shall not be treated as consideration for the performance of services unless such organization clearly indicated its intent to so treat such benefit.

(B) Excess benefit.—The term "excess benefit" means the excess referred to in subparagraph (A).

(2) Authority to include certain other private inurement.—To the extent provided in regulations prescribed by the Secretary, the term "excess benefit transaction" includes any transaction in which the amount of any economic benefit provided to or for the use of a disqualified person is determined in whole or in part by the revenues of 1 or more activities of the organization but only if such transaction results in inurement not permitted under paragraph (3) or (4) of section 501(c), as the case may be. In the case of any such transaction, the excess benefit shall be the amount of the inurement not so permitted.

(d) Special Rules.—For purposes of this section—

(1) Joint and several liability.—If more than 1 person is liable for any tax imposed by subsection (a) or subsection (b), all such persons shall be jointly and severally liable for such tax.

(2) Limit for management.—With respect to any 1 excess benefit transaction, the maximum amount of the tax imposed by subsection (a)(2) shall not exceed $10,000. [Increased to 20,000 in 2006]

(e) Applicable Tax–Exempt Organization.—For purposes of this subchapter, the term "applicable tax-exempt organization" means—

(1) any organization which (without regard to any excess benefit) would be described in paragraph (3) or (4) of section 501(c) and exempt from tax under section 501(a), and

(2) any organization which was described in paragraph (1) at any time during the 5–year period ending on the date of the transaction.

Such term shall not include a private foundation (as defined in section 509(a)).

(f) Other Definitions.—For purposes of this section—

(1) Disqualified person.—The term "disqualified person" means, with respect to any transaction—

(A) any person who was, at any time during the 5–year period ending on the date of such transaction, in a position to exercise substantial influence over the affairs of the organization,

(B) a member of the family of an individual described in subparagraph (A), and

(C) a 35–percent controlled entity.

(2) Organization manager.—The term "organization manager" means, with respect to any applicable tax-exempt organization, any officer, director, or trustee of such organization (or any individual

having powers or responsibilities similar to those of officers, directors, or trustees of the organization).

(3) 35–percent controlled entity.—

(A) In general.—The term "35–percent controlled entity" means—

(i) a corporation in which persons described in subparagraph (A) or (B) of paragraph (1) own more than 35 percent of the total combined voting power,

(ii) a partnership in which such persons own more than 35 percent of the profits interest, and

(iii) a trust or estate in which such persons own more than 35 percent of the beneficial interest.

(B) Constructive ownership rules.—Rules similar to the rules of paragraphs (3) and (4) of section 4946(a) shall apply for purposes of this paragraph.

(4) Family members.—The members of an individual's family shall be determined under section 4946(d); except that such members also shall include the brothers and sisters (whether by the whole or half blood) of the individual and their spouses.

(5) Taxable period.—The term "taxable period" means, with respect to any excess benefit transaction, the period beginning with the date on which the transaction occurs and ending on the earliest of—

(A) the date of mailing a notice of deficiency under section 6212 with respect to the tax imposed by subsection (a)(1), or

(B) the date on which the tax imposed by subsection (a)(1) is assessed.

(6) Correction.—The terms "correction" and "correct" mean, with respect to any excess benefit transaction, undoing the excess benefit to the extent possible, and taking any additional measures necessary to place the organization in a financial position not worse than that in which it would be if the disqualified person were dealing under the highest fiduciary standards.

On appeal, the Fifth Circuit reversed the decision of the Tax Court and ruled for the taxpayer. [*Caracci v. Comm.*, 456 F.3d 444 (5th Cir. 2006)] However, the decision of the Fifth Circuit was based on the Tax Court's acceptance of an appraiser's determination of the fair market value of the assets transferred to the for profit entity and not on the Tax Court's interpretation of § 4958. The First Circuit decided the transferred assets had no net fair market value because it decided the liabilities exceeded the value of the assets.

Questions

1. Legal standards imposed on directors of nonprofit corporations by state law generally cause a director to be liable for violation of fiduciary standards of conduct only if the director's actions or failures to act constitute gross negligence. Further, a director may engage in a conflict of interest

transaction that is "fair" to the corporation without liability under state law. However, federal standard of conduct provisions as set out in §§ 4941 of the Internal Revenue Code subject directors who represent § 501(c)(3) organizations that are classified as private foundations for tax purposes (discussion in Chapter 7) to substantial penalties if they engage in *any* conflict of interest transactions. Should state conflict of interest provisions follow the concept of § 4941 of the Internal Revenue Code and prohibit all conflict of interest transactions?

2. Officers and directors of § 501(c)(3) organizations that qualify as public charities (discussion in Chapter 6) and of social welfare organizations exempt under § 501(c)(4) of the Internal Revenue Code (discussion in Chapter 4) are subject to substantial penalty taxes should they obtain "excess" benefits from conflict of interest transactions. Should the more strict federal standards of conduct imposed on §§ 501(c)(3) and (4) organizations cause courts and state legislatures to reconsider the less exacting state standards imposed on directors of nonprofit organizations?

3. Do you think the imposition of more stringent standards of conduct on the actions of board members of nonprofit organizations would cause individuals to refuse to serve on, or withdraw from, nonprofit boards? Or are more demanding requirements needed to prevent the director abuses that have surfaced in some nonprofit organizations?

4. What bearing do you think the enactment of § 4958 will have on volunteer service on boards of charitable and social welfare organizations?

5. The payment of excessive compensation to officers and directors of public charities and § 501(c)(4) organizations is an "excess benefit" that can cause the officer or director receiving "excessive" compensation to be subject to the penalty tax under § 4958. Do you think compensation paid to many university presidents and to chief executive officers and physicians of hospitals is excessive? If so, is the enactment of § 4958 an appropriate means to control such salaries? Do you think enactment of § 4958 will affect the size of compensation packages offered the chief executive officers of nonprofit organizations?

Notes

1. Regulations issued pursuant to § 4958 exempt governmental units or affiliates from the provisions of § 4958. See Treas. Reg. § 53.4958–2(a)(2)(ii).

2. The Regulations, § 53.4958–3(a)(1), define a "disqualified person" as "any person who was in a position to exercise substantial influence over the affairs of an applicable tax-exempt organization at any time during the five-year period ending on the date of the transaction." Persons deemed to have "substantial influence" include voting members of the governing body; presidents, chief executive officers, or chief operating officers; treasurers and chief financial officers; and persons with a material financial interest in a provider-sponsored organization. See Treas. Reg. § 53.4958–3(c).

3. The Regulations pursuant to § 4958 exempt from the definition of an excess benefit transaction an "initial contract" that provides for a "fixed payment." See Treas. Reg. § 53.4958–4(a)(3)(i). An "initial contract" is

defined as a binding written contract between an applicable tax-exempt organization and a person who was not a disqualified person immediately prior to entering into the contract. A "fixed payment" is defined as "an amount of cash or other property specified in the contract, or determined by a fixed formula specified in the contract, which is to be paid or transferred in exchange for the provision of specified services or property." A fixed formula may incorporate an amount dependent upon future specified events or contingencies so long as no person can exercise discretion when calculating the amount of the payment or deciding whether to make a payment (such as a bonus). The Regulations give as an example a tax-exempt organization entering into a five year contract to employ a chief financial officer at a salary of $200,000. Because the financial officer, as a new employee, would not be a disqualified person at the time of the contract, the contract would qualify as an "initial contract" subject to a fixed payment and § 4958 would not be applicable. However, if the chief financial officer is subsequently promoted to chief executive officer at a salary increase of $40,000, the changes in the employment relationship would constitute material changes in the initial contract so that the board will have entered into a new contract with a then disqualified person and § 4958 would be applicable. [See Treas. Reg. § 53.4958–4(a)(3)(vii) Examples 1 and 4.]

4. The Regulations, Treas. Reg. § 4958–5, provide for a rebuttable presumption that a transaction is not an excess benefit transaction if the following conditions are satisfied: (1) The compensation arrangement or terms of the property transfer are approved in advance by an authorized body of the applicable tax exempt organization composed entirely of individuals who do not have a conflict of interest with respect to the compensation arrangement or property transfer; (2) The authorized body obtained and relied upon appropriate data as to comparability prior to making its determination; and (3) The authorized body adequately documented the basis for its determination concurrently with making its determination. An authorized body has appropriate data as to comparability if, given the knowledge and expertise of its members, it has information sufficient to determine whether the compensation arrangement is reasonable in its entirety or the property transfer is at fair market value. In the case of compensation, relevant information includes compensation levels paid by similarly situated organizations, both taxable and tax-exempt, for functionally comparable positions; the availability of similar services in the geographic area of the applicable tax-exempt organization; current compensation surveys compiled by independent firms; and actual written offers from similar institutions competing for the services of the disqualified person. For organizations with annual gross receipts (including contributions) of less than $1 million, the authorized body will be considered to have appropriate data as to comparability if it has data on compensation paid by three comparable organizations in the same or similar communities for similar services. For property transfers, relevant information includes current independent appraisals of the value of all property to be transferred and offers received as part of an open and competitive bidding process.

5. Many state public universities are not subject to § 4958. The Regulations, § 53.4958–1(a)(2)(ii), exempt governmental entities and their affiliates from the provisions of § 4958. Thus, any public university that is a

governmental entity whose income is not taxed pursuant to § 115 of the Code is not subject to § 4958.

6. The IRS sought to impose penalties pursuant to § 4958 on trustees of the Bishop's Estate, which manages the Kamehameha Schools in Hawaii. The Bishop's Estate was created in 1884 upon the death of Princess Bernice Pauahi Bishop with assets and funds worth in excess of $1.2 billion. Trustees of the Estate lobbied members of Congress to prevent the enactment of § 4958. Trustees of the Estate had been paid annual salaries in excess of $900,000, and some had entered into conflict of interest transactions with the Estate that benefitted them substantially. The State Attorney General charged the trustees with gross mismanagement of the estate and petitioned a court to remove all the trustees. The Bishop's Estate signed a closing agreement with the IRS in 2002 wherein the Estate agreed to pay the IRS approximately $17 million (plus interest) allegedly to correct information from a previously filed tax return. Its for-profit subsidiaries agreed to pay the IRS approximately $55.5 million in taxes (plus interest) to settle all other tax matters. (See discussion in a book on the subject entitled *Broken Trust* by Samuel P. King and Randall W. Roth.)

Problem

The salary of the CEO of a nonprofit hospital is being renegotiated. Members of the hospital board propose to increase the CEO's annual salary from $600,000 to $900,000. The compensation package will include a housing allowance and the use of automobile. Members of a committee of the board have reviewed compensation packages for CEOs of hospitals in surrounding communities and have concluded that the compensation package they are proposing would not provide the CEO with an "excess benefit." The CEO asks you, her attorney, to give her a written opinion that the proposed compensation package will not cause her to be penalized under § 4958. Discuss whether or not you could give her such a written opinion. How would you draft your opinion?

Chapter 4

CHARITABLE ORGANIZATIONS

I. BACKGROUND

Since its initial enactment, the Internal Revenue Code has continuously recognized that some organizations should not to be subject to income taxes. [See I.R.C. §§ 401(a), 501(c)(1)–(27), 501(d)–(f), (k), (n), 521, 526–528.] Without doubt, the most important are charitable organizations exempt under § 501(c)(3). More than one-half of all tax-exempt organizations are § 501(c)(3) organizations. [The IRS Data Book Publication Table 22, indicates that of the 1.7 million tax-exempt organizations, 1,045,979 are exempt under § 501(c)(3).]

There are four principal reasons for the importance of § 501(c)(3) organizations. The obvious first reason is that charitable organizations, like all tax-exempt organizations, are not required to pay income taxes. This benefit, however, is more apparent than real. Many § 501(c)(3) organizations do not have taxable income, at least in meaningful amounts. Boris Bittker, one of the most famous and insightful tax professors made this argument in his and George Rahdert's often cited article "The Exemption of Nonprofit Organizations from Federal Income Taxation," 85 Yale L.J. 299 (1976).

The second reason is that a § 501(c)(3) may elect not to pay federal unemployment taxes. Again, this benefit cannot support the wide-spread acceptance of § 501(c)(3) organizations. For smaller organizations, the amount of the tax is not large; many larger § 501(c)(3) organizations choose to pay the tax as a fringe benefit for their employees.

The third reason is the principal basis for establishing a § 501(c)(3) organization. Donors to such organizations are permitted to deduct the amount of their gifts. (See discussion in Chapter 8.) Moreover, most private foundations and governmental agencies will make grants only to § 501(c)(3) organizations. Thus, a § 501(c)(3) exemption is a fund-raising device.

The final reason concerns state taxation. Most states exempt from taxation organizations that have § 501(c)(3) status. Still, like the exemption from federal income taxes, this benefit, alone, does not justify the importance of a § 501(c)(3) exemption for charitable organizations.

The special status given to charitable organizations is as old as taxation itself. (See James McGovern, "The Exemption Provisions of Subchapter F," 29 Tax Law Rev. 527 (1976).) In fact, charities have always held a special place within our legal system as a whole. In spite of, or perhaps because of, this recognition no general theory supporting tax exemption for charities has evolved. Rather, several theories have been articulated to defend exemption from taxation for charities. See Rob Atkinson, "Theories of the Federal Income Tax Exemption for Charities: Thesis, Antithesis, and Synthesis, 18 Stetson L.Rev. 395, 402–424, in which Professor Atkinson surveys these theories.

II. SECTION 501(c)(3) ELEMENTS

To attain tax exempt status under § 501(c)(3), an organization must satisfy five statutory elements:

1. The organization must be a corporation, community chest, fund, or foundation. This element is discussed in Chapters 1 and 2.

2. and 3. The organization must be (a) organized and (b) operated exclusively for charitable purposes. These two elements are the topics of this chapter.

4. The organization must not violate the private inurement prohibition. This element is discussed in the next chapter.

5. The organization may not be an action organization. This element also is discussed in the next chapter.

Case law has added a sixth requirement. An organization must not violate public policy. This requirement is discussed in the next chapter.

III. ORGANIZATIONAL AND OPERATIONAL TESTS

The basic difference between the organizational and operational tests is timing. The organizational test measures the organization's purpose, as stated in its enabling documents, to determine whether those stated purposes are charitable in nature. The operational test considers the organization's conduct in attempting to fulfill its charitable objectives. Thus, the operational test looks to the organization's activities and compares them to its stated purposes. It questions whether those activities are in furtherance of the charitable purpose stated in the organization's enabling documents.

The Internal Revenue Service decides whether an organization has satisfied the organizational test by reviewing the organization's enabling documents, usually its articles of incorporation or trust agreement. Generally, the IRS's position is that it will not look beyond the organization's articles. [See Treas. Reg. § 1.501(c)(3)–1(b)(1)(i) and Internal Revenue Manual § 3.1.4(2).] Some courts, however, have permitted evidence from other documents, such as bylaws, or activities. [See

Dillingham Transp. v. United States, 146 F.Supp. 953 (Ct.Cl.1957); *Samuel Friedland Foundation v. United States,* 144 F.Supp. 74 (D.N.J. 1956); *Colorado State Chiropractic Soc'y v. Commissioner,* 93 T.C. 487 (1989).]

An entity's articles must state that the organization is organized exclusively for charitable purposes under § 501(c)(3) and must not permit the organization to engage in substantial activities that do not further the organization's stated purposes. [Treas. Reg. § 1.501(c)(3)-1(b)(1)(i).] The articles may be as general as stating that the organization is organized for charitable purposes under § 501(c)(3) or may be very specific, so long as the purposes detailed are not broader that those permitted under § 501(c)(3). [Treas. Reg. § 1.501(c)(3)-1(b)(1)(ii).] The articles also should have clauses that preclude the organization from violating the private inurement prohibition, prevent it from becoming an action corporation, and comply with the private foundation rules. These provisions will be discussed in chapters 5 and 7.

When an organization applies for tax exemption, usually only the organizational test is applicable. The organization has not been operating long enough for the IRS to determine whether the operational test has been met. Thus, the operational test is normally the basis for revocation of an organization's exempt status, assuming that the organization has met the organizational test. The different reasons for violating the operational test are covered in the next chapter.

In determining whether an organization has satisfied the organization and operational tests, the IRS ask two questions: Is the organization pursuing a *charitable purpose* and is the organization pursuing that purpose *exclusively*?

The following case, *Better Business Bureau,* is the leading decision defining "exclusively." Although the case addressed the exemption from the requirement to pay social security tax, the Court's analysis applies equally to tax exemption under § 501(c)(3).

BETTER BUSINESS BUREAU v. UNITED STATES
United States Supreme Court, 1945
326 U.S. 279, 66 S.Ct. 112, 90 L.Ed. 67

Mr. Justice MURPHY delivered the opinion of the Court.

Here our consideration is directed to the question of whether the petitioner, the Better Business Bureau of Washington, D.C., Inc., is exempt from social security taxes as a corporation organized and operated exclusively for scientific or educational purposes within the meaning of Section 811(b)(8) of the Social Security Act.

From the stipulated statement of facts it appears that petitioner was organized in 1920 as a non-profit corporation under the laws of the District of Columbia. It has no shares of stock and no part of its earnings inures to the benefit of any private shareholder or individual. Its officers are elected annually from its membership; they have merely nominal duties and are paid no salary. Only the managing director and a small number of employees are paid. Membership is open to 'any person, firm, corporation or association interested in better business ethics' as may be elected by the board of trustees and pay 'voluntary subscriptions' or dues. The charter of petitioner states that "the object for which it is formed is for the mutual welfare, protection and improvement of business methods among merchants and other persons engaged in any and all business or professions and occupations of every description whatsoever that deal directly or indirectly with the public at large, and for the educational and scientific advancements of business methods among persons, corporations or associations engaged in business in the District of Columbia so that the public can obtain a proper, clean, honest and fair treatment in its dealings or transactions with such merchants, tradesmen, corporations, associations or persons following a profession and at the same time protecting the interest of the latter classes of businesses to enable such as are engaged in the same to successfully and profitably conduct their business and for the further purpose of endeavoring to obtain the proper, just, fair and effective enforcement of the Act of Congress approved May 29th, 1916 (39 Stat. 165), otherwise known as 'An Act to prevent fraudulent advertising in the District of Columbia.'"

In carrying out its charter provisions, petitioner divides its work roughly into five subdivisions:

(1) Prevention of fraud by informing and warning members and the general public of the plans and schemes of various types of swindlers.

(2) Fighting fraud by bringing general and abstract fraudulent practices to the attention of the public.

(3) Elevation of business standards by showing and convincing merchants that the application of 'the doctrine of caveat emptor is not good business' and by showing and convincing them that misleading advertising, extravagant claims and price comparisons are not good business.

(4) Education of consumers to be intelligent buyers.

(5) Cooperation with various governmental agencies interested in law enforcement.

Information which the petitioner compiles is available to anyone without charge and is communicated to the members and the public by means of the radio, newspapers, bulletins, meetings and interviews. This information is also exchanged with the approximately eighty-five other Better Business Bureaus in the United States.

After paying the social security taxes for the calendar years 1937 to 1941, inclusive, petitioner filed claims for refunds, which were disallowed. This suit to recover the taxes paid was then filed by petitioner in the District Court, which granted a motion for summary judgment for the United States. The court below affirmed the judgment, 79 U.S.App.

D.C. 380, 148 F.2d 14, and we granted certiorari, the Tenth Circuit Court of Appeals having reached a contrary result in Jones v. Better Business Bureau of Oklahoma City, 10 Cir., 123 F.2d 767.

Petitioner claims that it qualifies as a corporation 'organized and operated exclusively for * * * scientific * * * or educational purposes * * * no part of the net earnings of which inures to the benefit of any private shareholder or individual' within the meaning of Section 811(b)(8) of the Social Security Act and hence is exempt from payment of social security taxes. No serious assertion is made, however, that petitioner is devoted exclusively to scientific purposes. The basic contention is that all of its purposes and activities are directed toward the education of business men and the general public. Merchants are taught to conduct their businesses honestly, while consumers are taught to avoid being victimized and to purchase goods intelligently. We join with the courts below in rejecting this contention.

It has been urged that a liberal construction should be applied to this exemption from taxation under the Social Security Act in favor of religious, charitable and educational institutions. Cf. Trinidad v. Sagrada Orden de Predicatores De La Provincia Del Santisimo Rosario de Filipinas, 263 U.S. 578, 44 S.Ct. 204, 68 L.Ed. 458; Helvering v. Bliss, 293 U.S. 144, 55 S.Ct. 17, 79 L.Ed. 246, 95 A.L.R. 207. But it is unnecessary to decide that issue here. Cf. Hassett v. Associated Hospital Service Corporation of Massachusetts, 1 Cir., 125 F.2d 611. Even the most liberal of constructions does not mean that statutory words and phrases are to be given unusual or tortured meanings unjustified by legislative intent or that express limitations on such an exemption are to be ignored. Petitioner's contention, however, demands precisely that type of statutory treatment. Hence it cannot prevail.

In this instance, in order to fall within the claimed exemption, an organization must be devoted to educational purposes exclusively. This plainly means that the presence of a single non-educational purpose, if substantial in nature, will destroy the exemption regardless of the number or importance of truly educational purposes. It thus becomes unnecessary to determine the correctness of the educational characterization of petitioner's operations, it being apparent beyond dispute that an important if not the primary pursuit of petitioner's organization is to promote not only an ethical but also a profitable business community. The exemption is therefore unavailable to petitioner.

The commercial hue permeating petitioner's organization is reflected in its corporate title and in the charter provisions dedicating petitioner to the promotion of the 'mutual welfare, protection and improvement of business methods among merchants' and others and to the securing of the 'educational and scientific advancements of business methods' so that merchants might 'successfully and profitably conduct their business.' Petitioner's activities are largely animated by this commercial purpose. Unethical business practices and fraudulent merchandising schemes are investigated, exposed and destroyed. Such efforts to cleanse the business system of dishonest practices are highly commendable and may even serve incidentally to educate certain persons. But they are directed fundamentally to ends other than that of education. Any claim that education is the sole aim of petitioner's organization is thereby destroyed. See Better Business Bureau v. District Unemployment Compensation Board, D.C.Mun.App., 34 A.2d 614.

Finally, a Treasury regulation defining an educational organization as 'one designed primarily for the improvement or development of the capabilities of the individual' for purposes of Section 101(6) of the Internal Revenue Code was in effect at the time when Congress used that section in framing Section 811(b)(8) of the Social Security Act. An identical definition has been promulgated under Section 811(b)(8) and petitioner admittedly does not meet its terms. Under the circumstances the administrative definition is 'highly relevant and material evidence of the probable general understanding of the times and of the opinions of men who probably were active in the drafting of the statute.' White v. Winchester Country Club, 315 U.S. 32, 41, 62 S.Ct. 425, 430, 86 L.Ed. 619. It lends persuasive weight to the conclusion we have reached. Article 101(6)–1 of Treasury Regulations 86. Article 12 of Treasury Regulations 91; Section 402.215 of Treasury Regulations 106. The definition further states that 'under exceptional circumstances' an educational organization 'may include an association whose sole purpose is the instruction of the public, or an association whose primary purpose is to give lectures on subjects useful to the individual and beneficial to the community, even though an association of either class has incidental amusement features.' No 'exceptional circumstances' are apparent in petitioner's case and, moreover, neither exceptional category fits the petitioner.

For the foregoing reasons the judgment of the court below is affirmed.

* * *

Questions

1. Exclusively commonly means solely. Is that the definition the Supreme Court gave to the word? Does "exclusively" *plainly* mean that the presence of a substantial non-exempt purpose destroys the exemption? Pay special attention to the eighth paragraph in *Better Business Bureau*. See Treas. Reg. § 1.501(c)(3)–1(c)(1), which defines "exclusively" as meaning "primarily." Primarily, however, means principally, inferring that there are other factors. Why do the Supreme Court and the regulations give a less restrictive meaning to the Code's requirement?

2. Assuming that Better Business Bureau had two purposes, were not both exempt purposes? This question should draw your attention to the difference between a § 501(c)(3) purpose and other § 501 exempt purposes.

3. The test commonly posited for the application of the exclusivity requirement is that an organization may not engage more than insubstantially in activities that do not further its charitable purposes. Treas. Reg.

§ 1.501(c)(3)–1(c)(1). See Universal Life Church, Inc. v. United States, 13 Cl.Ct. 567 (1987), *aff'd without opinion,* 862 F.2d 321 (Fed.Cir.1988) and Church by Mail, Inc. v. Commissioner, 765 F.2d 1387 (9th Cir.1985). Does "exclusively" really mean "substantially?"

IV. THE CHARITABLE PURPOSE TEST

Section 501(c)(3) lists the following purposes as exempt purposes: religious, charitable, scientific, testing for public safety, literary, educational, fostering national or international amateur sports competition, and preventing cruelty to children or animals. Treasury Regulations then interpret "charitable" according to its generally accepted legal meaning. Charitable includes relief of the poor and distressed or the underprivileged, advancement of religion or education or science, erecting and maintenance of public buildings, the lessening of the burdens or the government, and the promotion of social welfare. [See Treas. Reg. § 1.501(c)(3)–1(d)(2).]

The regulations borrow from the Restatement, Second, of Trusts § 358, which includes the generally accepted meaning of a charitable purpose. Section 358 includes the following as charitable purposes: relief of poverty, advancement of education and religion, promotion of health, governmental purposes, and purposes that benefit the community. The one Restatement purpose not in the regulations is the promotion of health. Health, however, has been accepted as charitable for purposes under § 501(c)(3). (See Rev. Rul. 69–545, 1969–2 C.B. 117.) Because of the expansive definition of "charity," it is common to classify all § 501(c)(3) purposes as charitable purposes. Chapters 10, 11, and 12 analyze educational, religious and health purposes more specifically. This chapter provides a conceptual framework for all § 501(c)(3) ("charitable") purposes.

All § 501(c)(3) purposes have in common the notion that they benefit the community ("community benefit" standard) and do not serve private interests more than incidentally.

Compare the following two cases. Why is the Monterey Parking Corporation exempt, while the Columbia Park and Recreation Association is not?

MONTEREY PUBLIC PARKING CORP. v. UNITED STATES

District Court, Northern District, California, 1970
321 F.Supp. 972

WOLLENBERG, District Judge.

This is an action for a refund of moneys paid as corporation income taxes for the years 1964, 1965, and 1967 * * * Most briefly summarized * * * plaintiff is a non-profit California corporation operating solely in the city of Monterey. It was formed in late1962 for the purpose of constructing and operating a public automobile off-street parking facility. Prior to plaintiff's incorporation, there had been considerable discussion by city authorities and private groups concerning the need for parking facilities in the central business district of Monterey. Like many older cities, Monterey was faced with the impending decay of center-city neighborhoods rendered crowded and uncomfortable by narrow streets; increasing vehicular traffic, and a lack of off-street parking facilities. Monterey's municipal government, in the opinion of many, could not expeditiously finance and construct needed parking facilities, and as a result several private business and professional persons organized plaintiff corporation. Plaintiff negotiated leases, demolished certain structures, and put up a parking lot which is open to the use of the public. A validation stamp system had been set up, allowing the rental of parking spaces for some seven cents per hour less than cash rates. Any business or private person can take advantage of these special rates.

The income which defendants claim should be the subject of taxation arose in 1964, 1965, and 1967. By far the largest yearly income to plaintiff was that realized in 1964, when it leased back a portion of its lot to the Monterey Savings and Loan Association. The consideration for this arrangement totaled some $30,000, and the parties agree that this is a 'non-recurrent type of income' * * * 'Taxable' income for the other relevant years was $2,462.47 (1965) and $1,725.68 (1967) * * *

Plaintiff does not argue that it is an exempt organization as defined in 26 U.S.C. § 501(c)(6), i.e. the section referring to 'business leagues, chambers of commerce, real-estate boards, boards of trade, (etc)'. Rather, plaintiff contends that its right to exemption may be grounded in either § 501(c)(3)(a corporation organized exclusively for religious or charitable purposes) or § 501(c)(4) (a civic organization not organized for profit but operated exclusively for the promotion of social welfare). Section 501(c)(4) of the Internal Revenue Code provides an exemption from federal income taxes for 'civic leagues or organizations not organized for profit but operated exclusively for the promotion of social welfare'. Plaintiff's initial application for exemption was based on this section. The Internal Revenue Service denied this application, however, basing itself upon applicable regulations interpreting the key phrase, 'not organized for profit'. Said regulations bar exemption for organizations whose 'primary activity is * * * carrying on a business with the general pubic in a manner similar to organizations which are operated for profit'. Regulations § 1.501(c)(4)–1. Section 501(c)(3) of the Code provides an alternate basis for organizational exemption from income taxes. 'Corporations * * * organized and operated exclusively for * * * charitable * * * purposes * * * no part of the earnings of which inures to the benefit of any private shareholder or individual (shall be exempt under 501(a))'. . .

Defendant's opposition to the § 501(c)(3) claim does not center on Plaintiff's asserted operation of a profit-making business, since the 'not operated for profit' language of § 501(c)(4) does not appear in § 501(c)(3). Rather, it is argued that the totality of the circumstances herein indicate that 'more than an insubstantial part of its activities is not in furtherance of an exempt purpose.' Regulations § 1.501(c)(3)–1. The government asserts that the primary, or at least a substantial, goal of plaintiff corporation is to encourage the general public to patronize those businesses which participate in plaintiff's validation stamp system. This, it is said, constitutes a direct private benefit to certain individuals, with only an incidental benefit to the public.

The tenor of the government's argument is that each of the claimed grounds for exemption must be considered separately from the other. The Court, as regards the 'charitable organization' ground of § 501(c)(3), is asked to consider whether the stamp validation system and the circumstances surrounding Plaintiff's operation indicate a substantial non-exempt purpose. Insofar as the 'social welfare organization' exemption under § 501(c)(4) is concerned, the government contends that plaintiff's operation of a commercial enterprise, i.e., a fee-charging parking facility, constitutes a per se bar to exemption.

The Court finds that the distinction between the two subsections of § 501 is more apparent than real. It is true that applicable regulations seem to allow the carrying on of a business for profit by a (c)(3) organization, while barring such operations for (c)(4) organizations. The Regulations are, of course, given considerable weight by the Courts. But the Regulations must be seen in light of applicable case law, which, in this area at least, has concentrated more on the philosophy behind § 501 as a whole, rather than on variations in the language employed in each subsection thereof. * * *

Thus, if this Court were convinced that plaintiff's organizers, by giving themselves special advertising rights, or by restricting the validation stamp system to certain businesses, were in fact primarily interested in their own ends rather than in those of the public, exemption under neither (c)(4) nor (c)(3) would be possible. Similarly, the operation of a commercial enterprise not in furtherance of an exempt purpose would bar consideration under both subsections. In short, the Regulations aim at discovering whether asserted civic or charitable ends are but subterfuges for what is fundamentally a private enterprise. If they are not, the case law under both subsections has made it clear that they will not destroy the exemption claimed . . . * * *

This Court cannot say that plaintiff corporation, organizationally or operationally, subserves, in any substantial way, private interests. There is no question that all but one of plaintiff's organizers were businessmen whose establishments would tend to suffer if the traffic problems of downtown Monterey were not soon resolved. Customers, finding themselves unable to find convenient parking, would avoid the center city in favor of suburban shopping centers. But this was a threat not only to plaintiffs, but to all the City of Monterey, and the deliberations of the City Council so state.

The City of Monterey, therefore, was the primary beneficiary when plaintiff succeeded in constructing public parking facilities without any significant outlay of public funds. The provision of public parking can clearly be regarded as a burden of local government, and when this is accomplished by private individuals, this burden is lessened within the meaning of Regulation § 1.501(c)(3)–1. It also results in the promotion of social welfare within the intendment of Regulation § 1.501(c)(4)–1. * * *

Plaintiff's organizers were also undeniable benefitted. But this benefit is indistinguishable from that which inhered to the community as a whole. Their profits may have been enhanced or maintained as customers continued to shop in the downtown area, but this observation applies equally to the profits of all downtown businessmen, to the property values of all property owners there, and to the value of the tax base of the entire City of Monterey. The validation stamp system is available to all persons and businesses, not just to the organizers. No profits, direct or indirect, and no advertising advantages have accrued to plaintiff's organizers which have not also accrued to non-organizers. The Court therefore finds that the benefits to plaintiff's organizers do not constitute a substantial non-exempt purpose under either of the subsections of § 501 invoked herein.

Nor under either subsection is the simple conduct of a business fatal to exemption. What is crucial is the manner of such conduct. If dividends are paid to the members or shareholders of the organization, the Courts will ignore protestations of charitable intent * * * Or if there is substantial possibility that upon dissolution, accumulated assets will find their way into private hands, exemption is barred. Regulations § 1.501(c)(3)–1(b)(4). Likewise unqualified for exemption under either subsection are corporations which carry on commercial enterprises which are unrelated to their charitable purposes; the fact that profits therefrom are later fed into an exempt organization is not relevant ... Further examples of the kind of conduct which is deemed to run counter to the general philosophy of the § 501 exemption include the unreasonable accumulation of income or surpluses * * *; and the restriction of corporate services and benefits to members of the exempt group ...

Plaintiff's manner of operation is not such as to run afoul of any of the above specific examples of conduct deemed to be for private gain rather than public good. Plaintiff, by its articles of incorporation and by-laws, restricted itself to aiding and assisting the City of Monterey in establishing and operating public parking facilities ... All future profits have been given over to, and accepted by, the City of and are to be used for further such facilities ... Upon dissolution, 'remaining assets shall be distributed to a nonprofit fund, foundation (ect.) organized and operated exclusively for charitable, educational, religious, and/or scientific purposes and which has established its tax-exempt status under Section 501(c)(3) of the Internal Revenue Code' ... There is no indication of unreasonably accumulated surpluses, and, as noted above, there are no special benefits accruing to plaintiff's organizers which do not also accrue to the community as a whole.

In short, the preponderance of the evidence is that not only are plaintiff's tangible assets and profits devoted to exempt purposes, but also that the business itself 'obviously bears a close and intimate relationship' to those purposes ... Plaintiff has none of the indicia by which Courts have exposed bad faith attempts to take advantage of § 501: no dividends for private persons, no under the table distributions of assets, no advertising advantages or special prices for a privileged few. The business activity itself is similar to that which others engage in for private profit, but it is not carried on in the same manner; it is carried on only because it is necessary for the attainment of an undeniably public end.

Accordingly, the Court finds that plaintiff qualifies for exemption from federal income taxes both as a charitable corporation under § 501(c)(3) and as a social welfare organization under § 501(c)(4) of the Internal Revenue Code, 26 U.S.C.

Note

In affirming the District Court, 481 F.2d 175, the Ninth Court of Appeals stated:

> The District Court made a quantitative comparison of the private versus the public benefits derived from the organization and operation of the plaintiff corporation. Thereby, it was determined that the "social welfare" and "charitable purpose" requirements of the two respective sections were adequately fulfilled. We cannot disagree.

COLUMBIA PARK AND RECREATION ASS'N v. COMMISSIONER

United States Tax Court, 1987
88 T.C. 1

GERBER, JUDGE:

This is an action for declaratory judgment pursuant to section 7428. By a final adverse ruling dated March 21, 1984, respondent determined that petitioner is neither organized nor operated exclusively for exempt purposes within the meaning of section 501(c)(3). Petitioner invokes the jurisdiction of this Court and challenges respondent's adverse determination seeking a declaratory judgment.

The issue for our consideration is whether petitioner, a section 501(c)(4) organization, qualifies as a section 501(c)(3) charitable organization. * * *

OPINION

General Background

Columbia Park and Recreation Association, Inc. (petitioner or Association), was incorporated as a nonprofit organization under the laws of the State of Maryland on December 10, 1965. At the time its petition was filed, petitioner was located (had its 'principal place of business') in

Columbia, Maryland. Petitioner was created by the developers of Columbia, Howard Research and Development Corporation (the Development Corporation), as an integral part of Columbia.

Columbia (Columbia or the Development) is a large, private development of residential, commercial and industrial real property located in Howard County, Maryland. Columbia is an unincorporated part of Howard County and is not a political subdivision. The residents of Columbia look to Howard County as the lowest level of public governmental authority. The Development covers 14,600 acres with a projected 'full occupancy' population of approximately 110,000. Conceived as an experiment in city planning, Columbia is comprised of a number of residential villages which are designed to provide housing opportunities for high, moderate and low income groups. The master plan requires each village to be serviced by or provided with roads, utilities, facilities, amenities, and employment and industrial areas, all of which are crucial to the establishment of self-sufficient communities. Neighborhoods, which are components of villages, share common educational and recreational facilities concentrated around a centrally located retail, office and commercial core. The commercial core is composed of business and industrial property which overall represents about $130 million of the Development's $600 million assessable real property. Approximately 20 percent of the 14,600 acres (2,920 acres) is designated for industrial purposes.

The Development Corporation intended to and did develop Columbia as a community that offered a new living style: 'a job opportunity for every residence; a dwelling for every job situation: houses and apartments in a wide variety of size and cost, and a chance to live, work, shop and play in the same place * * *.' Petitioner was created in an effort to achieve some of these goals. Additionally, and in furtherance of these goals, the Development Corporation transferred 1,400 of Columbia's 14,600 acres to petitioner without receiving any consideration in exchange.

Petitioner's purposes as set forth in its Articles of Incorporation, are as follows:

THIRD: * * *

To organize and operate a civic organization which shall not be organized or operated for profit, but which shall be organized and operated exclusively for the promotion of the common good and social welfare of the people of the community of Columbia and its environs * * *.

* * *

For the general purpose aforesaid, and limited to that purpose * * *, the corporation shall have the following SPECIFIC purposes:

(1) To aid, promote, and provide for the establishment, advancement and perpetuation of any and all utilities, systems, services and facilities within Columbia which tend to promote the general welfare

of its people with regard to health, safety, education, culture, recreation, comfort or convenience to the extent and in the manner deemed desirable by the Board of Directors;

(2) To exercise all the rights, powers and privileges, and to perform all of the duties and interests of the Corporation * * *.

* * *

(5) To do any and all lawful things and acts that the Corporation may from time to time, in its discretion, deem to be FOR THE BENEFIT OF COLUMBIA AND THE INHABITANTS THEREOF or advisable, PROPER OR CONVENIENT FOR THE PROMOTION OF THE INTERESTS OF SAID INHABITANTS with regard to health, safety, education, culture, recreation, comfort or convenience. [Emphasis supplied.]

Facilities and Services

Petitioner owns and maintains pedestrian and bicycle pathways, parks and open-space areas, 15 neighborhood centers, 16 neighborhood pools, 4 village community centers, 2 tennis clubs, 10 tennis courts, 4 softball fields, a horse center, 2 athletic clubs, 2 golf courses, boat docks, an indoor swim complex, a children's zoo, an ice rink, a visual arts center, and a transportation system. The services offered include a free monthly magazine, a before and after-school program, a day care program, senior citizen activities, adult education, and a variety of community events and festivals. Of these facilities and services the following do not have user fees and are open to the public: Pathways, parks, open-space areas, swim complex, one golf course, tennis courts and community festivals. The transportation system is available for public use, but a fare is charged for its use. The system operates 8 buses on 9 routes within Columbia. Howard County has been instrumental in securing both state and Federal funding for the system, which constituted 60 percent of Columbia's 1982 operating budget. Howard County replaced the older buses with wheelchair-equipped buses to make the system more accessible.

The before and after-school program has been available in Columbia's 14 elementary schools since 1972. This program is designed to provide care and supervision on a regular basis for school-age children of parents residing in Columbia who either work, attend school or training programs, or have special needs. Children enrolled in the program must be registered, and fees paid one month in advance of attendance. The fee structure is based on operating a break-even service, including administrative overhead and an energy surcharge. Families may qualify for a half-price fee for this service.

Financing—Assessments, Fees and Debt

Part of the cost of providing the desired facilities and services is financed through liens and assessments on all real property in Columbia. The lien secures petitioner's right to collect assessments arising out of the requirement that every property owner pay an annual assessment at a rate not to exceed $.75 per $100 of 'assessed valuation.' Petitioner pledged its future assessment revenues to secure repayment of bonds issued to finance the construction of its facilities, and to cover its operating deficits. The assessment system is petitioner's principal source of revenue. The required annual assessment is embodied in the ownership of property in Columbia. This right to ownership carries an inherent right to use the facilities and services offered by petitioner. The payment of the assessed fees is the equivalent of a quid pro quo for the owner's right to use the facilities and services petitioner offers.

In addition to the assessment system, and as a major source of revenue, petitioner has developed a system of user fees. Under this system members pay a stated fee, generally set in excess of cost, for the use of some recreational facilities and services. The use of the terms 'member' or 'membership' does not denote any exclusivity as to who is eligible to participate in the user fees program. Residents of Columbia, whether owners or lessees of residential, commercial or industrial properties, are considered members of petitioner for purposes of sharing the services and facilities offered. Nonresidents may, however, become members of petitioner by paying the required user fees. Nonresidents of Columbia who are not employed in the Development pay a higher fee than residents, because petitioner's facilities and services are financially backed by the assessment system. Columbia's lower income families who are unable to pay the user fees may work in public service jobs to earn the use of these facilities through petitioner's Earn-a-Membership Program. In addition to its Earn-a-Membership Program, petitioner offers half-price membership to residents whose household income falls within certain guidelines. Residents and nonresidents alike may use the facilities designated as 'public' free of charge. Even though petitioner has incurred substantial operating losses, the level of income generated by assessments and recreational facilities has steadily increased, and it is anticipated that as the community develops, a sufficient level of revenues will be achieved to finance its operations and to meet its debt service requirements.

Petitioner has incurred substantial debt for construction and operation of its facilities. As of the fiscal year 1982 long-term debt totaled $45,647,000, an increase of $1,613,000 from 1981 long-term debt of $44,034,000. Of the 1982 long-term debt $39,121,000 (85.7 percent) was directly incurred to finance the facilities and services offered. Petitioner's 1982 debt service was $4,680,000 or 37.7 percent of total expenses.

Use of Funds and Revenues

All funds collected by petitioner must be applied as mandated by Article IV of the 'Deed, Agreement and Declaration of Covenants, Easements, Charges and Liens' (Declaration), which provides, as follows:

Use of Funds

Section 4.01. [Columbia Park and Recreation Association] shall apply all funds received by it pursuant to these Restrictions, and all other funds and property received by it from any source * * * to the following, pro tanto and in the order stated:

(i) the payment of all principal and interest, when due, on all loans borrowed by [Columbia Park and Recreation Association] * * *; (ii) the costs and expenses of [Columbia Park and Recreation Association]; and (iii) FOR THE BENEFIT OF THE PROPERTY, OWNERS AND RESIDENTS by devoting the same to the acquisition, construction, reconstruction, conduct, alteration, enlargement, laying, renewal, replacement, repair, maintenance, operation and subsidizing of such of the following as the Board, in its discretion, may from time to time any or all projects, services, facilities, studies, programs, systems and properties relating to: parks, recreational facilities or services; drainage systems; streets, roads, highways, walkways * * * and any and all other improvements, facilities and services that the Board shall find to be necessary, desirable or beneficial to the interest of the Property, Owners and Residents. [Emphasis supplied.]

* * *

Distribution of Petitioner's Assets in the Event of Dissolution

Petitioner's Articles of Incorporation provide that 'no member, director, or officer of the Corporation, or any private person shall be entitled to share in the distribution of the corporate assets upon dissolution of the Corporation or otherwise.' Article Five further provides:

(2) In the event of the liquidation or winding up of the Corporation (whether voluntary or involuntary) all of the assets of the Corporation (after payment of debts) shall be transferred to and contributed to and shall vest in (a) Howard County, Maryland, a body politic and corporate and a political subdivision of the State of Maryland, or the agency, subdivision or instrumentality of said County appropriate to take title to each of such assets, or (b) any of the Associations or other non-profit civic organizations which are devoted to the social welfare of Columbia or a part thereof as the Board of Directors shall determine.

Moreover, the Declaration provides that petitioner shall have the power to assign its rights created under the Declaration to any successor non-profit membership corporation, and upon such assignment the successor corporation shall have all the rights and be subject to all the duties of petitioner. It further provides:

If for any reason [Columbia Park and Recreation Association] shall cease to exist without having first assigned its rights hereunder to a Successor Corporation, the covenants, easements, charges and liens imposed hereunder shall nevertheless continue and any Owner may petition a court of competent jurisdiction to have a trustee appointed for the purpose of organizing a non-profit membership corporation and assigning the rights of [Columbia Park and Recreation Association] hereunder with the same force and effect, and subject to the same conditions, as provided in this Section 7.04 with respect to an assignment and delegation by [Columbia Park and Recreation Association] to a Successor Corporation.

Procedural History

Petitioner sought exemption from Federal income tax under section 501(a), which was granted on November 24, 1970, based on respondent's determination that it qualified as a social welfare organization within the meaning of section 501(c)(4). Petitioner now believes that it is more appropriately described as a charitable organization within the meaning of section 501(c)(3), and seeks tax-exempt status as such. On October 22, 1982, the Association submitted its Form 1023, Application for Recognition of Exemption, to the District Director of the Internal Revenue Service, Baltimore, Maryland. After exchanges of written materials and a conference on July 28, 1983, petitioner exhausted its administrative remedies to respondent's initial adverse determination. Respondent then issued a final adverse ruling on March 21, 1984, denying petitioner section 501(c)(3) status. The reasons for respondent's determination were stated as follows:

> You are neither organized nor operated exclusively for exempt purposes as required by section 501(c)(3). You do not satisfy the organizational test because your organizing instrument does not limit your purposes to exempt ones within the meaning of section 501(c)(3 and your assets are not permanently dedicated to exempt purposes within the meaning of section 501(c)(3). Further, you do not satisfy the operational test because you possess enforcement and regulatory powers of a governmental nature. In addition, you are operated in furtherance of a substantial non-exempt purpose because you serve private interests.

Respondent's final adverse ruling has no effect upon the Association's current section 501(c)(4) status.

Legal Discussion

Petitioner's central motivation in seeking section 501(c)(3) qualification is to become eligible to use the proceeds of tax-exempt bonds which might be issued for its benefit by Howard County, or by any other instrumentality of the State of Maryland. Petitioner has the burden of proof and must demonstrate that respondent's determination is erroneous. Hancock Academy of Savannah, Inc. v. Commissioner, 69 T.C. 488 (1977); Rule 217(c)(2)(I).

Section 501(c)(3) provides, in relevant part, that an organization shall be exempt from taxation under section 501(a) if the organization is organized and operated exclusively for certain specified exempt purposes, if no part of its net earnings inures to the benefit of a private shareholder or individual, and if no substantial part of its activities consists of political or lobbying activities. * * * These requirements are stated in the conjunctive; failure to satisfy any one of them is fatal to qualification under section 501(c)(3). * * *

The requirement that the organization be 'organized and operated exclusively for an exempt purpose' involves two mutually exclusive tests: (1) The organizational test and (2) the operational test, both of which must be satisfied. See sec. 1.501(c)(3)–1(a)(1), (b) and (c), Income Tax Regs. * * * To satisfy the organizational test, the articles of organization must limit the organization's purpose to one or more exempt purposes and not expressly empower such organization to engage, except insubstantially, in activities which do not further its exempt purpose. Sec. 1.501(c)(3)–1(b)(1), Income Tax Regs. The existence, therefore, of a substantial nonexempt purpose is fatal to section 501(c)(3) qualification. Better Business Bureau v. United States; 326 U.S. 279 (1945); Moreover, an organization will not qualify as being 'organized exclusively for one or more exempt purposes' unless its assets are dedicated to an exempt purpose. Sec. 1.501(c)(3)-1(b)(4), Income Tax Regs. Section 1.501(c)(3)-1(b)(4), Income Tax Regs., provides in pertinent part:

> An organization's assets will be considered dedicated to an exempt purpose, for example, if, upon dissolution, such assets would, by reason of a provision in the organization's articles or by operation of law, be distributed for one or more exempt purposes, or to the Federal government, or to a State or local government, for a public purpose, or would be distributed by a court to another organization to be used in such manner as in the judgment of the court will best accomplish the general purposes for which the dissolved organization was organized. However, an organization does not meet the organizational test if its articles or the law of the State in which it was created provide that its assets would, upon dissolution, be distributed to its members or shareholders.

Respondent argues that petitioner fails the organizational test, in part, because its Articles do not limit its purpose to an exempt purpose within the meaning of section 501(c)(3) and that petitioner serves a substantial nonexempt purpose that is expressly permitted by its Articles. Respondent also argues that petitioner fails the organizational test because of its 'distribution of assets on dissolution' provision. Petitioner, on the other hand, argues that it meets the organizational test because its Articles limit its purpose to a charitable purpose within the meaning of section 501(c)(3). Petitioner further contends that its Articles do not permit and it does not substantially engage in activities which do not further an exempt purpose. Additionally, petitioner argues that its 'distribution of assets on dissolution' provision qualifies under the organizational test. After careful examination of the administrative record, we agree with respondent.

Sec. IV **THE CHARITABLE PURPOSE TEST** 193

ORGANIZATIONAL TEST
CHARITABLE PURPOSE WITHIN THE MEANING OF SEC. 501(c)(3)

Respondent contends that petitioner was created, as set forth in its Articles, for the purpose of providing substantial recreational facilities and community services to its property owners/members. This, respondent argues, is not an exempt purpose within the meaning of section 501(c)(3. We agree.

Petitioner takes the position that because it qualifies as a social welfare organization within the meaning of section 501(c)(4) and is not an 'action' organization it must qualify as a charitable organization within the meaning of section 501(c)(3). Petitioner relies on section 1.501(c)(4)–1(a)(2), Income Tax Regs., as support for this argument. Petitioner's reliance is misplaced. Section 1.501(c)(4)–1(a)(2)(i), Income Tax Regs., provides in pertinent part that a social welfare organization within the meaning of section 501(c)(4) will qualify for exemption as a charitable organization if (1) IT FALLS WITHIN THE DEFINITION OF 'CHARITABLE' AS SET FORTH IN SECTION 1.501(c)(3)–1(d)(2), INCOME TAX REGS., and (2) is not an 'action' organization as set forth in section 1.501(c)(3)–1(c)(3), Income Tax Regs. Consequently petitioner must meet the definition of 'charitable' independently of its 'social welfare' status. Petitioner has failed in this regard.

Section 1.501(c)(3)–1(d)(2), Income Tax Regs., provides as follows:

'charitable' is used in section 501(c)(3) in its generally accepted legal sense and is, therefore, not to be construed as limited by the separate enumeration in section 501(c)(3) of other tax-exempt purposes which may fall within the broad outlines of 'charity' as developed by judicial decisions. Such term includes: Relief of the poor and distressed or of the underprivileged; advancement of religion; advancement of education or science; erection or maintenance of public buildings, monuments, or works; lessening of the burdens of Government; AND PROMOTION OF SOCIAL WELFARE BY ORGANIZATIONS DESIGNED TO ACCOMPLISH ANY OF THE ABOVE PURPOSES, OR (i) TO LESSEN NEIGHBORHOOD TENSIONS; (ii) TO ELIMINATE PREJUDICE AND DISCRIMINATION; (iii) TO DEFEND HUMAN AND CIVIL RIGHTS SECURED BY LAW; OR (iv) TO COMBAT COMMUNITY DETERIORATION AND JUVENILE DELINQUENCY. * * * [Emphasis supplied.]

Petitioner's interpretation of section 1.501(c)(3)–1(d)(2), Income Tax Regs., ignores the statutory language requiring that petitioner be created for and limited (except insubstantially) to one or more of the purposes enumerated therein. We find that petitioner's promotion of the social welfare of the people of Columbia does not accomplish any of the purposes enumerated in section 1.501(c)(3)–1(d)(2), Income Tax Regs.

The purpose for which an organization was created, as used in the organizational test, refers to the real substance and intent of the organization. * * * Accordingly, the purpose for which petitioner was created may be determined from examining its Articles and the circumstances surrounding its creation. This is a question of fact to be determined by the objectives motivating petitioner, as well as petitioner's subsequent conduct. * * * A careful reading of petitioner's Articles and a close examination of the surrounding circumstances do not support petitioner's argument that it was organized principally for a charitable purpose within the meaning of section 501(c)(3).

Petitioner's Articles provide that petitioner was created for the general purpose of promoting the common good and social welfare of the people of Columbia, in addition to the following specific purposes:

(1) To aid, promote; and provide for the establishment, advancement and perpetuation of any and all utilities, systems, services and facilities within Columbia which tend to promote the general welfare of its people with regard to health, safety, education, culture, RECREATION, COMFORT OR CONVENIENCE * * *;

(2) To exercise all the rights, powers and privileges AND TO PERFORM ALL OF THE DUTIES AND OBLIGATIONS OF THE CORPORATION * * *. [Emphasis supplied.]

We find these purposes to be substantially nonexempt within the meaning of section 501(c)(3).

Petitioner contends, that because of its size and diversity, its purpose must be understood from the benefit it provides through its overall operations. We have carefully considered the scope of petitioner's operations and agree that the magnitude of its operations cannot be ignored. The estimated 110,000 residents of Columbia represent a cross-section of economic, social, and racial classes. They are served by petitioner who integrates these different classes while nourishing human growth. This, however, is incidental to petitioner's primary purpose, which is to promote the common good and social welfare of the residents of Columbia. Petitioner is an integral part of the Development and was created to serve Columbia, its residents and property owners. As petitioner's Articles demonstrate, Columbia and its residents are the justification for petitioner's existence. Accordingly, any benefit to the community as a whole is merely incidental and relatively insubstantial. Columbia approximates the size of Manhattan, and has the second largest population in the State of Maryland. It is a new experiment in city planning where its developers sought to balance social goals and private profit. Columbia, despite its size, has remained a private development designed to offer its residents a new living style: a job opportunity for every resident; a dwelling for every job situation; houses and apartments in a wide variety of sizes and cost; and a chance to live, work, shop and play in the same place. This new lifestyle could not be offered in its entirety without the creation of petitioner or a similar organization. Indeed, petitioner was organized by the developers of Columbia as an integral part of the Development, and it so functions. Accordingly, we find that petitioner was created as the component necessary for molding the social and physical environment desired for the Development.

We emphasize that the term 'charity,' from a legal perspective, is comprised of four principal divisions: (1) Relief of poverty; (2) advancement of education; (3) advancement of religion; and (4) other purposes (not falling within any of the preceding divisions) that are beneficial to the public or the community at large. * * *

Petitioner contends that the size of the Development it benefits is so large that it qualifies under the 'catch all' category of 'charitable,' i.e., a benefit to the public or the community at large. In essence, petitioner argues that its size causes it to be inherently charitable. We find this argument unpersuasive. Petitioner benefits what is merely an aggregation of homeowners and tenants bound together in a structural unit formed as an integral part of a plan for the development of real estate. We do not perceive such a group of people as the 'community at large' within the 'charitable' context because it lacks a sufficient public element. To hold otherwise would negate the requirement that petitioner must serve a public rather than a private interest. Sec. 1.501(c)(3)–1(d)(1)(ii), Income Tax Regs.

Columbia was planned as a new town and is referred to as a city. We agree that Columbia resembles a city in both geographic size and population and that it operates, to a large extent, like a city. Nevertheless, Columbia has remained nothing more than a private development, albeit a massive one. We should not be guided merely by petitioner's size because qualitative not quantitative factors are more determinative of the charitable purpose of an organization. The size of an organization is meaningless if it is not fully integrated with a public element. Mere size does not transform an otherwise noncharitable, private organization to a 'charitable' one. If Columbia were a development of greatly reduced size with a small population, it would be easier to see why petitioner does not qualify as a 'charitable' organization within the meaning of section 501(c)(3). The results do not change with petitioner's size. To the extent that Columbia is owned and controlled by the homeowners and residents within its boundaries, free from any governmental or other outside influence, we find that it is an unusually large aggregation of private interests.

Were petitioner operating primarily for a public rather than private interest, the people financing its operation would not have a right, based upon property ownership, to receive the benefits it offers. On the contrary, once financed, petitioner would offer its facilities and service programs primarily to those in need regardless of their place of residence. Unlike the instant case, no quid pro quo exists in an organization that is operating primarily for a public purpose.

Another important factor which serves to undercut petitioner's position is the fact that petitioner's method of financing is dissimilar from typical public organizations. Petitioner does not solicit or receive voluntary contributions from the public. Rather, its source of revenue is from the members whom it serves. Petitioner thus lacks this normal trait of a section 501(c)(3) organization or, more specifically, an organization which operates primarily for a public interest.

Additionally, petitioner's facilities and services which are open to the public constitute a small percentage of petitioner's total assets and a rather limited percentage of petitioner's budget, in amounts approximately as follows: Columbus system—2 percent of revenues and 2-1/2 percent of expenditures; open-space areas, parks and pathways—1/2 percent of revenues and 6 percent of expenditures; community service programs, including before and after-school care and day care—3 percent of revenues and 2 percent of expenditures. Also negating petitioner's contention that it exists primarily to serve a public interest is the small number of families that qualify for reduced and earned membership fees. Columbia, with an estimated population of 110,000, has approximately: 190 families qualifying for one-half price membership; 50 families qualifying for 'earned membership' and 13 families approved for one-half price before and after-school care. Families of Howard County or, more broadly, the State of Maryland are not eligible for such reduced prices. A significant requirement is that such recipients be residents of Columbia. These facts reflect that petitioner's activities are substantially for the promotion and protection of the interest of its members; this is a substantial nonexempt purpose within the meaning of section 501(c)(3).

We note that Columbia may be able to avail itself of the very section 501(c)(3) tax benefits it seeks, by incorporation as a city. To do this, however, might divest petitioner and its members of the right to manage and control Columbia in accordance with their desires. Columbia cannot be a city for purposes of availing itself of tax benefits that were intended for organizations of a public nature and, at the same time, be a privately owned and controlled development. Petitioner is bound by the consequences of its choice. We do not find persuasive petitioner's argument that its charitable purpose is to lessen the burdens of government. Petitioner contends that it provides a wide range of services and facilities to the residents of Columbia which, in petitioner's absence, would have to be provided by the local or state government. We reject this argument. The mere assertion that, in petitioner's absence, government would have to assume the activities in question does not mean that the activities are in fact the burdens of government. See Child v. United States, 540 F.2d 579 (2d Cir.1976). Before petitioner can be classified as having the charitable purpose of lessening the burdens of government, it must demonstrate that the State of Maryland and/or Howard County accepts the activities conducted by petitioner as their responsibility and recognize petitioner as acting on their behalf. Petitioner must further establish that its activities actually lessen the burden of the state or local government. Petitioner has failed to so demonstrate, and has even advanced the argument that it does not act on the behalf of either the State of Maryland or Howard County. Neither does it possess any governmental power, delegated or otherwise. Petitioner cannot have its classification both ways: as a surrogate government for some purposes and the representative of a private development for others.

OPERATIONAL TEST

In further support of his adverse determination, respondent argues that petitioner fails the operational test because it engages primarily in activities that further a nonexempt purpose by substantially serving the private interest of its owners/members. Petitioner maintains that any benefit resulting to the residents of Columbia is merely incidental to the benefit to the community as a whole. We agree with respondent.

In order to satisfy the operational test an organization must engage extensively in activities which accomplish one or more of the exempt purposes specified in section 501(c)(3). Sec. 1.501(c)(3), Income Tax Regs; * * *. The existence of a substantial nonexempt purpose, even if coexisting with an exempt purpose, precludes qualification under section 501(c)(3). Sec. 1.501(c)(3)–1(c)(l), Income Tax Regs.; * * *. Whether the operational test has been satisfied is a question of fact. * * * We find that petitioner does not satisfy the operational test but rather operated for the substantial nonexempt purpose of providing comfort and convenience to Columbia's residents.

The user fees and the assessments each generate an estimated 48 percent of petitioner's total revenues. Approximately 33 percent of petitioner's expenditures is spent on maintaining and managing the recreational facilities, with an additional 38 percent expended to service the debt incurred primarily for the construction of these facilities. In contrast, various nonrecreational activities represent an approximate percentage of total revenue, as follows: Community service programs—3 percent; transportation—2 percent; community centers—2 percent; land management—less than 1 percent. Conversely, expenditures for maintenance of various activities represent an approximate percentage of total expenditures, as follows: Community centers—6 percent; community service programs—2 percent; transportation—3 percent; and open space—6 percent. Petitioner's pattern of expenditure is dictated by its Articles. Pursuant to the Articles, all funds must be expended primarily for the payment of all debt principal and interest due, petitioner's administrative costs and expenses, and for the benefit of the property, owners and residents of Columbia. The net effect of this is the maintenance of an organization that operates substantially for the benefit of the residents and property owners of Columbia.

Apparently, petitioner interprets the 'private benefit' element of section 1.501(c)(3)–1(c)(2), Income Tax Regs., to be present only if one of its Board members or officers derives some prohibited benefit. We disagree with this interpretation. Section 1.501(a)–1(c), Income Tax Regs., provides that a private interest exists if any person having a private or personal interest in petitioner's activities is the focus of petitioner's benefit.

We find it difficult to accept petitioner's contention that the residents and property owners do not have a personal interest in petitioner and the 'new life style' petitioner was organized to provide. Petitioner's operations are controlled by the residents and property owners of Columbia. In addition, residents' advisory committees participate in formulating petitioner's budget and defining its goals and policies. Moreover, a substantial number of petitioner's activities are solely for the purpose of providing the 'new life style' promised to the residents of the Development. We, therefore, find that the residents and property owners of Columbia are the intended beneficiaries of petitioner's facilities and services and that they have a personal interest in petitioner's activities.

The retail, office and commercial core of the Development was integrated into the master plan to provide the residents with the opportunity to 'work and shop' in the same place. Petitioner was incorporated to provide all the necessary facilities that would enable the residents to 'play' in the same place, thus, completing the new living style that was intended by the developers. Indeed, petitioner engages substantially in activities which provide for the comfort and convenience of the residents of Columbia to 'play' in the same community in which they live, shop and work. To hold otherwise would ignore the contents of the administrative record.

Not only is petitioner operated by the residents and property owners of the Development but it is also financed by them in return for the benefits petitioner makes available to them. About 96 percent of petitioner's revenues is supplied by the residents and property owners of Columbia from property assessments or fees paid for admission to facilities or programs. In exchange, petitioner constructed and maintains facilities valued at approximately $20 million to be used at all times for the benefit and common good of the residents of this commercial development. We cannot be oblivious to the fact that residents, property owners and employees of businesses located in Columbia must pay an admission fee to the facilities. We accord this little weight, however, because resident fees are lower than nonresident fees. The residents are considered to have paid the remaining portion through the assessment levied against their property.

Petitioner argues that the activities in which it engages have been held to be charitable in nature, and therefore it engages substantially in activities which qualify under section 501(c)(3). In support of its position, petitioner enumerates activities such as maintaining public parks and playgrounds, open-space areas, swimming pools and other recreational facilities preschool education public transportation, community centers municipal planning and safety, center for visual arts, senior citizen activities, recreational and athletic programs, lakes, and public meetings and forums. We agree that the activities in the cases and rulings cited by petitioner were held to be 'charitable' within the meaning of section 501(c)(3). Petitioner, however, overlooks a major qualifying element in all these cases. The activities were not found to be charitable per se. Rather, they qualified because the various organizations involved were found to be organized for a charitable purpose and such activities accomplished that purpose. Our holding that petitioner was not organized for a charitable purpose precludes the same result as the cited cases and rulings because without the exempt purpose the activities do not come within the 'charitable umbrella' of an exempt organization. In applying the operational test, the purpose towards which an organization's activities are directed, and not the nature of the activities, is determinative. * * *

Petitioner, in serving Columbia, does produce socially desirable results. Nonetheless, the scope of our consideration does not include a determination of the success or effectiveness of petitioner or Development, but to decide whether petitioner should be afforded the statutory privileges of section 501(c)(3) status. The tax relief to which petitioner is already entitled under section 501(a) is unaffected by our holding that respondent did not err in denying section 501(c)(3) status to petitioner.

An appropriate order will be entered.

Reviewed by the Court.

* * *

Questions

Are the two courts defining "social welfare" differently? Were the Monterey merchants not beneficiaries to the same extent as Columbia Park residents? What was the charitable purpose in *Monterey*?

Notes

1. Generally, a determination of whether an organization satisfies the community benefit standard depends on who the organization's beneficiaries are. If the organization's beneficiaries are indefinite and sufficiently large, the organization, assuming it satisfies the other tests for exemption, probably will have a charitable purpose.

2. The court followed *Columbia Park and Recreation Ass'n*, in *American Campaign Academy v. Commissioner*, 92 T.C. 1053 (1989), cited in Chapter 5. The Republican Party established the American Campaign Academy to train individuals to participate in political campaigns. The Tax Court decided that the purpose of the academy was to advance the interests of the Republican Party and ruled that such a limited purpose did not benefit the community at large.

V. SOCIAL WELFARE ORGANIZATIONS

Closely related to § 501(c)(3) is § 501(c)(4). You were introduced to that relationship in *Monterey Public Parking Corp.* and *Columbia Park*. Section 501(c)(4) exempts organizations that are operated "exclusively for the promotion of social welfare." As is the case with § 501(c)(3), "exclusively," for purposes of § 501(c)(4) means "primarily." [See Treas. Reg. § 1.501(c)(4)–1(a)(2)(I).] Recall that the definition of charity in § 501(c)(3) includes the promotion of social welfare. Thus, the question: What is the difference between a § 501(c)(3) organization and a § 501(c)(4) social welfare organization?

The regulations provide some help. First, they state that an organization, to promote social welfare, must further "in some way the common good and general welfare of the community." [Treas. Reg. § 1.501(c)(4)–1(a)(2).] Like § 501(c)(3), benefitting the community is the basic standard. Recognizing this, the regulations conclude that a § 501(c)(4) organization can also be a § 501(c)(3) organization so long as the organization is not involved in political activities. Thus, the difference between § 501(c)(3) and § 501(c)(4) is not the inherent definition of a social welfare purpose, but the consequences of choosing one or the other classification. Contributions to § 501(c)(3) organizations are deductible, but contributions to § 501(c)(4) organizations are not. On the other hand, a § 501(c)(4) organization may engage in political campaigns [Treas. Reg. § 1.501(c)(4)–1(a)(2)(ii)], while a § 501(c)(3) organization may not.

Taxation with Representation, which follows, upheld the constitutionality of the limitations against political activity by § 501(c)(3) organizations.

REGAN v. TAXATION WITH REPRESENTATION

United States Supreme Court, 1983
461 U.S. 540, 103 S.Ct. 1997, 76 L.Ed.2d 129

Justice REHNQUIST delivered the opinion of the Court.

Appellee Taxation With Representation of Washington (TWR) is a nonprofit corporation organized to promote what it conceives to be the "public interest" in the area of federal taxation. It proposes to advocate its point of view before Congress, the Executive Branch, and the Judiciary. This case began when TWR applied for tax exempt status under § 501(c)(3) of the Internal Revenue Code, 26 U.S.C. § 501(c)(3). The Internal Revenue Service denied the application because it appeared that a substantial part of TWR's activities would consist of attempting to influence legislation, which is not permitted by § 501(c)(3).

TWR then brought this suit in District Court against the appellants, the Commissioner of Internal Revenue, the Secretary of the Treasury, and the United States, seeking a declaratory judgment that it qualifies for the exemption granted by § 501(c)(3). It claimed the prohibition against substantial lobbying is unconstitutional under the First Amendment and the equal protection component of the Fifth Amendment's Due Process Clause. The District Court granted summary judgment for appellants. On appeal, the *en banc* Court of Appeals for the District of Columbia Circuit reversed, holding that § 501(c)(3) does not violate the First Amendment but does violate the Fifth Amendment. 219 U.S.App. D.C. 117, 676 F.2d 715 (C.A.D.C.1982). Appellants appealed pursuant to 28 U.S.C. § 1252, and TWR cross-appealed. We noted probable jurisdiction of the appeal, 459 U.S. 819, 103 S.Ct. 47, 74 L.Ed.2d 55 (1982).

TWR was formed to take over the operations of two other non-profit corporations. One, Taxation With Representation Fund, was organized to promote TWR's goals by publishing a journal and engaging in litigation; it had tax exempt status under § 501(c)(3). The other, Taxation

With Representation, attempted to promote the same goals by influencing legislation; it had tax exempt status under § 501(c)(4). Neither predecessor organization was required to pay federal income taxes. For purposes of our analysis, there are two principal differences between § 501(c)(3) organizations and § 501(c)(4) organizations. Taxpayers who contribute to § 501(c)(3) organizations are permitted by § 170(c)(2) to deduct the amount of their contributions on their federal income tax returns, while contributions to § 501(c)(4) organizations are not deductible. Section 501(c)(4) organizations, but not § 501(c)(3) organizations, are permitted to engage in substantial lobbying to advance their exempt purposes.

In this case, TWR is attacking the prohibition against substantial lobbying in § 501(c)(3) because it wants to use tax-deductible contributions to support substantial lobbying activities. To evaluate TWR's claims, it is necessary to understand the effect of the tax exemption system enacted by Congress.

Both tax exemptions and tax-deductibility are a form of subsidy that is administered through the tax system. A tax exemption has much the same effect as a cash grant to the organization of the amount of tax it would have to pay on its income. Deductible contributions are similar to cash grants of the amount of a portion of the individual's contributions. The system Congress has enacted provides this kind of subsidy to non profit civic welfare organizations generally, and an additional subsidy to those charitable organizations that do not engage in substantial lobbying. In short, Congress chose not to subsidize lobbying as extensively as it chose to subsidize other activities that non profit organizations undertake to promote the public welfare.

It appears that TWR could still qualify for a tax exemption under § 501(c)(4). It also appears that TWR can obtain tax deductible contributions for its non-lobbying activity by returning to the dual structure it used in the past, with a § 501(c)(3) organization for non-lobbying activities and a § 501(c)(4) organization for lobbying. TWR would, of course, have to ensure that the § 501(c)(3) organization did not subsidize the § 501(c)(4) organization; otherwise, public funds might be spent on an activity Congress chose not to subsidize.* * *

TWR contends that Congress' decision not to subsidize its lobbying violates the First Amendment. It claims, relying on *Speiser v. Randall*, 357 U.S. 513, 78 S.Ct. 1332, 2 L.Ed.2d 1460 (1958), that the prohibition against substantial lobbying by § 501(c)(3) organizations imposes an "unconstitutional condition" on the receipt of tax-deductible contributions. In *Speiser,* California established a rule requiring anyone who sought to take advantage of a property tax exemption to sign a declaration stating that he did not advocate the forcible overthrow of the Government of the United States. This Court stated that "[t]o deny an exemption to claimants who engage in speech is in effect to penalize them for the same speech." *Id.,* at 518, 78 S.Ct., at 1338.

TWR is certainly correct when it states that we have held that the government may not deny a benefit to a person because he exercises a constitutional right. * * * But TWR is just as certainly incorrect when it claims that this case fits the *Speiser-Perry* model. The Code does not deny TWR the right to receive deductible contributions to support its non-lobbying activity, nor does it deny TWR any independent benefit on account of its intention to lobby. Congress has merely refused to pay for the lobbying out of public monies. This Court has never held that the Court must grant a benefit such as TWR claims here to a person who wishes to exercise a constitutional right.

This aspect of the case is controlled by *Cammarano v. United States,* 358 U.S. 498, 79 S.Ct. 524, 3 L.Ed.2d 462 (1959), in which we upheld a Treasury Regulation that denied business expense deductions for lobbying activities. We held that Congress is not required by the First Amendment to subsidize lobbying. *Id.,* at 513, 79 S.Ct., at 533. In this case, like in *Cammarano,* Congress has not infringed any First Amendment rights or regulated any First Amendment activity. Congress has simply chosen not to pay for TWR's lobbying. We again reject the "notion that First Amendment rights are somehow not fully realized unless they are subsidized by the State." *Id.,* at 515, 79 S.Ct., at 534 (Douglas, J., concurring). * * *

We have already explained why we conclude that Congress has not violated TWR's First Amendment rights by declining to subsidize its First Amendment activities. The case would be different if Congress were to discriminate invidiously in its subsidies in such a way as to "'aim[ ] at the suppression of dangerous ideas.'" *Cammarano, supra,* 358 U.S., at 513, 79 S.Ct., at 533, quoting *Speiser, supra,* at 519, 78 S.Ct., at 1338. But the veterans' organizations that qualify under § 501(c)(19) are entitled to receive tax-deductible contributions regardless of the content of any speech they may use, including lobbying. We find no indication that the statute was intended to suppress any ideas or any demonstration that it has had that effect. The sections of the Internal Revenue Code here at issue do not employ any suspect classification. The distinction between veterans' organizations and other charitable organizations is not at all like distinctions based on race or national origin.

The Court of Appeals nonetheless held that "strict scrutiny" is required because the statute "*affect[s]* First Amendment rights on a discriminatory basis." * * * (emphasis supplied). Its opinion suggests that strict scrutiny applies whenever Congress subsidizes some speech, but not all speech. This is not the law. Congress could, for example, grant funds to an organization dedicated to combatting teenage drug abuse, but condition the grant by providing that none of the money received from Congress should be used to lobby state legislatures. Under *Cammarano,* such a statute would be valid. Congress might also enact a statute providing public money for an organization dedicated to combatting teenage alcohol abuse, and impose no condition against using funds obtained from Congress for lobbying. The existence of the second statute would not make the first statute subject to strict scrutiny.

Congressional selection of particular entities or persons for entitlement to this sort of largesse "is obviously a matter of policy and discretion not open to judicial review unless in circumstances which here we are not able to find. * * * For the purposes of this case appropriations are comparable to tax exemptions and deductions, which are also "a matter of grace [that] Congress can, of course, disallow ... as it chooses." *Commissioner v. Sullivan,* 356 U.S. 27, 78 S.Ct. 512, 2 L.Ed.2d 559 (1958).

These are scarcely novel principles. We have held in several contexts that a legislature's decision not to subsidize the exercise of a fundamental right does not infringe the right, and thus is not subject to strict scrutiny. *Buckley v. Valeo,* 424 U.S. 1, 96 S.Ct. 612, 46 L.Ed.2d 659 (1976), upheld a statute that provides federal funds for candidates for public office who enter primary campaigns, but does not provide funds for candidates who do not run in party primaries. We rejected First Amendment and equal protection challenges to this provision without applying strict scrutiny. *Id.,* at 93–108, 96 S.Ct., at 670–677. *Harris v. McRae,* 448 U.S. 297, 100 S.Ct. 2671, 65 L.Ed.2d 784 (1980), and *Maher v. Roe,* 432 U.S. 464, 97 S.Ct. 2376, 53 L.Ed.2d 484 (1977), considered legislative decisions not to subsidize abortions, even though other medical procedures were subsidized. We declined to apply strict scrutiny and rejected equal protection challenges to the statutes.

The reasoning of these decisions is simple: "although government may not place obstacles in the path of a [person's] exercise of ... freedom of [speech], it need not remove those not of its own creation." *Harris, supra,* 448 U.S., at 316, 100 S.Ct., at 2688. Although TWR does not have as much money as it wants, and thus cannot exercise its freedom of speech as much as it would like, the Constitution "does not confer an entitlement to such funds as may be necessary to realize all the advantages of that freedom." *Id.,* at 318, 100 S.Ct., at 2688. As we said in *Maher,* "[c]onstitutional concerns are greatest when the State attempts to impose its will by force of law...." 432 U.S., at 476, 97 S.Ct., at 2383. Where governmental provision of subsidies is not "aimed at the suppression of dangerous ideas," *Cammarano, supra,* 358 U.S., at 513, 79 S.Ct., at 533, its "power to encourage actions deemed to be in the public interest is necessarily far broader." *Maher, supra,* at 476, 97 S.Ct., at 2383.

We have no doubt but that this statute is within Congress' broad power in this area. TWR contends that § 501(c)(3) organizations could better advance their charitable purposes if they were permitted to engage in substantial lobbying. This may well be true. But Congress— not TWR or this Court—has the authority to determine whether the advantage the public would receive from additional lobbying by charities is worth the money the public would pay to subsidize that lobbying, and other disadvantages that might accompany that lobbying. It appears that

Congress was concerned that exempt organizations might use tax-deductible contributions to lobby to promote the private interests of their members. See 78 Cong.Rec. 5861 (1934) (remarks of Senator Reed); *Id.*, at 5959 (remarks of Senator La Follette). It is not irrational for Congress to decide that tax exempt charities such as TWR should not further benefit at the expense of taxpayers at large by obtaining a further subsidy for lobbying.

It is also not irrational for Congress to decide that, even though it will not subsidize substantial lobbying by charities generally, it will subsidize lobbying by veterans' organizations. Veterans have "been obliged to drop their own affairs and take up the burdens of the nation," *Boone v. Lightner,* 319 U.S. 561, 575, 63 S.Ct. 1223, 1231, 87 L.Ed. 1587 (1943), "subjecting themselves to the mental and physical hazards as well as the economic and family detriments which are peculiar to military service and which do not exist in normal civil life." *Johnson v. Robison,* 415 U.S. 361, 380, 94 S.Ct. 1160, 1172, 39 L.Ed.2d 389 (1974). Our country has a long standing policy of compensating veterans for their past contributions by providing them with numerous advantages. * * * This policy has "always been deemed to be legitimate." *Personnel Administrator v. Feeney,* 442 U.S. 256, 279, n. 25, 99 S.Ct. 2282, 2296, n. 25, 60 L.Ed.2d 870 (1979).

The issue in this case is not whether TWR must be permitted to lobby, but whether Congress is required to provide it with public money with which to lobby. For the reasons stated above, we hold that it is not. Accordingly, the judgment of the Court of Appeals is *Reversed.*

The leading case discussing the elements of § 501(c)(4), especially the meaning of "promotion of social welfare," is *Peoples Educ. Camp Society, Inc. v. Commissioner,* which follows.

PEOPLE'S EDUCATIONAL CAMP SOCIETY, INC. v. COMMISSIONER

United States Court of Appeals, Second Circuit, 1964
331 F.2d 923

WATERMAN, Circuit Judge.

This is a petition to review a decision of the Tax Court of the United States which upheld the Commissioner of Internal Revenue's determination of a deficiency of $25,784.43 in the federal income tax of petitioner, People's Educational Camp Society, Inc., for its fiscal year ending September 30, 1956. The Tax Court rejected petitioner's claim that it was exempt from the income tax under Section 501(c)(4) of the Internal Revenue Code of 1954 as a nonprofit civic organization operated exclusively for the promotion of social welfare, rejecting it on the ground that such an exemption was precluded because of the relationship which petitioner's operation of a large commercial resort bore to its totality of activities. We agree that petitioner was not entitled to the exemption. A complete statement of the facts surrounding petitioner's operations, including a detailed breakdown of its financial activities, can be found in the opinion of the Tax Court, reported at 39 T.C. 756. Our summary thereof follows:

Petitioner is a New York membership corporation with its principal offices in New York City. It was organized in 1920 by persons associated with the Rand School of Social Science, an institution then operated by the American Socialist Society and engaged in conducting adult classes and presenting lectures and programs related to the dissemination of information on the labor movement and socialist principles. During 1920 officials and friends of the Rand School became interested in purchasing a tract of 2,196 acres of land in the Pocono mountains of Pennsylvania, with an eye toward developing on the tract a campsite where the Rand School's faculty, students and friends might gather during the summers to carry on their studies and develop programs in which they were interested. After the school's executive secretary had acquired an option to purchase the land for about $21,000, petitioner was organized to take title to the property and develop the summer camp, which was eventually given the name 'Tamiment,' the name of a lake nearby.

Petitioner, organized as a New York membership corporation, has never issued any shares of stock and has never had any stockholders. Its operations are conducted by a group of individuals known as members, whose number may never exceed 35 and whose election to membership is governed by petitioner's by-laws. Any person may be elected to membership who has publicly endorsed the principles of socialism for at least two years, and whose membership has been recommended by petitioner's Board of Directors and has been approved by those persons already members. None of petitioner's officers or directors receive any salary or other compensation, but the managing director and associate director, who conduct petitioner's day-to-day operations, do receive salaries as do petitioner's other employees.

When petitioner was organized its certificate of incorporation set forth its objects in the following terms:

'To organize, conduct and maintain summer camps and centers for instructive and recreative purposes; to build, purchase, own, lease, manage and operate camps, dormitories, dining halls, recreation rooms, play grounds, reading rooms, halls and other buildings for the purpose of said corporation as herein set forth; to diffuse a general knowledge of literature, art and science through the medium of lectures, publications and dramatic performances; to borrow money for the corporate purposes of the corporation and to issue bonds, notes or other evidences of indebtedness therefor; to assist other educational, civic, political and economic movements and organizations; to cooperate with such organizations and movements and to initiate such movements, but said purposes shall not extend to those objects for which corporations may be formed pursuant to the Education Law, nor shall any activities of the said corporation be conducted for pecuniary profit to its members.

As of the time of the Tax Court proceedings below, petitioner's by-laws provided that upon dissolution all its property was to revert to the American Socialist Society, although that Society, along with its Rand School of Social Science, had ceased to exist in 1956. As of this time no steps had been taken to amend the portion of the by-laws relating to the disposition of petitioner's property upon dissolution, nor had any alternative plan for dissolution been contemplated. From the opening of Camp Tamiment for occupancy in July of 1921, it began to experience considerable growth. During its first twenty years its growth was steady though moderate. By 1941 the camp's annual gross income had increased to $281,633.87, and the value of its fixed assets had increased to $398,663.93. Except for the years 1925 and 1932, when small losses were incurred, Tamiment has each year consistently shown a profit, and, except for the period from 1921 to 1923 when petitioner received contributions, it has been entirely self-sustaining. In January of 1936, and again in January of 1939, petitioner obtained rulings from the Commissioner of Internal Revenue that, on the basis of facts then available, petitioner was entitled to an exemption under the then existing provisions of the tax laws, provisions which later came to be embodied in substantially the same form in Section 501(c)(4) of the 1954 Code.

Tamiment's operations from 1941 through the taxable year 1956 represented a second distinct phase of its development, one marked by a growth much more rapid and substantial than that previously experienced. This was manifested by considerable increases in operating expenses and in the value of petitioner's fixed assets and accumulated surplus. An analysis of petitioner's balance sheet figures for these years shows that petitioner's assets, which stood at $398,663.93 in 1941, had increased to $1,124,229.91 by 1951. By the end of the taxable year 1956, the year here under discussion, these assets had grown to $2,301,604.74. During these same periods petitioner's surplus, designated in its balance sheet as 'reserves,' had increased from $311,079.97 in 1941, to $1,573,452.14 in 1951, and to $2,226,080.50 in 1956. Petitioner's annual revenues showed like increases after 1941, with the figures for petitioner's total gross revenues from all sources for 1941, 1951, and 1956 being, respectively, $290,804.60, $840,364.23, and $942,632.55. The overwhelming portion of petitioner's gross revenues and expenses during the period under examination, as well as of the increase in the value of its assets, was connected solely with the operation of Tamiment.

By the year 1956 Tamiment had become the largest and one of the most modern summer vacation resorts in Pennsylvania, with rates ranging from $12 to $19 per day per person. As already noted, the American Socialist Society and the Rand School of Social Science, the motivating forces behind the creation of Tamiment as a site for summer retreats, had both ceased to exist. The resort was open to the public and competed with other vacation resorts in the Poconos. It employed more than 400 persons during the peak season and it advertised itself through newspapers, magazines and brochures as 'Tamiment in the Poconos.'

Tamiment's principal guest quarters in 1956 consisted of more than 160 furnished cottages, capable of accommodating about 900 persons, and located adjacent to a dining hall with a seating capacity of 1000. Set apart from the main complex of cottages was a group of bungalows known as Sandyville, designed for use by families with children, and which adjoined a play school and a small store. The other physical facilities which dotted Tamiment's grounds were of the type not uncommon to luxury vacation resorts catering to a young adult clientele: an administration building; a library; a lecture and concert hall; a ballroom building; an 18–hole golf course with a clubhouse containing a cocktail lounge; another clubhouse and dining terrace overlooking Lake Tamiment; a theater building; and facilities for various outdoor sports.

Also, Tamiment's activities included organized programs in the fields of drama, music and art, all available to guests of the resort free of charge. On Saturday evenings and Sunday afternoons the theater building was the scene of a dramatic or musical production staged by a theater group employed by petitioner for that purpose, and throughout the rest of the week the building was used for the exhibition of motion pictures. Orchestras hired on theater evenings to play for musical comedies and revues were customarily used after the performances to provide music at dances. Each week during the summer season vocalists and musicians performed concerts or gave recitals, and a lecture dealing with a topic connected with the arts or with public affairs was also weekly fare for those staying at the resort. Throughout each summer season an art director employed by petitioner gave free art instruction to interested guests, and professional artists were invited to display their works there and offer them for sale.

The most outstanding single cultural attraction at Tamiment was presented each year early in the summer vacation season, a chamber music festival featuring an orchestra and string quartet. The festival was open to members of the general public as well as Tamiment's paying guests, but a moderate fee was charged those attending who were not staying at the resort. Though the operation of Tamiment constituted the great bulk of petitioner's activities during the period under review, petitioner also carried on other activities at the time, chiefly in New York City. In 1951 it acquired from the American Socialist Society a building in the city which housed the Rand School of Social Science, the school's library, the offices of an independent publication called the New Leader, and the principal corporate office of petitioner. When the American Socialist Society was dissolved in March of 1956, and the operations of the Rand School accordingly ceased, petitioner acquired all of the assets of the school's library and, after renovating it and hiring personnel to staff it, began itself to maintain and operate the library. Containing one of the largest and most complete collections of material dealing with the labor movement, Socialism, and Communism, the library was made freely available to all persons engaged in research in those fields.

Acting under the name of 'Tamiment Institute,' petitioner also undertook to sponsor and promote various other programs of public interest, mostly in New York City. In order to stimulate interest in American string quartet composition, petitioner promoted annual composition contests in this field of music, awarding prizes to original works adjudged the best. An annual book award luncheon was conducted, at which a prize was awarded by petitioner for the best biographical book of the year. Petitioner launched several programs to foster thought and discussion about important public issues. It discussed such issues from time to time in public service advertisements which it sponsored, and in pamphlets which it published and circulated itself. It also conducted numerous essay contests for college and university students. An annual public forum was held at which prominent citizens aired their views on matters of public concern, and, along these same lines, annual seminars were sponsored at Tamiment before the opening of the resort's summer season at which scholarly papers were read and discusses.

On March 3, 1956, the Commissioner of Internal Revenue wrote to petitioner, ruling that, inasmuch as petitioner was primarily engaged in operating a commercial enterprise, it was no longer to be accorded an exemption from federal income taxes. Petitioner filed a corporate income tax return for its fiscal year 1956 but claimed exemption from the tax, and the Commissioner asserted against it a deficiency of $25,784.13. In the Tax Court proceedings below petitioner did not contest the correctness of the deficiency figure, but unsuccessfully defended on the sole ground that it was not liable for any tax at all since it was entitled to an exemption under Section 501(c)(4) of the 1954 Code. Section 501(c)(4) provides for an exemption from the income tax in the case of:

> (4) Civic leagues or organizations not organized for profit but operated exclusively for the promotion of social welfare, or local associations of employees, the membership of which is limited to the employees of a designated person or persons in a particular municipality, and the net earnings of which are devoted exclusively to charitable, educational, or recreational purposes. Petitioner, of course, seeks to take advantage of that part of the subsection exempting 'civic leagues or organizations not organized for profit but operated exclusively for the promotion of social welfare. To do so, petitioner must meet the three statutory conditions set forth in the subsection and demonstrate that: (1) it is a civic league or organization; (2) it is not organized for profit; (3) it is operated exclusively for the promotion of social welfare.

Conditions (1) and (2) do not require extensive treatment. While at least one court has given the subsection a rather limited construction by defining the initial word 'civic' narrowly and then regarding it as modifying both 'leagues' and 'organizations,' * * * neither party to these proceedings has raised any question as to the emphasis to be placed upon the word 'civic' or the interpretation to be accorded it in construing Section 501(c)(4). Rather, they have both tacitly assumed that, even if the term does connote a limited genre of exempt organizations characterized by something other than social welfare operations, petitioner may be so classified, and they have confined themselves to an analysis of whether petitioner's operations in 1956 were exclusively of a social welfare nature.

This emphasis on the broader term 'social welfare' is in line with the current regulations covering the subsection, which do not appear to give the word 'civic' any real independent limiting effect but which only deal with organizations 'operated primarily for the purpose of bringing about civic betterment and social improvements,' Reg. § 1.501(c)(4)-(1) (a) (2), and is also in line with revenue rulings interpreting this and predecessor subsections, e.g., Rev.Rul. 55–495, 1955–2 Cum.Bull. 259; Rev.Rul. 55–439, 1955–2 Cum.Bull. 257; GCM 24100, 1944 Cum.Bull. 192. This emphasis on the social welfare aspect of the subsection is also in accord with the weight of judicial authority; some courts apparently have not viewed the word 'civic' as modifying 'organizations' along with 'leagues,' and have therefore simply concerned themselves with whether an organization has been exclusively conducting social welfare operations, * * * courts have reached about the same result by talking about 'civic organizations' but not defining 'civic' in the limited sense of 'municipal' or 'community sponsored' but in broader terms closely related to the general concept of the promotion of social welfare. * * * This view is also supported by the little legislative history one finds in explanation of the provision, for when it was first made a part of the tax laws, * * * it was apparently included as a result of a belief that the provision then exempting religious, charitable or educational organizations was not broad enough to cover many nonprofit organizations whose activities benefitted the general public. * * * Therefore, we, too, will assume that petitioner is a 'civic league or organization,' and, as it also appears that petitioner makes no profit which inures to the benefit of any private individual, we now concern ourselves with whether petitioner has operated exclusively for the promotion of social welfare. * * *

Certain of petitioner's activities, not involving the commercial operation of the Tamiment resort, were found by the Tax Court to constitute the promotion of social welfare. These activities, which we have already outlined in some detail, were largely conducted in the New York City area and included such things as the maintenance of a free library on Socialism, Communism and the labor movement, the sponsorship of public forums and symposia, the promotion of musical composition and essay contest, and the circulation of pamphlets discussing important matters of public interest. We agree that these activities involved the promotion of social welfare as that term is used in Section 501(c)(4) of the Code. This court has characterized the promotion of social welfare as involving the serving of 'purposes beneficial to the community as a whole,' or the promotion of the 'welfare of mankind' in the manner generally of the charitable, educational and religious organizations exempted by like provisions of the Code. ...These activities of petitioner, designed in the main to stimulate increased interests in the arts and public affairs and to provide the general citizenry with means for becoming better informed as to matters of public concern, amounted, we think, to the furthering of the beneficial interests of the community as a whole and therefore served to promote social welfare.

Petitioner further urges us to characterize, as promoting social welfare, the various cultural activities which were conducted at Tamiment, and which were connected with that area's operation as a commercial vacation resort. Our attention is directed to the lectures, concerts, plays, and art exhibits which were regularly held during the resort's summer season, and to Tamiment's annual four-day chamber music festival. We agree with the Tax Court, however, that these activities, considered in their relation to the total operation of Tamiment, did not involve the promotion of social welfare at all. They were simply part and parcel of Tamiment's operation as a commercial resort, and were necessary features of a luxury vacation spot catering to a young adult intellectual clientele. As the director of Pennsylvania's state tourist promotion agency testified below, such cultural programs, while perhaps of a higher quality at Tamiment, were not unusual programs for ordinary commercial resorts in the Poconos that sought to draw the type of guests who frequented Tamiment. These activities, while no doubt broadening and beneficial to Tamiment's paying guests who enjoyed them, and, therefore, in a very remote sense, doubtless of some incidental aid to the general community of which these guests were members, cannot by any stretch of the imagination be considered any more beneficial to the community as a whole or any more promotive of the general welfare, as those terms have been used to define the statutory phrase, than Tamiment's golfing, swimming, or dancing activities . . .

We come now to the important question of whether petitioner's operation of the resort Tamiment, not in itself an activity involving the promotion of social welfare, prevents the petitioner from obtaining a Section 501(c)(4) exemption as an organization operated exclusively for the promotion of social welfare. The word 'exclusively' as used in the statute has not been given a strict interpretation, so as to foreclose every operation for a non-exempt purpose no matter how insubstantial, but rather has been interpreted to mean 'primarily.' . . . Stated another way, 'the presence of a single * * * (non-exempt) purpose, if substantial in nature, will destroy the exemption regardless of the number or importance of truly * * *.

It was the nature of petitioner's operation of Tamiment as a commercial resort in active competition with other such businesses in the Poconos area, coupled with the relationship which the running of Tamiment bore to the total aggregation of petitioner's activities, that caused the Tax Court to conclude that petitioner was not operating exclusively for the promotion of social welfare. That court laid particular stress upon the fact that petitioner's expenditures for genuine social welfare activities constituted but a small fraction of its total revenues and paled in comparison with the total accumulated surplus which petitioner carried and which it had consistently increased over the years. . .

Moreover, petitioner spent substantial portions of its revenues in expanding and improving the facilities at Tamiment, with an extremely large addition to those facilities having been made during 1956, the taxable year here under review. During that year petitioner spent a total of $221,302.34 for capital additions. A comparison between petitioner's balance sheet figures for that year and those for the previous year indicates that of the total amount spent for capital additions, more than $200,000 was spent at Tamiment for buildings, equipment, and 'permanent inventory,' with the remainder being spent on books and equipment for petitioner's New York library.

We agree with the Tax Court that, under these circumstances, petitioner's operations at Tamiment foreclosed a determination that it is an organization operated exclusively for the promotion of social welfare ... True, none of petitioner's revenues from Tamiment have ever been turned over as profits to any private person, and petitioner's formally declared purpose as originally set forth in its certificate of incorporation when it was organized in 1920 was to conduct activities of a social welfare nature. Moreover, it may well be that the persons currently responsible for directing petitioner's operations sincerely and honestly believe that their organization's primary purpose is still the promotion of social welfare. Nevertheless, the exemption granted to social welfare and like organizations is made in recognition of the benefit which the public derives from their social welfare activities... and we think it only fair to determine a particular organization's right to an exemption largely on the basis of the effect its operations have on the public. In terms of petitioner's purpose as demonstrated by the fact of its operations, and as demonstrated by the actual effect which those operations have on the community of which it is a part, petitioner cannot be regarded as primarily a social welfare organization entitled to a Section 501(c)(4) exemption, but rather it must be viewed as an organization whose primary purpose has in fact become the running of a commercial resort.
* * *

Affirmed.

HAYS, Circuit Judge (dissenting).

Chapter 5

OBTAINING AND MAINTAINING TAX EXEMPT STATUS

Nonprofit organizations are not automatically exempt from federal income taxation. With the exception of churches and certain other religious organizations (discussion in Chapter 10), unless a nonprofit organization has received a determination letter or a Revenue Ruling informing it of its exempt status, the organization is subject to tax liability. Sections 501(c), (d), (e), (f), 521, 527, 528, and 529 describe those nonprofit organizations that qualify for tax exempt status and classify them into different categories.[1] The majority of nonprofit organizations qualifying for tax exempt status are classified under § 501(c). Each particular classification of tax exempt organization under this Section has a specific tax designation. For example, charitable organizations, both public charities and private foundations (discussed in Chapters 6 and 7) are called § 501(c)(3) organizations, social welfare organizations, such as the League of Women Voters, are § 501(c)(4) organizations, social clubs and country clubs are § 501(c)(7) organizations (discussed in Chapter 13); fraternal societies are § 501(c)(8) and (10) organizations; nonprofit cemetery companies are § 501(c)(13) organizations; trade and professional organizations are § 501(c)(6) organizations (discussed in Chapter 14); and war veterans' organizations are § 501(c)(19) organizations. Farm cooperatives obtain tax exempt status under § 521, political organizations qualify under § 527 (discussed in Chapter 15), and homeowners' association under § 528 (discussed in Chapter 16).

Rules differ for each of the classifications of tax exempt organizations. Donations to § 501(c)(3), (13), and (19) and under certain conditions to (8) and (10) organizations provide donors with charitable contribution deductions, whereas contributions to the other exempt organizations do not. Some organizations are taxed on investment income; most are not (discussion in Chapter 9).

---

1. Governmental entities are not treated as nonprofit organizations. They are automatically exempt from income taxation under § 115 of the Internal Revenue Code.

I. OBTAINING TAX EXEMPT STATUS

An organization seeking recognition of exempt status under § 501 or 521 must file an application with the key District Director for the Internal Revenue District in which the principal place of business or principal office of the organization is located. Application for tax exempt status is initiated for most organizations by filing either Form 1023 [for charitable organizations that qualify under § 501(c)(3) and for cooperative hospital service organizations qualifying under § 501(e)] or Form 1024.[2] Farmers' cooperatives file for exempt status under § 521 on Form 1028.

Most organizations seek tax exempt status under § 501(c)(3). The § 501(c)(3) organization was discussed in Chapter 4. As noted in chapter 4, a § 501(c)(3) organization must be organized and operated exclusively for one or more "charitable" purposes. A § 501(c)(3) organization files form 1023 to obtain tax exempt status but also to inform the Internal Revenue Service that it qualifies as a public charity (discussion in Chapter 6) or, in the alternative, is a private foundation (discussion in Chapter 7). The organization provides information on Form 1023 to demonstrate to the Service that it is "organized" for charitable purposes. The entity must file Form 1023 within 27 months after it is organized or its exempt status will be recognized only from the date the application is received by the Service. A § 501(c)(3) organization that is not a private foundation need not file for exemption if its gross receipts are normally not more than $5,000 annually [Treas. Reg. § 1.508–1(a)(3)].

Recognition of exempt status is retroactive for § 501(c)(4) organizations regardless of when Form 1024 is filed (assuming the organization qualifies for exempt status during the prior period). A § 501(c)(3) organization that does not file Form 1023 within the 27 month period then should seek qualification as a § 501(c)(4) organization prior to the date the Service receives its application for § 501(c)(3) status on Form 1023.

II. MAINTAINING TAX EXEMPT STATUS

To maintain exempt status, a nonprofit organization must be "operated" to carry out its exempt purpose or purposes. In chapter 4, you were introduced to the operational test for § 501(c)(3) organizations. This test requires that an organization's activities substantially further its charitable purposes. If the organization engages more than insubstantially in activities that do not advance its charitable purposes, it risks

---

2. If a nonprofit organization is controlled by a central organization, a group exemption letter may be issued to cover both the central organization and its affiliates. See Rev. Proc. 80–27, 1980–1 C.B. 677. The central organization is one that supervises one or more subordinates, such as a chapter, local, post, or unit of the central organization. The central must first obtain recognition of its own exemption. It then makes application for its subordinates by letter instead of by filing Form 1023 or 1024.

loss of its exempt status. The operational test, therefore, considers both the quality and quantity of an organization's activities. Activities that do not further the organization's charitable purposes are inconsistent with the operational test. If those activities are more than insubstantial, they are quantitatively in violation of the operational test. Thus, substantial unrelated activities do not pass the operational test.

The regulations classify the operational test for § 501(c)(3) organizations into four components: (1) commercial activity, (2) the private benefit limitation, (3) the private inurement prohibition, and (4) political activity. Great overlap exists among the first three. They determine whether the organization is pursuing as its primary purpose a charitable objective. Judicial decisions have added a fifth component: Activities in violation of public policy are not in furtherance of a charitable purpose. [See *Bob Jones University v. Simon*, 416 U.S. 725, 94 S.Ct. 2038, 40 L.Ed.2d 496 (1974), cited in Chapter 11.] If a § 501(c)(3) organization fails to meet requirements of the operational test, it can lose its tax-exempt status.

Tax exempt organizations, other than § 501(c)(3) organizations, must satisfy some of the components of the above noted operational test for § 501(c)(3) organizations. The prohibition on substantial commercial activity and the private inurement prohibition also apply to other tax exempt organizations. This chapter will consider the requirements to maintain tax exempt status in the context of the § 501(c)(3) organization, but some of the conditions may apply in some context to other tax exempt organizations.

A. Commercial Activity

It is not unusual for a charitable organization to engage in commercial activities. Profits from those activities produce resources that support the organization's charitable purposes.

An organization may engage in commercial activities for one or more of three reasons. First, the commercial activity itself may be related to the organization's exempt purposes.

According to the regulations: An organization may meet the requirements of § 501(c)(3) although it operates a trade or business as a substantial part of its activities, if the operation of such trade or business is in furtherance of the organization's exempt purpose or purposes and the organization is not organized or operated for the primary purpose of carrying on an unrelated trade or business.... [Treas. Reg. § 1.501(c)(3)–1(e).]

Note

Nonprofit hospitals are the classic example of organizations that engage in commercial activities related to their exempt purpose as they charge for the medical services they provide. Other examples include nonprofit educational institutions that impose tuition for the educational services they provide (tuition is the sales price for the educational services provided to students); nonprofit theater groups that charge admission for their productions; and nonprofit social service organizations funded by state and federal contracts, that in return deliver social services to covered individuals. In each of these examples, the nonprofit organization competes with for-profit organizations. Yet, Congress and the courts have always accepted that these organizations should be tax exempt.

A second reason why an organization engages in commercial activities is to raise funds to support its exempt activities. These commercial activities themselves are not related to the organization's exempt purposes. Unlike the first group of exempt activities in which the commercial activities not only finance, but also are related to, the organization's charitable purposes, some organizations will conduct commercial activities only to generate funds. Nonetheless the funds will be dedicated to the organization's charitable purposes. Use of income from commercial activities solely to finance charitable activities does not further the organization's exempt purpose. Thus, such commercial activity can cost the organization its exempt status.

Note

The classic example of an organization involved in commercial activities solely to generate funds was New York University School of Law's ownership of Mueller Macaroni as well as other businesses. [(See *C.F. Mueller Co. v. Commissioner*, 190 F.2d 120 (3d Cir.1951).] The income from these businesses was exempt from tax under the theory that the income was destined to finance exempt activities. With the tax-free profits earned from these businesses, the law school was able to fund its legal education activities.

What became known as the "destination of income test," wherein the destination of funds was the ultimate test of exemption, was effectively repealed by the Revenue Act of 1950. Section 502 of the Internal Revenue Code expressly states that a organization owned by a charitable organization (a so-called "feeder" organization) is not exempt from taxation merely because all of its profits are dedicated to the charitable organization. Section 513, in defining an "unrelated trade or business," indicates that a trade or business operated by a charitable organization is not related to the organization's exempt purposes just because the income is used by the charitable organization to support its exempt purposes.

The destination of income test is considered in more detail in chapter 9, which discusses the taxation of unrelated business income of an otherwise tax exempt organization. For an explanation of the test, see Boris I. Bittker & George K. Rahdert, "The Exemption of Nonprofit Organizations from Federal Income Taxation," 85 Yale L. J. 299 (1976); Robert J. Desiderio, "The Profitable Nonprofit Corporation," 1 N. M. L. Rev. 563 (1971); Kenneth Eliasberg, "Charity and Commerce: Section 501(c)(3)—How Much Unrelated Business Activity?" 21 Tax L. Rev. 53 (1965).

The third reason that an exempt organization may engage in commercial activities is simply to operate a business to make a profit. Obviously, engaging in commercial activities under this third scenario is improper because, at a minimum, the organization has a purpose that is not charitable or is not a tax exempt purpose. Tax exempt organizations conduct such business activities because they believe the activities are related to their tax exempt purposes or they have some nefarious purpose. Distinguishing the reason for which an organization in fact engages in commercial activity has been the substance of numerous cases and revenue rulings. Consider the reasons in the following cases.

LIVING FAITH, INC. v. COMMISSIONER

United States Court of Appeals, Seventh Circuit, 1991
950 F.2d 365

FLAUM, Circuit Judge.

Living Faith, Inc. (Living Faith) appeals the Tax Court's affirmance of a determination by the Commissioner of the Internal Revenue Service (Commissioner) that Living Faith was not operated for exempt purposes within the meaning of § 501(c)(3) of the Internal Revenue Code (I.R.C.), 26 U.S.C. § 501(c)(3). This Court has jurisdiction to review the Tax Court's ruling pursuant to I.R.C. § 7482, 26 U.S.C. § 7482. Because this case was submitted to the Tax Court for decision on a stipulated administrative record, the record is presumed true for purposes of this appeal. Upon review of the record, we find that the Tax Court's determination was not clearly erroneous and affirm its decision.

I.

Living Faith was incorporated as a not-for-profit corporation on September 4, 1986, under the laws of Illinois. According to its articles of incorporation, Living Faith was established for the purpose of keeping with the doctrines of the Seventh-day Adventist Church. Living Faith is a member of the Association of Self–Supporting Institutions of the Seventh-day Adventist Church, but, like all members, is independent from the church and receives no direct funding. Seventh-day Adventists believe that the concept of health is permeated with religious meaning. Good health, according to Seventh-day Adventists, promotes virtuous conduct, and is furthered by a vegetarian diet and abstention from tobacco, alcohol, and caffeine. Ill health, in contrast, promotes sin, with the original sin consisting of eating food condemned by God.

Living Faith operates two vegetarian restaurants and health food stores, in Oak Brook Terrace, Illinois, and Glen Ellyn, Illinois, in a manner consistent with these religious beliefs. These two facilities—the subject of this litigation—are open to the public, and operate under the name "Country Life." Country Life is a worldwide chain of independently operated restaurants and food stores. Living Faith is licensed to use the name, without charge, by Oak Haven, Inc., a wholesale food distributor. Oak Haven's guidelines require Country Life facilities to employ

Seventh-day Adventist management and maintain a good working relationship with the local Seventh-day Adventist Church. They also require that management have business ability, undergo six months training in operating a Country Life restaurant, and maintain good business relations with suppliers and the community.* * *

The Oak Brook Terrace facility operates out of a 3,200 square foot leased space in a shopping center, of which 2,400 square feet is used for the restaurant. Its hours of operation are:

Restaurant

Tuesday, Wednesday, Thursday 11:30 a.m.–7:30 p.m.

Monday 11:30 a.m.–4:00 p.m.

Friday 11:30 a.m.–2:00 p.m.

Saturday Closed

Health Food Store

Thursday 10:00 a.m.–8:00 p.m.

Friday 10:00 a.m.–3:00 p.m.

Saturday Closed

Operations at the Glen Ellyn facility are substantially similar to those at Oak Brook Terrace. Living Faith sets its meal and food prices at market rates. Buffet prices at its restaurants are set at approximately three times the wholesale cost of food, a formula commonly used in the food business, and retail prices at its health food stores are maintained at levels recommended by its wholesalers. According to Living Faith, its prices are similar to, and in some instances higher than, other vegetarian restaurants and health food stores. Products sold at the health food stores include grocery items, such as packaged and bulk foods, as well as vitamins, spices, and toiletries.

In addition to purveying food and health products, Living Faith disseminates various informational materials which promote both "[t]he healing message of Jesus Christ" and the "world famous" Country Life restaurants.* * * The literature is placed by the counter, the door, at the end of the buffet line, and on each table. Living Faith also offers books on religious subjects at no charge to its patrons. Customers are not required to take or read the literature. Living Faith states that its "literature evangelism" is currently limited to this in-store distribution, and estimates that 10 to 12 people have joined the Seventh-day Adventist Church as a result of its efforts.

Each day before the facilities open, Living Faith conducts a devotional talk by a staff member, hymn singing, and a Bible reading for workers. One Saturday each month, Living Faith provides the public an opportunity to sample vegetarian cooking by offering free meals. Those who attend may also peruse the Seventh-day Adventist literature and obtain information about the Church. Living Faith offers to the public a five-week cooking school which promotes vegetarian cooking. Classes meet on a weekly basis, during hours when the restaurants and food stores are closed, and are priced at $20 per person, or $25 per married couple, plus $15 for a cookbook. The organization also offers weekly Bible study class, free of charge, during hours when the facilities are closed. It occasionally provides meals to the needy in exchange for chores, such as washing dishes, and has collected and donated to charity approximately 100 plastic bags of used clothing.

Living Faith's financial statements for the 12–month periods ending September 30, 1987, and September 30, 1988, show the following results:

	1987	1988
Sales revenue	$73,134.78	$280,104.38
Cost of sales	34,576.03	158,340.22
Gross profit	38,558.75	121,705.99
General & administrative expenses	91,190.80	155,220.85
Operating loss	(52,632.05)	(33,514.86)
Donations	101,062.63	46,226.73
Miscellaneous income	6,999.20	
Net income	48,430.58	19,711.07

Stipends for Living Faith's five-member staff totalled $25,663.67 for the fiscal year ending September 30, 1987,* * * and increased to $63,673.93 the following fiscal year. According to Living Faith, its staff is composed of people who otherwise might have difficulty in finding employment. Several staff members also serve as officers and directors of Living Faith. Three of these—the president, vice president, and secretary—are ordained deacons of the Seventh-day Adventist Church. The chairperson, who is not on the staff, is an ordained Elder of the Church.

According to Living Faith, any profits realized from its operations will be used to expand its health ministry in accordance with Seventh-day Adventist tenets. Its application for § 501(c)(3) tax exemption states that its future plans include the establishment of an "outpost evangelism program" where people "may live in harmony with the principles of the Bible and the writings of Ellen G. White," a founder of the Seventh-day Adventist Church ... However, its current operations are limited to the two restaurants and health food stores.

Living Faith filed its application for tax-exempt status on March 29, 1988. The Commissioner denied Living Faith's application, finding that it was not operated exclusively for exempt purposes within the meaning of § 501(c)(3). Living Faith timely protested the ruling, and the Commissioner subsequently sent notice of the final adverse ruling. Living Faith filed a petition for a declaratory judgment with the Tax Court, pursuant to I.R.C. § 7428(a), requesting tax-exempt status pursuant to § 501(a) as an organization described in § 501(c)(3).

The Tax Court upheld the Commissioner's ruling, finding that Living Faith conducts its operations with a substantial commercial purpose and therefore does not qualify as a tax-exempt organization. *Living Faith, Inc. v. Commissioner,* 60 T.C.M. (CCH) 710 (1990). We now examine the Tax Court's decision.

II.

Living Faith contends that it operates its restaurants and health food stores with the exclusive, tax-exempt purpose of furthering the religious work of the Seventh-day Adventist Church as a health ministry. As the taxpayer claiming the exemption, Living Faith bears the burden of proving entitlement to it. * * * Section 501(c)(3) establishes a tax exemption, pursuant to § 501(a), for organizations "organized and operated exclusively for religious, charitable . . . or educational purposes, . . . no part of the net earnings of which inures to the benefit of any private shareholder or individual. . . ." To comport with these provisions, an entity must be both "organized and operated exclusively" for at least one of the listed exempt purposes. Treas. Reg. § 1.501(c)(3)1(a). The parties do not dispute that Living Faith satisfies the "organizational" test, or that its net earnings do not inure to any individual's benefit. The sole issue, therefore, is whether Living Faith is "operated exclusively" for exempt purposes within the meaning of § 501(c)(3).

In evaluating this issue, we focus on "the purposes toward which an organization's activities are directed, and not the nature of the activities." *B.S.W. Group, Inc. v. Commissioner,* 70 T.C. 352, 356–57 (1978). The purposes need not be solely religious; courts recognize that a nonexempt purpose, even "somewhat beyond a de minimis level," may be permitted without loss of exception. * * * The nonexempt purpose, however, cannot be substantial. "The presence of a single non-exempt purpose, if substantial in nature, will destroy the exemption regardless of the number or importance of truly [exempt] purposes." *American Ass'n of Christian Schools Voluntary Employees Beneficiary Ass'n Welfare Plan Trust v. United States,* 850 F.2d 1510, 1513 (11th Cir.1988) (quoting *Better Business Bureau v. United States,* 326 U.S. 279, 283, 66 S.Ct. 112, 114, 90 L.Ed. 67 (1945)); *see also* Treas. Reg. § 501(c)(3)1(c)(1) (organization not "operated exclusively" for exempt purposes "if more than an insubstantial part of its activities is not in furtherance of an exempt purpose.").

A single activity may be carried on for more than one purpose. The fact that an organization's primary activity may constitute a trade or business does not, of itself, disqualify it from classification under § 501(c)(3), provided the trade or business furthers or accomplishes an exempt purpose. Treas. Reg. § 1.501(c)(3)–1(c)(1),–1(e)(1); * * * If one of the activity's purposes, however, is substantial and nonexempt (*e.g.*, commercial), the organization will be denied exempt status under § 501(c)(3), even if its activity also furthers an exempt (*e.g.*, religious) purpose. * * *

Living Faith contends that the Tax Court erred in upholding the Commissioner's determination that its operations have a substantial commercial purpose. It makes essentially three claims. First, Living Faith argues the Tax Court applied an incorrect legal standard, therefore requiring this Court to undertake a plenary review of the decision. Second, Living Faith maintains that, even under a clearly erroneous standard, the Tax Court's determination was incorrect. Finally, Living Faith asserts that the Tax Court unconstitutionally discriminated against it by judging the merits of its beliefs in denying it tax-exempt status. We first determine the proper standard of review.

A.

Whether an activity has a substantial nonexempt purpose is a question of fact to be determined under the facts and circumstances of each case. * * * The Tax Court's factual finding that an organization is not operated exclusively for exempt purposes cannot be disturbed on appeal unless clearly erroneous. * * * Here, however, Living Faith argues that we should apply a *de novo* standard of review, apparently on the ground that the Tax Court's finding of fact that Living Faith has a substantial commercial purpose is predicated on a misunderstanding of the governing rule of law. * * *

Living Faith bases its contention on essentially two arguments, neither of which we find persuasive. It first claims that the Tax Court effectively established a new legal standard by using the phrase "essential ingredient" in examining the role of religion in Living Faith's operations. The Tax Court stated, for example, that it was "not persuaded that [Living Faith's religious] beliefs were an essential ingredient of [its] operations." 60 T.C.M. (CCH) at 715. Living Faith contends that the court's "essential ingredient" approach improperly emphasized the nature of Living Faith's activities, rather than its purposes, thereby permitting the court to determine whether the means Living Faith selected to pursue its beliefs were the most effective available to further the health principles of the Church. We disagree.

In more than one instance, the Tax Court stated the proper standard, that "[t]he critical inquiry is whether petitioner's activity encompasses a substantial nonexempt purpose irrespective of the presence of other exempt purposes." 60 T.C.M. (CCH) at 713.* * * This analysis demonstrates that it found Living Faith's activities to be imbued with a substantial commercial purpose. Although the Tax Court did not clearly delineate how it used the "essential ingredient" phraseology, we cannot conclude, as Living Faith seems to suggest, that the court elevated the phrase into a *de facto* legal standard in place of the insubstantiality test—especially given that "[n]either the Internal Revenue Code, the regulations, nor the case law provides a general definition of 'insubstantial' for purposes of section 501(c)(3)." 60 T.C.M. (CCH) at 713.* * *

Here, the "essential ingredient" phrase employed by the Tax Court helped in determining whether religion was the primary purpose—*i.e.,* the "essential ingredient"—of Living Faith's operations.

Living Faith also contends that the Tax Court failed to consider all of the relevant factors used by courts to determine the existence of a substantial nonexempt purpose. It asserts, for example, that the court neglected to address its "good faith" religious belief and "good works," and contends that the court focused solely upon its finances and competition with other businesses. A review of the Tax Court opinion, however, indicates that the court did consider these other factors. The court explicitly acknowledged that Living Faith conducted such activities as disseminating literature about the Seventh-day Adventist religion and after-hours Bible reading, but found these activities "clearly peripheral and incidental to the substantial commercial purpose" of its restaurants and health food stores. 60 T.C.M. (CCH) at 713–14.

Because we find that the Tax Court based its factual findings on a proper legal standard, we accept them unless clearly erroneous. The critical inquiry, therefore, is whether sufficient evidence exists in the record to support the Tax Court's finding that Living Faith operates for a substantial commercial purpose.

B.

When undertaking this inquiry, we look to various objective indicia. The particular manner in which an organization's activities are conducted, the commercial hue of those activities, competition with commercial firms, and the existence and amount of annual or accumulated profits, are all relevant evidence in determining whether an organization has a substantial nonexempt purpose. * * * Living Faith argues that the Tax Court unduly relied on such factors, however, and inordinately emphasized the nature of its activities. Living Faith maintains that "great weight [should] be given to the assertions of religious purpose made in good faith on behalf of the organization." * * * In this regard, it asserts that good health is an especially important component of the Seventh-day Adventist Church, and that its Country Life operations further this religious purpose.

While we agree with Living Faith that an organization's good faith assertion of an exempt purpose is relevant to the analysis of tax-exempt status, we cannot accept the view that such an assertion be dispositive. Put simply, saying one's purpose is exclusively religious doesn't necessarily make it so.

This Court and others have consistently held that an organization's purposes may be inferred from its manner of operations. * * * An organization's activities, and not solely its members' devotion to their work, determines entitlement to tax exemption. * * * Indeed, this Court previously has stated that "it is necessary and proper ... to survey all the activities of [an] organization, in order to determine whether what the organization in fact does is to carry out a religious mission or to engage in commercial business." *United States v. Dykema*, 666 F.2d 1096, 1100 (7th Cir.1981), *cert. denied*, 456 U.S. 983, 102 S.Ct. 2257, 72 L.Ed.2d 861 (1982); * * *. While "the inquiry must remain that of determining the purpose to which the ... business activity is directed," *Presbyterian & Reformed Publishing Co. v. Commissioner,* 743 F.2d 148, 156 (3d Cir.1984), the activities provide a useful indicia of the organization's purpose or purposes. Thus, keeping in mind Living Faith's good faith assertion of a religious purpose, we examine Living Faith's activities and manner of operations.

Although an organization is not disqualified from tax-exempt status solely because its primary activity constitutes a business, when it conducts a business with an apparently commercial character as its primary activity, "that fact weighs heavily against exemption." *B.S.W. Group,* 70 T.C. at 359. Living Faith, whose primary activity consists of operating restaurants and food stores, engages in precisely such conduct. Its operations are "as presumptively commercial" as the sale of prescription drugs to the general public and holders of special VIP cards, *see Federation Pharmacy Servs., Inc. v. Commissioner,* 625 F.2d 804, 808 (8th Cir.1980), the sale of consulting services, *see B.S.W.,* 70 T.C. at 358, "or the sale of any other product." *Federation Pharmacy,* 625 F.2d at 808.

It is significant that Living Faith is in direct competition with other restaurants. "Competition with commercial firms is strong evidence of the predominance of non-exempt commercial purposes." *B.S.W. Group,* 70 T.C. at 358; * * *. Living Faith has failed to demonstrate that its business, which operates in a shopping center, does not compete with other restaurants and food stores. Living Faith's prices, for example, are set "competitively with area businesses," * * * using pricing formulas common in the retail food business. This lack of below-cost pricing militates against granting an exemption. * * * Indeed, the profit-making price structure looms large in our analysis of its purposes. * * *

That Living Faith competes with other commercial enterprises is also indicated by its informational materials, which are apparently promotional as well. The use of promotional materials and "commercial catch phrases" to enhance sales are relevant factors in determining whether an organization "operate[s] in the same manner as that of any profitable commercial enterprise." *United Missionary Aviation,* 60 T.C.M. (CCH) at 1156. A few examples are illustrative. A tract dated June 1988 contains not only religious references ("The Lord has helped us to provide a haven of rest to nourish body, mind and soul"), but significant commercial overtones as well ("If you bring this story to our restaurant we will give you one meal free when you buy one. Limit one meal per story.").... A mailing distributed by Living Faith states its religious purpose ("Country Life is a 'not for profit' health ministry whose goal is to help people achieve a better life through the intelligent application of the laws of health and spiritual renewal in Christ"), but also contains language that is clearly commercial in nature (Country Life offers "[w]orld famous restaurants, superb vegetarian cuisine since 1963") ..... Another tract promotes Living Faith's various activities, including the Bible study classes and vegetarian cooking classes, and states, "We want to serve you better with expanded hours and services.".... These materials contain a strong "commercial hue," *see*

B.S.W. Group, 70 T.C. at 357, and thus provide an indicia of a forbidden commercial purpose.* * *

Living Faith's advertising—totalling $15,500 over a two-year period—is another relevant factor in determining that it is engaging in activities for a nonexempt purpose. * * * So, too, is its lack of plans to solicit contributions. * * * Although Living Faith states that it has received donations from members of the Seventh-day Adventist Church (its financial statements show that it received approximately $101,000 in "donations" for the 1987 operating year and $46,000 for 1988), the record does not document the sources of these donations. Living Faith relies exclusively on its own financial statements, and on memoranda it submitted to the Commissioner during the application process. However, its own arguments and statements, solely by virtue of being included in the administrative record, are insufficient to establish the source of the donations.* * * Similarly, although Living Faith states that it occasionally provides free meals to the needy, in exchange for chores, and has provided more than 100 bags of clothing to charity, the record provides no documentation other than Living Faith's own statements. * * *

Living Faith's financial statements show that its operations grossed $280,000 from paying customers during the 1988 fiscal year. Despite these gross profits, Living Faith asserts that its lack of net profits indicates that its purpose is indeed tax exempt. Although Living Faith is correct that a failure to show a profit is relevant in determining the presence or absence of commercial purposes, * * *, it is only one factor among several, and does not per se entitle an organization to exempt status. * * * This is especially so where, as here, the lack of profits occur during an organization's early period of existence. *See Schoger Found.,* 76 T.C. at 387 n. 6 (even if petitioner were operating at a deficit "during this early period of existence," it would not counterbalance the other facts indicating nonexempt purpose). * * *

Other factors reveal additional evidence of a commercial purpose. Living Faith's hours of operation, for example, are substantially competitive with other commercial enterprises; although closed on Saturdays, the Sabbath for members of the Seventh-day Adventist Church, its Country Life restaurants are open 40 hours each week, and the health food stores for 55. The various activities sponsored by Living Faith, such as the Bible study classes and the free meals periodically offered to the public, are offered after hours and thus do not interfere with routine business operations.

In urging us to reverse the Tax Court's determination, Living Faith relies heavily upon *Golden Rule Church Association v. Commissioner,* 41 T.C. 719 (1964). The petitioners in *Golden Rule* were a church and two of its subsidiaries, one which operated several businesses as vehicles for spreading the church's religious doctrines, and the other which held property for the church. The Commissioner sought to tax income the property-holding subsidiary had derived from the sale of timber on property it had purchased. In denying a tax exemption, the Commissioner relied on various other activities, unrelated to the timber sale, which had given rise to net operating losses over a period of more than ten years. The Tax Court reversed the Commissioner's adverse determination. Living Faith argues that *Golden Rule* is analogous to the instant case, and maintains further that

> *Golden Rule* appeared to give "controlling significance" to the petitioners' good faith assertion of religious purpose. * * *

We find the scenario in *Golden Rule* distinguishable from the present case. First, unlike Living Faith, which conducts the primary activity of operating two restaurants and health food stores, the organization in *Golden Rule* operated a variety of small businesses, the very purpose of which was to illustrate to the public that the "golden rule" can be applied to one's daily business activities. * * * Indeed, the petitioners in *Golden Rule* had closed at least one of these businesses, because it had turned out to be "a poor illustration of the concepts the church tried to demonstrate to the public." * * * Additionally, the petitioners had sustained "consistent and substantial" operating losses for most of the businesses over an eleven-year period. * * * In contrast, Living Faith's financial figures—which include its fledgling period—reflect a substantial increase in gross profits, from $73,000 for the fiscal year ending September 30, 1987, to $280,000 the following year, and a decline in operating losses during the same periods. Moreover, the businesses in *Golden Rule* were operated by "student ministers," who, unlike the Living Faith "volunteers," received no salaries and whose total time was under ecclesiastical direction. Living Faith's records indicate it paid salaries of more than $25,000 in fiscal year 1987 and $63,000 in 1988. Finally, the student ministers in *Golden Rule* were rotated among various projects "to maximize the variety of their experiences with the public," and the organization made no effort to create specialists in order to foster efficiency of operation. The Country Life guidelines under which Living Faith operates, however, require that, among other things, its management have business ability and six months training in a Country Life store. Given the numerous distinguishing factors, the result in *Golden Rule* is not compelled here.

We also reject Living Faith's claim that the Tax Court in *Golden Rule* gave "controlling significance" to the petitioners' assertion of religious purpose. Although the court recognized the petitioners' espoused purpose, it specifically stated that it "must always be guided by the character of the organization and its activities," and further noted that "[i]t does not necessarily follow that we must accept all claims that activities are religious simply because those claims are sincere."

Living Faith's situation is closer to that of the organization denied exempt status in *Schoger Foundation v. Commissioner,* 76 T.C. 380 (1981). The petitioner in *Schoger,* a not-for-profit corporation, operated a lodge located in the mountains of Colorado, and promoted the facility as a lodge "for Christian families." The lodge offered various recreational activities. It also offered religious activities—operated without a set program—including daily devotions and Scripture reading after breakfast, Sunday morning worship for guests requesting the service, and discussion seminars, Christian song sessions, and "share sessions" conducted by staff members. Attendance at both the recreational and religious activities was strictly optional. Although the lodge conducted only minimal advertising, a brochure—which referenced recreational activities and accommodations as well as religion—was provided to potential guests. While the court recognized that "specific mandatory religious activities are not necessarily required" to obtain exempt status, it added:

> [T]here must be something more than the fact that Christ Haven Lodge is promoted as a lodge "for Christian families." ... It is difficult to see how that experience differs, if it does, from the same experience one can have at any quiet inn or lodge located in the beautiful mountains of Colorado.

Similarly, it is difficult to see how the experience of dining or shopping at Living Faith's restaurant and health food stores differs, if it does, from the same experience one might have while dining or shopping at other vegetarian restaurants and health food stores. Granting a tax exemption to Living Faith would necessarily disadvantage its for-profit competitors. * * * We do not doubt the sincerity of Living Faith's beliefs, and we recognize its good faith in asserting a religious purpose of health promotion. Based on the record before us, however, we must uphold the Tax Court's determination that Living Faith operates with a substantial commercial purpose as well, and is therefore not entitled to § 501(c)(3) tax-exempt status.

* * * *

We find that the Tax Court's decision that Living Faith operates for a substantial commercial purpose and does not qualify as a tax-exempt organization under § 501(c)(3) is not clearly erroneous, but is supported by substantial evidence in the administrative record. The decision of the Tax Court is

AFFIRMED.

Questions

1. The court in *Living Faith* concludes that Living Faith, Inc. was operating restaurants for purposes unrelated to its educational, nutritional, and religious purposes. Do you agree?

2. The court, among its reasons, indicates that Living Faith was competing with other for-profit restaurants. The Revenue Act of 1950 did list uncompetitive activity by exempt organizations as the primary reason for the need for statutory change. However, the statute does not refer to uncompetitive activity at all. Still, the regulations pursuant to § 513, in defining an unrelated trade or business, indicate that competition is a relevant factor. [See Treas. Reg. § 1.513–1(b).] The court determined that Living Faith's restaurants were competing in an impermissible manner. Do nonprofit

hospitals or nonprofit educational institutions also compete with for-profit entities? Should these organizations be treated differently?

Note

The requirement that a tax-exempt organization be organized and operated exclusively for its specific exempt purposes presupposes that the organization will not engage in activities of a commercial nature that are unrelated to the tax-exempt purpose of the organization. Nonetheless a tax-exempt organization is regarded as being operated exclusively for its exempt purpose so long as its activities are primarily those that are carried on to accomplish its exempt purpose or purposes and if not more than an "insubstantial" part of its activities furthers a nonexempt purpose. Thus, an insubstantial amount of commercial, nonexempt activity will not disqualify most nonprofit organizations for tax-exempt status. There are no definitive guidelines as to how much commercial activity is "substantial" and, thus, could jeopardize the tax-exempt status of an organization.

B. Private Benefit

Although § 501(c)(3) does not explicitly limit private benefit, the section, by disallowing more than insubstantial unrelated activity, infers that conferring a "private benefit" can prejudice an organization's exempt status. The regulations expressly state the limitation:

> An organization is not organized or operated exclusively for one or more ... [charitable] purposes unless it serves a public rather than a private interest. Thus, to meet the requirement of this subdivision, it is necessary for an organization to establish that it is not organized or operated for the benefit of private interests.... [Treas. Reg. § 1.501(c)(3)–1(d)(1)(ii)].

AMERICAN CAMPAIGN ACADEMY v. COMMISSIONER

United States Tax Court, 1989
92 T.C. 1053

NIMS, CHIEF JUDGE:

Petitioner seeks a declaratory judgment under section 7428(a)* * * that it is exempt from Federal income taxation under section 501(a) as an organization meeting the requirements of section 501(c)(3). Further, should we declare petitioner to satisfy the requirements of section 501(c)(3), we are requested to also determine whether petitioner is classified as 'other than a private foundation' by reason of sections 509(a)(1) and 170(b)(1)(A)(ii). Based upon our holding that petitioner is nonexempt under section 501(c)(3), we do not reach the latter issue.

Pursuant to Rule 122, the case was submitted for decision with the stipulated administrative record, as defined in Rule 210(b)(11). For purposes of this proceeding, we accept the facts and representations contained in the administrative record as true and incorporate them herein by this reference. Petitioner has exhausted its administrative remedies within the Internal Revenue Service as required by section 7428(b)(2) and Rule 210(c)(4), received a final adverse ruling mailed on December 15, 1987, and invoked the jurisdiction of this Court by petition filed March 11, 1988.

FACTUAL BACKGROUND

Petitioner, American Campaign Academy (also referred to hereinafter as petitioner or the Academy), is a Virginia corporation incorporated by Jan W. Baran, General Counsel of the National Republican Congressional Committee, on January 24, 1986, exclusively for charitable and educational purposes, including:

>   A. Organizing and operating a school to train individuals for careers as campaign managers, communications directors, finance directors or other political campaign professionals;
>
>   B. Sponsoring research and publishing instructional materials, reports, newsletters, pamphlets or books relating to the conduct of a political campaign;
>
>   C. Sponsoring research, to include public opinion research or polling, concerning the public's attitude toward political issues or problems and the publishing of reports, pamphlets, books or other materials to be made available to the general public;
>
>   D. Elevating the standards of professionalism, ethics and morality that prevail in the conduct of campaigns for election to public office at the national, state and local levels.

At the time petitioner filed its petition, its principal place of business was located in Arlington, Virginia.

As its primary activity, petitioner operates a school to train individuals for careers as political campaign professionals. Petitioner's school maintains a regularly scheduled curriculum, a regular faculty, and a full-time enrolled student body at the facilities it occupies. Petitioner claims that it is the only school to exclusively offer a highly concentrated and extensive campaign training curriculum. Similar campaign management courses are offered by American University, Kent State University, Westminster College in Utah, Georgia State University, North Florida State, San Francisco State College, University of California–Davis, University of Southern California and Bernard Baruch College in New York. Seminars offering campaign training are also sponsored by such groups as the Republican National Committee Campaign Management College, United States Campaign Academy, The Leadership Institute, Committee for the Survival of a Free Congress, and the Democratic National Committee. Petitioner has no connection with any of these training programs.

Prior to the organization of the Academy, the National Republican Congressional Committee (NRCC), an unincorporated association comprised of Republican members of the United States House of Representatives, sponsored programs designed to train candidates and to train and subsequently place campaign professionals in Republican campaigns. A campaign professional works for a candidate. Campaign professionals typically occupy such strategic campaign positions as communications director, finance director, or campaign manager.

The Academy stated on its Application for Recognition of Exemption (Form 1023) that it was an 'outgrowth' of the course of instruction run by the NRCC. NRCC contributed physical assets such as furniture and computer hardware to the Academy. Two of the Academy's six full-time faculty were previously involved in the NRCC's training program. One of the Academy's three initial directors, Joseph Gaylord, is the Executive Director of the NRCC. Another initial director, John C. McDonald, is a member of the Republican National Committee.

NRCC continues to offer training for Republican candidates and staff members of incumbent Republican congressmen. The administrative record does not reveal to what extent, if any, NRCC continues to offer training to campaign professionals.

The Academy program for training campaign professionals differs from its predecessor NRCC program. Significantly, unlike the NRCC, the Academy limits its students to 'campaign professionals.' The Academy does not train candidates nor participate in, nor intervene in, any political campaign on behalf of any candidate. Neither does the Academy engage in any activities tending to influence legislation. Moreover, while the Academy actively refers resumes and provides recommendations of graduates to requesting campaigns, it assumes no formal placement responsibilities. Nonetheless, in June, 1986, after the first 1986 primary elections were completed, the Academy included in its newsletter (see discussion infra) the following invitation to all graduates:

LOST YOUR PRIMARY?

Hate your candidate? Can't deal with the weather? The primary's over, you lost. NEED A NEW JOB?

Having troubles finding that new job because someone's unfairly trashing your work? Nobody's listening to your side of the story? NEED HELP?

Call your friends at the ACA.

Just because we don't send you checks on Fridays doesn't mean we don't still stand ready to try to help you out of those sticky professional wickets.

Think about it—it's in our best interest that you do well. The success of the Academy can only be based on the contributions of our students. Our futures are inextricably linked.

* * *

Thanks to you all and the good work you're doing out there on the battlefields of democracy, the world is pretty aware that the Academy exists. More than that, that same world does call us looking for good folks to fill their urgent campaign needs.

If the need arises, call us up, send us a current resume, we'll see what we can do about getting you off the streets.

* * *

At least 15 graduates secured new campaign positions with Congressional and Senatorial candidates following publication of petitioner's invitation.

No training materials developed by the NRCC are used by the Academy. Rather, the Academy has generally hired its own faculty, developed its own courses and enhanced the training curriculum. The Academy's faculty consists of 5–6 full-time members and approximately 141 adjunct members. Training materials used by students include compilations and handouts, published textbooks, trade books and articles, and faculty-prepared lecture materials.

The Academy has more applicants for admission than its physical facilities can accommodate. Thus, its admissions criteria are competitive. The Academy seeks to admit applicants who have a strong commitment to professional campaign involvement on the Congressional level. The Academy believes committed applicants will possess at least four of the following qualifications:

    1. PAID CAMPAIGN EXPERIENCE. Applicant should have worked on a political campaign as a campaign staff member with considerable responsibility on the local, state or federal level.

    2. VOLUNTEER CAMPAIGN EXPERIENCE. Applicant should have volunteered time to a campaign to assist the efforts of the campaign.

    3. JOURNALISM/PUBLIC RELATIONS BACKGROUND. Applicant should have either a journalism background or practical experience working for a newspaper, radio or television station, advertising agency or political consulting firm.

    4. COLLEGE GRADUATE.

    5. POLITICAL EXPERIENCE. Applicant should have worked in a congressional office, state office, trade association, state or national political committee.

    6. CIVIC RESPONSIBILITY. Applicant should have actively served in a civic/volunteer organization or campus political organization.

    7. FUNDRAISING EXPERIENCE. Applicant should have worked in a fundraising campaign (for an organization, school, political campaign, etc.), preferably in a management or direct solicitation role.

    8. ORGANIZATIONAL EXPERIENCE. Applicant should have played a principle role in the production of a program, event,

organization, etc., which required coordinating people and resources in a defined time frame.

Each applicant provides the Academy with the details of his or her qualifications in each applicable category. In addition, applicants are asked to provide at least two political and two professional references. And while applicants are not required to formally declare their political affiliation to attend the Academy, such affiliations may often be deduced from the campaign experiences and political references contained in the application. Applicants may freely volunteer their political party affiliation. The Academy maintains no records indicating the number of applicants who are Republicans, Democrats, associated with other parties, or independent.

Completed applications for admission to the Academy are evaluated by an admission panel. The Academy has no requirement that a member of the admission panel be affiliated with any particular political party. However, the Academy believes that a substantial number of the members of its admission panel are affiliated with the Republican party. The Academy does not discriminate on the basis of race, color, national, or ethnic origin in admitting students, in administering its educational policies and school-sponsored programs, or in granting financial assistance.

The Academy's curriculum presents a considerable body of knowledge to be learned and skills to be mastered in preparing the student to perform effectively as a campaign professional. Initially, the curriculum offered by the Academy was divided into two parts. In part one of the curriculum, each student enrolled in an intensive overview course, lasting several weeks, designed to highlight the major elements of a political campaign. In part two of the curriculum, each student would enroll in one of three training programs providing specialized instruction in campaign management, campaign finance, or campaign communications.

Based upon feedback from its earliest graduating class, the Academy determined that a single unified curriculum, rather than a two-part specialized approach, would best prepare students to meet the challenges faced by campaign professionals. The Academy presently offers a single 10-week general program to all students. Current courses of instruction explore such topics as campaign strategy, the American political system and its environment, research techniques, organization basics, campaign strategy, professional ethics, Federal Election Commission rules and regulations, campaign financing techniques, voter surveying, vote targeting, issue development, media communications, speechwriting, volunteer recruiting and organizing, budgeting, coalition building and basic computer applications. Discussions concerning 'How some Republicans have won Black votes,' 'NRCC/RNC/NRSC/State Party naughtiness,' and 'Use of GOP allies' are included in the campaign strategy and organizational courses.

Students are expected to master the campaign fundamentals taught in the curriculum. Mastery of coursework requires students to attend daily classes from 9:00 a.m. to 5:30 p.m., and to complete demanding case studies, role playing assignments, research projects and various homework exercises. Periodic evaluations are given to measure each student's performance. Students who fail to adequately perform may be dismissed from the program. To encourage students to concentrate their efforts on mastering the presented materials, students are prohibited from holding full or part-time jobs during their 10–week enrollment. Students admitted to the Academy are not charged tuition and receive a nominal weekly stipend during their course of study.

Following graduation, Academy students are expected to apply their newly acquired knowledge and skills in a political campaign. If a graduate fails to put forth a good faith effort to secure a position in a campaign, the Academy may withhold its recommendation. Approximately 80 percent of the Academy's graduates served on political campaigns during 1986.

Beginning June 6, 1986, the Academy began publishing a monthly newsletter entitled 'A Hundred Battles.' The first newsletter announced that on May 16, 1986, the last students for the 1986 campaign year were graduated, bringing the total graduates to 120. During the months of June through September 1986, the newsletter tracked the activities of 119 of the Academy's 120 graduates. As reported in the four newsletters, 85 graduates participated in the campaigns of Congressional or Senatorial candidates, four graduates were employed by the NRCC or Republican National Committee Field Divisions, 10 graduates participated in gubernatorial or other statewide or local campaigns, at least three graduates were employed by various State Republican parties, and several graduates worked as political consultants. Many graduates whose candidates were defeated in the 1986 primary elections joined the campaigns of other candidates. In total, Academy graduates filled important positions in approximately 98 Congressional and Senatorial campaign positions during the 1986 election cycle. In addition, one graduate worked in a presidential campaign in a foreign country.

On September 16, 1986, respondent requested petitioner to provide additional information regarding several matters. One matter concerned the affiliation of the candidates served by petitioner's graduates. Specifically, respondent asked:

> Of the individuals that have already graduated from your programs, how many (to the best of your knowledge) are currently working for Republican candidates? How many are working for Democratic candidates? Other parties?

On October 3, 1986, petitioner answered respondent's inquiry as follows:

> We do not require students to remain in contact with the Academy following graduation. Of those who chose to do so, some have informed the Academy of the identity of the candidate(s) for

whom they are working. (See the [attached] newsletters * * *.) To the best that can be determined, the predominant party affiliation of the candidates for whom Academy graduates are working in 1986 is Republican, but the Academy has no exact numbers.

Following the 1986 Federal election, approximately 46 percent of the Academy's graduates were either unemployed or employed in nonpolitical positions.

Funding for the Academy's activities has been exclusively provided by the National Republican Congressional Trust (NRCT), an organization that collects political contributions and uses such funds for purposes approved by the Federal Election Commission. No funding has been received from any candidate's campaign committee. NRCT funding through August, 1987, reached $972,000. The Academy has estimated that 90 percent of its funding is expended to run its school. The remaining 10 percent of funding has been dedicated to research and the publishing of reports, pamphlets, books, or other materials to be made available to the general public.

DISCUSSION

Section 501(a) exempts organizations described in section 501(c) from Federal income tax. In order to qualify for an exemption under section 501(c)(3), an organization must satisfy four criteria: (1) it must be organized and operated exclusively for certain specified exempt purposes, including educational purposes; (2) no part of its net earnings may inure to the benefit of a private shareholder or individual; (3) no part of its activities may constitute intervention or participation in any political campaign on behalf of any candidate for public office; and (4) no substantial part of its activities may consist of political or lobbying activities. Section 501(c)(3). These requirements are stated in the conjunctive. Petitioner's failure to satisfy any of the four requirements is fatal to its qualification under section 501(c)(3). * * * In addition to satisfying each condition specified in section 501(c)(3), petitioner must also establish that its purpose is not contrary to public policy. * * *

The responsibility for ruling on the section 501(c)(3) exempt status of an organization lies with respondent, who, based upon the uninvestigated statements of fact submitted by the taxpayer, must determine whether each of the prescribed requirements is met. * * * Respondent discharges his responsibility pursuant to highly detailed administrative procedures. See Statement of Procedural Rules (SPR hereinafter), 26 C.F.R. section 601.201(n) (1988); section 1.508–1, Income Tax Regs. If in respondent's judgment the organization fails to qualify for exempt status, the reasons for disqualification are normally (and were in the case at bar) articulated in a notice of final determination issued to the organization. The organization which has properly exhausted its administrative remedies may thereafter timely petition for judicial review of respondent's denial by this Court, the United States Claims Court, or the

United States District Court for the District of Columbia. Section 7428 and SPR, 26 C.F.R. section 601.201(n)(5)-(7).

A timely petition made under section 7428(a) confers jurisdiction on this Court to declare whether the petitioning organization initially qualifies or continues to qualify under section 501(c)(3) as an exempt section 501(a) entity. In making our declaration, we do not, however, engage in a de novo review of the administrative record. * * * Rather, we 'base [our] determination upon the reasons provided by the Internal Revenue Service in its notice to the party making the request for a determination, or based upon any new argument which the Service may wish to introduce at the time of the trial.' See H. Rept. 94–658, at 285 (1976), 1976-3 C.B. (Vol. 2) 977. Thus, the scope of our inquiry and declaration is limited to the propriety of the reasons given by respondent for denying petitioner's application for exempt status. * * *

Respondent concedes that (1) petitioner is organized exclusively for exempt purposes, i.e., educational purposes, (2) no part of petitioner's net earnings inure to the benefit of a private shareholder or individual, (3) no substantial part of petitioner's activities consists of political or lobbying activities and (4) petitioner is not involved in any proscribed campaign activities. Likewise, respondent makes no contention that the activities of the Academy are contrary to established public policy. Rather, respondent rests his denial of the Academy's application for exempt status solely on the Academy's alleged failure to operate exclusively for exempt purposes. Specifically, respondent's final ruling letter states:

> You have failed to establish that you are operated exclusively for exempt purposes as required by section 501(c)(3). You are operated for a substantial non-exempt private purpose. You benefit Republican Party entities and candidates more than incidentally. Also, your activities serve the private interests of Republican Party entities rather than public interests exclusively. Respondent does not assert at this proceeding any additional bases for denying petitioner's application.

We note at the outset that petitioner bears the burden of overcoming the grounds set forth in respondent's final ruling letter. Rule 217(c)(2)(i). To prevail herein, petitioner must show, based upon the materials in the administrative record, that it does not operate to benefit Republican Party entities and candidates more than incidentally or that such benefits do not serve a private rather than a public interest. * * *

OPERATIONAL TEST

The operational test of section 1.501(c)(3)-1(c)(1), Income Tax Regs., is designed to insure that the organization's resources and activities are devoted to furthering exempt purposes. The operational test examines the actual purpose for the organization's activities and not the nature of the activities or the organization's statement of purpose. * * * In testing compliance with the operational test, we look beyond the four corners of the organization's charter to discover 'the actual objects motivating the organization and the subsequent conduct of the organization.' Taxation with Representation v. United States, 585 F.2d 1219, 1222 (4th Cir. 1978), citing Samuel Friedland Foundation v. United States, 144 F.Supp. 74, 85 (D.N.J.1956); * * * What an organization's purposes are and what purposes its activities support are questions of fact. * * * We may draw factual inferences from the administrative record in the performance of our review function. * * *

The Treasury Regulations specify three conditions which must be satisfied for an organization to meet the operational test. * * * First, the organization must be primarily engaged in activities which accomplish one or more of the exempt purposes specified in section 501(c)(3). Section 1.501(c)(3)–1(c)(1), Income Tax Regs. Second, the organization's net earnings must not be distributed in whole or in part to the benefit of private shareholders or individuals. Section 1.501(c)(3)–1(c)(2), Income Tax Regs. Third, the organization must not be an 'action' organization, i.e., one which devotes a substantial part of its activities attempting to influence legislation, or participates or intervenes, directly or indirectly, in any political campaign. Section 1.501(c)(3)–1(c)(3), Income Tax Regs.

Respondent does not contend that petitioner's earnings inure to the benefit of private shareholders or individuals, or that petitioner is an action organization. Rather, respondent recognizes on brief that 'Academy would * * * be described in section 501(c)(3) so long as it serves a public interest as required by section 1.501(c)(3)–1(d)(1)(ii) [Income Tax Regs.].' Thus, the sole issue for declaration is whether respondent properly determined that petitioner failed to satisfy the first condition of the operational test by not primarily engaging in activities which accomplish exempt purposes.

OPERATING PRIMARILY FOR EXEMPT PURPOSES

To establish that it operates primarily in activities which accomplish exempt purposes, petitioner must establish that no more than an insubstantial part of its activities does not further an exempt purpose. Section 1.501(c)(3)–1(c)(1), Income Tax Regs. The presence of a single substantial nonexempt purpose destroys the exemption regardless of the number or importance of the exempt purposes. * * *

When an organization operates for the benefit of private interests such as designated individuals, the creator or his family, shareholders of the organization, or persons controlled, directly or indirectly, by such private interests, the organization by definition does not operate exclusively for exempt purposes. Section 1.501(c)(3)–1(d)(1)(ii), Income Tax Regs.* * * Prohibited private benefits may include an 'advantage; profit; fruit; privilege; gain; [or] interest.' Retired Teachers Legal Fund v. Commissioner, 78 T.C. 280, 286 (1982). Occasional economic benefits flowing to persons as an incidental consequence of an organization pursuing exempt charitable purposes will not generally constitute prohibited private benefits. * * * Thus, should petitioner be shown to benefit private interests, it will be deemed to further a nonexempt purpose under section 1.501(c)(3)–1(d)(1)(ii), Income Tax Regs. This nonexempt purpose will prevent petitioner from operating primarily for exempt purposes absent a showing that no more than an insubstantial part of its activities further the private interests or any other nonexempt purposes. Section 1.501(c)(3)–1(c)(1), Income Tax Regs.

Respondent contends that petitioner's activities substantially benefit the private interests of Republican party entities and candidates, thereby advancing a nonexempt private purpose. Petitioner counters that respondent erred in denying its exemption application by incorrectly applying the private benefit analysis of section 1.501(c)(3)–1(d)(1)(ii), Income Tax Regs., to persons other than a 'private shareholder or individual' within the meaning of section 1.501(a)–1(c), Income Tax Regs. Section 1.501(a)–1(c), Income Tax Regs., defines the words 'private shareholder or individual' as persons having a personal and private interest in the activities of the organization (hereinafter private shareholders or individuals are sometimes referred to as 'insiders'). Alternatively, petitioner argues that the private benefits, if any, conferred on various Republican entities and candidates were incidental to the exempt public educational purposes its activities further.

UNRELATED PARTIES AND PRIVATE INTERESTS

We begin our analysis by considering whether an organization may transgress the 'public rather than a private interest' mandate of section 1.501(c)(3)–1(d)(1)(ii), Income Tax Regs., by conferring benefits on persons not having a personal and private interest in the activities of the organization. See sections 1.501(c)(3)–1(c)(2) and 1.501(a)–1(c), Income Tax Regs. Petitioner maintains that the prohibition against private benefit is limited to situations in which an organization's insiders are benefitted.

Petitioner further contends that since 'Republican Party entities and candidates' cannot be construed as insiders of its organization, no transgression of the operational test exists.

In support of limiting the private benefit analysis to insiders, petitioner compares the language of section 1.501(c)(3)–1(d)(1)(ii), Income Tax Regs...., to the statutory and regulatory language prohibiting the inurement of organizational earnings to private shareholders and individuals. Section 501(c)(3) and sections 1.501(c)(3)–1(c)(2) and 1.501(a)–1(c), Tax Income Regs. Petitioner asserts that the class of persons illustrated in section 1.501(c)(3)–1(d)(1)(ii), Income Tax Regs. (i.e., designated individuals, the creator or his family, shareholders of the organization or persons controlled directly or indirectly by such private interests), overlaps with the class of persons identified by section 501(c)(3) and section 1.501(a)–1(c), Income Tax Regs., as insiders in the private inurement context (i.e., persons having a personal and private interest in the activities of the organization). Petitioner believes that this overlap 'clearly indicates' that both the prohibition against private inurement and the prohibition against conferral of substantial private benefits exclusively target the same class of persons.

Petitioner reasons that because this Court has explicitly excluded unrelated third parties from the ambit of the term 'private shareholder or individual' in the earnings inurement context, * * * unrelated third parties must likewise be excluded from the class of private persons whose receipt of a substantial benefit would cause the organization to be operated other than exclusively for exempt purposes. Section 1.501(c)(3)-1(d)(1)(ii), Income Tax Regs. Accordingly, petitioner concludes that since Republican entities and candidates are not interested insiders, the private benefit analysis of section 1.501(c)(3)-1(d)(1)(ii), Income Tax Regs., is inapplicable in the case at bar. We do not agree.

Petitioner misconstrues the overlapping characteristics of the private benefit and private inurement prohibitions. We have consistently recognized that while the prohibitions against private inurement and private benefits share common and often overlapping elements, * * * the two are distinct requirements which must independently be satisfied. * * * Nonetheless, we have often observed that the prohibition against private inurement of net earnings appears redundant, since the inurement of earnings to an interested person or insider would constitute the conferral of a benefit inconsistent with operating exclusively for an exempt purpose. * * * In other words, when an organization permits its net earnings to inure to the benefit of a private shareholder or individual, it transgresses the private inurement prohibition and operates for a nonexempt private purpose.

The absence of private inurement of earnings to the benefit of a private shareholder or individual does not, however, establish that the organization is operated exclusively for exempt purposes. Therefore, while the private inurement prohibition may arguably be subsumed within the private benefit analysis of the operational test, the reverse is not true. Accordingly, when the Court concludes that no prohibited inurement of earnings exists, it cannot stop there but must inquire further and determine whether a prohibited private benefit is conferred. * * *

Moreover, an organization's conferral of benefits on disinterested persons may cause it to serve 'a private interest' within the meaning of section 1.501(c)(3)–1(d)(1)(ii), Income Tax Regs. * * * In this connection, we use 'disinterested' to distinguish persons who are not private shareholders or individuals having a personal and private interest in the activities of the organization within the meaning of section 1.501(a)–1(c), Income Tax Regs.

PRESENCE OF PRIVATE BENEFITS

Having determined that nonincidental benefits conferred on disinterested persons may serve private interests, we now consider whether respondent erred in determining that petitioner conferred nonincidental private benefits upon Republican entities and candidates. Section

1.501(c)(3)–1(d)(1)(ii), Income Tax Regs. Petitioner contends that Rev. Rul. 76–456, 1976–2 C.B. 151, prescribes the proper characterization of all benefits conferred by organizations engaging in its type of activities. In this revenue ruling, an organization collected, collated and disseminated information concerning general campaign practices on a nonpartisan basis. The organization also furnished 'teaching aids' to political science and civics teachers. Emphasizing the organization's nonpartisan nature, respondent determined that the organization exclusively served a public purpose by encouraging citizens to increase their knowledge and understanding of the election process and participate more effectively in their selection of government officials.

We note that revenue rulings are not binding precedent on this Court, but rather are viewed as contentions of respondent. * * * However, where a revenue ruling incorporates a long-standing administrative practice sanctioned by the Courts or the Congress, it may acquire the force of law. * * * Furthermore, it seems self-evident that in general a taxpayer may rely on a revenue ruling where parallel facts place the ruling in the posture of a concession by the Commissioner as to the analogous taxpayer. Nevertheless, because we distinguish petitioner from the organization described in Rev. Rul. 76–456, 1976–2 C.B. 151, we need not evaluate the significance of the position respondent espouses therein.

In contrast to the nonpartisan activities conducted by the organization in Rev. Rul. 76–456, supra, respondent determined and we find that petitioner conducted its educational activities with the partisan objective of benefiting Republican candidates and entities. Petitioner was incorporated by Jan W. Baran, General Counsel of the NRCC on January 24, 1986. In April, 1986, petitioner stated in its Application for Recognition of Exemption that its training program was an outgrowth of the program run by the NRCC.

Petitioner's activities have been exclusively funded by the National Republican Congressional Trust. Two of petitioner's three initial directors had significant ties to the Republican party: Joseph Gaylord as Executive Director of NRCC and John C. McDonald as a member of the Republican National Committee. Petitioner's bylaws empowered this Republican majority of the Board to 'have general charge of the affairs, property and assets of the Corporation.' Under their general charge the Academy instituted a curriculum that included studies of the 'Growth of NRCC, etc.' and 'Why are people Republicans.'

Following the reorganization of petitioner's curriculum after the 1986 election, additional partisan topics such as 'Other Republican givers lists,' 'How some Republicans have won Black votes,' and 'NRCC/RNC/NRSC/State Party naughtiness' were added. The Academy's curriculum failed to counterbalance the Republican party focus of these courses with comparable studies of the Democratic or other political parties.

Petitioner does not require that its admission panel members be affiliated with a particular political party, but believes that a substantial number of the panel members are affiliated with the Republican party. Likewise, while no particular political affiliation is required of students, the two political references solicited by petitioner on its application for admission often permit the admission panel to deduce the applicant's political affiliation. In turn, knowledge of an applicant's political affiliation provides the admission panel with a means of limiting enrollment to applicants who are likely to subsequently work in Republican organizations and campaigns.

Petitioner was asked by respondent to identify the affiliation of the candidates served by its graduates. Petitioner responded that although graduates are not required to remain in contact with Academy following graduation, 'some' graduates chose to report their whereabouts. To the 'best' that petitioner could determine, these graduates served on campaigns of candidates who were predominantly affiliated with the Republican party.

The administrative record reveals that 119 of 120 graduates reported their whereabouts to petitioner. These addresses were reported by petitioner in its June, 1986, monthly newsletter. The addresses of graduates working in Congressional or Senatorial campaigns contained the name of the political committee or organization of the candidate; e.g., Bruce Long for Congress, Friends of Bill Emerson, Jim Hansen Committee, People for Dio Guardi, etc. The June–September, 1986, newsletters disclosed that 85 Academy graduates worked in approximately 98 Congressional and Senatorial candidate campaigns. The newsletters did not, however, specify the political affiliations of the respective candidates.

The political affiliations of the candidates served by petitioner's graduates were readily available to petitioner from the public records maintained by the Federal Election Commission. See Election Campaign Act of 1971 (as amended by Pub. L. 96–187, 93 Stat. 1354), 2 U.S.C. sections 431, 433, 434 and 438 (Supp. IV 1986), which generally require political committees authorized by a candidate to register with and disclose financial and affiliation information, including the party affiliation of the candidate, to the Federal Election Commission, which in turn must compile and index such information and make it available to the public.

As we have delineated under the heading FEDERAL BACKGROUND ..., Federal Election Commission rules and regulations are one of the topics which petitioner's course of study explores, so petitioner would have to concede that it is peculiarly positioned to have knowledge and awareness of the ready availability of data from the Commission's public records. Accordingly, we infer that petitioner's 'best determination' regarding the predominant Republican party affiliation of the candidates for whom Academy graduates were working in

1986 reflects the political affiliations disclosed in the Federal Election Commission's public records.

A showing that petitioner's graduates served in Congressional and Senatorial campaigns of candidates from both major political parties in substantial numbers would have significantly aided petitioner's contention that its activities only benefited nonselect members of a charitable class. Nevertheless, petitioner did not see fit to include in the administrative record any specific example of a graduate working for a Democratic Senatorial or Congressional candidate. We cannot assume that information regarding the placement of Academy graduates, not shown to be unavailable, would have been favorable to petitioner; i.e., would have reflected nonpartisan placement. In fact the contrary is true. * * * Consequently, it is reasonable to infer from petitioner's omission that the affiliation information, had it been included, would have revealed the Republican affiliation of the candidates.

Based upon our review of the administrative record, we find that petitioner operated to advance Republican interests. We also find that the placement of 85 of petitioner's graduates in the campaigns of 98 Republican Senatorial and Congressional candidates conferred a benefit on those candidates. Petitioner's partisan purpose distinguishes the case at bar from Rev. Rul. 76–456. Likewise, petitioner's partisan purpose differs significantly from the nonpartisan educational purpose advanced by a university through means of a political science course which required each student to participate for a two-week period in the political campaign of a candidate of his or her choice. See Rev. Rul. 72–512, 1972–2 C.B. 246.

Petitioner next contends that because all educational programs inherently benefit both the student by increasing his or her skills and future earnings and the eventual employer who profits from the services of trained individuals, the educational benefits it provides should not be construed as prohibited private benefits. (Hereinafter, we will refer to the benefits conferred on the students as primary private benefits and the benefits conferred on the employers as secondary benefits.) In support of this contention, petitioner cites several revenue rulings granting exempt status to training programs and educational facilities sponsored by various industry and professional organizations.

The aforementioned revenue rulings cited by petitioner are: Rev. Rul. 72–101, 1972–1 C.B. 144 (six-week, full-time training program created as a result of collective agreements and funded by industry employers to train individuals working or desiring to work in that industry).

Rev. Rul. 67–72, 1967–1 C.B. 125 (organization created as a result of collective bargaining and funded jointly by labor and management to conduct an industry-wide apprentice training program for interested individuals seeking to qualify for employment as journeymen anywhere in the industry). Rev. Rul. 68–504, 1968–2 C.B. 211 (organization with a membership open to all bank employees in a particular urban area operated to conduct an educational program and publish a professional magazine).

Rev. Rul. 75–196, 1975–1 C.B. 155 (organization supported by a local bar association to maintain a law library for the use of bar association members and their designees).

Petitioner argues that the above rulings establish that organizations which restrict benefits to identified classes demarked by industrial or geographic limitations may, nonetheless, qualify as exempt if the benefited class is broad enough to represent the community. Moreover, petitioner argues that since Republican entities and candidates arguably represent the interests of a class consisting of hundreds of organizations and millions of citizens, the benefits accruing to this class should be construed as public in nature.

Respondent does not quarrel with the notion that exempt educational organizations must inherently confer private benefits on participating individuals. Indeed, he recognizes that an educational organization exists to confer primary private benefits by instructing or training individuals for the purpose of improving or developing his or her capabilities. Section 1.501(c)(3)–1(d)(3)(i), Income Tax Regs. Moreover, respondent does not assert that the pool of potential students is so narrowly drawn that the Academy would confer a proscribed primary private benefit.
* * *

Instead, respondent objects to the secondary benefit accruing exclusively to the Republican entities and candidates who employ petitioner's skilled alumni. Respondent contends that where the training of individuals is focused on furthering a particular targeted private interest, the conferred secondary benefit ceases to be incidental to the providing organization's exempt purposes. By contrast, respondent contends that when secondary benefits are broadly distributed, they become incidental to the organization's exempt purposes.

Respondent asserts that the case at bar differs from the circumstances described in revenue rulings cited by petitioner. Significantly, respondent contends that the secondary benefit provided in each ruling was broadly spread among members of an industry (i.e., employers of union members within an industry, banks within an urban area, members and designees of a local bar association), as opposed to being earmarked for a particular organization or person. The secondary benefit in each of the cited rulings was therefore incidental to the providing organization's exempt purpose.

Based upon his determination that petitioner targeted Republican entities and candidates to receive the secondary benefit through employing its alumni, respondent concludes that the secondary benefit provided by petitioner was not incidental and that more than an insubstantial part of petitioner's activities were performed to further a nonexempt purpose. We agree with respondent.

The question of whether a benefit is private in nature, within the meaning of 1.501(c)(3)–1(d)(1)(ii), Income Tax Regs., was explored by this Court in Aid to Artisans, Inc. v. Commissioner, 71 T.C. 202, 215–216 (1978). In that case, the Commissioner asserted that the organization's purchase of handicrafts from disadvantaged artisans served the private interests of the artisans selling their works. In evaluating the merit of the Commissioner's contention, we stated that:

> The questions whether an organization serves private interests within the meaning of [section 1.501(c)(3)–1(d)(1)(ii), Income Tax Regs.] and whether an organization's activities are conducted for private gain * * * may be resolved * * * by examining the definiteness and charitable nature of the class to be benefited and the overall purpose for which the organization is operated. [71 T.C. at 215.]

Upon finding that (1) the disadvantaged artisans receiving the benefits of the organization's purchases comprised a charitable class, (2) the organization's method of selecting handicrafts for purchase indicated no selectivity with regard to individual artisans to be benefited, and (3) the organization's overall purpose was to benefit disadvantaged communities, we declared the Aid to Artisans organization exempt. * * * Similarly, we have found that organizations which further exempt purposes through sponsoring legal or medical referral services did not confer private benefits so long as the referral service was open to a broad representation of professionals and no select group of professionals were the primary beneficiaries of the service. * * *

To prevail herein, petitioner must establish that the Republican entities and candidates benefiting from the employment of its graduates are members of a charitable class, and within that charitable class do not comprise a select group of members earmarked to receive benefits. With regard to the charitable nature of Republican entities and candidates, petitioner contends that because the Republican party is comprised of millions of individuals with like 'political sympathies,' benefits conferred by the Academy on Republican entities and candidates should be deemed to benefit the community at large. We are not persuaded by petitioner's argument.

Petitioner cites no authority in support of its contention that size alone transforms a benefited class into a charitable class. On the contrary, we believe a qualitative as opposed to a quantitative analysis is more appropriate in assessing the charitable characteristics of a benefited class. In Columbia Park & Recreation Assn. v. Commissioner, 88 T.C. 1, 18–21 (1987), affd. without published opinion 838 F.2d 465 (4th Cir.1988), an organization, formed to provide recreational and other benefits to a membership comprised of approximately 110,000 homeowners and tenants of a real estate development, contended that the magnitude and breath of the benefited class caused it to be inherently charitable. We were not persuaded by the recreation association's per se charitable contention. Rather, we stated that in evaluating qualified organizations:

> We should not be guided merely by petitioner's size [i.e., number of benefited residents] because qualitative not quantitative factors are more determinative of the charitable purpose of an organization. The size of an organization is meaningless if it is not fully integrated with a public element. Mere size does not transform an otherwise noncharitable, private organization to a 'charitable' one. [88 T.C. at 19.]

Finding that the recreation association benefited private members, albeit 110,000, we refused to declare the organization inherently exempt based solely upon its size.

We recognize that Republican entities and candidates differ from the organization at issue in Columbia Park. Nonetheless, we find the principle that size alone fails to confer charitable status applicable to the case at hand. Class size is only one factor to be considered in our qualitative analysis; it is not the sole determinant. Accordingly, petitioner must show that Republican entities and candidates possess charitable characteristics in order that the entities and candidates be deemed members of a charitable class. See section 1.501(c)(3)–1(d)(2), Income Tax Regs., for a noninclusive list of charitable characteristics: poor, distressed, underprivileged, religious, educational, scientific, etc. The large size of the Republican party, which petitioner submits is ultimately benefited by its graduates, does not diminish the need for such showing. Petitioner has not established that the specific Republican entities and candidates which benefited by its educational programs were members of a charitable class.

Moreover, even were we to find political entities and candidates to generally comprise a charitable class, petitioner would bear the burden of proving that its activities benefited the members of the class in a nonselect manner. * * * The administrative record and the partisan affiliation of the candidates served fail to establish that petitioner broadly distributed its secondary benefits among political entities and candidates in a nonselect manner.

Petitioner contends that the infusion of competent campaign workers into the overall political system will benefit the entire community by bolstering confidence in the American electorate. We do not disagree. It is clear, however, that not all organizations which incidentally enhance the public good will be classified as 'public' organizations within the meaning of section 501(c)(3). One need only glance at the other types of organizations described in section 501(c) for examples of 'nonpublic' organizations which often do much to enhance the public good: private clubs, fraternal societies, veterans' organizations, labor organizations, cemetery companies, etc. * * *

We think it is significant that Congress enacted special exemption provisions for certain types of organizations which would be unable to meet the stricter section 501(c)(3) tests which require service to public interests rather than to private ones. * * * Thus, while petitioner may incidentally benefit the public, we conclude that the administrative record and the partisan affiliation of the candidates served by petitioner's graduates in the 1986 election fully support respondent's determination that petitioner confers substantial private benefits on Republican entities and candidates.

Petitioner contends that should we determine that a private benefit is conferred on Republican entities and candidates, such benefit is incidental and collateral to its primary purpose of benefiting the general public. In support of this contention, petitioner argues that a benefit which it cannot control must be incidental in nature. Petitioner observes that 'while it is undoubtedly [petitioner's hope] that its alumni eventually will work for Republican organizations and candidates, Petitioner has in fact no control over whether they will do so or not.' Petitioner reasons that absent an ability to control the employment of its students, it lacks the ability to control the conferral of secondary benefits attributable to such employment. Therefore, the secondary benefits conferred on Republicans are the result of happenstance and should in the opinion of petitioner be treated as merely incidental to its exempt purpose of educating campaign professionals.

Petitioner cites no compelling authority in support of its contention that nonincidental benefits must be controllable by the organization. Moreover, as discussed previously, we find the administrative record supports respondent's contention that petitioner was formed with a substantial purpose to train campaign professionals for service in Republican entities and campaigns, an activity previously conducted by NRCC. Petitioner has failed to persuade us that this is not the case. Secondary benefits which advance a substantial purpose cannot be construed as incidental to the organization's exempt educational purpose. Indeed, such a construction would cloud the focus of the operational test, which probes to ascertain the purpose towards which an organization's activities are directed and not the nature of the activities themselves. * * * Had the record established that the Academy's activities were nonpartisan in nature and that its graduates were not intended to primarily benefit Republicans, we would have a different case. We are not, however, deciding such a case.

Accordingly, we conclude that petitioner is operated for the benefit of private interests, a nonexempt purpose. Because more than an insubstantial part of petitioner's activities further this nonexempt purpose, petitioner has failed to establish that it operates exclusively for exempt purposes within the meaning of section 501(c)(3). Consequently, petitioner is not entitled to an exemption from taxation under section 501(a).

Decision will be entered for the respondent.

Question

Does a tax-exempt organization's involvement in a partnership or joint venture with outside investors or with a for-profit organization constitute private benefit that would jeopardize the nonprofit's tax exempt status? Consider the following case.

PLUMSTEAD THEATRE SOCIETY v. COMMISSIONER

Court of Appeals, Ninth Circuit, 1982
675 F.2d 244

Before GOODWIN and TANG, Circuit Judges, and SOLOMON, District Judge.

PER CURIAM.

The Commissioner appeals the Tax Court's ruling that Plumstead Theatre Society, Inc. is organized and operated exclusively for charitable and educational purposes under I.R.C. § 501(c), 26 U.S.C. s 501(c)(3), notwithstanding its participation in a limited partnership with investors who would have made a profit if the undertaking had not lost money.

The facts, as stated in 74 T.C. 1324 (September 18, 1980) are substantially as follows: "Petitioner is a nonprofit corporation formed to promote and foster the performing arts, particularly the theatre. Its initial proposed activities include the presentation of dramatic theatre productions, the formation of a workshop for new American playwrights, and the establishment of a fund to assist the new and established playwrights. Petitioner co-produced a play with the John F. Kennedy Center for the Performing Arts, entitled 'First Monday in October.'"

In order to meet its obligations under the agreement with the Kennedy Center regarding the shared capitalization costs of the First Monday in October venture, Plumstead sold a portion of its rights in the production to outside investors through a limited partnership. The limited partners, two individuals and a for-profit corporation, provided capital in exchange for an interest in the profits of First Monday in October.

The Commissioner abandoned at trial his initial argument that Plumstead's net earnings inure to the benefit of private individuals. The issue on appeal is whether the Tax Court erred when it found as a fact that Plumstead is not operated for the benefit of private individuals in violation of 26 C.F.R. section 1.501(c)(3)–1(d)(1)(ii).

The Tax Court's finding was not clearly erroneous.* * * The private investors were limited partners in the First Monday venture only, not shareholders in or officers or directors of Plumstead itself. The partnership agreement expressly reserved full management control to Plumstead. The arrangement in question was no more indicative of impermissible service of private interests than that approved in Broadway Theatre League of Lynchburg, Va., Inc. v. United States, 293 F.Supp. 346 (W.D.Va.1968) (contract with a booking agent under which the agent was paid a percentage of the membership dues did not interfere with the theatre's exempt purposes).

We therefore affirm the Tax Court's conclusion that Plumstead is operated exclusively for charitable and educational purposes within the meaning of section 501(c)(3) and therefore qualifies for tax exempt status.

Affirmed.

Note

The issue of whether involvement of a tax exempt organization in a partnership with outside investors or with for-profit entities will jeopardize the organization's tax exempt status is discussed further in Chapter 12 with respect to joint ventures between a tax exempt hospital and physicians or for-profit health care organizations.

C. Private Inurement

Section 501(c)(3) provides that "no part of the earnings of . . . [the charitable organization] inures to the benefit of any private shareholder or individual." This prohibition is similar to the private benefit limitation in that it prohibits the conferring of a benefit on private interests. It differs, however, in two important ways. First, the private inurement prohibition is absolute; it applies even if the inurement is insubstantial. Second, it applies to private shareholders or other individuals. Other individuals have come to mean "insiders," who generally are persons who has some control over the organization. The *Church of Scientology* and *United Cancer Council* cases develop the elements and limits of the private inurement prohibition.

CHURCH OF SCIENTOLOGY OF CALIFORNIA v. COMMISSIONER

United States Court of Appeals, Ninth Circuit, 1987
823 F.2d 1310

TANG, Circuit Judge:

The Church of Scientology (Church) appeals a judgment of the Tax Court which affirmed the Commissioner's assessment of tax deficiencies and late filing penalties against the Church for the years 1970, 1971 and 1972. At issue is whether the Commissioner properly revoked the Church's tax exempt status.

I.

The Church was incorporated as a nonprofit corporation in the State of California in 1954. In 1957, the Commissioner recognized it as a tax exempt organization under § 501(c)(3) of the Internal Revenue Code of 1954. The Commissioner revoked the Church's tax exempt status in 1967. The letter of revocation stated that the Church was "engaged in a business for profit," and was "operated in a manner whereby a portion of [its] earnings inure[d] to the benefit of a private individual," and was "serving a private, rather than a public interest." The letter instructed the Church to file federal income tax returns. The IRS subsequently published a notice of revocation in the Internal Revenue Service bulletin, and removed the Church from the Service's official roster of organizations eligible to receive tax deductible charitable donations. The Church did not file income tax returns for the years 1970 through 1972, instead, it submitted Form 990, information returns. On December 28, 1977, after auditing the Church's records, the IRS sent a Notice of Deficiency for the years 1970, 1971, and 1972. The IRS calculated the deficiency to be $1,150,458.87 and imposed an additional $287,614.71 in late filing penalties.

On March 28, 1978, the Church filed suit in United States Tax Court challenging the Commissioner's determination of tax deficiency. In an extensive opinion, the Tax Court substantially upheld the determination of the Commissioner, 83 T.C. 381 (1984). It held that the Church did not qualify for exemption from taxation under §§ 501(a) & 501(c)(3) because: (1) the Church was operated for a substantial commercial purpose; (2) its earnings inured to the benefit of L. Ron Hubbard, his family, and OTC, a private non-charitable corporation controlled by key Scientology officials; and (3) it violated well defined standards of public policy by conspiring to prevent the IRS from assessing and collecting taxes owed by the Church. The Court also upheld the validity of the Notice of Deficiency. Finally, the Court upheld the penalties for failure to file tax returns.

II.

During the years in question, the Church of Scientology of California was the "Mother Church" of the many Scientology churches around the country. The Church propagated the Scientology faith, a religion founded by L. Ron Hubbard, through such means as the indoctrination of laity, training and ordination of ministers, creation of congregations, and provision of support to affiliated organizations.

Scientology teaches that the individual is a spiritual being having a mind and body. Part of the mind, called the "reactive mind" is unconscious and filled with mental images that are frequently the source of irrational behavior. Through the administration of a process known as "auditing" a parishioner, called a "pre-clear," is helped to erase his or her reactive mind and gain spiritual awareness. Auditing is administered individually by a trained "auditor." The auditor poses questions to the pre-clear and measures the latter's response with an electronic device call an "E–Meter" that is attached to the skin. The E–Meter assists in the identification of spiritual difficulty. Scientology teaches that spiritual awareness is achieved in stages. A disciple achieves different levels of awareness through additional auditing. The religion also offers courses to train auditors.

Scientology teaches that people should pay for whatever of value they receive. This is called the "Doctrine of Exchange." Toward the realization of this doctrine, branch churches exacted a "fixed donation" for training and auditing. Fixed donations were not based on ability to pay and with few exceptions, services were not given for free.

Scientology is an international religion with numerous churches around the world. In the 1970's, these churches were organized along hierarchical lines according to the level of services they were authorized to provide. Churches that delivered services at the lowest levels were called "franchises" and later "missions." "Class IV orgs" delivered auditing through "grade IV" and training through "level IV." "St. Hill organizations" and "advanced organizations" offered intermediate and higher level services. The branch known as "Flag" offered the highest level of training and auditing.

The California Church consisted of several divisions. The San Francisco Organization and the Los Angeles Organization were both class IV organizations. The American St. Hill Organization was located in Los Angeles and offered intermediate auditing and training. The Advanced Organization of Los Angeles provided high levels of auditing and training to persons who had completed services at a class IV organization. The Flag Operations Liaison Office, located in Los Angeles, was an administrative unit of the California Church.

In addition to auditing and training, the Church provided assistance to prisoners, ex-offenders, the elderly, the mentally ill and drug addicts. On occasion the Church assisted the poor and the sick. The Church performed christenings, funerals and wedding ceremonies free of charge, and conducted regular Sunday services. The Church's chaplain provided marriage and family counseling free of charge. The Church also provided free, a specialized form of auditing geared to help people in crisis.

Flag was the highest division of the California Church. It provided spiritual leadership. It also acted as the Church's administrative center. The Flag division was headquartered aboard the ship *Apollo,* which cruised the Mediterranean Sea and docked in various countries along its shores. L. Ron Hubbard, his wife, Mary Sue, and their family lived aboard the *Apollo* with other members of the ship's crew and staff. Besides performing the highest levels of auditing and training, Flag staff members performed a variety of management functions. The Church's other divisions and other Scientology churches sent reports on a regular basis to Flag. These reports supplied information, often in statistical form, about the organization's operations. Flag staff, on the basis of the review of these reports, issued policy letters, directives, and other kinds of administrative advice geared to improving local church operations. Flag personnel also researched and developed programs for improving the administration of local churches. Flag sent teams of specialists to help other units or churches experiencing management difficulties.

The Church derived income from four sources: (1) auditing and training; (2) sales of Scientology literature, recordings and E-meters; (3) franchise operations; and (4) management services. Franchise operators were required to remit ten percent of gross income to the Church. The

Church offered its managerial services to branch organizations around the world for a fixed fee.

One of the policy directives of the Church was to "MAKE MONEY". The Church frequently engaged in aggressive promotion of its products and services. This promotion included market surveys and advertisements. In addition, the Church trained staff members in salesmanship techniques.

L. Ron Hubbard officially resigned his position as executive head of the California and other Scientology churches in 1966. Despite his official resignation, the Tax Court found that he continued to exert significant control over the Church by making policy statements, directives, and orders. In addition, his approval was required for all financial planning. He was the sole trustee of a major Scientology trust fund into which the Church made substantial payments. He or Mary Sue Hubbard were signatories on many Church bank accounts.

During the tax years at issue, L. Ron Hubbard and Mary Sue Hubbard received salaries from the California Church and its affiliate, the United Kingdom Church, in the following amounts:

	1970	1971	1972
California Church			
L. Ron Hubbard	$ 4,932	$ 9,368	$ 35,000
Mary Sue Hubbard	$ 3,017	$ 2,430	$ 25,000
United Kingdom Church			
L. Ron & Mary Sue Hubbard			
Combined	$12,300	$37,850	$ 55,680
TOTAL	$20,249	$49,648	$115,680

During these years, L. Ron Hubbard, Mary Sue Hubbard and their four children resided for the most part aboard the *Apollo*. While aboard ship, the Church provided the Hubbards with free lodging, food, laundry, medical services and vitamins.

The Church made royalty payments to L. Ron Hubbard for sales of his books, tapes and E-meters. The royalties amounted to ten percent of the retail price. The Church, for example, made $104,618.27 in royalty payments to Hubbard in 1972. Additionally, Church policy required that all work pertaining to Scientology and Dianetics be copyrighted to L. Ron Hubbard. As the result of this policy, a number of publications copyrighted by L. Ron Hubbard were actually written by others. For example, Ruth Mitchell wrote the book *Know Your People* and Peter Gillum wrote the book *How to be Successful*. Additionally, a series of books called the OEC series contained policy letters, some written by L. Ron Hubbard and others written by paid employees of the Church. L. Ron Hubbard received royalty payments on the sale of all of these publications.

During the 1960's, Scientology organizations around the world were required to pay directly to L. Ron Hubbard, ten percent of their income. These payments were termed "debt repayments" because they were designed to compensate Hubbard for his work in originating the Scientology religion. The Tax Court concluded that during 1971–1972 the Church continued to make debt repayments to Hubbard.

In 1968, L. Ron Hubbard, Mary Sue Hubbard, and Leon Steinberg incorporated a Panamanian corporation called Operation Transport Corp., Ltd. (OTC). OTC was a for-profit corporation. Shortly after the corporation's formation, Hubbard, Mary Sue Hubbard and Steinberg resigned and were replaced by three Flag employees. During the years in question, the new directors performed only one function. In the summer of 1972, they approved L. Ron Hubbard's decision to transfer approximately two million dollars from an OTC bank account in Switzerland to the *Apollo*. The money was stored in a locked file cabinet to which Mary Sue Hubbard had the only set of keys.

Between 1971 and 1972, the Church made payments in excess of three and a half million dollars to OTC. During these years, the Church also made payments totaling nearly $175,000 to the Central Defense and Dissemination Fund. According to the Church, these payments were placed in the United States Church of Scientology Trust of which L. Ron Hubbard was the sole trustee. The trust funds were deposited in several Swiss bank accounts. L. Ron Hubbard and Mary Sue Hubbard were signatories of the accounts and L. Ron Hubbard kept the trust checkbooks.

III.

A. *Tax Exemption*

Internal Revenue Code § 501 exempts certain organizations from taxation. Section 501(c)(3) exempts:

> corporations and any community chest, fund, or foundation, organized and operated exclusively for religious ... purposes, ... no part of the net earnings of which inures to the benefit of any private shareholder or individual....

To qualify for exemption, a church must show that it is (1) organized, and (2) operated, exclusively for religious or charitable purposes. *Hall v. Commissioner*, 729 F.2d 632, 634 (9th Cir.1984).

The Church strenuously argues that the trial court failed to recognize it as a bona fide religion. This argument goes to whether the Church meets the organizational test. Neither the Commissioner, nor the Tax Court, nor this court questions that the Church of Scientology of California was organized for a bona fide religious purpose. The only question before the court, is whether the Church met the second requirement for tax exempt status, the operational test.

Four elements compose the operational test. First, the organization must engage primarily in activities which accomplish one or more of the exempt purposes specified in § 501(c)(3). Treas.Reg. § 1.501(c)(3)–1(c)(1); *Church by Mail, Inc. v. Commissioner,* 765 F.2d 1387, 1391 (9th Cir.1985). Second, the organization's net earnings may not inure to the benefit of private shareholders or individuals. Treas.Reg. § 1.501(c)(3)–1(c)(2); * * *. Third, the organization must not expend a substantial part of its resources attempting to influence legislation or political campaigns. Treas.Reg. § 1.501(c)(3)–1(c)(3) * * *. Courts have imposed a fourth element. Organizations seeking exemption from taxes must serve a valid public purpose and confer a public benefit. *Bob Jones University v. United States,* 461 U.S. 574, 585–92, 103 S.Ct. 2017, 2025–29, 76 L.Ed.2d 157 (1983). If an organization fails to comply with any one of these four elements, it will fail the operational test and lose its eligibility for tax exempt status. * * *

We conclude that the Church failed to establish that "no part of the net earnings ... inures to the benefit of any private shareholder or individual...." 26 U.S.C. § 501(c)(3). Because we may affirm the Tax Court on this ground, we do not reach the questions of whether the Church operated for a substantial commercial purpose or whether it violated public policy.

B. *Inurement*

Congress conferred tax exemption on churches and other organizations in recognition of the benefit society derives from the activities of these organizations. * * * The government leaves funds in the hands of charitable organizations rather than taxing them and spending the funds on public projects. Implicit in this purpose is that charities must promote the public good to qualify for tax exemption. * * *

Section 501(c)(3) embodies this policy. Churches are eligible for tax exempt status only if no part of their net earnings inure to the benefit of private individuals. Each phrase of the statute has significance. The term "no part" is absolute. The organization loses tax exempt status if even a small percentage of income inures to a private individual. * * * The sole beneficiary of the church's activities must be the public at large. * * *

Courts have construed broadly the term "net earnings". * * * "Net earnings" includes more than gross receipts minus disbursements as shown on the books of the organization. * * * Only those ordinary expenses necessary to the operation of the church are not included in net earnings. * * *

The heart of § 501(c)(3) tax exempt status is the phrase "inures to the benefit." Payment of reasonable salaries to church officials does not constitute inurement. *Bubbling Well Church of Universal Love v. Commissioner,* 670 F.2d 104, 105 (9th Cir.1981). However, payment of excessive salaries will result in a finding of inurement. Inurement can also result from distributions other than the payment of excessive salaries. * * * Unaccounted for diversions of a charitable organization's resources by one who has complete and unfettered control can constitute inurement. * * *

Finally, the regulations define "private shareholder or individual" broadly as any person "having a personal and private interest in the activities of the organization." 26 C.F.R. 1.501(a)–1(c).

While we remain solicitous of Congress' intent to confer tax exempt status on religious organizations, this court has previously affirmed the denial of tax exemption where church income inures to private individuals. In *Church by Mail,* the Commissioner denied the Church's application for tax exempt status. Two individuals, Reverend Ewing and Reverend McElrath, ran a church that mailed printed sermons to several million homes. They also owned Twentieth Century Advertising Agency which provided the Church's printing and mailing services. We found that the salaries paid to Reverend Ewing and Reverend McElrath by the Church and Twentieth Century were excessive. We rejected the Church's argument that the income paid by Twentieth Century should not be included because Twentieth Century, a for-profit company, simply funneled church income to Reverends Ewing and McElrath. 765 F.2d at 1393. Similarly, in *Hall,* we held that William and Lorna Hall were not entitled to a charitable donation deduction for money donated to the Church of the United Brotherhood (CUB). CUB failed to qualify as a charitable organization because its major purpose was to funnel rental income to the Halls. 729 F.2d at 634. In *Bubbling Well Church,* we upheld the Tax Court's denial of the Church's application for tax exempt status. Three members of one family were the sole employees and voting directors of the Church. The Church paid a substantial portion of its income to the three family members. We held that the Church failed to carry its burden to prove that the salary and benefits paid to the family members were reasonable. 670 F.2d at 106. These cases emphasize that excessive compensation and potential for abuse, even absent a showing of actual abuse, will constitute inurement.

The finding of the Tax Court that a portion of the Church's net earnings inured to the benefit of L. Ron Hubbard, his family, and OTC, a private for-profit corporation, is a factual finding. * * * We review this finding for clear error. *Bubbling Well Church,* 670 F.2d at 106.

The taxpayer has the burden to demonstrate that it is entitled to tax exempt status. * * * This is especially true in situations where there is a great potential for abuse created by one individual's control of the church. * * * The Church must come forward with candid disclosure of the facts bearing on the exemption application. *Id.* Doubts will be resolved in favor of the government. * * *

In finding that a portion of the Church's net earnings inured to the benefit of L. Ron Hubbard, his family and OTC, the court isolated two indicia of inurement, overt and covert. The overt indicia included salaries, living expenses, and royalties. The covert indicia included "debt repayments" and L. Ron Hubbard's unfettered control over millions of dollars of Church assets. The court concluded that these indicia, when viewed in light of the self-dealing associated with them, coupled with the Church's failure to carry its burden of proof and to disclose the facts candidly, proved conclusively that the Church was operated for the benefit of L. Ron Hubbard and his family.

The Church challenges the overt indicia of inurement on the ground that the salaries, expenses and royalties, were reasonable. It notes that the court did not find them unreasonable, considered separately. The Church questions the logic of the finding that several reasonable payments add up to inurement.

The Church paid L. Ron Hubbard and Mary Sue Hubbard combined salaries of $20,249 in 1970, $49,648 in 1971 and $115,680 in 1972. We cannot say that these salaries were excessive.

In addition to Hubbard's salary, the Church paid for all of the Hubbards' living and medical expenses aboard the cruise ship *Apollo*. These expenses amounted to about $30,000 per year. Because it is unnecessary to our decision, we express no opinion on whether supporting a Church's founder and his family aboard a yacht cruising the Mediterranean constitutes a reasonable Church expense.

The Church also paid substantial royalties to L. Ron Hubbard for his books, recordings and E-meters. Churches, especially less established ones, rely on the distribution of church literature to propagate their beliefs. Financing church operations through the sale of religious literature does not necessarily violate the requirements for tax exemption. * * * Furthermore, a church may pay the author reasonable compensation in the form of royalties for his literary works. However, the payments in this case, cross the line between reasonable and excessive. Here, the evidence indicates that Hubbard used the Church to generate copyrighted literature and market his products. Scientology policy mandated that any book on Dianetics and Scientology be copyrighted in the name of L. Ron Hubbard. Pursuant to this policy, a number of publications copyrighted by L. Ron Hubbard were actually written by Church employees. Furthermore, the Church encouraged its staff members to market aggressively his products. We agree with the Tax Court that the royalty payments support a finding of inurement.

The Church argues that the evidence does not support the Tax Court's finding of covert inurement. However, the record reveals that L. Ron Hubbard had unfettered control over millions of dollars in Church assets. The Church transferred several million dollars to OTC during 1970–72. These payments were designated as "charter mission expenses." L. Ron Hubbard and Mary Sue Hubbard controlled OTC funds. Sometime during 1972, OTC transferred approximately two million dollars from OTC bank accounts in Switzerland to the *Apollo*. The finding that OTC was a sham corporation is sustained. During the tax years in question OTC funneled millions of dollars of Church assets to L. Ron Hubbard. * * *

The record also supports the Tax Court's conclusion that L. Ron Hubbard had unfettered control over Church of Scientology Trust Fund assets. The Church deducted payments of $28,930.34 in 1970, $67,892.40 in 1971, and $77,986.62 in 1972 to the Central Defense and Dissemination Fund. According to the Church, these payments were made to the United States Church of Scientology Trust. L. Ron Hubbard was the sole trustee of the Trust during the years in question. Trust funds were deposited in several Swiss bank accounts. L. Ron Hubbard and Mary Sue Hubbard were two of the three signatories on the Trust accounts. L. Ron Hubbard kept the Trust checkbooks. In 1972, over a million dollars was withdrawn from the Trust accounts in Switzerland and brought aboard the *Apollo* where it was kept in a locked file cabinet. Mary Sue Hubbard had the only keys to the cabinet.

The Church disputes that control over assets compels a finding of inurement. It argues that every Sunday morning pastors all over America collect money from parishioners and hold that money for Church uses. It asserts that OTC funds were used for expenses associated with operation of the *Apollo* and in providing banking services for Flag. Witnesses testified that the Church used Trust monies to defend Scientology against attack and to propagate the religion. Finally, the Church argues that the three million dollars brought aboard the *Apollo* from the OTC and Trust accounts remained on the *Apollo* during the years in question. It cites the testimony of a Trust accountant who counted the cash aboard the *Apollo* and testified that none of it was missing.

We find these arguments unpersuasive. Unlike the typical Saturday or Sunday when parishioners donate their money to the church, here the Church transferred millions of dollars to bank accounts controlled by a private individual who had no official responsibility for managing church assets. Although witnesses testified that the money was used for Church purposes, the Church presented little documentation to show that the majority of Trust or OTC money was actually spent on bona-fide Church activities. Finally, the self-serving testimony of a Church employee that the three million dollars remained in the *Apollo* safe proves nothing. The fact that there were three million dollars in the safe on the day the Church accountant checked, is not inconsistent with the Tax Court's finding that L. Ron Hubbard had unfettered control over millions of dollars in money that originated with the Church. The Church failed to come forward with testimony from key individuals such as L. Ron Hubbard and Mary Sue Hubbard and failed to present the documentation necessary to trace the source and use of OTC and Trust monies. In sum, the Church failed to carry its burden of proof in a situation where "the potential for abuse created by the [founder's] control of the Church required open and candid disclosure of facts bearing on the exemption application." * * *

The Tax Court found that Church income inured to the benefit of L. Ron Hubbard in a "grand scale" in the form of "debt repayments." During the 1950's, Hubbard was paid a portion of the gross income of Scientology congregations, franchises and organizations. * * * This compensation scheme was called the "proportional pay plan." During the

1960's these tithes became known as "Founding Debt Payments" (sometimes also called "LRH RR" or "LRH 10").

Although the form changed, the payments continued through the years at issue in this case. Church records indicate that between October 9, 1972 and December 28, 1972, it made debt repayments totaling $19,324.41. A policy letter dated September 7, 1972 entitled "Repayment or Due Money Collected for LRH Personally" set out a program to reimburse Hubbard for past use of Hubbard's personal income and capital; research and development of the technology of Dianetics and Scientology; and the use of Hubbard's goodwill and high credit rating. The letter establishes the post of "LRH accounts officer" to monitor collection of debt repayments.

The Church argues that the Tax Court's finding of continued debt repayments is clearly erroneous. The policy letter establishing the post of "LRH accounts officer" was canceled two days after it was promulgated. According to the Church, the only credible evidence of payments were the checks issued between October and December 1972. It contends that these payments, even though invoiced in the Church's records as "Per HCO Policy Letter 7 Sept. 72", "LRH Repayments," and "Founding Debt Payment," were actually deposited in an OTC bank account for the benefit of the Church. Finally, even if the evidence is believed, argues the Church, it accounts for only a four-month period and is insufficient to support revocation of tax exemption for all three years.

These arguments are unavailing. Even though the payments were called debt repayments, the Church produced no evidence of bona fide indebtedness. The typical indicia of a debt are a sum certain payable over a specific period of time at a stipulated rate of interest. Here, the evidence indicates a continuing obligation to make uncertain payments based on a percentage of the Church's total receipts. In enforcing federal tax laws, courts look to the substance of a transaction rather than its form. * * * These payments more closely resemble tithes to L. Ron Hubbard than debt repayments. It makes no difference whether the $19,000 was the tip of the iceberg, as the Tax Court concluded, or the total of all debt repayments made by the Church. *No part* of the Church's income could inure to L. Ron Hubbard if it was to maintain tax exempt status. * * * Even if the money went into an OTC account, it inured to the benefit of L. Ron Hubbard because he had unrestrained and unaccounted for access to that account. * * * The Church failed to come forward with credible proof that the funds were actually spent on behalf of the Church. * * *

In sum, we hold that significant sums of Church money inured to the benefit of L. Ron Hubbard and his family during the tax years 1970, 1971 and 1972. Although neither the salaries nor the living expenses necessarily constituted evidence of inurement, the cumulative effect of Hubbard's use of the Church to promote royalty income, Hubbard's unfettered control over millions of dollars of church assets, and his receipt of untold thousands of dollars worth of "debt repayments" strongly demonstrate inurement. We find no clear error.

* * *

IV.

We affirm the Tax Court decision upholding the Commissioner's revocation of the Church of Scientology of California's tax exempt status on the ground that a portion of its income inured to the benefit of L. Ron Hubbard and others.

Note

The Internal Revenue Service has contended payment of an excessive fee to a professional fundraiser can be inurement, or, in the alternative, that a charity may bestow a "private benefit" on a professional fundraiser who charges an excessive fee for solicitation on behalf of the charity. Consider this issue as you review the following case. The issue is addressed further in Chapter 8 on fundraising.

UNITED CANCER COUNCIL, INC. v. COMMISSIONER

United States Court of Appeals, Seventh Circuit, 1999
165 F.3d 1173

POSNER, Chief Judge.

The United Cancer Council is a charity that seeks, through affiliated local cancer societies, to encourage preventive and ameliorative approaches to cancer, as distinct from searching for a cure, which has been the emphasis of the older and better-known American Cancer Society, of which UCC is a splinter. The Internal Revenue Service revoked UCC's charitable exemption and the Tax Court upheld the revocation, precipitating this appeal.

So far as relates to this case, a charity, in order to be entitled to the charitable exemption from federal income tax, and to be eligible to receive tax-exempt donations, must be "organized and operated exclusively for ... [charitable] purposes" and "no part of the net earnings of [the charity may] inure[ ] to the benefit of any private shareholder or individual." 26 U.S.C. §§ 501(c)(3) (exemption); 170(c)(2)(B), (C) (receipt of donations); 26 C.F.R. § 1.501(a)–1(c), 1.501(c)(3)–1(d)(1)(i), (ii). The IRS claims that UCC (which is defunct) was not operated exclusively for charitable purposes, but rather was operated for, or also for, the private benefit of the fundraising company that UCC had hired, Watson & Hughey Company (W & H). The Service also claims that part of the charity's net earnings had inured to the benefit of a private shareholder or individual—W & H again. The Tax Court upheld the Service's second ground for revoking UCC's exemption—inurement—and did not reach the first ground, private benefit. The only issue before us is whether the court clearly erred, * * *, in finding that a part of UCC's net earnings inured to the benefit of a private shareholder or individual.

It is important to understand what the IRS does not contend. It does not contend that any part of UCC's earnings found its way into the pockets of any members of the charity's board; the board members, who were medical professionals, lawyers, judges, and bankers, served without compensation. It does not contend that any members of the board were owners, managers, or employees of W & H, or relatives or even friends of any of W & H's owners, managers, or employees. It does not contend that the fundraiser was involved either directly or indirectly in the creation of UCC, or selected UCC's charitable goals. It concedes that the contract between charity and fundraiser was negotiated at an arm's length basis. But it contends that the contract was so advantageous to W & H and so disadvantageous to UCC that the charity must be deemed to have surrendered the control of its operations and earnings to the noncharitable enterprise that it had hired to raise money for it.

The facts are undisputed. In 1984, UCC was a tiny organization. It had an annual operating budget of only $35,000, and it was on the brink of bankruptcy because several of its larger member societies had defected to its rival, the American Cancer Society. A committee of the board picked W & H, a specialist in raising funds for charities, as the best prospect for raising the funds essential for UCC's survival. Another committee of the board was created to negotiate the contract. Because of UCC's perilous financial condition, the committee wanted W & H to "front" all the expenses of the fundraising campaign, though it would be reimbursed by UCC as soon as the campaign generated sufficient donations to cover those expenses. W & H agreed. But it demanded in return that it be made UCC's exclusive fundraiser during the five-year term of the contract, that it be given co-ownership of the list of prospective donors generated by its fundraising efforts, and that UCC be forbidden, both during the term of the contract and after it expired, to sell or lease the list, although it would be free to use it to solicit repeat donations. There was no restriction on W & H's use of the list. UCC agreed to these terms and the contract went into effect.

Over the five-year term of the contract, W & H mailed 80 million letters soliciting contributions to UCC. Each letter contained advice about preventing cancer, as well as a pitch for donations; 70 percent of the letters also offered the recipient a chance to win a sweepstake. The text of all the letters was reviewed and approved by UCC. As a result of these mailings, UCC raised an enormous amount of money (by its standards)—$28.8 million. But its expenses—that is, the costs borne by W & H for postage, printing, and mailing the letters soliciting donations, costs reimbursed by UCC according to the terms of the contract—were also enormous—$26.5 million. The balance, $2.3 million, the net proceeds of the direct-mail campaign, was spent by UCC for services to cancer patients and on research for the prevention and treatment of cancer. The charity was permitted by the relevant accounting conventions to classify $12.2 million of its fundraising expenses as educational expenditures because of the cancer information contained in the fundraising letters.

Although UCC considered its experience with W & H successful, it did not renew the contract when it expired by its terms in 1989. Instead, it hired another fundraising organization—with disastrous results. The following year, UCC declared bankruptcy, and within months the IRS revoked its tax exemption retroactively to the date on which UCC had signed the contract with W & H. The effect was to make the IRS a major creditor of UCC in the bankruptcy proceeding. The retroactive revocation did not, however, affect the charitable deduction that donors to UCC since 1984 had taken on their income tax returns. * * *

The term "any private shareholder or individual" in the inurement clause of section 501(c)(3) of the Internal Revenue Code has been interpreted to mean an insider of the charity. * * * A charity is not to siphon its earnings to its founder, or the members of its board, or their families, or anyone else fairly to be described as an insider, that is, as the equivalent of an owner or manager. The test is functional. It looks to the reality of control rather than to the insider's place in a formal table of organization. The insider could be a "mere" employee—or even a nominal outsider, such as a physician with hospital privileges in a charitable hospital * * *.

The Tax Court's classification of W & H as an insider of UCC was based on the fundraising contract. Such contracts are common. Fundraising has become a specialized professional activity and many charities hire specialists in it. If the charity's contract with the fundraiser makes the latter an insider, triggering the inurement clause of section 501(c)(3) and so destroying the charity's tax exemption, the charity sector of the economy is in trouble. The IRS does not take the position that every such contract has this effect. What troubles it are the particular terms and circumstances of UCC's contract. It argues that since at the inception of the contract the charity had no money to speak of, and since, therefore, at least at the beginning, all the expenses of the fundraising campaign were borne by W & H, the latter was like a founder, or rather refounder (UCC was created in 1963), of the charity. The IRS points out that 90 percent of the contributions received by UCC during the term of the contract were paid to W & H to defray the cost of the fundraising campaign that brought in those contributions, and so argues that W & H was the real recipient of the contributions. It argues that because W & H was UCC's only fundraiser, the charity was totally at W & H's mercy during the five-year term of the contract—giving W & H effective control over the charity. UCC even surrendered the right to rent out the list of names of donors that the fundraising campaign generated. The terms of the contract were more favorable to the fundraiser than the terms of the average fundraising contract are.

Singly and together, these points bear no relation that we can see to the inurement provision. The provision is designed to prevent the siphoning of charitable receipts to insiders of the charity, not to empower the IRS to monitor the terms of arm's length contracts made by charitable organizations with the firms that supply them with essential inputs, whether premises, paper, computers, legal advice, or fundraising services.

Take the Service's first point, that W & H defrayed such a large fraction of the charity's total expenses in the early stages of the contract that it was the equivalent of a founder. Pushed to its logical extreme, this argument would deny the charitable tax exemption to any new or small charity that wanted to grow by soliciting donations, since it would have to get the cash to pay for the solicitations from an outside source, logically a fundraising organization. We can't see what this has to do with inurement. The argument is connected to another of the Service's points, that W & H was UCC's only fundraiser during the period of the contract. If UCC had hired ten fundraisers, the Service couldn't argue that any of them was so large a recipient of the charity's expenditures that it must be deemed to have controlled the charity. Yet in terms of the purposes of the inurement clause, it makes no difference how many fundraisers a charity employs. W & H obtained an exclusive contract, and thus was the sole fundraiser, not because it sought to control UCC and suck it dry, but because it was taking a risk; the exclusive contract lent assurance that if the venture succeeded, UCC wouldn't hire other fundraisers to reap where W & H had sown.

And it was only at the beginning of the contract period that W & H was funding UCC. As donations poured into the charity's coffers as a result of the success of the fundraising campaign, the charity began paying for the subsequent stages of the campaign out of its own revenues. True, to guarantee recoupment, the contract with W & H required UCC to place these funds in an escrow account, from which they could be withdrawn for UCC's charitable purposes only after W & H recovered the expenses of the fundraising campaign. But this is a detail; the important point is that UCC did not receive repeated infusions of capital from W & H. All the advances that W & H had made to UCC to fund the fundraising campaign were repaid. Indeed, it is an essential part of the government's case that W & H profited from the contract.

The other point that the Service makes about the exclusivity provision in the contract—that it put the charity at the mercy of the fundraiser, since if W & H stopped its fundraising efforts UCC would be barred from hiring another fundraiser until the contract with W & H expired—merely demonstrates the Service's ignorance of contract law. When a firm is granted an exclusive contract, the law reads into it an obligation that the firm use its best efforts to promote the contract's objectives. * * * If W & H folded its tent and walked away, it would be in breach of this implied term of the contract and UCC would be free to terminate the contract without liability.

The Service also misses the significance of the contract's asymmetrical treatment of the parties' rights in the donor list. The charitable-fundraising community distinguishes between "prospect files" and "housefiles." A prospect file is a list of people who have not given to the charity in question but are thought sufficiently likely to do so to be placed on the list of addressees of a direct-mail fundraising campaign. If the prospect responds with a donation, his or her name is transferred to the housefile, that is, the list of people who have made a donation to the charity. A housefile is very valuable, because people who have already donated to a particular charity are more likely to donate to it again than mere prospects are likely to donate to it for the first time. The housefile's value to the charity is thus as a list of people who are good prospects to respond favorably to future solicitations. Its value to the fundraiser is quite different. The fundraiser is not a charity. The value to it of a housefile that it has created is the possibility of marketing it (as a prospect file—but as a prospect file in which all the prospects are charitable donors rather than a mere cross-section of potential donors) to another charity that hires it. So it made perfect sense for the contract to give the fundraiser the exclusive right to use the UCC housefile that it created in raising money for other charities, while reserving to UCC the right to use the housefile to solicit repeat donations to itself.

The Service's point that has the most intuitive appeal is the high ratio of fundraising expenses, all of which went to W & H because it was UCC's only fundraiser during the term of the contract, to net charitable proceeds. Of the $28–odd million that came in, $26–plus million went right back out, to W & H. These figures are deceptive, because UCC got a charitable "bang" from the mailings themselves, which contained educational materials (somewhat meager, to be sure) in direct support of the charity's central charitable goal. A charity whose entire goal was to publish educational materials would spend all or most of its revenues on publishing, but this would be in support rather than in derogation of its charitable purposes.

Even if this point is ignored, the ratio of expenses to net charitable receipts is unrelated to the issue of inurement. For one thing, it is a ratio of apples to oranges: the *gross* expenses of the fundraiser to the *net* receipts of the charity. For all that appears, while UCC derived a net benefit from the contract equal to the difference between donations and expenses plus the educational value of the mailings, W & H derived only a modest profit; for we know what UCC paid it, but not what its expenses were. The record does contain a table showing that W & H incurred postage and printing expenses of $12.5 million, but there is nothing on its total expenses.

To the extent that the ratio of net charitable proceeds to the cost to the charity of generating those proceeds has any relevance, it is to a different issue, one not presented by this appeal, which is whether charities should be denied a tax exemption if their operating expenses are a very high percentage of the total charitable donations that they receive. To see that it's a different issue, just imagine that UCC had spent $26 million to raise $28 million but that the $26 million had been scattered among a host of suppliers rather than concentrated on one.

There would be no issue of inurement, because the Service would have no basis for singling out one of these suppliers as being in "control" of UCC (or the suppliers as a group, unless they were acting in concert). But there might still be a concern either that the charity was mismanaged or that charitable enterprises that generate so little net contribution to their charitable goals do not deserve the encouragement that a tax exemption provides. Recall that most of UCC's fundraising appeals offered the recipient of the appeal a chance to win a sweepstake, a form of charitable appeal that, we are told, is frowned upon. There may even be a question of how reputable W & H is (or was). * * * But these points go to UCC's sound judgment, not to whether W & H succeeded in wresting control over UCC from the charity's board.

UCC's low net yield is no doubt related to the terms of the fundraising contract, which were more favorable to the fundraiser than the average such contract. But so far as appears, they were favorable to W & H not because UCC's board was disloyal and mysteriously wanted to shower charity on a fundraiser with which it had no affiliation or overlapping membership or common ownership or control, but because UCC was desperate. The charity drove (so far as the record shows) the best bargain that it could, but it was not a good bargain. Maybe desperate charities should be encouraged to fold rather than to embark on expensive campaigns to raise funds. But that too is a separate issue from inurement. W & H did not, by reason of being able to drive a hard bargain, become an insider of UCC. If W & H was calling the shots, why did UCC refuse to renew the contract when it expired, and instead switch to another fundraiser?

We can find nothing in the facts to support the IRS's theory and the Tax Court's finding that W & H seized control of UCC and by doing so became an insider, triggering the inurement provision and destroying the exemption. There is nothing that corporate or agency law would recognize as control. A creditor of UCC could not seek the satisfaction of his claim from W & H on the ground that the charity was merely a cat's paw or alter ego of W & H, as in *Pepper v. Litton*, 308 U.S. 295, 311–12, 60 S.Ct. 238, 84 L.Ed. 281 (1939), or *Freeman v. Complex Computing Co.*, 119 F.3d 1044, 1051–53 (2d Cir.1997). The Service and the Tax Court are using "control" in a special sense not used elsewhere, so far as we can determine, in the law, including federal tax law. It is a sense which, as the amicus curiae briefs filed in support of UCC point out, threatens to unsettle the charitable sector by empowering the IRS to yank a charity's tax exemption simply because the Service thinks the charity's contract with its major fundraiser too one-sided in favor of the fundraiser, even though the charity has not been found to have violated any duty of faithful and careful management that the law of nonprofit corporations may have laid upon it. The resulting uncertainty about the charity's ability to retain its tax exemption—and receive tax-exempt donations—would be a particular deterrent to anyone contemplating a donation, loan, or other financial contribution to a new or small charity. That is the type most likely to be found by the IRS to have surrendered control over its destiny to a fundraiser or other supplier, because it is the type of charity that is most likely to have to pay a high price for fundraising services. "Developments in the Law—Nonprofit Corporations," 105 *Harv. L.Rev.* 1578, 1649–51 (1992). It is hard enough for new, small, weak, or marginal charities to survive, because they are likely to have a high expense ratio, and many potential donors will be put off by that. The Tax Court's decision if sustained would make the survival of such charities even more dubious, by enveloping them in doubt about their tax exemption.

We were not reassured when the government's lawyer, in response to a question from the bench as to what standard he was advocating to guide decision in this area, said that it was the "facts and circumstances" of each case. That is no standard at all, and makes the tax status of charitable organizations and their donors a matter of the whim of the IRS.

There was no diversion of charitable revenues to an insider here, nothing that smacks of self-dealing, disloyalty, breach of fiduciary obligation or other misconduct of the type aimed at by a provision of law that forbids a charity to divert its earnings to members of the board or other insiders. What there may have been was imprudence on the part of UCC's board of directors in hiring W & H and negotiating the contract that it did. Maybe the only prudent course in the circumstances that confronted UCC in 1984 was to dissolve. Charitable organizations are plagued by incentive problems. Nobody owns the right to the profits and therefore no one has the spur to efficient performance that the lure of profits creates. Donors are like corporate shareholders in the sense of being the principal source of the charity's funds, but they do not have a profit incentive to monitor the care with which the charity's funds are used. Maybe the lack of a profit motive made UCC's board too lax. Maybe the board did not negotiate as favorable a contract with W & H as the board of a profitmaking firm would have done. And maybe tax law has a role to play in assuring the prudent management of charities. Remember the IRS's alternative basis for yanking UCC's exemption? It is that as a result of the contract's terms, UCC was not really operated exclusively for charitable purposes, but rather for the private benefit of W & H as well. Suppose that UCC was so irresponsibly managed that it paid W & H twice as much for fundraising services as W & H would have been happy to accept for those services, so that of UCC's $26 million in fundraising expense $13 million was the equivalent of a gift to the fundraiser. Then it could be argued that UCC was in fact being operated to a significant degree for the private benefit of W & H, though not because it was the latter's creature. That then would be a route for using tax law to deal with the problem of improvident or extravagant expenditures by a charitable organization that do not, however, inure to the benefit of insiders.

That in fact is the IRS's alternative ground for revoking the exemption, the one the Tax Court gave a bye to. It would have been better had the court resolved that ground as well as the inurement ground, so that the case could be definitively resolved in one appeal. But it did not, and so the case must be remanded to enable the court to consider it. We shall not prejudge the proceedings on remand. The usual "private benefit" case is one in which the charity has dual public and private goals, see, e.g., *Better Business Bureau v. United States*, 326 U.S. 279, 283, 66 S.Ct. 112, 90 L.Ed. 67 (1945); *Living Faith, Inc. v. Commissioner*, 950 F.2d 365 (7th Cir.1991); *American Campaign Academy v. Commissioner, supra*, 92 T.C. at 1064–65, and that is not involved here. However, the board of a charity has a duty of care, just like the board of an ordinary business corporation, * * *, and a violation of that duty which involved the dissipation of the charity's assets might (we need not decide whether it would—we leave that issue to the Tax Court in the first instance) support a finding that the charity was conferring a private benefit, even if the contracting party did not control, or exercise undue influence over, the charity. This, for all we know, may be such a case.

REVERSED AND REMANDED.

Note

Private inurement issues have been prevalent in a hospital's or a community's recruitment of physicians. Many times these physicians are offered large incentive packages to entice them to join a hospital. See Revenue Ruling 97–21, 1997–1 C.B. 121 (discussed in detail in Chapter 12), which addresses the area and provides some safe-harbor for hospitals.

D. Excess Benefit Transaction

Although charitable organizations continue to worry about private inurement, in fact, relatively few organizations have lost their exempt status because of inurement. There are egregious cases, such as *Church of Scientology*. [See also, *Kemper Military School v. Crutchley*, 274 F. 125 (W.D.Mo.1921) (distribution of assets to insider) and *The Church of Eternal Life & Liberty, Inc. v. Commissioner*, 86 T.C. 916 (1986) (excessive compensation).] The reason why private inurement's "bark is greater than its bite" is twofold. First, the only penalty is loss of tax exemption with the consequence that the beneficiaries of the organization are the real victims. The public loses. Second, the insider, who actually benefitted from the illicit transaction, is not required to repay the benefit. Thus, only in the more serious cases do the IRS and courts believe that the benefits from loss of exemption outweigh the loss to the beneficiaries. This position, however, accepted that inurement would go uncorrected.

In 1996, Congress responded by adding § 4958 to the Code. [Taxpayer Bill of Rights 2, Pub. L. 104–168, 104th Cong. 2d Sess. (July 30, 1996).] (Section 4958 was discussed earlier in Chapter 3.) Section 4958 enacted "intermediate sanctions" for activity that amounts to inurement. The sanctions involve a serious of taxes imposed on insiders who enter into transactions with the charitable organization, which transactions result in an "excess benefit" to the insider. The sanctions are intermediate in that they lie between loss of exemption and doing nothing. Moreover, they are imposed on the offending insiders, not the organization. Accordingly, with § 4958, Congress reacted to both problems inherent in the private inurement prohibition.

Congress, however, did not repeal the inurement doctrine with the enactment of § 4958. Both the private inurement prohibition of § 501(c)(3) and the intermediate sanctions can apply to an inurement-type transaction. The organization can lose its exempt status and the insider can be taxed under § 4958. The more likely situation, however, is that the intermediate sanctions will be imposed in lieu of revocation of an organization's exemption. Congress articulated this likelihood in the committee report to § 4958:

> In general, the intermediate sanctions are the sole sanction imposed on those cases in which the excess benefit does not rise to a level where it calls into question whether, on the whole, the organization functions as a charitable ... organization. In practice, revocation of tax-exempt status, with or without the imposition of excise taxes, would occur only when the organization no longer operates as a charitable organization.

H.R. No. 506, 104th Cong., 2d Sess. 53, 56–50 (1996).

(See *Carraci v. Commissioner*, cited in Chapter 3, wherein sanctions were imposed on persons receiving "excess benefits," but the court did not terminate tax exempt status of the organization.)

Section 4958 replicates the self-dealing rules of § 4941; § 4958 imposes excise taxes on disqualified persons who engage in impermissible activities. Section 4941 is discussed in Chapter 3, with respect to federal standards of conduct for directors of nonprofit organizations, and in Chapter 7, along with other private foundation penalty taxes. Note, however, as pointed out in Chapter 3, § 4958 does not apply to a private foundation. The reason is that private foundation activity that would violate § 4958 already is prohibited by the self-dealing provisions of § 4941. According, § 4958 would be repetitive.

Structurally, § 4958 includes four elements: (1) the organizations to which the section applies; (2) the persons to whom the section applies; (3) the transactions prohibited; and (4) the taxes levied if the section is violated. With respect to the first element—targeted organizations—§ 4958 applies to §§ 501(c)(3) and (4) organizations [I.R.C. § 4958(e)(1)].

The intermediate sanctions of § 4958 apply to disqualified persons and organization managers [I.R.C. § 4958(a)]. A "disqualified person" is any person "in a position to exercise substantial influence over the affairs of the organization" [I.R.C. § 4958 (f)(1)(A)]. Compare this definition to the definition of an "insider." The essence of both an insider and a disqualified person is substantial control over the charitable organization. A disqualified person is an insider. [See Treas. Reg. § 53.4958–3(e)(2).] They are those persons who have substantial control of the organization—voting members of the organization's board, the president, chief executive officer, the chief operating officer, and the chief financial officer. A disqualified person also includes a member of the family of a person who has substantial influence over the organization and an entity in which such a person owns at least 35 percent [I.R.C. § 4859(f)(1)(B), (C)].

Organization managers include officers, directors, trustees, or other persons who have similar power or responsibilities with respect to the organization [I.R.C. § 4958(f)(2)]. Again, such persons are insiders under the private inurement prohibitions.

Section 4958 applies to "excess benefit transactions." An "excess benefit transaction" is "any transaction in which an economic benefit is provided by an applicable tax-exempt organization directly or indirectly to or for the use of any disqualified person if the value of the economic benefit provided exceeds the value of the consideration (including the performance of services) received for providing such benefit" [I.R.C. § 4958(c)(1)(A)]. In other words, an excess benefit transaction is private inurement; therefore, § 4958 applies to private inurement activities.

Section 4958 levies three levels of taxes on disqualified persons or organization managers who participate in a excess benefit transaction. Unless abated, a disqualified person is subject to a tax equal to 25 percent of the amount of excess benefit [I.R.C. § 4958(a)(1)]. The tax may be abated by the IRS if the disqualified person corrects the transaction and the IRS determines that the transaction was the result of reasonable conduct and not willful neglect [I.R.C. § 4962(a)]. Correction means rescinding the illicit transaction [I.R.C. § 4958(f)(6)].

A disqualified person who does not correct the transaction, is subject to an additional tax equal to 200 percent of the excess benefit [I.R.C. § 4958(b)]. Like the initial tax, this additional tax may be abated [Treas. Reg. § 4958–1(c)(2)(iii)].

Multiple disqualified persons who participate in the same excess benefit transactions are jointly and severally liable for both taxes [I.R.C. § 4958(d)(1)].

An organization manager who knowingly and willfully joins a disqualified person in an excess benefit transaction is subject to tax of 10 percent of the amount of the excess benefit [I.R.C. § 4958(a)(2)]. The maximum tax is $20,000. If more than one organization manager participates in the excess benefit transaction, then each organization manager is jointly and severally liable for the tax [I.R.C. § 4958(d)(1)].

In sum, § 4958 attempts to accomplish a couple of goals. First, it provides some certainty to the meaning of private inurement and an insider. Under § 4958, the former is an excess benefit transaction and the latter are disqualified persons and organization managers. In addition, by means of the three tiers of taxes, Congress seeks, through § 4958, to deter any inurement and to correct inurement if it does occur. These goals are sought without revocation of the organization's exempt

E. Action Organization

Under § 501(c)(3), "no substantial part of the activitie[s of an] organization may involve] carrying on propaganda, or otherw[is]ing to influence legislation (except as otherwise provided in subsection (h)) . . . " Further, a § 501(c)(3) organization is one "which does not participate in, or otherwise intervene in . . . , any political campaign on behalf of (or in opposition to) any candidate for public office." The regulations label an organization that engages in lobbying or political activity an "action organization" [Treas. Reg. § 1.501(c)(3)–1(3)]. An action organization, then, is an organization that either lobbies for or against legislation or is involved in a political campaign.

The constitutionality of restrictions against political activity was upheld in *Regan v. Taxation with Representation*, cited in Chapter 4.

1. Lobbying Activity

The regulations take a very expansive interpretation of lobbying activity. Lobbying includes contacting legislators or their staff, urging the public to contact legislators or their staff, or otherwise advocating the adoption or repeal of legislation.

Lobbying is defined in the Regulations under § 501(c)(3) [Treas. Reg. § 1.501(c)(3)–1(c)(3)] as an attempt to influence legislation by propaganda or otherwise. An organization "attempts to influence legislation" if it contacts, or urges the public to contact, members of a legislative body for the purpose of proposing or supporting legislation, or if it advocates adoption or rejection of legislation. The term "legislation" is defined in the Regulations as any action by Congress, by any state legislature, by any local council or similar governing body, or by the public in referendum, initiative, constitutional amendment, or similar procedure. Any attempt to influence legislation through communication with any member or employee of a "legislative body," or with any government official or employee who may participate in formulation of the legislation, is lobbying.

Lobbying does not include nonpartisan analysis, study, or research, including making the results available to the public; technical assistance or advice to a governmental body in response to a request by the governmental body; and appearance before, or communication with, any legislative body with respect to a decision of the legislative body that would adversely affect the organization [Treas. Reg. §§ 56.4911–2(c) and 53.4945–2(d)].

Although the definition of lobbying in the Regulations includes only action by legislative bodies, i.e., Congress, State legislatures, local councils or similar governing body, or by the public in a referendum, initiative, constitutional amendment, or similar procedure, the IRS has ruled that legislation also includes administrative decisions. (See Rev.

Rul. 67–6, 1967–1 C.B. 135, *modified,* Rev. Rul. 76–147, 1976–1 C.B. 40.) As indicated in *Christian Echoes National Ministry,* courts have approved the IRS's interpretation.

CHRISTIAN ECHOES NATIONAL MINISTRY, INC. v. UNITED STATES

United States Court of Appeals, Tenth Circuit, 1972
470 F.2d 849

BARRETT, Circuit Judge.

Christian Echoes sued for refund of Federal Insurance Contribution Act (FICA) taxes for 1961 and 1963 through 1968 amounting to $103,493.08 plus statutory interest. On June 24, 1971 the District Court held that the taxpayer qualified for tax exemption under 26 U.S.C.A. Section 501(c)(3). The Government appealed to the United States Supreme Court which vacated the judgment and remanded for entry of a new decree. United States v. Christian Echoes National Ministry, Inc., 404 U.S. 561, 92 S.Ct. 663, 30 L.Ed.2d 716 (1972). The District Court entered the same decision on February 24, 1972. The Government takes this appeal therefrom.

Christian Echoes is a nonprofit religious corporation organized in 1951 under the laws of Oklahoma by Dr. Billy James Hargis, its president, chief spokesman and an ordained minister. The Articles of Incorporation state in part that the corporation is founded "to establish and maintain weekly religious, radio and television broadcasts, to establish and maintain a national religious magazine and other religious publications, to establish and maintain religious educational institutions, . . ." Article III of the Articles of Faith in the corporate by-laws reads as follows:

> "We believe in God, Supreme and Eternal, and in Jesus Christ as His Son, perfect Deity, and in the Holy Comforter and Challenger of this age, The Holy Ghost, and in the Bible as the inspired Word of God.
>
> We believe that the solution of the World's problems, economic, political and spiritual, is found by the application of Christian Teachings in the lives of men and nations rather than in political ideologies of any kind.
>
> We believe in the Twentieth Century Reformation to combat apostate conditions with the Church.
>
> We realize atheistic world forces seek the destruction and overthrow of all the religions of the World, including particularly that founded upon the teachings of Jesus Christ. The same forces seek also the destruction of all free governments, in which the lives and property of the people are protected by civil, moral and spiritual law. We associate ourselves together to educate and proclaim the essential truths of Christianity, and the doctrine: Jesus Christ is the Hope

of the World and America is God's Greatest Nation under the Living Son.

We believe in the real spiritual unity in Christ of all redeemed by His precious blood.

We believe in constitutional government, whereby religious as well as other freedoms of mankind are preserved and protected.

We believe in the fundamentals of New Testament Christianity, and we propose to promulgate the eternal truths thereof at all costs."

The activities of the organization have been addressed to that theology ever since the date of incorporation.

Christian Echoes maintains religious radio and television broadcasts, authors publications, and engages in evangelistic campaigns and meetings for the promotion of the social and spiritual welfare of the community, state and nation. Dr. Hargis has stated that its mission is a battle against Communism, socialism and political liberalism, all of which are considered arch enemies of the Christian faith. Dr. Hargis testified that Christian Echoes supports "Christian conservative statesmen ..." without regard to party political labels. The organization publishes a monthly anti-Communist magazine, *Christian Crusade*, a weekly "intelligence report", *Weekly Crusader*, and a newspaper column, "For and Against". It also distributes pamphlets, leaflets and broadcast reprints on aspects of anti-Communist activity; it distributes tapes and records of selected broad casts; and it conducts an annual anti-Communist leadership school whose goal is to answer the question, "What can my community do to stem the forces of liberalism and thus stop the growth of socialism and communism?" In 1962 it established a Summer Anti–Communist University and formed youth groups, Torchbearer Chapters, to educate the public on the threat of Communism. In 1964 Christian Echoes encouraged adults to organize local Christian Crusade chapters. Christian Echoes appealed for contributions from the public to carry on its campaign. It earned money from the sale of its publications, tapes, films and admission fees at rallies. From 1961 through 1966 its gross receipts ranged from about $677,000 to $1,000,000 per year. It spent 52% of this income on radio, television, publications and postage.

On March 12, 1953 the Internal Revenue Service ruled that Christian Echoes qualified as a tax-exempt religious and educational organization under Section 501(c)(3) of the 1954 Code, formerly Section 101(6) of the 1939 Code. Section 501(c)(3) states as follows:

"Corporations, and any community chest, fund, or foundation, organized and operated exclusively for religious, charitable, scientific, testing for public safety, literary, or educational purposes, or for the prevention of cruelty to children or animals, no part of the net earnings of which inures to the benefit of any private shareholder or individual, *no substantial part of the activities of which is carrying on propaganda, or otherwise attempting, to influence legislation, and which does not participate in, or intervene in (including the publishing or distributing of statements), any political campaign on behalf of any candidate for public office."* (Emphasis ours.)

In 1962 and 1963 the National Office of the Internal Revenue Service requested that the activities and financial affairs of Christian Echoes be re-examined. The IRS agents recommended no change in its exempt status. The National Office, after reviewing and analyzing the activities of Christian Echoes, recommended that the exemption be revoked. On November 13, 1964 the District Director in Oklahoma City advised Christian Echoes in a letter of the revocation of its exemption and of its protest rights. Christian Echoes filed a formal protest on June 25, 1965 after conferences with the District Director and the National Office. The District Director notified Christian Echoes on September 22, 1966 that its exempt status was being revoked for three reasons: (1) it was not operated exclusively for charitable, educational or religious purposes; (2) it had engaged in substantial activity aimed at influencing legislation; and (3) it had directly and indirectly intervened in political campaigns on behalf of candidates for public office. Christian Echoes filed further protests without avail. It paid the taxes as assessed. Christian Echoes then filed this refund suit, claiming its right to exemption.

The District Court held that the taxpayer was entitled to tax-exempt status under Section 501(c)(3). The Court ruled that Christian Echoes qualified in that no substantial part of its activities had been devoted to attempts to influence legislation or intervene in political campaigns. The Court found that the only activity of Christian Echoes relating to an attempt to influence legislation was in support of the Becker Amendment urging support of restoration of prayers in the public schools. The Trial Court accepted Dr. Hargis's interpretation of the "attempts to influence legislation" prohibition in 501(c)(3), wherein Dr. Hargis testified on cross-examination that:

> "... it's my interpretation that as long as I don't lobby in Washington, which I never have, as long as I don't get behind a bill or a-post a bill which I never have, as long as I don't endorse a political candidate, which I never have ... that by no stretch of the imagination could you say what I am doing is political, ..."

It also held that all of its activities were motivated by sincere religious convictions; that the First Amendment prohibits the Government and courts from determining whether the activities are religious or political; and that the IRS had revoked Christian Echoes' exempt status without evidence to support its action and without constitutionally justifiable cause in violation of the First Amendment. It found that the taxpayer had been denied its right to due process under the Fifth Amendment because the Government had arbitrarily selected it from organizations engaged in similar activities and had violated its published administrative procedures in the steps leading to the revocation.

The Government appealed directly to the United States Supreme Court which dismissed the appeal for lack of jurisdiction, vacated the District Court's judgment and remanded for entry of a new decree. The IRS appeals from the District Court's holding in favor of Christian Echoes following remand.

The Government contends that: (1) the taxpayer failed to qualify as tax-exempt under Section 501(c)(3); (2) its interpretation and application of Section 501(c)(3) did not violate the taxpayer's rights under the First Amendment; (3) its revocation of tax-exempt status to the taxpayer under Section 501(c)(3) did not violate the taxpayer's rights of due process under the Fifth Amendment; and (4) the Commissioner did not abuse his discretion in revoking the exemption with retroactive effect.

I.

The Government contends that Christian Echoes failed to qualify as tax-exempt under Section 501(c)(3) because: (1) a *substantial* part of its activities consisted of carrying on propaganda, or otherwise attempting to influence legislation; and (2) it participated or intervened in political campaigns on behalf of candidates for public office. The issue raises the interpretation and application of Section 501(c)(3).

Almost since the earliest days of the federal income tax, Congress has exempted certain corporations from taxation. The exemption to corporations organized and operated exclusively for charitable, religious, educational or other purposes carried on for charity is granted because of the benefit the public obtains from their activities and is based on the theory that:

> "... the Government is compensated for the loss of revenue by its relief from financial burden which would otherwise have to be met by appropriations from public funds, and by the benefits resulting from the promotion of the general welfare." H.R.Rep.No.1860, 75th Cong., 3d Sess. 19 (1939).

Tax exemptions are matters of legislative grace and taxpayers have the burden of establishing their entitlement to exemptions. Dickinson v. United States, 346 U.S. 389, 74 S.Ct. 152, 98 L.Ed. 132 (1953). The limitations in Section 501(c)(3) stem from the Congressional policy that the United States Treasury should be neutral in *political affairs and that substantial activities directed to attempts to influence legislation or affect a political campaign should not be subsidized.*

The limitation in Section 501(c)(3) originated in the Revenue Act of 1934, allowing tax exempt status to organizations, if "no substantial part of the activities of which is carrying on propaganda, or otherwise attempting, to influence legislation." The case which led to the 1934 legislation was Slee v. Commissioner of Internal Revenue, 42 F.2d 184 (2d Cir. 1930). There the Court held that the American Birth Control League was not entitled to a charitable exemption because it disseminated propaganda to legislators and the public aimed at the repeal of laws preventing birth control. The IRS denied tax exempt status because the

Birth Control League's purposes were not exclusively charitable, educational or scientific. In 1954 Congress attached a further condition to exempt status by adding the bar against participation or intervention in political campaigns on behalf of candidates for public office.

A religious organization that engages in substantial activity aimed at influencing legislation is disqualified from tax exemption, whatever the motivation. The Government has at all times recognized Christian Echoes as a religious organization. Indeed, the Government acknowledges that in all of its activities, Christian Echoes has been religiously motivated.

The critical issue is whether the limitation on attempts to influence legislation should be given the narrow interpretation applied by the District Court or a broader construction. The District Court held that the only attempt to influence legislation by Christian Echoes was in its support of the Becker Amendment relating to restoration of prayers in the public schools. By this construction, there must be specific legislation before Congress in order for the "attempt to influence legislation" prohibition to come into play. We disagree. We hold that the Trial Court was clearly erroneous in this interpretation of law.

Treasury Regulation 1.501(c) (3)–1(c)(3)(ii) states that an organization will be regarded as attempting to influence legislation if the organization:

> "(a) Contacts, or urges the public to contact, members of a legislative body for the purpose of proposing, supporting, or opposing legislation; or
>
> (b) Advocates the adoption or rejection of legislation."

Legislation is defined in the regulations as:

> "... action by the Congress, by any State legislature, by any local council or similar governing body, or by the public in a referendum, initiative, constitutional amendment, or similar procedure." Treas.Reg. 1. 501(c)(3)-1(c)(3)(ii)(b).

The Regulation goes well beyond the District Court's interpretation of Section 501(c)(3). It includes direct and indirect appeals to legislators and the public in general. Cammarano v. United States, 358 U.S. 498, 79 S.Ct. 524, 3 L. Ed.2d 462 (1959). We hold that the Regulation properly interprets the intent of Congress. A capsule review of the "substantial" activities of Christian Echoes will adequately demonstrate, we believe, that Congress intended that the limitations be given a broad or liberal interpretation.

Christian Echoes' publications, such as the *Christian Crusade*, contained numerous articles attempting to influence legislation by appeals to the public to react to certain issues. These articles were either authored by Dr. Hargis, members of his organization, solicited contributors, or unsolicited authors-but all such articles had the stamp of approval of Dr. Hargis before acceptance for publication. The fact that specific legislation was not mentioned does not mean that these attempts to influence public opinion were not attempts to influence legislation. For example, Christian Echoes appealed to its readers to: (1) write their Congressmen in order to influence the political decisions in Washington; (2) work in politics at the precinct level; (3) support the Becker Amendment by writing their Congressmen; (4) maintain the McCarran–Walter Immigration law; (5) contact their Congressmen in opposition to the increasing interference with freedom of speech in the United States; (6) purge the American press of its responsibility for grossly misleading its readers on vital issues; (7) inform their Congressmen that the House Committee on UnAmerican Activities must be retained; (8) oppose an Air Force Contract to disarm the United States; (9) dispel the mutual mistrust between North and South America; (10) demand a congressional investigation of the biased reporting of major television networks; (11) support the Dirksen Amendment; (12) demand that Congress limit foreign aid spending; (13) discourage support for the World Court; (14) support the Connally Reservation; (15) cut off diplomatic relations with communist countries; (16) reduce the federal payroll by discharging needless jobholders, stop waste of public funds and balance the budget; (17) stop federal aid to education, socialized medicine and public housing; (18) abolish the federal income tax; (19) end American diplomatic recognition of Russia; (20) withdraw from the United Nations; (21) outlaw the Communist Party in the United States; and (22) to restore our immigration laws.

The taxpayer also attempted to mold public opinion in civil rights legislation, medicare, the Postage Revision Act of 1967, the Honest Election Law of 1967, the Nuclear Test Ban Treaty, the Panama Canal Treaty, firearms control legislation, and the Outer Space Treaty. These appeals urging the readers to action all appeared in Christian Echoes' publications between 1961 and 1968. They were all attempts to influence legislation through an indirect campaign to mold public opinion. This was directly evidenced by Dr. Hargis' keynote address delivered at the Anti–Communist Leadership School on February 11, 1963, entitled "Counter Strategy for Counter Attack". After setting forth a 10–point program, he stated that "Your opinion isn't worth a nickel without your action to back it up."

The political activities of an organization must be balanced in the context of the objectives and circumstances of the organization to determine whether a *substantial* part of its activities was to influence or attempt to influence legislation. * * * A percentage test to determine whether the activities were substantial obscures the complexity of balancing the organization's activities in relation to its objectives and circumstances. * * * An essential part of the program of Christian Echoes was to promote desirable governmental policies consistent with its objectives through legislation. * * * The activities of Christian Echoes in influencing or attempting to influence legislation were not incidental, but were substantial and continuous. The hundreds of exhibits demonstrate this. These are the activities which Congress intended should not be carried on by exempt organizations.

In addition to influencing legislation, Christian Echoes intervened in political campaigns. Generally it did not formally endorse specific candidates for office but used its publications and broadcasts to attack candidates and incumbents who were considered too liberal. It attacked President Kennedy in 1961 and urged its followers to elect conservatives like Senator Strom Thurmond and Congressmen Bruce Alger and Page Belcher. It urged followers to defeat Senator Fulbright and attacked President Johnson and Senator Hubert Humphrey. The annual convention endorsed Senator Barry Goldwater. These attempts to elect or defeat certain political leaders reflected Christian Echoes' objective to change the composition of the federal government.

* * * *

Reversed.

Notes

1. An organization is not an action organization if its activities involve presentation of issues in a nonpartisan manner for the purpose of educating the public. (See Rev. Rul. 66–256, 1966–2 C.B. 210.) In contrast, an organization whose purpose can be accomplished by the enactment or repeal of certain legislation is an action organization. (See Rev. Rul. 62–71, 1962–1 C.B. 85.) Advocacy groups have presented a perplexing Issues: Are they involved in education or impermissible propaganda? This issue was raised in Chapter 1 with Big Momma Rag v. United States, National Alliance v. United States and Nationalist Foundation v. Commissioner. The IRS promulgated the methodology test it introduced in National Alliance in Rev. Proc. 86–43, 1986–2 C.B. 729. The Tax Court held that the constitutional vagueness issue raised by Big Momma Rag was cured by Rev. Proc. 86–43. [Nationalist Movement v. Commissioner, 102 T.C. 558 (1994), *aff'd* 37 F.3d 216 (5th Cir.1994)].

2. Section 501(c)(3) restricts only substantial lobbying activity. Neither the Code nor the regulations give any guidance as to when activity becomes substantial. The IRS in unpublished General Counsel Memorandum provides some standards.

Consider these issues in the General Counsel Memorandum.

GENERAL COUNSEL MEMORANDUM

34798

IN RE: FACTORS FOR DETERMINING THE EXTENT TO WHICH 501(c)(3) ORGANIZATIONS ARE ATTEMPTING TO INFLUENCE LEGISLATION

March 2, 1972

HAROLD T. SWARTZ

Assistant Commissioner (Technical)

Attention: Director, Miscellaneous and Special Provisions Tax Division

Your memorandum (T:MS:EO:CR–EDC) dated January 29, 1969, referred a proposed Revenue Ruling on the above subject for our consideration. Although we have given the matter extensive consideration, it has recently been agreed by representatives of our respective offices that it would be preferable to have this subject dealt with by regulations rather than by a published ruling. Consequently, pursuant to an informal agreement with Lawrence B. Jerome, Chief of the Exempt Organizations Branch, we have transferred your memorandum to us and your administrative file to the Chairman of the Task Force to Revise Section 501(c)(3) Regulations (Chief Counsel Project No. 4 in book of Exempt Organizations Administration Program Objectives) with the suggestion that this matter be incorporated in the proposed regulations.

* * *

The proposed Revenue Ruling has not been considered by Chief Counsel. It sets forth factors to be considered in determining the extent to which an organization is carrying on propaganda, or otherwise attempting, to influence legislation for purposes of section 501(c)(3) of the Code.

The factors were previously incorporated in a proposed Revenue Procedure that was considered at the Assistant Commissioner's (Technical) Position Meeting of 10–23–68. At that meeting it was decided to (1) restructure the document in a Revenue Ruling format, (2) eliminate the test relative to impact on public opinion and the affected legislative body, and (3) place the proposed Revenue Ruling in normal Briefing channels.

* * *

REV. RUL.

Advice has been requested concerning factors to be considered in determining the extent to which an organization is carrying on propaganda, or otherwise attempting, to influence legislation for purposes of section 501(c)(3) of the Internal Revenue Code of 1954.

Section 501(c)(3) of the Code provides that an organization does not qualify for exemption from Federal income tax if a substantial part of its activities is carrying on propaganda, or otherwise attempting, to influence legislation.

Section 1.501(c)(3)–1(c)(3) of the Income Tax Regulations provides that an organization is not operated exclusively for one or more exempt purposes if it is an 'action' organization. An organization is an 'action' organization if a substantial part of its activities is attempting to influence legislation by propaganda or otherwise.

However, an organization is not precluded from qualifying for exemption under section 501(c)(3) of the Code merely because in carrying out its purposes it advocates social or civic changes or presents opinion on controversial issues with the intention of molding public opinion or creating public sentiment to an acceptance of its views so long as it is not an 'action' organization. See section 1.501(c)(3)–1(d)(2) of the regulations.

Furthermore, an organization may qualify as 'educational' under section 501(c)(3) of the Code even though it advocates a particular position or viewpoint if it presents a sufficiently full and fair exposition of the pertinent facts as to permit an individual or the public to form an independent opinion or conclusion. See section 1.501(c)(3)–1(d)(3)(i) of the regulations.

The term 'legislation', as used in section 501(c)(3) of the Code, includes action by the Congress, by any State legislature, by any local council or similar governing body, or by the public in a referendum, initiative, constitutional amendment, or similar procedure. The phrase 'attempting to influence legislation' encompasses all activities undertaken and carried on by an organization for the purpose of proposing, supporting, or opposing legislation. An organization's attempts to influence legislation may consist of direct or indirect attempts, or both. See section 1.501(c)(3)-1(c)(3)(ii) of the regulations.

Examples of attempts to influence legislation are set forth below:

1. Contacting, or urging the public to contact, members of a legislative body for the purpose of proposing, supporting, or opposing legislation. See section 1.501(c)(3)–1(c)(3)(ii)(a) of the regulations.

2. Contacting, or urging members of the public to contact, members of the executive branch of a governmental body to request them to propose, support, or oppose legislation.

3. Researching, deliberating, and disseminating information and opinions that are integral and essential to a legislative program. See League of Women Voters v. United States, 180 F. Supp. 379 (1960); and Kuper v. Commissioner, 332 F. 2d 562 (1964). However, an organization's research, deliberation, and dissemination activities are not attempts to influence legislation if they are conducted to educate the public about the nature and ramifications of a legislative proposal rather than to advocate a legislative position. See Rev. Rul. 64–195, C.B. 1964–2, 138.

4. Advocating in any other manner the adoption or rejection of legislation.

Section 501(c)(3) of the Code precludes exemption only if the carrying on of propaganda, or otherwise attempting, to influence legislation is a substantial part of an organization's activities. This requires a comparison of the legislative activities with the organization's activities in furtherance of its exempt purposes. What constitutes a 'substantial part' must be decided from the facts and circumstances of each case. Because of the nature of the factors to be considered it is not feasible to establish a percentage or other mathematical standard to serve as a precise measure of what is substantial in a particular case. The facts relating to each factor must be developed and evaluated. Then an overall appraisal of the legislative activity based on all factors is required to determine its substantiality in relation to the exempt activities of the organization.

Many factors may be considered in determining whether an activity is substantial. Those relating to costs and time or physical effort are generally the most significant.

1. Cost—The dollar cost of the legislative activity in relation to the cost of carrying on the organization's exempt activities can be very important in cases where dollar expenditures accurately reflect the extent and scope of an organization's activities. Costs attributable to the conduct of an unrelated trade or business should not be included in the comparison. Likewise, receipts and expenditures for products or services with respect to which the members pay the cost, in whole or in part, may not be entirely reflective of organizational activities. For example, an organization may arrange for the sale of a book to members at a special price. In such case the dollars involved in the sales price of the book and the payment to the publisher or distributor do not necessarily reflect actual organizational activities.

2. Time or Physical Effort—Actual manhours devoted to an organization's activities may be used as an aid in determining substantiality. Where a substantial amount of volunteer time or effort is involved, this comparison may be more meaningful than the cost comparison discussed above. Here, as with costs, comparison should be between the legislative activities and the exempt activities of the organization. Furthermore, it may be appropriate on occasion to consider the caliber of the time and effort expended. For instance, the time of an executive officer of the organization or an important public figure acting pursuant to a request from the organization may far outweigh comparable hours of clerical or routine work. Consequently, a mere comparison of total hours expended is not sufficient.

Other factors such as those described below may be considered in determining the substantiality of an organization's legislative activities.

1. Importance—The importance an organization attaches to its legislative activities as compared to its exempt activities can be significant. In addition to cost and time or effort previously discussed, importance may be indicated by:

(a) the emphasis and priority given the activity by key people in the organization;

(b) the amount of personal attention given to the activity by key people;

(c) the amount and nature of assistance sought from outside the organization in support of the activity;

(d) the content of documents and publications prepared by the organization in support of the activity, and the extent of dissemination of such materials; and

(e) the level of authority toward which the activity is directed.

2. Frequency of Legislative Activities—The frequency with which an organization attempts to influence legislation may be indicative of the organization's underlying purposes. If an organization frequently engages in attempts to influence various pieces of proposed legislation, it may be indicative that such activities are, in fact, a regular, formal, and purposeful part of the organization's overall operation.

The factors discussed above are not necessarily the only ones that will be taken into consideration. In specific cases, additional factors may have a material bearing on the question of substantiality. If so, they also will be included in determining the extent to which an organization is carrying on propaganda, or otherwise attempting, to influence legislation.

Notes

1. The revenue ruling referenced in the GCM was never issued, nor were regulations promulgated.

2. If an organization fails the substantially test, it not only may lose its tax exemption, but it also may be subject to a penalty tax of five percent on all lobbying expenditures [I.R.C. § 4912(c)]. In addition, an organization manager who agreed to the lobbying expenditures knowing that those expenditures were in violation of the substantiality test, may be liable for a tax of five percent on the amount of expenditures [I.R.C. § 4912(b)]. This additional tax is imposed on an organization manager only if the manager acted willfully and unreasonable.

3. An organization that is denied § 501(c)(3) status because its application indicates that it would be an action organization, may seek exemption under § 501(c)(4). Section 501(c)(4) organizations may engage in lobbying activity. However, if the organization has been granted § 501(c)(3) status and then that status is revoked because of political activity, the organization cannot revert to § 501(c)(4) status [I.R.C. § 504(a)].

Because of the uncertainty inherent in the substantiality test, Congress enacted § 501(h) in 1976 to permit charitable organizations, other than churches and private foundations, to engage in a limited amount of lobbying activity. [See Revenue Act of 1976, Pub. L. No. 94–455, 94th Cong. 2d Sess. § 1307(a) (Oct. 4, 1976).] Section 501(h) distinguishes between "general lobbying" and "grass roots lobbying." General lobbying involves direct contact with legislators, while grass roots lobbying includes attempts to influence legislation through public opinion. An organization that elects under § 501(h) may expend for general lobbying activity the lesser of $1 million or a certain percentage of its exempt function expenditures, i. e., those expenditures incurred for exempt purposes (as set out below). Of that amount, 25 percent may be expended on grass roots lobbying.

A § 501(c)(3) organization elects under § 501(h) by filing Form 5768. The election, once made, is effective until revoked.

The permissible lobbying expenditures for an electing § 501(c)(3) organization are set out in § 4911 of the Code and are as follows:

1) Twenty percent of exempt purpose expenditures up to $500,000;

2) $100,000, plus fifteen percent of the excess of exempt purpose expenditures over $500,000 and up to $1,000,000;

3) $175,000, plus ten percent of the excess exempt purpose expenditures over $1,000,000 up to $1,500,000; or

4) $225,000, plus five percent of excess purpose expenditures over $1,500,000. (In no event may the permitted level exceed $1,000,000 for one year.)

The limit for total lobbying expenditures for electing § 501(c)(3) organizations for a year applies to all expenditures, both for direct lobbying and for grass roots lobbying (attempts to influence the general public), but the amount of permitted grass roots lobbying expenditures is subject to a further limitation of twenty-five percent of the total permitted amount. There is a twenty-five percent penalty tax on expenditures for lobbying and/or grass roots lobbying in excess of the permissible amounts.

Example. City Foundation has exempt purpose expenditures (expenditures to accomplish its exempt purpose) for the year of $580,000. Its nontaxable lobbying expenditures may not exceed $112,000 [20 percent of $500,000 ($100,000) plus 15 percent of $80,000 ($12,000)]. However, any grass roots lobbying expenditures may not exceed $28,000 (25 percent of $112,000).

As noted previously, lobbying expenditures for electing § 501(c)(3) organizations are divided into expenditures for "direct" lobbying communications and for "grass roots" communications. A direct lobbying communication is any attempt to influence legislation through communication with any member or employee of a legislative body or any government official or employee who may participate in formulation of legislation (but only if the principal purpose of the communication is to influence legislation). A communication with a legislator or governmental official will be treated as a direct lobbying communication only if the communication refers to specific legislation and reflects a view on such legislation. Grass roots lobbying is the influencing of legislation through any attempt to affect opinions of the general public. A communication is treated as grass roots lobbying communication only if the communication (a) refers to specific legislation, (b) reflects a view on such legislation, and (c) encourages the recipient of the communication to take action with respect to the legislation.

Problem

State University Foundation has exempt purpose expenditures for the year of $1,000,000. It expended $200,000 for attempts to influence Congress regarding a pending bill and $80,000 to inform the general public of the pending bill (but it did not encourage members of the public to take action). Will State University Foundation be subject to a penalty tax on its lobbying and grass roots lobbying expenditures and, if so, what is the amount of the penalty tax?

Note

1. A § 501(c)(3) organization will not meet the operational test (which requires the organization to be operated for an exempt purpose) if it engages

in substantial lobbying activities or, if it is an electing organization under § 501(h) of the Code, should its lobbying expenditures exceed 150 percent of the permitted amounts of lobbying under § 4911 of the Code set out above.

2. A § 501(c)(3) organization that does not elect under § 501(h) is subject to a subjective test, i.e., it may not engage in "substantial" lobbying. Because the term substantial is not defined, nonelecting organizations face considerable uncertainty as to the amount of lobbying expenditures they can incur without jeopardizing their exempt status.

3. If two or more § 501(c)(3) organizations are members of an affiliated group of organizations and the organizations have elected under § 501(h) of the Code, the organizations are treated as one for purposes of determining whether the organizations had excess lobbying expenditures. An organization is a member of an affiliated group if (a) the governing instrument of the organization requires it to be bound by decisions of another organization on legislative issues or (b) the governing board of one organization includes persons who are specifically designated representatives of another organization or are members of the governing board, officers, or paid executive staff members of the other organization and, if by aggregating their votes, such persons have sufficient voting power to cause or prevent action on legislative issues by the first organization. Thus, two organizations are affiliated if one organization can control action on legislative issues by the other by reason of interlocking governing boards or by reason of provisions of the governing instruments of the controlled organization. The ability of one organization to control action on legislative matters of another organization is sufficient to cause the organizations to be affiliated. It is not necessary that control be exercised. See Treas. Reg. § 56.4911–7(a).

4. A § 501(c)(3) organization, whether electing or not, must report its lobbying expenditures annually on Schedule A of Form 990. Schedule A sets out the expenditure limitations for electing organizations.

5. Pursuant to the Lobbying Disclosure Act, 2 U.S.C. §§ 1601 et. seq., an exempt organization that engages in substantial lobbying (lobbying expenditures in excess of $20,000) must register with the Secretary of the Senate and the Clerk of the House of Representatives [2 U.S.C. § 1602(10), 1603]. If the organization has employees who are paid to lobby and who spend more than 20 percent of their time engaged in lobbying activities, the organization must register within 45 days after the lobbyist employee makes a "lobbying contact." The Lobbying Disclosure Act applies only to Federal lobbying activities. It does not include attempts to influence legislation by any state legislature or by any local governing body.

Problem

A nonelecting § 501(c)(3) organization devoted twenty percent of its time and efforts to lobbying. Has it engaged in "substantial" lobbying so that the Internal Revenue Service could revoke its tax exempt status. See Seasongood v. Comm., 227 F.2d 907 (6th Cir.1955) and Haswell v. U.S., 500 F.2d 1133 (Ct.Cl.1974).

2. Political Campaigns

Section 501(c)(3) prohibits an organization from engaging in political campaigns even at a de minimis level. The substantiality test does not apply to this prohibition. Generally, a political campaign includes supporting or opposing a candidate for public office [Treas. Reg. § 1.501(c)(3)–1(c)(3)(iii)]. Political campaigning, however, does not include nonpartisan, voter education. Revenue Ruling 78–248, 1978–1 C.B. 154 provides illustrations of the partisan and nonpartisan activities.

Again, an organization that loses its § 501(c)(3) exempt status cannot then seek exemption under § 501(c)(4) [I.R.C. § 504(a)].

An organization that engages in prohibited political campaign activity, besides losing its tax exemption, may be subject to a multi-tier tax. (See I.R.C. § 4955.) The tax is imposed on "political expenditures," which includes amounts spent for the candidate's speeches, travel, any polls or surveys, advertising, publicity, or fund raising. The tax initially includes a tax of 10 percent on the political expenditures (I.R.C. § 4955). If the organization does not correct the impermissible activity, an additional tax of 100 percent on the amount of the political expenditures is imposed. Finally, any manager who knowingly approves of the expenditure is liable for a tax equal to 2 1/2 percent of the political expenditures [I.R.C. § 4955(a)(2)]. The maximum initial tax for which a manager is liable for each expenditure is $5,000. And if the manager does not correct the expenditures, the activity is subject to an additional tax of 50 percent of the political expenditures with a maximum of $10,000.

Note

Section 4955 provides the Internal Revenue Service with a method of imposing intermediate sanctions on a § 501(c)(3) organization that incurs a limited and often unintentional amount of political campaign expenditure. This provides an alternative means to sanctioning a § 501(c)(3) organization for involvement in political activities so that the Service is not limited, as it was prior to Congress' enactment of § 4955, to revocation of the organization's tax exempt status.

The IRS may seek to have an organization enjoined from continuing to engage in political campaign activity when the activity is flagrant [I.R.C. § 7409(a)(2)]. The federal district court in which the organization has its principal place of business has the jurisdiction to issue an injunction. The IRS has the burden of proving by clear and convincing evidence that the organization's activity is flagrant and that an injunction is an appropriate remedy.

Notes

1. Most tax-exempt organizations, other than § 501(c)(3) organizations, may incur political campaign expenditures, but such expenditures, unless incurred through a separate, segregated fund, are subject to a tax under § 527 of the Code. The tax, which is the highest tax rate for corporations, is imposed on the lesser of the organization's net investment income or the amounts expended for campaign activities. The organization can avoid the § 527 tax by establishing a separate, segregated fund to

receive and disburse all funds related to the nomination of, or opposition to, candidates for public office. The fund is treated as a political organization (a PAC) and is not taxed on its exempt function income. Funds collected must be placed directly into the separate, segregated fund. (See further discussion in Chapter 15 on political organizations.)

2. Although § 501(c)(3) organizations are prohibited from making any political campaign expenditures and may not establish a separate fund for this purpose, a § 501(c)(3) organization can establish a separate, segregated fund to influence the selection, nomination or appointment of individuals to nonelective offices. Such expenditures are lobbying expenditures, but they are not political campaign expenditures because they are not incurred on behalf of, or in opposition to, a "candidate for a public office," i.e., an "elective" office. The expenditures are covered by § 527, however, and will be subject to the § 527 tax unless they are placed directly in a separate, segregated fund. (See discussion in Chapter 15.)

F. Public Policy

Courts have imposed a fifth requirement for a charitable organization to obtain and maintain tax-exempt status. A charitable organization seeking tax exempt status must serve a valid public purpose and must confer a public benefit. If the primary purpose of an organization is contrary to public policy, it cannot qualify as a § 501(c)(3) organization even if no provision in the law prohibits it.

Consider the public policy requirement in *Bob Jones University v. United States,* 461 U.S. 574, 103 S.Ct. 2017, 76 L.Ed.2d 157, cited in Chapter 11.

Questions

1. The Supreme Court agreed with the IRS that the tax exempt status of Bob Jones University should be revoked. The regulations dealing with education indicate that an educational purpose includes instruction or training for purposes of improving or developing a student's capabilities [Treas. Reg. § 1.501(c)(3)–1(d)(3)(i)(a)]. Refer to *Bob Jones University v. United States,* cited in Chapter 11. Did not Bob Jones University meet this definition? If so, what was the basis for the Supreme Court's conclusion that Bob Jones University was not entitled to exemption under § 501(c)(3)?

2. The IRS has applied the public policy doctrine to few cases other than to those involving racial discrimination cases. However, in Revenue Ruling 75–384, 1975–2 C.B. 204, the IRS ruled that an anti-war organization was not entitled to exempt status because the organization advocated civil disobedience. Even in the context of racial discrimination, other than with respect to private schools, the IRS has used the public policy doctrine only with respect to recreational facilities (Rev. Rul. 67–325, 1967–2 C.B. 113) and scholarship funds. [See *Virginia Education Fund v. Commissioner,* 85 T.C. 743 (1985), *aff'd,* 799 F.2d 903 (4th Cir.1986).] For IRS procedures dealing with non discrimination, see Revenue Procedure 75–50, 1975–2 C.B. 567. See further discussion with respect to private schools in Chapter 11.

Chapter 6

PUBLIC CHARITIES

You were introduced to § 501(c)(3) organizations in Chapters 4 and 5. As noted in those chapters, a § 501(c)(3) organization must be "organized" and "operated" for a charitable purpose. There are, however, additional concerns for the founders and directors of § 501(c)(3) organizations. Section 501(c)(3) organizations are classified for tax purposes either as public charities or as private foundations. The tax treatment of a § 501(c)(3) organization is determined by this classification system. A public charity is treated more favorably for tax purposes than is a private foundation.

A public charity is a church, school, hospital, or some other form of charitable organization, such as a museum or symphony, that has broad public support or that actively functions in a supporting relationship to other charitable organizations having broad public support. A private foundation, on the other hand, is a § 501(c)(3) organization, other than a church, school, or hospital, that is supported, and often controlled, by a small number of donors. Because private foundations are controlled by a few donors, they are closely supervised by the Internal Revenue Service and are subject to substantial penalties for engaging in certain prohibited acts. In addition, private foundations must pay an excise tax, and donors to private nonoperating foundations receive less favorable tax treatment for their contributions (discussion of charitable contributions in Chapter 8). Private foundations are discussed in Chapter 7. This chapter considers public charity status for § 501(c)(3) organizations.

I. REQUIREMENTS FOR PUBLIC CHARITY STATUS

Section 509 of the Internal Revenue Code sets out the requirements for public charity status. It does so by defining a private foundation in a negative context. Section 509 defines a "private foundation" as all § 501(c)(3) organizations *except* those listed in § 509(a)(1), (2) (3) or (4). Thus, § 509 actually defines those § 501(c)(3) organizations that qualify as public charities. A public charity is a § 501(c)(3) organization that is also a § 509(a)(1), (2), (3), or (4) organization. All other § 501(c)(3) organizations are private foundations.

A § 501(c)(3) organizations obtains public charity status at the same time it applies for tax exempt status—by filing Form 1023. It declares on the form the status it seeks under § 509 of the Code.

II. SECTION 509(a) ORGANIZATIONS

Section 509 provides as follows:

§ 509. Private foundation defined.

For purposes of this title, the term "private foundation" means a domestic or foreign organization described in section 501(c)(3) **other than—**

    (1) an organization described in section 170(b)(1)(A) (other than in clauses (vii) and (viii));

    (2) an organization which—

        (A) normally receives more than one-third of its support in each taxable year from any combination of—

            (i) gifts, grants, contributions, or membership fees, and

            (ii) gross receipts from admissions, sales of merchandise, performance of services, or furnishing of facilities, in an activity which is not an unrelated trade or business (within the meaning of section 513), not including such receipts from any person, or from any bureau or similar agency of a governmental unit (as described in section 170(c)(1)), in any taxable year to the extent such receipts exceed the greater of $5,000 or 1 percent of the organization's support in such taxable year, from persons other than disqualified persons (as defined in section 4946) with respect to the organization, from governmental units described in section 170(c)(1), or from organizations described in section 170(b)(1)(A) (other than in clauses (vii) and (viii)), and

        (B) normally receives not more than one-third of its support in each taxable year from the sum of—

            (i) gross investment (as defined in subsection (e)), and

            (ii) the excess (if any) of the amount of the unrelated business taxable income (as defined in section 512) over the amount of the tax imposed by section 511;

    (3) an organization which—

        (A) is organized, and at all times thereafter is operated, exclusively for the benefit of, to perform the functions of, or to carry out the purposes of one or more specified organizations described in paragraph (1) or (2),

(B) is—

(i) operated, supervised, or controlled by one or more organizations described in paragraph (1) or (2),

(ii) supervised or controlled in connection with one or more such organizations, or

(iii) operated in connection with one or more such organizations, and

(C) is not controlled directly or indirectly by one or more disqualified persons (as defined in section 4946) other than foundation managers and other than one or more organizations described in paragraph (1) or (2); and

(4) an organization which is organized and operated exclusively for testing for public safety.

Public charities are referred to by their § 509(a) classification as well as their § 501(c)(3) classification. In addition, if a charity seeks public charity status under § 509(a)(1), it is further classified under § 170(b)(1)(A) of the Code. [Note from § 509(a)(1) quoted above, that § 509(a)(1) organizations are those organizations described in § 170(b)(1)(A).] Thus, a § 509(a)(1) organization also is referred to by its classification under § 170(b)(1)(A).

A. Section 509(a)(1) Organizations

An organization will qualify automatically as a public charity under § 509(a)(1) if it is a church [described in § 170(b)(1)(A)(i)], a school [defined in § 170(b)(1)(A)(ii)], or a hospital [qualified under § 170(b)(1)(A)(iii)]. Other charitable organizations [those qualified under § 170(b)(1)(A)(iv) and (vi)] must satisfy a support test, set out in the regulations under § 170(b)(1)(A)(vi) [Treas. Reg. § 1.170A–9(e)(9)]. These charitable organizations must seek contributions from the general public annually to maintain public charity status.

1. Churches

A "church" qualifies automatically for public charity status under §§ 509(a)(1) and 170(b)(1)(A)(i). The term "church" as described in § 170(b)(1)(A)(i) includes a religious order or a religious organization if the organization is an integral part of a church and is engaged in performing functions of a church. Churches and other religious organizations are discussed at length in Chapter 10.

2. Educational Organizations

An educational organization, which qualifies automatically for public charity status under §§ 509(a)(1) and 170(b)(1(A(ii), is defined in § 170(b)(1)(A)(ii) as an organization that has as its primary function the presentation of formal instruction and that normally maintains a regular faculty and curriculum. It generally must have a regularly enrolled body of pupils or students in attendance at the location where its educational activities are regularly performed. Primary, secondary, preparatory, high schools, colleges and universities qualify. Organizations that are engaged both in educational and noneducational activities do not qualify unless the latter are merely incidental to the educational activities [Treas. Reg. § 1.170A–9(b)(1)]. Schools are discussed at length in Chapter 11.

3. Hospitals and Medical Research Organizations

A hospital or medical research organization qualifies for public charity status under §§ 509(a)(1) and 170(b)(1)(A)(iii). Federal hospitals and state, county, and municipal hospitals are included. A rehabilitation institution, outpatient clinic, or community mental health or drug treatment center may qualify as a hospital if the principal function of the institution is the providing of hospital or medical care. A skilled nursing facility will qualify as a hospital if the principal purpose or function is the providing of hospital or medical care. Convalescent homes or homes for children or the aged, or institutions training disabled individual to pursue some vocation do not qualify as hospitals [Treas. Reg. § 1.170A–9(c)]. An organization that provides medical education or medical research is not a hospital unless it also is actively engaged in providing medical or hospital care to patients on its premises or in its facilities.

To qualify for public charity status as a hospital, a medical research organization must be engaged directly in the continuous active conduct of medical research in conjunction with a hospital and must have medical research in conjunction with a hospital as its primary function. To be engaged primarily in medical research, an organization must either devote a substantial part of its assets to, or expend a significant percentage of its endowment for, such purposes. An organization that devotes more than one-half of its assets to the continuous active conduct of medical research will meet this requirement [Treas. Reg. § 170A–9(c)(2)].

Hospitals are discussed at length in Chapter 12.

4. Organizations for the Benefit of Colleges and Universities

A public charity, which qualifies under §§ 509(a)(1) and 170(b)(1)(A)(iv), is an entity that is organized and operated exclusively to receive, hold, invest, and administer property and to make expenditures to or for the benefit of a college or university. The college or university it supports must be an educational organization that qualifies for public charity status under §§ 509(a)(1) and 170(b)(1)(A)(ii). This type organization must receive a substantial part of its support from governmental units or from the general public. It must meet a one-third support test, which also is required of § 170(b)(1)(A)(vi) organizations. The one-third support test is described below with respect to § 170(b)(1)(A)(vi) organizations.

5. Governmental Units

Governmental units qualify for public charity status under §§ 509(a)(1) and 170(b)(1)(A)(v). However, these organizations generally do not apply for tax exempt status as their income is automatically exempt under § 115.

6. Publicly Supported Organizations

An organization qualifies for public charity status under § 509(a)(1) if it meets the requirements of a publicly supported organization under § 170(b)(1)(A)(vi). Organizations that may qualify under this provision include museums; libraries; community centers; organizations providing facilities for the support of an opera, symphony orchestra, ballet, or repertory drama; or organizations providing some other direct service to the general public, such as the Red Cross or the United Fund.

An organization is treated as a publicly supported organization if the total amount of support the organization normally receives (over a four year period) from governmental units or from the general public is at least one-third of the total support normally received by the organization.

One-Third Support Test

A charitable organization will satisfy the support test, which is required for §§ 170(b)(1)(A)(iv) and 170(b)(1)(A)(vi) organizations, if the total amount of support the organization normally receives (as an average over a four-year period) from governmental units or from the general public is at least 33 1/3 percent of the organization's total support. This support test is referred to as the "one-third support test." [Treas. Reg. § 1.170A–9(e)(3).] It is computed in the form of a fraction. The numerator is "qualified" support from governmental units and individuals, and the denominator is the organization's total support excluding gross receipts. To qualify as a public charity, the fraction must compute to at least 1/3. Support, for this purpose, does not include amounts received for services, i. e., gross receipts. Amounts received for services rendered are excluded from both the numerator and the denominator of the one-third support fraction.

Gifts from "disqualified persons" are counted in full in the denominator of the one-third fraction but are counted in the numerator only to the extent of two percent of total support. This is to assure that support will be from the general public rather than from a few substantial donors.

Disqualified persons include an organization's manager and its substantial contributors—those who contributed more than $5,000 during a taxable year if that amount is more than two percent of total contributions and bequests received by the organization during the year.[1]

---

1. "Disqualified persons" are defined in I.R.C. § 4946. If a corporation, partnership, or trust contributed more than $5,000 to the organization and if that amount is more than two percent of total contribution received by the organization during the year, any more than 20 percent owner of such an entity would also be a disqualified person.

The following examples illustrate the computation of the one-third support test.

Example 1. State University Foundation received support of $4,100,000 in the past four years from the following sources:

Investment Income	$ 800,000
Admission Fees for Charitable Events	200,000
Governmental Unit	40,000
United Fund	60,000
Contributions	3,000,000
	$4,100,000

Total support is $3,900,000 [$4,100,000 − $200,000 (admission fees)]. (Admission fees or gross receipts are not counted in either the numerator or the denominator of the support fraction.) Included in the $3,000,000 contributions are donations from eight contributors of $250,000 each. These were in excess of two percent of total support of $3,900,000, which is $78,000.

State University Foundation would qualify as a § 509(a)(1) organization because it received in excess of one-third of its support from governmental units and from the general public. The numerator of the fraction to determine if State University Foundation meets the one-third support test would be $1,724,000, computed as follows: the $3,900,000 of total support is reduced by investment income of $800,000 and by $1,376,000, which is the amount of the contributions from the eight disqualified persons that exceeded two percent of total support. [The contribution from each contributor was $250,000. This amount from each exceeded two percent of total support by $172,000 [$250,000 (total contribution for each of the eight persons)—$78,000 (2 percent of total support of $3,900,000)]. For the eight contributors, the excess would be $1,376,000 ($172,000 x 8).] The numerator of the one-third fraction then would be $1,724,000 [$3,900,000 (total support)—$800,000 (investment income)—$1,376,000 (contributions from disqualified persons in excess of two percent of total support)]. The denominator of the fraction would be $3,900,000. Thus, the fraction would be $1,724,000/$3,900,000, which computes to 44.2 percent. As this exceeds 33 1/3 percent, State University Foundation currently qualifies for public charity status.

Example 2. Assume in the above example that Rachel Martin gave $5,000,000 to State University Foundation. Total support then would be $8,900,000. Of the contributions from the eight disqualified persons, in Example 1, $576,000 now would be excluded from

Further, such entities will be disqualified persons if any person having a more than 35 percent interest in the entity is a disqualified person. The family members of a disqualified person, but including only spouse, ancestors, lineal descendants and spouses of lineal descendants, are also disqualified persons.

the numerator of the fraction. Two percent of total support of $8,900,000 is $178,000. The excess of each contribution of $250,000 over this amount is $72,000 ($250,000—$178,000 = $72,000). This excess amount, $72,000, multiplied by 8, equals $576,000. The contribution from Rachel would be included in the numerator only as to $178,000. Thus, of her contribution, $4,822,000 ($5,000,000—$178,000) would be excluded from the numerator. The numerator of the fraction then would be $2,702,000 [$8,900,000 (total support)—$800,000 (investment income)—$576,000 (amount excluded from eight contributors)—$4,822,000 [contribution from Rachel in excess of two percent of total support ($5,000,000—$178,000)]. Thus, the fraction would be $2,702,000/$8,900,000, which computes to 30.3 percent. As this amount is less than 1/3, or 33 1/3 percent, State University Foundation would not meet the one-third support test.

The above examples illustrate the problem when a charity accepts an exceptionally large gift from one person or entity. The large gift may cause it to be deemed to be supported by only a few donors.

Facts and Circumstances Test

State University Foundation, in Example 2 above, might meet an alternative publicly supported test and, thus, continue to qualify as a public charity under § 509(a)(1). Although it could not meet the "one-third support test," it might meet the alternative "facts and circumstances test" [Treas. Reg. § 1.170A–9(e)(3)(i-v)].

The facts and circumstances test permits an organization that does not meet the one-third support test but that normally receives a substantial part of its support from governmental units and from the general public, to qualify as a § 509(a)(1) organization if the organization meets certain other requirements demonstrating that it is, in fact, publicly oriented. To meet the facts and circumstances test, an organization must receive at least ten percent of total support from governmental units and the general public. Other "facts and circumstances" are then considered in addition to the ten percent support test. The organization must be organized and operated to attract new and additional public or governmental support on a continuous basis. (This requirement is met if the organization maintains a continuous and bona fide program for solicitation of funds from the general public, community, or membership groups involved, or if it carries on activities designed to attract support from governmental units or other charitable organizations.)

In determining whether an organization has met the facts and circumstances, the following factors are considered: (1) the percentage of support received from the public or governmental sources, (2) the sources of support (whether principally from a few persons or from the general public), (3) whether the organization has a representative governing body (rather than principal donors and family members of a major donor or donors), and (4) the availability of the organization's facilities or services to the public, as well as the amount of public participation in its programs [Treas. Reg. § 1.170A–9(e)(3)].

Unusual Grants

State University Foundation, in Example 2 above, could seek to exclude the gift from Rachel from both the numerator and denominator of the fraction as an unusual grant [Treas. Reg. § 1.170A–9(e)(6)(ii)].

If a large gift qualifies as an unusual grant, it can be excluded from both the numerator and the denominator of a § 509(a)(1) organization. Thus, if a large contribution can qualify as an unusual grant, the gift would not adversely affect the public charity status of a charitable organization. An unusual grant is a substantial contribution or bequest from a disinterested party that was attracted by reason of an organization's publicly supported nature, that is unusual or unexpected as to its amount, and that, by reason of its size, would affect adversely an organization's public charity status. A grant may be considered an unusual grant without need of an advance ruling from the Internal Revenue Service if the grant was not made by a person (or related person) who created the organization or who was a substantial contributor prior to the grant; the grant was not made by a person in a position of authority; the grant is in the form of cash or readily marketable securities; the grantor did not impose any material restrictions on the organization; and the organization had met the required publicly supported test before the year in which it received the grant [Treas. Regs. §§ 1.170A–9(e)(6)(ii) and 1.509(a)–3(c)(3), (4)].

Problem

City Hospital Foundation received $2,300,000 support from the following sources in the previous four years: Investment income, $200,000; admission fees for charitable events, $300,000; contributions from the public, $1,700,000; contribution from City, $60,000; and contribution from United Fund, $40,000. Included in the $1,700,000 of contributions from the public were contributions from five persons of $200,000 each. Will the foundation qualify as a public charity? Would it qualify if it had eight persons who gave $200,000 each?

In the current year, Sandra Parker Smith wants to make a donation of a ranch worth $8,000,000 that cost her $700,000 thirty years ago. Does the foundation have a problem in accepting the gift?

B. Section 509(a)(2) Organizations

A § 501(c)(3) organization that receives support from the general public in the form of receipts for services rendered or for other activities related to the organization's exempt functions may qualify as a public charity under § 509(a)(2). Section 509(a)(2) treats as public charities charitable organizations that are supported by gross receipts from the public or governmental agencies and that could not meet the § 509(a)(1) publicly-supported tests. The organizations include orchestras, some art groups, and the Boys and Girls Scouts. A § 509(a)(2) organization qualifies as a public charity because it provides *services* to the general public whereas a § 509(a)(1) organizations qualifies because it receives *donations* from the general public. Generally, it is more advantageous for an organization to qualify as a public charity under § 509(a)(1), than § 509(a)(2). The regulations recognize this by indicating that an organization that satisfies the requirements of both § 509(a)(1) and § 509(a)(2), will be treated as public charity under § 509(a)(1).

A § 509(a)(1) organization must meet two tests—a one-third support test and a not more than one-third gross investment test.

1. One–Third Support Test

Like a § 509(a)(1) organization, a § 509(a)(2) organization must meet a more than one-third support test. As is the case with a § 509(a)(1) organization, a fraction is necessary, the denominator of which is total support and the numerator of which is public support. Total support, the denominator, is defined in § 509(d) and has the same meaning as used in § 590(a)(1). The meaning of "public support," is what distinguishes a § 509(a)(2) organization from a § 509(a)(1) organization. Under § 509(a)(2), public support includes gifts, grants, contributions, membership fees, and gross receipts from activities relating to the organization's charitable purposes.

In determining whether an organization meets the one-third support test under § 509(a)(2), gifts from disqualified persons cannot be counted at all in the numerator of the support fraction. In addition, gross receipts from performance of the organization's exempt functions are included in the numerator, for any one individual or entity, only to the extent receipts from that person or entity do not exceed the greater of $5,000 or one percent of the organization's support for a taxable year. A § 509(a)(2) organization also cannot receive more than a third of its support from gross investment income.

Example 3. City Research Foundation received $1,200,000 support from the following sources in the current year:

Governmental Bureau, for services rendered	$ 120,000
Bill Brown, for services rendered	100,000
General public, for services rendered	400,000
Gross investment income	80,000
Contributions from individual substantial contributors (all disqualified persons)	500,000
	$1,200,000

Because the $120,000 from Governmental Bureau and the $100,000 from Bill Brown exceed $5,000 or one percent of City Foundation's total support, each amount may be included in the one-third support fraction only to the extent of $12,000 [the greater of $5,000 or one percent of total support (which would be $12,000)]. Contributions from substantial contributions may not be included at all in the numerator. Thus, the numerator of the fraction is

$424,000 [$1,200,000 (total support) − $196,000 [gross receipts from Governmental Bureau ($120,000) and Bill Brown ($100,000) in excess of $12,000 for each, or $24,000 total, i.e. $220,000−$24,000]− $80,000 (gross investment income) − $500,000 (contributions from disqualified persons)]. The fraction, 424,000/1,200,000 is 35.3 percent; thus, City Foundation meets the one-third support test for the current year. [This test, however, is computed over a four-year period except that the gross receipts limitation (wherein gross receipts from any one person or entity are excluded from the numerator to the extent they exceed the greater of $5,000 or one percent) is computed on an annual basis with respect to support for each year.]

Questions

1. Is it preferable for an organization to receive a grant or to receive the same amount of money from gross receipts? The usual answer is that grant funds are preferable. Why?

2. What is the difference between funds received as a grant and as gross receipts? Both generally require the organization to perform some type of service in return for the funds. [See discussion at Treas. Reg. § 1.509(a)−3(f)(2), (g)(2) (gross receipts) and § 1.509(a)−3(g)(1).]

3. The difference between membership dues and gross receipts may also be troublesome. If a member is entitled to some privilege at no extra cost–for example, attendance at a theatrical presentation—are the member's dues really gross receipts? [See Treas. Reg. § 1.509(a)−3(h)(i), Example 2.]

2. One–Third Investment Income Test

City Research Foundation, in the example above, also must meet a not more than one-third gross investment test. Gross investment income includes interest, dividends, rents, and some royalties. It is income that we generally term "passive" or "portfolio" income. Not more than one-third of total support for a § 509(a)(2) organization can be from gross investment income.

The numerator of the fraction in the above example would be $80,000 (gross investment income) and the denominator would be $1,200,000. The fraction, $80,000/$1,200,000, is 6.66 percent; thus, City Research Foundation also meets the gross investment test.

Because City Research Foundation meets both the one-third support test and the not more than one-third gross investment test, it qualifies in the current year as a § 509(a)(2) organization.

Note

1. There is no alternative "facts and circumstances" test for a § 509(a)(2) organization. Thus, if an organization does not meet the one-third support test as set out above, it cannot qualify under § 509(a)(2).

2. A large grant also could prevent an organization from qualifying under § 509(a)(2). No contributions from disqualified persons (which in-

cludes substantial donors as noted above) can be counted in the numerator in determining whether one-third of the organization's support is from the general public. However, if the grant qualifies as an unusual grant, as discussed above for § 509(a)(1) organizations, it can be excluded from both the numerator and the denominator of the support fraction [as is the case for a § 509(a)(1) organization].

Problem

Refer to the previous problem in which you were asked to determine if City Hospital Foundation could qualify as a public charity under § 509(a)(1). Determine now whether it can qualify as a public charity under § 509(a)(2). For purposes of this problem, assume the $60,000 contributed by City was for services rendered. (Even though you would compute the amount of the contribution from City that can be included in the numerator on an annual basis, make your computation for purposes of this problem based on total support as stated in the problem.)

C. Section 509(a)(3) Organizations

An organization that receives little, if any, support from the general public may be able to qualify as a public charity under § 509(a)(3) of the Internal Revenue Code if it supports (is operated exclusively for the benefit of) either a § 509(a)(1), or a § 509(a)(2) public charity, a § 501(c)(4) social welfare organization, a § 501(c)(5) labor organization, or a § 501(c)(6) business league. Thus, a supporting organization for a church, school, hospital, or for an organization that either meets the one-third support test under § 509(a)(1) or the one-third support test and gross investment tests under § 509(a)(2), could qualify as a public charity under § 509(a)(3) even though the supporting organization was created and funded by only a few donors. A § 509(a)(3) organization must meet an organizational and an operational test.

1. Organizational Test

A § 509(a)(3) organization must be organized exclusively for the benefit of, to perform the functions of, or to carry out the purposes of, one or more *specified* § 509(a)(1) or (2) organization. The articles of incorporation of a § 509(a)(3) organization must so limit its purposes and must not expressly empower the organization to engage in activities that are not in furtherance of these purposes. The articles must state the specified publicly supported organization (or organizations) on whose behalf the supporting organization is operated and must not expressly empower the supporting organization to operate or benefit any other organization. An organization will not qualify under § 509(a)(3) if any part of its activities is in furtherance of a purpose other than supporting or benefitting its specified publicly supported charity or charities.

2. Operational Test

A § 509(a)(3) organization must be engaged solely in activities that support or benefit its specified publicly supported charity or charities. Section 509(a)(3) supporting organizations must be responsive to the needs and demands of the public charity or charities they are designated to support and must constitute an integral part of, or maintain a significant involvement in, operations of the supported charities.

The relationship between a supporting organization and its supported charity or charities requires either (1) the presence of a substantial degree of direction by the supported charity over conduct of the supporting organization, (2) the presence of common supervision or control among governing bodies of the organizations involved, or (3) a supporting organization responsive to, and significantly involved in, operations of the supported public charity or charities [Treas. Reg. § 509(a)–4].

To meet the relationship test, one of the following three types of relationships must exist between the supporting organization and its supported charity or charities.

1. The supporting organization must be operated, supervised, or controlled by the supported organization. This type relationship requires a substantial degree of direction by the publicly supported charity over conduct of the supporting organization. The relationship is comparable to that of a parent corporation and its subsidiary.

2. The supporting organization must be supervised or controlled in connection with the publicly supported charity. This relationship requires the presence of common supervision or control among governing bodies of the supporting and the supported charities. Control or management of the supporting organization must be vested in the same persons who control or manage the publicly supported charity.

3. The supporting organization must be operated in connection with the supported charity. This test requires that the supporting charity meet a responsiveness test and an integral part test.

The responsiveness test requires that the supporting organization be responsive to the needs and demands of its publicly supported charity. At least one of its officers, directors, or trustees must be elected or appointed by officers, directors, trustees, or members of the supported charity. In addition, at least one of the members of the governing bodies of the publicly supported charity must hold some important office in the supporting organization. Finally, there must be a close and continuous working relationship with officers, directors, or trustees of the supporting organization and the publicly supported public charity.

The integral part test requires that a supporting organization maintain a significant involvement in operations of its supported charity and that its designated supported charity be dependent in some manner upon the supporting organization for the type of support it provides [Treas. Reg. § 1.509(a)–4].

Section 509(a)(3) organizations may not be controlled directly or indirectly by disqualified persons (other than foundation managers) [Treas. Reg. § 1.509(a)–4(j)]. A supporting organization will be controlled if voting power of disqualified persons is 50 percent or more of the total voting power of the organization's governing body or if one or more of these persons has the right to exercise veto power over actions of the organization.

LAPHAM FOUNDATION, INC. v. COMMISSIONER

United States Court of Appeals, Sixth Circuit, 2004
389 F.3d 606

DAUGHTREY, Circuit Judge.

The petitioner, Lapham Foundation, Inc., appeals from a Tax Court judgment classifying it as a private foundation under 26 U.S.C. section 509(a)(3). The Tax Court based its decision on a finding that the Foundation did not meet the "integral part" test set forth in 26 C.F.R. section 1.509(a)–4(i)(3). On appeal, the Foundation argues that it does meet the requisite test and is therefore a supporting organization, rather than a private organization. The Commissioner of Internal Revenue, in response, claims that the Tax Court was correct in holding that the Foundation did not meet the "integral part" test and that, even if the Foundation does meet that test, the Tax Court's decision should be affirmed because the Foundation has not shown that it is not controlled by disqualified persons, as required by 26 U.S.C. section 509(a)(3)(C) in order to be classified as a supporting organization. The Tax Court did not address the latter question and, because we conclude that the Tax Court's ruling on the Foundation's failure to meet the integral part test was correct, we likewise find it unnecessary to address the issue raised under section 509(a)(3)(C)).

I

Factual and Procedural Background

Lapham Foundation, Inc. (the Foundation), is a Michigan non-profit corporation, organized under its articles "to operate exclusively for the benefit of the American Endowment Foundation" in a manner intended to "enable [it] to qualify as a supporting organization of the American Endowment Foundation within the meaning of Section 509(a)(3) of the Code." In turn, the American Endowment Foundation (AEF) is an Ohio non-profit corporation that the IRS has recognized both as tax-exempt as an organization described in section 501(c)(3) and as a publicly supported entity under section 509(a)(1). AEF runs a donor-advised fund program through which the donors have the right to advise AEF on how they wish their contributions to be distributed, but AEF is not obligated to follow the recommendations and retains control over the timing, manner, and recipients of the distributions. The Foundation's sole asset was a promissory note, payable to Charles and Maxine Lapham, in a face amount of $1,554,244. The maker of the note was Estate Storage Co., a corporation owned by the Laphams, and it was collateralized with real estate owned by Estate Storage. The principal amount was due in full no later than December 30, 2013. The interest rate on the note was 7.75%, to be paid in equal quarterly payments of $30,113.48. In exchange for the note, the Laphams received a gift annuity, under which the Foundation agreed to pay them $116,568 annually over their joint lives. In July 1999, the Foundation filed Form 1023 with the IRS, seeking to be recognized as a tax-exempt organization under section 501(c)(3) and as a supporting organization under section 509(a)(3). The application indicated that the Foundation would support AEF "by receiving and administering funds for the benefit of [AEF]" and listed its sources of financial support as "[d]onations from the Lapham family and its friends, including individuals and businesses," and interest on investments. On a financial disclosure form, the Foundation noted that it had received $1,554,244 in 1998 (the promissory note) and that it expected to receive $5,000 a year in gifts, grants, and contributions in 1999 and 2000. The form also noted that the entity anticipated receipt of $120,454 in gross investment income in 1999 and in 2000, and that it had a gift annuity obligation of $116,568 per year. The Foundation thus expected an excess of revenue over expenses of $8,886 per year for 1999 and 2000. Because it intended to give at least 85 percent of its income to the supported organization, the application estimated a donation of $7,600 annually to AEF.

During the administrative process, the Foundation reported that it would receive outright testamentary gifts of approximately $693,000 at the death of the Laphams, which it estimated would occur in 25.5 years, and that it was the beneficiary of a charitable lead trust under the revocable living trusts of Charles and Maxine Lapham, which, if certain assumptions proved to be true, would distribute $355,834 annually for 17 years after the Laphams' deaths.

The report also indicated that the Laphams had pledged an additional $207,733 to the Foundation contingent upon the approval of its status under section 501(c)(3) and section 509(a)(3).

In a later communication to the IRS, the Foundation stated that it would recommend that AEF use one-third of the support provided through the donor-advised fund to expand its representation in Southeastern Michigan, and the remaining two-thirds to support charities in Northville, Michigan. It also estimated that AEF's total annual income was $7,997,910, although the Tax Court later determined that, in 1998, AEF received total contributions in the amount of $7,350,000 but had income of only $650,000.

On April 19, 2000, the IRS recognized the Foundation as exempt from taxation as a section 501(c)(3) organization but determined that it was a private foundation, rather than a supporting organization under section 509(a)(3). In response, the Foundation offered to make various changes in its organizational structure in order to achieve supporting organization status. The Tax Court found it unclear from the administrative record whether any of the proposed changes were actually made, although it appears that the Foundation did amend its by-laws concerning the make-up of the board of directors. The Foundation nonetheless received an adverse ruling as to its request for a supporting organization classification under section 509(a)(3). The IRS explained that the Foundation had failed to meet the "attentiveness" test under the "integral part" test found in section 1.509(a)–4(i)(3)(iii) of the Income Tax Regulations, and that it had also failed to meet the test for control by disqualified persons set forth in section 1.509(a)–4(j)(1) of the Regulations. The IRS further explained, as to the control test, that the Foundation's primary asset was a promissory note payable by a corporation controlled by disqualified persons and secured by assets of that corporation. It found, therefore, that "[d]isqualified persons are in a position to control [the Foundation] by means of the power they exercise, through their corporation, with respect to [the Foundation's] primary asset."

Dissatisfied with this ruling, the Foundation filed a petition for declaratory judgment in the Tax Court, seeking a determination that it was a supporting organization as described in section 509(a)(3), rather than a private foundation. The case was submitted for a decision on the basis of the pleadings and the administrative record. The Tax Court found that the Foundation did not meet the "integral part" test and, because that decision was fatal to the Foundation's claim that it was a supporting organization, did not reach the issue of whether the Foundation was controlled by disqualified persons.

* * *

II

We have held that the determination that an organization is not "organized and operated exclusively for" exempt purposes, for purposes of section 501(c)(3), is a question of fact.* * * It could be argued that the question of whether an organization is operated "in connection" with another organization is similar in kind to the question of whether it is operated exclusively for certain purposes. On the other hand, what is being reviewed here is not actually the existence of a fact, but the application of the law to the facts, a situation requiring de novo review.

* * *

III

Under 26 U.S.C. section 509(a), a section 501(c)(3) organization is a "private foundation" unless it meets one of the exemptions specified in section 509(a)(1)-(4). Private foundations are subject to various taxes, such as an excise tax based on investment income and taxes on self-dealing and failure to distribute income. See 26 U.S.C. section 4940–4948. "Public charities [are] excepted from private foundation status on the theory that their exposure to public scrutiny and their dependence on public support [will] keep them from the abuses [of the tax-exempt status] to which private foundations [are] subject." * * * The Foundation claims that it should not be classified as a private foundation because it is a supporting organization, as described in section 509(a)(3). Supporting organizations are exempt from private foundation status "in so far as they are subject to the scrutiny of a public charity." * * * "The Treasury Regulations therefore provide that the supporting organization must be responsive to the needs of the public charity and intimately involved in its operations."

Under section 509(a)(3), an organization is exempt from private foundation status if it: (A) is organized, and at all times thereafter is operated, exclusively for the benefit of, to perform the functions of, or to carry out the purposes of one or more specified organization described in paragraph (1) or (2), (B) is operated, supervised, or controlled by or in connection with one or more organizations described in paragraph (1) or (2), and (C) is not controlled directly or indirectly by one or more disqualified persons (as defined in section 4946) other than foundation managers and other than one or more organizations described in paragraph (1) or (2); * * * The Commissioner contends that Lapham fails to meet the criteria of subsections (B) and (C); subsection (A) is not at issue in this case.

In order to qualify under section 509(a)(3)(B), an organization must be "(i) [o]perated, supervised, or controlled by, (ii) [s]upervised or controlled in connection with, or (iii) [o]perated in connection with, one or more publicly supported organizations." 26 C.F.R. 1.509(a)–4(f)(2). The Foundation claims that it is operated in connection with AEF and therefore fulfills the third of these relationships. However, the Treasury Regulations further elaborate that an organization will only be considered to be operated "in connection with" a publicly supported organization if it meets a "responsiveness test" and an "integral part test." See 26 C.F.R. section 1.509(a)–4(i)(1). The Tax Court found that the Foundation's structure satisfied the responsiveness test, and the Commissioner does not challenge that finding on appeal. Thus, the only question that remains with regard to section 509(a)(3)(B) is whether the Foundation meets the "integral part" test.

That test "is designed to insure that the publicly supported organization will be attentive to the supporting organization." * * * A supporting organization meets the integral part test if "it maintains a significant involvement in the operations of one or more publicly supported organizations and such publicly supported organizations are in turn dependent upon the supporting organization for the type of support which it provides." 26 C.F.R. 1.509(a)-4(i)(3)(i).

There are two ways in which an organization can fulfill the integral part test: by meeting either the "but for" test set out in 26 C.F.R. 1.509(a)–4(i)(3)(ii) or the "attentiveness" test described in 26 C.F.R. 1.509(a)-4(i)(3)(iii).

A. The Attentiveness Test

The "attentiveness" test focuses on whether the supported organization will be attentive to the supporting operation. In order to satisfy this test, the supporting organization must donate substantially all of its income to the supported organization, and the amount of support received by the supported organization must be "sufficient to insure the attentiveness of such organization to the operations of the supporting organization." 26 C.F.R. 1.509(a)–4(i)(3)(iii)(a). In order for the amount of support received to be considered sufficient, either the amount of support must "represent a sufficient part of the [supported] organization's total support so as to insure such attentiveness," or it must be demonstrated that "in order to avoid the interruption of the carrying on of a particular function or activity, the beneficiary organization will be sufficiently attentive to the operations of the supporting organization." 26 C.F.R. 1.509(a)-4(i)(3)(iii)(b). "This may be the case where either the supporting organization or the beneficiary organization earmarks the support received from the supporting organization for a particular program or activity, even if such program or activity is not the beneficiary organization's primary program or activity so long as such program or activity is a substantial one." In determining whether the amount of support received is sufficient, "[a]ll pertinent factors, including the number of beneficiaries, the length and nature of the relationship between the beneficiary and supporting organization and the purpose to which the funds are put" will be considered. 26 C.F.R. 1.509(a)-4(i)(3)(iii)(d). "[E]vidence of actual attentiveness by the beneficiary organization is of almost equal importance" with the substantiality of the amount involved in determining the attentiveness of the supported organization.

With regard to the first way of satisfying "attentiveness," the Tax Court pointed out that the Foundation anticipated giving only $7,600 per year to AEF in the near future and concluded that such a small contribution was insufficient to ensure AEF's attentiveness. The Foundation argues that the Tax Court erred by over-emphasizing the amount AEF would be receiving in the Foundation's first two years of operation, while failing to take into consideration the nearly $7 million the Laphams had pledged to the Foundation on a long-term basis, at least 85 percent of which the Foundation intended to donate to AEF. It points out that taxpayers often establish charitable-giving programs that are modest during their lifetimes but significant after death, and that such programs are beneficial in that they allow taxpayers to teach a charitable philosophy to their children and help to avoid post-mortem litigation by enabling taxpayers to address potential IRS objections during their lifetimes. The Foundation contends that we should follow the analysis used in National Foundation, Inc. v. United States, 13 Cl.Ct. 486 (1987), a case in which a foundation was given section 501(c)(3) status based on proposed activities, and that we allow a "declaratory judgment based upon proposed activities before substantial time and resources have been committed toward actual operations."

Although the Laphams have pledged significant funds to the Foundation, and although the Foundation has indicated that it will distribute at least 85 percent of its future income to AEF, we agree with the Tax Court's determination that the future contributions are not sufficient to fulfill the "attentiveness" test, given how far in the future AEF anticipates receiving them. It is difficult to believe that AEF will give the Foundation the sort of regular oversight contemplated by the test when it will not be receiving substantial support from the organization for another two decades.

Furthermore, although the relevant documents recording the various trusts set up by the Laphams are not in the record, it appears that the trust through which the Foundation will supposedly receive $355,834 a year for 17 years is, in fact, revocable. If this is the case, there is no assurance that the Foundation, and through it AEF, will ever receive those contributions. Finally, as the Commissioner has pointed out, once AEF actually receives enough support to ensure its attentiveness, i.e., once the Laphams have died and the Foundation begins to receive their funds and make donations to AEF, then the Foundation can petition, under 26 U.S.C. section 507(b)(1)(B), to convert from a private organization into a supporting organization.

With regard to the second method of fulfilling the "attentiveness" test, the Foundation asserts that AEF intends to place contributions from the Foundation in a special account for making grants to support charitable activities in southeastern Michigan in general and in Northville, Michigan, in particular.

Without its support, the Foundation argues, the donations in those areas would likely cease. In other words, it is arguing that, without its support, the "particular function or activity" of giving charitable donations in southeastern Michigan would be "interrupted." As the Tax Court points out, however, the regulations specify that the program or activity to which the Foundation has earmarked its funds must be a "substantial" one; it must be important enough to the supported organization that the fear of its loss will cause the supported organization to be properly attentive to the supporting organization. Supporting charitable organizations in Michigan is not a substantial part of AEF's work. In 1998, for example, of $1,300,000 it distributed to organizations similar to those the Foundation proposes to recommend, AEF distributed only $5,500 in Michigan. Furthermore, the Foundation's contributions can hardly be said to be earmarked for a specific program or activity when the Foundation has simply named a geographic area in which it wants the funds to be spent, rather than naming specific charities to which it wants the funds distributed and when, in any case, AEF does not have to abide by the Foundation's recommendations.

Finally, the Foundation claims that it has demonstrated actual attentiveness on the part of AEF. In particular, it points out that AEF appointed one of the Foundation's directors, that this director has access to all of the Foundation's financial information, that the Foundation sends financial reports to AEF, and that the Foundation and AEF have had ongoing communications. Although 26 C.F.R. 1.509(a)–4(i)(3)(iii)(d) uses the imposition of the requirement that the supporting organization furnish reports to the supported organization as an example of evidence of actual attentiveness, there is no evidence here that AEF requires the

Foundation to furnish such reports, nor that the requirement is in the Foundation's by-laws or articles of incorporation. Absent more specific evidence about the communications between the Foundation and AEF, we, like the Tax Court, "remain unconvinced that the [ ] features highlighted portend the type of ongoing monitoring and attentiveness envisaged in the regulation."

For all these many reasons, we conclude that the Tax Court was correct in finding that the Foundation does not meet the "attentiveness" test.

B. *The But–For Test*

The "integral part" test is also fulfilled if "[t]he activities engaged in for or on behalf of the publicly supported organizations are activities to perform the functions of, or to carry out the purposes of, such organizations, and, but for the involvement of the supporting organization, would normally be engaged in by the publicly supported organizations themselves." 26 C.F.R. 1.509(a)–4(i)(3)(ii). We conclude that the Foundation does not meet this test any more than it meets the "attentiveness" test. To begin with, it is unclear that the Foundation is engaging in any activity "for or on behalf" of AEF, given that its only activity is contributing money to AEF. Even if donating money to AEF was considered an activity "for" AEF, it is not an activity AEF itself would be doing but for the Foundation. The Foundation similarly fails the but-for test if its activity is viewed as giving grants to charitable organizations, which it does by giving money to its donor-advised fund at AEF. As the Tax Court pointed out, "such grant-making activities cannot properly be characterized as something in which AEF would be engaged but for petitioner's support. Rather, distributing grant moneys is something in which AEF is and will continue to be engaged regardless of support from petitioner." If the Foundation's activity is construed as giving grants within Southeastern Michigan, it still cannot be said that but for the Foundation's involvement, AEF would engage in the activity itself. As described above, absent significant funding from the Foundation, AEF distributes very little money in Michigan.

Conclusion

Because we agree with the Tax Court's determination that the Foundation fails to qualify as a supporting organization under 26 U.S.C. section 509(a)(3)(B), we also conclude that it is unnecessary to address the contention that the Foundation also fails to qualify under subsection (C). The failure to meet the requirements of any one of the three subsections of section 509(a)(3) is a sufficient basis on which to deny the petitioner status as a supporting organization. For the reasons set out above, we AFFIRM the judgment of the Tax Court in all respects.

* * *

Note

Even though the amount of support a charity receives from a supporting organization does not represent a sufficient part of the supported charity's total support, the support it receives may be sufficient for the supporting organization to meet the integral part test if the supporting charity can demonstrate that in order to avoid the interruption of a particular function of activity, the supported charity will be sufficiently attentive to the supporting organization's operations. This may occur when either the supporting organization or the supported charity earmarks the support, which the charity will receive from the supporting organization, for a particular program or activity even though the program or activity may not be the supported charity's primary program or activity. An example would be an organization that pays all of its annual net income to a university for a chair the supporting organization has established at the university. Without the supporting organization's continued support, the university might not continue to maintain the chair. Under these circumstances, the supporting organization will be treated as providing the university with a sufficient portion of the university's total support to assure the university's attentiveness to the operations of the supporting organization. The supporting organization, in this instance, will meet the integral part test.

Example 4. Patrick and Katy Ryan want to form The Ryan Family Supporting Foundation to support City Private School. They want the foundation to qualify as a public charity for tax purposes but they want to have input as to activities and operations of the foundation. They have decided the foundation will seek nonprofit corporation status and that its articles of incorporation will set out its purpose as supporting activities for the benefit of, or to carry out the purposes of, City Private School. Its board will consist of nine persons—Patrick and Katy Ryan, their two adult children, three members of the general public, and two members to be appointed by City Private School. One member of the board of City Private School will serve as Vice-President of Ryan Foundation. The Foundation will provide significant funds to the school to fund a scholarship program and to provide operating funds for the school lunch program. The Ryan Family Supporting Foundation will qualify as a public charity under § 509(a)(3) as "operated in connection with" its supported charity. It is not controlled by the Ryans (disqualified persons), and it will be operated solely to support City Private School. Although the Ryans do not control the board, they will have input as four of the nine board members are family members. There is significant involvement by the Ryan Foundation in the operations of the City Private School, and City Private School will be dependent on the foundation to continue the scholarship program and to cover costs of its school lunch program. The foundation will bear the family name, but will not have the disadvantages of private foundation status (discussed in Chapter 7).

Note

Section 509(f) was added to the Internal Revenue code pursuant to the Pension Protection Act of 2006 to cover concerns such as those addressed in *Lapham*. Section 509(f) writes into the Code the responsiveness test, which previously was only set out in treasury regulations. Section 509(a)(3) organizations that are operated in connection with a § 509(a)(1)or (2) organization, such as the Lapham Foundation, now are referred to as "type III supporting organizations." Pursuant to new § 509(f)(1)(A) a type III supporting organization is not considered to be operated in connection with a supported organization [and thus, will not qualify under § 509(a)(3)] if the supporting organization does not provide its supported organization(s) with information the IRS may require to ensure that the supporting organization is responsive to the needs or demands of its supported organization(s).

Section 509(a)(3) organizations now are designated as "type I," those operated, supervised, or controlled by one or more § 509(a)(1) or (2) organizations, "type II," those supervised or controlled in connection with one or more § 509(a)(1) or (2) organizations, and "type III," those operated in connection with one or more § 509(a)(1) or (2) organizations. [See IRC § 4942(g)(4)(B)]. Section 509(f) provides that a "type I" or "type II" organization will cease to qualify under § 509(a)(3) if the "type I" or "type II" organization accepts any gift or contribution from a person (or that person's 35 percent or more controlled entity) who directly or indirectly controls the § 509(a)(3)'s supported organization.

Any type III supporting organization (other than a functionally integrated type III supporting organization), as well as a " type I" or "type II" organization that accepts a gift or contribution from a person who directly or indirectly controls the § 509(a)(3)'s supported organization, now will be treated as a private foundation for purposes of § 4943 of the Code (discussion of § 4943 in Chapter 7).

Section 4943 defines a "type III supporting organization" as a § 509(a)(3) organization that is operated in connection with one or more § 509(a)(1) or (2) organizations. It defines a "functionally integrated type III organizations" as a type III supporting organization that is not required, pursuant to regulations to be issued by the Treasury, to make payments to the supported organization because of the activities of the supported organization related to performing its functions.

D. Section 509(a)(4) Organizations

Section 509(a)(4) excludes from private foundation status those § 501(c)(3) entities that are organized and operated for the purpose of testing products for public safety. These organizations generally are those that test consumer products to determine their acceptability for use by the general public.

E. Filing Requirements

Section 501(c)(3) organizations that qualify as public charities under § 509 and that have total gross receipts normally exceeding $25,000 must file annual returns on Form 990 (or Form 990EZ if gross receipts for the year are less than $100,000 and total assets at the end of the year are less than $250,000). Schedule A to Form 990 (or Form 990EZ) also must be filed annually. It requires information relating to the activities of the § 501(c)(3) organization so that the IRS can determine if the organization can continue to qualify as a public charity. For example, publicly supported organizations claiming public charity status under

§ 509(a)(1) and 170(b)(1)(A)(iv) or (vi) or under § 509(a)(2) must disclose their sources of support on Schedule A for the previous four years. Section 501(c)(3) organizations also must file Schedule B to Form 990 (or Form 990EZ) to report substantial contributions during the year from any one donor (generally $5,000 or more).

(Section 501(c)(3) organizations that do not qualify as public charities, and thus are private foundations for federal income tax purposes, must file Form 990PF, which is discussed in Chapter 7.)

Form 990 and Schedule A provide a complete accounting of the financial activities of a § 501(c)(3) organization.

Organizations other than § 501(c)(3) organizations also must file Form 990 annually. However, other tax exempt organizations do not file the Schedule A to Form 990. Form 990 now is used as a national uniform annual report and, thus, may be used in most states in place of all or a part of the State's required financial report form for nonprofit organizations.

Note

The Pension Protection Act of 2006 added § 6033(i) to the Internal Revenue Code to provide that any organization, which is not required to file annual returns because their income is less than $25,000, must furnish the IRS annually, in electronic form, the legal name of the organization, the name under which it operates or does business, its mailing address and Internet web address (if any), its taxpayer identification number, the name and address of a principal officer, and evidence of the continuing basis for its exemption from filing requirements.

Section 6033(j) was added to the Code to provide for the revocation of tax exempt status for organizations that fail to file an annual return or the notice required in § 6033(i) for three consecutive years.

Chapter 7

PRIVATE FOUNDATIONS

Section 501(c)(3) organizations that cannot meet the requirements for public charity status (as discussed in Chapter 6) are private foundations. A private foundation is subject to substantial restrictions and reporting requirements as well as to an excise tax on net investment income and to penalty taxes for failure to comply with certain restrictions set out in the Internal Revenue Code. Private foundations receive most of their support from a small number of contributors and normally are controlled by their founders or substantial donors. Because such organizations provide their donors with tax deductions for their contributions while being responsive to private groups rather than to the public, the Internal Revenue Service closely supervises their operations to make certain there are no abuses relating to tax-exempt status and to tax benefits donors receive for their contributions.

A gift to a private nonoperating foundation receives less favorable tax treatment than a gift to a public charity, but a private operating foundation (discussed below) is treated like a public charity for purposes of determining the charitable contributions deduction for donors.[1] (The tax treatment of gifts to public charities and to private foundations is discussed in Chapter 8.)

Pursuant to §§ 4941–4945 of the Internal Revenue Code, private foundations are subject to five two-tier excise taxes for engaging in certain prohibited acts or for failing to perform certain required acts. The prohibited acts, or failures to act, are (1) self-dealing (§ 4941), (2) failure to distribute income (§ 4942), (3) having excess business holdings (§ 4943), (4) making investments that jeopardize the charitable purpose

---

1. I.R.C § 170(b)(1)(E)(i). In addition, a private foundation that distributes, by the 15th day of the third month after the close of the foundation's year, 100 percent of all contributions received during the year, is also treated in the same manner as a public charity for purposes of determining the charitable contribution deduction for donors. Treas. Reg. § 1.170A–9(g)(1). A private foundation maintaining a common fund wherein all contributions received are pooled also qualifies donors for the same contribution deduction benefits available to public charities. Treas. Reg. § 1.170A–9(h)(1).

of the foundation (§ 4944), and (5) making certain improper "taxable" expenditures (§ 4945).

Once an organization is classified as a private foundation, it will continue as such until its status is terminated pursuant to § 507 of the Internal Revenue Code. Failure to comply with the requirements of § 507 also will subject a private foundation to substantial penalty taxes.

Section 508(e) of the Code requires that the governing instrument of a private foundation contain special provisions that prohibit it from acting, or refraining from acting, in a manner that would make it liable for penalty taxes under §§ 4941–4945. Specific reference to these sections must be included in the governing instrument unless equivalent language is used that the Service considers to have the same force and effect. This requirement is waived if state law requires that a private foundation act, or refrain from acting, so that it will not be liable for any of the taxes imposed on the prohibited transactions or if it treats the required provisions as though they were contained in the foundation's governing instrument.

All private foundations must file Form 990PF by the 15th day of the 5th month following the close of the foundation's year. The form is subject to public inspection, and the foundation must furnish a copy to the appropriate State Attorney General.

I. PRIVATE OPERATING FOUNDATION

If an organization is involved directly in charitable activities but was created and is funded by only a few donors, the organization may not be able to qualify as a public charity. However, such an organization generally can meet requirements to qualify it for special private foundation status as a private "operating" foundation. A private operating foundation is one that uses its funds "directly" in furtherance of its exempt purposes. Donations to private operating foundation receive identical tax treatment as donations to public charities. In addition, a private operating foundation may be the recipient of qualifying distributions from a private "nonoperating" foundation.

A private operating foundation must satisfy an income test. This test requires it to make qualifying distributions "directly" for the active conduct of its exempt activities equal in value to substantially all (85 percent or more) of the lesser of its adjusted net income or its "minimum investment return." "Minimum investment return" is five percent of the excess of the fair market value of all its noncharitable assets over any acquisition indebtedness on the property. A private operating foundation also must satisfy either an assets, endowment, or support test for any three years during a four-year period.

The assets test is met if 65 percent or more of the foundation's assets are devoted directly to the active conduct of its exempt purposes. The endowment test is met if the foundation makes qualifying distributions directly for the active conduct of its exempt activities of an amount not less than two-thirds of its minimum investment return. The support test is met if 85 percent of support (other than gross investment income) is normally received from the general public and from five or more exempt organizations.[2]

> **Example.** Martin Perry Art History Museum was established by Martin Perry and receives no support from the general public. As the museum cannot qualify as a public charity, members of the board want the museum to be classified as a private operating foundation. Income for the current year was $1,000,000. Expenses relating to the production of its income were $250,000. Reasonable expenses of managing the museum were $450,000. The museum purchased an artifact costing $200,000 during the year. The museum's building and its contents, along with other properties used in activities directly to perform the museum's exempt purposes, are valued at $4,000,000. The Martin Perry Art History Museum has a farm that is not used to perform its exempt purposes valued at $1,000,000. The museum would qualify as a private operating foundation. Its adjusted net income is $750,000 ($1,000,000—$250,000) and its minimum investment return is $50,000 [$1,000,000 (assets not used to perform its exempt purposes) x 5%]. Qualifying distributions total $650,000 [$450,000 (reasonable expenses of managing the museum) + $200,000 (cost of artifact)]. The qualifying distributions were substantially more than the required 85 percent of the lesser of adjusted net income ($750,000) or minimum investment return ($50,000). In addition, the assets test was satisfied as 80 percent of its assets [$4,000,000 (assets used for exempt purposes)/$5,000,000 (total assets)] were devoted directly to the active conduct of activities constituting the museum's exempt purpose.

II. EXCISE TAX

A private foundation is subject to an excise tax of two percent of its net investment income. Net investment income is the amount by which the sum of gross investment income and any net capital gain exceeds the ordinary and necessary expenses paid or incurred for the production or collection of gross investment income or for the management, conservation, or maintenance of property held for the production of investment income. Gross investment income is the gross amount of income from interest, dividends, rents, and royalties, excluding any amounts that were subject to the tax on unrelated business taxable income (discussed in Chapter 9). Income of this category derived from assets devoted to charitable activities also is included in gross investment income. In computing net capital gains on sales of assets, only those gains and

---

2. Treas. Reg. § 53.4942(b)–2(c)(1). For purposes of the support test, a foundation cannot receive more than 25 percent of its support from any one exempt organization and cannot receive more than half its support from gross investment income. Support from any one exempt organization is counted only if the foundation receives support from no fewer than five exempt organizations.

losses from the sale of property held for investment purposes and for the production of unrelated business income are included in the computation of gross investment income. Tax-exempt interest on governmental obligations and expenses incurred related to production of such income are excluded from the computation. A foundation may deduct only expenses relating to its investment activities. Expenses that are incurred for both investment and exempt purposes are allocated between the two. Depreciation computed using the straight-line method is deductible.

The tax is reduced to one percent for any tax year in which the private foundation's qualifying distributions equal or exceed the sum of the foundation's assets times the average percentage payout for a base period (preceding five years) plus one percent of the foundation's net investment income for the year.[3] Further, a private operating foundation will be exempt from the excise tax if the foundation has been publicly supported for at least ten years, has a governing body that at all times during the year consisted of individuals at least 75 percent of whom were not disqualified persons, and is broadly representative of the general public [I.R.C. § 4940(d)]. None of the foundation officers of such an "exempt operating foundation" can be a disqualified person.

Note

An operating foundation must obtain a ruling letter from the Internal Revenue Service recognizing its special exempt operating foundation status. A copy of the ruling letter is attached to the foundation's annual return on Form 990PF.

Problem

State University Foundation had the following income during the current year.

Interest on State of Texas bonds	$25,000
Dividends on stock investments	75,000
Interest on savings accounts	65,000
Capital gain from sale of securities	25,000

Its expenses that were directly related to producing its income totaled $30,000. The foundation also had a loss on the sale of its securities in the amount of $5,000. What is its excise tax liability under § 4940 of the Code for the current year?

ZEMURRAY FOUNDATION v. UNITED STATES

United States Court of Appeals, Fifth Circuit, 1982
687 F.2d 97

JOHNSON, Circuit Judge:

This is a civil action for recovery of excise taxes assessed and collected by the Internal Revenue Service (IRS) from the Zemurray

---

3. I.R.C. § 4940(e). The tax reduction from two percent to one percent is not available if the foundation was liable during any base period for the penalty tax under § 4942 on undistributed income.

Foundation (Foundation) for calendar year 1974. On March 31, 1978, the IRS assessed an excise tax deficiency of $112,317 plus interest against the Foundation for sale of an undivided one-half interest in timberland. The district court, 509 F.Supp. 976, however, determined that the sale of the timberland did not fall under the excise tax provisions of 26 U.S.C. § 4940, and entered judgment in favor of the Foundation. The Government appeals.

I. Background

The Foundation is a tax exempt private foundation subject to an excise tax on its net investment income under 26 U.S.C. § 4940, Internal Revenue Code, enacted as part of the Tax Reform Act of 1969 (Reform Act) (Pub.L. 91–172, 83 Stat. 487). On November 30, 1961, Samuel Zemurray died, bequeathing the Foundation naked ownership of an undivided one-half interest in 12,746 acres of timberland in Tangipahoa Parish, Louisiana. His wife, Sarah Zemurray, received a usufruct interest for life in the Foundation's undivided one-half interest.[4] The Foundation received possession of its interest by a judgment of possession on June 16, 1970.

The timberland surrounded a private lodge and 100 to 150 acres of flower gardens. The flower gardens and parts of the timberland were open to the public for sightseeing, fishing, and hunting. The timberland was carefully managed to harvest timber on a sustained-yield basis, although actual income from timber sales fluctuated from year to year. * * * All of the income from these timber sales went to Mrs. Zemurray as usufructuary.

On February 16, 1974, Mrs. Zemurray donated her usufruct interest in the timberland to the Foundation. She was ninety-one years old at the time. Five days later, on February 21, 1974, the Foundation agreed to sell its entire one-half interest in the timberland to an unrelated third party, and the sale was consummated in June of that year. The Foundation did not receive any income from timber sales between February 16, 1974 and the date of the sale to the unrelated third party.

The value of the one-half interest in the timberland, including the usufruct, was $2,716,540 as of December 31, 1969. * * * The Foundation received $5,525,000 for this one-half interest in June of 1974. On March 31, 1978, the Commissioner of the IRS assessed a tax deficiency against the Zemurray Foundation of $112,317 plus interest of $23,797.62. The Commissioner contended that net capital gain on the sale of the timberland was "net investment income" subject to a four percent excise tax under 26 U.S.C. § 4940 and Treas.Reg. § 53.4940–1(f)(1) promulgated thereunder. The Foundation paid the asserted deficiency, interest, and penalty and then filed a claim for refund. When this claim was neither

---

4. A "naked ownership" is an imperfect ownership subject to a usufruct. LSA–C.C. Art. 490 (West 1973). Usufruct is the right of enjoying a thing, the property of which is vested in another, and to draw from the same all the profit, utility, and advantages which it may produce, provided it be without altering the substance of the thing. LSA–C.C. Art. 533 (West 1973).

approved nor disallowed, the Foundation brought the instant action in the federal district court on March 23, 1979.

After a bench trial, the district court awarded the Foundation a refund of the excise tax plus statutory interest on grounds the Foundation never actually used the timberland to produce net investment income. In arriving at this result, the district court held that Treas.Reg. § 53.4940–1(f)(1) was invalidly overbroad in allowing taxation of property merely susceptible to use for production of net investment income, whether or not it was actually used for that purpose. The district court never actually determined whether timberland qualified as a type of property from which investment income could be produced. On appeal, the Government contends that Treas.Reg. § 53.4940–1(f)(1) validly applies to the taxation of capital gains from the sale of the timberland and that the gains are taxable.

II. Taxability of Property for Purposes Set Forth In 26 U.S.C. § 4940

At the time of the timberland sale, 26 U.S.C. § 4940(c)(4)(A) imposed an excise tax of four percent on the "net investment income" of charitable foundations.[5] 26 U.S.C. § 4940(c)(1) defines two types of net investment income: (1) "gross investment income" and (2) "net capital gain." Gross investment income is ordinary income from "interest, dividends, rents, and royalties." 26 U.S.C. § 4940(c)(2). Net capital gain includes "gains and losses from the sale or other disposition of property used for the production of interest, dividends, rents, and royalties," and certain other property involved in the tax of unrelated business income. 26 U.S.C. § 4940(c)(4) (emphasis added).[6]

At issue in the instant case is whether the timberland sold by the Foundation is taxable as "net capital gain." Treas.Reg. § 53.4940–1(f)(1), T.D. 7250, 1973–1 C.B. 469, 472, interprets net capital gain as follows:

> (f) Capital gain and losses-(1) General rule. In determining capital gain net income (net capital gain for taxable years beginning before January 1, 1977) for purposes of the tax imposed by section 4940, there shall be taken into account only capital gains and losses from the sale or other disposition of property held by a private foundation for investment purposes (other than program-related investments, as defined in section 4944(c)), and property used for the production of income included in computing the tax imposed by section 511 except to the extent gain or loss from the sale or other disposition of

---

5. Section 4940, as originally enacted in 1969, levied a 4% excise tax on net investment income. A 1978 amendment changed the tax rate to 2%. See Revenue Act of 1978, Pub.L. 95–600, § 520(a), 92 Stat. 2763.

6. 26 U.S.C. § 4940(c)(4), recites, in pertinent part:

(4) Capital gains and losses.-For purposes of paragraph (1) in determining capital gain net income-

(A) There shall be taken into account only gains and losses from the sale or other disposition of property used for the production of interest, dividends, rents, and royalties, and property used for the production of income included in computing the tax imposed by section 511 (except to the extent gain or loss from the sale or other disposition of such property is taken into account for purposes of such tax).

such property is taken into account for purposes of such tax. For taxable years beginning after December 31, 1972, property shall be treated as held for investment purposes even though such property is disposed of by the foundation immediately upon its receipt, if it is property of a type which generally produces interest, dividends, rents, royalties, or capital gains through appreciation (for example, rental real estate, stock, bonds, mineral interests, mortgages, and securities).

The regulation excludes gains and losses from the sale or other disposition of property used for the exempt (i.e., charitable) purposes of the private foundation. * * *

The Foundation had only a naked ownership interest in the timberland for several years, during all of which time the income from the timberland went to the usufructuary, Mrs. Zemurray; the Foundation received no income from the timberland production prior to the sale; the Foundation sold no timber and received no income from the timberland after Mrs. Zemurray donated her usufruct interest. The Government nevertheless contends, in accordance with 26 U.S.C. § 4940 and Treas. Reg. § 53.4940–1(f)(1), that the Foundation's timberland was of a type "which generally produces" the applicable types of investment income. The language "generally produces" in the regulation interprets the term "used" in 26 U.S.C. § 4940(c)(4) to allow taxation so long as the property sold is usable to produce the applicable types of income, regardless of whether the property is actually used to produce income or not. The district court, however, determined that Treas.Reg. § 53.4940–1(f)(1) invalidly broadened the term "used" to the extent that the regulation taxed property not actually used to produce taxable investment income, and held that the excise tax did not therefore apply to the Foundation's sale of the timberland.

This Court must determine whether the district court properly held Treas.Reg. § 53.4940–1(f)(1) invalid with respect to its interpretation of "used" in 26 U.S.C. § 4940(c)(4). A Treasury regulation is presumed to be valid unless it can be demonstrated that the regulation is unreasonable and plainly inconsistent with the statute. * * * The Treasury regulation's interpretation in the instant case is not perceived as unreasonable or plainly inconsistent with the statute. The language of the statute is susceptible to at least two reasonable interpretations of the term "used": the IRS interpretation and the Foundation's interpretation.[7] Furthermore, several canons of statutory construction give support

---

7. The Tax Court in Friedman Foundation, Inc. v. Commissioner, 71 T.C. 40, 50 (1978) observed that the term "use" in s 4940(c)(4) is capable of several constructions:

For example, we might conclude that the term "use" referred to is use of the property by the foundation.... On the other hand, we might conclude that use by either the foundation or its donors is sufficient for taxation under Section 4940. Alternatively, relying on part 2 of the Ways and Means Committee Report, we might conclude that a holding for investment income consisting of capital gain is sufficient for taxation under section 4940 (here, too, we might conclude that the relevant holding must be that of the foundation alone or that the relevant holding may be that of either the founda-

to the IRS interpretation. First, the administrative regulation was a substantially contemporaneous interpretation of 26 U.S.C. § 4940(c)(4) and therefore entitled to even greater weight than is otherwise accorded to a regulation. * * * Second, congressional reaction appears to support the administrative interpretation. Since the regulation's adoption, Congress has amended 26 U.S.C. § 4940 on three separate occasions-each time without materially changing the provisions of section 4940(c)(4)(A). Congressional approval is reflected by virtue of subsequent re-enactments without material changes. * * *

The Government's interpretation is also supported by the broad congressional purpose underlying 26 U.S.C. § 4940. The Reform Act was passed to ensure that private foundations promptly and properly use their funds for charitable purposes. * * * Congress created the excise tax in 26 U.S.C. § 4940 as an audit fee to be paid by foundations to finance government supervision of a foundation's investment income activity. The intent of both the Reform Act in general and the excise tax in particular was to prevent abuse resulting from the tax exempt status of charitable foundations.[9] Any ambiguity or susceptibility of the language of the statute to more than one interpretation, therefore, should be broadly interpreted.

III. Taxability of Property Held for "Capital Gains Through Appreciation"

The question remains whether the Foundation's timberland is the type of property subject to the excise tax. Treas.Reg. § 53.4940–1(f)(1) is made applicable to gains on property used for interest, dividends, rents, and royalties. Treas.Reg. § 53.4940–1(f)(1) expands upon the four categories (interest, dividends, rents, and royalties) of taxable property by adding a fifth category effective December 31, 1972:

> ... if it is property of a type which generally produces interest, dividends, rents, royalties, or capital gains through appreciation (for example, rental real estate, stock, bonds, mineral interests, mortgages, and securities.) (emphasis added). The district court made no finding of fact as to whether the Foundation's timberland was property which generally produces interest, dividends, rents, or

---

tion or donor). As another possibility, we might conclude that the pattern of statutory materials requires the line be drawn between the foundation's "charitable assets" and its "noncharitable assets." Other alternatives may suggest themselves after careful perusal of the statute and its legislative history.

The court in Friedman ultimately determined that sale of stock by a foundation immediately upon receipt was taxable, even though the stock produced no income stream from dividends before the sale.

9. The broad purpose in enacting s 4940 is set forth in H.R.Rep.No.91–413, Pt. 1, 91st Cong., 1st Sess. at 19 (1969), U.S.Code Cong. & Admin.News 1969, at 1663:

> Your Committee believes that since the benefits of government are available to all, the costs should be borne, at least to some extent, by all of those able to pay. Your committee believes that this is as true for private foundations as it is for taxpayers generally. Also, it is clear that vigorous and extensive administration is needed in order to provide appropriate assurances that private foundations will promptly and properly use their funds for charitable purposes. This tax, then, may be viewed as being in part a user fee.

royalties. Rather, the district court determined that it was not necessary to decide this issue, since the Foundation had failed to actually use the land for production of income before the sale.

Under these circumstances, this cause must be remanded to the district court for findings of fact on whether the timberland was property which generally produces interest, dividends, rents, or royalties. * * * The district court, however, has complicated this course of action by finding that the timberland is the "type of property that generally produces capital gains through appreciation." The district court further held that Treas.Reg. § 53.4940–1(f) (1) is invalid to the extent it subjects to the excise tax any property which generally produces "capital gains through appreciation." We again hold that the district court erred.

Read in isolation, 26 U.S.C. § 4940(c)(4) might appear to extend only to property used for the production of "interest, dividends, rents, and royalties." Statutory meaning, however, is to be derived not from reading of a single sentence or section, but from the provisions of the whole law, and its object and policy. * * *

A narrow reading of the phrase "... if it is property of a type which generally produces interest, dividends, rents, royalties, or capital gains through appreciation (for example, rental real estate, stock, bonds, mineral interests, mortgages, and securities)" appears to underscore the interpretation previously made by this Court of the word "used." The regulation simply recognizes that property usable for interest, dividends, rents, or royalties may sometimes be held simply for capital gains through appreciation. Growth stocks would be a prime example, see Friedman Foundation, supra, and the regulation lists several others. Interpreted in this manner, this phrase in the regulation is neither unreasonable nor inconsistent with 26 U.S.C. § 4940(c)(4), and, therefore, must be presumed valid. * * *

On remand, the district court should make a factual determination on whether the timberland is the type of property which generally produces interest, dividends, rents, or royalties. * * * Even if the timberland is property held for capital gains through appreciation, the district court should treat it as property used for interest, dividends, rents, or royalties if the property is susceptible for use in this manner. * * *

The judgment of the district court is reversed and this cause is remanded for further proceedings consistent with this opinion.

REVERSED AND REMANDED.

GEE, Circuit Judge, dissenting:

The law applicable to this sale by a charity of a capital asset provides, in pertinent part, that a tax is due upon the gain from such a sale of "property used for the production of interest, dividends, rents, and royalties...." 26 U.S.C. § 4940(c)(4)(A). Since it is undisputed that this charity did not use the property concerned for any such production, the late Judge Gordon held that no tax was due. * * * We hold that because the property may have been usable for such purposes its sale may be taxable and remand for such a determination. With deference, and for the reasons stated in his opinion, it seems to me that Judge Gordon has the better of the argument. * * *

There is nothing ambiguous about the word "used," and it simply does not mean "usable." * * * Had Congress meant the latter, it could easily have said so. Though it did not, Treasury decrees that this is what it meant, and we agree. I see no more justification for this than for a decision by us that had Congress instead said "usable," it really meant "used." Why is one amendment preferable to the other?

More than most others, tax laws are literally received and applied. A reason for this is that tax impositions and exemptions are matters of legislative grace and of compromises-compromises typically ending hard fights between advocates of opposing forces and policies. To a considerable extent they simply represent where the contending forces exhausted themselves and the legislative struggle came to an end. To reopen the contest in the judicial branch, in the name of an internal consistency that seems satisfying to us, and declare a different outcome seems to me an action beyond the warrant of our office and especially inappropriate in the tax field. I respectfully dissent.

GREENACRE FOUNDATION v. UNITED STATES

United States Court of Appeals, Federal Circuit, 1985
762 F.2d 965

Davis, Circuit Judge.

The question is whether a tax-exempt private foundation is liable (under the special tax imposed by 26 U.S.C. § 4940) with respect to capital gains from sales of stocks donated to the foundation and shortly sold pursuant to a pre-existing plan. In this refund suit, the Claims Court (Kozinski, C.J.) somewhat reluctantly held that such gains were to be included in the tax. 6 Cl. Ct. 113 (1984). On taxpayer's appeal, we affirm on the ground that the pertinent Treasury Department regulations validly so provide.

Appellant-taxpayer Greenacre Foundation (Greenacre) is a nonprofit New York corporation and is tax-exempt as a private operating foundation under the Internal Revenue Code. During 1973–75, Greenacre received, by donation, a number of shares of stock which were very shortly thereafter sold (in 1974, 1975, and 1976) with realization of capital gains. Greenacre did not include that gain in computing the tax on private foundations levied by 26 U.S.C. § 4940(a). The Internal Revenue Service (IRS), of the view that these gains should have been included, imposed deficiencies which taxpayers paid. Greenacre filed refund claims which were denied; it then timely filed this refund suit in the Claims Court.

The parties stipulated the following facts: The securities now involved (entirely stock shares) were never used or intended for use by

Greenacre for the production of interest, dividends, rents, or royalties, and no interest, dividends, rents, or royalties were received by Greenacre on those securities during the period it held them. Greenacre intended to sell those securities immediately on receipt in order to fund its operations and endowment. However, the securities are property of the type which generally produces interest, dividends, royalties, or capital gains through appreciation; the companies that issued these securities were publicly traded and all except one security admittedly paid dividends at one time or another in the years 1972–1976. Greenacre's sale of the stocks came within a few days after receipt, the longest holding period being 30 days.

* * *

Section 4940(c) defines "net investment income" as including "gross investment income" plus "net capital gains" less allowable deductions. In turn, the statute provides [§ 4940(c)(4)(A)] that in determining "net capital gains":

> There shall be taken into account only gains and losses from the sale or other disposition of *property used for the production of interest, dividends, rents, and royalties,* and property used for the production of income included in computing the tax imposed by section 511 [the unrelated business income tax] (except to the extent gain or loss from the sale or other disposition of such property is taken into account for purposes of such tax). [Emphasis added.]

Treasury Regulations § 53.4940–1(f)(1), implementing the tax statute, provide, *inter alia:*

> For taxable years beginning after December 31, 1972, *property shall be treated as held for investment purposes even though such property is disposed of by the foundation immediately upon its receipt, if it is property of a type which generally produces interest, dividends, rents, royalties,* or capital gains through appreciation (for example, rental real estate, stocks, bonds, mineral interests, mortgages, and securities). Under this subparagraph, gains and losses from the sale or other disposition of property used for the exempt purposes of the private foundation are excluded.... [Emphasis added.]

The stipulated facts * * * show that the stock in issue here falls within the emphasized portion of Treas. Reg. § 53.4940–1(f)(1), *supra,* though those securities did not actually produce dividends during the short period they were held by Greenacre and though the stocks were not held for that purpose. The issue, therefore, is whether this part of the regulation is a valid implementation of the taxing statute, § 4940(c)(4)(A), *supra.* That is the question decided by the Claims Court and argued to us by both sides.

* * *

Greenacre insists, too, that the regulation's interpretation of § 4940(c)(4)(A) runs against the legislative history of the tax imposed by

§ 4940, and for that reason cannot be accepted (even though it might otherwise be consistent with Congress' wording). We do not see any such conflict.

Taxpayer's point is that (1) the House of Representatives' bill proposed to lay a flat percentage tax on a foundation's net investment income (H. Rep. No. 413, 91st Cong., 1st Sess. (1969), 1969–3 Cum. Bull. 200, 213–14) while the Senate planned a user or audit fee measured by a percentage of a foundation's noncharitable assets (A. Rep. No. 552, 91st Cong. 1st Sess., 27 (1969), U.S. Code Cong. & Admin. News 1969, p. 1645, 1969–3 Cum. Bull. 423, 441–42); and (2) the full Congress adopted the House approach and its language taxing investment income, rather than the Senate's. The conclusion taxpayer draws is that the Treasury Regulation reinstates the rejected Senate version of a tax on the noncharitable assets by (it is claimed) imposing a tax on all noncharitable assets.

Unlike taxpayer, we find no help (for our present problem) in this history. The House proposal and the statute both impose a tax on "net investment income" (including "net capital gain"), as does the Treasury Regulation which permits inclusion of stocks only if they were "held for investment purposes." When the regulation goes on to define property "of a type which generally produces ... dividends" as being automatically "held for investment purposes," the regulation does not conflict at all with the legislative history taxpayer invokes—a history which wholly fails to cover or allude to that precise point. The Treasury Department was not adopting the Senate plan, but simply defining as "held for investment purposes" a class of property which normally does produce the kinds of income specified in the statute and which is often held for investment.

Nor is there adequate reason, in our view, to doubt that the regulation serves the statutory purpose. The Claims Court observed that it is "difficult to discern how these purposes will be served" in this instance, 6 Ct. Cl. At 114, but that position seems based on the mistaken premise that the purpose of the § 4940(a) tax was to curb abuses by private foundations and to assure that such foundations' investments were not jeopardized by financial speculation. Those were indeed the objectives of other parts of the 1969 legislation respecting private foundations (e.g., self-dealing; failure to distribute income; excess business holdings; investments jeopardizing charitable purposes), but they were not the purposes of the § 4940(a) tax which was to impose a type of user fee or tax to help pay for the administration of private foundations. For that special kind of tax, there is no reason to think that Congress desired to exclude donated stock which the foundation promptly sells and from which it reaps a good capital gain.

* * *

AFFIRMED.

Note

In computing gain or loss on a private foundation's sale of its property, the tax basis to the foundation of donated property would the lesser of the fair market value of the property on the date of the gift or the donor's tax basis. Tax basis is determined pursuant to § 1015 of the Code, which generally provides a foundation with a carryover of the donor's basis.

III. SELF–DEALING

Each act of self-dealing between a disqualified person and a private foundation is subject to an excise tax (I.R.C. § 4941). The tax is imposed upon the disqualified person who participated in the act (rather than upon the private foundation) and applies regardless of whether the disqualified person was aware that the act was one of self-dealing. The tax on self-dealing is ten percent of the "amount involved" for each year, but if the act is not corrected, 200 percent of the amount involved. The foundation manager is subject to an initial tax of five percent of the amount involved (maximum of $20,000) if the foundation manager knew the act was self-dealing and the manager willfully participated. An additional tax of 50 percent of the amount involved (maximum of $20,000) is imposed on the manager if the manager refused to agree to a part or all of the correction of the self-dealing act.

The term "self-dealing" refers to transactions, direct or indirect, between a private foundation and a disqualified person. It includes sales or exchanges of property, leases, and loans between a private foundation and a disqualified person; provision of goods, services, or facilities by a private foundation to a disqualified person; a disqualified person's use of a private foundation's income or assets; and a private foundation's payment of "unreasonable" compensation to a disqualified person. A transaction between a private foundation and a disqualified person constitutes "self-dealing" regardless of whether the transaction is fair to the private foundation.

The "amount involved" is the greater of the amount of money and the fair market value of other property given or the amount of money and the fair market value of other property received.

Notes

1. Where the use of property is involved, the "amount involved" is the greater of the amount paid for such use or the fair market value of the use for the period for which the property is used. Assume a substantial donor to a private foundation leases office space in a building owned by the foundation at an annual rental of $12,000. The fair rental of the office space is $24,000 per year. The "amount involved" under § 4941 for purposes of computing the self-dealing penalty tax is $24,000 for each year or partial year.

2. The public recognition benefits a substantial contributor will derive from a publicity campaign conducted by a charity generally are incidental and tenuous and, thus, will not result in a penalty for self-dealing if the

charity does not encourage the purchase of services or products of the contributor.

ESTATE OF REIS v. COMMISSIONER
United States Tax Court, 1986
87 T.C. 1016

Swift, Judge.

* * *

The issues in this case arise out of the widely publicized and much litigated Estate of Mark Rothko (hereinafter sometimes referred to as the estate). Mark Rothko was a well-known American abstract expressionist painter who died in 1970. Bernard J. Reis, decedent (Reis), was one of the executors of the Estate of Mark Rothko. Reis also was one of the directors of the Mark Rothko Foundation (the foundation). The foundation was established by Mark Rothko in 1967. In his will, after making certain specific requests to family members, Mark Rothko bequeathed all of his remaining property to the foundation.

Reis also was an officer and employee of the Marlborough Gallery, Inc. (the gallery). In May of 1970, shortly after Mark Rothko's death, the executors of the estate, including Reis, entered into contracts on behalf of the estate with the gallery under which the paintings of Mark Rothko (which comprised the bulk of the estate's assets) could be sold only by the gallery or its affiliated corporations, offices of which were located throughout the world. The contracts were to last 12 years, and the gallery was to receive a commission of 50 percent of the proceeds from the sale of each painting. * * *

In New York State courts, the surviving members of Mark Rothko's family sued the estate, the executors thereof (including Reis), and the gallery. The foundation intervened and became a party to the State court proceedings. The litigation, insofar as pertinent to the motions before us, sought to void the 12-year exclusive sales contract between the estate and the gallery, to remove Reis as an executor of the estate, and to recover monetary damages. * * *

Much of the legal relief sought by the surviving family of Mark Rothko was granted in the New York litigation. Reis and the other executors of the estate were removed, the contract with the gallery was voided, and monetary damages were awarded to the estate.

The New York litigation did not go unnoticed by the Internal Revenue Service. Respondent's representatives audited the foundation and determined that Reis was liable for various self-dealing excise taxes under section 4941 for the years 1970 through 1974 in the total amount of $18,582,500, and additions to tax under sections 6651 and 6684 for the same years in the respective total amounts of $518,125 and $2,112,500.

Petitioner's motion for summary judgment is based on the following three alternative legal arguments: (1) That section 4941(d)(1)(E) and the related provisions are so vague and imprecise that they are unconstitutional and void; (2) that the assets of the estate were separate and distinct from the assets of the foundation and therefore that any improper, non-arm's length conduct that occurred in administering the assets of the estate do not also constitute self-dealing in the use of the assets of the foundation; and (3) that whatever misuse of the assets of the foundation may have occurred, under the undisputed facts of this case, such misuse did not constitute self-dealing by Reis because the assets of the foundation were not used for the benefit of or transferred to Reis.

* * *

Petitioner argues that in light of the large amounts of Federal excise taxes (e.g., the approximate $21 million at issue herein) that can be assessed against an individual for self-dealing with respect to the assets of a private foundation, it is particularly important that the statutory language be clear and precise. If ambiguous, petitioner argues that the Court should not be hesitant to void the statute as unconstitutional. Petitioner submits that subparagraph (E) of section 4941(d)(1) is so vague that it should be held unconstitutional. * * *

Although based on slightly different reasons, the constitutionality of the self-dealing excise taxes of section 4941 and the underlying regulations previously have been upheld. * * * A number of court opinions have discussed the statutory scheme of the self-dealing excise taxes, and each opinion has recognized those provisions as a valid legislative response to perceived abuses in the use of private foundations. * * * We find no basis for holding any of the provisions of section 4941 unconstitutional.

Petitioner contends that under New York law the paintings of Mark Rothko that were the subject matter of the May 1970 contracts entered into by Reis and the other executors on behalf of the estate and the gallery constituted, at that time, property of the estate, not assets of the foundation. Petitioner thus contends that regardless of the propriety of those contracts, as a matter of law, the contracts could not have constituted acts of self-dealing by Reis with respect to assets of the foundation.

Respondent contends that because the foundation was a beneficiary under Mark Rothko's will, the foundation had a vested beneficial interest in the property of the estate. Respondent contends that Reis' acts with respect to the property of the estate simultaneously and adversely affected the foundation's beneficial interest therein and thereby constituted an indirect use by or for the benefit of Reis of the assets of the foundation. Respondent cites section 53.494(d)–1(b)(3), Excise Tax Regs., as authority for the general proposition that acts of self-dealing with respect to property of an estate also will be regarded as acts of self-dealing with respect to assets of a private foundation that has a beneficial interest in the property of the estate. For the reasons explained below, we agree with respondent on this issue.

Section 53.4941(d)-(b)(3), Excise Tax Regs., clearly contemplates that the interest of a private foundation in the property of an estate, as a beneficiary thereof, will be treated as an "asset" of the private foundation under section 4941(d)(1)(E). Accordingly, acts of self-dealing with respect to property of an estate may also constitute acts of self-dealing with respect to assets of a private foundation which is a beneficiary of the estate. Section 53.4941(d)–1(b)(3), Excise Tax Regs., provides, however, an exception to what otherwise is considered acts of self-dealing if, among other requirements, the transaction is approved by a probate court and if the transaction reflects an exchange at fair market value.

* * *

Regardless of whether the foundation is considered to have had a vested or merely an expectancy interest under New York law in the property of the Mark Rothko Estate, under section 4941 and the relevant Treasury regulations, the expectancy interest the foundation had in the estate is treated as an asset of the foundation, and transactions affecting property of the estate are treated as affecting assets of the foundation. Such transactions are excepted from the definition of acts of self-dealing under section 4941 only if they qualify for the exception described in section 53.4941(d)–1(b)(3), Excise Tax Regs., or under one of the other available exceptions (e.g., the exception for transactions which provide only incidental benefits to disqualified persons). Sec. 53.4941(d)–2(f)(2), Excise Tax Regs.

Petitioner's third argument in support of its motion for summary judgment is that the alleged acts of self-dealing only could have benefitted Reis in a nonpecuniary manner and that under any proper reading of section 4941, that section does not reach nonpecuniary benefits. We disagree.

The language of section 4941(d)(1)(E) does not suggest that it is limited to pecuniary benefits, and we find no basis for imposing such a limitation. Section 4941(d) enumerates in detail those categories of activities that will constitute acts of self-dealing. The purpose of that enumeration was to clarify what acts would be considered acts of self-dealing and to minimize the need to use subjective standards in evaluating potential acts of self-dealing. S. Rept. 91–552 (1969), 1969–3 C.B. 423, 442–443; Rockefeller v. United States, 572 F. Supp. 9, 12–13 (E.D.Ark.1982).

Petitioner argues that respondent's interpretation of section 494(d)(1)(E) is erroneous because it is too broad and fails adequately to distinguish between significant and insignificant personal benefits accruing to a disqualified person. We again disagree. Implicit in the statutory language of subparagraph (E) of section 4941(d)(1) is the requirement that the benefits accruing to the disqualified person be significant. That reading of the statute is supported by Treasury regulations which expressly provide that incidental or tenuous benefits accruing to a disqualified person will not constitute acts of self-dealing. See sec. 53.4941(d)–2(f)(2), Excise Tax Regs.

We also note that respondent contends that the benefits accruing to Reis as a result of the alleged acts of self-dealing were pecuniary in nature and were substantial. Although such allegation does not establish either of those facts, we must assume such facts to be true for purposes of deciding petitioner's motion for summary judgment. *Espinoza v. Commissioner*, 78 T.C. 412 (1982). If petitioner establishes in a subsequent trial herein that Reis, as a disqualified person, received tenuous benefits from his use of the assets of the foundation, section 53.4941(d)–2(f)(2), Excise Tax Regs., will protect petitioner from imposition of the self-dealing taxes.

For the reasons set forth above, petitioner's motion for summary judgment against respondent will be denied.

* * *

Problems

1. Claire Kelly, the director of the Southern History Museum, which is located on an old Southern plantation, would like to move into the plantation home. She believes she could help preserve the mansion by living it and could prevent possible vandalism and thefts on the plantation grounds. The Southern History Museum is a private operating foundation for tax purposes. Would Claire's living in the plantation home be an act of self-dealing?

2. Funds of a private foundation were used to pay the cost of transporting art works of Grace Mayfield, a board member who is a substantial contributor to the foundation, and for providing a forum for exhibition of her art. The foundation openly used its resources to solicit interest in Grace's works. Is use of foundation funds for these purposes self-dealing?

3. Michael Reece, a member of the board of directors of Art Museum, periodically takes valuable paintings from the museum collection and hangs them at his private residence or at his office. Art Museum is a private operating foundation for tax purposes. Has Michael engaged in self-dealing?

IV. FAILURE TO DISTRIBUTE INCOME

A private nonoperating foundation must distribute its income to public charities or to private operating foundations (I.R.C. § 4942). Failure to do so will subject a nonoperating foundation to an initial penalty tax of 30 percent of any "undistributed income." There is an additional tax of 100 percent of undistributed income remaining at the earlier of the mailing of a notice of a tax deficiency for the initial tax or the date on which the initial tax is assessed. To avoid the tax on undistributed income, a foundation must distribute, in the form of qualifying distributions, the required amount of income for a taxable year, not later than the close of the following tax year. "Undistributed income" is a "distributable" amount reduced by "qualifying distributions," the two percent excise tax on net investment income, and any regular taxes paid by the foundation. It is not reduced by penalty taxes. "Distributable" amount is the "minimum investment return" reduced by the sum of any regular taxes imposed on the foundation and the two percent excise tax on net investment income tax. Minimum investment return is five percent of the excess of the fair market value of all noncharitable assets of a foundation (those not used in performing the foundation's exempt functions) over any acquisition indebtedness on the property. Qualifying distributions are expenditures for administrative expenses and for charitable purposes. It includes amounts set aside for charitable projects.

Note

1. A foundation can "set aside" amounts for a specific project and have the amounts treated as qualifying distributions if the foundation will complete the project in five years and it can better complete or accomplish the project by set-aside funds than by the immediate payment of any funds. Generally the Internal Revenue Service must approve set-asides in advance; thus, a foundation normally would seek a revenue ruling prior to using set-aside funds as qualifying distributions. I.R.C. § 4942(g)(2).

2. A private nonoperating foundation must state annually on Form 990PF its grant or donation policy, including how a public charity or private operating foundation can apply to it for a grant or donation. Because nonoperating foundations will incur penalty taxes under § 4942 if they fail to distribute the required amount of their income annually to public charities or private operating foundations, the information provided on the Form 990PF is especially beneficial to public charities and private operating foundations that seek grant funds.

Problem

Sydney Masters donated publicly traded stock to a private nonoperating foundation that supports City University. The stock was valued at $2,000,000. Annual dividend income from the stock generally has been approximately $40,000. The private foundation had other income of $20,000 from interest on investments. The foundation plans to distribute all of its current net income from investments to City University next year, but members of the board expressed some concern about the penalty tax under § 4942 of the Internal Revenue Code because dividend income on the stock has averaged only above 2 percent. Is there a problem?

Note

A private nonoperating foundation can make qualifying distributions to a private operating foundation as well as to a public charity.[4] Suppose an

---

4. Pursuant to § 4942(g)(4), which was added to the Code by the Pension Protection Act of 2006, a private foundation cannot count as a "qualifying distribution" any amount the private foundation paid to the following § 509(a)(3) public charities: a type III supporting organization, which is not a functionally integrated type III organization (definition of "functionally integrated type III organization in chapter 6) and a type I or II supporting organization if a disqualified person of the private foundation directly or indirectly controls the § 509(a)(3) or its supported organization.

individual creates a museum that will qualify as a private operating foundation. The individual also establishes a trust, which is a private nonoperating foundation for tax purposes, to which the individual donates funds to be used to support the museum the individual created. The trust instrument provides that funds of the nonoperating foundation can be used only to support the museum. Later the museum ceases to qualify as a private operating foundation. How can trustee of the trust follow the dictates of the trust instrument but also avoid penalty taxes under § 4942?

Consider the issues in the following case.

IN RE ESTATE OF JOHN A. HERMANN

Supreme Court, Pennsylvania, 1973
454 Pa. 292, 312 A.2d 16

POMEROY, Justice.

Pittsburgh National Bank, as corporate trustee of a charitable trust established by John A. Hermann, Jr., now deceased, petitioned the Orphans' Court Division of the Court of Common Pleas of Allegheny County for approval of an interim account of the affairs of the trust. Appellants, individual trustees of another charitable trust of the same settlor, filed exceptions which were overruled by the court below in an order which approved the bank's second and partial account. Hence this appeal.

There are involved here two separate trusts, although only one is presently before the Court in this proceeding. The first is an inter vivos trust created in 1939 by a conveyance of the settlor, John A. Hermann, Jr., to five individual trustees, including himself. By this deed of trust Mr. Hermann established the John A. Hermann, Jr. Memorial Art Museum, intended to be a free 'public art museum', conveying to the trustees thereof his personal collection of paintings, ivories, bronzes and other objects d'art, together with a plot of land and a residence thereon situated in the borough of Bellevue, Pennsylvania. * * * We will refer to this trust as the 'museum trust'.

The second trust is a testamentary trust created by Mr. Hermann in his will, executed in 1940 (the testator died in 1942). Under the terms of this trust, $75,000 was transferred to Peoples–Pittsburgh Trust Co., predecessor of the present accountant, as trustee to hold, invest and reinvest, and to pay the net income to the museum trustees 'for the maintenance, repair and improvement of the museum and real property connected therewith.' * * * The trustee of this testamentary trust, appellee here, is not, it should be noted, a trustee of the museum trust.

The inter vivos trust which created the museum was in perpetuity. The testamentary trust, however, provided that '(i)f ever the Art Museum shall cease to exist the principal and any unused income shall be held thereafter by Peoples–Pittsburgh Trust Company, as Trustee, for the same uses and purposes as are herein set forth for my residuary estate.'

In 1954 the trustees of the museum trust instituted proceedings in the Court of Common Pleas of Allegheny County to have the trust terminated. The residence in which the art collection was housed had become dilapidated and expensive to maintain, and income was insufficient to build a new building or to undertake a major renovation of the old one. The petition sought, in terminating the trust, to have the trustee of the testamentary trust take over all the objets d'art of the museum. The trust company opposed the petition, arguing that it was a trustee only of funds totalling $100,000, and that it was not responsible for what might become of the settlor's art collection. The court refused to declare a termination, but by its order, entered August 16, 1955, authorized the individual trustees of the museum to sell the land and building (this was done, producing $91,300), to transfer the art to a floor of the public library building in Bellevue, Pennsylvania, and to conduct the activities of the museum at that site. The museum has remained at this location until the present time. The income of the invested assets since 1955 has consistently far exceeded maintenance expenses.

Following enactment of the federal Tax Reform Act of 1969, Pub.L. 91—172, 83 Stat. 502, the corporate fiduciary, as trustee of principal funds of $100,000, * * * refused to pay over to the individual trustees of the art museum the income received by the bank for the last quarter of 1970 and all subsequent quarters to date. Its reason for refusing was not that the purpose of the trust of which it was trustee had failed or that the purpose of the museum trust had failed; its refusal to pay over income was based, rather, on its opinion that income so distributed to the museum trustees would be considered as made to an entity which was not an 'operating foundation', with the result that its income payments would not qualify as tax exempt 'qualifying distributions' and so would be subject to a severe federal tax under section 4942 of the Internal Revenue Code of 1954, as amended by the Tax Reform Act of 1969, Pub.L. 91—172.[4]

Suffice it to say that there is no dispute here that the John A. Hermann, Jr. Memorial Art Museum is other than a 'private foundation' within these statutory provisions. As such, it must, to avoid payment of a tax, be an 'operating foundation'; that is to say, must make 'qualifying distributions; of its income 'directly for the active conduct of the activities constituting the purpose or function for which it is organized. The reason that the appellee thought the museum not to be an 'operating foundation' was that since the sale of the original building with court approval in 1955 and transfer of the settlor's collection to a floor of the library building in Bellevue, income of the bank trust had far exceeded expenses associated with maintaining the museum in such reduced surroundings. It would follow that the excess would not be expended 'directly for the active conduct of the activities constituting the purpose

---

4. Section 4942 of the Internal Revenue Code is entitled 'Taxes Failure to Distribute Income.' It applies to a 'private foundation' which is defined as an organization generally exempt from income taxation under section 501 of the I.R.C. of 1954, but within the definition of section 509 of the I.R.C. of 1954, added by Pub.L. 91—172.

Sec. IV   FAILURE TO DISTRIBUTE INCOME   323

(of the museum).' 26 U.S.C. § 4942(j)(3) (1970). If it is not an 'operating foundation', then under § 4942(a), its nondistributed income is subject to a 15% Tax, and, if the income so taxed is not distributed by the end of a 'correction period' (defined, generally, as three months after receipt of a deficiency notice), the provision of § 4942(b) taxes the remainder to the extent of 100%. It was the position of the corporate fiduciary that if it distributed income to the trustees of the museum, these payments would not be 'qualifying distributions' because made 'to ... a private foundation which is not an operating foundation', § 4942(g)(1) (A), that such distributions would be income subject to the 15% Tax (if not the 100% Tax), and that therefore such nonqualifying distributions should not be made.

The individual trustees of the museum sought to allay the bank's fears that the museum was not an entity to which 'qualifying distributions' might be made by requesting, on May 24, 1971, a federal tax ruling on the matter. Under § 4942(g)(2) of the I.R.C. of 1954, as amended, the Secretary of the Treasury (or his designate) is empowered to authorize a 'set-a-side' of undistributed income (otherwise taxable under § 4942) if the 'set-aside' is to be expended on a specific project within 5 years, the project is one associated with the purposes of the foundation, and the project is one better accomplished through accumulation. The project proposed by the individual trustees was the acquisition of suitable land and the construction of a museum building within the next five years. Proposed expenditure for land was $50,000 and for the building was $250,000. On March 16, 1972—after the first hearing before the auditing judge in this matter, but before the second—the Secretary's designate responded and approved a 'set-aside' of $8,400 for 1972 and indicated that upon submission of evidence of further planning (option to purchase real estate, architect's drawings, cost estimates, etc.), he would extend the authorization to set-aside income for four additional years.

The account of the appellee-trustee indicated the fact of withholding the accumulated income, and its petition for distribution, after reciting most of the foregoing history, sought approval of the account and the proposed 'deviation' from the terms of the trust. * * * The learned auditing judge considered, as stated in his opinion, that the petition 'raises the question as to whether or not the Museum is still in existence', and concluded that 'the purposes of the Museum trust have failed. There is no question about this.' In a later portion of his opinion the court stated the conclusion that 'the Museum (has) ceased to exist.'

* * *

It was the premise of the appellee-corporate trustee in filing its account here in audit that should trust income distributed to the museum trustees be taxable under section 4942 of the Internal Revenue Code (see Note 4, Supra), then it would be justified in refusing to make distributions commanded by the trust instrument. We do not think that the conclusion necessarily follows. Should such distributions precipitate the first step, or 15% income tax, we doubt that the corporate trustees would thereby be justified in refusing further distributions. The mere fact of imposition of a tax is insufficient reason to conclude that the settlor would want his trustees to cease making all distributions. * * * Should such distributions further result in a 100% taxation of the income, a considerably more difficult question would arise. It is, however, not necessary for us here to grapple with new legal issues caused by the impact of section 4942 of the I.R.C. on the law of charitable trusts in Pennsylvania, and particularly whether that impact could be said to render the purpose of the trust 'indefinite or impossible or impractical of fulfillment'. * * * It is enough to observe that the ruling obtained from the Internal Revenue Service by the museum trustees, approving a 'set-aside' and thus staying the imposition of a section 4942 tax, has caused any such issues to disappear from this proceeding. The income which the appellee-corporate trustee has withheld is, for our purposes today, as immune to taxation as it was before the enactment of section 4942.

As to the learned auditing judge's conclusion that 'the Museum (has) ceased to exist', with all respect, we do not agree that failure of the testamentary trust is even raised by the petition for distribution. The penultimate paragraph of the petition, reproduced in the margin, * * * while perhaps not as lucid as one might wish, is not an allegation of failure of purpose or of cessation of the museum or the museum trust to exist. It is rather a suggestion to the auditing judge that there was no present need for the court to examine, by appointment of a master or otherwise, whether the purpose of the trust had failed, in view of the fact that the Secretary of the Treasury, in undertaking to act upon the 'Request for Approval of Set–Aside' filed by the museum trustees, would necessarily examine the manner of operation of the museum.

Not only was the question of continued existence of the museum trust not presented by the petition for distribution, but there was no attempt by the corporate trustee to offer any proof for such a proposition; it adduced no evidence whatever beyond the averments of the petition for distribution. The only witness called at the audit was an individual trustee of the museum trust. His testimony dealt solely with his efforts to obtain a favorable tax ruling from the Internal Revenue Service. The only evidence, if it can be called that, relied upon by the appellee to support the finding of failure is a statement in the petition of the museum trustees in 1955 for leave to terminate the trust. It was there alleged that the museum and its objets d'art 'have been almost totally ignored by the public during the past five years, the current rate of visitation thereto by the general public being one person per month.' * * * But this petition was refused, as noted above, and the court directed that, with modification, 'the Trust known as the John A. Hermann Jr. Memorial Art Museum Shall continue in being.' (Emphasis added.) Appellee also points to a statement at audit by appellant's counsel that, 'I would not kid the court, the art is miserable.' Counsel, of course, is no more qualified than is the court to make such a judgment, and this offhand, perhaps jocular remark cannot be considered evidence against the client, the museum trust. * * * The lower court terminated this trust for the sole reason that the art it is designated to support 'does not warrant the maintenance of a building' and that the public continues to ignore the display. It is difficult to conceive of a subject less appropriate for judicial review than the quality of an artistic work; certainly judicial condemnation is nowise justified by this record. * * * If Mr. Hermann's collection is as poor as the appellee contends, it well may be that he entertained a certain insensitivity toward prevailing tastes in 'art.' There is no indication in his trust instruments nor precedent in the law for judicial review of the question whether Mr. Hermann's museum 'does (or does) not warrant the maintenance of a building.' * * *

In sum, our review of the record is that there was no evidence that the purpose of the trust had been made impossible of fulfillment or that the trust res, the museum, had ceased to exist. * * * To the contrary, the record evidence does establish that the museum trust has principal and assets of approximately $250,000, of which $108,000 represents undistributed income. * * * It is apparent that the objets d'art exist, that adequate funds are now on hand to acquire land and to construct a building, and that the individual museum trustees intend so to act within the next five years.

The balance for distribution should be decreed back to the appellee Pittsburgh National Bank as trustee, as the court below did by its decree here appealed from, but not for administration pursuant to the court's opinion of June 27, 1972; rather, the accountant should be directed to hold and administer the trust funds in accordance with the terms of the testamentary trust of the decedent, viz., to invest and reinvest the same and pay over all income to the trustees of the museum trust.

Decree reversed and case remanded for entry of a decree in accordance with this opinion. Costs on appellee as trustee.

Question

The *Hermann* decision was rendered in 1973, four years after § 4942 was added to the Code (by the Tax Reform Act of 1969). Do you agree with the solution the court offered to the problem the trustee of the Hermann testamentary trust faced when the museum the trust was required to support no longer qualified as an operating foundation? Do you think the court fully understood the consequences of a private nonoperating foundation failing to make adequate qualifying distributions as required by the then new § 4942 of the Code?

V. EXCESS BUSINESS HOLDINGS

The combined holdings of a private foundation and all its disqualified persons may not exceed 20 percent of the voting stock of a business enterprise (or profits interest in a partnership or joint venture), but if control of the business is in persons other than disqualified persons, permitted holdings can be as much as 35 percent (I.R.C. § 4943). A private foundation may exclude the interests of disqualified persons if the foundation, and all related or controlled foundations, have in the aggregate no more than two percent of the voting stock and not more than two percent of the value of all outstanding shares of all classes of stock in a corporation. Should a private foundation's business holdings exceed the permissible amount, an initial penalty of ten percent of the value of the foundation's holdings is imposed under § 4943 of the Code. Further, if the foundation continues to have excess holdings after the earlier of a mailing of a notice of deficiency for the initial tax or the date on which the initial tax is assessed, a second-tier penalty tax of 200 percent is imposed on excess holdings.

Note

Because a private foundation's permissible holdings in a partnership or corporation is measured by its holdings and those of all its disqualified persons, the trustees or directors of a private foundation must carefully monitor annually the holdings of its disqualified persons. For example, assume a private foundation owns ten per cent of the stock of a for-profit corporation and one of its disqualified persons owns nine percent. Should the disqualified person purchase an additional two percent interest in the corporation to increase that person's interest to eleven percent, the private foundation would have excess business holdings of one percent in the corporation. The foundation would be subject to the initial penalty tax under § 4943.

VI. JEOPARDIZING INVESTMENTS

If a private foundation makes investments that could jeopardize financially the organization's performance of its exempt functions, both the foundation and the foundation manager can become liable for taxes on such investments (I.R.C. § 4944). There is an initial tax of ten percent of the amount invested and an addition tax of 25 percent if investments are not removed from jeopardy. In addition, there is a five percent penalty imposed upon the manager and an additional penalty tax of five percent (maximum of $20,000) if the manager refuses to agree to removal of part or all of the foundation's investments from jeopardy.

Note

The jeopardizing effect of each investment is determined on an individual basis, considering the foundation's portfolio as a whole. No category of investment is treated as per se jeopardizing. Certain investments are scrutinized closely. Trading in securities on margin, trading in commodity futures, investments in working interests in oil and gas wells, purchase of "puts" and "calls," purchase of warrants, and selling short are mentioned in Regulation § 53.4944–1(a)(1) as being speculative investments that could jeopardize a foundation's financial status. The determination of whether an investment is speculative is made at the time of the investment and not subsequently on the basis of hindsight.

VII. TAXABLE EXPENDITURES

A private foundation that incurs any "taxable expenditures" is subject to an initial penalty tax of twenty percent of the amount involved (I.R.C. § 4945). If the expenditures are not corrected (within the earlier of the date of the mailing of a notice of deficiency as to the initial twenty percent penalty tax or the date on which the twenty percent penalty is assessed), a second tier penalty tax of 100 percent of the amount of the expenditures is imposed. (A foundation corrects a taxable expenditures by recovering part or all of the expenditures to the extent possible.) There is an initial tax of five percent of the amount involved (maximum of $10,000) imposed on the foundation manager if the manager knowingly and willfully agreed to the expenditure. In addition, there is a tax of 50 percent of the amount involved (maximum of $20,000) imposed on the foundation manager if the manager refuses to agree to part or all of the correction of the expenditures.[5]

Taxable expenditures include amounts expended for lobbying; to make grants to an individual unless certain requirements are satisfied; to make grants to an organization other than a public charity qualified under § 509(a)(1), (2), or (3) unless expenditure responsibility is exercised; and for any other purpose that is not a charitable purpose [as defined in § 501(c)(3) of the Code].

Grants to individuals are taxable expenditures unless the foundation obtains advance approval of the foundation's grant procedures from the Internal Revenue Service. Grants to organizations other than public charities are taxable expenditures unless the foundation exercises expenditure responsibility.[6] A foundation exercises expenditure responsibility by exerting all reasonable efforts, and establishing adequate procedures, to make certain all grants are spent solely for the purposes for which they were made. The foundation most obtain a full and complete report from each grantee on how the funds were spent. It must then make a full, detailed report to the Internal Revenue Service.

MANNHEIMER CHARITABLE TRUST v. COMMISSIONER
United States Tax Court, 1989
93 T.C. 35

RAUM, JUDGE:

The Commissioner determined that petitioner, taxable as a private foundation, is liable for the 10 percent private foundation excise tax

---

5. Relying on the advice of counsel will protect a manager if the manager made full disclosure of the factual situation to legal counsel and had a reasoned written legal opinion that the expenditure was not a taxable one.

6. Section 4945(d)(4)(ii), which was added to the Code by the Pension Protection Act of 2006, requires a private foundation to exercise expenditure responsibility for a grant to a § 509(a)(3) public charity if it is classified as a type III supporting organization (and is not a "functionally integrated type III organization) or is a type I or II and a disqualified person of the private foundation directly or indirectly controls the § 509(a)(3) or its supported organization.

under section 4945(a)(1) * * * in the amounts of $42,184 in 1981, $41,205 in 1982, and $26,173 in 1983, in respect of grants which it made to two other private foundations. The issue is whether such grants were 'taxable expenditures' under section 4945(d)(4), which in turn depends upon whether petitioner exercised 'expenditure responsibility' with respect to the grants within the meaning of section 4945(h). The case was submitted on the basis of a stipulation of facts.

Petitioner, the Hans S. Mannheimer Charitable Trust ('Trust'), was located in Newark, New Jersey, at the time it filed the petition herein. It was created to advance Hans S. Mannheimer's interests in the care and study of animals, especially primates. Pursuant to the terms of the Agreement of Trust, as amended, a portion of the trust income is to be paid to Animal Care Fund, Inc. (Animal Care), and the balance is to be paid to Mannheimer Primatological Foundation (Mannheimer Primatological). Both Animal Care and Mannheimer Primatological (grantees or donees) are and have been 'not for profit' corporations classified as tax exempt organizations under section 501(c)(). Both were established by Hans S. Mannheimer, as was petitioner.

Animal Care provides an animal shelter for the care and prevention of cruelty to animals. It is located in East Smithfield, Pennsylvania. Mannheimer Primatological is involved in the research and development of breeding programs for the purpose of preserving endangered species of nonhuman primates and is involved in the advancement and promotion of the study of the physical and behavioral structure and patterns of nonhuman primates. Mannheimer Primatological also provides assistance to charitable, scientific or educational agencies or institutions. It is located in Homestead, Florida.

* * *

Pursuant to the requirements of section 6033, petitioner filed information returns, Forms 990–PF Return of Private Foundation, for each of the years in question, namely, 1981, 1982, and 1983. On each of these returns, the responses to the questions relating to the section 4945 taxes on taxable expenditures were incorrect. Item 14(a)(4) on each Form 990–PF called for an answer to the following question: 'During the year did you pay or incur any amount to provide a grant to an organization, other than a charitable, etc., organization described in section 509(a)(1), (2) or (3)?' Petitioner's response to this question for each of the years at issue was 'No.' The correct answer was 'Yes,' since Animal Care and Mannheimer Primatological received monies from petitioner but are not section 509(a)(1), (2), or (3) organizations. As a result of the incorrect answer to item 14(a)(4), the related questions in 14(b) and (c) were marked 'N/A'. The correct answer to both 14(b) and 14(c) was 'Yes' rather than 'N/A,' and a 'Yes' answer to 14(c) would have called for the attachment of the 'statement required.' No such statement was attached in any of the three returns.

Such required statement obviously referred to the provisions of section 53.4945–5(d)(1) and (2) of the regulations, which provide that the foundation must make a report 'with respect to each grant.' * * * (Emphasis added.) In addition to supplying the name and address of the grantee, the grantor was obligated to set forth detailed information in that report as to a number of pertinent matters, including the date and the amount of each grant, the purposes of the grant, and the results of any verification of the grantee's reports to the grantor. All of the requirements could be satisfied by submitting with the foundation's return a report from the grantee if the required information is contained in such report. Although petitioner's returns did identify Mannheimer Primatological and Animal Care as the grantees and did report an amount paid to each of them, they did not otherwise supply the information asked for in the 'statement' required. For example, although the returns reported the AGGREGATE amounts paid to each of the two named grantees, there was no breakdown or even any clue as to the purpose for which the payments or any specified portion thereof was made.

Animal Care filed information returns, Forms 990-PF, on a fiscal year basis for the years ending September 30, 1981, 1982, 1983, and 1984. Mannheimer Primatological also filed information returns, Forms 990-PF, for the years at issue on a calendar year basis. In their returns, the donees stated the total amounts received as 'contributions, gifts, grants, etc.' and specifically listed the aggregate amount received from petitioner. * * *

The Commissioner determined that petitioner was liable for the 10 percent tax imposed by section 4945(a)(1). Whether he erred in that determination, as contended by petitioner, depends upon the applicability of section 4945(d) and (h), as will be developed more fully hereinafter. Preliminarily, it is important that section 4945 be considered in proper context.

Section 4945 first appeared in the Code in 1969. It was part of subchapter A of an entirely new chapter 42 that was added to the Code by the Tax Reform Act of 1969. * * * Subchapter A of chapter 42 dealt exclusively with private foundations. One can hardly read the extensive and highly detailed new provisions of subchapter A (sections 4940–4948) without concluding that Congress was determined to put an end, as far as it reasonably could, to the abuses and potential abuses associated with private foundations. As the Report of the House Committee on Ways and Means, H. Rept. 91–413 at 39 (1969) stated:

> [Y]our committee has determined that organizations should not receive substantial and continuing tax benefits in exchange for the promise of their contributions to society, and then avoid the carrying out of those responsibilities. * * *

Accord, Senate Finance Committee, S. Rept. 91–552 at 55 (1969), 1969–3 C.B. 423, 459.

The 10 percent excise imposed on each taxable expenditure by section 4945(a)(1), involved in this case, was merely a first step. Section 4945(a)(2) imposes a two and one-half percent tax on management. The (a)(1) and the (a)(2) taxes are sometimes referred to as the 'first tier' excise taxes. A pair of second tier of excise taxes captioned 'additional taxes,' of much greater severity, are imposed by section 4945(b)(1) and (2). The 'additional tax' in (b)(1) is upon the foundation at 100 percent of each taxable expenditure, and in (b)(2) upon management at 50 percent. * * * The (b)(1) tax is imposed, however, only where the taxable expenditure is not 'corrected' within the taxable period, a word that is defined in section 4945(i)(1). And the (b)(2) tax is imposed on any foundation manager who refuses to agree to part or all of the correction where there is a (b)(1) tax. Subchapter C is concerned with the abatement of second tier taxes, both (b)(1) and (b)(2), where there is correction. However, the 'first tier' taxes, (a)(1) and (a)(2), are mandatory and may not be avoided by subsequent remedial action by the Foundation. * * * The relationship between the first and second tier taxes was characterized by this Court in that case as follows (p. 745):

> [T]he initial tax is a spur designed to remind the foundation that it has been remiss. Subsequent compliance with the rules enables the foundation to avoid the real whip of section 4945(b)(1), but cannot undo the punishment for its initial infraction.

It is not feasible within the limits of this opinion even to outline the scope of all the extensive and comprehensive provisions of subchapter A to show the nature of the Congressional concern about preventing abuses associated with private foundations. * * * It is sufficient here to note, as did the court in Jackson v. Statler Foundation, 496 F.2d 623, 633 (2d Cir.1974) that while section 4945 is intrusive, it is also necessary:

> Congress attempted in section 4945 to prevent * * * the use of foundation assets for private purposes.

* * *

Such an intrusive and detailed scheme was deemed necessary to prevent the use of foundations' assets for a wide range of private purposes, * * * and to ensure that the fruits of exemption benefit the public.

Very extensive and detailed regulations have been promulgated by the Treasury to implement section 4945, involved herein. By complying with these regulations and the new statutory provisions a private foundation can avoid triggering these new taxes. To the extent that such regulations relate to those statutory provisions involved in this case (particularly, section 4945(d)(4) and (h)), they will be dealt with hereinafter. We now proceed to consider the specific statutory provisions and the related regulations as applied to the facts here.

Section 4945(a)(1) imposes a 10 percent excise tax on each 'taxable expenditure' made by a private foundation. * * * A 'taxable expenditure' is defined in section 4945(d). As in effect during the years at issue, section 4945(d) provided:

SEC. 4945. TAXES ON TAXABLE EXPENDITURES.

* * *

(d) Taxable Expenditure.—For purposes of this section, the term 'taxable expenditure' means any amount paid or incurred by a private foundation—

(1) to carry on propaganda, or otherwise to attempt, to influence legislation, within the meaning of subsection (e),

(2) except as provided in subsection (f), to influence the outcome of any specific public election, or to carry on, directly or indirectly, any voter registration drive,

(3) as a grant to an individual for travel, study, or other similar purposes by such individual, unless such grant satisfies the requirements of subsection (g),

(4) as a grant to an organization (other than an organization described in paragraph (1), (2), or (3) of section 509(a)) unless the private foundation exercises expenditure responsibility with respect to such grant in accordance with subsection (h).

* * *

Paragraphs (1), (2), and (3) of subsection (d) are not involved here, and as to paragraph (4), it is undisputed that the two grantees are not and have not been organizations described in paragraph (1), (2), or (3) of section 509(a). Thus, in order to avoid the excise tax imposed by section 4945(a)(1), petitioner must show that, in accordance with subsection (h) of section 4945, it exercised 'expenditure responsibility,' over the funds distributed to the two grantees in 1981, 1982, and 1983.

Section 4945(h) defines 'expenditure responsibility' as follows:

(h) Expenditure Responsibility.—The expenditure responsibility referred to in subsection (d)(4) means that the private foundation is responsible to exert all reasonable efforts and to establish adequate procedures—

(1) to see that the grant is spent solely for the purpose for which made,

(2) to obtain full and complete reports from the grantee on how the funds are spent, and

(3) to make full and detailed reports with respect to such expenditures to the Secretary.

Each paragraph under subsection (h) of section 4945 requires a grantor to take affirmative action in order to avoid the 10 percent excise tax imposed by section 4945(a)(1). Moreover, the three requirements are in the conjunctive; petitioner must satisfy all three. Although the regulations (section 53.4945–5(b)(1)) make clear that a private foundation is not an insurer of the activity of the organization to which it makes a grant, section 4945(h) of the Code nevertheless requires that a private foundation, at the very least, 'exert all reasonable efforts and * * *

establish adequate procedures' to see that the three requirements are met. We hold that petitioner has failed to show that it 'exert[ed] all reasonable efforts and * * * establish[ed] adequate procedures 'to comply with any one of the three requirements or that it has in fact complied with any one of those requirements. We consider each of them separately.

SECTION 4945(h)(1). Section 4945(h)(1) requires a grantor to take affirmative steps 'to see that the grant is spent solely for the purposes for which [the grant was] made.' The regulations provide that as a first step, prior to making a grant, a private foundation should conduct a limited inquiry concerning the potential grantee and, as a second step, must obtain a written commitment signed by an appropriate officer, director, or trustee of the grantee organization. The detailed provisions relating to the first step are set forth in section 53.4945–5(b)(2)), which is captioned 'Pre-grant inquiry,' and the second in section 53.4945–5(b)(3), which is captioned 'Terms of grants.' We find that, although petitioner did not run afoul of the requirements of the first, it completely failed to comply with those of the second, and thus failed to meet the demands of section 4945(h)(1) of the statute.

A. PRE–GRANT INQUIRY. The pre-grant inquiry is described by section 53.4945–5(b)(2)(i) of the regulations as a 'limited inquiry' which should concern itself with the identity, prior history, and experience of the grantee organization and its managers and any knowledge which the private foundation has concerning management, activities, and practices of the grantee organization. The scope of the pre-grant inquiry will vary from case to case 'depending upon the size and purpose of the grant, the period over which it is to be paid, and the prior experience which the grantor has had with respect to the capacity of the grantee to use the grant for the proper purposes.' Section 53.4945–5(b)(2)(i).

Petitioner was created in 1969 by Hans S. Mannheimer to advance his interests in the care and study of animals by distributing funds to Animal Care and Mannheimer Primatological, two organizations created by him in 1967 and 1968, respectively. Petitioner and the two grantees share at least two common trustees—Warren Lloyd Lewis and Lesley A. Sinclair—who would have had some personal knowledge of the activities of all three organizations, although the extent of their involvement is unclear from the record. Further, both Animal Care and Mannheimer Primatological have received funds from petitioner in the past and these funds have been spent for the proper purposes of the grant. Under these circumstances, we hold that petitioner had sufficient information about the two grantees to satisfy the limited pre-grant inquiry described in section 53.4945–5(b)(2)(i) of the regulations.

B. WRITTEN COMMITMENT. Section 53.4945–5(b)(3) of the regulations states that 'a private foundation MUST require that each grant to an organization, * * * BE MADE SUBJECT TO A WRITTEN COMMITMENT signed by an appropriate officer, director or trustee of the grantee organization.' (Emphasis added.) The prescribed nature and content of that commitment are then set forth in detail as follows:

Such commitment MUST INCLUDE AN AGREEMENT by the grantee—

(i) To repay any portion of the amount granted which is not used for the purposes of the grant,

(ii) To submit full and complete annual reports on the manner in which the funds are spent and the progress made in accomplishing the purposes of the grant, except as provided in paragraph (c)(2) of this section,

(iii) To maintain records of receipts and expenditures and to make its books and records available to the grantor at reasonable times, and

(iv) Not to use any of the funds—

(a) To carry on propaganda, or otherwise to attempt, to influence legislation (within the meaning of section 4945(d)(1)),

(b) To influence the outcome of any specific public election, or to carry on, directly or indirectly, any voter registration drive (within the meaning of section 4945(d)(2)), or

(c) To make any grant which does not comply with the requirements of section 4945(d)(3) or (4), or

(d) To undertake any activity for any purpose other than one specified in section 170(c)(2)(B).

The agreement must also clearly specify the purposes of the grant. Such purposes may include contributing for capital endowment, for the purchase of capital equipment, or for general support provided that neither the grants nor the income therefrom may be used for purposes other than those described in section 170(c)(2)(B).

Moreover, section 53.4945-5(d)(3)(i) provides that the foundation shall make available to the IRS at the foundation's principal office a copy of the foregoing required agreement 'covering each 'expenditure responsibility' grant made during the taxable year.'

Thus, petitioner bears the burden of showing that all grants were made subject to a written agreement which met the content requirements of section 53.4945-5(b)(3) and that all such written agreements were made available to the IRS for inspection at petitioner's principal office pursuant to section 53.4945-5(d)(3)(i). This petitioner has failed to do.

Petitioner contends that it 'more than adequately fulfilled' the written commitment requirement 'through numerous documents executed by officers, directors, or trustees and exchanged by and circulated among the parties including the Agreement of Trust, certificates of incorporation (specifically stating the corporation would not make any taxable expenditures), bylaws, minutes, detailed monthly and annual reports and information returns.' However, there is no evidence before us that any of these documents contained the agreements required by section 53.4945–5(b)(3) of the regulations, or that any of them was made available for inspection at petitioner's principal office, as required by section 53.4945–5(d)(3)(i). The only such documents in evidence are the Trust instrument (with amendments) establishing petitioner and the information returns (Forms 990 PF) for the years involved on behalf of petitioner and the two grantees. They do not contain the commitments required by section 53.4945–5(b)(3) of the regulations.

That there were not in fact any such written commitments as were required by the regulations emerges quite plainly from a stipulated affidavit of one of the trustees to the effect that he and the 'other trustees and officers of the grantees * * * have always been willing to provide the form of written commitment deemed required.' And in an obvious attempt to belittle the failure to comply with the requirements of the regulations, the affidavit states further that 'any non-compliance was entirely technical.' But such non-compliance can hardly be characterized as merely 'technical.' Thus, even if some sort of 'commitment' on the part of the grantees could be implied on the basis of the materials in evidence, we have no way of knowing whether such 'commitments' included even an informal undertaking to repay any grant or portion thereof that is not in fact used for purposes of the grant. The commitment to repay in such circumstances goes to the very heart of the Congressional objective of curbing abuses associated with private foundations.

Petitioner also seems to argue that somehow or other the existence of the required commitment is established by the fact that there were common officers, directors, and trustees of petitioner and the two grantees, and that they 'obtained and exchanged personal knowledge in their various capacities.' How this circumstance can satisfy the requirement for a written commitment available for inspection at petitioner's principal office (as required by section 53.4945–5(d)(3)) completely eludes us.

Petitioner also argues that since the funds received by grantees from petitioner were spent appropriately, no harm was done. However, 'Section 4945(a)(1) states simply that a tax is 'hereby imposed' on the taxable expenditure; unlike section 4945(b)(1), it contains no language indicating that the liability is conditional.' * * * Where a grantor fails to satisfy any or all of the expenditure responsibility requirements of section 4945(h), the section 4945(a)(1) excise tax is mandatory regardless of the harm or lack thereof resulting from the failure. Petitioner did not obtain the required agreements from the two grantees, nor did it introduce evidence of efforts made by it to obtain the written agreements or otherwise see that the grants were spent solely for the purposes for which made. We hold that petitioner has failed to carry its burden of showing that it exercised 'expenditure responsibility' pursuant to section 4945(h)(1).

SECTION 4945(h)(2). Section 4945(h)(2) of the Code requires the foundation to exert all reasonable efforts and to establish adequate procedures 'to obtain full and complete reports from the grantee on how the funds are spent.' And the regulations, in section 53.4945–5(c)(1), (2), (3), and (4), contain highly specific provisions calculated to give meaningful effect to section 4945(h)(2) of the Code.

Notwithstanding petitioner's representations on brief that the grantees 'accurately maintained and kept current its books and records' and that 'full and detailed reports * * * were made by the grantees to the grantor,' the evidence completely fails to support such bold assertions. They may or may not be true, but the record is barren of any proof to that effect. We need not belabor the point further—even though we could point out that petitioner's position in respect of section 4945(h)(2) is fatally defective in other respects under the statute and regulations.

SECTION 4945(h)(3). Section 4945(h)(3) imposes a duty upon petitioner 'to make full and detailed reports with respect to [its] * * * expenditures to the Secretary.' And section 53.4945–5(d)(2) of the regulations explains in detail what such a report should contain, as follows:

> (2) Contents of report. The report required by this paragraph shall include the following information:
>
> (i) The name and address of the grantee,
>
> (ii) The date and amount of the grant,
>
> (iii) The purpose of the grant,
>
> (iv) The amounts expended by the grantee (based upon the most recent report received from the grantee),
>
> (v) Whether the grantee has diverted any portion of the funds (or the income therefrom in the case of an endowment grant) from the purpose of the grant (to the knowledge of the grantor),
>
> (vi) The dates of any reports received from the grantee, and
>
> (vii) The date and results of any verification of the grantee's reports undertaken pursuant to and to the extent required under paragraph (c)(1) of this section by the grantor or by others at the direction of the grantor.

It is undisputed in petitioner's brief * * * that the information required by the statute and the regulations was not in petitioner's information returns, nor was it submitted to the Secretary in a separate statement. It is also undisputed, not only that the questions on petitioner's returns relating to section 4945 taxes on taxable expenditures (questions 14(a)(4), 14(b), and 14(c)) were answered incorrectly but also, as pointed out above, that the returns failed to include the attached statement required in connection with question 14(c). However, petitioner's returns did contain the name, address, and aggregate amount of money distributed to each grantee for each of the years at issue. As to the purpose for which the grants were made, petitioner merely stated, on each return that it was '[t]o pay net income to Mannheimer Primatological Foundation and Animal Care.' Such a summary or conclusory statement hardly qualifies even as substantial compliance with the requirements calling for the specific items of information meticulously set forth in subparagraphs (i) through (vii) listed above.

Petitioner argues, however, that it was not necessary to include all of the required information in its returns because 'the Internal Revenue Service was advised * * * of the expenditure, to whom and the purpose for which it was made and had in its possession the donees' returns, thus the Service was given sufficient information to trace, with little effort, the expenditure and insure compliance.' In support of this argument, petitioner attempts to draw an analogy between section 4945 and section 6501(e).

* * *

* * * We do not accept the notion that the tax here in issue can be avoided merely by petitioner's disclosure of the names and addresses of the grantees in its returns. We do not understand Congress to have intended to require the IRS to conduct a fishing expedition into the returns of the grantees to obtain at most only some of the information that petitioner itself was directly obligated to report to the IRS.

We also note that had the Secretary even followed the 'clue' (i.e., names and addresses of the two grantees) and obtained the grantees' returns from presumably different IRS service centers (Animal Care and Mannheimer Primatological were located in Pennsylvania and Florida, respectively), he still would not have obtained all of the information required by section 53.4945(d)(1) and (2) of the regulations. Among other difficulties that would be encountered in attempting to extract the required information from the grantees' returns is the fact that substantial amounts were received by them from sources other than petitioner in the form of contributions, gifts, fees, etc. It is thus impossible in all of the returns of Mannheimer Primatological and some of the returns of Animal Care to correlate the amounts received from petitioner with any of the expenditures made by the grantees, although in the case of the remaining returns of Animal Care it is possible to make such correlation but only with respect to some of the payments. Furthermore, wholly apart from what the IRS might have been able to uncover from the grantees' returns, petitioner's failure to make the required reports to the IRS left unrevealed not only a statement as to the purpose of the grants, but also any information with respect to whatever actions, if any, that petitioner may have taken to verify the grantees' reports, as required by section 53.4945–5(d)(2)(iii) and (vii) of the regulations quoted supra, pp. 18–19. We totally reject not only petitioner's contention that the returns of the grantees, which the Secretary would have to ferret out, constituted reports which petitioner itself was required to make, but also any implication from such contention that the grantees' returns contained all the significant information that petitioner was required to supply in ITS reports to the IRS.

In sum, we find that petitioner has not carried its burden of showing that it satisfied even one of three requirements of section 4945(h) of the Code in respect of its 'expenditure responsibility' which was necessary pursuant to section 4945(d)(4) to relieve it of tax on 'taxable expenditures.'

The conclusion that we thus reach is not affected by a 1984 amendment to section 4945(d)(4) upon which petitioner seems to rely. * * * Apart from other possible impediments here, that amendment is applicable only with respect to grants made after December 31, 1984 (sec. 302(c), 98 Stat. 779, 781). It has no relevance to petitioner's years 1981, 1982, and 1983 that are before us in this case.

* * * *

Throughout petitioner's briefs there is a recurring note that its failure to comply with the statute was 'technical,' that in any event there was 'substantial compliance,' that the repeated incorrect answers in its three successive annual returns were merely the result of 'oversight,' 'inadvertence,' etc. None of these points, if they can seriously be considered as such, has any validity. Section 4945(h) reflects a Congressional determination to leave no loophole by imposing strict and detailed conditions to make sure that a private foundation's grants would not be used for proscribed purposes.

We are aware that petitioner and its two grantees were the creatures of Hans S. Mannheimer, established for the purpose of promoting his interests in what could plainly qualify as tax exempt fields. And it could well be that they did not engage in any activities that could fairly be characterized as the kind of abuses that gave rise to the Congressional concern reflected in section 4945. However, Congress was obviously fed up with widespread abusive practices by private foundations, and it reacted by enacting extensive and strict provisions that it thought were necessary to put an end to such practices. Thus, although it is conceivable that petitioner may not have been 'guilty' of any such abuses, it was nevertheless covered by and subject to the provisions that Congress enacted. In short, this may be but another instance of where 'a legislature seeking to catch a particular abuse may find it necessary to cast a wider net.' Commissioner v. Pepsi–Cola Niagara Bottling Corp., 399 F.2d 390, 392 (2d Cir.1968). Petitioner had the opportunity of avoiding the tax by complying with the statutory requirements which were deliberately intended to be strict and the regulations carrying out the legislative purpose. Petitioner failed to do so and of necessity must take the consequences. What we said on another occasion in an entirely different context is also pertinent here: 'We need not speculate upon whether Congress, if it had given consideration to the unusual kind of situation before us might have drawn a more sophisticated type of line so as to produce a result favorable to [petitioner]. The point is that it chose to legislative (sic) in terms of a hard and fast rule.' Wiese v. Commissioner, T.C. Memo. 1976–362, 35 TCM 1641, 1652, 45 P–H Memo T.C. par. 76,362 at 76–1617, 76–1628 (1976), affd. per curiam Anderson v. Commissioner, 614 F.2d 535 (5th Cir.1980), cert. denied 449 U.S. 841 (1980). Similarly in the present case, we have no alternative but to follow the all-embracing provisions enacted that were so obviously intended to apply to every private foundation. As was stated by the District Court in John Q. Shunk Association, Inc. v. United States, 626 F. Supp. 564, 571 (S.D.Ohio 1985), in applying other provisions of section 4945, while recognizing that '[the] plaintiff's omission was indisputably inadvertent':

> Plaintiff's uncontested assurances that it was not one of those tax exempt foundations at which the tax reforms were directed is irrelevant. The provisions of the law apply to every private foundation receiving tax benefits from the United States government.

A like result is required here.

Decision will be entered for the respondent.

VIII. TERMINATION OF PRIVATE FOUNDATION STATUS

A private foundation must terminate its status pursuant to § 507 of the Internal Revenue Code or it will be subjected to substantial penalty taxes. A private foundation can terminate its status by either transferring all net assets to one or more § 509(a)(1) public charities or it can itself convert to public charity status. If a private foundation chooses to terminate by transferring its assets to a public charity, it must make certain the public charity is one described in § 509(a)(1) and that it has qualified under that section for at least 60 months immediately preceding the distribution. A private foundation also may qualify itself as a public charity, either a § 509(a)(1), (2) or (3) public charity, for a continuous 60–month period after notice of its intent to terminate private foundation status. The foundation must notify the Internal Revenue Service of its intent to accomplish its termination by qualifying as a public charity.

If a private foundation is involuntarily terminated, § 507(c) subjects it to a penalty tax of the lesser of (1) the total amount of all tax benefits (income, estate, and gift) derived by all substantial contributors since the foundation's inception plus the increase in taxes imposed upon the foundation had it been a taxable organization, or (2) the value of the net assets of the foundation.

GLADNEY v. COMMISSIONER
United States Court of Appeals, Fifth Circuit, 1984
745 F.2d 955

TIMBERS, Circuit Judge.

The Commissioner of Internal Revenue appeals from a decision of the United States Tax Court, Herbert L. Chabot, *Judge*, 45 T.C. Mem. 280 (1982), holding that the taxpayers (appellees) were not liable for federal excise taxes under § 4945 as transferees of taxable expenditures made by a private foundation, i.e. by the board of trustees of a home for elderly men. A Louisiana state court had ordered the transfer of assets from the private foundation to the heirs of the residuary legatees under a will in which the decedent originally had created the foundation. The Tax Court concluded, contrary to the arguments of the IRS, that the state court judgment operated to terminate the board's private foundation status and that reports filed by the board subsequent to the transfer satisfied the statutory notice requirements.

For the reasons stated below, we hold that the decision of the Tax Court is not supported by the 1969 Act, particularly in light of its legislative history. We reverse and remand.

* * *

Lelia Bonner Dwyer died testate on June 22, 1905. In her will, Mrs. Dwyer directed that the real estate she owned be sold. She further directed that a portion of the proceeds be used by a group of named individuals as trustees to found and maintain in New Orleans a home for aged and infirm men to be called the John M. Bonner Memorial Home (the Home). Mrs. Dwyer's first cousins in due course became her substitute residuary legatees. They were placed in possession of all property remaining after payment of specific legacies named in Mrs. Dwyer's will. The heirs on this appeal are descendants of those first cousins.

On July 13, 1905, the surviving trustees named in the will organized a charitable corporation known as the Board of Trustees of the John M. Bonner Memorial Home (the Board). The surviving trustees under the will were the trustees or the Board. The Board completed construction of the Home in 1915. The Home operated at a capacity of about twenty resident men until the early 1950's. During the 1950's, the number of residents of the Home began to decrease. The Home at this time also experienced financial difficulties. It began to draw upon its endowment to pay operating expenses.

In 1963, the heirs sued the Board in the Louisiana Civil District Court. They alleged that the trust had been completely fulfilled and no longer could be operated as originally contemplated. They requested that the trust be dissolved and that the remaining assets be delivered to them. The court's judgment in favor of the Board and against the heirs was affirmed on appeal. The Court of Appeal of Louisiana, Fourth Circuit, in affirming, pointed out that five men remained in the home and that funds were available to care for them, even though only for a few more years. *Bonner v. Board of Trustees*, 181 So.2d 255, 258 (La.App.1965), *writ denied*, 248 La. 915, 182 So.2d 664 (1966).

In 1970, the Board responded to a letter from the IRS by filing a statement that the Board was a private foundation within the meaning of § 509(a) and claimed that it was an operating foundation within the meaning of § 4942(j)(3).

On July 1, 1971, the Board closed the Home because the cost of operations significantly exceeded the revenues of the trust fund. At that time the Home had only two residents.

In a letter dated July 9, 1971, the IRS notified the Board that it was waiting for promulgation of Treasury Regulations under § 509 before it could rule on the Board's request for foundation status for the Home. In a letter dated October 5, 1971, the IRS informed the Board that it had been classified as a private foundation under § 509(a) and as an operating foundation under § 4942(j)(3).

On November 5, 1971, the heirs filed a petition in a declaratory judgment action in the Louisiana Civil District Court requesting that the trust be dissolved because of non-performance of the conditions imposed by the donor and that the heirs be declared entitled to the remaining assets. The Board responded that the Home had been closed, it was impractical to continue the trust, and the trust established by Mrs. Dwyer had been fulfilled satisfactorily. The Board left to the court the decision whether the remaining assets should be delivered to the heirs or diverted to another cause under the doctrine of cy pres. On December 23, 1971, the court entered its judgment. It agreed with the heirs and ordered the assets distributed to them. One of the trustees concluded and recommended to the Board that the judgment was based on a factual determination and thus there was no basis for an appeal. Accordingly, on January 18 and March 13, 1972, the Board delivered the remaining assets, valued at $200,596, to the heirs in equal parts. After delivery of the assets to the heirs, the Board carried on only minimum ministerial functions.

* * *

On March 21, 1977, the IRS mailed notices to each of the heirs asserting excise tax liability. The notices stated that the excise tax liability of the heirs resulted from their status as transferees of non-charitable expenditures by a private foundation as provided for in § 4945. The notices asserted liability in the amount of $30,081.28 against each heir-transferee, or a total of $210,568.96.

In June 1977, the heirs filed petitions in the Tax Court challenging the Commissioner's determination that the Board had incurred § 4945 excise tax liability and his assertion that the heirs were liable as transferees of the Board's assets.

On December 6, 1982, the Tax Court filed its memorandum decision holding that the heirs were not liable as transferees because the Board was not liable for the § 4945 excise tax. *Gladney v. Commissioner*, 45 T.C.M. 280 (1982).

The Tax Court held that the Board's private foundation status was terminated upon the entry of the 1971 judgment of the Louisiana Civil District Court and that transfers of assets in accordance with that judgment did not give rise to tax liability. The Tax Court also held that any federal statutory notification requirements were satisfied by Board's filings after the distributions of the assets. The Commissioner's post-decision motions were denied by the Tax Court. He now appeals from that decision and the Bonner heirs cross-appeal.

* * *

Under § 501(c)(3), organizations, like the Home, which provide desirable social and charitable functions, are exempt from federal income taxes. As in any other area where both people and taxes are involved, however, abuses did occur. Prior to the enactment of the 1969 Act, the sole penalty for abuse was the loss of an organization's exempt status. In §§ 4940–4945 of the 1969 Act, Congress enacted a series of excise taxes designed to regulate the activities of tax exempt organizations. Section 4945, the provision before us in this case, imposes taxes on amounts expended by the foundation for other than specified (charitable or the like) purposes.

Under § 507, an organization may terminate its status as a private foundation by notifying the IRS. Under that section, however, a tax is imposed on an organization which has terminated its private foundation status.

The Tax Court concluded that the Board's private foundation status was terminated in the instant case upon the entry of the 1971 judgment of the Louisiana Civil District Court. The Tax Court based its conclusion on three facts or circumstances:

> At the time the District Court judgment was entered and the Board determined not to appeal, (1) the Board's charitable operation had been closed down for about six months, (2) the Board's section 507(c) tax was zero, and (3) respondent had not taken any public position in furtherance of his statutory obligation under section 507(a)(1) to prescribe by regulations the time and manner in which an organization was to notify respondent of an intention to terminate its private foundation status.

Gladney v. Commissioner, supra, 45 T.C.M. at 288. In addition to these facts or circumstances, the Tax Court stated that its conclusion was 'consistent with the Congress' clear policy of imposing regulatory-type burden in exchange for tax benefits.' * * *

In view of our interpretation of the statutory provisions in question and their underlying purposes, as explained below, we find the circumstances relied on by the Tax Court to be unconvincing, its statement of Congressional policy to be not altogether accurate, and its conclusion to be erroneous.

We shall first review the facts and circumstances of the case relied on by the Tax Court. The fact that the Board's charitable operation had been closed for six months prior to the judgment of the Louisiana Civil District Court in our view is irrelevant to the issue before us. We agree with the IRS that "termination" as used in § 507 is a statutory term of art which refers only to the organization's legal status, not to its operational status. The Tax Court ignored this critical distinction.

* * *

We hold that the failure of the IRS to promulgate regulations under § 507(a)(1) by the time the Board made the challenged distributions did not relieve the Board of its duty under the statutory notice requirement. The statute on its face clearly requires notice before termination of private foundation tax status can take place. *The fact is that two years elapsed between the time of the alleged termination (the date of the state court judgment) and the time the Board gave any notice whatsoever.* It might be different if the IRS were asserting that the Board's notice of termination did not conform to regulations which were not as yet promulgated at the time of the notice. That is not this case. Here, by failing to give the Secretary timely notice, *in any manner*, the Board did not comply with the statutory requirement of § 507.

The final factual circumstance relied on by the Tax Court—that the Board had no § section 507(c) tax benefits—dovetails with the court's interpretation of the policy behind the notice requirement. The court concluded that the policy is to permit the IRS to compute the termination tax under § 507(c), i.e., to impose regulatory type burdens in exchange for tax benefits. That tax would have been zero in this case. If computation of the § 507(c)termination tax were the sole purpose of the notice, then it might be said that only the most slavish reading of the statute would require the taxpayers to pay the excise tax. We hold, however, that the notice requirement, as part of a larger statutory scheme, has other important purposes which the Tax Court wholly overlooked.

* * *

In the instant case, the informational purpose of the Congressional plan was thwarted. Untimely notification to the IRS resulted in no notification to State officials that the Board was prepared to turn over its assets to private parties. If State officials had been notified, the State might have intervened in the state court action as *parens patriae* to protect the charity. Speculation as to what State officials might have done here is not essential to our holding. We find it is sufficient that (1) the Commissioner has shown that a taxable expenditure took place before the Board notified the IRS under § 507 and (2) there is a clear Congressional intent to require private foundations to comply with the information regulations—even a foundation which has no "termination tax" liability. The IRS was unaware of the dissolution of this foundation for two years. To affirm the Tax Court decision and therefore to allow foundations to act without the knowledge of the IRS or State officials would constitute a precedent striking a severe blow at the carefully articulated information purpose of the Congressional plan. We decline to do so.

Sec. VIII TERMINATION OF PRIVATE FOUNDATION STATUS 343

Appellees advance two additional arguments. First, they argue that the Board substantially complied with § 507. Second, they argue that the IRS was not prejudiced by the Board's failure to notify the IRS of its intention to terminate. These closely related arguments are based for the most part on the same mistaken interpretation of the Congressional policy underlying § 507 which the Tax Court relied upon. They can be dismissed in light of the broader legislative history analysis set forth above. We nevertheless add a few comments.

On the issue of substantial compliance, appellees cite *Rickey v. United States*, 592 F.2d 1251 (5th Cir. 1979) (substantial compliance doctrine applicable where taxpayer failed to comply with filing date requirements set forth in regulations relating to waiver of § 318 attribution rules). In *Rickey*, we rejected a 'crabbed reading of the Code when the [Congressional] rationale for applying a rule is absent'. *Id.* At 1258. In the instant case, on the contrary, there is a clear Congressional rationale for applying the notice requirements. In light of the information gathering rationale, after-the-fact notification is not substantial compliance.

On the issue of prejudice, appellees argue that the procedural notification requirement does not relate to the substance of § 507. As explained above, failure to notify the IRS and, indirectly, State officials, does relate to the very heart of the Congressional plan to give these authorities sufficient information.

We find these two arguments, as well as appellees' other related contentions regarding the applicability of § 4945, to be without merit.

* * *

For the reasons set forth above, we reverse the decision of the Tax Court and remand the case to that court for further proceedings according to law.

Politz, Circuit Judge, dissenting:

* * *

We have before us taxpayers who have inherited what is effectively a residual estate. Under Louisiana law, as applied by the Louisiana courts, these taxpayers were declared owners of the remainder of property which had been placed in a testamentary charitable trust by an ancestor. The trust was established by the last will and testament of Lelia Bonner Dwyer who died on June 22, 1905. The trustees were directed to take the proceeds from the sale of certain property and "found and maintain in New Orleans a home for aged and infirm men to be called the John M. Bonner Memorial Home".

In 1905 there were no federal estate, gift, or income taxes. No taxes were evaded or avoided by the creation of the trust. Over the years the trustees determined that a non-profit corporation would be a better vehicle for administration of the trust. As reflected by the stipulation of the parties, at no time did the existence or operation of the trust result in an avoidance or evasion of income tax. All income was used for unchallenged trust expenses. A half-century or so after its creation it became apparent that the purpose of the trust could no longer be achieved. The occupancy of the home had dwindled almost to naught. The heirs of Lelia Bonner Dwyer sought and secured a judgment declaring the trust at an end, and recognizing them as the persons entitled to ownership of the remaining trust assets. Those assets were accordingly distributed.

The facts to me are simple and clear. Property was placed in a charitable trust for a stated purpose. At that point in time no estate or gift tax was imposed, thus none was avoided. At no time during the life of the trust was there any taxable income, thus no income tax was avoided. But when the court terminated the trust and recognized the heirs as owners, the tax consequences exploded like a dreaded landmine. According to the majority opinion, which accepts the commissioner's position, because the trustees failed to notify the Secretary timely of their intent to dissolve the corporation and distribute the residual assets as per the judgment of the Louisiana court, the heirs/taxpayers must pay to the government 110% of the amount received. The tax court disagreed with the commissioner. So do I.

* * *

The obvious intent of Congress in adopting § 4945 was to reduce, if not eliminate, the opportunity for individuals to create tax-free organizations for the pursuit of their private purposes. Private after-tax dollars ought to be used for those pursuits, not tax dollars. But that is not the case here presented. Lelia Bonner Dwyer did not provide for the creation of the John M. Bonner Memorial Home as part of a grand design or scheme to avoid estate, gift or income taxes; in 1905 no such taxes existed. There has been no manipulation by the taxpayers for their own gain or advantage. When it became apparent that the trust purpose had expired, the taxpayers exercised their rights under Louisiana law and sought a declaration of termination of the trust and a distribution of residual assets. The commissioner concedes that if the trustees had simply given prior notice of this intention there would be no basis for any tax payment or penalty. Notice after the distribution came too late, says the commissioner. So says today's majority. In this particular case, in this particular setting, I would not say so. Under these peculiar facts, I would find the belated preregulation notice adequate.

I respectfully dissent.

Note

The foundation in *Gladney* was not subject to a penalty tax under § 507(c) as there were no tax benefits to the founder. The foundation was created in 1905 before there were federal estate, gift, or income taxes. However, any distribution not for charitable purposes will be a taxable expenditure and subject to penalty taxes under § 4945. A distribution upon dissolution of foundation assets to heirs of the founder would be a taxable expenditure under § 4945.

Problem

The Scott and Cara Reid Foundation, Inc. is a § 501(c)(3) nonprofit corporation and a private nonoperating foundation for tax purposes. Scott and Cara Reid, founders of the organization, question whether the foundation can become a public charity. They are concerned about the extensive reporting requirements for the foundation and about the possibility of penalties for prohibited acts. They are willing to relinquish control of the foundation but want to remain on the board of directors so that they still may have some input into activities of the foundation. How may the foundation qualify as a public charity under these circumstances?

Chapter 8

FUNDRAISING

I. THE IMPORTANCE OF FUNDRAISING

Like for-profit associations, nonprofit organizations must finance their operations. Many acquire needed funds from gifts and grants. As noted in Chapter 1, these nonprofits are known as "donative organizations." Your university foundation, to which you make contributions to support your university, is a classic example of a donative organization. Others generate revenues by means of commercial activities. These organizations are termed "commercial organizations." Hospitals are probably the best example of commercial organizations. Other than gifts, grants and receipts from commercial activities, a nonprofit organization's only other sources of finances are investment income and debt. Nonprofit organizations do not sell equity interests in the organization.

The focus of this chapter is on private contributions, with special emphasis on the factors of which a § 501(c)(3) organization should be aware when it solicits contributions. The subsequent chapter will consider commercial activities and investment income.

Recall from Chapter 6 that § 501(c)(3) organizations, which qualify as public charities under § 509(a)(1) and § 170(b)(1)(A)(vi), must continually solicit contributions from the general public to retain public charity status. Thus, these charities must engage in annual fundraising activities even if they have received substantial contributions from a few donors and are not in need of donations from the general public.

Many factors motivate donors to make donations to charitable organizations. Because each donor has different reasons for giving to a particular charity, a list of the myriad factors is not feasible. Suffice it to say that altruism is a primary motivation for all donors. Donors give because of their desire to support some particular charitable purpose or organization. Thus, a charity learns to target donors who have an affinity for the charity's purpose. Altruism, however, may not be the sole factor. Donors generally want some recognition for their contributions. The public esteem that may come from recognition can be considered as a form of "quid pro quo" for the gift. In most cases, moreover, donors give only to organizations that entitle them to some tax benefit. The tax benefit reduces the actual cost of the gift to the donor, and at the same time provides the donor with the recognition of having made a donation in the face amount transferred to the charitable organization. This chapter addresses issues of which directors of charitable organizations must be aware in assuring donors that their donations will provide them with a charitable contribution deduction.

As charities have growing needs for donations, many have engaged professional solicitors to help them in their fundraising activities. Many states have become concerned that such solicitors may retain an exorbitant amount of the donations they obtain in the name of a particular charity. Thus, some states have attempted to regulate the activities of professional solicitors through licensing requirements. This chapter also considers the constitutionality of state regulation of charitable giving.

II. REGULATION OF CHARITABLE SOLICITATIONS

A nonprofit organization must obtain whatever licenses or permits are required by a particular state, county, or city in order to conduct solicitation activities within that state. State and local governmental control over private philanthropy is a growing trend, and a number of states have enacted laws to control the solicitation of funds from the public.[1] Others have required that some form of permit or license be obtained before any solicitation can take place within the state. Generally any required permits are handled at the municipal level through local regulations or ordinances.

The constitutionality of ordinances requiring registration prior to registration often has been an issue in the courts. The Supreme Court has ruled unconstitutional state statutes prohibiting a charitable organization from paying more than a certain percentage of the amount raised to professional solicitors. Consider the issues in the following case.

RILEY v. NATIONAL FEDERATION OF BLIND OF NORTH CAROLINA

Supreme Court of the United States, 1988
487 U.S. 781, 108 S.Ct. 2667, 101 L.Ed.2d 669

Justice BRENNAN delivered the opinion of the Court.

The North Carolina Charitable Solicitations Act governs the solicitation of charitable contributions by professional fundraisers. As relevant here, it defines the prima facie "reasonable fee" that a professional fundraiser may charge as a percentage of the gross revenues solicited; requires professional fundraisers to disclose to potential donors the gross

---

1. See Uniform Supervision of Trustees for Charitable Purposes Act, 7, which has been adopted in several states, California, Illinois, Michigan, and Oregon being examples. See Cal Gov't. Code §§ 12580–12597; 760 ILCS 55/1–760 ILCS 55/14; MSA § 501.71 et seq; MCL § 14.251 et. seq.; Or Rev. Stat. §§ 128.610–128.990.

percentage of revenues retained in prior charitable solicitations; and requires professional fundraisers to obtain a license before engaging in solicitation. The United States Court of Appeals for the Fourth Circuit held that these aspects of the Act unconstitutionally infringed upon freedom of speech. We affirm.

I

Responding to a study showing that in the previous five years the State's largest professional fundraisers had retained as fees and costs well over 50% of the gross revenues collected in charitable solicitation drives, North Carolina amended its Charitable Solicitations Act in 1985. As amended, the Act prohibits professional fundraisers from retaining an "unreasonable" or "excessive" fee, * * * a term defined by a three-tiered schedule. * * * A fee up to 20% of the gross receipts collected is deemed reasonable. If the fee retained is between 20% and 35%, the Act deems it unreasonable upon a showing that the solicitation at issue did not involve the "dissemination of information, discussion, or advocacy relating to public issues as directed by the [charitable organization] which is to benefit from the solicitation." Finally, a fee exceeding 35% is presumed unreasonable, but the fundraiser may rebut the presumption by showing that the amount of the fee was necessary either (1) because the solicitation involved the dissemination of information or advocacy on public issues directed by the charity, or (2) because otherwise the charity's ability to raise money or communicate would be significantly diminished. As the State describes the Act, even where a prima facie showing of unreasonableness has been rebutted, the factfinder must still make an ultimate determination, on a case-by-case basis, as to whether the fee was reasonable—a showing that the solicitation involved the advocacy or dissemination of information does not alone establish that the total fee was reasonable. * * *

The Act also provides that, prior to any appeal for funds, a professional fundraiser must disclose to potential donors: (1) his or her name; (2) the name of the professional solicitor or professional fundraising counsel by whom he or she is employed and the name and address of his or her employer; and (3) the average percentage of gross receipts actually turned over to charities by the fundraiser for all charitable solicitations conducted in North Carolina within the previous 12 months. * * * Only the third disclosure requirement is challenged here.

A coalition of professional fundraisers, charitable organizations, and potential charitable donors brought suit against various government officials charged with the enforcement of the Act (hereinafter collectively referred to as North Carolina or the State), seeking injunctive and declaratory relief. The District Court for the Eastern District of North Carolina ruled on summary judgment that the foregoing aspects of the Act on their face unconstitutionally infringed upon freedom of speech (it also found the Act constitutional in other respects not before us now), and enjoined enforcement of the unconstitutional provisions. 635 F.Supp. 256 (1986). The Court of Appeals for the Fourth Circuit affirmed in a *per curiam* opinion. 817 F.2d 102 (judgment order), and we noted probable jurisdiction, 484 U.S. 911, 108 S.Ct. 256, 98 L.Ed.2d 214 (1987).

II

We turn first to the "reasonable fee" provision. In deciding this issue, we do not write on a blank slate; the Court has heretofore twice considered laws regulating the financial aspects of charitable solicitations. We first examined such a law in *Schaumburg v. Citizens for a Better Environment,* 444 U.S. 620, 100 S.Ct. 826, 63 L.Ed.2d 73 (1980). There we invalidated a local ordinance requiring charitable solicitors to use, for charitable purposes (defined to exclude funds used toward administrative expenses and the costs of conducting the solicitation), 75% of the funds solicited. We began our analysis by categorizing the type of speech at issue. The village argued that charitable solicitation is akin to a business proposition, and therefore constitutes merely commercial speech. We rejected hat approach and squarely held, on the basis of considerable precedent, that charitable solicitations "involve a variety of speech interests ... that are within the protection of the First Amendment," and therefore have not been dealt with as "purely commercial speech." * * * Applying standard First Amendment analysis, we determined that the ordinance was not narrowly tailored to achieve the village's principal asserted interest: the prevention of fraud. We concluded that some charities, especially those formed primarily to advocate, collect, or disseminate information, would of necessity need to expend more than 25% of the funds collected on administration or fundraising expenses. * * * Yet such an eventuality would not render a solicitation by these charities fraudulent. In short, the prevention of fraud was only "peripherally promoted by the 75–percent requirement and could be sufficiently served by measures less destructive of First Amendment interests." *Id.,* at 636–637, 100 S.Ct., at 835–836. We also observed that the village was free to enforce its already existing fraud laws and to require charities to file financial disclosure reports. * * *

We revisited the charitable solicitation field four years later in *Secretary of State of Maryland v. Joseph H. Munson Co.,* 467 U.S. 947, 104 S.Ct. 2839, 81 L.Ed.2d 786 (1984), a case closer to the present one in that the statute directly regulated contracts between charities and professional fundraisers. Specifically, the statute in question forbade such contracts if, after allowing for a deduction of many of the costs associated with the solicitation, the fundraiser retained more than 25% of the money collected. Although the Secretary was empowered to waive this limitation where it would effectively prevent the charitable organization from raising contributions, we held the law unconstitutional under the force of *Schaumburg.* We rejected the State's argument that restraints on the relationship between the charity and the fundraiser were mere "economic regulations" free of First Amendment implication. Rather, we viewed the law as "a direct restriction on the amount of money a charity can spend on fundraising activity," and therefore "a direct restriction on protected First Amendment activity." 467 U.S., at

967, and n. 16, 104 S.Ct., at 2852–2853, and n. 16. Consequently, we subjected the State's statute to exacting First Amendment scrutiny. Again, the State asserted the prevention of fraud as its principal interest, and again we held that the use of a percentage-based test was not narrowly tailored to achieve that goal. In fact, we found that if the statute actually prevented fraud in some cases it would be "little more than fortuitous." An "equally likely" result would be that the law would "restrict First Amendment activity that results in high costs but is itself a part of the charity's goal or that is simply attributable to the fact that the charity's cause proves to be unpopular." *Id.,* at 966–967, 104 S.Ct., at 2852.

As in *Schaumburg* and *Munson,* we are unpersuaded by the State's argument here that its three-tiered, percentage-based definition of "unreasonable" passes constitutional muster. Our prior cases teach that the solicitation of charitable contributions is protected speech, and that using percentages to decide the legality of the fundraiser's fee is not narrowly tailored to the State's interest in preventing fraud. * * * That much established, unless the State can meaningfully distinguish its statute from those discussed in our precedents, its statute must fall. The State offers two distinctions. First, it asserts a motivating interest not expressed in *Schaumburg* or *Munson:* ensuring that the maximum amount of funds reach the charity or, somewhat relatedly, to guarantee that the fee charged charities is not "unreasonable." Second, the State contends that the Act's flexibility more narrowly tailors it to the State's asserted interests than the laws considered in our prior cases. We find both arguments unavailing.

The State's additional interest in regulating the fairness of the fee may rest on either of two premises (or both): (1) that charitable organizations are economically unable to negotiate fair or reasonable contracts without governmental assistance; or (2) that charities are incapable of deciding for themselves the most effective way to exercise their First Amendment rights. Accordingly, the State claims the power to establish a single transcendent criterion by which it can bind the charities' speaking decisions. We reject both premises.

The first premise, notwithstanding the State's almost talismanic reliance on the mere assertion of it, amounts to little more than a variation of the argument rejected in *Schaumburg* and *Munson* that this provision is simply an economic regulation with no First Amendment implication, and therefore must be tested only for rationality. We again reject that argument; this regulation burdens speech, and must be considered accordingly. There is no reason to believe that charities have been thwarted in their attempts to speak or that they consider the contracts in which they enter to be anything less than equitable. * * * Even if such a showing could be made, the State's solution stands in sharp conflict with the First Amendment's command that government regulation of speech must be measured in minimums, not maximums.

The State's remaining justification—the paternalistic premise that charities' speech must be regulated for their own benefit—is equally unsound. The First Amendment mandates that we presume that speakers, not the government, know best both what they want to say and how to say it. * * * "The very purpose of the First Amendment is to foreclose public authority from assuming a guardianship of the public mind through regulating the press, speech, and religion." *Thomas v. Collins,* 323 U.S. 516, 545, 65 S.Ct. 315, 329, 89 L.Ed. 430 (1945) (Jackson, J., concurring). To this end, the government, even with the purest of motives, may not substitute its judgment as to how best to speak for that of speakers and listeners; free and robust debate cannot thrive if directed by the government. We perceive no reason to engraft an exception to this settled rule for charities.

The foregoing discussion demonstrates that the State's additional interest cannot justify the regulation. But, alternatively, there are several legitimate reasons why a charity might reject the State's overarching measure of a fundraising drive's legitimacy—the percentage of gross receipts remitted to the charity. For example, a charity might choose a particular type of fundraising drive, or a particular solicitor, expecting to receive a large sum as measured by total dollars rather than the percentage of dollars remitted. Or, a solicitation may be designed to sacrifice short-term gains in order to achieve long-term, collateral, or noncash benefits. To illustrate, a charity may choose to engage in the advocacy or dissemination of information during a solicitation, or may seek the introduction of the charity's officers to the philanthropic community during a special event (*e.g.,* an awards dinner). Consequently, even if the State had a valid interest in protecting charities from their own naivete or economic weakness, the Act would not be narrowly tailored to achieve it.

The second distinguishing feature the State offers is the flexibility it has built into its Act. The State describes the second of its three-tiered definition of "unreasonable" and "excessive" as imposing no presumption one way or the other as to the reasonableness of the fee, although unreasonableness may be demonstrated by a showing that the solicitation does not involve the advocacy or dissemination of information on the charity's behalf and at the charity's direction. The State points out that even the third tier's presumption of unreasonableness may be rebutted.

It is important to clarify, though, what we mean by "reasonableness" at this juncture. As we have just demonstrated, * * * the State's generalized interest in unilaterally imposing its notions of fairness on the fundraising contract is both constitutionally invalid and insufficiently related to a percentage-based test. Consequently, what remains is the more particularized interest in guaranteeing that the fundraiser's fee be "reasonable" in the sense that it not be fraudulent. The interest in protecting charities (and the public) from fraud is, of course, a sufficiently substantial interest to justify a narrowly tailored regulation. The question, then, is whether the added flexibility of this regulation is sufficient to tailor the law to this remaining interest. We conclude that it is not.

Despite our clear holding in *Munson* that there is no nexus between the percentage of funds retained by the fundraiser and the likelihood that the solicitation is fraudulent, the State defines, prima facie, an "unreasonable" and "excessive" fee according to the percentage of total revenues collected. Indeed, the State's test is even more attenuated than the one held invalid in *Munson,* which at least excluded costs and expenses of solicitation from the fee definition. * * * Permitting rebuttal cannot supply the missing nexus between the percentages and the State's interest. * * *

But this statute suffers from a more fundamental flaw. Even if we agreed that some form of a percentage-based measure could be used, in part, to test for fraud, we could not agree to a measure that requires the speaker to prove "reasonableness" case by case based upon what is at best a loose inference that the fee might be too high. Under the Act, once a prima facie showing of unreasonableness is made, the fundraiser must rebut the showing. Proof that the solicitation involved the advocacy or dissemination of information is not alone sufficient; it is merely a factor that is added to the calculus submitted to the factfinder, who may still decide that the costs incurred or the fundraiser's profit were excessive. Similarly, the Act is impermissibly insensitive to the realities faced by small or unpopular charities, which must often pay more than 35% of the gross receipts collected to the fundraiser due to the difficulty of attracting donors. * * * Again, the burden is placed on the fundraiser in such cases to rebut the presumption of unreasonableness.

According to the State, we need not worry over this burden, as standards for determining "[r]easonable fundraising fees will be judicially defined over the years." * * * Speakers, however, cannot be made to wait for "years" before being able to speak with a measure of security. In the interim, fundraisers will be faced with the knowledge that every campaign incurring fees in excess of 35%, and many campaigns with fees between 20% and 35%, will subject them to potential litigation over the "reasonableness" of the fee. And, of course, in every such case the fundraiser must bear the costs of litigation and the risk of a mistaken adverse finding by the factfinder, even if the fundraiser and the charity believe that the fee was in fact fair. This scheme must necessarily chill speech in direct contravention of the First Amendment's dictates. * * *

This chill and uncertainty might well drive professional fundraisers out of North Carolina, or at least encourage them to cease engaging in certain types of fundraising (such as solicitations combined with the advocacy and dissemination of information) or representing certain charities (primarily small or unpopular ones), all of which will ultimately "reduc[e] the quantity of expression." * * * Whether one views this as a restriction of the charities' ability to speak, * * *, or a restriction of the professional fundraisers' ability to speak, * * * the restriction is undoubtedly one on speech, and cannot be countenanced here.

In striking down this portion of the Act, we do not suggest that States must sit idly by and allow their citizens to be defrauded. North Carolina has an antifraud law, and we presume that law enforcement officers are ready and able to enforce it. Further North Carolina may constitutionally require fundraisers to disclose certain financial information to the State, as it has since 1981. * * * If this is not the most efficient means of preventing fraud, we reaffirm simply and emphatically that the First Amendment does not permit the State to sacrifice speech for efficiency. * * *

III

We turn next to the requirement that professional fundraisers disclose to potential donors, before an appeal for funds, the percentage of charitable contributions collected during the previous 12 months that were actually turned over to charity. Mandating speech that a speaker would not otherwise make necessarily alters the content of the speech. We therefore consider the Act as a content-based regulation of speech. * * *

The State argues that even if charitable solicitations generally are fully protected, this portion of the Act regulates only commercial speech because it relates only to the professional fundraiser's profit from the solicited contribution. Therefore, the State asks us to apply our more deferential commercial speech principles here. * * *

It is not clear that a professional's speech is necessarily commercial whenever it relates to that person's financial motivation for speaking. * * * But even assuming, without deciding, that such speech in the abstract is indeed merely "commercial," we do not believe that the speech retains its commercial character when it is inextricably intertwined with otherwise fully protected speech. Our lodestars in deciding what level of scrutiny to apply to a compelled statement must be the nature of the speech taken as a whole and the effect of the compelled statement thereon. This is the teaching of *Schaumburg* and *Munson,* in which we refused to separate the component parts of charitable solicitations from the fully protected whole. Regulation of a solicitation "must be undertaken with due regard for the reality that solicitation is characteristically intertwined with informative and perhaps persuasive speech ..., and for the reality that without solicitation the flow of such information and advocacy would likely cease." * * * Thus, where, as here, the component parts of a single speech are inextricably intertwined, we cannot parcel out the speech, applying one test to one phrase and another test to another phrase. Such an endeavor would be both artificial and impractical. Therefore, we apply our test for fully protected expression. * * *

North Carolina asserts that, even so, the First Amendment interest in compelled speech is different than the interest in compelled silence; the State accordingly asks that we apply a deferential test to this part of the Act. There is certainly some difference between compelled speech and compelled silence, but in the context of protected speech, the difference is without constitutional significance, for the First Amendment guarantees "freedom of speech," a term necessarily comprising the decision of both what to say and what *not* to say.

The constitutional equivalence of compelled speech and compelled silence in the context of fully protected expression was established in *Miami Herald Publishing Co. v. Tornillo, supra.* There, the Court considered a Florida statute requiring newspapers to give equal reply space to those they editorially criticize. We unanimously held the law unconstitutional as content regulation of the press, expressly noting the identity between the Florida law and a direct prohibition of speech. "The Florida statute operates as a command in the same sense as a statute or regulation forbidding appellant to publish a specified matter. Governmental restraint on publishing need not fall into familiar or traditional patterns to be subject to constitutional limitations on governmental powers." *Id.,* 418 U.S., at 256, 94 S.Ct., at 2839. That rule did not rely on the fact that Florida restrained the press, and has been applied to cases involving expression generally. For example, in *Wooley v. Maynard,* 430 U.S. 705, 714, 97 S.Ct. 1428, 1435, 51 L.Ed.2d 752 (1977), we held that a person could not be compelled to display the slogan "Live Free or Die." In reaching our conclusion, we relied on the principle that "[t]he right to speak and the right to refrain from speaking are complementary components of the broader concept of 'individual freedom of mind,'" as illustrated in *Tornillo.* 430 U.S., at 714, 97 S.Ct., at 1435 (quoting *West Virginia Board of Education v. Barnette,* 319 U.S. 624, 637, 63 S.Ct. 1178, 1185, 87 L.Ed. 1628 (1943)). * * *

These cases cannot be distinguished simply because they involved compelled statements of opinion while here we deal with compelled statements of "fact": either form of compulsion burdens protected speech. Thus, we would not immunize a law requiring a speaker favoring a particular government project to state at the outset of every address the average cost overruns in similar projects, or a law requiring a speaker favoring an incumbent candidate to state during every solicitation that candidate's recent travel budget. Although the foregoing factual information might be relevant to the listener, and, in the latter case, could encourage or discourage the listener from making a political donation, a law compelling its disclosure would clearly and substantially burden the protected speech.

We believe, therefore, that North Carolina's content-based regulation is subject to exacting First Amendment scrutiny. The State asserts as its interest the importance of informing donors how the money they contribute is spent in order to dispel the alleged misperception that the money they give to professional fundraisers goes in greater-than-actual proportion to benefit charity. To achieve this goal, the State has adopted a prophylactic rule of compelled speech, applicable to all professional solicitations. We conclude that this interest is not as weighty as the State asserts, and that the means chosen to accomplish it are unduly burdensome and not narrowly tailored.

Although we do not wish to denigrate the State's interest in full disclosure, the danger the State posits is not as great as might initially appear. First, the State presumes that the charity derives no benefit from funds collected but not turned over to it. Yet this is not necessarily so. For example, as we have already discussed in greater detail, where the solicitation is combined with the advocacy and dissemination of information, the charity reaps a substantial benefit from the act of solicitation itself. See *Munson, supra,* 467 U.S., at 963, 104 S.Ct., at 2850; *Schaumburg,* 444 U.S., at 635, 100 S.Ct., at 835.

Thus, a significant portion of the fundraiser's "fee" may well go toward achieving the charity's objectives even though it is not remitted to the charity in cash. * * * Second, an unchallenged portion of the disclosure law requires professional fundraisers to disclose their professional status to potential donors, thereby giving notice that at least a portion of the money contributed will be retained. * * * Donors are also undoubtedly aware that solicitations incur costs, to which part of their donation might apply. And, of course, a donor is free to inquire how much of the contribution will be turned over to the charity. Under another North Carolina statute, also unchallenged, fundraisers must disclose this information upon request. N.C.Gen.Stat. § 131C–16 (1986). Even were that not so, if the solicitor refuses to give the requested information, the potential donor may (and probably would) refuse to donate.

Moreover, the compelled disclosure will almost certainly hamper the legitimate efforts of professional fundraisers to raise money for the charities they represent. First, this provision necessarily discriminates against small or unpopular charities, which must usually rely on professional fundraisers. Campaigns with high costs and expenses carried out by professional fundraisers must make unfavorable disclosures, with the predictable result that such solicitations will prove unsuccessful. Yet the identical solicitation with its high costs and expenses, if carried out by the employees of a charity or volunteers, results in no compelled disclosure, and therefore greater success. Second, in the context of a verbal solicitation, if the potential donor is unhappy with the disclosed percentage, the fundraiser will not likely be given a chance to explain the figure; the disclosure will be the last words spoken as the donor closes the door or hangs up the phone. * * * Again, the predictable result is that professional fundraisers will be encouraged to quit the State or refrain from engaging in solicitations that result in an unfavorable disclosure.

IV

Finally, we address the licensing requirement. This provision requires professional fundraisers to await a determination regarding their license application before engaging in solicitation, while volunteer fundraisers, or those employed by the charity, may solicit immediately upon submitting an application.

Given our previous discussion and precedent, it will not do simply to ignore the First Amendment interest of professional fundraisers in speaking. It is well settled that a speaker's rights are not lost merely because compensation is received; a speaker is no less a speaker because he or she is paid to speak. * * * And the State's asserted power to license professional fundraisers carries with it (unless properly constrained) the power directly and substantially to affect the speech they utter. Consequently, the statute is subject to First Amendment scrutiny. * * *

Generally, speakers need not obtain a license to speak. However, that rule is not absolute. For example, States may impose valid time, place, or manner restrictions. * * * North Carolina seeks to come within the exception by alleging a heightened interest in regulating those who solicit money. Even assuming that the State's interest does justify requiring fundraisers to obtain a license before soliciting, such a regulation must provide that the licensor "will, within a specified brief period, either issue a license or go to court." *Freedman v. Maryland,* 380 U.S. 51, 59, 85 S.Ct. 734, 739, 13 L.Ed.2d 649 (1965). That requirement is not met here, for the Charitable Solicitations Act (as amended) permits a delay without limit. The statute on its face does not purport to require when a determination must be made, nor is there an administrative regulation or interpretation doing so. The State argues, though, that its history of issuing licenses quickly constitutes a practice effectively constraining the licensor's discretion. * * * We cannot agree. The history to which the State refers relates to the period before the 1985 amendments, at which time professional fundraisers were permitted to solicit as soon as their applications were filed. Then, delay permitted the speaker's speech; now, delay compels the speaker's silence. Under these circumstances, the licensing provision cannot stand. * * *

V

We hold that the North Carolina Charitable Solicitations Act is unconstitutional in the three respects before us. Accordingly, the judgment of the Court of Appeals is

Affirmed.

* * *

Question

The Supreme Court stated, in *Riley*, that in striking down a portion of the North Carolina Act, it did not "suggest that States must sit idly by and allow their citizens to be defrauded." How may a state constitutionally regulate solicitation within the state?

As a corollary to *Riley*, in the following decision, the Supreme Court ruled that states may maintain fraud actions when fundraisers make false or misleading representations designed to deceive donors about how their donations will be used.

MADIGAN v. TELEMARKETING ASSOCIATES, INC.
United States Supreme Court, 2003
538 U.S. 600, 123 S.Ct. 1829, 155 L.Ed.2d 793

Justice GINSBURG delivered the opinion of the Court.

This case concerns the amenability of for-profit fundraising corporations to suit by the Attorney General of Illinois for fraudulent charitable solicitations. The controversy arises from the fundraisers' contracts with a charitable nonprofit corporation organized to advance the welfare of Vietnam veterans; under the contracts, the fundraisers were to retain 85 percent of the proceeds of their fundraising endeavors. The State Attorney General's complaint alleges that the fundraisers defrauded members of the public by falsely representing that "a significant amount of each dollar donated would be paid over to [the veterans organization] for its [charitable] purposes while in fact the [fundraisers] knew that ... 15 cents or less of each dollar would be available" for those purposes. * * * Complementing that allegation, the complaint states that the fundraisers falsely represented that "the funds donated would go to further ... charitable purposes," * * * when in fact "the amount ... paid over to charity was merely incidental to the fund raising effort," which was conducted primarily "for the private pecuniary benefit of" the fundraisers, * * *

The question presented is whether those allegations state a claim for relief that can survive a motion to dismiss. In accord with the Illinois trial and appellate courts, the Illinois Supreme Court held they did not. That court was "mindful of the opportunity for public misunderstanding and the potential for donor confusion which may be presented with fundraising solicitations of the sort involved in th[is] case," *Ryan v. Telemarketing Associates, Inc.*, 198 Ill.2d 345, 363, 261 Ill.Dec. 319, 763 N.E.2d 289, 299 (2001); it nevertheless concluded that threshold dismissal of the complaint was compelled by this Court's decisions in *Schaumburg v. Citizens for a Better Environment*, 444 U.S. 620, 100 S.Ct. 826, 63 L.Ed.2d 73 (1980), *Secretary of State of Md. v. Joseph H. Munson Co.*, 467 U.S. 947, 104 S.Ct. 2839, 81 L.Ed.2d 786 (1984), and *Riley v. National Federation of Blind of N. C., Inc.*, 487 U.S. 781, 108 S.Ct. 2667, 101 L.Ed.2d 669 (1988). Those decisions held that certain regulations of charitable subscriptions, barring fees in excess of a prescribed level, effectively imposed prior restraints on fundraising, and were therefore incompatible with the First Amendment.

We reverse the judgment of the Illinois Supreme Court. Our prior decisions do not rule out, as supportive of a fraud claim against fundraisers, any and all reliance on the percentage of charitable donations fundraisers retain for themselves. While bare failure to disclose that information directly to potential donors does not suffice to establish fraud, when nondisclosure is accompanied by intentionally misleading statements designed to deceive the listener, the First Amendment leaves room for a fraud claim.

I

Defendants below, respondents here, Telemarketing Associates, Inc., and Armet, Inc., are Illinois for-profit fundraising corporations wholly owned and controlled by defendant-respondent Richard Troia. * * * Telemarketing Associates and Armet were retained by VietNow National Headquarters, a charitable nonprofit corporation, to solicit donations to aid Vietnam veterans. * * * In this opinion, we generally refer to respondents, collectively, as "Telemarketers."

The contracts between the charity, VietNow, and the fundraisers, Telemarketers, provided that Telemarketers would retain 85 percent of the gross receipts from donors within Illinois, leaving 15 percent for VietNow. Under the agreements, donor lists developed by Telemarketers would remain in their "sole and exclusive" control. * * * Telemarketers also brokered contracts on behalf of VietNow with out-of-state fundraisers; under those contracts, out-of-state fundraisers retained between 70 percent and 80 percent of donated funds, Telemarketers received between 10 percent and 20 percent as a finder's fee, and VietNow received 10 percent. * * * Between July 1987 and the end of 1995, Telemarketers collected approximately $7.1 million, keeping slightly more than $6 million for themselves, and leaving approximately $1.1 million for the charity. * * *

In 1991, the Illinois Attorney General filed a complaint against Telemarketers in state court. * * * The complaint asserted common-law and statutory claims for fraud and breach of fiduciary duty. It alleged, *inter alia,* that the 85 percent fee for which Telemarketers contracted was "excessive" and "not justified by expenses [they] paid." * * * Dominantly, however, the complaint concerned misrepresentation.

In the course of their telephone solicitations, the complaint states, Telemarketers misleadingly represented that "funds donated would go to further Viet[N]ow's charitable purposes." * * * Affidavits attached to the complaint aver that Telemarketers told prospective donors their contributions would be used for specifically identified charitable endeavors; typical examples of those endeavors include "food baskets given to vets [and] their families for Thanksgiving," * * *, paying "bills and rent to help physically and mentally disabled Vietnam vets and their families," * * * "jo[b] training," * * * and "rehabilitation [and] other services for Vietnam vets," * * *. One affiant asked what percentage of her contribution would be used for fundraising expenses; she "was told 90% or more goes to the vets." * * * Another affiant stated she was told her donation would not be used for "labor expenses" because "all members are volunteers." * * * Written materials Telemarketers sent to each donor represented that contributions would "be used to help and assist Viet[N]ow's charitable purposes." * * *

Telemarketers moved to dismiss the fraud claims, urging that they were barred by the First Amendment. The trial court granted the motion, * * * and the dismissal order was affirmed, in turn, by the Illinois Appellate Court and the Illinois Supreme Court. The Illinois courts placed heavy weight on three decisions of this Court: *Schaumburg v. Citizens for a Better Environment,* 444 U.S. 620, 100 S.Ct. 826, 63 L.Ed.2d 73 (1980); *Secretary of State of Md. v. Joseph H. Munson Co.,* 467 U.S. 947, 104 S.Ct. 2839, 81 L.Ed.2d 786 (1984); and *Riley v. National Federation of Blind of N. C., Inc.,* 487 U.S. 781, 108 S.Ct. 2667, 101 L.Ed.2d 669 (1988). Each of the three decisions invalidated state or local laws that categorically restrained solicitation by charities or professional fundraisers if a high percentage of the funds raised would be used to cover administrative or fundraising costs. * * *

The Illinois Supreme Court acknowledged that this case, unlike *Schaumburg, Munson*, and *Riley,* involves no prophylactic provision proscribing any charitable solicitation if fundraising costs exceeded a prescribed limit. Instead, the Attorney General sought to enforce the State's generally applicable antifraud laws against Telemarketers for "specific instances of deliberate deception." * * * "However," the court said, "the statements made by [Telemarketers] during solicitation are alleged to be 'false' only because [Telemarketers] retained 85% of the gross receipts and failed to disclose this information to donors." * * * The Attorney General's complaint, in the Illinois Supreme Court's view, was "in essence, an attempt to regulate [Telemarketers'] ability to engage in a protected activity based upon a percentage-rate limitation"—"the same regulatory principle that was rejected in *Schaumburg* [,] *Munson*, and *Riley.*"

"[H]igh solicitation costs," the Illinois Supreme Court stressed, "can be attributable to a number of factors." In this case, the court noted, Telemarketers contracted to provide a "wide range" of services in addition to telephone solicitation. For example, they agreed to publish a newsletter and to maintain a toll-free information hotline. * * * Moreover, the court added, VietNow received "nonmonetary benefits by having [its] message disbursed by the solicitation process," and Telemarketers were directed to solicit "in a manner that would 'promote goodwill' on behalf of VietNow." * * * Taking these factors into account, the court concluded that it would be "incorrect to presume ... [any] nexus between high solicitation costs and fraud." * * *

The Illinois Supreme Court further determined that, under *Riley,* "fraud cannot be defined in such a way that it places on solicitors the affirmative duty to disclose to potential donors, at the point of solicitation, the net proceeds to be returned to the charity." * * * Finally, the court expressed the fear that if the complaint were allowed to proceed, all fundraisers in Illinois would be saddled with "the burden of defending the reasonableness of their fees, on a case-by-case basis, whenever in the Attorney General's judgment the public was being deceived about the charitable nature of a fund-raising campaign because the fundraiser's fee was too high." * * * The threatened exposure to litigation costs and penalties, the court said, "could produce a substantial chilling effect on protected speech." We granted certiorari. * * *

II

The First Amendment protects the right to engage in charitable solicitation. See *Schaumburg,* 444 U.S., at 632, 100 S.Ct. 826 ("charitable appeals for funds ... involve a variety of speech interests—communication of information, the dissemination and propagation of views and ideas, and the advocacy of causes—that are within the protection of the First Amendment"); *Riley,* 487 U.S., at 788–789, 108 S.Ct. 2667. But the First Amendment does not shield fraud. * * * Like other forms of public deception, fraudulent charitable solicitation is unprotected speech. * * * The Court has not previously addressed the First Amendment's application to individual fraud actions of the kind at issue here. It has, however, three times considered prophylactic statutes designed to combat fraud by imposing prior restraints on solicitation when fundraising fees exceeded a specified reasonable level. Each time, the Court held the prophylactic measures unconstitutional.

In *Schaumburg,* decided in 1980, the Court invalidated a village ordinance that prohibited charitable organizations from soliciting contributions unless they used at least 75 percent of their receipts "directly for the charitable purpose of the organization." * * *

* * *

Four years later, in *Munson,* the Court invalidated a Maryland law that prohibited charitable organizations from soliciting if they paid or agreed to pay as expenses more than 25 percent of the amount raised. * * *

* * *

Third in the trilogy of cases on which the Illinois Supreme Court relied was our 1988 decision in *Riley.* The village ordinance in *Schaumburg* and the Maryland law in *Munson* regulated charities; the North Carolina charitable solicitation controls at issue in *Riley* directly regulated professional fundraisers. * * *

* * *

III

A

The Court's opinions in *Schaumburg, Munson,* and *Riley* took care to leave a corridor open for fraud actions to guard the public against false or misleading charitable solicitations. * * * As those decisions recognized, and as we further explain below, there are differences critical to First Amendment concerns between fraud actions trained on representations made in individual cases and statutes that categorically ban solicitations when fundraising costs run high. * * * Simply labeling an action one for "fraud," of course, will not carry the day. For example, had the complaint against Telemarketers charged fraud based solely on the percentage of donations the fundraisers would retain, or their failure to alert potential donors to their fee arrangements at the start of each telephone call, *Riley* would support swift dismissal. * * *

* * *

Fraud actions so tailored, targeting misleading affirmative representations about how donations will be used, are plainly distinguishable, as we next discuss, from the measures invalidated in *Schaumburg, Munson*, and *Riley:* So long as the emphasis is on what the fundraisers misleadingly convey, and not on percentage limitations on solicitors' fees *per se,* such actions need not impermissibly chill protected speech.

B

In *Schaumburg, Munson*, and *Riley,* the Court invalidated laws that prohibited charitable organizations or fundraisers from engaging in charitable solicitation if they spent high percentages of donated funds on fundraising—whether or not any fraudulent representations were made to potential donors. Truthfulness even of all representations was not a defense. * * * In contrast to the prior restraints inspected in those cases, a properly tailored fraud action targeting fraudulent representations themselves employs no "[b]road prophylactic rul[e]," * * * lacking any "nexus ... [to] the likelihood that the solicitation is fraudulent," *Riley,* 487 U.S., at 793, 108 S.Ct. 2667. Such an action thus falls on the constitutional side of the line the Court's cases draw "between regulation aimed at fraud and regulation aimed at something else in the hope that it would sweep fraud in during the process." *Munson,* 467 U.S., at 969–970, 104 S.Ct. 2839. The Illinois Attorney General's complaint, in this light, has a solid core in allegations that home in on affirmative statements Telemarketers made intentionally misleading donors regarding the use of their contributions. * * *

Of prime importance, and in contrast to a prior restraint on solicitation, or a regulation that imposes on fundraisers an uphill burden to prove their conduct lawful, in a properly tailored fraud action the State bears the full burden of proof. False statement alone does not subject a fundraiser to fraud liability. As restated in Illinois case law, to prove a defendant liable for fraud, the complainant must show that the defendant made a false representation of a material fact knowing that the representation was false; further, the complainant must demonstrate that the defendant made the representation with the intent to mislead the listener, and succeeded in doing so. * * *

Exacting proof requirements of this order, in other contexts, have been held to provide sufficient breathing room for protected speech. * * * As an additional safeguard responsive to First Amendment concerns, an appellate court could independently review the trial court's findings. * * * What the First Amendment and our case law emphatically do not require, however, is a blanket exemption from fraud liability for a fundraiser who intentionally misleads in calls for donations.

The Illinois Supreme Court in the instant case correctly observed that "the percentage of [fundraising] proceeds turned over to a charity is not an accurate measure of the amount of funds used 'for' a charitable purpose." * * * But the gravamen of the fraud action in this case is not high costs or fees, it is particular representations made with intent to mislead. If, for example, a charity conducted an advertising or awareness campaign that advanced charitable purposes in conjunction with its fundraising activity, its representation that donated funds were going to "charitable purposes" would not be misleading, much less intentionally so. Similarly, charitable organizations that engage primarily in advocacy or information dissemination could get and spend money for their activities without risking a fraud charge. * * *

The Illinois Attorney General here has not suggested that a charity must desist from using donations for information dissemination, advocacy, the promotion of public awareness, the production of advertising material, the development or enlargement of the charity's contributor base, * * * and the like. Rather, she has alleged that Telemarketers attracted donations by misleading potential donors into believing that a substantial portion of their contributions would fund specific programs or services, knowing full well that was not the case. * * * Such representations remain false or misleading, however legitimate the other purposes for which the funds are in fact used.

We do not agree with Telemarketers that the Illinois Attorney General's fraud action is simply an end run around *Riley's* holding that fundraisers may not be required, in every telephone solicitation, to state the percentage of receipts the fundraiser would retain. * * * It is one thing to compel every fundraiser to disclose its fee arrangements at the start of a telephone conversation, quite another to take fee arrangements into account in assessing whether particular affirmative representations designedly deceive the public.

C

Our decisions have repeatedly recognized the legitimacy of government efforts to enable donors to make informed choices about their charitable contributions. In *Schaumburg,* the Court thought it proper to require "disclosure of the finances of charitable organizations," thereby to prevent fraud "by informing the public of the ways in which their contributions will be employed." * * * In *Munson,* the Court reiterated that "disclosure of the finances of a charitable organization" could be required "so that a member of the public could make an informed decision about whether to contribute." * * * And in *Riley,* the Court said the State may require professional fundraisers to file "detailed financial disclosure forms" and may communicate that information to the public. * * *

In accord with our precedent, as Telemarketers and their *amici* acknowledge, in "[a]lmost all of [the] states and many localities," charities and professional fundraisers must "register and file regular reports on activities [,] particularly fundraising costs." * * * These reports are generally available to the public; indeed, "[m]any states have placed the reports they receive from charities and professional fundraisers on the Internet." * * * Telemarketers do not object on First Amendment grounds to these disclosure requirements. * * *

Just as government may seek to inform the public and prevent fraud through such disclosure requirements, so it may "vigorously enforce ... antifraud laws to prohibit professional fundraisers from obtaining money on false pretenses or by making false statements." * * * High fundraising costs, without more, do not establish fraud. * * * And mere failure to volunteer the fundraiser's fee when contacting a potential donee, without more, is insufficient to state a claim for fraud. * * * But these limitations do not disarm States from assuring that their residents are positioned to make informed choices about their charitable giving. Consistent with our precedent and the First Amendment, States may maintain fraud actions when fundraisers make false or misleading representations designed to deceive donors about how their donations will be used.

* * *

For the reasons stated, the judgment of the Illinois Supreme Court is reversed, and the case is remanded for further proceedings not inconsistent with this opinion.

It is so ordered.

Note

The Internal Revenue Service also has attempted to regulate professional solicitation. It has been concerned that excess solicitation fees constitutes inurement and has taken the position that a charitable organization can lose its tax exempt status for incurring excessive fundraising expenditures to professional solicitors.

Questions

1. Can a professional solicitor be an "insider" so that payment of excessive fees to a solicitor would be inurement?

2. Would the payment of unreasonable fees to a professional solicitor support a finding that a charity conferred a "private benefit" on the solicitor and, thus, that directors of the charity violated the standard of care.

Consider these questions in the following case, which was cited in more detail in Chapter 5 on the issue of loss of exempt status because of inurement.

UNITED CANCER COUNCIL INC. v. COMMISSIONER

United States Court of Appeals, Seventh Circuit, 1999
165 F.3d 1173

POSNER, Chief Judge.

The United Cancer Council is a charity that seeks, through affiliated local cancer societies, to encourage preventive and ameliorative approaches to cancer, as distinct from searching for a cure, which has been the emphasis of the older and better-known American Cancer Society, of which UCC is a splinter. The Internal Revenue Service revoked UCC's charitable exemption and the Tax Court upheld the revocation, precipitating this appeal.

So far as relates to this case, a charity, in order to be entitled to the charitable exemption from federal income tax, and to be eligible to receive tax-exempt donations, must be "organized and operated exclusively for ... [charitable] purposes" and "no part of the net earnings of [the charity may] inure[ ] to the benefit of any private shareholder or individual." 26 U.S.C. §§ 501(c)(3) (exemption); 170(c)(2)(B), (C) (receipt of donations); 26 C.F.R. § 1.501(a)–1(c), 1.501(c)(3)–1(d)(1)(i), (ii). The IRS claims that UCC (which is defunct) was not operated exclusively for charitable purposes, but rather was operated for, or also for, the private benefit of the fundraising company that UCC had hired, Watson & Hughey Company (W & H). The Service also claims that part of the charity's net earnings had inured to the benefit of a private shareholder or individual—W & H again. The Tax Court upheld the Service's second ground for revoking UCC's exemption—inurement—and did not reach the first ground, private benefit. The only issue before us is whether the court clearly erred, * * *, in finding that a part of UCC's net earnings inured to the benefit of a private shareholder or individual.

* * *

The facts are undisputed. In 1984, UCC was a tiny organization. It had an annual operating budget of only $35,000, and it was on the brink of bankruptcy because several of its larger member societies had defected to its rival, the American Cancer Society. A committee of the board picked W & H, a specialist in raising funds for charities, as the best prospect for raising the funds essential for UCC's survival. Another committee of the board was created to negotiate the contract. Because of UCC's perilous financial condition, the committee wanted W & H to "front" all the expenses of the fundraising campaign, though it would be reimbursed by UCC as soon as the campaign generated sufficient donations to cover those expenses. W & H agreed. But it demanded in return that it be made UCC's exclusive fundraiser during the five-year term of the contract, that it be given co-ownership of the list of prospective donors generated by its fundraising efforts, and that UCC be forbidden, both during the term of the contract and after it expired, to sell or lease the list, although it would be free to use it to solicit repeat donations. There was no restriction on W & H's use of the list. UCC agreed to these terms and the contract went into effect.

Over the five-year term of the contract, W & H mailed 80 million letters soliciting contributions to UCC. Each letter contained advice about preventing cancer, as well as a pitch for donations; 70 percent of the letters also offered the recipient a chance to win a sweepstake. The text of all the letters was reviewed and approved by UCC. As a result of these mailings, UCC raised an enormous amount of money (by its standards)—$28.8 million. But its expenses—that is, the costs borne by W & H for postage, printing, and mailing the letters soliciting donations, costs reimbursed by UCC according to the terms of the contract—were also enormous—$26.5 million. The balance, $2.3 million, the net proceeds of the direct-mail campaign, was spent by UCC for services to cancer patients and on research for the prevention and treatment of cancer. The charity was permitted by the relevant accounting conventions to classify $12.2 million of its fundraising expenses as educational expenditures because of the cancer information contained in the fundraising letters.

Although UCC considered its experience with W & H successful, it did not renew the contract when it expired by its terms in 1989. Instead, it hired another fundraising organization—with disastrous results. The following year, UCC declared bankruptcy, and within months the IRS revoked its tax exemption retroactively to the date on which UCC had signed the contract with W & H. The effect was to make the IRS a major creditor of UCC in the bankruptcy proceeding. * * *

The term "any private shareholder or individual" in the inurement clause of section 501(c)(3) of the Internal Revenue Code has been interpreted to mean an insider of the charity. * * * A charity is not to siphon its earnings to its founder, or the members of its board, or their families, or anyone else fairly to be described as an insider, that is, as the equivalent of an owner or manager. The test is functional. It looks to the reality of control rather than to the insider's place in a formal table of organization. The insider could be a "mere" employee—or even a nominal outsider, such as a physician with hospital privileges in a charitable hospital, * * *—though the court in that case rejected the argument that the fundraiser controlled the charity.

The Tax Court's classification of W & H as an insider of UCC was based on the fundraising contract. Such contracts are common. Fundraising has become a specialized professional activity and many charities hire specialists in it. If the charity's contract with the fundraiser makes the latter an insider, triggering the inurement clause of section 501(c)(3) and so destroying the charity's tax exemption, the charity sector of the economy is in trouble. The IRS does not take the position that every such contract has this effect. What troubles it are the particular terms and circumstances of UCC's contract. It argues that since at the inception of the contract the charity had no money to speak of, and since, therefore, at least at the beginning, all the expenses of the fundraising campaign were borne by W & H, the latter was like a founder, or rather refounder (UCC was created in 1963), of the charity. The IRS points out that 90 percent of the contributions received by UCC during the term of the contract were paid to W & H to defray the cost of the fundraising campaign that brought in those contributions, and so argues that W & H was the real recipient of the contributions. It argues that because W & H was UCC's only fundraiser, the charity was totally at W & H's mercy during the five-year term of the contract—giving W & H effective control over the charity. UCC even surrendered the right to rent out the list of names of donors that the fundraising campaign generated. The terms of the contract were more favorable to the fundraiser than the terms of the average fundraising contract are.

* * *

Take the Service's first point, that W & H defrayed such a large fraction of the charity's total expenses in the early stages of the contract that it was the equivalent of a founder. Pushed to its logical extreme, this argument would deny the charitable tax exemption to any new or small charity that wanted to grow by soliciting donations, since it would have to get the cash to pay for the solicitations from an outside source, logically a fundraising organization. We can't see what this has to do with inurement. The argument is connected to another of the Service's points, that W & H was UCC's only fundraiser during the period of the contract. If UCC had hired ten fundraisers, the Service couldn't argue that any of them was so large a recipient of the charity's expenditures that it must be deemed to have controlled the charity. Yet in terms of the purposes of the inurement clause, it makes no difference how many fundraisers a charity employs. W & H obtained an exclusive contract, and thus was the sole fundraiser, not because it sought to control UCC and suck it dry, but because it was taking a risk; the exclusive contract lent assurance that if the venture succeeded, UCC wouldn't hire other fundraisers to reap where W & H had sown.

* * *

The Service's point that has the most intuitive appeal is the high ratio of fundraising expenses, all of which went to W & H because it was UCC's only fundraiser during the term of the contract, to net charitable proceeds. Of the $28–odd million that came in, $26–plus million went right back out, to W & H. These figures are deceptive, because UCC got a charitable "bang" from the mailings themselves, which contained educational materials (somewhat meager, to be sure) in direct support of the charity's central charitable goal. A charity whose entire goal was to publish educational materials would spend all or most of its revenues on publishing, but this would be in support rather than in derogation of its charitable purposes.

Even if this point is ignored, the ratio of expenses to net charitable receipts is unrelated to the issue of inurement. For one thing, it is a ratio of apples to oranges: the *gross* expenses of the fundraiser to the *net* receipts of the charity. For all that appears, while UCC derived a net benefit from the contract equal to the difference between donations and expenses plus the educational value of the mailings, W & H derived only a modest profit; for we know what UCC paid it, but not what its expenses were. The record does contain a table showing that W & H incurred postage and printing expenses of $12.5 million, but there is nothing on its total expenses.

To the extent that the ratio of net charitable proceeds to the cost to the charity of generating those proceeds has any relevance, it is to a different issue, one not presented by this appeal, which is whether charities should be denied a tax exemption if their operating expenses are a very high percentage of the total charitable donations that they receive. To see that it's a different issue, just imagine that UCC had spent $26 million to raise $28 million but that the $26 million had been scattered among a host of suppliers rather than concentrated on one. There would be no issue of inurement, because the Service would have no basis for singling out one of these suppliers as being in "control" of UCC (or the suppliers as a group, unless they were acting in concert). But there might still be a concern either that the charity was mismanaged or that charitable enterprises that generate so little net contribution to their charitable goals do not deserve the encouragement that a tax exemption provides. Recall that most of UCC's fundraising appeals offered the recipient of the appeal a chance to win a sweepstake, a form of charitable appeal that, we are told, is frowned upon. There may even be a question of how reputable W & H is (or was). * * * But these points go to UCC's sound judgment, not to whether W & H succeeded in wresting control over UCC from the charity's board.

UCC's low net yield is no doubt related to the terms of the fundraising contract, which were more favorable to the fundraiser than the average such contract. But so far as appears, they were favorable to W & H not because UCC's board was disloyal and mysteriously wanted to shower charity on a fundraiser with which it had no affiliation or overlapping membership or common ownership or control, but because UCC was desperate. The charity drove (so far as the record shows) the best bargain that it could, but it was not a good bargain. Maybe desperate charities should be encouraged to fold rather than to embark on expensive campaigns to raise funds. But that too is a separate issue from inurement. W & H did not, by reason of being able to drive a hard bargain, become an insider of UCC. If W & H was calling the shots, why did UCC refuse to renew the contract when it expired, and instead switch to another fundraiser?

* * *

There was no diversion of charitable revenues to an insider here, nothing that smacks of self-dealing, disloyalty, breach of fiduciary obligation or other misconduct of the type aimed at by a provision of law that forbids a charity to divert its earnings to members of the board or other insiders. What there may have been was imprudence on the part of UCC's board of directors in hiring W & H and negotiating the contract that it did. Maybe the only prudent course in the circumstances that confronted UCC in 1984 was to dissolve. Charitable organizations are plagued by incentive problems. Nobody owns the right to the profits and therefore no one has the spur to efficient performance that the lure of profits creates. Donors are like corporate shareholders in the sense of being the principal source of the charity's funds, but they do not have a profit incentive to monitor the care with which the charity's funds are used. Maybe the lack of a profit motive made UCC's board too lax.

Maybe the board did not negotiate as favorable a contract with W & H as the board of a profitmaking firm would have done. And maybe tax law has a role to play in assuring the prudent management of charities. Remember the IRS's alternative basis for yanking UCC's exemption? It is that as a result of the contract's terms, UCC was not really operated exclusively for charitable purposes, but rather for the private benefit of W & H as well. Suppose that UCC was so irresponsibly managed that it paid W & H twice as much for fundraising services as W & H would have been happy to accept for those services, so that of UCC's $26 million in fundraising expense $13 million was the equivalent of a gift to the fundraiser. Then it could be argued that UCC was in fact being operated to a significant degree for the private benefit of W & H, though not because it was the latter's creature. That then would be a route for using tax law to deal with the problem of improvident or extravagant expenditures by a charitable organization that do not, however, inure to the benefit of insiders.

That in fact is the IRS's alternative ground for revoking the exemption, the one the Tax Court gave a bye to. It would have been better had the court resolved that ground as well as the inurement ground, so that the case could be definitively resolved in one appeal. But it did not, and so the case must be remanded to enable the court to consider it. We shall not prejudge the proceedings on remand. The usual "private benefit" case is one in which the charity has dual public and private goals, * * *, and that is not involved here. However, the board of a charity has a duty of care, just like the board of an ordinary business corporation, * * *, and a violation of that duty which involved the dissipation of the charity's assets might (we need not decide whether it would—we leave that issue to the Tax Court in the first instance) support a finding that the charity was conferring a private benefit, even if the contracting party did not control, or exercise undue influence over, the charity. This, for all we know, may be such a case.

REVERSED AND REMANDED.

Question

Would a donor have contributed to United Cancer Council if the donor had been aware that over ninety percent of the donation would be retained by the professional solicitor?

III. CHARITABLE CONTRIBUTION DEDUCTIONS

Three sections of the Internal Revenue Code govern the tax benefits to which a donor may be entitled: § 170 (income tax); § 2055 (estate tax); and § 2522 (gift tax). Section 170 is the most important section as it permits taxpayers to deduct the amount of their gifts in determining their taxable income. Thus, an individual donor (so long as the donor itemizes deductions) receives a reduction in income tax liability equal to the donor's marginal tax rate times the amount of the gift. The consequence of §§ 2055 and 2522 is to relieve the donor of estate or gift tax with respect to testamentary or inter vivos gifts.

As noted in previous chapters, contributions to § 501(c)(3) organizations that qualify as public charities under § 509 receive more favorable tax treatment than do contributions to § 501(c)(3) organizations that are private foundations. Sections 170(b) and (c) track the organizations to which donations will be tax deductible. Section 170(b) describes those organizations that qualify for more favorable tax treatment with respect to the annual limitations on donations. These organizations also are the § 501(c)(3) organizations that qualify for public charity status under § 509(a)(1). The regulations under § 170(b) set out the requirements for § 501(c)3) organizations to qualify for public charity status under § 509(a)(1). (See discussion in Chapter 6.)

The materials below first consider the rules governing a § 170 income tax charitable contribution deduction. These rules are too intricate and complicated for any more than a survey in a text on nonprofit organizations. For a more complete analysis of § 170, refer to Daniel Q. Posin; Federal Income Taxation of Individuals (7th Ed. 2005); Bruce R. Hopkins, The Tax Law of Charitable Giving (3rd Ed. 2005); and Arthur Andersen & Co., S.C., Tax Economics of Charitable Giving (12th Ed. 1995).

Section 170(a) permits a taxpayer to deduct any charitable contributions paid during the taxable year. This privilege is subject to limitations, some of which are addressed later in this chapter. The core of Section 170(a) is the meaning of a charitable contribution. A definition of sorts is found in Section 170(c).

Pursuant to § 170(c), a charitable contribution is "a contribution or gift to or for the use of" designated organizations. Those organizations, in general, are the § 501(c)(3) charitable organizations, governmental entities, veterans organizations exempt under § 501(c)(19), and cemetery companies exempt under § 501(c)(13) [I.R.C. § 170(c)]. The most important of these organizations are the § 501(c)(3) organizations. Thus this chapter concentrates on § 501(c)(3) organizations. Section 501(c)(3) organizations are discussed in detail in Chapters 4–7 and 10–12.

A. Quid Pro Quo

Cash donations are generally the least controversial form of gift. A donor who gives money (cash, check, or credit card payment) to a charity, will claim a charitable contribution deduction equal to the gift amount, subject to certain substantiation requirements and percentage limitations.

Charitable organizations, however, have devised marketing schemes that give a donor value in return for the donor's gift. For example, a public radio or television station usually gives a donor some gratuity (a mug, t-shirt, CD, video) in return for the donor's gift. The value of the gratuity increases with the amount of the gift. A charity may hold a fund-raising dinner and charge an attendee more than the cost of the dinner. In addition, the charity may conduct a raffle. What amount, if any, may the "donor" deduct when the donor receives some *quid pro quo* in return?

The basic rule for quid pro quo gifts is found in Treas. Reg. § 1.170 A–1(h). The *American Bar Endowment* case, Revenue Ruling 67–246, and Revenue Procedure 90–12 amplify that basic rule.

UNITED STATES v. AMERICAN BAR ENDOWMENT

Supreme Court of the United States, 1986
477 U.S. 105, 106 S.Ct. 2426, 91 L.Ed.2d 89

JUSTICE MARSHALL delivered the opinion of the Court.

The first issue in this case is whether income that a tax-exempt charitable organization derives from offering group insurance to its members constitutes "unrelated business income" subject to tax under §§ 511 through 513 of the Internal Revenue Code (Code), 26 U.S.C. §§ 511–153. The second issue is whether the organization's members may claim a charitable deduction for the portion of their premium payments that exceeds the actual cost to the organization of providing insurance.

I

Respondent American Bar Endowment (ABE) is a corporation exempt from taxation under § 501(c)(3) of the Code, which, with certain exceptions not relevant here, exempts organizations "organized and operated exclusively for ... charitable ... or educational purposes." ABE's primary purposes are to advance legal research and to promote the administration of justice, and it furthers these goals primarily through the distribution of grants to other charitable and educational groups. All members of the American Bar Association (ABA) are automatically members of ABE. The ABA is exempt from taxation as a "business league" under § 501(c)(6).

ABE raises money for its charitable work by providing group insurance policies, underwritten by major insurance companies, to its members. Approximately 20% of ABE's members participate in the group insurance program, which offers life, health, accident and disability policies. ABE negotiates premium rates with insurers and chooses which insurers shall provide the policies. It also compiles a list of its own members and solicits them, collects the premiums paid by its members, transmits those premiums to the insurer, maintains files on each policyholder, answers members' questions concerning insurance policies, and screens claims for benefits.

There are two important benefits of purchasing insurance as a group rather than individually. The first is that ABE's size gives it bargaining power that individuals lack. The second is that the group policy is experience-rated. This means that the cost of insurance to the group is based on that group's claims experience, rather than general actuarial tables. Because ABA members have favorable mortality and morbidity rates, experience-rating results in a substantially lower insurance cost. When ABE purchases a group policy for its members, it pays a negotiated premium to the insurance company. If, as is uniformly true, the insurance company's actual cost of providing insurance to the group is lower than the premium paid in a given year, the insurance company pays a refund of the excess, called a "dividend," to ABE. Critical to ABE's fundraising efforts is the fact that ABE requires its members to agree, as a condition of participating in the group insurance program, that they will permit ABE to keep all of the dividends rather than distributing them pro rata to the insured members.

It would be possible for ABE to negotiate lower premium rates for its members than the rates it has charged throughout the relevant period, and thus receive a lower dividend. However, ABE prices its policies competitively with other insurance policies offered to the public and to ABE members. 761 F.2d 1573, 1575 (CAFC 1985). In this way, ABE is able to generate large dividends to be used for its charitable purposes. In recent years the total amount of dividends has exceeded 40% of the members' premium payments. Ibid. ABE advises its insured members that each member's share of the dividends, less ABE's administrative costs, constitutes a tax-deductible contribution from the member to ABE. Thus the after-tax cost of ABE's insurance to its members is less than the cost of a commercial policy with identical coverage and premium rates.

In 1980 the Internal Revenue Service (IRS) advised ABE that it considered ABE's insurance plan an "unrelated trade or business" and that the profits thereon were subject to tax under §§ 511–513. Subsequently IRS audited ABE's tax returns for 1979 and 1980 and assessed a tax deficiency on ABE's net revenues from the insurance program. ABE paid those taxes, as well as taxes on the 1981 revenues. After exhausting administrative remedies, it brought an action for a refund in the Claims Court, arguing that its revenues from the insurance program were not subject to tax. At approximately the same time, the individual respondents, who were participants in the ABE insurance program but who had not originally deducted any part of the insurance premiums as charitable contributions, brought suit for refunds in the Claims Court as well. Individual respondents argued that they were entitled to charitable deductions for a portion of those premium payments. The two suits were consolidated for trial in the Claims Court.

The Claims Court entered judgment for ABE in its suit, finding that ABE's provision of insurance to its members did not constitute a "trade or business" subject to tax. * * * The Court of Appeals for the Federal Circuit affirmed as to ABE's taxes. * * * As to the individual respondents, however the court reversed and remanded for further factfinding. We granted the Government's petition for certiorari on both issues, * * *, and we now reverse.

II

* * *

[Note: The Supreme Court held that the income the ABE received from its group insurance program was unrelated business income.]

III

Section 170 of the Code provides that a taxpayer may deduct from taxable income any "charitable contribution," defined as "a contribution or gift to or for the use of" qualifying entities, § 170(c). The individual respondents contend that the excess of their premium payments over the cost to ABE of providing insurance constitutes a contribution or gift to ABE.

Many of the considerations supporting our holding that ABE's earnings from the insurance program are taxable also bear on the question whether ABE's members may deduct part of their premium payments. The evidence demonstrates, and the Claims Court found, that ABE's insurance is no more costly to its members than other policies—group or individual—available to them. Thus, as we have recognized, ABE's members are never faced with the hard choice of supporting a worthwhile charitable endeavor or reducing their own insurance costs.

A payment of money generally cannot constitute a charitable contribution if the contributor expects a substantial benefit in return. * * * However, as the Claims Court recognized, a taxpayer may sometimes receive only a nominal benefit in return for his contribution. Where the size of the payment is clearly out of proportion to the benefit received, it would not serve the purposes of § 170 to deny a deduction altogether. A taxpayer may therefore claim a deduction for the difference between a payment to a charitable organization and the market value of the benefit received in return, on the theory that the payment has the "dual character" of a purchase and a contribution. * * *

In Rev. Rul. 67–246, supra, the IRS set up a two-part test for determining when part of the "dual payment" is deductible. First, the payment is deductible only if and to the extent it exceeds the market value of the benefit received. Second, the excess payment must be "made with the intention of making a gift." * * * The Tax Court has adopted this test * * *.

The Claims Court applied that test in this case, and held that respondents Broadfoot, Boynton, and Turner and not established that they could have purchased comparable insurance for less money. Therefore, the court held, they had failed to establish that the value of ABE's insurance to them was less than the premiums paid. * * * Respondent Sherwood demonstrated that there did exist a group insurance program for which he was eligible and which offered lower premiums than ABE's insurance. However, Sherwood failed to establish that he was aware of that competing program during the years at issue. Sherwood therefore had failed to demonstrate that he met the second part of the above test—

that he had intentionally paid more than the market value for ABE's insurance because he wished to make a gift.

The Court of Appeals, in reversing, held that the Claims Court had focused excessively on the taxpayers' motivation. In the Court of Appeals' view, the necessary inquiry was whether "the transaction was ... of a business and not a charitable nature," considering all of the circumstances. * * * The Court of Appeals therefore remanded for redetermination under the standard.

We hold that the Claims Court applied the proper standard. The sine qua non of a charitable contribution is a transfer of money or property without adequate consideration. The taxpayer, therefore, must at a minimum demonstrate that he purposely contributed money or property in excess of the value of any benefit he received in return. The most logical test of the value of the insurance respondents received is the cost of similar policies. Three of the four individual respondents failed to demonstrate that they could have purchased similar policies for a lower cost, and we must therefore, assume that the value of ABE's insurance to those taxpayers at least equals their premium payments. Had respondent Sherwood known that he could purchase comparable insurance for less money, ABE's insurance would necessarily have declined in value to him. Because Sherwood did not have that knowledge however, we again must assume that he valued ABE's insurance equivalently to those competing policies of which he was aware. Because those policies cost as much as or more than ABE's Sherwood has failed to demonstrate that he intentionally gave away more that he received.

We further hold that the individual taxpayers have not established that any portion of their premium payments to ABE constituted a charitable contribution. Accordingly, we reverse the judgment of the Courts of Appeals and remand to that court with instructions to reverse the judgment of the Claims Court with respect to ABE and to affirm the judgment of the Claims Court with respect to the individual taxpayers.

It is so ordered.

* * *

REVENUE RULING 67–246

1967–2 C.B. 104

Deductibility, as charitable contributions under section 170 of the Internal Revenue Code of 1954, of payments made by taxpayers in connection with admission to or other participation in fund-raising activities for charity such as charity balls, bazaars, banquets, shows and athletic events.

Advice has been requested concerning certain fund-raising practices which are frequently employed by or on behalf of charitable organizations and which involve the deductibility, as charitable contributions under section 170 of the Internal Revenue Code of 1954, of payments in connection with admission to or other participation in fund-raising activities for charity such as charity balls, bazaars, banquets, shows, and athletic events.

Affairs of the type in question are commonly employed to raise funds for charity in two days. One is from profit derived from sale of admissions or other privileges or benefits connected with the event at such prices as their value warrants. Another is through the use of the affair as an occasion for solicitation of gifts in combination with the sale of the admissions or other privileges or benefits involved. In cases of the latter type the sale of the privilege or benefit is combined with solicitation of a gift or donation of some amount in addition to the sale value of the admission or privilege.

The need for guidelines on the subject is indicated by the frequency of misunderstanding of the requirements for deductibility of such payments and increasing incidence of their erroneous treatment for income tax purposes.

In particular, an increasing number of instances are being reported in which the public has been erroneously advised in advertisements or solicitations by sponsors that the entire amounts paid for tickets or other privileges in connection with fund-raising affairs for charity are deductible. Audits of returns are revealing other instances of erroneous advice and misunderstanding as to what, if any, portion of such payments is deductible in various circumstances. There is evidence also of instances in which taxpayers are being misled by questionable solicitation practices, which make it appear from the wording of the solicitation that taxpayer's payment is a "contribution," whereas the payment solicited is simply the purchase price of an item offered for sale by the organization.

Section 170 of the Code provides for allowance of deductions for charitable contributions, subjects to certain requirements and limitations. To the extent here relevant a charitable contribution is defined by that section as "a contribution or gift to or for the use of" certain specified types of organizations.

To be deductible as a charitable contribution for Federal income tax purposes under section 170 of the Code, a payment to or for the use of a qualified charitable organization must be a gift. To be a gift for such purposes in the present context there must be, among other requirements, a payment of money or transfer of property without adequate consideration.

As a general rule, where a transaction involving a payment is in the form of a purchase of an item of value, the presumption arises that no gift has been made for charitable contribution purposes, the presumption being that the payment in such case is the purchase price.

Thus, where consideration in the form of admissions or other privileges or benefits is received in connection with payments by patrons of fund-raising affairs of the type in question, the presumption is that the payments are not gifts. In such case, therefore, if a charitable contribution deduction is claimed with respect to the payment, the burden is on the taxpayer to establish that the amount paid is not the purchase price of the privileges or benefits and that part of the payment, in fact, does qualify as a gift.

In showing that a gift has been made, an essential element is proof that the portion of the payment claimed as a gift represents the excess of the total amount paid over the value of the consideration received therefore. This may be established by evidence that the payment exceeds the fair market value of the privileges or other benefits received by the amount claimed to have been paid as a gift.

Another element which is important in establishing that a gift was made in such circumstances, is evidence that the payment in excess of the value received was made with the intention of making a gift. While proof of such intention may not be an essential requirement under all circumstances, the intention to make a gift is, nevertheless, highly relevant in overcoming doubt in those cases in which there is a question whether an amount was in fact paid as a purchase price or as a gift.

Regardless of the intention of the parties, however, a payment of the type in question can in any event qualify as a deductible gift only to the extent that it is shown to exceed the fair market value of any consideration received in the form of privileges or other benefits.

In those cases in which a fund-raising activity is designed to solicit payments which are intended to be in part a gift and in part the purchase price of admission to or other participation in an event of the type in question, the organization conducting the activity should employ procedures which make clear not only that a gift is being solicited in connection with the sale of the admissions or other privileges related to the fund-raising event, but also, the amount of the gift being solicited. To do this, the amount properly attributable to the purchase of admissions or other privileges and the amount solicited as a gift should be determined in advance of solicitation. The respective amounts should be stated in making the solicitation and clearly indicated on any ticket, receipt, or other evidence issued in connection with the payment.

In making such a determination, the full fair market value of the admission and other benefits or privileges must be taken into account. Where the affair is reasonably comparable to events for which there are established charges for admission, such as theatrical or athletic performances, the established charges should be treated as fixing the fair market value of the admission or privilege. Where the amount paid is the same as the standard admission charge there is, of course, no deductible contribution, regardless of the intention of the parties. Where the event has no such counterpart, only that portion of the payment which exceeds a reasonable estimate of the fair market value of the admission or other privileges may be designed as a charitable contribution.

The fact that the full amount or a portion of the payment made by the taxpayer is used by the organization exclusively for charitable purposes has no bearing upon the determination to be made as to the value of the admission or other privileges and the amount qualifying as a contribution.

Also the mere fact that tickets or other privileges are not utilized does not entitle the patron to any greater charitable contribution deduction than would otherwise be allowable. The test of deductibility is not whether the right to admission or privileges is exercised but whether the right was accepted or rejected by the taxpayer. If a patron desires to support an affair, but does not intend to use the tickets or exercise the other privileges being offered with the event, he can make an outright gift of the amount he wishes to contribute, in which event he would not accept or keep any ticket or other evidence of any or the privileges related to the event connected with the solicitation.

The foregoing summary is not intended to be all inclusive of the legal requirements relating to deductibility of payments as charitable contributions for Federal income tax purposes. Neither does it attempt to deal with many of the refinements and distinctions, which sometimes arise in connection with questions of whether a gift for such purposes has been made in particular circumstances.

The principles stated are intended instead to summarize with as little complexity as possible, those basic rules, which govern deductibility of payments in the majority of the circumstances involved. They have their basis in section 170 of the Code, the regulations thereunder, and in court decisions. The observance of these provisions will provide greater assurance to taxpayer contributors that their claimed deductions in such cases are allowable.

Where it is disclosed that the public or the patrons of a fundraising affair for charity have been erroneously informed concerning the extent of the deductibility of their payments in connection with the affair, it necessarily follows that all charitable contribution deductions claimed with respect to payments made in connection with the particular event or affair will be subject to special scrutiny and may be questioned in audit of returns.

In the following examples application of the principles discussed above is illustrated in connection with various types of fund-raising activities for charity. Again, the examples are drawn to illustrate the general rules involved without attempting to deal with distinctions that sometimes arise in special situations. In each instance, the charitable organization involved is assumed to be an organization previously determined to be qualified to receive deductible charitable contributions under section 170 of the Code, and the references to deductibility are to deductibility as charitable contributions for Federal income tax purposes.

Example 1:

The M Charity sponsors a symphony concert for the purpose of raising funds for M's charitable programs. M agrees to pay a fee, which is calculated to reimburse the symphony for hall rental, musicians' salaries, advertising costs, and printing of tickets. Under the agreement,

M is entitled to all receipts from tickets sales. M sells tickets to the concert charging $5 for balcony seats and $10 for orchestra circle seats. These prices approximate the established admission charges for concert performances by the symphony orchestra. The tickets to the concert and the advertising material promoting ticket sales emphasize that the concert is sponsored by, and is for the benefit of M Charity.

Notwithstanding the fact that taxpayers who acquire tickets to the concert may think they are making a charitable contribution to or for the benefit of M Charity, no part of the payments made is deductible as a charitable contribution for Federal income tax purposes. Since the payments approximate the established admission charge for similar events, there is no gift. The result would be the same even if the advertising materials promoting ticket sales stated that amounts paid for tickets are "tax deductible" and tickets to the concert were purchased in reliance upon such statements. Acquisition of tickets or other privileges by a taxpayer in reliance upon statements made by a charitable organization that the amounts paid are deductible does not convert an otherwise nondeductible payment into a deductible charitable contribution.

Example 2:

The facts are the same as in Example 1, except that the M Charity desires to use the concert as an occasion for the solicitation of gifts. It indicates that fact in its advertising material promoting the event, and fixes the payments solicited in connection with each class of admission at $30 for orchestra circle seats and $15 for balcony seats. The advertising and the tickets clearly reflect the fact that the established admission charges for comparable performances by the symphony orchestra are $10 for orchestra circle seats and $5 for balcony seats, and that only the excess of the solicited amounts paid in connection with admission to the concert over the established prices is a contribution to M. Under these circumstances a taxpayer who makes a payment of $60 and receives two orchestra circle seat tickets can show that his payment exceeds the established admission charge for similar tickets to comparable performances of the symphony orchestra by $40. The circumstances also confirm that that amount of the payment was solicited as, and intended to be, a gift to M Charity. The $40, therefore, is deductible as a charitable contribution.

Example 3:

A taxpayer pays $5 for a balcony ticket to the concert described in Example 1. This taxpayer had no intention of using the ticket when he acquired it and he did not, in fact, attend the concert.

No part of the taxpayer's $5 payment to the M Charity is deductible as a charitable contribution. The mere fact that the ticket to the concert was not used does not entitle the taxpayer to any greater right to a deduction than if he did use it. The same result would follow if the taxpayer had made a gift of the ticket to another individual. If the taxpayer desired to support M, but did not intend to use the ticket to the concert, he could have made a qualifying charitable contribution by making a $5 payment to M and refusing to accept the ticket to the concert.

Example 4:

A receives a brochure soliciting contributions for the support of the M Charity. The brochure states: "As a grateful token of appreciation for your help, the M Charity will send to you your choice of one of the several articles listed below, depending upon the amount of your donation." The remainder of the brochure is devoted to a catalog-type listing of articles of merchandise with the suggested amount of donation necessary to receive each particular article. There is no evidence of any significant difference between the suggested donation and the fair market value of any such article. The brochure contains the further notation that all donations to M Charity are tax deductible.

Payments of the suggested amounts solicited by M Charity are not deductible as a charitable contribution. Under the circumstances, the amounts solicited, as "donations" are simply the purchase prices of the articles listed in the brochure.

Example 5:

A taxpayer paid $5 for a ticket, which entitled him to a chance to win a new automobile. The raffle was conducted to raise funds for the X Charity. Although the payment for the ticket was solicited as a "contribution" to the X Charity and designated as such on the face of the ticket, no part of the payment is deductible as a charitable contribution. Amounts paid for chances to participate in raffles, lotteries, or similar drawings or to participate in puzzle or other contests for valuable prizes are not gifts in such circumstances, and therefore, do not qualify as deductible charitable contributions.

Example 6:

A women's club, which serves principally as an auxiliary of the X Charity, holds monthly membership luncheon meetings. Following the luncheon and any entertainment that may have been arranged, the members transact any membership business, which may be required attendance of the luncheon meetings is promoted through the advance sale of tickets. * * *

While the ticket does not specifically state that the amount is tax deductible, the characterization of the $5.50 price of the ticket as a "donation" is highly misleading in that it is done in a context which suggests that the price of the ticket is a charitable contribution and, therefore, tax deductible. On the facts recited, no part of the payment is deductible, since there is no showing that any part of the price of the ticket is in fact a gift of an amount in excess of the fair market value of the luncheon and entertainment.

Example 7:

In support of its summer festival program of 10 free public concerts, the M Symphony, a charitable organization, mails out brochures soliciting contributions from its patrons. The brochure recites the purposes and activities of the organization, and as an inducement to contributors states that:

> "A contribution of $20 entitles the donor to festival membership for the season and free admission to the premiere showing of the motion picture * * * and * * *.

Cocktails—7:00 P.M. Curtain–8:15 P.M.

This special premiere performance is not open to the public.

* * *

"Your contribution will benefit an important community function; it also entitles you to choice reserved seats for all summer festival concerts and events."

The envelope furnished for mailing in payments contains the following:

> "Enclosed is my tax-deductible membership contribution to the M Symphony summer concert program in the amount of $_." Send me–tickets to the May 1 premiere performance. "I do not desire to attend the special premiere performance for festival members, but I am enclosing my contribution."

A taxpayer mails in a payment of $20, indicating on the envelope form that he desires a ticket to the premiere showing of the film.

No part of the payment is deductible as a charitable contribution. Payment of the $20 entitles an individual not only to the privilege of attending the cocktail party and the premiere showing of the film, but also the privilege of choice reserved seats for the summer festival concerts. Under the circumstances, no part of the payment qualifies as a gift, since there is no showing that the payment exceeds the fair market value of the privileges involved. Even if a "contributor" indicates he does not desire to attend the cocktail party and premiere showing of the film, it would still be incorrect for the organization to characterize the $20 payment as a deductible charitable contribution, since under these circumstances the fair market value of the privilege of having choice reserved seats for attending the concerts would, in all likelihood, exceed the amount of the payment. However, if the taxpayer wishes to support the M Symphony, and advises the organization that he does not desire the ticket to the premiere and does not want seats reserved for him, the amount contributed to M is deductible as a charitable contribution.

Example 8:

> In order to raise funds, W Charity plans a theater party consisting of admission to a premiere showing of a motion picture and an after-theater buffet. The advertising material and tickets to the theater party designate $5 as an admission charge and $10 as a gift to W Charity. The established admission charge for premiere showings of motion pictures in the locality is $5.

Notwithstanding W's representations respecting the amount designated as a gift, the specified $10 does not qualify as a deductible charitable contribution because W's allocation fails to take into account the value of admission to the buffet dinner.

Example 9:

The X Charity sponsors a fund-raising bazaar, the articles offered for sale at the bazaar having been contributed to X by persons desiring to support X's charitable programs. The prices for the articles sold at the bazaar are set by a committee of X with a view to charging the full fair market value of the articles.

A taxpayer who purchases articles at the bazaar is not entitled to a charitable contribution deduction for any portion of the amount paid to X for such articles. This is true even though the articles sold at the bazaar are acquired and sold without cost to X and the total proceeds of the sale of the articles are used by X exclusively for charitable purposes.

Example 10:

The members of the M Charity undertake a program of selling Christmas cards to raise funds for the organization's activities. The cards are purchased at wholesale prices and are resold at prices comparable to the prices at which similar cards are sold by regular retail outlets. On the receipts furnished to its customers, the difference between the amount received from the customer and the wholesale cost of the cards to the organization is designated by the organization as a tax-deductible charitable contribution.

The organization is in error in designating this difference as a tax-deductible charitable contribution. The amount paid by customers in excess of the wholesale cost of the cards to the organization is not a gift to the organization, but instead is part of the purchase price or the fair market value of the cards at the retail level.

Example 11:

In support of the annual fund-raising drive of the X Charity, a local department store agrees to award a transistor radio to each person who contributes $50 or more to the charity. The retail value of the radio is $15. B receives one of the transistor radios as a result of his contribution of $100 to X. Only $85 of B's payment to X qualifies as a deductible charitable contribution. In determining the portion of the payment to a charitable organization, which is deductible as a charitable contribution in these circumstances, the fair market value of any consideration received for the payment from any source must be subtracted from the total payment.

Example 12:

To assist the Charity in the promotion of a Halloween Ball to raise funds for Y's activities, several individuals in the community agree to pay the entire costs of the event, including the costs of the orchestra, publicity, and rental of the ballroom, refreshments, and any other necessary expenses. Various civic organizations and clubs agree to undertake the sale of tickets for the dance. The publicity and solicitations for the sale of the tickets emphasize the fact that the entire cost of the ball is being borne by anonymous patrons of Y and by the other community groups, and that the entire gross receipts from the sale of the tickets, therefore, will go to Y Charity. The price of the tickets, however, is set at the fair market value of admission to the event.

No part of the amount paid for admission to the dance is a gift. Therefore, no part is deductible as a charitable contribution. The fact that the event is conducted entirely without cost to Y Charity and that the full amount of the admission charge goes directly to Y for its uses has no bearing on the deductibility of the amounts paid for admission, but does have a bearing on the deductibility of the amounts paid by the anonymous patrons of the event. The test is not the cost of the event to Y, but the fair market value of the consideration received by the purchaser of the ticket or other privileges for his payment.

REVENUE PROCEDURE 90–12

1990–1 C.B. 471

SEC. 1. PURPOSE

These guidelines are intended to provide charitable organizations with help in advising their patrons of the deductible amount of contributions under section 170 of the Code when the contributors are receiving something in return for their contributions. These guidelines will also be used by agents in determining whether charities have provided accurate information about deductibility to their contributors.

SEC. 2. BACKGROUND

.01 Recently, the Congress expressed concern that charities do not accurately inform their patrons of the extent to which contributions are deductible. In expressing its concern, the Congress stated that it "anticipates that the Internal Revenue Service will monitor the extent to which taxpayers are being furnished accurate and sufficient information by charitable organizations as to the nondeductibility of payments to such organizations where benefits or privileges are received in return, so that taxpayers can correctly compute their Federal income tax liability." H.R. Rep. No. 100–391, 100th Cong., 1st Sess. 1608 (1987).

.02 In August 1988, the Service sent publication 1391, Deductibility of Payments Made to Charities Conducting Fund–Raising Events, to over 400,000 charities. Publication 1391 contains a message from the Commissioner of the Internal Revenue Service asking charities for help in informing contributors more accurately about the deductibility of contributions made in connection with fund-raising events and programs.

.03 Publication 1391 also contains a copy of Rev. Rul. 67–246, 1967–2 C.B 104, which discusses the rules that apply in determining the amount of the charitable contribution under section 170 of the Code when something of value is received in return for the contribution. Rev. Rul. 67–246 also sets forth a simple procedure that charities can use to provide "accurate and sufficient" information to their contributors.

.04 Rev. Rul. 67–246 asks charities to determine the fair market value of the benefits offered for contributions in advance of a solicitation and to state in the solicitation and in tickets, receipts, or other documents issued in connection with a contribution how much is deductible under section 170 of the Code and how much is not. If charities are unable to make an exact determination of the fair market value of the benefits, Rev. Rul. 67–246 indicates that they should use a reasonable estimate of fair market value.

.05 Many charities have suggested that this determination is difficult or burdensome particularly in the case of small items or other benefits that are of token value in relation to the amount contributed. The Service has determined that a benefit may be so inconsequential or insubstantial that the full amount of a contribution is deductible under section 170 of the Code. Under the following guidelines, charities offering certain small items or other benefits of token value may advise contributors that contributions are fully deductible under section 170.

SEC. 3. GUIDELINES

.01 Benefits received in connection with a payment to a charity will be considered to have insubstantial fair market value for purposes of advising patrons if the requirements of paragraphs 1 and 2 are met:

> 1. The payment occurs in the context of a fund-raising campaign in which the charity informs patrons how much of their payment is a deductible contribution, and either 2. (a) The fair market value of all of the benefits received in connection with the payment, is not more that 2 percent of the payment, or $50, whichever is less, or (b) The payment is $25 (adjusted for inflation as described below) or more and the only benefits received in connection with the payment are token items (bookmarks, calendars, key chains, mugs, posters, tee shirts, etc.) bearing the organization's name or logo. The cost (as opposed to fair market value) of all of the benefits received by a donor must, in the aggregate, be within the limits established for "low cost articles" under section 513(h)(2) of the Code. (Generally, under section 170, the deductible amount of the contribution is determined by taking into account the fair market value, not the cost to the charity, of any benefits received in return. For administrative reasons, however, in the limited circumstances of this subparagraph, the cost of the charity may be used in determining whether the benefits are insubstantial.)

.02 For purposes of paragraph 1 of section 3.02, above, a qualifying fund-raising campaign is one designed to raise tax-deductible contributions, in which the charity determines the fair market value of the benefits offered in return for contributions (using a reasonable estimate if an exact determination is not possible), and states in its solicitations (whether written, broadcast, telephoned, or in person)—as well as in tickets, receipts, or other documents issued in connection with contributions—how much is deductible under section 170 of the Code and how much is not. If a charity is providing only insubstantial benefits in return for a payment, fund-raising materials should include a statement to the effect that: "Under Internal Revenue Service guidelines the estimated value of the [the benefits received] is not substantial; therefore; the full amount of your payment is a deductible contribution."

03. There may be situations in which it is impractical to state in every solicitation how much of a payment is deductible. For example, where a nonprofit broadcasting organization offers a number premiums in an on-air fund-raising announcement, it may be unduly cumbersome to include information on the fair market value of each premium. If a charity believes that stating how much is deductible in every statement is impractical, it may seek a ruling from the Service concerning an alternative procedure. The Service will rule on whether the alternative procedure meets the Congressionally mandated goal of providing accurate and sufficient information to contributors. See Rev. Proc. 90–4 1990–2 I.R.B. 15.

.04 For purposes of paragraph 2 of section 3.01 above, newsletters or program guides (other than commercial quality publications) will be treated as if they do not have a measurable fair market value or cost if their primary purpose is to inform members about the activities of an organization and if they are not available to nonmembers by paid subscription or through newsstand sales. Whether a publication is considered a commercial quality publication depends upon all of the facts and circumstances. Generally, publications that contain articles written for compensation and that accept advertising will be treated as commercial quality publications having measurable fair market value or cost. Professional journals (whether or not articles are written for compensation and advertising is accepted) will normally be treated as commercial quality publications. For purposes of subparagraph (b) of paragraph 2, the cost of a commercial quality publication include the costs of production and distribution and must be computed without regard to income from advertising or newsstand or subscription sales.

.05 In applying paragraph 2, the total amount of a pledge payable in installments will be considered to be the amount of the payment. Also, benefits provided by charities in the form of cash or its equivalent will never be considered insubstantial.

.06 For purposes subparagraph (b) of paragraph 2, an item is a "low cost article" under section 513 (h)(2) of the Code if its cost does not exceed $5, increased for years after 1987 by a cost-of-living adjustment under section 1(f)(3). The $25 payment required in subparagraph (b) of paragraph 2 must also be increased, in the same manner. For calendar year 1990, the cost of a "low cost article" under section 513 (h)(2) cannot exceed $5.45. The adjusted required payment is $27.26. See Rev. Proc. 90–7, 1990–3 I.R.B. 8.

.07 For purposes of subparagraph (b) of paragraph 2, if items offered to contributors are donated to the charity or if services are donated in connection with the production of an item, the cost "to the organization" for purposes of section 513(h)(2) of the Code will be a reasonable estimate of the amount the organization would have to pay for the items or services in question.

.08 These guidelines describe a safe harbor; depending on the facts in each case, benefits received in connection with contributions may be "insubstantial" even if they do not meet these guidelines.

SEC. 4. EXAMPLES

The following examples illustrate the application of the guidelines. In each example, it is assumed that the charity is engaged in a fundraising campaign which informs patrons how much of their payment is tax deductible as required by paragraph 1 section 3.01.

Example 1. A zoo gives its patrons lapel pins reading "Friends of the Small City Zoo" in return for payments of $15. The fair market value of the lapel pin is $.25. Since the fair market value of the pin is less than 2 percent of the payment (and the fair market value of the pin is less than $50), the zoo may advise its patrons that the full amount of the payment is a deductible contribution.

Example 2. Assume the same facts as Example 1, except that the zoo also sends patrons a newsletter the primary purpose of which is to inform members about the activities of the zoo. The newsletter is not available to nonmembers by paid subscription or through newsstand sales. Moreover, it is not a "commercial quality publication" as described in section 3.04, above. Since the newsletter has no fair market value and the fair market value of the pin is less than 2 percent of the payment (and less than $50), the zoo may advise its patrons that the full amount of the payment is a deductible contribution.

Example 3. For a payment of $15, a museum sends its patrons a bulletin the primary purpose of which is to inform members about coming events at the museum. The bulletin is not available to nonmembers by paid subscription or through newsstand sales. The bulletin is written by a salaried staff member at the museum, but it accepts no advertising. It is printed on magazine quality paper and it is distributed on a quarterly basis. Under the facts and circumstances, the bulletin is not a "commercial quality publication" as described in section 3.04, above. Since the bulletin has no fair market value for purposes of paragraph 2 the museum may advise its patrons that the full amount of the payment is a deductible contribution.

Example 4. In 1990, a nonprofit broadcast organization sends its patrons a listener's guide for one year in return for a contribution of $30. The cost of production and distribution of the listener's guide is $4 per year per patron and its fair market value is $6. The listener's guide is not available to nonmembers by paid subscription or through newsstand sales. It is written by a salaried staff member at the broadcast organization and it accepts advertising. The listener's guide, therefore, is a "commercial quality publication" as described in section 3.04, above. However, since the cost of the listener's guide is $4 and it is received in return for a contribution of $30, the broadcast organization may advise its patrons that the full amount of the payment is a deductible contribution.

Example 5. Assume the same facts as Example 4, except that the nonprofit broadcast organization also gives its patrons a coffee mug with the organization's logo. The cost of a mug to the organization is $3. Its fair market value is $5. Since the listener's guide costs $4 and the coffee mug costs $3, their aggregate cost exceeds the 1990 limit of section 513(h)(2) of $5.45. The organization should inform its patrons that $19 of their contribution is deductible and $11 is not. The result would be the same even if these benefits were received separately in return for two separate contributions of $30 each. Under section 513(h)(2), the cost of all the low cost items received in one year is aggregated in determining whether the limit is exceeded.

* * *

Notes

1. For taxable years beginning in 2006, the $5, $25, and $50 guidelines in section 3 of Revenue Procedure 90–12, have been increased to $8.60, $44, and $86, respectively (Revenue Procedure 2005–70, I.R.B. 2005–47, 979).

2. Revenue Procedure 92–49, 1992–1 C.B. 987, amplified Revenue Procedure 90–12 by advising potential contributors that the full amount of a contribution is deductible under § 170 if the fundraising campaign follows the requirements of Revenue Procedure 90–12 and meets the following requirements:

(1) The charity mails or otherwise distributes free, unordered items to patrons. To meet this requirement, any item received by a patron must not have been distributed at the patron's request or with the express consent of the patron. Any item distributed must be accompanied by a request for a charitable contribution and by a statement that the patron may retain the item whether or not the patron makes a contribution.

(2) The cost (as opposed fair market value of all such items) in the aggregate, distributed by or on behalf of the organization to a single patron in a calendar year, is within the limits established for "low cost articles" in § 513(h) of the Code.

B. Services

Many individuals give their time, rather than their money or property, to charitable organizations. The value of those services is not deductible [Treas. Reg. § 1.170A–1(g), (h)(2)]. Reasonable expenses related to performing the services, however are deductible.

The reason for denial of services is not as draconian as it sounds. Most donors are cash-basis taxpayers. That means that they do not recognize any income or deductions until cash or cash equivalents are received or paid. Moreover, when an individual helps a charitable organization by donating her time, that time is either leisure time or forgone earnings opportunities. In either case, the individual has not earned income from which a matching deduction should be allowed.

If the service provider is a corporation, it will receive a deduction. As an entity, a corporation provides service through agents who receive compensation for their time and effort. The corporation is entitled to deduct the amount it pays to an agent either as a business deduction under § 162(a) or a charitable contribution under § 170(a).

C. Timing

A charitable contribution is deductible in the year it is paid regardless of the taxpayer's accounting method. [See Treas. Reg. § 1.170A–1(a).] An exception applies to certain corporations using the accrual method of accounting. [See IRC § 170(a)(2).] An accrual-based corporation may deduct a charitable contribution in the year it is accrued if the board of directors authorized the gift and pays for the gift by the 15th day of the fourth month in the subsequent taxable year.

D. Unconditional Gift

A charitable gift is deductible only if it is given unconditionally to a charity. An unconditional gift is made when it is delivered [Treas. Reg. § 1.170A–1(b)]. The regulations require that the delivery be absolute, that is, not subject to any conditions unless a condition is so remote as not likely to happen [Treas. Reg. § 170A–1(e)].

A check is delivered when it is given or mailed to the charitable organization, is given unconditionally, and clears in due course. A stock certificate is delivered when it is given or mailed to the charitable organization if it is given unconditionally and, if mailed, the organization receives the certificate in the ordinary course of the mails. If a donor gives the certificate to an agent of the issuing corporation, delivery occurs when the stock is transferred on the books of the corporation.

A pledge to a charitable organization is not deductible when the pledge is given. Payments in satisfaction of the pledge, however, are deductible in the year payments are made. (See Rev. Rul. 68–174, 1968–1 C.B. 81.) Similarly, a donation of a promissory note to a charitable organization is not deductible until payments are made. Payment of a gift by a credit card is deductible in the year the amount of the gift is charged to the donor's account (Rev. Rul. 78–38, 1978–1. C.B. 67).

E. Amount of Deduction

The amount of charitable contribution deduction a taxpayer may take depends upon two factors: (a) the amount of the charitable contribution and (b) the percentage limitations.

1. Amount of Contribution

Obviously, the amount of a cash charitable contribution is the amount of money delivered to the charitable organization. The problem area concerns gifts of property.

The starting point for gifts of property is the fair market value of the property [Treas. Reg. § 1.170A–1(c)(6)]. However, as noted below, a donor is not always entitled to deduct the fair market value of the property. The donor may be required to reduce the amount of the deduction by some or all of the property's appreciation, as noted below.

Property that a taxpayer donates normally has appreciated or depreciated in value since the date the taxpayer acquired the property. Because a gift of property is not a sale or exchange of the property, gain or loss is not recognized. The question, therefore, is whether the taxpayer should adjust the deductible amount of a property donation to recognize the difference between the fair market value of the property as of the date of the gift and the taxpayer's adjusted basis.[2] The answer is that the taxpayer may be required to reduce the deductible amount of the donation by the amount of any appreciation (I.R.C. § 170(e); Treas. Reg. § 1.170A–3].

Without a particular non-tax reason for making a gift, a taxpayer should never give to a charity property that has depreciated in value if the taxpayer could deduct a loss for tax purposes from the sale or exchange of the property. The taxpayer is better off selling the property and donating the proceeds to the charity. Why?

The consequence of donating property that has appreciated depends upon the kind of property: long-term capital gain property or ordinary income property.

2. Long–Term Capital Gain Property

Long-term capital gain property is property that qualifies as a capital asset and that the taxpayer has held for more than one year. [See I.R.C. § 1222(3).] A capital asset is property held for personal and investment purposes. However, for purposes of § 170(e), depreciable property used in trade or business (so-called § 1231 assets) qualify as long-term capital gain property except to the extent the property is subject to depreciation recapture. (A discussion of the depreciation recapture rules is beyond the scope of this text.)

Subject to two exceptions, a taxpayer is entitled to deduct the full value of long-term capital gain property. That is, no reduction is required.

The first exception is as follows. If a taxpayer donates personal property that is not related to a charity's exempt purpose, the amount of the charitable contribution is the property's adjusted basis [I.R.C. § 170

---

2. The "adjusted basis" of property is the property's cost (or other basis if the property was acquired by gift or by bequest) plus cost of any improvements to the property and less any depreciation allowed or allowable for tax purposes with respect to the property. See I.R.C. §§ 1011, 1012, 1014, 1015, and 1016.

(2)(1)(B)].[3] For example, a taxpayer who donates art to an exempt scientific organization may deduct only her basis (generally cost) in the art work.

The second exception applies to gifts of long-term capital gain property to a private nonoperating foundation (discussed in chapter 7). [See I.R.C. § 170(e)(1)(B)(ii).] A taxpayer must reduce a gift to a private nonoperating foundation by any gain the taxpayer would have recognized had the taxpayer sold the property. However, this exception does not apply to stock sold over an established securities market. [See I.R.C. § 170(e)(5).]

It is obvious then that the long-term capital gain property rule, wherein the donor may deduct the full fair market value of a property donation, applies to real estate, securities, intangibles that are capital assets, and related tangible personal property.

Note

Section 170(e)(1)(B)(iii) of the Internal Revenue Code limits the charitable contribution deduction for patents and other intellectual property to the lesser of the taxpayer's basis in the property or the property's fair market value. The limit applies to patents, copyrights, trademarks, trade names, trade secrets, know-how, software, and similar property. However, pursuant to § 170(m), a taxpayer who has donated such intellectual property may claim a charitable contribution deduction in later years equal to a percentage of the income that the charity receives from such patent or other intellectual property. In the first two years, the donor's addition contribution is 100 percent of the income received by the charity, but the percentage decreases 10 percent each year beginning in the third year so that in the eleventh and twelfth year, it is 10 percent of the charity's net income from the property. After the twelfth year, the donor cannot claim a charitable contribution deduction. Charitable donees must give the donor a report annually setting out the amount of net income it received from the donated property.

3. Ordinary Income Producing Property

Any property that is not long-term capital gain property produces ordinary income upon a sale. Such property includes a capital asset a taxpayer holds for less than one year, § 1231 assets to the extent of depreciation recapture, inventory, and other property that is not a capital asset. With the exceptions mentioned below, a taxpayer must reduce the fair market value of such property by the amount of ordinary gain the taxpayer would have realized had the taxpayer sold the property. [See I.R.C. § 170(e)(1)(A).]

The first exception to the above rule applies to certain corporate contributions of inventory to charities other than private foundations if

---

3. Congress added a third exception in IRC § 170(e)(B)(i). For contributions after September 1, 2006, the adjusted basis is the deductible amount if the donee transfers related tangible property and the donee dispenses of such property before the last day of the taxable year in which the contribution was made and the donee has not made a certification under IRC § 170(e)(7)(D).

(a) the inventory is related to the charity's exempt purpose; (b) the charity does not sell the inventory and uses it solely for the care of the ill, the needy, or infants; (c) the charity gives the taxpayer a written statement representing (a) and (b); and (d) with respect to property subject to the Federal Food, Drug and Cosmetic Act, the property satisfies the requirements of the Act and its regulations on the date of the gift and for 180 days prior to the date of the gift. [See I.R.C. § 170(e)(3)(A).] With respect to such property, the taxpayer must reduce the charitable contribution deduction by 50 percent of the amount that would have been a gain had the taxpayer sold the inventory. The 50 percent rule also applies to certain contributions of scientific property used for research [I.R.C. § 170(e)(4)] and certain contributions of computer technology and equipment for educational purposes [I.R.C. § 170(e)(6)].

4. Percentage Limitations

Congress has always thought that a donor should not be able to avoid payment of any income tax by means of charitable contributions. Consequently, over the years, Congress has enacted a series of extremely complicated rules to limit the amount of a deduction a donor-taxpayer may take in a tax year. Congress' response was not so much to disallow charitable contribution deductions as to spread them out so that a taxpayer could not bunch them into a single year. It did this by enacting annual limitation and carry forward rules, discussed below. The reason for annual limitations on the amount of a charitable contribution deduction relates to our progressive tax system and the worth of aggregating deductions in one year as opposed to spreading such deductions over many years.

An individual taxpayer first calculates the amount of a charitable contribution deduction by applying the rules discussed above. The taxpayer then must determine the maximum deduction for the current tax year. The amount of the percentage limitations for an individual depends upon the classification of the donee to whom a gift is made and the type of property donated. The annual limitation is a percentage of a taxpayer's "contribution base," defined as a taxpayer's "adjusted gross income (computed without regard to any net operating loss carryback to the taxable year under section 172)." [See I.R.C. § 170(b)(1)(F).]

The maximum deduction that a taxpayer may take for donations to public charities (discussed in Chapter 6) and private operating foundations (discussed in Chapter 7) is 50 percent of the taxpayer's contribution base. The deduction for gifts to private nonoperating foundations (discussed in Chapter 7) is limited to 30 percent of the taxpayer's contribution base. In no case, however, may a taxpayer deduct more than 50 percent of a taxpayer's contribution base. For example, assume that a taxpayer with a contribution base of $100,000 makes the following gifts in cash or check during the year:

(a) $10,000 to the university from which she graduated and $40,000 to the Family Private Foundation;

(b) $30,000 to the university from which she graduated and $30,000 to the Family Private Foundation;

(c) $50,000 to the university from which she graduated and $10,000 to the Family Private Foundation; and

(d) Nothing to the University and $50,000 to the Family Private Foundation.

Her maximum charitable contribution for the taxable year is:

(a) $30,000 ($10,000 to university and $30,000 to Foundation); (b) $50,000 ($30,000 to university and $20,000 to Foundation); (c) $50,000 (all attributed to gift to university); and (d) $30,000.

A specific limitation applies to long-term capital gain property that is not reduced pursuant to § 170(e). The maximum amount that a taxpayer may deduct is 30 percent of the taxpayer's contribution base. [See I.R.C. § 170(b)(1)(C)(i).] The taxpayer can elect, however, to have the amount of the contribution reduced by the amount of the appreciation and increase the maximum deduction to 50 percent of the taxpayer's contribution base. [See I.R.C. § 170(b)(1)(C)(ii).])

A gift of capital gain property to a private nonoperating foundation is subject to two restrictions. The first is the § 170(e) reduction for any appreciation over the adjusted basis of the property. The second is a specific percentage limitation under § 170(b). Section 170(b)(1)(D) limits the maximum deduction of such property to 20 percent of the taxpayer's contribution base. Because of these various percentage limitations, the Code requires that charitable contributions be considered in the following order:

(a) Gifts subject to 50 percent limitation;

(b) Gifts to private nonoperating foundations subject to the 30 percent limitation;

(c) Gifts of long-term capital gain property subject to the 30 percent limitation; and

(d) Gifts of capital gain property to private foundations subject to the 20 percent limitation.

The percentage limitation for corporate gifts of money is 10 percent of the corporation's taxable income. [See I.R.C. § 170 (b)(2).] A corporation calculates its taxable income without deducting organization expenses under § 248, any net operating loss carryback under § 172, and a capital loss carryback under § 1212 (a)(1).

5. Carryforward of Charitable Contribution Deduction

When the amount of a contribution exceeds the percentage limitations prescribed by § 170(b), the excess of the contribution over the allowable deduction may be carried forward for five years. [See I.R.C.

§ 170(d).] While this rule is easy enough to state, its application is more complicated especially when a taxpayer may carry over contributions from the different percentage limitation categories.

Carryforwards are deducted in the following order:

(a) Fifty-percent gifts in excess of current year 50–percent gifts. The carryover amounts are applied on an annual basis, the earliest year first.

(b) Carryovers of gifts to 30–percent charities.

(c) Carryovers of 30–percent capital gain property.

(d) Carryovers of 20–percent capital gain property.

Within each of the categories, the earliest year's carryforward is applied first, and then successive years.

Corporations also may carry forward any charitable contribution in excess of the 10 percent limitation for five years. [See I.R.C. 170(d)(2).] Current year charitable contributions are deducted first. If a corporation still has reductions capacity, a carry forward is deducted.

F. Appraisals of Donated Property

How does a donor determine the amount of a charitable contribution deduction for a donation of long-term capital gain property? As noted, previously, the amount of the deduction is the property's fair market value on the date of the gift. The donor's estimate of the fair market value may differ significantly from that of the Internal Revenue Service, particularly with respect to art objects, antiques, and other cultural property. A taxpayer is subject to substantial penalties should the donor claim a deduction that is substantially higher than the property's actual value. Thus, the donor is required to have property appraised prior to donating it to a charity if the property's value exceeds $5,000. (See Treas. Reg. § 170A–13.)

The Internal Revenue Service has published guidelines for making appraisals of donated properties such as art objects, literary manuscripts, and antiques.

REVENUE PROCEDURE 66–49

1966–2 C.B. 1257

A procedure to be used as a guideline by all persons making appraisals of donated property for Federal income tax purposes.

SECTION 1. PURPOSE.

The purpose of this procedure is to provide information and guidelines for taxpayers, individual appraisers, and valuation groups relative to appraisals of contributed property for Federal income tax purposes. The procedures outlined are applicable to all types of noncash property for which an appraisal is required such as real property, tangible or intangible personal property, and securities. These procedures are also appropriate for unique properties such as art objects, literary manuscripts, antiques, etc., with respect to which the determination of value often is more difficult.

SEC. 2. LAW AND REGULATIONS.

.01 Numerous sections of the Internal Revenue Code of 1954, as amended, give rise to a determination of value for Federal tax purposes; however, the significant section for purposes of this Revenue Procedure is section 170, Charitable, Etc., Contributions and Gifts.

.02 Value is defined in section 1.170—1(c) of the Income Tax Regulations as follows:

> * * *. The fair market value is the price at which the property would change hands between a willing buyer and a willing seller, neither being under any compulsion to buy or sell and both having reasonable knowledge of relevant facts. * * *

.03 This section further provides that:

> * * *. If the contribution is made in property of a type which the taxpayer sells in the course of his business, the fair market value is the price which the taxpayer would have received if he had sold the contributed property in the lowest usual market in which he customarily sells, at the time and place of contribution (and in the case of a contribution of goods in quantity, in the quantity contributed). * * *

.04 As to the measure of proof in determining the fair market value, all factors bearing on value are relevant including, where pertinent, the cost, or selling price of the item, sales of comparable properties, cost of reproduction, opinion evidence and appraisals. Fair market value depends upon value in the market and not on intrinsic worth.

.05 The cost or actual selling price of an item within a reasonable time before or after the valuation date may be the best evidence of its fair market value. Before such information is taken into account, it must be ascertained that the transaction was at arm's length and that the parties were fully informed as to all relevant facts. Absent such evidence, even the sales price of the item in question will not be persuasive.

.06 Sales of similar properties are often given probative weight by the courts in establishing fair market value. The weight to be given such evidence will be affected by the degree of similarity to the property under appraisal and the proximity of the date of sale to the valuation date.

.07 With respect to reproductive cost as a measure of fair market value, it must be shown that there is a probative correlation between the cost of reproduction and fair market value. Frequently, reproductive cost will be in excess of the fair market value.

.08 Generally, the weight to be given to opinion evidence depends on its origin and the thoroughness with which it is supported by experience and facts. It is only where expert opinion is supported by facts having strong probative value, that the opinion testimony will in itself be given appropriate weight. The underlying facts must corroborate the opinion; otherwise such opinion will be discounted or disregarded.

.09 The weight to be accorded any appraisal made either at or after the valuation date will depend largely upon the competence and knowledge of the appraiser with respect to the property and the market for such property.

SEC. 3. APPRAISAL FORMAT.

.01 When it becomes necessary to secure an appraisal in order to determine the values of items for Federal income tax purposes, such appraisals should be obtained from qualified and reputable sources, and the appraisal report should accompany the return when it is filed. The more complete the information filed with a tax return the more unlikely it will be that the Internal Revenue Service will find it necessary to question items on it. Thus, when reporting a deduction for charitable contributions on an income tax return, it will facilitate the review and the acceptance of the returned values if any appraisals which have been secured are furnished. The above-mentioned regulations prescribe that support of values claimed should be submitted and a properly prepared appraisal by a person qualified to make such an appraisal may well constitute the necessary substantiation. In this respect, it is not intended that all value determinations be supported by formal written appraisals as outlined in detail below. This is particularly applicable to minor items of property or where the value of the property is easily ascertainable by methods other than appraisal.

.02 In general, an appraisal report should contain at least the following:

(1) A summary of the appraiser's qualifications.

(2) A statement of the value and the appraiser's definition of the value he has obtained.

(3) The bases upon which the appraisal was made, including any restrictions, understandings, or covenants limiting the use or disposition of the property.

(4) The date as of which the property was valued.

(5) The signature of the appraiser and the date the appraisal was made.

.03 An example of the kind of data which should be contained in a typical appraisal is included below. This relates to the valuation of art objects, but a similar detailed breakdown can be outlined for any type of property. Appraisals of art objects, paintings in particular, should include:

(1) A complete description of the object, indicating the size, the subject matter, the medium, the name of the artist, approximate date created, the interest transferred, etc.

(2) The cost, date, and manner of acquisition.

(3) A history of the item including proof of authenticity such as a certificate of authentication if such exists.

(4) A photograph of a size and quality fully identifying the subject matter, preferably a 10" x 12" or larger print.

(5) A statement of the factors upon which the appraisal was based, such as:

>(a) Sales of other works by the same artist particularly on or around the valuation date.

>(b) Quoted prices in dealers' catalogs of the artist's works or of other artists of comparable statute.

>(c) The economic state of the art market at or around the time of valuation, particularly with respect to the specific property.

>(d) A record of any exhibitions at which the particular art object had been displayed.

>(e) A statement as to the standing of the artist in his profession and in the particular school or time period.

.04 Although an appraisal report meets these requirements, the Internal Revenue Service is not relieved of the responsibility of reviewing appraisals to the extent deemed necessary.

SEC. 4. REVIEW OF VALUATION APPRAISALS.

.01 While the Service is responsible for reviewing appraisals, it is not responsible for making appraisals; the burden of supporting the fair market value listed on a return is the taxpayer's. The Internal Revenue Service cannot accord recognition to any appraiser or group of appraisers from the standpoint of unquestioned acceptance of their appraisals. Furthermore, the Service cannot approve valuations or appraisals prior to the actual filing of the tax return to which the appraisal pertains and cannot issue advance rulings approving or disapproving such appraisals.

.02 In determining the acceptability of the claimed value of the donated property, the Service may either accept the value claimed based on information or appraisals submitted with the return or make its own determination as to the fair market value. In either instance, the Service may find it necessary to:

(1) contact the taxpayer and ask for additional information,

(2) refer the valuation problem to a Service appraiser or valuation specialist,

(3) recommend that an independent appraiser be employed by the Service to appraise the asset in question. (This latter course is frequently used by the Service when objects requiring appraisers of highly specialized experience and knowledge are involved.)

Sec. III   CHARITABLE CONTRIBUTION DEDUCTIONS   395

Note

The Service will provide a "Statement of Value," which can be used to substantiate the value of art for income, estate, or gift tax purposes. Revenue Procedure 96–15, 1996–1 C.B. 627, informs taxpayers how to obtain IRS review of a taxpayer's valuation of a work of art before filing a return.

G. Substantiation

To claim a charitable contribution deduction for a noncash gift in excess of $500, a donor must file Form 8283 on which the donor gives the IRS information about the gift. The donor must include the cost and date of acquisition, the fair market value of the gift, the method to determine fair market value, and the date of the contribution. The form requires the charity to acknowledge receipt of the gift. If the claimed value of donated property (other than donations of publicly traded stock) exceeds $5,000, the donor must include on the form a written independent appraisal of the property by a qualified appraiser. Appraisals must be made no earlier than 60 days before the date of the contribution and must be received before the due date of the return on which the deduction was first claimed. If the donee charity, or a successor donee, disposes of the property for which a donor has claimed a deduction in excess of $5,000, within three years of receipt, the charity must file Form 8282 and furnish to the Internal Revenue Service, with a statement to the donor, the name of the donor, the donor's tax identification number, a description of the property, the date of the contribution, the amount received on disposition of the property and the date of disposition. Failure to file Form 8282 can subject a charity to substantial penalties. Further, if the donor's claimed value for a gift of property to a charity exceeds the property's correct value (presumably established when the property is sold within two years by the selling price indicated on Form 8282), the overvaluation will subject the donor to a penalty of 20 percent to 40 percent of any tax underpayment. (See I.R.C. § 6662.)

Section 170(f) indirectly places upon charitable organizations the burden to substantiate all gifts of $250 or more. The section actually denies a deduction to a taxpayer for gifts of $250 or more unless the taxpayer "substantiates the contribution by a contemporaneous written acknowledgment of the contribution by the donee organization . . ." [See I.R.C. § 170(f)(8)(A).] Thus, a charitable organization must give to the taxpayer an acknowledgment so that the taxpayer can comply with the substantiation requirement. The written acknowledgment must state the amount of money the taxpayer has contributed and whether the taxpayer received any consideration in return. To be "contemporaneous," the taxpayer must receive the written acknowledgment no later than the date the taxpayer files a tax return or the due date including extensions of such return. Subject to the guidelines of Revenue Procedure 90–12, as amplified, when a quid pro quo gift exceeds $75, the charitable organization must also provide the taxpayer with a good faith estimate in writing of the values of the goods or services it gives taxpayers. (See I.R.C.

§ 6115.) "Goods or services" includes "cash, property, services, benefits, and privileges." [See Treas. Reg. § 1.170A–13(f)(5).]

Note

Section 170(f)(12) of the Internal Revenue Code provides that in the case of a contribution of a used motor vehicle, boat, or airplane wherein the claimed value exceeds $500, the amount of the donor's deduction is limited to the gross sales proceeds if the donee organization sells the vehicle without any significant intervening use or material improvement. In order to claim a deduction, the donee organization must substantiate the contribution by a contemporaneous written acknowledgment within 30 days of the contribution. The acknowledgment must include the name and taxpayer identification number of the donor, the vehicle identification number and, if the donee organization sells the vehicle, the gross proceeds from the sale, and a statement that the vehicle was sold in an arm's length transaction between unrelated parties. The acknowledgment also must state that the deductible amount may not exceed the amount of the gross proceeds.

Effective August 17, 2006, Congress added § 170(f)(16) and (17) to the Code. These new provisions place restrictions on the donation of "clothing and household items." Included within "household items" are furniture, furnishings, electronics, appliances and linens. Any clothing or household items must be "in good use condition or better."

H. Deferred Giving

The above discussion has addressed gifts of cash and a donor's total interest in property. Donors may want to defer gifts to a charity because they want to retain an interest in their property for a period of years. They may want to give a charitable organization certain of their property but only after the termination of their interest. The simplest way to accomplish their goal is to make a testamentary gift of property to a charitable organization. However, with a testamentary gift, charitable organizations risk the possibility that a donor may change her mind. The organizations would rather "lock in" the donor by means of any enforceable lifetime transfer. A donor, in turn, would prefer to complete a gift during his lifetime so that the donor may receive an income tax deduction as well as being able to exclude the value of the property from his gross estate to avoid paying estate taxes. The donor, however, wants to enjoy the property, usually by means of annual income, during the donor's life. To accomplish these goals is no mean feat because a third party, the federal government, has input as to whether donors and charitable organizations can attain the donative objectives.

Congress had two objectives in enacting provisions relating to deferred gifts. Congress wanted to encourage deferred gifts to charities, but, at the same time, Congress had to assure that charities would receive in current value the amount of the donation which the donor claimed as a tax deduction. Congress accomplished both objectives by a series of intricate statutes, which, in general, inform a donor that the safest way to make a deferred gift is by a charitable remainder trust or a charitable gift annuity. [The Code also permits pooled income trusts and charitable lead trusts. Under a lead trust, the charity receives an income interest for a term with the remainder going to the grantor or a third party. [See I.R.C. § 170(f)(1)(B) and Treas. Reg. § 1.170A–6(c).] A discussion of pooled income and charitable lead trusts is beyond the scope of this text.]

To accomplish its objectives, Congress disallowed a taxpayer a deduction for a gift of a future interest in tangible personal property until "all intervening interests in, and rights to the actual possession or enjoyment of, the property have expired or are held by persons other than the taxpayer or those related to the taxpayer." [See I.R.C. § 170 (a)(3).] Thus, an owner of a masterpiece cannot take a deduction if the owner retains a life interest in the art even though the owner gives the remainder interest to a museum. The result would be the same if the donor by will bequeaths a remainder interest in the artwork to the museum but gives lifetime enjoyment to a noncharitable third party.

A taxpayer generally is disallowed a charitable contribution deduction for any interest in property that consists of less than the donor's entire interest in the property unless the transfer is in the form of a charitable remainder trust. [See I.R.C. § 170(f)(3).] Thus, a taxpayer may not deduct the value of a remainder interest in property, such as an investment account, if the taxpayer retains an income interest in the account unless the donation is made in the form of a qualified charitable remainder trust. Section 170(f)(3)(B) permits three important exceptions to this limitation:

(1) the taxpayer gives a remainder interest in the taxpayer's personal residence or farm;

(2) the taxpayer donates an undivided portion of the taxpayer's entire interest in property, such as a one-third interest in a painting;

(3) the taxpayer gives a qualified conservation interest in real property.

1. Charitable Remainder Trusts

Except for the three exceptions listed above and a charitable gift annuity discussed below, the Code's safe harbor for deferred gifts is a charitable remainder trust. Section 170(f)(2)(A) permits a taxpayer to create either a charitable remainder unitrust or a charitable remainder annuity trust. [See § 644(d)(2) and (d)(1) for definitions of each trust.] Section 4947 treats these trusts as private foundations if the grantor claimed charitable contribution deductions for income, estate, or gift tax purposes. However, these so-called split-interest trusts are not subject to the two percent tax on net investment income imposed by § 4940 or to the excise tax on failure to distribute income under § 4942. Upon expiration of the noncharitable interest, such a trust will become a charitable trust and will be subject to the tax on investment income and the penalty tax under § 4942.

A charitable remainder trust provides for a specified distribution at least annually to one or more noncharitable beneficiaries for life or for a term of years not exceeding 20 years, with an irrevocable remainder interest held for the benefit of a charity. The specified distribution to be paid at least annually must be a definite sum. The amount paid to a noncharitable beneficiary cannot be less than 5 percent nor more than 50 percent of the initial net fair market value of all property placed in a charitable remainder annuity trust or the net fair market value of assets, valued annually, of a charitable remainder unitrust. The value of the remainder interest donated to charity must be at least 10 percent of the net fair market value of all property placed in a charitable remainder annuity trust and at least 10 percent of the net fair market value of the property of a charitable remainder unitrust as of the date property is contributed to the trust.

No amount may be paid to income beneficiaries other than the fixed amount. There also may not be a power to invade, alter, amend or revoke the trust for the beneficial use of anyone other than the public charity holding the remainder interest. Upon termination of the trust, the property must be transferred to the charity or held for its benefit and use. Thus, there are no probate costs upon the death of the grantor of the trust.

The governing instruments of a charitable remainder trust must provide that the annuity amount paid for the noncharitable beneficiary will be prorated on a daily basis for a short taxable year.

Whereas a charitable remainder annuity trust may not have additional contributions after the initial contributions, a unitrust may. If additional contributions are made to a unitrust after the initial contribution, the governing instrument must provide that the annuity payment to the noncharitable beneficiaries will be the fixed percentage (not less than 5 percent nor more than 50 percent) of the sum of the net fair market value of assets excluding any added assets and the value of the added assets times the percentage of time the added assets have been held during the year. A unitrust must require that should the net fair market value of the trust assets be incorrectly determined by the trustee, the trustee must pay the income recipient in the case of an undervaluation, or be repaid by the income recipient in the case of an overvaluation, in an amount equal to the difference. If the net income of a unitrust is less than the fixed percentage of the net fair market value of the assets of the fund valued for that year, the trust instrument may provide for payment of the lesser amount. This option is not available for a charitable remainder annuity trust.

Revenue Procedures 89–20 and 89–21 contain sample unitrust and annuity trust, respectively. If a charitable remainder trust meets Code qualifications, the present value of a charitable remainder interest is deductible for income, estate, and gift tax purposes.

Note the difference between a charitable remainder unitrust and a charitable remainder annuity trust as set out in the following Revenue Procedures.

REVENUE PROCEDURE 2005–52
2005–34 I.R.B. 326

SECTION 1. PURPOSE

This revenue procedure contains an annotated sample declaration of trust and alternate provisions that meet the requirements of § 664(d)(2) and (d)(3) of the Internal Revenue Code for an inter vivos charitable remainder unitrust (CRUT) providing for unitrust payments for one measuring life followed by the distribution of trust assets to a charitable remainderman.

SECTION 2. BACKGROUND

Previously, the Internal Revenue Service issued sample trust instruments for certain types of CRUTs. The Service is updating the previously issued samples and issuing new samples for additional types of CRUTs; annotations and alternate sample provisions are included as further guidance. In addition to the sample trust instrument included in this revenue procedure for an inter vivos CRUT providing for unitrust payments for one measuring life, samples are provided in other separate revenue procedures for:

(a) an inter vivos CRUT providing for unitrust payments for a term of years (see Rev. Proc. 2005–53);

(b) an inter vivos CRUT providing for unitrust payments payable consecutively for two measuring lives (see Rev. Proc. 2005–54, superseding section 4 of Rev. Proc. 90–30, 1990–1 C.B. 534, and section 5 of Rev. Proc. 90–31, 1990–1 C.B. 539);

(c) an inter vivos CRUT providing for unitrust payments payable concurrently and consecutively for two measuring lives (see Rev. Proc. 2005–55, superseding section 5 of Rev. Proc. 90–30 and section 6 of Rev. Proc. 90–31);

(d) a testamentary CRUT providing for unitrust payments for one measuring life (see Rev. Proc. 2005–56, superseding section 6 of Rev. Proc. 90–30 and section 7 of Rev. Proc. 90–31);

(e) a testamentary CRUT providing for unitrust payments for a term of years (see Rev. Proc. 2005–57);

(f) a testamentary CRUT providing for unitrust payments payable consecutively for two measuring lives (see Rev. Proc. 2005–58, superseding section 7 of Rev. Proc. 90–30 and section 8 of Rev. Proc. 90–31); and

(g) a testamentary CRUT providing for unitrust payments payable concurrently and consecutively for two measuring lives (see

Rev. Proc. 2005–59, superseding section 8 of Rev. Proc. 90–30 and section 9 of Rev. Proc. 90–31).

SECTION 3. SCOPE AND OBJECTIVE

Section 4 of this revenue procedure provides a sample declaration of trust for an inter vivos CRUT with one measuring life that is created by an individual who is a citizen or resident of the United States. Section 5 of this revenue procedure provides annotations to the provisions of the sample trust. Section 6 of this revenue procedure provides samples of certain alternate provisions concerning: (.01) the payment of part of the unitrust amount to an organization described in § 170(c); (.02) a qualified contingency; (.03) the last unitrust payment to the recipient; (.04) the restriction of the charitable remainderman to a public charity; (.05) a retained right to substitute the charitable remainderman; (.06) a power of appointment to designate the charitable remainderman; (.07) the net income method of calculating the unitrust amount; (.08) the net income with make-up method of calculating the unitrust amount; and (.09) a combination of methods for calculating the unitrust amount.

For transfers to a qualifying CRUT, as defined in § 664(d)(2) and, if applicable, § 664(d)(3), the remainder interest will be deductible by a citizen or resident of the United States under §§ 170(f)(2)(A), 2055(e)(2)(A), and 2522(c)(2)(A) for income, estate, and gift tax purposes, respectively, if the other requirements of §§ 170(f)(2)(A), 2055(e)(2)(A), and 2522(c)(2)(A) (that is, the requirements not relating to the provisions of the governing instrument) also are met. The Service will recognize a trust as a qualified CRUT meeting all of the requirements of § 664(d)(2) and, if applicable, § 664(d)(3), if the trust operates in a manner consistent with the terms of the trust instrument, if the trust is a valid trust under applicable local law, and if the trust instrument: (i) is substantially similar to the sample in section 4 of this revenue procedure; or (ii) properly integrates one or more alternate provisions from section 6 of this revenue procedure into a document substantially similar to the sample in section 4 of this revenue procedure. A trust that contains substantive provisions in addition to those provided in section 4 of this revenue procedure (other than properly integrated alternate provisions from section 6 of this revenue procedure or provisions necessary to establish a valid trust under applicable local law that are not inconsistent with the applicable federal tax requirements), or that omits any of the provisions of section 4 of this revenue procedure (unless an alternate provision from section 6 of this revenue procedure is properly integrated), will not necessarily be disqualified, but neither will that trust be assured of qualification under the provisions of this revenue procedure. The Service generally will not issue a letter ruling on whether an inter vivos trust created by an individual providing for unitrust payments for one measuring life qualifies as a CRUT. The Service, however, generally will issue letter rulings on the effect of substantive trust provisions, other than those contained in sections 4 and 6 of this revenue procedure, on the qualification of a trust as a CRUT.

SECTION 4. SAMPLE INTER VIVOS CHARITABLE REMAINDER UNITRUST—ONE LIFE

On this ___ day of ___, 20___, I, ___ (hereinafter "the Donor"), desiring to establish a charitable remainder unitrust within the meaning of Rev. Proc. 2005–52 and § 664(d)(2) of the Internal Revenue Code (hereinafter "the Code"), hereby enter into this trust agreement with ___ as the initial trustee (hereinafter "the Trustee"). This trust shall be known as the ___ Charitable Remainder Unitrust.

1. *Funding of Trust.* The Donor hereby transfers and irrevocably assigns, on the above date, to the Trustee the property described in Schedule A, and the Trustee accepts the property and agrees to hold, manage, and distribute the property, and any property subsequently transferred, under the terms set forth in this trust instrument.

2. *Payment of Unitrust Amount.* In each taxable year of the trust during the unitrust period, the Trustee shall pay to [*permissible recipient*] (hereinafter "the Recipient") a unitrust amount equal to [*a number no less than 5 and no more than 50*] percent of the net fair market value of the assets of the trust valued as of the first day of each taxable year of the trust (hereinafter "the valuation date"). The first day of the unitrust period shall be the date property is first transferred to the trust and the last day of the unitrust period shall be the date of the Recipient's death. The unitrust amount shall be paid in equal quarterly installments at the end of each calendar quarter from income and, to the extent income is not sufficient, from principal. Any income of the trust for a taxable year in excess of the unitrust amount shall be added to principal. If, for any year, the net fair market value of the trust assets is incorrectly determined, then within a reasonable period after the correct value is finally determined, the Trustee shall pay to the Recipient (in the case of an undervaluation) or receive from the Recipient (in the case of an overvaluation) an amount equal to the difference between the unitrust amount(s) properly payable and the unitrust amount(s) actually paid.

3. *Proration of Unitrust Amount.* For a short taxable year and for the taxable year during which the unitrust period ends, the Trustee shall prorate on a daily basis the unitrust amount described in paragraph 2, or, if an additional contribution is made to the trust, the unitrust amount described in paragraph 5.

4. *Distribution to Charity.* At the termination of the unitrust period, the Trustee shall distribute all of the then principal and income of the trust (other than any amount due the Recipient under the terms of this trust) to [*designated remainderman*] (hereinafter "the Charitable Organization"). If the Charitable Organization is not an organization described in §§ 170(c), 2055(a), and 2522(a) of the Code at the time when any principal or income of the trust is to be distributed to it, then the Trustee shall distribute the then principal and income to one or more organizations described in §§ 170(c), 2055(a), and 2522(a) of the Code as the Trustee shall select, and in the proportions as the Trustee shall decide, in the Trustee's sole discretion.

5. *Additional Contributions.* If any additional contributions are made to the trust after the initial contribution, the unitrust amount for the year in which any additional contribution is made shall be [*same percentage used in paragraph 2*] percent of the sum of (a) the net fair market value of the trust assets as of the valuation date (excluding the assets so added and any post-contribution income from, and appreciation on, such assets during that year) and (b) for each additional contribution during the year, the fair market value of the assets so added as of the valuation date (including any post-contribution income from, and appreciation on, such assets through the valuation date) multiplied by a fraction the numerator of which is the number of days in the period that begins with the date of contribution and ends with the earlier of the last day of the taxable year or the last day of the unitrust period and the denominator of which is the number of days in the period that begins with the first day of such taxable year and ends with the earlier of the last day in such taxable year or the last day of the unitrust period. In a taxable year in which an additional contribution is made on or after the valuation date, the assets so added shall be valued as of the date of contribution, without regard to any post-contribution income or appreciation, rather than as of the valuation date.

6. *Deferral of the Unitrust Payment Allocable to Testamentary Transfer.* All property passing to the trust by reason of the death of the Donor (hereinafter "the testamentary transfer") shall be considered to be a single contribution that is made on the date of the Donor's death. Notwithstanding the provisions of paragraphs 2 and 5 above, the obligation to pay the unitrust amount with respect to the testamentary transfer shall commence with the date of the Donor's death. Nevertheless, payment of the unitrust amount with respect to the testamentary transfer may be deferred from the date of the Donor's death until the end of the taxable year in which the funding of the testamentary transfer is completed. Within a reasonable time after the end of the taxable year in which the testamentary transfer is completed, the Trustee must pay to the Recipient (in the case of an underpayment) or receive from the Recipient (in the case of an overpayment) the difference between any unitrust amounts allocable to the testamentary transfer that were actually paid, plus interest, and the unitrust amounts allocable to the testamentary transfer that were payable, plus interest. The interest shall be computed for any period at the rate of interest, compounded annually, that the federal income tax regulations under § 664 of the Code prescribe for this computation.

7. *Unmarketable Assets.* Whenever the value of a trust asset must be determined, the Trustee shall determine the value of any assets that are not cash, cash equivalents, or other assets that can be readily sold or exchanged for cash or cash equivalents (hereinafter "unmarketable assets"), by either (a) obtaining a current "qualified appraisal" from a "qualified appraiser," as defined in § 1.170A–13(c)(3) and § 1.170A–13(c)(5) of the Income Tax Regulations, respectively, or (b) ensuring the valuation of these unmarketable assets is performed exclusively by an

"independent trustee," within the meaning of § 1.664–1(a)(7)(iii) of the Income Tax Regulations.

8. *Prohibited Transactions.* The Trustee shall not engage in any act of self-dealing within the meaning of § 4941(d) of the Code, as modified by § 4947(a)(2)(A) of the Code, and shall not make any taxable expenditures within the meaning of § 4945(d) of the Code, as modified by § 4947(a)(2)(A) of the Code.

9. *Taxable Year.* The taxable year of the trust shall be the calendar year.

10. *Governing Law.* The operation of the trust shall be governed by the laws of the State of _____. However, the Trustee is prohibited from exercising any power or discretion granted under said laws that would be inconsistent with the qualification of the trust as a charitable remainder unitrust under § 664(d)(2) of the Code and the corresponding regulations.

11. *Limited Power of Amendment.* This trust is irrevocable. However, the Trustee shall have the power, acting alone, to amend the trust from time to time in any manner required for the sole purpose of ensuring that the trust qualifies and continues to qualify as a charitable remainder unitrust within the meaning of § 664(d)(2) of the Code.

12. *Investment of Trust Assets.* Nothing in this trust instrument shall be construed to restrict the Trustee from investing the trust assets in a manner that could result in the annual realization of a reasonable amount of income or gain from the sale or disposition of trust assets.

13. *Definition of Recipient.* References to the Recipient in this trust instrument shall be deemed to include the estate of the Recipient with regard to all provisions in this trust instrument that describe amounts payable to and/or due from the Recipient. The prior sentence shall not apply to the determination of the last day of the unitrust period.

SECTION 5. ANNOTATIONS REGARDING SAMPLE INTER VIVOS CHARITABLE REMAINDER UNITRUST—ONE LIFE

* * *

SECTION 6. ALTERNATE PROVISIONS FOR SAMPLE INTER VIVOS CHARITABLE REMAINDER UNITRUST—ONE LIFE

* * *

REVENUE PROCEDURE 2005–53

2005–34 I.R.B. 339

SECTION 1. PURPOSE

This revenue procedure contains an annotated sample declaration of trust and alternate provisions that meet the requirements of § 664(d)(1) of the Internal Revenue Code for an inter vivos charitable remainder annuity trust (CRAT) providing for annuity payments for one measuring life followed by the distribution of trust assets to a charitable remainderman.

SECTION 2. BACKGROUND

Previously, the Internal Revenue Service issued sample trust instruments for certain types of CRATs. The Service is updating the previously issued samples and issuing new samples for additional types of CRATs; annotations and alternate sample provisions are included as further guidance. In addition to the sample trust instrument included in this revenue procedure for an inter vivos CRAT providing for annuity payments for one measuring life, samples are provided in separate revenue procedures for:

(a) an inter vivos CRAT providing for annuity payments for a term of years (see Rev. Proc. 2003–54);

(b) an inter vivos CRAT providing for annuity payments payable consecutively for two measuring lives (see Rev. Proc. 2003–55, superceding section 4 of Rev. Proc. 90–32, 1990–1 C.B. 546);

(c) an inter vivos CRAT providing for annuity payments payable concurrently and consecutively for two measuring lives (see Rev. Proc. 2003–56, superceding section 5 of Rev. Proc. 90–32);

(d) a testamentary CRAT providing for annuity payments for one measuring life (see Rev. Proc. 2003–57, superceding section 6 of Rev. Proc. 90–32);

(e) a testamentary CRAT providing for annuity payments for a term of years (see Rev. Proc. 2003–58);

(f) a testamentary CRAT providing for annuity payments payable consecutively for two measuring lives (see Rev. Proc. 2003–59, superceding section 7 of Rev. Proc. 90–32); and

(g) a testamentary CRAT providing for annuity payments payable concurrently and consecutively for two measuring lives (see Rev. Proc. 2003–60, superceding section 8 of Rev. Proc. 90–32).

SECTION 3. SCOPE AND OBJECTIVE

Section 4 of this revenue procedure provides a sample declaration of trust for an inter vivos CRAT with one measuring life that is created by an individual who is a citizen or resident of the United States. Section 5 of this revenue procedure provides annotations to the provisions of the sample trust. Section 6 of this revenue procedure provides samples of alternate provisions concerning: (.01) the statement of the annuity amount as a specific dollar amount; (.02) the payment of part of the annuity to an organization described in § 170(c); (.03) a qualified contingency; (.04) the last annuity payment to the recipient; (.05) the restriction of the charitable remainderman to a public charity; (.06) a retained right to substitute the charitable remainderman; and (.07) a power of appointment to designate the charitable remainderman.

For transfers to a qualifying CRAT, as defined in § 664(d)(1), the remainder interest will be deductible by a citizen or resident of the

United States under §§ 170(f)(2)(A), 2055(e)(2)(A), and 2522(c)(2)(A) for income, estate, and gift tax purposes, respectively, if the other requirements of §§ 170(f)(2)(A), 2055(e)(2)(A), and 2522(c)(2)(A) (that is, the requirements not relating to the provisions of the governing instrument) are also met. The Service will recognize a trust as a qualified CRAT meeting all of the requirements of § 664(d)(1) if the trust operates in a manner consistent with the terms of the trust instrument, if the trust is a valid trust under applicable local law, and if the trust instrument: (i) is substantially similar to the sample in section 4 of this revenue procedure; or (ii) properly integrates one or more alternate provisions from section 6 of this revenue procedure into a document substantially similar to the sample in section 4 of this revenue procedure. A trust instrument that contains substantive provisions in addition to those provided in section 4 of this revenue procedure (other than properly integrated alternate provisions from section 6 of this revenue procedure, or provisions necessary to establish a valid trust under applicable local law that are not inconsistent with the applicable federal tax requirements), or that omits any of the provisions of section 4 of this revenue procedure (unless an alternate provision from section 6 of this revenue procedure is properly integrated), will not necessarily be disqualified, but neither will that trust be assured of qualification under the provisions of this revenue procedure. The Service generally will not issue a letter ruling on whether an inter vivos trust created by an individual and with one measuring life qualifies as a CRAT. The Service, however, generally will issue letter rulings on the effect of substantive trust provisions, other than those contained in sections 4 and 6 of this revenue procedure, on the qualification of a trust as a CRAT.

SECTION 4. SAMPLE INTER VIVOS CHARITABLE REMAINDER ANNUITY TRUST—ONE LIFE

On this ___ day of ___, 20___, I, ___ (hereinafter "the Donor"), desiring to establish a charitable remainder annuity trust, within the meaning of Rev. Proc. 2003–53 and § 664(d)(1) of the Internal Revenue Code (hereinafter "the Code"), hereby enter into this trust agreement with ___ as the initial trustee (hereinafter "the Trustee"). This trust shall be known as the ___ Charitable Remainder Annuity Trust.

1. *Funding of Trust.* The Donor hereby transfers and irrevocably assigns, on the above date, to the Trustee the property described in Schedule A, and the Trustee accepts the property and agrees to hold, manage, and distribute the property under the terms set forth in this trust instrument.

2. *Payment of Annuity Amount.* In each taxable year of the trust during the annuity period, the Trustee shall pay to [*permissible recipient*] (hereinafter "the Recipient") an annuity amount equal to [*a number no less than 5 and no more than 50*] percent of the initial net fair market value of all property transferred to the trust, valued as of the above date (that is, the date of the transfer). The first day of the annuity period shall be the date the property is transferred to the trust and the last day

of the annuity period shall be the date of the Recipient's death. The annuity amount shall be paid in equal quarterly installments at the end of each calendar quarter from income, and to the extent income is not sufficient, from principal. Any income of the trust for a taxable year in excess of the annuity amount shall be added to principal. If the initial net fair market value of the trust assets is incorrectly determined, then within a reasonable period after the value is finally determined for federal tax purposes, the Trustee shall pay to the Recipient (in the case of an undervaluation) or receive from the Recipient (in the case of an overvaluation) an amount equal to the difference between the annuity amount(s) properly payable and the annuity amount(s) actually paid.

3. *Proration of Annuity Amount.* The Trustee shall prorate the annuity amount on a daily basis for any short taxable year. In the taxable year of the trust during which the annuity period ends, the Trustee shall prorate the annuity amount on a daily basis for the number of days of the annuity period in that taxable year.

4. *Distribution to Charity.* At the termination of the annuity period, the Trustee shall distribute all of the then principal and income of the trust (other than any amount due the Recipient or the Recipient's estate under the provisions above) to [*designated remainderman*] (hereinafter "the Charitable Organization"). If the Charitable Organization is not an organization described in §§ 170(c), 2055(a), and 2522(a) of the Code at the time when any principal or income of the trust is to be distributed to it, then the Trustee shall distribute the then principal and income to one or more organizations described in §§ 170(c), 2055(a), and 2522(a) of the Code as the Trustee shall select, and in the proportions as the Trustee shall decide, in the Trustee's sole discretion.

5. *Additional Contributions.* No additional contributions shall be made to the trust after the initial contribution.

6. *Prohibited Transactions.* The Trustee shall not engage in any act of self-dealing within the meaning of § 4941(d) of the Code, as modified by § 4947(a)(2)(A) of the Code, and shall not make any taxable expenditures within the meaning of § 4945(d) of the Code, as modified by § 4947(a)(2)(A) of the Code.

7. *Taxable Year.* The taxable year of the trust shall be the calendar year.

8. *Governing Law.* The operation of the trust shall be governed by the laws of the State of ___. However, the Trustee is prohibited from exercising any power or discretion granted under said laws that would be inconsistent with the qualification of the trust as a charitable remainder annuity trust under § 664(d)(*l*) of the Code and the corresponding regulations.

9. *Limited Power of Amendment.* This trust is irrevocable. However, the Trustee shall have the power, acting alone, to amend the trust from time to time in any manner required for the sole purpose of

ensuring that the trust qualifies and continues to qualify as a charitable remainder annuity trust within the meaning of § 664(d)(1) of the Code.

10. *Investment of Trust Assets.* Nothing in this trust instrument shall be construed to restrict the Trustee from investing the trust assets in a manner that could result in the annual realization of a reasonable amount of income or gain from the sale or disposition of trust assets.

SECTION 5. ANNOTATIONS REGARDING SAMPLE INTER VIVOS CHARITABLE REMAINDER ANNUITY TRUST—ONE LIFE

* * *

SECTION 6. ALTERNATE PROVISIONS FOR SAMPLE INTER VIVOS CHARITABLE REMAINDER ANNUITY TRUST—ONE LIFE

* * *

Note

A more detailed discussion of deferred giving is beyond the scope of this text.

2. Charitable Gift Annuity

A charitable gift annuity involves the transfer of money and property by a taxpayer to a charitable organization and in return the charitable organization promises to pay the donor an annual amount (an annuity) for a term of years, usually the donor's life. In effect, the taxpayer is making a quid pro quo gift. The amount of money or value of the property minus the present value of annuity is the deductible contribution. [See Treas. Reg. § 170A–1(d).] When the taxpayer receives each annuity payment, the taxpayer will pay tax on a portion of the annuity under the rules for taxation of annuities. (See I.R.C. § 72.)

The more difficult situation arises when the taxpayer transfers property that has appreciated in value for a annuity whose value is less than the total value of the property. The taxpayer should account for two tax consequences.

First, the taxpayer will be able to deduct as a charitable contribution the difference between the value of the property and the actuarial value of the annuity. Assuming the property is long-term capital gain property, the taxpayer's maximum deduction for this gift is 30 percent of the taxpayer's contribution base.

Second, the taxpayer must recognize gain on a portion of the property. Since the taxpayer is receiving value in return (the annuity) the taxpayer is deemed to be selling a portion of the property to the charitable organization. This is known as a "bargain sale."

A bargain sale occurs when a taxpayer transfers appreciated property to a charitable organization and receives consideration in return that is less than the value of the property. The Code requires that the taxpayer recognize the gain on the portion of the transfer that is deemed a sale. [See I.R.C. § 1011(b).] The taxpayer's adjusted basis in the property for purpose of the sale is determined by multiplying a fraction times the property's total adjusted basis. The numerator of the fraction is the value of the annuity and the denominator of the fraction is the total fair market value of the property.

For example, assume that a taxpayer transferred stock with a fair market of $100,000 to State University. The stock cost taxpayer $25,000 and State University promises to pay taxpayer $10,000 a year for 6 years. Assume for this example that the actuarial value of the annuity to taxpayer is $60,000. Taxpayer may deduct $40,000 as a charitable contribution ($100,000 fair market value of stock—$60,000 actuarial value of the annuity). Since the property transferred is stock, taxpayer's maximum deduction is 30 percent of the taxpayer's contribution base. Although taxpayer has a charitable contribution deduction, taxpayer also must recognize a taxable gain of $45,000 on the bargain sale. The amount taxpayer realized from the sale portion of the stock is $60,000, the value of the annuity. Taxpayer's adjusted basis in the portion of the stock sold would be $15,000 [$25,000 (total adjusted basis) X $60,000/$100,000]. The $60,000 numerator is the amount realized for the portion of the stock sold and the $100,000 denominator is the total fair market value of the stock.

IV. CY PRES DOCTRINE

Suppose that a donor has given a gift to a charitable organization for a specific purpose and that the organization is not able to fulfill the donor's purpose. Must the organization return the gift to the donor or the donor's estate or may the organization use the gift for other charitable purposes? If the donor indicated a more general intention to devote the property to charitable purposes, a court may apply the cy pres doctrine to direct that the property be applied to some charitable purpose that falls within the general charitable intention of the donor so that the gift will not fail.

Cy pres is included in this section on fundraising because the doctrine affects the resources a charitable organization has available to support its function. Not to apply cy pres may mean that a charitable organization will be required to divert funds supporting other functions to repay a gift, or the organization may be required to raise resources to fund a purpose that would otherwise be supported if a court would apply cy pres.

The following case illustrates the application of the cy pres doctrine.

UNITED STATES v. CERIO
United States District Court, Eastern District, Virginia, 1993
831 F.Supp. 530

ELLIS, District Judge.
MEMORANDUM OPINION.

This is a rare case. How often, after all, does the recipient of a generous bequest object to that bequest and threaten to reject it on the ground that it is too generous? Yet that is precisely what has occurred here. Indeed, this is essentially a case of looking the gift horse in the mouth and finding it too good to accept as is.

More particularly, this unique dispute concerns the validity and disposition of a retired Coast Guard Captain's testamentary gift to the United States Coast Guard Academy (the "Academy") for the purpose of establishing a trust fund, the annual income of which is to be awarded each year to the graduating cadet who attains the highest grade point average in chemistry and physics while enrolled at the Academy. So large is the gift—the trust corpus is estimated to be worth over $1 million—that the proposed cadet award would range from $65,000 to $130,000 annually. Such an annual cadet award, according to the Coast Guard, would seriously disrupt the Academy's operations and interfere with the attainment of its goals. Unless the trust is somehow modified, the Coast Guard claims it would be compelled to refuse the gift. Seeking to avoid this result, the United States brought this action on behalf of the Coast Guard seeking application of the equitable doctrine of *cy pres* to change the terms of the trust so that the Coast Guard Academy can accept the testamentary trust in a modified form. Not surprisingly, the testator's heirs-at-law, the defendants here, argue that the trust should either be performed as written or held to fail, in which event, the trust funds would pass to them under Virginia's intestate succession laws.

* * *

II.

FINDINGS OF FACT

Robert T. Alexander, a resident of the Commonwealth of Virginia, died testate on April 18, 1988. A retired Coast Guard Captain, Alexander had spent his entire thirty-four year professional career with the Coast Guard. He began his career with the Coast Guard as a cadet at the Academy in 1928, following in the footsteps of his half-brother, George C. Alexander, who graduated from the Academy in 1904. Captain Alexander graduated second in his Academy class, received a Bachelor of Science Degree in Engineering, and went on to become a successful Coast Guard officer. By the time he retired from the Coast Guard in 1962, Captain Alexander had risen to the rank of Captain. During his Coast Guard career, Captain Alexander also earned a Master of Science degree in Physics from the University of Michigan in 1940, and a second Bachelor of Science degree in Engineering from the George Washington University in 1953.

Captain Alexander's assignments as a Coast Guard officer during his thirty-four year career often required application of his engineering and scientific skills. Three years after his graduation, Captain Alexander formally requested assignment to the Academy as an instructor. This request was granted, and, in 1935, he was assigned to the Academy as an instructor in chemistry and physics. Captain Alexander remained as an instructor at the Academy for five years. During this period, he also served as Head of the Chemistry Department. In addition to his tour of duty as an Academy instructor, Captain Alexander served in many other billets requiring scientific and engineering expertise including, *inter alia,* his tenure as: (1) Chief of Staff, 12th Coast Guard District, from 1961 to 1962; (2) Chief, Civil Engineering Division, from 1954 to 1958; and (3) Chief, Testing and Development Division, from 1947 to 1952. He also maintained memberships in the American Society of Civil Engineers, the Society of Naval Engineers, and the American Society of Military Engineers.

Captain Alexander distinguished himself as a Coast Guard officer, receiving numerous commendations and awards, including, *inter alia:* (1) the Bronze Star Medal, awarded in the name of the President of the United States, for "distinguishing himself by meritorious conduct as a Commanding Officer of a U.S. Navy vessel during operations against enemy-held islands in the Southwest Pacific Area . . . ;" (2) the American Defense Service Medal; (3) the American Campaign Medal; (4) the Asiatic–Pacific Campaign Medal; (5) the European-African–Middle Eastern Campaign Medal; (6) the World War II Victory Medal; and (7) the National Defense Service Medal. In 1962, a disability forced Captain Alexander to retire from the Coast Guard. But following his retirement, and up until the time of his death in April 1988, Captain Alexander maintained a close attachment to the Coast Guard, faithfully attending Coast Guard functions on virtually a monthly basis. Although the exact number of Coast Guard functions attended by Captain Alexander is unknown, his close friend and fellow Coast Guard officer, Admiral Cowart, estimated that they attended approximately 6–8 functions each year together.

Although Captain Alexander enjoyed a distinguished career in the Coast Guard, he was not selected for flag rank. The heirs rely chiefly on this event in their attempt to paint a picture of Captain Alexander as a man embittered against the Coast Guard for failure to acknowledge his merit. The attempt fails; the testimony paints a different picture. No doubt, Captain Alexander was profoundly disappointed when he was not selected for flag rank. Yet, Admiral Cowart testified convincingly that Captain Alexander shared with him a sincere life-long affection for the Coast Guard. According to the Admiral, Captain Alexander never complained about the Coast Guard; he loved it. Mrs. Mahoney, Captain Alexander's personal secretary and assistant in his final years, noted that all the Captain talked about was his years as a Coast Guard officer. She never heard him say anything negative about the Coast Guard or the Academy. Nor did she ever hear him express any bitterness over the Coast Guard's decision not to promote him to the rank of Admiral. Significantly, she noted that everyone addressed him as "Captain," hardly a title he would have retained had he been irreconcilably bitter.

This general theme was echoed by Mr. Cerio, the Captain's personal lawyer for twenty years, his neighbor for thirty and the executor of his estate. Significantly, Mr. Cerio testified that the Captain spoke highly of the Academy, noting that he felt privileged to have been a cadet there. Similarly, Mr. Cerio reported that Captain Alexander also spoke affectionately and often of the Coast Guard. As Mr. Cerio put it, "that's where his heart was."

At the time of his death in April 1988, Captain Alexander was a widower with no children. He was survived by no relatives of closer kinship than nieces and nephews or perhaps more accurately, half nieces and nephews. * * * Captain Alexander does not appear to have been particularly close to any surviving family members. Although it was established at trial that Donald Alexander had infrequent contacts with Captain Alexander, their relationship appears to have been far from intimate. It does appear that Captain Alexander, in his later years, may have sought to renew some family ties, but little seems to have come of this. * * *None of the potential heirs came to visit Captain Alexander in the hospital in the months immediately preceding his death. And only Donald D. Alexander attended Captain Alexander's funeral.

Following his death, Captain Alexander's will, dated April 28, 1986, was admitted to probate in the Circuit Court of the County of Arlington, Virginia. After providing for the payment of Captain Alexander's just debts, funeral expenses, estate administration costs, and estate and inheritance taxes, the will provided for monetary bequests to eleven specified individuals, including bequests of $50,000 each to Captain Alexander's half-nieces and nephews—Donald David Alexander, Nelson Earl Alexander, Julia Ann Farkas, and Mary Louise Brumbaugh. Captain Alexander's will did not provide for any of the surviving grand nieces or grand nephews. He devised the remainder of his estate to the Coast Guard Academy for the purpose of establishing a scholarship fund in his name and that of his half-brother George Alexander, also an Academy graduate. Paragraph THIRD of the will (the "Residuary Clause") provides as follows:

I hereby devise and bequeath all the remainder of my property, of every description and wherever located, that I now own or may hereafter acquire, to the UNITED STATES COAST GUARD ACADEMY LOCATED AT NEW LONDON, CONNECTICUT, FOR THE PURPOSE OF ESTABLISHING THE GEORGE C. ALEXANDER (CLASS OF 1904) AND ROBERT T. ALEXANDER SCHOLARSHIP FUND FOR EXCELLENCE IN CHEMISTRY AND PHYSICS,—THE ANNUAL NET INCOME FROM THE CORPUS OF THE SAID FUND IS TO BE AWARDED AND PAID TO THE GRADUATING CADET WHO HAS ATTAINED THE HIGHEST GRADE AVERAGE IN CHEMISTRY AND PHYSICS WHILE ENROLLED IN THE ACADEMY;

Pursuant to the terms of this Residuary Clause, Daniel Cerio, the executor of Captain Alexander's estate and drafter of the Will, delivered two checks to the Coast Guard following Captain Alexander's death.

Cerio delivered the first check, in the amount of $1 million, to the Coast Guard in January 1990, and he handed over the second check, in the amount of $154,204.42, in April 1993. These checks have been deposited in the United States Coast Guard's General Gift Fund, and the proceeds of these checks are currently earning interest. According to recent estimates, the annual net income from the trust, and thus, the proposed annual award to the graduating Cadet attaining the highest grade point average in chemistry and physics will range between $65,000 and $130,000 (or perhaps higher), depending on fluctuations in interest rated and inflation. These estimates are based on a trust corpus of $1.3 million, and interest rates ranging from 5 to 10 percent.

Upon realizing the size of the annual award called for by the terms of the testamentary trust, the Coast Guard determined that it would not be able to accept the trust gift as written. The award of such a large cash prize, in the eyes of the Coast Guard, would disrupt the Academy's educational program and unduly interfere with its mission of preparing young men and women for a life of public service in the Coast Guard. As such, the government, on behalf of the Coast Guard, initiated this suit seeking application of the *cy pres* doctrine.

Testimony at trial from Admiral Versaw, the Academy's current Superintendent, and Captain Gronlund, the head of the Academy's Science Department, showed convincingly that an annual award of $65,000 to $130,000 to a cadet would have unacceptably deleterious effects on the Academy's operations and prevent the attainment of its mission. * * * Asked to describe the Academy's mission, Admiral Versaw, without hesitation, recited the following litany he and all other Academy graduates over the decades learned as part of their plebe year indoctrination.

The Mission of United States Coast Guard academy is to graduate young men and women with sound bodies stout hearts, alert minds and a liking for the sea and its lore, and with that high sense of honor, loyalty and obedience which goes with trained initiative and leadership, well grounded in seamanship, sciences and the amenities and strong in the resolve to be worthy of the tradition of commissioned officers in the United States Coast Guard in the service of their country and humanity.

This mission, in Admiral Versaw's view, would be jeopardized if the proposed trust were enforced as written. Specifically, he noted that an annual award of $65,000 to $130,000 to a cadet would (i) engender intense, unhealthy competition among cadets, (ii) spawn honor code offenses, (iii) distort the competition to major in the sciences at the expense of other majors (iv) erode, if not destroy, the class and interpersonal relationships and esprit de corps so vital to the Academy's goal of instilling in cadets the value of teamwork and (v) serve to teach cadets, wrongly, that the reward for a job well done in a life of public service in the Coast Guard is cash rather than the personal satisfaction that comes from doing well one's duty as an officer. No student of human nature can seriously doubt the validity of Admiral's views in this regard.

Attempts at literal enforcement of the trust would fundamentally change the Academy in ways neither contemplated, nor desired by Captain Alexander.

III.
CONCLUSIONS OF LAW

Under Virginia law, the equitable doctrine of *cy pres* permits courts to alter a trust so as to carry out a testator's intent "as near as possible" when it is not possible to effectuate this intent in the exact manner specified by the testator. *See Va.Code* § 55–31 (1992). * * * For the doctrine of *cy pres* to be properly invoked, there must be: "(1) a valid charitable trust without a gift over, (2) an existing general charitable intent, *and* (3) the beneficiaries must be indefinite or uncertain, *or* (4) the purpose of the trust must be indefinite, impossible to perform, or so impracticable of performance as to characterize the fulfillment of the purpose as 'impossible.'" *Smith v. Moore,* 225 F.Supp. 434, 441 (E.D.Va. 1963), modified and remanded on other grounds, 343 F.2d 594 (4th Cir.1965) (emphasis in original). * * * In this case, the Coast Guard argues that *cy pres* should be applied to save Captain Alexander's charitable bequest from failing because it cannot accept or perform the trust as written. Defendant heirs, for their part, argue that *cy pres* is inapplicable, and that the failure of the gift results in the trust funds passing to them by intestate succession. In light of the trial evidence, however, it is clear that the requirements for application of the *cy pres* doctrine are met.

First, the Residuary Clause of Captain Alexander's will unmistakably creates a valid charitable trust without a gift over. Under to Va.Code § 55–26.1, a valid "charitable" trust is created by a devise or bequest for education or for charitable purposes. Instructive here is the Supreme Court of Virginia's expansive definition of "charity":

A charity, in a legal sense, may be described as a gift to be applied, consistently with existing laws, for the benefit of an indefinite number of persons, either by bringing their hearts under the influence of education or religion, by relieving their bodies from disease, suffering or constraint, by assisting them to establish themselves for life, or by erecting or maintaining public buildings or works, or otherwise lessening the burdens of government. It is immaterial whether the purpose is called charitable in the gift itself, if it is so described as to show that it is charitable. Generally speaking, any gift not inconsistent with existing laws which is promotive of science or tends to the education, enlightening, benefit or amelioration of mankind or the diffusion of useful knowledge, or is for the public convenience is a charity. * * * Given this definition, the proposed trust created by the Residuary Clause is a valid charitable trust because (i) its purpose is to benefit an indefinite number of cadets, * * * and (ii) the proposed trust lends itself to the advancement of education by encouraging academic excellence in chemistry and physics at the Academy. * * * Indeed, where, as here, a bequest has been made to establish a fund for the giving of prizes for achievement in education, courts have uniformly held such a bequest to be a valid charitable gift. Moreover, no "gift over" exists in Captain Alexander's will—*i.e.*, no provision appears in the will directing an alternative disposition of the trust funds should the proposed trust fail. The absence of such a "gift over" further compels the conclusion that the proposed trust at issue here is a valid charitable trust. * * *

The next inquiry is whether Captain Alexander possessed a general charitable intent to benefit education at the Academy, or whether he simply had a specific, charitable intent to benefit only those Academy graduates attaining the highest grade point averages in chemistry and physics. As a preliminary matter, it should be noted that courts, in construing the nature of a charitable gift, properly endeavor to find, a general charitable intent whenever possible. * * * By contrast, it is well established that courts will find a specific, charitable intent only where such intent is "clear, definite, and unambiguous." * * * Equally well established is that in Virginia, "charitable gifts are viewed with particular favor by the courts and every presumption consistent with the language contained in the instruments of gift will be employed in order to sustain them." * * * Put another way, once the charitable nature of a trust is established, all doubts will be resolved in favor of preserving its charitable character.

Given this, the crucial question that must be answered to ascertain the nature of Captain Alexander's charitable intent is whether (i) he would have preferred that his bequest be applied to a like charitable purpose in the event that his original scheme failed, or (ii) would he instead have desired that the unused funds be removed from charitable use entirely. * * * In light of the evidence offered at trial, it is clear that if Captain Alexander were alive today, he "probably would not direct that [the residue of his estate] be delivered to distant relatives in the event of the failure of the specific purpose set forth in his will." *Moore*, 225 F.Supp. at 439. Instead, Captain Alexander most likely would have preferred that the remainder of his estate be used for closely related charitable purposes if the precise terms of his original scheme could not be carried out.

Indeed, Captain Alexander's general, charitable intent is made manifest by the express language of the will itself. As noted, the Residuary Clause reads, in pertinent part:

> "I hereby devise and bequeath all the remainder of my estate ... *to the UNITED STATES COAST GUARD ACADEMY* FOR THE PURPOSE OF ESTABLISHING THE GEORGE C. ALEXANDER (CLASS OF 1904) AND ROBERT T. ALEXANDER (CLASS OF 1931) SCHOLARSHIP FUND...." (emphasis added).

Significantly, the express terms of the Residuary Clause direct the remainder of Captain Alexander's estate to be given "to the United States Coast Guard Academy" for the purpose of establishing a scholarship fund to provide an annual cadet award for excellence in chemistry and physics. Fairly construed, this language makes clear that Captain Alexander intended the Academy to be the beneficiary of his largesse, and that the particular manner in which the trust was to be performed was secondary to his dominant, general charitable intent to encourage academic excellence at the Academy in chemistry and physics.

The absence of any "gift over" provision in the will further supports this conclusion. No alternative disposition for the trust corpus appears anywhere in the Residuary Clause, nor does any alternative disposition appear elsewhere in the will. It is well established that

> "[t]he absence of a provision for forfeiture in case of noncompliance with a direction in a will with regard to a charitable trust is an indication that the testator did not intend that the gift should revert on failure to comply therewith while the carrying out of his general purpose is practicable."

* * *

Further evidence of this intent arises from the fact that Captain Alexander made specific, testamentary bequests of $50,000 to each of the half nieces and nephews. These specific, substantial bequests, coupled with the absence of a gift over provision in the will, are convincing proof that Captain Alexander would have wanted the residue of his estate to be used to further education at the Academy, even if the precise trust terms could not be effectuated. * * * Clearly then, one need not look beyond the four corners of the will document to discern Captain Alexander's general charitable intent.

Even assuming, *arguendo,* that such intent cannot be clearly discerned from the will itself, an examination of Captain Alexander's professional career and educational background supports a finding that he possessed a general, charitable intent to benefit the study of science, particularly of physics and chemistry, at the Academy. *See Moore,* 225 F.Supp. at 442 ("[t]he background of the testator, . . . his education and business acumen, may all be considered in determining his general charitable intent, unless the same is precluded by the precise language of the will"). As noted above, Captain Alexander spent his entire professional career in the Coast Guard, serving for a time as an Academy physics and chemistry instructor and as the Head of the Chemistry Department. Moreover, his pronounced interest in the sciences is further evident in his receipt of two additional degrees, a Masters degree in Physics from the University of Michigan and another Bachelors degree in engineering from the George Washington University. Also pertinent is that, as Captain Alexander rose through the ranks of the Coast Guard, he occupied various billets that called upon his scientific background and expertise. In addition, he was a member of the American Society of Civil Engineers, the Society of Naval Engineers, and the American Society of Military Engineers. Nor can there be any serious doubt that Captain Alexander had a deep and abiding love for the Coast Guard and the Academy. His post-retirement attachment to the Coast Guard is apparent from his relatively regular attendance at Coast Guard meetings and functions. It is accordingly clear that Captain Alexander possessed the requisite general intent to have the residue of his estate applied to charitable ends, namely the encouragement of academic excellence in the sciences at the Academy. It is equally clear that "he would attach so much more importance to the object of the gift than to the mechanism by which he intended to accomplish it that he would prefer to alter the mechanism to the extent necessary to save the object." * * *

But the *cy pres* analysis does not end here; a final issue must be resolved as *cy pres* applies only where a charitable trust is "indefinite, impossible to perform, or so impracticable of performance as to characterize the fulfillment of the purpose as 'impossible.'" * * * In this regard, the Coast Guard argues that, as written, the trust is fatally indefinite and legally, as well as practically impossible to perform. The indefiniteness argument, while not without same force, is not, in this context, an adequate predicate for the application of *cy pres*. Any ambiguities in the trust as written here could be resolved in a traditional action for aid and guidance of the Court. * * * The focus here, therefore, is on the Coast Guard's contentions (1) that the trust, as written, is impossible to perform because the law precludes the Coast Guard from giving cadets large cash prizes and (2) that the trust, as written, cannot achieve the testator's purposes because it would be so destructive of the Academy's operations and mission that it must be refused unless reformed.

Cy Pres does not require literal impossibility. That the Academy could conceivably carry out the terms of the trust does not bar application of the doctrine. It is enough that the gifts essential impracticality precludes performance. * * *

Particularly instructive in this regard is the New Jersey Supreme Court decision in *Howard Sav. Institution v. Peep,* 34 N.J. 494, 170 A.2d 39 (1961). In that case, the testator bequeathed money to Amherst College to be held in trust "to be used as a scholarship loan fund for deserving American born, Protestant, Gentile boys of good moral repute, not given to gambling, smoking, drinking, or similar acts." Amherst College desired to accept the gift, but only if it could do so free of the religious restrictions, which, while not illegal, were contrary to the College's policies. The potential heirs-at-law argued that if Amherst did not want to perform under the trust as written, the trust failed and its funds passed to them under intestate succession.

On these facts, the Supreme Court of New Jersey held that the doctrine of *cy pres* was applicable, and permitted Amherst to accept the gift free of religious restrictions. The court based its decision on a finding that such a result was closer to the testator's intent than was the proposal to give the trust funds to the heirs. Also cited in support of the ruling were specifically, the following findings: (1) the will contained no provisions for alternative control of the trust in the event the trust was not accepted by the College; (2) the testator had attended and graduated from Amherst; and (3) the only persons who could inherit in the event of intestacy were cousins with whom the testator had not had personal relations. *Howard* and the case at bar are strikingly similar. Both cry out for the application of *cy pres*.

In this case, the award of an annual cash prize ranging from $65,000 to $130,000 to a single cadet would plainly violate Academy policy. As Admiral Versaw's persuasive testimony made pellucidly clear, an annual award of this magnitude would wreak such havoc on the Academy that the Coast Guard would be compelled to refuse the gift in the absence of any change in its terms. The Academy, like the other service academies, strives to prepare young men and women for the challenges of public service, not only through academic preparation, but by building and maintaining a reverence for honor, a commitment to teamwork and an *esprit de corps*. Were cadets aware that achieving the highest grade point average in chemistry and physics would result in large monetary remuneration, the serious consequences anticipated by Admiral Versaw would doubtless come to pass. Given this, and in light of the Coast Guard's position that it would refuse the Captain Alexander's bequest rather than perform the trust as written, the gift is "so impracticable of performance as to characterize the fulfillment of [Captain Alexander's specific] purpose as 'impossible.'" * * * While this statute does not, by is express terms, limit the amount of "cash prizes," the application of the doctrine of *ejusdem generis* supports a finding that, fairly construed, the statute authorizes awards of only modest value, e.g., trophies, badges, and buttons. Under this statutory construction doctrine, when a particular class of things is enumerated in a statute, and general words follow, such general words are not to be construed broadly, but are to be held as applying only to things of the same general kind or class as those specifically mentioned. * * * Applied here, this statutory construction doctrine compels the conclusion that the general term "cash prizes" should be construed to encompass only cash awards similar in nature to those enumerated by the preceding specific terms, namely trophies and badges. As such, the Academy may be limited in the amount of monetary compensation it can bestow on a single cadet.

IV.

In sum then, it is clear: (i) that the proposed trust set forth in Captain Alexander's will is a valid charitable trust; (ii) that Captain Alexander possessed a general, charitable intent; and (iii) that it is "impossible" to carry out the precise terms of this proposed trust. Accordingly, application of *cy pres* doctrine is manifestly appropriate here so that "defects in the trust may be cured, beneficiaries selected and determined upon, purposes for the trust supplied, and suitable plans and details of execution and administration adopted". *Shenandoah*, 63 S.E.2d at 794–95. Importantly; courts undertaking to alter trusts pursuant to the *cy pres* doctrine must be mindful that their discretion is not unlimited. Rather, their discretion is limited and guided by the principle that preservation of the testator's purposes is paramount and that alterations to the trust fashioned to eliminate any impossibility or impracticality of performance, must, as much as possible, result in a trust that effectuates the testator's original purposes. With this guiding principle in mind, the Court concludes that the terms of the trust must be altered to provide as follows:

> The corpus of the reformed trust shall remain in the Coast Guard General Gift Fund pursuant to 10 U.S.C. § 2601(b)(4). The corpus shall be known as the "George C. Alexander (Class of 1904) and Robert T. Alexander (Class of 1931) Academic in Excellence in the Sciences Fund." The reformed trust shall be maintained in perpetuity; * * *

* * *

3. The annual net income of the reformed trust shall be applied as follows:

a. (i) First, a cash award of $750 shall be awarded to the graduating cadet or cadets who attain the highest cumulative grade point average in four or more physics courses taken during the cadet's four years at the Academy. To be eligible for this award, a cadet must take at least four physics courses over a four year Academy career. The Superintendent, with the advice of the Head of the Science Department, shall determine from time to time which Academy courses qualify as physics courses. A cadet's senior project in science, if substantially involving physics, may be included as a physics course for purposes of this award. This award is to be called the "George C. Alexander, Class of 1904 and Robert T. Alexander, Class of 1931 Prize in Physics". Funds from the trust are also to be used to purchase and install a plaque to be placed in an appropriate location at the Academy entitled, "The George C. Alexander, Class of 1904 and Robert T. Alexander, Class of 1931 Prize Winners in Physics." The name of each prize recipient is to be inscribed or engraved on the plaque. The case amount of this award may be increased from time to time at the direction and discretion of the Superintendent.

(ii) A cash award of $750 shall be awarded to the graduating cadet or cadets who attain the highest cumulative grade point average in four or more chemistry courses taken during the cadet's four years at the Academy. To be eligible for this award, a cadet must take at least four chemistry courses over a four year Academy career. The Superintendent, with the advice of the Head of the Science Department, shall determine from time to time which Academy courses qualify as chemistry courses. A cadet's senior project in science, if substantially involving chemistry, may be included as a chemistry course for purposes of this award. This award is to be called the "George C. Alexander, Class of 1904 and Robert T. Alexander, Class of 1931 Prize in Chemistry". Funds from the trust are also to be used to purchase and install a plaque to be placed in an appropriate location at the Academy entitled, "The George C. Alexander, Class of 1904 and Robert T. Alexander, Class of 1931 Prize Winners in

Chemistry." The names of all recipients of this prize are to be inscribed or engraved on the plaque. The cash amount of this award may be increased from time to time at the direction and discretion of the Superintendent.

b. Second, modest cash awards of $400 each shall be awarded annually to the cadet or cadets who attain the highest grade in each of the chemistry and physics courses offered at the Academy at any point in time. These awards are to be known as the "George C. Alexander (Class of 1904) and Robert T. Alexander (Class of 1931) Excellence in Chemistry and Physics Awards." One award of $400 will be established for each current chemistry and physics class, the number of awards to increase or decrease in subsequent years to correspond to future curriculum changes. Recipients of these awards will be selected annually, and all cadets at the Academy enrolled in these classes will be eligible for the prizes. The cash amount of these awards may be increased from time to time at the direction and discretion of the Superintendent.

c. Third, each year up to a total of $5000 of trust funds will be available to be awarded to one or more cadets to support senior projects in science. Recipients of these grants will be selected by the Superintendent, with the advice of the Academy's science faculty. Winners of these research grants will be selected on the basis of applications by cadets setting forth in appropriate detail the nature, scope and purpose of a science project to be undertaken and completed during the senior year. Applications for research grants must be submitted at a date during junior year to be set at the discretion of the Superintendent. The Superintendent may also publish more detailed criteria to guide cadets in the completion of applications for the research award. Also the number of research grants awarded may vary from year to year depending upon the level of interest among cadets and the quality and merit of the applications. Grant funds may only be used to defray expenses incurred directly in connection with the subject science project. These expenses may include payment for the purchase, repair or rental of machinery or equipment, the purchase of books, travel and miscellaneous administrative costs. Because these expenses may vary from project to project, the amount of each grant may vary at the discretion Superintendent in order to accommodate the requirements of the particular proposed project.

d. Fourth, up to $40,000 annually shall be available to establish the "Robert T. Alexander Coast Guard Academy Science and Teaching Graduate Fellowship" to fund the graduate studies of a Coast Guard Academy graduate who, following at least one tour of sea duty, wishes to pursue a Ph.D in the sciences, preferably chemistry or physics, and then return to the Academy to serve as an instructor. To be eligible, a Coast Guard officer must be an Academy graduate who is on active duty and who has served at least one tour of duty at sea. The Superintendent of the Academy, with the advice of the Academy faculty, shall select qualified Coast Guard Officers for the graduate fellowship on the basis of academic excellence, intellectual prowess, leadership, dedication and interest in the sciences, commitment to a career in the Coast Guard, and sincere desire to serve as an instructor at the Academy. Recipients of this fellowship are to be selected as often as the Superintendent of the Academy deems appropriate or necessary, although at least one recipient must be designated at least once every five years. Recipients of the fellowship are to receive tuition, expenses, and an appropriate stipend to fund their graduate studies. A plaque is to be placed in an appropriate location at the Academy in memory of Robert T. Alexander upon which the names of all recipients of the fellowship award are to be inscribed or engraved.

e. Fifth, up to $7,500 of trust funds shall be available annually to allow the Academy to invite distinguished professors, researchers and lecturers in the sciences from other universities and institutions to visit the Academy for the purpose of providing further instruction to cadets in science. These visiting professors, researchers or scientists shall be paid an appropriate honorarium plus their expenses and each shall be given the title of "Robert T. Alexander Visiting Fellow." Fellowship recipients will be selected from other universities and institutions on the basis of their potential to enhance cadets' understanding of science, in general and also the role of science in the formulation of sound public policy. It is contemplated that there may be more than one Robert T. Alexander Visiting Fellow per year and selected Fellows may remain at the Academy for periods of up to two weeks.

f. Sixth, any trust funds remaining in a given year after funding all of the various awards, prizes, grants and fellowships described in paragraphs (a) through (e), above, may be used to purchase or repair special scientific equipment or machinery, at the discretion of the Superintendent, with the advice of the science faculty. Trust funds may be expended only in connection with machinery or equipment that will be used directly by cadets in connection with their science studies. Each piece of machinery or equipment purchased shall include a permanent plaque or label identifying it as a "Gift of Robert T. Alexander, Class of 1931."

4. Finally, the Superintendent is directed to communicate by letter annually with a designated member or representative of the surviving members of Captain Alexander's family to advise them of the details of the disposition of trust funds for the year. Specifically, the Superintendent's letter should identify the recipients of all prizes, awards and fellowships and provide such additional information as may seem appropriate such as hometowns, ages, academic major, nature of study project, titles and copies of lectures given, physics or chemistry grades and, in the case of any equipment purchased, a description of the nature, uses and location of that equipment. Donald D. Alexander is designated as the family representative and

he shall have the discretion and authority to designate his successor in this capacity, which designation should be sent in writing to the Superintendent. Should it occur in the future that no representative is designated, the Superintendent is to undertake to locate a surviving family member to whom the report may be sent. For this effort, the Superintendent may expend up to $2000 of trust funds. Only if no family representative is located may this reporting requirement be omitted.

This alteration of the trust terms is fully in keeping with the spirit of Captain Alexander's charitable intent, and Captain Alexander undoubtedly would have approved the modification.

An appropriate order shall issue.

Notes

1. The generally accepted meaning of the cy pres doctrine is found in Restatement Second of Trusts § 399. The cy pres doctrine applies to charitable gifts when:

    a. a valid trust has been created;

    b. it becomes impossible or impracticable, or illegal to fulfill the charitable purpose and;

    c. the evidence shows that the donor's general intent was to give the property for a charitable purpose.

2. Once a court decides to apply cy pres, the court must then decide how to apply, or to whom to give, the gift. See *In re Bishop's College*, 151 B.R. 394 (1993), in which the Bankruptcy Court held that a gift was not part of the bankrupt estate and remanded the case to state court for determination of the cy pres doctrine. Comment (d) Restatement, Second, of Trusts § 399 states the basic principle:

> Under the circumstances stated in...[§ 399 of the Restatement], the court will direct the framing of a scheme to apply the trust property for some charitable purpose falling within the general charitable intention of the settlor. In framing a scheme, the court will consider evidence as to what would probably have been the wish of the settlor at the time when he created the trust if he had realized that the particular purpose could not be carried out.

Note that a court is exercising equitable powers when it applies the cy pres doctrine.

Questions

1. The Court in *Cerio* relies on the impossibility reason for using cy pres. To quote the court:

> Cy pres does not require literal impossibility. That the Academy could conceivably carry out the terms of the trust does not bar application of the doctrine. It is enough that the gifts essential impracticality precludes performance.

831 F.Supp. at 539. The leading case *refusing* to apply the cy pres doctrine on the basis of impractibility is *In re Estate of Beach*, No. 23257 [Ca. Super. Cl. Maren County, Aug. 15 1986) (reprinted in 21 U.S.F. L. Rev. 691 (1987)].

The court in *Ciero* refused to base its reason on illegality. Would illegality have been the more appropriate reason for applying cy pres to Captain Alexander's gift to the Coast Guard Academy?

2. Do you think Captain Alexander ever thought about the substitute trust set out by the *Ciero* court?

Note

In instances where a charitable trust would fail because restrictions of property placed in the trust make it impossible to administer the trust, a court may apply the doctrine of deviation, which is analogous to the cy pres doctrine, to ease administrative restraints the donor did not anticipate at the time of the gift.

Compare the cy pres doctrine with the doctrine of deviation in the following case.

NIEMANN v. VAUGHN COMMUNITY CHURCH

Supreme Court of Washington, 2005
154 Wash.2d 365, 113 P.3d 463

BRIDGE, J.

This case requires us to consider whether an alleged restrictive covenant in a deed transferring church property from one church to another, prevents the receiving church, Vaughn Community Church (VCC), from selling the original church property in order to relocate to a larger, nearby property. Petitioner Joyce Niemann, a parishioner at VCC, brought suit alleging the restrictive covenant in the deed prevented the proposed sale. The trial court ruled that the conveyance created a charitable trust, then granted VCC equitable relief, removing the alienation restriction from the trust. The Court of Appeals affirmed. We now affirm the grant of equitable relief, thereby modifying the charitable trust and permitting the sale of the church property. We hold the trial court correctly permitted deviation from the administrative trust provision, finding changed circumstances unanticipated by the settlor, and that the requested deviation furthered the charitable trust's primary purpose. * * *

I

In 1949, the Emmanuel Congregational Church of Vaughn (ECC) owned a parcel of real property located at 17616 Hall Road, Vaughn, Washington. * * * ECC was a Protestant evangelical church and held services on the property. Since at least 1899, the property had been continuously used for evangelical services by a series of churches. In 1949, ECC merged with the Christian Church of Vaughn to create a new church called the Vaughn Community Church in Christ (which later changed its name to Vaughn Community Church, referred to here as

VCC). As part of the merger, the trustees of ECC passed a resolution to transfer the subject property to VCC with the stipulation that "the property shall forever remain for the perpetual use of Protestant Evangelical Churches of the Community of Vaughn." * * * While VCC took possession and began holding services, the land was not formally deeded at that time.

In 1956, VCC needed to remodel the church building on the subject property to meet the needs associated with its recent growth. In order to obtain a loan to finance the remodel, on February 22, 1956, ECC formally conveyed the subject property to VCC by deed. It contained the following relevant language:

WHEREAS, on April 5, 1949, the Board of Trustees of [ECC] met in regular session and passed a resolution pursuant to the authority of the Special Congregation Meeting aforesaid, as follows, resolved that "The Emmanuel Congregational Church of Vaughn transfer (the) church property to the Vaughn Community Church of Christ, with the stipulation that said property shall forever remain for the perpetual use of Protestant Evangelical Churches of the Community of Vaughn".... * * *

VCC continued to grow. In fact, the pastor testified that average Sunday services grew from 30 participants in 1956 to approximately 180 participants by 1999. In the early 1980s, VCC was remodeled and expanded to its current condition, including expansion of the sanctuary and addition of a fellowship hall and classrooms. In 1991, only six years after the completion of the remodel, VCC commissioned a feasibility study to explore options for expanding capacity at the current site. The study concluded the current conditions were inadequate and further expansion was not feasible. On March 28, 1999, the majority of those present at the VCC congregational meeting, 79 percent, voted in favor of selling the church property. * * * VCC purchased a parcel of real property approximately 4.3 miles from the subject property and planned to use the proceeds from a sale of the subject property to fund construction of a new church facility.

Following a two-week bench trial, Judge Marywave Van Deren entered final judgment and made specific findings of fact and conclusions of law in favor of VCC. Based on the pretrial ruling that the 1956 deed created a charitable trust, the trial court, without distinguishing between the two, applied the similar yet distinct equitable doctrines of cy pres and equitable deviation to modify its terms and administration. The court sanctioned VCC's request to deviate from the trust terms to allow for the sale of the subject property to finance a new church building to serve the Protestant evangelical community of Vaughn. In addition to this grant of equitable relief, the court ruled that the Washington Law Against Discrimination (WLAD), * * * prohibited the restrictive covenant found in the habendum clause of the 1956 deed. Specifically, the court held that RCW 49.60.224 applies to charitable trusts and prohibits restraints on alienation of real property on the basis of creed. Secondly, in response to Niemann's argument challenging the constitutionality of the WLAD's application in this case, the trial court held that RCW 49.60.224 does not have a coercive effect on Niemann's practice of religion, that a compelling state interest exists, and that the statute is the least restrictive means of accomplishing that interest. * * *

The Court of Appeals, by a 2–1 majority, affirmed the trial court's rulings* * * We granted Niemann's petition for review.

II

We begin our analysis by addressing the trial court's grant of equitable relief, permitting modification of the charitable trust. * * *

* * *

On partial summary judgment, the trial court held that the 1956 deed created a charitable trust. * * * While this ruling was not appealed, the parties on appeal dispute the settlor's primary intent in deeding the property to VCC and thereby establishing the charitable trust.

The Court of Appeals concluded that substantial evidence supported the trial court's finding that the intent of the settlor was "to benefit the new church, VCC, and to provide for its 'success, growth, and endurance as a church, in ministering and spreading the gospel to the evangelical Protestants of the Vaughn community,' regardless of where the ministries were specifically located." * * *

Niemann correctly asserts that the creation and administration of a charitable trust lies with the settlor's intent. * * * But as VCC notes, the instrument which gave rise to the charitable trust here lacks the typical trust language and detail. As such, recognizing the various possible interpretations of the deed language, the trial court correctly found ambiguity existed. Finding ambiguity, the court looked to extrinsic evidence to construe the intent of the settlors. * * *

Niemann asserts that the purpose of the trust, based on the settlor's intent, was to maintain "this specific Church Property . . . for the use of the Protestant Evangelical Churches of Vaughn." * * * She bases her contention on two separate pieces of evidence before the trial court: (1) a 1998 affidavit signed by the two living grantors, and (2) ECC's articles of incorporation prior to merger. In the 1998 affidavit, grantors Harmon Van Slyke, Jr. and Richard Kroger stated that they believed the board of trustees of ECC "intended that the stipulations contained in that deed/indenture be binding and permanent, and prevent any use of said land other than for a Protestant evangelical church in the community of Vaughn." * * * Additionally, they stated that ECC would never [have] granted [the property] if the Board of Trustees ever understood that the Vaughn Community Church, or its successors . . . would have ever considered or acted to sell or gift this real property to a private party for profit making development; and/or any use other than that as a Protestant evangelical church of the community of Vaughn.

For Niemann's secondary support she cites the ECC articles of incorporation for the proposition that "[t]he purpose of the [ECC] was to hold real property for 'the promotion of regular and permanent meetings for religious worship in the Town of Vaughn, Pierce County, Washington....'" * * *

With regard to the grantors' 1998 affidavit the trial court considered sufficient and substantial evidence to disregard its application. First, while there is no dispute Kroger was a trustee of ECC in 1949 at the time of the merger, the trial court found it "unclear" as to whether Van Slyke, Jr. was also a trustee. * * * Nevertheless, the court accepted him as one of the grantors of the 1956 deed. At trial, Van Slyke, Jr. maintained that ECC intended the church to remain "in that spot" but he also testified that "the intent of the deed was to transfer the property to the Vaughn Community Church." * * * Also at trial, Kroger apparently denied ever believing the grantors intended a restriction on alienation. He testified that "[t]he intent of the deed restriction was not to preserve a particular piece of land or building. The intent was to perpetuate a Protestant Evangelical ministry in the Vaughn community and to insure that there was a Protestant Evangelical church available to the people of the Vaughn area." * * *

As to the ECC articles of incorporation, Niemann takes the cited statement of purpose out of context. The relevant portion is found in the articles' "Statement of Object and Purpose" and reads, in full:

The object of this corporation shall be to purchase, lease, receive by gift, legacy, bequest or otherwise, real and personal property wherever situated, and to sell, lease, mortgage or otherwise dispose of the same in any and every way that shall be useful to, and assist in, the promotion of the regular and permanent meetings for religious worship in the town of Vaughn, Pierce County, Washington, according to the principles and usages of the Congregational Churches of the United States. * * *

Thus, the articles fail to support her contention that the land was to remain and be used in specie.

The trial court concluded that the grantors had "one overriding and dominant intent in conveying the Subject Property to VCC" and that was "to benefit the new church." * * * Specifically, the court found that "[t]he primary aspect of this purpose was to assist and ensure the continuation of the Protestant evangelical ministries of the Vaughn community through VCC, regardless of where they were specifically located and regardless of the name of that church ... [and][t]o see that ministry carried on." * * *

While the trial court additionally found a specific intent to ensure that the subject property would be available for the Protestant evangelical churches of Vaughn, this purpose was secondary to the grantors' "overriding and dominant" intent. Based on the above conflicting evidence, we defer to the trial court's findings of fact regarding the grantors' intent and note only that the record contains sufficient evidence to support its findings. * * *

CY PRES VERSUS EQUITABLE DEVIATION

The Court of Appeals upheld the trial court's trust modification applying the doctrines of cy pres and equitable deviation. * * * The similar objective of these doctrines is to best effectuate the settlor's intent and purpose. While noting some differences in the two doctrines, the Court of Appeals failed to recognize the fundamental distinction. * * * The Restatement (Second) of Trusts commentary clarifies this distinction by providing that "[t]he rule stated in this Section [regarding equitable deviation] has to do with the powers and duties of the trustees of charitable trusts with respect to the administration of the trust; it has to do with the methods of accomplishing the purposes of the trust." RESTATEMENT (SECOND) OF TRUST section 381 cmt. a (1959). It goes on to distinguish it from cy pres:

> The question of the extent to which the court will permit or direct the trustee to apply the trust property to charitable purposes other than the particular charitable purpose designated by the settlor where it is or becomes impossible or illegal or impracticable to carry out the particular purpose involves the doctrine of cy pres....

In sum, courts apply equitable deviation to make changes in the manner in which a charitable trust is carried out while courts apply cy pres in situations where trustees seek to modify or redefine the settlor's specific charitable purpose. * * *

As there is a singular trust issue before the court, only one doctrine, and not the other, is applicable here. The threshold inquiry therefore is whether the term VCC seeks to modify concerns an "administrative" provision of the trust. VCC, as trustee, does not seek to modify the primary purpose of the trust, * * * apply the funds to an alternative objective, nor substitute beneficiaries. Rather, it hopes to remove the alleged restriction on alienation of the property in order to further the trust's primary purpose.

Courts have often classified restrictions on the sale of property as administrative provisions. * * * The Restatement commentary regarding deviation also supports this view.

> Where sale of land forbidden by terms of trust. If a testator devises land for the purpose of maintaining a school or other charitable institution upon the land, and owing to a change of circumstances it becomes impracticable to maintain the institution on the land, the court may direct or permit the trustee to sell the land and devote the proceeds to the erection and maintenance of the institution on other land, even though the testator in specific words directed that the land should not be sold and that the institution should not be maintained in any other place. * * *

TRUST DEVIATION PRINCIPLES

The Restatement (Second) standard provides a relatively narrow standard for applying deviation: The court will direct or permit the trustee of a charitable trust to deviate from a term of the trust if it appears to the court that compliance is impossible or illegal, or that owing to circumstances not known to the settlor and not anticipated by him compliance would defeat or substantially impair the accomplishment of the purposes of the trust. * * *

The Restatement's most recent rendition of the rule grants courts broader discretion to permit deviation. "The court may modify an administrative or distributive provision of a trust, or direct or permit the trustee to deviate from an administrative or distributive provision, if because of circumstances not anticipated by the settlor the modification or deviation will further the purposes of the trust." Restatement (Third) of Trusts section 66(1). While the first prong of the most recent version is substantially similar to the Restatement (Second), the second prong requires only that "modification or deviation will further the purposes of the trust." By requiring a lower threshold finding for equitable relief, this standard gives courts broader discretion in permitting deviation. * * *

Over 80 years ago we held that "[i]n the execution of [trusts in perpetuity] the courts look rather to the intent of the testator than to the method or mode prescribed for its execution." * * * We have also stated that "[w]hile courts, in construing the provisions of a charitable trust, ordinarily will not deviate from the plan outlined by the testator, they undoubtedly have the power to do so, if it is reasonably necessary in effectuating the primary purpose of the trust." * * *

The commentary accompanying the Restatements also provides insight into court's application of equitable deviation. It is important to recognize that the objective of equitable deviation is not to disregard the intention of the settlor, but rather to "give effect to what the settlor's intent probably would have been had the circumstances in question been anticipated." RESTATEMENT (THIRD) OF TRUSTS section 66 cmt. a. Deviation may be allowed with regards to the "provisions governing the management or administration of the trust estate." * * * Both versions contemplate deviation from express terms either directing or forbidding the sale of certain properties. * * *

The party seeking permission to deviate from the trust terms has the burden of showing either changed circumstances or that relevant circumstances were unknown to the settlor. * * * Upon a finding of unanticipated changed circumstances, the court must then determine whether a proposed modification or deviation "would tend to advance (or, instead, possibly detract from) the trust purposes."

III

Finding equitable deviation rather than cy pres applicable here, we next apply the appropriate standard to discern its permissibility according to the facts of the case. As set forth above, this is decided as a matter of law. * * * The trial court heard testimony and made several significant factual determinations supporting a finding of present-day material "circumstances not anticipated by the settlor." These include significant congregational growth, limitations with the building and property, stricter development and building codes, drastic changes in the "community of Vaughn," including growth, expansion, and relocation of its business core, and finally changes in the attitudes, expectations, and needs of parishioners compared with the 1950s. These findings support the conclusion that present day conditions present "circumstances not anticipated by the settlor[s]" in the maintenance of the church and its service to the Vaughn community. * * *

Niemann's contention that the current church location can and is being used for church functions, and thus VCC or another church could continue to occupy these premises, fails to directly address the proper legal standard and issue before the court.

VCC proffered substantial evidence showing the church's mission, and thus the trust's primary purpose, would in fact be substantially impaired by continued habitation of the specific parcel of property. Niemann disputes this finding and points to evidence in the record showing that nothing was physically wrong with the church property and that it could continue to be used as a viable church. When extrinsic evidence allows for conflicting reasonable inferences to be drawn, we generally defer to the trial court's determinations. * * *

The trial court determined that the settlor's primary intent was to convey the property to VCC, and its primary purpose in doing so was to "ensure VCC's success, growth, and endurance as a church, in ministering and spreading the gospel to the evangelical Protestants of the Vaughn community." * * * The housing of VCC at the specific parcel of property, at the time, may have seemed a necessary means of securing this intent. However, the primary trust purpose remained the same; the success of VCC as a church and the spread of the gospel within the community of Vaughn. The trial court made sufficient findings to support its conclusion that permitting deviation was reasonably necessary to effectuate and further the trust's primary purpose.

Based on substantial evidence introduced at trial, we now find, as a matter of law, that changed, unanticipated circumstances exist that are material to the trust's purpose, and permitting deviation from the alleged restriction on alienation would in fact further the primary purpose of the trust. As such, the facts of this case permit deviation.

IV

In conclusion, we affirm the Court of Appeals grant of equitable relief, modifying the charitable trust and permitting the sale of the church property. In so doing, we hold that deviation is permissible when, due to circumstances unanticipated by the settlor, modification of an administrative requirement would advance the trust's purpose. The trial court, as a matter of law, correctly permitted deviation from an administrative trust provision, finding circumstances unanticipated by the settlor and that deviation furthered the charitable trust's primary purpose.

Chapter 9

UNRELATED BUSINESS TAXABLE INCOME

Tax-exempt organizations are subject to income tax liability in the same manner as are for-profit entities if they engage in certain business activities that are unrelated to their exempt purposes. If a tax-exempt organization has "unrelated business taxable income" from such activities in excess of $1,000, it must file Form 990T by the 15th day of the 5th month following the close of its year and pay tax on that income. Tax liability on unrelated business income is computed in the same manner as for a taxable entity. If the organization is incorporated, it will be taxed at corporate rates. If it is a trust, it will be taxed in the same manner as a taxable trust.

Note

In *Sherwin-Williams, Employee Health Plan Trust v. United States*, 403 F.3d 793 (6th Cir. 2005), the court agreed with the Internal Revenue Service that a tax-exempt association organized as a trust was required to pay tax on its unrelated business taxable income at the higher rate applicable to trusts, rather than at the lower corporate income tax rate.

Except for certain mutual benefit organizations, such as social clubs and homeowners' associations, and the political organization, tax-exempt organizations are taxed on the following sources: (1) income from an unrelated trade or business, (2) net rentals from personalty, (3) a part of net investment income from a controlled organization, and (4) a percentage of net income from any "debt-financed" properties. Thus, with the exception of net rentals from personalty, a percentage of investment income from a controlled organization (other than dividend income), and investment income from debt-financed properties, tax exempt organizations are not taxed on investment income. This differs for the social club, the homeowners' association, and political organizations. These organizations are taxed on investment income. (The taxation of social clubs, homeowners' associations, and political organizations is discussed in Chapters 13, 15, and 16. These entities are taxed on all income except "exempt function income" or, as for social clubs, all income except income derived from its members.)

I. HISTORY OF THE UNRELATED BUSINESS INCOME TAX

A. Pre–Revenue Act of 1950

The history of the unrelated business income tax chronicles an "action-reaction" relationship between Congress and exempt organizations. For approximately the first fifty years of the Internal Revenue Code's existence, the majority view was that an exempt organization could engage in commercial activity and could earn a profit without putting its exempt status in jeopardy so long as the income earned from the business activity was used to further the organization's exempt purposes. [See, *e.g., Trinidad v. Sagrada Orden de Predicadores,* 263 U.S. 578, 44 S.Ct. 204, 68 L.Ed. 458 (1924); *Roche's Beach, Inc. v. Commissioner,* 96 F.2d 776 (2d Cir.1938); *C.F. Mueller Co. v. Commissioner,* 190 F.2d 120 (3d Cir.1951); *Sand Springs Home v. Commissioner,* 6 B.T.A. 198 (1927).] This liberal position became known as the "destination of income" test; tax exemption turned not on the relationship between the income-producing activity to an organization's exempt purposes, but on the use to which the income from the business activity was put.[1]

Not all courts agreed with the destination of income test. A small number rejected the test and used a "primary purpose" test. [See, *e.g., United States v. Community Services, Inc.,* 189 F.2d 421 (4th Cir.1951); *Scripture Press Foundation v. United States,* 285 F.2d 800 (Ct.Cl.1961); *Fides Publishers Ass'n v. United States,* 263 F.Supp. 924 (N.D.Ind.1967); *Golden Rule Church Ass'n v. Commissioner,* 41 T.C. 719 (1964).] Relying on *Better Business Bureau v. United States,* 326 U.S. 279, 66 S.Ct. 112, 90 L.Ed. 67 (1945), cited in Chapter 4, these courts concluded that an organization, which operated a business not functionally related to the exempt organization's exempt purposes, violated the operational test. The organization was engaging in activities that advanced two purposes; an exempt and a nonexempt (business) purpose.

Except for the few jurisdictions that rejected the destination of income test, exempt organizations had great incentive to engage in business activity before 1950. They could generate the funds needed to help meet their mission without depending exclusively on private philanthropy. Exempt organizations acquired very successful businesses but would not report their receipts from these businesses as income because they would dedicate the profits earned to their exempt functions. For example, the New York University School of Law owned a macaroni company, a leather company, a piston-ring company, and a chinaware

---

1. For a brief history of the pre–1950 history, see Robert J. Desiderio, *Planning Tax–Exempt Organizations,* §§ 15.02–15.05 (2005).

manufacturing operation.² Because the profits from these business ventures were not subject to income taxes (and other state taxes), business organizations complained that exempt organizations enjoyed an unfair competitive advantage over business organizations conducting similar business. Nonprofit organizations could charge lower prices for their products or services, have more resources to expand their business activities, or pay for marketing and advertising campaigns to promote their products. As a consequence, the theory espoused was that tax paying competitors would be driven out of the market, thus shrinking the tax base.³ (In an article on the subject⁴, Boris Bittker and George Rahdert argued that the shrinkage of the tax base was "overstated if not wholly erroneous.") In any case, Congress responded with the Revenue Act of 1950. (Chapter 994, 64 Stat. 906.)

B. The Revenue Act of 1950

Congress had two purposes in enacting provisions that provided for the unrelated business income tax ("UBIT"). The first, and most important, was to eliminate the favorable competitive environment in which exempt organizations operated. The second was to raise additional revenues. The Senate Finance Committee articulated the unfair competition justification for the Act:

> The problem at which the tax on unrelated business income is directed is primarily that of unfair competition. The tax-free status of organizations enables them to use their profits tax-free to expand operations, while other competitors can expand only with profits remaining after taxes....

(S. Rep. No. 2375, 81st Cong., 2d Sess. 28–29 (1950).)

The second reason for the Revenue Act of 1950 was to offset the revenue loss from reduction in the war excise taxes originally enacted to finance World War II. Congress decided to reduce the war excise taxes with the 1950 Act just as the Korean War was heating up. Both the House Ways and Means Committee [H.R. Rep. No. 2319, 81st Cong., 2d Sess. 1–3 (1950)] and the Senate Finance Committee [S. Rep. No. 2375, 81st Cong., 2d Sess. 1 (1950)] referred to UBIT as a means of negating the impact of the reduction in the war excise taxes.

The Revenue Act's attack on business activity was two fold. First, it prohibited a "feeder organization" from attaining tax exemption [I.R.C. § 502(a)].⁵ As a result of Congress enacting § 502 of the Code, tax-exempt organizations can no longer acquire the stock of profitable

---

2. See Richard L. Kaplan, "Intercollegiate Athletics and Unrelated business Income Tax," 80 Colum. L. Rev. 1430, 1432 (1980).

3. Kaplan, cited in note 2 at 1433.

4. Boris Bittker and George Rahdert,"The Exemption of Nonprofit Organizations from Federal Income Taxation," 85 Yale L.J. 299, 320 (1976).

5. A feeder organization is an "organization [usually a corporation] operated for the primary purpose of carrying on a trade or business for profit," but one that pays all its profits to an exempt organization. (See § 502.) The Mueller Macaroni Company, acquired by New York University School of Law, was a feeder corporation.

corporations and claim that such corporations are tax exempt because their profits are destined to support the exempt organization's purposes. The income earned by the for-profit is taxed so that only post-tax dollars are transferred from the for-profit entity to the exempt organization. In theory, taxing feeder organizations places these organizations on the same competitive footing as business organizations not owned by exempt organizations.

Congress next move was the enactment of §§ 511–513 of the Code, which provided for the unrelated business income tax (UBIT). The treatment of UBIT is akin to taxation of a feeder organization. A feeder organization is a separate entity owned by the exempt organization, while UBIT deals with business activity conducted by the exempt organization itself. The UBIT provisions tax business activity of an otherwise tax exempt organization if that activity does not further directly the organization's exempt purpose. If the only claim for exemption is that the income from the activity financially supports the organization's exempt purpose, the activity is an "unrelated trade or business" (I.R.C. § 513) and subject to normal corporate income taxes. (I.R.C. § 511).[6]

Interestingly, although Congress based the unrelated business amendments on unfair competition, unfair competition is not made an element for taxation, or, for that matter, not even mentioned in the legislation. The regulations, however, do rely on competition as a factor in determining whether commercial activity is related or unrelated. Treasury Regulation § 1.513–1(b) states that "the primary objective of adoption of the unrelated business income tax was to eliminate a source of unfair competition by placing the unrelated business activities of certain exempt organizations upon the same tax basis as the nonexempt endeavors with which they compete."

C. The Regulations

Treasury regulations go farther than the statute in restricting commercial activity. Sections 511–513 recognize the destination of income test to the extent that an organization does not lose its tax exemption if it engages in unrelated business activity. The result simply is that the income from that activity is taxed. The regulations appear, on the other hand, to rely on the pre–1950 minority view. Treasury regulations defining the operational test state that an organization which engages substantially in business activity that does not further the organization's exempt purpose, other than the profits from the activity being dedicated to those purposes, violates the operational test and, thus, is not entitled to tax exemption [Treas. Reg. § 1–501(c)(3)–1(e)].) The regulations, therefore, require that an exempt organization focus upon two questions: (1) whether the commercial activity is related or unrelated to its exempt purposes. If the commercial activities are related, the organization's exempt status is not put in jeopardy. If, on the other

---

6. See Robert J. Desiderio, "The Profitable, Nonprofit Corporation," 1 N.M. Law Rev. 1 (1979).

hand, the commercial activities are unrelated, the organization must face the second question. (2) Whether the commercial activities are substantial or insubstantial. An organization may lose its exemption if it engages substantially in commercial activities. If those activities are insubstantial, the organization will not lose its exemption, but it will be taxed on the income from those activities.

Questions

1. Are the regulations invalid because they go beyond the sanctions imposed by the Code on an unrelated trade or business? Should an exempt organization that engages in substantial unrelated commercial activity lose its tax exemption? Or may the regulations be justified under the Supreme Court's decision in *Better Business Bureau* (discussed in Chapter 4)?

II. ORGANIZATIONS TO WHICH 'UBIT' APPLIES

As originally enacted, UBIT applied only to § 501(c)(3) organizations, except churches, and to labor organizations, business leagues, and chambers of commerce. With the Tax Reform Act of 1969, Congress applied UBIT to virtually all § 501(c) organizations [I.R.C. § 511(a)(2)(A)]. Public colleges and university are subject to UBIT [I.R.C. § 511(a)(2)(B)] even though public institutions are not § 501 exempt organizations. Income from essential government functions earned by such institutions is exempt from taxation under § 115. Section 511, however, supersedes § 115; a public college or university can be taxed constitutionally on its unrelated taxable income. [See *Iowa State University v. United States,* 500 F.2d 508 (Ct.Cl.1974).] Feeder organizations, however, are not subject to UBIT. The reason is that feeders are already subject to tax as a result of § 502.

III. ELEMENTS OF THE UNRELATED BUSINESS INCOME TAX (UBIT)

The unrelated business income tax (UBIT) is imposed on an exempt organization's "unrelated business taxable income" [I.R.C. § 511(a)]. "Unrelated business taxable income" is defined as "the gross income derived by any organization from any unrelated trade or business (as defined in § 513) regularly carried on by it, less the deductions * * * which are directly connected with the carrying on of such trade or business, both computed with the modifications provided in subsection (b)." [See I.R.C. § 512(a)(1).] The elements of this definition are:

a. Gross income from an unrelated trade or business;

b. That is regularly carried on;

c. Less trade or business deductions; and

d. Adjusted for modifications.

A. Unrelated Trade or Business

The core of UBIT is the meaning of an unrelated trade or business. The definition of an "unrelated trade or business" is found in § 513(a), which defines it as "in the case of any organization subject to the tax imposed by § 511, any trade or business the conduct of which is not substantially related (aside from the need of such organization for income or funds or the use it makes of the profits derived) to the exercise or performance by the organization of its ... [charitable purpose]." To this definition is added the § 512 requirement that a trade or business must be regularly carried on. Accordingly, an unrelated trade or business is a trade or business, regularly carried on, that is not substantially related to an organization's exempt purposes.

PROFESSIONAL INSURANCE AGENTS v. COMMISSIONER

United States Court of Appeals, Sixth Circuit, 1984
726 F.2d 1097

MORTON, Chief District Judge.

Professional Insurance Agents of Michigan (PIA), is a trade association exempt from federal income taxation as a "business league" under Section 501(c)(6) of the Internal Revenue Code of 1954. PIA was formed in 1937, incorporated as a non-profit corporation under the laws of Michigan in 1956, and received an Internal Revenue Service ruling that it qualified as an exempt organization in 1958. PIA's Articles of Incorporation describe its objectives as follows: The object of this Association shall be to maintain and extend the American Agency System, which system is defined to be the production of insurance premiums and service of insurance contracts by insurance agents operating solely on a commission basis on their own account as independent contractors, owning their own expirations and who maintain their own offices separate from any insurance company; to promote the equitable rights of its members; to provide its members with increased knowledge through education in insurance underwriting and selling, loss prevention and agency management; to promote a high standard of ethics, friendship and cooperation among its members, to better serve the public, themselves, their companies and to professionalize the industry; to oppose bad practices of insurance and to cooperate with the Department of Insurance of the State of Michigan.

About 1,000 of the nearly 2,400 eligible Michigan insurance agents belonged to PIA. Many of the other agents belonged to a rival trade organization known as Independent Insurance Agents of Michigan. The average PIA member was a relatively small insurance agency with 3–5 employees, writing primarily personal lines of coverage such as automobile and homeowners' insurance.

An insurance agent, upon becoming a member of PIA, automatically became a member of the National Association of Professional Insurance

Agents (National Association). The National Association was a nationwide organization of insurance agents whose membership consisted of the members of its various state and regional affiliates. Despite their shared membership, PIA and the National Association were separate organizations operating independently of one another. The governing body of the National Association was a board of directors comprised of two or three directors elected by each local organization.

During the tax years at issue, PIA endorsed or promoted to its membership several different group insurance programs underwritten by private insurance companies. These programs were: (1) an "Errors and Omissions" liability policy sponsored by the National Association and underwritten by the Utica Mutual Insurance Company; (2) a group life and health insurance policy sponsored by PIA and underwritten by the Independent Liberty Life Insurance Company; and (3) a group life and disability policy sponsored by the National Association and underwritten by unspecified insurance companies. PIA also had at one time (prior to beginning its agreement with Independent Liberty) sponsored a group health, life, and disability program underwritten by the Time Insurance Company. PIA received a refund with respect to Time Insurance Company's program during its fiscal year ending September 30, 1975. The above three programs and the Time Insurance refund will now be discussed in turn.

Errors and Omissions Insurance (sponsored by the National Association).

Errors and Omissions (E & O) insurance is a type of professional malpractice insurance which protects the insurance agent from liability in the event his client suffers a loss as a result of errors made in writing a policy. The insurance is expensive and difficult to underwrite, and the insurance carriers who offer it prefer to spread their risk by selling to a national market on a group, rather than an individual, basis. As a result, the market for coverage on an individual basis was both limited and volatile, with insurance companies occasionally finding it necessary to discontinue the coverage soon after entering the market.

In order to increase the availability of the insurance and maintain continuity of coverage, the National Association agreed to sponsor an E & O program carried by the Utica Mutual Insurance Company. PIA also performed services in connection with the program, including putting certain brochures describing the program and schedules from which a member could calculate his premiums into the membership packets which PIA distributed to new and prospective members; promoting the insurance at educational seminars and in PIA's official magazine; and answering telephone inquiries concerning the program. However, the E & O program could have been available to the PIA's members through the National Association without PIA's participating therein. Utica Mutual paid the National Association a fee equal to 15 percent of gross premiums for the latter's sponsorship of the E & O program. The National Association in turn gave PIA an amount equal to 8 percent of the premiums paid by its members, as compensation for PIA's efforts in promoting the program. While the National Association was not contractually obligated to make these payments to PIA, PIA's executive vice president testified that if the National had stopped making them he would have recommended to PIA's board of directors that they drop the National's E & O insurance program entirely and look for an acceptable substitute sponsor.

During the years at issue approximately 75 to 80 percent of PIA's members subscribed to the E & O coverage sponsored by the National Association. Non-member insurance agents were also permitted to enroll in the plan. The fees received by PIA for its E & O promotional activities amounted to $21,242, $25,978, and $32,991, during the three taxable years here at issue.

Group health and life insurance (sponsored by PIA).

During the years at issue, PIA sponsored a group health and life insurance policy offered by the Independent Liberty Life Insurance Company. As the sponsor, PIA performed several promotional and administrative services for the insurance company, as set forth in a 1974 letter from the company to PIA:

The Association [PIA] will perform certain services on behalf of Independent Liberty such as: Publicizing the program and collecting applications, maintaining an inventory and issuing group certificates, reviewing all claims for submission to the company's claims department, disbursing claim drafts, coordinating communications between the company and the membership regarding underwriting and claim problems, and assisting the company in making other company products available to the general membership. Because these services are to be performed on behalf of Independent Liberty to provide better service for the association members, we will reimburse the Association for a portion of its increased administrative cost by paying a service fee of 6% of the monthly collected premium. The Association should receive the service fee shortly after the close of each month and will continue as long as the Association continues to provide the agreed upon services.

The above-mentioned six percent fee amounted to $16,709, $27,576, and $24,570, during the 3 taxable years here at issue.

Access to low cost group health and life insurance was important to PIA's member agencies because it helped them to compete for employees in the marketplace. However, several other multiple-employer group insurance plans were open to insurance agencies and were operating in Michigan during the years at issue.

Somewhere between 20 and 30 percent of the members participated in the Independent Liberty program. Those who did not do so generally fell into one of two groups: (1) those with few or no employees who had no need for group insurance benefits, or (2) those with 10 or more employees who chose to negotiate their own plan directly with an insurance company.

Group life and disability insurance (sponsored by the National Association).

PIA also promoted to its members several group life and disability insurance programs which were sponsored by the National Association and underwritten by various private insurance companies. The services PIA performed in connection with these plans were similar to the services it provided in connection with the National Association's E & O program, and included the mailing of descriptive brochures to new or prospective members as part of their membership packet. In return for its promotional efforts PIA received a fee from the National Association equal to 4 percent of all premiums paid by its members. This 4 percent fee amounted to $5,183, $8,103, and $7,294 during the 3 taxable years here at issue.

Experience rating reserve refund.

From 1964 through December 31, 1973, PIA directly, or through its nonexempt subsidiary, Agent's Service Exchange, provided a group health, life and disability insurance program to its members through a master group insurance policy with Time Insurance Company. One aspect of this policy was a provision permitting the insurance company to maintain an "experience rating reserve." An "experience rating reserve" is a sum, taken from the insured individuals' premium payments, that is set aside by the insurance company to protect it against the possibility that the claims made under the policy turn out to be larger than anticipated. In the event that larger-than-anticipated losses do not materialize, the insurance company refunds the reserve to the master policyholder.

By letter dated November 12, 1973, PIA notified Time Insurance that all policies between them would be cancelled as of January 1, 1974, the next quarterly renewal date. In its response, Time Insurance stated that it would make a final accounting to applicant concerning the experience rating reserve 1 year after the January 1, 1974, policy termination date. This 1–year claim-lag period was provided in order to insure that most, if not all, claims arising under the policy prior to the termination date were filed and settled before the balance remaining in the reserve was refunded.

In March 1975, representatives of PIA and Time Insurance executed the following agreement with respect to Time's refunding of the experience rating reserve:

> It is agreed that Time Insurance Company will refund to Michigan Association of Mutual Insurance Agents [PIA] a sum in the amount of $43,227.76, in accordance with the Experience Rating Refund formula, upon written acceptance of this release which provides for the following two stipulations:
>
> 1. The distribution of such funds to members of the Association is the sole obligation of the Association, and,

2. Any benefits yet to be paid under the above-named group contract shall be paid by Time Insurance Company only upon the receipt from the Association of the necessary funds. This stipulation shall not bind the Association to any sum, in aggregate, greater than the fund herewith returned.

Pursuant to this agreement, PIA received a refund check from Time Insurance in the amount of $43,227. PIA, however, did not segregate or otherwise earmark this sum to indicate that it was being held in trust. Instead, it deposited the refund check in its general checking account and enjoyed full use and control of the funds thereafter. PIA made no effort to distribute the funds to its members.

No additional claims under the Time Insurance Company policy were made following the expiration of the 1–year claim-lag period. Consequently, PIA was never called upon to return to Time Insurance any portion of its refund in order to meet any such claim.

The Professional Insurance Agents of Michigan (PIA) is a business league exempt from taxation under the provisions of 501(c)(6) of the Internal Revenue Code. The issue presented by this case is whether or not the income which had been received by PIA through the payment of a percentage of the insurance premium income constituted unrelated business income in accordance with Section 511 of the Internal Revenue Code. The income is taxable only if two conditions are present: (1) The income must be from a trade or business regularly carried on by the organization and (2) the trade or business must not be substantially related to the exempt purposes.

PIA, as previously stated, is a tax exempt business league under the provisions of Section 501(c)(6). Its operating income is derived from the splitting of insurance premiums with the sponsor of the insurance programs which were made available to the membership of PIA. Thus, at issue is the characterization and taxability of the revenue so produced. Section 511(a)(1), as previously stated, imposes a tax on unrelated business taxable income. Unrelated business income is defined in Section 512(a) as being gross income derived by any organization from any unrelated trade or business regularly carried on by it. Unrelated trade or business is defined in Section 513 of the Code as being such trade or business, the conduct of which is not substantially related to the exercise or performance by such organization of its function constituting the basis for its exemption under Section 501. As set forth in the regulations of the Internal Revenue Code, Treasury Regulation 1.513–1(a) defines three items which are to be used in determining whether the amounts received by the tax exempt organization constitute unrelated business tax income, to-wit: (1) if the income is from a trade or business; (2) if the trade or business is regularly carried on by the organization; and (3) if the conduct of the trade or business is not substantially related to the organization's performance of its exempt functions (other than through the production of funds). Treas.Reg. § 1.513–1(a).

Thus in determining whether or not PIA has income from a trade or business, the term trade or business includes any activity that is carried on for the production of income from the sale of goods or the performance of services, IRC Section 513(c), and generally conveys the same meaning it does in Section 162. Treas.Reg. 1.513–1(b).

PIA, of course, contends that its insurance premium revenue is not unrelated business taxable income. It further asserts that its insurance promotion does not rise to the level of a trade or business. It is beyond peradventure that the insurance premium payments to PIA are income. The language of the statute states that any activity which is carried on for the production of income is to be deemed a trade or business. IRC § 513(c). The phrase "carried on for the production of income" limits the type of activities covered. That phrase requires us to examine the exempt organization's underlying reasons for engaging in the questioned activity. If it has as its motive the production of income, the activity constitutes a trade or business under Section 513(c), so, the language of the Code prescribes the application of the motive test. The regulations under Section 513 strengthen this interpretation of the statute by incorporating the Section 162 meaning of the term trade or business. "It is well established that the existence of a genuine profit motive is the most important criterion for the finding that a given course of activity constitutes a trade or business." * * * In addition to the intent to earn a profit, Section 162's definition of "trade or business" connotes "extensive activity over a substantial period of time during which the taxpayer holds himself out as a provider of goods and services." * * *

It is the belief of this circuit that the "profit motive" standard is proper in that it is consistent with the language of Section 513, as well as the regulations thereunder. Section 513 and its regulations raise the question of motive in connection with any activity carried on for the production of income. The regulations which invoke Section 162 and its profit motive language confirm that motive is the key inquiry. Thus, the court must look to see whether PIA has engaged in extensive activity over a substantial period of time with intent to earn a profit. It seems clear to us that the record in this cause reflects that a profit motive existed. PIA selected the companies whose products and services would be endorsed and actively promoted among its members. PIA performed the day-to-day administrative services essential to the operation of those products and services. In fact, it would be difficult to imagine a more comprehensive involvement than that performed by PIA. Certainly it was rewarded for its efforts. Its activities were profitable and those profits are ever increasing. We hold that PIA's motive for offering the insurance policies at issue here, particularly in view of the statement of its president that absent a proper split of the insurance premiums a different company would have been selected, was one of profit sufficient to support a finding that the premiums it received were from a trade or business for the purpose of unrelated business tax income.

Having determined that the insurance activities of PIA constituted a trade or business under Section 513, the next step is to determine whether the trade or business is regularly carried on. Obviously, whatever the framework of the statute and regulations, PIA cannot argue that its activities are not ongoing and continuous.

Thus we must now address whether or not PIA's activities are substantially related to its exempt function. Unless its insurance activities are substantially related to its exempt function, the income will be taxed as unrelated business income. Section 513(a) states that the need of an exempt organization for income does not constitute the necessary substantial relationship; so we must turn to the regulations to determine what type of relationship qualifies as substantial. The relevant regulation provides as follows: Trade or business is "related" to exempt purposes, in the relevant sense, only where the conduct of the business activities has causal relationship to the achievement of exempt purposes (other than through the production of income); and it is "substantially related," for purposes of section 513, only if the causal relationship is a substantial one. Thus, for the conduct of trade or business from which a particular amount of gross income is derived to be substantially related to purposes for which exemption is granted, the production or distribution of the goods or the performance of the services from which the gross income is derived must contribute importantly to the accomplishment of those purposes.

Treas.Reg. § 1.513–1(d)(2). Regulations Section 1.513–1(d)(3) states further that "[i]n determining whether activities contribute importantly to the accomplishment of an exempt purpose, the size and extent of the activities involved must be considered in relation to the nature and extent of the exempt function which they purport to serve." Treas.Reg. § 1.513–1(d)(3).

The purpose of PIA is "to promote the organization and development of independent insurance agents through the maintenance and extension of the American agency system; to promote the equitable rights of its members, to provide its members with increased knowledge through education in insurance underwriting and selling, etc.; to better serve the public, themselves, their companies and to professionalize the industry; and to oppose bad practices of insurance."

Thus PIA's tax exempt purpose is to promote the agency system and through education to promote the common interest of its members in the insurance field. Therefore, to fall within the framework of the purposes of PIA, its activities must be substantially related to its stated purpose and must benefit its membership as a group, rather than in their individual capacities. Furthermore, the "substantial relationship" is a determination which is necessarily based upon the facts involved. Two factual elements are critical to the finding of the necessary substantial relationship between a business league's activities and its purposes: (1) the unique nature of the activities vis-a-vis the organizational function, and (2) the capacity in which benefits are received by the organization's members.

For the activities of an exempt business to be related to its exempt function, those activities must be unique to the organization's tax exempt purpose. Such services as educational training programs and promotion of learning within the insurance industry clearly satisfy this uniqueness test since they advance the purpose of the tax exempt entity. Thus, as can be seen, it is the educational ends that must be served if the activity is to be deemed substantially related. Educational and advertising services are peculiarly suitable activities for a business league because they further a common interest that unites the association members. Therefore, the providing of these services for a membership fee would bear a substantial relationship to its purpose. In evaluating the relationship of PIA's activities to its purposes as a business league, the capacity in which benefits are received by the organization's members is as important as the unique character of the organization's activities. For a substantial relationship to exist, any direct benefits flowing from a business league's activities must inure to its members in their capacities as members of the organization. Thus, where a business league's uniquely relevant activities produce inherently group benefits that accrue to its members qua members, a substantial relationship exists within the meaning of Section 513. * * *

Only those activities that benefit the independent insurance agents in their capacities as regular members of PIA can be substantially related to PIA's exempt function. This group benefit standard also accords with the requirement that a business league seek to improve the conditions of an entire line of business rather than perform discrete services for individuals. When the activities of a business league are directed toward the achievement of the common business interest of its members, the benefits that accrue to its members are inherently group benefits. A product or service that seeks to accomplish a truly tax exempt purpose does not assure the member that he will receive benefits directly proportional to the fees he pays. For instance, a portion of PIA's membership dues might have been used to sponsor lobbying efforts for legislation favorable to small insurance agencies. The benefits PIA's members might have received from such activities could have been negligible or far more valuable than the amount of their dues. A similar point can be made regarding educational seminars. A member attending PIA-sponsored seminars might receive far more or less than he paid for. The insurance at issue here, however, was strictly a quid pro quo proposition. A member received a benefit exactly proportional to the premium he paid. Services which render benefits according to the fee that is paid for them are taxable business activities, not tax exempt services. Were we to adopt another rule people would attempt to market all services and products under the aegis of a tax exempt organization.

Therefore, the activities that serve the interests of individual insurance agents according to what they pay produce individual benefits insufficient to fulfill the substantial relationship test, since those activities generally do not generate inherent group benefits that inure to the advantage of its members as members.

Since PIA's insurance premium benefits are basically a fund raising activity, it is by definition unrelated business activity under Section 513(a). It is not the sort of unique activity that satisfies the substantial relationship test, nor are its benefits inherently group related. Advising its members of the availability and desirability of insurance coverage does not fall within that category. We feel that PIA's endorsement of the insurance programs and the promotion thereof are not substantially related to its exempt functions. *See, Louisiana Credit Union League v. United States, supra.* In effect, whether a trade or business is substantially related to an exempt function of a tax exempt business requires an examination and a comparison of the services it renders and the purposes as set forth in its organizational charter. In this case, an examination of the activities reflects that as to its insurance premiums, PIA's purpose is entirely revenue raising. Such a financial relationship is by definition not substantially related to its tax exempt purposes.

* * *

UNITED STATES v. AMERICAN BAR ENDOWMENT

United States Supreme Court, 1986
477 U.S. 105, 106 S.Ct. 2426, 91 L.Ed.2d 89

[This case is reported in Chapter 8. Excluded from that report is the Court's discussion with respect to UBIT. That part of the Court's opinion follows.]

* * *

We recently discussed the history and structure of the unrelated business income provisions of the Code in *United States v. American College of Physicians,* 475 U.S. 834, 106 S.Ct. 1591, 89 L.Ed.2d 841 (1986). The Code imposes a tax, at ordinary corporate rates, on the income that a tax-exempt organization obtains from an "unrelated trade or business ... regularly carried on by it." §§ 512(a)(1), 511(a)(1). An "unrelated trade or business" is "any trade or business the conduct of which is not substantially related ... to the exercise or performance by such organization of its charitable, educational, or other purpose," § 513(a). The Code thus sets up a three-part test. ABE's insurance program is taxable if it (1) constitutes a trade or business; (2) is regularly carried on; and (3) is not substantially related to ABE's tax-exempt purposes. Treas.Reg. § 1.513–1(a), 26 CFR § 1.513–1(a) (1985); *American College of Physicians, supra,* at 838–839, 106 S.Ct., at 1594. ABE concedes that the latter two portions of this test are satisfied. 761 F.2d, at 1576. Its defense is based solely on the proposition that its insurance program does not constitute a trade or business.

A

In the Tax Reform Act of 1969, Pub.L. 91–172, 83 Stat. 487, Congress defined a "trade or business" as "any activity which is carried on for the production of income from the sale of goods or the performance of services," § 513(c). The Secretary of the Treasury has provided further clarification of that definition in Treas.Reg. § 1.513–1(b) (1985), which provides: "in general, any activity of [an exempt] organization which is carried on for the production of income and which otherwise possesses the characteristics required to constitute 'trade or business' within the meaning of section 162" is a trade or business for purposes of 26 U.S.C. §§ 511–513.

ABE's insurance program falls within the literal language of these definitions. ABE's activity is both "the sale of goods" and "the performance of services," and possesses the general characteristics of a trade or business. Certainly the assembling of a group of better-than-average insurance risks, negotiating on their behalf with insurance companies, and administering a group policy are activities that can be—and are—provided by private commercial entities in order to make a profit. ABE itself earns considerable income from its program. Nevertheless, the Claims Court and Court of Appeals concluded that ABE does not carry out its insurance program in order to make a profit. The Claims Court relied on the former Court of Claims holding, in *Disabled American Veterans v. United States,* 650 F.2d 1178, 1187 (1981), that an activity is a trade or business only if "operated in a competitive, commercial manner." * * * Because ABE does not operate its insurance program in a competitive, commercial manner, the Claims Court decided, that program is not a trade or business. The Court of Appeals adopted this reasoning. * * *

The Claims Court rested its conclusion on four factors. First, it found that "the program was devised as a means for fundraising and has been so presented and perceived from its inception." * * * Second, the court found that the program's phenomenal success in generating dividends for ABE was evidence of noncommercial behavior. The court noted that ABE's insurance program has provided $81.9 million in dividends in its 28 years of operation, and concluded that such large profits could not be the result of commercial success, but must proceed from the generosity of ABE's members. Third, and most important, in the court's view, was the fact that ABE's members collectively had the power to change ABE's conduct of the insurance program so as to drastically reduce premiums. That the members had not done so was strong evidence that they sought to further ABE's charitable purposes by paying higher insurance rates than necessary. Fourth, because ABE did not underwrite insurance or act as a broker, it was not competing with other commercial entities.

It appears, then, that the Claims Court viewed ABE as engaging in two separate activities—the provision of insurance and the acceptance of contributions in the form of dividends. If so, the unspoken premise of the Claims Court's decision is that ABE's income is not a result of the first activity, but of the second. There is some sense to this reasoning; should ABE sell a product to its members for more than that product's fair market value, it could argue to the IRS that the members intended to pay excessive prices as a form of contribution, and that some formula should be adopted to separate the income received into taxable profits and nontaxable contributions. Even if we viewed it as appropriate for the federal courts to engage in such a quasi-legislative activity, however, there is no factual basis for the Claims Court's attempt to do so in this case.

B

We cannot agree with the Claims Court that the enormous dividends generated by ABE's insurance program demonstrate that those dividends cannot constitute "profits." Were ABE's insurance markedly more expensive than other insurance products available to its members, but ABE nevertheless kept the patronage of those members, we might plausibly conclude that generosity was the reason for the program's success. The Claims Court did not find, however, that this was the case. ABE prices its insurance to remain competitive with the rest of the market. *Id.,* at 406. Thus ABE's members never squarely face the decision whether to support ABE or to reduce their own insurance costs.

The Claims Court concluded that "such profit margins [as ABE's] cannot be maintained year after year in a competitive market." * * * The court apparently reasoned that ABE's staggering success would inevitably induce other firms to offer similar programs to ABA members unless that success is the result of charitable intentions rather than price-sensitive purchasing decisions. It is possible, of course, that ABE's members genuinely intend to support ABE by paying higher premiums than necessary, and would pay those high premiums even if a competing group insurance plan offered very low premiums. But that is by no means the only possible explanation for the market's failure to provide competition for ABE. * * * Lacking a factual basis for concluding that generosity is at the core of ABE's success, we can easily view this case as a standard example of monopoly pricing. ABE has a unique asset—its access to the ABA's members and their highly favorable mortality and morbidity rates—and it has chosen to appropriate for itself all of the profit possible from that asset, rather than sharing any with its members.

The argument that ABE's members could change the insurance program and receive the bulk of the dividends themselves if they so desired is unconvincing. Were ABE to give each member a choice between retaining his pro rata share of dividends or assigning them to ABE, the organization would have a strong argument that those dividends constituted a voluntary donation. That, however, is not the case here. ABE requires its members to assign it all dividends as a condition for participating in the insurance program. It is simply incorrect to characterize the assignment of dividends by each member as "voluntary" simply because the members theoretically could band together and attempt to change the policy.

Again, the Claims Court put too much weight on an unsupported assumption. It found that the program was "operated with the approval and consent of the ABA membership," *ibid.*, observing that the program had met with "surprisingly little dissent," *id.*, at 411, even though there were "ample" opportunities for members to change policies with which they disagreed, *ibid.* We believe that those facts cannot carry the weight that the Claims Court put on them. Perhaps each member that purchases insurance would, given the option, pay excessive premiums in order to support ABE's charitable purposes; however, that is not the only possible explanation for the members' failure to change the program. Any given member might feel that the potential savings in insurance costs are not sufficient to justify the effort required to mount a challenge to ABE's leadership. Many might not want to "make waves" and upset a program that generates tax-free income for ABE and charitable deductions for their fellow members. The members' theoretical ability to change the program, therefore, is at best inconclusive.

The Claims Court also erred in concluding that ABE's insurance program did not present the potential for unfair competition. The undisputed purpose of the unrelated business income tax was to prevent tax-exempt organizations from competing unfairly with businesses whose earnings were taxed. * * * This case presents an example of precisely the sort of unfair competition that Congress intended to prevent. If ABE's members may deduct part of their premium payments as a charitable contribution, the effective cost of ABE's insurance will be lower than the cost of competing policies that do not offer tax benefits. Similarly, if ABE may escape taxes on its earnings, it need not be as profitable as its commercial counterparts in order to receive the same return on its investment. Should a commercial company attempt to displace ABE as the group policyholder, therefore, it would be at a decided disadvantage.

The Claims Court failed to find any taxable entities that compete with ABE, and therefore found no danger of unfair competition. It is likely, however, that many of ABE's members belong to other organizations that offer group insurance policies. Employers, trade associations, and financial services companies frequently offer group insurance policies. Presumably those entities are taxed on their profits, and their policyholders may not deduct any part of the premiums paid. Such entities may therefore find it difficult to compete for the business of any ABE members who are otherwise eligible to participate in these group insurance programs.

The only valid argument in ABE's favor, therefore, is that the insurance program is billed as a fundraising effort. That fact, standing alone, cannot be determinative, or any exempt organization could engage in a tax-free business by "giving away" its product in return for a "contribution" equal to the market value of the product. ABE further contends that it must prevail because the Claims Court found that ABE's profits represent contributions rather than business income; ABE argues that we may not upset that finding unless it is clearly erroneous. * * * The undisputed facts, however, simply will not support the inference that the dividends ABE receives are charitable contributions from its members rather than profits from its insurance program. Moreover, the Claims Court failed to articulate a legal rule that would permit it to split ABE's activities into the gratuitous provision of a service and the acceptance of voluntary contributions, and we find no such rule in the Code or regulations. Even if we assumed, however, that the court's failure to attach the label "trade or business" to ABE's insurance program constitutes a finding of fact, we would be constrained to hold that finding clearly erroneous.

* * *

Question

Is the insurance program in *ABE* different from the program in *Professional Insurance Agents*? Should both programs be subject to tax?

Note

Section 513 (c) defines a "trade or business" as "any activity which is carried on for the production of income from the sale of goods or the performance of services." The regulations then equate the meaning of trade or business for purposes of UBIT with the meaning of trade or business under § 162. However, the standard for whether a trade or business exists for purposes of § 162 is whether the taxpayer has a profit motive. See *Commissioner v. Groetzinger,* 480 U.S. 23, 35, 107 S.Ct. 980, 94 L.Ed.2d 25 (1987).

B. Regularly Carried On

The regularly carried on criterion is probably the closest the Code comes to recognizing unfair competition as a basis for UBIT. Other than to eliminate casual commercial activity, one wonders why the regularly carried on element was added to § 512. The regulations appear to answer the question with its interpretation of "regularly carried on:"

> regard must be had to the frequency and continuity with which the activities productive of the income are conducted and the manner in which they are pursued. *This requirement must be applied in light of the purpose of the unrelated business income tax to place exempt organization business activities upon the same tax basis as the nonexempt business endeavors with which they compete. Hence, for example, specific business activities of an exempt organization will ordinarily be deemed to be "regularly carried on" if they manifest a frequency and continuity, and are pursued in a manner, generally similar to comparable commercial activities if nonexempt organizations.*

Treas. Reg. § 1.51301(c)(1).

The following case is probably the most controversial case dealing with the regularly carried on requirement.

NATIONAL COLLEGIATE ATHLETIC ASS'N v. COMMISSIONER

United States Court of Appeals, Tenth Circuit, 1990
914 F.2d 1417

SEYMOUR, Circuit Judge.

The National Collegiate Athletic Association (NCAA), the petitioner in this case, appeals from the decision of the tax court, which determined a deficiency of $10,395.14 in unrelated business income tax due for the 1981–1982 fiscal year. On appeal, the NCAA challenges the court's conclusion that revenue received from program advertising constituted unrelated business taxable income under I.R.C. § 512, not excludable from tax as a royalty under section 512(b)(2), I.R.C. § 512(b)(2). We reverse.

I.

The NCAA is an unincorporated association of more than 880 colleges, universities, athletic conferences and associations, and other educational organizations and groups related to intercollegiate athletics, for which it has been the major governing organization since 1906. The NCAA is also an "exempt organization" under section 501(c)(3) of the Code, I.R.C. § 501(c)(3), and hence is exempt from federal income taxes. One of the purposes of the NCAA, as described in the organization's constitution, is "[t]o supervise the conduct of ... regional and national athletic events under the auspices of this Association." * * * Pursuant to this purpose, the NCAA sponsors some seventy-six collegiate championship events in twenty-one different sports for women and men on an annual basis. The most prominent of these tournaments, and the NCAA's biggest revenue generator, is the Men's Division I Basketball Championship. The tournament is held at different sites each year. In 1982, regional rounds took place at a variety of sites, and the Louisiana Superdome in New Orleans was the host for the "Final Four," the tournament's semifinal and final rounds. In that year, the Championship consisted of forty-eight teams playing forty-seven games on eight days over a period of almost three weeks. The teams played in a single-game elimination format, with each of the four regional winners moving into the Final Four.

The NCAA contracted with Lexington Productions, a division of Jim Host and Associates, Inc. ("Host" or "Publisher"), in 1981 to print and publish the program for the 1982 Final Four games. The purpose of such programs, according to the NCAA's then-director of public relations, is

> "to enhance the experience primarily for the fans attending the game.... [It also] gives the NCAA an opportunity to develop information about some of its other purposes that revolve around promoting sports [as a] part of higher education and demonstrating that athletes can be good students as well as good participants."

* * *

Prior to the middle of the 1970s, the host institution produced the Final Four program. The NCAA took over production until the late 1970s, when it began contracting with Host for the Final Four program. In 1982, Host began producing the programs for all rounds of the Championship. The motive for contracting the program production to Host was, according to the NCAA, to achieve consistency and quality at each round's game sites; making a profit was not the primary incentive.* * *

The "Official Souvenir Program" for the 1982 Final Four round of the tournament was some 129 pages long, and it featured pictures of NCAA athletes such as Michael Jordan and articles on the NCAA itself, on New Orleans, on individual athletes, on championships from prior years, and on the Final Four teams: Georgetown, Houston, Louisville, and North Carolina. Advertisements made up a substantial portion of the program, some of which were placed by national companies. Among the products and services so displayed were Buick automobiles, Miller beer, Texaco motor oil, Fuji film, Maxwell House coffee, Nike sneakers, McDonald's fast food, Coca-Cola soda, Xerox photocopiers, ESPN cable network, and Popeyes Famous Fried Chicken. Other advertisers were local New Orleans merchants. A number of the New Orleans advertisements, including those for restaurants, hotels, and rental cars, apparently were directed at out-of-town tournament attendees. But these advertisements were exceeded in number by those placed by New Orleans/Louisiana companies not specifically related to the tourist industry. Among the local advertisers were the Canal Barge Company, the National Bank of Commerce in Jefferson Parish, Breit Marine Surveying, Inc., Pontchartrain Materials Corp., McDermott Marine Construction, and Tri-Parish Construction & Materials, Inc...

The NCAA's total revenue from the 1982 Men's Division I Basketball Championship was $18,671,874 ... The NCAA reported none of this amount as unrelated business taxable income on its federal income tax return for the fiscal year ending August 31, 1982. The Commissioner mailed the NCAA a notice of deficiency in which he determined that the NCAA was liable for $10,395.14 in taxes on $55,926.71 of unrelated business taxable income from the program advertising revenue. The NCAA petitioned the tax court for a redetermination of the deficiency set forth by the Commissioner. The tax court determined that this revenue was unrelated business taxable income, and that it was not excludable from the tax as a royalty.

* * *

III.

Section 511 of the Code imposes a tax on the unrelated business taxable income of exempt organizations. Section 512(a)(1) of the Code defines the term "unrelated business taxable income" as "the gross income derived by any organization from any unrelated trade or business ... regularly carried on by it...." The term "unrelated trade or business" means "any trade or business the conduct of which is not substantially related ... to the exercise or performance by such organization" of its exempt function. I.R.C. § 513(a). Under the heading "Advertising, etc., activities," section 513(c) provides that "the term 'trade or business' includes any activity which is carried on for the production of income from the sale of goods or the performance of services.... [A]n activity does not lose identity as a trade or business merely because it is carried on ... within a larger complex of other endeavors which may, or may not, be related to the exempt purposes of the organization." I.R.C. § 513(c).

The NCAA's advertising revenue therefore must be considered unrelated business taxable income if: "(1) It is income from trade or business; (2) such trade or business is regularly carried on by the organization; and (3) the conduct of such trade or business is not substantially related (other than through the production of funds) to the organization's performance of its exempt functions." Treas.Reg. § 1.513–1(a); *see also United States v. American College of Physicians,* 475 U.S. 834, 838–39, 106 S.Ct. 1591, 1594–95, 89 L.Ed.2d 841 (1986). If a taxpayer shows that it does not meet any one of these three requirements, the taxpayer is not liable for the unrelated business income tax. * * *

The NCAA concedes that its program advertising was a "trade or business" not "substantially related" to its exempt purpose. The only question remaining, therefore, is whether the trade or business was "regularly carried on" by the organization. The meaning of the term "regularly carried on" is not defined by the language of the statute. Accordingly, we turn to the Treasury Regulations for assistance.

Section 1.513–1(c) of the Treasury Regulations provides a discussion of the phrase "regularly carried on." The general principles set out there direct us to consider "the frequency and continuity with which the activities productive of the income are conducted *and* the manner in which they are pursued." Treas.Reg. § 1.513–1(c)(1) (emphasis added). As a cautionary note, the regulations emphasize that whether a trade or business is regularly carried on must be assessed "in light of the purpose of the unrelated business income tax to place exempt organization business activities upon the same tax basis as the nonexempt business endeavors with which they compete."

The regulations then move beyond the general principles and set out a process for applying the principles to specific cases. The first step is to consider the normal time span of the particular activity, and then determine whether the length of time alone suggests that the activity is regularly carried on, or only intermittently carried on. *See id.* § 1.513–1(c)(2)(i). If the activity is "of a kind normally conducted by nonexempt commercial organizations on a *year-round* basis, the conduct of such [activity] by an exempt organization over a period of only a few weeks does not constitute the regular carrying on of trade or business." * * * As an example of a business not regularly carried on, the regulations describe a hospital auxiliary's operation of a sandwich stand for only two weeks at a state fair. In contrast, the regulations deem the operation of a commercial parking lot every Saturday as a regularly-carried-on activity.

If the activity is "of a kind normally undertaken by nonexempt commercial organizations only on a *seasonal* basis, the conduct of such activities by an exempt organization during a *significant portion* of the season ordinarily constitutes the regular conduct of trade or business." * * * The operation of a horse racing track several weeks a year is an example of a regularly-conducted seasonal business, because such tracks generally are open only during a particular season.

A primary point of contention in this case is whether the NCAA's advertising business is normally a seasonal or year-round one, and whether it is intermittent or not. The tax court noted that the Commissioner looked at the short time span of the *tournament,* concluded that it was as much a "seasonal" event as the operation of a horse racing track, and then argued that the time involved in the tournament program advertising made it a regularly carried on business. The court observed that the NCAA, which did not agree with the Commissioner's "season" conclusion, also focused on the tournament itself in contending that the event's short time span made the activity in question intermittent. The tax court rejected these arguments as "plac [ing] undue emphasis on the tournament itself as the measure for determining whether petitioner regularly carried on the business at issue.... Although sponsorship of a college basketball tournament and attendant circulation of tournament programs are seasonal events, the 'trade or business' of selling advertisements is not." * * *

We agree that to determine the normal time span of the activity in this case, we should consider the business of *selling advertising space,* since that is the business the Commissioner contends is generating unrelated business taxable income. There is no dispute that the tournament itself is substantially related to the NCAA's exempt purpose and so, unlike the horse racing track, it should not be the business activity in question. *See American College of Physicians,* 475 U.S. at 839, 106 S.Ct. at 1594–95 ("Congress has declared unambiguously that the *publication of paid advertising* is a trade or business activity *distinct* from the publication of accompanying ... articles") (emphasis added). Since the publication of advertising is generally conducted on a year-round basis, we conclude that if the NCAA's sale of program advertising was conducted for only a few weeks, that time period could not, standing alone, convert the NCAA's business into one regularly carried on.

In regard to the question of how long the NCAA conducted its advertising business, the tax court stated that "[i]t is inappropriate to decide whether the trade or business at issue is regularly carried on solely by reference to the time span of the tournament itself." * * * The tax court, observing that the agency relationship between the NCAA and Host allowed the court to attribute Host's activities to the NCAA, noted that the NCAA had "not produced any evidence ... regarding the extent or manner of Host's conduct in connection with the solicitation, sale, and publication of advertising for the tournament programs." * * * The court went on to conclude that "[w]ithout such evidence [the NCAA] has not proven that neither it nor Host carried on the activity of selling program advertising regularly. [The tax court] will not assume Host's conduct in this regard was infrequent or conducted without the competitive and promotional efforts typical of other commercial endeavors." * * * We believe the tax court focused its analysis in the wrong direction.

The tax court held, and the Commissioner argues, that the amount of preliminary time spent to solicit advertisements and prepare them for publication is relevant to the regularly-carried-on determination, and that the length of the tournament is not relevant. This position is contrary to the regulations and to existing case law. The language of the regulations alone suggests that preparatory time should not be considered. The sandwich stand example in the regulations, for instance, included a reference only to the two weeks it was operated at the state fair. See Treas.Reg. § 1.513–1(c)(a)(i). The regulations do not mention time spent in planning the activity, building the stand, or purchasing the alfalfa sprouts for the sandwiches.

The case closest to the one here also does not evaluate preparatory time. In that case, *Suffolk County Patrolmen's Benevolent Ass'n v. Commissioner,* 77 T.C. 1314 (1981), an exempt organization staged a professional vaudeville show every year as a fundraising event, using a company with which it had contracted. The organization derived the vast majority of its receipts from the sale of advertising in a program guide distributed to show patrons and to anyone who requested it. The shows generally consisted of three or four performances stretching over two weekends. The tax court found that preparation for the shows and the program, including the solicitation of advertisements, lasted eight to sixteen weeks, but it then emphasized that

> "nowhere in the regulations or the legislative history of the tax on unrelated business income is there any mention of time apart from the duration of the event itself.... The fact that an organization seeks to insure the success of its fundraising venture by beginning to plan and prepare for it earlier should not adversely affect the tax treatment of the income derived from the venture."
> * * *

As in *Suffolk County,* the advertising here was solicited for publication in a program for an event lasting a few weeks. The NCAA did put on evidence as to the duration of that event. While the length of the tournament is irrelevant for purposes of assessing the normal time span of the business of selling advertising space, we hold that, contrary to the tax court's conclusion, the tournament must be considered the actual time span of the business activity sought to be taxed here. The length of the tournament is the relevant time period because what the NCAA was selling, and the activity from which it derived the relevant income, was the publication of advertisements in programs distributed over a period of less than three weeks, and largely to spectators. Obviously, the tournament is the relevant time frame for those who chose to pay for advertisements in the program. This case is unlike *American College of Physicians,* 475 U.S. at 836, 106 S.Ct. at 1593, where advertisements were sold for each issue of a monthly medical journal. Accordingly, we conclude that the NCAA's involvement in the sale of advertising space was not sufficiently long-lasting to make it a regularly-carried-on business solely by reason of its duration.

The next step of the regulation's analysis is to determine whether activities which are intermittently conducted are nevertheless regularly carried on by virtue of the manner in which they are pursued. In general, according to the regulations, "exempt organization business activities which are engaged in only discontinuously or periodically will not be considered regularly carried on if they are conducted without the competitive and promotional efforts typical of commercial endeavors." Treas.Reg. § 1.513–1(c)(2)(ii). As an example of an activity not characteristic of commercial endeavors, the regulations refer to "the publication of *advertising in programs for sports events* or music or drama performances." * * * The NCAA places considerable emphasis on this latter sentence and criticizes the tax court, which stated only that there was insufficient evidence from which the court could draw conclusions on the manner of Host's conduct of its advertising activities. As the NCAA stresses, the tax court did not distinguish the 1982 Basketball Championship from the "sports events" referred to in the regulation above.

On appeal, the Commissioner initially agreed with the tax court that the record was devoid of evidence with which the NCAA could show that Host's efforts were not of a sufficiently competitive and promotional nature. But the Commissioner then went on to focus on the Final Four program, a part of the record. He characterized the program's advertisements as "typical print media advertisements," and distinguished them from the advertisements in the vaudeville show programs, which " 'more closely resembled complimentary contributions than commercial selling agents.' " * * * The sentence referring to sports events in the regulations was, according to the Commissioner, directed more at advertising in high school sports programs than at the type of advertising in the program here.

Addressing first the tax court's conclusion, we fail to see what evidence in addition to the advertisements themselves the tax court could require. The regulations discuss the business of advertising but refer only to advertisements published in programs, and not to any efforts to secure the advertisements. In *Suffolk County,* the tax court disregarded all but the advertisements themselves and stated that it is "entirely reasonable for an exempt organization to hire professionals in an effort to insure the success of a fundraiser, and there are no indications [in the applicable statutes and regulations] ... that the use of such professionals would cause an otherwise infrequent intermittent activity to be considered regularly carried on." * * *

The Commissioner's assertion that the advertisements themselves are of a commercial nature deserves more discussion. It is true that a number of the advertisements are virtually indistinguishable from those that might appear in magazines like *Sports Illustrated.* A substantial number of other advertisements, however, particularly those placed by Louisiana companies not engaged in the tourist industry, seem to us to resemble more closely the "complimentary contributions" of *Suffolk County.*

The difficult question of whether the NCAA's advertising is of the type envisioned as commercial in nature, or instead as consistent with that connected to the "sports events" referred to in the regulations, is not one which we must answer now, however. For the final step in the process spelled out by the regulations requires us to consider whether, promotional efforts notwithstanding, an intermittent activity occurs "so infrequently that neither [its] recurrence nor the manner of [its] conduct will cause [it] to be regarded as trade or business regularly carried on." Treas.Reg. § 1.513–1(c)(2)(iii). We conclude that the advertising here is such an infrequent activity. The programs containing the advertisements were distributed over less than a three-week span at an event that occurs only once a year. We consider this to be sufficiently infrequent to preclude a determination that the NCAA's advertising business was regularly carried on.

Our conclusion is buttressed by the regulation's admonition that we apply the regularly-carried-on test in light of the purpose of the tax to place exempt organizations doing business on the same tax basis as the comparable nonexempt business endeavors with which they compete. *See* Treas.Reg. § 1.513–1(c)(1). The legislative history of the unrelated business income tax also convinces us that we must consider the impact an exempt organization's trade or business might have on its competition. The tax was a response to the situation prevailing before 1950, when an exempt organization could engage in any commercial business venture, secure in the knowledge that the profits generated would not be taxed as long as the *destination* of the funds was the exempt organization. The *source* of those funds did not affect their tax status. * * * As more and more exempt organizations began acquiring and operating commercial enterprises, there were rumblings in Congress to do away with the perceived advantage enjoyed by these organizations. The case which most forcefully brought this point home was that involving the C.F. Mueller Co. That company, a leading manufacturer of macaroni products, was in 1947 acquired and organized for the purpose of benefitting the New York University's School of Law, a tax-exempt educational institution. * * * This acquisition prompted an outcry from a number of sources.

In President Truman's 1950 message to Congress, for example, he stated that " 'an exemption intended to protect educational activities has been misused in a few instances to gain competitive advantage over private enterprise through the conduct of business ... entirely unrelated to educational activities.'" Kaplan, *Intercollegiate Athletics and the Unrelated Business Income Tax,* 80 Colum.L.Rev. 1430, 1433 (1980) (quoting Message of the President, 96 Cong.Rec. 769, 771 (1950)). Primarily to "restrain the unfair competition fostered by the tax laws," *American College of Physicians,* 475 U.S. at 838, 106 S.Ct. at 1594 (citing H.R.Rep. No. 2319, 81st Cong., 2d Sess., 36–37 (1950)), Congress imposed a tax on the business income of exempt organizations, but only on that income substantially unrelated to the organization's exempt purposes. *See* Revenue Act of 1950, Pub.L. No. 814, § 301, 64 Stat. 906, 947.

Although we have observed that the purpose of the unrelated business income tax was to prevent unfair competition between companies whose earnings are taxed and those whose are not, it is not necessary to prove or disprove the existence of actual competition. * * * But analyzing the business in question in terms of its possible effect on prospective competitors helps to explain why an activity can occur "so infrequently" as to preclude a designation as a business regularly carried on. While the operation of a parking lot on a weekly basis occurs sufficiently frequently to threaten rival parking lot owners, the hospital auxiliary's annual sandwich stand is too infrequent a business to constitute a threat to sandwich shop owners. The competition in this case is between the NCAA's program and all publications that solicit the same advertisers. The competition thus includes weekly magazines such as *Sports Illustrated* and other publications which solicit automobile, beverage, photocopier, and fried chicken advertisements, to name a few. Viewed in this context, we conclude that the NCAA program, which is published only once a year, should not be considered an unfair competitor for the publishers of advertising. Application of the unrelated business tax here therefore would not further the statutory purpose. We hold that the NCAA's advertising business was not regularly carried on within the meaning of the Code.

The decision of the tax court is REVERSED.

Question

Do you think that the advertising in the Final Four program was not a regularly carried on trade or business?

C. Substantially Related

The regulations define "substantially related" as a relation that is causally related to and that contributes importantly to the organization's exempt purposes. The application of these standards involves analysis of the context in which the organization operates the trade and business, considering all the relevant facts. *American College of Physicians* is the leading case.

Sec. III UNRELATED BUSINESS INCOME TAX (UBIT) 455

UNITED STATES v. AMERICAN COLLEGE OF PHYSICIANS
United States Supreme Court, 1986
475 U.S. 834, 106 S.Ct. 1591, 89 L.Ed.2d 841

Justice MARSHALL delivered the opinion of the Court.

A tax-exempt organization must pay tax on income that it earns by carrying on a business not "substantially related" to the purposes for which the organization has received its exemption from federal taxation. The question before this Court is whether respondent, a tax-exempt organization, must pay tax on the profits it earns by selling commercial advertising space in its professional journal. The Annals of Internal Medicine.

I

Respondent, the American College of Physicians, is an organization exempt from taxation under § 501(c)(3) of the Internal Revenue Code. The purposes of the College, as stated in its articles of incorporation, are to maintain high standards in medical education and medical practice; to encourage research, especially in clinical medicine; and to foster measures for the prevention of disease and for the improvement of public health. * * * The principal facts were stipulated at trial. In furtherance of its exempt purposes, respondent publishes The Annals of Internal Medicine (Annals), a highly regarded monthly medical journal containing scholarly articles relevant to the practice of internal medicine. Each issue of Annals contains advertisements for pharmaceuticals, medical supplies, and equipment useful in the practice of internal medicine, as well as notices of positions available in that field. Respondent has a longstanding policy of accepting only advertisements containing information about the use of medical products, and screens proffered advertisements for accuracy and relevance to internal medicine. The advertisements are clustered in two groups, one at the front and one at the back of each issue.

In 1975, Annals produced gross advertising income of $1,376,322. After expenses and deductible losses were subtracted, there remained a net income of $153,388. Respondent reported this figure as taxable income and paid taxes on it in the amount of $55,965. Respondent then filed a timely claim with the Internal Revenue Service for refund of these taxes, and when the Government demurred, filed suit in the United States Claims Court.

The Claims Court held a trial and concluded that the advertisements in Annals were not substantially related to respondent's tax-exempt purposes. * * * Rather, after finding various facts regarding the nature of the College's advertising business, it concluded that any correlation between the advertisements and respondent's educational purpose was incidental because "the comprehensiveness and content of the advertising package is entirely dependent on each manufacturer's willingness to pay for space and the imagination of its advertising agency." Accordingly, the court determined that the advertising proceeds were taxable.

The Court of Appeals for the Federal Circuit reversed. 743 F.2d 1570 (1984). It held clearly erroneous the trial court's finding that the advertising was not substantially related to respondent's tax-exempt purpose. The Court of Appeals believed that the trial court had focused too much on the commercial character of the advertising business and not enough on the actual contribution of the advertisements to the education of the journal's readers. It held that respondent had established the requisite substantial relation and its entitlement to exemption from taxation. * * * We granted the Government's petition for certiorari, * * *, and now reverse.

II

The taxation of business income not "substantially related" to the objectives of exempt organizations dates from the Revenue Act of 1950, Ch. 994, 64 Stat. 906 (1950 Act). The statute was enacted in response to perceived abuses of the tax laws by tax-exempt organizations that engaged in profit-making activities. Prior law had required only that the profits garnered by exempt organizations be used in furtherance of tax-exempt purposes, without regard to the source of those profits. * * * As a result, tax-exempt organizations were able to carry on full-fledged commercial enterprises in competition with corporations whose profits were fully taxable. See Revenue Revision of 1950: Hearings before the House Committee on Ways and Means, Vol. I, 81st Cong., 2d Sess., 18–19 (1950) (hereinafter cited as 1950 House Hearings) (describing universities' production of "automobile parts, chinaware, and food products, and the operation of theatres, oil wells, and cotton gins"). Congress perceived a need to restrain the unfair competition fostered by the tax laws. * * *

Nevertheless, Congress did not force exempt organizations to abandon all commercial ventures, nor did it levy a tax only upon businesses that bore no relation at all to the tax-exempt purposes of an organization, as some of the 1950 Act's proponents had suggested. * * * Rather, in the 1950 Act it struck a balance between its two objectives of encouraging benevolent enterprise and restraining unfair competition by imposing a tax on the "unrelated business taxable income" of tax-exempt organizations. 26 U.S.C. § 511(a)(1).

"Unrelated business taxable income" was defined as "the gross income derived by any organization from any unrelated trade or business ... regularly carried on by it...." § 512(a)(1). Congress defined an "unrelated trade or business" as "any trade or business the conduct of which is not substantially related ... to the exercise or performance by such organization of its charitable, educational, or other purpose or function constituting the basis for its exemption...." § 513(a). Whether respondent's advertising income is taxable, therefore, depends upon (1) whether the publication of paid advertising is a "trade or business," (2) whether it is regularly carried on, and (3) whether it is substantially related to respondent's tax-exempt purposes.

III

A

Satisfaction of the first condition is conceded in this case, as it must be, because Congress has declared unambiguously that the publication of paid advertising is a trade or business activity distinct from the publication of accompanying educational articles and editorial comment.

In 1967, the Treasury promulgated a regulation interpreting the unrelated business income provision of the 1950 Act. The regulation defined "trade or business" to include not only a complete business enterprise, but also any component activity of a business. Treas.Reg. § 1.513–1(b), * * *. This revolutionary approach to the identification of a "trade or business" had a significant effect on advertising, which theretofore had been considered simply a part of a unified publishing business. The new regulation segregated the "trade or business" of selling advertising space from the "trade or business" of publishing a journal, an approach commonly referred to as "fragmenting" the enterprise of publishing into its component parts:

> "[A]ctivities of soliciting, selling, and publishing commercial advertising do not lose identity as a trade or business even though the advertising is published in an exempt organization periodical which contains editorial matter related to the exempt purposes of the organization." 26 CFR § 1.513–1(b) (1985).

In 1969, Congress responded to widespread criticism of those Treasury regulations by passing the Tax Reform Act of 1969, Pub.L. 91–172, 83 Stat. 487 (1969 Act). That legislation specifically endorsed the Treasury's concept of "fragmenting" the publishing enterprise into its component activities, and adopted, in a new § 513(c), much of the language of the regulation that defined advertising as a separate trade or business:

> "Advertising, etc., activities ... an activity does not lose identity as a trade or business merely because it is carried on ... within a larger complex of other endeavors which may, or may not, be related to the exempt purposes of the organization." 26 U.S.C. § 513(c).

The statute clearly established advertising as a trade or business, the first prong of the inquiry into the taxation of unrelated business income.

The presence of the second condition, that the business be regularly carried on, is also undisputed here. The satisfaction of the third condition, however, that of "substantial relation," is vigorously contested, and that issue forms the crux of the controversy before us.

B

According to the Government, Congress and the Treasury established a blanket rule that advertising published by tax-exempt professional journals can never be substantially related to the purposes of those journals and is, therefore, always a taxable business. Respondent, however, contends that each case must be determined on the basis of the characteristics of the advertisements and journal in question. Each party finds support for its position in the governing statute and regulations issued by the Department of the Treasury.

In its 1967 regulations, the Treasury not only addressed the "fragmentation" issue discussed above, but also attempted to clarify the statutory "substantially related" standard found in § 513(a). It provided that the conduct of a tax-exempt business must have a causal relation to the organization's exempt purpose (other than through the generation of income), and that "the production or distribution of the goods or the performance of the services from which the gross income is derived must *contribute importantly* to the accomplishment of [the exempt] purposes." Treas.Reg. § 1.513–1(d)(2), 26 CFR § 1.513–1(d)(2) (1985) (emphasis added). In illustration of its new test for substantial relation, the Treasury provided an example whose interpretation is central to the resolution of the issue before us. Example 7 of Treas.Reg. § 1.513–1(d)(4)(iv) involves "Z," an exempt association formed to advance the interests of a particular profession and drawing its membership from that profession. Z publishes a monthly journal containing articles and other editorial material that contribute importantly to the tax-exempt purpose. Z derives income from advertising products within the field of professional interest of the members:

> "Following a practice common among taxable magazines which publish advertising, Z requires its advertising to comply with certain general standards of taste, fairness, and accuracy; but within those limits the form, content, and manner of presentation of the advertising messages are governed by the basic objective of the advertisers to promote the sale of the advertised products. While the advertisements contain certain information, the informational function of the advertising is incidental to the controlling aim of stimulating demand for the advertised products and differs in no essential respect from the informational function of any commercial advertising. Like taxable publishers of advertising, Z accepts advertising only from those who are willing to pay its published rates. Although continuing education of its members in matters pertaining to their profession is one of the purposes for which Z is granted exemption, the publication of advertising designed and selected in the manner of ordinary commercial advertising is not an educational activity of the kind contemplated by the exemption statute; it differs fundamentally from such an activity both in its governing objective and in its method. Accordingly, Z's publication of advertising does not contribute importantly to the accomplishment of its exempt purposes; and the income which it derives from advertising constitutes gross income from unrelated trade or business." § 1.513–1(d)(4)(iv), Example 7.

The Government contends both that Example 7 creates a *per se* rule of taxation for journal advertising income and that Congress intended to adopt that rule, together with the remainder of the 1967 regulations, into law in the 1969 Act. We find both of these contentions unpersuasive.

Read as a whole, the regulations do not appear to create the type of blanket rule of taxability that the Government urges upon us. On the contrary, the regulations specifically condition tax exemption of business income upon the importance of the business activity's contribution to the particular exempt purpose at issue, and direct that "[w]hether activities productive of gross income contribute importantly to the accomplishment of any purpose for which an organization is granted an exemption depends *in each case* upon the facts and circumstances involved," § 1.513–1(d)(2) (emphasis added). Example 7 need not be interpreted as being inconsistent with that general rule. Attributing to the term "example" its ordinary meaning, we believe that Example 7 is best construed as an illustration of one possible application, under given circumstances, of the regulatory standard for determining substantial relation.

The interpretative difficulty of Example 7 arises primarily from its failure to distinguish clearly between the statements intended to provide hypothetical facts and those designed to posit the necessary legal consequences of those facts. Just at the point in the lengthy Example at which the facts would appear to end and the analysis to begin, a pivotal statement appears: "the informational function of the advertising is incidental to the controlling aim of stimulating demand for the advertised products." The Government's position depends upon reading this statement as a general proposition of law, while respondent would read it as a statement of fact that may be true by hypothesis of "Z" and its journal, but is not true of Annals.

We recognize that the language of the Example is amenable to either interpretation. Nevertheless, several considerations lead us to believe that the Treasury did not intend to set out a *per se* statement of law. First, when the regulations were proposed in early 1967, the Treasury expressed a clear intention to treat all commercial advertising as an unrelated business. * * * When the regulations were issued in final form, however, following much criticism and the addition of Example 7, they included no such statement of intention. 32 Fed.Reg. 17657 (1967). Second, a blanket rule of taxation for advertising in professional journals would contradict the explicit case-by-case requirement articulated in Treas.Reg. § 1.513–1(d)(2), and we are reluctant to attribute to the Treasury an intention to depart from its own general principle in the absence of clear support for doing so. Finally, at the time the regulations were issued, the 1950 Act had been interpreted to mean that business activities customarily engaged in by tax-exempt organizations would continue to be considered "substantially related" and untaxed. * * * A *per se* rule of taxation for the activity, traditional among tax-exempt journals, of carrying commercial advertising would have been a significant departure from that prevailing view. Thus, in 1967 the idea of a *per se* rule of taxation for all journal advertising revenue was sufficiently controversial, its effect so substantial, and its statutory authorization so tenuous, that we simply cannot attribute to the Treasury the intent to take that step in the form of an ambiguous example, appended to a subpart of a subsection of a subparagraph of a regulation.

It is still possible, of course, that, regardless of what the Treasury actually meant by its 1967 regulations, Congress read those regulations as creating a blanket rule of taxation, and intended to adopt that rule into law in the 1969 Act. The Government appears to embrace this view, which it supports with certain statements in the legislative history of the 1969 Act. For example, the Government cites to a statement in the House Report, discussing the taxation of advertising income of journals published by tax-exempt organizations:

> "Your committee believes that a business competing with taxpaying organizations should not be granted an unfair competitive advantage by operating tax free unless the business contributes importantly to the exempt function. It has concluded that by that standard, advertising in a journal published by an exempt organization is not related to the organization's exempt functions, and therefore it believes that this income should be taxed." H.R.Rep. No. 91–413, pt. 1, p. 50 (1969), U.S.Code Cong. & Admin.News 1969, pp. 1645, 1695.

Similar views appear in the Senate Report:

> "Present law.—In December 1967, the Treasury Department promulgated regulations under which the income from advertising and similar activities is treated as 'unrelated business income' even though such advertising for example may appear in a periodical related to the educational or other exempt purpose of the organization.
>
> "General reasons for change.—The committee agrees with the House that the regulations reached an appropriate result in specifying that when an exempt organization carries on an advertising business in competition with other taxpaying advertising businesses, it should pay a tax on the advertising income. The statutory language on which the regulations are based, however, is sufficiently unclear so that substantial litigation could result from these regulations. For this reason, the committee agrees with the House that the regulations, insofar as they apply to advertising and related activities, should be placed in the tax laws." S.Rep. No. 91–552, p. 75 (1969), U.S.Code Cong. & Admin.News 1969, p. 2104.

Based on this language, the Government argues that the 1969 Act created a *per se* rule of taxation for advertising income. The weakness of this otherwise persuasive argument, however, is that the quoted discussion appears in the Reports solely in support of the legislators' decision to enact § 513(c), the provision approving the fragmentation of "trade or business." Although § 513(c) was a significant change in the tax law that removed one barrier to the taxation of advertising proceeds, it cannot be construed as a comment upon the two other distinct conditions—"regularly carried on" and "not substantially related"—whose satisfaction is prerequisite to taxation of business income under the 1950 Act. Congress did not incorporate into the 1969 Act the language of the regulation defining "substantial relation," nor did the statute refer in any other way to the issue of the relation between advertising and exempt functions, even though that issue had been hotly debated at the hearings. * * * Thus, we have no reason to conclude from the Committee Reports that Congress resolved the dispute whether, in a specific case, a journal's carriage of advertising could so advance its educational objectives as to be "substantially related" to those objectives within the meaning of the 1950 Act.

It is possible that the Committees' discussion of advertising reflects merely an erroneous assumption that the "fragmentation" provision of § 513(c), without more, would establish the automatic taxation of journal advertising revenue. Alternatively, the quoted passages could be read to indicate the Committees' intention affirmatively to endorse what they believed to be existing practice, or even to change the law substantially. The truth is that, other than a general reluctance to consider commercial advertisements generally as substantially related to the purposes of tax-exempt journals, no congressional view of the issue emerges from the quoted excerpts of the Reports. Thus, despite the Reports' seeming endorsement of a *per se* rule, we are hesitant to rely on that inconclusive legislative history either to supply a provision *not* enacted by Congress, * * * or to define a statutory term enacted by a prior Congress. * * * We agree, therefore, with both the Claims Court and the Court of Appeals in their tacit rejection of the Government's argument that the Treasury and Congress intended to establish a *per se* rule requiring the taxation of income from all commercial advertisements of all tax-exempt journals without a specific analysis of the circumstances.

IV

It remains to be determined whether, in this case, the business of selling advertising space is "substantially related"—or, in the words of the regulation, "contributes importantly"—to the purposes for which respondent enjoys an exemption from federal taxation. Respondent has maintained throughout this litigation that the advertising in Annals performs an educational function supplemental to that of the journal's editorial content. * * * Testimony of respondent's witnesses at trial tended to show that drug advertising performs a valuable function for doctors by disseminating information on recent developments in drug manufacture and use. * * * In addition, respondent has contended that the role played by the Food and Drug Administration, in regulating much of the form and content of prescription-drug advertisements, enhances the contribution that such advertisements make to the readers' education. All of these factors, respondent argues, distinguish the advertising in Annals from standard commercial advertising. Respondent approaches the question of substantial relation from the perspective of the journal's subscribers; it points to the benefit that they may glean from reading the advertisements and concludes that that benefit is substantial enough to satisfy the statutory test for tax exemption. The Court of Appeals took the same approach. It concluded that the advertisements performed various "essential" functions for physicians, and found a substantial relation based entirely upon the medically related content of the advertisements as a group.

The Government, on the other hand, looks to the conduct of the tax-exempt organization itself, inquiring whether the publishers of Annals have performed the advertising services in a manner that evinces an intention to use the advertisements for the purpose of contributing to the educational value of the journal. Also approaching the question from the vantage point of the College, the Claims Court emphasized the lack of a comprehensive presentation of the material contained in the advertisements. It commented upon the "hit-or-miss nature of the advertising," 3 Cl.Ct., at 543, n. 3, and observed that the "differences between ads plainly reflected the advertiser's marketing strategy rather than their probable importance to the reader." "[A]ny educational function [the advertising] may have served was incidental to its purpose of raising revenue."

We believe that the Claims Court was correct to concentrate its scrutiny upon the conduct of the College rather than upon the educational quality of the advertisements. For all advertisements contain some information, and if a modicum of informative content were enough to supply the important contribution necessary to achieve tax exemption for commercial advertising, it would be the rare advertisement indeed that would fail to meet the test. Yet the statutory and regulatory scheme, even if not creating a *per se* rule *against* tax exemption, is clearly antagonistic to the concept of a *per se* rule *for* exemption for advertising revenue. Moreover, the statute provides that a tax will be imposed on "any trade or business the *conduct* of which is not substantially related," 26 U.S.C. § 513(a) (emphasis added), directing our focus to the manner in which the tax-exempt organization operates its business. The implication of the statute is confirmed by the regulations, which emphasize the "manner" of designing and selecting the advertisements. See Treas.Reg. § 1.513–1(d)(4)(iv), Example 7, 26 CFR § 1.513–1(d)(4)(iv), Example 7 (1985). Thus, the Claims Court properly directed its attention to the College's conduct of its advertising business, and it found the following pertinent facts:

> "The evidence is clear that plaintiff did not use the advertising to provide its readers a comprehensive or systematic presentation of any aspect of the goods or services publicized. Those companies willing to pay for advertising space got it; others did not. Moreover, some of the advertising was for established drugs or devices and was repeated from one month to another, undermining the suggestion that the advertising was principally designed to alert readers of recent developments [citing, as examples, ads for Valium, Insulin and Maalox]. Some ads even concerned matters that had no conceiv-

able relationship to the College's tax-exempt purposes." 3 Cl.Ct., at 534 (footnotes omitted).

These facts find adequate support in the record. * * * Considering them in light of the applicable legal standard, we are bound to conclude that the advertising in Annals does not contribute importantly to the journal's educational purposes. This is not to say that the College could not control its publication of advertisements in such a way as to reflect an intention to contribute importantly to its educational functions. By coordinating the content of the advertisements with the editorial content of the issue, or by publishing only advertisements reflecting new developments in the pharmaceutical market, for example, perhaps the College could satisfy the stringent standards erected by Congress and the Treasury. In this case, however, we have concluded that the Court of Appeals erroneously focused exclusively upon the information that is invariably conveyed by commercial advertising, and consequently failed to give effect to the governing statute and regulations. Its judgment, accordingly, is

Reversed.

Notes

1. In *American College of Physicians,* the Court references the "fragmentation rule." The rule is codified in § 513(c): "An activity does not lose identity as a trade or business merely because it is carried on within a larger aggregate of similar activities or within a larger complex of other endeavors which may, or may not, be related to the exempt purposes of the organization." The rule requires that an organization separate commercial activity from exempt activity and measure the relationship of the commercial to the exempt purposes distinct from the exempt activity. The purpose was to prevent an exempt organization from arguing that commercial activity, which otherwise would be an unrelated activity, is substantially related because it is part of some overall, larger activity. The best example, which *American College of Physicians* illustrates, involves advertisement included within an exempt organization's journal. Section 513(c), which is entitled "Advertising, etc. activities," was enacted primarily to deal with advertising income earned by an exempt organization.

2. The clearest example of related activity involves facilities that attract patrons, like a cafeteria run by a museum or a hospital (Rev. Rul. 74–399, 1974–2 C.B. 172; Rev. Rul. 69–268, 1969–1 C.B. 160), or for the convenience of its intended beneficiaries. [See, *e.g.,* Rev. Rul. 81–61, 1981–1 C.B. 355 (a beauty shop operated by a senior citizen's center).]

3. A facility owned by an exempt organization that is used for dual purposes is also subject to the substantially contributed requirement. For example, a museum that has a movie theater, which is used to show educationally-related films and also movies for public entertainment, is operating a trade of business as to the public entertainment films. [See Treas. Reg. § 1.513–1(d)(4).]

Problems

1. A university conducts travel tours for its professors, students, and alumni. Some of the tours have instruction or curricula related to destinations being visited and others do not. The history department sponsors travel tours to archaeological sites devoted to the study of ancient history and cultures. The tours are part of a coordinated educational program designed to educate tour participants about the ancient history of a particular region. The promotional materials do not refer to any particular recreational or sightseeing activities. Will the university be taxed on net income it derives from any of these tours?

2. A museum operates a restaurant for its visitors. Recently it has advertised the restaurant monthly in a local newspaper and has provided the general public access to the restaurant. Customers to the restaurant alone need not pay a museum admission fee charged visitors to the museum collections. Will the museum be taxed on net income from restaurant sales?

3. A hospital charges visitors a fee to park in its parking lot. Will the hospital be taxed on these fees?

4. An art museum sells several items in its gift shop, including reproductions of its collections, greeting cards containing artwork of famous painters, pharmaceuticals, toys, souvenirs of the city in which it is located, and books on art and history. Will the museum be taxed on income from sales of these items?

D. Exceptions to "UBIT"

Section 513 provides for eleven exceptions to UBIT: A trade or business is not subject to tax:

1. Where substantially all the work is performed by volunteers [I.R.C. § 513(a)(1)].

2. If it is operated by a § 501(c)(3) organization or by a state college or university and the trade or business is carried on primarily for the convenience of the organization's members, students, patients, officers, or employees [I.R.C. § 513(a)(2)].

3. If it involves the sale of merchandise, substantially all of which was donated to the organization [I.R.C. § 513(a)(3)].

4. If it involves public entertainment activities at a fair or exposition [I.R.C.§ 513(d)(1)-(2)].

5. If it involves certain convention and trade show activities [I.R.C. § 513(d)(3)].

6. If it involves providing certain hospital services [I.R.C. § 513(e)].

7. If it involves conducting certain bingo games [I.R.C. § 513(f)].

8. If it involves the distribution of low cost articles incidental to the solicitations of charitable contributions. [I.R.C. § 513(h)(1)(A)].

9. If it involves the rental of mailing lists by charitable and veterans' organizations to other such organizations [I.R.C. § 513(h)(1)(B)].

10. If it involves "qualified" sponsorship agreements [I.R.C. § 513(i)].

11. If it involves pole rentals and the organization is a mutual or cooperative telephone or electric company. [I.R.C. § 513(g).]

The requirements of each of these exceptions is beyond the scope of this casebook.[7] A few comments are in order, however. Most of these exceptions are justifiable on the theory that they involve activity that does not compete unfairly with comparable business organizations. The activity is the type that we usually expect of the particular type of exempt organization.

An exception, probably, is the exclusion for corporate sponsorships. That exception excludes from unrelated business taxable income the moneys earned by granting sponsorships to for-profit entities for such activities as the Rose Bowl, Fiesta Bowl, Orange Bowl and Sugar Bowl. Congress enacted the exception for sponsorships in 1997, after a continuing battle between the IRS and exempt organizations. The exception, set out in § 513(i) provides a safe harbor for "qualified sponsorship payments" [H.R. Rep. 2014, 1015 Cong., 1st Sess. § 915(a) (1997)]. Congress' response was an attempt to end the battle, while recognizing that sponsorships, especially in the collegiate athletic arena, was a major source of funds for the organizations operating the events.

A second point is that the IRS has interpreted these exceptions strictly. [See, *e.g., Waco Lodge No. 166 v. Commissioner,* T.C. Memo 1981–546, *aff'd. on other grounds,* 696 F.2d 372 (5th Cir.1983) (the IRS denied the volunteer exception when volunteers were given free drinks with a cash value of $.63.)] An organization that relies on one of the exceptions should be able to support its decision with evidence that shows it strictly meets the requirements of the exception.

Problems

1. An exempt orphanage operates a retail store and sells to the general public. Substantially all the work is performed by volunteers. Would the orphanage be taxed on net income from these sales?

2. A thrift shop operated by a tax exempt organization sells old clothing, books, and furniture contributed by the general public. Would the organization be taxed on net income from these sales?

3. A university provides facilities, instruction, and faculty supervision for a campus newspaper operated by students. In addition to news items and editorial commentary, the newspaper publishes paid advertising. Will the university be taxed on income generated by the advertising? The university

---

7. For a discussion of them, See 1 Marilyn Phelan, *Nonprofit Enterprises: Nonprofit Enterprises* §§ 11:05–11:11 (2003) and Robert J. Desiderio, *Planning Tax–Exempt Organizations,* § 15.09 (2002).

also has a radio station and sells advertising time and services to commercial advertisers in the manner of an ordinary commercial station. Will it be taxed on this advertising income?

4. Volunteers of an exempt organization sell advertising over a period of two months to raise funds for an exempt symphony orchestra. The organization publishes an annual concert book distributed at the orchestra's annual charity ball. Would the organization be taxed on this advertising income?

E. Modifications

Section 512(a) concludes its definition of unrelated business income with the caveat that gross income from an unrelated trade or business must be adjusted for "modifications." Section 512 then lists sixteen modifications [I.R.C. § 512(b)(1)-(13), (15)-(17)], seven of which involve passive income [I.R.C. § 512((b)(1)-(5), (13), (16)], four exclude certain income [I.R.C. § 512(b)(7)-(9), (15)], four provide for certain deductions [I.R.C. § 512(b)(6), (10)-(12)], and one prescribes that certain income is unrelated business income [I.R.C. § 512(b)(17)]. Of these sixteen, the most important are those dealing with passive income.

Passive income has been excluded from UBIT since the enactment of the Revenue Act of 1950. As the Senate Finance Committee recognized:

> Dividends, interest, royalties, most rents, capital gains and losses and similar items are excluded from the base of the tax on unrelated income because your committee believes that they are "passive" in character and are not likely result in serious competition for taxable businesses having similar income. Moreover, investment-producing incomes of these types have long been recognized as a proper source of income for educational and charitable organizations and trusts.

S. Rep. No. 2375, 81st Cong., 2d Sess. 30 (1950).

The regulations state that dividends and interest are "income from ordinary and routine investments [Treas. Reg. § 1.512(b)–1(a)(1)]. Accordingly, dividends from equity investments and interest on bank accounts, bonds, certificates of deposit and annuities are excluded from UBIT, no matter how large the amount may be. Rents and royalties cause more difficulty.

1. Rents

Rents from the lease of real property generally are excluded. [See Treas. Reg. § 1.512(b)–1(c)(2)(ii)(a).] Rents from the lease of personal property are not excluded unless the personal property is leased in conjunction with real property and the rents attributable to the personal property are an incidental amount of the total rents from the lease [Treas. Reg. § 1.512(b)–1(c)(2)(ii)(b)]. Rents attributable to personal property are considered as an incidental amount of the total rents if the rents are 10 percent or less of total rents from the leased property. This is determined at the time the personal property is first placed in service by the lessee. Rents from real property will not be excluded from unrelated business income if more than 50 percent of the total rents received are attributable to personal property determined at the time the personal property first is placed in service by the lessee [I.R.C. § 512(b)(3)(B); Treas. Reg. § 1.512(b)–1(c)(1)(iii)(a)]. In addition, if the amount of rent from real property depends in whole or in part on the income or profits derived from the property leased, other than an amount based on a fixed percentage of gross receipts or sales, the rents will not be excluded from unrelated business income [Treas. Reg. § 1.512(b)–1(c)(2)(iii)(b)].

A problem arises when the exempt organization renders services along with leasing property. Payments for services provided the occupant (lessee) are not excluded if the services are "primarily for ... (the occupant's convenience and are other than those usually or customarily rendered in connection with the rental of rooms or other space for occupancy only." [See Treas. Reg. § 1.512(b)(1)–1(c)(5).] The regulations state that "the supplying of maid service ... constitutes such service, whereas the furnishing of heat and light, the cleaning of public entrances, exits, stairways, and lobbies, the collection of trash, etc., are not considered as services rendered to the occupant." The latter provision takes care of most dormitory type facilities.

Note

The IRS has limited a university from renting its athletics facilities to a professional athletic team. If the university provides ground maintenance, dressing room, linen and stadium security services for the team, the Service has ruled that payment to the university is for services and is not rent. (See Rev. Rul. 80–298, 1980–2 C.B. 197.)

2. Royalties

Although not defined in the Code and regulations, the IRS has adopted the ordinary definition of a royalty, that is, a payment "for the use of a valuable intellectual property right." (See Rev. Rul. 81–178, 1981–2 C.B. 135, 136.) Royalties are payments for the right to use copyrights, trademarks, trade names, lists and similar intangible property rights. The courts have accepted this definition. [See, *e.g, Sierra Club v. Commissioner,* 86 F.3d 1526, 1530 (9th Cir.1996), *aff'g in part, rev'g in part, and remanding,* 103 T.C. 307 (1994) and T.C. Memo 1993–199 and *Common Cause v. Commissioner,* 112 T.C. 332, 339 (1999).] Royalties also include payments for mineral rights. [See I.R.C. § 512(b)(2).]

Similar to the situation with rent, if the exempt organization-owner of the intellectual property right performs services for the licensee that are related to the marketing of the property right, the payment from the licensee will be a payment for services rendered rather than a royalty. Assume an exempt organization gives a marketing company its membership list in return for a fee. As a condition of the fee, the organization must maintain the list. Is the fee payment for use of the use of the list or the service related to maintenance of the lists?

For over twenty years, the IRS and exempt organization have litigated this issue with respect to mailing lists and the right to use the exempt organization's name and logo on credit cards ("affinity cards"). [See, *Disabled American Veterans v. Commissioner,* 650 F.2d 1178 (Ct.Cl. 1981); *National Water Well Ass'n, Inc. v. Commissioner,* 92 T.C. 75 (1989); *Sierra Club v. Commissioner (Sierra Club I),* T.C. Memo 1993–199, *aff'd,* 86 F.3d 1526 (9th Cir.1996); and *(Sierra Club II),* 103 T.C. 307 (1994), *aff'd in part, rev'd in part, and remanded,* 86 F.3d 1526 (9th Cir.1996); *Alumni Ass'n of Univ. of Oregon v. Commissioner,* T.C. Memo 1996–63, *aff'd sub nom.,* 193 F.3d 1098 (9th Cir.1999); *Oregon State Alumni Ass'n v. Commissioner,* T.C. Memo. 1996–34, *aff'd,* 86 F.3d 1098 (Fed.Cir.1996); *Mississippi State Univ. Alumni, Inc. v. Commissioner,* T.C. Memo. 1997–397).] The *Sierra Club* cases best reflect the conflict. The Tax Court opinion for *Sierra Club II* follows.

SIERRA CLUB, INC. v. COMMISSIONER
United States Tax Court, 1994
103 T.C. 307

HALPERN, Judge:

We have previously issued a report in this case: *Sierra Club, Inc. v. Commissioner,* T.C.Memo. 1993–199 (Sierra Club I). In that report, we dealt with the question of whether income from petitioner's rental of its mailing lists constituted unrelated business taxable income within the meaning of section 512(a)(1) (hereafter, UBTI). We held that, since the mailing lists are intangible property, all consideration received for the use of those lists did not constitute UBTI because it constituted royalty income within the meaning of section 512(b)(2). We granted petitioner's motion for partial summary judgment with regard to that question. * * * The parties, however, have filed additional motions for partial summary judgment, which we address in this report.

* * *

History of the Affinity Card Program

The affinity card program in issue (the affinity card program or, simply, the program) is the product of numerous agreements among various parties. Among those parties are petitioner and a corporation named American Bankcard Services, Inc. (ABS). In 1980, petitioner was approached by a predecessor of ABS and entered into the negotiations that resulted in the agreements in question. In its initial proposal to petitioner, the predecessor of ABS described how affinity card programs work in essentially the following terms: Simply stated, the affinity group contracts with a financial institution to issue credit cards to its members and supporters. In return for encouraging its members and supporters to accept and use the credit cards, the financial institution pays the affinity group a percentage of the monthly sales volume resulting from transactions made with the cards. The financial institution provides the affinity group with certain other benefits and services.

* * *

Discussion

* * *

We believe that the income received from the affinity card program during the years in issue *did* constitute royalties within the meaning of section 512(b)(2), and, therefore, was exempt from the tax on UBTI. See sec. 512(a)(1). Our reasons are as follows.

III. *Analysis*

A. *Business Arrangements*

1. *Marketing Efforts*

It is clear that the agreements described above (the agreements) establish an arrangement to be carried out for the mutual (but perhaps separate) profit of the parties thereto. Indeed, the parties have stipulated that, after the agreements were entered into (1) written marketing plans were prepared, setting forth a strategy to market Sierra Club Visa cards to members, (2) solicitations for such cards were sent to members, and (3) advertisements for such cards appeared in *Sierra* magazine. Apparently, those marketing efforts met with some success. The parties have stipulated that, for petitioner's 1986 and 1987 tax years, it had gross receipts from its participation in the affinity card program of $6,021 and $303,225, respectively.

2. *Credit Cards*

Many people hold and use credit cards, and the use of credit cards has become a familiar aspect of contemporary American life. Stipulated documents establish the general nature of the arrangements underlying the use of credit cards. Most cardholders no doubt understand that, in consideration of their agreeing to pay the credit card bill when it comes due, a financial institution is extending to them credit, which they may use to purchase goods and services. Generally, no interest charge is stated to the cardholder if the credit card bill is paid promptly. If the credit card bill is not paid promptly, however, the cardholder accesses the "credit reserve" feature of her card, and a stated charge for further credit is incurred. Participating vendors allow the financial institution a discount on the amount billed in exchange for prompt payment by the financial institution.

3. *Compensation of Petitioner*

Respondent states that banks that issue credit cards normally receive a discount of about 3 percent from participating vendors. Respondent also states that Chase Lincoln "agreed to share with SC the revenues it received from merchants when individual holders of SC credit cards made purchases." * * *

B. *Questions Presented*

That parties to a profitable arrangement may mutually, but separately, profit is not unusual. An author and her publisher may mutually profit from sales of the author's book. The author may earn a royalty based on the number of books sold; the publisher will profit if receipts from sales exceed costs. Petitioner's position, simply put, is that, with regard to the affinity card program, petitioner was in a position like that of the author, merely receiving a royalty for use of an intangible asset: "Sierra Club received royalty payments in exchange for the license of the use of intangible assets—Sierra Club's name and logo, and, perhaps, use of its mailing list."

Respondent's position is less precise: "During the years in issue, SC was in the trade or business of promoting acquisition and use of its VISA credit card." Respondent explains her position as follows: In the alternative, petitioner (1) as a joint venturer with Chase Lincoln (or with Chase Lincoln and ABS), was in the business of "selling credit card goods and services" or (2) as a sole proprietor, was in the business of providing its "services in marketing and endorsing SC's credit card". The revenues produced by such a business, respondent would add, simply do not constitute royalties. Respondent's position seems to come down to the following: If petitioner was a joint venturer or sole proprietor in the business described, the income received from the affinity card activities could not have been royalties.

We will address, first, whether petitioner participated in a joint venture with regard to the affinity card program. Since we conclude that it did not, we will then examine the scope of petitioner's activities to determine whether petitioner engaged in the business described or, alternatively, simply engaged in a licensing transaction.

C. *Joint Venture*

1. *Introduction*

In *Beck Chem. Equip. Corp. v. Commissioner,* 27 T.C. 840, 848–849 (1957), we gave extensive consideration to the issue of whether the taxpayer had associated with another party in a joint venture during the year in controversy. We said:

> The legal relationship known as a joint venture has been defined as a "special combination of two or more persons, where in some specific venture a profit is jointly sought without any actual partnership or corporate designation," and also as "an association of persons to carry out a single business enterprise for profit." * * *

Those definitions are still pertinent. * * *

Under section 7701(a)(2), a joint venture is one of the various unincorporated associations included within the broad definition of a partnership "through or by means of which any business, financial operation, or venture is carried on". As we said in *Beck Chem. Equip. Corp. v. Commissioner, supra* at 849: "The Code thus makes its own classification and prescribes its own standards for qualification as a 'partnership,' and to the extent thereof, it supersedes local law for Federal income tax purposes. * * * [currently, pars. (b) and (c), sec.

301.7701-1, Proced. & Admin. Regs.]; *Commissioner v. Tower,* 327 U.S. 280 (1946)." Therefore, our use of the term "partnership" is a reference to that term as it is defined for Federal income tax purposes.

2. A. *Question of Intent*

The landmark cases setting forth what constitutes a valid partnership for Federal income tax purposes are *Commissioner v. Tower,* 327 U.S. 280 (1946), and *Commissioner v. Culbertson,* 337 U.S. 733 (1949). In *Tower,* the Supreme Court, in upholding this Court's conclusion that a partnership had not been established, stated:

> When the existence of an alleged partnership arrangement is challenged by outsiders, the question arises whether the partners really and truly intended to join together for the purpose of carrying on business and sharing in the profits or losses or both. And their intention is a question of fact, to be determined from testimony disclosed by their "agreement, considered as a whole, and by their conduct in execution of its provisions". * * *

In *Culbertson,* the Supreme Court elaborated on the factors to be considered in determining the intent of the partners to form a partnership:

> whether, considering all the facts—the agreement, the conduct of the parties in execution of its provisions, their statements, the testimony of disinterested persons, the relationship of the parties, their respective abilities and capital contributions, the actual control of income and the purposes for which it is used, and any other facts throwing light on their true intent—the parties in good faith and acting with a business purpose intended to join together in the present conduct of the enterprise. * * *

Those principles and commentary are equally applicable where the kind of partnership is an alleged joint venture within the purview of section 7701(a)(2). * * * Thus, the inquiry we must make is whether petitioner and Chase Lincoln (or petitioner, Chase Lincoln, and ABS) "really and truly intended to join together for the purpose of carrying on business and sharing in the profits or losses or both." See *Commissioner v. Tower, supra* at 287.

4. *Conclusion*

Based on the various agreements described above and the other stipulated facts and exhibits, we conclude that petitioner and Chase Lincoln (or petitioner, Chase Lincoln, and ABS) did not "really and truly intend to join together for the purpose of carrying on business and sharing in the profits or losses or both." * * * Petitioner did not participate in a joint venture with regard to the affinity card program. Petitioner was not, on account of the affinity card program, a partner with Chase Lincoln (or Chase Lincoln and ABS) for tax purposes.

* * *

E. *License*

1. *Introduction*

Having determined that petitioner neither participated in a joint venture with regard to the affinity card program nor engaged in the business of selling financial services to members, we are left to determine whether the financial consideration that petitioner received pursuant to the agreement properly is to be characterized as royalties.

2. *Definition of Royalties*

Our report in Sierra Club I contains an extended discussion of the term "royalties", as that term is used in section 512(b)(2). We will not repeat that discussion here. Suffice it to say that we have accepted the following definition of the term "royalties" for purposes of section 512(b)(2): "payments for the use of valuable intangible property rights".
* * *

3. *Petitioner's Position*

Pursuant to section 2.1 of the agreement, petitioner is obligated: "to cooperate with ABS on a continuing basis in the solicitation and encouragement of SC members to utilize the Services provided by ABS". In consideration thereof, pursuant to section 4.1 of the agreement, ABS agrees to pay to petitioner "a royalty fee". Petitioner argues that the agreement constitutes a license of its name and logo, and permission to use its membership mailing list, for which it received "royalties", as that term is used in section 512(b)(2).

4. *Respondent's Position*

Respondent's position is fundamentally inconsistent with the notion that petitioner received *anything* (whether as a royalty or otherwise) from ABS pursuant to the agreement. Respondent insists on her agency theory: "Because it was SC's business, use of SC's name and logo in connection therewith did not give rise to royalty income." "In reality," respondent explains, "SC was paying ABS for performing services in connection with the * * * [agreement]." Respondent further insists that the agreement is "unambiguous in *not* creating a licensing agreement for the use of SC's name, logo or mailing list." If the Court determines any ambiguity in the agreement, respondent argues that there is thus a material fact at issue and a trial is required.

* * *

On the basis of the agreement and stipulated exhibits, we conclude that the agreement made available for ABS's use petitioner's name, marks, and mailing list. Such items are intangible property, and the financial consideration received by petitioner under the agreement was in consideration of such use. Such financial consideration was not in consideration of services performed by ABS or property other than valuable intangible property. Such consideration thus constitutes royalties within the meaning of section 512(b)(2). * * *

IV. *Conclusion*

Petitioner has moved for partial summary judgment that its income from the affinity card program for the years in dispute constituted royalties within the meaning of section 512(b)(2). Respondent has objected on the grounds that (1) her own motion for partial summary judgment (to the contrary) should be granted and (2) alternatively, there are unresolved genuine issues of material fact requiring a trial. We have decided that there is no genuine issue as to any material fact requiring a trial. We have also decided that the income in question *did* constitute royalties within the meaning of section 512(b)(2) and *did not* constitute either (1) a share of profits from selling credit card goods and services received by petitioner as a joint venturer with Chase Lincoln (or with Chase Lincoln and ABS) or (2) payments for services performed as a sole proprietor by petitioner in connection with its activities in marketing and endorsing its credit card. Accordingly, we will grant petitioner's motion for partial summary judgment and, by necessity, deny respondent's motion for partial summary judgment.

An appropriate order will be issued.

Note

The Code places another limitation on passive income. An exempt organization could avoid UBIT by creating a subsidiary organization that it would control. The exempt organization would then transfer its unrelated trade or business to the subsidiary organization and take from the subsidiary interest, royalties, or rents. Section 512(b)(13) prevents an exempt organization from pursuing this scenario. Section 512(b)(13) provides that interest, annuities, interest and rents (but not dividends) an exempt organization receives from a controlled organization are unrelated business income. Control for this purpose is control (by vote or value) of more than 50 percent of the stock in a corporation, or more than 50 percent ownership of the profits or capital interests of a partnership, or ownership of more than 50 percent of the beneficial interests in any other case.

3. Unrelated Debt–Financed Income

To prevent a for-profit organization from using the exempt status of a nonprofit organization to shield income taxation (by buying a business through debt financing, leasing it and paying off the debt with nontaxable rent income), § 514 was added to the Code to cause income from a tax-exempt organization's debt-financed property to be taxed in proportion to the amount of acquisition debt on the property. The following case illustrates why Congress decided an exempt organization's income from debt-financed property should be taxed.

UNIVERSITY HILL FOUNDATION
v. COMMISSIONER

United States Tax Court, 1969
51 T.C. 548

TANNENWALD, Judge:

These consolidated proceedings involve income and excess profits taxes for the fiscal years ended April 30, 1952, through April 30, 1965, in the aggregate amount of $10,070,677.25. The principal questions in issue are whether petitioner is exempt from Federal income tax under sections 501(c)(3) of the 1954 Code and 101(6) of the 1939 Code; whether petitioner is a 'feeder organization' within the meaning of sections 502 and 101 of the 1954 and 1939 Codes, respectively; and what part, if any, of petitioner's income is taxable as 'unrelated business taxable income' within the meaning of sections 511–513 of the 1954 Code and 421–422 of the 1939 Code. If any of those questions are decided against petitioner, there are several remaining questions which will require consideration.

FINDINGS OF FACT

Petitioner is a California corporation. Its principal office was located at 218 North Juanita Avenue, Los Angeles, at the time its petition herein was filed. Its returns were filed with the district director of internal revenue at Los Angeles.

Petitioner, hereinafter sometimes called the foundation, was organized April 26, 1945, under the General Non-Profit Corporation Law of the State of California for the sole purpose of raising funds for Loyola University of Los Angeles. Its founders were Lorenzo M. Malone, hereinafter called Father Malone, a Catholic priest of the Jesuit Order (Society of Jesus), and Daniel G. Marshall and J. P. Carroll, prominent Catholic laymen living in Los Angeles.

Under its articles of incorporation the foundation had broad powers to conduct various charitable and educational activities, to contribute funds to other tax-exempt organizations, to engage in various fund-raising business transactions such as acquiring, selling, or leasing real and personal property, and—

In general to do all things authorized to be done by the laws relating to non-profit corporations of the state of California, whether or not specifically set forth in these articles of incorporation, and to do all acts necessary or expedient for the administration of its affairs but the corporation shall not have the authority to do anything which would deprive it of exemption from federal income tax under Section 101(6) of the Internal Revenue Code.

Loyola University, hereinafter sometimes called the university, is an educational institution and at all times relevant herein has been exempt from Federal income tax under section 101(6) of the 1939 Code and section 501(c)(3) of the 1954 Code. It was organized by the Jesuit order and has always been under its management and control. It maintains a full time university for male students located at 7101 West 80th Street, Los Angeles, and a school of law in the downtown Los Angeles area.

The foundation's original bylaws provided for three directors, one of whom was to be nominated by the president of the university. All three of the directors were to be nominated or approved by the Jesuit Order. There has always been a close relationship and complete unanimity of interest between the foundation and the university. The university made the foundation an initial gift of $10,000 at the time of its organization.

Father Malone became associated with the university prior to 1935, after having taught for several years at St. Ignatius High School in San Francisco. His whole remaining life, until his death in 1956, was devoted principally to Loyola University and the education of young men. He was untiring in his efforts to raise funds for the financial needs and growth of the university. He served as its treasurer and director of development. He organized a number of university-supporting various fund-raising guilds and he was constantly soliciting and obtaining private donations for the university.

Father Malone had been a banker before he entered the Catholic priesthood. The financial survival of Loyola University and the success of the foundation in its fund-raising operation was due largely to his extraordinary business acumen and capacity for work and his personal charm and persuasiveness. In his later years, he came to be known as the symbol, or patron saint, of Loyola University. He never received any compensation for his services to Loyola University or to the foundation. As a Jesuit priest, he was subject to the vows common to Catholic orders, of chastity, poverty, and obedience.

About 1942 Father Malone, with the help of Mildred Spencer, prepared a mailing list of about 5,000 names of Southern California businessmen from whom they began soliciting donations to the university. Mildred was a recent Catholic convert whose husband had died in 1941. After becoming acquainted with Father Malone, she volunteered to help him with his work on behalf of the university and remained associated with him until his death. She was a woman of independent means and never received any compensation of her services from Father Malone, the university, or the foundation.

The idea of forming a nonprofit corporation to raise money for Loyola University was first suggested to Father Malone by Joseph W. Drown, a successful California businessman with whom Father Malone had become acquainted in 1942. Through Father Malone, Drown became interested in the university and made substantial contributions to it and to the foundation. He told Father Malone that he owned a valuable income-producing hotel property which he would be willing to sell to such a corporation under a plan which he thought would be helpful in raising money for the university.

After further conferences, in which Father Malone and Drown and others connected with or interested in Loyola University participated, the foundation was formed and soon thereafter purchased the hotel property.

The property was the U.S. Grant Hotel, located in downtown San Diego, Calif. It was then the largest hotel in San Diego. It was owned by H. C. Fryman Hotel Co., whose stock was all owned by Drown. The hotel was then in a prosperous condition with an annual net profit, before depreciation, of approximately $1 million. Essentially, the plan agreed upon, which will be discussed in more detail below, was for the foundation to purchase the H. C. Fryman Hotel Co. stock, dissolve the corporation, then lease the hotel properties back to the operators and pay the balance of the purchase price for the stock out of the rentals from the lessee. Under this plan it was contemplated that the tax-exempt foundation would incur no tax liability on the receipt of the rental payments, that the operating group would be able to deduct the rent as a business expense, and that the profit on the sale of the stock would be taxed to Drown at capital gains rates.

The acquisition of the U.S. Grant Hotel property was the first of a series of transactions of the same general character in which the foundation purchased the assets or the stock ownership of a going business and leased the assets back to the former operators, or others, without any disrupting change in the conduct of the business. One of the chief architects of the plan, as later developed, was Paul Cote. It came to be known as the Cote formula. Cote was a Los Angeles attorney and Catholic layman who had assisted in organizing the foundation. He had attended school with Father Malone and they had remained close friends and associates. He served as legal counsel for the foundation from its inception and as its president and a member of its board of directors from 1947 until his death in November 1956. The foundation's business affairs were conducted from his office. He received no compensation for his services to the foundation prior to 1953. From 1953 to 1956, he was paid $1,000 per month, and from July 1956 until his death, $1,500 per month, for his legal services to the foundation.

J. P. Carroll became president of the foundation in 1957 to succeed Paul Cote and has continued to serve in that capacity. He has also served as a director since the foundation's inception. Carroll is a successful businessman and is president and a majority stockholder of J. P. Carroll Co., a large paint-contracting firm located in Los Angeles. The foundation's business affairs are conducted from his offices. He has never received directly any compensation for his services to the foundation but since 1959 the foundation has paid the J. P. Carroll Co. from $15,000 to $25,000 per year for office space and services and to compensate for the loss of time spent by Carroll on behalf of the foundation.

Following is a list of the principal properties acquired by the foundation over the period November 11, 1945, to October 31, 1954, showing the type of business, the year acquired, and the year sold: * * *

The assets acquired included land, buildings, machinery and equipment, current assets, trade names, goodwill, etc., comprising generally all of the assets used in the going business.

The outstanding liabilities of the acquired businesses were usually assumed by the foundation. Most of the businesses were operating profitably at the time and continued to do so. Others proved unprofitable and were disposed of by the foundation, some at considerable losses. A few of them are still owned by the foundation, as shown in the above table, and are still producing income. * * *

* * *

In most instances, a new corporation was formed to operate the business under lease from the foundation. The new companies usually had a comparatively small equity capitalization. Former owners and key employees who were to continue with the business acquired interests in some of the operating companies. The former owners were limited to a minority interest of not more than 48 percent. While the leases remained in force, the majority interest in the lessees was required to be held by persons approved in writing by the foundation.

Prior to the enactment of the unrelated business taxable income and business lease provisions of the 1950 Revenue Act, the terms of the lease usually exceeded 5 years and some carried renewal options. Thereafter new leases were limited to a term of not more than 5 years with no renewal options, and the existing leases were so amended.

The lessees usually agreed to pay the foundation rentals of 80 percent of the defined net profits of the business, sometimes reduced to 60 percent after total payments had reached a specified amount, and the foundation agreed to pay to the former owners on the purchase price a percentage of the rentals received, from the lessee, usually 90 percent, plus the proceeds from the sale of any capital assets. In determining net profits the lessees were limited to the payment of reasonable salaries and bonuses to their employees. Any assets found not to be needed in the operation of the businesses were withdrawn from the leased properties and sold or otherwise disposed of by the foundation. * * *

* * *

The current assets acquired by the foundation in the purchase of the businesses were usually sold to the lessees at full value in return for their promissory notes. Such notes were received by the foundation over the 1947–54 period in the aggregate amount of $4,473,577.69. At the close of the foundation's fiscal year, ended April 30, 1965, there were only two unpaid notes with a principal balance due of $603,979.79 and unpaid interest in the amount of $171,598.58.

All of the lease agreements purported to establish a strict lessor-lessee relationship between the foundation and its lessees and conformed, in most respects, to the usual lease pattern. The lessees had the right to exclusive use of the assets for the term of the lease. Neither the foundation nor any of its officers or directors took any active part in the actual day-to-day operation of the businesses. Business management was left to the lessees. The foundation reserved the right to inspect the premises and the books and records of the lessees and also the right of approval of any assignee of the lessee.

* * *

None of the sellers of the assets acquired by the foundation were officers or directors of the foundation and no officer or director of the foundation had any proprietary interest in any of the businesses or assets acquired by the foundation.

In several instances, the lessee companies sold shares of their stock, or partnership interests, to Paul Cote's wife or his two minor children or to Father Malone's secretary or her nephew. In each instance the shares (interests) were paid for by the person to whom they were issued in the same proportionate amount as was paid by other participants. The interests were minor.

Generally the foundation was required to make purchase-money payments only out of the rentals received, with the shares acquired by the foundation and/or the underlying assets being pledged as security for payment. As a result, the foundation generally had no personal liability for the unpaid purchase price. The lessees were obligated to pay rentals to the foundation only out of net profits. In a few instances, minimum payments and minimum rentals were required, regardless of profits. However, the lessees were not unconditionally liable to pay such minimum rentals but their failure to do so gave the foundation the right to cancel the lease. Other than through the receipt of rentals, or its failure to receive rentals, the foundation did not share in the operating profits or losses. The lessee agreed to exert its best efforts to produce the highest possible net profits consistent with good judgment and sound business practices. The salaries and bonuses payable to the lessees' officers and employees were limited to fair and reasonable amounts and in some instances limitations were prescribed in the lease agreements. It was generally understood that the foundation reserved the right to repossess assets not required in the operation of the business and there was a specific reservation of that right in some of the leases. * * *

* * *

Each of the foundation's above-described acquisitions had an origin similar to that of the U.S. Grant Hotel. Generally, the opportunity for the investment was brought to the attention of Father Malone or Paul Cote by their friends or business acquaintances, some of whom had previously made donations to the foundation or the university. In some instances, the approach was through professional brokers who had learned of the foundation's activities along that line. Father Malone usually made the final decision.

In each transaction, there was a bona fide arm's-length negotiation between representatives of the foundation and the sellers and the

Sec. III UNRELATED BUSINESS INCOME TAX (UBIT) 479

purchase price arrived at was considered fair and reasonable by both parties. The parties herein have stipulated that in all instances the purchase prices were reasonably commensurate with the fair market value of the properties acquired. * * *

* * *

The only other distribution by the foundation was a donation to Loyola High School, another nonprofit organization under the jurisdiction of the Jesuit order.

The reduction in the contributions to the university after 1956 was on the advice of its counsel, pending settlement of the within tax dispute. It is the foundation's intention to distribute at least $4 million of its accumulated funds to the university if and when the present controversy is settled favorably. A resolution to that effect was adopted by the foundation's board of directors held March 29, 1966. * * *

* * *

Soon after its organization the foundation filed with the Commissioner an application for income tax exemption, which was granted on a temporary basis on June 15, 1945. A final tax ruling was issued by the Commissioner on November 19, 1946, and continued in effect until revoked by the Commissioner April 4, 1956. The letter of revocation summarized the methods of operations of the foundation, already set forth in these findings of fact and went on to state:

> In order to be entitled to exemption under section 101(6) of the 1939 Code, or section 501(c)(3) of the 1954 Code, an organization must be both organized and operated exclusively for one or more of the purposes stated therein.
>
> Further, certain organizations described in such sections of the law shall be denied exemption for the taxable year if the amounts accumulated out of income during the taxable year or any prior year and not actually paid out by the end of the year are unreasonable in amount or duration in order to carry out the charitable, educational, or other purpose or function constituting the basis for exemption under section 501(c)(3) or 101(6). (Section 504 of the 1954 Code corresponding to section 3814 of the 1939 Code.)
>
> It is the opinion of this office that by engaging in the transactions referred to above that you have not been engaged exclusively in educational or charitable activities. In comparison with the business transaction engaged in and the financial operations attendant thereto, your funds and activities attributable to your educational or charitable undertakings are nominal. It is apparent that your primary activities and principal expenditures are concerned with your business ventures and that your exempt activities are incidental.
>
> It is the further opinion of this office, that in addition to not being operated exclusively for exempt purposes, you are precluded from exemption by reason of section 504 of the Code. As stated

above, at April 30, 1954 you were indebted to the extent of approximately nineteen and one-half million dollars. We have concluded that the amount of income used to liquidate such indebtedness is an unreasonable accumulation within the meaning of section 504.

Accordingly, it is held that beginning with the fiscal year ended April 30, 1952 and for subsequent fiscal years you are not entitled to exemption from Federal income tax. Our ruling of November 19, 1946 is modified in accordance herewith. You are required, therefore, to file income tax returns on Form 1120 for the fiscal year ended April 30, 1952 and subsequent fiscal years with the District Director of Internal Revenue at Los Angeles, California, who is being advised of this action.

Pursuant to the Commissioner's instruction, the foundation filed returns on Form 1120 for each of the fiscal years ended April 30, 1952, to April 30, 1965, inclusive, although it continued to assert its claim for tax-exempt status. In due course, deficiency notices for all of such years were sent to the foundation and the petitions herein were filed.

OPINION

The purchase- and lease-type of transaction which gives rise to the within litigation was the product of a plan constructed by Paul Cote and has often been described as the Cote formula. Under this plan, all of the shares of a corporation, engaged in active business operations, were purchased by petitioner against a small down payment and an agreement to pay the balance of the agreed purchase price through the remittance by petitioner of 90 percent of the amounts received by it from the 'lease' of the business. The shares and/or the assets of the corporation were pledged by the petitioner as security for, and as the sole source of payment of, the purchase price by petitioner. Petitioner thus had no personal liability for the unpaid purchase price. Simultaneously with, or immediately after, the acquisition of the shares, the corporation was completely liquidated and all of its assets transferred to petitioner. Petitioner then transferred the current assets of the business to certain persons in exchange for an interest-bearing promissory note and entered into what was described as a lease agreement covering the physical and other assets, including tradenames, goodwill, etc. Under that agreement, petitioner was to receive as 'rent,' 80 percent of the net profits of the business; sometimes provision was made for a downward reduction in this percentage at a later date. The owners of the leases were usually different from those who previously owned the shares of the corporation, such previous owners holding at most minority interests. Some 21 of such transactions are involved herein covering a wide variety of businesses. The bulk of petitioner's income was derived from the 'rents' it received. The economic effect of these devices was to divide the net profits of each business: 20 percent to the operators, 8 percent to petitioner, and 72 percent to the sellers, with the operators claiming a deduction for the rentals as business expenses, the sellers reporting their profit on the sale as capital gains, and the petitioner claiming exemptions from tax as a charitable organization on the amounts received by it.

Respondent's principal challenges in the past, in his more than 15–year litigating activities involving purchase-and-lease transactions by entities claiming exemption as charitable organizations under the Internal Revenue Code, have been directed against the private parties involved through challenges to the capital gains treatment to the seller of the gain from the 'sale' and to the deductibility of the 'rent' by the lessee. This time, respondent has challenged the claimed exemption and, alternatively, the status of the 'rent' as 'unrelated business taxable income.' Respondent's position is that the statutory language reflects the intention of Congress to proscribe, or at least limit, the tax-free fruits of the type of purchase-and-lease transactions involved herein and that, by engaging in such transactions, petitioner has wandered from the Elysian fields of tax exemption into the everyday world of taxable business profits. Petitioner vigorously counters with the assertion that its activities clearly fit the statutory language and that to accede to respondent's blandishments would, therefore, be an unwarranted intrusion into the legislative arena. In essence, we are called upon herein to chart a course on the sea of judicial interpretation which will avoid the reefs of judicial legislation. Under the circumstances, the task is made even more difficult by the fact that, in many of its aspects, this case is one of first impression. * * *

There are two primary questions which require decision. The first is whether, during the 14–year period involved, petitioner was entitled to exemption as a charitable organization under sections 101(6) and 501(c)(3) of the 1939 and 1954 Codes, respectively. Intertwined with this question is the further question of the impact of the 'feeder' provisions of section 101 of the 1939 Code (added by section 301(b) of the Revenue Act of 1950 (Pub. L. No. 814, 81st Cong., 2d Sess.)) and contained in section 502 of the 1954 Code. The second question is what part, if any, of petitioner's income constitutes 'unrelated business taxable income' within the meaning of section 422(a) of the 1939 Code (added by section 301(a) of the Revenue Act of 1950, supra) and contained in section 512(a) and (b)(3) of the 1954 Code. Common to both questions is the issue of whether under the Internal Revenue Code, the payments received by petitioner from the 'lease' transactions were 'rents' or 'rental' and, if so, whether they constituted rent from 'real property (including personal property leased with real property)'.

* * *

The basic exemption of a charitable organization is conferred by section 501(c)(3) which requires that the organization be 'organized and operated exclusively' for exempt purposes. There is no question that petitioner meets the 'organized' requirement. The 'operated' test presents a more difficult problem.

Respondent makes some veiled references to the fact that various friends and relatives of petitioner's sponsors participated in the profits of some of the operating concerns and appears to claim that, under section 503(c)(3), and regardless of our decision on the other elements involved, this would deprive petitioner of its right to exemption. As far as the record shows, however, these persons made the same proportionate investment (albeit sometimes nominal in absolute amount) in the operating concerns as the unrelated persons and there was no discrimination in their favor with respect to their share in the earnings of these concerns. If they had not participated, the amount of the 'rent' remitted to the petitioner (80 percent of net profits) would not have been changed one iota; in the absence of their participation, the nonrelated persons would simply have received a greater share of the earnings. Under these circumstances, we cannot say that any part, much less a 'substantial part of the net earnings' of petitioner inured 'to the benefit of any private shareholder or individual' so as to bring the proscription of section 501(c)(3) into play.

As our findings of fact show, practically all of petitioner's income was disbursed to Loyola University, a concededly exempt institution. Prior to the Revenue Act of 1950, if the organization distributed its income exclusively for charitable purposes, it was entitled to exemption under the judicially established 'destination of income' rule (p. 562, supra) even though its primary or indeed sole activity consisted of carrying on active business operations. Thus, if it were not for the Revenue Act of 1950, petitioner would be in the clear. The enactment of section 301(b) of that Act (now section 502) constructed a new roadblock along petitioner's path to exemption. * * *

Respondent asserts that petitioner actively carried on the trade or business of the operating companies by virtue of its continuing control and participation in those companies after the assets were 'leased.' We disagree. Petitioner's activities, for the most part, were conducted by Father Malone and Paul Cote, neither of whom appears to have had any experience with or knowledge of the type of businesses involved or, for that matter, with the operations of businesses generally. It is highly unlikely that they could have contributed much to the success of the businesses if they had attempted to participate in the day-to-day management. The evidence is clear, and we have so found, that petitioner did not itself, or through any of its officers or representatives, take part in the day-to-day operations of the businesses. Nor does the fact that petitioner retained the rights of inspection, approval of 'lease' assignments, and veto with respect to charging asset acquisitions against the 'rent' payments due it, change our conclusion. These rights were not inconsistent with the simple objective of an owner of property in making certain that the value of this ownership and his right to receive the payments due him not be dissipated by a third party in possession. Certainly they should not be equated with active, direct participation in the carrying on of a business.

Respondent's principal thrust with regard to the question whether petitioner was carrying on a trade or business is reflected in his contention that the so-called lease arrangements were in reality not leases but joint ventures or principal-agent contracts.

Whether a joint venture or a principal and agent relationship exists is essentially a question of fact and we are, of course, not bound by the nomenclature used by the parties. Among the critical elements, involved in the determination are the existence of controls over the venture and a risk of loss in the taxpayer, both of which elements are lacking herein. * * * We have already discussed our finding of fact that petitioner did not participate in the day-to-day operations of the leased businesses (see above) and, as will subsequently appear, we have concluded that the various rights retained by petitioner did not represent a degree of control abnormal to its status as lessor. Petitioner did share in expenses to a degree, since such expenses were charged against income in arriving at net profits and the 'rent' paid to petitioner was a percentage participation of profits. This element is often one indication of a joint venture but standing alone it is not enough. This is particularly true where, as is the case herein, petitioner was not required to contribute to losses. If losses occurred, petitioner simply did not collect any rent for the particular period.

When we turn to the so-called leases themselves, we find that the provisions, although sophisticated in many respects, are not so unusual in this day and age so as to require us to find that the 'leases' are something other than what they purport to be. In this connection we have adopted the approach of the parties and have posited our analysis in terms of the lease provisions generally rather than in terms of a piecemeal dissection of each lease separately. * * *

* * *

But our inquiry is not ended. We still must determine whether petitioner's leasing activity was of such a character that petitioner should be held to be 'operated for the primary purpose of carrying on a trade or business for profit' within the meaning of section 502. Petitioner argues that Congress had in mind, in enacting section 502, only those corporations which were actively engaged in direct commercial operations; that long-term leasing is not such an activity; and that, therefore, section 502 is generally inapplicable. Alternatively, petitioner contends that the transactions involved constituted leases of 'real property (including personal property leased with real property)' and that, therefore, by virtue of the second sentence of section 502, that section is inoperative herein.

Since we agree with petitioner's alternative argument, there is no need for us to dwell upon its assertion that, since leasing activities gave rise to 'passive' income such activities should not constitute 'carrying on a trade or business for profit' within the meaning of section 502. * * *

The second sentence of section 502 provides that 'the term 'trade or business' shall not include the rental by an organization of its real property (including personal property leased with real property).' With the exception of a very few situations, noted below, every lease involved herein encompassed real property, in the classical sense. Respondent argues, however, that, in many, if not most, of the leases, the real property constituted a very small percentage of the value of the total property (the percentages as derived by respondent ranged from 2.32 percent to 45.6 percent) and that Congress, in carving out the exception to section 502, had in mind only those situations, such as a hotel or an apartment building, where real property was the essential element of the lease, with the personal property being of only incidental significance. Concededly, Congress was concerned principally with protecting the right of exempt organizations to lease industrial and commercial real estate without tax consequences except with respect to certain leases extending over a period of more than 5 years. Secs. 512(b)(4) and 514; H. Rept. No. 2319, supra at 36–40, 108–115; S. Rept. No. 2375, supra at 26–33, 106–115. But this does not justify our reading into the language used a quantitative, statistical, or mathematical formula pursuant to which some leases of personal property with real property would be sheltered and others would be beyond the pale.

There is not the slightest indication that Congress intended that such an approach be used. If Congress had wanted to distinguish between various types of leases involving real property in the manner suggested by respondent, it would have been easy for it to have done so—for example, by indicating that the exclusion of leases of personal property would apply only if the real property was the 'primary' or 'principal' subject matter of the lease, or by providing some guidelines as to whether the exclusionary formula should be based upon cost, fair market value, depreciated value, or some other basis of valuation of the leased assets.

Indeed, the difficulties which inhere in the development of such a formula are highlighted by the realization that, in many cases, the real property, although small in terms of absolute relative values, may be the critical operational element. By way of contrast to these difficulties, the courts can readily deal with situations where the real property is so clearly insignificant as to require the conclusion that the lease was not in fact a lease of real property. * * * Clearly the leases herein cannot be so categorized.

* * *

In summary, as far as section 502 is concerned, we think it clear that, whether or not petitioner was operated for the purpose of acquiring and leasing businesses and, therefore, in a broad sense, might be said to have been 'carrying on a trade or business for profit,' the types of transactions in which it was engaged were within the exclusionary provisions of the second sentence of section 502. Such being the case, section 502 does not apply. Since there is no question that all of petitioner's income was destined for charitable purposes, petitioner is therefore exempt under section 501(c)(3).

Even though petitioner is exempt under section 501(c)(3), it may still be subject to tax on unrelated business taxable income. The extent to which it may be so subject depends upon whether petitioner derived income from 'any unrelated trade or business * * * regularly carried on by it' (section 512(a)) and the applicability of section 512(b)(3), which excludes from 'unrelated business taxable income' ' * * * all rents from real property (including personal property leased with real property).'

Our discussion of the foregoing clause in connection with the applicability of section 502 is equally applicable here for the reasons previously expressed. We think the leasing activities of petitioner fell within the exception contained in section 512(b)(3). * * *

* * *

To respondent's suggestion that such a construction of the statutory phrase 'real property' embodies a 'peppercorn' approach which will open the floodgates of tax avoidance, there is a twofold answer: (1) The area of sham transactions furnishes the courts with ample opportunity to stem the flow substantially, if not entirely (cf. Emanuel N. (Manny) Kolkey, supra) and (2) it is always open to the Congress to provide more precise guidance if it so desires.

We are required herein to reconcile the tax consequences of purchase-and-lease transactions to an otherwise exempt organization with detailed statutory provisions which have been enacted gingerly and have been most carefully drawn against a background of historical bias in favor of the charitable exemption which still survives with the luster of its public-service emblem untarnished. In Commissioner v. Brown, supra, the Supreme Court was required to reconcile the tax consequences to the seller in such transactions with the specific provisions of the Internal Revenue Code dealing with capital gains. The Supreme Court was concerned with the impact of an unusual construction of the word 'sale' on other provisions of the Code where that word is used. In this case, although the use in the Code of the words 'rents' and 'lease' is perhaps not as frequent as that of the word 'sale,' a similar problem exists. * * * Under all the circumstances herein, we are constrained to follow the lead of the Supreme Court, which expressed itself as follows (380 U.S. at 579):

> The problems involved in the purchase of a going business by a tax-exempt organization have been considered and dealt with by the Congress. Likewise, it has given its attention to various kinds of transactions involving the payment of the agreed purchase price for property from the future earnings of the property itself. In both situations it has responded, if at all, with precise provisions of narrow application. We consequently deem it wise to 'leave to the Congress the fashioning of a rule which, in any event, must have wide ramifications.' American Automobile Assn. v. United States, 367 U.S. 687, 697. * * *

We hold that petitioner was exempt from tax by virtue of sections 501(c)(3) and 502 and that, with the exception of a small amount which petitioner concedes as taxable by virtue of section 514, it did not have any 'unrelated business taxable income' within the meaning of section 512.

Reviewed by the Court

Decision will be entered under Rule 50.

Note

1. The Ninth Circuit reversed the Tax Court decision in *University Hill Foundation v. Commissioner,* 446 F.2d 701 (9th Cir.1971), *cert. denied,* 405 U.S. 965, 92 S.Ct. 1172, 31 L.Ed.2d 240 (1972). Before the court of appeals issued its decision, Congress enacted the present unrelated debt-finance income rules of § 514. Those rules effectively halted 'bootstrap' transactions like those in *University Hill Foundation.*

2. The case that finally brought the bootstrap transaction to the forefront was *Commissioner v. Clay Brown,* 380 U.S. 563, 85 S.Ct. 1162, 14 L.Ed.2d 75 (1965). In *Clay Brown,* the Supreme Court ruled that a for-profit corporation was entitled to capital gain treatment on proceeds from the sale of business property to an exempt organization. The exempt organization purchased the assets by the use of debt and the leasing of those assets to a new corporation owned by the original seller. The exempt organization did not report the rental income as unrelated business income and the new corporation deducted the rents as business expenses. The exempt organization used the rental income to pay the acquisition indebtedness on the property. The IRS contended the purported sale was a sham, and the for-profit corporation was not entitled to capital gain treatment on the sale. The Supreme Court disagreed and permitted the transaction to stand.

Section 514 is too intricate to develop in detail in this casebook. For present purposes, we will just outline the statute. We emphasize that the purpose of § 514 is to prevent the bootstrap transaction by discouraging exempt organizations from purchasing income producing assets and paying for those assets with tax-free income earned from those assets.

Under § 514, an exempt organization includes in unrelated business income a certain percentage of its income from property not used to accomplish its exempt purposes that is financed by debt. Debt-financed property is any property held to produce income that is encumbered by "acquisition" indebtedness, which is indebtedness incurred to acquire or improve the property [I.R.C. § 514(b)(1), (c)(1)]. The amount of income that is included in unrelated debt-financed income is determined by applying a fraction to the income and related deductions from the property (the "debt/basis percentage") [I.R.C. § 514(a).] The numerator of the fraction is the average acquisition indebtedness, which is the average monthly principal balance outstanding on the debt incurred to acquire the property. The denominator is the average adjusted basis of the property determined by dividing the sum of the adjusted basis at the beginning of the year and the adjusted basis at the end of the year by two.

Sec. III   UNRELATED BUSINESS INCOME TAX (UBIT)

The resultant income and deductions from debt-financed property are netted against each other. The net income from the property times the debt/basis fraction is the amount of gain that is added to the organization's unrelated business income [Treas. Reg. § 1.514(a)–1(a)(1)(i)].

If property of an exempt organization is used in part for exempt purposes, an additional allocation is necessary to reflect the exempt use, which would not be taxed [I.R.C. § 514(e).]

Problem

An exempt organization purchased some land on January 2 of the current year for $500,000, using $300,000 of borrowed funds. Nothing was paid on the principal in the current year. The organization received net rental income from the land for the year of $30,000 (gross rental income of $50,000, less expenses to produce such income of $20,000). Would the $30,000 be taxed to the organization, and, if so, how would it be taxed? Assume the organization purchased a depreciable asset on January 2 of the current year for $500,000, using $300,000 of borrowed funds. Again, nothing was paid on the principal of the note, but depreciation on the asset of $100,000 was claimed for the year. How would the $30,000 net income from the asset be taxed to the exempt organization?

Question

What is included as "acquisition indebtedness" for purposes of § 514? Consider the definition of "indebtedness" in the following case.

MOSE AND GARRISON SISKIN MEMORIAL FOUNDATION v. UNITED STATES

United States Court of Appeals, Sixth Circuit, 1986
790 F.2d 480

CORNELIA G. KENNEDY, Circuit Judge.

This appeal presents the question whether the Internal Revenue Code's ("I.R.C.") "unrelated business income" provisions apply to income that a charitable organization derives by withdrawing the accumulated cash value of life insurance policies that the charitable organization owns and reinvesting the proceeds in marketable securities and other income paying investments. The District Court held that since the proceeds from the withdrawals against the accumulated cash value are "acquisition indebtedness" under I.R.C. § 514(c), the unrelated business income provisions apply. *Mose and Garrison Siskin Memorial Foundation, Inc. v. United States,* 603 F.Supp. 91 (E.D.Tenn.1984). For the reasons set forth below, we affirm.

Plaintiff-appellant, the Mose and Garrison Siskin Memorial Foundation, Inc. ("the Foundation"), a I.R.C. § 501(c)(3) tax-exempt organization, timely filed its 1979 Form 990–T, exempt organization business income tax return, reporting unrelated business taxable income of $134,501. The Foundation earned this income by withdrawing the accumulated cash value of approximately 800 life insurance policies that the

Foundation owned and reinvesting the proceeds in marketable securities and other income producing investments. The Foundation's Form 990–T reflected a tax liability of $42,160, which the Foundation paid to the Internal Revenue Service in installments of $21,500 on May 15, 1980 and $20,660 on August 15, 1980. On March 16, 1981, the Foundation filed an amended return, seeking the refund of the entire amount of unrelated business income tax paid, claiming the income was not taxable. The IRS disallowed the claim on January 13, 1983. Subsequently, the Foundation instituted this 28 U.S.C. § 1346(a)(1) action in the United States District Court for the Eastern District of Tennessee to recover the $42,160 in unrelated business income taxes that the Foundation had paid for the 1979 calendar year. Based on a joint stipulation of facts, the parties filed cross-motions for summary judgment. On December 4, 1984, the District Court entered an order overruling the Foundation's motion for summary judgment, sustaining the defendant's motion for summary judgment, and dismissing the case.

The Foundation, a Tennessee not-for-profit corporation, operates a rehabilitation facility and school for handicapped individuals. Contributors to the Foundation frequently donate life insurance policies, which name the Foundation as beneficiary. The Foundation holds these policies for investment purposes, while the contributors continue to pay the annual premiums. During 1979, the Foundation owned more than 800 life insurance policies covering the lives of more than 800 people. As of February 1, 1979, the life insurance policies had accumulated cash value of approximately $2,292,900. During 1979, the Foundation's officers decided that the investment in the life insurance policies could produce a higher yield if the Foundation withdrew the policies' accumulated cash value and reinvested the proceeds in marketable securities and other income producing investments. Accordingly, the Foundation withdrew the accumulated cash value and reinvested the proceeds. The Foundation paid a cost for withdrawing the cash value which averaged approximately five and a half percent per year. The Foundation, however, earned in excess of ten percent per year on the reinvestment of the proceeds. Accordingly, the reinvested proceeds earned $134,501, net of the insurance company charges for such withdrawals, during the 1979 calendar year. Although the Foundation could have surrendered the policies in exchange for the policies' cash surrender values, the donors of annual premiums for such policies would have reconsidered their gifts to the Foundation.

I.R.C. § 501(a) exempts charitable and educational organizations from federal income taxation. The Foundation undisputably qualifies as an "exempt organization" under I.R.C. § 501(c)(3). I.R.C. § 511(a), however, imposes a tax on an exempt organization's "unrelated business taxable income." I.R.C. § 511(a)(2). I.R.C. § 512 defines the term "unrelated business taxable income." As a general rule, I.R.C. § 512(b) excludes passive investment income, such as interest, dividends, and royalties from "unrelated business taxable income." I.R.C. § 512(b)(4), however, negates the exclusion "in the case of debt-financed property (as defined in section 514)." I.R.C. § 514(b) defines the term "debt-financed property" as "any property which is held to produce income and with respect to which there is an acquisition indebtedness (as defined in subsection (c)) at any time during the taxable year...." With respect to any debt-financed property, I.R.C. § 514(c)(1) defines the term "acquisition indebtedness" as the unpaid amount of:

(A) the indebtedness incurred by the organization in acquiring or improving such property;

(B) the indebtedness incurred before the acquisition or improvement of such property if such indebtedness would not have been incurred but for such acquisition or improvement; and

(C) the indebtedness incurred after the acquisition or improvement of such property if such indebtedness would not have been incurred but for such acquisition or improvement and the incurrence of such indebtedness was reasonably foreseeable at the time of such acquisition or improvement.

Essentially, we face the question whether withdrawals against the accumulated cash value of the life insurance policies are "indebtedness." If the withdrawals are not "indebtedness," there can be no "acquisition indebtedness" and hence no "debt-financed property." If there is no "debt-financed property," I.R.C. § 512(b)(4) would not negate the exclusion of passive investment income from "unrelated business taxable income."

Neither the I.R.C. nor the Treasury Regulations define "indebtedness." The Foundation, however, contends that the withdrawal of the accumulated cash value of a life insurance policy does not create "indebtedness." The Foundation argues that the withdrawals were not "loans" but rather "advances" of funds that the insurance companies would ultimately pay, in any event, to the Foundation. The Foundation contends that the "advances" did not create a debtor-creditor relationship because the Foundation did not have an obligation to repay the insurance companies. The Foundation further contends that the "loan interest" amounts paid the insurance companies were not "interest" but rather "charges" to maintain the face values of each insurance policy.

We conclude, however, that the withdrawals against the cash value of the policies are "indebtedness." Although the "typical" life insurance policy * * * labels a withdrawal against the cash value of the policy as a "loan," the policy describes such a withdrawal as "an advance (herein called a loan)." The "typical" life insurance policy, however, also uses such terms as "loan value," "loan interest," "indebtedness," and "loan repayment." Admittedly, the withdrawal against the accumulated cash value of a life insurance policy differs from an ordinary loan. * * * Nevertheless, in *Salley v. Commissioner,* 55 T.C. 896, 903 (1971), *aff'd,* 464 F.2d 479 (5th Cir.1972), while holding that the taxpayers could deduct, under I.R.C. § 163(a), the interest on loans attributable to the accumulated cash value of life insurance policies, the Tax Court stated:

The obligation on a life insurance policy loan is unique in the sense that the borrower assumes no personal liability, and the insurance company looks only to the cash surrender values for repayment of the loans. Nevertheless, this Court has recognized that the borrower becomes obligated in a sense to pay interest, and such obligation is sufficient to support a deduction for income tax purposes.

I.R.C. § 163(a) (emphasis added) allows a deduction for "all interest paid or accrued within the taxable year on *indebtedness.*" Furthermore, in *Minnis v. Commissioner,* 71 T.C. 1049, 1054 (1979), a case involving an annuity contract, the Tax Court stated "policy loans have generally been regarded as a valid form of indebtedness."

In addition, we note that in the Revenue Act of 1964, Pub.L. No. 88–272, § 215, 78 Stat. 19, 55 (1964), Congress amended I.R.C. § 264 to disallow a deduction for amounts paid or accrued on indebtedness incurred or continued to purchase or carry a life insurance policy under a financing arrangement that contemplates the systematic borrowing of part or all of the increases in the cash value of the policy. Although Congress intended to eliminate the interest deduction on insurance loans when used as a "tax-saving device," the legislative history explicitly acknowledges the desire to preserve the interest deduction on insurance loans in other situations. The House Report stated:

> Your committee recognizes, however, the importance of being able to borrow on insurance policies; and, therefore, while adopting a provision designed at minimizing the sale of insurance as a tax-saving device, it has been careful in this provision to provide for the retention of rights to borrow on insurance for other than tax-saving purposes without the loss of the interest deduction.

H.R.Rep. No. 749, 88th Cong., 2 Sess., *reprinted in* 1964 U.S. Code Cong. & Ad.News 1313, 1370. * * * Since Congress intended to preserve the interest deduction for payments on insurance loans, Congress implicitly considers withdrawals against the accumulated cash value of life insurance policies as "indebtedness" because without "indebtedness" a taxpayer cannot qualify for an interest deduction. Consequently, we hold that the withdrawals against the cash value of the life insurance policies involved in this case created "acquisition indebtedness" under I.R.C. § 514(c)(1).

Accordingly, we affirm the District Court's order overruling the Foundation's motion for summary judgment, sustaining the defendant's motion for summary judgment, and dismissing the action.

Note

Because the cash surrender value of the policies in *Mose and Garrison Siskin Memorial Foundation* would equal the cost of the securities and other assets in which the foundation invested, the total amount of earnings from such investments would be taxed. (The CSV of the policies would be the numerator of the debt/basis fraction and the cost of the investments would be the denominator. Because these two amounts would be the same, 100 percent of the net income from the investments would be taxed.)

Chapter 10

CHURCHES AND OTHER RELIGIOUS ORGANIZATIONS

Churches, synagogues, mosques, and other religious organizations are special forms of nonprofit organizations in that religious organizations are protected by the First Amendment from extensive governmental interference. For example, because of First Amendment constraints, a church and its related auxiliaries is not required to apply for and obtain recognition of federal income tax exempt status in order to qualify as a § 501(c)(3) organization [I.R.C. § 508(c)(1)(A)]. In addition, churches are exempt from the requirement of filing annual information returns with the Internal Revenue Service [I.R.C. § 6033(a)(2)].

I. DEFINITION OF A "CHURCH"

There are few definitions of a "church." Treasury Regulations [§ 1.511–2(a)(3)(ii)] describe a church as an organization the duties of which include the "ministration of sacerdotal functions and the conduct of religious worship."

FOUNDATION OF HUMAN UNDERSTANDING v. COMMISSIONER
United States Tax Court, 1987
88 T.C. 1341

GOFFE, JUDGE:

In 1965 the Internal Revenue Service issued a ruling letter which recognized that petitioner is exempt from Federal income tax as an organization described in section 501(c)(3). The Commissioner subsequently recognized petitioner as a non-private foundation because petitioner satisfied the requirements of a publicly supported organization described in section 509(a)(1) and 170(b)(1)(A)(vi). Petitioner later requested a ruling to modify its exemption so that it would be recognized as a non-private foundation under section 509(a)(1) because it is a 'church' within the meaning of section 170(b)(1)(A)(i). The Commissioner determined that petitioner is not a church, but this determination did not affect petitioner's exemption as a non-private foundation under sections 509(a)(1) and 170(b)(1)(A)(vi). Petitioner has challenged the determination of the Commissioner by invoking the jurisdiction of this Court for declaratory judgment pursuant to section 7428. The issue for decision is whether petitioner is a 'church' within the meaning of section 170(b)(1)(A)(I).

* * *

The Foundation of Human Understanding (petitioner) was established in 1961 by Roy Masters as the organizational vehicle whereby his doctrine concerning meditation, salvation, emotional self-control, and man's relation to God could be spread to the world. Roy Masters has summarized his beliefs, which are based upon Judeo–Christian principles, as follows: 'man is a fallen being, and hence is subject to his emotions. Through meditation and faith in Christ, it is possible for man to gain control of his emotions, to become self-disciplined, and hence a disciple of Christ.' In this regard, Roy Masters has developed a particular form of meditation that is used by his followers.

On January 15, 1963, Roy Masters, Ann Masters, his wife, and Patrick C. Shields executed articles of association whereby petitioner became a nonprofit unincorporated association organized for religious purposes under the laws of California. On May 27, 1963, petitioner was incorporated under the nonprofit corporation law of California. The original directors were Roy Masters, Ann Masters, and John Brill. The articles of incorporation stated that the purposes for which petitioner was formed were 'the promulgation of the religious, charitable, scientific, literary and educational aspects of mind over matter and spiritual health known as psychocatalysis.'

* * *

On May 15, 1972, the purpose clause of the articles of incorporation of petitioner was amended to indicate that petitioner was a church. Counsel for petitioner mailed the amendment to the articles of incorporation to the District Director of Internal Revenue. Thereupon, counsel for petitioner notified petitioner that '[t]he Foundation is now a church.'

As a result of the advice of counsel, petitioner believed that all steps necessary to change the nature of its exemption to that of a church had been completed. Accordingly, petitioner did not file information returns for the years 1973 through 1978. Ultimately, representatives of the IRS informed petitioner that it was not recognized as a church and that a formal application for such recognition would be necessary. Consequently, in 1979 petitioner prepared and filed Forms 990, Return of Organization Exempt from Income Tax, for the years 1973 through 1978 and requested a ruling that it was a church.

* * *

On September 12, 1979, petitioner again amended its articles of incorporation to include a charitable dedication provision and to amend its purposes and powers to read as follows:

(a) Purposes of the corporation:

> The sole purpose for which this church is formed is the promulgation of the religious, charitable, scientific, and literary and educational aspects of the theological concepts upon which this church was founded and is organized and operated exclusively for religious purposes within the meaning of Section 501(c)(3) of the Internal Revenue Code of 1954.

(b) Powers of the corporation:

> The general power of this church is to engage in any activity which is in furtherance of the above-stated specific purpose.

Petitioner's application was subsequently referred to the Exempt Organizations Division of the IRS National Office. On January 14, 1980, Roy Masters participated in a meeting in Washington, D.C., with IRS representatives regarding petitioner's exemption application. On March 13, 1980, the Commissioner issued an adverse determination letter denying petitioner's application to have its exemption classification modified to that of a church under sections 509(a)(1) and 170(b)(1)(A)(i).

On February 10, 1981, petitioner commenced an action in U.S. District Court for the Central District of California seeking declaratory relief from the adverse determination of the Commissioner. By agreement with the Assistant U.S. Attorney, the Department of Justice, and the Office of the Chief Counsel of the IRS, petitioner agreed to dismiss the district court suit without prejudice and requested a rehearing on its church status with the Exempt Organizations Division of the IRS National Office. On November 12, 1982, the Commissioner issued an adverse determination letter pursuant to the rehearing in which the Commissioner again refused to modify the non-private foundation status from that of a publicly supported organization described in sections 509(a)(1) and 170(b)(1)(A)(vi) to that of a church described in sections 509(a)(1) and 170(b)(1)(A)(i). Following a protest filed by petitioner, the Commissioner issued a final adverse determination letter on February 23, 1983.

At about the time petitioner was formed, Roy Masters, using his own resources, began purchasing radio air time to present a program entitled 'A Moment of Truth' during which he preached concerning his doctrine. Masters also began conducting discussion and teaching groups to educate people about his doctrine and meditation technique. After petitioner was incorporated, it continued to purchase radio air time to broadcast the pre-recorded 'A Moment of Truth' on various radio stations. Petitioner also began purchasing radio air time for a live show in Los Angeles hosted by Roy Masters using a call-in format whereby listeners telephone Masters with their questions, concerns, and problems and he responds with counseling in keeping with his doctrine and teachings. At one point these radio shows, including taped replays of the live call-in show, were broadcast 5 or 6 days a week over more than a dozen stations from New England to Hawaii. The programs are also broadcast every night on Satellite Radio Network by local cable television in many communities throughout the country. The estimated listening audience for these programs is approximately 2 million with a regular following of 30,000.

Petitioner has published several books and pamphlets written by Roy Masters. * * *

Petitioner publishes a magazine, 'The Iconoclast,' with 5,200 subscribers and an estimated readership of 15,000. Each issue features writings described as follows:

> [Iconoclast writings] focus on the role that illusions, false religious images, misplaced beliefs and disintegrating institutions play in our personal and inter-personal problems. * * * Once our illusions have been destroyed, the path to true religion is revealed.

More particularly, each issue contains an article by Masters plus features that keep readers informed of petitioner's activities, as well as materials and services offered by petitioner.

Petitioner owns and operates a building in Los Angeles, which at one time housed its headquarters. The building displays the name 'Foundation of Human Understanding' along with the following quote:

> 'Where there is no insight, the people perish.' The building contains facilities to record Roy Masters' radio programs and to duplicate tapes. The building also contains a meeting hall for followers of petitioner to congregate, as well as office space.

Petitioner conducts 'services' at its Los Angeles building three or four times a week. These services, which are open to the public, are conducted by one of the ministers of petitioner. The conducting minister is permitted to structure the service as he chooses, ranging from highly Scriptural exhortations to practical suggestions on overcoming sin, weakness, and depression. Afterwards, followers in the congregation are allowed to and regularly do share their recent experiences concerning the Scriptures, meditation, and God. Although ministers may discuss the meditation technique prescribed by Roy Masters, meditation is performed by petitioner's followers in solitude. Ministers have performed weddings; however, the beliefs of petitioner eschew other rites such as baptism and holy communion. Although petitioner does not require its followers to disavow membership in other churches or religious organizations, many of its followers look upon petitioner as their only church.

In October 1977, petitioner opened a school for children. Although general education is provided, classwork includes religious instruction based upon the beliefs of petitioner. Petitioner also operates one or more thrift stores where donated articles are sold.

In 1979 petitioner applied for authority to transact business in the State of Oregon. In the same year petitioner purchased 373 acres of land near Selma, Oregon, and constructed basic living quarters and facilities for milling wood ranching, farming, teaching, and conducting seminars and meetings. This property, called the Tall Timber Ranch, is operated by petitioner as a retreat and meeting facility. Although the number of people who have lived or worked at the Tall Timber Ranch has varied, approximately 50 persons were present in August 1981.

In 1982 petitioner purchased a church building, which formerly belonged to a Seventh Day Adventist congregation, in Grants Pass, Oregon. Petitioner relocated its headquarters to Grants Pass while retaining its building in Los Angeles. Petitioner encouraged its followers to relocate to Oregon and some did so. In Oregon, followers of petitioner attend services in the Grants Pass church, take part in activities at the Tall Timber Ranch, and are able to associate with other followers on a daily basis. Attendance at services at both Grants Pass and Los Angeles ranges from 50 to 350 people.

In 1981 petitioner had nine ordained ministers who were employed full time. The ministers included Roy Masters, his wife, Ann Masters, and his children, David Masters, Dianne Masters, and Michael Masters. In addition, there were five ministers in training. The ministerial training process is a 3 year apprenticeship under the personal tutelage of Roy Masters.

* * *

In the adverse determination letter issued on November 12, 1982, the Commissioner denied the request of petitioner to be classified as a church as follows:

> In determining whether a particular organization can be considered to be a 'church' within the meaning of section 170(b)(1)(A)(i) * * * the following criteria are taken into consideration: (1) a distinct legal existence; (2) a recognized creed and form of worship; (3) a definite and distinct ecclesiastical government; (4) a formal code of doctrine or discipline; (5) a distinct religious history; (6) a membership not associated with any church or denomination; (7) a complete organization of ordained ministers ministering to their congregations; (8) ordained ministers selected after completing prescribed courses of study; (9) a literature of its own; (10) established places of worship; (11) regular congregations; (12) regular religious services; (13) Sunday schools for the religious instruction of the young; and (14) schools for the preparation of its ministers. These criteria are not exclusive and are not mechanically applied, but, rather, serve as a list of some of the characteristics that may be used in determining whether an organization is a church * * * any other facts and circumstances which may bear upon an organization's claim that it is entitled to church status must also be taken into consideration.

* * *

The term 'church' is not defined in the Internal Revenue Code. Nor are the regulations promulgated under section 170 helpful in deciding what is a church. They simply restate the statutory language of section 170(b)(1)(A)(I). Sec. 1.170A–9(a), Income Tax Regs. It seems clear, however, that Congress intended that the word 'church' have a more restrictive definition than the term 'religious organization.' * * *

The Tax Reform Act of 1969 made several changes in the tax treatment of exempt organizations including repeal of the exemption given to churches from the tax on unrelated business income under section 511. Pub. L. No. 91–172, 83 Stat. 536. Following enactment of the Tax Reform Act of 1969, the Treasury proposed regulations defining 'church' for purposes of section 170 that closely resembled the definition found in section 1.511–2(a)(3)(ii), Income Tax Regulations. Sec. 1.170A–9(a), Proposed Income Tax Regs., 36 Fed. Reg. 9298 (May 22, 1971). Because of objections from the public, the proposed regulation defining 'church' under section 170 was never promulgated as final. Instead the current regulation merely provides that '[a]n organization is described in section 170(b)(1)(A)(i) if it is a church or a convention or association of churches.' Sec. 1.170A-9(a), Income Tax Regs. * * *

In the absence of guidance by Congress and a meaningful regulatory definition, it has been suggested that the term 'church' is to be interpreted in light of the generally accepted meaning and usage of the word. * * *

* * *

Although every church may be a religious organization, not every religious organization is a church. * * * To classify a religious organization as a church under the Internal Revenue Code, we should look to its religious purposes and, particularly, the means by which its religious purposes are accomplished. * * * The means by which an avowedly religious purpose is accomplished separates a 'church' from other forms of religious enterprise. * * * At a minimum, a church includes a body of believers or communicants that assembles regularly in order to worship. * * * When bringing people together for worship is only an incidental part of the activities of a religious organization, those limited activities are insufficient to label the entire organization a church. * * *

In its efforts to identify organizations that qualify for church status the IRS has developed 14 criteria. These criteria, which were first announced in a speech by a former Commissioner, were applied by the Commissioner in the instant case. * * *

In addition to the 14 criteria enumerated above, the IRS will consider '[a]ny other facts and circumstances which may bear upon the organization's claim for church status.' * * *

Although this Court has not adopted these 14 criteria in deciding whether an organization is a church, other courts have expressly adopted them or at least given them the appearance of judicial imprimatur. * * * It is recognized that few traditional churches could meet all of the criteria. None of the criteria is considered controlling* * *

Although the criteria developed by the IRS are helpful in deciding what is essentially a fact question, whether petitioner is a church, we do not adopt them as a test.

Petitioner, a nonprofit corporation incorporated under the laws of California, certainly has a distinct legal existence. Although based on Judeo–Christian principles, the emphasis on emotional self-control through a specific type of meditation as the key to salvation sets petitioner apart from other recognized religions. Petitioner provides regular religious services for established congregations that are served by an organized ministry. Worship takes the form of regular meetings of regular congregations at established places of worship, petitioner's Los Angeles headquarters and the Grant Pass, Oregon, church building. These services are open to the public. * * * These services were regularly conducted by the ministry for congregations consisting of 50 to 350 persons. Such activity is far from incidental. * * * Although petitioner does not require its followers to reject membership in other churches, many followers consider petitioner to be their only church. Although the regular services have no set structure or liturgy, they are conducted by petitioner's ordained ministers. Ministers ordained by petitioner must serve a three year apprenticeship under the personal tutelage of Roy Masters. Petitioner does not maintain separate physical facilities for the preparation of its ministers. Although petitioner does not separately provide for the religious instruction of the young, such as through Sunday School classes, its school includes religious instruction as part of the general education curriculum.

Petitioner clearly has a distinct, if relatively short, religious history. Petitioner first existed as an unincorporated association formed in 1961 as the vehicle to spread the beliefs of Roy Masters, its founder. The record is unclear as to when and how Roy Masters formulated his beliefs or had them revealed to him. Nonetheless, petitioner had existed, at the time the Commissioner made his final adverse determination, for more than 20 years as an association and a corporation.

Petitioner lacks a definite ecclesiastical government. The record does not reveal how religious or doctrinal decisions are made. However as founder, Roy Masters is clearly the leader of petitioner. He is also president of petitioner under civil corporate law. Furthermore, his ample writings illustrate fully the beliefs and doctrine of petitioner. Nonetheless, petitioner lacks a formal code of doctrine and discipline.

Petitioner does not possess all of the criteria. It does, however, possess most of the criteria to some degree. Moreover, most of the factors considered to be of central importance are satisfied. It possesses associational aspects that are much more than incidental. Despite the involvement of several members of Roy Master's family, petitioner is more than a one family church. * * * Furthermore, petitioner is not a sham organization created solely for tax purposes * * * Based upon all the facts and circumstances, we conclude that petitioner is a church within the meaning of section 170(b)(1)(A)(I).

We acknowledge that petitioner reaches far more people with its message of emotional self control through its radio broadcasts, books, pamphlets, and magazine. Petitioner's radio broadcasts have the potential to reach 2 million people with a regular listening audience of 30,000. Petitioner's magazine, The Iconoclast, has a subscription circulation of 5,200. In contrast, approximately 2,000 followers relocated to Oregon at petitioner's behest, leaving approximately that many in Los Angeles. Attendance at services at the Los Angeles and Grants Pass, Oregon locations, ranged from 50 to 350. In financial terms, petitioner's radio broadcast and publishing efforts constitute a large percentage of petitioner's total receipts and expenditures. Nevertheless, petitioner's substantial broadcasting and publishing activities do not overshadow the other indications that petitioner is a church. The call to evangelize or otherwise spread one's religious beliefs is, undeniably, an integral part of many faiths. The fact that in this case, the religious outreach was substantial both before and after petitioner began to possess many church-like characteristics does not change our conclusion. More importantly, despite the breadth of petitioner's broadcasting and publishing efforts, its associational aspects are much more than incidental. * * * We hold that petitioner has sufficient associational aspects to be considered a church. American Guidance Foundation, Inc. v. United States, supra;* * * We readily acknowledge that this case presents a close question. Our conclusion is based upon the particular facts of this case. At its inception petitioner was not a church, nor did it perceive itself as such. It was granted tax exempt status as a religious and educational organization described in section 501(c)(3). But as more people heard and began to follow the teachings of Roy Masters, petitioner began to adopt church-like characteristics. The means by which petitioner accomplished its admittedly religious purposes have developed such that we conclude that petition is now a church. We hasten to emphasize that by its use of the term 'church' Congress must have intended a more narrow classification than that embodied by a term such as 'religious organization.' Despite the lack of guidance from Congress, and in the absence of a more explicit regulatory definition of the term 'church,' we will continue our efforts to give a distinct meaning to this statutory classification.

* * *

Question

An "integrated auxiliary" of a church is exempt, along with a church, from the requirement of obtaining recognition of its tax-exempt status from the IRS and from the annual reporting requirements applicable to other tax-exempt organizations. What is an "integrated auxiliary" of a church?

LUTHERAN SOCIAL SERVICE OF MINNESOTA v. UNITED STATES

United States Court of Appeals, Eighth Circuit, 1985
758 F.2d 1283

ROSS, Circuit Judge.

Lutheran Social Service of Minnesota (LSS) filed this action to obtain a refund of a $700.00 penalty which had been assessed against it by the Internal Revenue Service (IRS) for failing to file a tax information reporting form (Form 990) on time. The appellant claimed that it was exempt from filing the form under 26 U.S.C. § 6033. The district court rejected LSS's position and this appeal followed. Jurisdiction in this court is based on 28 U.S.C. § 1291.

I. FACTS

The facts in this case are essentially undisputed, and are as follows. LSS is a tax-exempt, nonprofit social service agency that is affiliated with the various synods of the Lutheran Church. The board of directors of LSS is elected by the Minnesota representatives of the three major national Lutheran bodies: the American Lutheran Church, the Lutheran Church in America, and the Lutheran Church–Missouri Synod. It is a separate corporation from these bodies. The articles of incorporation of LSS provide that the purposes of the organization are:

1. To witness to the Gospel of Jesus Christ through ministrations of Christian love to those who may be served, in conformity with the faith and practice of the church bodies to which this corporation is responsible.

2. To develop and maintain a program of Christian social welfare, with appropriate facilities, as needs are demonstrated and resources permit.

3. To work in close cooperation with other health and welfare programs in the community.

4. To participate in coordinating programs which may be sponsored by the church or community.

The services LSS provides include child care and adoption services, family and individual counseling services, residential treatment services for the emotionally disturbed, residential treatment services for mentally retarded adolescents and mentally retarded adults, residential treatment services involving a community based correctional program for young male felons, a nutrition program for the aging, a camp for mentally and physically impaired individuals, community counseling programs, resettlement programs, and a chaplaincy program. LSS charges fees for its services according to its clients' ability to pay. Additionally, approximately 65 percent of its operating budget is derived from federal, state, and county funds.

LSS maintains that the services it provides are religious in that they are "religiously motivated, a manifestation of religious belief, a form of worship, and a means of propagation of the Christian faith, according to the tenets and practices of [the Lutheran Churches by which LSS is owned and controlled]." * * * LSS admits, however, that many of its services would be secular in nature if performed by secular organizations.

The dispute involved here arose when LSS filed a Form 990 (Return of Organization Exempt from Income Tax) with the IRS on July 24, 1979, for the tax year 1978. Since the form was due two months earlier, the IRS assessed a $700 late filing penalty pursuant to 26 U.S.C. § 6652(d). After paying the penalty, the plaintiff filed a claim for a refund arguing that it was exempt from the filing requirement pursuant to 26 U.S.C. § 6033(a)(2)(A)(i). The IRS eventually denied the claim giving rise to this lawsuit. The issue came before the district court for resolution on cross motions for summary judgment. The government's motion was granted, and the refund denied. This appeal followed. For the reasons stated herein we reverse.

* * *

II. ISSUE

The issue presented by this appeal is whether LSS, a church-affiliated tax-exempt organization, is exempt from filing annual informational returns pursuant to 26 U.S.C. § 6033(a)(2)(A)(i).

III. DISCUSSION

A. *Introduction*

The statute which requires tax exempt organizations to file informational returns provides:

§ 6033. Returns by exempt organizations

(a) Organizations required to file.—

> (1) In general.—Except as provided in paragraph (2), every organization exempt from taxation under section 501(a) shall file an annual return, stating specifically the items of gross income, receipts, and disbursements, and such other information for the purpose of carrying out the internal revenue laws as the Secretary may by forms or regulations prescribe * * *.

26 U.S.C. § 6033(a)(1). The statute excepts certain types of organizations from this filing requirement:

> (2) Exceptions from filing.—
>
> (A) Mandatory exceptions. Paragraph (1) shall not apply to—
>
> > (i) *churches, their integrated auxiliaries, and conventions or associations of churches,*

Sec. I DEFINITION OF A "CHURCH" 501

> (ii) any organization (other than a private foundation, as defined in section 509(a)) described in subparagraph (C), the gross receipts of which in each taxable year are normally not more than $5,000, or
>
> (iii) the exclusively religious activities of any religious order.

26 U.S.C. § 6033(a)(2)(A) (emphasis added). Additionally, organizations that are not separately incorporated from the churches with which they are affiliated are exempt under the mandatory exception for churches. *See* Treas.Reg. § 1.6033–2(g)(5)(iv), example 6. *Cf. St. Martin Evangelical Lutheran Church v. South Dakota,* 451 U.S. 772, 784, 101 S.Ct. 2142, 2149, 68 L.Ed.2d 612 (1981) (church-affiliated schools that have no separate legal existence from a church are exempt from Federal Unemployment Tax Act).

LSS contends that it is exempt from filing the Form 990 informational return because it is a "church" or a "convention or association of churches" within the meaning of section 6033(a)(2)(A)(i). Furthermore, although LSS concedes that it is not an integrated auxiliary of a church as the term is defined by the IRS, LSS asserts that the Treasury regulation which defines integrated auxiliary is invalid because it includes an exclusively religious purpose requirement not contained in the statute. *See* Treas.Reg. § 1.6033–2(g)(5)(i). Although we reject the appellant's position that LSS is a church or a convention or association of churches, we agree that the exclusively religious purpose requirement embodied in Treas.Reg. § 1.6033–2(g)(5)(i) is contrary to the legislative history of section 6033.

B. Church

The appellant contends that it is entitled to an exemption as a church within the meaning of 26 U.S.C. § 6033(a)(2)(A)(i). We do not agree. Section 6033 does not define the term "church," and the Treasury regulations to that section make no attempt to clarify the term. "Church" is, however, defined in Treasury Regulation § 1.511–2(a)(3)(ii), a regulation that pertains to organizations exempt from taxes on unrelated business income. The regulation provides in part:

> (ii) The term "church" includes * * * a religious organization if such * * * organization (a) is an integral part of a church, and (b) is engaged in carrying out the functions of a church, whether as a civil law corporation or otherwise. In determining whether a religious * * * organization is an integral part of a church, consideration will be given to the degree to which it is connected with, and controlled by, such church. A religious * * * organization shall be considered to be * * * carrying out the functions of a church if its duties include the *ministration of sacerdotal functions* and the *conduct of religious worship* * * * [which is to be determined based upon] the tenets and practices of a particular religious body constituting a church.

Treas.Reg. § 1.511–2(a)(3)(ii) (emphasis added). Additionally, the IRS has developed fourteen criteria which it applies to individual organizations when determining whether the organization is a church* * *

* * *

When we view the activities of LSS in light of the regulation and criteria set forth above, we believe that the district court was correct in concluding LSS is not a church. LSS's primary activities consist of providing social services to the public at large irrespective of their religious beliefs. Not only are the services available to persons of any religious belief, but LSS's counselors are not required to counsel with any particular religious orientation. Such services are secular in nature when performed by secular organizations, and cannot be transformed into "ministrations of sacerdotal functions" merely because they are performed by a religiously affiliated social service organization like LSS. * * * Additionally, as the district court found, while LSS does have a chaplaincy program whereby it enters into service contracts with hospitals, nursing homes, etc., to provide full or part-time chaplains, there is no evidence in the record that regular worship services are held.

Our reading of the record indicates that LSS is a social service agency, and it cannot become a church within the meaning of section 6033(a)(2)(A)(i) merely by being affiliated with a church.

* * *

C. *Convention or Association of Churches*

Just as the statute and regulations failed to define "church," they also fail to define "convention or association of churches." * * * LSS contends that a literal dictionary definition should be applied. Under the appellant's construction of the statute it would clearly be entitled to an exemption because LSS represents the association of three Lutheran churches. To accept appellant's position would be to exalt literalism over the historical usage of the phrase by Congress.

In the Revenue Act of 1950 Congress imposed a tax on unrelated business income of all 501(c)(3) organizations except churches and conventions or associations of churches. The term "convention or association of churches" was added to the statute at the urging of Baptist leaders. * * * This addition relieved concerns that the term "church" included hierarchical churches (such as the Catholic Church), but not congregational churches in which each local congregation is autonomous (such as with the Baptist). * * * Therefore, churches *and* conventions or associations of churches were exempted to give equal federal tax treatment to both hierarchical and congregational churches.

Since the legislative history to section 6033 is silent as to the meaning of "convention or association of churches," and Congress was aware of the meaning previously attributed to the phrase, we conclude that Congress intended the term to be construed in a manner consistent with its prior use. Congress uses the term "convention or association of churches" merely to refer to the organizational structures of congregational churches. Accordingly, and additionally, for the reasons stated in part B. of this opinion, LSS does not qualify for the "convention or association of churches" exemption contained in section 6033.

D. Integrated Auxiliary

Section 6033 also provides an exemption to integrated auxiliaries of a church. The Treasury has defined "integrated auxiliary" as follows:

> (5)(i) For purposes of this title, the term "integrated auxiliary of a church" means an organization:
>
> > (a) Which is exempt from taxation as an organization described in section 501(c)(3);
> >
> > (b) Which is affiliated (within the meaning of paragraph (g)(5)(iii) of this section) with a church; and
> >
> > (c) Whose principal activity is exclusively religious.

Treas.Reg. § 1.6033–2(g)(5)(i). The IRS concedes that LSS satisfies the first two requirements, but it has nonetheless denied LSS exempt status because the organization's principal activity is not "exclusively religious." Treasury Regulation § 1.6033–2(g)(5)(ii) defines "exclusively religious" as follows:

> (ii) An organization's principal activity will not be considered to be exclusively religious if that activity is educational, literary, charitable, or of another nature (other than religious) that would serve as a basis for exemption under section 501(c)(3).

LSS does not contend that its activities are exclusively religious, rather LSS asserts that the inclusion of an exclusively religious test in the definition of "integrated auxiliary" is invalid because it is contrary to the statute and to legislative intent. The appellant claims that nothing in the legislative history of section 6033 supports the inclusion of an exclusively religious test, and in fact, that the legislative history is to the contrary.

The Senate Finance Committee Report that accompanied the Tax Reform Act of 1969, did not define the term "integrated auxiliary;" it did, however, provide the following list of examples of organizations that were intended to be included in that category: Among the auxiliary organizations to which this exemption applies are the mission societies and the church's religious schools, youth groups, and men's and women's organizations, and interchurch organizations of local units qualifying as local auxiliaries. S.REP. NO. 552, 91st Cong., 1st Sess. 52, *reprinted in* 1969 U.S.CODE CONG. & AD.NEWS 1645, 2027, 2080 (hereinafter cited as S.Rep. No. 552). At the conference on the House and Senate versions of the 1969 Tax Reform Act, the Senate's version of section 6033 was adopted.** The Conference Committee Report stated:

The integrated auxiliary organizations to which this applies include the church's religious school, youth group, and men's and women's clubs.

H.R.REP. NO. 782, 91st Cong., 1st Sess. 286, *reprinted in* 1969 U.S. CODE CONG. & AD. NEWS 2392, 2400 (hereinafter cited as H.R.Rep. No. 782).

LSS argues that the types of organizations that are expressly exempted are no more "exclusively religious" in their activities than it is, and that by providing an exemption for such groups, Congress could not have intended that an "exclusively religious" test be applied to integrated auxiliaries.

In response, the government contends that the court must grant deference to Treasury regulations that implement the congressional mandate in a reasonable manner, and that the regulation in question must be sustained unless unreasonable and plainly inconsistent with the statute. * * * The IRS asserts that the exclusively religious test is not plainly inconsistent with the statute or legislative history, and therefore must be upheld.

While it is true that Treasury regulations are entitled to a great deal of deference, we cannot "rubber-stamp" the regulation if it will "frustrate the congressional policy underlying a statute." * * * A Treasury regulation that is inconsistent with the statute upon which it is based cannot be sustained. * * * In this case, both the plain language of section 6033 and the legislative history of section 6033 convince us that the IRS regulation is inconsistent with clear congressional policy.

Looking first to the language of the statute, we bear in mind that " '[w]here Congress includes particular language in one section of a statute but omits it in another section of the same [statute], it is generally presumed that Congress acts intentionally and purposely in the disparate inclusion or exclusion." * * * Here, while Congress specifically required that religious orders be "exclusively religious" to qualify for section 6033's mandatory exceptions, 26 U.S.C. § 6033(a)(2)(A)(iii), it did not mandate the same requirement with respect to integrated auxiliaries, *id.* at § 6033(a)(2)(A)(i). This omission on the part of Congress can only be viewed as an intentional and purposeful decision not to limit the group of integrated auxiliaries qualifying for the filing exception to those that are exclusively religious.

This conclusion is particularly compelling given that Congress' inclusion of the "exclusively religious" test with respect to religious orders and Congress' exclusion of this test with respect to integrated auxiliaries occur within the very same subsection of section 6033, rather than in two separate and unrelated subsections. Thus, it is clear that Congress had this test in mind when adopting section 6033, and as such had Congress intended the "exclusively religious" test to apply to integrated auxiliaries, "it presumably would have done so expressly as it did" with respect to religious orders. * * * The government's attempt to include an exclusively religious component in the definition of an integrated auxiliary unreasonably restricts the intended scope of the section's mandatory exceptions, is contrary to Congress' clear intent, and thus cannot be sustained.

* * *

The plain meaning of the words of the statute, combined with the legislative history, persuade us to hold that LSS falls within the purview of the statute. LSS is substantially connected with the Lutheran faith, and it performs functions of the church bodies to which it is related by satisfying the tenet of the Lutheran faith which requires the stimulation of works of mercy through social action ministries developed to promote human welfare. The IRS concedes that LSS is a nonprofit organization affiliated with a church in that it is "controlled by or associated with a church." * * * LSS is separately incorporated from a church, * * *, accordingly it must derive its exempt status as an integrated auxiliary.

* * *

IV. CONCLUSION

LSS is not a church or a convention or association of churches within the meaning of section 6033. However, it is entitled to an exemption under that section as an integrated auxiliary of a church. The exclusively religious test contained in the regulation defining "integrated auxiliary" is inconsistent with the legislative history of section 6033, and as such, cannot be relied upon to deny LSS exempt status. Accordingly, we reverse the judgment of the district court and remand for further proceedings consistent with this opinion.

Question

Must an organization demonstrate a belief in a "Supreme Being" in order to be considered a religious organization under § 501(c)(3)? Is a belief in a "Supreme Being" a requirement for an organization to be classified as a church? Consider the following case.

STRAYHORN v. ETHICAL SOCIETY OF AUSTIN

Court of Appeals, Texas, 2003
110 S.W.3d 458

MACK KIDD, Justice.

The Ethical Society of Austin ("the Ethical Society"), a congregation of individuals who meet regularly to practice a belief system known as "Ethical Culture," seeks tax-exempt status as a religious organization under the tax code. * * * The Texas Comptroller denied the application on the ground that the Ethical Society must demonstrate that it requires belief in a "God, Gods, or higher power" (hereinafter "the Supreme Being test") in order to qualify. The trial court found that the Ethical Society should not have been denied tax-exempt status because the Comptroller's test was unconstitutionally underinclusive and that the

Ethical Society should have qualified for the requested tax exemptions. We must now decide whether a state government may, consistent with the First Amendment to the United States Constitution, require a group to demonstrate its belief in a "Supreme Being" in order to be considered a religion for statutory purposes. Because the Comptroller's test fails to include the whole range of belief systems that may, in our diverse and pluralistic society, merit the First Amendment's protection, we will affirm the trial court's judgment.

Background

In 1995, the Ethical Society, then known as the "Ethical Culture Fellowship of Austin," organized the first ethical culture group in Texas. Society members characterize themselves as "ethical humanists," sharing the unifying belief that "within the human experience ethics is central." In 1996, the Society applied with the Comptroller's Office for tax-exempt status from sales, use, excise, hotel, and franchise taxes as a "religious" organization. See Tex. Tax Code Ann. section 171.058, 151.310(a)(1), 156.102.

The Society filed a tax exemption application accompanied by detailed information about its beliefs and activities. Initially, the Comptroller's office determined that the Society did not qualify for tax-exempt status. However, after receiving additional information the Comptroller's office set the application for a higher-level review. The Tax Policy Group, which comprises the highest ranking officials in the Comptroller's office, considered the entire application, including several citations to United States Supreme Court decisions that seemed to indicate that the Society was, indeed, a religious organization. Based on this record, Karey Barton, an official of the Comptroller's office, sent a letter to the Society indicating that it qualified for the requested tax exemptions.

Shortly after the Society received the letter granting it tax-exempt status, the local newspaper published a story detailing the determination made by the Comptroller's office. * * * Comptroller John Sharp learned about the Tax Policy Group's determination from the article. The Comptroller's office soon issued a "letter of correction," stating that the original determination applied and that the Society was not a "religious organization" for purposes of the tax code. Subsequently, the Comptroller confirmed that the Society did not qualify for a tax exemption because it failed to meet the definition of "religion," which the Comptroller construes to require worship of a Supreme Being for the purpose of interpreting the administrative rules.

The Ethical Society challenged the Comptroller's decision. Sitting without a jury, the trial court determined that, by using its formulation of the "Supreme Being" test as the primary basis for determining which organizations are "religious" for tax-exemption purposes, the Comptroller had violated the First Amendment. On appeal, the Comptroller contends that the "Supreme Being" test creates a necessary bright-line rule protecting the state from being required to award tax exemption to any group that calls itself "religious." Relying on language contained in the United States Supreme Court's opinion in Wisconsin v. Yoder, 406 U.S. 205, 92 S.Ct. 1526, 32 L.Ed.2d 15 (1972), the Comptroller asserts that its rule is consistent with the principle that "religious" beliefs must be clearly delineated from "personal or philosophical" beliefs. The Ethical Society, joined by various amici curiae, responds that the Comptroller's test too narrowly defines the scope of religion. Relying on several United States Supreme Court opinions that seem to include Ethical Culture within a group of religions, the Ethical Society argues that the "Supreme Being" test, when applied as the sole determining factor for granting tax exemptions, does not adequately account for the range of belief systems which comprise the broad spectrum of religious faith in contemporary society. We agree with the Ethical Society and will affirm.

DISCUSSION

* * *

The Legislature has provided that certain religious, educational, and charitable groups are exempt from the franchise, sales and use, and hotel taxes. See Tex. Tax Code Ann. section 171.058, 151.310(a)(1), 156.102. The Comptroller's implementing administrative rules require that a group be organized for the purpose of religious worship. See 34 Tex. Admin. Code section 3.161(a)(3), .322(a)(3), .541(c)(3) (2002). Because exempt status is not favored by state law, any organization seeking a tax exemption has the burden to show, without doubt, that it meets the applicable requirements and any doubt regarding the organization's qualifications will result in denial of the exemption. * * * The Comptroller assesses each application according to a non-exclusive set of factors set out in internal agency documents, most of which are objective factors, including whether the organization meets regularly for services, when and where services are held, the approximate number of people attending services, and whether the organization ordains clergy. In addition, the Comptroller has apparently made an informal determination, applied in this case, that an organization must meet what we have called the Supreme Being test, requiring belief in a "God, Gods, or higher power" in order to qualify for tax-exempt status. This Supreme Being requirement does not appear in the tax code or the administrative code. From the documents contained in the record, it appears that the Ethical Society met all of the objective requirements contained within the Comptroller's internal memorandum: among other things, it holds regular meetings, maintains a separate bank account that profits no individual, and undertakes only activities having to do with its congregational meetings. The Tax Policy Group, based on the Ethical Society's application, granted the exemption. It appears, then, that the Comptroller's decision was based entirely on the determination that Ethical Culture does not require belief in a Supreme Being.

As a background matter, we recognize that the State may, consistent with the Constitution, exempt religious groups from taxation. * * * We also recognize that the State has a compelling interest in insuring that only qualified religious organizations receive the tax exemption-it cannot be sufficient for a group simply to label itself as a religion in order to enjoy tax-exempt status. * * * However, this case involves a determination of whether the Comptroller's Supreme Being litmus test is a valid means for determining whether the Ethical Society is a religious group under the tax code.

Although Texas courts have not addressed this issue, the slate on which we write is not blank. Many courts and state administrative agencies have long determined that Ethical Culture is a religion for the purpose of interpreting various government regulations. * * * Although none of these determinations are based explicitly on First Amendment grounds, they all represent the reasoned application of statutes in light of contemporary cultural and religious values. This judicial history is persuasive in suggesting that the Comptroller's test and decision are out of step with the general understanding of the grant of tax exemptions to "religious" organizations in the United States.

The Comptroller relies on the supreme court's declaration in Wisconsin v. Yoder that a way of life, however virtuous and admirable, will not have First Amendment protection unless it is rooted in "religious belief." 406 U.S. 205, 215, 92 S.Ct. 1526, 32 L.Ed.2d 15 (1972). The Comptroller argues that only its Supreme Being test adequately distinguishes between personal and religious beliefs. Furthermore, because the test encompasses the generic concept of a supernatural reality, the Comptroller asserts that it is sufficiently broad to account for the various diverse religious views existing in contemporary society. The Comptroller's argument rests on its understanding of the development of the supreme court's interpretation of the First Amendment religious protections. Initially, the First Amendment was, indeed, understood to protect only those who believed in a monotheistic deity. * * * However, in two more recent cases interpreting the federal conscientious objector statute, United States v. Seeger, 380 U.S. 163, 85 S.Ct. 850, 13 L.Ed.2d 733 (1965), and Welsh v. United States, 398 U.S. 333, 90 S.Ct. 1792, 26 L.Ed.2d 308 (1970), the Court adopted a broader definition of religion. The Universal Military Training and Service Act exempted from military service persons "who by reason of their religious training and belief are conscientiously opposed to participation in war in any form." * * * The statute defined religious belief as "belief in a relation to a Supreme Being involving duties superior to those arising from any human relation." * * * In interpreting the statute, the Seeger court carefully examined a number of religious and philosophical viewpoints in order to avoid too narrow an analysis of individual belief. * * * Thus, in the context of interpreting a specific statutory provision, the Court saw fit to interpret the term "religion" broadly in order to take into account the breadth of religious opinion in American society. According to the Comptroller, however, in Yoder the Court took a step back from its position in Seeger and Welsh. Yoder involved an attempt by the state of Wisconsin to enforce its mandatory schooling provisions, which required children to

attend school until the age of sixteen, against a group of Old Order Amish, who maintained that it would offend their religious beliefs to require their children to attend a consolidated secondary school. The Court held that the state's interest in keeping the children in school did not outweigh the Amish community's interest in maintaining its religious independence. In making this determination, the Court observed that:[a] way of life, however virtuous and admirable, may not be interposed as a barrier to reasonable state regulation of education if it is based on purely secular considerations; to have the protection of the Religion Clauses, the claims must be rooted in religious belief.... Thus, if the Amish asserted their claims because of their subjective evaluation and rejection of the contemporary secular values accepted by the majority, much as Thoreau rejected the social values of his time and isolated himself at Walden Pond, their claims would not rest on a religious basis. Thoreau's choice was philosophical and personal rather than religious, and such belief does not rise to the demands of the Religion Clauses.
* * *

According to the Comptroller, this language counteracts any expansive reading of religion undertaken in the conscientious objector cases, because it focuses the First Amendment analysis squarely, and exclusively, on the distinction between religious and personal or philosophical beliefs. In support, the Comptroller cites several cases that have relied on this distinction in making the same analysis. * * * According to the Comptroller, the State has an overriding interest in determining with ease and clarity whether a group is actually "religious" or whether it merely labels itself as religious. * * * The Comptroller paints Ethical Culture as a belief system based only on the unifying belief that "within the human experience ethics is central." As one of its founding figures, Felix Adler, wrote: "Our ethical religion has its basis in the effort to improve the world and ourselves morally." Although Ethical Culture does not exclude individuals who profess a faith in a particular understanding of divinity or religion, it is also open to those who do not claim such beliefs. As the American Ethical Union, an umbrella group for Ethical Culture, reports, "The Ethical Societies have no creed of theology or metaphysics, no set doctrines concerning the unknown mysteries of life. There is no claim to a belief in a supernatural universe or Supreme Being." Consequently, members of the Ethical Society were reluctant to testify that the society was a "religion" under the Comptroller's definition because, for them, it dealt with human relationships. According to the Comptroller, statements like these, which emphasize "human experience," indicate that the Ethical Society is only focused on personal, philosophical beliefs because, by the Comptroller's own definition, the Ethical Society's principles do not embrace any reality beyond that perceived in human relationships.

The Ethical Society replies, as a preliminary matter, that the supreme court has, at least in passing, referred to Ethical Culture as a creedless religion. In Torcaso v. Watkins, 367 U.S. 488, 81 S.Ct. 1680, 6 L.Ed.2d 982 (1961), the Court invalidated a Maryland provision requiring notaries public to swear an oath "to God" on the grounds that such a requirement would "aid those religions based on a belief in the existence of God as against those religions founded on different beliefs." * * * In a footnote, the Court included Ethical Culture in a list with Buddhism and Taoism as an example of a religion that did not teach "what would generally be considered a belief in the existence of God." * * * Likewise, in Seeger, the Court mentioned Ethical Culture in describing the breadth of religious opinion in the United States. * * * The Ethical Society contends that, because the supreme court has twice referred to its faith system in addressing questions regarding the scope of the First Amendment's protections, we should consider it to be a religion.

Although the supreme court has not unambiguously declared that the practice of Ethical Culture is a religion protected by the First Amendment, it does not follow that under an appropriate First Amendment analysis Ethical Culture cannot qualify as a religion. We reject the Comptroller's reliance on the language regarding the distinction between personal and religious beliefs outlined in Yoder. While Yoder restates the principle that the First Amendment protects religions, as opposed to purely personal belief systems, it neither introduces a new concern into the Court's religion analysis nor articulates a workable test for distinguishing personal from religious beliefs. The protection of the freedom of religious conscience, without regard to majority opinion, has been an element of American law since the founding of the Republic. * * * Judges are not oracles of theological verity, and the Founders did not intend for them to be declarants of religious orthodoxy. * * * Any inquiry that delves too closely into the textual references made by a religion to the existence of God puts the courts in danger of making determinations based on dimly understood, and perhaps misconceived, characterizations of unfamiliar religions. * * * In sum, the Comptroller's position merely begs the question by looking to Yoder for a definitive test. Although Yoder reaffirms that the relevant question is whether a set of beliefs is religious or philosophical, it does not outline a useful test for making that determination.

Serious contemplation of the supreme court's commitment to protecting the full range of religious belief, as expressed in Seeger, requires us to reject the proposition that a narrowly defined "Supreme Being" test can account for the broad range of religious faith protected by the First Amendment. Although the Ethical Society's tenets and beliefs may not explicitly reference a divinity, they evidence enough of a sense of spiritual feeling that the Society's claim to religious status should be carefully assessed. The Comptroller's litmus test does not allow for a closer assessment of the Ethical Society's claims and, because it forecloses careful evaluation of the ways in which Ethical Humanism may be more religious than personal, it violates the First Amendment* * * Therefore, we hold that the Comptroller's reliance on a Supreme Being litmus test to determine whether an organization qualifies as a religion for purposes of the tax code is constitutionally infirm.

Having determined that the Comptroller's test is invalid under the First Amendment, we are left with the question of whether, under an appropriate analysis, the Ethical Society constitutes a religious group. Both parties refer us to the line of cases relying on the three-factor test laid out by Judge Adams in his concurrence in Malnak v.Yogi, 592 F.2d 197, 207–210 (3d Cir.1979) * * * and later applied by him in Africa v. Pennsylvania, 662 F.2d 1025, 1032 (3d Cir.1981). The Malnak test gives a court the basis on which to determine whether an unfamiliar religion is entitled to First Amendment protection by comparing it to familiar religions. The test requires that a set of beliefs: (1) address fundamental and ultimate questions having to do with deep and imponderable matters such as the meaning of life and death or man's role in the universe; (2) be broad in scope and comprehensive in nature; and (3) be accompanied by the presence of certain formal and external signs. * * * The Comptroller takes the position that Ethical Culture does not meet the Malnak test because the inclusion of a transcendental being or metaphysical experience is essential to making the case that a new religion is analogous to a traditionally recognized religion. The Ethical Society responds that, because it puts weight on external indicia of religious belief, the Malnak test supports its claim to religious status. While we have already concluded that the requirement of a belief in a Supreme Being cannot, by itself, serve as the litmus test for determining which organizations merit religious tax exemptions, we believe that the Malnak test provides an appropriate guideline for the Comptroller to apply and, further, that Ethical Culture meets the test's requirements.

* * *

The Ethical Society is part of the American Ethical Union ("the Ethical Union"), an umbrella group for Ethical Culture congregations founded in 1889. We must assess the Ethical Society's claims in context of its membership in the larger organization. The Ethical Union, rather than adopting a formal creed, allows each of its societies to develop relatively independently. Many of the societies take a less "spiritual" approach. However, other societies adopt the religious and metaphysical approach embraced by Felix Adler, one of Ethical Culture's seminal thinkers. Faced with what he considered to be the "definite and permanent disappearance of the individualistic conception of Deity," Adler sought to articulate the ethical underpinning he believed to be the foundation of all the great religions. Accordingly, he formulated the concept of a "spiritual and ethical ideal," now often referred to as the "Ethical Ideal" or "Ethical Manifold." For Adler, the attempt to reach this understanding reflected a fundamental, and therefore observable, transcendent reality underlying human thought and consciousness. He, and the members of the Ethical Culture movement, refused to adopt this position as an official doctrine because they were committed to the discovery of ethical principles by individuals learning from their own experiences. Ethical Culture, in its contemporary form, begins from the proposition that its members cannot simply accept a belief in a God or higher power as the basis of their religious experience. However, while it rejects the idea of "spiritual revelations," it does not follow that Ethical Culture rejects a religious approach to the ultimate questions facing humankind. In place of discussing a supernatural reality, Ethical Culturists see themselves as discovering religious value and direction from their lives and their relationships with other people. This is more than a simple statement that they consider "life" to be an example of religious experience; it is a commitment to an attempt to discover, through observance and debate, the transcendent moral truths that underlie human experience.

Our assessment of the scope of the questions posed by Ethical Culture might be debatable. There can be no doubt that Ethical Culture attempts to address the religious needs of its members without reference to a God or a supernatural reality. However, we believe that in its focus on situating each individual within a network of ethical decision-making as the central concern of that individual's human experience, Ethical Culture poses the kinds of questions that have been considered by other courts to be "ultimate" in nature.

* * *

* * * Ethical Culture has a developed body of literature and a set of principles. As the Ethical Union posits, "We define ethics not simply and solely in terms of what is right or wrong, but in the larger sense of what is good and what is true." Thus, according to the Ethical Union, any attempt to reduce its principles to a specific creed would violate its adherents' ability to articulate truth and goodness through the practices of Ethical Culture. Some Ethical Culture documents include injunctions to "treat each other as ends, not merely as means," that "self-reflection and our social nature require us to shape a more humane world," and that "life itself inspires religious response." Books and essays on Ethical Culture and its practice have been routinely published over the more than a century during which the movement has existed. Furthermore, beyond simply asserting the primacy of a particular narrow idea or assumption, Ethical Culture attempts to create a comprehensive response to the problems faced in life based on a common contemplative practice. While it is true that Ethical Culture congregations welcome leaders trained in other religious traditions, including priests and rabbis, such pluralism is not inconsistent with a wide religious viewpoint attempting to assimilate various opinions about religious faith. * * *

More fundamentally, the Ethical Union sees the totality of this debate, in both writing and observance, as an attempt to arrive at an understanding of "humanity's place in the universe." Ethical Culture is not merely a disassociated string of ethical commitments, but a commitment to a particular discipline of spiritual observation. The emphasis the Society places on what Adler described as the "reality producing functions of the mind" focuses its members on deriving moral commitment from an understanding of human psychological experience and offers an

Sec. I DEFINITION OF A "CHURCH" 513

absolute, and universal, basis on which Ethical Society members are to structure their own lives.

* * *

In ruling that organizations are not religions, courts often emphasize their lack of certain practices or characteristics. The organizations held not to be religions in the cases cited by the Comptroller have lacked many of the features that would have made them more akin to traditional religious practices. They have lacked life ceremonies, such as naming ceremonies and ceremonial marriage. * * * They have lacked trained clergy. * * * Nor have they been able to demonstrate a coherent and uniform body of literature supporting and elaborating on their religious ideals. * * * Most importantly, some of these organizations have not even bothered to set up a separate corporate entity and have funneled their funds, which they claim to have been used for religious purposes, into the private accounts of individuals who have used that money almost exclusively for personal expenses. * * *

By contrast, Ethical Culture has the marks of a traditional religious organization. Indeed, with a history dating back to 1876, Ethical Culture does appear to function in a way analogous to more established religious groups. It maintains a bona fide separate corporate existence. It possesses a coherent literature. Ethical Culture groups meet regularly, typically on Sundays, for services including ceremonial practices. Those services are led by a group of clergy, most of whom have been educated at theological institutes and seminaries. The same trained clergy perform life cycle rituals, including marriages and naming ceremonies. The services are supplemented with religious instruction for children. The Ethical Society of Austin has such meetings, coordinated by professional clergy, and meets regularly on Sundays. Taken together, these factors indicate to us a sincere attempt by the Ethical Society, and its sister groups, to undertake to provide the benefits of a traditional religion. In light of our understanding of the structure of Ethical Culture's principles, these external indications of religious faith mark an important factor for determining whether the Ethical Society is a religion.

Organizations such as the Ethical Society are entitled under the First Amendment to a careful assessment of their claim to religious status. Such an assessment requires careful analysis of all the factors we have discussed in this opinion. We do not conclude that the Comptroller may never consider whether an organization espouses a belief in a Supreme Being; such an inquiry may be instructive in evaluating the types of ideas espoused by a particular applicant group. Instead, we hold that belief in a supernatural reality must serve, at most, as part of a broader inquiry that investigates both an organization's beliefs and the means by which those beliefs are put into action. Ethical Culture's practices and beliefs, in our opinion, address ultimate concerns and present a comprehensive belief system. Without question, their practices and rituals constitute the external signs of a religion. In short, the Ethical Society manifests its spiritual beliefs through organized observance; we cannot say that this activity falls outside of the scope of the First Amendment's protection, and we believe, therefore, that it must fall within the legislature's intent in granting the tax exemptions in question. Having held that the Comptroller's requirement that a group believe in a Supreme Being, applied as the sole test for determining the grant of religious tax exemptions, violates the First Amendment, we now hold that, under the Malnak analysis, Ethical Culture qualifies as a religion for First Amendment purposes.

Conclusion

Because we understand the First Amendment to require a broader definition of what should be considered a religion than the simple Supreme Being litmus test offered by the Comptroller, and because we believe that under such an analysis Ethical Culture should be so considered, we affirm the trial court's judgment.

Question

Do you agree with the court in *Strayhorn*? Do you think a federal court would reach a different result if it were considering whether the Ethical Culture qualified as a church under § 501(c)(3)?

II. MEMBERSHIP

The jurisdiction of civil courts to review decisions of ecclesiastical tribunals regarding rights of members of a religious organization is limited by the First Amendment. As a general rule, the rights and status of members of a church or other religious organization depends upon the organization's form of government.

SERBIAN EASTERN ORTHODOX DIOCESE v. MILIVOJEVICH
United States Supreme Court, 1976
426 U.S. 696, 96 S.Ct. 2372, 49 L.Ed.2d 151

Mr. Justice BRENNAN delivered the opinion of the Court.

In 1963, the Holy Assembly of Bishops and the Holy Synod of the Serbian Orthodox Church (Mother Church) suspended and ultimately removed respondent Dionisije Milivojevich (Dionisije) as Bishop of the American-Canadian Diocese of that Church, and appointed petitioner Bishop Firmilian Ocokoljich (Firmilian) as Administrator of the Diocese, which the Mother Church then reorganized into three Dioceses. In 1964 the Holy Assembly and Holy Synod defrocked Dionisije as a Bishop and cleric of the Mother Church. In this civil action brought by Dionisije and the other respondents in Illinois Circuit Court, the Supreme Court of Illinois held that the proceedings of the Mother Church respecting Dionisije were procedurally and substantively defective under the internal regulations of the Mother Church and were therefore arbitrary and invalid. The State Supreme Court also invalidated the Diocesan reorganization into three Dioceses. 60 Ill.2d 477, 328 N.E.2d 268 (1975). We granted certiorari to determine whether the actions of the Illinois Supreme Court constituted improper judicial interference with decisions of the highest authorities of a hierarchical church in violation of the First and Fourteenth Amendments. 423 U.S. 911, 96 S.Ct. 770, 46 L.Ed.2d 634 (1975). We hold that the inquiries made by the Illinois Supreme Court into matters of ecclesiastical cognizance and polity and the court's actions pursuant thereto contravened the First and Fourteenth Amendments. We therefore reverse.

I

The basic dispute is over control of the Serbian Eastern Orthodox Diocese for the United States of America and Canada (American–Canadian Diocese), its property and assets. Petitioners are Bishops Firmilian, Gregory Udicki, and Sava Vukovich, and the Serbian Eastern Orthodox Diocese for the United States of America and Canada (the religious body in this country). Respondents are Bishop Dionisije, the Serbian Orthodox Monastery of St. Sava, and the Serbian Eastern Orthodox Diocese for the United States of America and Canada, an Illinois religious corporation. A proper perspective on the relationship of these parties and the nature of this dispute requires some background discussion.

The Serbian Orthodox Church, one of the 14 autocephalous, hierarchical churches which came into existence following the schism of the universal Christian church in 1054, is an episcopal church whose seat is the Patriarchate in Belgrade, Yugoslavia. Its highest legislative, judicial, ecclesiastical, and administrative authority resides in the Holy Assembly of Bishops, a body composed of all Diocesan Bishops presided over by a Bishop designated by the Assembly to be Patriarch. The Church's highest executive body, the Holy Synod of Bishops, is composed of the Patriarch and four Diocesan Bishops selected by the Holy Assembly. The Holy Synod and the Holy Assembly have the exclusive power to remove, suspend, defrock, or appoint Diocesan Bishops. The Mother Church is governed according to the Holy Scriptures, Holy Tradition, Rules of the Ecumenical Councils, the Holy Apostles, the Holy Faiths of the Church, the Mother Church Constitution adopted in 1931, and a "penal code" adopted in 1961. These sources of law are sometimes ambiguous and seemingly inconsistent. Pertinent provisions of the Mother Church Constitution provide that the Church's "main administrative division is composed of dioceses, both in regard to church hierarchical and church administrative aspect," Art. 12, and that "(d)ecisions of establishing, naming, liquidating, reorganizing, and the seat of the dioceses, and establishing or eliminating of position of vicar bishops, is decided upon by the (Holy Assembly), in agreement with the Patriarchal Council," Art. 16.

During the late 19th century, migrants to North America of Serbian descent formed autonomous religious congregations throughout this country and Canada. These congregations were then under the jurisdiction of the Russian Orthodox Church, but that Church was unable to care for their needs and the congregations sought permission to bring themselves under the jurisdiction of the Serbian Orthodox Church.

In 1913 and 1916, Serbian priests and laymen organized a Serbian Orthodox Church in North America. The 32 Serbian Orthodox congregations were divided into 4 presbyteries, each presided over by a Bishop's Aide, and constitutions were adopted. In 1917, the Russian Orthodox Church commissioned a Serbian priest, Father Mardary, to organize an independent Serbian Diocese in America. Four years later, as a result of Father Mardary's efforts, the Holy Assembly of Bishops of the Mother Church created the Eastern Orthodox Diocese for the United States of America and Canada and designated a Serbian Bishop to complete the formal organization of a Diocese. From that time until 1963, each bishop who governed the American–Canadian Diocese was a Yugoslav citizen appointed by the Mother Church without consultation with Diocesan officials.

* * *

Respondent Bishop Dionisije was elected Bishop of the American–Canadian Diocese by the Holy Assembly of Bishops in 1939. He became a controversial figure; during the years before 1963, the Holy Assembly received numerous complaints challenging his fitness to serve as Bishop and his administration of the Diocese.

During his tenure, however, the Diocese grew so substantially that Dionisije requested that the Patriarch and Holy Assembly appoint bishops to assist him but to serve under his supervision. Eventually, the Diocese sought its elevation by the Holy Assembly to the rank of Metropolia, that South America be added to the Diocese, and that several assistant bishops be appointed under Dionisije. Dionisije specifically recommended that petitioners Firmilian and Gregory Udicki, and one Stefan Lastavica be named assistant bishops. A delegation from the Diocese was sent to the May 1962 meeting of the Holy Assembly in Belgrade to urge adoption of these reorganization proposals, and on June 12, 1962, the Holy Synod appointed a delegation to visit the United States and study the proposals. The delegation was also directed to confer with Dionisije concerning the complaints made against him and his administration over the years.

The delegation remained in the United States for three months, visiting parishes throughout the Diocese and discussing both the reorganization proposals and the complaints against Dionisije. After completion of its survey, the delegation suggested to the Holy Synod the assignment of vicar bishops to the Diocese and recommended that a commission be appointed to conduct a thorough investigation into the complaints against Dionisije. However, the Holy Assembly on May 10, 1963, instead recommended that the Holy Synod institute disciplinary proceedings against Dionisije. The Holy Synod thereupon met immediately and suspended Dionisije pending investigation and disposition of the complaints. The Holy Synod appointed petitioner Firmilian, Dionisije's chief episcopal deputy since 1955 and one of Dionisije's candidates for assistant bishop, as Administrator of the Diocese pending completion of the proceedings.

* * *

On June 13 (1963), the Holy Synod appointed* * * a commission, composed of two Bishops and the Secretary of the Holy Synod. On July 5, the commission met with Dionisije, who reiterated his refusal to recognize his suspension or the Diocesan reorganization, and who demanded all accusations in writing. The commission refused to give Dionisije the written accusations on the ground that defiance of decisions of higher church authorities itself established wrongful conduct, and advised him that the Holy Synod would appoint a Bishop as court prosecutor to prepare an indictment against him.

On the basis of the commission's report and recommendations, which recited Dionisije's refusal to accept the decisions of the Holy Synod and Holy Assembly and his refusal to recognize the court of the Holy Synod or its competence to try him, the Holy Assembly met on July 27, 1963, and voted to remove Dionisije as Bishop. The minutes of the Holy Assembly meeting and the Patriarch's letter to Dionisije informing him of the Holy Assembly's actions made clear that the removal was based solely on his acts of defiance subsequent to his May 10, 1963, suspension, and his violation of his oath and loss of certain qualifications for Bishop under Art. 104 of the constitution of the Mother Church.

The Diocesan National Assembly, with Dionisije presiding despite his removal, met in August 1963 and issued a resolution repudiating the division of the Diocese into three Dioceses and demanding a revocation by the Mother Church of the decisions concerning that division. When the Holy Assembly refused to reconsider, the Diocesan National Assembly in November 1963 declared the Diocese completely autonomous and reinstated the provisions of the Diocesan constitution that provided for election of the Bishop of the Diocese itself and for amendments without the approval of the Holy Assembly.

* * *

The Holy Synod, on February 25, 1964, declared that it could not proceed further without Dionisije and referred the matter to the Holy Assembly, which tried Dionisije as a default case on March 5, 1964, because of his refusal to participate. The indictment was also amended at that time to include charges based on Dionisije's acts of rebellion such as those committed at the November meeting of the National Assembly which had declared the Diocese separate from the Mother Church. Considering the original and amended indictments, the Holy Assembly unanimously found Dionisije guilty of all charges and divested him of his episcopal and monastic ranks.

Even before the Holy Assembly had removed Dionisije as Bishop, he had commenced what eventually became this protracted litigation, now carried on for almost 13 years. Acting upon the threat contained in his May 27, 1963, press release, Dionisije filed suit in the Circuit Court of

Lake County, Ill., on July 26, 1963, seeking to enjoin petitioners from interfering with the assets of respondent corporations and to have himself declared the true Diocesan Bishop. Petitioners countered with a separate complaint, * * * seeking declaratory relief that Dionisije had been removed as Bishop of the Diocese and that the Diocese had been properly reorganized into three Dioceses, and injunctive relief granting petitioner Bishops control of the reorganized Dioceses and their property. After the trial court granted summary judgment for respondents and dismissed petitioners' counter complaint, the Illinois Appellate Court reversed and remanded for a hearing on the merits. * * *. * * *

Following a lengthy trial, the trial court filed an unreported memorandum opinion and entered a final decree which concluded that "no substantial evidence was produced ... that fraud, collusion or arbitrariness existed in any of the actions or decisions preliminary to or during the final proceedings of the decision to defrock Bishop Dionisije made by the highest Hierarchical bodies of the Mother Church," * * * that the property held by respondent corporations is held in trust for all members of the American–Canadian Diocese; that it was "improper and beyond the power of the Mother Church to take its action in dividing the whole American Diocese into three new Dioceses, changing its boundaries, and in appointing new bishops for said so-called new Dioceses," * * * and that "Firmilian was validly appointed by the Holy Episcopal Synod as temporary Administrator of the whole American Diocese in place of the defrocked Bishop Dionisije." * * *

On appeal, the Supreme Court of Illinois affirmed in part and reversed in part, essentially holding that Dionisije's removal and defrockment had to be set aside as "arbitrary" because the proceedings resulting in those actions were not conducted according to the Illinois Supreme Court's interpretation of the Church's constitution and penal code, and that the Diocesan reorganization was invalid because it was beyond the scope of the Mother Church's authority to effectuate such changes without Diocesan approval. * * * Although the court denied rehearing, it amended its original opinion to hold that, although Dionisije had been properly suspended, that suspension terminated by operation of church law when he was not validly tried within one year of his indictment. Thus, the court purported in effect to reinstate Dionisije as Diocesan Bishop.

II

The fallacy fatal to the judgment of the Illinois Supreme Court is that it rests upon an impermissible rejection of the decisions of the highest ecclesiastical tribunals of this hierarchical church upon the issues in dispute, and impermissibly substitutes its own inquiry into church polity and resolutions based thereon of those disputes. Consistently with the First and Fourteenth Amendments "civil courts do not inquire whether the relevant (hierarchical) church governing body has power under religious law (to decide such disputes).... Such a determination ... frequently necessitates the interpretation of ambiguous religious law and usage. To permit civil courts to probe deeply enough into the allocation of power within a hierarchical) church so as to decide ... religious law (governing church polity) ... would violate the First Amendment in much the same manner as civil determination of religious doctrine." * * * For where resolution of the disputes cannot be made without extensive inquiry by civil courts into religious law and polity, the First and Fourteenth Amendments mandate that civil courts shall not disturb the decisions of the highest ecclesiastical tribunal within a church of hierarchical polity, but must accept such decisions as binding on them, in their application to the religious issues of doctrine or polity before them. * * *

* * *

The conclusion of the Illinois Supreme Court that the decisions of the Mother Church were "arbitrary" was grounded upon an inquiry that persuaded the Illinois Supreme Court that the Mother Church had not followed its own laws and procedures in arriving at those decisions. We have concluded that whether or not there is room for "marginal civil court review" under the narrow rubrics of "fraud" or "collusion" when church tribunals act in bad faith for secular purposes, no "arbitrariness" exception in the sense of an inquiry whether the decisions of the highest ecclesiastical tribunal of a hierarchical church complied with church laws and regulations is consistent with the constitutional mandate that civil courts are bound to accept the decisions of the highest judicatories of a religious organization of hierarchical polity on matters of discipline, faith, internal organization, or ecclesiastical rule, custom, or law. For civil courts to analyze whether the ecclesiastical actions of a church judicatory are in that sense "arbitrary" must inherently entail inquiry into the procedures that canon or ecclesiastical law supposedly requires the church judicatory to follow, or else in to the substantive criteria by which they are supposedly to decide the ecclesiastical question. But this is exactly the inquiry that the First Amendment prohibits; recognition of such an exception would undermine the general rule that religious controversies are not the proper subject of civil court inquiry, and that a civil court must accept the ecclesiastical decisions of church tribunals as it finds them. * * *

* * *

Indeed, it is the essence of religious faith that ecclesiastical decisions are reached and are to be accepted as matters of faith whether or not rational or measurable by subjective criteria. Constitutional concepts of due process, involving secular notions of "fundamental fairness" or impermissible objectives, are therefore hardly relevant to such matters of ecclesiastical cognizance.

The constitutional evils that attend upon any "arbitrariness" exception in the sense applied by the Illinois Supreme Court to justify civil court review of ecclesiastical decisions of final church tribunals are manifest in the instant case. The Supreme Court of Illinois recognized that all parties agree that the Serbian Orthodox Church is a hierarchical church, and that the sole power to appoint and remove Bishops of the Church resides in its highest ranking organs, the Holy Assembly and the Holy Synod. Indeed, final authority with respect to the promulgation and interpretation of *all* makers of church discipline and internal organization rests with the Holy Assembly, and even the written constitution of the Mother Church expressly provides:

> "The Holy Assembly of Bishops, as the highest hierarchical body, is legislative authority in the matters of faith, officiation, church order (discipline) and internal organization of the Church, as well as the highest church juridical authority within its jurisdiction. * * *"

"All the decisions of the Holy Assembly of Bishops and of the Holy Synod of Bishops of canonical and church nature, in regard to faith, officiation, church order and internal organization of the church, are valid and final."

* * *

Yet having recognized that the Serbian Orthodox Church is hierarchical and that the decisions to suspend and defrock respondent Dionisije were made by the religious bodies in whose sole discretion the authority to make those ecclesiastical decisions was vested, the Supreme Court of Illinois nevertheless invalidated the decision to defrock Dionisije on the ground that it was "arbitrary" because a "detailed review of the evidence discloses that the proceedings resulting in Bishop Dionisije's removal and defrockment were not in accordance with the prescribed procedure of the constitution and the penal code of the Serbian Orthodox Church." * * * Not only was this "detailed review" impermissible under the First and Fourteenth Amendments, but in reaching this conclusion, the court evaluated conflicting testimony concerning internal church procedures and rejected the interpretations of relevant procedural provisions by the Mother Church's highest tribunals. * * * The court also failed to take cognizance of the fact that the church judicatories were also guided by other sources of law, such as canon law, which are admittedly not always consistent, and it rejected the testimony of petitioners' five expert witnesses that church procedures were properly followed, denigrating the testimony of one witness as "contradictory" and discounting that of another on the ground that it was "premised upon an assumption which did not consider the penal code," even though there was some question whether that code even applied to discipline of Bishops. The court accepted, on the other hand, the testimony of respondents' sole expert witness that the Church's procedures had been contravened in various specifics. We need not, and under the First Amendment cannot, demonstrate the propriety or impropriety of each of Dionisije's procedural claims, but we can note that the state court even rejected petitioners' contention that Dionisije's failure to participate in the proceedings undermined all procedural contentions because Arts. 66 and 70 of the penal code specify that if a person charged with a violation fails to participate or answer the indictment, the allegations are admitted and due process will be concluded without his participation; the court merely asserted that "application of this provision ... must be viewed from the perspective that Bishop Dionisije refused to participate because he maintained that the proceedings against him were in violation of the constitution and the penal code of the Serbian Orthodox Church." * * * The court found no support in any church dogma for this judicial rewriting of church law, and compounded further the error of this intrusion into a religious thicket by declaring that although Dionisije had, even under the court's analysis, been properly suspended and replaced by Firmilian as temporary administrator, he had to be reinstated as Bishop because church law mandated a trial on ecclesiastical charges within one year of the indictment. Yet the only reason more time then that had expired was due to Dionisije's decision to resort to the civil courts for redress without attempting to vindicate himself by pursuing available remedies within the church. Indeed, the Illinois Supreme Court overlooked the clear substantive canonical violations for which the Church disciplined Dionisije, violations based on Dionisije's conceded open defiance and rebellion against the church hierarchy immediately after the Holy Assembly's decision to suspend him (a decision which even the Illinois courts deemed to be proper) and Dionisije's decision to litigate the Mother Church's authority in the civil courts rather than participate in the disciplinary proceedings before the Holy Synod and the Holy Assembly. Instead, the Illinois Supreme Court would sanction this circumvention of the tribunals set up to resolve internal church disputes and has ordered the Mother Church to reinstate as Bishop one who espoused views regarded by the church hierarchy to be schismatic and which the proper church tribunals have already determined merit severe sanctions. In short, under the guise of "minimal" review under the umbrella of "arbitrariness," the Illinois Supreme Court has unconstitutionally undertaken the resolution of quintessentially religious controversies whose resolution the First Amendment commits exclusively to the highest ecclesiastical tribunals of this hierarchical church. And although the Diocesan Bishop controls respondent Monastery of St. Sava and is the principal officer of respondent property-holding corporations, the civil courts must accept that consequence as the incidental effect of an ecclesiastical determination that is not subject to judicial abrogation, having been reached by the final church judicatory in which authority to make the decision resides.

* * *

In short, the First and Fourteenth Amendments permit hierarchical religious organizations to establish their own rules and regulations for internal discipline and government, and to create tribunals for adjudicating disputes over these matters. When this choice is exercised and ecclesiastical tribunals are created to decide disputes over the government and direction of subordinate bodies, the Constitution requires that civil courts accept their decisions as binding upon them.

Reversed.

* * *

Note

Refer to the decision of the Supreme Court of Arkansas *Holiman v. Dovers,* 236 Ark. 211, 366 S.W.2d 197 (1963), discussed below, in which the Court recognized that courts will assume jurisdiction with respect to self-governing congregational churches. As the Court noted in *Holiman,* a local congregation is independent and autonomous. There is no recourse within the denomination. Congregational churches, unlike hierarchical churches, generally are governed by a majority vote of the membership.

III. ASSOCIATION STATUS

Many churches and other religious organizations operate as unincorporated associations. As noted in Chapter 2, associations are not recognized as legal entities. Under the common law, they are incapable of holding title to real property and the members can be personally liable for debts of the association.

A. Liability of Members of a Religious Organization

A contract entered into in the name of a religious association generally will be regarded as that of the individual member who either authorized or ratified the contract. Further, those members who incur debt for the association or who assent to its creation can be personally liable for such debts.

Notes

1. Those states that have adopted the Uniform Unincorporated Nonprofit Association Act have provided some protection for members of unincorporated religious organizations. See discussion of the Act and associations generally in chapter 2.

2. Members of an unincorporated religious association also may become subject to tort liability. Although freedom of belief is absolutely guaranteed by the First Amendment, freedom of action is not.

Consider possible tort claims arising from church discipline in the following case.

SMITH v. CALVARY CHRISTIAN CHURCH
Supreme Court, Michigan, 2000
462 Mich. 679, 614 N.W.2d 590

MICHAEL F. CAVANAGH, J.

In this case, we are asked to decide whether plaintiff's intentional tort claims arising from church discipline are barred by the religion clauses of the federal constitution. Even if those constitutional provisions do not provide any defense to plaintiff's claims, plaintiff cannot prevail in this action. Through his words and deeds, plaintiff consented to the religious discipline imposed on him, so his claims fail as a matter of tort law. Accordingly, we reverse the judgment of the Court of Appeals, and reinstate the trial court's grant of summary disposition under MCR 2.116(C)(10) for the defendants.

I

Plaintiff began attending Calvary Christian Church, a small, independent church, in August 1985. He formally became a church member in early 1986. When he became a member, plaintiff specifically consented not to cause division within the church, to be faithful to Matthew 18:15–17,[1] and to accept discipline imposed by the church.

Shortly after he began to attend the church, plaintiff requested a meeting with the church's pastor, Mark Byers. At that meeting, plaintiff disclosed that he previously had frequented prostitutes. Plaintiff apparently believed that this disclosure would be kept confidential.

Later, in 1991, plaintiff was formally removed from the church's membership. He was removed not because of his disclosure, but rather because he was causing division within the church by challenging church leaders over religious doctrine. Plaintiff requested that he be reinstated, but the pastor advised that before plaintiff could be reinstated, he had to confess his sins, including his past indiscretions with prostitutes, to the church board and to plaintiff's wife. Plaintiff complied and was reinstated, but the board warned him that if he did not end his divisive conduct, he would again be subject to discipline.

Despite this warning, plaintiff continued to cause division within the church. Therefore, the church decided to "mark" plaintiff according to Matthew 18:15–17, which involves singling out a person who is involved in sin and causing division within the church, and detailing the person's sins before the church congregation. The pastor advised plaintiff's wife and family that plaintiff would be marked on December 8, 1996, and cautioned them against attending services that day. By that time, plaintiff had submitted a letter withdrawing his formal membership in the church; however, he remained involved with the church, and was present at the church on the day chosen for his marking, apparently entering the church to dispute the pastor over religious doctrine. Later in the service, the pastor announced to the congregation that plaintiff had formerly visited prostitutes.

On the basis of this revelation, plaintiff filed suit, alleging several causes of action. First, he asserted that his disclosure was confidential,

---

1. This passage provides:

Moreover if thy brother shall trespass against thee, go and tell him his fault between thee and him alone; if he shall hear thee, thou has gained thy brother.

But if he will not hear *thee, then* take with thee one or two more, that in the mouth of two or three witnesses every word may be established.

And if he shall neglect to hear them, tell *it* unto the church; but if he neglect to hear the church, let him be unto thee as an heathen man and a publican. [*The Holy Bible,* Matthew 18:15–17 (King James Version).]

and that the pastor repeating it to the congregation violated M.C.L. § 600.2156; MSA 27A.2156.[2] He further asserted claims for breach of contract, invasion of privacy, and intentional infliction of emotional distress, and contended that the disclosure was not motivated by religious doctrine, but by the pastor's personal spite and his intent to humiliate plaintiff and cause dissension in his family.

After a hearing, the trial court granted summary disposition for the defendants on all counts. The court held that the statute was a rule of evidence and did not create a cause of action for the disclosure of private or privileged communications. It also held that plaintiff could not prove the elements of a breach of contract because there was no agreement that plaintiff's disclosure would be kept confidential. Finally, the trial court held that plaintiff had not adequately pleaded his tort claims, but added that even if he had, whether clergy must keep confidential a personal disclosure is a matter of religious doctrine that a civil court cannot decide.

The Court of Appeals affirmed on the statutory and contract claims, but reversed and remanded the tort claims. After reviewing cases discussing the First Amendment Free Exercise Clause in the context of religious discipline, doctrine, and polity, the Court remanded for a determination of whether plaintiff was a member of the church when he was marked. The Court reasoned that if plaintiff was a member, then judicial examination of the marking process would be barred by the Free Exercise Clause; however, if he was not a member, the Court reasoned that the church would have had no power to discipline plaintiff, and his tort claims may have been viable. 233 Mich.App. 96, 592 N.W.2d 713 (1998). Defendant appealed the remand order, and this Court granted leave. 461 Mich. 942, 607 N.W.2d 721 (2000).

II

Throughout this case, the defendants have argued that plaintiff's claims are barred by the First Amendment religion clauses. Briefly, the defendants' first argument is that this Court cannot decide plaintiff's claims without deciding matters of defendants' religious doctrine. Under the ecclesiastical abstention doctrine, apparently derived from both First Amendment religion clauses, "civil courts may not redetermine the correctness of an interpretation of canonical text or some decision relating to government of the religious polity." * * * Second, defendants argue that under the Free Exercise Clause, this Court cannot impose liability on them unless their actions in this case posed a threat to the public safety, peace, or order. * * * Accordingly, defendants argue that their actions did not pose such a threat.

---

2. This section is in chapter 21 of the Revised Judicature Act, which concerns evidence. The section provides:

No minister of the gospel, or priest of any denomination whatsoever, or duly accredited Christian Science practitioner, shall be allowed to disclose any confessions made to him in his professional character, in the course of discipline enjoined by the rules or practice of such denomination.

Plaintiff, of course, disputes these defenses. He argues that his claims do not involve any question of religious polity or doctrine, avoiding the ecclesiastical abstention doctrine. Further, he argues that because Michigan tort law is valid, neutral, and of general applicability, defendants do not have a free exercise defense. * * *

A

Although these competing claims present interesting and complex constitutional issues, we do not believe that resolving them is necessary to decide this case. Instead, we can simply assume without deciding that plaintiff is correct that these constitutional defenses do not apply. Similarly, because the defendants expressly waived any reliance on the Michigan Constitution, we need not decide whether its protections of religious freedom offer the defendants any shelter. Under the assumption that no constitutional defenses apply, plaintiff's claims fail as a matter of tort law.

B

Plaintiff alleges that the defendants committed the torts of invasion of privacy and intentional infliction of emotional distress. However, the extent of plaintiff's actions do not leave a genuine issue of material fact whether he consented to the defendants' allegedly tortious acts. Because plaintiff had consented to the church's practices, his claims fail as a matter of law and defendants are entitled to judgment under MCR 2.116(C)(10).

Plaintiff manifested his consent to the church's practices in several ways. First, he became actively engaged in the church in 1985, and shortly after, he explicitly consented in writing to obey the church's law, and to accept the church's discipline "with a free, humble, and thankful heart." Thus, plaintiff can be taken to have impliedly consented by his active engagement and participation in the church, or to have expressly consented through his writing. * * * Any doubt whether plaintiff appreciated the scope of his consent by his active engagement is certainly resolved by the explicit writing. Further, as the Supreme Court stated over 130 years ago, "[a]ll who unite themselves to such a body do so with an implied consent to this [church] government, and are bound to submit to it." * * *

However, plaintiff argues, relying on the Oklahoma court's decision in *Guinn v. Church of Christ*, 775 P.2d 766 (Okla., 1989), that he revoked consent when he resigned his church membership. In *Guinn*, the plaintiff's perceived misdeeds subjected her to the same marking process as the instant plaintiff. She resigned her church membership and disassociated herself from the church, but the church marked her anyway. Considering her intentional infliction of emotional distress claim, the *Guinn* court held that when a church member "removed herself from membership, [she] withdrew her consent, depriving the Church of the power actively to monitor her spiritual life through overt disciplinary acts." *Id.* at 779. The instant plaintiff claims that because he too revoked his membership in the defendant church, he revoked his consent to the defendants' practices.

We disagree with plaintiff's argument because church membership alone is not dispositive of whether plaintiff consented to the church's practices. For example, a person may be a full participant in a church, fully aware of and actively engaged in all of its practices, without ever having become a formal church member. Through knowledge and actions, a person so engaged with the church would indicate consent to the church's practices although the person never became a church "member." Further, "membership" is an amorphous concept. Indeed, many faiths do not include a concept of "membership" at all, and do not require membership for adherents to participate in the faith's formalities and customs. Therefore, we reject the proposition that whether a person is a member of the church or religious organization that allegedly invaded the person's rights is alone determinative of whether the person may bring an intentional tort claim against the alleged tortfeasor.

Instead, consent is the relevant consideration. As discussed, plaintiff consented to the church's practices, and specifically consented to accept discipline. His claim that he revoked consent by terminating membership is belied by his continued involvement with the church. Even after the plaintiff resigned his formal church membership, he remained actively engaged in the church. Particularly, he was present and participating in a doctrinal dispute in the church on the day he was marked. In the same vein, plaintiff is in a different position than the plaintiff in *Guinn*. There, the plaintiff not only resigned her church membership, but she "expressed no interest in continuing her association with the [church]." Further, she "posed no threat of continued adverse influence on any [church] congregation." *Id.* at 782. Although the instant plaintiff did resign his formal church membership, he continued an active association with the church, and specifically attempted to influence the church's congregation, even on the very day he was being marked.

Under tort law principles, a person who consents to another's conduct cannot bring a tort claim for the harm that follows from that conduct. Restatement, § 892A(1). This is because no wrong is done to one who consents. *Id.* comment a. Without a wrong, plaintiff has no compensable claim. Had the church taken its action toward a person more comparable to the plaintiff in *Guinn,* a more difficult question would be presented. Similarly, a more difficult question would be presented if the circumstances of the discipline were different, for example, if the discipline was in violation of the Michigan Penal Code. However, because plaintiff consented to the church's practices, and his active engagement with the church indicated his continuing consent, the church's actions disciplining plaintiff were not tortious.

III

In conclusion, we hold that because reasonable minds cannot disagree that plaintiff consented to the church's practices, and manifested his continuing consent by remaining actively engaged with the church, his intentional tort claims against the defendants fail as a matter of tort law. Because tort law disposes of the plaintiff's claims, we need not consider the constitutional defenses the defendants presented. The judgment of the Court of Appeals is reversed, and summary disposition for the defendants is reinstated.

Notes

1. In *Doe v. Corporation of the President of the Church of Jesus Christ of Latter–Day Saints*, 98 P.3d 429 (Utah App. 2004), the court ruled that a church does not have a duty to warn of alleged sexual abuse. A member of a church who held the position of "High Priest" and who was a scout leader within the church was allegedly sexually abusing children within his ward. The church failed to do anything in response to complaints and allegedly concealed the member's sexual abuse from its other members. In addition, the church permitted the member to continue to hold the positions of High Priest and scout leader. The court concluded that no special relationship existed between the church and the member at the time the member allegedly abused children that would give rise to a duty on the church's part to warn others about the member. The court noted that the sexual abuse occurred in the member's house and was unrelated to the church or any of its activities. The court held that because the member was not a church employee, agent, or clergy member, the church had no common law duty to warn others about the member's prior acts of child sexual abuse.

2. In *Elvig v. Ackles*, 123 Wash.App. 491, 98 P.3d 524 (2004), the court ruled that it could not adjudicate a sex discrimination case brought by a Presbyterian pastor against the Calvin Presbyterian Church without impermissibly examining decisions made by a church tribunal and undermining a church's inherent autonomy. The plaintiff pastor alleged that the defendant, her church's senior minister, made unwelcome sexual advances toward her shortly after she began her service at the church. She also alleged that the defendant retaliated against her by taking away her preaching assignments and expressing doubt about her continued employment. She then left the church but filed with the church a written statement accusing the defendant of sexual misconduct. The church referred the statement to an Investigating Committee composed of members from a different Presbyterian church. The Committee conducted a fact-finding inquiry and concluded that charges would not be filed against the defendant. Plaintiff appealed this decision to the Permanent Judicial Commission of the Presbytery, the highest Presbyterian adjudicatory body. This Commission affirmed the Investigating Committee's decision. The plaintiff then filed an EEOC charge of discrimination against the church, but the EEOC concluded that she failed to establish a civil rights violation. The presbytery later voted to dissolve her pastoral relationship with the church. When she sought permission from the presbytery's Committee on Ministry to seek other ministerial positions, committee officials allegedly told her that she could not seek another position until she resolved her issues with the Calvin Presbyterian Church. After receiving right-to-sue letters from the EEOC, plaintiff filed a civil action in federal court. The District Court dismissed her complaint on the grounds that considering the claims would entangle improperly the court with the

church's ecclesiastical decision-making process. The Ninth Circuit Court of Appeals reversed and remanded, holding that the portions of her claims that involved a church's freedom to make employment decisions about its ministers were precluded, but that her remaining claims could proceed. [*Elvig v. Calvin Presbyterian Church*, 375 F.3d 951 (9th Cir. 2004)] Upon the dismissal of her case from the federal district court, the plaintiff filed an action in the Washington district court. The Washington appellate court noted that in Washington, civil courts may adjudicate church-related disputes only if the dispute does not involve ecclesiastical or doctrinal issues. It further noted that if the church accused of wrongdoing is a member of a hierarchically-organized church that has ecclesiastical judicial tribunals, civil courts must defer to the highest church tribunal's resolution of the matter despite the fact that the dispute could be resolved by a civil court. It also noted that civil courts may not adjudicate matters involving a church's selection of its spiritual leaders. The court recognized that the Presbyterian Church is governed by its Book of Order which outlines the form of church government, the church's theology, and the member discipline and conflict resolution processes. It referred to the procedure for addressing disputes and to the Book of Order's procedure for the discharge of ministers, which were followed with respect to the plaintiff's complaint. The court ruled that it could not question and interpret the church's Book of Order; thus, it affirmed the trial court's order dismissing the plaintiff's claims against the church.

In *Elvig v. Calvin Presbyterian Church*, 375 F.3d 951 (9th Cir. 2004), the Ninth Circuit Court of Appeals ruled that the minister's sexual harassment claims, in which she alleged that the church terminated her employment and foreclosed her from seeking employment in any other parish, were barred by the ministerial exception to Title VII to the extent her claims implicated the church's ministerial employment decisions. However, the court held that her sexual harassment claim could succeed if she proved she suffered a hostile work environment and if the defendants could not prove she unreasonably failed to take advantage of available measures to prevent and correct that hostile environment. The court also ruled that her retaliation claim could succeed if she proved she suffered retaliatory harassment, in the form of verbal abuse and intimidation, because of her complaints to the church and to the EEOC. The Ninth Circuit noted the ministerial exception to Title VII, but decided that the plaintiff's claim could be litigated if it presented no great danger of substantive entanglement in ecclesiastical matters. The court ruled that sexual harassment itself is not a protected employment decision. The court stated that the plaintiff must prove her pastor's alleged conduct was severe and pervasive. It ruled that the church could be held vicariously liable for the alleged sexual harassment. The court also ruled that the retaliatory harassment plaintiff alleged–verbal abuse and intimidation–is not a protected employment decision. The court stressed, however, that in both the sexual harassment and retaliation contexts, the plaintiff could not rely on protected ministerial decisions as bases for the church's liability under Title VII.

B. Property Ownership

The question of title to property of an unincorporated religious association can be complex. Absent incorporation or the express establishment of a trust, a conveyance of property to a church, for example, is deemed to be held in an implied trust for members of the church.

Disputes over church property involve controversies both between a local church and the general church organization and between members of a particular local church. While the state has a legitimate interest in resolving property disputes and a civil court generally is the proper forum for such a resolution, special First Amendment problems arise when the disputes implicate controversies over religious doctrine and practice.

PRESBYTERIAN CHURCH IN UNITED STATES v. HULL PRESBYTERIAN CHURCH

United States Supreme Court, 1969
393 U.S. 440, 89 S.Ct. 601, 21 L.Ed.2d 658

Mr. Justice BRENNAN delivered the opinion of the Court.

Petitioner, Presbyterian Church in the United States, is an association of local Presbyterian churches governed by a hierarchical structure of tribunals which consists of, in ascending order, (1) the Church Session, composed of the elders of the local church; (2) the Presbytery, composed of several churches in a geographical area; (3) the Synod, generally composed of all Presbyteries within a State; and (4) the General Assembly, the highest governing body.

A dispute arose between petitioner, the general church, and two local churches in Savannah, Georgia—the respondents, Hull Memorial Presbyterian Church and Eastern Heights Presbyterian Church—over control of the properties used until then by the local churches. In 1966, the membership of the local churches, in the belief that certain actions and pronouncements of the general church were violations of that organization's constitution and departures from the doctrine and practice in force at the time of affiliation,[1] voted to withdraw from the general church and to reconstitute the local churches as an autonomous Presbyterian organization. The ministers of the two churches renounced the general church's jurisdiction and authority over them, as did all but two of the ruling elders. In response, the general church, through the Presbytery of Savannah, established an Administrative Commission to

---

1. The opinion of the Supreme Court of Georgia summarizes the claimed violations and departures from petitioner's original tenets of faith and practice as including the following: 'ordaining of women as ministers and ruling elders, making pronouncements and recommendations concerning civil, economic, social and political matters, giving support to the removal of Bible reading and prayers by children in the public schools, adopting certain Sunday School literature and teaching neo-orthodoxy alien to the Confession of Faith and Catechisms, as originally adopted by the general church, and causing all members to remain in the National Council of Churches of Christ and willingly accepting its leadership which advocated named practices, such as the subverting of parental authority, civil disobedience and intermeddling in civil affairs'; also 'that the general church has * * * made pronouncements in matters involving international issues such as the Vietnam conflict and has disseminated publications denying the Holy Trinity and violating the moral and ethical standards of the faith.' 224 Ga. 61, 62–63, 159 S.E.2d 690, 692 (1968).

seek a conciliation. The dissident local churchmen remained steadfast; consequently, the Commission acknowledged the withdrawal of the local leadership and proceeded to take over the local churches' property on behalf of the general church until new local leadership could be appointed.

The local churchmen made no effort to appeal the Commission's action to higher church tribunals—the Synod of Georgia or the General Assembly. Instead, the churches filed separate suits in the Superior Court of Chatham County to enjoin the general church from trespassing on the disputed property, title to which was in the local churches. The cases were consolidated for trial. The general church moved to dismiss the actions and cross-claimed for injunctive relief in its own behalf on the ground that civil courts were without power to determine whether the general church had departed from its tenets of faith and practice. The motion to dismiss was denied, and the case was submitted to the jury on the theory that Georgia law implies a trust of local church property for the benefit of the general church on the sole condition that the general church adhere to its tenets of faith and practice existing at the time of affiliation by the local churches.[2] Thus, the jury was instructed to determine whether the actions of the general church 'amount to a fundamental or substantial abandonment of the original tenets and doctrines of the (general church), so that the new tenets and doctrines are utterly variant from the purposes for which the (general church) was founded.' The jury returned a verdict for the local churches, and the trial judge thereupon declared that the implied trust had terminated and enjoined the general church from interfering with the use of the property in question. The Supreme Court of Georgia affirmed, 224 Ga. 61, 159 S.E.2d 690 (1968). We granted certiorari to consider the First Amendment questions raised.[3] * * * We reverse.

2. This theory derives from principles fashioned by English courts. See, e.g., Craigdallie v. Aikman, 1 Dow 1, 3 Eng.Rep. 601 (H.L.1813) (Scot.); Attorney General ex rel. Mander v. Pearson, 3 Mer. 353, 36 Eng.Rep. 135 (Ch. 1817). For the subsequent development of the implied trust theory in English courts, see Note, Judicial Intervention in Disputes Over the Use of Church Property, 75 Harv.L.Rev. 1142, 1148–1149 (1962).

3. We reject the contention of respondent local churches that no First Amendment issues were raised or decided in the state courts. Petitioner's answer and cross-claim in each case included an express allegation that the action of respondents in appropriating the church property to their use was 'in violation of the laws of Georgia, the United States of America, and the Southern Presbyterian Church.' (Italics supplied.) At trial, petitioners' counsel objected to the admission of all testimony 'pertaining to (the) alleged deviation from the faith and practice of the Presbyterian Church in the United States' because that question was 'exclusively within the right of the Presbyterian Church in the United States through its proper judicial body to determine.' On appeal, petitioners again contended 'that questions of an ecclesiastical nature concerning whether or not a church has abandoned its tenets (sic) and doctrines, or some of them, are exclusively within the jurisdiction of the church courts and should not be submitted to a jury for determination as this would destroy the doctrine of separation of church and state.' Petitioners thus clearly raised claims under the First Amendment as applied to the States by the Fourteenth Amendment. Kedroff v. St. Nicholas Cathedral of Russian Orthodox Church in North America, 344 U.S. 94, 116, 119, 73 S.Ct. 143, 97 L.Ed. 120 (1952). The Georgia Supreme Court considered and decided these claims. 'In considering this contention (that the petitions raise ecclesiastical questions which are exclusively within the jurisdiction of the

It is of course true that the State has a legitimate interest in resolving property disputes, and that a civil court is a proper forum for that resolution. Special problems arise, however, when these disputes implicate controversies over church doctrine and practice. The approach of this Court in such cases was originally developed in Watson v. Jones, 13 Wall. 679, 20 L.Ed. 666 (1872), a pre-Erie R. Co. v. Tompkins diversity decision decided before the application of the First Amendment to the States but nonetheless informed by First Amendment considerations.[4] There, as here, civil courts were asked to resolve a property dispute between a national Presbyterian organization and local churches of that organization. There, as here, the disputes arose out of a controversy over church doctrine. There, as here, the Court was asked to decree the termination of an implied trust because of departures from doctrine by the national organization. The Watson Court refused pointing out that it was wholly inconsistent with the American concept of the relationship between church and state to permit civil courts to determine ecclesiastical questions. * * *

* * *

church, not of civil courts, and therefore that respondents could not maintain their action),' the court said, 'we are mindful that 'The traditional American doctrine of freedom of religion and separation of church and state carries with it freedom of the church from having its doctrines or beliefs defined, interpreted, or censored by civil courts.' 224 Ga., at 68, 159 S.E.2d, at 695. The court concluded, however, that the trial court did not violate the doctrine. Citing Georgia Code Ann. s 22—408, which provides: 'Courts are reluctant to interpose in questions affecting the management of the temporalities of a church; but when property is devoted to a specific doctrine or purpose, the courts will prevent it from being diverted from the trust,' the court held that 'a trust (in favor of the general church) is conditioned upon the general church's adherence to its tenets of faith and practice existing when the local church affiliated with it and * * * an abandonment of, or departure from, such tenets is a diversion from the trust, which the civil courts will prevent.' 224 Ga., at 68, 159 S.E.2d, at 695.

4. 'Watson v. Jones, although it contains a reference to the relations of church and state under our system of laws, was decided without depending upon prohibition of state interference with the free exercise of religion. It was decided in 1871 (sic), before judicial recognition of the coercive power of the Fourteenth Amendment to protect the limitations of the First Amendment against state action. It long antedated the 1938 decisions of Erie R. Co. v. Tompkins and Ruhlin v. New York Life Ins. Co., 304 U.S. 64, 58 S.Ct. 817, 82 L.Ed. 1188, and 304 U.S. 202, 58 S.Ct. 860, 82 L.Ed. 1290 and, therefore, even though federal jurisdiction in the case depended solely on diversity, the holding was based on general law rather than Kentucky law.' Kedroff v. St. Nicholas Cathedral of Russian Orthodox Church in North America, 344 U.S. 94, 115—116, 73 S.Ct. 143, 154 (1952).

'In this country the full and free right to entertain any religious belief, to practice any religious principle, and to teach any religious doctrine which does not violate the laws of morality and property, and which does not infringe personal rights, is conceded to all. The law knows no heresy, and is committed to the support of no dogma, the establishment of no sect. * * * All who unite themselves to such a body (the general church) do so with an implied consent to (its) government, and are bound to submit to it. But it would be a vain consent and would lead to the total subversion of such religious bodies, if any one aggrieved by one of their decisions could appeal to the secular courts and have them (sic) reversed. It is of the essence of these religious unions, and of their right to establish tribunals for the decision of questions arising among themselves, that those decisions should be binding in all cases of ecclesiastical cognizance, subject only to such appeals as the organism itself provides for.' 13 Wall., at 728—729.

In Kedroff v. St. Nicholas Cathedral of Russian Orthodox Church in North America, 344 U.S. 94, 73 S.Ct. 143, 97 L.Ed. 120 (1952), the Court converted the principle of Watson * * * into a constitutional rule. Kedroff grew out of a dispute between the Moscow-based general Russian Orthodox Church and the Russian Orthodox churches located in North America over an appointment to St. Nicholas Cathedral in New York City. The North American churches declared their independence from the general church, and the New York Legislature enacted a statute recognizing their administrative autonomy. The New York courts sustained the constitutionality of the statute and held that the North American churches' elected hierarch had the right to use the cathedral. This Court reversed, finding that the Moscow church had not acknowledged the schism, and holding the statute unconstitutional. The Court said, * * *:

> 'The opinion (in Watson v. Jones) radiates * * * a spirit of freedom for religious organizations, an independence from secular control or manipulation—in short, power to decide for themselves, free from state interference, matters of church government as well as those of faith and doctrine. Freedom to select the clergy, where no improper methods of choice are proven, we think, must now be said to have federal constitutional protection as a part of the free exercise of religion against state interference.' * * *

And, speaking of the New York statute, the Court said further, * * *:

> 'By fiat it displaces one church administrator with another. It passes the control of matters strictly ecclesiastical from one church authority to another. It thus intrudes for the benefit of one segment of a church the power of the state into the forbidden area of religious freedom contrary to the principles of the First Amendment.' * * *

This holding invalidating legislative action was extended to judicial action in Kreshik v. St. Nicholas Cathedral, 363 U.S. 190, 80 S.Ct. 1037, 4 L.Ed.2d 1140 (1960), where the Court held that the constitutional guarantees of religious liberty required the reversal of a judgment of the New York courts which transferred control of St. Nicholas Cathedral from the central governing authority of the Russian Orthodox Church to the independent Russian Church of America.

Thus, the First Amendment severely circumscribes the role that civil courts may play in resolving church property disputes. It is obvious, however, that not every civil court decision as to property claimed by a religious organization jeopardizes values protected by the First Amendment. Civil courts do not inhibit free exercise of religion merely by opening their doors to disputes involving church property. And there are neutral principles of law, developed for use in all property disputes, which can be applied without 'establishing' churches to which property is awarded. But First Amendment values are plainly jeopardized when church property litigation is made to turn on the resolution by civil courts of controversies over religious doctrine and practice. If civil courts undertake to resolve such controversies in order to adjudicate the property dispute, the hazards are ever present of inhibiting the free development of religious doctrine and of implicating secular interests in matters of purely ecclesiastical concern. Because of these hazards, the First Amendment enjoins the employment of organs of government for essentially religious purposes, * * *; the Amendment therefore commands civil courts to decide church property disputes without resolving underlying controversies over religious doctrine. Hence, States, religious organizations, and individuals must structure relationships involving church property so as not to require the civil courts to resolve ecclesiastical questions.

The Georgia courts have violated the command of the First Amendment. The departure-from-doctrine element of the implied trust theory which they applied requires the civil judiciary to determine whether actions of the general church constitute such a 'substantial departure' from the tenets of faith and practice existing at the time of the local churches' affiliation that the trust in favor of the general church must be declared to have terminated. This determination has two parts. The civil court must first decide whether the challenged actions of the general church depart substantially from prior doctrine. In reaching such a decision, the court must of necessity make its own interpretation of the meaning of church doctrines. If the court should decide that a substantial departure has occurred, it must then go on to determine whether the issue on which the general church has departed holds a place of such importance in the traditional theology as to require that the trust be terminated. A civil court can make this determination only after assessing the relative significance to the religion of the tenets from which departure was found. Thus, the departure-from-doctrine element of the Georgia implied trust theory requires the civil court to determine matters at the very core of a religion—the interpretation of particular church doctrines and the importance of those doctrines to the religion. Plainly, the First Amendment forbids civil courts from playing such a role.

Since the Georgia courts on remand may undertake to determine whether petitioner is entitled to relief on its cross-claims, we find it appropriate to remark that the departure-from-doctrine element of Georgia's implied trust theory can play no role in any future judicial proceedings. The departure-from-doctrine approach is not susceptible of the marginal judicial involvement contemplated in Gonzalez. Gonzalez' rights under a will turned on a church decision, the Archbishop's, as to church law, the qualifications for the chaplaincy. It was the archbishopric, not the civil courts, which had the task of analyzing and interpreting church law in order to determine the validity of Gonzalez' claim to a chaplaincy. Thus, the civil courts could adjudicate the rights under the will without interpreting or weighing church doctrine but simply by engaging in the narrowest kind of review of a specific church decision—i.e., whether that decision resulted from fraud, collusion, or arbitrariness. Such review does not inject the civil courts into substantive ecclesiastical matters. In contrast, under Georgia's departure-from-doctrine approach, it is not possible for the civil courts to play so limited a role. Under this approach, property rights do not turn on a church decision as to church doctrine. The standard of departure-from-doctrine, though it calls for resolution of ecclesiastical questions, is a creation of state, not church, law. Nothing in the record suggests that this state standard has been interpreted and applied in a decision of the general church. Any decisions which have been made by the general church about the local churches' withdrawal have at most a tangential relationship to the state-fashioned departure-from-doctrine standard. A determination whether such decisions are fraudulent, collusive, or arbitrary would therefore not answer the questions posed by the state standard. To reach those questions would require the civil courts to engage in the forbidden process of interpreting and weighing church doctrine. Even if the general church had attempted to apply the state standard, the civil courts could not review and enforce the church decision without violating the Constitution. The First Amendment prohibits a State from employing religious organizations as an arm of the civil judiciary to perform the function of interpreting and applying state standards. See School District of Township of Abington, Pa. v. Schempp, supra. Thus, a civil court may no more review a church decision applying a state departure-from-doctrine standard than it may apply that standard itself.

The judgment of the Supreme Court of Georgia is reversed, and the case is remanded for further proceedings not inconsistent with this opinion. * * *

HOLIMAN v. DOVERS

Supreme Court, Arkansas, 1963
236 Ark. 211, 366 S.W.2d 197

GEORGE ROSE SMITH, Justice.

This is a dispute between two factions in the Landmark Missionary Baptist Church of Traskwood, Arkansas. The appellants, the minority group, brought suit to enjoin the pastor, Elder A. Z. Dovers, and the majority group from using the church property for the preaching and teaching of doctrines fundamentally contrary to the Landmark Missionary Baptist faith. The chancellor refused to grant the relief sought, finding that the deviations which had occurred were not of sufficient consequence to call for the intervention of equity.

This church was organized in 1902 and had existed for almost sixty years when the present controversy, centering upon the pastor's theological views, reached a crisis in 1961. At a church meeting in August of that year the majority, by a vote of 54 to 47, defeated a motion to dismiss the pastor. An ensuing attempt to censure the minority failed, but a week later the majority directed the church clerk to notify the minority members that they would have no voting privileges in the church until they had apologized for their conduct. The minority reacted to that letter by filing this suit a few days later.

Before turning to the proof we may note that the controlling principles of law are not open to serious dispute. The civil courts are not concerned with mere schisms stemming from disputations over matters of religious doctrine, not only because such questions are essentially ecclesiastical rather than judicial but also because of the separation between the church and the state. And even when property rights are involved the rival factions may be remitted to their remedy within the denomination if its form of government is such as to permit an appeal to higher ecclesiastical authority.

The situation is different, however, in the case of self-governing congregational churches, such as the Landmark Missionary Baptists. Here the courts do not hesitate to assume jurisdiction when a schism affects property rights, for in this form of church government each local congregation is independent and autonomous. * * * There is no recourse within the denomination. * * *

Although congregational churches are governed by a majority vote of the membership, the church property must be devoted to church purposes. We mentioned this matter in Hatchett v. Mt. Pleasant Baptist Church, 46 Ark. 291, saying: 'In a congregational church, the majority, if they adhere to the organization and to the doctrines, represent the church.' In a later case we added that the majority controls unless there has been 'such an abrupt departure from congregational principles' as to discredit the ruling group. * * *

It is firmly settled that the controlling faction will not be permitted to divert the church property to another denomination or to the support of doctrines, usages, and practices basically opposed to those characteristic of the particular church. * * * As the court said in Dix v. Pruits, 194 N.C. 64, 138 S.E. 412: 'In other words, a majority in a Baptist Church is supreme, or a 'law unto itself' so long as it remains a Baptist Church or true to the fundamental usages, customs, doctrine, practice, and organization of Baptists. For instance, if a majority of a Baptist Church should attempt to combine with a Methodist or Presbyterian Church, or in any manner depart from the fundamental faiths, usages, and customs which are distinctively Baptist and which mark out that denomination as a separate entity from all others, then, in such case, the majority could not take the church property with them, for the reason that they would not be acting in accordance with distinctively Baptist principles. Or suppose a majority of a Baptist Church should determine to abandon immersion and receive members without either an individual profession of faith or baptism, such majority could not take possession of the church property and exclude the minority who remained true to the fundamental faith and practice.' In harmony with these views equitable relief was granted, in Franke v. Mann, 106 Wis. 118, 81 N.W. 1014, 48 L.R.A. 856, where, as in the case at bar, the controlling group engaged a minister whose beliefs were contrary to those of the sect in question.

The extensive record before us consists mainly of testimony explaining the Landmark Missionary Baptist articles of faith. Among the plaintiffs' many witnesses were nine leading clergymen of this particular sect, whose total ministerial experience exceeded 230 years. These men were in complete agreement about a number of basic doctrines of the church, such as the view that a person who has been saved cannot later become lost, the belief that the unpardonable sin (the rejection of Christ) can be committed only by the unsaved, and several other religious tenets that we need not enumerate.

Elder Dovers was the only witness for the defendants. He was thirty-five years old at the time of the trial. His background of experience included an eighth-grade education, seven years work in a filling station, a half year of study in a Missionary Baptist seminary, and seven years in the ministry. Elder Dovers testified at great length and was entirely candid in conceding that he believed and preached doctrines contrary to the Landmark faith as understood by the plaintiffs' witnesses. This pastor derived many of his beliefs from his own study of the Bible. He taught his flock that a person who has been saved can later be lost, that the saved can be guilty of the unpardonable sin, and that he interpreted a number of other articles of faith in a way that differed from the orthodox Landmark Missionary Baptist thinking.

It being substantially undisputed that Elder Dovers' beliefs were contrary to the accepted doctrines and usages of the church, the only remaining question is whether the differences are so important as to justify the intervention of a court of equity. As we have indicated, the variance must be fundamental; relief will not be granted where the division is based upon doctrinal distinctions that are not vital or substantial. * * *

Whether particular articles of belief are so fundamental as to be of the very essence of a given creed is evidently a question to be decided by the church itself; the civil courts cannot assume independent authority to arbitrate the niceties of ecclesiastical disputations. Hence we must be guided solely by the evidence in the case, as it sheds light upon the position traditionally taken by the Landmark Missionary Baptist Church.

We find the decided weight of the testimony to be against the chancellor's conclusion that the doctrinal differences disclosed by the evidence are unimportant. Witness after witness testified that these are cardinal beliefs in this church, that anyone who rejects them is not a Landmark Baptist, and that the teachings of Elder Dovers are heresy. Several of the minority group felt so strongly about the matter that they had withdrawn from the Traskwood church before the trial. The situation is rather like that described in Parker v. Harper, 295 Ky. 686, 175 S.W.2d 361: 'The evidence in the case at bar is that both local groups do regard the grounds upon which they have divided as very vital and substantial. Other than their declarations, the sorry fact is that they have proven to be important and potent enough to break up the struggling little church * * *. We are of the opinion there was such departure from the faith of the founders of the church at Martin as calls for the protection of their property rights by the courts.'

In reaching our conclusion we stress the fact that we have no concern whatever with the merits of the theological differences between these parties. The majority members of this church or of any church are of course at liberty to adopt any religious belief they choose, whether it be a liberal Baptist theology, Presbyterianism, Greek Catholicism, or Mohammedanism. Moreover, the majority members have a similar right to engage a pastor who will preach the doctrines of their choice. But the vital point is that the majority are not entitled to devote the property of the Landmark Missionary Baptist Church at Traskwood to a faith contrary to that for which it was dedicated. We are aware of no case holding that the majority members of a church have the absolute power to use its property for any purpose they select; certainly no such case has been cited. If the courts are not to afford any protection for property rights in such a situation then there is literally no limit to the purposes to which the majority might divert the church property.

The decree must be reversed, but it seems unnecessary for the appellants to be granted the sweeping relief sought by their complaint, by which all the majority members would be enjoined from taking part in the control of the church property. We think it to be sufficient for Elder Dovers, whose ministry has been the central point of controversy, to be restrained from acting as pastor of the church. This limitation upon the court's decree may aid the congregation in regaining its original unity.

Reversed.

* * *

MILLS v. BALDWIN

Supreme Court, Florida, 1978
362 So.2d 2

SUNDBERG, Justice.

This cause is a petition for writ of certiorari to review a decision of the District Court of Appeal, First District, reported at 344 So.2d 259, which is alleged to be in conflict with St. John's Presbytery v. Central Presbyterian Church, 102 So.2d 714 (Fla.1958) and Froelich v. Rowley, 102 So.2d 720 (Fla.1958). On petition for rehearing of our prior denial of writ of certiorari in this cause, we have concluded that this Court is possessed of jurisdiction under Article V, Section 3(b)(3), of the Florida Constitution.

Essentially this case involves a dispute over the ownership of property of the Madison Presbyterian Church in Madison, Florida, or stated more accurately, a controversy as to who constitutes the Madison Presbyterian Church in Madison, Florida. The dispute is occasioned by the withdrawal of a majority of the congregation from the Presbyterian

Church in the United States (PCUS) and its claim of title to the church property as against the claim of the minority of the congregation who did not withdraw but remained faithful to the parent church. Applying "neutral principles of law" the majority of the district court concluded that there was no implied trust in favor of the mother church as was found to exist in Central Presbyterian Church, supra, and, accordingly, held the property of the church to be vested in the withdrawing members. * * *

* * *

A Church Session is the governing body of a local church. A Presbytery is composed of several churches in a geographical area; a Synod is generally composed of all Presbyteries within a state or other designated geographical area and the General Assembly is the highest governing body in the hierarchical spiritual structure of the Presbyterian Church.

The first Presbyterian Church was established in America on the Virginia coast in 1607. Originally there was one main body of Presbyterianism which was known as the Presbyterian Church in the United States of America. (PCUSA) The Madison Presbyterian Church located at Madison, Florida was founded in 1840. It was originally a part of the Presbytery of Georgia but later became a congregation of the Presbytery of Florida. It is, and at all times has been, an unincorporated entity. Since its formation in 1840 all of the church property has been held by trustees elected by a majority of the congregation of the church. The primary church property was acquired by deed executed in March of 1851 to the "Trustees of the Presbyterian Church at Madison aforesaid and their successors in office * * * To Have and To Hold the said lots of land to and for the use of the Presbyterian Church at Madison." In 1861 the Presbytery of Florida met at the Madison Presbyterian Church in Madison and unanimously adopted a resolution severing its affiliation with the Presbyterian Church in the United States of America (PCUSA) and concurred in a call for Commissioners for the organization of a General Assembly with power to organize a new church. The Madison Church sent a delegate to the meeting of the General Assembly held in 1861 (held incidentally at the Madison Church) at which time a resolution was unanimously adopted by which a denomination was formed bearing the name Presbyterian Church in the Confederate States of America. Thereafter, the name of that denomination was changed to the Presbyterian Church of the United States (PCUS). The parties have stipulated that neither the General Assembly of the Presbyterian Church in the United States nor the Synod of Florida nor the Presbytery of Florida has ever contributed any property to the Madison Presbyterian Church, nor has it provided any funds with which the property of said church was acquired.

On March 11, 1973, John P. Baldwin, then the regular ordained and installed Pastor of the Madison Presbyterian Church, presided over a meeting of the congregation. Upon a vote taken at such meeting, a petition was adopted requesting the Presbytery of Florida to dismiss the Madison church and its property from the Presbytery and to dismiss and dissolve the relationship between Rev. Baldwin and the Presbytery of Florida and the PCUS. Following various intra-church maneuvers a resolution was adopted by the congregation of the Madison Presbyterian Church on May 20, 1973 withdrawing from and severing all relationship with the Presbytery of Florida and the PCUS. On June 5, 1973 the Presbytery of Florida removed the name of John Baldwin from the roll of the Presbytery and declared the pulpit of the Madison Presbyterian Church to be vacant. The Presbytery declared and recognized Messrs. Beck and Ragans, among others, as constituting the Church Session of the Madison Presbyterian Church with full authority to assume control of the congregation and all land, buildings, personal property and monies of the local church.

On August 7, 1973 plaintiffs (petitioners) filed an action in Circuit Court asking that the individual defendants (respondents) and all others associated with them be restrained from interfering with the plaintiffs and other members of the PCUS in the use of the property of the Madison Presbyterian Church; from using or attempting to use the property of the Madison Presbyterian Church for any purpose except in conformity with and subject to the government and discipline of the PCUS; from selling, disposing of or encumbering the property of the Madison Presbyterian Church; from paying or delivering to any person or corporation any money, funds, bonds, securities, or other property in their possession or under their control constituting the property of the Madison Presbyterian Church and from occupying the Manse of the Madison Presbyterian Church. The foundation of the plaintiffs' cause of action as alleged in their complaint was a trust "originally imposed upon said property (of the Madison Presbyterian Church) for the promulgation of the trusts and doctrines of the Presbyterian Church in the United States * * * " At the conclusion of a lengthy trial, final judgment was entered for the plaintiffs.

* * *

The majority below determined that the structure of the Presbyterian Church, being hierarchical as opposed to congregational, was immaterial to its resolution of the case because, through application of "neutral principles of law" to the facts, neither form of accepted implied trust (constructive or resulting) could be recognized. This conclusion of the district court was based primarily upon its finding that no funds were provided by either the Presbytery of Florida or PCUS with which any of the property of the Madison Church was acquired. Consequently, the necessary ingredient for a constructive trust was absent. Likewise, there was no evidence at trial that any of the properties conveyed to the Madison Church "were intended to be conveyed for the benefit of any entity other than the congregation of the Madison Presbyterian Church" and therefore, no resulting trust could arise. Its position with respect to the absence of a resulting trust was bolstered by the fact that PCUS did not come into existence until some 21 years after the Madison Church was organized. St. John's Presbytery v. Central Presbyterian Church and Froelich v. Rowley, supra, were distinguished by the district court on the premise that the facts in those cases demonstrated the existence of elements necessary to support a constructive trust.

* * *

The first question presented is whether or not the majority of the congregation of a Presbyterian Church in the United States can withdraw from said church and the presbytery and claim title to the church property as against the claim of title of the minority group who did not withdraw but remained faithful to the parent church. This is the identical question that was presented and decided in St. John's Presbytery v. Central Presbyterian Church of St. Petersburg. What we said in that case concludes the point raised here contrary to the contention of appellants (the withdrawing majority).

* * *

In short, a careful reading of the cases makes clear that the issue in a case such as this is not who owns the property. The Madison Presbyterian Church of Madison, Florida, owns the property. The true issue is who represents the Madison Presbyterian Church? The authorities from Watson v. Jones forward clearly respond that petitioners represent that church because of the structure and government of PCUS. As pointed out in Judge Smith's dissent, the fact that PCUS was formed by the secession of Presbyterian churches in the Confederacy a generation after organization of the Madison Church affects not at all the commitment of the Madison Presbyterian Church to PCUS in 1861 and continuously for generations thereafter.

Accordingly, the petition for certiorari is granted, the opinion of the District Court of Appeal, First District, is quashed and the dissenting opinion is adopted as the opinion of this Court.

Note

In approaching issues of title to church property, it is imperative to examine the policies, procedures, and internal government of the church or other religious organization involved. The Roman Catholic Church and the Church of the Latter–Day Saints permit the Bishop of the various dioceses in the Catholic Church or the presiding Bishop in the Church of Latter–Day Saints to hold title in trust for benefit of the church. A deed from the Bishop passes good title to the property. A Book of Discipline governs the sale or mortgage of real estate held by the Methodist Church. It prescribes certain procedures that must be followed in conveying land belonging to the Methodist Church. The Presbyterian Church is governed by the Book of Church Order which designates the deacons as having charge of church property; however, the deacons cannot act without consent of the congregation under supervision of a board in the church consisting of the pastor and the ruling elders. Congregational churches often designate the deacons or elders as trustees to hold title to church property. However, conveyance of property should be approved by a meeting of members conducted after proper notice has been given the membership.

WOOD v. BENEDICTINE SOCIETY OF ALABAMA

Supreme Court, Alabama, 1988
530 So.2d 801

ADAMS, Justice.

The plaintiff, Kathryn Wood, appeals from judgments based on directed verdicts entered for the defendants, Bishop Joseph G. Vath, a corporation sole; Abbot Hilary Dreaper; and the Benedictine Society of Alabama, Inc. The defendants cross-appealed. We affirm.

On June 15, 1984, Father Edward Markley entered an abortion clinic in Huntsville, Alabama, with two cans of red paint he had purchased with his own money. After entering the clinic, he damaged three suction machines and injured Kathryn Wood. Ms. Wood filed a lawsuit against Father Markley on March 17, 1986, to recover for the injuries she had received. She also sued Bishop Joseph G. Vath, both individually and as a corporation sole; Abbot Hilary Dreaper; and the Benedictine Society, on the theory that these parties were the principals or masters of Father Markley.

* * *

[A] corporation sole has very specific functions, see Ala.Code 1975, § 10–4–4, which relate to conducting a business, not ecclesiastical duties. Section 10–4–4 sets forth the particular powers of a corporation sole. These powers include, for example, holding and conveying real and personal property, succession in its corporate name, borrowing money, and appointing officers to conduct business. Because the powers of a corporation sole are limited by statute, unless the substance of the Bishop's letters involved a function specified in § 10–4–4, then even if the Bishop intended to sign the letters as "a corporation sole" it would not necessarily create liability on the part of the corporation sole.

In the instant case, three letters were admitted into evidence containing the signature and title "Most Reverend Bishop Joseph G. Vath, D.D., Bishop of Birmingham in Alabama." In one of the letters, the Bishop reprimanded Father Markley for using violent conduct to achieve his goals. In another letter, the Bishop accepted Father Markley's resignation as pro-life coordinator. In the final letter, the Bishop noted that Father Markley would be returning to the Abbey and thanked him for his services as pastor of Our Lady of the Shoals Catholic Church. None of these letters contains a reference to anything that could be construed as a business activity within the meaning of § 10–4–1. Therefore, even if it were the Bishop's intent to sign his letters to Father Markley as a corporation sole, without more, we find no basis for liability on the part of Bishop Vath, a corporation sole. Therefore, we conclude that the verdict in favor of Bishop Vath, a corporation sole, was properly directed.

As to the directed verdicts for Abbot Dreaper and the Benedictine Society, the plaintiff's entire argument on appeal is as follows:

> As to Dreaper and the Society, plaintiff's evidence affirmatively established that Markley was a member of the Society and, as such, was subject to Dreaper's orders as it related to his 24-hour life as a monk, including the authority to recall him to the abbey. The evidence established that Dreaper knew of at least one previous act of violence on Markley's part, but failed or refused to exercise any discipline over him because of it. Finally, it established that Markley was driving a Society-owned car when he went to Huntsville and attacked the plaintiff. All these facts constitute more than the requisite scintilla of evidence necessary for the case to have gone to the jury.

We disagree.

The Benedictine Society is a clerical order. Father Markley is a monk in that Society and Abbot Dreaper is his superior. However, the relationship between Father Markley and the Society was ecclesiastical and did not necessarily create a legal master/servant or principal/agent relationship. * * * Furthermore, the fact that Father Markley is a monk—and also a priest—24 hours a day, does not necessarily mean that his membership in the Society makes the Society liable for all of his actions. In ruling on Abbot Dreaper's motion for a directed verdict, the trial court made the following comments:

> THE COURT: This Court finds not a scintilla of evidence of agency as to Abbot Dreaper. There is no evidence to the effect that Abbot Dreaper was in authority in a master-servant relationship with Edward Markley at the time of the events in question. This Court understands the law with regard to ecclesiastical orders, religious societies to be that the relationship is essentially ecclesiastical in nature. I would analogize this to situations where a young man may be in a seminary and the seminary be asked to supply a preacher or a minister for a congregation. The fact that the young minister may have some alma mater does not make the seminary responsible for his behavior in the event he elects to commit a burglary or some other act which he might consider to be ordained by divine aegis or providence. It would [not] in and of itself make the seminary responsible for his behavior. The Abbot in question in this case, absent some proof in the record to the effect that the behavior of Edward Markley was in the line and scope of employment for the abbey, would not be responsible as principal, and I find no scintilla of evidence to that effect. I find that the oath was an ecclesiastical oath, that even if it had any bearing, it was not an oath to Abbot Dreaper in this case.

Furthermore, in directing a verdict for the Benedictine Society, the court stated:

> Well, in viewing the evidence as it relates to the Benedictine Society-Defendant, in the face of the motion for directed verdict, this Court

finds that there is no scintilla of evidence that the Benedictine Society was acting in a principal-agency capacity with the Defendant Edward Markley. Further, the Court finds that there was no employment as that term implies or no employment in the sense required for a negligent employment.

* * *

We concur with the trial court's reasoning. In order to prove that the Society or Abbot Dreaper was responsible for Father Markley's actions, the plaintiff must have evidence in addition to the fact that Father Markley was a member of the Benedictine Society of monks.

Furthermore, even if this Court were to hold that Abbot Dreaper or the Benedictine Society was the master or principal of Father Markley, the plaintiff presented no evidence that Father Markley was acting within the scope of his authority when he damaged the machines and injured Ms. Wood.

Finally, the plaintiff claimed that the fact that Father Markley was driving a Society-owned car when he drove to the clinic was sufficient evidence to meet the scintilla rule. However, Father Markley had access to the car for both personal and business use; therefore, the mere fact that he was driving the car does not, standing alone, constitute a scintilla of evidence that the Society was responsible for Father Markley's actions.

For the foregoing reasons, the directed verdicts for Bishop Vath, a corporation sole; Abbot Dreaper; and the Benedictine Society are due to be affirmed.

* * *

IV. INCORPORATION OF RELIGIOUS ASSOCIATIONS

Many of the legal difficulties inherent in the unincorporated associational structure are eliminated if a religious organization incorporates. The requisite formalities of the corporate structure provide for continuity by perpetual succession and clear designation of authorization to act on behalf of a religious organization. Members of the organization are given greater protection in the form of limited liability, and an orderly system for determining property rights is established.

MURPHY v. TRAYLOR
Supreme Court, Alabama, 1974
292 Ala. 78, 289 So.2d 584

MERRILL, Justice.

This appeal is from a decree vesting title in Equality United Methodist Church, a corporation, to 2 1/2 acres of land near the church.

The trustees of Equality Methodist Church and Equality United Methodist Church, a corporation, filed a declaratory judgment proceeding to establish the owner of the land in question.

Fred Raht Whitaker died testate on August 1, 1953. Under Paragraph 2 of his will, Whitaker provided that:

'All of the real estate which I shall own at my death, I give and devise to my beloved wife, Dorma Jewell Whitaker, if she shall survive me, for her natural life time; and if she shall not survive me, then I give and devise the same to Josie L. Yates, my wife's aunt and step-mother, for the term of her natural life time. And if both my wife and the said Josie L. Yates shall survive me, and if then my said wife shall die, leaving the said Josie L. Yates surviving, then in that event I give and devise the same to the said Josie L. Yates for her life time. If neither of them shall survive me, or on the death of the survivor of them, I give and devise the same to the Equality Methodist Church, in fee simple, the same to be used by said church for such purposes as it shall see fit.'

At the time of the death of Whitaker, the church was an unincorporated association. It was incorporated more than ten months prior to the trial.

The question presented to the trial court and here, on appeal, is whether the devise to the church is valid, inasmuch as the church was not incorporated when the testator died but was incorporated before the trial.

The pertinent part of the trial court's decree follows:

'That the Equality Methodist Church was at the time of the termination of the life estate an unincorporated religious body with a board of trustees consisting of Herbert Traylor, Charles Selman, R. W. Granger, Thomas W. Barkely, Bobby Granger, William C. Wilson and Morris Wilbanks.

'The Court having understood and considered the evidence in this cause, it is the opinion of the Court that the Equality Methodist Church was without legal capacity to receive and hold real property at the time of the termination of the life estate created by Fred Raht Whitaker. The Court is also of the opinion that such incapacity could be abrogated by a subsequent legal incorporation of the church under appropriate provisions of law, and that this incorporation was in fact accomplished by the church prior to the Court hearing this cause.

'It is the further opinion of the Court that when the life estate was terminated by the death of Dorma J. Whitaker the fee simple title to this real property vested in the hereinabove named trustees of the Equality Methodist Church in trust until such time as the church acquired legal capacity to receive and hold real property in its own name as an incorporated body.'

Sec. IV INCORPORATION OF RELIGIOUS ASSOCIATIONS

The appellant argues that an unincorporated religious society is without capacity to acquire or hold title to realty and cites McLean v. Church of God, 254 Ala. 134, 47 So.2d 257, and other cases which so hold. In McLean, this court stated in part:

'We have no statute nor have we recognized charitable or religious societies as having a quasi corporate existence with power to hold land, as has been done in some jurisdictions. * * * On the contrary, our cases have reiterated that such societies are incapable of acquiring and holding title to land. Authorities supra.'

But this rule is not absolute. While this court has held that an unincorporated religious society cannot maintain an action in the nature of ejectment in the name of the society, * * *, it has also held that an unincorporated religious society can maintain a bill for injunction to require respondents to remove a fence on its property and from further trespassing on church property, * * *; and that an incorporated church, by and through its trustees and deacons, can maintain a bill to quiet title to their church property, * * *. This court has also held that equity has power to compel specific performance of an agreement to convey land made to trustees of a religious society before it was incorporated, upon application of the church after it became incorporated. * * *

In Hundley v. Collins, 131 Ala. 234, 32 So. 575, this court said:

' * * * A church or religious society may exist for all the purposes for which it was organized independently of any incorporation of the body under the statutes of the state; and, it is a matter of common knowledge that many do exist and are never incorporated. For the promotion of religion and charity, they may subserve all the purposes of their organization, and, generally, need no incorporation except incidentally to further these objects. They do not place themselves beyond the pale of the protection of the law as to properties, for the lack of incorporation. It is the province of a court of equity to protect such organizations in what they hold, in order to sustain trusts, because of their charitable uses, which would otherwise be held void. * * * '

This court has dealt with deeds to unincorporated religious societies several times. The author of McLean, 254 Ala. 134, 47 So.2d 257 (1950), also authored Johnson v. Sweeney's Lane Church of God, 270 Ala. 260, 116 So.2d 899 (1959). In the latter case, Delia v. Bowen deeded property to an unincorporated religious society, but which, as here, subsequently became incorporated, and this court quoted from Gewin v. Mt. Pilgrim Baptist Church, 166 Ala. 345, 51 So. 947:

"The unincorporated society was without capacity to acquire or hold title. * * * Nor did the conveyance to trustees—or, rather, the agreement to convey—for the unincorporated society in strictness create a charitable use. Nevertheless, the jurisdiction of the chancery court over such voluntary associations and their property is maintained in this state, independently of the English statute of charitable uses and of any prerogative power of the court, on the ground of the trust nature of the property, the charitable uses for which it is designed, and the inadequacy of legal remedies. * * * Equity must therefore have power to compel a conveyance to the incorporated church. This will not involve the court in the impossible function of making a contract for the parties, nor require the performance of a contract differently from its agreed terms. An organization, under the statute, by the majority of a society, operates ipso facto as a transfer of the rights and interests of individual members to the corporation hereby created.—Happy v. Morton, 33 Ill. 398. The incorporated church has succeeded to all the rights of the unincorporated church. * * * "

This court also quoted from Hope of Alabama Lodge of Odd Fellows v. Chambless, 212 Ala. 444, 103 So. 54:

"A court of equity treats the active members of a voluntary nonbusiness association as the owners of its properties in trust for the community interest of the unincorporated society or association. This was in effect, the result of First Nat. Bank (of Gadsden) v. Winchester, 119 Ala. 168, 172, 24 So. 351, 72 Am.St.Rep. 904, as dealing with corporate property and the stockholders' interest therein, where the corporation was in abeyance. When there is an incorporation of such society or association, participated in and authorized by a majority of its membership, the legal title passes to the corporation. * * *; such is the result as to the legal title to the community property, if incorporated by a majority of the association's members. If incorporation is participated in and authorized by less than a majority of the lodge membership, the title to said properties would not vest in the corporation, but remain in trust for the majority membership, or in abeyance for the association unincorporated. This is the theory of our unincorporated church cases. * * * "

Then this court wrote:

' * * * Nevertheless, equity has jurisdiction over voluntary unincorporated associations and their property in this state. If the legal title never passed out of Delia v. Bowen, in equity she held such title as trustee for The Church of God of Prichard, and when that church was incorporated, the legal title passed to the incorporated church regardless of whether it was in Delia v. Bowen or the individual members of the unincorporated church. * * * '

All the justices concurred in the opinion in Johnson, and three of them had participated in the McLean decision. So, it appears that in equity this court does allow a conveyance to an unincorporated religious society to stand where the society is later incorporated in order to secure title to the property.

We fail to see any material distinction in a grant by deed and a devise by will in an attempt to convey property to an unincorporated religious society that is later incorporated. A deed is effective upon delivery and a will speaks as of the death of the testator. But if the grantor in a deed has named an improper grantee, he can redraft his deed, but the testator cannot redraft his will. And there are numerous instances where courts have upheld devises to people not then in esse. Here, the unincorporated church was in existence, the congregation occupies a building; it owns the church property, a parsonage and a cemetery, and it is the same church, incorporated, as it was unincorporated, and still a part of the North Alabama Conference, and the pastor is appointed by the bishop. Also, it was the unquestioned intention of the testator to convey the property to his church.

In MacGregor v. Commissioner of Corporations and Taxation, 327 Mass. 484, 99 N.E.2d 468, it was said:

> 'Voluntary associations were not regarded at common law as legal entities and so could not as such take title to real or personal property either for their own benefit or in trust for others. Scott, Trust, s 97. The gifts, however, would not fail for want of a trustee, and any technical difficulty that might exist as to the legal title might easily be removed by the appointment of a trustee. * * *'

In Frazier v. St. Luke's Church, 147 Pa. 256, 23 A. 442, the court said:

> '* * * A devise to an unincorporated association is a devise to nobody. But the devise in this instance did not fail, and why? Because it was for a charitable or religious use, and the beneficiaries were the real owners. A gift to the lame, the halt, and the blind, is not to fail in the nineteenth century because the legal title is given to a person or corporation incapable of taking it, or even forbidden by law to take it. Chancery here steps in to enforce the charity, and commits it to some one who may lawfully administer it. * * *'

In Restatement, Second, Trust, s 397, Comment f, the rule as to a devise to an unincorporated charitable association is stated as follows:

> 'If the owner of property devises or bequeaths it to an unincorporated charitable association, a charitable trust may be created although the purposes of the trust are not mentioned in the will. If the association is incapable of taking title to the property and administering the trust, the court will appoint a trustee to take the title and administer the trust for the purposes of the association. * * *'

In Schneider v. Kloepple, 270 Mo. 389, 193 S.W. 834, several Missouri cases are cited for the rule 'since the corporate character of the devisee is not necessary to the validity of a charitable devise' made to an unincorporated religious society.

* * *

We think it appropriate to note that it is general knowledge that in the organization of the United Methodist Church, title to real property is not in the local churches but in the respective Annual Conferences. In 1 Page on Wills, s 17.14, at 835, the author says:

'A devise to an unincorporated association, which is an agency of an incorporated church, is treated as a devise to the church in trust for such agency. * * * '

The cases cited in support of the rule so hold. Had proof been made that the Annual Conference was incorporated or that it held title to the property of the local church, this would have been an additional reason for affirming the decree of the trial court.

Applying the rule of our cases heretofore cited, we hold (paraphrasing the language of Johnson, 270 Ala. 260, 116 So.2d 899, and authorities cited therein), that the legal title to the property passed under the will to the incorporated church regardless of whether it was held in trust by the trustees of the church, individual members of the unincorporated church, or the next of kin of the testator, and passed to the church when it was incorporated.

Affirmed.

* * *

Notes

1. There are problems relating to incorporating religious organization. Some religious organizations object to having a corporate structure, which is deemed to be a "creature of the state" and, thus, is subject to laws of the state. Many state laws on nonprofit corporations do not distinguish religious corporations from other corporations even though constitutional and policy distinctions are substantially different. For example, a provision requiring that a nonprofit corporation have three directors can pose difficulties for a church that may be managed by a pastor, a board of deacons or elders, or by a majority vote of all members. Hierarchical churches may operate under agency or subsidiary role structures.

2. Some state statutes specifically address the incorporation of religious associations. These statutes range from lengthy objectives occupying an entire volume of the state's code (see, e.g. N.Y. Relig. Corp. Law) to very limited provisions embodied in a few pages of the state's statutes. The statutes may include all religious organizations within a general incorporating plan or it may contain specific provisions for many named religious groups. (See N.J. Rev. Stat. §§ 16.1–1 to 16:15A–4). Among those statutes that particularize for different churches, the distinctions may be based on hierarchical affiliation, traditional ethnic segregation, or doctrinal differences. Most Western states have not adopted denomination specific provisions, this being a characteristic in the older Eastern jurisdictions. (See, as examples, the California Nonprofit Religious Corporation Law, Cal. Corp. Code §§ 9110–9690, and Utah Code § 16–7–1 to 16–7–11, which has special provisions for forming a corporation sole.)

See discussion of a corporation sole in *Wood v. Benedictine Society of Alabama,* text, *supra.*

In News Release 2004–81, the IRS noted that it had become aware some promoters were urging use of the corporation sole statutes for tax evasion. Individuals would incorporate under the pretext of being a "bishop" of a religious organization or society. The individuals then would not report their income because they supposedly were entitled to tax exempt status as a § 501(c)(3) organizations. These individuals were told that current or future creditors would not reach their assets. The Service warned that these promotions are not legitimate and that it is taking vigorous action to stop them.

In Rev. Rul. 2004–27, 2004–1 C.B. 625, the IRS warned that a taxpayer cannot avoid income tax by establishing a corporation sole. The Service commented that it was aware some taxpayers were attempting to reduce their federal tax liability by taking the position their income was earned by a "corporation sole" created by the taxpayer. It noted that it was aware promoters, including tax return preparers, had been advising or recommending that taxpayers take frivolous position based on this argument. Some promoters were marketing a package, a kit, or other materials that claimed to show taxpayers how they could avoid paying income taxes through establishing a "corporation sole." The Service stated that a corporation sole may be used only by a bona fide religious leader for a specific, limited purposes relating to the religious leader's office. The argument that a taxpayer's income can be assigned to a corporation sole and, thus, be exempted from taxation has no merit and is frivolous according to the Service. The Service warned that in addition to having to pay the actual tax due on unreported income transferred to a "corporation sole," plus statutory interest, individuals who claim tax benefits on their returns based on a "corporation sole" scheme face substantial civil and criminal penalties.

3. Incorporation of religious organizations is prohibited in Virginia. See Va. Const. Art IV, § 14. However, church powers, such as conveyance of property, are provided legal effect without the necessity of formal incorporation. See Va. Code § 57-7.

V. SPECIALIZED TAX ISSUES RELATING TO RELIGIOUS ORGANIZATIONS

A. Involvement in Political Activities

BRANCH MINISTRIES v. ROSSOTTI
United States Court of Appeals, D.C. Circuit, 2000
211 F.3d 137

BUCKLEY, Senior Judge:

Four days before the 1992 presidential election, Branch Ministries, a tax-exempt church, placed full-page advertisements in two newspapers in which it urged Christians not to vote for then-presidential candidate Bill Clinton because of his positions on certain moral issues. The Internal Revenue Service concluded that the placement of the advertisements violated the statutory restrictions on organizations exempt from taxation and, for the first time in its history, it revoked a bona fide church's tax-exempt status because of its involvement in politics. Branch Ministries and its pastor, Dan Little, challenge the revocation on the grounds that

(1) the Service acted beyond its statutory authority, (2) the revocation violated its right to the free exercise of religion guaranteed by the First Amendment and the Religious Freedom Restoration Act, and (3) it was the victim of selective prosecution in violation of the Fifth Amendment. Because these objections are without merit, we affirm the district court's grant of summary judgment to the Service.

I. BACKGROUND

A. Taxation of Churches

The Internal Revenue Code ("Code") exempts certain organizations from taxation, including those organized and operated for religious purposes, provided that they do not engage in certain activities, including involvement in "any political campaign on behalf of (or in opposition to) any candidate for public office." 26 U.S.C. § 501(a), (c)(3) (1994). Contributions to such organizations are also deductible from the donating taxpayer's taxable income. *Id.* § 170(a). Although most organizations seeking tax-exempt status are required to apply to the Internal Revenue Service ("IRS" or "Service") for an advance determination that they meet the requirements of section 501(c)(3), *id.* § 508(a), a church may simply hold itself out as tax exempt and receive the benefits of that status without applying for advance recognition from the IRS. *Id.* § 508(c)(1)(A).

The IRS maintains a periodically updated "Publication No. 78," in which it lists all organizations that have received a ruling or determination letter confirming the deductibility of contributions made to them. *See* Rev. Proc. 82–39, 1982–1 C.B. 759, §§ 2.01, 2.03. Thus, a listing in that publication will provide donors with advance assurance that their contributions will be deductible under section 170(a). If a listed organization has subsequently had its tax-exempt status revoked, contributions that are made to it by a donor who is unaware of the change in status will generally be treated as deductible if made on or before the date that the revocation is publicly announced. * * * Donors to a church that has not received an advance determination of its tax-exempt status may also deduct their contributions; but in the event of an audit, the taxpayer will bear the burden of establishing that the church meets the requirements of section 501(c)(3). * * *

The unique treatment churches receive in the Internal Revenue Code is further reflected in special restrictions on the IRS's ability to investigate the tax status of a church. The Church Audit Procedures Act ("CAPA") sets out the circumstances under which the IRS may initiate an investigation of a church and the procedures it is required to follow in such an investigation. 26 U.S.C. § 7611. Upon a "reasonable belief" by a high-level Treasury official that a church may not be exempt from taxation under section 501, the IRS may begin a "church tax inquiry." * * * A church tax inquiry is defined, rather circularly, as any inquiry to a church (other than an examination) to serve as a basis for determining whether a church—

(A) is exempt from tax under section 501(a) by reason of its status as a church, or

(B) is ... engaged in activities which may be subject to taxation....

If the IRS is not able to resolve its concerns through a church tax inquiry, it may proceed to the second level of investigation: a "church tax examination." In such an examination, the IRS may obtain and review the church's records or examine its activities "to determine whether [the] organization claiming to be a church is a church for any period." * * *

B. Factual and Procedural History

Branch Ministries, Inc. operates the Church at Pierce Creek ("Church"), a Christian church located in Binghamton, New York. In 1983, the Church requested and received a letter from the IRS recognizing its tax-exempt status. On October 30, 1992, four days before the presidential election, the Church placed full-page advertisements in *USA Today* and the *Washington Times*. Each bore the headline "Christians Beware" and asserted that then-Governor Clinton's positions concerning abortion, homosexuality, and the distribution of condoms to teenagers in schools violated Biblical precepts. The following appeared at the bottom of each advertisement:

> This advertisement was co-sponsored by the Church at Pierce Creek, Daniel J. Little, Senior Pastor, and by churches and concerned Christians nationwide. Tax-deductible donations for this advertisement gladly accepted. Make donations to: The Church at Pierce Creek. [mailing address]. * * *

The advertisements did not go unnoticed. They produced hundreds of contributions to the Church from across the country and were mentioned in a *New York Times* article and an Anthony Lewis column which stated that the sponsors of the advertisement had almost certainly violated the Internal Revenue Code. * * *

The advertisements also came to the attention of the Regional Commissioner of the IRS, who notified the Church on November 20, 1992 that he had authorized a church tax inquiry based on "a reasonable belief ... that you may not be tax-exempt or that you may be liable for tax" due to political activities and expenditures. Letter from Cornelius J. Coleman, IRS Regional Commissioner, to The Church at Pierce Creek (Nov. 20, 1992)* * *. The Church denied that it had engaged in any prohibited political activity and declined to provide the IRS with certain information the Service had requested. On February 11, 1993, the IRS informed the Church that it was beginning a church tax examination. Following two unproductive meetings between the parties, the IRS revoked the Church's section 501(c)(3) tax-exempt status on January 19, 1995, citing the newspaper advertisements as prohibited intervention in a political campaign.

The Church and Pastor Little (collectively, "Church") commenced this lawsuit soon thereafter. This had the effect of suspending the revocation of the Church's tax exemption until the district court entered its judgment in this case. See 26 U.S.C. § 7428(c). The Church challenged the revocation of its tax-exempt status, alleging that the IRS had no authority to revoke its tax exemption, that the revocation violated its right to free speech and to freely exercise its religion under the First Amendment and the Religious Freedom Restoration Act of 1993, 42 U.S.C. § 2000bb ("RFRA"), and that the IRS engaged in selective prosecution in violation of the Equal Protection Clause of the Fifth Amendment. After allowing discovery on the Church's selective prosecution claim, *Branch Ministries, Inc. v. Richardson*, 970 F.Supp. 11 (D.D.C. 1997), the district court granted summary judgment in favor of the IRS. *Branch Ministries v. Rossotti*, 40 F.Supp.2d 15 (D.D.C.1999).

* * *

II. ANALYSIS

The Church advances a number of arguments in support of its challenges to the revocation. We examine only those that warrant analysis.

A. *The Statutory Authority of the IRS*

The Church argues that, under the Internal Revenue Code, the IRS does not have the statutory authority to revoke the tax-exempt status of a bona fide church. It reasons as follows: section 501(c)(3) refers to tax-exempt status for religious organizations, not churches; section 508, on the other hand, specifically exempts "churches" from the requirement of applying for advance recognition of tax-exempt status, *id.* § 508(c)(1)(A); therefore, according to the Church, its tax-exempt status is derived not from section 501(c)(3), but from the lack of any provision in the Code for the taxation of churches. The Church concludes from this that it is not subject to taxation and that the IRS is therefore powerless to place conditions upon or to remove its tax-exempt status as a church.

We find this argument more creative than persuasive. The simple answer, of course, is that whereas not every religious organization is a church, every church is a religious organization. More to the point, irrespective of whether it was required to do so, the Church applied to the IRS for an advance determination of its tax-exempt status. The IRS granted that recognition and now seeks to withdraw it. CAPA gives the IRS this power.

That statute, which pertains exclusively to churches, provides authority for revocation of the tax-exempt status of a church through its references to other sections of the Internal Revenue Code. The section of CAPA entitled "Limitations on revocation of tax-exempt status, etc." provides that the Secretary of the Treasury may "determine that an organization is not a church which [ ] (i) is exempt from taxation by reason of section 501(a), or (ii) is described in section 170(c)." 26

U.S.C.§ 7611(d)(1)(A)(i), (ii). Both of these sections condition tax-exempt status on non-intervention in political campaigns. Section 501(a) states that "[a]n organization described in subsection (c) ... shall be exempt from taxation...." *Id.* § 501(a). Those described in subsection (c) include corporations ... organized and operated exclusively for religious ... purposes ... which do[ ] not participate in, or intervene in (including the publishing or distributing of statements), any political campaign on behalf of (or in opposition to) any candidate for public office.

Id. § 501(c)(3). Similarly, section 170(c) allows taxpayers to deduct from their taxable income donations made to a corporation organized and operated exclusively for religious ... purposes ... which is not disqualified for tax exemption under section 501(c)(3) by reason of attempting to ... intervene in (including the publishing or distributing of statements), any political campaign on behalf of (or in opposition to) any candidate for public office.

Id. § 170(c)(2)(B), (D).

The Code, in short, specifically states that organizations that fail to comply with the restrictions set forth in section 501(c) are not qualified to receive the tax exemption that it provides. Having satisfied ourselves that the IRS had the statutory authority to revoke the Church's tax-exempt status, we now turn to the free exercise challenges.

B. *First Amendment Claims and the RFRA*

The Church claims that the revocation of its exemption violated its right to freely exercise its religion under both the First Amendment and the RFRA. To sustain its claim under either the Constitution or the statute, the Church must first establish that its free exercise right has been substantially burdened. * * * 42 U.S.C. § 2000bb–1(a),(b) "Government shall not substantially burden a person's exercise of religion" in the absence of a compelling government interest that is furthered by the least restrictive means.). We conclude that the Church has failed to meet this test.

The Church asserts, first, that a revocation would threaten its existence. * * * ("The Church at Pierce Creek will have to close due to the revocation of its tax exempt status, and the inability of congregants to deduct their contributions from their taxes."). The Church maintains that a loss of its tax-exempt status will not only make its members reluctant to contribute the funds essential to its survival, but may obligate the Church itself to pay taxes.

The Church appears to assume that the withdrawal of a conditional privilege for failure to meet the condition is in itself an unconstitutional burden on its free exercise right. This is true, however, only if the receipt of the privilege (in this case the tax exemption) is conditioned

> upon conduct proscribed by a religious faith, or ... denie[d] ... because of conduct mandated by religious belief, thereby putting

substantial pressure on an adherent to modify his behavior and to violate his beliefs.

* * * Although its advertisements reflected its religious convictions on certain questions of morality, the Church does not maintain that a withdrawal from electoral politics would violate its beliefs. The sole effect of the loss of the tax exemption will be to decrease the amount of money available to the Church for its religious practices. The Supreme Court has declared, however, that such a burden "is not constitutionally significant." * * *

In actual fact, even this burden is overstated. Because of the unique treatment churches receive under the Internal Revenue Code, the impact of the revocation is likely to be more symbolic than substantial. As the IRS confirmed at oral argument, if the Church does not intervene in future political campaigns, it may hold itself out as a 501(c)(3) organization and receive all the benefits of that status. All that will have been lost, in that event, is the advance assurance of deductibility in the event a donor should be audited. *See* 26 U.S.C. § 508(c)(1)(A); Rev. Proc. 82–39 § 2.03. Contributions will remain tax deductible as long as donors are able to establish that the Church meets the requirements of section 501(c)(3).

Nor does the revocation necessarily make the Church liable for the payment of taxes. As the IRS explicitly represented in its brief and reiterated at oral argument, the revocation of the exemption does not convert bona fide donations into income taxable to the Church. *See* 26 U.S.C. § 102 ("Gross income does not include the value of property acquired by gift...."). Furthermore, we know of no authority, and counsel provided none, to prevent the Church from reapplying for a prospective determination of its tax-exempt status and regaining the advance assurance of deductibility—provided, of course, that it renounces future involvement in political campaigns.

We also reject the Church's argument that it is substantially burdened because it has no alternate means by which to communicate its sentiments about candidates for public office. In *Regan v. Taxation With Representation,* 461 U.S. 540, 552–53, 103 S.Ct. 1997, 76 L.Ed.2d 129 (1983) (Blackmun, J., concurring), three members of the Supreme Court stated that the availability of such an alternate means of communication is essential to the constitutionality of section 501(c)(3)'s restrictions on lobbying. The Court subsequently confirmed that this was an accurate description of its holding. * * *

In *Regan,* the concurring justices noted that "TWR may use its present § 501(c)(3) organization for its nonlobbying activities and may create a § 501(c)(4) affiliate to pursue its charitable goals through lobbying." * * *

The Church has such an avenue available to it. As was the case with TWR, the Church may form a related organization under section 501(c)(4) of the Code. * * * Such organizations are exempt from taxation; but unlike their section 501(c)(3) counterparts, contributions to them are not deductible. * * * Although a section 501(c)(4) organization is also subject to the ban on intervening in political campaigns, *see* 26 C.F.R. § 1.501(c)(4)–1(a)(2)(ii) (1999), it may form a political action committee ("PAC") that would be free to participate in political campaigns. *Id.* § 1.527–6(f), (g) ("[A]n organization described in section 501(c) that is exempt from taxation under section 501(a) may, [if it is not a section 501(c)(3) organization], establish and maintain such a separate segregated fund to receive contributions and make expenditures in a political campaign.").

At oral argument, counsel for the Church doggedly maintained that there can be no "Church at Pierce Creek PAC." True, it may not itself create a PAC; but as we have pointed out, the Church can initiate a series of steps that will provide an alternate means of political communication that will satisfy the standards set by the concurring justices in *Regan*. Should the Church proceed to do so, however, it must understand that the related 501(c)(4) organization must be separately incorporated; and it must maintain records that will demonstrate that tax-deductible contributions to the Church have not been used to support the political activities conducted by the 501(c)(4) organization's political action arm. * * *

That the Church cannot use its tax-free dollars to fund such a PAC unquestionably passes constitutional muster. The Supreme Court has consistently held that, absent invidious discrimination, "Congress has not violated [an organization's] First Amendment rights by declining to subsidize its First Amendment activities." * * *

Because the Church has failed to demonstrate that its free exercise rights have been substantially burdened, we do not reach its arguments that section 501(c)(3) does not serve a compelling government interest or, if it is indeed compelling, that revocation of its tax exemption was not the least restrictive means of furthering that interest.

Nor does the Church succeed in its claim that the IRS has violated its First Amendment free speech rights by engaging in viewpoint discrimination. The restrictions imposed by section 501(c)(3) are viewpoint neutral; they prohibit intervention in favor of all candidates for public office by all tax-exempt organizations, regardless of candidate, party, or viewpoint. * * *

C. *Selective Prosecution (Fifth Amendment)*

The Church alleges that the IRS violated the Equal Protection Clause of the Fifth Amendment by engaging in selective prosecution. In support of its claim, the Church has submitted several hundred pages of newspaper excerpts reporting political campaign activities in, or by the pastors of, other churches that have retained their tax-exempt status. These include reports of explicit endorsements of Democratic candidates by clergymen as well as many instances in which favored candidates have been invited to address congregations from the pulpit. The Church complains that despite this widespread and widely reported involvement by other churches in political campaigns, it is the only one to have ever had its tax-exempt status revoked for engaging in political activity. It attributes this alleged discrimination to the Service's political bias.

To establish selective prosecution, the Church must "prove that (1) [it] was singled out for prosecution from among others similarly situated and (2) that [the] prosecution was improperly motivated, i.e., based on race, religion or another arbitrary classification." * * * This burden is a demanding one because "in the absence of clear evidence to the contrary, courts presume that [government prosecutors] have properly discharged their official duties." * * *.

At oral argument, counsel for the IRS conceded that if some of the church-sponsored political activities cited by the Church were accurately reported, they were in violation of section 501(c)(3) and could have resulted in the revocation of those churches' tax-exempt status. But even if the Service could have revoked their tax exemptions, the Church has failed to establish selective prosecution because it has failed to demonstrate that it was similarly situated to any of those other churches. None of the reported activities involved the placement of advertisements in newspapers with nationwide circulations opposing a candidate and soliciting tax deductible contributions to defray their cost. As we have stated,

> [i]f ... there was no one to whom defendant could be compared in order to resolve the question of [prosecutorial] selection, then it follows that defendant has failed to make out one of the elements of its case. Discrimination cannot exist in a vacuum; it can be found only in the unequal treatment of people in similar circumstances.
> * * *

Because the Church has failed to establish that it was singled out for prosecution from among others who were similarly situated, we need not examine whether the IRS was improperly motivated in undertaking this prosecution.

III. CONCLUSION

For the foregoing reasons, we find that the revocation of the Church's tax-exempt status neither violated the Constitution nor exceeded the IRS's statutory authority. The judgment of the district court is therefore

Affirmed.

Notes

1. See further discussion of the prohibition of § 501(c)(3) organizations being involved in political activities in Chapters 4 and 5.

2. In TAM 200437040 the Service ruled that a church would not lose its tax exempt status because of statements made by its minister who opposed a person's candidacy for President, but it decided the church would be subject to a penalty tax under § 4955. The Service stated that the

minister's statements were imputed to the church when they were set out in official programs of the church. The only exception would be where the church clearly informed the members prior to the statements that the publication or program did not speak for the church and that the church did not utilize the minister or the publication to represent the views of the church. The Service held that the church would be liable for a 10 percent tax on the amount of each political expenditure and, because the church "did not clearly and unequivocally acknowledge" that the minister's statements about the presidential election might have been inappropriate until months later, the church was liable for a 100 percent tax on the amount of each political expenditure. In addition, it ruled that the minister would be liable for a 2 ½ percent tax initially and a 50 percent tax on the amount of each political expenditure.

3. In *Tax Analysts v. Internal Revenue Service and Christian Broadcasting*, 410 F.3d 715 (D.C. Cir. 2005), a publisher of tax materials, sued the IRS and Christian Broadcasting Network, Inc. (CBN) under the Freedom of Information Act (FOIA)and the Internal Revenue Code in an attempt to obtain copies of a closing agreement between the IRS and CBN concerning CBN's filing for tax exempt status. CBN had been a § 501(c)(3) organization since 1961. However, in 1985 and 1986, CBN allegedly engaged in political activities in support of presidential candidate and CBN founder Pat Robertson. The IRS audited CBN regarding CBN's past and continued eligibility for tax-exempt status. After CBN filed a Form 1023 in 1998, the IRS granted § 501(c)(3) status to CBN retroactive to 1987. CBN then issued a press release announcing that it had entered into an agreement with the IRS to conclude an audit and to preserve its tax exempt status. The press release announced both the closing agreement regarding previous taxable years and the Form 1023 regarding the period subsequent to those years. The publisher of tax materials then send a FOIA request to the IRS seeking a copy of all closing agreements it had with CBN. The court, however, ruled that the withheld documents were exempt from FOIA's disclosure requirements. The FOIA includes a number of exceptions from disclosure, one of which excludes documents specifically exempted by statute. Section 6103 of the Internal Revenue Code protects the confidentiality of tax return information including closing agreements so long as the information is not subject to disclosure under § 6104 of the Code. The Regulations pursuant to § 6104 except from disclosure information relating to applications for tax exempt status.

B. Tax Audits of Churches

Because of the limited governmental intervention in the affairs of churches and certain other religious organizations and the exemption of churches from the requirements of filing annual information returns with the Internal Revenue Service, some individuals have abused the tax system by seeking to utilize the church form of organization to evade taxes. While the Service actively investigates and examines church organizations to determine if there is abuse, First Amendment constraints require limitations on the ability of the Service to conduct such investigations.

Section 7611 of the Internal Revenue Code prohibits a church tax examination unless the regional commissioner of the Internal Revenue Service or a higher Treasury official reasonably believes (on the basis of facts and circumstances recorded in writing) that the organization in question may not qualify as a church or may be engaged in an unrelated trade or business or otherwise should be subject to income taxation. The Service must given written notice to the church organization before beginning the tax inquiry and must explain in the notice the concerns that gave rise to the inquiry as well as the general subject matter of the inquiry. The notice also must explain the applicable administrative and constitutional provisions regarding the inquiry as well as a statement that the church has the right to a conference with the Service before any examination of church records. The Service must give the church a second notice (at least fifteen days before the beginning of the examination) if it chooses to examine church records and church religious activities. The notice must be sent to both the church and to an appropriate regional counsel of the Internal Revenue Service and must notify the church that it has a reasonable time to participate in a conference should the church request such preexamination conference. The second notice must include a copy of the original church tax inquiry notice, a description of the church records and activities which the Service seeks to examine, an offer to have a conference between the church and the Service in an attempt to resolve any concerns, and a copy of all documents that were collected or prepared by the Service for use in the examination where disclosure of such documented is required by the Freedom of Information Act (5 U.S.C. § 552). The Service must not give the second notice to the church before the fifteenth day after the date of the first notice. The regional counsel for the Service has fifteen days from the date of the second notice to file an advisory objection to the examination.

If the Service does not send a second notice to the church after it gave the church the initial tax inquiry notice, the Service must complete the inquiry and must make a final determination within ninety days after the tax inquiry notice date. If the Service gives the church a second notice, the Service must complete the examination and make a final determination within two years after the date of the second notice. This two-year period is suspended for any period during which a judicial proceeding either is brought by the church or by the Service to compel compliance with its request for examination of records or during a period in which the Service is unable to act because of an order issued in a judicial proceeding involving access to third party records.

The Service may examine church records only to the extent necessary to determine the liability for any federal income tax. It may inquire into religious activities only to the extent necessary to determine whether the organization is in fact a church. The Service is limited to the three most recent tax years preceding the date on which it sent the second notice of examination to determine whether the organization qualifies as a church. If the Service determines the organization does not qualify as a church, it then may examine records and assess tax as part of the same audit for the six-year period preceding the examination notice date.

A church may bring a declaratory judgment action to have tax exempt status determined by a court. For this purpose, the final report of an Internal Revenue agent proposing to revoke or deny tax exempt status is treated as a final adverse determination so that the church is deemed to have exhausted administrative remedies to authorize it to petition a court.

Once the Service has audited a church, it may not again conduct an audit on the same or similar issues for a period of five years unless the first audit resulted in a revocation of tax exemption, an assessment of tax, or a request by the Service for a significant change in the operational practices of the church.

C. Other Tax Issues

Churches became subject to the tax on unrelated business taxable income in 1969. The rules applicable to a determination on unrelated business taxable income generally are the same for churches as for other nonprofit organizations. (See discussion in Chapter 9.) However, each parish, individual church, district, or other local unit of a church, such as a diocese, province of a religious order or convention or association of churches, is allowed one specific deduction of $1,000.

Religious organizations often operate child care centers. If religious training is part of the day care center activities, income is related to the exempt purposes of the religious organization. However, if only child care is provided with no religious training, the income from such services is subject to tax. Religious organizations that operate bookstores and gift shops can exclude income from sale of religious books and materials but not from sales of other articles. Still, if the bookstore is operated by volunteer labor, the income will not be taxed.

Churches must pay social security taxes on wages paid their employees unless the church organization (newly formed) elects before the first date on which a quarterly employment tax return would otherwise be due to oppose the payment of social security taxes based on its certification that it is opposed to the payment of social security taxes on religious grounds. Elementary or secondary schools controlled by a church or a convention or association of churches qualify for the exclusion. See I.R.C. § 3121(w). If the church organization makes a qualified election to have salaries paid its employees exempt from social security taxes, the salaries will be treated as self-employment income to the employees.

Regardless of whether a religious organization makes an election, services performed by a duly ordained, commissioned, or licensed minister, in his or her capacity as a minister, are considered self-employment income and are subject to self-employment tax. Still, those ministers of a religious order who have taken a vow of poverty are exempt from payment of self-employment taxes. Those ministers who have not taken such a vow and Christian Science practitioners will be exempt from payment of the tax only if they are individually conscientiously opposed to accepting any public insurance for their ministerial services or they are members of a religious denomination that opposes such insurance. The exemption does not cover services performed in other than a ministerial capacity. A minister who is not exempt from payment of self-employment tax must include as self-employment income the rental value of a parsonage furnished the minister or a rental allowance even though the allowance is not subject to income tax.

Problem

There have been major disagreements among members of a local Baptist church. A majority of the members have voted to dissolve the church corporation and to liquidate and distribute its assets to local churches (none are Baptists), a nondenominational Christian school, a retirement center, and a Baptist Church in another state. The majority want to give the church building to the Christian school located in their city. A few members of the church are adamant that assets of the church, including the church building, should remain and that they should be permitted to continue services in the church building as Baptists. Can the minority prevent the withdrawing majority from selling and distributing church assets?

Chapter 11

SCHOOLS

I. ROLE OF PRIVATE SCHOOLS

Courts have long held compulsory school laws to be constitutional. The requirement of a public school education is a valid exercise of the police power of the state. In this respect, the natural rights of parents to the custody and control of their children are subordinate to the power of the state and may be restricted and regulated by state laws. Still, states cannot require that children may attend only a public school. Such a requirement would interfere with the liberty of parents and guardians to direct the education of the children under their control, as noted in the following case.

PIERCE v. SOCIETY OF THE SISTERS OF HOLY NAMES OF JESUS AND MARY
United States Supreme Court, 1925
268 U.S. 510, 45 S.Ct. 571, 69 L.Ed. 1070

Mr. Justice McREYNOLDS delivered the opinion of the Court.

These appeals are from decrees, based upon undenied allegations, which granted preliminary orders restraining appellants from threatening or attempting to enforce the Compulsory Education Act* * * adopted November 7, 1922 (Laws Or. 1923, p. 9), under the initiative provision of her Constitution by the voters of Oregon. Judicial Code, § 266 (Comp. St. § 1243). * * *

The challenged act, effective September 1, 1926, requires every parent, guardian, or other person having control or charge or custody of a child between 8 and 16 years to send him 'to a public school for the period of time a public school shall be held during the current year' in the district where the child resides; and failure so to do is declared a misdemeanor. There are exemptions—not specially important here—for children who are not normal, or who have completed the eighth grade, or whose parents or private teachers reside at considerable distances from any public school, or who hold special permits from the county superintendent. The manifest purpose is to compel general attendance at public schools by normal children, between 8 and 16, who have not completed the eighth grade. And without doubt enforcement of the statute would seriously impair, perhaps destroy, the profitable features of appellees' business and greatly diminish the value of their property.

Appellee the Society of Sisters is an Oregon corporation, organized in 1880, with power to care for orphans, educate and instruct the youth, establish and maintain academies or schools, and acquire necessary real and personal property. It has long devoted its property and effort to the secular and religious education and care of children, and has acquired the valuable good will of many parents and guardians. It conducts interdependent primary and high schools and junior colleges, and maintains orphanages for the custody and control of children between 8 and 16. In its primary schools many children between those ages are taught the subjects usually pursued in Oregon public schools during the first eight years. Systematic religious instruction and moral training according to the tenets of the Roman Catholic Church are also regularly provided. All courses of study, both temporal and religious, contemplate continuity of training under appellee's charge; the primary schools are essential to the system and the most profitable. It owns valuable buildings, especially constructed and equipped for school purposes. The business is remunerative—the annual income from primary schools exceeds $30,000—and the successful conduct of this requires long time contracts with teachers and parents. The Compulsory Education Act of 1922 has already caused the withdrawal from its schools of children who would otherwise continue, and their income has steadily declined. The appellants, public officers, have proclaimed their purpose strictly to enforce the statute.

After setting out the above facts, the Society's bill alleges that the enactment conflicts with the right of parents to choose schools where their children will receive appropriate mental and religious training, the right of the child to influence the parents' choice of a school, the right of schools and teachers therein to engage in a useful business or profession, and is accordingly repugnant to the Constitution and void. And, further, that unless enforcement of the measure is enjoined the corporation's business and property will suffer irreparable injury.

Appellee Hill Military Academy is a private corporation organized in 1908 under the laws of Oregon, engaged in owning, operating, and conducting for profit an elementary, college preparatory, and military training school for boys between the ages of 5 and 21 years. The average attendance is 100, and the annual fees received for each student amount to some $800. The elementary department is divided into eight grades, as in the public schools; the college preparatory department has four grades, similar to those of the public high schools; the courses of study conform to the requirements of the state board of education. Military instruction and training are also given, under the supervision of an army officer. It owns considerable real and personal property, some useful only for school purposes. The business and incident good will are very

Sec. I ROLE OF PRIVATE SCHOOLS 563

valuable. In order to conduct its affairs, long time contracts must be made for supplies, equipment, teachers, and pupils.

Appellants, law officers of the state and county, have publicly announced that the Act of November 7, 1922, is valid and have declared their intention to enforce it. By reason of the statute and threat of enforcement, appellee's business is being destroyed and its property depreciated; parents and guardians are refusing to make contracts for the future instruction of their sons, and some are being withdrawn.

The Academy's bill states the foregoing facts and then alleges that the challenged act contravenes the corporation's rights guaranteed by the Fourteenth Amendment and that unless appellants are restrained from proclaiming its validity and threatening to enforce it irreparable injury will result. The prayer is for an appropriate injunction.

No answer was interposed in either cause, and after proper notices they were heard by three judges (Judicial Code, § 266 [Comp. St. § 1243]) on motions for preliminary injunctions upon the specifically alleged facts. The court ruled that the Fourteenth Amendment guaranteed appellees against the deprivation of their property without due process of law consequent upon the unlawful interference by appellants with the free choice of patrons, present and prospective. It declared the right to conduct schools was property and that parents and guardians, as a part of their liberty, might direct the education of children by selecting reputable teachers and places. Also, that appellees' schools were not unfit or harmful to the public, and that enforcement of the challenged statute would unlawfully deprive them of patronage and thereby destroy appellees' business and property. Finally, that the threats to enforce the act would continue to cause irreparable injury; and the suits were not premature.

No question is raised concerning the power of the state reasonably to regulate all schools, to inspect, supervise and examine them, their teachers and pupils; to require that all children of proper age attend some school, that teachers shall be of good moral character and patriotic disposition, that certain studies plainly essential to good citizenship must be taught, and that nothing be taught which is manifestly inimical to the public welfare.

The inevitable practical result of enforcing the act under consideration would be destruction of appellees' primary schools, and perhaps all other private primary schools for normal children within the state of Oregon. Appellees are engaged in a kind of undertaking not inherently harmful, but long regarded as useful and meritorious. Certainly there is nothing in the present records to indicate that they have failed to discharge their obligations to patrons, students, or the state. And there are no peculiar circumstances or present emergencies which demand extraordinary measures relative to primary education.

Under the doctrine of Meyer v. Nebraska, 262 U. S. 390, 43 S. Ct. 625, 67 L. Ed. 1042, 29 A. L. R. 1146, we think it entirely plain that the Act of 1922 unreasonably interferes with the liberty of parents and guardians to direct the upbringing and education of children under their control. As often heretofore pointed out, rights guaranteed by the Constitution may not be abridged by legislation which has no reasonable relation to some purpose within the competency of the state. The fundamental theory of liberty upon which all governments in this Union repose excludes any general power of the state to standardize its children by forcing them to accept instruction from public teachers only. The child is not the mere creature of the state; those who nurture him and direct his destiny have the right, coupled with the high duty, to recognize and prepare him for additional obligations.

* * *

The suits were not premature. The injury to appellees was present and very real, not a mere possibility in the remote future. If no relief had been possible prior to the effective date of the act, the injury would have become irreparable. Prevention of impending injury by unlawful action is a well-recognized function of courts of equity.

The decrees below are affirmed.

Questions

As the Supreme Court noted in *Society of the Sisters of Holy Names of Jesus and Mary*, parents have a constitutional right to send their children to a private school. Can a state exert control over the educational program of a private school? If the private school is a religious institution, would state control over the school's secular education violate the free exercise clause of the First Amendment? Would it violate the establishment clause of the First Amendment?

NEW LIFE BAPTIST CHURCH ACADEMY v. EAST LONGMEADOW

United States Court of Appeals, First Circuit, 1989
885 F.2d 940

BREYER, Circuit Judge.

This case raises questions about the extent to which the First Amendment permits a religious group to refuse to comply with state rules and procedures for determining the adequacy of the secular education that the religious group provides to children. The present controversy arises because a child cannot satisfy Massachusetts' compulsory school attendance laws by attending a private school unless the local school committee "approves" the education that the private school provides. Mass.Gen.L. ch. 76, § 1. A school committee must "approve" the private school when the school meets certain minimal statutory criteria and also offers a secular education comparable to that provided in the town's public schools. The New Life Baptist Church Academy, together with several of its members and related persons (the plaintiffs, whom we shall collectively call the "Academy"), believe that it is a sin to "submit" their educational enterprise to a secular authority for approval. The Academy claims that the First Amendment therefore forbids the School Committee of the Town of East Longmeadow, Massachusetts (the "School Committee") to "approve" the school, particularly if the School Committee, in doing so, follows its proposed procedures for evaluating the school, procedures which essentially consist of gathering written information from the Academy, reviewing the academic credentials of the Academy's teachers, and visiting the school once (or, in the absence of adequate teacher credentials, more than once) to observe the quality of the teaching. In the Academy's view, those proposed procedures unnecessarily burden the free exercise of religion when compared with the Academy's preferred alternative, an approach that depends upon standardized pupil testing. The Academy brought this law suit to prevent the School Committee from carrying out its proposed approval process.

* * *

I.

Background

A. *State law.* Massachusetts state law requires nearly all children to attend school. Mass.Gen.L. ch. 76, § 1. They may attend a "public day school . . . or some other day school;" but any "other day school" (i.e., private school, whether secular or parochial) must be "approved by the school committee" of the town in which the school is located. The school committee must approve a private school when satisfied that the instruction in all the studies required by law equals in thoroughness and efficiency, and in the progress made therein, that in the public schools in the same town; but shall not withhold such approval on account of religious teaching. The "studies required by law" include orthography, reading, writing, the English language and grammar, geography, arithmetic, drawing, music, the history and Constitution of the United States, the duties of citizenship, health education, physical education, and good behavior. * * * If children between the ages set by the state Department of Education do not attend a public school or an "approved" private school (or receive official permission to work or to be educated in some other setting), the state may prosecute their parents under Mass.Gen.L. ch. 76, § 2; and any person (including a town) may initiate a civil proceeding under Mass.Gen.L. ch. 119, § 24, to compel education for the children or even to remove the children from their parents.

B. *The School Committee's proposal.* The School Committee, complying with the statute, intends to evaluate, and then to approve or disapprove, the Academy's secular education. The Committee has developed a set of procedures to help it decide whether or not to approve a private school such as the Academy. It has modified those procedures somewhat in an effort to accommodate the Academy's religious beliefs.

* * *

C. *The Academy.* The Academy is a school operated by an independent congregation of which the individual plaintiffs are members. * * * The Academy's religion teaches its members that God is the sovereign and the final authority in all human conduct, [and] to submit their educational ministry for the prior or continued approval of secular authorities would violate the sovereignty of Christ over his church and would, therefore, be a sin. * * * The Academy has said it has no religious objection to:

(a) complying with state health, safety and zoning rules* * *;

(b) submitting written information to the School Committee about the number of its students, the number of hours and days taught, the curriculum, texts, the number of teachers, and the criteria for hiring teachers, * * *;

(c) permitting School Committee officials to visit the Academy, at least occasionally, to meet administrators and teachers, to read texts, and to observe classes, * * *;

(d) teaching the subjects required by state law, and holding classes the number of days required by state law, * * *;

(e) hiring teachers with adequate credentials, provided the state does not specify the credentials or whom the Academy must hire or discharge, * * *;

(f) being incorporated under Massachusetts law (which it is), * * *.

The Academy does object on religious grounds, however, to taking many of these same steps if they are part of a School Committee "approval" procedure, for the Academy does not want to admit or recognize, in any way, that the state has the authority to approve or disapprove the Academy's educational program. * * *

The Academy has proposed what it sees as a "less restrictive" way for the School Committee to proceed. It has proposed (1) that it furnish to the School Committee, on a voluntary basis, information about its activities, curriculum, students and teachers; (2) that it see that its students voluntarily take annual standardized examinations prepared by an outside source; (3) that it see that the School Committee obtain the exam results for review; and (4) that it provide or assist in arranging "follow-up" sessions (including discussions among students, teachers, parents, and School Committee representatives, and further testing) for students whose test results are poor. * * *

D. *The decision below.* After holding evidentiary hearings, the district court held that the School Committee's proposed procedures violated the "free exercise" clause of the First Amendment.

* * *

II.

FREE EXERCISE OF RELIGION

For ease of analysis, we shall consider the Academy's constitutional "free exercise" claim by asking two distinct questions: First, does the

First Amendment's Free Exercise Clause forbid the state (i.e., the School Committee) to insist upon approving the secular education offered by a religious school that believes it sinful to submit even its secular education program to the approval of secular authorities? Second, if not, does the Free Exercise Clause forbid the School Committee to follow its proposed approval procedures rather than the "standardized testing" procedures that the Academy prefers?

To answer each of these questions, we must determine (1) whether the Academy's religious beliefs are sincerely held, * * * (2) whether (and the extent to which) the relevant regulation burdens the exercise of those beliefs, * * * (3) if so, whether the regulation nonetheless serves a compelling, or overriding, governmental interest, * * * and (4) if so, whether the School Committee might nonetheless adequately serve that interest in a "less restrictive," *i.e.,* a less burdensome, way, * * *.

A. *The First Question: Approval in General.* We believe the legal answer to the first question is clear. The Free Exercise Clause does not prohibit the School Committee from enforcing, through appropriate means, a state law that requires "approval" of the Academy's secular education program. We concede that the Academy has a sincere, relevant religious belief that it ought not participate in any such secular approval process. * * * We also agree with the Academy that the very existence of a state approval requirement will burden the exercise of its religion by placing it under "substantial pressure ... to modify [its] behavior and to violate [its] beliefs." * * * That is to say, given the adverse consequences that would attend a failure to obtain approval, the state requirement could well lead the Academy to participate, at least to some degree, in the approval process, thereby violating, at least to some degree, its religious principles.

Nonetheless, the state's interest in making certain that its children receive an adequate secular education is "compelling." * * * And no one in this case suggests any "less burdensome" way to guarantee the adequacy of the Academy's secular education than to subject it to *some form* of state evaluation process.

We therefore conclude that the many cases holding that the Free Exercise clause allows a state reasonably to regulate private secular education (including secular education offered by religious institutions) govern here. They make clear that the state of Massachusetts may, as a general matter, authorize its towns to approve or disapprove the Academy's secular education, as provided in the state statute. * * *

Of course, the standards the School Committee applies in deciding whether to approve or to disapprove the secular education program must be reasonable. * * * But, at this stage of the proceeding, before the School Committee has presented or applied its precise standards (other than the standards contained in the statute), we have no reason to think that the substantive content of those standards will prove constitutionally impermissible.

B. *The Second Question: The Proposed Procedures.* The second question—that of comparative means—is more difficult. Does the Free Exercise Clause permit the School Committee to use its preferred "information gathering" procedures (written information/teacher credentials/visits), or does it prohibit the Committee from doing so, because another procedure—the Academy's preferred method (standardized testing)—is a less restrictive alternative? Again, we take the Academy's profession of its religious beliefs as sincere. And we also are willing to accept the district court's finding that the Committee's proposals would burden the Academy in exercising its religious beliefs (perhaps because, compared with standardized testing, the Academy believes the Committee's procedures would involve the school more deeply in the approval process). Moreover, the state's educational interest is "compelling."

But the question remains whether or not "standardized testing" is a "less restrictive" way to achieve the state's legitimate, "compelling" goals. In answering this question, we begin with the Supreme Court's requirement that when a state chooses to attain its goals in a way which imposes a burden upon the free exercise of religion, the state must show that "it is *the least restrictive means* of achieving some compelling state interest," * * *

The term "least restrictive means," however, is not self-defining. In applying that term, one must pay heed to Justice Blackmun's caution, offered in another context, that " 'least drastic means' is a slippery slope . . . [, for a] judge would be unimaginative indeed if he could not come up with something a little less 'drastic' or a little less 'restrictive' in almost any situation, and thereby enable himself to vote to strike legislation down." * * *

* * *

In reviewing the record, we have kept in mind* * * the fact that Massachusetts' legitimate interest extends, not only to the existence of private school education, but also to its quality. * * * We have also taken note of the district court's finding that the School Committee had "a reasonable basis to be concerned about the qualifications of at least some New Life [Academy] teachers to instruct children." * * * As a result, we have concluded that the First Amendment does not preclude the School Committee from employing its approval procedures; the record reveals too many potential educationally-related difficulties, and too little alleviation of the burden on religion, to justify the district court's conclusion that standardized testing is a "less restrictive alternative." We believe, in other words, that the testing proposal would "materially detract," * * *

First consider the educational difficulties. The standardized testing system that the district court preferred is a voluntary system; but how can the School Committee find assurance that a child will receive an adequate secular education through reliance on a monitoring system that is *voluntary?* How can the Academy make certain the students and their parents agree to the testing plan? Suppose they do not. Suppose a parent refuses to permit the Academy to give the Committee the test results. Suppose a parent refuses to permit his child to participate in the testing, or in the remedial "follow-up." (Suppose, for example, a parent decided that doing so amounted to impermissible cooperation with secular authorities.) Is the School Committee then to enforce truancy laws against the individual parent? Is it to demand expulsion of the child? Is it to "disapprove" the entire Academy? And consider these problems if several parents withdraw their children from the testing scheme. It is difficult to see how a purely voluntary system for monitoring nonpublic education can serve the state's interest in assuring educational quality. * * * Yet a system that relies heavily upon state laws to force testing requirements on individual parents threatens to burden their own religious freedom. * * *

Moreover, the testing plan provides for the School Committee to conduct remedial "follow-up" for children who test poorly; but how can the School Committee administer the individual child remedial "follow-up" without running afoul of the First Amendment's Establishment Clause, a Clause that may prohibit state-funded counseling, testing, and special remedial education, at least when provided on the private school's premises? * * *

Further, can the School Committee safely rely upon standardized testing to determine what *will* occur in the classroom? Teacher credentials, review of written curricula, and school visits offer the Committee a way of finding out what does actually occur in respect to teaching; tests, at best, reveal what *has* occurred. Can the Committee satisfactorily relate the results to past teaching? Does an average Academy-pupil score lower than an average public-school-pupil score reflect inadequate teaching, inappropriate subject matter, a different student body background, or other factors having nothing to do with the "thoroughness and efficiency" of this private school, compared with public schools? Do equivalent test results mean comparable teaching or worse (or better) teaching to different kinds of student bodies? How is the School Committee to interpret results that differ in different subject matter areas? Can it be certain that good results reflect good teaching, *i.e.,* the teaching of intellectual skills, discipline and complete subject matter, rather than simply teaching the answers to questions the teachers believe will appear on tests? And how can testing measure those important aspects of an adequate education that do not readily reduce themselves to standardized test questions, aspects such as practical vocational skills, the "basic tools by which individuals might lead economically productive lives," * * *; or the values of civic participation that are "necessary to the maintenance of a democratic political system," * * *

We ask these questions not to suggest they cannot be answered. Indeed, some states have answered them and use testing as a means for monitoring the quality of education in nonpublic schools, though such states may have different educational quality objectives than does Massachusetts, and we can find *no state* that uses a *voluntary* testing system, the "alternative" system at issue here. * * * Rather, we ask these questions in order to indicate the type of obstacles, and the significant additional administrative problems, that the need to answer them would create for, and impose upon, this School Committee: one that intends to use a written information/credentials/visit basis for determining approval, but one that is not familiar with, and is skeptical of, a system of standardized testing. * * * And, of course, those potential obstacles are potentially aggravated where a court imposes a *legal* requirement to use such a system, for then, presumably, a religious group much like the Academy, using only slightly different religious reasoning to find the written information/credentials/visit system less burdensome than the "standardized test" system, would have a similar legal right to force the School Committee to use the *former* system in its case. Legally obligated to employ the method preferred by each religious group, the towns of Massachusetts might find it difficult to implement a coherent system of furthering the state's compelling interest in educational quality; but even in the absence of multiple competing demands, the questions we have raised indicate the formidable administrative hardships that the effort to develop a standardized testing system would impose upon the School Committee.

Second, consider the comparative religious "burden." The Academy's religious objection is to the fact of secular sanction of its secular education program; it objects to any *recognition* of the fact that state authorities may approve or disapprove its program. The Academy has specifically stated that it does not object to supplying the School Committee with the written information that it seeks, adding that the Committee is "welcome to visit at anytime." Letter from Pastor Chase* * * It objects to those procedures only as they are part of an "approval" process. Thus, its religiously-based preference for the "standardized testing" *method* for obtaining approval must rest upon a belief that this alternative involves the Academy less, implicates the Academy less, in the secular *approval* granting process.

The standardized testing alternative, however, undeniably involves and implicates the Academy, at least to a degree, in the very approval process to which it objects. The Academy will have to obtain the School Committee's approval for the type of tests it gives, and the conditions in which it gives them. It will have to negotiate with the Committee about what conclusions to draw from test results, as well as the nature of "follow-up" or other remedial measures for individual students who do badly on the tests. It may have to negotiate about the changes it might make in its own programs should too many students do badly. And, since testing of each student will take place annually, this involvement potentially will take place every year. Hence the Academy will have to endure state "approval" of the education it provides to each student each year.

Moreover, the "testing" plan risks imposing still greater burdens upon individual parents or children, insofar as it foresees the School Committee enforcing testing or remedial or alternative schooling obligations upon individual families, potentially through use of the courts, and potentially under circumstances where the Academy itself retains the state's approval. That is, unless purely voluntary, it foresees the Committee applying coercive criminal and civil enforcement measures to the parents of children who test poorly. * * * Given the fact that the Academy has expressed a preference for standardized testing and the fact that the Academy is the best judge of its own religious needs and interests, we cannot say that standardized testing is *no* less burdensome than the School Committee's proposal, but neither can we see how it *substantially* alleviates the burden upon the free exercise of religion, nor how it could represent a *major* improvement.

Finally, the weight of legal precedent is strongly against the Academy's position. Some cases specifically state that the Constitution does not require a state to employ a "standardized testing" approach in evaluating the secular education provided at private religious schools. * * * Other cases uphold the constitutionality of "approval" requirements for private religious schools that seem at least as burdensome as those present here. * * * Still other cases simply uphold the state approval statute itself. * * * And some cases uphold regulations applied to religious "home school" education. * * *.

At the same time, this case differs significantly from the leading case in which the courts have upheld a "free exercise" claim against a state effort to control secular education provided by a religious institution. In that case, *Wisconsin v. Yoder,* the Supreme Court held that the First Amendment required a partial exemption (for students aged 14 to 16) from the state's compulsory school attendance law, where continued attendance for those two additional years threatened "the continued survival of Amish communities," * * * where compulsory attendance after the eighth grade "would gravely endanger" the exercise of basic Amish religious beliefs, * * * and where the Amish community's own system of education for children over age fourteen was close to "ideal," * * *. Here, unlike the case of the Amish, and as the district court noted, * * * the School Committee's proposed procedures do not threaten interference with religious practices, prayer, or religious teaching; and the record, while indicating a sincere religious scruple, does not suggest that enforcement of the proposed School Committee procedures would destroy a religious community's way of life. * * * Nor does the record support the view that the Academy, left on its own, would provide "ideal" or even adequate secular education. * * * All these factors make this case quite unlike *Yoder.* * * *

The only other significant case that we have found arguably relevant and helpful to the Academy is *State v. Whisner,* 47 Ohio St.2d 181, 351 N.E.2d 750 (1976), which invalidated state regulation of a private school where the regulations at issue provided that the board of education could control "all activities" of the private school, * * * the court found these regulations "so pervasive and all-encompassing" that they would "effectively eradicate the distinction between public and non-public education," * * * and it therefore held them unconstitutional. The case before us does not involve any so burdensome, all-encompassing, regulation.

In sum, given the "standardized testing" alternative's voluntary (and thus unsatisfactory) nature, the difficult administrative problems that it threatens to impose, its uncertain potential for achieving the state's legitimate "educational quality" objectives, and the limited extent to which it will alleviate the burden the "approval requirement" itself imposes upon the Academy's free exercise of religion, we conclude that, in the factual context of this case, the "standardized testing" alternative is not a "less restrictive alternative" for First Amendment "free exercise" purposes. The First Amendment, therefore, does not prevent the School Committee from using its preferred written information/teacher credential/school visit method. We add that we now consider these latter methods only as the School Committee has proposed them here, in outline form; we are not examining their actual implementation.

Our answer to the second question, together with our answer to the first question, means that the School Committee's proposals do not violate the First Amendment's Free Exercise Clause.

III.

Establishment of Religion

The "Establishment Clause" question in this case is whether the state "approval" requirement or the School Committee's proposed methods of gathering the information needed to decide the approval question will "foster an excessive government entanglement with religion." * * *

The relevant elements of the proposed state activities include: a) the act of approving or disapproving; b) obtaining written information about secular teaching programs from the Academy; c) examining the teaching credentials of those who teach secular subjects; d) one or more occasional visits to the school, and e) the making of suggestions to the Academy about how it might obtain approval if it initially fails to do so. The Academy does not argue that the first two of these elements pose entanglement concerns. The review of credentials appears to be of concern only as it indicates a need for the School Committee to visit the school, and insofar as it might lead the School Committee to insist that the Academy hire different teachers. The visits will consist of at least one initial visit where the visitors (who represent the School Committee) will read texts, examine teaching plans for secular courses, consider curricula, observe some classes, and discuss these matters with the school administration. The School Committee foresees additional visits only if the teaching credentials are inadequate. Since the Academy has no religious objection to hiring teachers with adequate credentials, and since such teachers seem available, * * * additional visits might not take place, though the School Committee may well insist that the Academy hire better-credentialed faculty. Any School Committee suggestions for improvement will concern only secular topics; neither observations nor suggestions will consider religious matters; indeed, Massachusetts law forbids the School Committee to rest its approval or disapproval upon "religious teaching." * * *

In determining whether this "involvement" amounts to impermissible "excessive entanglement," we assume that the Committee will implement its procedures reasonably. We assume at this point that any visits, or suggestions, will comply with the statute's proscription against basing approval decisions on "religious teaching." (We also note that the "standardized testing" alternative also means state involvement, for example, in remedial programs for individual students.) We have kept in mind that the law prohibits only "excessive" entanglements, not all state contacts with religious institutions. * * * We have then compared the School Committee's proposals with the factual circumstances at issue in those cases where the courts have found impermissible entanglements. And, having done so, we can find no controlling similarities; the degree of relevant state involvement here is significantly less.

The approval requirement and procedures do not involve state provisions of financial aid nor, on any reasonable interpretation of the School Committee's proposals, do they involve, to any significant degree, state funding of educational services. * * * Nor (interpreting the Committee's proposals reasonably) do the Committee's methods involve any "pervasive state presence in the sectarian schools," or "frequent contacts between [state and private school] teachers," * * * The state intends no "comprehensive, discriminating and continuing state surveillance" of the sort at issue in *Lemon,* 403 U.S. at 619, 91 S.Ct. at 2114. The School Committee's visitors will not "assess [ ] or compar[e] ... religious curricula," * * * they will not express religious views, or express either approval or disapproval of any religious matter, * * * nor, in any other way that we can see, will they seek to monitor the separation between religious and secular activities, * * *. Given the simple "checkup" purpose of the visit, and interpreting the proposal reasonably, we cannot now say that the state is embarking upon the kind of mission that seems likely to force it to "examine the content and curricula of religious programs," * * * or to evaluate the "religious content" of the Academy's teaching, * * *. Certainly the School Committee will not exercise the overarching control of the school's possibly religiously-motivated choices that was struck down in *NLRB v. Catholic Bishop of Chicago,* 440 U.S. 490, 502–03, 99 S.Ct. 1313, 1319–20, 59 L.Ed.2d 533 (1979) (rejecting NLRB jurisdiction over labor disputes at religious high schools, because NLRB would have to resolve unfair labor practice claims in which the school asserted that its decisions were motivated by religious creeds, decide what religious educational activities were mandatory subjects of collective bargaining, and engage in an intrusive "process of inquiry" into the religious bases of church-employee disputes), and *Surinach v. Pesquera de Busquets,* 604 F.2d 73, 79 (1st Cir.1979) (rejecting government's continuing control over detailed expenditures of Catholic schools, because such control would "permit [the government] to intrude upon decisions of religious authorities as to how much money should be expended and how funds should be allotted to serve the religious goals of the students").

We can imagine how the School Committee might, in practice, enforce the approval requirement and implement its proposed procedures (particularly the observation of classes) in ways that would unreasonably and unnecessarily entangle it with the religious aspect of teaching. But one might find similar theoretical possibilities lurking within virtually any state approval procedure. Here, the proposal to observe classes is primarily a proposal to visit the school, to see if the school teaches what it says it teaches, and to observe children being taught such secular subjects as mathematics, geography, spelling, reading and writing. Additional visits will occur as an accommodation to the Academy only if the school fails to meet standards for its teachers' credentials, and then simply to see whether teachers, say, lacking university degrees, are able adequately to teach secular subjects. * * * We are aware of no case that goes so far as to find an Establishment Clause violation in such circumstances. * * * Indeed, since the School Committee now has simply proposed, in outline form, the possibility of a future "checkup" visit, to say that the Establishment Clause forbids the proposal would amount to saying that the Clause forbids *any* classroom observation or "checkup," a holding that could significantly inhibit the state's efforts to evaluate the secular education provided by religious schools (or home schools), evaluations that (as we observed in Part II above) are of critical importance to the state. * * *

Since the proposal for one visit involving observing classes appears to be reasonably necessary to the state's furtherance of its compelling interest in assuring the quality of secular education, since it involves no monitoring of the uses to which secular aid will be put, * * * and since there is now no reason to believe that additional visits will improperly entangle the School Committee in religious matters, we have no reason now to believe that the School Committee will implement its proposals in an unconstitutional way. We conclude that the School Committee's procedures for gathering information for its "approval" decision, as currently proposed, do not pose any "reasonable likelihood" of excessive entanglements, *Surinach,* 604 F.2d at 76 (citation omitted), resembling the kinds of entanglements found unconstitutional in prior cases. We therefore cannot find a violation of the First Amendment's Establishment Clause.

For these reasons the judgment of the district court is

Reversed.

Question

To what extent can a state provide subsidies to private schools and/or parents of children who attend private schools? What if the private school is a religious school?

ZELMAN v. SIMMONS–HARRIS
United States Supreme Court, 2002
536 U.S. 639, 122 S.Ct. 2460, 153 L.Ed.2d 604

Chief Justice REHNQUIST delivered the opinion of the Court.

The State of Ohio has established a pilot program designed to provide educational choices to families with children who reside in the Cleveland City School District. The question presented is whether this program offends the Establishment Clause of the United States Constitution. We hold that it does not.

There are more than 75,000 children enrolled in the Cleveland City School District. The majority of these children are from low-income and minority families. Few of these families enjoy the means to send their children to any school other than an inner-city public school. For more than a generation, however, Cleveland's public schools have been among the worst performing public schools in the Nation. In 1995, a Federal District Court declared a "crisis of magnitude" and placed the entire Cleveland school district under state control. See *Reed v. Rhodes,* No. 1:73 CV 1300 (ND Ohio, Mar. 3, 1995). Shortly thereafter, the state auditor found that Cleveland's public schools were in the midst of a "crisis that is perhaps unprecedented in the history of American education." Cleveland City School District Performance Audit 2–1 (Mar. 1996). The district had failed to meet any of the 18 state standards for minimal acceptable performance. Only 1 in 10 ninth graders could pass a basic proficiency examination, and students at all levels performed at a dismal rate compared with students in other Ohio public schools. More than two-thirds of high school students either dropped or failed out before graduation. Of those students who managed to reach their senior year, one of every four still failed to graduate. Of those students who did graduate, few could read, write, or compute at levels comparable to their counterparts in other cities.

It is against this backdrop that Ohio enacted, among other initiatives, its Pilot Project Scholarship Program, Ohio Rev.Code Ann. §§ 3313.974–3313.979 (Anderson 1999 and Supp.2000) (program). The program provides financial assistance to families in any Ohio school district that is or has been "under federal court order requiring supervision and operational management of the district by the state superintendent." § 3313.975(A). Cleveland is the only Ohio school district to fall within that category.

The program provides two basic kinds of assistance to parents of children in a covered district. First, the program provides tuition aid for students in kindergarten through third grade, expanding each year through eighth grade, to attend a participating public or private school of their parent's choosing. §§ 3313.975(B) and (C)(1). Second, the program provides tutorial aid for students who choose to remain enrolled in public school. § 3313.975(A).

The tuition aid portion of the program is designed to provide educational choices to parents who reside in a covered district. Any private school, whether religious or nonreligious, may participate in the program and accept program students so long as the school is located within the boundaries of a covered district and meets statewide educational standards. § 313.976(A)(3). Participating private schools must agree not to discriminate on the basis of race, religion, or ethnic background, or to "advocate or foster unlawful behavior or teach hatred of any person or group on the basis of race, ethnicity, national origin, or religion." § 3313.976(A)(6). Any public school located in a school district adjacent to the covered district may also participate in the program. § 3313.976(C). Adjacent public schools are eligible to receive a $2,250 tuition grant for each program student accepted in addition to the full amount of per-pupil state funding attributable to each additional student. §§ 3313.976(C), 3317.03(I)(1). * * * All participating schools, whether public or private, are required to accept students in accordance with rules and procedures established by the state superintendent. §§ 3313.977(A)(1)(a)-(c).

Tuition aid is distributed to parents according to financial need. Families with incomes below 200% of the poverty line are given priority and are eligible to receive 90% of private school tuition up to $2,250. §§ 3313.978(A) and (C)(1). For these lowest-income families, participating private schools may not charge a parental co-payment greater than $250. § 3313.976(A)(8). For all other families, the program pays 75% of tuition costs, up to $1,875, with no co-payment cap. §§ 3313.976(A)(8), 3313.978(A). These families receive tuition aid only if the number of available scholarships exceeds the number of low-income children who choose to participate. * * * Where tuition aid is spent depends solely upon where parents who receive tuition aid choose to enroll their child. If parents choose a private school, checks are made payable to the parents who then endorse the checks over to the chosen school. § 3313.979.

The tutorial aid portion of the program provides tutorial assistance through grants to any student in a covered district who chooses to remain in public school. Parents arrange for registered tutors to provide assistance to their children and then submit bills for those services to the State for payment. §§ 3313.976(D), 3313.979(C). Students from low-income families receive 90% of the amount charged for such assistance up to $360. All other students receive 75% of that amount. § 3313.978(B). The number of tutorial assistance grants offered to students in a covered district must equal the number of tuition aid scholarships provided to students enrolled at participating private or adjacent public schools. § 3313.975(A).

The program has been in operation within the Cleveland City School District since the 1996–1997 school year. In the 1999–2000 school year, 56 private schools participated in the program, 46 (or 82%) of which had a religious affiliation. None of the public schools in districts adjacent to Cleveland have elected to participate. More than 3,700 students participated in the scholarship program, most of whom (96%) enrolled in religiously affiliated schools. Sixty percent of these students were from families at or below the poverty line. In the 1998–1999 school year, approximately 1,400 Cleveland public school students received tutorial aid. This number was expected to double during the 1999–2000 school year.

The program is part of a broader undertaking by the State to enhance the educational options of Cleveland's schoolchildren in response to the 1995 takeover. That undertaking includes programs governing community and magnet schools. Community schools are funded under state law but are run by their own school boards, not by local school districts. §§ 3314.01(B), 3314.04. These schools enjoy academic independence to hire their own teachers and to determine their own curriculum. They can have no religious affiliation and are required to accept students by lottery. During the 1999–2000 school year, there were 10 start-up community schools in the Cleveland City School District with more than 1,900 students enrolled. For each child enrolled in a community school, the school receives state funding of $4,518, twice the funding a participating program school may receive.

Magnet schools are public schools operated by a local school board that emphasize a particular subject area, teaching method, or service to students. For each student enrolled in a magnet school, the school district receives $7,746, including state funding of $4,167, the same amount received per student enrolled at a traditional public school. As of 1999, parents in Cleveland were able to choose from among 23 magnet schools, which together enrolled more than 13,000 students in kindergarten through eighth grade. These schools provide specialized teaching methods, such as Montessori, or a particularized curriculum focus, such as foreign language, computers, or the arts.

In 1996, respondents, a group of Ohio taxpayers, challenged the Ohio program in state court on state and federal grounds. The Ohio Supreme Court rejected respondents' federal claims, but held that the enactment of the program violated certain procedural requirements of the Ohio Constitution. * * * The state legislature immediately cured this defect, leaving the basic provisions discussed above intact.

In July 1999, respondents filed this action in United States District Court, seeking to enjoin the reenacted program on the ground that it violated the Establishment Clause of the United States Constitution. In August 1999, the District Court issued a preliminary injunction barring further implementation of the program, 54 F.Supp.2d 725 (N.D.Ohio), which we stayed pending review by the Court of Appeals, 528 U.S. 983, 120 S.Ct. 443, 145 L.Ed.2d 346 (1999). In December 1999, the District Court granted summary judgment for respondents. 72 F.Supp.2d 834. In December 2000, a divided panel of the Court of Appeals affirmed the judgment of the District Court, finding that the program had the "primary effect" of advancing religion in violation of the Establishment Clause. * * * The Court of Appeals stayed its mandate pending disposition in this Court. App. to Pet. for Cert. in No. 01–1779, p. 151. We granted certiorari, * * * and now reverse the Court of Appeals.

The Establishment Clause of the First Amendment, applied to the States through the Fourteenth Amendment, prevents a State from enacting laws that have the "purpose" or "effect" of advancing or inhibiting religion. *Agostini v. Felton,* 521 U.S. 203, 222–223, 117 S.Ct. 1997, 138 L.Ed.2d 391 (1997) ("[W]e continue to ask whether the government acted with the purpose of advancing or inhibiting religion [and] whether the aid has the 'effect' of advancing or inhibiting religion" (citations omitted)). There is no dispute that the program challenged here was enacted for the valid secular purpose of providing educational assistance to poor children in a demonstrably failing public school system. Thus, the question presented is whether the Ohio program nonetheless has the forbidden "effect" of advancing or inhibiting religion.

To answer that question, our decisions have drawn a consistent distinction between government programs that provide aid directly to religious schools, * * * and programs of true private choice, in which government aid reaches religious schools only as a result of the genuine and independent choices of private individuals, *Mueller v. Allen,* 463 U.S. 388, 103 S.Ct. 3062, 77 L.Ed.2d 721 (1983); *Witters v. Washington Dept. of Servs. for Blind,* 474 U.S. 481, 106 S.Ct. 748, 88 L.Ed.2d 846 (1986); *Zobrest v. Catalina Foothills School Dist.,* 509 U.S. 1, 113 S.Ct. 2462, 125 L.Ed.2d 1 (1993). While our jurisprudence with respect to the constitutionality of direct aid programs has "changed significantly" over the past two decades, * * * our jurisprudence with respect to true private choice programs has remained consistent and unbroken. Three times we have confronted Establishment Clause challenges to neutral government programs that provide aid directly to a broad class of individuals, who, in turn, direct the aid to religious schools or institutions of their own choosing. Three times we have rejected such challenges.

In *Mueller,* we rejected an Establishment Clause challenge to a Minnesota program authorizing tax deductions for various educational expenses, including private school tuition costs, even though the great majority of the program's beneficiaries (96%) were parents of children in religious schools. We began by focusing on the class of beneficiaries, finding that because the class included *"all* parents," including parents with "children [who] attend nonsectarian private schools or sectarian private schools," * * * the program was "not readily subject to challenge under the Establishment Clause," * * * Then, viewing the program as a whole, we emphasized the principle of private choice, noting that public funds were made available to religious schools "only as a result of numerous, private choices of individual parents of school-age children." * * * This, we said, ensured that " 'no imprimatur of state approval' can be deemed to have been conferred on any particular religion, or on religion generally."* * * We thus found it irrelevant to the constitutional inquiry that the vast majority of beneficiaries were parents of children in religious schools, saying:

"We would be loath to adopt a rule grounding the constitutionality of a facially neutral law on annual reports reciting the extent to which various classes of private citizens claimed benefits under the law." * * *

That the program was one of true private choice, with no evidence that the State deliberately skewed incentives toward religious schools, was sufficient for the program to survive scrutiny under the Establishment Clause.

In *Witters,* we used identical reasoning to reject an Establishment Clause challenge to a vocational scholarship program that provided tuition aid to a student studying at a religious institution to become a pastor. Looking at the program as a whole, we observed that "[a]ny aid . . . that ultimately flows to religious institutions does so only as a result of the genuinely independent and private choices of aid recipients." * * * We further remarked that, as in *Mueller,* "[the] program is made available generally without regard to the sectarian-nonsectarian, or public-nonpublic nature of the institution benefited." * * * In light of these factors, we held that the program was not inconsistent with the Establishment Clause. * * *

Five Members of the Court, in separate opinions, emphasized the general rule from *Mueller* that the amount of government aid channeled to religious institutions by individual aid recipients was not relevant to the constitutional inquiry. * * * Our holding thus rested not on whether few or many recipients chose to expend government aid at a religious school but, rather, on whether recipients generally were empowered to direct the aid to schools or institutions of their own choosing.

Finally, in *Zobrest,* we applied *Mueller* and *Witters* to reject an Establishment Clause challenge to a federal program that permitted sign-language interpreters to assist deaf children enrolled in religious schools. Reviewing our earlier decisions, we stated that "government programs that neutrally provide benefits to a broad class of citizens defined without reference to religion are not readily subject to an Establishment Clause challenge." * * * Looking once again to the challenged program as a whole, we observed that the program "distributes benefits neutrally to any child qualifying as 'disabled.'" * * * Its "primary beneficiaries," we said, were "disabled children, not sectarian schools." * * *

We further observed that "[b]y according parents freedom to select a school of their choice, the statute ensures that a government-paid interpreter will be present in a sectarian school only as a result of the private decision of individual parents." * * * Our focus again was on neutrality and the principle of private choice, not on the number of program beneficiaries attending religious schools. * * * Because the program ensured that parents were the ones to select a religious school as the best learning environment for their handicapped child, the circuit between government and religion was broken, and the Establishment Clause was not implicated.

Mueller, Witters, and *Zobrest* thus make clear that where a government aid program is neutral with respect to religion, and provides assistance directly to a broad class of citizens who, in turn, direct government aid to religious schools wholly as a result of their own genuine and independent private choice, the program is not readily subject to challenge under the Establishment Clause. A program that shares these features permits government aid to reach religious institutions only by way of the deliberate choices of numerous individual recipients. The incidental advancement of a religious mission, or the perceived endorsement of a religious message, is reasonably attributable to the individual recipient, not to the government, whose role ends with the disbursement of benefits. * * * It is precisely for these reasons that we have never found a program of true private choice to offend the Establishment Clause.

We believe that the program challenged here is a program of true private choice, consistent with *Mueller, Witters,* and *Zobrest,* and thus constitutional. As was true in those cases, the Ohio program is neutral in all respects toward religion. It is part of a general and multifaceted undertaking by the State of Ohio to provide educational opportunities to the children of a failed school district. It confers educational assistance directly to a broad class of individuals defined without reference to religion, *i.e.,* any parent of a school-age child who resides in the Cleveland City School District. The program permits the participation of *all* schools within the district, religious or nonreligious. Adjacent public schools also may participate and have a financial incentive to do so. Program benefits are available to participating families on neutral terms, with no reference to religion. The only preference stated anywhere in the program is a preference for low-income families, who receive greater assistance and are given priority for admission at participating schools.

There are no "financial incentive[s]" that "ske[w]" the program toward religious schools. * * * Such incentives "[are] not present ... where the aid is allocated on the basis of neutral, secular criteria that neither favor nor disfavor religion, and is made available to both religious and secular beneficiaries on a nondiscriminatory basis." * * * The program here in fact creates financial *dis*incentives for religious schools, with private schools receiving only half the government assistance given to community schools and one-third the assistance given to magnet schools. Adjacent public schools, should any choose to accept program students, are also eligible to receive two to three times the state funding of a private religious school. Families too have a financial disincentive to choose a private religious school over other schools. Parents that choose to participate in the scholarship program and then to enroll their children in a private school (religious or nonreligious) must copay a portion of the school's tuition. Families that choose a community school, magnet school, or traditional public school pay nothing. Although such features of the program are not necessary to its constitutionality, they clearly dispel the claim that the program "creates ... financial incentive[s] for parents to choose a sectarian school." * * *

Respondents suggest that even without a financial incentive for parents to choose a religious school, the program creates a "public perception that the State is endorsing religious practices and beliefs." * * * But we have repeatedly recognized that no reasonable observer would think a neutral program of private choice, where state aid reaches religious schools solely as a result of the numerous independent decisions of private individuals, carries with it the *imprimatur* of government endorsement. * * * The argument is particularly misplaced here since "the reasonable observer in the endorsement inquiry must be deemed aware" of the "history and context" underlying a challenged program. * * * Any objective observer familiar with the full history and context of the Ohio program would reasonably view it as one aspect of a broader undertaking to assist poor children in failed schools, not as an endorsement of religious schooling in general.

There also is no evidence that the program fails to provide genuine opportunities for Cleveland parents to select secular educational options for their school-age children. Cleveland schoolchildren enjoy a range of educational choices: They may remain in public school as before, remain in public school with publicly funded tutoring aid, obtain a scholarship and choose a religious school, obtain a scholarship and choose a nonreligious private school, enroll in a community school, or enroll in a magnet school. That 46 of the 56 private schools now participating in the program are religious schools does not condemn it as a violation of the Establishment Clause. The Establishment Clause question is whether Ohio is coercing parents into sending their children to religious schools, and that question must be answered by evaluating *all* options Ohio provides Cleveland schoolchildren, only one of which is to obtain a program scholarship and then choose a religious school.

Justice SOUTER speculates that because more private religious schools currently participate in the program, the program itself must somehow discourage the participation of private nonreligious schools. * * * But Cleveland's preponderance of religiously affiliated private schools certainly did not arise as a result of the program; it is a phenomenon common to many American cities. See U.S. Dept. of Ed., National Center for Education Statistics, Private School Universe Survey: 1999–2000, pp. 2–4 (NCES 2001–330, 2001) (hereinafter Private School Universe Survey)* * *. Indeed, by all accounts the program has captured a remarkable cross-section of private schools, religious and nonreligious. It is true that 82% of Cleveland's participating private schools are religious schools, but it is also true that 81% of private schools in Ohio are religious schools. * * * To attribute constitutional significance to this figure, moreover, would lead to the absurd result that a neutral school-choice program might be permissible in some parts of Ohio, such as Columbus, where a lower percentage of private schools are religious schools, * * * but not in inner-city Cleveland, where Ohio has deemed such programs most sorely needed, but where the preponderance of religious schools happens to be greater. * * * Likewise, an identical private choice program might be constitutional in some States, such as

Maine or Utah, where less than 45% of private schools are religious schools, but not in other States, such as Nebraska or Kansas, where over 90% of private schools are religious schools. *Id.,* at 15–16 (citing Private School Universe Survey).

Respondents and Justice SOUTER claim that even if we do not focus on the number of participating schools that are religious schools, we should attach constitutional significance to the fact that 96% of scholarship recipients have enrolled in religious schools. They claim that this alone proves parents lack genuine choice, even if no parent has ever said so. We need not consider this argument in detail, since it was flatly rejected in *Mueller,* where we found it irrelevant that 96% of parents taking deductions for tuition expenses paid tuition at religious schools. Indeed, we have recently found it irrelevant even to the constitutionality of a direct aid program that a vast majority of program benefits went to religious schools. * * *

This point is aptly illustrated here. The 96% figure upon which respondents and Justice SOUTER rely discounts entirely (1) the more than 1,900 Cleveland children enrolled in alternative community schools, (2) the more than 13,000 children enrolled in alternative magnet schools, and (3) the more than 1,400 children enrolled in traditional public schools with tutorial assistance. * * * Including some or all of these children in the denominator of children enrolled in nontraditional schools during the 1999–2000 school year drops the percentage enrolled in religious schools from 96% to under 20%. * * * The 96% figure also represents but a snapshot of one particular school year. In the 1997–1998 school year, by contrast, only 78% of scholarship recipients attended religious schools. * * * The difference was attributable to two private nonreligious schools that had accepted 15% of all scholarship students electing instead to register as community schools, in light of larger per-pupil funding for community schools and the uncertain future of the scholarship program generated by this litigation. * * * Many of the students enrolled in these schools as scholarship students remained enrolled as community school students,* * * thus demonstrating the arbitrariness of counting one type of school but not the other to assess primary effect, * * * In spite of repeated questioning from the Court at oral argument, respondents offered no convincing justification for their approach, which relies entirely on such arbitrary classifications. * * *

Respondents finally claim that we should look to *Committee for Public Ed. & Religious Liberty v. Nyquist,* 413 U.S. 756, 93 S.Ct. 2955, 37 L.Ed.2d 948 (1973), to decide these cases. We disagree for two reasons. First, the program in *Nyquist* was quite different from the program challenged here. *Nyquist* involved a New York program that gave a package of benefits exclusively to private schools and the parents of private school enrollees. Although the program was enacted for ostensibly secular purposes, * * * we found that its "function" was "*unmistakably* to provide desired financial support for nonpublic, sectarian institutions," * * * Its genesis, we said, was that private religious schools faced "increasingly grave fiscal problems." * * * The program thus provided direct money grants to religious schools. * * * It provided tax benefits "unrelated to the amount of money actually expended by any parent on tuition," ensuring a windfall to parents of children in religious schools. * * * It similarly provided tuition reimbursements designed explicitly to "offe[r] ... an incentive to parents to send their children to sectarian schools." * * * Indeed, the program flatly prohibited the participation of any public school, or parent of any public school enrollee. * * * Ohio's program shares none of these features.

Second, were there any doubt that the program challenged in *Nyquist* is far removed from the program challenged here, we expressly reserved judgment with respect to "a case involving some form of public assistance (*e.g.*, scholarships) made available generally without regard to the sectarian-nonsectarian, or public-nonpublic nature of the institution benefited." * * * That, of course, is the very question now before us, and it has since been answered, first in *Mueller,* * * * ("[A] program ... that neutrally provides state assistance to a broad spectrum of citizens is not readily subject to challenge under the Establishment Clause" * * * To the extent the scope of *Nyquist* has remained an open question in light of these later decisions, we now hold that *Nyquist* does not govern neutral educational assistance programs that, like the program here, offer aid directly to a broad class of individual recipients defined without regard to religion. * * *

In sum, the Ohio program is entirely neutral with respect to religion. It provides benefits directly to a wide spectrum of individuals, defined only by financial need and residence in a particular school district. It permits such individuals to exercise genuine choice among options public and private, secular and religious. The program is therefore a program of true private choice. In keeping with an unbroken line of decisions rejecting challenges to similar programs, we hold that the program does not offend the Establishment Clause.

The judgment of the Court of Appeals is reversed.

* * *

Notes

1. In *Locke, Governor of Washington v. Davey*, 540 U.S. 712, 124 S.Ct. 1307, 158 L.Ed.2d 1 (2004), Washington State established a Promise Scholarship Program to assist academically gifted students with postsecondary education expenses. In accordance with the State Constitution, students could not use the scholarship to pursue a devotional theology degree. Davey was awarded a Promise Scholarship and chose to attend a private, church-affiliated institution that was eligible under the program. However, when Davey chose a major in pastoral ministries, the state informed him he could not use his scholarship to pursue that degree. He filed suit in federal district court contending that the denial of his scholarship violated the First Amendment Free Exercise and Establishment Clauses. The Ninth Circuit reversed the District Court's rejection of his claim. However, the Supreme Court ruled that Washington's exclusion of the pursuit of a devotional theology

degree from its otherwise-inclusive scholarship aid program does not violate the Free Exercise Clause. The Supreme Court decided that the state's interest in not funding the pursuit of devotional degrees was substantial and the exclusion of such funding placed a relatively minor burden on Promise Scholars.

In Eulitt v. Maine, 386 F.3d 344 (1st Cir. 2004), the court ruled that parents did not have standing to challenge a Maine statute, which provided that only nonsectarian schools were eligible for receipt of public funds for tuition purposes. The court did state that the statute did not violate the Free Exercise Clause.

2. The Supreme Court in *Zelman*, text, *supra*, ruled that a state does not violate the "Establishment Clause" by establishing a voucher program that includes religious schools in the program. It ruled in *Locke v. Davey*, *supra*, that a state does not violate the "Free Exercise Clause" by excluding religious organizations from a scholarship program.

II. TAX EXEMPT STATUS OF PRIVATE SCHOOLS

A private school is tax exempt under § 501(c)(3) and qualifies as a public charity under § 509(a)(1) and 170(b)(2)(A)(ii) if it presents formal instruction and normally maintains a regular faculty and curriculum with a regularly enrolled body of students in attendance at the place where it carries on its educational activities. Although there is no requirement in the code or the regulations that private schools maintain a nondiscriminatory admission policy, since 1970, the Internal Revenue Service has denied tax-exempt status to private schools that have racially discriminatory admission policies.

BOB JONES UNIVERSITY v. UNITED STATES
United States Supreme Court, 1983
461 U.S. 574, 103 S.Ct. 2017, 76 L.Ed.2d 157

Chief Justice BURGER delivered the opinion of the Court.

We granted certiorari to decide whether petitioners, nonprofit private schools that prescribe and enforce racially discriminatory admissions standards on the basis of religious doctrine, qualify as tax-exempt organizations under § 501(c)(3) of the Internal Revenue Code of 1954.

I

A

Until 1970, the Internal Revenue Service granted tax-exempt status to private schools, without regard to their racial admissions policies, under § 501(c)(3) of the Internal Revenue Code, 26 U.S.C. § 501(c)(3), and granted charitable deductions for contributions to such schools under § 170 of the Code, 26 U.S.C. § 170.

On January 12, 1970, a three-judge District Court for the District of Columbia issued a preliminary injunction prohibiting the IRS from according tax-exempt status to private schools in Mississippi that discriminated as to admissions on the basis of race. *Green v. Kennedy,* 309 F.Supp. 1127 (D.D.C.), *app. dismissed sub nom. Cannon v. Green,* 398 U.S. 956, 90 S.Ct. 2169, 26 L.Ed.2d 539 (1970). Thereafter, in July 1970, the IRS concluded that it could "no longer legally justify allowing tax-exempt status [under § 501(c)(3)] to private schools which practice racial discrimination." IRS News Release (7/10/70), * * *. At the same time, the IRS announced that it could not "treat gifts to such schools as charitable deductions for income tax purposes [under § 170]." * * * By letter dated November 30, 1970, the IRS formally notified private schools, including those involved in this case, of this change in policy, "applicable to all private schools in the United States at all levels of education." * * *

On June 30, 1971, the three-judge District Court issued its opinion on the merits of the Mississippi challenge. *Green v. Connally,* 330 F.Supp. 1150 (D.D.C.), *aff'd sub nom. Coit v. Green,* 404 U.S. 997, 92 S.Ct. 564, 30 L.Ed.2d 550 (1971) (*per curiam*). That court approved the IRS' amended construction of the Tax Code. The court also held that racially discriminatory private schools were not entitled to exemption under § 501(c)(3) and that donors were not entitled to deductions for contributions to such schools under § 170. The court permanently enjoined the Commissioner of Internal Revenue from approving tax-exempt status for any school in Mississippi that did not publicly maintain a policy of nondiscrimination.

The revised policy on discrimination was formalized in Revenue Ruling 71–447, 1971–2 Cum.Bull. 230:

> "Both the courts and the Internal Revenue Service have long recognized that the statutory requirement of being 'organized and operated exclusively for religious, charitable, . . . or educational purposes' was intended to express the basic common law concept [of 'charity'].... All charitable trusts, educational or otherwise, are subject to the requirement that the purpose of the trust may not be illegal or contrary to public policy." * * *

Based on the "national policy to discourage racial discrimination in education," the IRS ruled that "a private school not having a racially nondiscriminatory policy as to students is not 'charitable' within the common law concepts reflected in sections 170 and 501(c)(3) of the Code." * * *

B

Bob Jones University is a nonprofit corporation located in Greenville, South Carolina. Its purpose is "to conduct an institution of learning . . . , giving special emphasis to the Christian religion and the ethics revealed in the Holy Scriptures." * * * The corporation operates a school with an enrollment of approximately 5,000 students, from kindergarten through college and graduate school. Bob Jones University is not affiliated with any religious denomination, but is dedicated to the teaching and propagation of its fundamentalist Christian religious beliefs. It is both a religious and educational institution. Its teachers are required to be devout Christians, and all courses at the University are taught according to the Bible. Entering students are screened as to their religious beliefs, and their public and private conduct is strictly regulated by standards promulgated by University authorities.

The sponsors of the University genuinely believe that the Bible forbids interracial dating and marriage. To effectuate these views, Negroes were completely excluded until 1971. From 1971 to May 1975, the University accepted no applications from unmarried Negroes, but did accept applications from Negroes married within their race.

Following the decision of the United States Court of Appeals for the Fourth Circuit in *McCrary v. Runyon*, 515 F.2d 1082 (C.A.4 1975), *aff'd* 427 U.S. 160, 96 S.Ct. 2586, 49 L.Ed.2d 415 (1976), prohibiting racial exclusion from private schools, the University revised its policy. Since May 29, 1975, the University has permitted unmarried Negroes to enroll; but a disciplinary rule prohibits interracial dating and marriage. That rule reads:

There is to be no interracial dating

1. Students who are partners in an interracial marriage will be expelled.

2. Students who are members of or affiliated with any group or organization which holds as one of its goals or advocates interracial marriage will be expelled.

3. Students who date outside their own race will be expelled.

4. Students who espouse, promote, or encourage others to violate the University's dating rules and regulations will be expelled. * * *

The University continues to deny admission to applicants engaged in an interracial marriage or known to advocate interracial marriage or dating. * * *

Until 1970, the IRS extended tax-exempt status to Bob Jones University under § 501(c)(3). By the letter of November 30, 1970, that followed the injunction issued in *Green v. Kennedy, supra,* the IRS formally notified the University of the change in IRS policy, and announced its intention to challenge the tax-exempt status of private schools practicing racial discrimination in their admissions policies.

After failing to obtain an assurance of tax exemption through administrative means, the University instituted an action in 1971 seeking to enjoin the IRS from revoking the school's tax-exempt status. That suit culminated in *Bob Jones University v. Simon*, 416 U.S. 725, 94 S.Ct. 2038, 40 L.Ed.2d 496 (1974), in which this Court held that the Anti–Injunction Act of the Internal Revenue Code, 26 U.S.C. § 7421(a), prohibited the University from obtaining judicial review by way of injunctive action before the assessment or collection of any tax.

Thereafter, on April 16, 1975, the IRS notified the University of the proposed revocation of its tax-exempt status. On January 19, 1976, the IRS officially revoked the University's tax-exempt status, effective as of December 1, 1970, the day after the University was formally notified of the change in IRS policy. The University subsequently filed returns under the Federal Unemployment Tax Act for the period from December 1, 1970, to December 31, 1975, and paid a tax totalling $21.00 on one employee for the calendar year of 1975. After its request for a refund was denied, the University instituted the present action, seeking to recover the $21.00 it had paid to the IRS. The Government counterclaimed for unpaid federal unemployment taxes for the taxable years 1971 through 1975, in the amount of $489,675.59, plus interest.

The United States District Court for the District of South Carolina held that revocation of the University's tax-exempt status exceeded the delegated powers of the IRS, was improper under the IRS rulings and procedures, and violated the University's rights under the Religion Clauses of the First Amendment. 468 F.Supp. 890, 907 (D.S.C.1978). The court accordingly ordered the IRS to pay the University the $21.00 refund it claimed and rejected the IRS counterclaim.

The Court of Appeals for the Fourth Circuit, in a divided opinion, reversed. 639 F.2d 147 (C.A.4 1980). Citing *Green v. Connally, supra,* with approval, the Court of Appeals concluded that § 501(c)(3) must be read against the background of charitable trust law. To be eligible for an exemption under that section, an institution must be "charitable" in the common law sense, and therefore must not be contrary to public policy. In the court's view, Bob Jones University did not meet this requirement, since its "racial policies violated the clearly defined public policy, rooted in our Constitution, condemning racial discrimination and, more specifically, the government policy against subsidizing racial discrimination in education, public or private." *Id.,* at 151. The court held that the IRS acted within its statutory authority in revoking the University's tax-exempt status. Finally, the Court of Appeals rejected petitioner's arguments that the revocation of the tax exemption violated the Free Exercise and Establishment Clauses of the First Amendment. The case was remanded to the District Court with instructions to dismiss the University's claim for a refund and to reinstate the Government's counterclaim.

C

No. 81–1, Goldsboro Christian Schools, Inc. v. United States

Goldsboro Christian Schools is a nonprofit corporation located in Goldsboro, North Carolina. Like Bob Jones University, it was established "to conduct an institution of learning . . . , giving special emphasis to the Christian religion and the ethics revealed in the Holy scriptures." * * * The school offers classes from kindergarten through high school, and since at least 1969 has satisfied the State of North Carolina's requirements for secular education in private schools. The school requires its high school students to take Bible-related courses, and begins each class with prayer.

Since its incorporation in 1963, Goldsboro Christian Schools has maintained a racially discriminatory admissions policy based upon its interpretation of the Bible. Goldsboro has for the most part accepted only Caucasians. On occasion, however, the school has accepted children from racially mixed marriages in which one of the parents is Caucasian.
* * *

Goldsboro never received a determination by the IRS that it was an organization entitled to tax exemption under § 501(c)(3). Upon audit of Goldsboro's records for the years 1969 through 1972, the IRS determined that Goldsboro was not an organization described in § 501(c)(3), and therefore was required to pay taxes under the Federal Insurance Contribution Act and the Federal Unemployment Tax Act.

Goldsboro paid the IRS $3,459.93 in withholding, social security, and unemployment taxes with respect to one employee for the years 1969 through 1972. Thereafter, Goldsboro filed a suit seeking refund of that payment, claiming that the school had been improperly denied § 501(c)(3) exempt status. The IRS counterclaimed for $160,073.96 in unpaid social security and unemployment taxes for the years 1969 through 1972, including interest and penalties.

The District Court for the Eastern District of North Carolina decided the action on cross-motions for summary judgment. * * * In addressing the motions for summary judgment, the court assumed that Goldsboro's racially discriminatory admissions policy was based upon a sincerely held religious belief. The court nevertheless rejected Goldsboro's claim to tax-exempt status under § 501(c)(3), finding that "private schools maintaining racially discriminatory admissions policies violate clearly declared federal policy and, therefore, must be denied the federal tax benefits flowing from qualification under Section 501(c)(3)." * * * The court also rejected Goldsboro's arguments that denial of tax-exempt status violated the Free Exercise and Establishment Clauses of the First Amendment. Accordingly, the court entered summary judgment for the Government on its counterclaim.

The Court of Appeals for the Fourth Circuit affirmed, 644 F.2d 879 (CA4 1981) (*per curiam*). That court found an "identity for present purposes" between the *Goldsboro* case and the *Bob Jones University* case, which had been decided shortly before by another panel of that court, and affirmed for the reasons set forth in *Bob Jones University*.

We granted certiorari in both cases, * * *, and we affirm in each.

II

A

In Revenue Ruling 71–447, the IRS formalized the policy first announced in 1970, that § 170 and § 501(c)(3) embrace the common law "charity" concept. Under that view, to qualify for a tax exemption pursuant to § 501(c)(3), an institution must show, first, that it falls within one of the eight categories expressly set forth in that section, and second, that its activity is not contrary to settled public policy.

Section 501(c)(3) provides that "[c]orporations ... organized and operated exclusively for religious, charitable ... or educational purposes" are entitled to tax exemption. Petitioners argue that the plain language of the statute guarantees them tax-exempt status. They emphasize the absence of any language in the statute expressly requiring all exempt organizations to be "charitable" in the common law sense, and they contend that the disjunctive "or" separating the categories in § 501(c)(3) precludes such a reading. Instead, they argue that if an institution falls within one or more of the specified categories it is automatically entitled to exemption, without regard to whether it also qualifies as "charitable." The Court of Appeals rejected that contention and concluded that petitioners' interpretation of the statute "tears section 501(c)(3) from its roots." * * *

It is a well-established canon of statutory construction that a court should go beyond the literal language of a statute if reliance on that language would defeat the plain purpose of the statute:

> "The general words used in the clause ... , taken by themselves, and literally construed, without regard to the object in view, would seem to sanction the claim of the plaintiff. But this mode of expounding a statute has never been adopted by any enlightened tribunal—because it is evident that in many cases it would defeat the object which the Legislature intended to accomplish. And it is well settled that, in interpreting a statute, the court will not look merely to a particular clause in which general words may be used, *but will take in connection with it the whole statute ... and the objects and policy of the law....*" * * *

Section 501(c)(3) therefore must be analyzed and construed within the framework of the Internal Revenue Code and against the background of the Congressional purposes. Such an examination reveals unmistakable evidence that, underlying all relevant parts of the Code, is the intent that entitlement to tax exemption depends on meeting certain common law standards of charity—namely, that an institution seeking tax-exempt status must serve a public purpose and not be contrary to established public policy.

This "charitable" concept appears explicitly in § 170 of the Code. That section contains a list of organizations virtually identical to that contained in § 501(c)(3). It is apparent that Congress intended that list to have the same meaning in both sections. In § 170, Congress used the list of organizations in defining the term "charitable contributions." On its face, therefore, § 170 reveals that Congress' intention was to provide tax benefits to organizations serving charitable purposes. The form of § 170 simply makes plain what common sense and history tell us: in enacting both § 170 and § 501(c)(3), Congress sought to provide tax benefits to charitable organizations, to encourage the development of private institutions that serve a useful public purpose or supplement or take the place of public institutions of the same kind.

Tax exemptions for certain institutions thought beneficial to the social order of the country as a whole, or to a particular community, are deeply rooted in our history, as in that of England. The origins of such exemptions lie in the special privileges that have long been extended to charitable trusts. * * *

More than a century ago, this Court announced the caveat that is critical in this case:

"[I]t has now become an established principle of American law, that courts of chancery will sustain and protect ... a gift ... to public charitable uses, *provided the same is consistent with local laws and public policy....*" Perin v. Carey, 24 How. 465, 501, 16 L.Ed. 701 (1861) (emphasis added).

Soon after that, in 1878, the Court commented:

"A charitable use, *where neither law nor public policy forbids,* may be applied to almost any thing *that tends to promote the well-doing and well-being of social man.*" Ould v. Washington Hospital for Foundlings, 95 U.S. 303, 311, 24 L.Ed. 450 (1878) (emphasis added).
* * *

In 1891, in a restatement of the English law of charity which has long been recognized as a leading authority in this country, Lord MacNaghten stated:

" 'Charity' in its legal sense comprises four principal divisions: trusts for the relief of poverty; *trusts for the advancement of education;* trusts for the advancement of religion; and trusts for *other purposes beneficial to the community,* not falling under any of the preceding heads." Commissioners v. Pemsel, [1891] A.C. 531, 583 (emphasis added). See, *e.g.,* 4 A. Scott, The Law of Trusts § 368, at 2853–2854 (3d ed. 1967) (hereinafter Scott).

These statements clearly reveal the legal background against which Congress enacted the first charitable exemption statute in 1894: charities were to be given preferential treatment because they provide a benefit to society.

* * *

A corollary to the public benefit principle is the requirement, long recognized in the law of trusts, that the purpose of a charitable trust may not be illegal or violate established public policy. In 1861, this Court stated that a public charitable use must be "consistent with local laws and public policy," * * * Modern commentators and courts have echoed that view. See, *e.g.,* Restatement (Second) of Trusts, § 377, comment c (1959); 4 Scott § 377, and cases cited therein; Bogert § 378, at 191–192.

When the Government grants exemptions or allows deductions all taxpayers are affected; the very fact of the exemption or deduction for the donor means that other taxpayers can be said to be indirect and vicarious "donors." Charitable exemptions are justified on the basis that the exempt entity confers a public benefit—a benefit which the society or the community may not itself choose or be able to provide, or which supplements and advances the work of public institutions already supported by tax revenues. History buttresses logic to make clear that, to warrant exemption under § 501(c)(3), an institution must fall within a category specified in that section and must demonstrably serve and be in harmony with the public interest. The institution's purpose must not be so at odds with the common community conscience as to undermine any public benefit that might otherwise be conferred.

B

We are bound to approach these questions with full awareness that determinations of public benefit and public policy are sensitive matters with serious implications for the institutions affected; a declaration that a given institution is not "charitable" should be made only where there can be no doubt that the activity involved is contrary to a fundamental public policy. But there can no longer be any doubt that racial discrimination in education violates deeply and widely accepted views of elementary justice. Prior to 1954, public education in many places still was conducted under the pall of *Plessy v. Ferguson,* 163 U.S. 537, 16 S.Ct. 1138, 41 L.Ed. 256 (1896); racial segregation in primary and secondary education prevailed in many parts of the country. See, *e.g.,* Segregation and the Fourteenth Amendment in the States (B. Reams & P. Wilson, eds. 1975).[20] This Court's decision in *Brown v. Board of Education,* 347 U.S. 483, 74 S.Ct. 686, 98 L.Ed. 873 (1954), signalled an end to that era. Over the past quarter of a century, every pronouncement of this Court and myriad Acts of Congress and Executive Orders attest a firm national policy to prohibit racial segregation and discrimination in public education.

* * *

In *Norwood v. Harrison,* 413 U.S. 455, 468–469, 93 S.Ct. 2804, 2812, 37 L.Ed.2d 723 (1973), we dealt with a non-public institution:

"[A] private school—even one that discriminates—fulfills an important educational function; *however, . . . [that] legitimate educational function cannot be isolated from discriminatory practices . . . [D]is-*

---

20. In 1894, when the first charitable exemption provision was enacted, racially segregated educational institutions would not have been regarded as against public policy. Yet contemporary standards must be considered in determining whether given activities provide a public benefit and are entitled to the charitable tax exemption. In *Walz v. Tax Comm'n,* 397 U.S. 664, 672–673, 90 S.Ct. 1409, 1413, 25 L.Ed.2d 697 (1970), we observed:

"Qualification for tax exemption is not perpetual or immutable; some tax-exempt groups lose that status when their activities take them outside the classification and new entities can come into being and qualify for the exemption."

Charitable trust law also makes clear that the definition of "charity" depends upon contemporary standards. See, *e.g.,* Restatement (Second) of Trusts, § 374, comment a (1959); Bogert § 369, at 65–67; 4 Scott § 368, at 2855–2856.

criminatory treatment exerts a pervasive influence on the entire educational process." (Emphasis added).

* * *

Congress, in Titles IV and VI of the Civil Rights Act of 1964, Pub.L. 88–352, 78 Stat. 241, 42 U.S.C. §§ 2000c et seq., 2000c–6, 2000–d et seq., clearly expressed its agreement that racial discrimination in education violates a fundamental public policy. Other sections of that Act, and numerous enactments since then, testify to the public policy against racial discrimination. See, *e.g.,* the Voting Rights Act of 1965, Pub.L. 89–110, 79 Stat. 437, 42 U.S.C. §§ 1971 *et seq.;* Title VIII of the Civil Rights Act of 1968, Pub.L. 90–284, 82 Stat. 81, 42 U.S.C. §§ 3601 * * *.

The Executive Branch has consistently placed its support behind eradication of racial discrimination. Several years before this Court's decision in *Brown v. Board of Education, supra,* President Truman issued Executive Orders prohibiting racial discrimination in federal employment decisions, Exec. Order No. 9980, 3 CFR 720 (1943–1948 Comp.), and in classifications for the Selective Service, Exec. Order No. 9988, *id.* 726, 729. In 1957, President Eisenhower employed military forces to ensure compliance with federal standards in school desegregation programs. Exec. Order No. 10730, 3 CFR 389 (1954–1958 Comp.). And in 1962, President Kennedy announced:

> "[T]he granting of federal assistance for ... housing and related facilities from which Americans are excluded because of their race, color, creed, or national origin is unfair, unjust, and inconsistent with the public policy of the United States as manifested in its Constitution and laws." Exec. Order No. 11063, 3 CFR 652 (1959–1963 Comp.).

* * *

Few social or political issues in our history have been more vigorously debated and more extensively ventilated than the issue of racial discrimination, particularly in education. Given the stress and anguish of the history of efforts to escape from the shackles of the "separate but equal" doctrine of *Plessy v. Ferguson, supra,* it cannot be said that educational institutions that, for whatever reasons, practice racial discrimination, are institutions exercising "beneficial and stabilizing influences in community life," * * *, or should be encouraged by having all taxpayers share in their support by way of special tax status.

There can thus be no question that the interpretation of § 170 and § 501(c)(3) announced by the IRS in 1970 was correct. That it may be seen as belated does not undermine its soundness. It would be wholly incompatible with the concepts underlying tax exemption to grant the benefit of tax-exempt status to racially discriminatory educational entities, which "exer[t] a pervasive influence on the entire educational process." * * * Whatever may be the rationale for such private schools' policies, and however sincere the rationale may be, racial discrimination in education is contrary to public policy. Racially discriminatory educational institutions cannot be viewed as conferring a public benefit within the "charitable" concept discussed earlier, or within the Congressional intent underlying § 170 and § 501(c)(3).

C

Petitioners contend that, regardless of whether the IRS properly concluded that racially discriminatory private schools violate public policy, only Congress can alter the scope of § 170 and § 501(c)(3). Petitioners accordingly argue that the IRS overstepped its lawful bounds in issuing its 1970 and 1971 rulings.

Yet ever since the inception of the tax code, Congress has seen fit to vest in those administering the tax laws very broad authority to interpret those laws. In an area as complex as the tax system, the agency Congress vests with administrative responsibility must be able to exercise its authority to meet changing conditions and new problems. Indeed as early as 1918, Congress expressly authorized the Commissioner "to make all needful rules and regulations for the enforcement" of the tax laws. Revenue Act of 1918, ch. 18, § 1309, 40 Stat. 1057, 1143 (1919). The same provision, so essential to efficient and fair administration of the tax laws, has appeared in tax codes ever since, see 26 U.S.C. § 7805(a) (1976); and this Court has long recognized the primary authority of the IRS and its predecessors in construing the Internal Revenue Code, * * *.

Congress, the source of IRS authority, can modify IRS rulings it considers improper; and courts exercise review over IRS actions. In the first instance, however, the responsibility for construing the Code falls to the IRS. Since Congress cannot be expected to anticipate every conceivable problem that can arise or to carry out day-to-day oversight, it relies on the administrators and on the courts to implement the legislative will. Administrators, like judges, are under oath to do so.

In § 170 and § 501(c)(3), Congress has identified categories of traditionally exempt institutions and has specified certain additional requirements for tax exemption. Yet the need for continuing interpretation of those statutes is unavoidable. For more than 60 years, the IRS and its predecessors have constantly been called upon to interpret these and comparable provisions, and in doing so have referred consistently to principles of charitable trust law. In Treas. Reg. 45, art. 517(1) (1921), for example, the IRS denied charitable exemptions on the basis of proscribed political activity before the Congress itself added such conduct as a disqualifying element. In other instances, the IRS has denied charitable exemptions to otherwise qualified entities because they served too limited a class of people and thus did not provide a truly "public" benefit under the common law test. * * * Some years before the issuance of the rulings challenged in these cases, the IRS also ruled that contributions to community recreational facilities would not be deductible and that the facilities themselves would not be entitled to tax-exempt status, unless those facilities were open to all on a racially nondiscriminatory basis. See Rev.Rul. 67–325, 1967–2 Cum.Bull. 113. These rulings reflect the Commissioner's continuing duty to interpret and apply the Internal Revenue Code. * * *

Guided, of course, by the Code, the IRS has the responsibility, in the first instance, to determine whether a particular entity is "charitable" for purposes of § 170 and § 501(c)(3). This in turn may necessitate later determinations of whether given activities so violate public policy that the entities involved cannot be deemed to provide a public benefit worthy of "charitable" status. We emphasize, however, that these sensitive determinations should be made only where there is no doubt that the organization's activities violate fundamental public policy.

On the record before us, there can be no doubt as to the national policy. In 1970, when the IRS first issued the ruling challenged here, the position of all three branches of the Federal Government was unmistakably clear. The correctness of the Commissioner's conclusion that a racially discriminatory private school "is not 'charitable' within the common law concepts reflected in ... the Code," Rev.Rul. 71–447, 1972–2 Cum.Bull., at 231, is wholly consistent with what Congress, the Executive and the courts had repeatedly declared before 1970. Indeed, it would be anomalous for the Executive, Legislative and Judicial Branches to reach conclusions that add up to a firm public policy on racial discrimination, and at the same time have the IRS blissfully ignore what all three branches of the Federal Government had declared. Clearly an educational institution engaging in practices affirmatively at odds with this declared position of the whole government cannot be seen as exercising a "beneficial and stabilizing influenc[e] in community life," * * * and is not "charitable," within the meaning of § 170 and § 501(c)(3). We therefore hold that the IRS did not exceed its authority when it announced its interpretation of § 170 and § 501(c)(3) in 1970 and 1971.

* * *

The evidence of Congressional approval of the policy embodied in Revenue Ruling 71–447 goes well beyond the failure of Congress to act on legislative proposals. Congress affirmatively manifested its acquiescence in the IRS policy when it enacted the present § 501(i) of the Code, Act of October 20, 1976, Pub.L. 94–568, 90 Stat. 2697 (1976). That provision denies tax-exempt status to social clubs whose charters or policy statements provide for "discrimination against any person on the basis of race, color, or religion."[26] Both the House and Senate committee reports on that bill articulated the national policy against granting tax exemptions to racially discriminatory private clubs. S.Rep. No. 1318,

---

26. Prior to the introduction of this legislation, a three-judge district court had held that segregated social clubs were entitled to tax exemptions. *McGlotten v. Connally,* 338 F.Supp. 448 (D.D.C.1972). Section 501(i) was enacted primarily in response to that decision. See S.Rep. No. 1318, 94th Cong., 2d Sess., 7–8 (1976); H.R.Rep. No. 1353, 94th Cong., 2d Sess., 8 (1976), U.S.Code Cong. & Admin.News 1976, p. 6051.

94th Cong., 2d Sess., 8 (1976); H.R.Rep. No. 1353, 94th Cong., 2d Sess., 8 (1976), U.S.Code Cong. & Admin.News 1976, p. 6051.

Even more significant is the fact that both reports focus on this Court's affirmance of *Green v. Connally, supra,* as having established that "discrimination on account of race is inconsistent with an *educational institution's* tax exempt status." S.Rep. No. 1318, *supra,* at 7–8 and n. 5; H.R.Rep. No. 1353, *supra,* at 8 and n. 5 (emphasis added), U.S.Code Cong. & Admin. News, p. 6058. These references in Congressional committee reports on an enactment denying tax exemptions to racially discriminatory private social clubs cannot be read other than as indicating approval of the standards applied to racially discriminatory private schools by the IRS subsequent to 1970, and specifically of Revenue Ruling 71–447.

* * *

Petitioner Bob Jones University, however, contends that it is not racially discriminatory. It emphasizes that it now allows all races to enroll, subject only to its restrictions on the conduct of all students, including its prohibitions of association between men and women of different races, and of interracial marriage. Although a ban on intermarriage or interracial dating applies to all races, decisions of this Court firmly establish that discrimination on the basis of racial affiliation and association is a form of racial discrimination, * * * We therefore find that the IRS properly applied Revenue Ruling 71–447 to Bob Jones University. The judgments of the Court of Appeals are, accordingly,

Affirmed.

Question

The Supreme court announced in *Bob Jones* a "public policy" limitation on the right of individuals to obtain tax exempt status for "charitable" organizations. How would you, as a governmental official, apply such a limitation to organizations seeking nonprofit status and/or tax exempt status?

Notes

1. The IRS subjected Bob Jones University to payment of unemployment taxes as a result of its loss of tax exempt status. Section 501(c)(3) organizations are not subject to unemployment taxes. See I.R.C. § 3606(c)(8) and Treas. Reg. § 31.3306(c)(8)–1.

2. The Court in *Bob Jones* referred to § 501(i) of the Internal Revenue Code which prohibits a social club, which is tax exempt under § 501(c)(7) of the Code, from having a *written* policy that provides for racial discrimination. The section makes no mention of a club's *operation* under a racial discriminatory policy nor does it prohibit gender discrimination in social clubs. (See discussion in Chapter 13.)

3. Based on a "public policy" limitation as sanctioned by the Supreme Court in *Bob Jones*, the Internal Revenue Service now posits that a private school must have a racially nondiscriminatory policy to qualify as a

§ 501(c)(3)organization. Tax audits of private schools are directed toward a determination of whether the school has a nondiscriminatory policy and whether the school is, in fact, operating under the nondiscriminatory policy.

A private school must show affirmatively both that it has adopted a racially nondiscriminatory policy as to its students and that the policy is made known to the general public. (See Rev. Proc. 75–50, 1975–2 C.B, 587.) The Service considers discrimination on the basis of race to include discrimination on the basis of color and national or ethnic origin. A private school must include a statement in its charter, bylaws, or other governing instrument, or in a resolution of its governing body, that it has a racially nondiscriminatory policy as to students. Every private school must include the statement in its brochures and catalogues dealing with student admissions, programs and scholarships. In addition, the school must include a reference to its racially nondiscriminatory policy in other written advertising that it issues as a means of informing prospective students of its programs. Its racially nondiscriminatory policy must be publicized either by references in a newspaper of general circulation that serves all racial segments of the community or by broadcast media if this use makes such nondiscriminatory policy known to all segments of the general community the school serves. Records, including brochures and catalogues, indicating the racial composition of the student body, faculty and administrative staff for each academic year must be retained for three years. However, the Service will not require a private school to release personally identifiable records or person information that would violate the Family Educational Rights and Privacy Act of 1974 (20 U.S.C. § 1232g, discussed *infra*). Failure to maintain or to produce upon proper request the required records and information will create a presumption that the school has failed to comply with the Service's guidelines.

4. A private school must not only have a written policy prohibiting racial discrimination; it also must operate in a nondiscriminatory manner. See *Calhoun Academy v. Comm.*, 94 T.C. 284 (1990) in which the Tax Court concluded that a private school did not carry its burden to demonstrate that it operated in good faith in accordance with its nondiscriminatory policy toward African American Students. The court concluded the school did not qualify for § 501(c)(3) status. The court noted that there was not a single African American student in the school and that the school had no plausible explanation of its inability to attract African American students.

DOE v. KAMEHAMEHA SCHOOLS/BERNICE PAUAHI BISHOP ESTATE

United States Court of Appeals, Ninth Circuit, 2004
416 F.3d 1025

Before BEEZER, GRABER, and BYBEE, Circuit Judges.

BYBEE, Circuit Judge.

Since 1887, the Kamehameha Schools have operated as the charitable legacy of Princess Bernice Pauahi Bishop, the last direct descendant of King Kamehameha I. Private and non-sectarian, the Kamehameha Schools give preference to students who are of native Hawaiian ancestry.

As a result of this policy, attendance at the Kamehameha Schools is effectively limited to those descended from the Hawaiian race. The issue considered here is a significant one in our statutory civil rights law: May a private, nonsectarian, commercially operated school, which receives no federal funds, purposefully exclude a student qualified for admission solely because he is not of pure or part aboriginal blood? The parties agree that this is a case of first impression in our circuit.

The plaintiff, John Doe, appeals the district court's grant of summary judgment in favor of defendants, the Kamehameha Schools and the Bernice Pauahi Bishop Estate and its individual trustees. He argues that he was denied entry to the Kamehameha Schools because of his race in violation of 42 U.S.C. section 1981, which forbids racial discrimination in the making and enforcement of contracts. For the following reasons, we agree with Doe and find that the Schools' admissions policy, which operates in practice as an absolute bar to admission for those of the non-preferred race, constitutes unlawful race discrimination in violation of section 1981. Accordingly, we reverse the district court's decision granting summary judgment to the Kamehameha Schools.

I

The facts are not in dispute. The Kamehameha Schools comprises a system of private, nonsectarian schools which are dispersed among the Hawaiian Islands. See EEOC v. Kamehameha Schs./Bishop Estate, 990 F.2d 458, 461 (9th Cir.1993). The school system was founded in 1887 under a "charitable testamentary trust established by the last direct descendent of [Hawaii's] King Kamehameha I, Princess Bernice Pauahi Bishop." Burgert v. Lokelani Bernice Pauahi Bishop Trust, 200 F.3d 661, 663 (9th Cir.2000). At the time of her death in 1884, Princess Pauahi Bishop was the largest landowner in Hawai'i, owning approximately one-tenth of the aggregate lands. Her will provided that the bulk of her estate should be placed in a charitable trust "to erect and maintain in the Hawaiian Islands two schools, each for boarding and day scholars, one for boys and one for girls, to be known as, and called the Kamehameha Schools." Will of Bernice Pauahi Bishop, reprinted in Wills And Deeds Of Trust 17–18 (3d ed.1957) (hereinafter "Pauahi Bishop Will"). See also Kamehameha Schs./Bishop Estate, 990 F.2d at 459.

Under the direction of the original trustees, chaired by Pauahi's husband, Charles Reed Bishop, both schools opened shortly after her death; the boys' school in the Fall of 1887 and the girls' in the Fall of 1894. The two schools were consolidated into one coeducational institution during the 1965–66 academic year. Currently, the Kamehameha Schools operate K–12 campuses on three separate islands, Kapalama (O'ahu), Pukalani (Maui), and Kea'au (Island of Hawai'i), enrolling more than 16,000 children annually. While the Schools subsidize much of the educational costs through funds held in trust, annual tuition remains at $1,784 for K–12th grade students, with approximately sixty-five percent of those enrolled receiving some form of financial aid. * * *

Pauahi's will contains several instructions pertaining to the administration of the Kamehameha Schools, none of which establish race as an admissions criteria. She directs that all students attending the Kamehameha Schools should be provided "first and chiefly a good education in the common English branches, and also instruction in morals and in such useful knowledge as may tend to make good and industrious men and women" and, in addition, that "the teachers of said schools shall forever be persons of the Protestant religion." Pauahi Bishop Will at 18–19. * * * She further instructs that a portion of the trust's annual income should be devoted "to the support and education of orphans, and others in indigent circumstances, giving the preference to Hawaiians of pure or part aboriginal blood." * * * While this racial preference is expressly listed as a criterion for the administration of estate resources charitably directed to orphans and indigents, the Will is notably devoid of any mention of race as a criterion for admission into the Kamehameha Schools.

As the Schools' 1885 Prospectus observed: "The noble minded Hawaiian chiefess who endowed the Kamehameha Schools, put no limitations of race or condition on her general bequest.

Instruction will be given only in English language, but The Schools will be opened to all nationalities." * * * Rather than institute race as an admissions prerequisite, Pauahi left to her Trustees the discretion "to regulate the admission of pupils" and "to make all such rules and regulations as they may deem necessary for the government" of the Kamehameha Schools. * * * The original trustees determined, however, that it was Pauahi's intent to prefer students of native Hawaiian ancestry. Specifically, the policy articulated by Charles Bishop was that "boys and girls of pure or part aboriginal blood ... should have preference; that is[,] they should have the first right." Accordingly, the admissions process at Kamehameha currently proceeds in two phases: first, the applicant must demonstrate that he possesses the minimum qualifications necessary to meet the Schools' rigorous academic standards and, second, he must complete an "Ethnic Ancestry Survey" designed to verify his aboriginal blood. The Schools forthrightly admit that as long as there are qualified students who possess at least some native Hawaiian ancestry, they will be admitted before even the most qualified of those who lack aboriginal blood. It is this "Hawaiians first" admissions policy that motivates the instant controversy.

The plaintiff-appellant, John Doe, twice sought admission to the Kamehameha Schools and, having met the academic requirements for admission, was twice determined to be a "competitive applicant." After completing the Ethnic Ancestry Survey, in which he acknowledged that he possessed no aboriginal blood, his application was each time, as expected, denied. Still desiring to attend the Kamehameha Schools, Doe filed suit alleging that the Schools' admissions policy violates 42 U.S.C. section 1981, as amended by the Civil Rights Act of 1991, Pub.L. No. 102–166, 105 Stat. 1071. Concluding that the admissions policy constituted a valid race-conscious remedial affirmative action program, the district court entered summary judgment in favor of the Kamehameha Schools and the Bernice Pauahi Bishop Estate. * * * This appeal followed.

II

Before proceeding to analyze the question presented in this appeal, it is worth clarifying those which are not. Specifically, the Kamehameha Schools does not contest, and candidly admits, that its admissions process is based upon an express racial classification. * * * The School does not attempt to justify its admissions policy by appealing to a First Amendment right to freedom of association, * * * nor does it explicitly argue for a relaxed level of scrutiny by appealing to the political nature of classifications premised on membership in a federally recognized Indian tribe.

* * *

* * * We are, likewise, not presented with a challenge to the racially discriminatory admissions policy of a public school or a school which accepts federal funding. See, e.g., Gratz v. Bollinger, 539 U.S. 244, 275–76 & n. 23, 123 S.Ct. 2411, 156 L.Ed.2d 257(2003) (applying strict scrutiny to a racial preference challenged under the Equal Protection Clause); Grutter v. Bollinger, 539 U.S. 306, 343, 123 S.Ct. 2325, 156 L.Ed.2d 304 (2003) (same).

Instead, we are confronted with a question of statutory origin: whether a private school, receiving no federal funds, may legitimately restrict admission to those of the native Hawaiian race. In other words, does the Kamehameha Schools' "Hawaiians first" admissions policy constitute invidious discrimination in violation of section 1981? The district court concluded that it does not. Because the issue is one of law, we review that decision de novo. * * *

III

Because the Kamehameha Schools admits that its admissions process is premised upon an express racial classification, we must first identify the standard of scrutiny that should be applied to proffered justifications for the racially discriminatory program. Two obvious contenders exist: strict scrutiny, such as that used to analyze challenges brought under the Fourteenth Amendment's Equal Protection Clause; or the more deferential form of scrutiny employed to resolve challenges brought pursuant to Title VII of the Civil Rights Act of 1964, 42 U.S.C. section 2000e et seq. (2004).

If strict scrutiny applies to the plaintiff's section 1981 challenge, the Schools must demonstrate that its admissions program is a "narrowly tailored measure[ ] that further[s] compelling governmental interests." * * * On the other hand, if Title VII scrutiny applies to this section 1981 suit, the Schools must merely "present evidence that the plaintiff was rejected, or the other applicant was chosen, for a legitimate nondiscriminatory reason." * * *

The plaintiff-appellant argues that strict scrutiny is the only method of review sufficiently rigorous to enforce the substantive commands of section 1981. He urges that although the McDonnell Douglas burden-shifting framework and order of proof is frequently applied to section 1981 suits, Title VII's substantive legal standards are inapplicable in this context. See McDonnell Douglas Corp. v. Green, 411 U.S. 792, 93 S.Ct. 1817, 36 L.Ed.2d 668 (1973). We disagree. * * *

* * *

Under our well-established framework, the plaintiff has the initial burden of proving, by a preponderance of the evidence, a prima facie case of discrimination. . . . Once the plaintiff establishes a prima facie case, an inference of discrimination arises. In order to rebut this inference, the employer must present evidence that the plaintiff was rejected, or the other applicant was chosen, for a legitimate nondiscriminatory reason. . . . At this point, as our prior cases make clear, petitioner retains the final burden of persuading the jury of intentional discrimination. Although petitioner retains the ultimate burden of persuasion, our cases make clear that she must also have the opportunity to demonstrate that respondent's proffered reasons for its decision were not its true reasons. * * *

We find this treatment particularly instructive because the Court's discussion appears to approve the use of, in the arena of section 1981 employment discrimination claims, not only the McDonnell Douglas order of proof, but also the nature of the proof that a private defendant in a Title VII action is required to adduce. * * * This Court has applied the 'framework' developed in Title VII cases to claims brought under [section 1981]." * * * While the Court could have suggested that a section 1981 defendant must demonstrate that race-based action is narrowly tailored to further a compelling governmental interest, * * * it stated instead that the employer must show merely "that the plaintiff was rejected, or the other applicant was chosen, for a legitimate nondiscriminatory reason," * * *.

* * *

Contrary to the appellant's argument, we do not find the Court's recent decisions in the "Michigan Affirmative Action Cases" relevant to our analysis. See Grutter, 539 U.S. at 343, 123 S.Ct. 2325 (concluding that the University of Michigan Law School's admissions program satisfied strict scrutiny under the Equal Protection Clause and, therefore, that it also satisfied Title VI and section 1981); Gratz, 539 U.S. at 275–76 n. 23, 123 S.Ct. 2411 (concluding that the University of Michigan's undergraduate admissions program failed strict scrutiny under the Equal Protection Clause and, therefore, that it also violated Title VI and section 1981). Aside from the fact that both cases involved a challenge to a public university's use of racial preferences in admissions, neither case presented the Court with an occasion to address, at any length, the appropriate standard of scrutiny for a section 1981 challenge. Because the preference in Grutter satisfied strict scrutiny, it necessarily would satisfy a lower standard; as the preference in Gratz failed strict scrutiny, the invalidity of the university's admissions program rendered it unnecessary for the Court to consider whether it could satisfy a lower standard. * * *

IV

It is undisputed that the Kamehameha Schools employs an express racial classification designed to deny admission to all students possessing no aboriginal blood, so long as qualified native Hawaiian applicants seek admission in sufficient number to fill the positions. * * * Accordingly, the issue becomes whether the Schools can articulate a legitimate nondiscriminatory reason justifying this racial preference. Toward this end, the Schools urge that its policy constitutes a valid affirmative action plan rationally related to redressing present imbalances in the socioeconomic and educational achievement of native Hawaiians, producing native Hawaiian leadership for community involvement, and revitalizing native Hawaiian culture.

The Supreme Court has held that Title VII's prohibition against racial discrimination "does not condemn all private, voluntary, race-conscious affirmative action plans." Weber, 443 U.S. at 208, 99 S.Ct. 2721. Consequently, in the Title VII context, if the challenged employment decision was made pursuant to such a plan, the existence of an affirmative action plan itself can form the basis of a legitimate nondiscriminatory rationale. * * * We assume, absent objection from the parties, that the same principle applies to a section 1981 suit against a purely private school. * * *

As a preliminary matter, we note that the plaintiff generally bears the burden of establishing the invalidity of an affirmative action plan challenged under Title VII. * * *

The starting point for our analysis is the Court's seminal decision in United Steelworkers of America v. Weber, 443 U.S. 193, 99 S.Ct. 2721, 61 L.Ed. 2d 480 (1979). * * *

* * *

Appellees argue * * * that the need is so great that the Schools should be permitted to admit only native Hawaiians until the educational deficits affecting that community disappear. They present abundant evidence demonstrating that native Hawaiians are over-represented in negative socioeconomic statistics such as poverty, homelessness, child abuse and neglect, and criminal activity; they are more likely to live in economically disadvantaged neighborhoods and attend low-quality schools; and, because of low levels of educational attainment, they are severely under-represented in professional and managerial positions, and over-represented in low-paying service and labor occupations. In sum, they urge, even though the admissions policy creates an "absolute bar," it is necessary for the Schools to "trammel" the interests of non-aboriginal applicants in order to reach its goal. To accept this argument, however, is to completely abolish what we perceive to be an important limitation embodied in Weber's second principle: fairness to applicants of the non-preferred race. Even if we assumed that some, limited racial preferences might be appropriate in order for the Schools to advance its mission, an absolute bar on the basis of race alone exceeds any reasonable application of Weber * * * Indeed, the sub-text to the Schools' policy-that of all those who are found in poverty, homelessness, crime and other socially or economically disadvantaged circumstances, only native Hawaiians count—"perpetuate[s] the notion that race matters most" and " 'may exacerbate the very [conditions that Kamehameha's policy is intended] to counteract.' " * * *

As we emphasized in Coral Construction Co. v. King County, "race conscious programs must be designed to minimize-if not avoid-burdens upon nonculpable third parties." 941 F.2d 910, 917 (9th Cir.1991). We cannot agree with the district court's conclusion that the challenged program constitutes a valid affirmative action plan supplying a legitimate nondiscriminatory reason for the Schools' racially exclusionary admissions policy. Under the principles we find controlling, the Schools' absolute bar to admission on the basis of race is invalid.

* * *

Appellees urge that Congress's intent is essential to guiding our interpretation of how section 1981 applies to a particular set of facts. They argue that because Congress has given native Hawaiians in general, and the Kamehameha Schools in particular, preferences in the context of education, see 20 U.S.C. section 7901 et seq.; 20 U.S.C. section 7511 et seq., our analysis must harmonize these enactments by according the Schools greater deference under section 1981. Appellees argue that it is inconceivable that the same Congress that enacted preferences for native Hawaiians would think that the Schools preferences violate section 1981; additionally, they argue that we can give section 1981 this more generous reading because section 1981 was amended in the Civil Rights Act of 1991. We have located no authority for the proposition that congressional intent, as manifested by scattered statutes adopted specially for the benefit of native Hawaiians, is sufficient to modify the standards embodied in a statute of general applicability. We cannot imagine the task of trying to harmonize all of the various acts of Congress-a prodigious output that is ever expanding and contracting-with statutes of general applicability such as section 1981. * * *

Judge GRABER, in dissent, urges us to consider 20 U.S.C. section 4905(a) (1991) (repealed 1994) as evidence of Congress's intent to abrogate the otherwise plain language of section 1981 as it applies to the Kamehameha Schools' racially exclusionary admissions policy. We are told that because the now repealed section 4905(a) authorized grants to the Kamehameha Schools to develop a demonstration program to support native Hawaiians who choose to attend college, it follows as an "inescapable conclusion" that Congress intends the Schools to refuse to admit, into its K–12 program, anyone without aboriginal blood. * * * Even assuming, arguendo, the premise that section 1981 may affect parties differently when Congress so directs, we cannot agree that a statute adopted in 1988 and repealed in 1994 created a native Hawaiian carve-out for section 1981. * * *

Absent proof that Congress has validly exempted the Schools-or the class of native Hawaiians as a whole-from the substantive commands of section 1981, we can ascertain no basis for subjecting a private school's racial preference premised on aboriginal blood to a wholly different standard than all other racial preferences challenged under the statute. We thus turn to the question of whether Congress has implicitly exempted the Schools from section 1981.

* * *

V

We emphasize that our ruling today is a narrow one. We conclude only that the plaintiff-appellant has met his burden of establishing the invalidity of the racially exclusionary affirmative action plan in place at the Kamehameha Schools, as that plan currently operates as an absolute bar to admission for those of the non-preferred race. Nothing in our decision, however, implicates the validity of the Pauahi Bishop Will, as we do not read that document to require the use of race as an admissions prerequisite. Consequently, we affirm the entry of summary judgment for the Bernice Pauahi Bishop Estate and its individual trustees.

For the foregoing reasons, the decision of the district court granting summary judgment to the Kamehameha Schools is reversed. In all other respects, the judgment is affirmed. The case is remanded for proceedings consistent with this opinion.

AFFIRMED IN PART; REVERSED IN PART.

GRABER, Circuit Judge, concurring in part and dissenting in part:

I respectfully dissent from the majority's conclusion that 42 U.S.C. section 1981 bars the admissions policy of the Kamehameha Schools. Our only task is to discern Congress' intent with respect to the application of section 1981 to a wholly private, Hawaiian institution that educates Native Hawaiian children in Hawaii. Although I have no quarrel with many of the general principles set forth so gracefully in the majority opinion—and, indeed, I concur in the opinion insofar as it applies Title VII principles, rather than strict scrutiny, to admissions preferences by a private school—I cannot agree with the opinion's narrow perspective on congressional intent.

When Congress first enacted section 1981 in 1866, the Hawaiian Islands were still a sovereign kingdom. But in 1991, when Congress revisited and reenacted section 1981 in the Civil Rights Act of 1991, Pub.L. No. 102–166, section 101, 105 Stat. 1071, Congress' view of the statute's proper scope presumptively was informed by the body of law that had developed in the interim. * * * It is our duty to harmonize section 1981, to the extent possible, with the statutory context in which Congress acted. * * *

In 1988, just three years before its reenactment of section 1981, Congress recognized the United States government's unique relationship with Native Hawaiians, acknowledged the severe socioeconomic and educational disadvantages experienced by Native Hawaiians, and authorized federal money for private entities-including the Kamehameha Schools-to provide loans and scholarships exclusively to Native Hawaiians. * * *

The majority holds that section 1981 forbids all exclusive racial preferences (whether remedial or not) and suggests that political status is the only alternative justification for the Schools' exclusive preference for Native Hawaiians. * * * Thus, the Schools' concession that "Native Hawaiian" is a racial category, for purposes of this case, dooms its policy under the majority's view. * * * I do not perceive such a dichotomy between the racial and the political aspects of the Schools' preference for Native Hawaiian applicants. That is, if "Native Hawaiian" is indeed a racial category, then Congress has shown by its actions that an exclusive, remedial, racial preference can be permissible, at least when it is employed to remedy demonstrable and extreme educational and socioeconomic deficiencies that are faced by a racial group that (a) is descended from people whose sovereignty and culture were upended and nearly destroyed, in part by the actions of the United States, and (b) consequently enjoys a special trust relationship with the United States government that parallels (but is not identical to) that between the federal government and Native Americans. These factors distinguish Native Hawaiians from the other racial groups mentioned by the majority, * * * who have received special funding. In other words, we need not decide that Native Hawaiians have any particular political status in order to recognize, as Congress has, that the Kamehameha Schools pursue unique remedial objectives and may, consistent with congressional intent, employ special remedial tools.

The Supreme Court has not established "a rigid formula for testing the validity of an affirmative action plan" applied by a private employer, Johnson v. Transp. Agency, 770 F.2d 752, 757 (9th Cir.1985), nor has it spoken at all to the operation of section 1981 with respect to remedial preferences at a private school. In the absence of more specific Supreme Court guidance, we should look directly to congressional intent. Congress clearly meant to allow for the private education of Native Hawaiian children at the Kamehameha Schools. Because the statutory context demonstrates that Congress did not intend for section 1981 to bar all exclusive preferences to remedy the severe educational deficits suffered by Native Hawaiians, a population unique within this country, and because Kamehameha Schools has amply demonstrated that its admission preference is regularly reviewed and currently required to combat those deficits, I respectfully dissent from the majority's contrary conclusion.

Note

The Ninth Circuit agreed to rehear this case by the en banc court. See *Doe v. Kamehameha Schools*, 441 F.3d 1029 (9th Cir. 2006).

III. RIGHTS OF STUDENTS

A. Suspension of Students

Courts generally will not intrude into disciplinary procedures of private schools unless the state is involved in the school's activities in a meaningful way. Still, a private school can be subject to legal action for dismissal of a student under a contract theory or by application of the principles of the law of association. A court will prevent a private school from expelling a student arbitrarily, unreasonably, or in bad faith.

The dismissal of a student for academic reasons is seldom subject to judicial review. Courts assume that decisions regarding grades and qualifications for degrees are matters wholly within the jurisdiction of school authorities who alone are qualified to make such determinations. A court will review academic dismissals only to determine if school authorities were motivated by bad faith or acted arbitrarily.

HARRIS v. TRUSTEES OF COLUMBIA UNIVERSITY

Supreme Court, Appellate Division, New York, 1983
98 A.D.2d 58, 470 N.Y.S.2d 368

ASCH, Justice.

Petitioner has lived in a Columbia University-owned apartment building at 601 West 115th Street since 1971 pursuant to a series of one-year leases, renewed annually, which contained an "affiliation clause" requiring him to maintain an affiliation with the University as a condition to continuing his tenancy. Petitioner had been Chief Reference Book Editor of Columbia University Press from 1969–1975, mainly as Editor-in-Chief of the Columbia Encyclopedia. Upon the completion of the Encyclopedia project he left Columbia's employ. In what was admittedly a tactic to retain his University affiliation and *ergo* his residence, Harris began working part time and informally in 1975 as a consultant to the Columbia University Library, basically in the School of International Affairs, aiding foreign students in their research and in their difficulties with the English language, for a "modest annual honorarium." Harris allegedly continued in this capacity from 1975 through 1980.

The University sought documentation of petitioner's affiliation status in 1978 and Dr. George Lowy, since retired, sent a statement as to Harris' consultant status. A similar request for proof of affiliation was made on October 1, 1980, and Harris submitted a letter from one "Donald Chang, Chief, Research Facilities–South Asian Division, School of International Affairs," dated October 6, 1980, which stated that Harris was employed as a "consultant to the Center for South Asian Studies." Petitioner was advised that this letter was not sufficient proof of affiliation and a Notice to Vacate was served on him on November 7, 1980.

In December of 1980, petitioner was admitted as a full-time Ph.D. candidate student in the University's Graduate School of Arts and Sciences. His lease was renewed until December 31, 1982. Thereafter, the University became aware that there was no "Donald Chang" employed by the South Asia Institute. Raymond Anderson, Associate Dean of the Graduate School of Arts and Sciences, wrote petitioner on June 30, 1981, advising him that disciplinary action may be taken because of his submission of this allegedly fraudulent letter. Anderson asked petitioner to make an appointment with him to "discuss the matter" and "make any representations on your own behalf."

A meeting was then held between Anderson and Harris on August 17, 1981. Anderson termed it a "hearing" while Harris characterized it as a "stern headmaster dressing down an adolescent student." It appears that what transpired was, in fact, a face to face meeting between only Anderson and Harris in Anderson's office, at which Anderson informed Harris that he believed the "Chang" letter to be a forgery prepared by Harris and Harris replied by denying that it was a forgery and stating that he obtained the letter by means of a telephone conversation with an unknown person in the School of International Affairs.

Anderson wrote Harris a letter on August 17, 1981, memorializing the meeting, and stated in it that he considered the explanation "implausible" but would give Harris the "benefit of the doubt" and consider his action "gross negligence." As a consequence, Anderson stated that Harris would have two weeks to "submit persuasive evidence" that the letter "represented a bona fide affiliation with the University acceptable to the Office of the General Counsel." If Harris could not make such a showing, Anderson would then "request that your lease not be renewed upon its termination."

Harris replied by a letter dated August 28, 1981, explaining his long-term affiliation with the University, including his current status as student, and reiterating his story concerning the letter and his innocence in obtaining it. He also claimed that his lease was renewed in December based upon his new status as student, and not upon any effect of this letter.

Anderson immediately replied by rejecting this letter as "reminding me of what I already know" and not as "persuasive evidence." Anderson stated that "I consider the issue closed" (letter of August 31, 1981).

Columbia instituted a holdover proceeding in Civil Court on April 7, 1982, to recover possession of the apartment. On May 6, 1982, this proceeding was discontinued due to the existing extension of Harris' lease until December 1982 (claimed to be a clerical error).

On July 7, 1982, in another attempt to get Harris out of the apartment, Anderson wrote Harris, claiming that he "took advantage" of this clerical error "to evade my directive" in "a flagrant breach of discipline." Anderson informed him that unless Harris *vacated the apartment* by September 1, 1982, he "would not be permitted, for disciplinary reasons, to enroll in the University in the future, and that fact will be noted on your permanent academic record."

On August 2, 1982, Harris' attorney, Harry Kresky, responded to the July 7 letter, stating that Harris had a valid lease until December 31, 1982 on the basis of being a bona fide student and not because of the allegedly fraudulent letter of October 1980.

By letter dated September 17, 1982, Anderson dismissed Harris from the University for disciplinary reasons for failure to comply with the prior directive to vacate the apartment.

Harris then instituted this instant Article 78 proceeding challenging this determination.

The application was denied and the petition dismissed by Special Term on the grounds that petitioner did not show that the University abused its discretion, violated due process or acted contrary to law. It found that petitioner had notice and an opportunity to be heard and that also he did not exhaust his administrative appeals. Finally, Special Term found that because of the allegedly underlying fraud of the Chang letter, petitioner was barred from relief under the clean hands doctrine.

The majority of this court disagrees with Special Term and would reverse.

It is undisputed that the actions of a private university against a student are subject to Article 78 review and that the courts will intervene if the disciplinary dismissal of a student is arbitrary * * * However, it is equally well settled that "when a university, in expelling a student, acts within its jurisdiction, not arbitrarily but in the exercise of an honest discretion based on facts within its knowledge that justify the exercise of discretion, a court may not review the exercise of its discretion" * * *

In matters concerning a student's academic qualifications, the determination of the school is granted great weight and courts are reluctant to intervene, as such determinations are within the expertise of the university and rest upon the subjective professional judgment of trained educators * * * But in cases involving expulsion for causes unrelated to academic achievement, courts must look more closely at the matter * * *.

In the case at bar, the factual background, given at some length *supra*, shows that Columbia University was acting throughout not as an academic aerie of higher education. Dean Anderson appeared primarily concerned with getting petitioner out of a rent-stabilized apartment on behalf of the landlord, Columbia. To that end, he held the threat of Harris' status as a Columbia student as a sword of Damocles over petitioner's head. The issue presented is simply put—was Anderson, acting on behalf of the University, arbitrary when he dismissed Harris for failure to comply with a directive to vacate an apartment to which

Harris had a legal right? I note that although the University speaks of Harris' fraud vis-a-vis the letter he submitted, the express reason he was dismissed was his failure to leave his apartment despite his lease and despite the fact Columbia had discontinued the holdover proceeding in Civil Court. When the University acts as a university, this court should be mindful of the restrictions placed upon judicial scrutiny of its actions in expelling or disciplining students. When, however, the University acts as a landlord, then this court must be more mindful of the rights of the student *qua* tenant. It offends the basic sense of fairness for the college to use its disciplinary power to strengthen its bargaining position as a landlord.

In the instant case it is true that the submission of the "Chang letter" was probably a fraudulent act, even though Columbia did not conclusively prove so. Harris' explanation was implausible, but Columbia did not rebut it or investigate the matter further. However, we will assume that the letter *was* fraudulently submitted by Harris.

The incident occurred *before* Harris was admitted as a student. It also did not affect his tenant status, as the University rejected the letter as a basis for a lease renewal and only later renewed Harris' lease based on his affiliation as a student (although it claims such renewal was a "clerical error").

It was almost a year later before the matter was brought to the attention of Dean Anderson. Petitioner complains that the action that Dean Anderson took deprived him of due process. However, Anderson did afford him a meeting in his office and offered him a chance to give his side of the story. In private university procedures, due process does not envision a full hearing but rather only an informal opportunity to be heard by students, *i.e.,* "to present their version of the case and to make such showing as they desire to the person or group of persons who have the authorized responsibility of determining the facts of the case and the nature of the action, if any, to be taken" * * *

After this meeting, Anderson meted out the penalty: that Harris vacate his apartment. It is unclear whether an Associate Dean of a division of the University has the authority to make such a landlord decision, in the course of fulfilling his "academic duties."

Columbia backed up this determination by bringing an action in Civil Court to evict Harris. Harris won this action, as, upon a showing of his valid lease, Columbia was forced to discontinue the action.

It was only thereafter, now two years after Harris was a student, that Anderson made a determination to expel him and forbid him to register as a student. Anderson claimed that Harris "took advantage" of the alleged "clerical error" of the renewed lease to "evade his directive." The expulsion of petitioner for this avowed reason was arbitrary and capricious.

Harris merely properly defended in court the eviction proceeding against him, presenting his valid lease, obtained on the basis of his affiliated status as a student. The decision to expel him as a student was a punitive measure aimed to strip him of his affiliated status and thus his apartment, where he resided for eleven years. No disciplinary action against him *qua* student was taken in 1981 when the allegedly forged letter was considered and then the matter closed. If the University had taken its action then, upon that basis, the result might well be different.

There are very few reported cases dealing with judicial review of university expulsion of a student for non-academic discipline, but most of them have upheld the university action.

In *Goldstein v. New York University,* 76 App.Div. 80, 78 N.Y.S. 739, plaintiff was expelled from NYU Law School for the indiscretion of passing a letter to a woman classmate "expressing a desire to make her acquaintance" and "thinking it uncourteous to present myself without your assent, I ask if I may do so in the classroom." The woman reported the letter to the dean, and the plaintiff lied and denied writing it when he was confronted. Plaintiff had a full hearing on the matter, and this court found "such a person would be unfit to remain a member of the law school" and upheld the expulsion.

In the case of *Samson v. Trustees of Columbia University,* 101 Misc. 146, 167 N.Y.S. 202, * * * plaintiff, a Columbia undergraduate, attended a demonstration against General Leonard Wood in 1916 and made an antidraft speech at an Emma Goldman rally in 1917. Columbia refused to allow him to register for the upcoming term on the grounds of moral unfitness, and the court upheld the action. After moralizing about the necessity of the draft and the evils of socialism, the court stated that "[m]isconduct perhaps refers more particularly to demeanor within the walls of the institution or in connection with the ordinary activities of student life, and of improper practices by the plaintiff in that regard there is no claim made here. But the implied stipulation of good conduct ... is not ... to receive the restricted construction that the student's conduct may be the subject of control only in so far as it relates to his actions in his capacity and status as student.... [A]ny conduct that may interfere with or injure the university, or lessen its proper control over its student body, or impair its influence for good upon its students and the community [may be disciplined]." * * *

In *Anthony v. Syracuse University,* 224 App.Div. 487, 489, 231 N.Y.S. 435, the court upheld the expulsion of a student because of rumors about her life style that did not make her a "typical Syracuse girl."

* * *

The more modern trend has been to extend the court's discretionary power to overrule the arbitrary exercise of university discipline.

In *Tedeschi v. Wagner College, supra,* the Court of Appeals sent the matter back to the university for a hearing when a student was dismissed for emotional problems. In *Ryan v. Hofstra University,* 67 Misc.2d 651, 324 N.Y.S.2d 964, a student was dismissed for an alleged act of vandalism, throwing a rock through the bookstore window. The court held that he could not be disciplined without full due process and that expulsion as a student was too severe a penalty for this non-academic misconduct. In *Morales v. New York University,* 83 A.D.2d 811, 442 N.Y.S.2d 12, * * *, this Court held that where the institution exercises its discretion arbitrarily, judicial intervention is warranted even in controversies involving academic standards.

In the matter currently before this court, the allegedly fraudulent letter was sent before petitioner became a student. The only misconduct alleged against him during the time he was a student was his alleged failure to comply with the directive of Anderson and vacate his housing. No misconduct was alleged against him as a student. The Graduate School of Arts and Sciences bulletin,*i.e.,* the student handbook which is the basis of Columbia's action against him under a contract basis, or as a member of an association (see *Tedeschi v. Wagner College, supra*), merely contains a rule that a student's continuation in the university is "strictly subject to the disciplinary powers of the university." There is no specific rule that he was alleged to have violated. Under the general disciplinary powers of the University, this extreme and capricious punishment for conduct totally unrelated to his continuation as a student can be deemed "arbitrary."

Special Term held that relief should also be barred for petitioner's failure to exhaust his administrative appeals. However, Dean Anderson in his expulsion letter did not advise petitioner of any avenues of appeal (although admittedly petitioner was told on the eve of bringing this action that he could appeal to the Dean of the Graduate School of Arts and Sciences). In *Ryan v. Hofstra University, supra,* the expulsion letter was termed "permanent and complete." The court there held that "[t]he law does not require exercises in futility. The authorities in New York are plain that where the end result is apparent, and administrative proceedings are moot, they need not be carried to their technical end." (*Ryan, supra,* 67 Misc. at 657, 324 N.Y.S.2d 964).

Special Term was also in error in applying the "clean hands" doctrine as an alternative ground for denying relief. This doctrine is applicable when the immoral or unconscionable conduct complained of is directly related to the subject matter in litigation and the party invoking the doctrine was injured by such conduct (see *Islamic Republic of Iran v. Pahlavi,* 116 Misc.2d 590, 598–9, 455 N.Y.S.2d 987). As noted above, the submission of an allegedly fraudulent letter concerning his apartment was not "immoral or unconscionable" conduct related to his status as a student.

Accordingly, the order and judgment (one paper) of Supreme Court, New York County, entered January 13, 1983, denying petitioner's application and dismissing the petition, should be reversed, on the law and facts, without costs, the petition reinstated and the application granted.

* * *

Note

In *Jackson v. Birmingham Board of Education*, 544 U.S. 167, 125 S.Ct. 1497, 161 L.Ed.2d 361 (2005), the Supreme Court ruled that there is a private right of action for retaliation for persons who, although not themselves the victims of gender discrimination, suffer retaliation because they have complained about gender discrimination suffered by another. Thus, it held that a coach had a private right of action under Title IX for alleged retaliation, in removing him from his coaching position, for complaining about a school's differential treatment of girls' teams.

B. Privacy Rights

The Family Educational Rights and Privacy Act, 42 U.S.C. § 1232g, establishes the privacy rights of students with regard to educational records. The Act permits the inspection, review, and amendment of educational records by a student (or the student's parents if the student is under 18) and requires, in most instances, prior consent from the student for disclosure of such records to third parties. The Act denies federal funds to an institution that has a policy of permitting the release of personally identifiable records or files of students except for directory information (student's name, address, telephone number, date and place of birth, major field of study, participation in officially recognized activities and sports, weight and height of members of athletic teams, dates of attendance, degrees and awards received, most recent previous institution attended by the student, and other similar information[2]), without the written consent of the student, to any individual, agency or organization. A student may have a hearing, either formal or informal, to challenge the content of the student's educational records in order to assure that the record is not misleading, inaccurate, or that otherwise inappropriate data are not contained in the record.[3] The student may insert in the record a written explanation of any information in the student's file. A student may waive rights of access to confidential statements if the student is notified of the names of all persons making confidential recommendations and the recommendations are used solely for the purpose for which they were specifically intended. A school may not require students to waive their rights of access to confidential statements as a condition for admission to, receipt of financial aid, or receipt of any other services of benefits from the school.[4]

---

2. Directory information may be released without the prior consent of the student if the school gives public notice of the categories of personally identifiable information the school has designated as directory information and has given the student (or parent if the student is under 18) the right to refuse to permit the release of such information.

3. The hearing process does not entitle a student to challenge a grade per se. Still students (or parents if the student is under 18) may contest the recording of a grade that they believe has been inaccurately entered in the record.

4. Records may be released to the following persons or organizations without the consent of the student (or the parent if the student is under 18): other school officials, including teachers within the school determined by the school to have legitimate educational interests; officials of other schools or school systems in which the student seeks to enroll upon the condition that the student be notified of the transfer of any records, unless the transfer is initiated by

Note

The Supreme Court pointed out, in *Gonzaga University v. John Doe*, 536 U.S. 273, 122 S.Ct. 2268, 153 L.Ed.2d 309 (2002), that the Family Educational Rights and Privacy Act (FERPA) does not create individual rights. The Court foreclosed a plaintiff's claim under 42 U.S.C. § 1983 for an alleged violation of the Act. The Court commented that federal spending legislation does not confer enforceable rights and noted that the mechanism Congress chose in FERPA to provide for enforcement of its nondisclosure provisions involves an administrative review procedure under the Secretary of Education.

C. Right of Expression

Students do not shed their constitutional rights to freedom of speech or expression at the school house gate.[5] Still, the states and the school authorities have comprehensive authority to prescribe and control conduct in the schools.[6] Problems occur in public schools when students' exercise of their First Amendment rights collide with the school. This is less of a problem in a private school. Still, public schools can place reasonable restrictions on the time, place, and manner of speech as such restrictions generally are necessary for discipline and orderly processes in the school.

Question

Do students and faculty members have expressive association rights? Consider this question in light of the following case.

RUMSFELD v. FORUM FOR ACADEMIC AND INSTITUTIONAL RIGHTS, INC.

United States Supreme Court, 2006
___ U.S. ___, 126 S.Ct. 1297, 164 L.Ed.2d 156

ROBERTS, C. J., delivered the opinion of the Court, in which all other Members

joined, except ALITO, J., who took no part in the consideration or decision of the case.

Chief Justice ROBERTS delivered the opinion of the Court.

When law schools began restricting the access of military recruiters to their students because of disagreement with the Government's policy on homosexuals in the military, Congress responded by enacting the

---

the student or the school has given notice in its policies and procedures that it forwards students' records on request to a school in which a student seeks to enroll without further notice of transfer; and certain authorized representatives of the government for educational purposes or to protect the health or safety of the student or other individuals.

5. *Tinker v. Des Moines Independent Community School Dist.*, 393 U.S. 503, 89 S.Ct. 733, 21 L.Ed.2d 731 (1969).

6. *Bethel School Dist. v. Fraser*, 478 U.S. 675, 106 S.Ct. 3159, 92 L.Ed.2d 549 (1986).

Solomon Amendment. See 10 U.S.C.A. section 983 (Supp.2005). That provision specifies that if any part of an institution of higher education denies military recruiters access equal to that provided other recruiters, the entire institution would lose certain federal funds. The law schools responded by suing, alleging that the Solomon Amendment infringed their First Amendment freedoms of speech and association. The District Court disagreed but was reversed by a divided panel of the Court of Appeals for the Third Circuit, which ordered the District Court to enter a preliminary injunction against enforcement of the Solomon Amendment. We granted certiorari.

Student Forum for Academic and Institutional Rights, Inc. (FAIR), is an association of law schools and law faculties. * * * Its declared mission is "to promote academic freedom, support educational institutions in opposing discrimination and vindicate the rights of institutions of higher education." * * * FAIR members have adopted policies expressing their opposition to discrimination based on, among other factors, sexual orientation. They would like to restrict military recruiting on their campuses because they object to the policy Congress has adopted with respect to homosexuals in the military. * * * The Solomon Amendment, however, forces institutions to choose between enforcing their nondiscrimination policy against military recruiters in this way and continuing to receive specified federal funding.

In 2003, FAIR sought a preliminary injunction against enforcement of the Solomon Amendment, which at that time-it has since been amended-prevented the Department of Defense (DOD) from providing specified federal funds to any institution of higher education "that either prohibits, or in effect prevents" military recruiters "from gaining entry to campuses." * * * FAIR considered the DOD's interpretation of this provision particularly objectionable. Although the statute required only "entry to campuses," the Government-after the terrorist attacks on September 11, 2001–adopted an informal policy of " 'requir[ing] universities to provide military recruiters access to students equal in quality and scope to that provided to other recruiters.' " * * * Prior to the adoption of this policy, some law schools sought to promote their nondiscrimination policies while still complying with the Solomon Amendment by having military recruiters interview on the undergraduate campus. * * * But under the equal access policy, military recruiters had to be permitted to interview at the law schools, if other recruiters did so.

FAIR argued that this forced inclusion and equal treatment of military recruiters violated the law schools' First Amendment freedoms of speech and association. According to FAIR, the Solomon Amendment was unconstitutional because it forced law schools to choose between exercising their First Amendment right to decide whether to disseminate or accommodate a military recruiter's message, and ensuring the availability of federal funding for their universities.

* * *

FAIR appealed the District Court's judgment, arguing that the recently amended Solomon Amendment was unconstitutional for the same reasons as the earlier version. A divided panel of the Court of Appeals for the Third Circuit agreed. * * * According to the Third Circuit, the Solomon Amendment violated the unconstitutional conditions doctrine because it forced a law school to choose between surrendering First Amendment rights and losing federal funding for its university. * * * As a result, the Court of Appeals reversed and remanded for the District Court to enter a preliminary injunction against enforcement of the Solomon Amendment. * * * We granted certiorari. * * *

The Solomon Amendment denies federal funding to an institution of higher education that "has a policy or practice ... that either prohibits, or in effect prevents" the military "from gaining access to campuses, or access to Students ... on campuses, for purposes of military recruiting in a manner that is at least equal in quality and scope to the access to campuses and to students that is provided to any other employer." 10 U.S.C.A. section 983(b) (Supp.2005). The statute provides an exception for an institution with "a longstanding policy of pacifism based on historical religious affiliation." * * * The Government and FAIR agree on what this statute requires: In order for a law school and its university to receive federal funding, the law school must offer military recruiters the same access to its campus and students that it provides to the nonmilitary recruiter receiving the most favorable access.

* * *

The Constitution grants Congress the power to "provide for the common Defence," "[t]o raise and support Armies," and "[t]o provide and maintain a Navy." Art. I, section 8, cls. 1, 12–13. Congress' power in this area "is broad and sweeping," * * * and there is no dispute in this case that it includes the authority to require campus access for military recruiters. That is, of course, unless Congress exceeds constitutional limitations on its power in enacting such legislation. * * * But the fact that legislation that raises armies is subject to First Amendment constraints does not mean that we ignore the purpose of this legislation when determining its constitutionality; as we recognized in Rostker, "judicial deference ... is at its apogee" when Congress legislates under its authority to raise and support armies. * * *

Although Congress has broad authority to legislate on matters of military recruiting, it nonetheless chose to secure campus access for military recruiters indirectly, through its Spending Clause power. The Solomon Amendment gives universities a choice: Either allow military recruiters the same access to students afforded any other recruiter or forgo certain federal funds. Congress' decision to proceed indirectly does not reduce the deference given to Congress in the area of military affairs. Congress' choice to promote its goal by creating a funding condition deserves at least as deferential treatment as if Congress had imposed a mandate on universities. Congress' power to regulate military recruiting under the Solomon Amendment is arguably greater because universities are free to decline the federal funds. In Grove City College v. Bell, 465 U.S. 555, 575–576, 104 S.Ct. 1211, 79 L.Ed.2d 516 (1984), we rejected a private college's claim that conditioning federal funds on its compliance with Title IX of the Education Amendments of 1972 violated the First Amendment. We thought this argument "warrant[ed] only brief consideration" because "Congress is free to attach reasonable and unambiguous conditions to federal financial assistance that educational institutions are not obligated to accept." * * * We concluded that no First Amendment violation had occurred-without reviewing the substance of the First Amendment claims-because Grove City could decline the Government's funds. * * *

* * *

This case does not require us to determine when a condition placed on university funding goes beyond the "reasonable" choice offered in Grove City and becomes an unconstitutional condition. It is clear that a funding condition cannot be unconstitutional if it could be constitutionally imposed directly. * * * Because the First Amendment would not prevent Congress from directly imposing the Solomon Amendment's access requirement, the statute does not place an unconstitutional condition on the receipt of federal funds.

* * *

The Solomon Amendment neither limits what law schools may say nor requires them to say anything. Law schools remain free under the statute to express whatever views they may have on the military's congressionally mandated employment policy, all the while retaining eligibility for federal funds. * * * As a general matter, the Solomon Amendment regulates conduct, not speech. It affects what law schools must do-afford equal access to military recruiters-not what they may or may not say.

* * *

Having rejected the view that the Solomon Amendment impermissibly regulates speech, we must still consider whether the expressive nature of the conduct regulated by the statute brings that conduct within the First Amendment's protection. In O'Brien, we recognized that some forms of " 'symbolic speech' " were deserving of First Amendment protection. 391 U.S., at 376, 88 S.Ct. 1673. But we rejected the view that "conduct can be labeled 'speech' whenever the person engaging in the conduct intends thereby to express an idea." Instead, we have extended First Amendment protection only to conduct that is inherently expressive. In Texas v. Johnson, 491 U.S. 397, 406, 109 S.Ct. 2533, 105 L.Ed.2d 342 (1989), for example, we applied O'Brien and held that burning the American flag was sufficiently expressive to warrant First Amendment protection.

Unlike flag burning, the conduct regulated by the Solomon Amendment is not inherently expressive. Prior to the adoption of the Solomon

Amendment's equal-access requirement, law schools "expressed" their disagreement with the military by treating military recruiters differently from other recruiters. But these actions were expressive only because the law schools accompanied their conduct with speech explaining it. For example, the point of requiring military interviews to be conducted on the undergraduate campus is not "overwhelmingly apparent." * * * An observer who sees military recruiters interviewing away from the law school has no way of knowing whether the law school is expressing its disapproval of the military, all the law school's interview rooms are full, or the military recruiters decided for reasons of their own that they would rather interview someplace else.

The expressive component of a law school's actions is not created by the conduct itself but by the speech that accompanies it. The fact that such explanatory speech is necessary is strong evidence that the conduct at issue here is not so inherently expressive that it warrants protection under O'Brien. If combining speech and conduct were enough to create expressive conduct, a regulated party could always transform conduct into "speech" simply by talking about it. For instance, if an individual announces that he intends to express his disapproval of the Internal Revenue Service by refusing to pay his income taxes, we would have to apply O'Brien to determine whether the Tax Code violates the First Amendment. Neither O'Brien nor its progeny supports such a result.

* * *

The Solomon Amendment does not violate law schools' freedom of speech, but the First Amendment's protection extends beyond the right to speak. We have recognized a First Amendment right to associate for the purpose of speaking, which we have termed a "right of expressive association." See, e.g., Boy Scouts of America v. Dale, 530 U.S. 640, 644, 120 S.Ct. 2446, 147 L.Ed.2d 554 (2000). The reason we have extended First Amendment protection in this way is clear: The right to speak is often exercised most effectively by combining one's voice with the voices of others. See Roberts v. United States Jaycees, 468 U.S. 609, 622, 104 S.Ct. 3244, 82 L.Ed.2d 462 (1984). If the government were free to restrict individuals' ability to join together and speak, it could essentially silence views that the First Amendment is intended to protect.

FAIR argues that the Solomon Amendment violates law schools' freedom of expressive association. According to FAIR, law schools' ability to express their message that discrimination on the basis of sexual orientation is wrong is significantly affected by the presence of military recruiters on campus and the schools' obligation to assist them. Relying heavily on our decision in Dale, the Court of Appeals agreed. * * *

In Dale, we held that the Boy Scouts' freedom of expressive association was violated by New Jersey's public accommodations law, which required the organization to accept a homosexual as a scoutmaster. After determining that the Boy Scouts was an expressive association, that "the forced inclusion of Dale would significantly affect its expression," and that the State's interests did not justify this intrusion, we concluded that the Boy Scout's First Amendment rights were violated. * * *

The Solomon Amendment, however, does not similarly affect a law school's associational rights. To comply with the statute, law schools must allow military recruiters on campus and assist them in whatever way the school chooses to assist other employers. Law schools therefore "associate" with military recruiters in the sense that they interact with them. But recruiters are not part of the law school. Recruiters are, by definition, outsiders who come onto campus for the limited purpose of trying to hire students-not to become members of the school's expressive association. This distinction is critical. Unlike the public accommodations law in Dale, the Solomon Amendment does not force a law school " 'to accept members it does not desire.' " * * * The law schools say that allowing military recruiters equal access impairs their own expression by requiring them to associate with the recruiters, but just as saying conduct is undertaken for expressive purposes cannot make it symbolic speech, * * * so too a speaker cannot "erect a shield" against laws requiring access "simply by asserting" that mere association "would impair its message." * * *

FAIR correctly notes that the freedom of expressive association protects more than just a group's membership decisions. For example, we have held laws unconstitutional that require disclosure of membership lists for groups seeking anonymity, * * * or impose penalties or withhold benefits based on membership in a disfavored group, * * *. Although these laws did not directly interfere with an organization's composition, they made group membership less attractive, raising the same First Amendment concerns about affecting the group's ability to express its message. The Solomon Amendment has no similar effect on a law school's associational rights. Students and faculty are free to associate to voice their disapproval of the military's message; nothing about the statute affects the composition of the group by making group membership less desirable. The Solomon Amendment therefore does not violate a law school's First Amendment rights. A military recruiter's mere presence on campus does not violate a law school's right to associate, regardless of how repugnant the law school considers the recruiter's message.

* * *

In this case, FAIR has attempted to stretch a number of First Amendment doctrines well beyond the sort of activities these doctrines protect. The law schools object to having to treat military recruiters like other recruiters, but that regulation of conduct does not violate the First Amendment. To the extent that the Solomon Amendment incidentally affects expression, the law schools' effort to cast themselves as just like the schoolchildren in Barnette, the parade organizers in Hurley, and the Boy Scouts in Dale plainly overstates the expressive nature of their activity and the impact of the Solomon Amendment on it, while exaggerating the reach of our First Amendment precedents.

Because Congress could require law schools to provide equal access to military recruiters without violating the schools' freedoms of speech or association, the Court of Appeals erred in holding that the Solomon Amendment likely violates the First Amendment. We therefore reverse the judgment of the Third Circuit and remand the case for further proceedings consistent with this opinion.

It is so ordered.

Note

The right of association is discussed further in Chapter 13.

Chapter 12

HOSPITALS

I. ORGANIZATIONAL STRUCTURE

Hospitals are organized both as profit and as nonprofit entities. Nonprofit hospitals are exempt from income tax under § 501(c)(3) and qualify as public charities under §§ 509(a)(1) and 170(b)(1)(A)(iii).

Nonprofit hospitals are managed by a governing body, corresponding to a board of directors; an administrator, corresponding to a president of a nonprofit corporation; and a medical staff. Although members of the medical staff generally are independent of the hospital, they make many administrative decisions for the hospital.

Hospitals are subject to extensive governmental regulation. They must be licensed and most are accredited. Various functions of a hospital in delivering health care to patients are heavily regulated. The dispensing of drugs and participation in the Medicare program are examples. Further, financing and construction of hospital buildings have been subject to extensive federal and state regulation.

Questions

1. Do consumers prefer nonprofit hospitals? See Robert Charles Clark, Does the Nonprofit Form Fit the Hospital Industry? 93 Harv. L. Rev. 1417 (1980). The author considered whether physicians prefer practicing in nonprofit hospitals because they can relate better to trustees who have no personal stake in the hospital's financial performance than to hospitals responsive to shareholder demands. The author questioned whether nonprofit hospitals actually provide a higher quality of patient care and discussed efforts to counterbalance physician dominance of nonprofit hospitals by more consumer control of the governance structure of nonprofit hospitals.

2. Should there be more consumers on the boards of nonprofit hospitals? Consider this issue in the following case.

AMERICAN HOSPITAL ASSOCIATION v. HANSBARGER

United States District Court, West Virginia, 1984
600 F.Supp. 465, aff'd 783 F.2d 1184, cert. denied, 479
U.S. 820, 107 S.Ct. 85, 93 L.Ed.2d 38 (1986)

KIDD, District Judge.

* * *

The plaintiffs, American Hospital Association, et al., filed this civil action on June 25, 1984, seeking declaratory and injunctive relief against the State of West Virginia and the Commissioner of Health, L. Clark Hansbarger. The complaint seeks a judgment declaring W.Va.Code § 16-5B-6a (hereinafter "the Act") unconstitutional. Plaintiffs also seek injunctive relief prohibiting the defendant from enforcing the Act. Defendant answered, *inter alia,* that the Act is not unconstitutional and therefore plaintiffs should be denied all relief.

* * *

W.Va.Code § 16-5B-6a requires that on or before July 1, 1984, at least forty percent (40%) of the board of directors of all non-profit and local governmental hospitals located in West Virginia must be composed of an equal proportion of "consumer representatives" from "[s]mall businesses, organized labor, elderly persons, and persons whose income is less than the national median income" and that "[s]pecial consideration shall be made to select women, racial minorities and handicapped persons" for such positions and authorizes defendant Hansbarger and private citizens to enforce its provisions. The entire text of W.Va.Code 16-5B-6a is as follows:

(a) The legislature declares that a crisis in health care costs exists, and that one important approach to deal with this crisis is to have widespread citizen participation in hospital decision-making, and that many hospitals in West Virginia exclude from their boards important categories of consumers, including small businesses, organized labor, elderly persons and lower-income consumers. The legislature further declares that non-profit hospitals receive such major revenue from public sources and are so crucial in health planning and development that it is necessary to require consumer representatives on their boards of directors. Therefore, the legislature determines that non-profit hospitals and hospitals owned by local governments should have boards of directors representative of the communities they serve.

(b) As used in this section, "applicable hospitals" means all non-profit hospitals and all hospitals owned by a county, city or other political subdivision of the State of West Virginia.

(c) At least 40 percent of the boards of directors of applicable hospitals shall, on or before the first day of July, 1984, be composed of an equal proportion of consumer representatives from each of the following four categories: Small businesses, organized labor, elderly persons and persons whose income is less than the national median income. Special consideration shall be made to select women, racial minorities and handicapped persons.

(d) The provisions of this section may be enforced by the director of health, or by any citizen of the county wherein any offending hospital is located, by the filing of an action at law in the circuit court of such county.

* * *

Equal Protection Clause

Plaintiff alleges in Count One of its complaint that the Act is unconstitutional because it does not apply uniformly with respect to the class of all non-profit corporations in the State of West Virginia, more specifically being limited in its applicability by its terms to all non-profit corporations owning and operating hospitals in the State of West Virginia, and the classification attempted by such statute bears no rational relationship to any legitimate interest of the State of West Virginia. This claim is based upon the Equal Protection Clause of the Fourteenth Amendment of the United States Constitution and Section 1, Article XI of the Constitution of West Virginia. * * *

Plaintiffs argue that the Act employs a classification of non-profit and local governmental hospitals on one hand and for-profit and state owned hospitals on the other hand in order to achieve its stated purpose of dealing with health care costs. Further, the plaintiffs argue that such classification bears upon the members of the Sisters of the Pallottine Missionary Society's fundamental right of Freedom of Association.

The Act declares that "a crisis in health care costs exists, that one important approach to deal with this crisis is to have widespread participation in hospital decision making . . ." Under the Act, at least forty percent (40%) of boards of directors of all non-profit and local governmental hospitals located in West Virginia must be composed of an equal proportion of consumer representatives from small business, organized labor, elderly persons, and persons whose income is less than the national median income. The Act also provides that special consideration must be given to women, racial minorities, and handicapped persons. The legislature enacted W.Va.Code § 16–5B–6a with the goal of curbing the rising costs of health care within the state by giving greater citizen participation in hospital decision making. It is the hope and intent of the Legislature that greater citizen participation on the boards of non-profit and local government supported hospitals will result in greater scrutiny over the cost of health care in the state. Since the Act does not apply to profit and state owned hospitals, as opposed to non-profit and local government hospitals, the Court must determine if the classifications in the Act are reasonable in light of the Act's purpose. In *Eisenstadt v. Baird*, 405 U.S. 438, 446, 92 S.Ct. 1029, 1034, 31 L.Ed.2d 349, the

United States Supreme Court referred to *Reed v. Reed,* 404 U.S. 71, 75–76, 92 S.Ct. 251, 253–254, 30 L.Ed.2d 225 (1972), which held:

> In applying that clause, this Court has consistently recognized that the Fourteenth Amendment does not deny to States the power to treat different classes of persons in different ways. * * * The Equal Protection Clause of that amendment does, however, deny to States the power to legislate that different treatment be accorded to persons placed by a statute into different classes on the basis of criteria wholly unrelated to the objective of that statute. A classification "must be reasonable, not arbitrary, and must rest upon some ground of difference having a fair and substantial relation to the object of the legislation, so that all persons similarly circumstanced shall be treated alike." * * *

The Court, in equal protection analysis, must look to the classification or interest involved. * * * Whenever a state act is being challenged as violative of the Equal Protection Clause, the Court must look to one of two constitutional tests. If the legislation creates a suspect classification or impinges upon a fundamental right based upon inherently suspect criteria, then the proper standard of review is strict scrutiny. There must be some showing of a compelling state interest and that the means chosen to achieve that purpose is the least restrictive alternative to meet the standards of strict scrutiny. * * * If no suspect classification exists, or there is no infringement of a fundamental right, then the appropriate standard is the rational basis test. Under the rational basis standard there must be some showing that the classification is rationally related to a legitimate state purpose. * * *

Plaintiffs have a heavy burden. Clearly W.Va.Code 16–5B–6a is an economic regulation. Indeed, the purpose set forth in the Act states specifically that the Legislature's intent in passing such legislation is to attempt to control the rising costs of health care. * * * The Court declines to declare that W.Va.Code 16–5B–6a is an impingement so fundamental that it justifies the protections of strict judicial scrutiny.

In applying W.Va.Code 16–5B–6a, the West Virginia Legislature distinguished between making the Act applicable to non-profit and local government hospitals and not applying the Act to profit and state owned hospitals. Local government hospitals receive their appropriations from political subdivisions of the state. Non-profit hospitals receive a favorable tax status which is clearly a benefit. Indeed, the recognition as a non-profit organization under the tax laws is an indirect grant of public monies or considered as an indirect donation by the public at large:

> When the Government grants exemptions or allows deductions all taxpayers are effected; the very fact of the exemption or deduction for the donor means that other taxpayers can be said to be indirect and vicarious "donors". Charitable exemptions are justified on the basis that the exempt entity confers a public benefit—a benefit which the society or the community may not itself choose or be able

to provide or which supplements and advances the work of public institutions already supported by tax revenues....

Bob Jones University v. United States, 461 U.S. 574, 591, 103 S.Ct. 2017, 2028, 76 L.Ed.2d 157 (1983). There is recognition that organizations are entitled to preferential treatment and tax benefits because they provide a benefit to society. *Bob Jones University v. United States, supra.* Clearly, non-profit hospitals are conferred an advantageous benefit which for-profit hospitals do not receive. Further, W.Va.Code 16–5B–6a does not apply to state hospitals because state hospitals are governed by the director of health and the state rather than a board of directors.

Courts have traditionally exercised judicial restraint to legislative judgment regarding public purpose or purposes based upon the general good. The Court has given great deference to the Legislature's judgment and finds that the Legislature's enactment of W.Va.Code 16–5B–6a has a rational basis. "The Equal Protection Clause does not require that a State must choose between attacking every aspect of a problem or not attacking the problem at all." *Dandridge v. Williams,* 397 U.S. 471, 486, 90 S.Ct. 1153, 1162, 25 L.Ed.2d 491 (1970).

FREEDOM OF ASSOCIATION

The next issue is whether W.Va.Code 16–5B–6a violates the right of association guaranteed to the Sisters of the Pallottine Missionary Society by the First and Fourteenth Amendments of the United States Constitution. The plaintiff, Pallottine Missionary Society, is a religious society of the Roman Catholic Church and is organized as a corporation under the laws of West Virginia. The Pallottine Missionary Society, hereinafter referred to as "the Society," owns and operates St. Joseph's Hospital, in Buckhannon, West Virginia. The Society argues that the Act requiring consumer representation on the boards of non-profit hospitals infringes upon their First Amendment right of Freedom of Association.

The Society is a corporation with a board of governors and provincial council which oversees its operations. St. Joseph's Hospital is not a separate corporation from the Society but is property of the Society and subject to control of the provincial council. However, St. Joseph's Hospital does have its own local board of directors whose members are appointed by the provincial council. The provincial council, composed only of Sisters of the Society, retains the power to approve or disapprove all major actions of the local board. The by-laws of St. Joseph's Hospital local board of directors requires that at least seventy percent (70%) of the local board be members of the Society of Sisters. The Society argues that they are uncertain whether W.Va.Code 16–5B–6a requires consumer representatives on its provincial council or on the local board of St. Joseph's Hospital, or both.

The Act provides that consumer representatives be placed upon "the boards of directors of applicable hospitals." Clearly, the goal is to give greater access and input into the decision making process of hospital boards in hopes of curbing the rising costs of health care. The Sisters of the Pallottine Missionary Society is a religious order of nuns of the Roman Catholic Faith whose purpose is to foster the ideals and beliefs of the Roman Catholic Faith. While the Society may have title and possession over certain hospitals, their primary purpose is the fostering of religious principles protected by the First Amendment. Indeed, the operation of a hospital would seem to be secondary to their religious obligations though the two are very compatible. It is difficult for this Court to believe that the Legislature intended to require consumer representatives on the board of directors of religious orders. The constitutionality of such legislation would be very questionable. Looking to the purpose and the plain language of the Act it appears to the Court that the Act would only require consumer representatives on the local board of directors of the hospital and the Act would not be applicable to the religious society or its governing board.

* * *

* * * The plaintiffs entered an area which is highly regulated and were aware of the regulatory system when they entered the health services area. Further, the main purpose for operating a hospital is to provide health care. While the operation of a hospital and the right to exercise one's religious beliefs or vocation may be compatible, the primary purpose of operating a hospital is to provide health services to the public. The Act does not require Catholic hospitals to alter their creed or beliefs, nor does it prevent them from excluding individuals with ideologies or philosophies different from those of its existing members. * * * Indeed, testimony revealed that the plaintiffs do not exclude members of the categories set forth in the Act and that some board members of Catholic Hospitals qualify in at least one or more categories set forth in the statute. Testimony of Sister Mary Diane Bushee revealed that St. Joseph's Hospital had developed a plan to comply with the Act but had not implemented such plan because of the pending litigation. * * *

The Court recognizes a difference between the First Amendment right of a religious society to associate for the advancement of its beliefs and ideas and the operation of a hospital. Clearly, the operation of a hospital, pursuant to the corporate laws of the state, is not essential to the expression or advocacy of one's religious beliefs. * * *

* * *

Due Process Clause

The plaintiffs argue that the Act is (1) unreasonable, arbitrary and capricious because it bears no real relationship to hospital cost containment control; (2) unreasonably and arbitrarily restricts the ability of hospitals to discharge their legal responsibility to quality as well as cost efficient health care; and (3) takes the Sisters of the Pallottine Missionary Society's property without compensation; and (4) is vague, ambiguous, and overbroad. The Court will address these issues in the order presented.

Plaintiffs argue that the Act has no relationship to the containment of hospital costs. The Legislature passed this Act in hopes of curbing rising hospital costs. Certainly, there is a rational relationship between the operation of a hospital and its board of directors. In fact, the board of directors establish the policy and guidelines which ultimately determine the cost and quality of services to be provided by a hospital. The Legislature apparently was of the opinion that placing consumer representatives on hospital boards would allow the consumer a greater input into the overall operation of hospitals and ultimately result in closer scrutiny of financial operations. The Court gives great deference to the Legislature in this matter and is of the opinion that there is a relationship between the composition of hospital boards and the containment of hospital costs. The Court is of the opinion that it should not infringe upon the powers of the Legislature.

The next issue concerns whether the Act restricts the ability of hospitals to maintain effective governance and to discharge their legal responsibility to qualify as well as cost efficient health care. Plaintiffs contend that the Act's establishment of specified percentages for consumer representation on hospital boards without regard to qualification and commitment regarding the discharge of their duties constitutes an arbitrary and unreasonable restriction in violation of the Due Process Clause of the Fourteenth Amendment. There is no reason to believe that the average consumer is not qualified to serve as a hospital board member. The ultimate decision regarding the selection of individuals to serve on hospital boards rests solely upon the hospital itself. When selecting board members the hospital may continue to use the criteria and standards for selection of board members as it has done in the past. The only difference is that the hospital must now be sensitive to the four categories set forth in the Act. Certainly, there are individuals within those categories who would make excellent board members. In fact, testimony revealed that some members who are presently serving on hospital boards would come within one or more of the four categories set forth in the Act. The ultimate responsibility lies, as it has in the past, with the hospital to recruit and select only those individuals who would make good board members. For these reasons, the Court is of the opinion that this issue is without merit.

The plaintiffs have also raised the question of whether there is a taking of property without compensation. It is argued that there is a taking of the Sisters of the Pallottine Missionary Society's property without compensation and therefore in violation of the Due Process Clause of the Fourteenth Amendment.

The Fourteenth Amendment of the United States Constitution provides that no person shall be deprived of his property without due process of law. However, it has been held that every governmental regulation of uses of private property was not a taking for public use. * * * In *Troy Ltd. v. Renna,* 727 F.2d 287, 302 (3d Cir.1984), it was held that "regulations of the use of private property frequently involve costs to the owner. They are nevertheless not deemed to be takings." Where there is a common exercise of regulatory power then courts have tended to sustain government action. * * * In *Pennsylvania Coal Co. v. Mahon,* 260 U.S. 393, 413, 43 S.Ct. 158, 159, 67 L.Ed. 322 (1922), the court held that:

> [G]overnment regulation—by definition—involves the adjustment of rights for the public good. Often this adjustment curtails some potential for the use or economic exploitation of private property. To require compensation in all such circumstances would effectively compel the government to regulate by purchase.
>
> "Government hardly could go on if to some extent values incident to property could not be diminished without paying for every such change in the general law."

The court went on to indicate that "the greatest weight is given to the judgment of the legislature, but it always is open to interested parties to contend that the legislature has gone beyond its constitutional power." * * * A taking occurs in the ordinary sense when government controls a person's use of property so tightly that, although some uses remain to the owner, the property's value has been virtually destroyed. * * * In *Penn Central Transportation Company v. City of New York,* 438 U.S. 104, 98 S.Ct. 2646, 57 L.Ed.2d 631 (1978), the court set forth guidelines on determining when a taking has occurred:

> In engaging in these essentially ad hoc, factual inquiries, the Court's decisions have identified several factors that have particular significance. The economic impact of the regulation on the claimant and, particularly, the extent to which the regulation has interfered with distinct investment-backed expectations are, of course, relevant considerations.
>
> ... So, too, is the character of the governmental action. A "taking" may more readily be found when the interference with property can be characterized as a physical invasion by government ... than when interference arises from some public program adjusting the benefits and burdens of economic life to promote the common good.

The Act establishes certain guidelines or regulations for the common good in the hopes of containing health care costs. The regulated hospitals are either directly supported by the state or indirectly supported through certain tax exemptions. Irregardless of the method of financial support, non-profit and local government hospitals receive such benefits because of their commitment to public service. Clearly, the state has not appropriated or taken governing control of these hospitals. Hospitals, and the health field in general, have been a highly regulated field. The plaintiffs were aware of that fact when they entered the hospital business. The Act challenged here is a method or attempt to regulate hospital costs.

* * *

On the basis of the testimony adduced at the hearing on plaintiffs' "Motion for Preliminary Injunction", the parties respective memorandums of law and reply, the Court finds that W.Va.Code 16–5B–6a does not violate the Constitution of the United States and the Constitution of the State of West Virginia.

Judgment shall be accordingly ORDERED.

Notes

1. States, vis-a-vis their power to promote public health, regulate hospitals through licensing requirements. Licensure is used both to assure that hospitals meet minimum quality standards of health care and also to control the rising costs of health care.

2. Most hospitals seek accreditation by the Joint Commission on Accreditation of Healthcare Organizations (JCAHO). The Joint Commission is a nonprofit corporation formed in 1951 for the purpose of creating and maintaining professional standards for evaluating hospital performance. The JCAHO standards are published in its Accreditation Manual. Both federal and state governments have relied upon standards of the Joint Commission as a guarantee of high quality of medical care. Hospitals accredited by JCAHO generally will meet the conditions of participation required for a hospital to qualify as a provider in the Medicare and Medicaid programs (42 U.S.C. §§ 1395 et. seq.).

II. REORGANIZATIONS OF NONPROFIT HOSPITALS

Nonprofit hospital corporations have been engaged in extensive reorganizations to meet the growing demands of the health care industry and to prevent nonprofit hospitals from losing their tax exempt status by too much involvement in activities that produce unrelated business taxable income. These reorganizations have included the formation of multicorporate structures, generally other nonprofit corporations (to perform fund-raising activities and to engage in various health-related programs) and the formation of for-profit corporations (to perform activities that would produce unrelated business taxable income to a tax exempt hospital). Such reorganizations reportedly have provided hospitals with additional income, have enhanced their ability to attract physicians, have provided more effective reimbursement management through segregation of nonhospital functions, and have improved cost reporting procedures.

To retain valued physicians, hospitals often have entered into partnership arrangements with members of the hospital staff and with profit organizations to manage and operate office buildings in which members of the hospital staff can lease offices. Hospitals have entered into agreements with for-profit research corporations whereby the for-profit corporation receives rights to any patentable technology developed through research performed in the hospital and, in turn, remits a portion of the profits from marketing the results of the research to the hospital. Nonprofit hospitals also have engaged in reorganizations that are structured so that a parent nonprofit corporation, generally one that either is involved in health educational programs or that performs fund-raising activities, becomes a holding company for the nonprofit hospital and for the various other nonprofit health-related organizations formed to engage in related exempt functions, such as outpatient services; care facilities for the aged; nursing homes; day care centers; rehabilitation programs, including speech therapy; and billing, data processing, collection, laundry and consulting services. The parent nonprofit corporation may control a profit corporation established, as examples, to operate a pharmacy, a home nursing care organization, or a surgical center; to operate a printing or graphics service; to sell laboratory services to physicians for use in their private practices; or to acquire and maintain a medical office building. In addition, the parent organization may control a nonprofit fund-raising organization.

The creation and operation of separate corporations related to a nonprofit hospital must center around a concern to retain public charity status for the nonprofit corporations within the controlled group. Thus, the differing problems relating to each type of public charity—the § 509(a)(1) under § 170(b)(1)(A)(vi), the § 509(a)(2) charity, and the § 509(a)(3), must be considered. The hospital would qualify under § 509(a)(1) and 170(b)(1)(A)(iii). As noted in Chapter 6, a § 509(a)(1) organization under § 170(b)(1)(A)(vi) must obtain more than one-third of its support from the general public. Gross receipts from the performance of services are not counted in the computation of the one-third support fraction. As a result, service organizations would have difficulty maintaining public charity status under § 509(a)(1). The service organizations that provide a variety of health care services, such as care facilities for the aged, outpatient services, community health programs, and nursing care, or home health agencies should be established as § 509(a)(2) organizations. Because a § 509(a)(2) organization may not receive more than a third of its income from investment sources, fund raising activities and the investment of general funds should be carried on by a § 509(a)(1) organization under § 170(b)(1)(A)(vi) or by a supporting organization under § 509(a)(3).

Dividends from profit corporations within a health care group can be returned to a parent nonprofit corporation tax-free because dividends are not taxed as unrelated business taxable income. (See Chapter 9.)

While the provision of health care is a "charitable" tax-exempt purpose, some hospitals have had difficulty in maintaining their tax exempt status when they failed to provide health care without charge to indigents, when they formed partnerships with for-profit entities to maximize profits, and when they provided excessive incentives to recruit private physicians.

Question

What incentives can a hospital provide private physicians, to encourage them to join its medical staff or to relocate to a community to provide medical services, without jeopardizing the hospital's tax exempt status?

Sec. II   REORGANIZATIONS OF NONPROFIT HOSPITALS   629

REVENUE RULING 97–21
1997–1 C.B. 121

ISSUE

Whether, under the facts described below, a hospital violates the requirements for exemption from federal income tax as an organization described in § 501(c)(3) of the Internal Revenue Code when it provides incentives to recruit private practice physicians to join its medical staff or to provide medical services in the community.

FACTS

All of the hospitals in the situations described below have been recognized as exempt from federal income tax under § 501(a) as organizations described in § 501(c)(3) and operate in accordance with the standards for exemption set forth in Revenue Ruling 69–545, 1969–2 C.B. 117. The physicians described in the following recruiting transactions do not have substantial influence over the affairs of the hospitals that are recruiting them. Therefore, they are not disqualified persons as defined in § 4958, nor do they have any personal or private interest in the activities of the organizations that would subject them to the inurement proscription of § 501(c)(3). Furthermore, in Situations 1, 2, and 4, the physicians have no pre-existing relationship with the hospital or the members of its board. For purposes of this revenue ruling, the physician recruiting activities described in Situations 1, 2, 3, and 4 are assumed to be lawful. However, because the Internal Revenue Service does not have jurisdiction regarding whether the activities described in Situations 1, 2, 3, and 4 are lawful under the Medicare and Medicaid anti-kickback statute, 42 U.S.C. § 1320a–7b(b), taxpayers may not rely upon the facts or assumptions described in this ruling for purposes relating to that statute.

Situation 1

Hospital A is located in County V, a rural area, and is the only hospital within a 100 mile radius. County V has been designated by the U.S. Public Health Service as a Health Professional Shortage Area for primary medical care professionals (a category that includes obstetricians and gynecologists). Physician M recently completed an ob/gyn residency and is not on Hospital A's medical staff. Hospital A recruits Physician M to establish and maintain a full-time private ob/gyn practice in its service area and become a member of its medical staff. Hospital A provides Physician M a recruitment incentive package pursuant to a written agreement negotiated at arm's-length. The agreement is in accordance with guidelines for physician recruitment that Hospital A's Board of Directors establishes, monitors, and reviews regularly to ensure that recruiting practices are consistent with Hospital A's exempt purposes. The agreement was approved by the committee appointed by Hospital A's Board of Directors to approve contracts with hospital medical staff. Hospital A does not provide any recruiting incentives to Physician M other than those set forth in the written agreement.

In accordance with the agreement, Hospital A pays Physician M a signing bonus, Physician M's professional liability insurance premium for a limited period, provides office space in a building owned by Hospital A for a limited number of years at a below market rent (after which the rental will be at fair market value), and guarantees Physician M's mortgage on a residence in County V. Hospital A also lends Physician M practice start-up financial assistance pursuant to an agreement that is properly documented and bears reasonable terms.

Situation 2

Hospital B is located in an economically depressed inner-city area of City W. Hospital B has conducted a community needs assessment that indicates both a shortage of pediatricians in Hospital B's service area and difficulties Medicaid patients are having obtaining pediatric services. Physician N is a pediatrician currently practicing outside of Hospital B's service area and is not on Hospital B's medical staff. Hospital B recruits Physician N to relocate to City W, establish and maintain a full-time pediatric practice in Hospital B's service area, become a member of Hospital B's medical staff, and treat a reasonable number of Medicaid patients. Hospital B offers Physician N a recruitment incentive package pursuant to a written agreement negotiated at arm's-length and approved by Hospital B's Board of Directors. Hospital B does not provide any recruiting incentives to Physician N other than those set forth in the written agreement.

Under the agreement, Hospital B reimburses Physician N for moving expenses as defined in § 217(b), reimburses Physician N for professional liability "tail" coverage for Physician N's former practice, and guarantees Physician N's private practice income for a limited number of years. The private practice income guarantee, which is properly documented, provides that Hospital B will make up the difference to the extent Physician N practices full-time in its service area and the private practice does not generate a certain level of net income (after reasonable expenses of the practice). The amount guaranteed falls within the range reflected in regional or national surveys regarding income earned by physicians in the same specialty.

Situation 3

Hospital C is located in an economically depressed inner city area of City X. Hospital C has conducted a community needs assessment that indicates indigent patients are having difficulty getting access to care because of a shortage of obstetricians in Hospital C's service area willing to treat Medicaid and charity care patients. Hospital C recruits Physician O, an obstetrician who is currently a member of Hospital C's medical staff, to provide these services and enters into a written agreement with Physician O. The agreement is in accordance with guidelines for physician recruitment that Hospital C's Board of Directors establishes, monitors, and reviews regularly to ensure that recruiting practices are consistent with Hospital C's exempt purpose. The agreement was approved by the officer designated by Hospital C's Board of Directors to enter into contracts with hospital medical staff. Hospital C does not provide any recruiting incentives to Physician O other than those set forth in the written agreement. Pursuant to the agreement, Hospital C agrees to reimburse Physician O for the cost of one year's professional liability insurance in return for an agreement by Physician O to treat a reasonable number of Medicaid and charity care patients for that year.

Situation 4

Hospital D is located in City Y, a medium to large size metropolitan area. Hospital D requires a minimum of four diagnostic radiologists to ensure adequate coverage and a high quality of care for its radiology department. Two of the four diagnostic radiologists currently providing coverage for Hospital D are relocating to other areas. Hospital D initiates a search for diagnostic radiologists and determines that one of the two most qualified candidates is Physician P.

Physician P currently is practicing in City Y as a member of the medical staff of Hospital E (which is also located in City Y). As a diagnostic radiologist, Physician P provides services for patients receiving care at Hospital E, but does not refer patients to Hospital E or any other hospital in City Y. Physician P is not on Hospital D's medical staff. Hospital D recruits Physician P to join its medical staff and to provide coverage for its radiology department. Hospital D offers Physician P a recruitment incentive package pursuant to a written agreement, negotiated at arm's-length and approved by Hospital D's Board of Directors. Hospital D does not provide any recruiting incentives to Physician P other than those set forth in the written agreement.

Pursuant to the agreement, Hospital D guarantees Physician P's private practice income for the first few years that Physician P is a member of its medical staff and provides coverage for its radiology department. The private practice income guarantee, which is properly documented, provides that Hospital D will make up the difference to Physician P to the extent the private practice does not generate a certain level of net income (after reasonable expenses of the practice). The net income amount guaranteed falls within the range reflected in regional or national surveys regarding income earned by physicians in the same specialty.

Situation 5

Hospital F is located in City Z, a medium to large size metropolitan area. Because of its physician recruitment practices, Hospital F has been found guilty in a court of law of knowingly and willfully violating the Medicare and Medicaid anti-kickback statute, 42 U.S.C. § 1320a–7b(b), for providing recruitment incentives that constituted payments for referrals. The activities resulting in the violations were substantial.

LAW

* * *

Section 1.501(c)(3)–1(d)(1)(ii) states that an organization is not organized exclusively for any of the purposes specified in § 501(c)(3) unless it serves public, rather than private interests. Thus, an organization applying for tax exemption under § 501(c)(3) must establish that it is not organized or operated for the benefit of private interests.

Rev. Rul. 69–545, 1969–2 C.B. 117, holds that a non-profit hospital that benefits a broad cross section of its community by having an open medical staff and a board of trustees broadly representative of the community, operating a full-time emergency room open to all regardless of ability to pay, and otherwise admitting all patients able to pay (either themselves, or through third party payers such as private health insurance or government programs such as Medicare) may qualify as an organization described in § 501(c)(3). The same standard has been used by the courts as the basis for evaluating whether health maintenance organizations qualify for exemption as organizations described in § 501(c)(3). Sound Health Association v. Commissioner, 71 T.C. 158 (1978), acq. 1981–2 C.B. 2; Geisinger Health Plan v. Commissioner, 985 F.2d 1210 (3d Cir.1993), rev'g 62 T.C.M. (CCH) 1656 (1991).

Rev. Rul. 72–559, 1972–2 C.B. 247, holds that an organization that provides subsidies to recent law school graduates during the first three years of their practice to enable them to establish legal practices in economically depressed communities that have a shortage of available legal services and to provide free legal service to needy members of the community may qualify as an organization described in § 501(c)(3).

Rev. Rul. 73–313, 1973–2 C.B. 174, holds that attracting a physician to a community that had no available medical services furthered the charitable purpose of promoting the health of the community. In Rev. Rul. 73–313, residents of an isolated rural community had to travel a considerable distance to obtain care. Faced with the total lack of local services, the community formed an organization to raise funds and build a medical office building to attract a doctor to the locality. (No hospitals or existing medical practices were involved.) The ruling states that certain facts are particularly relevant: (1) the demonstrated need for a physician to avert a real and substantial threat to the community; (2) evidence that the lack of a suitable office had impeded efforts to attract a physician; (3) the arrangements were completely at arm's-length; and (4) there was no relationship between any person connected with the organization and the recruited physician. The ruling states that, under all the circumstances, the arrangement used to induce the doctor to locate a practice in the area "bear[s] a reasonable relationship to promotion and protection of the health of the community" and any private benefit to the physician is incidental to the public purpose achieved. It concludes that the activity furthers a charitable purpose and the organization qualifies for exemption as an organization described in § 501(c)(3).

Rev. Rul. 75–384, 1975–2 C.B. 204, holds that an organization whose primary activity is sponsoring antiwar protest demonstrations in which demonstrators are urged to commit violations of local ordinances and breaches of the public order does not qualify as an organization described in § 501(c)(3) because its activities demonstrate an illegal purpose that is inconsistent with charitable purposes.

Rev. Rul. 80–278, 1980–2 C.B. 175, and Rev. Rul. 80–279, 1980–2 C.B. 176, discuss the qualification as organizations described in § 501(c)(3) of organizations that conduct environmental litigation and environmental dispute mediation. In holding that these organizations may qualify, the rulings state that, in determining whether an organization meets the operational test, the issue is whether the particular activity undertaken by the organization appropriately furthers the organization's exempt purpose. The rulings state that an organization's activities will be considered permissible under § 501(c)(3) if the following conditions are met: (1) the purpose of the organization is charitable; (2) the activities are not illegal, contrary to a clearly defined and established public policy, or in conflict with express statutory restrictions; and (3) the activities are in furtherance of the organization's exempt purpose and are reasonably related to the accomplishment of that purpose.

ANALYSIS

In order to meet the requirements of § 501(c)(3), a hospital that provides recruitment incentives to physicians must provide those incentives in a manner that does not cause the organization to violate the operational test of § 1.501(c)(3)–1. Whether the recruitment incentives cause the organization to violate the operational test is determined based on all relevant facts and circumstances. When a § 501(c)(3) hospital recruits a physician for its medical staff who is to perform services for or on behalf of the organization, the organization meets the operational test by showing that, taking into account all of the benefits provided the physician by the organization, the organization is paying reasonable compensation for the services the physician is providing in return. A somewhat different analysis must be applied when a § 501(c)(3) hospital recruits a physician for its medical staff to provide services to members of the surrounding community but not necessarily for or on behalf of the organization. In these cases, a violation will result from a failure to comply with any of the following four requirements:

First, the organization may not engage in substantial activities that do not further the hospital's exempt purposes or that do not bear a reasonable relationship to the accomplishment of those purposes. As discussed in Rev. Rul. 80–278 and Rev. Rul. 80–279, in determining whether an organization meets the operational test, the issue is whether the particular activity undertaken by the organization is appropriately in furtherance of the organization's exempt purpose.

Second, the organization must not engage in activities that result in inurement of the hospital's net earnings to a private shareholder or individual. An activity may result in inurement if it is structured as a device to distribute the net earnings of the hospital. See Lorain Avenue Clinic v. Commissioner, 31 T.C. 141 (1958); Birmingham Business College, Inc. v. Commissioner, 276 F.2d 476 (5th Cir.1960).

Third, the organization may not engage in substantial activities that cause the hospital to be operated for the benefit of a private interest rather than public interest so that it has a substantial non-exempt purpose. Section 1.501(c)(3)–1(d)(1)(ii).

Finally, the organization may not engage in substantial unlawful activities. As discussed in Rev. Rul. 75–384, Rev. Rul. 80–278, and Rev. Rul. 80–279, the conduct of an unlawful activity is inconsistent with charitable purposes. An organization conducts an activity that is unlawful, and therefore not in furtherance of a charitable purpose, if the organization's property is to be used for an objective that is in violation of the criminal law. Activities can accomplish an unlawful purpose through either direct or indirect means.

Situation 1

Like the organization described in Rev. Rul. 73–313, Hospital A has objective evidence demonstrating a need for obstetricians and gynecologists in its service area and has engaged in physician recruitment activity bearing a reasonable relationship to promoting and protecting the health of the community in accordance with Rev. Rul. 69–545. As with the subsidies provided to the recent law school graduates in Rev. Rul. 72–559, the payment of a bonus, the guarantee of a mortgage, the reimbursement of professional liability insurance and provision of subsidized office space for a limited time, and the lending of start-up financial assistance as recruitment incentives are reasonably related to causing Physician M to become a member of Hospital A's medical staff and to establish and maintain a full-time private ob/gyn practice in Hospital A's service area. The provision of the incentives under the circumstances described furthers the charitable purposes served by the hospital and is consistent with the requirements for exemption as an organization described in § 501(c)(3).

Situation 2

Like Hospital A in Situation 1, Hospital B has objective evidence demonstrating a need for pediatricians in its service area and has engaged in physician recruitment activity bearing a reasonable relationship to promoting and protecting the health of the community in much the same manner as the organization described in Rev. Rul. 73–313. As with the recruitment incentive package provided by Hospital A, the payment of moving expenses, the reimbursement of professional liability "tail" coverage, and the provision of a reasonable private practice income guarantee as recruitment incentives are reasonably related to causing Physician N to become a member of Hospital B's medical staff and to establish and maintain a full-time private pediatric practice in Hospital B's service area. Thus, the recruitment activity described furthers the charitable purposes served by the hospital and is consistent with the requirements for exemption as an organization described in § 501(c)(3).

Situation 3

In accordance with the standards for exemption set forth in Rev. Rul. 69–545, Hospital C admits and treats Medicaid patients on a nondiscriminatory basis. Hospital C has identified a shortage of obstetricians willing to treat Medicaid patients. The payment of Physician O's professional liability insurance premiums in return for Physician O's agreement to treat a reasonable number of Medicaid and charity care patients is reasonably related to the accomplishment of Hospital C's exempt purposes. Because the amount paid by Hospital C is reasonable and any private benefit to Physician O is outweighed by the public purpose served by the agreement, the recruitment activity described is consistent with the requirements for exemption as an organization described in § 501(c)(3)

Situation 4

Hospital D has objective evidence demonstrating a need for diagnostic radiologists to provide coverage for its radiology department so that it can promote the health of the community. The provision of a reasonable private practice income guarantee as a recruitment incentive that is conditioned upon Physician P obtaining medical staff privileges and providing coverage for the radiology department is reasonably related to the accomplishment of the charitable purposes served by the hospital. A significant fact in determining that the community benefit provided by the activity outweighs the private benefit provided to Physician P is the determination by the Board of Directors of Hospital D that it needs additional diagnostic radiologists to provide adequate coverage and to ensure a high quality of medical care. The recruitment activity described is consistent with the requirements for exemption as an organization described in § 501(c)(3).

Situation 5

Hospital F has engaged in physician recruiting practices resulting in a criminal conviction. As in Rev. Rul. 75–384, the recruiting activities were intentional and criminal, not isolated or inadvertent violations of a regulatory statute. An organization that engages in substantial unlawful activities, including activities involving the use of the organization's property for an objective that is in violation of criminal law, does not qualify as an organization described in § 501(c)(3). Because Hospital F has knowingly and willfully conducted substantial activities that are inconsistent with charitable purposes, it does not comply with the requirements of § 501(c)(3) and § 1.501(c)(3)–1.

HOLDING

The hospitals in Situations 1, 2, 3, and 4 have not violated the requirements for exemption from federal income tax as organizations described in § 501(c)(3) as a result of the physician recruitment incentive agreements they have made because the transactions further charitable purposes, do not result in inurement, do not result in the hospitals serving a private rather than a public purpose, and are assumed to be lawful for purposes of this revenue ruling.

Hospital F in Situation 5 does not qualify as an organization described in § 501(c)(3) because its unlawful physician recruitment activities are inconsistent with charitable purposes.

* * *

Question

Under what circumstances will a hospital jeopardize its tax exempt status by entering into a joint venture with a for-profit entity?

REVENUE RULING 98–15

1998–1 C.B. 718

ISSUE

Whether, under the facts described below, an organization that operates an acute care hospital continues to qualify for exemption from federal income tax as an organization described in § 501(c)(3) of the Internal Revenue Code when it forms a limited liability company (LLC) with a for-profit corporation and then contributes its hospital and all of its other operating assets to the LLC, which then operates the hospital.

FACTS

Situation 1

A is a nonprofit corporation that owns and operates an acute care hospital. A has been recognized as exempt from federal income tax under § 501(a) as an organization described in § 501(c)(3) and as other than a private foundation as defined in § 509(a) because it is described in § 170(b)(1)(A)(iii). B is a for-profit corporation that owns and operates a number of hospitals.

A concludes that it could better serve its community if it obtained additional funding. B is interested in providing financing for A's hospital, provided it earns a reasonable rate of return. A and B form a limited liability company, C. A contributes all of its operating assets, including its hospital to C. B also contributes assets to C. In return, A and B receive ownership interests in C proportional and equal in value to their respective contributions.

C's Articles of Organization and Operating Agreement ("governing documents") provide that C is to be managed by a governing board consisting of three individuals chosen by A and two individuals chosen by B. A intends to appoint community leaders who have experience with hospital matters, but who are not on the hospital staff and do not otherwise engage in business transactions with the hospital. * * *

The governing documents require that C operate any hospital it owns in a manner that furthers charitable purposes by promoting health for a broad cross section of its community. The governing documents explicitly provide that the duty of the members of the governing board to operate C in a manner that furthers charitable purposes by promoting health for a broad cross section of the community overrides any duty they may have to operate C for the financial benefit of its owners. Accordingly, in the event of a conflict between operation in accordance with the community benefit standard and any duty to maximize profits, the members of the governing board are to satisfy the community benefit standard without regard to the consequences for maximizing profitability.

The governing documents further provide that all returns of capital and distributions of earnings made to owners of C shall be proportional to their ownership interests in C. The terms of the governing documents are legal, binding, and enforceable under applicable state law.

C enters into a management agreement with a management company that is unrelated to A or B to provide day-to-day management services to C. The management agreement is for a five-year period, and the agreement is renewable for additional five-year periods by mutual consent. The management company will be paid a management fee for its services based on C's gross revenues. The terms and conditions of the management agreement, including the fee structure and the contract term, are reasonable and comparable to what other management firms receive for similar services at similarly situated hospitals. C may terminate the agreement for cause.

None of the officers, directors, or key employees of A who were involved in making the decision to form C were promised employment or any other inducement by C or B and their related entities if the transaction were approved. None of A's officers, directors, or key employees have any interest, including any interest through attribution determined in accordance with the principles of § 318, in B or any of its related entities.

Pursuant to § 301.7701–3(b) of the Procedure and Administrative Regulations, C will be treated as a partnership for federal income tax purposes.

A intends to use any distributions it receives from C to fund grants to support activities that promote the health of A's community and to help the indigent obtain health care. Substantially all of A's grantmaking will be funded by distributions from C. A's projected grantmaking program and its participation as an owner of C will constitute A's only activities.

Situation 2

D is a nonprofit corporation that owns and operates an acute care hospital. D has been recognized as exempt from federal income tax under § 501(a) as an organization described in § 501(c)(3) and as other than a private foundation as defined in § 509(a) because it is described in § 170(b)(1)(iii). E is a for-profit hospital corporation that owns and operates a number of hospitals and provides management services to several hospitals that it does not own.

D concludes that it could better serve its community if it obtained additional funding. E is interested in providing financing for D's hospital, provided it earns a reasonable rate of return. D and E form a limited liability company, F. D contributes all of its operating assets, including its hospital to F. E also contributes assets to F. In return, D and E receive ownership interests proportional and equal in value to their respective contributions.

F's Articles of Organization and Operating Agreement ("governing documents") provide that F is to be managed by a governing board consisting of three individuals chosen by D and three individuals chosen by E. D intends to appoint community leaders who have experience with hospital matters, but who are not on the hospital staff and do not otherwise engage in business transactions with the hospital.

The governing documents further provide that they may only be amended with the approval of both owners and that a majority of board members must approve certain major decisions relating to F's operation * * *.

F's governing documents provide that F's purpose is to construct, develop, own, manage, operate, and take other action in connection with operating the health care facilities it owns and engage in other health care-related activities. The governing documents further provide that all returns of capital and distributions of earnings made to owners of F shall be proportional to their ownership interests in F.

F enters into a management agreement with a wholly-owned subsidiary of E to provide day-to-day management services to F. The management agreement is for a five-year period, and the agreement is renewable for additional five-year periods at the discretion of E's subsidiary. F may terminate the agreement only for cause. E's subsidiary will be paid a management fee for its services based on gross revenues. The terms and conditions of the management agreement, including the fee structure and the contract term other than the renewal terms, are reasonable and comparable to what other management firms receive for similar services at similarly situated hospitals.

As part of the agreement to form F, D agrees to approve the selection of two individuals to serve as F's chief executive officer and chief financial officer. These individuals have previously worked for E in hospital management and have business expertise. They will work with the management company to oversee F's day-to-day management. Their compensation is comparable to what comparable executives are paid at similarly situated hospitals.

Pursuant to § 301.7701–3(b). F will be treated as a partnership for federal tax income purposes.

D intends to use any distributions it receives from F to fund grants to support activities that promote the health of D's community and to help the indigent obtain health care. Substantially all of D's grantmaking will be funded by distributions from F. D's projected grantmaking program and its participation as an owner of F will constitute D's only activities.

LAW

* * *

Section 1.501(c)(3)–1(d)(2) provides that the term "charitable" is used in § 501(c)(3) in its generally accepted legal sense. The promotion of health has long been recognized as a charitable purpose. See Restatement (Second) of Trusts, §§ 368, 372 (1959); 4A Austin W. Scott and William F. Fratcher, The Law of Trusts §§ 368, 372 (4th ed. 1989). However, not every activity that promotes health supports tax exemption under § 501(c)(3). For example, selling prescription pharmaceuticals certainly promotes health, but pharmacies cannot qualify for recognition of exemption under § 501(c)(3) on that basis alone. Federation Pharmacy Services, Inc. v. Commissioner, 72 T.C. 687 (1979), aff'd, 625 F.2d 804 (8th Cir.1980) ("Federation Pharmacy"). Furthermore, "an institution for the promotion of health is not a charitable institution if it is privately owned and is run for the profit of the owners." 4A Austin W. Scott and William F. Fratcher, The Law of Trusts § 372.1 (4th ed. 1989). See also Restatement (Second) of Trusts, § 376 (1959). This principle applies to hospitals and other health care organizations. As the Tax Court stated, "[w]hile the diagnosis and cure of disease are indeed purposes that may furnish the foundation for characterizing the activity as 'charitable,' something more is required." Sonora Community Hospital v. Commissioner, 46 T.C. 519, 525–526 (1966), aff'd 397 F.2d 814 (9th Cir.1968) ("Sonora"). See also Sound Health Association v. Commissioner, 71 T.C. 158 (1978), acq. 1981–2 C.B. 2 ("Sound Health"); Geisinger Health Plan v. Commissioner, 985 F.2d 1210 (3d Cir., 1993), rev'g 62 T.C.M. 1656 (1991) ("Geisinger").

In evaluating whether a nonprofit hospital qualifies as an organization described in § 501(c)(3), Rev. Rul. 69–545, 1969–2 C.B. 117, compares two hospitals. The first hospital discussed is controlled by a board of trustees composed of independent civic leaders. In addition, the hospital maintains an open medical staff, with privileges available to all qualified physicians; it operates a full-time emergency room open to all regardless of ability to pay; and it otherwise admits all patients able to pay (either themselves, or through third party payers such as private health insurance or government programs such as Medicare). In contrast, the second hospital is controlled by physicians who have a substantial economic interest in the hospital. This hospital restricts the number of physicians admitted to the medical staff, enters into favorable rental agreements with the individuals who control the hospital, and limits emergency room and hospital admission substantially to the patients of the physicians who control the hospital. Rev. Rul. 69–545 notes that in considering whether a nonprofit hospital is operated to serve a private benefit, the Service will weigh all the relevant facts and circumstances in each case, including the use and control of the hospital. The revenue ruling concludes that the first hospital continues to qualify as an organization described in § 501(c)(3) and the second hospital does not because it is operated for the private benefit of the physicians who control the hospital.

Section 509(a) provides that the term "private foundation" means a domestic or foreign organization described in § 501(c)(3) other than an organization described in § 509(a)(1), (2), (3), or (4). The organizations described in § 509(a)(1) include those described in § 170(b)(1)(A)(iii). An organization is described in § 170(b)(1)(A)(iii) if its principal purpose is to provide medical or hospital care.

* * *

In Plumstead Theatre Society, Inc. v. Commissioner, 74 T.C. 1324 (1980), aff'd, 675 F.2d 244 (9th Cir.1982) ("Plumstead"), the Tax Court held that a charitable organization's participation as a general partner in a limited partnership did not jeopardize its exempt status. The organization co-produced a play as one of its charitable activities. Prior to the opening of the play, the organization encountered financial difficulties in raising its share of costs. In order to meet its funding obligations, the organization formed a limited partnership in which it served as general partner, and two individuals and a for-profit corporation were the limited partners. One of the significant factors supporting the Tax Court's holding was its finding that the limited partners had no control over the organization's operations.

In Broadway Theatre League of Lynchburg, Virginia, Inc. v. U.S., 293 F.Supp. 346 (W.D.Va.1968) ("Broadway Theatre League"), the court held that an organization that promoted an interest in theatrical arts did not jeopardize its exempt status when it hired a booking organization to arrange for a series of theatrical performances, promote the series and sell season tickets to the series because the contract was for a reasonable term and provided for reasonable compensation and the organization retained ultimate authority over the activities being managed.

In Housing Pioneers v. Commissioner, 65 T.C.M. (CCH) 2191 (1993), aff'd, 49 F.3d 1395 (9th Cir.1995), amended 58 F.3d 401 (9th Cir.1995) ("Housing Pioneers"), the Tax Court concluded that an organization did not qualify as a § 501(c)(3) organization because its activities performed as co-general partner in for-profit limited partnerships substantially furthered a non-exempt purpose, and serving that purpose caused the organization to serve private interests. The organization entered into partnerships as a one percent co-general partner of existing limited partnerships for the purpose of splitting the tax benefits with the for-profit partners. Under the management agreement, the organization's authority as co-general partner was narrowly circumscribed. It had no management responsibilities and could describe only a vague charitable function of surveying tenant needs. * * *

* * *

ANALYSIS

For federal income tax purposes, the activities of a partnership are often considered to be the activities of the partners. See, e.g., Butler. Aggregate treatment is also consistent with the treatment of partnerships for purpose of the unrelated business income tax under § 512(c). See H.R. No. 2319, 81st Cong., 2d Sess. 36, 110–112 (1950); S.Rep. No. 2375, 81st Cong., 2d Sess. 26, 109–110 (1950); § 1.512(c)–1. In light of the aggregate principle discussed in Butler and reflected in § 512(c), the aggregate approach also applies for purposes of the operational test set forth in § 1.501(c)(3)–1(c). Thus, the activities of an LLC treated as a partnership for federal income tax purposes are considered to be the activities of a nonprofit organization that is an owner of the LLC when evaluating whether the nonprofit organization is operated exclusively for exempt purposes within the meaning of § 501(c)(3).

A § 501(c)(3) organization may form and participate in a partnership, including an LLC treated as a partnership for federal income tax purposes, and meet the operational test if participation in the partnership furthers a charitable purpose, and the partnership arrangement permits the exempt organization to act exclusively in furtherance of its exempt purpose and only incidentally for the benefit of the for-profit partners. See Plumstead and Housing Pioneers. Similarly, a § 501(c)(3) organization may enter into a management contract with a private party giving that party authority to conduct activities on behalf of the organization and direct the use of the organization's assets provided that the organization retains ultimate authority over the assets and activities being managed and the terms and conditions of the contract are reasonable, including reasonable compensation and a reasonable term. See Broadway Theatre League. However, if a private party is allowed to control or use the non-profit organization's activities or assets for the benefit of the private party, and the benefit is not incidental to the accomplishment of exempt purposes, the organization will fail to be organized and operated exclusively for exempt purposes. See * * * § 1.501(c)(3)–1(c)(1); and § 1.501(c)(3)–1(d)(1)(ii).

Situation 1

After A and B form C, and A contributes all of its operating assets to C, A's activities will consist of the health care services it provides through C and any grantmaking activities it can conduct using income distributed to C. A will receive an interest in C equal in value to the assets it contributes to C, and A's and B's returns from C will be proportional to their respective investments in C. The governing documents of C commit C to providing health care services for the benefit of the community as a whole and to give charitable purposes priority over maximizing profits for C's owners. Furthermore, through A's appointment of members of the community familiar with the hospital to C's board, the board's structure, which gives A's appointees voting control, and the specifically enumerated powers of the board over changes in activities, disposition of assets, and renewal of the management agreement, A can ensure that the assets it owns through C and the activities it conducts through C are used primarily to further exempt purposes. Thus, A can ensure that the benefit to B and other private parties, like the management company, will be incidental to the accomplishment of charitable purposes. Additionally, the terms and conditions of the management contract, including the terms for renewal and termination are reasonable. Finally, A's grants are intended to support education and research and give resources to help provide health care to the indigent. All of these facts and circumstances establish that, when A participates in forming C and contributes all of its operating assets to C, and C operates in accordance with its governing documents, A will be furthering charitable purposes and continue to be operated exclusively for exempt purposes.

Because A's grantmaking activity will be contingent upon receiving distributions from C, A's principal activity will continue to be the provision of hospital care. As long as A's principal activity remains the provision of hospital care. A will not be classified as a private foundation in accordance with § 509(a)(1) as an organization described in § 170(b)(1)(A)(iii).

Situation 2

When D and E form F, and D contributes its assets to F, D will be engaged in activities that consist of the health care services it provides through F and any grantmaking activities it can conduct using income distributed by F. However, unlike A, D will not be engaging primarily in activities that further an exempt purpose. "While the diagnosis and cure of disease are indeed purposes that may furnish the foundation for characterizing the activity as 'charitable,' something more is required." Sonora, 46 T.C. at 525–526. See also Federation Pharmacy; Sound Health; and Geisinger. In the absence of a binding obligation in F's governing documents for F to serve charitable purposes or otherwise provide its services to the community as a whole, F will be able to deny care to segments of the community, such as the indigent. Because D will share control of F with E, D will not be able to initiate programs within F to serve new health needs within the community without the agreement of at least one governing board member appointed by E. As a business enterprise, E will not necessarily give priority to the health needs of the community over the consequences for F's profits. The primary source of information for board members appointed by D will be the chief executives, who have a prior relationship with E and the management company, which is a subsidiary of E. The management company itself will have broad discretion over F's activities and assets that may not always be under the board's supervision. For example, the management company is permitted to enter into all but "unusually large" contracts without board approval. The management company may also unilaterally renew the management agreement. Based on all these facts and circumstances, D cannot establish that the activities it conducts through F further exempt purposes. "[I]n order for an organization to qualify for exemption under § 501(c)(3) the organization must 'establish' that it is neither organized nor operated for the 'benefit of private interests.'" Federation Pharmacy, 625 F.2d at 809. Consequently, the benefit to E resulting from the activities D conducts through F will not be incidental to the furtherance of an exempt purpose. Thus, D will fail the operational test when it forms F, contributes its operating assets to F, and then serves as an owner to F.

HOLDING

A will continue to qualify as an organization described in § 501(c)(3) when it forms C and contributes all of its operating assets to C because A has established that A will be operating exclusively for a charitable purpose and only incidentally for the purpose of benefiting the private interests of B. Furthermore, A's principal activity will continue to be the provision of hospital care when C begins operations. Thus, A will be an organization described in § 170(b)(1)(A)(iii) and thus, will not be classified as a private foundation in accordance with § 509(a)(1), as long as hospital care remains its principal activity.

D will violate the requirements to be an organization described in § 501(c)(3) when it forms F and contributes all of its operating assets to F because D has failed to establish that it will be operated exclusively for exempt purposes.

* * *

REDLANDS SURGICAL SERVICES v. COMMISSIONER

United States Tax Court, 1999
113 T.C. 47

THORNTON, J.

Petitioner brought this action for a declaratory judgment, pursuant to section 7428 and Title XXI of this Court's Rules. Petitioner requests the Court to determine the correctness of respondent's adverse determination with respect to its initial qualification as a tax-exempt organization under section 501(c)(3).

FINDINGS OF FACT

Petitioner is a California nonprofit public benefit corporation with its principal place of business in Redlands, California. It is a wholly owned subsidiary of Redlands Health Systems, Inc. (RHS), a California nonprofit public benefit corporation that has been recognized as exempt under section 501(c)(3) of the Code and as a public charity within the meaning of section 509(a). RHS is the parent corporation of three subsidiaries in addition to petitioner, namely Redlands Community Hospital (Redlands Hospital) and Redlands Community Hospital Foundation (Redlands Foundation), both of which are California nonprofit public benefit corporations that have been recognized as exempt under section 501(c)(3); and Redlands Health Services, a for-profit corporation.

As described in more detail below, and as reflected schematically in the appendix hereto, in 1990 RHS became co-general partner with a for-profit corporation, Redlands–SCA Surgery Centers, Inc. (SCA Centers), in a general partnership formed to acquire a 61–percent interest in an existing outpatient surgical center in Redlands, California, two blocks from the Redlands Hospital facility. This general partnership in turn became sole general partner in the California limited partnership that owns and operates the surgical center. Under a long-term management contract, SCA Management Co. (SCA Management)—a for-profit affiliate of SCA Centers—manages the day-to-day operations of the surgical center, in return for a percentage of gross revenues. Several months after forming the general partnership, RHS formed petitioner to succeed to its interest in it.

Petitioner has no activity other than its involvement with the partnerships. The question is whether petitioner is operated exclusively for exempt purposes within the meaning of section 501(c)(3). We hold that it is not.

Redlands Hospital

Since its founding in 1929, Redlands Hospital has been recognized by respondent as a charitable organization described in section 501(c)(3) and as a "hospital" described in section 170(b)(1)(A)(iii). Its mission includes providing necessary medical care free of charge, or at a discount, to individuals without insurance or other means of paying.

Redlands Hospital has its own outpatient surgery program within the hospital facility. It also maintains a 24–hour emergency room that provides emergency medical services for all patients regardless of their ability to pay. It maintains an open medical staff and is governed by a community-based board of directors. It does not discriminate on the basis of race, gender, age, color, national origin, or disability.

Inland Surgery Center, L.P.

Since its inception in 1983, the Inland Surgery Center Limited Partnership (the Operating Partnership) has operated a freestanding ambulatory surgery center (the Surgery Center) in a 12,000–square foot building within two blocks of Redlands Hospital. During the 1980's, the Operating Partnership was a successful for-profit venture, serving only surgical patients who were able to pay, by insurance or otherwise. Prior to its affiliation with the General Partnership, the Operating Partnership comprised Beaver Medical Clinic, Inc., and some 30 physician partners, who were also physicians on the medical staff of Redlands Hospital.

The Affiliation of Redlands Hospital With the Surgery Center

Before 1990, Redlands Hospital desired to increase its outpatient surgery capacity but lacked the capital resources and experience to develop and operate its own freestanding outpatient facility. In addition, such a facility would have been in competition with the existing Surgery Center, and there was concern that the Redlands community could not sustain both.

On March 1, 1990, RHS and SCA Centers entered into a general partnership agreement to acquire jointly a 61–percent general partnership interest in the Surgery Center. The partnership is known as Redlands Ambulatory Surgery Center (the General Partnership).

SCA Centers is a for-profit, wholly owned subsidiary of Surgical Care Affiliates, Inc. (SCA), a publicly held corporation based in Nashville, Tennessee, and specializing in owning and managing ambulatory surgery centers. Prior to formation of the General Partnership, neither SCA nor any of its affiliated entities had any relationship, contractual or otherwise, with RHS or any of its affiliated entities, or with the Surgery Center.

* * *

The General Partnership is the sole general partner of the Operating Partnership. There are 32 limited partners. Except for Beaver Medical Clinic, Inc., the limited partners are all physicians who are also on the medical staff of Redlands Hospital. Two of the limited partners are board members of Redlands Hospital and RHS. The amended Operating Partnership agreement contains no statement of charitable purpose and imposes no requirement that the Operating Partnership operate for a charitable purpose. * * *

* * *

As indicated in * * * the General Partnership agreement, * * * overall management of the General Partnership, except for questions of medical standards and medical policies, is vested in its managing directors, consisting of four persons, two of whom are appointed by petitioner, and two of whom are appointed by SCA Centers. * * *

* * *

Medical Advisory Group

Pursuant to * * * of the Operating Partnership agreement * * *%, all questions regarding medical standards and policies at the Surgery Center are determined by a Medical Advisory Group, which also reviews procedures being performed at the Surgery Center. The Medical Advisory Group is composed of six physicians who are all limited partners of the Operating Partnership. The managing directors of the General Partnership select three members of the medical advisory group; Beaver Medical Clinic—which is a limited partner in the Operating Partnership—selects the other three members. Prior to the affiliation of the General Partnership with the Surgery Center, the Medical Advisory Group was inactive.

Redlands Surgical Services (Petitioner)

On August 1, 1990, 5 months after entering into the General Partnership agreement, RHS incorporated petitioner as a California nonprofit public benefit corporation. On September 30, 1990, RHS transferred its interest in the General Partnership to petitioner.

RHS formed petitioner with the intent that petitioner's sole planned activity would be its efforts with respect to the Operating Partnership. The decisions to incorporate petitioner as a separate corporate entity and to transfer the interests in the General Partnership to petitioner were made to protect Redlands Hospital and Redlands Foundation from potential creditors of the Surgery Center and to keep petitioner's and the Surgery Center's activities free of the debt covenants of Redlands Hospital.

* * *

Petitioner's sole source of financial support is its share of the revenues from the Operating Partnership. Petitioner has no paid or salaried employees. The president of Redlands Hospital serves concurrently as petitioner's president.

The Surgery Center's Operations

The Surgery Center operates on a nondiscriminatory basis both as to doctors and patients. There are no restrictions as to whether a surgical patient can be operated on at the Surgery Center, other than a review as to the appropriateness of conducting the surgical procedure in an outpatient setting and the overall medical condition of the patient. There is practically a 100–percent overlap between surgeons who operate at Redlands Hospital and at the Surgery Center. * * *

Procedures Authorized To Be Performed at the Surgery Center

The General Partnership agreement specifies the types of medical services and procedures to be available at the Surgery Center, which include: Arthroscopic surgeries, laproscopic surgeries (including hysterectomies and appendectomies), conizations, tonsillectomies, herniorrhaphy and eye surgeries. When such procedures involve a higher-risk patient, they are performed at Redlands Hospital or another acute-care hospital. The decision to perform surgery at a hospital rather than at the Surgery Center is exclusively a medical decision.

* * *

OPINION

I. *The Parties' Positions*

Respondent contends that petitioner is not operated exclusively for charitable purposes because it operates for the benefit of private parties and fails to benefit a broad cross-section of the community. In support of its position, respondent contends that the partnership agreements and related management contract are structured to give for-profit interests control over the Surgery Center. Respondent contends that both before and after the General Partnership acquired an ownership interest in it, the Surgery Center was a successful profit-making business that never held itself out as a charity and never operated as a charitable health-care provider.

Petitioner argues that it meets the operational test under section 501(c)(3) because its activities with regard to the Surgery Center further its purpose of promoting health for the benefit of the Redlands community, by providing access to an ambulatory surgery center for all members of the community based upon medical need rather than ability to pay, and by integrating the outpatient services of Redlands Hospital and the Surgery Center. Petitioner argues that its dealings with the for-profit partners have been at arm's length, and that its influence over the activities of the Surgery Center has been sufficient to further its charitable goals. Petitioner further contends that it qualifies for exemption because it is organized and operated to perform services that are integral to the exempt purposes of RHS, its tax-exempt parent, and Redlands Hospital, its tax-exempt affiliate.

II. *Applicable Legal Principles*

A. *Operational Test*

To qualify for exemption from Federal income tax, an organization must be "organized and operated exclusively for * * * charitable * * * purposes". Sec. 501(c)(3); see *Church of Scientology v. Commissioner*, 823 F.2d 1310, 1315 (9th Cir.1987), affg. 83 T.C. 381 (1984).

* * *

B. *Promotion of Health as a Charitable Purpose*

Section 501(c)(3) specifies various qualifying exempt purposes, including "charitable" purposes. The term "charitable" is not defined in section 501(c)(3), but is used in its generally accepted legal sense. * * * In applying this standard, courts have looked to the law of charitable trusts. * * *

The promotion of health for the benefit of the community is a charitable purpose. * * * As applied to determinations of qualification for tax exemption, the definition of the term "charitable" has not been static. * * * Suffice it to say that, in recognition of changes in the health-care industry, the standard no longer requires that "the care of indigent patients be the primary concern of the charitable hospital, as distinguished from the care of paying patients". * * * Rather, the standard reflects "a policy of insuring that adequate health care services are actually *delivered* to those in the community who need them." *Id.* at 180–181. Under this standard, health-care providers must meet a flexible community benefit test based upon a variety of indicia, one of which may be whether the organization provides free care to indigents. Cf. *id.* at 184–185 (subsidized dues program was an indicium of charitable purposes).

To benefit the community, a charity must serve a sufficiently large and indefinite class; as a corollary to this rule, private interests must not benefit to any substantial degree. See *id.* at 181.

C. *Proscription Against Benefiting Private Interests*

An organization does not operate exclusively for exempt purposes if it operates for the benefit of private interests such as designated individuals, the creator or his family, shareholders of the organization, or persons controlled, directly or indirectly, by such private interests. See sec. 1.501(c)(3)–1(d)(1)(ii), Income Tax Regs. The private benefit proscription inheres in the requirement that an organization operate exclusively for exempt purposes.

* * *

The mere fact that an organization seeking exemption enters into a partnership agreement with private parties that receive returns on their capital investments does not establish that the organization has impermissibly conferred private benefit. The question remains whether the organization has a substantial nonexempt purpose whereby it serves private interests. Compare *Plumstead Theatre Socy., Inc. v. Commissioner,* 675 F.2d 244 (9th Cir.1982), affg. per curiam 74 T.C. 1324 (1980) (a nonprofit arts organization furthered its charitable purposes by participating as sole general partner in a partnership with private parties to produce a play), with *Housing Pioneers, Inc. v. Commissioner,* 49 F.3d 1395 (9th Cir.1995), affg. T.C. Memo.1993–120 (a nonprofit corporation's participation as co-general partner in low-income housing partnerships, structured to trade off its tax exemption to secure tax benefits for its for-profit partners, had a substantial nonexempt purpose and impermissibly served private interests).

The proscription against private benefit corresponds to a similar proscription in the law of charitable trusts. "A trust is not a charitable trust if the property or the income therefrom is to be devoted to a private use." 2 Restatement, Trusts 2d, sec. 376 (1959). An organization's property may be impermissibly devoted to a private use where private interests have control, directly or indirectly, over its assets, and thereby secure nonincidental private benefits.

For instance, in *est of Hawaii v. Commissioner,* 71 T.C. 1067 (1979), several for-profit 'est' organizations that had no formal structural control over the nonprofit entity in question nevertheless exerted "considerable control" over its activities. The for-profit organizations set fees that the nonprofit charged the public for training sessions, required the nonprofit to carry on certain types of educational activities, and provided management personnel paid for and responsible to one of the for-profits. Under a licensing agreement with the for-profits, the nonprofit was allowed to use certain intellectual property for 10 years, and at the end of the licensing agreement, all copyrighted material, including new material developed by the nonprofit, was required to be turned over to the for-profits. The nonprofit was required to use its excess funds for the development of 'est' or related research. The for-profits also required that trainers and local organizations sign an agreement not to compete with 'est' for 2 years after terminating their relationship with 'est' organizations.

In *est of Hawaii v. Commissioner*, * * *, this Court agreed with respondent that the nonprofit was "part of a franchise system which is operated for private benefit and * * * its affiliation with this system taints it with a substantial commercial purpose." We found that the "ultimate beneficiaries" of the nonprofit's activities were the for-profit corporations, and that the nonprofit "was simply the instrument to subsidize the for-profit corporations and not vice versa". *Id.* at 1082. This Court held that the nonprofit was not operated exclusively for exempt purposes. * * *

III. *Petitioner's Claim to Exemption on a "Stand–Alone" Basis*

Applying the principles described above, we next consider whether petitioner has established that respondent improperly denied it tax-exempt status as a section 501(c)(3) organization.

* * *

Respondent asserts that petitioner has ceded effective control over its sole activity—participating as a co-general partner with for-profit parties in the partnerships that own and operate the Surgery Center—to the for-profit partners and the for-profit management company that is an affiliate of petitioner's co-general partner. Respondent asserts that this arrangement is indicative of a substantial nonexempt purpose, whereby petitioner impermissibly benefits private interests.

Without conceding that private parties control its activities, petitioner challenges the premise that the ability to control its activities determines its purposes. Petitioner argues that under the operational test, "the critical issue in determining whether an organization's purposes are noncharitable is *not* whether a for profit or not for profit entity has control. Rather, the critical issue is the sort of conduct in which the organization is actually engaged." On brief, the parties agree that under an aggregate theory of partnership taxation, the partnerships' activities are considered petitioner's own activities. Petitioner's brief states: "The evidence in the administrative file demonstrates that * * * [the Operating Partnership] has been operated in an exclusively charitable manner since 1990." Therefore, petitioner concludes, it should be deemed to operate exclusively for charitable purposes.

We disagree with petitioner's thesis. It is patently clear that the Operating Partnership, whatever charitable benefits it may produce, is not operated "in an exclusively charitable manner." As stated by Justice Cardozo (then Justice of the New York Court of Appeals), in describing one of the "ancient principles" of charitable trusts, "It is only when income may be applied to the profit of the founders that business has a beginning and charity an end." *Butterworth v. Keeler,* 219 N.Y. 446, 449–450, 114 N.E. 803, 804 (1916). The Operating Partnership's income is, of course, applied to the profit of petitioner's co-general partner and the numerous limited partners. It is no answer to say that none of petitioner's income from this activity was applied to private interests, for the activity is indivisible, and no discrete part of the Operating Partnership's income-producing activities is severable from those activities that produce income to be applied to the other partners' profit.

Taken to its logical conclusion, petitioner's thesis would suggest that an organization whose main activity is passive participation in a for-profit health-service enterprise could thereby be deemed to be operating exclusively for charitable purposes. Such a conclusion, however, would be contrary to well-established principles of charitable trust law.

Frequently, a business enterprise may have charitable effects. * * * A private hospital relieves sickness and suffering. * * * However, the primary object of these institutions is the pecuniary gain of the operators. Hence trusts to aid in the founding or maintenance of private hospitals or clinics * * *, which are business enterprises operated for the purpose of making profits for stockholders or owners, are not charitable even though they involve incidentally some public benefits. "It is not charity to aid a business enterprise." [Bogert & Bogert, The Law of Trusts and Trustees, sec. 364 (Rev.2d ed.1991) (quoting *Butterworth v. Keeler,* 219 N.Y. at 449, 114 N.E. at 804); fn. refs. omitted.]

Clearly, there is something in common between the structure of petitioner's sole activity and the nature of petitioner's purposes in engaging in it. An organization's purposes may be inferred from its manner of operations; its "activities provide a useful indicia of the organization's purpose or purposes." *Living Faith, Inc. v. Commissioner,* 950 F.2d 365, 372 (7th Cir.1991), affg. T.C. Memo.1990–484. The binding commitments that petitioner has entered into and that govern its participation in the partnerships are indicative of petitioner's purposes. To the extent that petitioner cedes control over its sole activity to for-profit parties having an independent economic interest in the same activity and having no obligation to put charitable purposes ahead of profit-making objectives, petitioner cannot be assured that the partnerships will in fact be operated in furtherance of charitable purposes. In such a circumstance, we are led to the conclusion that petitioner is not operated exclusively for charitable purposes.

Based on the totality of factors described below, we conclude that petitioner has in fact ceded effective control of the partnerships' and the Surgery Center's activities to for-profit parties, conferring on them significant private benefits, and therefore is not operated exclusively for charitable purposes within the meaning of section 501(c)(3).

* * *

IV. *Petitioner's Claim to Exemption Under the Integral Part Doctrine*

Petitioner argues that even if it does not qualify for tax exemption on a "stand alone" basis, it qualifies for exemption under the integral part doctrine.

The integral part doctrine is not codified, but rather is the outgrowth of judicial opinions, rulings, and regulations. The precise contours of this doctrine are not clearly defined. The seminal case of *Squire v. Students Book Corp.*, 191 F.2d 1018 (9th Cir.1951), held that an organization that operated a bookstore on the premises of a college for the accommodation of students and faculty was exempt because it bore a "close and intimate relationship" to the functioning of the college itself.
* * *

Shortly after the decision in *Squire,* Treasury regulations acknowledged the existence of the integral part doctrine in providing an exception to the feeder organization rules under section 502.

Section 1.502–1(b), Income Tax Regs., provides as follows:

(b) If a subsidiary organization of a tax-exempt organization would itself be exempt on the ground that its activities are an integral part of the exempt activities of the parent organization, its exemption will not be lost because, as a matter of accounting between the two organizations, the subsidiary derives a profit from its dealings with its parent organization, for example, a subsidiary organization which is operated for the sole purpose of furnishing electric power used by its parent organization, a tax-exempt educational organization, in carrying on its educational activities. However, the subsidiary organization is not exempt from tax if it is operated for the primary purpose of carrying on a trade or business which would be an unrelated trade or business (that is, unrelated to exempt activities) if regularly carried on by the parent organization. For example, if a subsidiary organization is operated primarily for the purpose of furnishing electric power to consumers other than its parent organization (and the parent's tax-exempt subsidiary organizations), it is not exempt since such business would be an unrelated trade or business if regularly carried on by the parent organization. Similarly, if the organization is owned by several unrelated exempt organizations, and is operated for the purpose of furnishing electric power to each of them, it is not exempt since such business would be an unrelated trade or business if regularly carried on by any one of the tax-exempt organizations. For purposes of this paragraph, organizations are related only if they consist of—

(1) A parent organization and one or more of its subsidiary organizations; or

(2) Subsidiary organizations having a common parent organization. An exempt organization is not related to another exempt organization merely because they both engage in the same type of exempt activities.

Since *Squire,* only a relatively small number of cases have applied the integral part doctrine. These cases are fact-specific. See *Geisinger Health Plan v. Commissioner,* 30 F.3d 494, 501 (3d Cir.1994), affg. 100 T.C. 394 (1993), and cases cited therein. As applied in a number of these cases, the integral part doctrine requires the organization in question to provide "necessary and indispensable" services solely to an exempt organization to which it bears some legal or significant operational relationship. * * * As applied in these cases, the integral part doctrine operates to recognize a derivative exemption of an organization which serves only another exempt organization and performs essential services that the client organization otherwise would have performed for itself to accomplish its own exempt purposes. * * *

Consistent with this rationale, professional group practices serving exempt entities have been granted tax exemption under the integral part doctrine. * * * These cases involved anesthesiology services or faculty medical activities that were provided solely to the served hospital or medical school and that were essential to the operation of the hospital or medical school. See *Geisinger Health Plan v. Commissioner,* 100 T.C. 394 (1993).

In *Geisinger Health Plan v. Commissioner, supra,* this Court denied a claim for tax exemption asserted by an HMO under the integral part theory. We reasoned that the group-practice line of cases was not controlling because, unlike the exempt organizations in those cases, the HMO had a population of subscribers that did not overlap substantially with the patients of the related exempt entities. In considering whether the HMO's activities would have constituted an unrelated business if conducted by its affiliate, we noted that section 513(a) defines "unrelated trade or business" by reference to conduct that is "not substantially related" to the organization's exempt functions. We stated that the determination whether conduct is "substantially related" in this context "considers the degree to which income is earned from services rendered or sales made to persons who are not patients of the exempt affiliated entity." *Id.* at 405. Noting that entities related to the HMO provided 80 percent of the hospital services rendered to the HMO's patients, we held that the record in *Geisinger* did not justify a conclusion as to whether the instances in which the HMO's subscribers were served by unrelated entities were substantial or insubstantial. See *id.* at 406. Accordingly, we held that the HMO failed to establish that its activities comprised an integral part of its affiliate's exempt activities.

Similarly, in the instant case, petitioner has failed to establish that the Surgery Center's patient population overlaps substantially with that of Redlands Hospital. The record does not reveal what percentage of persons served at the Surgery Center are patients of Redlands Hospital.

Clearly, however, the Surgery Center was performing ambulatory surgery on a for-profit basis for its own patients before petitioner was ever involved and presumably continued to do so afterward.

Even if we were to assume, arguendo, that the patient populations of the Surgery Center and Redlands Hospital overlap substantially, this circumstance would not suffice to confer exemption on petitioner under the integral part doctrine. In all the precedents cited above in which courts have applied the integral part doctrine to recognize a derivative exemption, the organization has been under the supervision or control of the exempt affiliate (or a group of exempt affiliates with common exempt purposes) or otherwise expressly limited in its purposes to advancing the interests of the affiliated exempt entity or entities, and serving no private interests. For instance, in *Squire v. Student Book Corp.*, 191 F.2d 1018, 1019 (9th Cir.1951), all actions of the bookstore's board of trustees were submitted to the president of the college for approval, and the college comptroller acted as ex officio treasurer of the bookstore. The bookstore paid no rebates and no part of its earnings inured to private benefit. It seems clear that such considerations are central to the court's holding in *Squire* that the bookstore's business enterprise "bears a close and intimate relationship to the functioning of the College itself."

By contrast, as previously discussed, petitioner's sole activity (the Surgery Center) is effectively controlled by for-profit parties. The operations of the Surgery Center plainly are not dedicated to advancing the interests of petitioner's exempt affiliates other than as those interests might happen to coincide with the commercial interests of petitioner's for-profit partners. Moreover, as previously discussed, petitioner impermissibly serves private interests. Petitioner's activity is not so substantially and closely related to the exempt purposes of its affiliates that these private interests may be disregarded. See *Geisinger Health Plan v. Commissioner*, 100 T.C. at 406, 407. Accordingly, petitioner is not entitled to exemption under the integral part doctrine.

Remaining contentions not addressed herein we deem irrelevant, without merit, or unnecessary to reach.

To reflect the foregoing,

Decision will be entered for respondent.

Note

In *St. David's Health Care System v. U.S.*, 349 F.3d 232 (5th Cir. 2003), the Fifth Circuit overturned a district court's summary judgment ruling in favor of a nonprofit hospital that had its tax-exempt status revoked by the Internal Revenue Service because of a partnership it formed with a for-profit health care organization. The Fifth Circuit agreed with the Internal Revenue Service that St. David's would not be operated exclusively for charitable purposes if the for-profit organization had either formal or effective control over the partnership's activities. The Fifth Circuit ruled that the determining factor as to whether St. David's could retain its tax exempt status was whether it or the for-profit controlled the partnership. The Fifth Circuit stated that if a nonprofit enters into a partnership with a for-profit entity and retains control, the non-profit's activities via the partnership would primarily further exempt purposes. The court decided there were genuine issues of material fact that had to be resolved before it could determine whether St. David's had ceded control to the for-profit entity. Thus, the court vacated the district court's grant of summary judgment in favor of St. David's and remanded the case for further proceedings. The Fifth Circuit referred to the Tax Court's decision in *Redlands Surgical Services v. Commissioner*, 113 T.C. 47 (1999), in which the Tax Court rejected the taxpayer's argument that the central issue was not one of control but rather whether the partnership in fact performed charitable work, and to Rev. Rul. 98–15, in which the IRS noted the requirements to show that a non-profit retained control of the partnership.

Upon remand, a jury in the U.S. District Court for the Western District of Texas (No. 101CV–046) decided that St. David's was entitled to tax-exempt status despite its partnership with a for-profit.

Question

Must a hospital provide substantial health care services to indigents to qualify for § 501(c)(3) status?

Notes

1. When Congress enacted the Tax Reform Act of 1969, P.L. 91–172, and added § 509 to the Code (to prescribe the requirements for public charity status for § 501(c)(3) organizations), framers of the Act recognized that IRS agents had been challenging the exempt status of hospitals "on the sole ground" that hospitals were "accepting insufficient numbers of patients at no charge or at rates substantially below cost." 1969 U.S.C.A.N.N. p. 1688. Drafters of the Act commented that the "bill removes uncertainty by establishing hospitals as a separate exempt category" under the now § 509(a)(1).

2. The court in *Redlands* commented that "in recognition of changes in the health-care industry," the standard to be applied in determining whether a health-care entity serves a "charitable purpose" no longer requires that "the care of indigent patients be the primary concern of the charitable hospital, as distinguished from the care of paying patients." Rather, the court opined, the standard reflects "a policy of insuring that adequate health care services are actually *delivered* to those who need them." Subsequent to the decision in *Redlands*, *t*he Internal Revenue Service ruled that a hospital does not qualify for tax exempt status under § 501(c)(3) if it cannot demonstrate that its stated policies to provide health care services to the indigent actually result in the delivery of significant health care services to the indigent. (See FSA 200110030.) The Service stated that a hospital does not qualify for § 501(c)(3) status merely because it promotes health. Rather, it must benefit the community primarily to qualify for § 501(c)(3) status.

III. EXEMPTION FROM PROPERTY TAXES

Most state statutes exempt charitable organizations from property taxes. However, some appraisal districts have challenged property tax exemptions for hospitals.

Question

Must a hospital provide medical care without regard to a patient's ability to pay to qualify for a property exemption? Consider in the following cases the differing opinions, both rendered in 1985, of the Texas appellate court and the Utah Supreme Court on this issue.

LAMB COUNTY APPRAISAL DISTRICT v. SOUTH PLAINS HOSPITAL–CLINIC
Court of Appeals, Texas, 1985
688 S.W.2d 896

DODSON, Justice.

The trial court rendered a declaratory judgment determining that certain property owned by the South Plains Hospital–Clinic, Inc. is exempt from ad valorem taxes pursuant to Tex. Tax Code Ann. § 11.18 (Vernon 1982) and Tex. Const. art. VIII, § 2. * * * Concluding that the appraisal district's points of error do not present cause for disturbing the judgment, we affirm.

By its first three points of error, the appraisal district claims the evidence is factually insufficient to support the trial court's findings that: (1) the hospital is organized exclusively to perform charitable purposes by providing medical care without regard to the beneficiaries' ability to pay; (2) the hospital is operated in a way that does not result in realization of private gain resulting from payment for salary or other compensation in excess of a reasonable allowance for salaries or other compensation for services rendered or realization of any other form of private gain; and (3) any non-charitable functions performed by the hospital are only incidental to the organization's charitable functions.

* * *

Tex. Const. art. VIII, § 2 provides, in part, that the Legislature may, by general law, exempt certain property from taxation, including all buildings used exclusively and owned by institutions of purely public charity. The phrase "institution of purely public charity" is not defined in the Constitution. However, in *City of Houston v. Scottish Rite Benev. Ass'n*, 111 Tex. 191, 230 S.W. 978, 981 (1921), the court suggested the following definition:

> [T]he Legislature might reasonably conclude that an institution was one of "purely public charity" where: First, it made no gain or profit; second, it accomplished ends wholly benevolent; and, third, it

benefited persons, indefinite in numbers and in personalities, by preventing them, through absolute gratuity, from becoming burdens to society and to the state.

The court further explained that:

Charity need not be universal to be public. It is public when it affects all the people of a community or state, by assuming, to a material extent, that which otherwise might become the obligation or duty of the community or the state. The care of those unable to provide for themselves certainly may devolve on those of the same community or state. [emphasis added]

Since the court's decision in *City of Houston,* numerous Supreme Court decisions have acknowledged, reaffirmed, and further explained the suggested guidelines. In that regard, the most recent decision by the Supreme Court is *City of McAllen v. Ev. Luth. Good Sam. Soc.,* 530 S.W.2d 806 (Tex.1975). That case and others will be discussed in this opinion as we resolve the appraisal district's points of error and contentions.

Pursuant to the constitutional provisions, the above-stated guidelines and the court's explanations and interpretations of those guidelines, the Legislature implemented article VIII, section 2 of the Constitution by enacting section 11.18 of the Texas Tax Code Annotated. Section 11.18(a) provides that a qualified charitable organization is entitled to the ad valorem tax exemption on buildings and tangible personal property owned by the organization which are used exclusively by the organization. However, in regard to exclusive use, the exemption is not lost where the property is used by persons who do not qualify as charitable organizations, if that use is *incidental* to the qualified charitable organization's use and that use is limited to activities that benefit the beneficiaries of the qualified charitable organization which owns or uses the property.

To qualify as a charitable organization under section 11.18(c) and 11.18(d) of the statute, the organization must:

(1) Be organized exclusively to perform charitable purposes and engage exclusively in providing medical care without regard to the beneficiaries' ability to pay; provided however, in regard to *exclusive* purpose and performance, the charitable organization's exemption is not lost by performing non-charitable functions, if those functions are *incidental* to the organization's charitable functions;

(2) Be operated in a way that does not result in accrual of distributable profits, realization of private gain resulting from payment of compensation in excess of a reasonable allowance for salary or other compensation for services rendered, or realization of any other form of private gain; and

(3) By charter, bylaws, or other regulation adopted to govern the organization's affairs, pledge its assets for use in performing the organization's charitable functions and "direct that on discontinu-

ance of the organization by dissolution or otherwise, the assets are to be transferred to this State or to an educational, religious, charitable or other similar organization that is qualified as a charitable organization under Section 501(c)(3), Internal Revenue Code of 1954, as amended."

In this instance, the record shows that the hospital is located in Amherst, Lamb County, Texas. The town of Amherst has approximately 900 to 1000 people. The hospital was originally chartered as a non-profit cooperative hospital in 1940 or 1941. * * *

* * *

The appraisal district further argues that the hospital facilities are not exclusively used for the hospital's stated purpose because the hospital has no stated admissions policy or policy for determining charity status. However, the record shows that patients are admitted to the hospital on the medical staff's directions when the patient's doctor determines that the patient needs hospital care. When that medical determination is made, the patient is admitted to the hospital without regard to the patient's ability to pay. Since the hospital cannot practice medicine, per se, only its staff doctors can make the medical determination as to whether a patient needs hospital care.

The patient's charity status is determined from the staff's knowledge of the patient's ability to pay (*i.e.*, by the patient's prior ability to pay for previous treatment) and from information furnished by the patient in the "Information Sheet" which includes information as to employment, insurance, and other similar matters. Thus, the record shows that the hospital's admission policy and its implementation of that policy in actual practice does not contravene the hospital's stated purpose. Consequently, after considering all of the evidence in favor of and contrary to the trial court's first finding of fact, we conclude that the challenged finding is not so against the great weight and preponderance of the evidence as to be manifestly wrong and unjust. The appraisal district's first point of error is overruled.

* * *

Next, the appraisal district argues that the doctors' compensation arrangement with the hospital constitutes "private gain" to the doctors because the hospital retains only ten percent of the doctors' collectible fees for overhead services furnished the doctors rather than a forty percent amount which doctors normally have to pay for overhead in private practice. However, in that regard, section 11.18(c)(2) provides that the organization must be operated in a way that does not result in "realization of private gain resulting from payment of compensation in excess of a reasonable allowance for salary or other compensation for services rendered."

In this instance, the record shows, as we stated above, that Amherst is a town of approximately 900 to 1000 inhabitants. The town is located approximately fifty miles from Lubbock in a rural area of Texas. It is extremely difficult to obtain and retain the services of doctors in Amherst. It is a matter of common knowledge and the record in this instance shows that it is not feasible to operate a hospital without doctors. Thus, from the evidence, we are persuaded that the hospital's compensation arrangement with the doctors is reasonable and not excessive under the circumstances. Consequently, after considering all of the evidence in favor of and contrary to the trial court's third finding of fact, we conclude that the challenged finding is not so against the great weight and preponderance of the evidence as to be manifestly wrong or unjust. The appraisal district's second point of error is overruled.

By its third point of error, the appraisal district challenges the trial court's seventh finding of fact. That finding reads: "Any noncharitable functions performed by South Plains Hospital–Clinic, Inc., are only incidental to the organization's charitable functions." Under this point of error, the appraisal district contends that the trial court's third finding of fact is "against the great weight of the evidence" because the evidence establishes beyond any doubt that: (1) the hospital's only source of income is from paying patients; (2) the hospital's so-called "charity" is its fifteen percent of uncollectible bills; and (3) that the hospital's small percentage of charity patients shows that the hospital's primary purpose is to treat paying patients and that any "charity" is purely incidental to its primary purpose.

We acknowledge that the record shows that the hospital's only source of income is from paying patients; however, that fact does not destroy the hospital's charity status. * * * We disagree that the evidence establishes that "the hospital's so-called 'charity' is its fifteen percent of uncollectible bills." The record shows that in addition to the usual fifteen percent rate of uncollectible bills, the hospital provided charity to 517 persons in the year of 1980 alone and that over a two-and-one-half-year period beginning in January 1980 and ending in June 1982, the hospital provided $248,307.76 of services to charity patients.

We further disagree that the hospital's small percentage of charity patients shows that the hospital's primary purpose is to treat paying patients and that any "charity" is purely incidental to its primary purpose. The record shows that eight to fifteen percent of the hospital's patients were charity patients. However, as the court stated in *City of McAllen:*

> [I]t is well settled *that the fact that paying patients predominate over those unable to pay does not detract from the charitable nature of the service rendered.... Reliance upon percentages of paying patients versus non-paying patients, however, should not be the controlling factor.* With the advent of present day social security and welfare programs, the traditional concept of charity, involving the extension of free services to the poor and alms-giving, will be rarely found since wide ranging assistance is available to the poor under such programs. Furthermore, the courts have defined charity to be some-

thing more than mere alms-giving or the relief of poverty and distress. [emphasis added]

* * * The ultimate consideration is whether this organization has assumed "to a material extent, that which otherwise might become the obligation or duty of the community or state." *Id.* In this instance, the evidence shows that the hospital has assumed that obligation to a material extent.

* * *

By its third contention under this point of error, the appraisal district renews the claim that the hospital's facilities are not exclusively used for the hospital's alleged charity functions. In that regard, the appraisal district argues that the use is not exclusive because the doctors are provided office space in the hospital facilities and other services necessary to conduct a private medical practice. In that connection, the district claims the furnishing of office space and the other services is tantamount to a lease of the hospital facilities which destroys the property's exempt status. To support its position, the appraisal district relies on City of Longview v. Markham–McRee Memorial Hosp., 137 Tex. 178, 152 S.W.2d 1112 (1941).

In *City of Longview,* the court determined that the organization did not qualify for tax-exempt status because two doctors rented office space from the organization for $100.00 per month and conducted their independent, private medical practice from those office facilities. In that regard, the court pointed out that even though the doctors performed certain functions of house physician, they were not, in fact, house physicians or subsidiaries of the charitable owners, but that the charitable organization had turned over to the doctors a substantial part of the facilities to be used by the doctors for their own private purposes.

In this instance, and as the court pointed out in *Santa Rosa Infirmary v. City of San Antonio,* 259 S.W. at 932, "there is no claim here that any part of the hospital building was leased out in the ordinary sense." In that connection, the record shows there is no landlord-tenant relationship between the hospital and the doctors. Furthermore, the evidence shows that the doctors performed all of the functions of house physicians. The hospital owns and operates all of the facilities. The record does not show that the hospital has turned over to the doctors any part of its facilities.

We acknowledge that the doctors do practice at the hospital facilities, that the hospital provides the doctors with the necessary services for the doctors to treat patients at the hospital facilities, and that the hospital retains ten percent of the collectible fees charged for the doctor's services rendered to the patients. However, that arrangement does not destroy the hospital's tax-exempt status, since the doctors' services are essential and incidental to the hospital's charitable functions. *See* section 11.18(a).

* * *

In summary, we overrule the appraisal district's five points of error and affirm the judgment of the trial court.

UTAH COUNTY v. INTERMOUNTAIN HEALTH CARE

Supreme Court, Utah, 1985
709 P.2d 265

DURHAM, Justice:

Utah County seeks review of a decision of the Utah State Tax Commission reversing a ruling of the Utah County Board of Equalization. The Tax Commission exempted Utah Valley Hospital, owned and operated by Intermountain Health Care (IHC), and American Fork Hospital, leased and operated by IHC, from *ad valorem* property taxes. At issue is whether such a tax exemption is constitutionally permissible. We hold that, on the facts in this record, it is not, and we reverse.

* * *

IHC is a nonprofit corporation that owns and operates or leases and operates twenty-one hospitals throughout the intermountain area, including Utah Valley Hospital and American Fork Hospital. IHC also owns other subsidiaries, including at least one for-profit entity. It is supervised by a board of trustees who serve without pay. It has no stock, and no dividends or pecuniary profits are paid to its trustees or incorporators. Upon dissolution of the corporation, no part of its assets can inure to the benefit of any private person.

IHC's policy with respect to all of its hospitals is to make charges to patients for hospital services whenever it is possible to do so. Hospital charges are paid either by patients, by private insurance companies such as Blue Cross and Blue Shield, or by governmental programs such as Medicare and Medicaid. IHC and its individual hospitals also are the recipients of private bequests, endowments, and contributions in amounts not established in the record.

Utah County seeks the resolution of two issues: (1) whether U.C.A., 1953, §§ 59-2-30 (1974) and 59-2-31 (1974), which exempt from taxation hospitals meeting certain requirements, constitute an unconstitutional expansion of the charitable exemption in article XIII, section 2 of the Utah Constitution; and (2) whether Utah Valley Hospital and American Fork Hospital are exempt from taxation under article XIII, section 2 of the Utah Constitution.

Utah County does not seriously dispute that the two hospitals in this case comply with sections 59-2-30 and 59-2-31, but contends instead that these statutes unlawfully expand the charitable exemption granted by article XIII, section 2 of the Utah Constitution (1895, amended 1982), which provides in pertinent part:

> The property of the state, cities, counties, towns, school districts, municipal corporations and public libraries, lots with the buildings

thereon used exclusively for either religious worship or charitable purposes, ... shall be exempt from taxation.

In ruling upon the validity of a statute which purports to define the meaning of a constitutional provision, we are obligated to scrutinize the language of the Constitution with considerable care. It is true, as explained in Justice Howe's dissent, that a significant degree of deference is due to a legislative construction of the meaning of a constitutional term. But his opinion itself, in accord with well-established principles of judicial review, acknowledges that this Court's obligation is to serve as the "final arbiter" of the question of what constitutes "charitable purposes." "Section 2 of art. XIII grants a charitable exemption and our statutes cannot *expand* or *limit* the scope of the exemption or defeat it. To the extent the statutes have that effect, they are not valid." * * *

The power of state and local governments to levy property taxes has traditionally been limited by constitutional and statutory provisions such as those at issue in this case that exempt certain property from taxation. These exemptions confer an indirect subsidy and are usually justified as the *quid pro quo* for charitable entities undertaking functions and services that the state would otherwise be required to perform. A concurrent rationale, used by some courts, is the assertion that the exemptions are granted not only because charitable entities relieve government of a burden, but also because their activities enhance beneficial community values or goals. Under this theory, the benefits received by the community are believed to offset the revenue lost by reason of the exemption.

A consideration of the reasons for exemption provisions is important in determining the proper standards under which they should be reviewed.

A liberal construction of exemption provisions results in the loss of a major source of municipal revenue and places a greater burden on nonexempt taxpayers, thus, these provisions have generally been strictly construed. For the same reasons parties seeking an exemption bear the burden of proving their entitlement to it. The doctrine of strict construction and the difficulties taxpayers have in bearing the burden of proof explain why taxation has been the rule and exemption has been the exception. In some jurisdictions, however, the doctrine of strict construction has been eroding. Courts in these jurisdictions pay "lip service" to the doctrine but fail to apply it to exemption provisions.

* * *

Unlike the courts described in the foregoing comment, this Court recently reaffirmed its commitment to the doctrine of strict construction as applied to the charitable exemption provision contained in the Utah Constitution. In *Loyal Order of Moose,* 657 P.2d at 264, we determined that the clause exempting property "used exclusively for ... charitable purposes" is to be strictly construed, Utah Const. art. XIII, § 2. *Accord*

Salt Lake County v. Tax Commission ex rel. Laborers Local No. 295, Utah, 658 P.2d 1192, 1194 (1983).

An entity may be granted a charitable tax exemption for its property under the Utah Constitution only if it meets the definition of a "charity" or if its property is used exclusively for "charitable" purposes. Essential to this definition is the element of gift to the community.

> Charity is the *contribution* or *dedication* of something of value ... to the common good.... By exempting property used for charitable purposes, the constitutional convention sought to encourage individual or group sacrifice for the welfare of the community. An essential element of charity is an *act of giving.*

Salt Lake County v. Tax Commission ex rel. Greater Salt Lake Recreational Facilities, Utah, 596 P.2d 641, 643 (1979) (emphasis added). A gift to the community can be identified either by a substantial imbalance in the exchange between the charity and the recipient of its services or in the lessening of a government burden through the charity's operation. * * * In *Friendship Manor Corp. v. Tax Commission,* 26 Utah 2d 227, 487 P.2d 1272 (1971), this Court declined to exempt from taxation property used as a home for the elderly because the alleged givers of the charity also constituted its sole beneficiaries. We were unable in that case to find any gift to the general public. We there quoted with approval *United Presbyterian Association v. Board of County Commissioners,* 167 Colo. 485, 503, 448 P.2d 967, 976 (1968): "[W]here material reciprocity between alleged recipients and their alleged donor exists—then charity does not." *Friendship Manor,* 26 Utah 2d at 238, 487 P.2d at 1279. Similarly, in *Laborers Local No. 295,* 658 P.2d at 1196, we held that a union was not entitled to a tax exemption for condominium office space because the primary purpose of this use was to benefit union members, and there was no gift to the general public.

Given the complexities of institutional organization, financing, and impact on modern community life, there are a number of factors which must be weighed in determining whether a particular institution is in fact using its property "exclusively for ... charitable purposes." Utah Const. art. XIII, § 2 (1895, amended 1982). These factors are: (1) whether the stated purpose of the entity is to provide a significant service to others without immediate expectation of material reward; (2) whether the entity is supported, and to what extent, by donations and gifts; (3) whether the recipients of the "charity" are required to pay for the assistance received, in whole or in part; (4) whether the income received from all sources (gifts, donations, and payment from recipients) produces a "profit" to the entity in the sense that the income exceeds operating and long-term maintenance expenses; (5) whether the beneficiaries of the "charity" are restricted or unrestricted and, if restricted, whether the restriction bears a reasonable relationship to the entity's charitable objectives; and (6) whether dividends or some other form of financial benefit, or assets upon dissolution, are available to private interests, and whether the entity is organized and operated so that any commercial activities are subordinate or incidental to charitable ones. These factors provide, we believe, useful guidelines for our analysis of whether a charitable purpose or gift exists in any particular case. We emphasize that each case must be decided on its own facts, and the foregoing factors are not all of equal significance, nor must an institution always qualify under all six before it will be eligible for an exemption.

Because the "care of the sick" has traditionally been an activity regarded as charitable in American law, and because the dissenting opinions rely upon decisions from other jurisdictions that in turn incorporate unexamined assumptions about the fundamental nature of hospital-based medical care, we deem it important to scrutinize the contemporary social and economic context of such care. We are convinced that traditional assumptions bear little relationship to the economics of the medical-industrial complex of the 1980's. Nonprofit hospitals were traditionally treated as tax-exempt charitable institutions because, until late in the 19th century, they were true charities providing custodial care for those who were both sick and poor. The hospitals' income was derived largely or entirely from voluntary charitable donations, not government subsidies, taxes, or patient fees.

The function and status of hospitals began to change in the late 19th century; the transformation was substantially completed by the 1920's. "From charities, dependent on voluntary gifts, [hospitals] developed into market institutions financed increasingly out of payments from patients." The transformation was multidimensional: hospitals were redefined from social welfare to medical treatment institutions; their charitable foundation was replaced by a business basis; and their orientation shifted to "professionals, and their patients," away from "patrons and the poor."

The magnitude and character of the change in hospital care is suggested by a number of factors. (1) The social composition of hospital patients appears to have changed until by the early 20th century it became quite similar to the population at large. Paul Starr, *The Social Transformation of American Medicine* at 159 (1982). The change in hospital architecture (large wards were replaced with private rooms) suggests the same movement away from the poor to paying patients. (2) The number and percentage of paying patients increased as did the percentage of revenue derived from patient fees. This revenue amounted to over 65 percent for general hospitals in the country as a whole by 1922. Public appropriations amounted to about 18 percent; endowment income amounted to 3.6 percent; and donations added 5.7 percent. (3) The practice of not permitting physicians to charge private patients for their services in hospitals was abandoned during this period. In 1880, according to one study, no hospital permitted physician fees. By 1905, 47 of 52 New England hospitals surveyed permitted physicians to charge for services to private patients. (4) Before 1880, less than 2 percent of physicians had hospital privileges; by 1933, 5 of 6 physicians had hospital privileges. (5) The number of hospitals increased, according to census figures, from 178 in 1872 to over 4,000 in 1910. (6) Between 1890 and

1920 there was a substantial growth in for-profit hospitals, organized by physicians and corporations, as the opportunity for profit in the hospital business improved. All of the above factors indicate a substantial change in the nature of the hospital; a part of that change was the gradual disappearance of the traditional charitable hospital for the poor.

Also of considerable significance to our review is the increasing irrelevance of the distinction between nonprofit and for-profit hospitals for purposes of discovering the element of charity in their operations. The literature indicates that two models, described below, appear to describe a large number of nonprofit hospitals as they function today.

(1) The "physicians' cooperative" model describes nonprofit hospitals that operate primarily for the benefit of the participating physicians. Physicians, pursuant to this model, enjoy power and high income through their direct or indirect control over the nonprofit hospitals to which they bring their patients. The nonprofit form is believed to facilitate the control by physicians better than the for-profit form. Pauley & Redisch, *The Not–For-Profit Hospital as a Physicians' Cooperative,* 63 Am.Econ.Rev. 87, 88–89 (1973). This model has also been called the "exploitation hypothesis" because the physician "income maximizing" system is hidden behind the nonprofit facade of the hospital. Clark, *Does the Nonprofit Form Fit the Hospital Industry?,* 93 Harv.L.Rev. 1416, 1436–37 (1980). A minor variation of the above theory is the argument that many nonprofit hospitals operate as "shelters" within which physicians operate profitable businesses, such as laboratories. Starr, *supra,* at 438.

(2) The "polycorporate enterprise" model describes the increasing number of nonprofit hospital chains. Here, power is largely in the hands of administrators, not physicians. Through the creation of holding companies, nonprofit hospitals have grown into large groups of medical enterprises, containing both for-profit and nonprofit corporate entities. Nonprofit corporations can own for-profit corporations without losing their federal nonprofit tax status as long as the profits of the for-profit corporations are used to further the nonprofit purposes of the parent organization. (IHC owns at least one for-profit subsidiary.) The emergence of hospital organizations with both for-profit and nonprofit components has increasingly destroyed the charitable pretensions of nonprofit organizations:

> "The extension of the voluntary hospital into profit-making businesses and the penetration of other corporations into the hospital signal the breakdown of the traditional boundaries of voluntarism. Increasingly, the polycorporate hospitals are likely to become multi-hospital systems and competitors with profit-making chains, HMO's and other health care corporations."

The foregoing discussion of the economic environment in which modern hospitals function is critical to our analysis in this case because it is an analysis which is generally not present in any of the cases relied upon by the dissenting opinions. Those cases, in our view, do not take into account the revolution in health care that has transformed a "healing profession" into an enormous and complex industry, employing millions of people and accounting for a substantial proportion of our gross national product. Dramatic advances in medical knowledge and technology have resulted in an equally dramatic rise in the cost of medical services. At the same time, elaborate and comprehensive organizations of third-party payers have evolved. Most recently, perhaps as a further evolutionary response to the unceasing rise in the cost of medical services, the provision of such services has become a highly competitive business. Furthermore, even the more recent cases cited by the dissenting opinions contradict the rule this Court has adopted strictly construing our constitutional provision, *Loyal Order of Moose,* 657 P.2d at 264, and requiring every charity to show an element of gift. *Community Memorial Hospital v. City of Moberly,* Mo., 422 S.W.2d 290 (1967), as an example, contains no mention of the element of gift that this Court has held crucial to the meaning of charity. It appears that the hospital in *Moberly* was granted its tax exemption largely on the basis of its nonprofit structure, for the Missouri court held it of no account that the hospital gave charity in an amount less than 1.4 percent of the amount collected from paying patients, that this so-called "charity" included some bad debts, and that for four of the eight years at issue no charity at all was given by the hospital. Similarly, *Vick v. Cleveland Memorial Medical Foundation,* 2 Ohio St.2d 30, 206 N.E.2d 2 (1965), does not insist on identifying the element of gift in an organization's practices before it can be held to be a charity. Both *Moberly* and *Vick,* as well as other cases cited in the dissents, are therefore inconsistent with the holdings of this Court. * * *

Having discussed the standards for the application of Utah's constitutional exemption for property used for charitable purposes, and the economic and historic context in which we conduct this review, we now examine the record respecting the two hospitals ("the defendants") whose eligibility has been challenged by Utah County. We note that this examination focuses exclusively on what the record before us demonstrates regarding these two hospitals, and only these hospitals. The policies, practices, and structure of Intermountain Health Care, Inc., are relevant to this examination insofar as they have been shown in this case to affect the operations of these hospitals. Evidence concerning the functions and operations of other hospitals in the IHC system appears to be entirely irrelevant, as the exempt status of the property used by those hospitals is not now before us.

The stated purpose of IHC regarding the operation of both hospitals clearly meets at least part of the first criterion we have articulated for determining the existence of a charitable use. Its articles of incorporation identify as "corporate purposes," among other things, the provision of "care and treatment of the sick, afflicted, infirm, aged or injured within and/or without the State of Utah." The same section prevents any "part of the net earnings of this Corporation" to inure to the private benefit of any individual. Furthermore, under another section, the assets of the corporation upon dissolution likewise may not be distributed to benefit any private interest.

The second factor we examine is whether the hospitals are supported, and to what extent, by donations and gifts. The findings of the Tax Commission are ambiguously worded in regard to this element, since they do not make any distinction between patient charges, third-party payments from private insurers and government entitlement programs, and "gifts (wills, endowments and contributions)." The finding reads: "The sources of revenue of IHC are derived primarily from patient charges, third parties (Blue Cross, Blue Shield, Medicare, Medicaid), and gifts (wills, endowments and contributions)." Therefore, we have examined the testimony and exhibits in evidence on this question. The latter demonstrate that current operating expenses for both hospitals are covered almost entirely by revenue from patient charges. Although a substantial donation to capital was identified in the case of Utah Valley Hospital, there was no demonstration of the impact of that donation on the current support, maintenance, and operation of that hospital in the tax year in question in this lawsuit. The evidence was that both hospitals charge rates for their services comparable to rates being charged by other similar entities, and no showing was made that the donations identified resulted in charges to patients below prevailing market rates. Presumably such differentials, if they exist, could be quantified and introduced into evidence. The defendants have failed to provide such evidence, and it is they who bear the burden of showing their eligibility for exemption.

Justice Stewart's dissenting opinion argues that the element of charitable giving from private donors and benefactors to a nonprofit entity, without more, satisfies the requirement of "gift" in the definition of "charitable purpose" under the Utah Constitution. Although that argument is attractive, we believe that it is inconsistent with our precedent, the language of the Constitution, and public policy.

Many institutions are largely or partly created and supported by gifts, but do not therefore automatically qualify for tax exemptions for their property. Examples might include private, nonprofit schools, museums, research organizations, libraries, planetariums, zoos, scientific consulting groups, environmental research agencies, professional associations, and so forth.

One of the most significant of the factors to be considered in review of a claimed exemption is the third we identified: whether the recipients of the services of an entity are required to pay for that assistance, in whole or in part. The Tax Commission in this case found as follows:

> The policy of [IHC's hospitals] is to collect hospital charges from patients whenever it is reasonable and possible to do so; however, no person in need of medical attention is denied care solely on the basis of a lack of funds.

The record also shows that neither of the hospitals in this case demonstrated any substantial imbalance between the value of the services it provides and the payments it receives apart from any gifts, donations, or endowments. The record shows that the vast majority of the services provided by these two hospitals are paid for by government programs, private insurance companies, or the individuals receiving care. Collection of such remuneration does not constitute giving, but is a mere reciprocal exchange of services for money. Between 1978 and 1980, the value of the services given away as charity by these two hospitals constituted less than one percent of their gross revenues. Furthermore, the record also shows that such free service as did exist was deliberately not advertised out of fear of a "deluge of people" trying to take advantage of it. Instead, every effort was made to recover payment for services rendered. Utah Valley Hospital even offered assistance to patients who claimed inability to pay to enter into bank loan agreements to finance their hospital expenses.

The defendants argue that the great expense of modern hospital care and the universal availability of insurance and government health care subsidies make the idea of a hospital solely supported by philanthropy an anachronism. We believe this argument itself exposes the weakness in the defendants' position. It is precisely because such a vast system of third-party payers has developed to meet the expense of modern hospital care that the historical distinction between for-profit and nonprofit hospitals has eroded. For-profit hospitals provide many of the same primary care services as do those hospitals organized as nonprofit entities. They do so at similar rates as those charged by defendants. The doctors and administrators of nonprofit hospitals have the same opportunity for personal remuneration for their services as do their counterparts in for-profit hospitals. * * *

The dissent of Justice Stewart suggests that the fact that "ability to pay" is not a criterion for admission to IHC's facilities is dispositive of the question of "charitable purpose," regardless of the actual amount of free care provided therein. This argument overlooks the fact that for-profit institutions may well implement similar policies, either for public relations reasons or by virtue of regulations mandated by their receipt of federal-or state-funded payments. Institutions constructed with Hill–Burton funds, for example, were required to provide free care to qualify under that act. Furthermore, many for-profit service providers both provide free care and write off "bad debts," thereby satisfying this criterion. The dissent's reasoning would therefore require that *any* health care provider that accepted patients regardless of ability to pay be deemed eligible for a charitable exemption unless the for-profit/nonprofit distinction is to become the sole means of identifying "charitable purposes" under the Utah Constitution. This Court rejected that unilateral test in *William Budge Memorial Hospital v. Maughan*, 79 Utah 516, 3 P.2d 258 (1931), and we are not persuaded that we should adopt it now.

The fourth question we consider is whether the income received from all sources by these IHC hospitals is in excess of their operating and maintenance expenses. Because the vast majority of their services are paid for, the nonprofit hospitals in this case accumulate capital as do their profit-seeking counterparts. The record indicates that this accumulated capital is used for the construction of additional hospitals and other facilities throughout the IHC system and the provision of expanded services. The record before us is undeveloped on this point, but there is nothing therein to indicate that the capital accumulated by either of the defendant hospitals is even earmarked in any way for use in their facilities or even in Utah County. In view of the fact that Intermountain Health Care owns and operates facilities, for-profit and nonprofit, throughout this state and in other states, we are particularly concerned that there is no showing on the record that surplus funds generated by one hospital in the system will not be utilized for the benefit of facilities in other counties, outside the state of Utah, or purely for administrative costs of the system itself.

Indeed, it is difficult to see a significant difference between the *operation* (as opposed to the form of corporate structure) of defendants' facilities and the operation of the for-profit hospital in *Budge,* where William Budge Memorial Hospital had a similar policy of collecting charges, in all cases where it was possible, for the services and accommodations furnished its patients. 79 Utah at 521, 3 P.2d at 260. In *Budge,* we were unable to find a single distinctive charitable feature that marked Budge Memorial as a charitable institution, even though no benefits or profit had ever actually been distributed to or received by the shareholders of the owner corporation. 79 Utah at 528, 3 P.2d at 263. The only apparent difference between Budge Memorial and the defendants is that the hospitals in this case have adopted a nonprofit corporate format in their legal organization. Yet *Budge* decisively rejected, as we have already noted, the contention that all nonprofit corporations are entitled to a charitable exemption for purposes of property taxes. * * * The significant difference between for-profit and nonprofit hospital corporations is, in effect, the method of distribution of assets upon dissolution of the corporation, which is itself a rare occurrence.

A large portion of the profits of most for-profit entities is used for capital improvements and new, updated equipment, and the defendant hospitals here similarly expend their revenues in excess of operational expenses. There can be no doubt, in reviewing the references in the record by members of IHC's administrative staff, that the IHC system, as well as the two hospitals in question, has consistently generated sufficient funds in excess of operating costs to contribute to rapid and extensive growth, building, competitive employee and professional salaries and benefits, and a very sophisticated management structure. While it is true that no financial benefits or profits are available to private interests in the form of stockholder distributions or ownership advantages, the user *entity* in this case clearly generates substantial "profits" in the sense of income that exceeds expenses. This observation is not intended to imply that an institution must consume its assets in order to be eligible for tax exemption—the requirement of charitable giving may obviously be met before that point is reached. However, there is a serious question regarding the constitutional propriety of subsidies from

Utah County taxpayers being used to give certain entities a substantial competitive edge in what is essentially a commercial marketplace. None of the defendants in this case made any effort to demonstrate that they would suffer any operating losses or have to discontinue any services if they are ineligible for exemption from property taxes. Justice Stewart's assertion that the taxes levied by the county would have to be passed on to patients in the form of higher charges is without any foundation in the evidence. The far more logical assumption is that *growth of the IHC system* would possibly be slowed, but there is no indication of a likelihood that current and future levels of care would be jeopardized.

The final two factors we address are whether the beneficiaries of the services of the defendants are "restricted" in any way and whether private interests are benefited by the organization or operation of the defendants. Although the policy of IHC is to impose no restrictions, there were some incidents recounted in the testimony which suggested that these institutions do not see themselves as being in the business of providing hospital care "for the poor," an activity which was certainly at the heart of the original rationale for tax exemptions for charitable hospitals. Otherwise, it appears that they meet this criterion. On the question of benefits to private interests, certainly it appears that no individuals who are employed by or administer the defendants receive any distribution of assets or income, and some, such as IHC's board of trustees members, volunteer their services. We have noted, however, that IHC owns a for-profit entity, as well as nonprofit subsidiaries, and there is in addition the consideration that numerous forms of private commercial enterprise, such as pharmacies, laboratories, and contracts for medical services, are conducted as a necessary part of the defendants' hospital operations. The burden being on the taxpayer to demonstrate eligibility for the exemption, the inadequacies in the record on these questions cannot be remedied by speculation in the defendants' favor.

In summary, after reviewing the facts in this case in light of the factors we have identified, we believe that the defendants in this case confuse the element of gift to the community, which an entity must demonstrate in order to qualify as a charity under our Constitution, with the concept of community benefit, which any of countless private enterprises might provide. We have no quarrel with the assertion that Utah Valley Hospital and American Fork Hospital meet great and important needs of persons within their communities for medical care. Yet this meeting of a public need by a provision of services cannot be the sole distinguishing characteristic that leads to an automatic property tax exemption. "[T]he usefulness of an enterprise is not sufficient basis for relief from the burden of sharing essential costs of local government." *In re Marple Newtown School District,* 39 Pa.Commw. 326, 336, 395 A.2d 1023, 1028 (1978). Such a "usefulness" rule would have to be equally applied to for-profit hospitals and privately owned health care entities, which also provide medical services to their patients. We note, for example, that the increasing emphasis on competition in health care services is resulting in significant expansion of the activities and roles of health care providers generally, including hospitals, both for-profit and nonprofit. Laboratory services, pharmaceutical services, "birthing" centers, and outpatient surgical units are becoming common adjuncts to traditional hospital care. It would be impossible to justify a distinction, within the constitutional boundaries of "charitable" activities, between outpatient surgical services, for example, provided on property owned by an IHC hospital and those provided on privately owned property, where both are identical and are remunerated at the same rate. As we have pointed out, there was no showing in the record that either of the hospitals in question uses billing rates which differ materially from rates charged for the same services by for-profit hospitals, or that the defendants' rates or services would change if they were required to pay county property taxes.

Furthermore, if the "importance" of the public benefit resulting from the operation of an enterprise were to become the primary constitutional test for a charitable purpose, as the dissents imply, this Court would be required to accomplish the impossible task of determining the relative value to the public or to the community of any function performed by any entity and its consequent entitlement to a "charitable" tax exemption. * * * This cannot be the rule under our precedents established in *Loyal Order of Moose,* 657 P.2d 257, and *Laborers Local No. 295,* 658 P.2d 1192. It may very well be, as a matter of public policy, that *all* hospitals, for-profit and nonprofit, should be granted a tax exemption because of the great public need they serve. But it is beyond the power of the Legislature to grant such a public policy-based exemption under the language of the Utah Constitution as it now reads. This Court has clearly and recently affirmed the necessity of identifying the element of "gift," a nonreciprocal contribution to the community. *Laborers Local No. 295,* 658 P.2d at 1195. The dissenting opinions fail to acknowledge that, however worthy the principles of public policy they articulate may be, the standards they advocate would require us to overrule or ignore both the construction given to the "charitable purpose" language in the past by this Court and the strict analytical approach we have used in such construction. Under these circumstances, the extensive references to authority from other jurisdictions in the dissent are not persuasive on the question before us; they would only become so if we were to contemplate abandonment of our own precedent, an approach that is not openly sought here by either the defendants or the dissenting members of the Court.

Neither can we find on this record that the burdens of government are substantially lessened as a result of the defendants' provision of services. The record indicates that Utah County budgets approximately $50,000 annually for the payment of hospital care for indigents. Furthermore, the evidence described two instances within a three-month period where, after a Utah County official had declined to authorize payment for a person in the emergency room, Utah Valley Hospital refused to admit the injured person on the basis of that person's inability to pay. The county official was told in these instances to either authorize payment or to "come and get" the person. Such behavior on the hospital's part is inconsistent with its argument that it functions to relieve government of a burden. Likewise, as we have pointed out, there has been no showing that the tax exemption is a significant factor in permitting these defendants to operate, thereby arguably relieving government of the burden of establishing its own medical care providers. In fact, government is already carrying a substantial share of the operating expenses of defendants, in the form of third-party payments pursuant to "entitlement" programs such as Medicare and Medicaid.

As we noted in the introduction to this opinion, the "burden" theory of tax exemptions has been traditionally based on the notion that a charitable organization should be eligible for exemption because it performs a task which the government would otherwise have to perform. The basis for the tax exemption is a *quid pro quo:* "private charities perform functions that the state would be required to undertake and tax exemption is granted as a quid pro quo for the performance of these functions and services." * * * A hospital, whether nonprofit or for-profit, that provides its services to paying patients relieves no public burden because, in its absence, the government would not (or would have no duty to) provide free health care to patients able to pay for treatment. * * * If nonprofit hospitals, which charge fully for their services, were to be made tax exempt under the "burden" theory, for-profit hospitals logically ought to be treated in the same manner since both provide the public with the same service. Indeed, it might be argued that for-profit hospitals relieve a greater portion of the public "burden" because they provide medical care without public subsidy. All hospitals use tax-supported public services, including road construction and maintenance, police protection, fire protection, water and sewer maintenance, and waste removal, to name a few. Exempt hospitals use those services at the expense of nonexempt health care providers and other taxpayers, commercial and individual. Furthermore, nonprofit hospitals that generate a surplus from their operations ought not to be tax exempt under the "burden" theory because they are not passing along the benefit of the exemption to the public unless they are charging less for services than would be required absent the tax exemption: "Even if the organization uses such surplus to expand its public benefit services, thereby remaining within the definition of nonprofitability, it does so at the expense of the beneficiaries whom it was created to serve." * * *

While the practice of courts has often deviated from the strict logic of the "burden" theory, the general pattern is that "burden" jurisdictions generally require some degree of almsgiving or unpaid services for the granting of a charitable tax exemption. "Consequently in these states operations financed primarily or entirely with funds supplied by the beneficiaries are classified as noncharitable." * * *

We cannot find, on this record, the essential element of gift to the community, either through the nonreciprocal provision of services or through the alleviation of a government burden, and consequently we hold that the defendants have not demonstrated that their property is being used exclusively for charitable purposes under the Utah Constitution.

Because we so hold, it follows that U.C.A., 1953, § 59–2–31 provides no safe harbor for defendants. In *Loyal Order of Moose*, 657 P.2d 257, we reiterated the principle that our statutes cannot expand the scope of the tax exemption granted by article XIII, section 2 of our Constitution. "To the extent the statutes have that effect, they are not valid." *Id.* at 261. *Accord Laborers Local No. 295*, 658 P.2d at 1193–94. Property used exclusively for hospital purposes is not *automatically* being used for charitable purposes, even where the hospital is nonprofit.

We reverse the Tax Commission's grant of an *ad valorem* property tax exemption to defendants as being unconstitutional. We emphasize, contrary to the assertions of the dissents, that this opinion is no more than an extension of the principles of strict construction set forth in *Loyal Order of Moose*, 657 P.2d 257. This is a "record" case, and we make no judgment as to the ability of these hospitals or any others to demonstrate their eligibility for constitutionally permissible tax exemptions in the future. We note, however, that reliance on automatic exemptions granted heretofore, and on the kind of minimal efforts to show charity reflected in this record, will no longer suffice.

The circumstances of this decision are very similar to those in *Loyal Order of Moose*, 657 P.2d 257, which gave rise to that case's holding respecting its effective date. The defendants here have relied for many years on a statutory interpretation of a constitutional provision, and this opinion resolves a difficult question of first impression. Because of the substantial delay entailed in the litigation process, retroactive application requiring the assessment of back taxes might well result in an unreasonable burden on the defendants in this case and on other similarly situated entities. Substantial changes in their operating budgets, record-keeping, and admission policies may result from our holding. It may be that adjustments in accounting practices and other policies will enable these defendants and other hospitals to qualify in the future for the constitutional exemption. In order to avoid the unreasonable burden that might otherwise be placed on them, we hold that the ruling of this case shall be applied prospectively only, with an effective date of January 1, 1986.

Notes

1. Uninsured patients filed over forty class-action lawsuits in 23 states against hospitals that allegedly had not provided medical care without regard to patients' ability to pay. Four of the reported cases are *Burton v. William Beaumont Hospital*, 347 F.Supp.2d 486 (E.D. Mich. 2004), *Kizzire v. Baptist Health System, Inc.*, 343 F.Supp.2d 1074 (N.D. Ala. 2004), *Lorens v. Catholic Health Care Partners*, 356 F.Supp.2d 827 (N.D. Ohio 2005), and *Valencia v. Mississippi Baptist Medical Center*, 363 F.Supp.2d 867 (S.D. Miss. 2005). In *Burton*, the uninsured patients alleged the hospital breached a charitable trust for failing to provide medical care without regard to patients' ability to pay. The plaintiffs in the Michigan case contended that because the Internal

Revenue Service has granted hospitals tax exempt status under § 501(c)(3) of the code, hospitals have a duty to provide free or discounted medical care to the insured. They contended that hospitals have entered into a "public charitable trust to provide mutually affordable medical care to its uninsured patients" by virtue of their tax exempt status. They maintained that they, as uninsured patients, are the intended beneficiaries of the alleged charitable trust. The Michigan district court ruled that, even if the plaintiffs could establish the existence of a charitable trust and a breach, they were not the proper parties to prosecute the breach because, as the court asserted, the Attorney General is the proper party to enforce a charitable trust. Thus, the Michigan district court held that the patients could not maintain an action for the hospital's alleged breach of charitable trust. In *Lorens*, the court ruled that a hospital's tax exempt status does not create a contractual obligation to uninsured patients; that, even if it did, the patient lacked standing to sue under the alleged contract; and that a hospital's tax exemption does not create a charitable trust that would support the patient's breach of charitable trust claim. In *Valencia* the court ruled that there is no contract by which the government extends tax free status in return for a hospital's nondiscriminatory billing of indigents and that there is no charitable trust that requires equitable charging.

2. The Internal Revenue Service began an extensive investigation of tax-exempt hospitals in 2006 to determine whether nonprofit hospitals were denying care to the uninsured. It sent a compliance check questionnaire to 550 tax exempt hospitals in which it inquired as to whether the questioned hospital denied medical services to uninsured patients and/or to those on medicare and medicaid, the hospital's policy on uncompensated care, its billing practices, its community programs, and its compensation practices.

* * *

IV. ABANDONMENT OF NONPROFIT HOSPITAL STATUS

Problems surface when a hospital seeks to abandon its nonprofit status. What restrictions, if any, should be imposed in the event that charitable assets of a nonprofit hospital are sold to a for-profit entity? May a nonprofit hospital convert to some other form of health care provider? Consider some of the issues in the following case.

QUEEN OF ANGELS HOSPITAL v. YOUNGER
Court of Appeals, California, 1977
66 Cal.App.3d 359, 136 Cal.Rptr. 36

KAUS, Presiding Justice.

Plaintiffs in this action are the Queen of Angels Hospital, a California corporation ('Queen'), and the Franciscan Sisters of the Sacred Heart, an unincorporated association ('Motherhouse').

FACTS

The facts are not disputed; the materiality of some of the facts is.

Plaintiff Queen of Angels Hospital is a non-profit corporation, first incorporated in 1927. Plaintiff Franciscan Sisters—the Motherhouse—is a religious order, based in Illinois, composed of women of the Roman Catholic faith.

The hospital was established in 1927. In 1932, Queen added a ten-floor wing to its main building. A clinic moved into the new wing. In 1948, the Sisters took over operation of the clinic, which remained a separate corporation until 1958. The treatment of clinic patients was supervised by physicians from Queen's medical staff. The overall operation of the hospital included instructing nurses and medical students, operating the clinic, and performing general charitable work.

John Brandlin became Queen's attorney in 1964 or 1965. He was also a lay member of Queen's board of directors. In April 1971 * * * Queen's board of directors approved a lease to be effective May 1, 1971, between Queen as lessor and W.D.C. Services, Inc., hospital entrepreneurs, as lessee. Queen leased the hospital, excepting the outpatient clinic and a convent house, to W.D.C. for 25 years with two options for ten additional years each. The minimum annual rental guaranteed Queen was $800,000 for the first two years and one million dollars a year thereafter.

Queen intends to use a substantial portion of the lease proceeds to establish and operate additional medical clinics in East and South Central Los Angeles, which clinics will dispense free medical care, aid and advice to the poor and needy. It is not disputed that an outpatient clinic is not functionally equivalent to a hospital.

* * *

DISCUSSION

* * * The Attorney General contends that under its articles of incorporation, Queen held its assets in trust primarily for the purpose of operating a hospital, and the use of those assets exclusively for outpatient clinics would constitute an abandonment of Queen's primary charitable purpose and a diversion of charitable trust assets. As noted, it is not disputed that a 'hospital' is not the functional equivalent of an 'outpatient clinic.'

The rules governing the use of the assets of a non-profit charitable organization are well established: '(A)ll the assets of a corporation organized solely for charitable purposes must be deemed to be impressed with a charitable trust by virtue of the express declaration of the corporation's purposes, and notwithstanding the absence of any express declaration by those who contribute such assets as to the purpose for which the contributions are made.... It follows that ... (a non-profit corporation cannot) legally divert its assets to any purpose other than charitable purposes, and said property (is) therefore 'irrevocably dedicated' to exempt purposes within the meaning of the welfare exemption.'

(Pacific Home v. County of Los Angeles, 41 Cal.2d 844, 852, 264 P.2d 539, 543.)

* * *

With this apparent agreement in principle we turn to an examination of the articles of incorporation and the relevant undisputed facts.

The articles of incorporation, as amended in 1941, provides in relevant part as follows:

'First: That the name of said corporation is

QUEEN OF ANGELS HOSPITAL

"Second: That the purposes for which said corporation is formed are:

> (1) To establish, ... own, ... maintain, ... and operate a hospital in the City of Los Angeles, ... to furnish, ... hospital care, ... and medical and surgical treatment of every kind and character, and to receive, treat and care for patients, invalids, the aged and infirm, and generally to conduct and carry on, and to do all things necessary or advisable in conducting and carrying on a hospital; * * *

* * *

In brief, whatever else Queen of Angels Hospital Corporation may do under its articles of incorporation, it was intended to and did operate a hospital and cannot, consistent with the trust imposed upon it, abandon the operation of the hospital business in favor of clinics.

* * *

That the issue is not the desirability of the new use to which Queen wishes to put the trust assets is illustrated by Holt v. College of Osteopathic Physicians & Surgeons, 61 Cal.2d 750, 40 Cal.Rptr. 244, 394 P.2d 932. In Holt the purposes stated in the articles of incorporation were to establish and conduct an osteopathic medical and surgical college. * * * The college operated as an osteopathic school from 1914 until about May 1961, when the trustees decided to delete the word 'osteopathic' and to become an allopathic medical school. * * *

Although it was not suggested that the teaching of allopathic medicine was in any way a less desirable use of charitable funds than the teaching of osteopathic medicine, the court held: 'We have concluded that the complaint states a cause of action for enjoining a threatened breach of a charitable trust. If the allegations of the complaint are true, the charitable purpose of COPS is primarily to conduct a college of osteopathy,' and there is 'a distinction between osteopathic and allopathic medicine.' * * *

We think the principle of Holt is controlling; here, as in Holt, the issue is not whether the new and different purpose is equal to or better than the original purpose, but whether that purpose is authorized by the articles.

* * *

V. CONVERSION TO FOR-PROFIT STATUS

Several nonprofit hospitals, as well as health maintenance organizations (HMOs), have dissolved and have distributed their assets to for-profit entities. There have been concerns that there is a great potential for abuse in these transactions.

STATE OF FLORIDA v. ANCLOTE MANOR HOSPITAL
Court of Appeals, Florida, 1990
566 So.2d 296

PER CURIAM.

The appellant, State of Florida, *ex rel.* Robert Butterworth, Attorney General of the State of Florida, on behalf of the citizens of the State of Florida appeals a final judgment entered in an action brought against the appellees, Anclote Manor Hospital, Inc., a for-profit Florida corporation; * * * Directors of Anclote Psychiatric Center, Inc., a not-for-profit Florida corporation, and Anclote Manor Hospital, Inc.; and Anclote Psychiatric Center, Inc. The appellees have cross-appealed. We affirm.

This dispute arose out of the sale of the assets of Anclote Psychiatric Center, Inc., a nonprofit Florida corporation which operated Anclote Manor Hospital. On May 9, 1983, the corporation sold the hospital and two undeveloped parcels of land to Anclote Manor Hospital, Inc., a for-profit corporation, for approximately $6.3 million. This corporation was formed and wholly owned by the sole directors and members of Anclote Psychiatric Center, Inc. In October 1985, Anclote Manor Hospital, Inc., sold the hospital to American Medical International for a sum in excess of $29 million.

In 1987, the State of Florida upon the relation of Robert A. Butterworth, Attorney General (attorney general), on behalf of Anclote Psychiatric Center, Inc., and the citizens of the State of Florida, filed the instant action. The attorney general alleged that the twelve defendant directors of Anclote Psychiatric Center, Inc., breached their fiduciary duty to the corporation and violated its articles of incorporation when they sold the corporation's assets to Anclote Manor Hospital, Inc., a corporation that they owned, for less than fair market value. * * *

The trial court, prior to trial, held that the attorney general had no standing to sue in a derivative capacity on behalf of Anclote Psychiatric Center, Inc., because he was not a member or stockholder of the corporation. That corporation was, accordingly, dismissed as a party plaintiff, and the action proceeded to trial under section 617.09, Florida

Statutes (1983), which allows the Department of Legal Affairs to institute proceedings to revoke a corporation's charter or to prevent the corporation from being used for purposes inconsistent with its charter.

At the conclusion of a nonjury trial, the court found that the evidence did not establish any act that would invalidate the corporation's status as an exempt organization under 26 U.S.C. section 501(c)(3). The court, however, after considering conflicting evidence, found that the corporate assets of Anclote Psychiatric Center, Inc., were sold to its directors as stockholders of a for-profit corporation at less than the fair market price on May 9, 1983. Based upon this finding, the court held that the sale was not in compliance with section 607.124(1)(c), Florida Statutes (1983). The court then declined to dissolve the corporation as authorized by section 617.09 but issued an injunction prohibiting improper use of Anclote Psychiatric Center, Inc., in the future. The appellant filed a timely notice of appeal from the judgment and the subsequent order denying costs. The appellees have cross-appealed.

The trial court properly held that the attorney general had no standing to sue in a derivative capacity on behalf of Anclote Psychiatric Center, Inc., and properly dismissed the corporation as a party plaintiff. Assuming that the 1983 sale was voidable at the instance of the corporation because it violated section 607.124, Florida Statutes (1983), no creditor, officer, director, or shareholder complained of the sale or sought to have it set aside either individually or by a request that the attorney general institute an action on their behalf.

The appellees contend that the trial court erred by not finding that the attorney general had failed to prove a case against them under section 617.09. The attorney general on the other hand contends that section 617.09 granted broad authority to the attorney general to take all legal and equitable action to prevent the improper use of charitable corporations, and that the trial court erred in failing to afford appropriate equitable or legal relief by refusing to disgorge the appellees' profits. We disagree with both parties' contentions.

At all material times, section 617.09 provided:

617.09 Proceedings to revoke articles of incorporation or charter or prevent its use.—In the event any member or citizen shall complain to the Department of Legal Affairs that any corporation organized under this chapter was organized or is being used as a cover to evade any of the laws against crime, or for purposes inconsistent with those stated in its articles of incorporation or charter, and shall submit prima facie evidence to sustain such charge, together with sufficient money to cover court costs and expenses, the said department forthwith shall institute and in due course prosecute to final judgment such legal or equitable proceedings as may be considered advisable either to revoke the articles of incorporation or charter or prevent its improper use.

The law provides a remedy for the improper use of the articles of incorporation of a corporation. The court may either prevent its improper use or, if necessary, dissolve the corporation.

In this case, the Department of Legal Affairs received a complaint that the corporation was being used for purposes inconsistent with those stated in its articles of incorporation and determined that there was prima facie evidence to sustain that charge. The attorney general, therefore, upon receiving a sufficient deposit to cover court costs and expenses, had the duty to file the instant action. *See Miami Retreat Foundation v. Ervin,* 62 So.2d 748 (Fla.1952); *State ex rel. Landis v. S.H. Kress & Co.,* 155 So. 823, 155 Fla. 189 (1934).

The attorney general presented sufficient competent evidence to sustain the trial court's finding that the appellees improperly used the corporation's articles of incorporation when they sold the corporation's assets in 1983 and, accordingly, had the authority to enter an injunction prohibiting them from doing so in the future.

We reject the appellees' contention that the court has no authority to enter an injunction unless the improper use is being carried on at the time of the litigation. To so hold would allow a corporation to improperly use their articles of incorporation until litigation was threatened. The privilege to operate under articles of incorporation is a privilege granted by the state. The state has the right, and the attorney general has the duty, if the requirements of section 617.09 are met to see that this privilege is being properly used at all times.

The court also held that since there was no improper use of the articles of incorporation since 1983 and that since nothing had been done to invalidate the corporation's status as a section 501(c)(3) corporation because the Internal Revenue Service had accepted the transaction as it was culminated, it was not necessary to dissolve the corporation. We cannot find that the court abused its discretion by failing to apply the remedy of dissolving the corporation.

The attorney general contends that in addition to permitting the court to enjoin the improper use of articles of incorporation or revoking said articles, the statute authorizes him to recover any profits the appellees might have received from the sale of Anclote Psychiatric Center, Inc.'s assets. We disagree. Section 617.09 allows the Department of Legal Affairs to institute such legal or equitable proceedings as may be considered advisable either to revoke the articles of incorporation or charter or prevent its improper use. Such legal or equitable proceedings must, however, be appropriate as a means to accomplish the end of either preventing the improper use of the articles or revoking said articles. The statute is not directed to nor does it authorize a suit to disgorge profits by those who might choose to improperly use the grant of a corporate charter. It only provides a way to insure its proper use or to remove the grant from them.

We realize that this statute has been amended since this matter was decided by the trial court and that the statute now provides the remedy sought herein by the attorney general. Ch. 89–78, Laws of Fla. § 1. We decline to hold that the amended statute is just a restatement of the original intent set forth in the statute. Courts cannot construe an unambiguous statute in a way which would extend, modify, or limit its express terms or its reasonable and obvious implications. *Holly v. Auld*, 450 So.2d 217 (Fla.1984).

* * *

Affirmed.

Questions

Why did the court in *Anclote* deny the Attorney General standing to sue in a derivative capacity on behalf of Anclote Psychiatric Center? How do you reconcile this decision with *In re Estate of Stern*, cited in Chapter 3? Consider the denial of standing to the Attorney General in *Anclote* in conjunction with the ruling of the Virginia Supreme Court in *Commonwealth of Virginia v. The Jaco Foundation*, cited in Chapter 1.

Notes

1. The assets of Anclote Psychiatric Center were sold for $4.59 million plus liabilities, for a total of $6.3 million, to a for-profit in which all of the stock was owned by the directors of Anclote. Two years later, the for-profit sold the hospital's operating assets for nearly $30 million. As a § 501(c)(3) organization, Anclote was required to distribute its assets, upon dissolution, to another § 501(c)(3) hospital. [See Treas. Reg. § 1.501(c)(3)–4.] The Florida court in *Anclote* found that the evidence did not establish any act that would invalidate the § 501(c)(3) tax exempt status of Anclote Psychiatric Center. Later, however, the IRS did revoke the corporation's tax exempt status because it contended the sale at less than fair market value provided a private benefit to the individuals involved. See *Anclote Psychiatric Center, Inc. v. Comm.*, 76 T.C.M. 175, T.C. Memo 1998–273 (1998), aff'd, 190 F.3d 541 (11th Cir.1999).

2. Directors of nonprofit hospitals can be subject to the excess benefits penalty tax under § 4958 for disposing of hospital assets for less than fair market value if the directors have an interest in the purchasing entity. See *Caracci v. Comm.*, 118 T.C. 379 (2002), rev'd based on valuation issues Caracci v. Comm., 456 F.3d 444 (5th Cir. 2006) cited in Chapter 3.

3. The health maintenance organization (HMO) evolved in the 1970s to provide a solution to the escalating costs of medical care as well as to increase the quality and availability of health care. The HMO is a form of prepaid health plan. The consumer pays a fixed fee to a functionally integrated group of doctors in exchange for the group's agreement to provide any medical treatment that the subscriber needs. Both Congress and numerous state legislatures have enacted comprehensive HMO legislation. See 42 U.S.C. § 300e. In the past HMOs qualified for § 501(c)(3) status. However, § 501(m), which was added to the Internal Revenue Code in 1986, presents questions regarding the tax-exempt status of health plans that provide commercial-type insurance resembling indemnity-type arrangements. Section 501(m) denies tax exempt status to §§ 501(c)(3) and (4) organizations if a substantial part of their activities consist of providing commercial-type insurance.

Chapter 13

SOCIAL CLUBS

I. NATURE OF SOCIAL CLUBS

Social clubs are membership organizations. A social club generally is organized and operated primarily to permit individuals to join together to provide recreational or social facilities on a mutual basis and to furnish goods and services to its members. Thus, a social club, which benefits its members, differs substantially from a charitable organization, which benefits members of the public. In those states that classify nonprofit corporations as public benefit or mutual benefit organizations, the social club would be a mutual benefit corporation. Whether or not classified as a mutual benefit corporation, in most states a social club can make distributions to its members upon dissolution.

A social club that is organized and operated exclusively for pleasure or recreation is qualified for tax exempt status under § 501(c)(7). Generally, distributions to members upon dissolution will not cause a social club to lose its tax exempt status.

REVENUE RULING 58-501
1958-2 C.B. 262

Where a social club, qualified for tax exemption under section 501(c)(7) of the Internal Revenue Code of 1954, finds it impracticable to continue to conduct its exempt activities and, as a result, sells its property and liquidates, such sale is incidental to its exempt purposes and the club is still to be considered as operated exclusively for pleasure, recreation and similar purposes up through the date of the sale and distribution of the liquidated assets to its active members.

Advice has been requested whether a tax exempt social club which is unable to continue its exempt activities will be deprived of its exemption because a profit was realized on the sale of all the club's property upon liquidation.

A club was incorporated, as a corporation without stock, under the laws of the state in which it was located, for the purpose of operating a golf club exclusively on a nonprofit basis for the pleasure and recreation of its members. The club membership was composed of two groups, the regular members, who held certificates of indebtedness in the Club's property and a small number of associate members, who were proposed by and approved of in the same manner as the regular members, but who were not to share in the distribution of the assets of the club. As the years progressed, it became apparent that the club was in peril due to the urbanization of the immediate surrounding area. Among the problems faced by the club were increased real estate assessments; rearrangement of its golf course made necessary by the city's street-building activities; and the imminent possibility of further condemnation of additional golf property for the widening of a boulevard which would render the club facilities useless for club purposes. Several offers were received from builders who desired to use the property for residential development and finally, on recommendation of the board of directors, prospective purchasers were invited to submit bids. After negotiations, an offer for purchase of the property was accepted and a contract of sale was executed. The price was payable in part upon execution of the contract, in part upon closing date, and the balance was secured by a purchase money mortgage at four and one-half percent interest payable in three years. After an agreed date there were no club activities except to collect interest on notes and to defend the club from claims of past members. A committee had been appointed, while the sale was still being negotiated, to find a new location for the club, but no adequate facilities were found and no serious action was taken in this respect. The personal property was also sold. Shortly after the sale of the property, the club passed a resolution to dissolve and commenced distribution of the proceeds to the certificate holders, who were entitled to the amounts. The mortgage was paid in full at maturity.

To qualify for exemption from Federal income tax under section 501(c)(7) of the Internal Revenue Code of 1954, a social club must be organized and operated exclusively for pleasure, recreation and other nonprofit purposes and no part of its net earnings may inure to the benefit of any private shareholder. Section 1.501(c)(7)–1(b) of the Income Tax Regulations states that an incidental sale of property will not deprive the club of its exemption. It has also been held that sales of property at a profit will not cause a social club to lose its exemption provided the sale is incidental to the club's purpose. * * *

In determining whether the transaction in the present case is an incidental sale or a sale primarily for profit, it is necessary to examine the circumstances under which the sale was made and determine the primary purpose of the sale. The extensive urbanization of the area surrounding the club, the increased taxes and expenses occasioned thereby, the probable condemnation of a large section of the land and continued trespasses all indicate that the further continuance of the club would not be possible. Therefore, the sale of the club property was for the purpose of facilitating its dissolution and not primarily for a profit. In G.C.M. 19465, C.B. 1938–1, 172, it is held that a social club does not lose its exemption by reason of the sale at a profit of its club properties to avoid financial burden. The sale of the property and the distribution of its assets are important transactions in the dissolution of a club and, as such, these activities do not form a basis on which to deprive the club of its exemption. This transaction was obviously a singular event in the club's history and to facilitate the dissolution does not convert a social club into a real estate business. The sale was incidental to the club's purpose.

The fact that a portion of the profit resulting from the sale was distributed to the members does not cause the club to lose its exemption. Every social and recreational group has a prospect of eventually being disbanded and dissolved. Therefore, the fact that the assets of a club will, upon dissolution, be paid to members or shareholders is not alone sufficient to make the organization liable to render income tax returns.
* * *

Another aspect of this case is whether the holding of the mortgage note and the collection of interest were something more than a mere incident to the sale and liquidation, that is, whether it became a profit making venture for the club which would cause the club to lose its exemption. The receipt of interest on its purchase money mortgage did not deprive the taxpayer of its exempt status. The method of settlement on this sale of land was as practical and reasonable a method of payment as could be expected and it resulted in the fastest possible liquidation without depriving the taxpayer of a just price by the necessity of demanding full payment in cash. As long as no repeated extensions of the mortgage note were granted and there being no other evidence to show an investment purpose, the settlement under the facts herein stated is considered an ordinary and reasonable method of settlement and an integral part of the sale. As such, it does not affect the taxpayer's exempt status.

As to the possibility of considering this as a sale for profit rather than a sale for liquidation because of the fact that an effort was made to locate a new site, the taxpayer would not lose its tax status because the conversion of property to other property better suited to serve the operations of a club is a valid purpose within the contemplation of the Code. * * *

Accordingly, it is held that where a social club, qualified for tax exemption under section 501(c)(7) of the Code, finds it impracticable to continue to conduct its exempt activities and, as a result, sells its property and liquidates, such sale is incidental to its exempt purposes. The club is still to be considered as operated exclusively for pleasure, recreation, and similar purposes up through the date of the sale and distribution of the liquidated assets to its active members. The profit from the sale by the club of all its property in conjunction with the termination of its activities and liquidation does not deprive the club of the exemption provided by section 501(c)(7) of the Code.

* * *

Note

A social club can have several types of memberships, including regular or active members, associate members, and corporate or corporate-sponsored memberships. A regular member has the right to vote and to determine the management, operation and control of the club. A regular member can share in the assets of the club should it be dissolved. An associate member generally does not have a right to vote and would not share in the assets of the club upon dissolution. Associate members may be entitled to the use and enjoyment of all club facilities or may be limited to only a part of the facilities, such as tennis or golf. A corporate member is a membership issued to a corporation, which then designates those officers or employees who may use the club facilities. A corporate-sponsored membership involves a bona fide membership of individuals rather than a business entity, as is the case for the corporate membership.

II. RIGHT OF ASSOCIATION

The First Amendment protects membership in a private social club by granting a right to associate with others in the pursuit of activities of a private club. However, implicit in the right to associate with persons of the club members' own choosing is the right to exclude others. Those persons who are denied membership in a particular private social club may experience injurious discrimination. Thus, courts have ruled that, while members of a club have a right of association, they lack the right to practice invidious racial and gender discrimination.

BOARD OF DIRECTORS, ROTARY INTERNATIONAL v. ROTARY CLUB OF DUARTE

United States Supreme Court, 1987
481 U.S. 537, 107 S.Ct. 1940, 95 L.Ed.2d 474

Justice POWELL delivered the opinion of the Court.

We must decide whether a California statute that requires California Rotary Clubs to admit women members violates the First Amendment.

I

A

Rotary International (International) is a nonprofit corporation founded in 1905, with headquarters in Evanston, Illinois. It is "an organization of business and professional men united worldwide who provide humanitarian service, encourage high ethical standards in all vocations, and help build goodwill and peace in the world." Rotary Manual of Procedure 7 (1981) (hereinafter Manual), App. 35. Individual members belong to a local Rotary Club rather than to International. In turn, each local Rotary Club is a member of International. *Ibid.* In August 1982, shortly before the trial in this case, International comprised 19,788 Rotary Clubs in 157 countries, with a total membership of about 907,750. * * *

Individuals are admitted to membership in a Rotary Club according to a "classification system." The purpose of this system is to ensure "that each Rotary Club includes a representative of every worthy and recognized business, professional, or institutional activity in the community." 2 Rotary Basic Library, Club Service 67–69 (1981) * * *. Each active member must work in a leadership capacity in his business or profession. The general rule is that "one active member is admitted for each classification, but he, in turn, may propose an additional active member, who must be in the same business or professional classification." * * *. Thus, each classification may be represented by two active members. In addition, "senior active" and "past service" members may represent the same classifications as active members. * * * There is no limit to the number of clergymen, journalists, or diplomats who may be admitted to membership. * * *

Subject to these requirements, each local Rotary Club is free to adopt its own rules and procedures for admitting new members. * * * International has promulgated Recommended Club By-laws providing that candidates for membership will be considered by both a "classifications committee" and a "membership committee." The classifications committee determines whether the candidate's business or profession is described accurately and fits an "open" classification. The membership committee evaluates the candidate's "character, business and social standing, and general eligibility." * * * If any member objects to the candidate's admission, the final decision is made by the club's board of directors.

Membership in Rotary Clubs is open only to men. * * * Herbert A. Pigman, the General Secretary of Rotary International, testified that the exclusion of women results in an "aspect of fellowship ... that is enjoyed by the present male membership," * * * and also allows Rotary to operate effectively in foreign countries with varied cultures and social mores. Although women are not admitted to membership, they are permitted to attend meetings, give speeches, and receive awards. Women relatives of Rotary members may form their own associations, and are authorized to wear the Rotary lapel pin. Young women between 14 and 28 years of age may join Interact or Rotaract, organizations sponsored by Rotary International.

B

In 1977 the Rotary Club of Duarte, California, admitted Donna Bogart, Mary Lou Elliott, and Rosemary Freitag to active membership. International notified the Duarte Club that admitting women members is contrary to the Rotary constitution. After an internal hearing, International's board of directors revoked the charter of the Duarte Club and terminated its membership in Rotary International. The Duarte Club's appeal to the International Convention was unsuccessful.

The Duarte Club and two of its women members filed a complaint in the California Superior Court for the County of Los Angeles. The complaint alleged, *inter alia,* that appellants' actions violated the Unruh Civil Rights Act, Cal.Civ.Code Ann. § 51 (West 1982). Appellees sought to enjoin International from enforcing its restrictions against admitting women members, revoking the Duarte Club's charter, or compelling delivery of the charter to any representative of International. Appellees also sought a declaration that appellants' actions had violated the Unruh Act. After a bench trial, the court concluded that neither Rotary International nor the Duarte Club is a "business establishment" within the meaning of the Unruh Act. The court recognized that "some individual Rotarians derive sufficient business advantage from Rotary to warrant deduction of Rotarian expenses in income tax calculations, or to warrant payment of those expenses by their employers.... * * * But it found that "such business benefits are incidental to the principal purposes of the association ... to promote fellowship ... and ... 'service' activities." The court also found that Rotary clubs do not provide their members with goods, services, or facilities. On the basis of these findings and conclusions, the court entered judgment for International.

The California Court of Appeal reversed. 178 Cal.App.3d 1035, 224 Cal.Rptr. 213 (1986). It held that both Rotary International and the Duarte Rotary Club are business establishments subject to the provisions of the Unruh Act. For purposes of the Act, a " 'business' embraces everything about which one can be employed," and an "establishment" includes "not only a fixed location, ... but also a permanent 'commercial force or organization' or a 'permanent settled position (as in life or business).' " * * * The Court of Appeal identified several "businesslike attributes" of Rotary International, including its complex structure, large staff and budget, and extensive publishing activities. The court held that the trial court had erred in finding that the business advantages afforded by membership in a local Rotary Club are merely incidental. It stated that testimony by members of the Duarte Club "leaves no doubt that business concerns are a motivating factor in joining local clubs," and that "business benefits [are] enjoyed and capitalized upon by Rotarians and their businesses or employers." * * * The Court of Appeal rejected the trial court's finding that the Duarte Club does not provide goods, services, or facilities to its members. In particular, the court noted that members receive copies of the Rotary magazine and numerous other Rotary publications, are entitled to wear and display the Rotary emblem, and may attend conferences that teach managerial and professional techniques.

The court also held that membership in Rotary International or the Duarte Club does not give rise to a "continuous, personal, and social" relationship that "take[s] place more or less outside public view." Ibid. * * * The court further concluded that admitting women to the Duarte Club would not seriously interfere with the objectives of Rotary International. Finally, the court rejected appellants' argument that their policy of excluding women is protected by the First Amendment principles set out in *Roberts v. United States Jaycees,* 468 U.S. 609, 104 S.Ct. 3244, 82 L.Ed.2d 462 (1984). It observed that "[n]othing we have said prevents, or can prevent, International from adopting or attempting to enforce membership rules or restrictions outside of this state." *Id.,* 178 Cal. App.3d, at 1066, 224 Cal.Rptr., at 231. The court ordered appellants to reinstate the Duarte Club as a member of Rotary International, and permanently enjoined them from enforcing or attempting to enforce the gender requirement against the Duarte Club.

The California Supreme Court denied appellants' petition for review. We postponed consideration of our jurisdiction to the hearing on the merits. 479 U.S. 929, 107 S.Ct. 396, 93 L.Ed.2d 350 (1986). We conclude that we have appellate jurisdiction, and affirm the judgment of the Court of Appeal.

II

In *Roberts v. United States Jaycees, supra,* we upheld against First Amendment challenge a Minnesota statute that required the Jaycees to admit women as full voting members. *Roberts* provides the framework for analyzing appellants' constitutional claims. As we observed in *Roberts,* our cases have afforded constitutional protection to freedom of association in two distinct senses. First, the Court has held that the Constitution protects against unjustified government interference with an individual's choice to enter into and maintain certain intimate or private relationships. Second, the Court has upheld the freedom of individuals to associate for the purpose of engaging in protected speech or religious activities. In many cases, government interference with one form of protected association will also burden the other form of association. In *Roberts* we determined the nature and degree of constitutional protection by considering separately the effect of the challenged state action on individuals' freedom of private association and their freedom of expressive association. We follow the same course in this case.

A

The Court has recognized that the freedom to enter into and carry on certain intimate or private relationships is a fundamental element of liberty protected by the Bill of Rights. Such relationships may take various forms, including the most intimate. * * * We have not attempted to mark the precise boundaries of this type of constitutional protection. The intimate relationships to which we have accorded constitutional protection include marriage, * * *; the begetting and bearing of children, * * *; child rearing and education, * * *; and cohabitation with relatives, * * *. Of course, we have not held that constitutional protection is restricted to relationships among family members. We have emphasized that the First Amendment protects those relationships, including family relationships, that presuppose "deep attachments and commitments to the necessarily few other individuals with whom one shares not only a special community of thoughts, experiences, and beliefs but also distinctively personal aspects of one's life." *Roberts v. United States Jaycees, supra,* 468 U.S., at 619–620, 104 S.Ct., at 3250. But in *Roberts* we observed that "[d]etermining the limits of state authority over an individual's freedom to enter into a particular association ... unavoidably entails a careful assessment of where that relationship's objective characteristics locate it on a spectrum from the most intimate to the most attenuated of personal attachments." * * * In determining whether a particular association is sufficiently personal or private to warrant constitutional protection, we consider factors such as size, purpose, selectivity, and whether others are excluded from critical aspects of the relationship. 468 U.S., at 620, 104 S.Ct., at 3250.

The evidence in this case indicates that the relationship among Rotary Club members is not the kind of intimate or private relation that warrants constitutional protection. The size of local Rotary Clubs ranges from fewer than 20 to more than 900. * * * There is no upper limit on the membership of any local Rotary Club. About 10 percent of the membership of a typical club moves away or drops out during a typical year. * * * The clubs therefore are instructed to "keep a flow of prospects coming" to make up for the attrition and gradually to enlarge the membership. *Ibid.* The purpose of Rotary "is to produce an inclusive, not exclusive, membership, making possible the recognition of all useful local occupations, and enabling the club to be a true cross section of the business and professional life of the community." * * * The membership undertakes a variety of service projects designed to aid the community, to raise the standards of the members' businesses and professions, and to improve international relations. Such an inclusive "fellowship for service based on diversity of interest," *ibid.*, however beneficial to the members and to those they serve, does not suggest the kind of private or personal relationship to which we have accorded protection under the First Amendment. To be sure, membership in Rotary Clubs is not open to the general public. But each club is instructed to include in its membership "all fully qualified prospective members located within its territory," to avoid "arbitrary limits on the number of members in the club," and to "establish and maintain a membership growth pattern."
* * *

Many of the Rotary Clubs' central activities are carried on in the presence of strangers. Rotary Clubs are required to admit any member of any other Rotary Club to their meetings. Members are encouraged to invite business associates and competitors to meetings. At some Rotary Clubs, the visitors number "in the tens and twenties each week." * * * Joint meetings with the members of other organizations, and other joint activities, are permitted. The clubs are encouraged to seek coverage of their meetings and activities in local newspapers. In sum, Rotary Clubs, rather than carrying on their activities in an atmosphere of privacy, seek to keep their "windows and doors open to the whole world." * * * We therefore conclude that application of the Unruh Act to local Rotary Clubs does not interfere unduly with the members' freedom of private association.

B

The Court also has recognized that the right to engage in activities protected by the First Amendment implies "a corresponding right to associate with others in pursuit of a wide variety of political, social, economic, educational, religious, and cultural ends." *Roberts v. United States Jaycees,* 468 U.S., at 622, 104 S.Ct., at 3252. * * * For this reason, "[i]mpediments to the exercise of one's right to choose one's associates can violate the right of association protected by the First Amendment...." * * * In this case, however, the evidence fails to demonstrate that admitting women to Rotary Clubs will affect in any significant way the existing members' ability to carry out their various purposes.

As a matter of policy, Rotary Clubs do not take positions on "public questions," including political or international issues. * * * To be sure, Rotary Clubs engage in a variety of commendable service activities that are protected by the First Amendment. But the Unruh Act does not require the clubs to abandon or alter any of these activities. It does not require them to abandon their basic goals of humanitarian service, high ethical standards in all vocations, good will, and peace. Nor does it require them to abandon their classification system or admit members who do not reflect a cross section of the community. Indeed, by opening membership to leading business and professional women in the community, Rotary Clubs are likely to obtain a more representative cross section of community leaders with a broadened capacity for service.

Even if the Unruh Act does work some slight infringement on Rotary members' right of expressive association, that infringement is justified because it serves the State's compelling interest in eliminating discrimination against women. * * * On its face the Unruh Act, like the Minnesota public accommodations law we considered in *Roberts,* makes no distinctions on the basis of the organization's viewpoint. Moreover, public accommodations laws "plainly serv[e] compelling state interests of the highest order." 468 U.S., at 624, 104 S.Ct., at 3253. In *Roberts* we recognized that the State's compelling interest in assuring equal access to women extends to the acquisition of leadership skills and business contacts as well as tangible goods and services. *Id.,* at 626, 104 S.Ct., at 3254. The Unruh Act plainly serves this interest. We therefore hold that application of the Unruh Act to California Rotary Clubs does not violate the right of expressive association afforded by the First Amendment.

III

Finally, appellants contend that the Unruh Act is unconstitutionally vague and overbroad. We conclude that these contentions were not properly presented to the state courts. It is well settled that this Court will not review a final judgment of a state court unless "the record as a whole shows either expressly or by clear implication that the federal claim was adequately presented in the state system." * * * Appellants did not present the issues squarely to the state courts until they filed their petition for rehearing with the Court of Appeal. The court denied the petition without opinion. When "the highest state court has failed to pass upon a federal question, it will be assumed that the omission was due to want of proper presentation in the state courts, unless the aggrieved party in this Court can affirmatively show the contrary." * * * Appellants have made no such showing in this case.

IV

The judgment of the Court of Appeal of California is affirmed.

* * *

Question

What private social clubs should be classified as "places of accommodation" so that the members' "right of association" becomes limited?

NEW YORK STATE CLUB ASSOCIATION, INC. v. CITY OF NEW YORK

United States Supreme Court, 1988
487 U.S. 1, 108 S.Ct. 2225, 101 L.Ed.2d 1

Justice WHITE delivered the opinion of the Court.

New York City has adopted a local law that forbids discrimination by certain private clubs. The New York Court of Appeals rejected a facial challenge to this law based on the First and Fourteenth Amendments. We sit in review of that judgment.

I

In 1965, New York City adopted a Human Rights Law that prohibits discrimination by any "place of public accommodation, resort or amusement." This term is defined broadly in the Law to cover such various places as hotels, restaurants, retail stores, hospitals, laundries, theaters, parks, public conveyances, and public halls, in addition to numerous other places that are specifically listed. N.Y.C. Admin.Code § 8–102(9) (1986). Yet the Law also exempted from its coverage various public educational facilities and "any institution, club or place of accommodation which proves that it is in its nature distinctly private." *Ibid.* The city adopted this Law soon after the Federal Government adopted civil rights legislation to bar discrimination in places of public accommodation, Civil Rights Act of 1964, Title II, 78 Stat. 243, 42 U.S.C. § 2000a(e).

In 1984, New York City amended its Human Rights Law. The basic purpose of the amendment is to prohibit discrimination in certain private clubs that are determined to be sufficiently "public" in nature that they do not fit properly within the exemption for "any institution, club or place of accommodation which is in its nature distinctly private." As the City Council stated at greater length:

"It is hereby found and declared that the city of New York has a compelling interest in providing its citizens an environment where all persons, regardless of race, creed, color, national origin or sex, have a fair and equal opportunity to participate in the business and professional life of the city, and may be unfettered in availing themselves of employment opportunities. Although city, state and federal laws have been enacted to eliminate discrimination in employment, women and minority group members have not attained equal opportunity in business and the professions. One barrier to the advancement of women and minorities in the business and professional life of the city is the discriminatory practices of certain membership organizations where business deals are often made and personal contacts valuable for business purposes, employment and professional advancement are formed. While such organizations may avowedly be organized for social, cultural, civic or educational purposes, and while many perform valuable services to the community, the commercial nature of some of the activities occurring therein and the prejudicial impact of these activities on business, professional and employment opportunities of minorities and women cannot be ignored." Local Law No. 63 of 1984, § 1, App. 14–15.

For these reasons, the City Council found that "the public interest in equal opportunity" outweighs "the interest in private association asserted by club members." * * * It cautioned, however, that it did not purpose "to interfere in club activities or subject club operations to scrutiny beyond what is necessary in good faith to enforce the human rights law," and the amendments were not intended as an attempt "to dictate the manner in which certain private clubs conduct their activities or select their members, except insofar as is necessary to ensure that clubs do not automatically exclude persons from consideration for membership or enjoyment of club accommodations and facilities and the advantages and privileges of membership, on account of invidious discrimination." * * *

The specific change wrought by the amendment is to extend the antidiscrimination provisions of the Human Rights Law to any "institution, club or place of accommodation [that] has more than four hundred members, provides regular meal service and regularly receives payment for dues, fees, use of space, facilities, services, meals or beverages directly or indirectly from or on behalf of nonmembers for the furtherance of trade or business." N.Y.C.Admin.Code § 8–102(9) (1986). Any such club "shall not be considered in its nature distinctly private." Nonetheless, the city also stated that any such club "shall be deemed to be in its nature distinctly private" if it is "a corporation incorporated under the benevolent orders law or described in the benevolent orders law but formed under any other law of this state, or a religious corporation incorporated under the education law or the religious corporations law." The City Council explained that it drafted the amendment in this way so as to meet the specific problem confronting women and minorities in the city's business and professional world: "Because small clubs, benevolent orders and religious corporations have not been identified in testimony before the Council as places where business activity is prevalent, the Council has determined not to apply the requirements of this local law to such organizations." * * *

Immediately after the 1984 Law became effective, the New York State Club Association filed suit against the city and some of its officers in state court, seeking a declaration that the Law is invalid on various state grounds and is unconstitutional on its face under the First and Fourteenth Amendments and requesting that defendants be enjoined from enforcing it. On cross-motions for summary judgment, the trial court upheld the Law against all challenges, including the federal constitutional challenges. The intermediate state appellate court affirmed this judgment on appeal; one judge dissented, however, concluding that the exemption for benevolent orders violates the Equal Protection Clause because it fails to accord equal protection to similarly situated persons. * * *

The State Club Association appealed this decision to the New York Court of Appeals, which affirmed in a unanimous opinion. * * * The court rejected the First Amendment challenge to Local Law 63, relying heavily on the decisions in *Roberts v. United States Jaycees,* 468 U.S. 609, 104 S.Ct. 3244, 82 L.Ed.2d 462 (1984), and *Board of Directors of Rotary Int'l v. Rotary Club,* 481 U.S. 537, 107 S.Ct. 1940, 95 L.Ed.2d 474 (1987). It ruled that any infringement on associational rights is amply justified by the city's compelling interest in eliminating discrimination against women and minorities. In addition, the Law employs the least restrictive means to achieve its ends because it interferes with the policies and activities of private clubs only "to the extent necessary to ensure that they do not automatically exclude persons from membership or use of the facilities on account of invidious discrimination." 69 N.Y.2d, at 223, 513 N.Y.S.2d, at 355, 505 N.E.2d, at 921. The court denied relief on the equal protection claim without discussing it.

The State Club Association appealed to this Court. We noted probable jurisdiction, * * * and we now affirm the judgment below, upholding Local Law 63 against appellant's facial attack on its constitutionality.

II

The initial question in this case is whether appellant has standing to challenge the constitutionality of Local Law 63 in this Court. We hold that it does.

Appellant is a nonprofit corporation, which essentially consists of a consortium of 125 other private clubs and associations in the State of New York, many of which are located in New York City. In *Hunt v. Washington Apple Advertising Comm'n,* 432 U.S. 333, 343, 97 S.Ct. 2434, 2441, 53 L.Ed.2d 383 (1977), we held that an association has standing to sue on behalf of its members "when (a) its members would otherwise have standing to sue in their own right; (b) the interests it seeks to protect are germane to the organization's purpose; and (c) neither the claim asserted nor the relief requested requires the participation of individual members in the lawsuit." * * * Appellees focus on the first part of this test; they read the requirement that the association's members "would otherwise have standing to sue in their own right" as meaning that appellant's member associations must have standing to sue only on behalf of themselves, and not on behalf of anyone else, such as their own individual members.

This reading of *Hunt* is incorrect. Under *Hunt,* an association has standing to sue on behalf of its members when those members would have standing to bring the same suit. It does not matter what specific analysis is necessary to determine that the members could bring the same suit, for the purpose of the first part of the *Hunt* test is simply to weed out plaintiffs who try to bring cases, which could not otherwise be brought, by manufacturing allegations of standing that lack any real foundation. Here, however, the appellant consortium has standing to sue on behalf of its member associations as long as those associations would have standing to bring the same challenge to Local Law 63. In this regard, it is sufficient to note that appellant's member associations would have standing to bring this same suit on behalf of their own individual members, since those individuals "are suffering immediate or threatened injury" to their associational rights as a result of the Law's enactment. * * * Thus the case is properly before us.

III

New York City's Human Rights Law authorizes the city's Human Rights Commission or any aggrieved individual to initiate a complaint against any "place of public accommodation, resort or amusement" that is alleged to have discriminated in violation of the Law. N.Y.C.Admin.Code § 8–109(1) (1986). The Commission investigates the complaint and determines whether probable cause exists to find a violation. When probable cause is found, the Commission may settle the matter by conciliatory measures, if possible; if the matter is not settled, the Commission schedules a hearing in which the defending party may present evidence and answer the charges against it. After the hearing is concluded, the Commission states its findings of fact and either dismisses the complaint or issues a cease-and-desist order. § 8–109(2). Any person aggrieved by an order of the Commission is entitled to seek judicial review of the order, and the Commission may seek enforcement of its orders in judicial proceedings. § 8–110.

None of these procedures has come into play in this case, however, for appellant brought this suit challenging the constitutionality of the 1984 Law on its face before any enforcement proceedings were initiated against any of its member associations. Although such facial challenges are sometimes permissible and often have been entertained, especially when speech protected by the First Amendment is at stake, to prevail on a facial attack the plaintiff must demonstrate that the challenged law either "could never be applied in a valid manner" or that even though it may be validly applied to the plaintiff and others, it nevertheless is so broad that it "may inhibit the constitutionally protected speech of third parties." * * * Properly understood, the latter kind of facial challenge is an exception to ordinary standing requirements, and is justified only by the recognition that free expression may be inhibited almost as easily by the potential or threatened use of power as by the actual exercise of that power. * * * Both exceptions, however, are narrow ones: the first kind of facial challenge will not succeed unless the court finds that "every application of the statute created an impermissible risk of suppression of ideas," *Taxpayers for Vincent, supra,* 466 U.S., at 798, n. 15, 104 S.Ct., at 2125 n. 15, and the second kind of facial challenge will not succeed unless the statute is "substantially" overbroad, which requires the court to find "a realistic danger that the statute itself will significantly compromise recognized First Amendment protections of parties not before the Court." * * *

We are unpersuaded that appellant is entitled to make either one of these two distinct facial challenges. Appellant conceded at oral argument, understandably we think, that the antidiscrimination provisions of the Human Rights Law certainly could be constitutionally applied at least to some of the large clubs, under this Court's decisions in *Rotary* and *Roberts.** * * The clubs that are covered under the Law contain at least 400 members. They thus are comparable in size to the local chapters of the Jaycees that we found not to be protected private associations in *Roberts,* and they are considerably larger than many of the local clubs that were found to be unprotected in *Rotary,* some which included as few as 20 members. * * * The clubs covered by Local Law 63 also provide "regular meal service" and receive regular payments "directly or indirectly from or on behalf of nonmembers for the furtherance of trade or business." N.Y.C.Admin.Code § 8–102(9) (1986). The city found these two characteristics to be significant in pinpointing organizations which are "commercial" in nature, "where business deals are often made and personal contacts valuable for business purposes, employment and professional advancement are formed." * * *

These characteristics are at least as significant in defining the nonprivate nature of these associations, because of the kind of role that strangers play in their ordinary existence, as is the regular participation of strangers at meetings, which we emphasized in *Roberts* and *Rotary.* * * * It may well be that a considerable amount of private or intimate association occurs in such a setting, as is also true in many restaurants and other places of public accommodation, but that fact alone does not afford the entity as a whole any constitutional immunity to practice discrimination when the government has barred it from doing so. * * * Although there may be clubs that would be entitled to constitutional protection despite the presence of these characteristics, surely it cannot be said that Local Law 63 is invalid on its face because it infringes the private associational rights of each and every club covered by it.

The same may be said about the contention that the Law infringes upon every club member's right of expressive association. The ability and the opportunity to combine with others to advance one's views is a powerful practical means of ensuring the perpetuation of the freedoms the First Amendment has guaranteed to individuals as against the government. "Effective advocacy of both public and private points of view, particularly controversial ones, is undeniably enhanced by group association, as this Court has more than once recognized by remarking upon the close nexus between the freedoms of speech and assembly." * * * This is not to say, however, that in every setting in which individuals exercise some discrimination in choosing associates, their selective process of inclusion and exclusion is protected by the Constitution. * * *

On its face, Local Law 63 does not affect "in any significant way" the ability of individuals to form associations that will advocate public or private viewpoints. *Rotary,* 481 U.S., at 548, 107 S.Ct., at 1947. It does not require the clubs "to abandon or alter" any activities that are protected by the First Amendment. *Ibid.* If a club seeks to exclude individuals who do not share the views that the club's members wish to promote, the Law erects no obstacle to this end. Instead, the Law merely prevents an association from using race, sex, and the other specified characteristics as shorthand measures in place of what the city considers to be more legitimate criteria for determining membership. It is conceivable, of course, that an association might be able to show that it is organized for specific expressive purposes and that it will not be able to advocate its desired viewpoints nearly as effectively if it cannot confine its membership to those who share the same sex, for example, or the same religion. In the case before us, however, it seems sensible enough to believe that many of the large clubs covered by the Law are not of this kind. We could hardly hold otherwise on the record before us, which contains no specific evidence on the characteristics of *any* club covered by the Law.

The facial attack based on the claim that Local Law 63 is invalid in all of its applications must therefore fail. Appellant insists, however, that there are some clubs within the reach of the Law that are "distinctively private" and that the Law is therefore overbroad and invalid on its face. But as we have indicated, this kind of facial challenge also falls short.

* * *

Appellant claims, however, that the Law erects an "irrebuttable" presumption that the clubs covered under it are not private in nature, and contends that its member associations will not be permitted to raise the constitutionality of the Law in individual administrative and judicial proceedings. * * * Even if this were a correct interpretation of what the Law says—and the decisions below at least suggest the contrary view—it does not affect our analysis. Although the city's Human Rights Commission may not be empowered to consider the constitutionality of the statute under which it operates, under accepted legal principles it would be quite unusual if the Commission "could not construe its own statutory mandate in the light of federal constitutional principles." * * * And even if this were also true, nothing in the Law purports to preclude judicial review of constitutional claims that may be raised on appeal from the administrative enforcement proceedings. * * * These opportunities for individual associations to contest the constitutionality of the Law as it may be applied against them are adequate to assure that any overbreadth under the Law will be curable through case-by-case analysis of specific facts.

IV

Appellant also contends that the exemption in Local Law 63 for benevolent and religious corporations, which deems them to be "distinctly private" in nature, violates the Equal Protection Clause. Since, as just discussed, it has not been demonstrated that the Law affects "in any significant way" the fundamental interests of any clubs covered by the Law, heightened scrutiny does not apply. * * * On this state of the record, the equal protection challenge must fail unless the city could not reasonably believe that the exempted organizations are different in relevant respects from appellant's members.

As written, the legislative classification on its face is not manifestly without reasoned support. The City Council explained that it limited the Law's coverage to large clubs and excluded smaller clubs, benevolent orders, and religious corporations because the latter associations "have not been identified in testimony before the Council as places where business activity is prevalent." Local Law No. 63, § 1, App. 15. This explanation echoes the logic of the decision in *New York ex rel. Bryant v. Zimmerman,* 278 U.S. 63, 49 S.Ct. 61, 73 L.Ed. 184 (1928), which upheld a New York law that exempted benevolent orders from having to file certain documents with the State that must be filed by most other corporations and associations. See N.Y.Civ.Rights Law § 53 (McKinney 1976). The Court rejected a claim that the statute violated the Equal Protection Clause, finding on the evidence before it that the legislative distinction was justified because benevolent orders were judged not to pose the same dangers as other groups that were required to file the documents. * * * In addition, New York State law indicates that benevolent orders and religious corporations are unique and thus that a rational basis exists for their exemption here. For well over a century, the State has extended special treatment in the law to these associations, and each continues to be treated in a separate body of legislation. * * * It is plausible that these associations differ in their practices and purposes from other private clubs that are now covered under Local Law 63. As the Appellate Division in this case pointed out, the benevolent orders are organized under the relevant law " 'solely for the benefit of [their] membership and their beneficiaries,' " and thus are not "public" organizations. * * * Similarly, religious organizations are " 'created for religious purposes' " and are "patently not engaged in commercial activity for the benefit of non-members." * * *

Appellant contends, however, that the benevolent and religious corporations exempted in the Law are in fact no different in nature from the other clubs and associations that are now made subject to the city's antidiscrimination restrictions. Because the Equal Protection Clause "is essentially a direction that all persons similarly situated should be treated alike," * * *

In support of its argument, appellant observes that appellees offered no evidence to support the city's position that benevolent and religious groups are actually different from other private associations. Legislative classifications, however, are presumed to be constitutional, and the burden of showing a statute to be unconstitutional is on the challenging party, *not* on the party defending the statute: "those challenging the legislative judgment must convince the court that the legislative facts on which the classification is apparently based could not reasonably be conceived to be true by the governmental decision maker." * * * In a case such as this, the plaintiff can carry this burden by submitting evidence to show that the asserted grounds for the legislative classification lack any reasonable support in fact, but this burden is nonetheless a considerable one. * * *

The City Council's explanation for exempting benevolent orders and religious corporations from the Local Law 63's coverage reflects a view that these associations are different in kind, at least in the crucial respect of whether business activity is prevalent among them, from the associations on whose behalf appellant has brought suit. Appellant has the burden of showing that this view is erroneous and that the issue is not truly debatable, a burden that appellant has failed to carry. There is no evidence in the record to indicate that a detailed examination of the practices, purposes, and structures of benevolent orders and religious corporations would show them to be identical in this and other critical respects to the private clubs that are covered under the city's antidiscrimination provisions. Without any such showing, appellant's facial attack on the Law under the Equal Protection Clause must founder.

We therefore affirm the judgment below.

* * *

Questions

1. Does the prohibition against discrimination in public accommodation laws include § 501(c)(3) organizations?

2. Does the prohibition include discrimination based on sexual orientation?

BOY SCOUTS OF AMERICA v. DALE

United States Supreme Court, 2000
530 U.S. 640, 120 S.Ct. 2446, 147 L.Ed.2d 554

Chief Justice REHNQUIST delivered the opinion of the Court.

Petitioners are the Boy Scouts of America and the Monmouth Council, a division of the Boy Scouts of America (collectively, Boy Scouts). The Boy Scouts is a private, not-for-profit organization engaged in instilling its system of values in young people. The Boy Scouts asserts that homosexual conduct is inconsistent with the values it seeks to instill. Respondent is James Dale, a former Eagle Scout whose adult membership in the Boy Scouts was revoked when the Boy Scouts learned that he is an avowed homosexual and gay rights activist. The New Jersey Supreme Court held that New Jersey's public accommodations law requires that the Boy Scouts readmit Dale. This case presents the question whether applying New Jersey's public accommodations law in this way violates the Boy Scouts' First Amendment right of expressive association. We hold that it does.

I

James Dale entered Scouting in 1978 at the age of eight by joining Monmouth Council's Cub Scout Pack 142. Dale became a Boy Scout in 1981 and remained a Scout until he turned 18. By all accounts, Dale was an exemplary Scout. In 1988, he achieved the rank of Eagle Scout, one of Scouting's highest honors.

Dale applied for adult membership in the Boy Scouts in 1989. The Boy Scouts approved his application for the position of assistant scoutmaster of Troop 73. Around the same time, Dale left home to attend Rutgers University. After arriving at Rutgers, Dale first acknowledged to himself and others that he is gay. He quickly became involved with, and eventually became the copresident of, the Rutgers University Lesbian/Gay Alliance. In 1990, Dale attended a seminar addressing the psychological and health needs of lesbian and gay teenagers. A newspaper covering the event interviewed Dale about his advocacy of homosexual teenagers' need for gay role models. In early July 1990, the newspaper published the interview and Dale's photograph over a caption identifying him as the copresident of the Lesbian/Gay Alliance.

Later that month, Dale received a letter from Monmouth Council Executive James Kay revoking his adult membership. Dale wrote to Kay requesting the reason for Monmouth Council's decision. Kay responded by letter that the Boy Scouts "specifically forbid membership to homosexuals." * * *

In 1992, Dale filed a complaint against the Boy Scouts in the New Jersey Superior Court. The complaint alleged that the Boy Scouts had violated New Jersey's public accommodations statute and its common law by revoking Dale's membership based solely on his sexual orientation. New Jersey's public accommodations statute prohibits, among other things, discrimination on the basis of sexual orientation in places of public accommodation. N.J. Stat. Ann. §§ 10:5–4 and 10:5–5 (West Supp.2000) * * *.

The New Jersey Superior Court's Chancery Division granted summary judgment in favor of the Boy Scouts. The court held that New Jersey's public accommodations law was inapplicable because the Boy Scouts was not a place of public accommodation, and that, alternatively, the Boy Scouts is a distinctly private group exempted from coverage under New Jersey's law. The court rejected Dale's common-law claim, holding that New Jersey's policy is embodied in the public accommodations law. The court also concluded that the Boy Scouts' position in respect of active homosexuality was clear and held that the First Amendment freedom of expressive association prevented the government from forcing the Boy Scouts to accept Dale as an adult leader.

The New Jersey Superior Court's Appellate Division affirmed the dismissal of Dale's common-law claim, but otherwise reversed and remanded for further proceedings. 308 N.J.Super. 516, 706 A.2d 270 (1998). It held that New Jersey's public accommodations law applied to the Boy Scouts and that the Boy Scouts violated it. The Appellate Division rejected the Boy Scouts' federal constitutional claims.

The New Jersey Supreme Court affirmed the judgment of the Appellate Division. It held that the Boy Scouts was a place of public accommodation subject to the public accommodations law, that the organization was not exempt from the law under any of its express exceptions, and that the Boy Scouts violated the law by revoking Dale's membership based on his avowed homosexuality. After considering the state-law issues, the court addressed the Boy Scouts' claims that application of the public accommodations law in this case violated its federal constitutional rights " 'to enter into and maintain ... intimate or private relationships ... [and] to associate for the purpose of engaging in protected speech.' " * * * With respect to the right to intimate association, the court concluded that the Boy Scouts' "large size, nonselectivity, inclusive rather than exclusive purpose, and practice of inviting or allowing nonmembers to attend meetings, establish that the organization is not 'sufficiently personal or private to warrant constitutional protection' under the freedom of intimate association." * * * With respect to the right of expressive association, the court "agree[d] that Boy Scouts expresses a belief in moral values and uses its activities to encourage the moral development of its members." * * * But the court concluded that it was "not persuaded ... that a shared goal of Boy Scout members is to associate in order to preserve the view that homosexuality is immoral." * * * Accordingly, the court held "that Dale's membership does not violate the Boy Scouts' right of expressive association because his inclusion would not 'affect in any significant way [the Boy Scouts'] existing members' ability to carry out their various purposes.' " * * * The court also determined that New Jersey has a compelling interest in eliminating "the destructive consequences of discrimination from our society," and that its public accommodations law abridges no more speech than is necessary to accomplish its purpose. * * * Finally, the court addressed the Boy Scouts' reliance on *Hurley v. Irish–American Gay, Lesbian and Bisexual Group of Boston, Inc.,* 515 U.S. 557, 115 S.Ct. 2338, 132 L.Ed.2d 487 (1995), in support of its claimed First Amendment right to exclude Dale. The court determined that *Hurley* did not require deciding the case in favor of the Boy Scouts because "the reinstatement of Dale does not compel Boy Scouts to express any message." * * *

We granted the Boy Scouts' petition for certiorari to determine whether the application of New Jersey's public accommodations law violated the First Amendment. * * *

II

In *Roberts v. United States Jaycees,* 468 U.S. 609, 622, 104 S.Ct. 3244, 82 L.Ed.2d 462 (1984), we observed that "implicit in the right to engage in activities protected by the First Amendment" is "a corresponding right to associate with others in pursuit of a wide variety of political, social, economic, educational, religious, and cultural ends." This right is crucial in preventing the majority from imposing its views on groups that would rather express other, perhaps unpopular, ideas. * * * Government actions that may unconstitutionally burden this freedom may take many forms, one of which is "intrusion into the internal structure or affairs of an association" like a "regulation that forces the group to accept members it does not desire." * * * Forcing a group to accept certain members may impair the ability of the group to express those views, and only those views, that it intends to express. Thus, "[f]reedom of association ... plainly presupposes a freedom not to associate."

The forced inclusion of an unwanted person in a group infringes the group's freedom of expressive association if the presence of that person affects in a significant way the group's ability to advocate public or private viewpoints. *New York State Club Assn., Inc. v. City of New York,* 487 U.S. 1, 13, 108 S.Ct. 2225, 101 L.Ed.2d 1 (1988). But the freedom of expressive association, like many freedoms, is not absolute. We have held that the freedom could be overridden "by regulations adopted to serve compelling state interests, unrelated to the suppression of ideas, that cannot be achieved through means significantly less restrictive of associational freedoms." * * *

To determine whether a group is protected by the First Amendment's expressive associational right, we must determine whether the group engages in "expressive association." The First Amendment's protection of expressive association is not reserved for advocacy groups. But to come within its ambit, a group must engage in some form of expression, whether it be public or private.

Because this is a First Amendment case where the ultimate conclusions of law are virtually inseparable from findings of fact, we are obligated to independently review the factual record to ensure that the state court's judgment does not unlawfully intrude on free expression. * * * The record reveals the following. The Boy Scouts is a private, nonprofit organization. According to its mission statement:

> "It is the mission of the Boy Scouts of America to serve others by helping to instill values in young people and, in other ways, to prepare them to make ethical choices over their lifetime in achieving their full potential.

* * *

Thus, the general mission of the Boy Scouts is clear: "[T]o instill values in young people." The Boy Scouts seeks to instill these values by having its adult leaders spend time with the youth members, instructing and engaging them in activities like camping, archery, and fishing. During the time spent with the youth members, the scoutmasters and assistant scoutmasters inculcate them with the Boy Scouts' values—both expressly and by example. It seems indisputable that an association that seeks to transmit such a system of values engages in expressive activity. * * * ("Even the training of outdoor survival skills or participation in community service might become expressive when the activity is intended to develop good morals, reverence, patriotism, and a desire for self-improvement").

Given that the Boy Scouts engages in expressive activity, we must determine whether the forced inclusion of Dale as an assistant scoutmaster would significantly affect the Boy Scouts' ability to advocate public or private viewpoints. This inquiry necessarily requires us first to explore, to a limited extent, the nature of the Boy Scouts' view of homosexuality.

The values the Boy Scouts seeks to instill are "based on" those listed in the Scout Oath and Law. * * * The Boy Scouts explains that the Scout Oath and Law provide "a positive moral code for living; they are a list of 'do's' rather than 'don'ts.'" * * * The Boy Scouts asserts that homosexual conduct is inconsistent with the values embodied in the Scout Oath and Law, particularly with the values represented by the terms "morally straight" and "clean."

Obviously, the Scout Oath and Law do not expressly mention sexuality or sexual orientation. * * * And the terms "morally straight" and "clean" are by no means self-defining. Different people would attribute to those terms very different meanings. For example, some people may believe that engaging in homosexual conduct is not at odds with being "morally straight" and "clean." And others may believe that engaging in homosexual conduct is contrary to being "morally straight" and "clean." The Boy Scouts says it falls within the latter category.

The New Jersey Supreme Court analyzed the Boy Scouts' beliefs and found that the "exclusion of members solely on the basis of their sexual orientation is inconsistent with Boy Scouts' commitment to a diverse and 'representative' membership ... [and] contradicts Boy Scouts' overarching objective to reach 'all eligible youth.'" * * * The court concluded that the exclusion of members like Dale "appears antithetical to the organization's goals and philosophy." But our cases reject this sort of inquiry; it is not the role of the courts to reject a group's expressed values because they disagree with those values or find them internally inconsistent. * * *

The Boy Scouts asserts that it "teach[es] that homosexual conduct is not morally straight," * * * and that it does "not want to promote homosexual conduct as a legitimate form of behavior." * * * We accept the Boy Scouts' assertion. We need not inquire further to determine the nature of the Boy Scouts' expression with respect to homosexuality. But because the record before us contains written evidence of the Boy Scouts' viewpoint, we look to it as instructive, if only on the question of the sincerity of the professed beliefs.

A 1978 position statement to the Boy Scouts' Executive Committee, signed by Downing B. Jenks, the President of the Boy Scouts, and Harvey L. Price, the Chief Scout Executive, expresses the Boy Scouts' "official position" with regard to "homosexuality and Scouting":

"Q. May an individual who openly declares himself to be a homosexual be a volunteer Scout leader?

"A. No. The Boy Scouts of America is a private, membership organization and leadership therein is a privilege and not a right. We do not believe that homosexuality and leadership in Scouting are appropriate. We will continue to select only those who in our judgment meet our standards and qualifications for leadership."
* * *

Thus, at least as of 1978—the year James Dale entered Scouting—the official position of the Boy Scouts was that avowed homosexuals were not to be Scout leaders.

A position statement promulgated by the Boy Scouts in 1991 (after Dale's membership was revoked but before this litigation was filed) also supports its current view:

"We believe that homosexual conduct is inconsistent with the requirement in the Scout Oath that a Scout be morally straight and in the Scout Law that a Scout be clean in word and deed, and that homosexuals do not provide a desirable role model for Scouts." * * *

This position statement was redrafted numerous times but its core message remained consistent. For example, a 1993 position statement, the most recent in the record, reads, in part:

"The Boy Scouts of America has always reflected the expectations that Scouting families have had for the organization. We do not believe that homosexuals provide a role model consistent with these expectations. Accordingly, we do not allow for the registration of avowed homosexuals as members or as leaders of the BSA." * * *

The Boy Scouts publicly expressed its views with respect to homosexual conduct by its assertions in prior litigation. For example, throughout a California case with similar facts filed in the early 1980's, the Boy Scouts consistently asserted the same position with respect to homosexuality that it asserts today. * * * We cannot doubt that the Boy Scouts sincerely holds this view.

We must then determine whether Dale's presence as an assistant scoutmaster would significantly burden the Boy Scouts' desire to not "promote homosexual conduct as a legitimate form of behavior." * * * As we give deference to an association's assertions regarding the nature of its expression, we must also give deference to an association's view of what would impair its expression. * * * That is not to say that an expressive association can erect a shield against antidiscrimination laws simply by asserting that mere acceptance of a member from a particular group would impair its message. But here Dale, by his own admission, is one of a group of gay Scouts who have "become leaders in their community and are open and honest about their sexual orientation." * * * Dale was the copresident of a gay and lesbian organization at college and remains a gay rights activist. Dale's presence in the Boy Scouts would, at the very least, force the organization to send a message, both to the youth members and the world, that the Boy Scouts accepts homosexual conduct as a legitimate form of behavior.

Hurley is illustrative on this point. There we considered whether the application of Massachusetts' public accommodations law to require the organizers of a private St. Patrick's Day parade to include among the marchers an Irish–American gay, lesbian, and bisexual group, GLIB, violated the parade organizers' First Amendment rights. We noted that the parade organizers did not wish to exclude the GLIB members because of their sexual orientations, but because they wanted to march behind a GLIB banner. We observed:

> "[A] contingent marching behind the organization's banner would at least bear witness to the fact that some Irish are gay, lesbian, or bisexual, and the presence of the organized marchers would suggest their view that people of their sexual orientations have as much claim to unqualified social acceptance as heterosexuals.... The parade's organizers may not believe these facts about Irish sexuality to be so, or they may object to unqualified social acceptance of gays and lesbians or have some other reason for wishing to keep GLIB's message out of the parade. But whatever the reason, it boils down to the choice of a speaker not to propound a particular point of view, and that choice is presumed to lie beyond the government's power to control." * * *

Here, we have found that the Boy Scouts believes that homosexual conduct is inconsistent with the values it seeks to instill in its youth members; it will not "promote homosexual conduct as a legitimate form of behavior." * * * As the presence of GLIB in Boston's St. Patrick's Day parade would have interfered with the parade organizers' choice not to propound a particular point of view, the presence of Dale as an assistant scoutmaster would just as surely interfere with the Boy Scouts' choice not to propound a point of view contrary to its beliefs.

The New Jersey Supreme Court determined that the Boy Scouts' ability to disseminate its message was not significantly affected by the forced inclusion of Dale as an assistant scoutmaster because of the following findings:

> "Boy Scout members do not associate for the purpose of disseminating the belief that homosexuality is immoral; Boy Scouts discourages its leaders from disseminating *any* views on sexual issues; and Boy Scouts includes sponsors and members who subscribe to different views in respect of homosexuality." * * *

We disagree with the New Jersey Supreme Court's conclusion drawn from these findings.

First, associations do not have to associate for the "purpose" of disseminating a certain message in order to be entitled to the protections of the First Amendment. An association must merely engage in expressive activity that could be impaired in order to be entitled to protection. For example, the purpose of the St. Patrick's Day parade in *Hurley* was not to espouse any views about sexual orientation, but we held that the parade organizers had a right to exclude certain participants nonetheless.

Second, even if the Boy Scouts discourages Scout leaders from disseminating views on sexual issues—a fact that the Boy Scouts disputes with contrary evidence—the First Amendment protects the Boy Scouts' method of expression. If the Boy Scouts wishes Scout leaders to avoid questions of sexuality and teach only by example, this fact does not negate the sincerity of its belief discussed above.

Third, the First Amendment simply does not require that every member of a group agree on every issue in order for the group's policy to be "expressive association." The Boy Scouts takes an official position with respect to homosexual conduct, and that is sufficient for First Amendment purposes. In this same vein, Dale makes much of the claim that the Boy Scouts does not revoke the membership of heterosexual Scout leaders that openly disagree with the Boy Scouts' policy on sexual orientation. But if this is true, it is irrelevant. The presence of an avowed homosexual and gay rights activist in an assistant scoutmaster's uniform sends a distinctly different message from the presence of a heterosexual assistant scoutmaster who is on record as disagreeing with Boy Scouts policy. The Boy Scouts has a First Amendment right to choose to send one message but not the other. The fact that the organization does not trumpet its views from the housetops, or that it tolerates dissent within its ranks, does not mean that its views receive no First Amendment protection.

Having determined that the Boy Scouts is an expressive association and that the forced inclusion of Dale would significantly affect its expression, we inquire whether the application of New Jersey's public accommodations law to require that the Boy Scouts accept Dale as an assistant scoutmaster runs afoul of the Scouts' freedom of expressive association. We conclude that it does.

State public accommodations laws were originally enacted to prevent discrimination in traditional places of public accommodation—like inns and trains. * * * Over time, the public accommodations laws have expanded to cover more places. New Jersey's statutory definition of " '[a] place of public accommodation' " is extremely broad. The term is said to "include, but not be limited to," a list of over 50 types of places. * * * Many on the list are what one would expect to be places where the public is invited. For example, the statute includes as places of public accommodation taverns, restaurants, retail shops, and public libraries. But the statute also includes places that often may not carry with them open invitations to the public, like summer camps and roof gardens. In this case, the New Jersey Supreme Court went a step further and applied its public accommodations law to a private entity without even attempting to tie the term "place" to a physical location. As the definition of "public accommodation" has expanded from clearly commercial entities, such as restaurants, bars, and hotels, to membership organizations such as the Boy Scouts, the potential for conflict between state public accommodations laws and the First Amendment rights of organizations has increased.

We recognized in cases such as *Roberts* and *Duarte* that States have a compelling interest in eliminating discrimination against women in public accommodations. But in each of these cases we went on to conclude that the enforcement of these statutes would not materially interfere with the ideas that the organization sought to express. In *Roberts,* we said "[i]ndeed, the Jaycees has failed to demonstrate ... any serious burdens on the male members' freedom of expressive association." * * * In *Duarte,* we said:

> "[I]mpediments to the exercise of one's right to choose one's associates can violate the right of association protected by the First Amendment. In this case, however, the evidence fails to demonstrate that admitting women to Rotary Clubs will affect in any significant way the existing members' ability to carry out their various purposes." * * *.

We thereupon concluded in each of these cases that the organizations' First Amendment rights were not violated by the application of the States' public accommodations laws.

In *Hurley,* we said that public accommodations laws "are well within the State's usual power to enact when a legislature has reason to believe that a given group is the target of discrimination, and they do not, as a general matter, violate the First or Fourteenth Amendments." * * * But we went on to note that in that case "the Massachusetts [public accommodations] law has been applied in a peculiar way" because "any contingent of protected individuals with a message would have the right to participate in petitioners' speech, so that the communication produced by the private organizers would be shaped by all those protected by the law who wished to join in with some expressive demonstration of their own." * * * And in the associational freedom cases such as *Roberts, Duarte,* and *New York State Club Assn.,* after finding a compelling state interest, the Court went on to examine whether or not the application of the state law would impose any "serious burden" on the organization's rights of expressive association. So in these cases, the associational interest in freedom of expression has been set on one side of the scale, and the State's interest on the other.

Dale contends that we should apply the intermediate standard of review enunciated in *United States v. O'Brien,* 391 U.S. 367, 88 S.Ct. 1673, 20 L.Ed.2d 672 (1968), to evaluate the competing interests. There the Court enunciated a four-part test for review of a governmental regulation that has only an incidental effect on protected speech—in that case the symbolic burning of a draft card. A law prohibiting the destruction of draft cards only incidentally affects the free speech rights of those who happen to use a violation of that law as a symbol of protest. But New Jersey's public accommodations law directly and immediately affects associational rights, in this case associational rights that enjoy First Amendment protection. Thus, *O'Brien* is inapplicable.

In *Hurley,* we applied traditional First Amendment analysis to hold that the application of the Massachusetts public accommodations law to a parade violated the First Amendment rights of the parade organizers. Although we did not explicitly deem the parade in *Hurley* an expressive association, the analysis we applied there is similar to the analysis we apply here. We have already concluded that a state requirement that the Boy Scouts retain Dale as an assistant scoutmaster would significantly burden the organization's right to oppose or disfavor homosexual conduct. The state interests embodied in New Jersey's public accommodations law do not justify such a severe intrusion on the Boy Scouts' rights to freedom of expressive association. That being the case, we hold that the First Amendment prohibits the State from imposing such a requirement through the application of its public accommodations law.

Justice STEVENS' dissent makes much of its observation that the public perception of homosexuality in this country has changed. * * * Indeed, it appears that homosexuality has gained greater societal acceptance. * * * But this is scarcely an argument for denying First Amendment protection to those who refuse to accept these views. The First Amendment protects expression, be it of the popular variety or not. * * *

* * *

We are not, as we must not be, guided by our views of whether the Boy Scouts' teachings with respect to homosexual conduct are right or wrong; public or judicial disapproval of a tenet of an organization's expression does not justify the State's effort to compel the organization to accept members where such acceptance would derogate from the organization's expressive message. "While the law is free to promote all sorts of conduct in place of harmful behavior, it is not free to interfere with speech for no better reason than promoting an approved message or discouraging a disfavored one, however enlightened either purpose may strike the government." *Hurley,* 515 U.S., at 579, 115 S.Ct. 2338.

The judgment of the New Jersey Supreme Court is reversed, and the case is remanded for further proceedings not inconsistent with this opinion.

* * *

Note

The Internal Revenue Service addresses the issue of discrimination in its audits of social clubs. Section 501(i) of the Internal Revenue Code prohibits a tax-exempt social club from having a written policy statement in its charter, bylaws, or other governing instruments that contains a provision providing for discrimination against any person on the basis of race, color, or religion. Still, a club can have a written policy relating to discrimination on the basis of religion if the club limits its membership to members of a particular religion or in good faith limits its membership to members of a particular religion in order to further the teachings or principles of that religion and not to exclude individuals of a particular race or color.

Section 501(i) does not include a prohibition against gender discrimination or discrimination based on sexual orientation.

III. TAXATION OF SOCIAL CLUBS

Nonprofit social clubs can be exempt or nonexempt. Taxable membership organizations are subject to § 277 of the Internal Revenue Code, which provides that deductions attributable to furnishing services, insurance, goods, or other items of value to members are permitted only to the extent of income from transactions with members.

Social clubs, as mutual benefit nonprofit organizations, are tax exempt in a substantially different manner than are public benefit nonprofit organizations. A social club is exempt from tax on receipts from its members. Because the tax exemption for social clubs is designed to permit individuals to join together to provide social and recreational facilities on a mutual basis, without tax consequences, the tax exemption operates only when sources of income of the organization are limited to receipts from the membership. Under such circumstances, an individual member is in substantially the same position as if the member had spent income on social or recreational activities outside the intervening membership club. However, when the club receives income from sources outside the membership, such as income from investments and transactions with nonmembers, the members receive a benefit in that untaxed funds can be used by the club to provide social and recreational activities. If outside income were not taxed, the gross amount of outside income could be used tax free to reduce the cost, or to increase the services, the club can provide to its members. Thus, income not related to the exempt function of the club is taxed.

Section 512(a)(3) of the Code provides that exempt function income that is not subject to tax includes a club's income from dues, fees, charges, or similar amounts paid by member, their dependents, or guests, for goods, facilities, or services. Any other income, including investment income and income from providing services to nonmembers, is taxed. However, if a social club uses its investment income for charitable purposes, that portion of its investment income will not be taxed.

Because unrelated business taxable income is defined as all income that is not "exempt function income," less deductions allowed which are "directly connected" with the production of that income, the question arose whether deductions attributable to serving nonmembers in excess of income from such services could offset income from investments.

PORTLAND GOLF CLUB v. COMMISSIONER

United States Supreme Court, 1990
497 U.S. 154, 110 S.Ct. 2780, 111 L.Ed.2d 126

Justice BLACKMUN delivered the opinion of the Court.

This case requires us to determine the circumstances under which a social club, in calculating its liability for federal income tax, may offset losses incurred in selling food and drink to nonmembers against the income realized from its investments.

I

Petitioner Portland Golf Club is a nonprofit Oregon corporation, most of whose income is exempt from federal income tax under § 501(c)(7) of the Internal Revenue Code of 1954, 26 U.S.C. § 501(c)(7). Since 1914 petitioner has owned and operated a private golf and country club with a golf course, restaurant and bar, swimming pool, and tennis courts. The great part of petitioner's income is derived from membership dues and other receipts from the club's members; that income is exempt from tax. Portland Golf also has two sources of nonexempt "unrelated business taxable income": sales of food and drink to nonmembers, and return on its investments.

The present controversy centers on Portland Golf's federal income tax liability for its fiscal years ended September 30, 1980, and September 30, 1981, respectively. Petitioner received investment income in the form of interest in the amount of $11,752 for fiscal 1980 and in the amount of $21,414 for fiscal 1981. * * * It sustained net losses of $28,433 for fiscal 1980 and $69,608 for fiscal 1981 on sales of food and drink to nonmembers. Petitioner offset these losses against the earnings from its investments and therefore reported no unrelated business taxable income for the two tax years. In computing these losses, petitioner identified two different categories of expenses incurred in selling food and drink to nonmembers. First, petitioner incurred *variable* (or direct) expenses, such as the cost of food, which varied depending on the amount of food and beverages sold (and therefore would not have been incurred had no sales to nonmembers been made). For each year in question, petitioner's gross income from nonmember sales exceeded these variable costs. Petitioner also included as an unrelated business expense a portion of the *fixed* (or indirect) overhead expenses of the club—expenses which would have been incurred whether or not petitioner had made sales to nonmembers. In determining what portions of its fixed expenses were attributable to nonmember sales, petitioner employed an allocation formula, described as the "gross-to-gross method," based on the ratio that nonmember sales bore to total sales. When fixed expenses, so calculated, were added to petitioner's variable costs, the total exceeded Portland Golf's gross income from nonmember sales.

On audit, the Commissioner took the position that petitioner could deduct expenses associated with nonmember sales up to the amount of receipts from the sales themselves, but that it could not use losses from those activities to offset its investment income. The Commissioner based that conclusion on the belief that a profit motive was required if losses from these activities were to be used to offset income from other sources, and that Portland Golf had failed to show that its sales to nonmembers were undertaken with an intent to profit. The Commissioner therefore determined deficiencies of $1,828 for 1980 and $3,470 for 1981; these deficiencies reflected tax owed on petitioner's investment income. * * *

Portland Golf sought redetermination in the Tax Court. That court ruled in petitioner's favor. 55 TCM 212 (1988), ¶ 88,076 P–H Memo TC. The court assumed, without deciding, that losses incurred in the course of sales to nonmembers could be used to offset other nonexempt income only if the sales were undertaken with an intent to profit. The court, however, held that Portland Golf had adequately demonstrated a profit motive, since its gross receipts from sales to nonmembers consistently exceeded the variable costs associated with those activities. The court therefore held that "petitioner is entitled to offset its unrelated business taxable income from interest by its loss from its nonmember food and beverage sales computed by allocating a portion of its fixed expenses to the nonmember food and beverage sales activity in a manner which respondent agrees is acceptable." * * *

The United States Court of Appeals for the Ninth Circuit remanded. * * * The Court of Appeals held that the Tax Court had applied an incorrect legal standard in determining that Portland Golf had demonstrated an intent to profit from sales to nonmembers. The appellate court relied on its decision in *North Ridge Country Club v. Commissioner,* 877 F.2d 750 (1989), where it had ruled that a social club "can properly deduct losses from a non-member activity only if it undertakes that activity with the intent to profit, where profit means the production of gains in excess of all direct and indirect costs." * * * The same court in the present case concluded: "Because Portland Golf Club could have reported gains in excess of direct and indirect costs, but did not do so, relying on a method of allocation stipulated to be reasonable by the Commissioner, we REMAND this case to the tax court for a determination of whether Portland Golf Club engaged in its non-member activities with the intent required under *North Ridge* to deduct its losses from those activities."

The basis for the Court of Appeals' remand order is not entirely clear to us. It appears, however, that the court left open the possibility that petitioner could establish its intent to profit by using some other method of allocating fixed costs (such as the "actual use" method* * *), while continuing to use the gross-to-gross formula in computing actual losses. Both parties interpret the Court of Appeals' decision in this manner, and both express disapproval of that approach. * * * Our disposition of the case makes unnecessary precise interpretation of the Court of Appeals' opinion.

Because of a perceived conflict with the decision of the Sixth Circuit in *Cleveland Athletic Club, Inc. v. United States,* 779 F.2d 1160 (1985) and because of the importance of the issue, we granted certiorari. * * *

II

Virtually all tax-exempt business organizations are required to pay federal income tax on their "unrelated business taxable income." The law governing social clubs, however, is significantly different from that governing other tax-exempt entities. As to exempt organizations other than social clubs, the Code defines "unrelated business taxable income" as "the gross income derived by any organization from any unrelated trade or business (as defined in section 513) regularly carried on by it, less the deductions allowed by this chapter which are directly connected with the carrying on of such trade or business." 26 U.S.C. § 512(a)(1). As to social clubs, however, "unrelated business taxable income" is defined as "the gross income (excluding any exempt function income), less the deductions allowed by this chapter which are directly connected with the production of the gross income (excluding exempt function income)." § 512(a)(3)(A). The salient point is that § 512(a)(1) (which applies to most exempt organizations) limits "unrelated business taxable income" to income derived from a "trade or business," while § 512(a)(3)(A) (which applies to social clubs) contains no such limitation. Thus, a social club's investment income is subject to federal income tax, while the investment income of most other exempt organizations is not.

In the Tax Reform Act of 1969, Congress extended the tax on "unrelated business income" to social clubs. As to these organizations, however, Congress defined "unrelated business taxable income" to include income derived from investments. Our review of the present case must therefore be informed by two central facts. First, Congress intended that the investment income of social clubs should be subject to federal tax, and indeed Congress devised a definition of "unrelated business taxable income" with that purpose in mind. Second, the statutory scheme for the taxation of social clubs was intended to achieve tax *neutrality,* not to provide these clubs a tax advantage: Even the exemption for income derived from members' payments was designed to ensure that members are not disadvantaged as compared with persons who pursue recreation through private purchases rather than through the medium of an organization.

III

Petitioner's principal argument is that it may deduct losses incurred through sales to nonmembers without demonstrating that these sales were motivated by an intent to profit. In the alternative, petitioner contends (and the Tax Court agreed) that if the Code does impose a profit-motive requirement, then that requirement has been satisfied in this case. We address these arguments in turn.

A

We agree with the Commissioner and the Court of Appeals that petitioner may use losses incurred in sales to nonmembers to offset investment income only if those sales were motivated by an intent to profit. The statute provides that, as to social clubs, "the term 'unrelated business taxable income' means the gross income (excluding any exempt function income), less the deductions *allowed by this chapter* which are directly connected with the production of the gross income (excluding exempt function income)." § 512(a)(3)(A) (emphasis added). As petitioner concedes, the italicized language limits deductions from unrelated business income to expenses allowable as deductions under Chapter 1 of the Code. * * * In our view, the deductions claimed in this case—expenses for food, payroll, and overhead in excess of gross receipts from nonmember sales—are allowable, if at all, only under § 162 of the Code. * * * Section 162(a) provides a deduction for "all the ordinary and necessary expenses paid or incurred during the taxable year in carrying on any trade or business." Although the statute does not expressly require that a "trade or business" must be carried on with an intent to profit, this Court has ruled that a taxpayer's activities fall within the scope of § 162 only if an intent to profit has been shown. * * * Thus, the losses that Portland Golf incurred in selling food and drink to nonmembers will constitute "deductions allowed by this chapter" only if the club's nonmember sales were performed with an intent to profit.

We see no basis for dispensing with the profit-motive requirement in the present case. Indeed, such an exemption would be in considerable tension with the statutory scheme devised by Congress to govern the taxation of social clubs. Congress intended that the investment income of social clubs (unlike the investment income of most other exempt organizations) should be subject to the same tax consequences as the investment income of any other taxpayer. To allow such an offset for social clubs would run counter to the principle of tax neutrality which underlies the statutory scheme.

Petitioner concedes that "[g]enerally a profit motive is a necessary factor in determining whether an activity is a trade or business." * * * Petitioner contends, however, that by including receipts from sales to nonmembers within § 512(a)(3)(A)'s definition of "unrelated business taxable income," the Code has defined nonmember sales as a "trade or business," and has thereby obviated the need for an inquiry into the taxpayer's intent to profit. We disagree. In our view, Congress' use of the term "unrelated *business* taxable income" to describe all receipts other than payments from the members hardly manifests an intent to define as a "trade or business" activities otherwise outside the scope of § 162. Petitioner's reading would render superfluous the words "allowed by this chapter in § 512(a)(3)(A): If each taxable activity of a social club is "deemed" to be a trade or business, then *all* of the expenses "directly connected" with those activities would presumably be deductible. Moreover, Portland Golf's interpretation ignores Congress' general intent to tax the income of social clubs according to the same principles applicable to other taxpayers. We therefore conclude that petitioner may offset losses incurred in sales to nonmembers against investment income only if its nonmember sales are motivated by an intent to profit.[16]

B

Losses from Portland Golf's sales to nonmembers may be used to offset investment income only if those activities were undertaken with a profit motive—that is, an intent to generate receipts in excess of costs. The parties and the other courts in this case, however, have taken divergent positions as to the range of expenses that qualify as costs of the nonexempt activity and are to be considered in determining whether petitioner acted with the requisite profit motive. In the view of the Tax Court, petitioner's profit motive was established by the fact that the club's receipts from nonmember sales exceeded its variable costs. Since Portland Golf's fixed costs, by definition, have been incurred even in the absence of sales to nonmembers, the Tax Court concluded that these costs should be disregarded in determining petitioner's intent to profit.

The Commissioner has taken no firm position as to the precise manner in which Portland Golf's fixed costs are to be allocated between member and nonmember sales. Indeed, the Commissioner does not even insist that any portion of petitioner's fixed costs must be attributed to nonmember activities in determining intent to profit. He does insist, however, that the *same* allocation method is to be used in determining petitioner's intent to profit as in computing its actual profit or loss. * * * In the present case the parties have stipulated that the gross-to-gross method provides a reasonable formula for allocating fixed costs, and Portland Golf has used that method in calculating the losses incurred in selling food and drink to nonmembers. The Commissioner contends that petitioner is therefore required to demonstrate an intent to earn gross receipts in excess of fixed and variable costs, with the allocable share of fixed costs being determined by the gross-to-gross method.

* * *

16. The Code distinguishes a social club's "exempt function income" from its "unrelated business taxable income" by looking to the source of the payment: "[E]xempt function income" is limited to money received from the members. § 512(a)(3)(B). However, a social club could easily organize events whose primary purpose was to benefit the membership, yet arrange for nonmembers to make modest contributions toward the cost of the events. Those contributions would constitute "unrelated business taxable income"; but if losses incurred in such activities could be used to offset investment income, it would be relatively easy for clubs to avoid taxation on their investments. The general rule that losses incurred in a not-for-profit activity may not be used to offset unrelated income rests on the recognition that one who incurs expenses without an intent to profit presumably derives some intrinsic pleasure or benefit from the activity. The Code's limitation on deductibility (expenses may be deducted up to, but not above, the gross income produced by the activity) reflects the view that taxpayers should not be allowed to deduct what are, in essence, personal expenses simply because the activity in question generates some receipts. Just as an individual taxpayer may not offset personal expenses against income from other sources, a social club should not be allowed to deduct expenses incurred for the benefit of the membership from unrelated business income.

We conclude that the Commissioner's position is the correct one. Portland Golf's argument rests, as the Commissioner puts it, on an "inherent contradiction." * * * Petitioner's calculation of actual losses rests on the claim that a portion of its fixed expenses is properly regarded as attributable to the production of income from nonmember sales. Given this assertion, we do not believe that these expenses can be ignored (or, more accurately, attributed to petitioner's exempt activities) in determining whether petitioner acted with the requisite intent to profit. Essentially the same criticism applies to the Court of Appeals' approach. That court required petitioner to include *some* portion of fixed expenses in demonstrating its intent to profit, but it left open the possibility that petitioner could employ an allocation method different from that used in calculating its actual losses. Under that approach, some of petitioner's fixed expenses could be attributed to exempt functions in determining intent to profit and to nonmember sales in establishing the club's actual loss. This, like the rationale of the Tax Court, seems to us to rest on an "inherent contradiction."

Petitioner's principal response is that § 162 requires an intent to earn an *economic* profit, and that this is quite different from an intent to earn *taxable income.* Portland Golf emphasizes that numerous provisions of the Code establish deductions and preferences which do not purport to mirror economic reality. Therefore, petitioner argues, taxpayers may frequently act with an intent to profit, even though the foreseeable (and, indeed, the intended) result of their efforts is that they suffer (or achieve) tax losses. Much of the Code, in petitioner's view, would be rendered a nullity if the mere fact of tax losses sufficed to show that a taxpayer lacked an intent to profit, thereby rendering the deductions unavailable. In Portland Golf's view, the parties have stipulated only that the gross-to-gross formula provides a reasonable method of determining what portion of fixed expenses is "directly connected" with the nonexempt activity for purposes of computing *taxable income.* That stipulation, Portland Golf contends, is irrelevant in determining the portion of fixed expenses that represents the *actual economic cost* of the activity in question.

We accept petitioner's contention that § 162 requires only an intent to earn an economic profit. We acknowledge, moreover, that many Code provisions are designed to serve purposes (such as encouragement of certain types of investment) other than the accurate measurement of economic income. A taxpayer who takes advantage of deductions or preferences of that kind may establish an intent to profit even though he has no expectation of realizing taxable income. The fixed expenses that Portland Golf seeks to allocate to its nonmember sales, however, are deductions of a different kind. The Code does not state that fixed costs are allocable on a gross-to-gross basis irrespective of economic reality. Rather, petitioner's right to use the gross-to-gross method rests on the club's assertion that this allocation formula reasonably identifies those expenses that are "directly connected" to the nonmember sales, § 512(a)(3)(A), and are "the ordinary and necessary expenses paid or incurred" in selling food and drink to nonmembers, see § 162(a). Language such as this, it seems to us, reflects an attempt to measure economic income—not an effort to use the tax law to serve ancillary purposes. Having calculated its actual losses on the basis of the gross-to-gross formula, petitioner is therefore foreclosed from attempting to demonstrate its intent to profit by arguing that some other allocation method more accurately reflects economic reality.

IV

We hold that any losses incurred as a result of petitioner's nonmember sales may be offset against its investment income only if the nonmember sales were undertaken with an intent to profit. We also conclude that in demonstrating the requisite profit motive, Portland Golf must employ the same method of allocating fixed expenses as it uses in calculating its actual loss. Petitioner has failed to show that it intended to earn gross income from nonmember sales in excess of its total (fixed plus variable) costs, where fixed expenses are allocated using the gross-to-gross method. The judgment of the Court of Appeals is therefore affirmed.

* * *

Notes

1. Section 277 was added to the Code because certain membership organizations were servicing their members at less than cost and were then offsetting the book loss against investment and business income so that investment income and business income were virtually untaxed. Section 277 eliminates the possibility of social clubs giving up tax exempt status in order to deduct losses from sales to members as against investment income. The effect of § 277 for nonexempt social clubs is essentially the same as the effect of § 512(a)(3) for tax exempt social clubs. Both sections prevent membership organizations from escaping tax on their investment income and nonmember income by offsetting this income with losses incurred in providing goods and services to members.

2. Gain on the sale of exempt property of a social club will be taxed; however, the gain can be postponed if other property is acquired to be used in the performance of the club's exempt functions within a period beginning one year before the date of the sale and ending three years after that date. If such property is acquired, gain from the sale will be recognized only to the extent the sales price of the property sold exceeds the cost of the property acquired. [See I.R.C. § 512(a)(3)(D).] If property is not used exclusively for a club's exempt purpose, only that part of the gain allocable to the portion of the property used for that purpose will be subject to nonrecognition treatment.

IV. BUSINESS USE OF A SOCIAL CLUB

A club that is organized and operated in a manner that is a subterfuge for doing business with the public will not qualify for tax exempt status. Advertising for public patronage of a club's facilities is evidence that the club is engaging in business.

REVENUE PROCEDURE 71-17
1971-1 C.B. 683

This Revenue Procedure sets forth guidelines for determining the effect gross receipts derived from use of a social club's facilities by the general public have on the club's exemption from Federal income tax under section 501(c)(7) of the Internal Revenue Code of 1954. These guidelines will be used in connection with the examination of annual returns on Forms 990 and 990—T filed by social clubs. This Revenue Procedure also describes the records required when nonmembers use a club's facilities and the circumstances under which a host-guest relationship will be assumed, which are relevant both for purposes of determining adherence to the exemption requirements and for computing exempt function income under section 512(a)(3) of the Code. However, his Revenue Procedure does not deal with other factors bearing on the exempt status of clubs.

SEC. 2. BACKGROUND.

.01 General statement.—Use of a club's facilities by the general public is significant for two reasons. It may indicate the existence of a nonexempt purpose; or, if not of sufficient substantiality to result in loss of exemption, it may make the club liable for unrelated business income tax. The term 'general public' as used in this Revenue Procedure means persons other than members of a club or their dependents or guests. The member's spouse is treated as a member.

.02 Nonexempt purpose.—In the examination of information returns of clubs, the problem frequently is to determine under what circumstances and to what extent the fact that a club makes its facilities available to the general public is to be relied upon by the Service as indicating the existence of a nonexempt purpose.

Where a club makes its facilities available to the general public to a substantial degree, the club is not operated exclusively for pleasure, recreation, or other nonprofitable purposes. See Rev. Rul. 60—324, C.B. 1960—2, 173; and Rev. Rul. 69—219, C.B. 1969—1, 153. However, this does not mean that all dealings with the general public are necessarily inconsistent with the club's purposes. See Rev. Rul. 58—589, C.B. 1958—2, 266; Rev. Rul. 68—119, C.B. 1968—1, 268; and Rev. Rul. 69—636, C.B. 1969—2, 126.

* * *

SEC. 3. GUIDELINES.

.01 Minimum gross receipts standard.—A significant factor reflecting the existence of a nonexempt purpose is the amount of gross receipts derived from use of a club's facilities by the general public. As an audit standard, this factor alone will not be relied upon by the Service if annual gross receipts from the general public for such use is $2,500 or less or, if more than $2,500, where gross receipts from the general public for such use is five percent or less of total gross receipts of the organization. This minimum gross receipts standard reflects the audit experience of the Service that gross receipts at or below this level do not, standing alone, usually demonstrate a nonexempt purpose. Even though gross receipts from the general public exceed this standard, it does not necessarily establish that there is a nonexempt purpose. A conclusion that there is a nonexempt purpose will be based on all the facts and circumstances, including but not limited to the gross receipts factor. This audit standard relates only to determinations of exempt status. There is no minimum audit tolerance with respect to unrelated business taxable income.

.02 Meaning of the term 'total gross receipts'.—For the purpose of the minimum gross receipts standard established in section 3.01 above, 'total gross receipts' means receipts from normal and usual activities of the club including charges, admissions, membership fees, dues, and assessments. Excluded for this purpose are (a) initiation fees and capital contributions, (b) interest, dividends, rents, and similar receipts, and (c) unusual amounts of income such as amounts derived from nonrecurring sales of club assets.

.03 Assumption as to status of nonmembers.

1. Where a group of eight or fewer individuals, at least one of whom is a member, uses club facilities, it will be assumed for audit purposes that the nonmembers are the guests of the member, provided payment for such use is received by the club directly from the member or the member's employer.

2. Where 75 percent or more of a group using club facilities are members, it will likewise be assumed for audit purposes that the nonmembers in the group are guests of members, provided payment for such use is received by the club directly from one or more of the members or the member's employer.

3. Solely for purposes of section 3.03 1 and 3.03 2, above, payment by a member's employer will be assumed to be for a use that serves a direct business objective of the employee-member.

4. In all other situations, a hostguest relationship will not be assumed but must be substantiated. See section 4, below, for the records required.

SEC. 4. RECORDKEEPING REQUIREMENTS.

.01 With respect to the situation described in section 3.03 1, above, the records specified in section 4.03, below, need not be maintained by the club. However, the club must maintain adequate records to substantiate that the group was comprised of eight or fewer individuals, that at least one of them was a member, and that payment was received by the club directly from members or their employers. Where payment is made directly to the club by the member, the club is under no obligation to inquire about reimbursement.

.02 With respect to the situation described in section 3.03 2, above, the records specified in section 4.03, below, need not be maintained by the club. However, the club must maintain adequate records to substantiate that 75 percent or more of the persons in the group were, in fact, members of the club at the time of such use and that payment was received by the club directly from members or their employers. Where payment is made directly to the club by the member, the club is under no obligation to inquire about reimbursement.

.03 With respect to all other occasions involving use by nonmembers, the club must maintain books and records of each such use and the amount derived therefrom. This requirement applies even though the member pays initially for such use. In each instance the record must contain the following information:

1. The date;
2. The total number in the party;
3. The number of nonmembers in the party;
4. The total charges;
5. The charges attributable to nonmembers;
6. The charges paid by nonmembers;
7. Where a member pays all or part of the charges attributable to nonmembers, a statement signed by the member indicating whether he has been or will be reimbursed for such nonmember use and, if so, the amount of the reimbursement:
8. Where the member's employer reimburses the member or makes direct payment to the club for the charges attributable to nonmembers, a statement signed by the member indicating the name of his employer; the amount of the payment attributable to the nonmember use; the nonmember's name and business or other relationship to the member; and the business, personal, or social purpose of the member served by the nonmember use. (The use of club facilities must serve some personal or social purpose of the employee-member or some direct business objective of the employee-member; the mere use of club facilities for the accommodation of the member's employer does not serve a business, personal, or social purpose of the member.) If a large number of nonmembers are involved and they are readily identifiable as a particular class of individuals, the member may record such class, rather than all of the names; and
9. Where a nonmember, other than the employer of the member, makes payment to the club or reimburses a member and a claim is made that the amount was paid gratuitously for the benefit of a member, a statement signed by the member indicating the donor's name and relationship to the member, and containing information

to substantiate the gratuitous nature of the payments or reimbursement.

.04 Failure to maintain such records or make them available to the Service for examination will preclude use of the minimum gross receipts standard and audit assumptions set forth in this Revenue Procedure.

* * *

Note

A tax exempt social club can receive up to 35 percent of its gross receipts, including investment income, from sources outside its membership without losing its tax-exempt status. Within this 35 percent, not more than 15 percent of the gross receipts can be derived from the use of a club's facilities or services by the general public. (S. Rep. No. 94–1318, 1976–2 C.B. 597, 599) Income from serving guests of members is treated as member income.

V. FRATERNITIES AND SORORITIES

College fraternities and sororities operating chapter houses for students are classified as social clubs under § 501(c)(7). Although a fraternity could technically qualify under § 501(c)(10), which applies to domestic fraternal societies, orders, or associations operating under the lodge system, regulations under § 501(c)(10) expressly state that national college fraternities do not qualify under § 501(c)(10). The difference in classification is important because tax exempt social clubs are taxed on net investment income whereas § 501(c)(10) fraternities are not. In addition, tax exempt social clubs cannot engage in a business. Their sole function must be the providing of social and recreational activities for their members.

ZETA BETA TAU FRATERNITY v. COMMISSIONER
United States Tax Court, 1986
87 T.C. 421

SWIFT, JUDGE:

In a timely statutory notice of deficiency respondent determined a deficiency in the unrelated business income tax of petitioner for its taxable year ending June 30, 1971, in the amount of $1,936. The only issue for decision is whether petitioner, a tax-exempt social club described in section 501(c)(7), also qualifies as a tax-exempt domestic fraternal society described in section 501(c)(10). If so, petitioner's income from investments is not taxable as unrelated business income and petitioner is not liable for an underpayment of tax.

FINDINGS OF FACT

* * *

Under the provisions of its national constitution and code of rules, the officers and directors of Zeta Beta's governing body, the supreme council, are selected by representatives of the local chapters who meet annually at a national convention. The supreme council meets periodically and acts as the legislative, executive, and judicial authority of Zeta Beta. Zeta Beta also employs an administrative staff. The principal purpose of Zeta Beta's central staff is to serve as the coordinating and governing organization of the local chapters, house corporations, and private foundations that comprise the Zeta Beta national college fraternity.

Zeta Beta also provides various programs, services, and publications to the local chapters, their members, and the house corporations. The services and publications provided by Zeta Beta include a philanthropic and social service programming guide, a dance marathon guide, a fraternity magazine, awards to local chapters and members for scholastic and public service achievements, information concerning scholarship and emergency student loan programs, a leadership school for undergraduate members, and a monthly newsletter containing articles on professional schools, study tips, financial aid information, and social news from local chapters throughout the United States. Zeta Beta itself does not engage in significant social activities.

Each local chapter of Zeta Beta adopts its own constitution and bylaws and generally exercises substantial autonomy in the governance of its affairs. The local chapter may not, however, adopt any rule that contravenes Zeta Beta's constitution or code of rules. Generally, each local chapter does not incorporate as a separate entity. Each chapter, however, files its own annual Federal tax returns (Forms 990, Return of Organization Exempt from Tax). The assets, liabilities, receipts, and expenses of local chapters are not included on Zeta Beta's Federal tax returns. Zeta Beta also does not file a separate group information return with respondent on behalf of local chapters.

Each house corporation associated with Zeta Beta is separately incorporated and serves as the owner and manager of the local fraternity house. The house corporations individually file annual Federal tax returns (Forms 990), and Zeta Beta does not include the assets, liabilities, receipts, or expenses of the individual house corporations in its Federal tax returns. Each house corporation is, however, subordinate to Zeta Beta and subject to its general supervision.

* * *

The parties agree that Zeta Beta and its subordinate local chapters operate under the lodge system and do not pay insurance benefits to members within the meaning of section 501(c)(10). Zeta Beta concedes that (together with its subordinate local chapters and house corporations) it is a national college fraternity within the meaning of section 1.501(c)(10)–1, Income Tax Regs.

On August 18, 1972, Zeta Beta filed a Return of Organization Exempt from Tax (Form 990) for its taxable year ended June 30, 1971. On June 15, 1973, Zeta Beta filed its Exempt Organization Business Income Tax Return (Form 990–T) for its taxable year ended June 30, 1971. In November of 1975, Zeta Beta filed with respondent an application for a determination that it was tax exempt as a domestic fraternal society under section 501(c)(10). Zeta Beta's application was denied on June 26, 1976. In his letter denying the application, respondent noted that Zeta Beta had 'always operated * * * exclusively for educational, charitable, or fraternal purposes,' but that as a national college fraternity, it was precluded from tax exemption under section 501(c)(10) by section 1.501(c)(10)–1, Income Tax Regs.

On July 8, 1976, Zeta Beta protested respondent's denial of its application for tax-exempt classification as a domestic fraternal society under section 501(c)(10), and requested reconsideration thereof. On September 30, 1977, respondent reaffirmed its denial of Zeta Beta's application. Respondent's notice of deficiency at issue herein followed.

Respondent's computation of the deficiency herein is based on his inclusion in Zeta Beta's unrelated business income the investment income Zeta Beta received in its taxable year ending June 30, 1971.

OPINION

Generally, tax-exempt organizations described in section 501(c) are taxed at regular corporate rates on unrelated business income. Sec. 511(a). The term 'unrelated business taxable income' is defined as the gross income derived from any unrelated trade or business regularly carried on by an organization, less allowable deductions that are directly connected with the conduct of the trade or business. Sec. 512(a). In general, investment income such as dividends, interest, annuities, royalties, rents derived from real property, and capital gains, are excluded from the exempt organization's unrelated business income. Sec. 512(b)(1).

Unrelated business income is described differently, however, for, among other organizations, tax-exempt social clubs described in section 501(c)(7). In the case of a section 501(c)(7) social club, unrelated business taxable income includes all income generated by the organization other than 'exempt function income' less expenses related to exempt function income. Sec. 512(a)(3)(A). Exempt function income is defined as the gross income derived from dues, fees, charges, or similar amounts received from organization members or their guests for goods, facilities, or services in furtherance of the tax-exempt purposes of the organization. Sec. 512(a)(3)(B). The result of this difference in the computation of unrelated business taxable income is that investment income of section 501(c)(7) social clubs is taxed as unrelated business income, whereas investment income of section 501(c)(10) fraternal organizations generally is not taxed as unrelated business income. * * *

Zeta Beta, as the central organization of a national college fraternity, received its long-standing tax exemption under the predecessor of section 501(c)(7). Zeta Beta argues, however, that it also properly may be classified as a domestic fraternal society under section 501(c)(10), and that its investment income, therefore, should not be subject to the unrelated business income tax.

Section 501(c)(10), a new category of tax-exempt organizations that was added to the Internal Revenue Code by the Tax Reform Act of 1969, Pub. L. 91–172, 83 Stat. 487 (hereinafter sometimes referred to as the '1969 Act'), provides a tax exemption for—

(10) Domestic fraternal societies, orders, or associations, operating under the lodge system—

(A) the net earning of which are devoted exclusively to religious, charitable, scientific, literary, educational, and fraternal purposes, and

(B) which do not provide for the payment of life, sick, accident, or other benefits.

Treasury regulations relating to section 501(c)(10) expressly state that national college fraternities do not qualify under section 501(c)(10). Section 1.501(c)(10)–1, Income Tax Regs., provides as follows:

CERTAIN FRATERNAL BENEFICIARY SOCIETIES.

(a) For taxable years beginning after December 31, 1969, an organization will qualify for exemption under section 501(c)(10) if it—

(1) Is a domestic fraternal beneficiary society order, or association, described in section 501(c)(8) and the regulations thereunder except that it does not provide for the payment of life, sick, accident, or other benefits to its members, and

(2) Devotes its net earnings exclusively to religious, charitable, scientific, literary, educational, and fraternal purposes.

Any organization described in section 501(c)(7), such as, for example, a national college fraternity, is not described in 501(c)(10) and this section. * * *

Zeta Beta argues that it is an organization that is precisely described by the language of section 501(c)(10) because it is a fraternal society that operates under the lodge system, it does not provide insurance benefits to members, and because its net earnings are devoted exclusively to religious, charitable, scientific, literary, educational, and fraternal purposes. Zeta Beta further argues that it cannot be distinguished factually from organizations such as the Masons, Moose, or Elks clubs which usually are classified by respondent as tax exempt under section 501(c)(10). Zeta Beta, therefore, contends that section 1.501(c)(10)–1, Income Tax Regs., in its exclusion of national college fraternities from tax exemption under section 501(c)(10), establishes an arbitrary distinction that discriminates between two similarly situated taxpayers (namely, national college fraternities and organizations such as the Masons) and is, therefore, to that extent invalid.

Zeta Beta also contends that its classification as a tax-exempt organization described in section 501(c)(7) does not preclude its additional classification under section 501(c)(10). Zeta Beta concludes that if it meets the precise description of a section 501(c)(10) organization, there is no express or implied legislative policy that would deny it an exemption thereunder just because it also may be classified as a section 501(c)(7) social club.

Respondent argues that Zeta Beta is not an organization described in section 501(c)(10) because of the clear congressional intent that national college fraternities be exempt from tax as social clubs under section 501(c)(7). Respondent contends that national college fraternities such as Zeta Beta are fundamentally different from those fraternal organizations, such as the Masons, that Congress intended to qualify for tax exemption under section 501(c)(10). Finally, respondent argues that even if a national college fraternity could qualify for tax exemption under section 501(c)(10), the net earnings of Zeta Beta herein are not exclusively devoted to the exempt purposes listed in section 501(c)(10)(A). For the above reasons, respondent argues that Zeta Beta properly may be classified only as a section 501(c)(7) tax-exempt social club.

After careful review of the relevant statutory provisions, the legislative history thereof, and the facts of this case, we agree with respondent that a national college fraternity such as Zeta Beta may not properly be classified as a domestic fraternal society described in section 501(c)(10).

Contrary to Zeta Beta's contention, the relevant statutory language is not clear and unambiguous. As we recently stated—

Trying to understand the various exempt organization provisions of the Internal Revenue Code is as difficult as capturing a drop of mercury under your thumb. There are currently 23 categories of exempt organizations under section 501(c) and five categories of organizations recognized as qualified donees of tax deductible contributions under section 170(c). Rarely is it clear that an organization would qualify only under one of the categories of section 501(c), and often it is clear that an organization would qualify under a number of the categories, even though a particular organization may have applied for and actually received its exemption letter under a single provision of section 501(c). * * * (Weingarden v. Commissioner, 86 T.C. No. 669, 675 (1986).

* * *

As explained, the tax exemption for domestic fraternal organizations in section 501(c)(10) had its genesis in the Tax Reform Act of 1969 and arose specifically out of the imposition of the unrelated business income tax on investment income of membership organizations described in sections 501(c)(7) and (c)(9). Congress recognized that a tax-exempt social club or similar group organized for recreational or social purposes merely was an extension of the individual members and that it would be inappropriate to impose a tax on the social club as a separate entity. S. Rept. No. 91–552 (1969), 1969–3 C.B. 423, 429. One court summarized the rationale as follows:

> Congress has determined that in a situation where individuals have banded together to provide recreational facilities on a mutual basis, it would be conceptually erroneous to impose a tax on the organization as a separate entity. The funds exempted are received only from the members and any 'profit' which results from overcharging for the use of the facilities still belongs to the same members. No income of the sort usually taxed has been generated; the money has simply been sifted from one pocket to another, both within the same pair of pants. * * * (McGlotten v. Connally, 338 F. Supp. 448, 458 (D.D.C.1972).

Where, however, the tax-exempt membership organization receives investment income and uses the tax free income to pay for recreational services offered to its members, the members receive an unintended benefit. As explained in the Senate committee report—

> (W)here the organization receives income from sources outside the membership, such as income from investments (or in the case of employee benefit associations, from the employer), upon which no tax is paid, the membership receives a benefit not contemplated by the exemption in that untaxed dollars can be used by the organization to provide pleasure or recreation (or other benefits) to its membership. For example, if a social club were to receive $10,000 of untaxed income from investment in securities, it could use that $10,000 to reduce the cost or increase the services it provides to its members. In such a case, the exemption is no longer simply allowing individuals to join together for recreation or pleasure without tax consequences. Rather, it is bestowing a substantial additional advantage to the members of the club by allowing tax-free dollars to be used for their personal recreational or pleasure purposes. The extension of the exemption to such investment income is, therefore, a distortion of its purpose. (S. Rept. No. 91–552, supra at 470.)

The House report accompanying the Tax Reform Act of 1969 notes similar concern with respect to fraternal societies, as follows:

> The receipt of untaxed income by fraternal beneficiary societies for use in providing recreational or social facilities in furtherance of the organization's fraternal purpose creates a similar problem to that of social clubs. * * * (H. Rept. No. 91–413 (1969), 1969–3 C.B. 199, 231.)

Congress recognized, however, that investment income also could be used by tax exempt membership organizations to further the exempt purposes of the organizations and that in such cases the tax on investment income would be inappropriate. Accordingly, the statutory exception found in section 512(a)(3)(B)(i) and (ii) for such income was enacted. As originally proposed by the House, only investment income of fraternal beneficiary associations and employees' beneficiary associations would have been eligible to qualify for this exception. In the Senate Finance Committee, however, the House version was changed to include investment income of social clubs where the investment income of social clubs was set aside for educational or charitable purposes. The Senate committee report explains the change as follows:

> In extending the exemption, the committee intends in the case of National organizations of college fraternities and sororities that amounts set aside for scholarships, student loans, loans on local chapter housing, leadership and citizenship schools and services, and similar activities, be classified as amounts used for educational or charitable purposes under this provision. * * *

S. Rept. No. 91–552, supra at 470. * * *

The express reference in the above legislative history to investment income of 'national organizations of college fraternities and sororities,' makes it very clear that Congress considered the investment income of such organizations to be generally subject to the new unrelated business income tax provisions.

In the general explanation of the 1969 Act issued in 1970 by the Joint Committee on Taxation it was expressly noted that the tax on investment income would apply to national organizations of college fraternities and sororities, unless the investment income thereof is set aside for certain educational or charitable purposes. Staff of Joint Comm. on Taxation, 91st Cong., 1st Sess., General Explanation of the Tax Reform Act of 1969 at 70 (J. Comm. print 1970).

In 1976, Congress reiterated its intention that national college fraternities be tax exempt under the provisions for social clubs described in section 501(c)(7). Certain amendments were made in 1976 to section 501(c)(7), not germane to the issue herein, concerning the scope of a social club's exempt activities and the discriminatory practices of some social clubs. Act of September 28, 1976, Pub. L. 94–568, 90 Stat. 2697. In the Committee report explaining those amendments, national college fraternities were expressly identified as the type of organizations described in section 501(c)(7), as follows—

> The House-passed bill, H.R. 1144, amends the requirements for tax exemption for Social clubs and similar organizations (including college fraternities and sororities) in two respects. * * * (S. Rept. No. 94–1318 (1976), 1976–2 C.B. 597. * * *)

That same committee report refers to national college fraternities and sororities several additional times in connection with their tax-exempt classification under section 501(c)(7). For example:

> In addition, the 1969 Act extended the unrelated business income tax, in the case of these social clubs and national organizations of college fraternities and sororities, to cover investment income as well as unrelated business income. * * * (S. Rept. No. 94–1318, supra at 598. * * *)

and

It is intended that a social club, national organization of a college fraternity or sorority, and any other organization exempt under section 501(c)(7), may receive the full 35–percent amount of its gross receipts from investment income sources * * *. (S. Rept. No. 94–1318, supra at 599. * * *)

* * *

Zeta Beta's emphasis on its similarity to section 501(c)(10) organizations such as the Masons also is not persuasive. Clearly, like the Masons, Zeta Beta operates under the lodge system and its local chapters engage in some activities that concededly further the charitable and educational goals of the fraternity. We agree with respondent, however, that the predominant purpose of Zeta Beta and its local chapters is to provide housing, board, and social activities for its undergraduate student members. In that respect, Zeta Beta is fundamentally different from fraternal organizations such as the Masons.

Even if we could find no relevant distinction between the purposes and activities of Zeta Beta and the Masons, it is not for this Court to counteract by judicial decision what we conclude is the congressional intent to treat national college fraternities in a manner different from fraternal organizations such as the Masons. Congress has 'broad latitude in creating classifications and distinctions in tax statutes.' Regan v. Taxation with Representation of Washington, 461 U.S. 540, 547–548 (1983).

Zeta Beta argues that its existing tax exemption under section 501(c)(7) does not preclude it from receiving an additional tax-exempt classification under section 501(c)(10), if it meets the qualifications thereof. As we stated earlier, in some situations an organization may qualify for tax exemption under a number of paragraphs of section 501(c). We have concluded, however, that national college fraternities are intended by Congress to be treated as exempt under section 501(c)(7) and not under section 501(c)(10).

Zeta Beta concedes that college fraternities historically have been granted tax-exempt classification under section 501(c)(7). If Congress had intended in 1969 to change that policy and to allow national college fraternities to be exempt under section 501(c)(10), it is reasonable to conclude that some mention of such a policy change would have been made in the extensive legislative history that accompanied the passage of the Tax Reform Act of 1969. To the contrary, that history (as well as the legislative history accompanying the 1976 amendments to section 501(c)(7)) reiterates the long-standing treatment of national college fraternities as tax-exempt organizations under section 501(c)(7) and the predecessors thereof.

* * *

The prohibition in section 1.501(c)(10)–1, Income Tax Regs., on national college fraternities obtaining their tax exemption under section 501(c)(10) is a valid and reasonable interpretation of the statutory provisions as explained above. Treasury regulations must be sustained unless unreasonable and plainly inconsistent with the language, history, and purpose of a statute. * * *

In light of the congressional intent that national college fraternities qualify for their tax-exempt status under section 501(c)(7), and not section 501c)(10), we agree with respondent that Zeta Beta is not an organization described in section 501(c)(10), and that Zeta Beta is taxable on its investment income under section 512(a)(3)(A).

* * *

Problem

Southern University Alumni Association operates to serve former students of Southern University through social events and other activities involving university alumni. Its members, former students at Southern University, pay annual dues to the association. Some of the association's funds are used to provide scholarships for current students at the university. Would Southern University Alumni Association qualify as a § 501(c)(3) organization or is it a social club tax exempt under § 501(c)(7)? What difference will it make to the association if it qualifies under § 501(c)(7) rather than § 501(c)(3)?

Chapter 14

TRADE AND PROFESSIONAL ORGANIZATIONS

I. TRADE ASSOCIATION STATUS

A trade association is a nonprofit organization whose membership consists of business groups. Trade associations are formed to provide a forum to advance common interests of a trade, business or profession and to exchange information on industry problems. They include employers' associations, boards of trade, manufacturing associations, chambers of commerce, better business bureaus, and professional societies, such as legal and medical associations.

Section 501(c)(5) provides for tax exempt status for agricultural and horticultural organizations. Section § 501(c)(6) provides tax exempt status for professional organizations, business leagues, chambers of commerce, real estate boards, boards of trade, and professional sports leagues. Agricultural and horticultural organizations must have as their objective the betterment of the conditions of persons engaged in the pursuit of agriculture or horticulture, the improvement of the grade of their products, and the development of a higher degree of efficiency in their respective organizations. Professional organizations and business leagues exempt under § 501(c)(6) are associations of persons who have some common business interest. These organizations must have as their purpose the promotion of the common interests of their members. Their activities should be directed to the improvement of business conditions of one or more lines of business as distinguished from the performance of particular services for individual persons. To be tax exempt, the organization must be industry wide.

NATIONAL MUFFLER DEALERS ASSOCIATION, INC. v. UNITED STATES
United States Supreme Court, 1979
440 U.S. 472, 99 S.Ct. 1304, 59 L.Ed.2d 519

Mr. Justice BLACKMUN delivered the opinion of the Court.

Petitioner, National Muffler Dealers Association, Inc. (Association), as its name indicates, is a trade organization for muffler dealers. The issue in this case is whether the Association, which has confined its membership to dealers franchised by Midas International Corporation (Midas), and its activities to the Midas muffler business, and thus is not "industrywide," is a "business league" entitled to the exemption from federal income tax provided by § 501(c)(6) of the Internal Revenue Code of 1954, 26 U.S.C. § 501(c)(6).

I

In 1971, during a contest for control of Midas, Midas muffler franchisees organized the Association under the New York Not-for-Profit Corporation Law. The Association's purpose was to establish a group to negotiate unitedly with Midas management. Its principal activity has been to serve as a bargaining agent for its members in dealing with Midas. It has enrolled most Midas franchisees as members. The Association was successful in negotiating a new form of franchise agreement which prevents termination during its 20-year life except for cause. It also persuaded Midas to eliminate its requirement that a customer pay a service charge when a guaranteed Midas muffler is replaced. And the Association sponsors group insurance programs, holds an annual convention, and publishes a newsletter for members.

The Association sought the exemption from federal income tax which § 501(c)(6) provides for a "business league." Treasury Regulation § 1.501(c)(6)–1, 26 CFR § 1.501(c)(6)–1 (1978), states that the activities of a tax exempt business league "should be directed to the improvement of business conditions of one or more lines of business." In view of that requirement, the Internal Revenue Service initially rejected the Association's exemption application, stating that § 501(c)(6) "would not apply to an organization that is not industry wide."

The Association then (in October 1972) amended its bylaws and eliminated the requirement that its members be Midas franchisees. Despite that amendment, and despite the Association's announced purpose to promote the interests of individuals "engaged in business as muffler dealers," it neither recruited nor acquired a member who was not a Midas franchisee.

In 1974, after the Internal Revenue Service had issued a final rejection of the Association's exemption application, the Association filed income tax returns for its fiscal years 1971, 1972, and 1973, and, thereafter, claims for refund of the taxes paid with those returns. The 1972 claim was formally denied. Subsequent to that denial, and after more than six months had passed since the filing of the 1971 and 1973 claims, see § 6532(a)(1) of the 1954 Code, 26 U.S.C. § 6532(a)(1), the Association brought this suit in the United States District Court for the Southern District of New York asserting its entitlement to a refund for the income taxes paid for the three fiscal years. The District Court found: "There is no evidence that [the Association] confers a benefit on the muffler industry as a whole or upon muffler franchisees as a group."

* * * It then concluded that "Midas Muffler franchisees do not constitute a 'line of business,'" and held that the Association was not a "business league" within the meaning of § 501(c)(6), and thus was not entitled to the claimed refund. * * *

The United States Court of Appeals for the Second Circuit affirmed. 565 F.2d 845 (1977). It confronted what it called the "lexicographer's task of deciding what is meant by a 'business league'." Finding no direct guidance in the statute, the court applied the maxim *noscitur a sociis* ("[i]t is known from its associates," Black's Law Dictionary 1209 (Rev. 4th ed. 1968)), and looked "at the general characteristics of the organizations" with which business leagues were grouped in the statute, that is, chambers of commerce and boards of trade. The court agreed with the Service's determination, in § 1.501(c)(6)–1 of the regulations, that a business league is an "organization of the same general class as a chamber of commerce or board of trade." Reasoning that it was the "manifest intention" of Congress by the statute "to provide an exemption for organizations which promote some aspect of the general economic welfare rather than support particular private interests," the court concluded that the "line of business" requirement set forth in the regulations is "well suited to assuring that an organization's efforts do indeed benefit a sufficiently broad segment of the business community." * * * The court noted that any success the Association might have in improving business conditions for Midas franchisees, and any advantage it might gain through tax exemption, would come at the expense of the rest of the muffler industry, and concluded that the Association's purpose was too narrow to satisfy the line-of-business test.

The court, * * *, explicitly refused to follow the decision in *Pepsi-Cola Bottlers' Assn. v. United States,* 369 F.2d 250 (C.A.7 1966). There, the Seventh Circuit, by a divided vote, had upheld the exempt status of an association composed solely of bottlers of a single brand of soft drink. It did so on the ground that the line-of-business requirement unreasonably narrowed the statute.

We granted certiorari to resolve this conflict. * * *

II

The statute's term "business league" has no well-defined meaning or common usage outside the perimeters of § 501(c)(6). It is a term "so general . . . as to render an interpretive regulation appropriate." *Helvering v. Reynolds Co.,* 306 U.S. 110, 114, 59 S.Ct. 423, 425, 83 L.Ed. 536, 540 (1939). In such a situation, this Court customarily defers to the regulation, which, "if found to 'implement the congressional mandate in some reasonable manner,' must be upheld." *United States v.Cartwright,* 411 U.S. 546, 550, 93 S.Ct. 1713, 1716, 36 L.Ed.2d 528, 532 (1973), quoting *United States v. Correll,* 389 U.S. 299, 307, 88 S.Ct. 445.

* * *

III

* * *

The history of Treas.Reg. § 1.501(c)(6)–1 and its "line of business" requirement provides much that supports the Government's view that the Association, which is not tied to a particular community and is not industrywide, should not be exempt. The exemption for "business leagues" from federal income tax had its genesis at the inception of the modern income tax system with the enactment of the Tariff Act of October 3, 1913, 38 Stat. 114, 172. In response to a House bill which would have exempted, among others, "labor, agricultural, or horticultural organizations," the Senate Finance Committee was urged to add an exemption that would cover nonprofit business groups. Both the Chamber of Commerce of the United States and the American Warehousemen's Association, a trade association for warehouse operators, submitted statements to the Committee. The Chamber's spokesman said:

> "The commercial organization of the present day is not organized for selfish purposes, and performs broad patriotic and civic functions. Indeed, it is one of the most potent forces in each community for the improvement of physical and social conditions. While its original reason for being is commercial advancement, it is *not in the narrow sense of advantage to the individual, but in the broad sense of building up the trade and commerce of the community as a whole....*" (Emphasis added.) Briefs and statements on H.R. 3321 filed with the Senate Committee on Finance, 63d Cong., 1st Sess., 2002 (1913) (hereinafter Briefs and Statements).

The Chamber's written submission added:

> "These organizations receive their income from dues ... which business men pay that they *may receive in common with all other members of their communities or of their industries* the benefits of cooperative study of local development, of civic affairs, of industrial resources, and of local, national, and international trade." (Emphasis added.) *Id.*, at 2003.

The Committee was receptive to the idea, but rejected the Chamber's proposed broad language which would have exempted all "commercial organizations not organized for profit." Instead, the Committee, and ultimately the Congress, provided that the tax would not apply to

> "business leagues, nor to chambers of commerce or boards of trade, not organized for profit or no part of the net income of which inures to the benefit of the private stockholder or individual." Tariff Act of Oct. 3, 1913, § II G(a), 38 Stat. 172.

Congress has preserved this language, with few modifications, in each succeeding Revenue Act.

The Commissioner of Internal Revenue had little difficulty determining which organizations were "chambers of commerce" or boards of trade" within the meaning of the statute. Those terms had commonly understood meanings before the statute was enacted. "Business league," however, had no common usage, and in 1919 the Commissioner undertook to define its meaning by regulation. The initial definition was the following:

> "A business league is an association of persons having some common business interest, which limits its activities to work for such common interest and does not engage in a regular business of a kind ordinarily carried on for profit. Its work need not be similar to that of a chamber of commerce or board of trade." Treas.Regs. 45, Art. 518 (1919).

This language, however, proved too expansive to identify with precision the class of organizations Congress intended to exempt. The Service began to cut back on the last sentence of the material just quoted when, in 1924, the Solicitor of Internal Revenue invoked *noscitur a sociis* to deny an exemption requested by a stock exchange. He reasoned that, while a stock exchange conceivably could come within the definitions of a "business league" or "board of trade," it lacked the characteristics that a "business league," "chamber of commerce," and "board of trade" share in common and that form the basis for the exemption. Congress must have used those terms, he said, "to indicate organizations of the same general class, having for their primary purpose the promotion of business welfare." The primary purpose of the stock exchange, by contrast, was "to afford facilities to a limited class of people for the transaction of their private business." L.O. 1121, III–1 Cum.Bull. 275, 280–281 (1924). The regulation was then amended so as specifically to exclude stock exchanges. T.D. 3746, IV–2 Cum.Bull. 77 (1925).

In 1927, the Board of Tax Appeals, in a reviewed decision with some dissents, applied the principle of *noscitur a sociis* and denied a claimed "business league" exemption to a corporation organized by associations of insurance companies to provide printing services for member companies. *Uniform Printing & Supply Co. v. Commissioner*, 9 B.T.A. 251, aff'd, 33 F.2d 445 (CA7), cert. denied, 280 U.S. 591, 50 S.Ct. 38, 74 L.Ed. 639 (1929). In 1928, Congress revised the statute so as specifically to exempt real estate boards that local revenue agents had tried to tax. The exclusion of stock exchanges, however, was allowed to remain.

In 1929, the Commissioner incorporated the principle of *noscitur a sociis* into the regulation itself. The sentence, "Its work need not be similar to that of a chamber of commerce or board of trade," was dropped and was replaced with the following qualification:

> "It is an organization of the same general class as a chamber of commerce or board of trade. Thus, its activities should be directed to the improvement of business conditions or to the promotion of the general objects of one or more lines of business as distinguished from the performance of particular services for individual persons." Treas.Regs. 74, Art. 528 (1929).

This language has stood almost without change for half a century through several re-enactments and one amendment of the statute.

During that period, the Commissioner and the courts have been called upon to define "line of business" as that phrase is employed in the regulation. True to the representation made by the Chamber of Commerce, in its statement to the Senate in 1913, that benefits would be received "in common with all other members of their communities or of their industries," *supra*, at 1308, the term "line of business" has been interpreted to mean either an entire industry, * * *, or all components of an industry within a geographic area, * * *.

Most trade associations fall within one of these two categories. The Commissioner consistently has denied exemption to business groups whose membership and purposes are narrower. Those who have failed to meet the "line of business" test, in the view of the Commissioner, include groups composed of businesses that market a single brand of automobile, or have licenses to a single patented product, or bottle one type of soft drink. The Commissioner has reasoned that these groups are not designed to better conditions in an entire industrial "line," but, instead, are devoted to the promotion of a particular product at the expense of others in the industry.

In short, while the Commissioner's reading of § 501(c)(6) perhaps is not the only possible one, it does bear a fair relationship to the language of the statute, it reflects the views of those who sought its enactment, and it matches the purpose they articulated. It evolved as the Commissioner administered the statute and attempted to give to a new phrase a content that would reflect congressional design. The regulation has stood for 50 years, and the Commissioner infrequently but consistently has interpreted it to exclude an organization like the Association that is not industrywide. The Commissioner's view therefore merits serious deference.

* * *

In sum, the "line of business" limitation is well grounded in the origin of § 501(c)(6) and in its enforcement over a long period of time. The distinction drawn here, that a tax exemption is not available to aid one group in competition with another within an industry, is but a particular manifestation of an established principle of tax administration. Because the Association has not shown that either the regulation or the Commissioner's interpretation of it fails to "implement the congressional mandate in some reasonable manner," *United States v. Correll*, 389 U.S., at 307, 88 S.Ct. at 450, the Association's claim for a § 501(c)(6) exemption must be denied.

The judgment of the Court of Appeals is affirmed.

* * *

GUIDE INTERNATIONAL CORPORATION v. UNITED STATES

United States Court of Appeals, Seventh Circuit, 1991
948 F.2d 360

KANNE, Circuit Judge.

Guide International Corporation is a nonprofit organization whose purpose is to develop data processing products and services, and to provide a forum for the exchange and dissemination of information concerning data processing equipment and systems. In 1971, the Internal Revenue Service determined that Guide was exempt from tax as a nonprofit business league under § 501(c)(6) of the Internal Revenue Code, 26 U.S.C. § 501(c)(6). However, Revenue Ruling 83–164, 1983–2 C.B. 95 put Guide's tax-exempt status into question. To obtain a binding determination of its tax-exempt status, Guide filed income tax returns for the years 1984, 1985, and 1986, and, thereafter, filed for refund of taxes paid with those returns. No action was taken on Guide's claim and Guide brought suit. On cross-motions for summary judgment, the district court found that Guide failed to qualify as a business league and granted summary judgment in favor of the government. Guide appeals and we affirm.

A number of circuits have held that the determination whether an association is a business league under § 501(c)(6) is a mixed question of fact and law, which is reviewed *de novo*. * * * We adopt this standard of review. Accordingly, the district court's grant of summary judgment in favor of the government is appropriate under Rule 56 of the Federal Rules of Civil Procedure only if there is no genuine issue as to any material fact and the government is entitled to judgment as a matter of law. * * *

The facts are undisputed. Guide was formed in 1956 and incorporated in Missouri in 1969 as a nonprofit association. Guide's purposes, as set forth in its Articles of Incorporation, are the following:

(a) The promotion of sound professional practices with respect to the uses of data processing equipment and systems.

(b) The exchange and dissemination of information concerning data processing equipment and systems.

(c) The participation with manufacturers of data processing equipment (including hardware, software and peripheral equipment) in the improvement and development of products, standards, and education.

Guide's By-laws state that its primary purposes include "communicat[ing] to the IBM Corporation user needs in all technical areas of interest" and "review [ing], comment[ing] and exchang[ing] information on products and services related to the equipment needed to qualify for GUIDE membership." The By-laws restrict membership to organizations who own large-scale computer equipment manufactured by International Business Machines (IBM mainframes).

Guide's membership includes major corporations from diverse fields, as well as educational and governmental organizations. Many of the members compete against each other, and some compete against IBM. Guide is managed by a board of directors, who are members of the organization. Guide's principal activity is the sponsorship of week-long conferences that are held three times a year and focus on data processing matters. Representatives of IBM and other persons are invited to speak at the conferences on topics chosen by Guide's management. Although IBM and manufacturers of compatible peripheral equipment present data processing products at the conferences, all sales and recruitment activities are prohibited. IBM provides administrative personnel, a personal computer, copiers and refreshments at the meetings. The information presented and discussed at the conferences is communicated to IBM.

Guide also conducts research involving data processing equipment manufactured by IBM and other companies. Project papers and other resource materials prepared by Guide are maintained in a library and are generally available to all interested parties, including non-members.

Guide argues that the district court erred in determining it was not a business league under § 501(c)(6). The principal issue before the district court was whether Guide satisfies the requirement of Treasury Regulation § 1.501(c)(6)–1 (26 C.F.R. § 1.501(c)(6)–1) that its activities "be directed to the improvement of business conditions of one or more lines of business as distinguished from the performance of particular services for individual persons."

Relying on *National Muffler Dealers Ass'n, Inc. v. United States*, 440 U.S. 472, 99 S.Ct. 1304, 59 L.Ed.2d 519 (1979), the district court found that Guide fails to meet the line of business test because it primarily serves the interests of IBM and the users of IBM computers rather than the data processing industry as a whole. * * *

Here, the district court acknowledged that although Guide's stated purpose is to facilitate the use and exchange of information regarding data processing equipment in general, the primary benefit inures to IBM which is only *a segment* (70 to 75%) of the mainframe computer business, not a line of business.

Guide argues that this case is distinguishable from *National Muffler* because its activities improve several lines of business by enabling its members to perform data processing more efficiently. This argument is in direct conflict with Revenue Ruling 83–164 and was rejected in *National Prime Users Group, Inc. v. United States*, 667 F.Supp. 250 (D.Md.1987). Revenue Ruling 83–164 held that an organization that directs its activities to the users of one brand of computers improves the business conditions in only segments of the various lines of business to which its members belong. Similarly, in *National Prime Users Group*, the court denied a tax exemption to an association whose members consisted of users of computers of a single manufacturer because the association only improved conditions for members in those lines of businesses that used the particular computers. The court found an inherent competitive advantage for the computer manufacturer. We believe that the Revenue Ruling and the decision of the district court in Maryland were correct.

Therefore, while Guide's members reflect a wide variety of businesses, no single business is enhanced and Guide only benefits IBM and those individuals within various lines of business who use IBM mainframes. Moreover, the district court found that Guide *primarily* advances IBM's interests and that any benefit to its members and other data processing companies who use information prepared by Guide is incidental.

We agree with the district court's characterization of Guide as a powerful marketing tool for IBM. Guide's conferences provide IBM customers with the opportunity to learn about IBM products and services and IBM receives feedback about those products and services which influences product development. The district court properly found that Guide fails to qualify as an exempt business league under § 501(c)(6).

The judgment of the district court is AFFIRMED.

II. TRADE SHOWS

Qualified convention and trade show activities conducted by a § 50(c)(5) or § 501(c)(6) organization are not unrelated trade or business activities. A qualified convention or trade show activity includes any activity designed to attract persons to an industry show for the purpose of displaying industry products, to stimulate interest in and demand for industry products or services, or to educate persons engaged in the industry in the development of new products and services or new matters affecting the industry. The event must be sponsored by a §§ 501(c)(5) or (6) organization that regularly conducts as one of its exempt purposes a show that stimulates interest in, or demand for, the products and services of the particular industry. [See I.R.C. § 513(d).]

III. POLITICAL ACTIVITIES

A § 501(c)(6) organization is not prohibited from engaging in any amount of legislative activity that is germane to the common business interests of its members. However, the organization must conduct such activities through a separate, segregated fund, that would become a political organization subject to § 527 of the Internal Revenue Code (discussion in Chapter 15) or the organization will be taxed on its direct political expenditures pursuant to § 527(f) of the Code (discussion in Chapter 15).

Members of a § 501(c)(6) organization generally may deduct their dues to the organization as an ordinary and necessary business expense under § 162 of the Code. However, they may not deduct that portion of their dues to the organization attributable to expenses for lobbying or for participation or intervention in a political campaign on behalf of, or in opposition to, any candidate for public office. [See I.R.C. § 162(e).] Trade associations and similar organizations must provide annual information disclosure to their members estimating the portion of member dues allocable to lobbying.[1] The organization must disclose on its annual tax return both the total amount of its lobbying and political expenditures and the total amount of dues allocable to such expenditures. The organization also is required to provide notice to each person paying dues, at the time of assessment or payment of such dues, of the portion of the dues the organization reasonably estimates will be allocable to the organization's lobbying expenditures during the year and that, therefore, is not deductible by the payor. The reporting is not required for in-house expenditures if the expenditures do not exceed $2,000. An organization may elect to pay a 35 percent proxy tax on the organization's lobbying and political expenditures paid or incurred during the year in lieu of sending disclosure notices to its members. An organization that fails to report, or under reports, the total amount of its lobbying expenditures is required to pay the 35 percent proxy tax.

AMERICAN SOCIETY OF ASSOCIATION EXECUTIVES v. UNITED STATES

United States Court of Appeals, D.C. Circuit, 1999
195 F.3d 47

STEPHEN F. WILLIAMS, Circuit Judge:

Before its amendment by the Omnibus Budget Reconciliation Act of 1993, Pub.L. No.103–66 (the "1993 Act" or the "Act"), § 162(e) of the Internal Revenue Code ("I.R.C.") allowed businesses to deduct their direct lobbying expenditures as business expenses. In the 1993 Act, Congress amended I.R.C. § 162(e) so that lobbying expenses would no longer be deductible. 26 U.S.C. § 162(e) (1994).

It also enacted several additional provisions to ensure that taxpayers could not evade the force of the Act by paying dues to tax-exempt organizations that would then conduct the desired lobbying activities. The American Society of Association Executives, a tax-exempt trade association that lobbies on behalf of its members, filed suit, alleging that these provisions placed an affirmative burden on its right to lobby, in violation of the First Amendment. The district court rejected the constitutional challenge and granted the government's motion for summary judgment; we affirm.

* * *

---

1. I.R.C. § 6033(e). Disclosure is not required for an organization that incurs only de minimis amounts of in-house lobbying expenditures (less than $2,000), elects to pay a proxy tax on its lobbying expenditures incurred during a taxable year, or establishes that substantially all its dues monies are paid by members not entitled to deduct such dues in computing their taxable income. The waiver is available if the organization receives 90 percent or more of its dues (or similar payments) from persons not entitled to deduct such payments. See Rev. Proc. 95–35, 1995–2 C.B. 391.

Under the 1993 Act, a tax-exempt organization that engages in lobbying activities and is funded in part by membership dues and other contributions may either pay a tax on its lobbying activities (the so-called "proxy tax"), or may follow "flow-through provisions" aimed at making sure no contributor or dues payer takes a deduction with respect to funds used for lobbying. 26 U.S.C. § 6033(e) (1994).

The proxy tax, if the tax-exempt organization chooses that route, falls on all lobbying expenses as defined in § 162(e)(1) and is imposed at the highest marginal rate of the corporate income tax under I.R.C. § 11, now 35%. *Id.* § 6033(e)(2)(A)(ii). If the organization chooses the flow-through alternative, it is required to provide donors, at the time of "assessment or payment" of dues or other contributions, with a "reasonable estimate" of the portion of the dues or contributions that is allocable to § 162(e)(1) expenditures. *Id.* § 6033(e)(1)(A)(ii). Donors are not allowed to take a deduction for the portion of their dues and contributions allocable to such expenditures. *Id.* § 162(e)(3).

To prevent organizations from circumventing the purpose of the flow-through provisions by artificially allocating their dues to non-lobbying activities, Congress enacted an "allocation provision." *Id.* § 6033(e)(1)(C)(i). This provision dictates that lobbying expenditures will be considered paid out of membership dues or "other similar amounts" to the extent that they exist. *Id.* So as to preclude the analogous manipulation across years (e.g., an organization might "prepay" lobbying expenses in excess of dues in one year and reduce its lobbying expenses below that received from dues in the following years, thereby artificially increasing the deductions for which its members are eligible), a "carryover" provision dictates that any lobbying expenditures in excess of the dues or other amounts paid to the organization in one year will be treated as expenditures incurred during the following year and payable out of dues received during that year. *Id.* § 6033(e)(1)(C)(ii).

The organization must include on its annual tax returns the lobbying expenditures that it has incurred as well as the total amount of dues "to which such expenditures are allocable." *Id.* § 6033(e)(1)(A)(i). If a tax-exempt organization trying to follow the flow-through method in fact incurs lobbying expenditures in excess of the aggregate amount covered as nondeductible by its notices to dues payers for the year, the discrepancy will be subject to the flat 35% tax. *Id.* § 6033(e)(2)(A). The Secretary may (but evidently need not) "waive" this tax if the organization agrees to correct its mistaken estimate by "carrying over" the excess to the following year and allocating it to dues paid in that year. *Id.* § 6033(e)(2)(B).

The American Society of Association Executives is a nonprofit professional association that lobbies on behalf of about 23,000 association executives and staff members. It is tax-exempt under 26 U.S.C. § 501(c)(6), as a "[b]usiness league[ ] ... not organized for profit." Thus it is subject to the lobbying tax provisions at issue in this case.

For its fiscal year ending June 30, 1994, the Society chose to apply the "proxy tax" to its lobbying expenditures, thus allowing its members and contributors full deductibility. On November 7, 1994 it submitted an amended tax return, requesting a refund of the $56,900 paid as proxy tax, and claiming that the tax scheme was unconstitutional. After six months passed without action on the refund claim by the Internal Revenue Service, the Society brought suit in district court. It alleged that the scheme placed a burden on its freedom of expression in violation of the First Amendment, and that it discriminated against lobbying associations and in favor of individual businesses and private persons, in contravention of the Fifth Amendment.

The district court granted the government's motion for summary judgment, rejecting both the Society's claims. See *American Soc'y of Ass'n Executives v. United States,* 23 F.Supp.2d 64 (D.D.C.1998). On appeal, the Society argues only its First Amendment theory.

* * *

The Society and the government agree on certain general principles. Although the government has no obligation to subsidize speech, * * * the courts will subject to "strict scrutiny" any affirmative burden that the government places on speech on the basis of its content. * * * The Society points to various effects of the proxy and flow-through choices that in its view affirmatively burden lobbying.

First, at least for association members in relatively low brackets, the flat 35% rate necessarily places a higher effective burden on lobbying through an association than the generally applicable corporate tax—a graduated rate starting at 15% and capped at 35%—places on direct lobbying. The government counters (in part) that a dues payer in the 35% bracket, and even well below, can get more lobbying per pretax dollar by contributing to a lobbying association than by doing its own lobbying. This is because the dues payer gets a deduction for its *full* contribution to the entity, including the amount devoted to the tax payment itself. Whereas a dues payer can buy $100 worth of lobbying for $135 (i.e., $100 plus the $35 proxy tax), a corporation that is taxed at a 35% rate would have to use up $154 of pre-tax income in order to spend $100 on lobbying (65% of $154 = $100). The Society contests these calculations, but we need not resolve the dispute, partly because the government figures would still leave dues payers in tax brackets lower than the effective rate of the proxy tax (brackets lower than 26% by the government's calculations) more burdened by the proxy tax than by the treatment of direct lobbying. An additional reason we need not resolve it is that, as we shall see, associations like the Society have an option that avoids any such possible burden.

Alternatively, argues the Society, the flow-through method subjects lobbying to a risk of non-neutral treatment. If an association *over*estimates its lobbying expenses, its dues payers will forfeit part of their deduction for nonlobbying business activities, without the possibility of recovering this deduction in the future. And if it *under*estimates lobbying expenditures, it is exposed to the proxy tax, from which it can escape only if the Secretary chooses to "waive" the tax and allow "carryover" treatment. The Secretary has failed to adopt regulations setting forth clear sufficient conditions for the waiver. According to the Society, his only official statement on the subject consists of instructions for Form 990 (the income tax return for associations), in which he says that he *may* permit a waiver if the association's estimate was reasonable and the association agrees to add the excess to the following year's amount. See IRS Form 990, line 85h and Instructions (1998). The Society argues that, in light of the First Amendment right to lobby, the Secretary's discretion is far too broad to survive strict scrutiny.

Finally, the Society says that the allocation rules, by treating the association's lobbying expenditures as funded by dues or similar payments (to the extent available), regardless of their actual source, in effect limit the deductions that members can take for dues that the association spends on ordinary business activities. This, it says, violates the principle that the government may not condition the receipt of an otherwise available benefit on an entity's refraining from the exercise of its freedom of speech. * * *

We do not reach these arguments, however, because a tax-exempt organization that engages in lobbying activities can altogether sidestep the specified dilemmas. A § 501(c)(6) association can avoid any alleged burden on its First Amendment rights by splitting itself into two § 501(c)(6) organizations—one that engages exclusively in lobbying on behalf of its members and one that completely refrains from lobbying. Whereas the lobbying wing can be funded by dues and contributions, for which members will not be able to take a deduction, the non-lobbying affiliate can be funded, at least in part, by deductible dues. This system achieves precisely what the Society says the Constitution demands: a generally applicable tax system that, although it does not subsidize lobbying, imposes no burden on it by comparison with other activities.

If this option is available, the treatment of lobbying contested here is subject only to "rational basis" scrutiny, and, as we shall see, handily survives. In *Regan v. Taxation With Representation,* 461 U.S. 540, 103 S.Ct. 1997, 76 L.Ed.2d 129 (1983), the Supreme Court considered the operation of I.R.C. §§ 170(c)(2), 501(c)(3) and 501(c)(4). Sections 501(c)(3) and (4) define the characteristics of certain tax-exempt organizations, the key difference (for our purposes) being that "no substantial part of the activities" of a § 501(c)(3) organization may consist of lobbying, whereas no such limit applies to § 501(c)(4) organizations. The tradeoff is that § 170(c)(2) permits taxpayers to deduct any contributions made to § 501(c)(3) organizations, but not to organizations that are tax-exempt under § 501(c)(4). Because the plaintiff organization in *Taxation With Representation* could conduct its lobbying activities through a § 501(c)(4) affiliate, and continue to receive deductible contributions as a § 501(c)(3) organization, the Court applied rational basis review and upheld the statute. * * * In contrast with the situation in *Taxation With Representation,* the Court in *FCC v. League of Women*

Voters, 468 U.S. 364, 104 S.Ct. 3106, 82 L.Ed.2d 278 (1984), invalidated a grant conditioned on a broadcasting station's not "engag [ing] in editorializing," on the basis that the station could not "segregate its activities according to the source of its funding." *Id.* at 400–01, 104 S.Ct. 3106.

In *Taxation With Representation* the Court noted that the taxpayer organization must show that its § 501(c)(3) wing does not subsidize its § 501(c)(4) affiliate, so as to ensure that "no tax-deductible contributions are used to pay for substantial lobbying." * * * The Court found, however, that the IRS's only requirements to that end—that the two organizations be "separately incorporated and keep records adequate to show that tax-deductible contributions are not used to pay for lobbying"—were not "unduly burdensome." * * *

An organization like the Society can similarly split into two § 501(c)(6) associations. Neither affiliate would forfeit its tax-exempt status, as the non-lobbying wing would clearly continue to be a "business league" for purposes of the statute, and the lobbying wing, so long as its activity is directed at furthering a business interest, would also remain tax-exempt under § 501(c)(6). See Rev. Rul. 61–177, 1961–2 C.B. 117 (stating that a corporation whose sole activity is to influence legislation relevant to a business interest is exempt under § 501(c)(6) if it otherwise meets the requirements of that section).

The Society argues, however, that the regulations promulgated in response to the 1993 Act block such a remedy. It points in particular to the Treasury Department's regulation precluding a taxpayer from "structur[ing] its activities with a principal purpose of achieving results that are unreasonable in light of the purposes of section 162(e)(1)(A) and section 6033(e)." Treas. Reg. § 1.162–29(f)(1995). Assuming that this applies to an organization that formally segregates its lobbying from its nonlobbying activities through dual incorporation, we see no indication that this is in any way more onerous than the separation criteria referred to in *Taxation With Representation*. So long as the organization does not attempt to evade § 162(e)(1)(A)—by funneling resources to the lobbying wing from the non-lobbying wing—we do not see how it could run afoul of the regulation. In fact, a dual-entity structure is entirely consistent with Congress's intent in enacting the 1993 Act: to withdraw the deduction for lobbying expenses without affirmatively burdening the right to lobby.

Apart from its claims that the regulations unduly hamper the dual-entity strategy, the Society invokes *Minneapolis Star & Tribune Co. v. Minnesota Comm'r of Revenue,* 460 U.S. 575, 587–88, 103 S.Ct. 1365, 75 L.Ed.2d 295 (1983), for the idea that differential tax treatment of the press is subject to heightened scrutiny even when the taxpayer cannot prove the differential burdensome. Similarly, any subjection of lobbying to differential treatment must meet heightened scrutiny. But *Taxation with Representation,* and the other cases cited above and using only rational basis scrutiny, were all decided after *Minneapolis Star* (indeed, *Taxation with Representation* was decided later the same Term). The

Court evidently regards the dual incorporation option as obviating the need for heightened scrutiny. Even if we reframe the Society's objection as a claim that the need to adopt a dual incorporation is itself a "differential" (after all, non-lobbying associations that have multiple functions commonly need not subdivide), the Court's decisions necessarily reject the notion.

Accordingly, we ask simply whether the provisions bear "a rational relation to a legitimate governmental purpose." *Taxation With Representation*, 461 U.S. at 547, 103 S.Ct. 1997. The parties agree on the legitimacy of withholding the benefits of tax deductibility from lobbying. And the scheme overall clearly bears a rational relation to that goal. For instance, the estimation provision, § 6033(e)(1)(A)(ii), allows taxpayers to continue to take a deduction for dues paid to tax-exempt organizations not allocable to lobbying. The carryover and allocation provisions, § 6033(e)(1)(C) ensure that taxpayers may not circumvent the Act by taking deductions for money that will fund lobbying activities, directly or indirectly. We find no constitutional violation.

* * *

The district court's order granting summary judgment for the defendant is

Affirmed.

IV. ANTITRUST REGULATIONS

Activities of trade associations are vulnerable to antitrust infractions. There is no language in the Sherman Act that would prevent its application to nonprofit organizations. (See 15 U.S.C. §§ 7, 15.)

GOLDFARB v. VIRGINIA STATE BAR
United States Supreme Court, 1975
421 U.S. 773, 95 S.Ct. 2004, 44 L.Ed.2d 572

Mr. Chief Justice BURGER delivered the opinion of the Court.

We granted certiorari to decide whether a minimum-fee schedule for lawyers published by the Fairfax County Bar Association and enforced by the Virginia State Bar violates § 1 of the Sherman Act, 26 Stat. 209, as amended, 15 U.S.C. § 1. The Court of Appeals held that, although the fee schedule and enforcement mechanism substantially restrained competition among lawyers, publication of the schedule by the County Bar was outside the scope of the Act because the practice of law is not 'trade or commerce,' and enforcement of the schedule by the State Bar was exempt from the Sherman Act as state action as defined in Parker v. Brown, 317 U.S. 341, 63 S.Ct. 307, 87 L.Ed. 315 (1943).

I

In 1971 petitioners, husband and wife, contracted to buy a home in Fairfax County, Va. The financing agency required them to secure title insurance; this required a title examination, and only a member of the Virginia State Bar could legally perform that service. * * * Petitioners therefore contacted a lawyer who quoted them the precise fee suggested in a minimum-fee schedule published by respondent Fairfax County Bar Association; the lawyer told them that it was his policy to keep his charges in line with the minimum-fee schedule which provided for a fee of 1% of the value of the property involved. Petitioners then tried to find a lawyer who would examine the title for less than the fee fixed by the schedule. They sent letters to 36 other Fairfax County lawyers requesting their fees. Nineteen replied, and none indicated that he would charge less than the rate fixed by the schedule; several stated that they knew of no attorney who would do so.

The fee schedule the lawyers referred to is a list of recommended minimum prices for common legal services. Respondent Fairfax County Bar Association published the fee schedule although, as a purely voluntary association of attorneys, the County Bar has no formal power to enforce it. Enforcement has been provided by respondent Virginia State Bar which is the administrative agency through which the Virginia Supreme Court regulates the practice of law in that State; membership in the State Bar is required in order to practice in Virginia. Although the State Bar has never taken formal disciplinary action to compel adherence to any fee schedule, it has published reports condoning fee schedules, and has issued two ethical opinions indicating that fee schedules cannot be ignored. The most recent opinion states that 'evidence that an attorney habitually charges less than the suggested minimum fee schedule adopted by his local bar Association, raises a presumption that such lawyer is guilty of misconduct....'

Because petitioners could not find a lawyer willing to charge a fee lower than the schedule dictated, they had their title examined by the lawyer they had first contacted. They then brought this class action against the State Bar and the County Bar alleging that the operation of the minimum-fee schedule, as applied to fees for legal services relating to residential real estate transactions, constitutes price fixing in violation of § 1 of the Sherman Act. Petitioners sought both injunctive relief and damages.

After a trial solely on the issue of liability the District Court held that the minimum-fee schedule violated the Sherman Act. 355 F.Supp. 491 (ED Va.(1973). The court viewed the fee-schedule system as a significant reason for petitioners' failure to obtain legal services for less than the minimum fee, and it rejected the County Bar's contention that as a 'learned profession' the practice of law is exempt from the Sherman Act.

Both respondents argued that their actions were also exempt from the Sherman Act as state action. Parker v. Brown, supra. The District Court agreed that the Virginia State Bar was exempt under that doctrine because it is an administrative agency of the Virginia Supreme Court, and more important, because its 'minor role in this matter ... derived from the judicial and 'legislative command of the State and was not intended to operate or become effective without that command.'' The County Bar, on the other hand, is a private organization and was under no compulsion to adopt the fee schedule recommended by the State Bar. Since the County Bar chose its own course of conduct the District Court held that the antitrust laws 'remain in full force and effect as to it.' The court enjoined the fee schedule, 15 U.S.C. § 26, and set the case down for trial to ascertain damages. 15 U.S.C. § 15.

The Court of Appeals reversed as to liability. 497 F.2d 1 (C.A.4 1974). Despite its conclusion that it 'is abundantly clear from the record before us that the fee schedule and the enforcement mechanism supporting it act as a substantial restraint upon competition among attorneys practicing in Fairfax County,' id., at 13, the Court of Appeals held the State Bar immune under Parker v. Brown, supra, and held the County Bar immune because the practice of law is not 'trade or commerce' under the Sherman Act. There has long been judicial recognition of a limited exclusion of 'learned professions' from the scope of the antitrust laws, the court said; that exclusion is based upon the special form of regulation imposed upon the professions by the States, and the incompatibility of certain competitive practices with such professional regulation. It concluded that the promulgation of a minimum-fee schedule is one of 'those matters with respect to which an accord must be reached between the necessities of professional regulation and the dictates of the antitrust laws.' The accord reached by that court was to hold the practice of law exempt from the antitrust laws.

Alternatively, the Court of Appeals held that respondents' activities did not have sufficient effect on interstate commerce to support Sherman Act jurisdiction. Petitioners had argued that the fee schedule restrained the business of financing and insuring home mortgages by inflating a component part of the total cost of housing, but the court concluded that a title examination is generally a local service, and even where it is part of a transaction which crosses state lines its effect on commerce is only 'incidental,' and does not justify federal regulation.

We granted certiorari, * * * and are thus confronted for the first time with the question of whether the Sherman Act applies to services performed by attorneys in examining titles in connection with financing the purchase of real estate.

II

Our inquiry can be divided into four steps: did respondents engage in price fixing? If so, are their activities in interstate commerce or do they affect interstate commerce? If so, are the activities exempt from the Sherman Act because they involve a 'learned profession?' If not, are the activities 'state action' within the meaning of Parker v. Brown, 317 U.S. 341, 63 S.Ct. 307, 87 L.Ed. 315 (1943), and therefore exempt from the Sherman Act?

A

The County Bar argues that because the fee schedule is merely advisory, the schedule and its enforcement mechanism do not constitute price fixing. Its purpose, the argument continues, is only to provide legitimate information to aid member lawyers in complying with Virginia professional regulations. Moreover, the County Bar contends that in practice the schedule has not had the effect of producing fixed fees. The facts found by the trier belie these contentions, and nothing in the record suggests these findings lack support.

A purely advisory fee schedule issued to provide guidelines, or an exchange of price information without a showing of an actual restraint on trade, would present us with a different question, * * *. The record here, however, reveals a situation quite different from what would occur under a purely advisory fee schedule. Here a fixed, rigid price floor arose from respondents' activities: every lawyer who responded to petitioners' inquiries adhered to the fee schedule, and no lawyer asked for additional information in order to set an individualized fee. The price information disseminated did not concern past standards, * * * but rather minimum fees to be charged in future transactions, and those minimum rates were increased over time. The fee schedule was enforced through the prospective professional discipline from the State Bar, and the desire of attorneys to comply with announced professional norms, * * *; the motivation to conform was reinforced by the assurance that other lawyers would not compete by underbidding. This is not merely a case of an agreement that may be inferred from an exchange of price information, * * * for here a naked agreement was clearly shown, and the effect on prices is plain. * * *

Moreover, in terms of restraining competition and harming consumers like petitioners the price-fixing activities found here are unusually damaging. A title examination is indispensable in the process of financing a real estate purchase, and since only an attorney licensed to practice in Virginia may legally examine a title, * * * consumers could not turn to alternative sources for the necessary service. All attorneys of course, were practicing under the constraint of the fee schedule. See generally United States v. Container Corp., supra, at 337, 89 S.Ct. at 512. The County Bar makes much of the fact that it is a voluntary organization; however, the ethical opinions issued by the State Bar provide that any lawyer, whether or not a member of his county bar association, may be disciplined for 'habitually charg(ing) less than the suggested minimum fee schedule adopted by his local bar Association....' * * * These factors coalesced to create a pricing system that consumers could not realistically escape. On this record respondents' activities constitute a classic illustration of price fixing.

B

The County Bar argues, as the Court of Appeals held, that any effect on interstate commerce caused by the fee schedule's restraint on legal services was incidental and remote. In its view the legal services, which are performed wholly intrastate, are essentially local in nature and therefore a restraint with respect to them can never substantially affect interstate commerce. Further, the County Bar maintains, there was no showing here that the fee schedule and its enforcement mechanism increased fees, and that even if they did there was no showing that such an increase deterred any prospective homeowner from buying in Fairfax County.

These arguments misconceive the nature of the transactions at issue and the place legal services play in those transactions. As the District Court found, 'a significant portion of funds furnished for the purchasing of homes in Fairfax County comes from without the State of Virginia,' and 'significant amounts of loans on Fairfax County real estate are guaranteed by the United States Veterans Administration and Department of Housing and Urban Development both headquartered in the District of Columbia.' Thus in this class action the transactions which create the need for the particular legal services in question frequently are interstate transactions. The necessary connection between the interstate transactions and the restraint of trade provided by the minimum-fee schedule is present because, in a practical sense, title examinations are necessary in real estate transactions to assure a lien on a valid title of the borrower. In financing realty purchases lenders require, 'as a condition of making the loan, that the title to the property involved be examined....' Thus a title examination is an integral part of an interstate transaction and this Court has long held that

> 'there is an obvious distinction to be drawn between a course of conduct wholly within a state and conduct which is an inseparable element of a larger program dependent for its success upon activity which affects commerce between the states.' United States v. Frankfort Distilleries, 324 U.S. 293, 297, 65 S.Ct. 661, 663, 89 L.Ed. 951 (1945).

* * *

Given the substantial volume of commerce involved, and the inseparability of this particular legal service from the interstate aspects of real estate transactions, we conclude that interstate commerce has been sufficiently affected. * * *

The fact that there was no showing that home buyers were discouraged by the challenged activities does not mean that interstate commerce was not affected. Otherwise, the magnitude of the effect would control, and our cases have shown that, once an effect is shown, no specific magnitude need be proved. * * * Nor was it necessary for petitioners to prove that the fee schedule raised fees. Petitioners clearly proved that the fee schedule fixed fees and thus 'deprive(d) purchasers or consumers of the advantages which they derive from from competition.' Apex Hosiery Co. v. Leader, 310 U.S. 469, 501, 60 S.Ct. 982, 996, 84 L.Ed. 1311 (1940). * * *

Where, as a matter of law or practical necessity, legal services are an integral part of an interstate transaction, a restraint on those services may substantially affect commerce for Sherman Act purposes. Of course, there may be legal services that involve interstate commerce in other fashions, just as there may be legal services that have no nexus with interstate commerce and thus are beyond the reach of the Sherman Act.

C

The County Bar argues that Congress never intended to include the learned professions within the terms 'trade or commerce' in s 1 of the Sherman Act, and therefore the sale of professional services is exempt from the Act. No explicit exemption or legislative history is provided to support this contention; rather, the existence of state regulation seems to be its primary basis. Also, the County Bar maintains that competition is inconsistent with the practice of a profession because enhancing profit is not the goal of professional activities; the goal is to provide services necessary to the community. That, indeed, is the classic basis traditionally advanced to distinguish professions from trades, businesses, and other occupations, but it loses some of its force when used to support the fee control activities involved here.

In arguing that learned professions are not 'trade or commerce' the County Bar seeks a total exclusion from antitrust regulation. Whether state regulation is active or dormant, real or theoretical, lawyers would be able to adopt anticompetitive practices with impunity. We cannot find support for the proposition that Congress intended any such sweeping exclusion. The nature of an occupation, standing alone, does not provide sanctuary from the Sherman Act, Associated Press v. United States, 326 U.S. 1, 7, 65 S.Ct. 1416, 1418, 89 L.Ed. 2013 (1945), nor is the public-service aspect of professional practice controlling in determining whether s 1 includes professions. United States v. National Assn. of Real Estate Boards, 339 U.S., at 489, 70 S.Ct., at 714. Congress intended to strike as broadly as it could in s 1 of the Sherman Act, and to read into it so wide an exemption as that urged on us would be at odds with that purpose.

The language of § 1 of the Sherman Act, of course, contains no exception. 'Language more comprehensive is difficult to conceive.' United States v. South–Eastern Underwriters Assn., 322 U.S. 533, 553, 64 S.Ct. 1162, 1174, 88 L.Ed. 1440 (1944). And our cases have repeatedly established that there is a heavy presumption against implicit exemptions, * * * Indeed, our cases have specifically included the sale of services within § 1. * * * Whatever else it may be, the examination of a land title is a service; the exchange of such a service for money is 'commerce' in the most common usage of that word. It is no disparagement of the practice of law as a profession to acknowledge that it has this business aspect, and § 1 of the Sherman Act '(o)n its face ... shows a carefully studied attempt to bring within the Act every person engaged in business whose activities might restrain or monopolize commercial intercourse among the states.' * * *

In the modern world it cannot be denied that the activities of lawyers play an important part in commercial intercourse, and that anticompetitive activities by lawyers may exert a restraint on commerce.

D

In Parker v. Brown, 317 U.S. 341, 63 S.Ct. 307, 87 L.Ed. 315 (1943), the Court held that an anticompetitive marketing program which 'derived its authority and its efficacy from the legislative command of the state' was not a violation of the Sherman Act because the Act was intended to regulate private practices and not to prohibit a State from imposing a restraint as an act of government. * * * Respondent State Bar and respondent County Bar both seek to avail themselves of this so-called state-action exemption.

Through its legislature Virginia has authorized its highest court to regulate the practice of law. That court has adopted ethical codes which deal in part with fees, and far from exercising state power to authorize binding price fixing, explicitly directed lawyers not 'to be controlled' by fee schedules. The State Bar, a state agency by law, argues that in issuing fee schedule reports and ethical opinions dealing with fee schedules it was merely implementing the fee provisions of the ethical codes. The County Bar, although it is a voluntary association and not a state agency, claims that the ethical codes and the activities of the State Bar 'prompted' it to issue fee schedules and thus its actions, too, are state action for Sherman Act purposes.

The threshold inquiry in determining if an anticompetitive activity is state action of the type the Sherman Act was not meant to proscribe is whether the activity is required by the State acting as sovereign. * * * Here we need not inquire further into the state-action question because it cannot fairly be said that the State of Virginia through its Supreme Court Rules required the anticompetitive activities of either respondent. Respondents have pointed to no Virginia statute requiring their activities; state law simply does not refer to fees, leaving regulation of the profession to the Virginia Supreme Court; although the Supreme Court's ethical codes mention advisory fee schedules they do not direct either respondent to supply them, or require the type of price floor which arose from respondents' activities. Although the State Bar apparently has been granted the power to issue ethical opinions, there is no indication in this record that the Virginia Supreme Court approves the opinions. Respondents' arguments, at most, constitute the contention that their activities complemented the objective of the ethical codes. In our view that is not state action for Sherman Act purposes. It is not enough that, as the County Bar puts it, anticompetitive conduct is 'prompted' by state action; rather, anticompetitive activities must be compelled by direction of the State acting as a sovereign.

III

We recognize that the States have a compelling interest in the practice of professions within their boundaries, and that as part of their power to protect the public health, safety, and other valid interests they have broad power to establish standards for licensing practitioners and regulating the practice of professions. We also recognize that in some instances the State may decide that 'forms of competition usual in the business world may be demoralizing to the ethical standards of a profession.' * * * The interest of the States in regulating lawyers is especially great since lawyers are essential to the primary governmental function of administering justice, and have historically been 'officers of the courts.' * * * In holding that certain anticompetitive conduct by lawyers is within the reach of the Sherman Act we intend no diminution of the authority of the State to regulate its professions.

The judgment of the Court of Appeals is reversed and the case is remanded to that court with orders to remand to the District Court for further proceedings consistent with this opinion.

* * *

NATIONAL COLLEGIATE ATHLETIC ASSOC. v. UNIVERSITY OF OKLAHOMA

United States Supreme Court, 1984
468 U.S. 85, 104 S.Ct. 2948, 82 L.Ed.2d 70

Justice STEVENS delivered the opinion of the Court.

The University of Oklahoma and the University of Georgia contend that the National Collegiate Athletic Association has unreasonably restrained trade in the televising of college football games. After an extended trial, the District Court found that the NCAA had violated § 1 of the Sherman Act and granted injunctive relief. * * * The Court of Appeals agreed that the statute had been violated but modified the remedy in some respects. 707 F.2d 1147 (C.A.10 1983). We granted certiorari, * * *, and now affirm.

I

The NCAA

Since its inception in 1905, the NCAA has played an important role in the regulation of amateur collegiate sports. It has adopted and promulgated playing rules, standards of amateurism, standards for academic eligibility, regulations concerning recruitment of athletes, and rules governing the size of athletic squads and coaching staffs. In some sports, such as baseball, swimming, basketball, wrestling, and track, it has sponsored and conducted national tournaments. It has not done so in the sport of football, however. With the exception of football, the NCAA has not undertaken any regulation of the televising of athletic events.

The NCAA has approximately 850 voting members. The regular members are classified into separate divisions to reflect differences in size and scope of their athletic programs. Division I includes 276 colleges with major athletic programs; in this group only 187 play intercollegiate football. Divisions II and III include approximately 500 colleges with less extensive athletic programs. Division I has been subdivided into Divisions I–A and I–AA for football.

Some years ago, five major conferences together with major football-playing independent institutions organized the College Football Association (CFA). The original purpose of the CFA was to promote the interests of major football-playing schools within the NCAA structure. The Universities of Oklahoma and Georgia, respondents in this Court, are members of the CFA.

History of the NCAA Television Plan

In 1938, the University of Pennsylvania televised one of its home games. From 1940 through the 1950 season all of Pennsylvania's home games were televised.** That was the beginning of the relationship between television and college football.

On January 11, 1951, a three-person "Television Committee," appointed during the preceding year, delivered a report to the NCAA's annual convention in Dallas. Based on preliminary surveys, the committee had concluded that "television does have an adverse effect on college football attendance and unless brought under some control threatens to seriously harm the nation's overall athletic and physical system." * * * The report emphasized that "the television problem is truly a national one and requires collective action by the colleges." * * * As a result, the NCAA decided to retain the National Opinion Research Center (NORC) to study the impact of television on live attendance, and to declare a moratorium on the televising of football games. A television committee was appointed to implement the decision and to develop an NCAA television plan for 1951. * * *

The committee's 1951 plan provided that only one game a week could be telecast in each area, with a total blackout on 3 of the 10 Saturdays during the season. A team could appear on television only twice during a season. The plan also provided that the NORC would conduct a systematic study of the effects of the program on attendance. * * * The plan received the virtually unanimous support of the NCAA membership; only the University of Pennsylvania challenged it. Pennsylvania announced that it would televise all its home games. The council of the NCAA thereafter declared Pennsylvania a member in bad standing and the four institutions scheduled to play at Pennsylvania in 1951 refused to do so. Pennsylvania then reconsidered its decision and abided by the NCAA plan. * * *

During each of the succeeding five seasons, studies were made which tended to indicate that television had an adverse effect on attendance at college football games. During those years the NCAA continued to exercise complete control over the number of games that could be televised. * * *

From 1952 through 1977 the NCAA television committee followed essentially the same procedure for developing its television plans. It would first circulate a questionnaire to the membership and then use the responses as a basis for formulating a plan for the ensuing season. The plan was then submitted to a vote by means of a mail referendum. Once approved, the plan formed the basis for NCAA's negotiations with the networks. Throughout this period the plans retained the essential purposes of the original plan. * * * Until 1977 the contracts were all for either 1– or 2–year terms. In 1977 the NCAA adopted "principles of negotiation" for the future and discontinued the practice of submitting each plan for membership approval. Then the NCAA also entered into its first 4–year contract granting exclusive rights to the American Broadcasting Cos. (ABC) for the 1978–1981 seasons. ABC had held the exclusive rights to network telecasts of NCAA football games since 1965. * * *

THE CURRENT PLAN

The plan adopted in 1981 for the 1982–1985 seasons is at issue in this case. This plan, like each of its predecessors, recites that it is intended to reduce, insofar as possible, the adverse effects of live television upon football game attendance. It provides that "all forms of television of the football Games of NCAA member institutions during the Plan control periods shall be in accordance with this Plan." * * * The plan recites that the television committee has awarded rights to negotiate and contract for the telecasting of college football games of members of the NCAA to two "carrying networks." * * * In addition to the principal award of rights to the carrying networks, the plan also describes rights for a "supplementary series" that had been awarded for the 1982 and 1983 seasons, as well as a procedure for permitting specific "exception telecasts."

In separate agreements with each of the carrying networks, ABC and the Columbia Broadcasting System (CBS), the NCAA granted each the right to telecast the 14 live "exposures" described in the plan, in accordance with the "ground rules" set forth therein. Each of the networks agreed to pay a specified "minimum aggregate compensation to the participating NCAA member institutions" during the 4–year period in an amount that totaled $131,750,000. In essence the agreement authorized each network to negotiate directly with member schools for the right to televise their games. The agreement itself does not describe the method of computing the compensation for each game, but the practice that has developed over the years and that the District Court found would be followed under the current agreement involved the setting of a recommended fee by a representative of the NCAA for different types of telecasts, with national telecasts being the most valuable, regional telecasts being less valuable, and Division II or Division III games commanding a still lower price. The aggregate of all these payments presumably equals the total minimum aggregate compensation set forth in the basic agreement. Except for differences in payment between national and regional telecasts, and with respect to Division II and Division III games, the amount that any team receives does not change with the size of the viewing audience, the number of markets in which the game is telecast, or the particular characteristic of the game or the participating teams. Instead, the "ground rules" provide that the carrying networks make alternate selections of those games they wish to televise, and thereby obtain the exclusive right to submit a bid at an essentially fixed price to the institutions involved. * * *

The plan also contains "appearance requirements" and "appearance limitations" which pertain to each of the 2–year periods that the plan is in effect. The basic requirement imposed on each of the two networks is that it must schedule appearances for at least 82 different member institutions during each 2–year period. Under the appearance limitations no member institution is eligible to appear on television more than a total of six times and more than four times nationally, with the appearances to be divided equally between the two carrying networks. * * * The number of exposures specified in the contracts also sets an absolute maximum on the number of games that can be broadcast.

Thus, although the current plan is more elaborate than any of its predecessors, it retains the essential features of each of them. It limits the total amount of televised intercollegiate football and the number of games that any one team may televise. No member is permitted to make any sale of television rights except in accordance with the basic plan.

Background of this Controversy

Beginning in 1979 CFA members began to advocate that colleges with major football programs should have a greater voice in the formulation of football television policy than they had in the NCAA. CFA therefore investigated the possibility of negotiating a television agreement of its own, developed an independent plan, and obtained a contract offer from the National Broadcasting Co. (NBC). This contract, which it signed in August 1981, would have allowed a more liberal number of appearances for each institution, and would have increased the overall revenues realized by CFA members. * * *

In response the NCAA publicly announced that it would take disciplinary action against any CFA member that complied with the CFA–NBC contract. The NCAA made it clear that sanctions would not be limited to the football programs of CFA members, but would apply to other sports as well. On September 8, 1981, respondents commenced this action in the United States District Court for the Western District of Oklahoma and obtained a preliminary injunction preventing the NCAA from initiating disciplinary proceedings or otherwise interfering with CFA's efforts to perform its agreement with NBC. Notwithstanding the entry of the injunction, most CFA members were unwilling to commit themselves to the new contractual arrangement with NBC in the face of the threatened sanctions and therefore the agreement was never consummated. * * *

* * *

II

There can be no doubt that the challenged practices of the NCAA constitute a "restraint of trade" in the sense that they limit members' freedom to negotiate and enter into their own television contracts. In that sense, however, every contract is a restraint of trade, and as we have repeatedly recognized, the Sherman Act was intended to prohibit only unreasonable restraints of trade.

It is also undeniable that these practices share characteristics of restraints we have previously held unreasonable. The NCAA is an association of schools which compete against each other to attract television revenues, not to mention fans and athletes. As the District Court found, the policies of the NCAA with respect to television rights are ultimately controlled by the vote of member institutions. By participating in an association which prevents member institutions from competing against each other on the basis of price or kind of television rights that can be offered to broadcasters, the NCAA member institutions have created a horizontal restraint—an agreement among competitors on the way in which they will compete with one another. A restraint of this type has often been held to be unreasonable as a matter of law. Because it places a ceiling on the number of games member institutions may televise, the horizontal agreement places an artificial limit on the quantity of televised football that is available to broadcasters and consumers. By restraining the quantity of television rights available for sale, the challenged practices create a limitation on output; our cases have held that such limitations are unreasonable restraints of trade. Moreover, the District Court found that the minimum aggregate price in fact operates to preclude any price negotiation between broadcasters and institutions, thereby constituting horizontal price fixing, perhaps the paradigm of an unreasonable restraint of trade.

Horizontal price fixing and output limitation are ordinarily condemned as a matter of law under an "illegal per se" approach because the probability that these practices are anticompetitive is so high; a per se rule is applied when "the practice facially appears to be one that would always or almost always tend to restrict competition and decrease output." Broadcast Music, Inc. v. Columbia Broadcasting System, Inc., 441 U.S. 1, 19–20, 99 S.Ct. 1551, 1562, 60 L.Ed.2d 1 (1979). In such circumstances a restraint is presumed unreasonable without inquiry into the particular market context in which it is found. Nevertheless, we have decided that it would be inappropriate to apply a per se rule to this case. This decision is not based on a lack of judicial experience with this type of arrangement, on the fact that the NCAA is organized as a nonprofit entity, or on our respect for the NCAA's historic role in the preservation and encouragement of intercollegiate amateur athletics. Rather, what is critical is that this case involves an industry in which horizontal restraints on competition are essential if the product is to be available at all.

As Judge Bork has noted: "[S]ome activities can only be carried out jointly. Perhaps the leading example is league sports. When a league of professional lacrosse teams is formed, it would be pointless to declare their cooperation illegal on the ground that there are no other professional lacrosse teams." R. Bork, The Antitrust Paradox 278 (1978). What the NCAA and its member institutions market in this case is competition itself—contests between competing institutions. Of course, this would be completely ineffective if there were no rules on which the competitors agreed to create and define the competition to be marketed. A myriad of rules affecting such matters as the size of the field, the number of players on a team, and the extent to which physical violence is to be encouraged or proscribed, all must be agreed upon, and all restrain the manner in which institutions compete. Moreover, the NCAA seeks to market a particular brand of football—college football. The identification of this "product" with an academic tradition differentiates college football from and makes it more popular than professional sports to which it might otherwise be comparable, such as, for example, minor league baseball. In order to preserve the character and quality of the "product," athletes must not be paid, must be required to attend class, and the like. And the integrity of the "product" cannot be preserved except by mutual agreement; if an institution adopted such restrictions unilaterally, its effectiveness as a competitor on the playing field might soon be destroyed. Thus, the NCAA plays a vital role in enabling college football to preserve its character, and as a result enables a product to be marketed which might otherwise be unavailable. In performing this role, its actions widen consumer choice—not only the choices available to sports fans but also those available to athletes—and hence can be viewed as procompetitive.

Broadcast Music squarely holds that a joint selling arrangement may be so efficient that it will increase sellers' aggregate output and thus be procompetitive. * * * Similarly, as we indicated in Continental T.V., Inc. v. GTE Sylvania Inc., 433 U.S. 36, 51–57, 97 S.Ct. 2549, 2558–2561, 53 L.Ed.2d 568 (1977), a restraint in a limited aspect of a market may actually enhance marketwide competition. Respondents concede that the great majority of the NCAA's regulations enhance competition among member institutions. Thus, despite the fact that this case involves restraints on the ability of member institutions to compete in terms of price and output, a fair evaluation of their competitive character requires consideration of the NCAA's justifications for the restraints.

Our analysis of this case under the Rule of Reason, of course, does not change the ultimate focus of our inquiry. Both per se rules and the Rule of Reason are employed "to form a judgment about the competitive significance of the restraint." * * * A conclusion that a restraint of trade is unreasonable may be "based either (1) on the nature or character of the contracts, or (2) on surrounding circumstances giving rise to the inference or presumption that they were intended to restrain trade and enhance prices. Under either branch of the test, the inquiry is confined to a consideration of impact on competitive conditions." * * *

Per se rules are invoked when surrounding circumstances make the likelihood of anticompetitive conduct so great as to render unjustified further examination of the challenged conduct. But whether the ultimate finding is the product of a presumption or actual market analysis, the essential inquiry remains the same—whether or not the challenged restraint enhances competition. Under the Sherman Act the criterion to be used in judging the validity of a restraint on trade is its impact on competition.

III

Because it restrains price and output, the NCAA's television plan has a significant potential for anticompetitive effects. The findings of the District Court indicate that this potential has been realized. The District Court found that if member institutions were free to sell television rights, many more games would be shown on television, and that the NCAA's output restriction has the effect of raising the price the networks pay for television rights. Moreover, the court found that by fixing a price for television rights to all games, the NCAA creates a price structure that is unresponsive to viewer demand and unrelated to the prices that would prevail in a competitive market. And, of course, since as a practical matter all member institutions need NCAA approval, members have no real choice but to adhere to the NCAA's television controls. * * *

The anticompetitive consequences of this arrangement are apparent. Individual competitors lose their freedom to compete. Price is higher and output lower than they would otherwise be, and both are unresponsive to consumer preference. * * * This latter point is perhaps the most significant, since "Congress designed the Sherman Act as a 'consumer welfare prescription.' " * * * A restraint that has the effect of reducing the importance of consumer preference in setting price and output is not consistent with this fundamental goal of antitrust law. * * * Restrictions on price and output are the paradigmatic examples of restraints of trade that the Sherman Act was intended to prohibit. * * * At the same time, the television plan eliminates competitors from the market, since only those broadcasters able to bid on television rights covering the entire NCAA can compete.** Thus, as the District Court found, many telecasts that would occur in a competitive market are foreclosed by the NCAA's plan.

Petitioner argues, however, that its television plan can have no significant anticompetitive effect since the record indicates that it has no market power—no ability to alter the interaction of supply and demand in the market. * * * We must reject this argument for two reasons, one legal, one factual.

As a matter of law, the absence of proof of market power does not justify a naked restriction on price or output. To the contrary, when there is an agreement not to compete in terms of price or output, "no elaborate industry analysis is required to demonstrate the anticompetitive character of such an agreement." * * * Petitioner does not quarrel with the District Court's finding that price and output are not responsive to demand. Thus the plan is inconsistent with the Sherman Act's command that price and supply be responsive to consumer preference. We have never required proof of market power in such a case. This naked restraint on price and output requires some competitive justification even in the absence of a detailed market analysis. * * *

As a factual matter, it is evident that petitioner does possess market power. The District Court employed the correct test for determining whether college football broadcasts constitute a separate market—whether there are other products that are reasonably substitutable for televised NCAA football games. Petitioner's argument that it cannot obtain supracompetitive prices from broadcasters since advertisers, and hence broadcasters, can switch from college football to other types of programming simply ignores the findings of the District Court. It found that intercollegiate football telecasts generate an audience uniquely attractive to advertisers and that competitors are unable to offer programming that can attract a similar audience. These findings amply support its conclusion that the NCAA possesses market power. Indeed, the District Court's subsidiary finding that advertisers will pay a premium price per viewer to reach audiences watching college football because of their demographic characteristics is vivid evidence of the uniqueness of this product. Moreover, the District Court's market analysis is firmly supported by our decision in International Boxing Club of New York, Inc. v. United States, 358 U.S. 242, 79 S.Ct. 245, 3 L.Ed.2d 270 (1959), that championship boxing events are uniquely attractive to fans and hence constitute a market separate from that for non-championship events. * * * Thus, respondents have demonstrated that there is a separate market for telecasts of college football which "rest [[[s] on generic qualities differentiating" viewers. * * * It inexorably follows that if college football broadcasts be defined as a separate market—and we are convinced they are—then the NCAA's complete control over those broadcasts provides a solid basis for the District Court's conclusion that the NCAA possesses market power with respect to those broadcasts. "When a product is controlled by one interest, without substitutes available in the market, there is monopoly power." * * *

Thus, the NCAA television plan on its face constitutes a restraint upon the operation of a free market, and the findings of the District Court establish that it has operated to raise prices and reduce output. Under the Rule of Reason, these hallmarks of anticompetitive behavior place upon petitioner a heavy burden of establishing an affirmative defense which competitively justifies this apparent deviation from the operations of a free market. * * * We turn now to the NCAA's proffered justifications.

IV

Relying on Broadcast Music, petitioner argues that its television plan constitutes a cooperative "joint venture" which assists in the marketing of broadcast rights and hence is procompetitive. While joint ventures have no immunity from the antitrust laws, as Broadcast Music indicates, a joint selling arrangement may "mak[e] possible a new product by reaping otherwise unattainable efficiencies." Arizona v. Maricopa County Medical Society, 457 U.S. 332, 365, 102 S.Ct. 2466, 2484, 73 L.Ed.2d 48 (1982) * * * The essential contribution made by the NCAA's arrangement is to define the number of games that may be televised, to establish the price for each exposure, and to define the basic terms of each contract between the network and a home team. The NCAA does not, however, act as a selling agent for any school or for any conference of schools. The selection of individual games, and the negotiation of particular agreements, are matters left to the networks and the individual schools. Thus, the effect of the network plan is not to eliminate individual sales of broadcasts, since these still occur, albeit subject to fixed prices and output limitations. Unlike Broadcast Music's blanket license covering broadcast rights to a large number of individual compositions, here the same rights are still sold on an individual basis, only in a non-competitive market.

The District Court did not find that the NCAA's television plan produced any procompetitive efficiencies which enhanced the competitiveness of college football television rights; to the contrary it concluded that NCAA football could be marketed just as effectively without the television plan. There is therefore no predicate in the findings for petitioner's efficiency justification. Indeed, petitioner's argument is refuted by the District Court's finding concerning price and output. If the NCAA's television plan produced procompetitive efficiencies, the plan would increase output and reduce the price of televised games. The District Court's contrary findings accordingly undermine petitioner's position. In light of these findings, it cannot be said that "the agreement on price is necessary to market the product at all." * * * In Broadcast Music, the availability of a package product that no individual could offer enhanced the total volume of music that was sold. Unlike this case, there was no limit of any kind placed on the volume that might be sold in the entire market and each individual remained free to sell his own music without restraint. Here production has been limited, not enhanced. No individual school is free to televise its own games without restraint. The NCAA's efficiency justification is not supported by the record.

V

Throughout the history of its regulation of intercollegiate football telecasts, the NCAA has indicated its concern with protecting live attendance. This concern, it should be noted, is not with protecting live attendance at games which are shown on television; that type of interest is not at issue in this case. Rather, the concern is that fan interest in a televised game may adversely affect ticket sales for games that will not appear on television.

Although the NORC studies in the 1950's provided some support for the thesis that live attendance would suffer if unlimited television were permitted, the District Court found that there was no evidence to support that theory in today's market. Moreover, as the District Court found, the television plan has evolved in a manner inconsistent with its original design to protect gate attendance. Under the current plan, games are shown on television during all hours that college football games are played. The plan simply does not protect live attendance by ensuring that games will not be shown on television at the same time as live events. * * *

There is, however, a more fundamental reason for rejecting this defense. The NCAA's argument that its television plan is necessary to protect live attendance is not based on a desire to maintain the integrity of college football as a distinct and attractive product, but rather on a fear that the product will not prove sufficiently attractive to draw live attendance when faced with competition from televised games. At bottom the NCAA's position is that ticket sales for most college games are unable to compete in a free market. The television plan protects ticket sales by limiting output—just as any monopolist increases revenues by reducing output. By seeking to insulate live ticket sales from the full spectrum of competition because of its assumption that the product itself is insufficiently attractive to consumers, petitioner forwards a justification that is inconsistent with the basic policy of the Sherman Act. "[T]he Rule of Reason does not support a defense based on the assumption that competition itself is unreasonable." Professional Engineers, 435 U.S., at 696, 98 S.Ct., at 1368.

* * *

The NCAA plays a critical role in the maintenance of a revered tradition of amateurism in college sports. There can be no question but that it needs ample latitude to play that role, or that the preservation of the student-athlete in higher education adds richness and diversity to intercollegiate athletics and is entirely consistent with the goals of the Sherman Act. But consistent with the Sherman Act, the role of the NCAA must be to preserve a tradition that might otherwise die; rules that restrict output are hardly consistent with this role. Today we hold only that the record supports the District Court's conclusion that by curtailing output and blunting the ability of member institutions to respond to consumer preference, the NCAA has restricted rather than enhanced the place of intercollegiate athletics in the Nation's life. Accordingly, the judgment of the Court of Appeals is

Affirmed.

* * *

V. MEMBERSHIP IN TRADE ASSOCIATIONS

Because many business leagues, particularly professional organizations, control a practice or trade, courts have reviewed the application and expulsion practices and procedures of such organizations.

AUSTIN v. AMERICAN ASSOCIATION OF NEUROLOGICAL SURGEONS
United States Court of Appeals, Seventh Circuit, 2001
253 F.3d 967

POSNER, Circuit Judge.

Donald C. Austin, a neurosurgeon, was suspended for six months by the American Association of Neurological Surgeons, a voluntary association incorporated under Illinois law as a not-for-profit corporation, to which he belonged (he has since resigned). He brought this suit against the Association claiming that he had been suspended in "revenge" for having testified as an expert witness for the plaintiff in a medical malpractice suit brought against another member of the Association, a Dr. Ditmore. Austin argues that the suspension violated Illinois law (federal jurisdiction is based on the parties' being citizens of different states) and seeks damages measured by the decline in his expert-witness income as a consequence of the suspension. He also seeks an injunction expunging the record of the suspension, but he does not seek reinstatement to membership.

Ordinarily a dispute between a voluntary association and one of its members is governed by the law of contracts, the parties' contractual obligations being defined by the charter, bylaws, and any other rules or regulations of the association that are intended to create legally enforceable obligations. See, e.g., * * * (2001); *Robinson v. Kansas State High School Activities Ass'n, Inc.*, 260 Kan. 136, 917 P.2d 836, 844 (1996); 2 Marilyn E. Phelan, *Nonprofit Enterprises: Corporations, Trusts, and Associations* § 14:03, p. 14–12 (2000). Austin does not argue that in suspending him the Association was violating any of its contractual obligations to him. But recognizing that membership in good standing in a professional association may be essential to a professional's livelihood, Illinois like other states has conferred additional legal rights on members of voluntary associations (not limited to professional associations). A member who can show that the association's action of which he complains substantially impaired an "important economic interest" of his can base suit on procedural irregularities (denial of "due process") or bad faith as well as on the usual contractual grounds. * * * The cases add to the list of grounds for such a suit violation of the association's charter or bylaws and contravention of public policy, but the former ground (violation of charter or bylaws) is just another way of assimilating voluntary-association law to contract law (see, besides the cases cited earlier, * * * and the latter too, since illegality is a conventional basis in contract law for rescinding a contract, * * * including a bylaw or charter provision pursuant to which a member of a voluntary association has been expelled. * * * What "bad faith" adds to the litany of grounds is obscure; it can be regarded either as a component of the due process analysis, analogous to the requirement of an impartial tribunal in an ordinary due process case, or as an implied term in the contract between the association and its members.

There were no procedural irregularities here—Austin received notice and a full hearing (with counsel) before a panel of Association members not implicated in his dispute with Ditmore. The complaint is rather that the Association acted in bad faith because it never disciplines members who testify on behalf of malpractice defendants as distinct from malpractice plaintiffs and that it is against public policy for a professional association to discipline a member on the basis of trial testimony unless the testimony was intentionally false.

Austin had been retained to testify on behalf of a woman whose recurrent laryngeal nerve was permanently damaged in the course of an anterior cervical fusion performed by Dr. Ditmore, resulting in a paralyzed vocal cord, difficulty in swallowing, and shortness of breath that ultimately required her to undergo a tracheostomy. An anterior cervical fusion is an operation to repair a herniated spinal disc at the back of the neck. The operation is called "anterior" because the surgeon cuts into the spine from the front, that is, through the neck, being careful to push aside ("retract," in medical lingo) the tissues in front of the spine. According to the testimony that Austin was permitted to give at trial, he believes and "the majority of neurosurgeons" would concur that the plaintiff could not have suffered a permanent injury to her recurrent laryngeal nerve unless Dr. Ditmore had been careless, because she had no anatomical abnormality that might have enabled such an injury to result without negligence on the surgeon's part—though in the disciplinary hearing it emerged that, because the recurrent laryngeal nerve is difficult to see, and often is not seen during the operation, it may be impossible to determine whether the particular patient's nerve is unusually susceptible to injury. Austin testified that Ditmore must have rushed the operation (though there was no other evidence of that) and as a result retracted the tissues adjacent to the recurrent laryngeal nerve too roughly. As Ditmore pointed out at the hearing, however, Austin could hardly be considered an expert on anterior cervical fusion, having performed only 25 to 30 of them in more than 30 years in practice, although he had performed a large number of other cervical operations. Ditmore in contrast had performed 700 anterior cervical fusions—with exactly one case of permanent damage to a patient's recurrent laryngeal nerve, namely the case of the patient who had sued him.

Dr. Austin claimed at the hearing that he had based his opinion on an article by a Dr. Ralph Cloward, described by Austin as the "father" of anterior cervical fusion, which had concluded that "serious complications are avoidable and can be prevented by the surgeon adhering strictly to the surgical technique described for" an anterior cervical fusion; and on another article, which Austin did not date, or identify other than by the last name of the author, Watkins, which states that "the key to prevention of traction injuries to the [recurrent laryngeal] nerve is not to retract vigorously into the soft tissues." Although neither side's lawyer appears to have been aware of the fact, both articles are reprinted in full in the appellate record—in fact twice. The citations are Ralph B. Cloward, "Complications of Anterior Cervical Disc Operation and Their Treatment," 69 *Surgery* 175, 182 (1971); Robert G. Watkins, "Cervical, Thoracic, and Lumbar Complications—Anterior Approach," in *Complications of Spine Surgery* 211, 221 (Steven R. Garfin ed. 1989).

Neither article supports Austin's testimony. Cloward was making a general statement of reassurance about the avoidability of serious complications of his pet operation, not anything specifically to do with the risk of permanent damage to the recurrent laryngeal nerve. Watkins never suggested that all traction injuries to the recurrent laryngeal nerve could be prevented by gentle retraction. Austin admitted that he hadn't discussed the matter with any other medical professionals. Expert evidence contrary to Austin's was given and the jury returned a verdict for Ditmore. That was in 1995. Ditmore promptly complained to the Association and Austin was suspended in 1997 following a hearing at which he and Ditmore testified, the latter to the effect that Austin had no basis for testifying that most neurosurgeons agreed with his view. This suit followed quickly on the heels of the suspension, and the district court granted summary judgment in favor of the Association.

* * *

The dismissal of Austin's suit was unquestionably correct. To begin with, he failed to show that an "important economic interest," as the Illinois cases interpret the term, is at stake. Membership in the American Association of Neurological Surgeons is not a precondition to the practice of neurosurgery. The AANS is not even the only association of such surgeons, though we were told without contradiction that it is the premier one. Austin continues to practice neurosurgery notwithstanding his suspension and subsequent voluntary resignation from the Association, and he doesn't even seek reinstatement—only damages and expungement of the record of his disciplinary suspension. Indeed, despite the suspension, he continues to testify extensively as an expert witness in medical malpractice cases. True, his income from testifying has fallen to 35 percent of what it was before the suspension, when it was more than $220,000 a year. Austin's brief describes this drop in income as "disastrous" and "catastrophic," but that is a hyperbolic characterization. Thirty-five percent of $220,000 is a healthy $77,000—and this is merely as it were Dr. Austin's moonlighting income, income from a sideline to his primary profession, which is that of a neurosurgeon, not an expert witness (he does not claim the dubious title of "professional expert witness"). That is not the kind of professional body blow that the cases have in mind when they speak of an "important economic interest" jeopardized by the action of a voluntary association. * * * At the very least, the association's action must jeopardize the principal source of the professional's livelihood, and not a mere sideline. * * * Where membership is optional, expulsion (or suspension, or denial of admission) is not deemed the invasion of an important economic interest. * * *

But there is much more that is wrong with this suit. There is no basis for Austin's claim that the Association entertains only complaints against members who testify on behalf of malpractice plaintiffs. What is true is that to date all complaints (but there have been very few) have been against such members; but the reason is at once obvious and innocent. If a member of the Association is sued for malpractice and another member gives testimony for the plaintiff that the defendant believes is irresponsible, it is natural for the defendant to complain to the Association; a fellow member has irresponsibly labeled him negligent. If a member of the Association who testifies for a plaintiff happens to believe that the defendant's expert witness was irresponsible, he is much less likely to complain, because that expert (and fellow member of the Association) has not accused *him* of negligence or harmed him in his practice or forced him to stand trial or gotten him into trouble with his liability insurer. The asymmetry that Austin points to as evidence of bad faith is thus no evidence of bad faith at all; and he has no other evidence of bad faith.

In support of his further claim that it is against public policy for a professional association to sanction one of its members for irresponsible (as distinct from knowingly false) testimony, Austin argues that the threat of such sanctions is a deterrent to the giving of expert evidence and so a disservice to, indeed an interference with, the cause of civil justice. We disagree and think the courts of Illinois would likewise; this kind of professional self-regulation rather furthers than impedes the cause of justice. By becoming a member of the prestigious American Association of Neurological Surgeons, a fact he did not neglect to mention in his testimony in the malpractice suit against Ditmore, Austin boosted his credibility as an expert witness. The Association had an interest—the community at large had an interest—in Austin's not being able to use his membership to dazzle judges and juries and deflect the close and skeptical scrutiny that shoddy testimony deserves. It is no answer that judges can be trusted to keep out such testimony. Judges are not experts in any field except law. Much escapes us, especially in a highly technical field, such as neurosurgery. When a member of a prestigious professional association makes representations not on their face absurd, such as that a majority of neurosurgeons believe that a particular type of mishap is invariably the result of surgical negligence, the judge may have no basis for questioning the belief, even if the defendant's expert testifies to the contrary.

* * *

AFFIRMED.

* * *

Chapter 15

POLITICAL ORGANIZATIONS

A political organization is a party, committee, association, fund, or other organization (whether or not incorporated) organized and operated primarily for the purpose of accepting, directly or indirectly, contributions, or making expenditures, for the purpose of promoting the nomination of an individual for an elective public office in a primary election or in a meeting or caucus of a political party. A segregated fund established and maintained by an individual may qualify as a political organization. A political organization qualifies under § 527 of the Code as a tax exempt organization with respect to its receipt of political contributions, membership fees, dues, and assessments (discussion *infra*).

I. REGULATION OF POLITICAL ORGANIZATIONS

Political committees, including clubs, associations, or groups of persons, that receive contributions or make expenditures aggregating in excess of $1,000 during a calendar year to nominate or elect candidates to federal offices are subject to regulation under the Federal Election Campaign Act of 1971 (2 U.S.C. §§ 431–455). The act imposes limitations on the contributions and expenditures of funds in political campaigns for federal offices and is implemented by the Federal Election Commission. For example, contributions to a candidate for federal office, and to the candidate's political committee for election to a federal office, are limited to $2,100 per person [2 U.S.C. §§ 441a(1)(A)]. However, a person may contribute up to $26,700 in a year to the political committees established and maintained by a national political party (that are not the authorized political committees of any candidate), or up to $5,000 for any other political committee [2 U.S.C. §§ 441a(1)(B) and (C)]. A corporation or a labor organization is prohibited from making any political contributions or expenditures unless it establishes a separate, segregated fund for such purposes [2 U.S.C. § 441b].

FEDERAL ELECTION COMMISSION v. BEAUMONT
United States Supreme Court, 2003
539 U.S. 146, 123 S.Ct. 2200, 156 L.Ed.2d 179

Justice SOUTER delivered the opinion of the Court.

Since 1907, federal law has barred corporations from contributing directly to candidates for federal office. We hold that applying the prohibition to nonprofit advocacy corporations is consistent with the First Amendment.

I

The current statute makes it "unlawful ... for any corporation whatever ... to make a contribution or expenditure in connection with" certain federal elections, 90 Stat. 490, as renumbered and amended, 2 U.S.C. § 441b(a), "contribution or expenditure" each being defined to include "anything of value," § 441b(b)(2). The prohibition does not, however, forbid "the establishment, administration, and solicitation of contributions to a separate segregated fund to be utilized for political purposes." § 441b(b)(2)(C); see § 431(4)(B). Such a PAC (so called after the political action committee that runs it) may be wholly controlled by the sponsoring corporation, whose employees and stockholders or members generally may be solicited for contributions. See §§ 441b(b)(4)(B)-(C); *Federal Election Comm'n v. National Right to Work Comm.*, 459 U.S. 197, 200, n. 4, 103 S.Ct. 552, 74 L.Ed.2d 364 (1982). While federal law requires PACs to register and disclose their activities, §§ 432–434; see *Federal Election Comm'n v. Massachusetts Citizens for Life, Inc.*, 479 U.S. 238, 253–254, 107 S.Ct. 616, 93 L.Ed.2d 539 (1986), the law leaves them free to make contributions as well as other expenditures in connection with federal elections, § 441b(b)(2)(C).

Respondents are a corporation known as North Carolina Right to Life, Inc., three of its officers, and a North Carolina voter (here, together, NCRL), who have sued the Federal Election Commission, the independent agency set up to "administer, seek to obtain compliance with, and formulate policy with respect to" the federal electoral laws. § 437c(b)(1). NCRL challenges the constitutionality of § 441b and the FEC's regulations implementing that section, 11 CFR §§ 114.2(b), 114.10 (2003), but only so far as they apply to NCRL. The corporation is organized under the laws of North Carolina to provide counseling to pregnant women and to urge alternatives to abortion, and as a nonprofit advocacy corporation it is exempted from federal taxation by § 501(c)(4) of the Internal Revenue Code, 26 U.S.C. § 501(c)(4).* * * It has no shareholders and, although it receives some donations from traditional business corporations, it is "overwhelmingly funded by private contributions from individuals." * * *. NCRL has made contributions and expenditures in connection with state elections, but not federal, owing to 2 U.S.C. § 441b. Instead, it has established a PAC, the North Carolina Right to Life, Inc., Political Action Committee, which has contributed to federal candidates. See *North Carolina Right to Life, Inc. v. Bartlett,* 168 F.3d 705, 709 (C.A.4 1999), cert. denied, 528 U.S. 1153, 120 S.Ct. 1156, 145 L.Ed.2d 1069 (2000).

The District Court granted summary judgment to NCRL and held § 441b unconstitutional as applied to the corporation, both as to direct contributions and independent expenditures. 137 F.Supp.2d 648 (E.D.N.C.2000). A divided Court of Appeals for the Fourth Circuit affirmed, 278 F.3d 261 (2002), relying primarily on *Massachusetts Citizens for Life,* in which this Court held it unconstitutional to apply the statute to independent expenditures by Massachusetts Citizens for Life, Inc., a nonprofit advocacy corporation in some respects like NCRL. The Court of Appeals ruled, first, that the prohibition on independent expenditures may not be applied to NCRL. Although the panel acknowledged that Massachusetts Citizens for Life, unlike NCRL, had a formal policy against accepting corporate donations, see *Massachusetts Citizens for Life, supra,* at 263–264, 107 S.Ct. 616 (describing this feature of the organization as "essential to our holding"), it nevertheless treated NCRL as materially indistinguishable from Massachusetts Citizens for Life.

To the point for present purposes, the Court of Appeals went on to hold the ban on direct contributions likewise unconstitutional as applied to NCRL. While the majority of the divided court recognized that regulation of campaign contributions has received greater deference under First Amendment cases than regulation of independent expenditures,* * * it held the ban on direct contributions unjustified as applied to "[*Massachusetts Citizens for Life*]-type corporations," which it thought "pose[d] no risk of 'unfair deployment of wealth for political purposes.'" * * * The Court of Appeals reasoned that "[t]he rationale utilized by the Court in *[Massachusetts Citizens for Life]* to declare prohibitions on independent expenditures unconstitutional as applied to [the advocacy corporation involved there] is equally applicable in the context of direct contributions." * * * Judge Gregory dissented from the others on this point, since he saw no way to square their conclusion with this Court's reasoning in *National Right to Work.* * * *

After the Fourth Circuit divided 7 to 4 in denying rehearing en banc, the FEC petitioned for certiorari solely as to the constitutionality of the ban on direct contributions.* * * Because on that issue the Fourth Circuit is in conflict with the Sixth, see *Kentucky Right to Life, Inc. v. Terry,* 108 F.3d 637, 645–646 (1997) (upholding a provision of Kentucky law analogous to § 441b), we granted certiorari, * * *. We now reverse.

II

A

Any attack on the federal prohibition of direct corporate political contributions goes against the current of a century of congressional efforts to curb corporations' potentially "deleterious influences on federal elections," which we have canvassed a number of times before. * * *

The current law grew out of a "popular feeling" in the late 19th century "that aggregated capital unduly influenced politics, an influence not stopping short of corruption." * * * A demand for congressional action gathered force in the campaign of 1904, which made a national issue of the political leverage exerted through corporate contributions, and after the election and new revelations of corporate political overreaching, President Theodore Roosevelt made banning corporate political contributions a legislative priority. * * * Although some congressional proposals would have "prohibited political contributions by [only] certain classes of corporations," * * * the momentum was "for elections 'free from the power of money,' * * * and Congress acted on the President's call for an outright ban, not with half measures, but with the Tillman Act, ch. 420, 34 Stat. 864. This "first federal campaign finance law" * * * banned "any corporation whatever" from making "a money contribution in connection with" federal elections * * *.

Since 1907, there has been continual congressional attention to corporate political activity, sometimes resulting in refinement of the law, sometimes in overhaul.* * * One feature, however, has stayed intact throughout this "careful legislative adjustment of the federal electoral laws," * * * and much of the periodic amendment was meant to strengthen the original, core prohibition on direct corporate contributions. The Foreign Corrupt Practices Act of 1925, for example, broadened the ban on contributions to include "anything of value," and criminalized the act of receiving a contribution to match the criminality of making one.* * * So, in another instance, the 1947 Labor Management Relations Act drew labor unions permanently within the law's reach and invigorated the earlier prohibition to include "expenditure[s]" as well.* * *

Today, as in 1907, the law focuses on the "special characteristics of the corporate structure" that threaten the integrity of the political process. *National Right to Work,* 459 U.S., at 209, 103 S.Ct. 552; see *id.,* at 207, 103 S.Ct. 552; see also *Austin v. Michigan Chamber of Commerce,* 494 U.S. 652, 658–659, 110 S.Ct. 1391, 108 L.Ed.2d 652 (1990); *Massachusetts Citizens for Life,* 479 U.S., at 257–258, 107 S.Ct. 616; *Federal Election Comm'n v. National Conservative Political Action Comm.,* 470 U.S. 480, 500–501, 105 S.Ct. 1459, 84 L.Ed.2d 455 (1985). As we explained it in *Austin,*

> "State law grants corporations special advantages—such as limited liability, perpetual life, and favorable treatment of the accumulation and distribution of assets—that enhance their ability to attract capital and to deploy their resources in ways that maximize the return on their shareholders' investments. These state-created advantages not only allow corporations to play a dominant role in the Nation's economy, but also permit them to use 'resources amassed in the economic marketplace' to obtain 'an unfair advantage in the political marketplace' " * * *

Hence, the public interest in "restrict[ing] the influence of political war chests funneled through the corporate form." *National Conservative Political Action Comm., supra,* at 500–501, 105 S.Ct. 1459; * * * .

As these excerpts from recent opinions show, not only has the original ban on direct corporate contributions endured, but so have the original rationales for the law. In barring corporate earnings from conversion into political "war chests," the ban was and is intended to "preven[t] corruption or the appearance of corruption." * * * But the ban has always done further duty in protecting "the individuals who have paid money into a corporation or union for purposes other than the support of candidates from having that money used to support political candidates to whom they may be opposed." * * *

Quite aside from war-chest corruption and the interests of contributors and owners, however, another reason for regulating corporate electoral involvement has emerged with restrictions on individual contributions, and recent cases have recognized that restricting contributions by various organizations hedges against their use as conduits for "circumvention of [valid] contribution limits." * * * To the degree that a corporation could contribute to political candidates, the individuals "who created it, who own it, or whom it employs," * * * could exceed the bounds imposed on their own contributions by diverting money through the corporation, * * *. As we said on the subject of limiting coordinated expenditures by political parties, experience "demonstrates how candidates, donors, and parties test the limits of the current law, and it shows beyond serious doubt how contribution limits would be eroded if inducement to circumvent them were enhanced." * * *

In sum, our cases on campaign finance regulation represent respect for the "legislative judgment that the special characteristics of the corporate structure require particularly careful regulation." * * * And we have understood that such deference to legislative choice is warranted particularly when Congress regulates campaign contributions, carrying as they do a plain threat to political integrity and a plain warrant to counter the appearance and reality of corruption and the misuse of corporate advantages. * * * As we said in *Colorado Republican,* "limits on contributions are more clearly justified by a link to political corruption than limits on other kinds of ... political spending are (corruption being understood not only as *quid pro quo* agreements, but also as undue influence on an officeholder's judgment, and the appearance of such influence)." * * *

B

That historical prologue would discourage any broadside attack on corporate campaign finance regulation or regulation of corporate contributions, and NCRL accordingly questions § 441b only to the extent the law places nonprofit advocacy corporations like itself under the general ban on direct contributions. But not even this more focused challenge can claim a blank slate, for Judge Gregory rightly said in his dissent that our explanation in *National Right to Work* all but decided the issue against NCRL's position.

National Right to Work addressed the provision of § 441b restricting a nonstock corporation to its membership when soliciting contributions to its PAC,* * * and we considered whether a nonprofit advocacy corporation without members of the usual sort could be held to violate the law by soliciting a donation to its PAC from any individual who had at one time contributed to the corporation.* * * We sustained the FEC's position that a fund drive as broad as this went beyond the solicitation of "members" permitted by § 441b, and we invoked the history distilled above in holding that the statutory restriction was no infringement on those First Amendment associational rights closely akin to speech.* * * We concluded that the congressional judgment to regulate corporate political involvement "warrants considerable deference" and "reflects a permissible assessment of the dangers posed by [corporations] to the electoral process." * * *

It would be hard to read our conclusion in *National Right to Work,* that the PAC solicitation restrictions were constitutional, except on the practical understanding that the corporation's capacity to make contributions was legitimately limited to indirect donations within the scope allowed to PACs.* * * In fact, we specifically rejected the argument made here, that deference to congressional judgments about proper limits on corporate contributions turns on details of corporate form or the affluence of particular corporations. In the same breath, we remarked on the broad applicability of § 441b to "corporations and labor unions without great financial resources, as well as those more fortunately situated," and made a point of refusing to "second-guess a legislative determination as to the need for prophylactic measures where corruption is the evil feared." * * *

Later cases have repeatedly acknowledged, without questioning, the reading of *National Right to Work* as generally approving the § 441b prohibition on direct contributions, even by nonprofit corporations "without great financial resources." In *National Conservative Political Action Committee,* for example, we not only spoke of *National Right to Work* as consistent with "the well-established constitutional validity of legislative regulation of corporate contributions to candidates for public office," but went on to reaffirm that the Court in that case had "rightly concluded that Congress might include, along with labor unions and corporations traditionally prohibited from making contributions to political candidates, membership corporations, though contributions by the latter might not exhibit all of the evil that contributions by traditional economically organized corporations exhibit." * * * Relying again on *National Right to Work,* we made a similar point in *Austin* when we sustained Michigan's ban on direct corporate contributions, even though the ban "include[d] within its scope closely held corporations that do not possess vast reservoirs of capital." * * * "Although some closely held corporations, just as some publicly held ones, may not have accumulated significant amounts of wealth, they receive from the State the special benefits conferred by the corporate structure and present the potential for distorting the political process. This potential for distortion justifies [the state law's] general applicability to all corporations." * * *

But *National Right to Work* does not stand alone in its bearing on the issue here, and equal significance must be accorded to *Massachusetts Citizens for Life,* the very case upon which NCRL and the Court of Appeals have placed principal reliance. There, we held the prohibition on independent expenditures under § 441b unconstitutional as applied to a nonprofit advocacy corporation. While the majority explained generally that the "potential for unfair deployment of wealth for political purposes" fell short of justifying a ban on expenditures by groups like Massachusetts Citizens for Life that "do not pose that danger of corruption," the majority's response to the dissent pointed to a different resolution of the present case. * * * THE CHIEF JUSTICE's dissenting opinion noted that Massachusetts Citizens for Life "was not unlike" the corporation at issue in *National Right to Work,* which he read as supporting the ban on independent expenditures. * * * Without disagreeing about the similarity of the two organizations, the majority nonetheless distinguished *National Right to Work* on the ground of its addressing regulation of contributions, not expenditures. * * *

C

The upshot is that, although we have never squarely held against NCRL's position here, we could not hold for it without recasting our understanding of the risks of harm posed by corporate political contributions, of the expressive significance of contributions, and of the consequent deference owed to legislative judgments on what to do about them. NCRL's efforts, however, fail to unsettle existing law on any of these points.

First, NCRL argues that on a class-wide basis "*[Massachusetts Citizens for Life]*-type corporations pose no potential of threat to the political system," so that the governmental interest in combating corruption is as weak as the Court held it to be in relation to the particular corporation considered in *Massachusetts Citizens for Life.* * * * But this generalization does not hold up. For present purposes, we will assume advocacy corporations are generally different from traditional business corporations in the improbability that contributions they might make would end up supporting causes that some of their members would not approve. * * * But concern about the corrupting potential underlying the corporate ban may indeed be implicated by advocacy corporations. They, like their for-profit counterparts, benefit from significant "state-created advantages," * * * and may well be able to amass substantial "political 'war chests,'" * * *. Not all corporations that qualify for favorable tax treatment under § 501(c)(4) of the Internal Revenue Code lack substantial resources, and the category covers some of the Nation's most politically powerful organizations, including the AARP, the National Rifle Association, and the Sierra Club.* * * Nonprofit advocacy corporations are, moreover, no less susceptible than traditional business companies to misuse as conduits for circumventing the contribution limits imposed on individuals. * * *

Second, NCRL argues that application of the ban on its contributions should be subject to a strict level of scrutiny, on the ground that § 441b does not merely limit contributions, but bans them on the basis of their source. * * * This argument, however, overlooks the basic premise we have followed in setting First Amendment standards for reviewing political financial restrictions: the level of scrutiny is based on the importance of the "political activity at issue" to effective speech or political association. * * * Going back to *Buckley v. Valeo,* 424 U.S. 1, 96 S.Ct. 612, 46 L.Ed.2d 659 (1976), restrictions on political contributions have been treated as merely "marginal" speech restrictions subject to relatively complaisant review under the First Amendment, because contributions lie closer to the edges than to the core of political expression. * * * "While contributions may result in political expression if spent by a candidate or an association ... , the transformation of contributions into political debate involves speech by someone other than the contributor." * * * This is the reason that instead of requiring contribution regulations to be narrowly tailored to serve a compelling governmental interest, "a contribution limit involving 'significant interference' with associational rights" passes muster if it satisfies the lesser demand of being " 'closely drawn' to match a 'sufficiently important interest.' " * * *

Indeed, this recognition that degree of scrutiny turns on the nature of the activity regulated is the only practical way to square two leading cases: *National Right to Work* approved strict solicitation limits on a PAC organized to make contributions, * * * whereas *Massachusetts Citizens for Life* applied a compelling interest test to invalidate the ban on an advocacy corporation's expenditures in light of PAC regulatory burdens,* * *. Each case involved § 441b, after all, and the same "ban" on the same corporate "sources" of political activity applied in both cases.

It is not that the difference between a ban and a limit is to be ignored; it is just that the time to consider it is when applying scrutiny at the level selected, not in selecting the standard of review itself. But even when NCRL urges precisely that, and asserts that § 441b is not sufficiently "closely drawn," the claim still rests on a false premise, for NCRL is simply wrong in characterizing § 441b as a complete ban. As we have said before, the section "permits some participation of unions and corporations in the federal electoral process by allowing them to establish and pay the administrative expenses of [PACs]." *National Right to Work, supra,* at 201, 103 S.Ct. 552 * * *. The PAC option allows corporate political participation without the temptation to use corporate funds for political influence, quite possibly at odds with the sentiments of some shareholders or members, and it lets the government regulate campaign activity through registration and disclosure, see §§ 432–434, without jeopardizing the associational rights of advocacy organizations' members, * * *

NCRL cannot prevail, then, simply by arguing that a ban on an advocacy corporation's direct contributions is bad tailoring. NCRL would have to demonstrate that the law violated the First Amendment in allowing contributions to be made only through its PAC and subject to a PAC's administrative burdens. But a unanimous Court in *National Right to Work* did not think the regulatory burdens on PACs, including restrictions on their ability to solicit funds, rendered a PAC unconstitutional as an advocacy corporation's sole avenue for making political contributions.* * * There is no reason to think the burden on advocacy corporations is any greater today, or to reach a different conclusion here.

III

The judgment of the Court of Appeals is reversed.

It is so ordered.

Campaigns for state and local offices are subject to state regulations regarding public disclosure of, and limitations on, campaign contributions and expenditures. However, the Federal Election Campaign Act has preempted state regulation of political contributions and expenditures by private individuals with respect to federal elections.

Each political committee that receives or expends in excess of $1,000 during a calendar year must file with the Federal Election Commission a statement of organization within ten days after its creation. Political committees must have a treasurer who must keep detailed records of all contributions made to or for the committee. Expenditures for or on behalf of a political committee may not be made without authorization of the treasurer or the treasurer's designated agent. Reports of receipts and expenditures must be filed with the Federal Election Commission.

Each individual who is a candidate for federal office must designate a political committee to serve as the candidate's principal campaign committee. Reports of receipts and expenditures of the candidate's principal campaign committee must be filed with the Federal Election Commission.

Note

1. All political committees that register and file reports with the FEC are 527 organizations, but not all 527 organizations are required to file with the FEC. Reporting requirements with the FEC apply only to political committees that solicit contributions or make expenditures for the major purpose of nominating or electing candidates or to expenditures by political committees made with authorization, consent or control of candidates. Thus, nonprofit advocacy organizations generally do not fall within the limited definition of a political committee and are not required to file with the FEC. However, these organizations nonetheless may be 527 organizations. As such, they now must file reports with the Internal Revenue Service. See discussion of § 527(i), *infra*, that lists the 527 organizations that are required to file with the IRS.

2. In *Chamber of Commerce of the United States v. Federal Election Commission*, 540 U.S. 93, 124 S.Ct. 619, 157 L.Ed.2d 491 (2003), the Supreme Court addressed the constitutionality of the Bipartisan Campaign Reform Act of 2002, which amended the Federal Election Campaign Act (BCRA) of 1971 "to purge national politics of what [is] conceived to be the pernicious influence of 'big money' campaign contributions." Congress sought to address three important developments since the Supreme Court's decision in *Buckley v. Valeo*, 424 U.S. 1, 96 S.Ct. 612, 46 L.Ed.2d 659 (1976): the increased importance of "soft money," the proliferation of "issue ads," and the 'disturbing' findings of a Senate investigation into campaign practices related to the 1996 federal elections. Title I of the BCRA regulates the use of soft money by political parties, officeholders, and candidates; Title II primarily prohibits corporations and unions from using general treasury funds for communications that are intended to, or have the effect of, influencing federal election outcomes; and Titles III, IV, and V set out other requirements. The Court ruled that Titles I and II (Congress' effort to plug the soft-money loophole and its regulation of electioneering communications) were constitutional. It ruled unconstitutional § 318 of the Act, which added FECA § 324 to prohibit individuals 17 years old or younger from making contributions to candidates and contributions or donations to political parties. The Supreme Court held that political parties and candidates can be banned from using "soft money" for federal election activities; the ban on part donations to tax exempt entities was generally valid; "soft money" cannot be used for issue ads which clearly identify a candidate; the statutory definition of "electioneering communications" was valid; the cost of third-party issue ads coordinated with a federal candidate's campaign could validly be considered as a contribution to those campaigns; labor union and corporations generally were required to pay for issue ads from separately segregated funds; the prohibition on political donations by minors was invalid; and the requirement that broadcasters disclose their records for air time political ads was valid.

II. TAXATION OF POLITICAL ORGANIZATIONS

Political committees and parties are treated as political organizations for tax purposes and must file income tax returns (on Form 1120–POL). They qualify for tax exempt status because political activity as such is not a trade or business that is appropriately subject to tax.

Political organizations are exempt from income taxes on their "exempt function income" pursuant to § 527 of the Internal Revenue Code. Exempt function income, which is not taxed to the organization, includes contributions of money or other property, or the receipt of membership fees, dues or assessments if the funds are segregated in separate accounts to be used solely for the nomination of political candidates. Expenditures from the fund to participate or intervene in political campaigns are exempt function expenditures and are not taxed pursuant to § 527(f) of the Internal Revenue Code.

Amounts expended by a political organization for an exempt function are not income to the individual on whose behalf the expenditures are made. However, should the political organization expend any other amount for the personal use of any individual, the amount is included in the individual's gross income. Any excess funds controlled by a political organization after a campaign or election are treated as expended for the personal use of the person having control over the ultimate use of the funds and, thus, are taxed to that individual. However, if the funds are transferred within a reasonable time to a public charity under § 509(a)(1) or (2), or to the general fund of the federal, state or local government, or are held in reasonable anticipation of being used by the political organization for future exempt functions, the funds will not be treated as excess funds. (See Treas. Reg. § 1.527–5.)

A political organization files a return annually on Form 1120–POL and pays tax on all income it receives other than exempt function income. The organization may deduct from its gross taxable income deductions that are directly incurred in connection with the production of the gross taxable income plus a specific deduction of $100. A political organization is not entitled to a net operating loss deduction. The organization's net taxable income is taxed at the highest corporation rate of 35 percent.

A political organization is required to file Form 1120–POL if it has taxable income in excess of the $100 deduction. A political organization with gross receipts of $25,000 or more is required to file Form 990 in addition to Form 1120–POL.[1] If the organization has gross receipts less than $100,000 and assets less than $25,000, it may file Form 990–EZ. Form 1120–POL is due on the 15th day of the third month after the close of the organization's taxable year. Form 990, or 990EZ, is due on the 15th day of the fifth month after the close of the organization's taxable year.

III. SEPARATE FUND FOR POLITICAL EXPENDITURES OF NONPROFIT ORGANIZATIONS

Although a tax exempt organization, other than § 501(c)(3) organizations, can engage in political activities, it will be subject to a tax under § 527(f) on its political expenditures unless it establishes a separate, segregated fund, which then will be treated as a political organization. Section 527(f) provides that any amount expended by a tax exempt organization for campaign activities will be taxed at the highest rate for corporations, which is 35 percent. The amount subject to tax under

---

1. For a "qualified" State or local political party (defined in footnote 3), the gross receipts threshold is $100,000. In addition, the following organizations are exempt from the information filing requirements: (1) a State or local committee of a political party, or a political committee of a State or local candidate, (2) a caucus or association of State or local officials, (3) an authorized committee of a candidate for Federal office, (4) a national committee of a political party, (5) a U.S. House of Representatives or U.S. Senate campaign committee of a political party committee, (6) a political committee required to report under the Federal Election Campaign Act of 1971, and (7) an organization described in § 501(c).

§ 527(f) is the lesser of the organization's net investment income or the amount expended for political purposes. However, if the organization establishes a separate, segregated fund to receive and disburse all funds related to the nomination of, or the opposition to, candidates for public office, the operation of such a segregated fund will remove the campaign type activities from the tax exempt organization's activities. The fund will be treated as an entity separate from the exempt organization that maintains the fund and will be treated as a political organization (a PAC). As such, it will not be taxed on its exempt function income.

Note

In Rev. Rul. 2004–6, the IRS ruled that because §§ 501(c)(4), (5), or (6) organizations, which publicly advocate positions on public policy issues, may include discussions of the positions of public official who are candidates for public office, a public policy advocacy communication may constitute an exempt function expenditure within the meaning of § 527(e)(2) and, thus, could be subject to tax under § 527(f). The Service stated that when an advocacy communication relating to a public policy issue does not advocate explicitly the election or defeat of a candidate, all the facts and circumstances must be considered to determine whether the expenditure is for an exempt function under § 527(e)(2). They are: (1) the communication identifies a candidate for a public office; (2) the timing of the communication coincides with an electoral campaign; (3) the communication targets voters in a particular election; (4) the communication identifies that candidate's position on the public policy issue which is the subject of the communication; (5) the position of the candidate on the public policy issue has been raised as distinguishing the candidate from others in the campaign, either in the communication itself or in other public communications; and (6) the communication is not part of an ongoing series of substantially similar advocacy communications by the organization on the same issue. Facts and circumstances that tend to show an advocacy communication on a public policy issue is not for an exempt function include, but are not limited to, the following: (2) the absence of any one or more of the six factors listed above; (2) the communication identifies specific legislation, or a specific event outside the control of the organization, that the organization hopes to influence; (3) the time of the communication coincides with a specific event outside the control of the organization that the organization hopes to influence; (4) the communication identifies the candidate solely as a governmental official who is a position to act on the public policy issue in connection with the specific event; and (5) the communication identifies the candidate solely in the list of key or principal sponsors of the legislation that is the subject of the communication.

Revenue Ruling 2004–6 also serves as a reminder that the Bipartisan Reform Act of 2002 (McCain–Feingold) does not replace the tax rules on public advocacy by tax-exempt organizations, such as those described in §§ 501(c)(4), (5), and (6). These organizations must adhere to both McCain–Feingold and the Internal Revenue Code.

IV. POLITICAL ACTIVITIES OF § 501(c)(3) ORGANIZATIONS

As discussed in Chapters 4 and 5, a § 501(c)(3) organization cannot participate or intervene, directly or indirectly, in any political campaign on behalf of, or in opposition to, any candidate for public office. [I.R.C. § 501(c)(3)] Establishing a segregated fund for these purposes is not permitted for a § 501(c)(3) organization.

Note

A § 501(c)(3) organization may establish a separate, segregated fund to avoid the § 527(f) tax on expenditures it might make for the purpose of influencing the selection, nomination or appointment of an individual to a *nonelective* public office, a federal judicial position, for example. Expenditures for supporting an nonelective candidate are not political campaign expenditures (because the expenditures are not incurred on behalf of, or in opposition to, a candidate for "elective" office), but they are deemed to constitute lobbying. As such, the expenditures will be taxed under § 527(f) unless they are incurred through a separate, segregated fund.[2]

Although a § 501(c)(3) organization cannot engage in political activities, it can establish another, completely separate entity, which would qualify for tax exempt status under another code section, such as § 501(c)(4), that could be involved in political activities.

BRANCH MINISTRIES v. ROSSOTTI
United States Court of Appeals, D.C. Circuit, 2000
211 F.3d 137

BUCKLEY, Senior Judge:

Four days before the 1992 presidential election, Branch Ministries, a tax-exempt church, placed full-page advertisements in two newspapers in which it urged Christians not to vote for then-presidential candidate Bill Clinton because of his positions on certain moral issues. The Internal Revenue Service concluded that the placement of the advertisements violated the statutory restrictions on organizations exempt from taxation and, for the first time in its history, it revoked a bona fide church's tax-exempt status because of its involvement in politics. Branch Ministries and its pastor, Dan Little, challenge the revocation on the grounds that (1) the Service acted beyond its statutory authority, (2) the revocation violated its right to the free exercise of religion guaranteed by the First

---

2. See Notice 88–76, 1988–2 C.B. 392 in which the IRS concluded that although attempts to influence the Senate confirmation of a federal judicial nominee would not constitute participation or intervention in a political campaign within the meaning of § 501(c)(3), any expenditures for that purpose would constitute lobbying. The IRS decided that a § 501(c)(3) organization would be taxed on such expenditures under § 527(f) unless it had established a separate, segregated fund to make such expenditures.

Amendment and the Religious Freedom Restoration Act, and (3) it was the victim of selective prosecution in violation of the Fifth Amendment. Because these objections are without merit, we affirm the district court's grant of summary judgment to the Service.

* * *

The Internal Revenue Code ("Code") exempts certain organizations from taxation, including those organized and operated for religious purposes, provided that they do not engage in certain activities, including involvement in "any political campaign on behalf of (or in opposition to) any candidate for public office." 26 U.S.C. § 501(a), (c)(3) (1994). Contributions to such organizations are also deductible from the donating taxpayer's taxable income. *Id.* § 170(a). * * *

* * *

Branch Ministries, Inc. operates the Church at Pierce Creek ("Church"), a Christian church located in Binghamton, New York. In 1983, the Church requested and received a letter from the IRS recognizing its tax-exempt status. On October 30, 1992, four days before the presidential election, the Church placed full-page advertisements in *USA Today* and the *Washington Times*. Each bore the headline "Christians Beware" and asserted that then-Governor Clinton's positions concerning abortion, homosexuality, and the distribution of condoms to teenagers in schools violated Biblical precepts. The following appeared at the bottom of each advertisement:

> This advertisement was co-sponsored by the Church at Pierce Creek, Daniel J. Little, Senior Pastor, and by churches and concerned Christians nationwide. Tax-deductible donations for this advertisement gladly accepted. Make donations to: The Church at Pierce Creek. [mailing address]. * * *

The advertisements did not go unnoticed. They produced hundreds of contributions to the Church from across the country and were mentioned in a *New York Times* article and an Anthony Lewis column which stated that the sponsors of the advertisement had almost certainly violated the Internal Revenue Code. * * *

The advertisements also came to the attention of the Regional Commissioner of the IRS, who notified the Church on November 20, 1992 that he had authorized a church tax inquiry based on "a reasonable belief ... that you may not be tax-exempt or that you may be liable for tax" due to political activities and expenditures. Letter from Cornelius J. Coleman, IRS Regional Commissioner, to The Church at Pierce Creek (Nov. 20, 1992)* * *. The Church denied that it had engaged in any prohibited political activity and declined to provide the IRS with certain information the Service had requested. On February 11, 1993, the IRS informed the Church that it was beginning a church tax examination. Following two unproductive meetings between the parties, the IRS revoked the Church's section 501(c)(3) tax-exempt status on January 19,

1995, citing the newspaper advertisements as prohibited intervention in a political campaign.

* * *

* * *Section 501(a) states that "[a]n organization described in subsection (c) ... shall be exempt from taxation...." *Id.* § 501(a). Those described in subsection (c) include corporations ... organized and operated exclusively for religious ... purposes ... which do[ ] not participate in, or intervene in (including the publishing or distributing of statements), any political campaign on behalf of (or in opposition to) any candidate for public office.

Id. § 501(c)(3). Similarly, section 170(c) allows taxpayers to deduct from their taxable income donations made to a corporation organized and operated exclusively for religious ... purposes ... which is not disqualified for tax exemption under section 501(c)(3) by reason of attempting to ... intervene in (including the publishing or distributing of statements), any political campaign on behalf of (or in opposition to) any candidate for public office.

Id. § 170(c)(2)(B), (D).

The Code, in short, specifically states that organizations that fail to comply with the restrictions set forth in section 501(c) are not qualified to receive the tax exemption that it provides.* * *

* * *

We also reject the Church's argument that it is substantially burdened because it has no alternate means by which to communicate its sentiments about candidates for public office. In *Regan v. Taxation With Representation,* 461 U.S. 540, 552–53, 103 S.Ct. 1997, 76 L.Ed.2d 129 (1983) (Blackmun, J., concurring), three members of the Supreme Court stated that the availability of such an alternate means of communication is essential to the constitutionality of section 501(c)(3)'s restrictions on lobbying. The Court subsequently confirmed that this was an accurate description of its holding. * * *

In *Regan,* the concurring justices noted that "TWR may use its present § 501(c)(3) organization for its nonlobbying activities and may create a § 501(c)(4) affiliate to pursue its charitable goals through lobbying." * * *

The Church has such an avenue available to it. As was the case with TWR, the Church may form a related organization under section 501(c)(4) of the Code. *See* 26 U.S.C. § 501(c)(4) (tax exemption for "[c]ivic leagues or organizations not organized for profit but operated exclusively for the promotion of social welfare"). Such organizations are exempt from taxation; but unlike their section 501(c)(3) counterparts, contributions to them are not deductible. * * * Although a section 501(c)(4) organization is also subject to the ban on intervening in political campaigns, *see* 26 C.F.R. § 1.501(c)(4)–1(a)(2)(ii) (1999), it may form a political action committee ("PAC") that would be free to participate in political campaigns.* * *

At oral argument, counsel for the Church doggedly maintained that there can be no "Church at Pierce Creek PAC." True, it may not itself create a PAC; but as we have pointed out, the Church can initiate a series of steps that will provide an alternate means of political communication that will satisfy the standards set by the concurring justices in *Regan*. Should the Church proceed to do so, however, it must understand that the related 501(c)(4) organization must be separately incorporated; and it must maintain records that will demonstrate that tax-deductible contributions to the Church have not been used to support the political activities conducted by the 501(c)(4) organization's political action arm. * * *

That the Church cannot use its tax-free dollars to fund such a PAC unquestionably passes constitutional muster. The Supreme Court has consistently held that, absent invidious discrimination, "Congress has not violated [an organization's] First Amendment rights by declining to subsidize its First Amendment activities." * * *

Because the Church has failed to demonstrate that its free exercise rights have been substantially burdened, we do not reach its arguments that section 501(c)(3) does not serve a compelling government interest or, if it is indeed compelling, that revocation of its tax exemption was not the least restrictive means of furthering that interest.

Nor does the Church succeed in its claim that the IRS has violated its First Amendment free speech rights by engaging in viewpoint discrimination. The restrictions imposed by section 501(c)(3) are viewpoint neutral; they prohibit intervention in favor of all candidates for public office by all tax-exempt organizations, regardless of candidate, party, or viewpoint. * * *

* * *

For the foregoing reasons, we find that the revocation of the Church's tax-exempt status neither violated the Constitution nor exceeded the IRS's statutory authority. The judgment of the district court is therefore

Affirmed.

Notes

1. Although a § 501(c)(3) organization can lose its tax exempt status for any involvement in a political campaign, small and often unintentional political campaign expenditures that may not cause a revocation of exempt status will be subject to a penalty tax under § 4955 of the Internal Revenue Code. Section 4955 provides the IRS a method of imposing sanctions on a § 501(c)(3) organization that incurs a limited, and often unintentional, amount of political campaign expenditures without having to revoke the organization's tax exempt status. The penalty tax initially is 10 percent of the amount of political campaign expenditures but will increase to 100

percent if the expenditure is not corrected. An expenditure is corrected if all or part, to the extent possible, is recovered and safeguards are established to prevent future expenditures.

2. In TAM 200437040 the Service ruled that a church would not lose its tax exempt status because of statements made by its minister who opposed a person's candidacy for President, but it decided the church would be subject to a penalty tax under § 4955. The Service stated that the minister's statements were imputed to the church when they were set out in official programs of the church. The only exception would be where the church clearly informed the members prior to the statements that the publication or program did not speak for the church and that the church did not utilize the minister or the publication to represent the views of the church. The Service held that the church would be liable for a 10 percent tax on the amount of each political expenditure and, because the church "did not clearly and unequivocally acknowledge" that the minister's statements about the presidential election might have been inappropriate until months later, the church was liable for a 100 percent tax on the amount of each political expenditure. In addition, it ruled that the minister would be liable for a 2 ½ percent tax initially and a 50 percent tax on the amount of each political expenditure.

V. REGISTRATION REQUIREMENTS FOR TAX EXEMPT POLITICAL ORGANIZATIONS

Since July 1, 2000, committees or organizations that engage in issue advocacy must register with the Internal Revenue Service. The Full and Fair Political Disclosure Act of 2000 added § 527(i) to the Code to require a political organization [except an organization that reasonably expects its annual gross receipts always to be less than $25,000, one that is required to report under the Federal Election Campaign Act of 1972, a "qualified"[3] State or local political organization, or an organization that has taxable income under § 527(f)] to notify the Internal Revenue Service that it is to be treated as a § 527 organization by filing Form 8871 within 24 hours of the date the organization is established. The organization reports on the form its name; address; electronic mailing address; purpose; the names and addresses of its officers, highly compensated employees, contact person, custodian of records, and members of its Board of Directors; and names and addresses of, and relationship to any related entities. Failure to file the form will cause the organization to be taxed on its exempt function income.

Every § 527 organization that accepts a contribution or makes an expenditure for an exempt function during the calendar year (except a

---

3. A "qualified" State or local political organization is an organization that does not engage in any exempt function activities other than to influence or attempt to influence the selection, nomination, election, or appointment of any individual to any State or local public office or office in a State or local political organization. In addition, the organization must be subject to a State law that requires the organization to report (and it does report) information regarding each separate expenditure and contribution that otherwise would be required to be reported to the Secretary.

political organization that is not required to file Form 8871 or a state or local committee of a political party or political committee of a state or local candidate) must file Form 8872 within 24 hours of the organization's formation and list the names of person who contributed $200 or more and the names of persons or entities to whom it made expenditures of $500 or more during a calendar year. The report is filed either quarterly (15th date after the last day of each calendar quarter in which the organization accepts a contribution or makes an expenditure) or monthly (20th day after the end of the month in which the organization accepts a contribution or makes an expenditure). In addition, the organization may be required to file a preelection report and a post-general election report. A preelection report must reflect all reportable contributions accepted and expenditures made through the 20th day before the election. The post-general election report must reflect all reportable contributions accepted and expenditures made through the 20th day after the general election. [An "election" means (a) any general, special, primary, or runoff election for a Federal office, (b) a convention or caucus of a political party that has authority to nominate a candidate for Federal office, (c) a primary election held for the selection of delegates to a national nominating convention of a political party, or (d) a primary election held for the expression of a preference for the nomination of individuals for election to the office of President.] A penalty of 35 percent of the total amount of contributions and expenditures that should have been reported is imposed on a § 527 organization for failure to file Form 8872 on the due date, or for failing to report all information required, or for reporting incorrect information. A political organization must make Form 8872 available for public inspection.

§ 527. Political organizations

* * *

(i) Organizations must notify Secretary that they are section 527 organizations.—

(1) In general.—Except as provided in paragraph (5), an organization shall not be treated as an organization described in this section—

(A) unless it has given notice to the Secretary, electronically and in writing, that it is to be so treated, or

(B) if the notice is given after the time required under paragraph (2), the organization shall not be so treated for any period before such notice is given or, in the case of any material change in the information required under paragraph (3), for a period beginning on the date on which the material change occurs and ending on the date on which such notice is given.

(2) Time to give notice.—The notice required under paragraph (1) shall be transmitted not later than 24 hours after the date on which the organization is established or, in the case of any material

change in the information required under paragraph (3), not later than 30 days after such material change.

(3) Contents of notice.—The notice required under paragraph (1) shall include information regarding—

    (A) the name and address of the organization (including any business address, if different) and its electronic mailing address,

    (B) the purpose of the organization,

    (C) the names and addresses of its officers, highly compensated employees, contact person, custodian of records, and members of its Board of Directors,

    (D) the name and address of, and relationship to, any related entities (within the meaning of section 168(h)(4)), and

    (E) whether the organization intends to claim an exemption from the requirements of subsection (j) or section 6033, and

    (F) such other information as the Secretary may require to carry out the internal revenue laws.

(4) Effect of failure.—In the case of an organization failing to meet the requirements of paragraph (1) for any period, the taxable income of such organization shall be computed by taking into account any exempt function income (and any deductions directly connected with the production of such income) or, in the case of a failure relating to a material change, by taking into account such income and deductions only during the period beginning on the date on which the material change occurs and ending on the date on which notice is given under this subsection. For purposes of the preceding sentence, the term "exempt function income" means any amount described in a subparagraph of subsection (c)93), whether or not segregated for use for an exempt function.

(5) Exceptions.—This subsection shall not apply to any organization—

    (A) to which this section applies solely by reason of subsection (f)(1), or

    (B) which reasonably anticipates that it will not have gross receipts of $25,000 or more for any taxable year, or

    (C) which is a political committee of a State or local candidate or which is a State or local committee of a political party.

(6) Coordination with other requirements.—This subsection shall not apply to any person required (without regard to this subsection) to report under the Federal Election Campaign Act of 1971 (2 U.S.C. 431 et seq.) as a political committee.

Note

In News Release 2004–110, the Service announced new steps to improve reporting and disclosure by § 527 political groups. The IRS noted that an organization which fails to report timely, fails to include all required information about contributions and disbursements, or that reports incorrect information will be required to pay 35 percent of the amount related to the failure. There is an exception for reasonable cause. The filings, as well as information on the filing requirements and upcoming dates, is available on the IRS website at www.irs.gov/polorgs. Form 8871, which is not available in paper form, is available on the above noted IRS website.

Chapter 16

HOMEOWNERS' ASSOCIATIONS

I. NATURE OF HOMEOWNERS' ASSOCIATIONS

The rise in land costs and the desire of homeowners to have recreational and other facilities that they could not afford alone led to the development of various forms of shared or "common" ownership of housing developments. The most common forms of shared ownership entities are condominiums, cooperatives, and planned residential real estate developments. A condominium is an interest in real property consisting of the exclusive ownership of an apartment or unit together with an undivided interest in common in the facilities of the building and grounds located on the property, which are used by all the residents. Real estate cooperatives are a form of apartments ownership, while planned residential real estate developments generally are composed of owners of single-family residential units located in a development area.

For federal tax purposes, a condominium management association and a residential real estate management association are treated the same. An incorporated homeowners' association may file as a regular corporation or may elect to be exempt from taxation under § 528 on its "exempt function income," which is income derived from owners of the residential units or lots in their capacity as members. An election to be taxed as a homeowners' association under § 528 is made by filing a properly completed Form 1120–H by the 15th day of the third month following the close of the association's taxable year. A separate election can be made each taxable year. An association is permitted a special deduction of $100, but is not permitted a net operating loss deduction.

To qualify under § 528, a homeowners' association must be organized and operated to provide for the acquisition, construction, management, maintenance, and care of association property. Substantially all the units, lots, or buildings must be used by individuals for residences. "Substantially all" means that at least 85 percent of the total square footage within the project must be used by individuals for residences or must be zoned for individuals' residences. (See Treas. Reg. § 1.518–4.) Unoccupied units constructed as residences, or last used as residences, will be considered used for residential purposes. Space used for auxiliary residential purposes, such as laundry rooms, parking spaces, recreational facilities and schools, are considered to be residential in nature. A unit that has a series of transient occupants, those who reside in the units for less than 30 days for at least one-half of the year, is not considered used for residential purposes.

Exempt function income includes income attributable to dues, fees, or assessments that arise solely from membership in the association. At least 60 percent of the association's gross income for the year must consist of these amounts. Dues, fees, and assessments based on the extent to which a member uses the facilities of the association are not exempt function income. Amounts received from nonmembers, from members for special use of the organization's facilities, interest earned on amounts set aside, amounts received for work performed on privately owned property that is not association property, and amounts received from members in return for transportation, are not exempt function income. The association will be taxed on these amounts.

At least 90 percent of an association's expenditures must be made for the acquisition, construction, management, maintenance, and care of association property. (See Treas. Reg. § 1.528–3.) Association property includes both real and personal property owned by the association or owned as tenants in common by members of the association. The property must be available for the common benefit of all members of the association and must be of a nature that tends to enhance the beneficial enjoyment of the private residences by their owners.

No part of the earnings of a homeowners' association may inure to the benefit of any private individual, other than by acquiring, constructing, or providing management, maintenance, and care of association property and other than by a rebate of excess membership dues, fees or assessments.

Note

Individuals making payments to homeowners' associations may deduct as itemized deductions that part of the payment which represents interest and taxes. The deduction is determined by dividing the number of shares owned by the individual by the total number of shares outstanding, including any shares held by the association, and multiplying the association's interest and taxes by this figure.

II. RIGHTS AND LIABILITIES OF MEMBERS

Members of homeowners' associations are subject to the covenants, restrictions, easements, conditions, and reservations set out in the declaration. In addition, they are governed by the bylaws of the association, which establish their responsibilities.

INWOOD NORTH HOMEOWNERS' ASSOCIATION, INC. v. HARRIS

Supreme Court, Texas, 1987
736 S.W.2d 632

ROBERTSON, Justice.

This case involves a suit between a homeowners' association and homeowners who are delinquent in their payment of neighborhood assessments. The issue before this court is whether the homestead laws of Texas protect the homeowners against foreclosure for their failure to pay the assessments.

The trial court granted a default judgment against the several homeowners in the amounts they were in arrears, but refused to allow the homeowners' association to foreclose on the homes to collect the sums due. The court of appeals affirmed, 707 S.W.2d 127. We reverse the judgment of the court of appeals.

In December 1980, Inwood North Associates filed a declaration of covenants and restrictions for the Inwood North subdivision in the Harris County real property records. The declaration provided that all the lots within the subdivision were impressed with certain covenants and restrictions and that such would run with the land and be binding upon all parties acquiring rights to any of the property therein. The declaration thereafter created Inwood North Homeowners' Association, a nonprofit corporation, to enforce the various restrictive covenants and to ensure the preservation of the uniform development plan. Under Article IV of the declaration, each person receiving a deed for a lot in the subdivision "is deemed to covenant and agree to pay the Association the following: (a) annual assessment or charges; and (b) special assessments for capital improvements." These assessments, plus interest and costs of collection, were designated to be "a charge on the land and shall be secured by a continuing Vendor's Lien upon the Lot against which such assessments or charges are made."

Many lots in the subdivision were bought between 1981–83, and the respondents here were among the purchasers. The deeds given to the various homeowners contained specific references to the maintenance charges, or in some cases to the property records where the declaration was filed. When some of the homeowners became lax in the payment of their assessment charges, the Association brought suit to recover the amounts due and sought to foreclose on the "Vendor's Lien" contained in the declaration. While many of the delinquent sums were subsequently received, several homeowners failed to settle their accounts. When these homeowners failed to appear at trial after being properly served, the trial court rendered a default judgment against them.

In upholding the trial court's refusal to order foreclosure, the court of appeals held that no proper vendor's lien was formed by the declarations, thus holding the homestead laws of this State precluded foreclosure. While we recognize that no vendor's lien was present, we disagree with the result reached by the court of appeals.

It is unquestioned that an owner of land may contract with respect to their property as they see fit, provided the contracts do not contravene public policy. * * * Therefore, the developer of the subdivision, as owner of all land subject to the declaration, is entitled to create liens on his land to secure the payment of assessments. * * * The declarations in question provided that the assessments "shall be secured by a continuing vendor's lien." It does not seem likely that a true vendor's lien exists in the present case because the assessment charges were not part of the purchase price of the property. Furthermore, there is no deed of trust which would have acknowledged the prior lien. * * * Much more probable is its existence as a contractual lien, as several older decisions hold that a contractual lien will be enforced regardless of the fact that it was improperly designated as a "vendor's lien." * * *

Creation of a contractual lien depends only on evidence apparent from the language of the agreement that the parties intended to create a lien. * * * Furthermore, under *Moore v. Smith,* 443 S.W.2d 552 (Tex. 1969), this court must consider the assessment provisions and lien as a whole and must not overthrow the clear and explicit intentions of the parties. * * * It seems clear from the language used in the agreement that the owner intended to provide for such liens, and we would be remiss in not conforming this decision to such an intent. With this decision made we turn to the crux of this case; the effect of Texas homestead law on the lien in question.

As a general rule, a homestead is protected against all debts of those who live in that homestead. * * *

* * *

* * * Homestead rights, however, may not be construed so as to avoid or destroy pre-existing rights. * * * It has long been held that an encumbrance existing against property cannot be affected by the subsequent impression of the homestead exception on the land. * * * As said by this court many years ago, "[A] previously acquired lien, whether general or special, voluntary or involuntary, cannot be subsequently defeated by the voluntary act of a debtor in attempting to make property his homestead." *Gage v. Neblett,* 57 Tex. 374, 378 (1882). Thus, we reaffirm that when the property has not become a homestead at the execution of the mortgage, deed of trust or other lien, the homestead protections have no application even if the property later becomes a homestead.

Thus, this case revolves around when the lien attached on the property. If it occurred simultaneously to or after the homeowners took title, there is authority which would deem the homestead right superior. * * * On the other hand, if the lien attached prior to the claimed homestead right and the lien is an obligation that would run with the land, there would be a right to foreclose.

In Texas, a covenant runs with the land when it touches and concerns the land; relates to a thing in existence or specifically binds the parties and their assigns; is intended by the original parties to run with the land; and when the successor to the burden has notice. * * * The covenant to pay maintenance assessments for the purpose of repairing and improving the common areas and recreational facilities of Inwood North touches and concerns the land. * * * The Declaration of Covenants evidences the intent of the original parties that the covenant run with the land, and the covenant specifically binds the parties, their successors and assigns. Because the property in question was conveyed in a succession of fee simple estates, the requirement of privity is satisfied. * * * Consequently, the covenant in question satisfies the requirements of a covenant running with the land. Furthermore, the deeds signed by each of the homeowners made reference to the assessments that would be due, thus each of the homeowners had notice of what their obligations were, and a purchaser with constructive notice of restrictive covenants becomes bound by them. * * * Moreover, a purchaser is bound by the terms of instruments in his chain of title. * * * Therefore, as the homeowners had constructive notice of the lien and foreclosure provisions in the declarations, they are bound by them.

The record discloses that the liens were contracted for several years before the homeowners took possession of their houses. Because the restrictions were placed on the land before it became the homestead of the parties, and because the restrictions contain valid contractual liens which run with the land, the homeowners were subject to the liens in question and an order of foreclosure would have been proper. * * *

Furthermore, a second and equally important theory supports our holding today. A homestead right in real property cannot rise any higher than the right, title or interest acquired by the homestead claimant. * * * A homestead may attach to an interest less than an unqualified fee simple title. A homestead may attach to any possessory interest, subject to the inherent characteristics and limitations of the right, title or interest in the property. * * * The homestead, however, will not operate to circumvent an inherent characteristic of the property acquired. * * * The concept of community association and mandatory membership is an inherent property interest. The declaration defines the rights and obligations of property ownership. The mutual and reciprocal obligation undertaken by all purchasers in Inwood Homes creates an inherent property interest possessed by each purchaser. The obligation to pay association dues and the corresponding right to demand that maximum services be provided within the association's budget are characteristics of that property interest. Moreover, the right to require that all property owners pay assessment fees is an inherent property right. That no owner has to pay more than a pro rata share is an essential characteristic of the property interest.

We see no distinction in pro rata fee simple ownership of common elements and in pro rata common ownership in an association, mandated by the declaration, which owns the common elements. The function of the association, with its attendant responsibilities, is the same in Inwood North as in *Johnson v. First Southern Properties, Inc.*, 687 S.W.2d 399 (Tex.App.—Houston [14th Dist.] 1985, writ ref'd n.r.e.)

The purchase of a lot in Inwood Homes carries with the purchase, as an inherent part of the property interest, the obligation to pay association fees for maintenance and ownership of common facilities and services. The remedy of foreclosure is an inherent characteristic of the property right. It is generally the only method by which other owners will not be forced to pay more than their fair share or be forced to accept reduced services. If we were not dealing with a homestead, no one would have a problem declaring that a lien exists to secure the payment of the Homeowners' Association assessments. Our focus in this case has been on whether the lien is enforceable against a homestead claim. In making that determination, we have considered the debt, the lien, the homestead claim, and the property interest to which the homestead attached. In so doing, we have found the lien in the present case to be superior, and worthy of protection against the homestead claim.

In conclusion, we hold that under the facts in the present case, the Homeowners' Association is entitled to the foreclosure of the contractual lien it has on the houses of delinquent owners. We recognize the harshness of the remedy of foreclosure, particularly when such a small sum is compared with the immeasurable value of a homestead. Under the laws of this state, however, we are bound to enforce the agreements into which the homeowners entered concerning the payment of assessments. Thus, the judgments of the trial court and court of appeals are reversed and we remand this cause to the trial court so that it may issue an order of foreclosure consistent with this opinion.

* * *

Question

Should there be limitations on the right of a homeowners' association to foreclose on property within the association for an owner's default in payment of assessments?

BROOKS v. NORTHGLEN ASSOCIATION

Supreme Court of Texas, 2004
141 S.W.3d 158

Justice JEFFERSON delivered the opinion of the court.

This is a declaratory judgment action involving eight property owners' challenge to their homeowners association's attempt to increase and accumulate annual assessments and impose late fees. The trial court held that chapter 204 of the Texas Property Code * * * authorized the Board to raise assessments unilaterally. The court of appeals affirmed the trial court's judgment in part and reversed in part. Both parties petitioned this Court for review. We granted the petitions to review the interplay between Texas Property Code chapter 204 and Northglen

Association's deed restrictions. We affirm the court of appeals' judgment in part, vacate in part, and reverse and render judgment in part.

Background

Northglen Association ("Northglen") is the homeowners association for six Harris County subdivisions or "sections" encompassing more than 1600 single-family residences. Each section is governed by a separate set of deed restrictions through which every property owner is a member of the Association. The restrictions subject each homeowner to an annual assessment that is deposited into a maintenance fund for such services as maintaining common areas, contracting for garbage disposal, and constructing parks. In 1994, Northglen's Board of Directors amended the deed restrictions to expand the Board and to assess late fees on unpaid assessments. Geneva Brooks and other Northglen property owners ("Brooks") organized a committee, called the Committee to Remove the Board, to remove certain Board members who, they complained, acted outside the bounds of the deed restrictions by adopting the amendments. Northglen responded by suing for injunctive and declaratory relief. Northglen sought an order enjoining the eight homeowners from conveying the false impression that Brooks's committee was formed pursuant to Northglen's bylaws and from other conduct designed to disrupt the Board's activities. Northglen also sought a judgment declaring that its actions in electing the Board and assessing late fees were valid exercises of its authority. Brooks counterclaimed for a declaratory judgment that Northglen had no authority to raise assessments or charge late fees without a vote of the property owners. Northglen eventually nonsuited its claims, and the case proceeded on Brooks's declaratory judgment action. The trial court granted summary judgment for Northglen, declaring that, without a vote of the homeowners, Northglen had the authority to: (1) raise the assessment for Sections One, Two, and Three; (2) raise the assessment for Sections Four, Five, and Six by ten percent each year or accumulate and assess the increase after a number of years; and (3) charge delinquent homeowners a $35 late fee. Finding that both parties had pursued legitimate interests, the trial court elected not to award attorney's fees.

The court of appeals affirmed the trial court's judgment in part and reversed in part. * * * It reversed as to Sections One, Two, and Three, holding that the deed restrictions did not permit annual assessments exceeding $120. As to Sections Four, Five, and Six, the court of appeals held that because the deed restrictions contained no language expressly forbidding accumulation, Northglen could accumulate previous assessments under Property Code section 204.010(16). * * * The court also held that section 204.010(10) gave Northglen the right to assess a $35 late fee in addition to the interest charge permitted by the deed restrictions. * * * Because the property owners did not have prior notice of the late fee, the court of appeals held that Northglen could not foreclose on any homesteads to collect those fees. The court of appeals affirmed the trial court's denial of attorney's fees. We hold that Northglen cannot accumulate unassessed fee increases because the language in the deed restrictions prevails over chapter 204, and we reverse that portion of the court of appeals' judgment. We affirm the portion of the court of appeals' judgment restricting increases in assessments to $120 and holding that Northglen has the authority to assess late charges for unpaid fees, in addition to the interest charges described in the deed restrictions. We conclude, however, that Northglen may not foreclose on the property if late charges are not paid. Finally, we affirm the court of appeals' judgment regarding attorney's fees.

* * *

Northglen deed restrictions subject each property owner to "an annual maintenance charge and assessment not to exceed $10 per month or $120 per annum, for the purpose of creating ... the 'maintenance fund'...." (Emphasis added.) The restrictions further provide that "[t]he rate at which each Lot will be assessed will be determined annually" by Northglen, and that "[s]aid rate and when same is payable may be adjusted from year to year by [Northglen] as the needs of the Subdivision may in the judgment of [Northglen] require." Northglen's argument does not survive the restrictions' plain language. First, the annual assessment is not to exceed $10 per month or $120 per year. The restrictions do not require that Northglen charge the maximum amount. Rather, Northglen may charge any amount so long as the amount does not exceed $120 per year. So, if Northglen had been assessing $50 per year and decided the next year that $120 was necessary, it has the authority to raise the rates unilaterally. Second, the deed restrictions neither contemplate nor permit an additional assessment once the maintenance fund is whole because the language says plainly that the assessment is not to exceed $10 per month or $120 per year. There is no language permitting an additional assessment beyond that which is included in the maintenance fund, aside from the special assessment for capital improvements. We hold that the court of appeals correctly concluded that Northglen cannot increase assessments beyond the $120 limitation set forth in the deed restrictions, and we affirm that part of the court of appeals' judgment.

* * *

Foreclosure

Because we hold that Northglen may charge late fees for unpaid fee assessments, we must address whether it has the authority to foreclose on the homestead if a property owner fails to pay the late fee. This Court has clarified that Texas' homestead laws authorize a homeowners association to foreclose on homesteads for the nonpayment of fee assessments. Inwood Homeowners' Ass'n v. Harris, 736 S.W.2d 632, 635–36 (Tex. 1987). In Inwood, we considered whether the homestead laws of Texas protect a homeowner against foreclosure for failure to pay homeowners association assessments. As a general rule, a homestead is protected against the debts of those who live in the homestead. However, the deed restrictions for the subdivision included a vendor's lien permitting foreclosure on the homestead for failure to pay the fee assessment. Because the property owner had notice when purchasing the property that a lien attached to the land, we held that foreclosure was permissible. The court of appeals, in our case, focused on the notice requirement and held that foreclosure was not a potential remedy against unpaid late charges. * * * The court noted that the lien to enforce the late charges attached to the property after the homestead was acquired because late charges were not included in the deed restriction. The court cited as authority an Attorney General opinion that said costs imposed upon property owners because of Chapter 204, which were not part of the deed restriction, could not be enforced through foreclosure. * * * The Attorney General concluded that, in determining whether foreclosure is a remedy, the issue is "whether the lien for those costs (i) attached to the property prior to the homestead right and (ii) is the result of a restriction that runs with the land." Tex. Att'y Gen.Op. LO–97–019. The court of appeals considered the two elements and held that because late charges were not part of the deed restrictions but rather a function of the statute, Northglen could not foreclose for failure to pay late charges. * * *

Northglen argues that a developer has the authority to create liens to ensure the payment of fee assessments, and under Inwood, an appropriate remedy for failure to pay assessments is foreclosure. Northglen also contends that because property owners were aware that delinquent assessments would be subject to late charges, in the form of an interest charge, the property owners had actual notice sufficient to satisfy Inwood. Thus, because the property owners had actual notice, Northglen asserts, the late charge should also run with the land as the interest charge does. We disagree with Northglen and agree with the court of appeals. Northglen's argument essentially amends the deed restrictions to include both late fees and interest charges. But the restrictions did not provide any notice that a late fee would be imposed in addition to the interest charge. As a result, the property owners did not have notice of the late charge. Therefore, in light of Inwood's notice requirement, foreclosure is not an appropriate remedy for a failure to pay the late charge. * * *

Non-profit Corporation Act

Northglen challenges that portion of the trial court's judgment providing hat "the bylaws may only be amended by the members...." Northglen argues that, even absent Property Code chapter 204, it had the authority to increase assessments because it may amend the bylaws unilaterally under the Texas Non–Profit Corporation Act. Tex. Rev. Civ. Stat. art. 1396–1.01 et seq. That statute provides, among other things, that a board of directors has the authority to amend bylaws unless the articles of incorporation reserve the power exclusively to the members. We cannot reach this issue. Northglen did not file a notice of appeal from the trial court's judgment, did not notice a cross-appeal, and did not petition this court for review on the point. Accordingly, Northglen did not preserve this issue for our review. * * *

TRUSTEES OF THE PRINCE CONDOMINIUM TRUST v. PROSSER

Supreme Judicial Court, Massachusetts, 1992
412 Mass. 723, 592 N.E.2d 1301

WILKINS, Justice.

The trustees of a condominium trust commenced this action pursuant to G.L. c. 183A, § 6 (1990 ed.), to collect unpaid common expenses lawfully assessed against the defendant Prosser, a unit owner, and to enforce a lien for those expenses against Prosser's condominium unit. On the summary judgment record before us, there is no dispute that Prosser owes the plaintiffs the amounts they claim. He argues that he has a valid claim against the trustees that he may use to offset any amounts due to them. Prosser asserts by counterclaim that since 1980 the plaintiffs have wrongfully denied him the right to use the garage parking space conveyed to him by the developer of the condominium in the 1976 deed by which Prosser also acquired his condominium unit. Prosser seeks payment of the fair rental value of the parking space and an order that the condominium trustees cease interfering with his right to the exclusive use of the parking space.

A judge of the Superior Court ruled that Prosser was obliged to pay his share of the lawfully assessed common expenses and could not exempt himself from doing so. The judge also ruled that the condominium trustees were not responsible for Prosser's loss of the use of his parking space. We transferred to this court Prosser's appeal from a summary judgment entered in favor of the condominium trustees on their complaint and on Prosser's counterclaim. We affirm the judgment.

1. The condominium trustees and the amicus curiae urge us to decide that the obligation of a condominium unit owner to pay any assessment of common expenses is an independent obligation not subject to offset. Because we conclude that the judgment can be affirmed simply on the ground that Prosser did not assert an enforceable claim against the condominium trustees, we do not have to decide the point. * * * We, therefore, elect to state our views on the point. * * *

In doing so, we agree with the Appeals Court's recent statement that there is no right to a set-off against a lawfully imposed condominium charge. * * * Such authority as there is elsewhere in this country also supports the proposition that a condominium unit owner may not properly withhold payment of lawfully assessed common area charges by asserting a right of offset against those charges. * * * The assessment is a lien on the unit enforceable as provided in G.L. c. 183A, § 6(c), and the financial obligations of a unit owner are covenants running with the land. Whatever grievance a unit owner may have against the condominium trustees must not be permitted to affect the collection of lawfully assessed common area expense charges. A system that would tolerate a unit owner's refusal to pay an assessment because the unit owner asserts a grievance, even a seemingly meritorious one, would threaten the financial integrity of the entire condominium operation. For the same reason that taxpayers may not lawfully decline to pay lawfully assessed taxes because of some grievance or claim against the taxing governmental unit, a condominium unit owner may not decline to pay lawful assessments. If there were to be an exception to this principle, it would be due to extraordinary circumstances not shown on the record before us.

2. Even if a unit owner could properly assert an offset against lawfully assessed common area charges, Prosser's claimed offset was not legally enforceable. It is important to understand the circumstances that resulted in Prosser's loss of his parking space. That parking space, which, as we have said, the developer of the condominium property and not the condominium trustees sold to Prosser, was located on top of the entrance to the building's boiler room. In 1980, the Boston fire department issued an abatement order directing the trustees to remove Prosser's vehicle from the parking space and to discontinue use of the space for parking. The trustees advised Prosser of the order, and he complied with it. Various attempts to find a solution to the problem have been unsuccessful.

Prosser argues that the condominium trustees unlawfully took his parking space without compensating him for his loss. The problem with this argument is that the condominium trustees did not cause Prosser's loss. It may be that the condominium developer purported to sell Prosser a space for parking that lawfully could not be used for that purpose. In any event, the Boston fire department issued the order that the space not be used for parking. The trustees simply carried out that order. Although Prosser paid for a parking space that he now cannot lawfully use, the condominium trustees are not responsible for any wrong the developer committed or for the consequences of an order of the Boston fire department. The trustees have not violated their obligations as trustees. They had no duty to provide Prosser with an alternative parking space.

* * *

Question

What recourse do homeowners have against arbitrary action on the part of directors of homeowners' associations?

ASHCREEK HOMEOWNER'S ASSOCIATION, INC. v. SMITH

Court of Appeals, Texas, 1995
902 S.W.2d 586

OLIVER–PARROTT, Chief Justice.

This is an appeal from a take-nothing judgment in a homeowner association's suit to enforce certain deed restrictions. We affirm.

* * *

The appellant, Ashcreek Homeowner's Association, Inc. ("Ashcreek") filed suit against the appellees, Michael Wayne Smith and Tzena Lynn Smith (collectively, "the Smiths") in 1991, seeking damages and attorneys' fees for violations of Ashcreek's deed restrictions. Specifically, Ashcreek alleged two violations: the absence of a backboard on the Smith's basketball goal, and a broken fence slat.

The suit was tried to the bench. After Ashcreek presented its case-in-chief, the Smiths presented one witness before making a motion for judgment, which the trial court granted. Ashcreek appeals * * *.

In their reply points, the Smiths contend that Ashcreek did not comply with the notice and hearing provisions of the deed restrictions. * * *

* * *

The trial court correctly interpreted the deed restrictions' notice provision. The purpose of giving notice is to allow the Smiths an opportunity to prepare and defend against the allegations, if they so choose. In order to properly prepare and defend themselves, the Smiths should have been apprised of the specific provision which they had allegedly violated. The purpose of affording a hearing is simply to give a homeowner a forum in which to defend against the association's allegations. We agree with the trial court's conclusion number nine, and hold that on the facts of this case, "notice" includes "a specification of the particular provision" alleged to have been violated, and that "afford a hearing" includes a fair opportunity to present evidence. We do not, as Ashcreek contends, require a full adversary hearing with findings of fact and conclusions of law. We merely require that the homeowner be informed in writing of the provision allegedly violated and given a fair opportunity to present evidence.

We now turn to the question of whether Ashcreek complied with the notice requirements as we have interpreted them. We hold that it did not.

* * *

Ashcreek introduced evidence that on December 21, 1990, it sent a letter to the Smiths notifying them that they were in violation of deed restriction section 3.13 The parties agree that this section relates to lot maintenance and the removal of trash from an owner's lot. However, at trial Ashcreek alleged that the Smiths had violated section 3.06, the nuisance provision. We hold that the Smiths were never given proper notice that their basketball goal violated section 3.06.

* * *

Ashcreek also argues that the Smiths were afforded a hearing. This contention is based on the fact that Michael Smith attended a regularly scheduled board meeting in June 1991. The minutes of this meeting are a part of the record, and they indicate:

> Mr. Smith questioned the Board's authority to enforce a basketball pole without a backboard and hoop. Mr. Smith stated that the deed restrictions do not specify what is considered trash and in his opinion a single upright pole is not trash or in need of repair. The Board did not agree with his assessment and indicated the project needed to be completed or removed.

Because we have already determined that the Smiths were never given "registered notice," we need not and do not address the question of whether the Smiths were "afforded a hearing." Nevertheless, we note that the minutes of the Board meeting show that the Smiths attended the meeting to contest what they thought was the Board's determination that the basketball goal was a violation of section 3.13, the section relating to grass, weeds, and trash on the lot. At trial, Ashcreek took the position that as long as it stated the subject of the violation (for example, the basketball goal or fence slat) it had no obligation to inform the Smiths of the particular provision of the deed restrictions being violated. This episode illustrates the unreasonableness of Ashcreek's position. Such a construction unfairly penalizes homeowners attempting to verify their compliance with the deed restrictions.

Because the Smiths were never given registered notice of the alleged violation which they were expected to defend against, we hold that the trial court correctly rendered judgment for the Smiths as to the basketball goal.

* * *

Ashcreek introduced evidence that it sent the Smiths registered notice regarding the broken fence slat on November 20, 1991. However, this suit was initiated August 27, 1991. In addition, the letter cited a provision of the deed restrictions that Ashcreek later admitted was inapplicable. Finally, Ashcreek's property manager admitted on cross-examination that the Smiths were never given a hearing on the fence slat, and that homeowners are not ever told of their right to a hearing. We hold that as to the fence slat, there was ample evidence for the judge to conclude that Ashcreek did not comply with section 10.04 of its deed restrictions, because it did not give the Smiths registered notice or a hearing prior to initiating this suit.

* * *

Consider provisions of the Texas Residential Property Owners Protection Act enacted by the Texas legislature in 2001, effective in 2002.

CHAPTER 209. TEXAS RESIDENTIAL PROPERTY OWNERS PROTECTION ACT

* * *

§ 209.006. Notice Required Before Enforcement Action

(a) Before a property owners' association may suspend an owner's right to use a common area, file a suit against an owner other than a suit to collect a regular or special assessment or foreclose under an association's lien, charge an owner for property damage, or levy a fine for a violation of the restrictions or bylaws or rules of the association, the association or its agent must give written notice to the owner by certified mail, return receipt requested.

(b) The notice must:

(1) describe the violation or property damage that is the basis for the suspension action, charge, or fine and state any amount due the association from the owner; and

(2) inform the owner that the owner:

(A) is entitled to a reasonable period to cure the violation and avoid the fine or suspension unless the owner was given notice and a reasonable opportunity to cure a similar violation within the preceding six months; and

(B) may request a hearing under Section 209.007 on or before the 30th day after the date the owner receives the notice.

§ 209.007. Hearing Before Board; Alternative Dispute Resolution

(a) If the owner is entitled to an opportunity to cure the violation, the owner has the right to submit a written request for a hearing to discuss and verify facts and resolve the matter in issue before a committee appointed by the board of the property owners' association or before the board if the board does not appoint a committee.

(b) If a hearing is to be held before a committee, the notice prescribed by Section 209.006 must state that the owner has the right to appeal the committee's decision to the board by written notice to the board.

(c) The association shall hold a hearing under this section not later than the 30th day after the date the board receives the owner's request for a hearing and shall notify the owner of the date, time, and place of the hearing not later than the 10th day before the date of the hearing. The board or the owner may request a postponement, and, if requested, a postponement shall be granted for a period of not more than 10 days. Additional postponements may be granted by agreement of the parties. The owner or the association may make an audio recording of the meeting.

(d) The notice and hearing provisions of Section 209.006 and this section do not apply if the association files a suit seeking a temporary restraining order or temporary injunctive relief or files a suit that includes foreclosure as a cause of action. If a suit is filed relating to a matter to which those sections apply, a party to the suit may file a motion to compel mediation. The notice and hearing provisions of Section 209.006 and this section do not apply to a temporary suspension of a person's right to use common areas if the temporary suspension is the result of a violation that occurred in a common area and involved a significant and immediate risk of harm to others in the subdivision. The temporary suspension is effective until the board makes a final determination on the suspension action after following the procedures prescribed by this section.

(e) An owner or property owners' association may use alternative dispute resolution services.

* * *

§ 209.009. Foreclosure Sale Prohibited in Certain Circumstances

A property owners' association may not foreclose a property owners' association's assessment lien if the debt securing the lien consists solely of:

(1) fines assessed by the association; or

(2) attorney's fees incurred by the association solely associated with fines assessed by the association.

§ 209.010. Notice After Foreclosure Sale

(a) A property owners' association that conducts a foreclosure sale of an owner's lot must send to the lot owner not later than the 30th day after the date of the foreclosure sale a written notice stating the date and time the sale occurred and informing the lot owner of the owner's right to redeem the property under Section 209.011.

(b) The notice must be sent by certified mail, return receipt requested, to the lot owner's last known mailing address, as reflected in the records of the property owners' association.

(c) Not later than the 30th day after the date the association sends the notice required by Subsection (a), the association must record an affidavit in the real property records of the county in which the lot is located, stating the date on which the notice was sent and containing a legal description of the lot. Any person is entitled to rely conclusively on the information contained in the recorded affidavit.

(d) The notice requirements of this section also apply to the sale of an owner's lot by a sheriff or constable conducted as provided by a judgment obtained by the property owners' association.

Question

Should there be statutory provisions governing the organization and operation of homeowners' associations?

2001 OREGON REVISED STATUTES
TITLE 10. PROPERTY RIGHTS AND TRANSACTIONS
CHAPTER 94. REAL PROPERTY DEVELOPMENT
PLANNED COMMUNITIES
GENERAL PROVISIONS

94.560. Legislative findings.

The Legislative Assembly finds that:

(1) In the State of Oregon there are hundreds of homeowners associations to which the Oregon Condominium Law (ORS chapter 100) does not apply.

(2) These homeowners associations have established a pattern of ownership in which ownership of a single unit makes the owner automatically a member of a homeowners association with responsibilities for management and maintenance.

(3) Many of these homeowners associations as associations and their members as individuals have experienced problems from the lack of statutory provisions. These problems which have arisen are usually the result of inexperience with this kind of ownership. This inexperience often leads to difficulties for the association when it assumes responsibility for the administration of the planned development because usually neither the developer who drafted the documents nor the local jurisdiction which may have reviewed them has realized the long term management implications of the restrictions imposed by the documents. The most serious and frequent error is imposing excessive voting requirements for any changes in the documents, a basic error that makes it and other errors unnecessarily difficult, if not impossible, to correct. Of almost equal importance is the lack of disclosure of significant differences this pattern of ownership imposes on the homeowner and the restrictions on choice that must be accepted.

(4) Oregon land conservation policies and the increasing cost of land will result in rapid growth of this kind of homeownership pattern.

(5) It is a matter of statewide concern that the Legislative Assembly address problems associated with homeowners associations in order to make this kind of homeownership pattern an acceptable choice and in order to assure proper maintenance of the

projects so that the investment of the owners and the appearance of Oregon communities are protected.

(6) It is essential that the Legislative Assembly establish basic statutory requirements for disclosure to first and subsequent buyers, for the organization of the homeowners association, and for a process by which administrative responsibility for the planned community is transferred from the developer to the association of individual owners.

(7) ORS 94.550 to 94.783 are intended to make developers, their legal counsel and homeowners in Oregon homeowners associations the beneficiaries of experience accumulated under Oregon's condominium law and gathered from members of existing Oregon homeowners associations and associations in parts of the country where the record of experience is longer than that in Oregon.

*

Index

References are to Pages

ACTION ORGANIZATIONS
Lobbying, 265–278
Political campaigns, 279–280

ACTIONS
Declaratory judgment actions, 559
Derivative actions, 89

ADVOCACY ORGANIZATIONS
Registration requirements, 15–27, 770, 772

AGRICULTURAL ORGANIZATIONS
Tax exempt status, 726

ANNUITIES
Charitable gift annuities, 407–408

ANTITRUST REGULATION
Trade and professional organizations, 740–756

APPRAISALS
Donated property, 391–395

APPRECIATION IN VALUE
Charitable Contribution Deductions (this index)

ART
Donation of, 388
IRS review of valuation, 395

ARTICLES OF INCORPORATION
Charitable organizations, 176–199
Nonprofit corporations, 61–90

ASSETS
Disposition upon dissolution, 119–125
Private foundations, assets test, 304
Section 1231 assets, 387

ASSOCIATION, RIGHT OF
Social clubs, 683–706

ASSOCIATIONS
Organizations as, 28–30
Trade and Professional Associations (this index)

ATTORNEY GENERAL
Fiduciary duties, enforcement of, 125

AUDITS
Churches and other religious organizations, 557–559

BUSINESS GROUPS
Trade and Professional Associations (this index)

BUSINESS JUDGMENT RULE
Generally, 105–106

BYLAWS
Nonprofit corporations, 65

CARRYFORWARD
Charitable contribution deductions, 368–408

CHAMBERS OF COMMERCE
Trade association status, 726

CHARITABLE CONTRIBUTION DEDUCTIONS
Generally, 368–408
Acknowledgment of receipt of gift, 395
Amount of deduction
    Generally, 386–389
    Contribution, amount of, 387
    Percentage limitations, 389–390
    Property, gift of, below
Appraisal of donated property, 391–395
Appreciation in value of property
    Generally, 387
    Bargain sales, 407
Art, donation of, 388
Bargain sale, 407
Carryforward of deduction, 390–391
Cash donations, 369
Charitable remainder trusts, 396–399, 403–407
Check, delivery of, 386
Computer technology, 389
Conditional gifts, 386
Contribution base, 389
Corporate gifts of money, percentage limitation, 390
Credit cards, use of, 386
Deferred giving
    Generally, 396–408
    Charitable gift annuities, 396–399, 403–407

CHARITABLE CONTRIBUTION DEDUCTIONS—Cont'd
Deferred giving—Cont'd
Charitable remainder trusts, 383, 384–385
Delivery of gift, 386
Depreciation in value of property, 387
Dinners, fund–raising, 370
Educational purposes, equipment for, 389
Exempt purpose, donated property not related to, 389
Filing requirements, noncash gifts, 395
Foreign organizations, 54–60
Foundation, private nonoperating, gift to, 388, 390
Free, unordered items, 385
Gratuities in exchange for donation
Generally, 369, 373
Good faith estimate of value, 395
Inventory, 387
IRS "Statement of Value," 395
Long–term capital gain property, 387–388
Maximum deduction, 389–390
Money, corporate gifts of, percentage limitation, 390
Ordinary income producing property, 388–389
Overvaluation, 395
Percentage limitations, 389–390
Pledges, 386
Private foundations, 369
Promissory notes, 386
Property, gift of
Art, 388
Depreciation in value, 387
Exempt purpose, property not related to, 387
Fair market value, 387
Long-term capital gain property, 387–388
Substantiation, noncash gifts, 395–396
Trade or business, depreciable property used in (§ 1231 assets), 387
Public charities vs. private foundations, 388–391
Quid pro quo gifts, 369–370,. 381
Raffles, 370
Scientific property used for research, 389
Services, expenses related to, 385
Statement of value, provision by IRS, 395
Stock certificate, delivery of, 386
Substantiation, noncash gifts, 395–396
Time, donation of, 386
Timing of deduction, 386
Trade or business, depreciable property used in (§ 1231 assets), 387
Unconditional nature of gift, 386

CHARITABLE ORGANIZATIONS
Generally, 176–199
Exclusivity of charitable purpose, 178
Operational tests, 177–178, 182
Organizational tests, 177–178
Public Charities (this index)

CHARITABLE ORGANIZATIONS—Cont'd
Section 501(c)(3) organizations
Benefits, 176
Elements, 177
Tax Exempt Status (this index)
Social welfare organizations
Generally, 199–200
Retroactivity of exempt status, 213

CHARITABLE SOLICITATIONS
Regulation of, 347

CHARITABLE TRUSTS
Nonprofit corporations, status as, 30
Organization as, 27–28
Remainder trusts, 396–399, 403–407
Uniform Supervision of Trustees for Charitable Purposes Act, 31–32

CHILD CARE CENTERS
Treatment of income from, 559

CHURCHES AND OTHER RELIGIOUS ORGANIZATIONS
Generally, 491–560
Association status, 522–543
Belief in a Supreme Being, 505–514
Bookstores, treatment of income from, 559
Child care centers, treatment of income from, 559
Contracts, liability under, 522
Debts, personal liability for, 522
Declaratory judgments, 559
Definition of church, 491
Duty to warn of sexual abuse, 527
Employment discrimination, 527–528
Incorporation, 543–549
Integrated auxiliary, 498–505
Liability of members, 522–528
Membership, 514–522
Notice of tax inquiry, 558–559
Political activities, involvement in, 549–557
Property ownership, 528–543
Public charity, status as, 283
Records, examination by IRS, 558–559
Self-employment tax, payment by ministers, 559–560
Social Security taxes on wages, 559
Tax audits, 557–559
Title to property, 540–543
Tort liability, 522
Unrelated business income tax, 559

CIVIC AND CULTURAL ORGANIZATIONS
Public charity, status as, 285

CLUBS
Social Clubs (this index)

COLLEGES AND UNIVERSITIES
Athletic facilities, renting to professional team, 467
Fraternities and sororities, 717–725
Organizations for the benefit of, 284
Public charity, status as, 283–284

INDEX

References are to Pages

COLLEGES AND UNIVERSITIES—Cont'd
Unrelated business income tax, 433

COMMERCIAL ACTIVITY
Engaging in, 214–216
Unrelated Business Income Tax (UBIT) (this index)

COMMUNITY CENTERS
Public charity, status as, 285

COMPUTER TECHNOLOGY
Charitable contribution deductions, 389

CONDOMINIUMS
Homeowners' Associations (this index)

CONFLICTS OF INTEREST
Directors, 108–109
Self–Dealing (this index)

CONSTITUTIONAL LAW
Charitable solicitations, registration requirements, 347
Social clubs, right of association, 683–706

CONSUMER PRODUCT TESTING ORGANIZATIONS
Public charity, status as, 301

CONTRACTS
Churches and other religious organizations, 522

CONTRIBUTIONS
Charitable Contribution Deductions (this index)

COOPERATIVES
Homeowners' Associations (this index)

CORPORATIONS
Gifts of money, percentage limitation, 390
Nonprofit Corporations (this index)
Sponsorships, 465

CREDIT CARDS
Affinity cards, royalties for use of name and logo, 467
Use of to make donation, deductibility, 386

CY PRES DOCTRINE
Generally, 122–125, 408–428

DEBT-FINANCED INCOME
Unrelated business income tax, 473

DEBTS
Personal liability of church member, 522

DECLARATORY JUDGMENTS
Church's tax exempt status, 559

DEDUCTIONS
Charitable Contribution Deductions (this index)
Dues paid to trade or professional organization, 734
Homeowners' associations, 781–782

DEDUCTIONS—Cont'd
Political organizations, 771

DEFINITIONS
Generally, 2
Charitable contribution, 369
Church, 491
Commercial nonprofits, 2
Contribution base, 389
Excess benefit transactions, 264
Royalties, 467
Self–dealing, 315
Substantially related, 454
Taxable expenditures, 327
Trade or business, 446
Undistributed income, 319
Unrelated trade or business, 433

DEPRECIATION IN VALUE
Charitable contribution deductions, 387

DEVIATION DOCTRINE
Generally, 422–428

DERIVATIVE ACTIONS
Nonprofit corporations, 89

DIRECTORS
Business judgment rule, 105–106
Conflict of interest, 108–109
Excess benefits transactions, 161–175, 262–265
Fiduciary obligations, 91–115, 125
General standards for, 108
Indemnification, 115–119
Negligence, liability for, 108
Nonprofit Corporations (this index)
Revised Model Nonprofit Corporation Act, 108–109
Self-dealing, 155–161

DISCRIMINATION
Private schools, racially nondiscriminatory policy, 595
Social clubs, racial or gender discrimination, 683

DISSOLUTION
Disposition of assets, 119–125

DIVIDENDS
Hospitals, dividends from profit corporations, 628
Unrelated business income tax (UBIT), 466

DONATIONS
Charitable Contribution Deductions (this index)

DONATIVE NONPROFITS
Defined, 2

EDUCATION
Tax deduction, equipment for educational purposes, 389

INDEX
References are to Pages

EDUCATIONAL ORGANIZATIONS
Public charity, status as, 283–284

EDUCATIONAL RECORDS
Family Educational Rights and Privacy Act, 611–612

ELECTIONS
Political Organizations and Activities (this index)

EXCESS BENEFIT TRANSACTIONS
Generally, 154–175, 262–265
Defined, 264
Disqualified person, 173, 263
Elements, 263–265
Hospitals, nonprofit, disposal of assets for less than fair market value, 679
Initial contract for fixed fee, 173–174
Intermediate sanction, 263
Rebuttable presumption, 174

FEDERAL STANDARDS OF CONDUCT
Excess benefits transactions, 161–175, 262–265
Self-dealing, 155–161

FIDUCIARY DUTIES
Generally, 92–115
Enforcement of, 125

FOREIGN NONPROFIT ORGANIZATIONS
Generally, 53
French law
    Generally, 48–53
    Associations, 48–50
    Corporate foundations, 50–52
    Foundations, 50
    Public interest foundations, 51
Italian law, 53

FOUNDATIONS
Private Foundations (this index)

FRATERNITIES
Generally, 717–725

FRENCH LAW
Foreign Nonprofit Corporations, this index

FUNDRAISING
Generally, 346–368
Cy pres doctrine, 122–125, 408–428
Deviation doctrine, 422–428
License or permit requirements, 347

FUNDS
Excess campaign funds, 771
Lobbying activity, segregated funds, 280
Prudent Management of Institutional Funds Act, 106–108
Separate funds for political activity. Political Organizations and Activities (this index)
Solicitations of funds, 347

FUNDS—Cont'd
Uniform Management of Institutional Funds Act, 106–108

GENDER DISCRIMINATION
Social clubs, 683

GIFT SHOPS
Treatment of income from, 464

GIFTS
Charitable Contribution Deductions (this index)

GOVERNANCE OF NONPROFIT ORGANIZATION
Generally, 91–175
Assets, disposition upon dissolution, 119–125
Corporate opportunity, 112–113
Dissolution, disposition of assets, 119–125
Excess benefits transactions, 161–175, 262–265
Federal standards of conduct
    Generally, 154–175
    Excess benefit transactions, 161–175
    Self-dealing, 155
Fiduciary obligations, 92–115, 125
Immunity of volunteers from liability, 154
Indemnification of directors, 115–119
Self-dealing, 155–161
State standards of conduct
    Generally, 91–154
    Fiduciary obligations, 91–115, 125
Volunteers, immunity from liability, 154

GOVERNMENTAL UNITS
Public charity, status as, 284

GRANTS
Taxable expenditures, grants as, 327

HEALTH MAINTENANCE ORGANIZATIONS
Tax-exempt status, 679

HOMEOWNERS' ASSOCIATIONS
Generally, 781–797
Auxiliary residential purposes, 782
Deductions, 782
Dues, fees, and assessments, 781–782
Exempt function income, 781–782
Expenditures, allowable, 782
Management associations, 781
Members, rights and liabilities, 782–797
Residential purposes, use for, 781–782
Tax exempt status (§ 528), 781–782
Transient occupancy, 782

HORTICULTURAL ORGANIZATIONS
Tax exempt status, 726

HOSPITALS
Generally, 619–679
Abandonment of nonprofit status, 673–676
Accreditation, 627
Conversion to for-profit status, 676

INDEX

References are to Pages

HOSPITALS—Cont'd
Consumers on hospital boards, 619
Dividends from profit corporations, treatment of, 628
Excess benefits penalty tax, disposing of assets for less than fair market value, 679
Health maintenance organizations (HMOs), 679
Holding companies, 628
Indigents, care for, 654–673
Joint ventures with for profit entities, 636–654
Organizational structure, 619–627
Parent organization, 627
Partnership arrangements with physicians, 636–643
Physician incentives, 628–636
Property taxes, exemption from, 655–672
Public charity, status as, 285
Reorganization of nonprofits, 627–628
Research corporations, for-profit, agreements with, 628
Types of tax-exempt status, choosing between, 628

IMMUNITY FROM LIABILITY
Volunteers, 154

INCOME TAX
Unrelated Business Income Tax (UBIT) (this index)

INDEMNIFICATION
Directors, 115–119

INDIGENTS
Care for by nonprofit hospitals, 654–673

INJUNCTIONS
Political campaign activity, 279

INSIDERS
Distributions to, 245, 261

INTEREST
Exclusion from unrelated business income tax, 467
Private foundations, 306

INTERNAL REVENUE CODE
Charitable Contribution Deductions (this index)
Difference between §§ 501(c)(3) and 501(c)(4), 199–200
Excess benefit transactions (§ 4958), 161–175, 262–265
Section 527 advocacy organizations, 770, 772
Section 528 homeowners' associations, 781–782
Section 509 organizations. Public Charities (this index)
Section 501(c)(5) and (6) organizations. Trade and Professional Organizations (this index)

INTERNAL REVENUE CODE—Cont'd
Section 501(c)(3) organizations
  Charitable Contribution Deductions (this index)
  Charitable Organizations (this index)
  Political activities, 279–280, 773–777
  Private Foundations (this index)
  Private schools. Schools (this index)
  Unemployment taxes, exemption from, 176
  Unrelated Business Income Tax (this index)
Section 501(c)(4) organizations, 199–201, 213

INTERNATIONAL LAW
Foreign Nonprofit Organizations (this index)
Nongovernmental organizations, 46–47

INVENTORY
Donation of, 387

INVESTMENTS
Private foundations, investments jeopardizing exemption, 326
Prudent Management of Institutional Funds Act, 106–108
Social clubs, taxation of investment income, 706
Uniform Prudent Investor Act, 107–108

ISSUE ADVOCACY
Registration requirements, 770, 772

ITALIAN LAW
Generally, 53

LEASES
Rents from, unrelated business income tax, 466–467

LIBRARIES
Public charity, status as, 285

LICENSES
Charitable solicitations, 347

LOBBYING ACTIVITY
  Generally, 265–278
Affiliated groups, 278
Definitions, 265
Excluded conduct, 265
Expenditure limits, 276
Federal disclosure requirements, 275
General lobbying, 276–277
Grass roots lobbying, 276–277
Nonpartisan activities, 265, 272
Political Organizations and Activities (this index)
Reporting requirements, 276
Segregated funds, 279
Substantiality test, 278
Trade and professional organizations, 735

INDEX

References are to Pages

LOCAL REGULATION
Charitable solicitations, 347

LONG-TERM CAPITAL GAIN PROPERTY
Donation of, tax deduction, 387–388

MAILING LISTS
Royalties for use of, 467

MEDICAL RESEARCH ORGANIZATIONS
Public charity, status as, 284

MEETINGS
Nonprofit Corporations (this index)

MEMBERS
Churches and other religious organizations, 514–528
Homeowners' associations, 782–797
Nonprofit Corporations (this index)
Trade and professional organizations, 757–760

MODEL ACTS
Nonprofit corporation acts, 30–31, 108–109

MUSEUMS
Public charity, status as, 285

MUTUAL BENEFIT CORPORATIONS
Defined, 2

NATURE OF NONPROFIT ORGANIZATION
Generally, 1–27
Definitions, 2

NEGLIGENCE
Liability of directors, 105

NONGOVERNMENTAL ORGANIZATIONS
Generally, 46–47
Foreign NGOs, 47–48

NONOPERATING FOUNDATIONS
Private Foundations (this index)

NONPARTISAN ACTIVITIES
Generally, 265, 272

NONPROFIT CORPORATIONS
Generally, 61–99
Articles of incorporation, 64–65
Bylaws, 65
Charitable trust, status as, 31–32
Creation, 64–66
Delegation of management activities, 71
Derivative actions, 89
Directors
    Generally, 66
    Meetings, 71
    Removal, 72
Management, 66
Meetings
    Directors, 71
    Members, 81
Members
    Generally, 76
    Derivative actions, 89

NONPROFIT CORPORATIONS—Cont'd
Members—Cont'd
    Meetings, 81
    Removal, 82
    Rights of, 77
Nature of, 61
Organization as, 30–32, 64–66
Other state, authorization to conduct affairs in, 66
Quorum requirements, 71, 82
Revised Model Nonprofit Corporation Act, 30, 108–109
Voting rights, 77

NOTICE
Member meetings, 82
Tax inquiry, notice of, 557–559

ORDINANCES
Charitable solicitations, regulation of, 347

ORGANIZATIONAL STRUCTURE
Generally, 27–46
Hospitals, 619–627

PASSIVE INCOME
Unrelated business income tax (UBIT), 466–467

PENALTIES
Hospitals, excess benefits penalty tax, 679
Political activity, 279–280, 776–777
Private Foundations (this index)

PERMITS
Charitable solicitations, 347

PHYSICIANS
Partnership arrangements with hospitals, 636–643

PLANNED UNIT DEVELOPMENTS
Homeowners' Associations (this index)

PLEDGES
Deduction for, 386

POLITICAL ORGANIZATIONS AND ACTIVITIES
Generally, 761–780
Bipartisan Reform Act of 2002, 770, 772
Churches and other religious organizations, 549–557, 773–777
Deductions, 771
Dues, deduction of, 735
Excess campaign funds, 771
Exempt function income, 770
Federal Election Campaign Act, 761, 770
Filing requirements, 771
Fund for political expenditures, 771
Issue advocacy organizations, registration requirements, 770, 772
Lobbying Activities (this index)
Nonelective candidates, expenditures on behalf of, 773
Penalty tax, 776–777
Public advocacy communication, 772

POLITICAL ORGANIZATIONS AND ACTIVITIES—Cont'd
Registration requirements, § 527 organizations, 769, 777–780
Regulation, 761–771
Section 527 organizations, registration requirements, 769–772
Section 501(c)(3) organizations, 279–280, 773–777
Separate fund
    Individual, fund maintained by, 761
    Nonprofit organization, establishment by, 771
    Section 501(c)(3) organizations, 773
Taxation, 770–771
Trade and professional organizations, 734–740

PRIVACY
Family Educational Rights and Privacy Act, 611–612

PRIVATE FOUNDATIONS
    Generally, 303–345
Assets test, 304
Business holdings, excess, 325–326
Compensation, unreasonable, to disqualified person, 315
Conversion to public charity status, 338
Deductible expenses, 306
Depreciation, 306
Disqualified person, self-dealing, 315
Donations to, tax treatment, 303
Endowment test, 304
Excess business holdings, 325
Excise tax
    Generally, 305–315
    Self-dealing with disqualified person, 315
Exempt operating foundations, 306
Expenses
    Deductible expenses, 306
    Taxable expenditures, 327–338
Failure to distribute income, 319–325
Filing requirements, 304
Governing instrument, 304
Grants as taxable expenditures, 327
Gross investment income, 305–306
Income, failure to distribute, 319–326
Income test, 304
Interest, tax-exempt, 306
Investments jeopardizing exemption, 326
Involuntary termination, 338
Jeopardizing investments, 326
Manager
    Investments jeopardizing exemption, 326
    Self-dealing, participation in, 315
Minimum investment return, 304, 320
Net capital gains, computation, 305–306
Net investment income, 305
Nonoperating foundations
    Filing requirements, 304

PRIVATE FOUNDATIONS—Cont'd
Nonoperating foundations—Cont'd
    Long-term capital gain property, gift of, 387–388
Operating foundations, 304–305
Penalty tax
    Excess business holdings, 325–326
    Investments jeopardizing exemption, 326
    Involuntary termination, 338
Self-dealing, 315
    Taxable expenditures, 327
    Undistributed income, 319
Public recognition benefits, 315
Qualifying distributions, 319–320
Reporting requirements, 304
Self-dealing, 315–319
Set asides for specific projects, 320
Speculative investments, 326
Support test, 305
Taxable expenditures, 327
Termination of status, 338–344
Undistributed income, penalty tax, 319

PRIVATE INUREMENT
    Generally, 245
Excess Benefit Transactions (this index)

PRIVATE SCHOOLS
Schools (this index)

PROFESSIONAL ORGANIZATIONS
Trade and Professional Organizations (this index)

PROFIT-MAKING ACTIVITIES
Engaging in, 214
Unrelated Business Income Tax (UBIT) (this index)

PROMISSORY NOTES
Deductibility, 386

PROPERTY
Donation of. Charitable Contribution Deductions (this index)

PROPERTY TAXES
Hospitals, exemption from, 655–672

PUBLIC BENEFIT CORPORATIONS
Defined, 2

PUBLIC CHARITIES
    Generally, 281–302
Churches, 283
Educational organizations, 283–284
Filing requirements, 301–302
Foundation, private, conversion of, 338
Governmental units, 285
Hospitals, 284
Medical research organizations, 284
Publicly supported organizations
    Generally, 285–288
    Facts and circumstances test, 287
    One-third support test, 285–287
    Unusual grants, 288–289

INDEX

References are to Pages

PUBLIC CHARITIES—Cont'd
Requirements, 281–302
Returns, filing requirements, 301–302
Section 509(a)(1) organizations, 283–288
Section 509(a)(2) organizations
    Generally, 288–291
    One-third investment income test, 290–291
    One-third support test, 289–290
Section 509(a)(3) organizations
    Generally, 291–301
    Operational test, 291–293
    Organizational test, 291
Section 509(a)(4) organizations, 301

PUBLIC POLICY
Tax exempt status, 280

QUORUMS
Nonprofit corporations, 71, 82

RACIAL DISCRIMINATION
Private schools, 595
Social clubs, 683

RELIGIOUS ORGANIZATIONS
Churches and Other Religious Organizations (this index)

REMAINDER INTEREST
Donation of, 396–408

RENTS
Unrelated business income tax, 466–467

RESTATEMENT
Charitable trusts, 28
Cy pres doctrine, 421

ROYALTIES
Unrelated business income tax, 467

SCHOOLS
Colleges and Universities (this index)
Compulsory school law, 561
Disciplinary procedures, 605–610
Expression, right of, 612–618
Family Educational Rights and Privacy Act, 611–612
Privacy rights of students, 611–612
Private schools
    Racially nondiscriminatory policy, 595–596
    Role of, 561–574
    Tax-exempt status, 584–596
Student rights
    Expression Rights, 612–618
    Privacy rights, 611–612
    Suspension or dismissal, 605
Voucher system, 575–585

SCIENTIFIC PROPERTY
Charitable contribution deductions, 389

SELF-DEALING
Federal standards of conduct, 155–161

SELF-DEALING—Cont'd
Private foundations, 315–319

SELF-EMPLOYMENT TAX
Ministers, payment by, 559–560

SEX DISCRIMINATION
Social clubs, 683

SOCIAL CLUBS
    Generally, 680–725
Association, right of, 683–706
Business use, 713–717
Discrimination racial or gender, 683–706
Exempt function income, 706
Exemption from taxation, 706–713
Fraternities and sororities, 717–725
Investment income, taxation, 706
Membership organizations, 713
Nature of, 680–683
Outside income, taxation, 706
Place of accommodation, 689–696
Sexual orientation discrimination, 696–705
Taxation, 706–713
Unrelated business taxable income, 706

SOCIAL SECURITY TAXES
Payment of, 559–560

SOCIAL WELFARE ORGANIZATIONS
    Generally, 199–200
Retroactivity of exempt status, 213

SOLICITATIONS OF FUNDS
Regulation of, 347

SORORITIES
Generally, 717–715

SPONSORSHIPS
Exclusion from unrelated business income tax, 465

STANDING TO SUE
Generally, 39–46, 128–153

STANDARDS OF CONDUCT
Governance of Nonprofit Organization (this index)

STUDENTS
Schools (this index)

TAX DEDUCTIONS
Charitable Contribution Deductions (this index)
Deductions (this index)

TAX EXEMPT STATUS
    Generally, 212–280
Action organizations, 265–278
Charitable Organizations (this index)
Commercial activity, 214–226
Destination of income test, 215
Insiders, distributions to
    Generally, 245, 261
    Excess benefit transactions, 262–265
Internal Revenue Code (this index)
Lobbying activity, 265–278

INDEX

References are to Pages

TAX EXEMPT STATUS—Cont'd
Maintaining, 213–280
Obtaining, 213
Political campaigns, 279–280
Private benefit, conferring, 226–245
Private inurement prohibition, 245–262
Private schools, 561–574
Profit-making activities, 214–215
Public policy, 280
Section 501(c)(4) organizations, 199–211

TAX LAWS
Internal Revenue Code (this index)

TAXABLE INCOME
Unrelated Business Income Tax (UBIT) (this index)

TERRORIST ORGANIZATIONS
Generally, 3

TITLE TO PROPERTY
Churches and other religious organizations, 540–543

TORT LIABILITY
Churches and other religious organizations, 522

TRADE AND PROFESSIONAL ORGANIZATIONS
Generally, 726–760
Antitrust regulations, 740–756
Conventions, 734
Lobbying activities, disclosure requirements, 735
Membership, 757–760
Political activities, 734–740
Proxy tax on lobbying and political expenditures, 735
Status as trade association, 726–734
Tax exemption, requirements for, 726
Trade shows, 734

TRUSTS AND TRUSTEES
Charitable remainder trusts, 396–399, 403–407
Charitable Trusts (this index)
Split-interest trusts, 403
Unitrusts, 397–403

UNEMPLOYMENT TAXES
Exemption from, 176

UNIFORM ACTS
Management of Institutional Funds Act, 106–107

UNIFORM ACTS—Cont'd
Prudent Management of Institutional Funds Act, 106–108
Prudent Investor Act, 107–108
Uniform Supervision of Trustees for Charitable Purposes Act, 31–32
Unincorporated nonprofit association act, 29, 522

UNINCORPORATED ASSOCIATIONS
Organization as, 28–29, 522

UNIVERSITIES
Colleges and Universities (this index)

UNRELATED BUSINESS INCOME TAX (UBIT)
Generally, 429–490
Bootstrap transactions, 486
Churches and other religious organizations, 559
Corporate sponsorships, 465
Debt-financed income, unrelated, 473
Destination of income test, 430, 432
Dividends, 466
Elements of tax
    Exceptions, 464–466
    Regularly carried on, 446–454
    Substantially related, 454–463
    Unrelated trade or business, 434–464
Exceptions, 464–466
Fragmentation rule, 463
History of UBIT
    Feeder organizations, 431–432
    Pre-Revenue Act of 1950, 430–431
    Revenue Act of 1950, 431–433
Interest, 467
Modifications, adjustments for, 466–473
Organizations to which UBIT applies, 433
Passive income, 466–467
Primary purpose test, 430
Rents, 466–467
Royalties, 467
Services rendered with leasing of property, 467
Substantial commercial activities, engaging in, 432–433
Treasury regulations, 432–433

VOLUNTEERS
Immunity from liability, 154

VOTER EDUCATION
Generally, 274

VOTING RIGHTS
Nonprofit corporations, 77